THE NEW
AMERICAN
COMMENTARY

An Exegetical and Theological
Exposition of Holy Scripture

THE NEW
AMERICAN
COMMENTARY

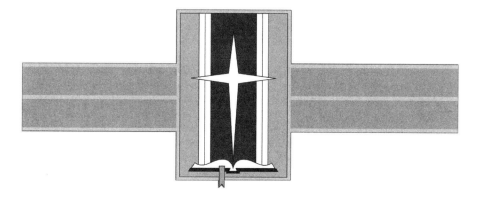

Volume
1B

GENESIS 11:27–50:26

Kenneth A. Mathews

PUBLISHING GROUP

Nashville, Tennessee

© Copyright 2005 • Broadman & Holman Publishers
All rights reserved
ISBN 978-0-8054-0141-7
Dewey Decimal Classification: 222.11
Subject Heading: BIBLE. O.T. GENESIS 11–50
Printed in the United States of America
16 15 14 13 12 8 7 6 5 4

To My Mother
Margaret Katherine Mathews
whose life teaches me to honor God's Word

Editors' Preface

God's Word does not change. God's world, however, changes in every generation. These changes, in addition to new findings by scholars and a new variety of challenges to the gospel message, call for the church in each generation to interpret and apply God's Word for God's people. Thus, THE NEW AMERICAN COMMENTARY is introduced to bridge the twentieth and twenty-first centuries. This new series has been designed primarily to enable pastors, teachers, and students to read the Bible with clarity and proclaim it with power.

In one sense THE NEW AMERICAN COMMENTARY is not new, for it represents the continuation of a heritage rich in biblical and theological exposition. The title of this forty-volume set points to the continuity of this series with an important commentary project published at the end of the nineteenth century called AN AMERICAN COMMENTARY, edited by Alvah Hovey. The older series included, among other significant contributions, the outstanding volume on Matthew by John A. Broadus, from whom the publisher of the new series, Broadman Press, partly derives its name. The former series was authored and edited by scholars committed to the infallibility of Scripture, making it a solid foundation for the present project. In line with this heritage, all NAC authors affirm the divine inspiration, inerrancy, complete truthfulness, and full authority of the Bible. The perspective of the NAC is unapologetically confessional and rooted in the evangelical tradition.

Since a commentary is a fundamental tool for the expositor or teacher who seeks to interpret and apply Scripture in the church or classroom, the NAC focuses on communicating the theological structure and content of each biblical book. The writers seek to illuminate both the historical meaning and contemporary significance of Holy Scripture.

In its attempt to make a unique contribution to the Christian community, the NAC focuses on two concerns. First, the commentary emphasizes how each section of a book fits together so that the reader becomes aware of the theological unity of each book and of Scripture as a whole. The writers, however, remain aware of the Bible's inherently rich variety. Second, the NAC is produced with the conviction that the Bible primarily belongs to the church. We believe that scholarship and the academy provide an indispensable foundation for biblical understanding and the service of Christ, but the editors and authors of this series have attempted to communicate the findings of their research in a manner that will build up the whole body of Christ. Thus, the commentary concentrates on theological exegesis while providing practical, applicable exposition.

THE NEW AMERICAN COMMENTARY's theological focus enables

the reader to see the parts as well as the whole of Scripture. The biblical books vary in content, context, literary type, and style. In addition to this rich variety, the editors and authors recognize that the doctrinal emphasis and use of the biblical books differs in various places, contexts, and cultures among God's people. These factors, as well as other concerns, have led the editors to give freedom to the writers to wrestle with the issues raised by the scholarly community surrounding each book and to determine the appropriate shape and length of the introductory materials. Moreover, each writer has developed the structure of the commentary in a way best suited for expounding the basic structure and the meaning of the biblical books for our day. Generally, discussions relating to contemporary scholarship and technical points of grammar and syntax appear in the footnotes and not in the text of the commentary. This format allows pastors and interested laypersons, scholars and teachers, and serious college and seminary students to profit from the commentary at various levels. This approach has been employed because we believe that all Christians have the privilege and responsibility to read and seek to understand the Bible for themselves.

Consistent with the desire to produce a readable, up-to-date commentary, the editors selected the *New International Version* as the standard translation for the commentary series. The selection was made primarily because of the NIV's faithfulness to the original languages and its beautiful and readable style. The authors, however, have been given the liberty to differ at places from the NIV as they develop their own translations from the Greek and Hebrew texts.

The NAC reflects the vision and leadership of those who provide oversight for Broadman Press, who in 1987 called for a new commentary series that would evidence a commitment to the inerrancy of Scripture and a faithfulness to the classic Christian tradition. While the commentary adopts an "American" name, it should be noted some writers represent countries outside the United States, giving the commentary an international perspective. The diverse group of writers includes scholars, teachers, and administrators from almost twenty different colleges and seminaries, as well as pastors, missionaries, and a layperson.

The editors and writers hope that THE NEW AMERICAN COMMENTARY will be helpful and instructive for pastors and teachers, scholars and students, for men and women in the churches who study and teach God's Word in various settings. We trust that for editors, authors, and readers alike, the commentary will be used to build up the church, encourage obedience, and bring renewal to God's people. Above all, we pray that the NAC will bring glory and honor to our Lord who has graciously redeemed us and faithfully revealed himself to us in his Holy Word.

SOLI DEO GLORIA
The Editors

Author's Preface

When a professional in the medical field asked me what my recent research concerned, I told him of the present Genesis commentary that had consumed my attention for now eight plus years. His remark was tellingly simple: "Don't we already have one of those?" Yes, I sighed, how do I know it! I am humbled by the number and by the excellence of Genesis commentaries available to students of the Bible today. Mine is one small voice among the many that have commented on the riches of the First Book of Moses. I have remarked selectively on those aspects of the text which I believed were important for understanding the literary shape and the message of the text. Many academic matters, such as detailed discussions of grammar, syntax, and textual criticism, are absent. I included only those items that I believed were most critical to determining the meaning of the text.

I gave more attention in this second volume to the compositional history of the text, but even here I limited myself to the most salient aspects of the discussion. I concluded in the first volume that Genesis exhibits in the main a primary composition authored in the second millennium, most likely during the wilderness sojourn of Israel (see vol. 1A, pp. 68–85). In the present volume I approach the compositional question for each literary unit under the subheading "Composition." I discovered that the literary unit under study normally exhibits literary coherence, which would suggest that the composition is the result of a single author. This coherence can be seen at the macro and micro levels of the text. The typical historical-critical reconstructions derived from source, form, and tradition criticisms entail complex literary growth that is unnecessary, when a simpler explanation is credibly defended at the exegetical level. Although the commentary cannot provide an exhaustive treatment of the debate for a passage, the composition discussions provide a survey of the major views and identify the major literary issues that have generated theories of multiple traditions. In doing so, I offered alternative explanations for what I considered the most compelling argument(s) presented by historical-critical scholars. The literary units that have created more discussion among scholars and/or are considered "classic" texts received more attention.

I am indebted to those persons who made the difference in the successful completion of this second volume. The most important were Dea Grayce Mathews, my wife and confidant, and E. Ray Clendenen, longstanding friend and able General Editor, who patiently encouraged me to continue despite some setbacks. My colleague of fifteen years, Frank Thielman, Professor of Divinity at Beeson Divinity School, persistently showed interest in the project and expressed words of encouragement. Timothy George, my friend and Dean of the Beeson Divinity School at Samford University, enthusiastically supported my research during two sabbatical leaves. Cheryl Cecil of the Samford University Library superbly assisted me in the acquisition of resources. Also, I am appreciative of the detailed attention given by Linda Scott at Broadman & Holman in the preparation of the manuscript for printing.

—Kenneth A. Mathews

Abbreviations

Bible Books

Gen	Isa	Luke
Exod	Jer	John
Lev	Lam	Acts
Num	Ezek	Rom
Deut	Dan	1, 2 Cor
Josh	Hos	Gal
Judg	Joel	Eph
Ruth	Amos	Phil
1, 2 Sam	Obad	Col
1, 2 Kgs	Jonah	1, 2 Thess
1, 2 Chr	Mic	1, 2 Tim
Ezra	Nah	Titus
Neh	Hab	Phlm
Esth	Zeph	Heb
Job	Hag	Jas
Ps (pl. Pss)	Zech	1, 2 Pet
Prov	Mal	1, 2, 3 John
Eccl	Matt	Jude
Song	Mark	Rev

Apocrypha

Add Esth	*The Additions to the Book of Esther*
Bar	*Baruch*
Bel	*Bel and the Dragon*
1,2 Esdr	*1, 2 Esdras*
4 Ezra	*4 Ezra*
Jdt	*Judith*
Ep Jer	*Epistle of Jeremiah*
1,2,3,4 Mac	*1, 2, 3, 4 Maccabees*
Pr Azar	*Prayer of Azariah and the Song of the Three Jews*
Pr Man	*Prayer of Manasseh*
Sir	*Sirach, Ecclesiasticus*
Sus	*Susanna*
Tob	*Tobit*
Wis	*The Wisdom of Solomon*

Commonly Used Sources

AASOR	Annual of the American Schools of Oriental Research
AAT	Ägypten und Altes Testament
AB	Anchor Bible
ABD	*Anchor Bible Dictionary,* ed. D. N Freedman
'Abot R. Nat.	*'Abot de Rabbi Nathan*
Abr.	*De Abrahamo,* Philo
ACCS	*Ancient Christian Commentary on Scripture: Old Testament II, Genesis 12–50,* ed. M. Sheridan
AcOr	*Acta orientalia*
Adv. Jud.	*Adversus Judaeos*
AEL	M. Lichtheim, *Ancient Egyptian Literature*
Ag. Ap.	*Against Apion,* Josephus
AHW	W. von Soden, *Akkadisches Handwörterbuch*
AJA	*American Journal of Archaeology*
AJBA	*Australian Journal of Biblical Archaeology*
AJSL	*American Journal of Semitic Languages and Literature*
Akk.	Akkadian
AnBib	Analecta Biblica
ANET	*Ancient Near Eastern Texts,* ed. J. B. Pritchard
Ant.	*Antiquities,* Josephus
AOAT	Alter Orient und Altes Testament
AOS	American Oriental Society
Apoc. Abr.	*Apocalypse of Abraham*
Ar.	Arabic
ARM	Archives royales de Mari
ArOr	Archiv orientální
AS	Assyriological Studies
As. Mos.	*Assumption of Moses*
ASOR	American Schools of Oriental Research
ASV	American Standard Version
ATD	Das Alte Testament Deutsch
ATR	*Anglican Theological Review*
AusBR	*Australian Biblical Review*
AUSS	*Andrews University Seminary Studies*
AV	Authorized Version
b.	*Babylonian Talmud*
BA	*Biblical Archaeologist*
BAGD	W. Bauer, W. F. Arndt, F. W. Gingrich, and F. W. Danker, *Greek-English Lexicon of the New Testament*
BALS	Bible and Literature Series
BAR	*Biblical Archaeology Review*
BASOR	*Bulletin of the American Schools of Oriental Research*
B. Bat.	*Baba Batra*
BBR	*Bulletin for Biblical Research*
BDB	F. Brown, S. R. Driver, and C. A. Briggs, *Hebrew and English Lexicon of the Old Testament*
BEATAJ	Beiträge zur Erforschung des Alten Testaments und des antiken Judentum
BECNT	Baker Exegetical Commentary on the New Testament

BETL	Bibliotheca ephemeridum theologicarum lovaniensium
BFT	Biblical Foundations in Theology
BHK	*Biblia Hebraica*, ed. R. Kittel
BHRG	*A Biblical Hebrew Reference Grammar*
BHS	*Biblia Hebraica Stuttgartensia*
Bib	*Biblica*
BibInt	*Biblical Interpretation*
BibOr	Biblica et orientalia
BibRev	*Bible Review*
BIS	Biblical Interpretation Series
BJRL	*Bulletin of the Johns Rylands University Library*
BJS	Brown Judaic Studies
BKAT	Biblischer Kommentar: Altes Testament
BMes	Bibliotheca mesopotamica
BMik	*Beth Mikra*
BN	*Biblische Notizen*
BO	*Bibliotheca orientalis*
BR	*Biblical Research*
BRev	*Bible Review*
BSac	*Bibliotheca Sacra*
BSC	Bible Student Commentary
BST	Bible Speaks Today
BT	*The Bible Translator*
BTB	*Biblical Theology Bulletin*
BThSt	Biblisch-theologische Studien
BurH	*Buried History*
BWANT	Beiträge zur Wissenschaft vom Alten und Neuen Testament
BZ	*Biblische Zeitschrift*
BZAW	Beihefte zur ZAW
CAD	*The Assyrian Dictionary of the Oriental Institute of the University of Chicago*
CAH	*Cambridge Ancient History*
CAT	Commentaire de l'Ancien Testament
CB	Century Bible
CBC	Cambridge Bible Commentary
CBQ	*Catholic Biblical Quarterly*
CBQMS	Catholic Biblical Quarterly Monograph Series
CBSC	Cambridge Bible for Schools and Colleges
CC	The Communicator's Commentary
CCK	*Chronicles of Chaldean Kings*, D. J. Wiseman
CCR	*Coptic Church Review*
CCSL	Corpus christianorum: series latina
CD	Cairo *Damascus Document*
CGTC	Cambridge Greek Testament Commentaries
CHAL	*Concise Hebrew and Aramaic Lexicon*, ed. W. L. Holladay
Comm.	J. Calvin, *Commentary on the First Book of Moses Called Genesis*, trans., rev. J. King
ConB	Coniectanea biblica
ConBOT	Coniectanea biblica, Old Testament Series
Congr.	*De Congressu eruditionis gratia*, Philo
COT	*Commentary on the Old Testament*, C. F. Keil and F. Delitzsch

CT	*Christianity Today*
CTM	*Concordia Theological Monthly*
CTR	*Criswell Theological Review*
CurTM	*Currents in Theology and Mission*
DBSup	*Dictionnaire de la Bible: Supplément,* ed. L. Pirot and A. Robert
DCH	*Dictionary of Classical Hebrew,* ed. D. J. A. Clines
DDD	*Dictionary of Deities and Demons in the Bible,* ed. K. van der Toorn, B. Becking, and P. W. van der Horst
Dial.	*Dialogus cum Tryphone*
DISO	C.-F. Jean and J. Hoftijzer, *Dictionnaire des inscriptions sémitiques de l'ouest*
DJD	Discoveries in the Judaean Desert
DSS	Dead Sea Scrolls
EAEHL	*Encyclopedia of Archaeological Excavations in the Holy Land,* ed. M. Avi-Yonah
EBC	Expositor's Bible Commentary
Ebib	Etudes bibliques
EDB	*Eerdmans Dictionary of the Bible,* ed. D. N. Freedman
EDBT	*Evangelical Dictionary of Biblical Theology,* ed. W. A. Elwell
EDT	*Evangelical Dictionary of Theology,* ed. W. A. Elwell (1984)
EE	*Enuma Elish*
EncJud	*Encyclopaedia Judaica* (1971)
ErIsr	*Eretz Israel*
ESV	English Standard Version
ETL	*Ephermerides theologicae lovanienses*
ETR	*Etudes théologiques et religieuses*
ETSMS	Evangelical Theological Society Monograph Series
EuroJTh	*European Journal of Theology*
EV(s)	English Version(s)
EvQ	*Evangelical Quarterly*
ExpTim	*Expository Times*
FB	Forschung zur Bibel
FOTL	Forms of Old Testament Literature
FRLANT	Forschungen zur Religion und Literatur des Alten und Neuen Testaments
Gen. Rab.	*Genesis Rabbah,* ed. J. Neusner
Gk.	Greek
GBH	P. Joüon, *A Grammar of Biblical Hebrew,* 2 vols., trans. and rev. T. Muraoka
GKC	Gesenius's Hebrew Grammar, ed. E. Kautzsch, trans. A. E. Cowley
GNB	Good News Bible
GTJ	*Grace Theological Journal*
HALOT	L. Koehler, W. Baumgartner, and J. J. Stamm, *The Hebrew and Aramaic Lexicon of the Old Testament*
HAR	*Hebrew Annual Review*
HAT	Handbuch zum Alten Testament
HCSB	Holman Christian Standard Bible
HBD	*Harper's Bible Dictionary,* ed. P. Achtemeier
HBT	*Horizons in Biblical Theology*
HKAT	Handkommentar zum Alten Testament

HL	Hittite Laws
HS	*Hebrew Studies*
HSM	Harvard Semitic Monographs
HT	Helps for Translators
HTR	*Harvard Theological Review*
HUCA	*Hebrew Union College Annual*
Ḥul.	*Ḥullin*
IB	*Interpreter's Bible*
ICC	International Critical Commentary
IBHS	B. K. Waltke and M. O'Connor, *Introduction to Biblical Hebrew Syntax*
IDB	*Interpreter's Dictionary of the Bible,* ed. G. A. Buttrick et al.
IEJ	*Israel Exploration Journal*
Int	*Interpretation*
INT	Interpretation: A Bible Commentary for Teaching and Preaching
IOS	*Israel Oriental Studies*
ISBE	*International Standard Bible Encyclopedia,* rev. ed., G. W. Bromiley
JAAR	*Journal of the American Academy of Religion*
JAARSup	*Journal of the American Academy of Religion,* Supplement
JANES	*Journal of Ancient Near Eastern Society*
JAOS	*Journal of the American Oriental Society*
Jastrow	*A Dictionary of the Targumim, the Talmud Babli and Yerushalmi, and the Midrashic Literature,* 2d ed., M. Jastrow
JBL	*Journal of Biblical Literature*
JBQ	*Jewish Bible Quarterly*
JBR	*Journal of Bible and Religion*
JCS	*Journal of Cuneiform Studies*
JEA	*Journal of Egyptian Archaeology*
JEOL	*Jaarbericht van het Vooraziatisch-Egyptisch Gezelschap (Genootschap) Ex oriente lux*
JETS	*Journal of the Evangelical Theological Society*
JJS	*Journal of Jewish Studies*
JNES	*Journal of Near Eastern Studies*
JNSL	*Journal of Northwest Semitic Languages*
Jos. Asen.	*Joseph and Aseneth*
JPOS	*Journal of Palestine Oriental Society*
JPS	Jewish Publication Society
JPSV	Jewish Publication Society Version
JPST	Jewish Publication Society Torah
JQR	*Jewish Quarterly Review*
JSOR	*Journal of the Society for Oriental Research*
JSOT	*Journal for the Study of the Old Testament*
JSOTSup	Journal for the Study of the Old Testament: Supplement Series
JSNTSup	Journal for the Study of the New Testament: Supplement Series
JSS	*Journal of Semitic Studies*
JTS	*Journal of Theological Studies*
JTSNS	*Journal of Theological Studies, New Series*
JTT	*Journal of Translation and Textlinguistics*
Jub.	*Jubilees*

J.W.	*Jewish War,* Josephus
KAI²	*Kanaanäische und aramäische Inschriften,* 2d ed. H. Donner and W. Röllig
KAT	Kommentar zum Alten Testament
KBL	L. Koehler and W. Baumgartner, *Lexicon in Veteris Testamenti libros,* 2d ed., 1958
L.A.B.	*Liber antiquitatum biblicarum* (Pseudo-Philo)
Leg.	*Legum allegoriae,* Philo
LSAWS	Linguistic Studies in Ancient West Semitic
LSJ	Liddell-Scott-Jones, *Greek-English Lexicon*
LW	*Luther's Works. Lectures on Genesis,* ed. J. Pelikan and D. Poellot, trans. G. Schick
LXX	Septuagint
m.	*Midrash*
MAL	Middle Assyrian Laws
Mek.	*Mekilta*
Migr.	*De migratione Abrahami,* Philo
Moʿed Qaṭ	*Moʿed Qaṭan*
MT	Masoretic Text
MS(S)	Manuscript(s)
NAB	New American Bible
NASB	New American Standard Bible
NAC	New American Commentary, ed. R. Clendenen
NBD	*New Bible Dictionary,* ed. J. D. Douglas
NBD³	*New Bible Dictionary,* 3d ed., ed. D. R. W. Wood (1996)
NCBC	New Century Bible Commentary
NEAEHL	*The New Encyclopedia of Archaeological Excavations in the Holy Land,* ed. E. Stern
NEB	New English Bible
Ned.	*Nedarim*
NIB	The New Interpreter's Bible
NICNT	New International Commentary on the New Testament
NICOT	New International Commentary on the Old Testament
NIDNTT	*New International Dictionary of New Testament Theology,* ed. C. Brown
NIDOTTE	*The New International Dictionary of Old Testament Theology and Exegesis,* ed. W. A. VanGemeren
NIV	New International Version
NJB	New Jerusalem Bible
NJPS	New Jewish Publication Society Version
NKJV	New King James Version
NLT	New Living Translation
NLT²	New Living Translation, 2d ed.
NovT	*Novum Testamentum*
NRSV	New Revised Standard Version
NRT	*La nouvelle revue théologique*
NTS	*New Testament Studies*
NTT	Norsk Teologisk Tidsskrift
OBO	Orbis biblicus et orientalis
OEAE	*The Oxford Encyclopedia of Ancient Egypt,* ed. D. B. Redford

OEANE	*The Oxford Encyclopedia of Archaeology in the Near East,* ed. E. M. Meyers
OL	Old Latin
Or	*Orientalia*
OrAnt	*Oriens antiquus*
OrBibLov	*Orientalia et biblica lovaniensia*
OTL	Old Testament Library
OTP	*The Old Testament Pseudepigrapha,* ed. J. H. Charlesworth
OTS	Old Testament Studies
OtSt	*Oudtestamentische Studiën*
par.	parallel (indicates textual parallels)
PEQ	*Palestine Exploration Quarterly*
Pirqe R. El.	*Pirqe Rabbi Eliezer*
POTT	*Peoples of Old Testament Times,* ed. D. J. Wiseman
POTW	*Peoples of the Old Testament World,* ed. A. E. Hoerth, G. L. Mattingly, and E. M. Yamauchi
Ps.-Philo	*Pseudo-Philo*
Pss. Sol	*Psalms of Solomon*
PTMS	Pittsburgh Theological Monograph Series
PTR	*Princeton Theological Review*
QE	*Quaestiones et solutiones in Exodum I, II,* Philo
RA	*Revue d'assyriologie et d'archéologie orientale*
RB	*Revue biblique*
REB	Revised English Bible
ResQ	*Restoration Quarterly*
RSV	Revised Standard Version
RTR	*Reformed Theological Review*
Šabb.	*Šabbat*
SANE	Sources from the Ancient Near East
Sanh.	*Sanhedrin*
SBF Analecta	Studium Biblicum Francisanum Analecta
SBJT	*Southern Baptist Journal of Theology*
SBLDS	Society of Biblical Literature Dissertation Series
SBLMS	Society of Biblical Literature Monograph Series
SBLSCS	Society of Biblical Literature Septuagint and Cognate Studies
SBLSP	Society of Biblical Literature Seminar Papers
SBT	Studies in Biblical Theology
SemeiaSt	Semeia Studies
SHANE	Studies in the History of the Ancient Near East
SHCANE	Studies in the History and Culture of the Ancient Near East
SJLA	Studies in Judaism in Late Antiquity
SP	Samaritan Pentateuch
SR	Studies in Religion/Sciences religieuses
ST	*Studia theologica*
STJD	Studies on the Texts of the Desert of Judah
Strom.	*Stromata*
SWBA	Social World of Biblical Antiquity
Syr.	Syriac
Ta'an.	*Ta'anit*
Tanḥ.	*Tanḥuma*
TDNT	*Theological Dictionary of the New Testament,* ed. G. Kittel and G. Friedrich

TDOT	*Theological Dictionary of the Old Testament,* ed. G. J. Botterweck and H. Ringgren
TEV	Today's English Version
Tg(s).	Targum(s)
Tg. Cant.	*Targum Canticles*
Tg. 1 Chr.	*Targum 1 Chronicles*
Tg. Esth. II	*First or Second Targum of Esther*
Tg. Onq.	*Targum Onqelos,* ed. B. Grossfeld
Tg. Neof.	*Targum Neofiti 1,* ed. M. McNamara
Tg. Ps.-J.	*Targum Pseudo-Jonathan,* ed. M. Mahler
T. Abr.	*Testament of Abraham*
T. Benj.	*Testament of Benjamin*
T.Levi	*Testament of Levi*
T. Reu.	*Testament of Reuben*
T. Naph.	*Testament of Naphtali*
TGUOS	Transactions of the Glasgow University Oriental Society
TJNS	Trinity Journal—New Series
TLOT	*Theological Lexicon of the Old Testament,* ed. E. Jenni and C. Westermann
TLZ	*Theologische Literaturzeitung*
TNTC	Tyndale New Testament Commentaries
TOTC	Tyndale Old Testament Commentaries
TrinJ	*Trinity Journal*
TS	*Theological Studies*
TWAT	*Theologisches Wörterbuch zum Alten Testament,* ed. G. J. Botterweck and H. Ringgren
TWOT	*Theological Wordbook of the Old Testament,* ed. R. Harris et al.
TynBul	*Tyndale Bulletin*
UF	*Ugarit-Forschungen*
Ug.	Ugaritic
UT	C. H. Gordon, *Ugaritic Textbook*
Vg.	Vulgate
VT	*Vetus Testamentum*
VTSup	Vetus Testamentum, Supplements
WBC	Word Biblical Commentaries
WMANT	Wissenschaftliche Monographien zum Alten und Neuen Testament
WTJ	*Westminster Theological Journal*
y.	Jerusalem Talmud
Yal.	*Yalquṭ*
YNER	Yale Near Eastern Researches
ZAH	*Zeitschrift für Althebräistik*
ZAW	*Zeitschrift für die alttestamentliche Wissenschaft*
ZDMG	*Zeitschrift der deutschen morgenländischen Gesellschaft*
ZDPV	*Zeitschrift des deutschen Palästina-Vereins*
ZPEB	*Zondervan Pictorial Encyclopedia of the Bible*
1 Clem	*1 Clement*
1QapGen	*Genesis Apocryphon* from Qumran Cave 1
1QS	*Rule of the Community* from Qumran Cave 1
2Bar.	*2 Baruch (Syriac Apocalypse)*
4Q225	psJub[a], *pseudoJubilees[a]* from Qumran Cave 4
4Q252	CommGen A, *Commentary on Genesis A* from Qumran Cave 4

Contents

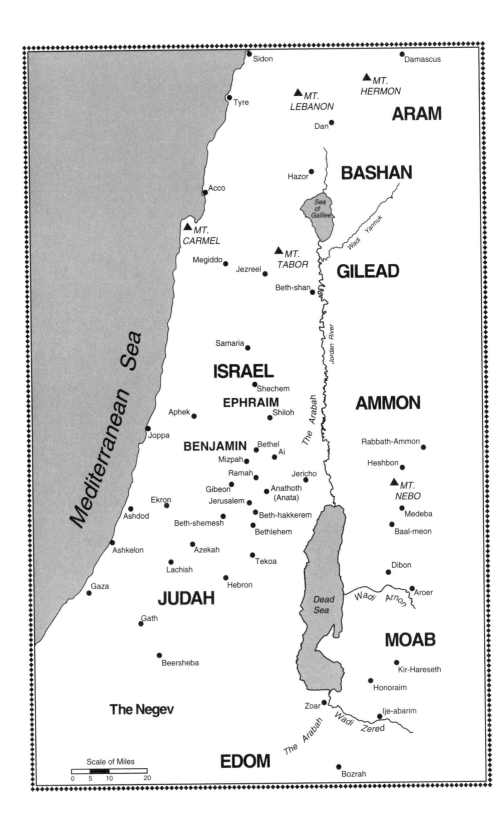

Genesis 11:27–50:26

INTRODUCTION

Genesis could well be entitled the Book of the Fathers, or as in Jewish tradition "The Book of the Upright" *(sēper ha-yāšār/yĕšārîm)*,[1] for it establishes the ancestral roots of Israel both historically and in terms of its spiritual heritage. We have already shown how Genesis functions as the prelude to the broader concern of the Pentateuch's attention on the Sinai covenant (vol. 1A, pp. 42–51). The identity of Israel's covenant-making God was expressed in the primal relationship between God and Israel's progenitors by the formulaic trilogy "the God of Abraham, the God of Isaac, and the God of Jacob" (e.g., Exod 3:6,15–16; 4:5; Ps 47:9) or by the collective "fathers" with *Yahweh* (LORD), "the LORD God of your fathers" (Deut 1:21; 6:3; 12:1; 27:3).[2] Similarly, the anticipated possession of the land was cast as the divine fulfillment of earlier promises made to the Fathers, "to Abraham, to Isaac, and to Jacob" (50:24; cp. Exod 2:24).[3]

Moses' commission to rescue the Hebrews and shepherd them to Canaan was explained theologically as God's response to his covenant made centuries earlier with Father Abraham and, importantly, with his "seed" (e.g., 15:18; 17:9; 22:17). It was this continuum between Abraham and his "seed," that is, the Mosaic audience, that provided for the claim of God on Israel and for its deliverance from Egypt. Yet the divine promises were not intended for *all* of Abraham's seed since Genesis carefully segregates the elect versus nonelect lines (e.g., 11:10–26; 21:12; Rom 9:7). When Moses' Israel later encountered the nations—including the Ishmaelites, Edomites, Ammonites, Moabites, and Keturah's children (Arabian tribes)—the nonelect offspring could prove a potential threat to the survival of the Hebrews. Genesis explained to later Israel the origins of these rival nations as their kinsmen and how they were disqualified or had discredited themselves.

By the time of the arrival of Moses' Israel at the banks of the Jordan, the challenge to the fulfillment of the covenant had long shifted from the question of descendants (barren Sarah) to suspense over Israel's possession of the promised real estate. The divine land grant found in Genesis had charted the territory reserved for Jacob's twelve tribes (e.g., 15:18–21). The Fathers experienced a

---

[1] Cp. "the Book of Jashar," Josh 10:13; 2 Sam 1:18; Num 23:10 counts Jacob, the namesake of Israel, as among the upright (יְשָׁרִים, *yĕšārîm;* NIV "righteous").

[2] Also in Genesis, see "the God of Abraham your father" (26:24); "the LORD God of Abraham your father, and the God of Isaac" (28:13); "the God of my father Abraham and God of my father Isaac" (32:9); and "the God of your father" (46:3; 49:25; 50:17).

[3] Also Exod 3:6,15–16; 4:5; 6:3,8; 32:13; 33:1; Lev 26:42; Num 32:11; Deut 1:8; 6:10; 9:5,27; 29:12; 30:20; 34:4.

roaming life, drifting in and out of the promised Canaan during excursions to Egypt and Paddan Aram, and finally resided in Egypt. But Genesis as a proto-type for later Israel's experience showed that the Fathers' experiences had set the typological groundwork for the future dispossession of Canaan's peoples. Examples are Abraham's armed victory over invading kings (chap. 14), Canaanite recognition of the patriarchs' rights to properties (e.g., Abimelech, chaps. 20; 26), the acquisition of a family burial site at Machpelah (23:17–20), and the heavenly assurance of Jacob's return and possession of Canaan from his self-imposed exile (28:13–15). Even a timetable for the dissolution of Canaan's inhabitants was found in the patriarchal stories (15:13–16). Although the Jacob family appeared well entrenched in Egypt at the book's end, Jacob's and Joseph's "deathbed" instructions for final interment with their fathers in Canaan looked expectantly toward the patriarchal homestead (49:29; 50:25). The very migratory movements of the patriarchs up and down the land served as a proleptic notice that the Hebrews were staking out their claim. This asso-ciation then of later Israel's possession of Canaan and the divine oath to the patriarchs was Israel's theological orthodoxy. Canaan was Israel's birthright and destiny by the appointment of God.

All of this is to underscore that the identity of Israel as a people, the nature of their relationship to God, and their claim on the fatherland had their anteced-ents in the story of the patriarchs. Such a historical and yet eschatological per-spective on their place among the nations made Genesis the necessary preamble to the birth of national Israel and its possession of Canaan (Exodus-Deuteronomy). The existence of the patriarchs and the historicity of their expe-riences were assumed by the ancient author of the Pentateuch. Since the histo-ricity of the patriarchal stories is in a "free-fall" among biblical critics today, we will address in this introduction whether in fact the purported history of Israel's ancestral roots is credible and hence whether the Pentateuch's theology is grounded in actual event or rests on muddled remembrances.

For the Christian expositor, the patriarchal history is of as great a conse-quence as it was for the synagogue. The opening verse of the New Testament announces it so: "A record of the genealogy of Jesus Christ the son of David, *the son of Abraham*" (Matt 1:1 [italics mine]). Matthew and Luke relied on the actual Abrahamic descent of Jesus of Nazareth as they showed that the long-awaited realization of the promises was found in the Messiah Jesus. This issue of Jesus' lineal credibility (which is commonly neglected by moderns) was a vital tenet for their case, showing that Jesus was the promised Savior of Jew and Gentile. Paul made explicit the *spiritual* significance of this kinship when he equated their spiritual descendants: "If you belong to Christ, then are you Abra-ham's seed, and heirs according to the promise" (Gal 3:29; cf. Gal 3:6–9; Rom 4:9–17). Simply put, the identity of Jesus of Nazareth and the character of the Christian gospel are enmeshed with the Hebrew Fathers and their claim that

God had declared an irrevocable allegiance to Abraham and his appointed descendants (e.g., Luke 1:73; Acts 7:17; Gal 3:16).

Moreover, the author of Genesis (and the Pentateuch) assumed that the God of Abraham, identified in Genesis as *El Shaddai* (17:1), was the same deity who revealed himself at Sinai as *Yahweh* (Exod 6:2–3). Was he wrong? Was the covenant deity of the patriarchs the clan deity *Shaddai?* Or the Canaanite deity *El?* Or were the God of Abraham and *Yahweh* one and the same? Was the use of *Yahweh* in Genesis anachronistic? We will pursue whether the genetic relationship between the religion of Abraham and that of Moses, as Genesis and Exodus depict it, was sound or a mistaken idea about the past.

Finally, related to the question of the patriarchal religion is the theme and motifs that make up the First Book. Our introduction therefore will conclude with a discussion of the literary-theological ideas that characterize the patriarchal narratives.

1. Historicity and History[4]

It is far beyond the scope of this introduction to discuss satisfactorily the historicity of the patriarchs. The scholarly literature is staggering, and the evidence put forward encompasses sources from two millennia derived from archaeological recoveries coming from virtually every significant corner of the ancient Near East. We will sketch the outline of the debate, point the reader to the major participants and views in the discussion, and conclude with our approach in this commentary.

Before the 1970s, biblical scholars typically relied on the testimony of the Old Testament for reconstructing the history of Israel, including the patriarchs. Today, some historians have all but eliminated the Old Testament as a reputable voice in the task of writing a history of Israel. F. Hartenstein explains that the hermeneutics of suspicion we see practiced today among some is the result of two leading factors.[5] First, the date of the writing of the Old Testament has been

---

[4] By "historicity" we mean historical actuality (i.e., authenticity); "history" is used commonly for two phenomena: (1) the process of events in the past and (2) the selective telling of past events, a verbal representation (i.e., historiography). The difference between "historiography" and "fiction" (i.e., fictional writing as a genre) is complex since the two overlap by sharing features of literary artistry and history (cf. nineteenth century historical novels, e.g., Sir Walter Scott's *Ivanhoe* [1820]). The core difference is the intention and constraints of the writing. Historiography requires the author to seek to represent authentic past events; the author may distort the past, in which case it may be deemed poor historiography (the standard is whether or not the verbal representation is a faithful reproduction), but it must still be considered history writing. Fiction writing, however, does not require the same standard of the author, whose works may not be referential to any external actuality. For a discussion of these terms, see V. P. Long, *The Art of Biblical History* (Grand Rapids: Zondervan, 1994), 58–87.

[5] F. Hartenstein, "Religionsgeschichte Israels—ein Überblick über die Forschung seit 1990," *Verkündigung und Forschung* 48 (2003): 2–28.

pushed down later and later, even some assigning the whole to the Persian period.[6] Second, archaeological investigation has produced a Syro-Palestinian history that does not correspond with the Bible's supposed "ancient Israel," its history and its religion. As V. P. Long observes, radical skepticism has resulted for some in assessing the biblical accounts as "inventions of Persian- and Hellenistic-period novelists."[7] Those who have rejected the biblical testimony as useful have been tagged as the "minimalists," and those who have maintained some appreciation for the witness of the Hebrew text are known as the "maximalists."[8] The debate concerning the historicity of ancient Israel or the patriarchs in particular, which is our concern, is shaped by an *a priori* decision about which kind of evidence should be given priority, the literary (Bible) or archaeological. Also, should the Bible be read as ancient texts customarily are, or should form-tradition methods be employed that reconstruct the traditions before evaluating their value as a witness? Is it a late composition (monarchic or exilic) shaped by succeeding waves of religio-political traditions, useful only as a witness to the traditions about the patriarchs but not the patriarchs themselves? Or is it a reliable ancient testimony that may serve adequately for understanding the persons and events of Israel's forefathers?

These methodological concerns have significant implications for the interpreter's task. If the biblical account is discredited, then we lose the sole evidence for the patriarchs themselves since the individuals Abraham, Isaac, and Jacob are not known in ancient sources outside of the Bible. If it is deemed that the narratives reflect traditions that have no correspondence to the persons of patriarchal Genesis, then the quest for establishing a historical context for the forefathers of Israel is pointless. The importance of this decision has been

---

[6] E.g., P. R. Davies, *In Search of "Ancient Israel,"* JSOTSup 148 (Sheffield: JSOT Press, 1992).

[7] V. P. Long, "Introduction," in *Windows into Old Testament History: Evidence, Argument, and the Crisis of "Biblical Israel"* (Grand Rapids: Eerdmans/Cambridge, U.K., 2002), 1.

[8] For the minimalists, e.g., see Davies, *In Search of "Ancient Israel"*; K. W. Whitelam, *The Invention of Israel: The Silencing of Palestinian History* (London: Routledge, 1996); L. L. Grabbe, ed., *Can a "History of Israel" Be Written?* JSOTSup 245 (Sheffield: Sheffield Academic Press, 1997); id., *"Like a Bird in a Cage": The Invasion of Sennacherib in 701 BCE,* JSOTSup 363 (London/New York: Sheffield Academic Press, 2003); N. P. Lemche, *The Israelites in History and Tradition* (Louisville: Westminster John Knox, 1998). For those who take the maximalist position and offer a critique of the opposing view, see V. P. Long, ed., *Israel's Past in Present Research: Essays on Ancient Israelite Historiography* (Winona Lake: Eisenbrauns, 1999); id., *Windows into Old Testament History;* D. M. Howard, Jr. and M. Grisanti, eds., *Giving the Sense: Understanding and Using Old Testament Historical Texts* (Grand Rapids: Kregel, 2003); I. W. Provan, V. P. Long, and T. Longman, *A Biblical History of Israel* (Louisville: Westminster John Knox, 2003); and W. G. Dever, *Who Were the Early Israelites and Where Did They Come From?* (Grand Rapids: Eerdmans, 2003). For a lively debate regarding historiographical method, see D. Henige, "Deciduous, Perennial or Evergreen? The Choices in the Debate over 'Early Israel,'" *JSOT* 47 (2003): 387–412 and the response of Provan, "Pyrrhon, Pyrrhus and the Possibility of the Past: A Response to David Henige," 413–38.

minimized by tradition critics. P. K. McCarter is slightly more optimistic than the minimalists when he contends that, unlike the Isaac and Jacob figures who were eponymous (fictitious) ancestors of clan groups, Abraham was an actual historical person, but he denies that we can know anything about when or where he lived.[9] Moreover, there is no benefit theologically for clinging to a historical individual since ultimately that person is irretrievable.[10]

There are limitations to what historical studies can achieve. In using solely historical tools, such as literary sources and material artifacts, no manner of documentation can show that God made himself known to Abraham and established exclusive promises with him and his family. Even if we were to recover from the Syro-Palestinian region a heap of cuneiform clay tablets bearing all the earmarks of authenticity that give a near contemporaneous history of the Abraham clan, it would still be outside the ability of historians to verify that the *interpretation* of those events as found in Genesis is true. For example, the historian cannot authenticate the narrator's interpretation of Abraham's faith (15:6). But we differ from T. L. Thompson, who insists that a nonhistorical Abraham does not undermine Christian faith: "In fact we can say that the faith of Israel is not a historical faith, in the sense of a faith based on historical event; it is rather a faith within history."[11] Historical integrity is teleologically essential for interpretation, and it is indefensible theologically that the faith of the Fathers is viable even if the Fathers were only a literary construct.

Both literary and historical studies together can show (not prove) whether the claims of the Genesis narratives have credibility or have been falsified.[12] Since the patriarchal narratives claim to be historical (and both Jewish and Christian traditions read them this way), there is the possibility of an intersection between the Genesis account and the historian's task. Neither Genesis nor ancient Near Eastern remains are exhaustive. It is not condemning that Genesis does not name Egypt's pharaoh, giving us a precise synchronic foothold, nor that the person Abraham is unattested in antiquity outside of the Bible. In fact there is no person in all of Genesis who is known from ancient extrabiblical sources. We remember, however, that it was only recently that the ancient Near East gave us the first extrabiblical testimony to the "House of David" with reference to an Aramean victory over the "king of Israel" in a ninth century stela

---

[9] P. K. McCarter, "The Historical Abraham," *Int* 42 (1988): 351–52.

[10] G. Ramsey makes this point for the elusive "historical Jacob," who, according to tradition critics, was not in fact the father of the twelve tribes and was originally unrelated to tribal Israel (*The Quest for the Historical Israel* [Atlanta: John Knox, 1981], 121–22). For examples in NT scholarship, see J. Fitzmyer, *Romans*, AB (New York: Doubleday, 1992), 379 and J. Walls, "The Flight from Truth in New Testament Scholarship," *CSR* 25 (1995): 180–96.

[11] T. L. Thompson, *The Historicity of the Patriarchal Narratives: The Quest for the Historical Abraham*, BZAW 133 (Berlin: de Gruyter, 1974), 328–29.

[12] See S. M. Warner, "The Patriarchs and Extra-Biblical Sources," *JSOT* 2 (1977): 50–61.

coming from Tell Dan.[13] Virtually no one until the minimalists would have thought to deny David's person and role as dynastic founder, so impressive is the weight of the biblical testimony.[14] Extrabiblical data are useful in evaluating the general historical and cultural background of the patriarchs, though it is difficult to assign a specific date on the basis of the historical and archaeological information alone.

(1) Historical Abraham or Abraham of Tradition

The dispute over story versus history in the interpretation of the patriarchs is both old and new. It is an old debate, for J. Wellhausen's nineteenth-century judgment was that no historical knowledge of the patriarchs could be obtained, only an understanding of the era in which the patriarchal stories were concocted (monarchic period).[15] Thus Abraham was not "a historical person; he might with more likelihood be regarded as a free creation of unconscious art."[16] The father of form criticism Hermann Gunkel continued the skepticism of Wellhausen, treating the patriarchal stories as folk stories (Sage) that might have contained a "historical echo" but were so overlaid with fancy and imagination that they could not serve as a reliable source for determining any patriarchal event or place.[17]

But the debate is also new because, though the distrust of the patriarchal nar-

---

[13] A. Biran and J. Naveh, "An Aramaic Stele Fragment from Tel Dan," *IEJ* 43 (1993): 81–98; and a popular summary in "David Found at Dan," *BAR* (1994): 26–39; D. N. Freedman and J. Geoghegan, "'House of David' Is There!" *BAR* 21 (1995): 78–79; and A. Lemaire, "The Tel Dan Stela as a Piece of Royal Historiography," *JSOT* 81 (1998): 3–14. Also cf. inscriptional evidence of biblical "Ekron" (1 Sam 6:17) and of a Philistine king whose Hebrew equivalent is "Achish," the name of a Philistine king in the Bible, in S. Gitin, T. Rothan, and J. Naveh, "Ekron Identity Confirmed: A Unique Royal Inscription Offers Clues to Early Philistine History," *Archaeology* 51 (1998): 30–31; Gitin dubs the inscription a "smoking gun" in "Israelite and Philistine Cult and the Archaeological Record in Iron Age II: The Smoking Gun Phenomenon," *Symbiosis, Symbolism, and the Power of the Past: Canaan, Ancient Israel, and Their Neighbors from the Late Bronze Age through Roman Palaestina* (Winona Lake: Eisenbrauns, 2003), 279–95; and see Z. Zevit, "Three Debates about Bible and Archaeology, *Bib* 83 (2002): 16.

[14] N. P. Lemche, T. L. Thompson, W. G. Dever, and P. K. McCarter, Jr., "Face to Face: Biblical Minimalists Meet Their Challengers," *BAR* 23 (1997): 26–42, 66.

[15] Dever observed: "These recent works [the minimalists] do not signal a new approach, much less a breakthrough in writing a history of Israel. Rather they mark a return full-circle to Wellhausen; they simply confirm the intellectual exhaustion, after a century and a half, of the philological method and the classic literary-critical apparatus that accompanied it" ("Philology, Theology and Archaeology: What Kind of History of Israel Do We Want, and What Is Possible?" *The Archaeology of Israel: Constructing the Past, Interpreting the Present*, JSOTSup 237 [Sheffield: Sheffield Academic Press, 1997], 294).

[16] J. Wellhausen, *Prolegomena to the History of Israel* (1885; Eng. reprint ed., Atlanta: Scholars Press, 1994), 320.

[17] H. Gunkel, *Genesis*, trans. M. Biddle (1910; 3d ed. Macon, Ga.: Mercer University Press, 1994), xiv–xvii.

ratives of the Wellhausenian sort diminished in influence in the mid-twentieth century, it has been revived with vigor in the last three decades. What had generated until recently the more favorable view of the Genesis narratives for identifying the patriarchal era was the collocation of the biblical text's general outlines of Israel's history and the remarkable epigraphic finds and archaeological advances since the 1930s. What is new is the tyranny of archaeological evidence over textual (biblical) evidence and the assumption that the biblical tradents could only produce "events of tradition," not information referential to past reality.[18]

The chief architects of the more favorable view of the patriarchal narratives during the mid-twentieth century were W. F. Albright and N. Glueck, followed by G. E. Wright and J. Bright, whose *History of Israel* gave this view wide circulation in America.[19] C. H. Gordon and E. A. Speiser were also leading spokesmen for the movement that identified the patriarchs with a particular historical period in the ancient Near East.[20] This "American school," as it was known, was given its finest defense, however, by French archaeologist R. de Vaux, and its view was held by others such as British scholar H. H. Rowley.[21] This is not to say that the American school accepted the Genesis narratives without employing source and tradition-history reconstructions,[22] but for them to argue that the patriarchal stories possessed a historical base that could be assigned to a particular period was a significant departure from Wellhausenian skepticism.

A. Alt and the tradition-critics M. Noth and G. von Rad took up the debate with the burgeoning "archaeological school" (as it was also known) in the

---

[18] Cf. the critique in J. B. Kofoed, "Epistemology, Historical Method, and the 'Copenhagen School,'" *Windows into Old Testament History,* 23–43; id., *Text and History* (Winona Lake: Eisenbrauns, 2005).

[19] E.g., W. F. Albright, *From the Stone Age to Christianity,* 2d ed. (Baltimore: Johns Hopkins Press, 1946), 179–89; *The Biblical Period from Abraham to Ezra* (New York: Harper & Row, 1963), 1–9; *Yahweh and the Gods of Canaan* (London: School of Oriental and African Studies, University of London, 1968), 53–109; N. Glueck, "The Age of Abraham in the Negeb," *BA* 18 (1955): 2–9; and *Rivers in the Desert: A History of the Negeb* (New York: Ferrar, Straus, Cudahy, 1959), 61–84, 102–7; G. E. Wright, *Biblical Archaeology,* rev. ed. (Philadelphia: Westminster/London: Duckworth, 1962), 40–52; and J. Bright, *A History of Israel,* 3d ed. (Philadelphia: Westminster, 1981), 67–103.

[20] C. H. Gordon, *Introduction to Old Testament Times* (Ventor, N.J.: Ventnor, 1953), 100–119; "The Patriarchal Age," *JBR* 21 (1953): 238–43; E. Speiser, "Wife-Sister Motif in the Patriarchal Narratives," in *Biblical and Other Studies* (Brandeis University, 1962), 15–28 = *Oriental and Biblical Studies: Collected Essays of E. A. Speiser* (Philadelphia: University of Pennsylvania Press, 1967), 62–82; and *Genesis,* AB (New York: Doubleday, 1964), xxxvii–lxii.

[21] R. de Vaux, *The Early History of Israel,* trans. D. Smith (London: Darton, Longman, & Todd; Philadelphia: Westminster, 1978 [1971, 1974]); also A. Parrot, *Abraham and His Times,* trans. J. Farley (Philadelphia: Fortress, 1968); H. Cazelles, "Patriarches," *IDBSup* 8:81–156; and H. H. Rowley, *The Servant of the Lord and Other Essays,* 2d ed. (Oxford: Blackwell, 1965), 281–318.

[22] E.g., de Vaux essentially agreed with Noth on the formation of the patriarchal traditions in their prehistory (*Early History of Israel,* 165–77).

heated decades of the 1950s and 1960s. Noth was conversant with the vast archaeological recoveries of his day, and he acknowledged that the patriarchs were actually historical persons but that not much could be known about their times, events, and personalities. As the archaeological school had argued, Noth agreed that the migrations of the early second millennium may have been the setting for the appearance of the patriarchs in Canaan,[23] but he opposed the optimism of those who had asserted that the authenticity of the broad outline of the patriarchal stories had been vindicated by the archaeologist's spade.

Renewed opposition to the Albright-Bright approach was fueled by two monographs presented in the mid–1970s in which, working independently, the authors repudiated the archaeological claims of the American school and concluded that the historical setting of the patriarchal narratives best fit in the first millennium. T. L. Thompson's *Historicity of the Patriarchal Narratives* put the Yahwist (J) narrative source in the early first millennium as was customary but returned to Wellhausen's skepticism that the traditions available to J were ancient and reliable.[24] More divergent was the conclusion of J. van Seters, who identified the period of J's composition as late as the exilic period; but he, like Thompson, also denied any value of the tradition for reconstructing a so-called "Patriarchal Age." The Genesis narratives possessed no authentic ancient memory of pre-Israelite times and reflected only the era of their composition.[25]

Recent histories of Israel welcomed the conclusions of Thompson and van Seters and took up the former view of Wellhausen and his successors, such as H. Gressman,[26] eliminating Genesis as a proper historical source for Israel's prehistory and dating its narratives to the exilic period.[27] G. W. Ahlström con-

---

[23] M. Noth, *The History of Israel*, trans. S. Godman (New York: Harper & Row, 1958), 120–26.

[24] Thompson, *Historicity of the Patriarchal Narratives*, 324–26. Subsequently, Thompson, in *The Origin Tradition of Ancient Israel*, JSOTSup 55 (Sheffield: JSOT Press, 1987), examined Gen 1 to Exod 23, observing that the Pentateuch is story, i.e., only Israel's self-understanding of its origins, and cannot be safely appropriated for historiography; he found five or six independent "complex-chain narratives" that were contemporaneous narrative chains brought together in the *Toledoth* by 600–550 B.C.

[25] J. van Seters, *Abraham in History and Tradition* (New Haven: Yale University Press, 1975), 120–22. He has since produced several works addressing Israelite historiography, contending that the core of the Pentateuch is authored by his exilic Yahwist (J): *In Search of History* (New Haven: Yale University Press, 1983); *Prologue to History: The Yahwist as Historian in Genesis* (Louisville: Westminster/John Knox, 1992); and *The Life of Moses* (Kampen: Kok, 1994).

[26] Gressman's (1910) attribution of the migrations and "history" of the patriarchal materials as imagination is quoted approvingly, e.g., by Thompson, Soggin, and Ahlström.

[27] E.g., both Lemche and Soggin conclude that nothing of historical value can be known from before the monarchy. See N. P. Lemche, *Ancient Israel: A New History of Israelite Society*, trans. F. Cryer (Sheffield: JSOT Press, 1988), 114–17, and J. Soggin, *An Introduction to the History of Israel and Judah*, trans. J. Bowden, 2d rev. ed. (Valley Forge: Trinity Press International, 1993), 89–99. J. M. Miller and J. Hayes comment that Genesis–Joshua "is an artificial and theologically influenced literary construction," making anything before the period of the Judges mere "guesswork" for historians (*A History of Ancient Israel and Judah* [Philadelphia: Westminster, 1986], 78).

cluded: "It is quite clear that the narrator of the Genesis stories did not have accurate knowledge about the prehistory of the Israelites. That was not necessary either, because his purpose was not to write history."[28] Today the chief spokesmen of the minimalists include members of the so-called "Copenhagen School" of Thompson, P. R. Davies, and N. P. Lemche. In their opinion, there were no "biblical Israelites." Lemche demurs "the Scholar's Israel," including the German and American Schools, by which he means "it was little more than a repetition of the image of Israel as found in the Old Testament, however, transferred into the historical world of which it had no part, being the creation of the imagination of the biblical authors."[29]

But the defense of the archaeological position, though modified at significant points, has been offered by many. The third edition of Bright's *History* did not stray from his earlier opinions and approach in this regard (1981).[30] A review of the archaeological and sociological evidence was undertaken in a collection of essays edited by A. R. Millard and D. J. Wiseman (1983), defending the historicity of the patriarchs and the antiquity of the biblical witness.[31] Millard upheld the case again in the *Anchor Bible Dictionary*,[32] and K. A. Kitchen concluded that the patriarchal accounts are historically reliable with their "roots in the early second millennium B.C."[33] Kitchen followed on his earlier studies with *On the Reliability of the Old Testament* (2003) in which he shows in a more comprehensive examination of the evidence that the patriarchal accounts depict an era that comports well with the political and cultural realities known in Syro-Palestine of the early second millennium.[34] Hermeneutical responses to the minimalist-maximalist debate have been forged especially by V. P. Long and I. W. Provan. Among major com-

---

[28] G. W. Ahlström, *The History of Ancient Palestine* (Minneapolis: Fortress/Sheffield: JSOT Press, 1993), 186.

[29] N. P. Lemche, *The Israelites in History and Tradition* (London: SPCK/Louisville: Westminster John Knox, 1998), 161.

[30] In his thorough review of the evidence, W. G. Dever concluded that ca. 2000–1800 was suitable for the "*nucleus* of the patriarchal traditions," but he distanced himself from the methodology and historical claims for the patriarchal traditions of the Albright-Wright-Bright school ("Palestine in the Second Millennium BCE: The Archaeological Picture," in *Israelite and Judean History* [Philadelphia: Westminster, 1977], 70–119, esp. 117–18.

[31] A. R. Millard and D. J. Wiseman, eds., *Essays on the Patriarchal Narratives* (Winona Lake: Eisenbrauns, 1983).

[32] A. R. Millard, "Abraham," *ABD* 1.35–41.

[33] K. A. Kitchen, "Genesis 12–50 in the Near Eastern World," in *He Swore an Oath: Biblical Themes from Genesis 12–50: Studies for D. J. Wiseman* (Cambridge: Tyndale House, 1993), 67–92; "The Patriarchal Age: Myth or History?" *BAR* 21 (1995): 48–57, 88, 90–92, 94–95.

[34] Id., *On the Reliability of the Old Testament* (Grand Rapids: Eerdmans/Cambridge, UK, 2003), 313–72.

mentaries on Genesis, N. Sarna and G. Wenham, for example, espoused the essential reliability of the narratives.[35] Recently, collections of essays, for example *Windows into Old Testament History* and *Giving the Sense,*[36] have challenged the evidential and methodological conclusions of the minimalists. In Part I of *A Biblical History of Israel,* entitled "History, Historiography, and Bible," Provan, Long, and Longman effectively dissent from the methodology and assumptions of the "biblical-history-is-dead" judgment and proceed to produce a biblical history that has "the biblical texts at the heart of its enterprise."[37]

(2) Text, Tradition, and Spade

The present impasse points up the problems historians face in considering the value of the biblical witness. First, what is the nature of the narratives (i.e., "traditions") and their relationship to the events they portray? And second, what is the proper place of archaeology's testimony? Moreover, can the archaeological record present a sufficiently clear picture so as to place the patriarchs in a defined era? Even more fundamental to this question is whether historians today should work within the biblical-historical framework.

We have already addressed the first concern regarding the literary composition of Genesis (see vol. 1A, pp. 68–85, and "Preface" in this volume), but here we will relate it specifically to the problem of the historicity of the patriarchs. A common belief is that the Genesis narratives are composite in nature, coming from the monarchic period and hence reflecting the milieu of the tenth century (the revisionists of this consensus have increased the gap down to the exilic/postexilic periods). Many scholars also assume on the basis of anthropological studies that the simple kinship of Abraham-Isaac-Jacob is a fiction, obscuring a complex historical situation, and expresses the relationship of diverse ethnic groups.[38] The persons of the genealogies supposedly were not individuals but eponymous heads who represented tribal groups.

The second issue that created this impasse is the methodological problems inherent in the tools of archaeology. The archaeological school argued for the reliability (not certitude) of the patriarchal traditions on the basis of these converging lines of evidence that pointed to the Middle Bronze period (ca. 2200–

---

[35] N. Sarna, בְּרֵאשִׁית *Genesis,* JPST (Philadelphia: Jewish Publication Society, 1989); G. Wenham, *Genesis 16–50,* WBC (Dallas: Word, 1995).

[36] See n. 8 above.

[37] Provan, Long, and Longman, *Biblical History,* 3.

[38] See R. Wilson, *Genealogy and History in the Biblical World,* YNER 7 (New Haven: Yale University Press, 1977) and, e.g., P. K. McCarter Jr., "The Patriarchal Age," *Ancient Israel* (Englewood Cliffs, N.J.: Prentice-Hall/Washington: Biblical Archaeology Society, 1988), 13–16, and Miller and Hayes, *History of Ancient Israel and Judah,* 59–60.

$1550)^{39}$ as the historical and cultural setting for the patriarchs:^{40}

1. The onomastica (names) of persons and towns in the Genesis narratives correspond to authentic early second-millennium names of the Amorite dialect that are attested in cuneiform texts coming from north Syria and Mesopotamia (see comments on Gen 11:26–31 and vol. 1A, pp. 497–500).

2. The migration of the Terah clan from Ur to Haran and the subsequent movements of Abraham in Canaan and the patriarchal descent into Egypt are thought to have a historical analogy from this early period in the widespread movements of the Amorites (see vol. 1A, p. 456).

3. Among these Amorite cities was the kingdom of Mari near Haran whose texts (eighteenth century) provided significant information about the political and social history of the Amorites. Mari's tribal life involved both sedentary life and pastoral migration, which has been termed "dimorphic." The pastoral life of the patriarchs is similar to the lifestyle evidenced at Mari among tribal groups named in the texts.

4. The settlements of Canaan during the early second millennium is consistent with the biblical portrait. Sites that were visited by the patriarchs were found to have existed during the twentieth to the eighteenth centuries; the central highlands and the Negeb where the patriarchs were said to traverse were sparsely populated, permitting them to move about unhindered.

5. Hurrian family law and customs depicted in the Nuzi tablets (Upper Mesopotamia), coming from the fifteenth and fourteenth centuries, showed remarkable parallels with patriarchal practices, indicating that they were of the same general historical and social milieu.

6. The distinctive features of patriarchal religion with its worship of *El* rather than *Yahweh* by name, was an authentic second-millennium memory.

Most advocates freely admit today that no one piece of evidence is conclusive and recognize that not all of the aforementioned arguments have stood up to continued scrutiny. Yet when the evidence is taken together—the onomastica, linguistic, and sociological evidence—the patriarchal narratives possess the trappings of authentic remembrances of a patriarchal time when pastoral tribal clans migrated to Canaan from among whose descen-

---

^{39} For the periodization of Syrian-Palestinian chronology, see *The New Encyclopedia of Archaeological Excavations in the Holy Land* (Jerusalem: Israel Exploration Society & Carta/New York: Simon & Schuster, 1993), in which Middle Bronze I = the distinctive period EBIV-MBI, 2200–2000 B.C. (for this revised nomenclature see W. G. Dever, "The EBIV-MBI Horizon in Transjordan and Southern Palestine," *BASOR* 210 [1973]: 37–63).

^{40} Within the archaeological school were alternative dates: C. H. Gordon suggested the fifteenth to fourteenth centuries due to the Nuzi evidence of the same period ("Biblical Customs and the Nuzu Tablets," *BA* 3 [1940]: 1–12 = *BAR* 2 [1964]: 21–33; *Introduction*, 103) and S. Herrmann argued for the end of the second millennium based on the narratives' Aramean connections (the Arameans became influential in the twelfth century; *A History of Israel in Old Testament Times*, trans. J. Bowden [Philadelphia: Fortress, 1975], 450).

dants the ancestors of Israel derived.

Many of the particulars challenging the claims of the archaeological school by Thompson (and others) rightly identified excesses, and we will reflect these later in our discussion of the evidence. Here, however, we want to address the revisionist movement in historiography calling for an independent approach to writing Israel's history—independent of the Bible as historiographic. This is due in large part to the increasing skepticism regarding the value of the Bible as a reliable testimony. Thompson, in his *Early History of the Israelite People,* showed that though the Alt-Noth and Albright-Bright positions differed about the literary sources and archaeology's merit, they still worked within a framework that looked to the biblical-historical witness as their reference point. Theirs was the ongoing attempt to write a history of the premonarchic period.[41] But now the minimalists are calling for a "secular" history without reference to or explicit dependence on the Hebrew Bible, using epigraphical and artifactual evidence, settlement patterns, and ecological studies in an interdisciplinary way.[42] Ahlström expressed the reason for the new aversion to the Bible: "Biblical historiography is a literary phenomenon whose primary goal is not to create a record of factual events. . . . Biblical historiography is not a product built on facts. It is the narrator's outlook and ideology rather than known facts."[43]

J. M. Miller answered the deconstructionists by showing the necessity of the Bible for interpreting the archaeological data and that they themselves rely upon it or a consensus based upon it in the writing of their new "secular" histories.[44] Written records usually take precedence, he argued, because whereas the new archaeology may give sociological data regarding a site or region, the literary sources provide the identity of the people and events. In the case of the archaeology of Syria-Palestine, the primary written source (and in many cases the only written evidence) is the biblical text. I. W. Provan rightly observed that

---

[41] Thompson proposes that Noth's opposition to Albright was due largely to his own rival historical thesis, a hypothetical proto-Aramean origin for the partriarchs ("Martin Noth and the History of Israel," in *The History of Traditions: The Heritage of Martin Noth,* JSOTSup182 [Sheffield: Sheffield Academic Press, 1994], 81–90).

[42] E.g., Ahlström, *History of Ancient Palestine*; R. B. Coote and K. W. Whitelam, *The Emergence of Early Israel in Historical Perspective,* SWBA 5 (Sheffield: Almond, 1987); G. Garbini, *History and Ideology in Ancient Israel* (New York: Crossroad, 1988); I. Finkelstein, *The Archaeology of the Israelite Settlement* (Jerusalem: Israel Exploration Society, 1988); and T. L. Thompson, *Early History of the Israelite People,* SHANE 4 (Leiden: Brill, 1992). See W. G. Dever, "The Death of a Discipline," *BAR* 21 (1995): 50–55, 70; O. Keel and C. Uehlinger (*Gods, Goddesses, and Images of God in Ancient Israel,* trans. T. Trapp [Minneapolis: Fortress, 1988]) present a history of Israel's religion based primarily on iconographic and archaeological material.

[43] G. W. Ahlström, "The Role of Archaeological and Literary Remains in Reconstructing Israel's History," in *The Fabric of History: Text, Artifact and Israel's Past,* JSOTSup 127 (Sheffield: Sheffield Academic Press, 1991), 118, 134.

[44] J. M. Miller, "Is It Possible to Write a History of Israel without Relying on the Hebrew Bible?" in *Fabric of History,* 93–102.

"testimony [from others] lies at the heart of our access to the past."[45] Without it we have little to nothing.

When we consider specifically the patriarchs, however, Miller himself condemned the biblical text as useless for the historian. What Miller has called for is a "critical" evaluation of the biblical materials. By this he meant that the folkloristic character of the patriarchal narratives, as the consensus of form-tradition criticism has shown, disqualifies it. In his coauthored history with J. Hayes, they considered the Hexateuch "an artificial and theologically influenced literary construct,"[46] and for this reason Miller and Hayes's history of Israel begins with the era of the Judges, a starting point which by the minimalists today is too optimistic.

Here we part with this skepticism among historians for two reasons. (1) The literary reconstruction produced by form-tradition criticism has not yet presented so compelling a case that the picture presented in the canonical text can be confidently ruled out (see vol. 1A, pp. 65–85). We will show in the commentary the literary unity of the narratives at the micro and macro levels. Literary and historical considerations point to a second-millennium setting and composition. (2) The biblical text is not weighed by critical scholars with the same measure as other ancient witnesses. E. Yamauchi showed how contemporary historiographers have failed to treat the biblical text in the same even-handed manner as they do other textual evidence.[47] Modern historians discount the Bible because of its religious and ideological features. Yet numerous appeals are made by these same scholars to Egyptian and Mesopotamian texts where religious references to deities are included. Moreover, most ancient literature was shaped by ideological concerns, reflecting the worldview of their creators. If applied consistently, this would virtually discredit all ancient literature. Kitchen illustrates this inconsistency by the skeptics' refusal to treat the war reported in Genesis 14 with the same openness to extrabiblical sources of analogous accounts: "The text of Yakhdun-lim of Mari [eighteenth century] shows striking affinities overall with the basics of the narrative in Gen 14. . . . It need only be added that Yakhdun-lim prefaces his entire account with a religious dedication to the god Shamash, who accompanied him on his campaigns." This account, although by appearances more overtly religious than Genesis 14, is given more credence despite "the plain, almost laconic Gen 14 report."[48] Furthermore, Millard observed that for many historians if any religious motive or

---

[45] I. W. Provan, "In the Stable with the Dwarves: Testimony, Interpretation, Faith, and the History of Israel," *Windows into Old Testament History*, 167; also "Ideologies, Literary and Critical: Reflections on Recent Writing in the History of Israel," *JBL* 114 (1995): 585–606.

[46] Miller and Hayes, *History of Ancient Israel and Judah*, 78.

[47] E. Yamauchi, "The Current State of Old Testament Historiography," in *Faith, Tradition, and History* (Winona Lake: Eisenbrauns, 1994), 1–36.

[48] Kitchen, *Reliability of the Old Testament*, 321.

explanation is given for an event in the Hebrew Bible, then it is rejected out of hand. But further he rightly indicated that while the Bible shows much in common with the reports of divine intervention among other ancient peoples, it exhibits throughout its tradition the consistent testimony to the correspondence of the divine word and the divine event of salvation rooted always in historical event. Hence, he made this appeal: "Israel's history cannot be fully comprehended without knowledge of her faith, nor can her faith be understood without a realistic portrayal of her history."[49]

Also Millard charged that scholars prejudge the biblical text as unique, requiring a speculative literary reconstruction, and refuse to treat it as a text in its own ancient context, as they typically do other texts originating from the ancient Near East.[50] It is standard to interpret any ancient text recovered from a site in the setting the text claims for itself. The patriarchal narratives speak of a time that antedated the founding of the nation, placing them in the second millennium. The Genesis narratives have similar features with ancient texts known from this period which have left remarkably reliable memories of the past. Millard remarked: "Repeatedly, traditional literature or records prove to report accurately events of long ago. In some cases this can be partially seen, as with Sargon and Naram-Sin, whatever fanciful overlay there may be. In other cases supporting evidence is more meagre, yet points in the same way, as with Gilgamesh."[51] Typically, the minimalists require external verification before a biblical claim can be accepted, and moreover what is considered satisfactory "verification" must run the gauntlet of extreme skepticism.[52] What is called for is not an "obscure 'verification test,'" variously defined and applied, but a reasonable standard of falsification.[53]

Moreover, code words such as "saga," "eponymous," "folk etymologies," "aetiologies," and "anachronisms" typically used to discount the biblical witness alleviate historians of taking seriously the biblical testimony and invite their own hypotheses, giving them more credence than the traditions of the Hebrews themselves. Millard observed that simply declaring an account, for example, "etiological" in a dogmatic way does not mean that it is necessarily

---

[49] Millard, "Story, History and Theology," *Faith, Tradition, and History*, 37–64, quote on p. 64.

[50] See Millard, "History and Legend in Early Babylonia," *Windows into Old Testament History*, 103–10: "The Hebrew histories are sober, unexciting by comparison with the Babylonian poems, and for that very reason may be deemed more credible" (p. 109).

[51] Millard, "Methods for Studying Patriarchal Narratives as Ancient Texts," *Essays on the Patriarchal Narratives*, 47.

[52] "In essence, the verificationist approach appears to be saying that every item of testimony must be externally verified, and *no verification of individual items will ever suffice to justify confidence in the testimony as a whole*. About all one can say to such an approach is that, were similar standards applied in a court of law, virtually no case could ever be decided" (Long, "The Future of Israel's Past: Personal Reflections," *Israel's Past in Present Research*, 583, n. 4.

[53] So Provan, "'In the Stable with the Dwarves,'" 170–75.

fictitious. Form-critical categories are not in themselves evidence against the events the narratives purport. Such assertions are often based on examples coming from unrelated societies and in many cases not ancient. Unless convincingly demonstrated to be false, there is no inherent reason why the Bible's explanation of a name or custom must be charged as patently false.

(3) Patriarchs in Historical Context

It follows from Millard's remarks that we should consider the biblical attestation itself for the proper period of investigation.[54] First, we must ask what kind of literature the Genesis narratives appear to be in their own context. Within the biblical-literary context, the patriarchs are historical individuals as the Genesis genealogies present them. There is no justification for insisting that they were personifications of tribal groups (e.g., Ishmael, Ammon, Moab) or became "ancestors" of peoples secondarily in the tradition,[55] for there is ample second-millennium evidence that ancient peoples attributed their origins to individuals. This genealogical consciousness is reflected in the Bible with its consistent reference to Abraham as forefather.[56] Against the backdrop of ancient stories, the Genesis narratives essentially stand apart since they tell of a single family's sojourn, without interest in detailing political events and persons. Kitchen found that the patriarchal stories are in part like ancient biographies and in part like historical legends, but they do not fall easily into any one attested genre from the past. Although they have much in common with historical legends, they do not have the fantastic as found in legend (excepting the patriarchs' ages). Wenham, reflecting on Kitchen's argument, noted, "But even were we to class them as legends, rather than biographies, oriental parallels would suggest that we are dealing with real historical figures, not make-believe."[57]

Second, the biblical testimony self-consciously sets the patriarchs in a time that antedated the Exodus/Sinai events, and patriarchal religious features and customs do not correspond to Mosaic worship or cultural practices. Evidence that the narratives come from an earlier period than the first millennium is the narrative's acceptance of practices that were taboo in Mosaic law, such as marrying one's half-sister, as in the case of Abraham and Sarah (20:12; Lev 18:11; 20:7; Deut 27:22). It is difficult to conceive of tradents creating out of whole cloth such practices while at the same time venerating the Fathers. If the narratives are first millennium, reflecting a later political and social setting, one won-

---

[54] See especially Millard's arguments in "Abraham," *ABD*.

[55] E.g., Gunkel, *Genesis*, xv.

[56] See D. Wiseman, "Abraham Reassessed," *Essays on the Patriarchal Narratives*, 153–58.

[57] G. Wenham, *Genesis 16–50*, WBC (Dallas: Word, 1995), xxii. For Kitchen see his *Bible in Its World* (Exeter: Paternoster, 1977), 64–65, cited in Wenham.

ders why the religious life and customs of the exilic period are not also refracted upon the Fathers.

Third, it still remains for us to discover how much earlier than the exodus the Bible puts the patriarchs. According to Exod 12:40–41 the Egyptian sojourn was 430 years,[58] which corresponds well with the approximation "400 years" given in 15:13.[59] There are two opinions about how the biblical text should be interpreted. (1) First Kings 6:1 indicates 480 years transpired between the exodus (1446 B.C.) and the dedication of Solomon's temple (966 B.C.), showing that Jacob's descent was 1876.[60] Embedded in Genesis are occasional chronological references that when correlated with 1 Kgs 6:1 produce a calculation for the birth of Abraham at 2166, making his departure for Canaan at 2091.[61] This kind of reconstruction, however, can only be held with sober caution. These references are not used by the biblical author in Genesis to date creation or the exodus (unlike 1 Kgs 6:1), and so a chronological system was not intended. (2) This late third-millennium date for Abraham assumes that "480 years" in 1 Kgs 6:1 is a literal figure as opposed to symbolic, representing twelve generations (12 x 40 years). Since twenty-five years is closer to an actual generation, twelve generations yield three hundred years. This duration accommodates the thirteenth-century dating for the exodus popularly held among scholars, and it places Joseph in Egypt ca. 1700.[62]

---

[58] It is common to question whether the biblical record is reliable since there is apparent incongruity within the biblical witness itself. First, textually the LXX adds at v. 40 καὶ ἐν γῇ Χανααν ("and in the land of Canaan"), thus including the settlement period as well as the Egyptian sojourn in the 430-year period (that is, 215 years each). But the MT reading is preferred since the verse concerns בְּנֵי יִשְׂרָאֵל ("the Israelite people"), which cannot describe the patriarchs but their tribal offspring. Second, although there are too few generations in Moses' genealogy (Exod 6:16–20; 1 Chr 5:27–29 [Eng 6:1–3]) between Levi and Moses/Aaron to accommodate 430 years, Joshua's genealogy (1 Chr 7:20–27) indicates twelve generations from Joseph to Joshua. Moses' genealogy is selective, as 1 Chr 7 for Joshua shows, including only Moses' tribe (Levi), clan (Kohath), and family (Amram). See K. A. Kitchen, *Ancient Orient and Old Testament* (Chicago: InterVarsity, 1966), 54–55 and W. C. Kaiser Jr., "Exodus," EBC (Grand Rapids: Zondervan, 1990), 380.

[59] Also 15:16, where "generation" דּוֹר is best taken as one hundred years (see comments there).

[60] This 480-year figure correlates well with the twelve generations in 1 Chr 5:29–41 [Eng 6:3–10] from Aaron to Johanan, the high priest at the time of Solomon's temple, yielding 12 x 40 years = 480. See J. A. Thompson, *1, 2 Chronicles*, NAC (Nashville: Broadman & Holman, 1994), 85.

[61] See E. H. Merrill, *Kingdom of Priests: A History of Old Testament Israel* (Grand Rapids: Baker, 1987), 25, 31, 66–79; he provides an exhaustive chronology of the patriarchs in "Chronology," *Dictionary of the Old Testament: Pentateuch* (Downers Grove: InterVarsity, 2003), 121. Abraham at seventy-five years migrated to Canaan (12:4). The descent of Jacob into Egypt was 1876, which is 215 years later (25 years + 60 + 130 = 215; see 21:5; 25:26; 47:9).

[62] Wright, *Biblical Archaeology*, 84, and Bright, *History*, 123. Kitchen argues on the basis of ancient parallels that the number 480 years (and 300 years, Judg 11:26) is an aggregate (*Ancient Orient*, 72–75), permitting a thirteenth-century exodus, but he defends the enslavement period (400/430 years) as an absolute number (pp. 53–55); also *Reliability of the Old Testament*, 307–8.

We can set the debate regarding the date of the exodus aside, however, if we reckon that whether one concludes the exodus is fifteenth or thirteenth century, Abraham would be dated to as early as the Middle Bronze I (2200–2000) or II periods (2000–1550). This places the patriarchs largely in the early second millennium, which as we saw has been seriously challenged by the revisionists. The question is whether the backdrop of the narratives better fits the earlier era as the Bible indicates or the first millennium. It is difficult to correlate the biblical information with a specific historical period. We can point only to a suitable context in ca. 2000–1550, one which accords better than what is known from later periods. As Millard concluded, the second-millennium date is permissible on the basis of archaeological evidence, even if not limited to that time.[63]

The cultural milieu of the patriarchal narratives bears the following marks of antiquity:

1. There is wide agreement that the kind of journeys undertaken by the patriarchs are known to have occurred in this early period. This is independent of the so-called "Amorite hypothesis." There is no reason to insist on a tie between the patriarchs and the Amorites since the Bible neither identifies them as Amorites nor indicates that Terah and Abraham were part of a mass migration.[64] If anything, a single family's movements would not be expected to leave any evidential remains, and such a family's movements would not likely receive mention among royal and cultic records. The question of the Amorite invasion is irrelevant. Kitchen compares the far-reaching movements of the Yaminite pastoral tribe (eighteenth century) with the biblical picture of the Terah migration: "From Larsa in the east to Amurru in the west, the wanderings of segments of the Mare-Yamina cover all but the extremities of the journeyings of Terah and Abraham from Ur to Canaan."[65]

2. Although the pastoral-sedentary ("dimorphic") life of the patriarchs is attested at different periods, it is challenging to conceive of such a lifestyle created by first-millennium tradents in what was their urban milieu. It must be remembered that the Bible contrasts the patriarchs' pastoral life with that of the urban Canaanites and distinguishes them from the fringe tribes of the Ishmaelites, Edomites, and Amalekites.[66] There are sufficient similarities between the social patterns of tribal life among the patriarchs (e.g., 21:22–32; 26:26–33) and what we know of the Mari tribes to warrant an analogy.[67] A. Malamat dem-

---

[63] Millard, "Abraham," *ABD* 1.40.

[64] Ezek 16:3, "Your father was an Amorite," refers to the Canaanite population and not the early Amorite groups migrating from north Mesopotamia.

[65] Kitchen, *Reliability of the Old Testament*, 317.

[66] de Vaux, *Early History of Israel*, 233.

[67] V. Matthews, "The Wells of Gerar," *BA* 49 (1986): 118–26; "Syria to the Early Second Millennium," *Mesopotamia and the Bible* (Grand Rapids: Baker, 2002), 168–90.

onstrated such typological connections by pointing out their similar linguistic terms for tribal institutions and customs, the patrimony by the Mari tribes and the biblical patriarchs,[68] shared connections in geography (e.g., Haran and Nahor are frequently mentioned at Mari), the mobility of tribal life as in the back-and-forth movements of the patriarchs, and tribal friction with urban centers (e.g., Gen 34). He said of the connections with Mari: "Significantly, this West Semitic terminology reflects, in one way or another, a thoroughly tribalistic milieu—mainly of non-urban populations but to some extent also of urban society. This is so at Mari as well as in early Israel, and it is only within these two sources—of all the documentary evidence of the ancient Near East till Islamic times—that tribal society manifests itself in full bloom."[69]

3. Does the description of the patriarchs' Canaan match what we know of second-millennium Palestine? Here we are dependent on correlations with the archaeological record. At issue is the archaeological evidence for settlements visited by the patriarchs. Not all archaeological sites can be identified with certainty (e.g., Bethel, Ai), and others have not been satisfactorily excavated. Moreover, the absence of material remains does not mean necessarily that a site was unoccupied since the earlier settlement may not have been found. Forty years ago de Vaux acknowledged the methodological problem here: "The narratives concerning the life of the patriarchs in the Negev (to say nothing of the Sinai) do not require, perhaps even exclude, an occupation of the kind attested by archaeology."[70] We simply have too little evidence to draw with confidence the settlement pattern in the second millennium. What appears more certain, however, is that the urban character of the first millennium does not suit the setting of the narratives. Here we have firm ground on which to evaluate the viability of the patriarchal picture as authentically situated in early second-millennium Canaan. From the geopolitical picture of Canaan in this period, when pastoralists moved about freely between city-owned territories and open pasturage, we find a corresponding description of the political setting of Abraham's travels. This depiction of Canaan has corroboration from Egyptian and Old Babylonian sources, leading Kitchen to conclude, "Thus for the patriarchal clan as transhumant pastoral folk, we have a rich backcloth of corresponding

---

[68] D. Fleming, based on the similarities of the Mari tribe Binu Yamin and the biblical tribe Benjamin, goes so far as to say that "Israel's tribe of Benjamin indicates *some kind of direct heritage* in the older tribal population that frequented southern and western Syria" (italics mine; "History in Genesis," *WTJ* 65 [2003]: 256); id., "Mari and the Possibilities of Biblical Memory," *RA* 92 (1998): 41–78.

[69] A. Malamat, *Mari and the Early Israelite Experience*, Schweich Lectures 1984 (London: Oxford University Press, 1989), 27–69, quote on p. 34. Dever concluded that the Mari analogy is the best evidence for putting the patriarchal traditions in the second millennium ("Palestine in the Second Millennium BCE," 104–18).

[70] R. de Vaux, "Method in the Study of Early Hebrew History," *The Bible in Modern Scholarship* (Nashville: Abingdon, 1965), 26.

conditions from the centuries preceding 1500." The picture of nation-states of the first millennium does not correspond with the Genesis depiction. "In that light the patriarchs and their lifestyle and world cannot possibly be a retrojection into the antiquity of the world of a settled, monarchic Israel as often claimed of old."[71]

4. As for the social customs found at Nuzi, the results are not as promising as first thought by Gordon and Speiser for dating the patriarchs. De Vaux and later Thompson recognized their value for establishing that the customs of the patriarchs were consistent with the broad social milieu of the Near East, but not for dating the patriarchs.[72] Van Seters attempted to use them, nevertheless, for dating the patriarchs to the first millennium but with no more success than those who hoped to place them exclusively in the second millennium. In a review of extrabiblical social customs, including the Nuzi evidence, M. Selman named thirteen parallels between extrabiblical law and biblical customs he believed valid.[73] He agreed that the Nuzi evidence could not be used to pinpoint the era of the patriarchs; rather, the value of the extrabiblical parallels is the evidence that patriarchal customs reflected the historically demonstrable practices of the second and first millennia. Patriarchal practices, he concluded, indicate in general terms the historical character of the patriarchal narratives, but no more.

5. The religious life of the patriarchs matches better the religious life known from the second millennium than the institutional life of first-millennium Israel. We will explore this matter in the discussion of the "Religion of the Patriarchs" that follows below.

In summary, we have said that the biblical evidence points to ca. 2200–1550 for the period of the patriarchs. The historical and sociological evidence cannot be correlated specifically with the patriarchs, but it does not falsify the Genesis depiction; and, if accepted, it offers a background in general terms in which the narratives can be read. Kitchen concluded, "It should be clear, finally, that the main features of the patriarchal narratives either fit specifically into the first half of the second millennium or are consistent with such a dating; some features common to that epoch and to later periods clearly must be taken with the early-second millennium horizon."[74]

(4) Anachronisms

Are there signs in the patriarchal stories that indicate they were composed in the monarchic period or later? Genesis shows a later editorial updating (e.g.,

---

[71] Kitchen, *Reliability of the Old Testament*, 335.

[72] So B. Eichler, "Nuzi and the Bible: A Retrospective," *DUMU-E2-DUB-BA-A: In Honor of A. Sjöberg* (Philadelphia: S. N. Kramer Fund/University Museum, 1989), 107–19.

[73] M. Selman, "Comparative Customs and the Patriarchal Age," *Essays on the Patriarchal Narratives*, 91–40; "The Social Environment of the Patriarchs," *TynBul* 27 (1976): 114–36.

[74] Kitchen, *Reliability of the Old Testament*, 372.

11:28,31; 14:14; 36:31), but these additions are isolated and of minimal importance for dating the composition (see vol. 1A, pp. 79–80).[75] The chief evidence advanced for a late date is proposed anachronisms detected in the narrative. Among the primary examples are references to the Philistines, the use of camels by the patriarchs, and the patriarchs' Aramean ancestry.

First, reference to the Philistines in the patriarchal narratives (21:32,34; 26:1,8,14–18) is usually explained as an anachronism,[76] since "Philistine" *(plšt)* does not occur until the twelfth century in Egyptian sources, which name the Philistines among the invading "Sea peoples." This dating plus the name of the Philistine king "Abimelech," which is Semitic whereas the Philistines were non-Semitic, have argued for relegating the Philistines to later editorial invention.[77] The Table of Nations attributes Philistine origins to the Casluhites (10:13), and the prophets indicate their location in Caphtor (= Crete; Amos 9:7; Jer 47:4). We have already shown how the biblical data including the early settlement of Philistines known in Genesis can be accounted for without resorting to emendation or anachronism (see vol. 1A, pp. 453–55). Here we only want to add that the incongruity of early Philistine features (in Genesis) and those of the later Philistines encountered by the judges (Judg 3:31; chaps. 13–16) contribute to the veracity of the Genesis depiction. The Genesis Philistines are not identified as constituting a pentapolis, nor is Abimelech, the "king *(melek)* of the Philistines," termed a *seren* ("tyrant, lord"), which is the customary term in the later biblical references for the rulers of the five Philistine cities (e.g., Josh 13:3; 1 Sam 7:16–18). Whereas van Seters recommends that this difference reflects a late exilic date, possible only after the pentapolis had dissolved, it is equally conceivable that this depiction of the Philistines in Genesis testifies to an earlier period in Philistine history before the better-known Philistine immigrants of the Late Bronze Age. After Kitchen observed evidence of Aegean peoples and culture migrating east to Canaan and the eastern Delta (Avaris) during the Middle Bronze period (2200–1550), he concluded that "Philistines" was a "blanket term for non-Canaanite Aegean people."[78] To pronounce the Philistine appearance in

---

[75] For the theological implications of limited, secondary updating, see M. Grisanti, "Inspiration, Inerrancy, and the OT Canon: The Place of Textual Updating in an Inerrant View of Scripture," *JETS* 44 (2001): 577–89.

[76] Also Exod 13:17; 15:14; 23:31; Josh 13:2–3; Judg 3:3. J. K. Hoffmeier proposes that "Philistines" may be a gloss, since Num 13:29 refers to "Canaanites" by the Mediterranean, when Exod 13:17 uses "Philistine" to describe the same coastal area. Thus "the Israelites understood that prior to the arrival of the Philistines in the early twelfth century B.C., the area had been occupied by Canaanites" (*Israel in Egypt: The Evidence for the Authenticity of the Exodus Tradition* [New York/Oxford: Oxford University Press, 1997], 202).

[77] E.g., de Vaux, *Early History of Israel*, 503–4; H. Katzenstein, "Philistine," *ABD* 5.326.

[78] Kitchen, *Reliability of the Old Testament*, 341; or, similarly, the patriarchs engaged Aegeans (the Minoans?), knowing them by a contemporary name of the Middle Bronze period; but later this term became unknown and the text of Genesis was updated by appealing to the name of another ethnic Aegean group known to the author/editor (suggested to me by Dr. S. M. Ortiz, New Orleans Baptist Theological Seminary, personal communication).

Genesis as unhistorical is not required by the facts and exposes the historian's priority of the Egyptian evidence and a cavalier dismissal of the biblical witness.

Second, the domestication of camels in Syria-Palestine is said to have occurred at the end of the second millennium, thus indicating that Genesis as a first-millennium composition has introduced an anachronism.[79] There is no evidence at Mari (ca. 1800), for example, that pastoral tribes bred camels. The pastoral life of the patriarchs included the breeding of small cattle, sheep, and goats (e.g., 13:5; 30:32–42). The donkey was the common beast of burden in Genesis (e.g., 22:3; 42:26–27; 45:23), and the camel was utilized for packing goods and for riding.[80] It is not at all certain, however, that the domesticated camel was unknown in Syria-Palestine in the early second millennium. Evidence for domestication is early and far reaching, including eastern Iran (ca. 2700) and the Indus Valley (ca. 2300) from which it may have spread to South Arabia.[81] Camel remains in Syria-Palestine from the early second millennium are fewer, and it is difficult to determine if they are the remains of wild or domesticated animals. It is presumptuous, however, to assert on the basis of such fragmentary evidence that the camel was undomesticated in Palestine. There are references to camels in the Old Babylonian period (ca. 2000–1700), some of which imply domestication. Bone fragments were retrieved from as early as 7000 B.C.[82] and from various Palestinian sites of the early second millennium.[83] If Genesis is a first-millennium product, the infrequency of the horse in Genesis is striking (47:17; 49:17; 50:9). On the theory of a late composition, we would expect the mention of the horse and not the camel. Sarna suggested that the domesticated camel was rare in Syria-Palestine and a possession of the wealthy.[84] This conforms to the role of the camel in Genesis as indicative of wealth and prestige and explains why it was not used regularly as a beast of burden.

Third, Aramean origins are obscure and therefore are suspect when marshaled as evidence for dating the patriarchal stories. The Bible suggests that the origin of the Arameans was not limited to one locale (cp. Amos 9:7). Because Aramean peoples were only first known confidently from royal Assyrian records of the twelfth century, the Aramean ancestry of the patriarchs in Genesis has been regularly considered anachronistic.[85] The widespread influence of

---

[79] E.g., de Vaux, *Early History of Israel*, 223–25; van Seters, *Abraham in History and Tradition*, 17.

[80] 12:16; 24:10(2x),19,20,22,30,31,32,44,61,63,64; 30:43; 31:17,34; 32:16; 37:25.

[81] J. Zarinis, "Camel," *ABD* 1.824–26.

[82] M. Ripinsky, "The Camel in Ancient Arabia," *Antiquity* 49 (1975): 295–98; also "The Camel in Dynastic Egypt," *JEA* 71 (1985): 134–41.

[83] Examples cited in Kitchen, *Ancient Orient*, 79–80.

[84] Sarna, *Genesis*, 96.

[85] E.g., Thompson, *Historicity of the Patriarchal Narratives*, 302–3; Soggin, *Introduction to the History of Israel and Judah*, 94.

Aramean culture was felt during the early first millennium down to the Persian period.

As for the Aramean connections of the patriarchs, Abraham resided in "Ur of the Chaldees" (11:28,31; 15:7), which refers to the place of the Aramean Chaldeans, who resided in southern Babylonia from the tenth to sixth centuries (see comments on 11:28). The home of the patriarchs is identified as Aram Naharaim (24:10) and Paddan Aram (e.g., 25:20; or "Paddan," 48:7). Isaac's wife was the daughter of "Bethuel the Aramean" and Laban, her brother, was identified as an "Aramean" (e.g., 25:20). "My father was a wandering Aramean" (Deut 26:5) acknowledges the Aramean ancestry of Israel (Jacob). The Table of Nations also attests to the kinship of the Hebrews and Arameans. Aram was descended from Shem (10:22), as was Eber the father of the Hebrews (10:21–25; 11:14–17), and there was Nahor, Abraham's brother, who was the father of Arameans and Chaldeans (22:20–24).

Although many have discounted the Aramean roots of Israel as pure fabrication, others have argued that there is a historical substratum to this association. M. Noth was the strongest proponent of a "Proto-Aramean" ancestry for Israel, that is, they were of the same root ancestry from which the Arameans later descended.[86] Noth attempted to justify his thesis on the basis of linguistic similarity between the early biblical names (e.g., Israel, Jacob) and the names of the preexilic/exilic period when Aramaic influence on Hebrew was at its greatest in the Old Testament period.[87] But his linguistic argument failed because it was not so distinctive as to specify an Aramean connection alone. De Vaux proposed the same association of the Arameans and early Amorites (which he assumed was the ethnic background of the patriarchs) on geographical and sociological correspondences. He concluded that Aramean ancestry "may be an anachronism, but is unconsciously linked with a reality, so that the Israelite could truthfully say, "My father was a wandering Aramean.""[88] A simple explanation by R. S. Hendel is that the Haran region, though Amorite ethnically during the era of the patriarchs, was Aramean during the updating of the tradition (ca. tenth century).[89]

Although the person and place names *Aramu* and *Ahlamu* (a name related to the Arameans) occur in early texts, they cannot be specifically linked with an Aramean people group. The association of "Aram" with an ethnic people is only first attested in the fourteenth century in Egyptian and Ugaritic texts,[90]

---

[86] See Thompson for discussion (*Historicity of the Patriarchal Narratives*, 75–76).

[87] The linguistic form is the verbal imperfect *yqtl*.

[88] de Vaux, *Early History of Israel*, 209; also Bright, *History of Israel*, 91–92 and W. Pitard, *Ancient Damascus* (Winona Lake: Eisenbrauns, 1987), 85–87.

[89] R. S. Hendel, "Finding Historical Memories in the Patriarchal Narratives," *BAR* 21 (1995): 59, 70.

[90] For details see de Vaux, *Early History of Israel*, 201–7, and A. R. Millard, "Arameans," *ABD* 1.348.

still too late for corroboration of an early second-millennium presence for an identifiable Aramean tribe. But is this Aramean ancestry claimed in the Bible for the patriarchs so far-fetched as to furnish an unquestionable anachronism?

As with the "Amorite migration" theory, scholars have tended to explain the identity of ethnic groups new to a region as the consequence of nomadic invaders from the desert who subdued the sedentary population and gradually took up the sedentary life of their predecessors. Similarly, the standard explanation for Aramean presence in Upper Mesopotamia was their arrival as newcomers, contributing to the fall of the Late Bronze Age cities (ca. 1250). W. Pitard reminds us that this old sociological paradigm of "nomadic" invasion has been found inadequate. The early Arameans resembled the Mari tribes (eighteenth century) that practiced a pastoral-village life, not nomadic tribes from the desert steppe. The Arameans were possibly the descendants of the Amorites who lived in the region throughout the second millennium.[91]

As Millard observed, the absence of inscriptional reference to an Aramean people group between the Bible (ca. 2000) and the Late Bronze Age gives a six-century gap. He pointed to other examples where such a gap is known for towns and other items, so as to show that the Aramean case is not unique. Moreover, he observed inherent problems in the alternative theory of a late composition for Genesis. During the first millennium the Arameans and Israelites experienced centuries of hostilities. The tolerance of Aram as Israel's parentage is difficult to explain unless it was an authentic memory.[92] And the depiction of an independent Aram in Genesis does not correspond to the first-millennium picture of small states that were made provinces in the successive empires of the Assyrians, Babylonians, and Persians. We agree with de Vaux that the biblical claims are truthful, but not with his notion that it was by odd historical coincidence; rather, the Hebrew people maintained an early memory of their roots in an Aramean kinship from which their ancestors eventually parted as they took up the language and material culture of their Canaanite habitat.

(5) Genesis 14

Special attention is required for this troubling chapter, for it has been largely assailed as legendary, some even viewing it as a late Jewish midrash. Although this chapter more so than any other patriarchal narrative comes close to yielding the kind of data cherished by modern historians, with its "mass of historical and

---

[91] W. Pitard, "Arameans," *Peoples of the Old Testament World* (Grand Rapids: Baker, 1994), 207–10.

[92] Pitard relegates the genealogical references to Aramean and Hebrew ancestry as legendary (10:22; 22:21) but agrees that the biblical insistence on the early connections between the two may well reflect an authentic association of these second-millennium peoples, though imprecisely (*Ancient Damascus*, 85–87).

geographical detail,"[93] its account of two warring coalitions has been deemed by many as historically and geographically impossible. Learned papers in their titles have admitted that it is a "riddle" and an "enigma"[94] due to its peculiar traits, among which are: a mixture of early and late features, antiquarian detail, the depiction of Abraham as a warrior, the mysterious Canaanite king-priest of Salem, and the only occasion of the description "Abram the Hebrew." This has led many scholars to treat the chapter as an independent source, unrelated to any of the traditional documents (J, E, D, P).

The competing schools of archaeology versus literary criticism came to the question of the chapter's historicity employing their respective tools. Albright, Glueck, and Speiser found sufficient corroboration from archaeology and epigraphic remains to posit an underlying historical foundation, while Noth, von Rad, and, more recently, Thompson, van Seters, and Soggin[95] dismissed it as an artificial creation, useless to the modern historian. The archaeological school argued that person and place names, the geographical route of the invading kings, and the narrative's archaic features (such as place names updated by glosses) evidenced an "authentic" and a "credible" account.[96] The literary school, on the other hand, delineated the chapter's form-tradition history, always looking for an ancient literary parallel, if not for the chapter as a whole, then for its parts. A popular appeal was to the pseudohistorical text of Sargon's legend, consisting of both a historical hero and fictitious elements.[97] Van Seters pointed to late Jewish stories such as *Judith* as the nearest parallel (as did Gunkel, Westermann).[98] O. Margalith identified its genre as *"para-mythe,"* a

---

[93] G. von Rad, *Genesis: A Commentary,* OTL, trans. J. Marks (Philadelphia: Westminster, 1972), 175.

[94] J. A. Emerton, "The Riddle of Genesis XIV," *VT* 21 (1971): 403–39; F. I. Andersen, "Genesis XIV: An Enigma," *Pomegranates and Golden Bells: Studies in Biblical, Jewish, and Near Eastern Ritual, Law, Literature in Honor of Jacob Milgrom* (Winona Lake: Eisenbrauns, 1995), 497–507.

[95] For Soggin see "Abraham and the Eastern Kings: On Genesis 14," *Solving Riddles and Untying Knots: Biblical, Epigraphic, and Semitic Studies in Honor of Jonas C. Greenfield,* (Winona Lake: Eisenbrauns, 1995), 283–91.

[96] Speiser, e.g., dated the battle to ca. 1800 (*Genesis,* 106, 109).

[97] As did de Vaux, *Early History of Israel,* 219–20.

[98] Van Seters, *Abraham in History and Tradition,* 305. For form-critical discussion see C. Westermann, *Genesis 12–36: A Commentary,* trans. J. Scullion (Minneapolis: Augsburg, 1985 [1981]), 187–93; Emerton, "The Riddle of Genesis XIV," 432–33. For a discussion of the history of interpretation, see Emerton, "Some False Clues in the Study of Genesis XIV," *VT* 21 (1971): 24–47. Thompson found modern Serbo-Croatian oral traditions concerning famous battles as the closest comparative material. For the Chedorlaomer text (ca. seventh–sixth centuries) of the Spartoli Tablets, which tells of a coalition of three kings opposing Babylon, see M. C. Astour, "Political and Cosmic Symbolism in Genesis 14 and Its Babylonian Sources," *Biblical Motifs. Origin and Transformation* (Cambridge: Harvard University Press, 1966), 65–112.

hero story that draws on pseudohistorical events for its background.[99]

Although our concern here is the larger question of the chapter's credibility as a historical account, it is necessary to address the literary question since it goes far to answering the issue of historicity. Form-tradition critics commonly treat the chapter as constituting three units: campaign report (vv. 1–11), the Abraham-Lot story (vv. 12–17,21–24), and the Melchizedek episode (vv. 18–20), which is usually taken as a late insertion to the Abraham story during the monarchic period. The final composition has been dated as late as the Maccabean period. Psalm 110, which alludes to Melchizedek, is taken as a late composition.[100] Margalith judged the chapter as "a badly-cobbled medley of episodes dimly remembered from past traditions."[101] Chapter 14, however, can be shown to be a literary whole, and the context for its composition is Genesis itself.[102] The account consists of two parts: the war of the eastern kings (vv. 1–12) and the rescue of Lot (vv. 13–24). The latter involves Abraham's encounter with three kings, namely, the defeat of (a) the eastern king Kedorlaomer, (b) the meeting with the king of Sodom, and (c) the blessing of the king-priest of Salem, Melchizedek.[103]

1. Our first section (vv. 1–12) tells of two coalitions of kings at war, the first made up of four eastern kings, led by the Elamite Kedorlaomer, and the second a coalition of five western kings from the region south of the Dead Sea, most notably the king of Sodom. Kedorlaomer initiated a punitive expedition against the rebellious western kings whose members were vassals to the Elamite for twelve years. The battle was disastrous for the western kings, and the booty taken by the eastern coalition included Lot and his dependants. Verse 12, which first mentions Abraham and Lot in the story, functions as a transition verse, tying the two halves together. For this reason it could as easily be viewed as belonging to the subsequent half of the chapter.

As noted already, many distinguish vv. 1–11 as a unit, understood as an independent source of unknown origin, most likely non-Israelite, which has been adapted to the Abraham-Lot story (vv. 12–17,21–24). There is, on the contrary, reason for taking vv. 1–11 as a part of a unified narrative in chap. 14. Although Abraham and Lot do not occur in vv. 1–11, repeated references to the "king of Sodom" (vv. 2,8,10) and the seizure of "all the goods of Sodom"

---

[99] O. Margalith dates the background in the turbulent thirteenth century ("The Riddle of Genesis 14 and Melchizedek," *ZAW* 112 [2000]: 501–8).

[100] So Soggin, "Abraham and the Eastern Kings," 291.

[101] Margalith, "The Riddle of Genesis 14," 504.

[102] See J. G. McConville, "Abraham and Melchizedek: Horizons in Genesis 14," *He Swore an Oath* (Cambridge: Tyndale, 1993), 93–118.

[103] G. Coats (*Genesis with an Introduction to Narrative Literature*, FOTL 1 [Grand Rapids: Eerdmans, 1983], 118) and Wenham (*Genesis 1–15*, 304) present a twofold outline: three battle reports in vv. 1–16 and the confrontation of Abram and the king of Sodom in vv. 17–24; both attribute the chapter to the J tradition as does Emerton ("Riddle," 406).

(v. 11), raising the question of Lot's involvement, echoes Lot's residence in "Sodom" in 13:12. This battle and Lot's capture are presupposed in the king of Sodom's offer to give Abraham the "goods" whereas he would retain the "people" (v. 21). To understand the tension concerning Lot's destiny, the battle report of vv. 1–11 must be assumed by the narrative. Wenham has demonstrated also how the vocabulary of vv. 11–12,15–16 recurs in vv. 21–24, showing that the Abraham-Lot aspect of the chapter must assume vv. 1–11. Moreover, the absence of vv. 1–11 would strikingly diminish the heroic efforts of Abraham. F. I. Andersen's analysis of the composition led him to observe, "If originally a separate story [vv. 17–24], the meeting between Abraham and Melchizedek has been woven tightly into the war epic."[104] In other words, the chapter appears to be made of one piece, not disparate parts.

2. Verses 13–24 constitute the second section with vv. 18–20 (Melchizedek episode) positioned as an embedded narrative. We have already said v. 12 is the hinge verse that anticipates Abraham's role and the outcome he will engineer. Abraham learned of Lot's predicament, gathered an army, and after a surprise attack liberated the possessions of the dispersed western kings and rescued nephew Lot. The king of Sodom went out to greet Abraham, but Melchizedek the king of Salem first blessed Abraham, who offered the king-priest a tenth part of the recovered possessions. After which the king of Sodom proposed a sharing of the spoil, keeping the people for himself and offering the goods to Abraham. The chapter ends with Abraham's pointed refusal, wishing nothing for himself lest he be perceived as indebted to the king of Sodom. Rather, he had sworn allegiance to the "LORD, God Most High, Creator of heaven and earth" (v. 22), trusting in him alone for his prosperity.

This story of Abraham as warrior is reckoned by many as so distinctive in the biblical portrait of the patriarch that it cannot be attributed to one of the traditional sources. Abraham is a local pastoralist, living in harmony with Canaanites; here he is portrayed as an international figure routing a formidable coalition of kings. Moreover the "clumsy" handling of vv. 11–12, as Emerton called it,[105] indicates that Lot was later added (vv. 11–12,16) to connect the chapter with the Abraham-Lot tradition (J source) in chaps. 13; 18–19. Westermann and Emerton both saw the Melchizedek episode as added to the original Abraham story (vv. 12–17,21–24) at the time of David either to legitimize new cultic practices (Westermann) or to encourage acceptance of the new religious synthesis and political center at Jerusalem during the reign of David (Emerton). For both, the international setting (vv. 1–11) was added to glorify Abraham all the more as a political figure.

McConville has shown, however, that such reconstructions are not convinc-

---

[104] Andersen, "Genesis XIV: An Enigma," 499.
[105] Emerton, "Riddle," 407.

ing. The assumption that the depiction of Abraham is radically different from what we know of him in Genesis is overstated. Abraham is found in the presence of Egyptian and Canaanite kings, and his decisions have a profound impact upon them (e.g., chaps. 12; 20). He is recognized at Hebron by the Hittites as a powerful leader (chap. 23).[106] In that sense he is viewed as a political figure. Also, excising "Lot" from the narrative will not do. As van Seters rightly observed, the removal of Lot would require a significantly altered account,[107] for without Lot's capture the military venture of Abraham has no motivation except possibly the "goods" that he refuses anyway. And, as Wenham noted, the Melchizedek appearance (vv. 18–20) can hardly be taken as a late insertion, for Abraham's speech to the king of Sodom (vv. 21–24) alludes to the Melchizedek episode.[108]

Further, there is no reason to look beyond Genesis itself for the proper setting since chap. 14 correlates well with chaps. 13 and 15.[109] Genesis 14 with chap. 13 presents the same focal characters (Abram, Lot) and location (plain of Jordan, Mamre). Also, chap. 14 explains two features of the Abraham-Lot narrative that are left unstated in chap. 13. First, the danger of Sodom is unknown to Lot (13:10), whereas chap. 14 suggests this in two ways. The names of the kings of Sodom and Gomorrah each entail the words for "evil" (Bera) and "wicked" (Birsha), respectively. Their names may be deliberately altered by the Hebrew author to ridicule the Canaanite kings, as with the Mesopotamian monarch Cushan-Rishathaim, meaning "Cushan doubly wicked" (Judg 3:8). Also the prominence of the king of Sodom and the marked contrast between him and Melchizedek implies the wickedness of Sodom that becomes focal in chaps. 18–19. And second, chap. 14 clarifies Abraham's relationship with Lot, since the two separated over disputed circumstances in chap. 13. The implications of this relationship bear on the integral narrative theme of the promissory blessings and the need of an heir (12:2–3; 15:1).[110] The relationship of chaps. 14 and 15 is also a natural association (see comments on chap. 15 for details), for both concern the question of family, inheritance, and land; chap. 15 shows the consequence of Abraham's reliance on God's provision rather than the beneficence of Sodom's king. The echo of "shield" *(māgēn)* in 15:1, "I am your shield," from 14:20, "who delivered *[miggēn]* your enemies into your hands" makes chap. 15's reiteration of the promise of a future heir (15:2–3) understandable as

---

[106] McConville, "Abram and Melchizedek," 102.

[107] van Seters, *Abraham in History and Tradition*, 298.

[108] See the details of Wenham's literary argument in *Genesis 1–15*, 305–7.

[109] See Y. Zakovitch, "Juxtaposition in the Abraham Cycle," *Pomegranates and Golden Bells*, 512–14.

[110] So McConville, "Abram and Melchizedek," 109, 112. Zakovitch thinks chap. 14 is useful to show the magnanimity of Abraham toward Lot despite the latter's conduct in chap. 13 ("Juxtaposition in the Abraham Cycle," 513).

the blessing (14:19–20) invoked by Melchizedek and as Abram's reward (14:22–23; 15:1). Moreover, both chaps. 14 and 15 involve defeat of foreigners by Abram or his descendants (14:13–16; 15:16,19–21).[111]

McConville demonstrated how the Melchizedek episode (vv. 18–20) contributes well to the thematic setting of Genesis's patriarchal narratives, indicating that it is best attributed to the Genesis context itself, not some extraneous work of Davidic or later origins serving a religio-political purpose.[112] (1) Abraham is a person of international import whose wealth is recognized as a gift from God; (2) Abraham will trust God for a descendant and not conscript Lot as his heir; (3) Abraham asserts his God is the one true "LORD" (Yahweh), known in Canaan as *Elyon;* and last (4) Abraham's proclamation of Yahweh, the Promise-Giver, as the God Most High finds realization of the promise of blessing upon the families of the earth in the deliverance of Sodom (cp. 12:3). Again, Andersen stated the obvious implication for the coherence of chap. 14 and Genesis: "If originally an independent unit, Genesis 14 has been woven into the rest of the Abraham story."[113] Since the chapter shows a literary unity and a vital link in its present literary context of Genesis, there is no need apart from some methodological purpose to judge the chapter a literary patchwork originally unrelated to the patriarchal narratives.

Although we have shown that the chapter possesses an inner literary integrity and an original setting in Genesis, there remains the question of its historical viability. When we look at its literary and historical features, we find that the account indicates an early date with some later updating of the place names (vv. 2–3,7–8,17). We have already found that chap. 14 contextually fits well within the Abraham narrative, contributing to the Abraham-Lot motif. There is ample evidence of archaic features that attest to the authenticity of the account: rare or unique terms and phrases (e.g., "trained men," *hānikîm*, 14:14); person and place names consistent with our knowledge of the early period (e.g., the four names of the eastern kings are genuine[114]); an accurate invasion route, following the trade route of the "King's Highway"; and accretions explaining old place names.[115]

The problem about whether these are truly archaic or merely archaisms cannot be resolved. Moreover, some elements can be taken as "inventive," such as the names of the western kings, their identity with historical persons, and the

---

[111] On ties between the two episodes, see D. Carr, *Reading the Fractures of Genesis: Historical and Literary Approaches* (Louisville: Westminster John Knox, 1996), 164–65.

[112] McConville, "Abram and Melchizedek," 111–16.

[113] Andersen, "Genesis 14: An Enigma," 500.

[114] Although the individuals are unattested in extrabiblical documents, this should not rule out the credibility of the account; e.g., the Mari corpus of thousands of texts "covers only about fifty to seventy years" (Kitchen, *Reliability of the Old Testament*, 320).

[115] See de Vaux, *Early History of Israel*, 217–19.

existence of a coalition headed by an Elamite king doing battle with the west (see comment on 14:1–4). Kitchen showed, however, that although the war of Genesis 14 is not known from ancient sources, an Elamite coalition and western campaign is consistent with what we know of east-west relations in the early second millennium. Such power alliances of kings in Mesopotamia is well attested for this period, which occurred in the power vacuum created by the fall of Ur III until the rise of Hammurapi.[116] Moreover, as Sarna showed, if chap. 14 is taken as an invention, it is difficult to square with some features of the story.[117] The expression "Abram the Hebrew" (v. 13) occurs only here and is therefore an unlikely imitation; if the names of the western kings are made up, it is inexplicable why no name was given to the king of Bela (v. 2); and the Amorite associates of Abraham (v. 13) would be an unexpected concoction since a Hebrew-Amorite alliance would violate Mosaic prohibitions (e.g., Deut 7; 20:17) and would be at tension with the depiction of the Amorites elsewhere in Genesis (15:16,21).

We cannot prove that the events of chap. 14 are authentic, but there is no clear evidence that falsifies the record of the persons and events, and they fit what we know of an early period. There is no compelling basis on form or tradition grounds to relegate it to pure fancy.

(6) Joseph in Egypt

The interpretation of the Joseph narrative (chaps. 37–50) requires a separate discussion. First, what is the literary character of the narrative? Second, what is its historical usefulness? And, last, if accepted as historical, what is the appropriate period in Egypt's history reflected in the narrative?

1. As to its literary composition, we will postpone a full discussion to the introduction to the Joseph section in the commentary. Suffice it to say here that most scholars are agreed that the Joseph narrative is a (redactional) unity composed by a single author.

2. The second issue is evaluating the story's historical value, which involves its date of composition and its marks of authentic memories. Until the last quarter of the twentieth century, scholars widely assigned the core of the story to the second millennium with the final form bearing evidence of the Solomonic

---

[116] Kitchen, *Ancient Orient*, 43–47; "Genesis 12–50 in the Near Eastern World," *He Swore An Oath*, 71–74; "The Patriarchal Age: Myth or History?" 56–57; and also recently, *Reliability of the Old Testament*, 320. R. S. Hendel's criticism ("Finding Historical Memories," 56–57) that alliances of kings, both in the west and east, is known as well in the first millennium made Kitchen's point. In each example presented by Hendel, a coalition of kings, whether in the east or west, is opposing the empire of Assyria. In Genesis 14, however, there are two alliances at war, no empire; Kitchen argued that the best setting for such a geopolitical situation would be when there was no formidable empire like those of the first millennium.

[117] Sarna, *Genesis*, 102–3.

era. Today, literary and historical "minimalists" conclude that the composition derived from the exilic or postexilic periods. The assessment that the work was late found support from some Egyptologists, especially D. Redford, who argued that the story's Egyptian background reflected the Saite (twenty-sixth dynasty) and Persian periods (i.e., seventh–fifth centuries).[118] The opposite voice among Egyptologists maintained that the Joseph narrative was set against a historical background that best fit within the second millennium. There is some disagreement about which quarter of the second millennium, but the precise period will not concern us here.[119]

Although the Joseph section as a whole shows a different literary style than chaps. 12–36, it is subsumed under the same literary framework of the *tôlĕdōt* ("generations") rubric (37:2 with 11:27; 25:19), which indicates that the Joseph narrative as it stands was the work of the person who shaped the book as a whole, or at least was adapted to the intentions of the book. What exactly the author/editor inherited, if anything, cannot be decided. Commonly, as we said above, the Joseph story has been assigned to the monarchic period of David-Solomon. We argued that the authorship of Genesis was second millennium, and this would apply to the Joseph piece as well (see vol. 1A, pp. 76–81). Redford's dating of the Joseph "novella" to the seventh-fifth centuries is at odds with the self-evident relationship of the story with the earlier patriarchal accounts.[120] Westermann rightly observed that scholarly emphasis on the uniqueness of the narrative has downplayed what it has in common with the patriarchal stories.[121] Redford is wrong to claim that the Joseph story can be omitted without seriously impairing the history of Israel's forefathers.[122] Such an omission leaves Jacob in Canaan, and the Pentateuch requires the events of the Joseph story to explain how Israel in light of the promise had its start in Egypt rather than Canaan. Only if one is willing to date the whole of the patriarchal narratives to a late period (as van Seters, Whybray) can this position be maintained. We contended earlier, however, that such a late date is unnecessary, if not untenable (see vol. 1A, pp. 77–79). Moreover, Redford's late dating of the Joseph story (and his rejection of the story as historically unreliable) on the basis of late Egyptian terms in the nar-

---

[118] D. Redford, *A Study of the Biblical Story of Joseph (Genesis 37–50)*, VTSup 20 (Leiden: Brill, 1970), 242.

[119] J. Vergote (*Joseph en Égypte: Genèse chap. 37–50 à la lumière des études égyptologiques récentes*, OrBibLov 3 (Louvain: Publications Universitaires, 1959) assigned it to the Nineteenth Dynasty (thirteenth century), and K. A. Kitchen contended for the late Middle Kingdom to the early Second Intermediate Period (eighteenth–seventeenth centuries) with a light updating in the thirteenth century, a position agreed with by Hoffmeier (see *Israel in Egypt*, 78, 98 and notes).

[120] Redford, *Joseph*, 242–50; *Canaan, Egypt, and Israel in Ancient Times* (Princeton: Princeton University Press, 1992), 422–29.

[121] Westermann, *Genesis 37–50*, 27–28.

[122] Redford, *Canaan, Egypt, and Israel*, 424.

rative has been answered in detail by Kitchen.[123]

As to the story's marks of authenticity, there is widespread agreement that it conveys an Egyptian background.[124] But do the narrative's features concur with the story's own claim of an early pre-Israelite era? Redford concluded that the author of the narrative was not as familiar with Egyptian life as has been generally perceived, and where there are authentic Egyptianisms they cannot be pinned down confidently to the Ramesside period or any one period. Kitchen has recently presented his fullest case for an early second-millennium milieu.[125] The details of personal names, titles, and customs show the author's authentic knowledge of early Egyptian culture. The common trafficking of Semite slaves in Egypt and the examples of "Asians" rising to political and social influence in the early second millennium argue for the general credibility of this early Egyptian era.[126] The Egyptian names "Zaphenath-Paneah" (41:45), "Asenath" (41:45), "Potiphera" (41:45), and "Potiphar" (37:36), according to Kitchen's reconstruction of their etymologies, suits best the early to mid-second millennium. The colonization of Avaris (Tell el-Dabʻa) and its environs in the eastern Delta and the city functioning as the capital of the Hyksos kings show that there was a populous Canaanite and Egyptian presence in this region at this time. To these can be added the details of a slave's purchase price (37:28), Joseph's rise to household overseer (39:2–5), his dreams and interpretations (chaps. 40–41), and the burials of Jacob and Joseph (50:2,26). All these are consistent with what we know of Egyptian culture in the early to mid-second millennium. Kitchen adds that some updating of Egyptian names (e.g., Potiphera) and the geographical notice "Rameses" (47:11) occurred in the thirteenth century (New Kingdom).

Redford argued that the Joseph figure at court reflects the common motif of "wiseman" found throughout Egyptian history. The "wiseman" motif involved a young man who overcame difficulties and arose unexpectedly to save the nation. But Redford argued that Joseph fits the *savior* "wiseman" figure of the first millennium better than that of the "wiseman" who is *magician* in earlier Egyptian periods.[127] Yet this assumes that Egypt's "wiseman" was the model for Joseph's character in the story. The biblical portrait of Joseph stands in contrast to the Egyptian "magician," and as for the idea of Joseph as the later savior figure, the motif of rescuer is so broadly used in the ancient Near East that it

---

[123] K. A. Kitchen, "Review of D. B. Redford," *A Study of the Biblical Story of Joseph (Genesis 37–50)* (Leiden: Brill, 1970)," *OrAnt* 12 (1973): 233–42, esp. 239–42.

[124] E.g., Vergote, *Joseph en Égypte*; J. Janssen, "Egyptian Remarks on the Story of Joseph in Genesis," *JAOL* 14 (1955–56): 63–72; for the skeptical views of Redford, see *Joseph*, 189–243.

[125] Kitchen, *Reliability of the Old Testament*, 343–51.

[126] Kitchen, "Genesis 12–50 in the Near Eastern World," 77–90; also "Joseph," *ISBE* 2.1126–30.

[127] Redford, *Canaan, Egypt, and Israel*, 427–28.

could fit many stories of diverse dates and places.

Joseph's story has no ancient parallel as a whole, and the individual parts and motifs that are claimed as Egyptian are not sufficiently specific to date the composition. The Egyptian "Tale of Two Brothers,"[128] for example, in which the younger brother rejects the seduction of the elder's wife, does not stand up as a true analogy. The motif of seduction only introduces the "Tale" having no further parallels to Joseph.[129] What they have in common at most is a general plot line of a married woman scorned by a young man who is threatened with death on the basis of the woman's false charges of rape. Not much can be derived from this broad similarity, and the dissimilarities are overwhelming.

Coats said of the Joseph story that it "employs historical verisimilitude effectively," while he denied its historical usefulness.[130] It is better to conclude that it appears historical because it *is* historical. The historical detail and historical nature of the story are recognizable because it authentically reflects historical events. No body of unassailable evidence falsifies the story's own claims for an Egyptian setting in the pre-Israelite period. Since the Egyptian evidence permits, if it does not assure, the early to mid-second millennium (Twelfth to Sixteenth Dynasties) date; and since the biblical picture itself claims this general period for the story's events, there is yet no compelling reason to deny their veracity.

3. This brings us to the third challenge for the expositor, narrowing the historical period in which to set Joseph. This determination would establish the end of the patriarchal era and therefore impinges on the dating of the later Exodus period. The two most likely Egyptian periods for Joseph are the Middle Kingdom (ca. 2100–1786) and the Second Intermediate era (ca. 1786–1550) in which the Hyksos kings ruled (ca. 1648–1540).[131] The Hyksos were Semitic invaders who exercised control of Lower Egypt from their capital city Avaris. The term "Hyksos" is a Greek rendering of the Egyptian word for "ruler(s) of foreign land(s)."[132]

Our earlier discussion of the date of Abraham included a chronological reconstruction that placed Abraham's birth at 2166 and set Joseph's lifespan (1916–1806) in the Twelfth Dynasty (1963–1786), with Jacob's descent into Egypt at 1876. E. Merrill argued that many features of the story can be better explained in this early Egyptian setting. The personal names are Egyptian, not Semitic (as Hyksos); Joseph shaved himself before facing Pharaoh, which fits Egyptian rather than Semitic custom (41:14); the story shows Egyptian preju-

---

[128] *ANET,* 23–25.

[129] Noted by Coats, "Joseph," 981.

[130] Ibid., 980–81.

[131] The beginning date of Hyksos rule is disputed as well as whether they infiltrated peacefully or invaded Egypt; for the Hyksos era, see M. Bietak, "Hyksos," *OEAE* 2.136–42.

[132] D. Redford, "Hyksos," *ABD* 3.341.

dice against Semites (43:32; 46:34); and the embalming process was Egyptian practice (50:2–3).[133] Also, as we noted earlier, there is ample evidence from the Middle Kingdom showing Semites entering Egypt and holding high positions, such as we find for biblical Joseph. M. W. Chavalas and M. R. Adamthwaite came to the same general conclusion but specified that Joseph's pharaoh was either Senusert (Sesostris) III (1862–1843) or Amenemhet III (1843–1798). Among the evidence they present is the land reforms of Senusert in which there was a centralization of authority under a vizier, similar to what is portrayed in Genesis 47. Afterward, the Hyksos regime reversed this policy by returning the governance of land to local districts.[134]

Many scholars who seek a specific historical setting point to the Hyksos regime.[135] This would conveniently explain why Joseph as a Semite gained acceptance among the aristocracy of an Egypt governed by the Semite Hyksos. Also Hyksos rule in the eastern Delta harmonizes well with the giving of nearby Goshen to their honored Semite guests (Jacob's family). The explanatory comment "Egyptian" in 39:1 for Potiphar suggests by inference the ruling elite were Hyksos. That the Egyptians found shepherds repugnant can also fit the Hyksos model (46:33–34) when the matter is explained by their social role as shepherds, not their ethnicity. Urban elitists such as the Hyksos rulers of Avaris despised the pastoralists who frequented the eastern Delta during periods of drought in Syria-Palestine.[136]

As to which of these eras is preferred is largely influenced by the chronology one adopts for the Exodus.[137] If taken as thirteenth century, the 400/430-year exile would put Joseph in Egypt at ca. 1700 (Thirteenth Dynasty), in the Second Intermediate period, just before the rise of the Hyksos era (ca. 1648). Kitchen provides a chronological scheme of 400/430 years, beginning with the Exodus at ca. 1260/1250, thus ca. 1720/1700 for Joseph and ca. 1690/1680 for Jacob's descent into Egypt.[138] If the fifteenth-century date (1446) is preferred, the nineteenth century (Middle Kingdom) would be appropriate.

We conclude that it is not possible to correlate the Joseph narrative confi-

---

[133] Merrill, *Kingdom of Priests,* 49–53.

[134] M. W. Chavalas and M. R. Adamthwaite, "Archaeological Light on the Old Testament," *The Face of Old Testament Studies,* 75–78, relying on J. R. Battenfield, "A Consideration of the Identity of the Pharaoh of Genesis 47," *JETS* 15 (1972): 77–85.

[135] E.g., G. E. Wright, *Biblical Archaeology,* 2d ed. (Philadelphia: Westminster, 1962), 54–58; R. K. Harrison, *Introduction to the Old Testament* (Grand Rapids: Eerdmans, 1969), 170–71; B. Halpern, "The Exodus and the Israelite Historians," *Eretz-Israel* 24 (1993): 89–95; and J. K. Hoffmeier, "Egyptians," *Peoples of the Old Testament World* (Grand Rapids: Baker, 1994), 286; id., *Israel in Egypt,* 98.

[136] J. K. Hoffmeier (personal communication).

[137] For a summary of the discussion see W. H. Shea, "The Date of the Exodus," *Giving the Sense,* 236–55.

[138] Kitchen, *Reliability of the Old Testament,* 359.

dently to a specific time based on the archaeological record alone. Semites were present in significant numbers at all periods in Egypt. "The material goods, cultic architecture, and religious practices of the Asiatics in the Delta during the Hyksos period reflect an amalgam of Syro-Palestinian and Egyptian features."[139] Thus we cannot be sure if the Egyptian practices reflected indicate an Egyptian regime or a Hyksos one that assimilated Egyptian culture. Until more information is recovered, a consensus is not in sight. Meanwhile, we think that the early date more closely conforms to the biblical picture of the exodus, and the archaeological evidence for the late date is inconclusive.

(7) Conclusion

For the purposes of this commentary, the theological exposition of the patriarchal narratives rests on a historical foundation of actual persons and events as self-evident by the composition itself. The precise historical era is difficult to correlate with a specific period on the basis of historical artifacts alone, but the biblical data point to the early second millennium, and the extrabiblical evidence permits this assessment (but cannot confirm it). The weight of the evidence for Israel's forefathers should be derived from the *final* form of the text (Pentateuch), which we have said is a unified composition coming from the second millennium (see vol. 1A, pp. 76–81).

2. Religion of the Patriarchs

The title of this discussion reflects the essential question faced by the interpreter in relating the cultic and family practices of the patriarchs to Mosaic orthodoxy and Christian norms. Although the Pentateuch shows a continuity in the worship of God between the patriarchs and later Israel, chiefly in the use of the divine name "LORD" (Yahweh),[140] there are significant differences in patriarchal religion that led many scholars to contend that the Hebrew Fathers observed a form of religion distinct from the Mosaic tradition of Yahwism. The primary distinction was "the God *(El)* of the Fathers" form of religious expression (e.g., "the God of Abraham and the God of Nahor," 31:53). Also traditional Judaism and traditional Christianity have believed that Israel's authentic religion from its beginnings was monotheistic, standing in contrast to the polytheism of all other nations. Modern scholarship, however, following the lead of J. Wellhausen, contends that Israel did not hold to a "pure monotheism" until the exilic time of Deutero-Isaiah. We will examine below the traits of patriarchal

---

[139] J. Weinstein, "Hyksos," *OEANE* 3.134.

[140] Among other hints of continuity, see Gen 19:5–6 with Lev 18:22; 20:13; Gen 34:14–17 with Exod 12:48–49; Gen 35:22 and 49:4 with Lev 18:18; 20:11; Deut 22:30; 27:20; Gen 38:1–11 with Deut 25:5–10.

religion and the question of monotheism, and we will conclude with comments on the relationship of patriarchal religion and Christian worship and practice.

(1) "God of the Fathers"

In the patriarchal narratives there is a high incidence of the divine names *Elohim, El,* and *El* compounds (e.g., *El Elyon*; *El Shaddai*), and conversely there is no person's name bearing the theophoric element *-yah* (e.g., *yĕhôšuaʿ*, Joshua) from the divine name *Yahweh* (possible exception, Jochebed [Exod 6:20]). According to the typical reconstruction by critical scholars, Exod 6:2–3 (Priestly source) has been usually understood to mean that the patriarchs did not know God by the name *Yahweh*, which was only first introduced to Israel by Moses (Exod 3:14–15, Elohist). Rather, the Fathers knew God as *El Shaddai* ("God Almighty," e.g., 17:1) and by the clan identification "God *(El)* of the Fathers" (e.g., 31:42). On the face of it, this contradicts the recurring use of *Yahweh* in early Genesis (e.g., 2:4b) and the particular notice that early humanity called on "the name of the LORD *[Yahweh]*" (4:26b, Yahwist). Although we discussed this issue in part elsewhere (vol. 1A, pp. 293–94), here it is appropriate to revisit the topic in the context of patriarchal religion.

Every modern discussion of patriarchal religion begins with A. Alt's *Der Gott der Väter* ("The God of the Fathers") published in 1929.[141] His central thesis became the accepted view among scholars in the twentieth century.[142] On the basis of hints, such as Exod 3:14 and Josh 24:2, Alt believed that Israel's ancestors observed a different form of religion that the biblical authors had camouflaged by equating the patriarchs' gods with Yahweh. Only a few passages still revealed this older form of family religion (e.g., 31:53; 46:1–3). Also by drawing on the analogy of the cult of ancestors observed among the Nabateans of Arabian heritage (first–second centuries A.D.), he concluded that Genesis retained in its earliest literary stratum remnants of the pre-Israelite form of religion, "the God of the Fathers."[143] Against his predecessors, Alt showed that "the God of the Fathers" was not an invention of the later Hebrew authors but was an authentic memory of Israel's earliest religion.

This "God of the Fathers" form of religion was characterized by an anonymous deity identified by the god's relationship to an individual whom the deity had adopted (e.g., "the God of Abraham and the Fear of Isaac," 31:42; cf. 28:13; 31:53; Exod 3:6,15–16). The deity was the benefactor of the ancestor and his clan, and the ancestor developed a cult perpetuating the worship of the

---

[141] A. Alt, "The God of the Fathers," *Essays on OT History and Religion*, trans. R. Wilson (Garden City: Doubleday, 1967), 3–100.

[142] For a critique of the history-of-traditions approach, beginning with Alt, see van Seters, *Abraham in History and Tradition*, 139–48.

[143] "God of my father," 31:5,42; 32:9; "God of your father," 26:24; 28:13; 31:29;43:23; 46:3; 50:17; "God of your fathers," e.g., Exod 3:14–16; Deut 1:11; "God of his father," 46:1.

deity. Early among the Israelite tribes were many such cults, according to Alt, including three dominant deities: "the God of Abraham" (31:53), "the Fear [paḥad] of Isaac" (31:42), and "the Mighty One [ʾābir] of Jacob" (49:24).[144] The nomadic lifestyle of these early cults made their deities portable who superintended the tribe's movements. When the Israelite tribes settled Canaan, they encountered local deities attached to shrines, such as *El Bethel* (31:13; 35:7). These two forms of religion, the *Elim* ("gods") and "the God of the Fathers," were assimilated by the biblical editors as they manufactured the sagas that told of how God revealed himself to the Fathers at holy places. A fictitious genealogy was fashioned to unite the disparate tribes (Abraham, Isaac, Jacob), and Yahwism, which had gained ascendancy, was imposed on the old stories so as to equate the deities with Israel's national God, Yahweh.

Alt's reconstruction was modified in subsequent studies that showed that "the God of the Fathers" was not anonymous nor migratory, but his view on the antiquity of the patriarchs' religion continued to be maintained by many.[145] The Nabatean analogy was deemed too remote, since by that time the Nabateans had become sedentary. More credible was the comparative material coming from the early second millennium. Old Assyrian evidence showed that the formulation "the god of the fathers" was not necessarily an anonymous deity (e.g., "May Ashur and Ilabrat, the God of our father, be witness," from Kanesh [ca. 1900]).[146] Genesis retained the *El* names because they were truly archaic and were in currency among the populations of Canaan. Moreover, since the religious practices of the Fathers differed from the Mosaic era (e.g., erecting pillars, 28:18; cf. Lev 26:1), it is evident that their customs were not of first-millennium innovation. Together, this picture of the Genesis author's fidelity to the archaic character of the stories supports the authenticity of his depiction of the religious faith of the patriarchs.

Following in the footsteps of W. F. Albright, F. M. Cross's work noted parallels between Canaanite *El* and biblical *El,* and he concluded that the *El* deity of the patriarchs was a form of the Canaanite *El*-religion they adopted. The *El* titles were the different names of the same patriarchal deity *(El Shaddai).* Since the patriarchs did not resist idolatry or conflict with the religions of the land, as we find it overtly condemned in the Torah and in the Prophets, Y. Kaufmann presumed that "there [was] no religious difference between the patriarchs and

---

[144] Also Ps 132:2,5; Isa 1:24 ("Mighty One of Israel"); 49:26; 60:16.

[145] See, e.g., J. Lewy, "Les Textes paléo-assyriens et l'Ancien Testament," *Revue l'historie des religions* 110 (1934): 29–65; F. M. Cross, *Canaanite Myth and Hebrew Epic: Essays in the History of the Religion of Israel* (Cambridge: Harvard University Press, 1973), 3–75; T. McComiskey, "The Religion of the Patriarchs: An Analysis of *The God of the Fathers* by Albrecht Alt," in *The Law and The Prophets: Old Testament Studies Prepared in Honor of O. T. Allis* (Nutley, N.J.: Presbyterian & Reformed, 1974), 195–206.

[146] Kitchen, *Reliability of the Old Testament*, 328–30.

their surroundings."[147] Thus monotheism was not a feature of patriarchal religion. Cross further proposed that originally *Yahweh* was an epithet for Canaanite *El,* and because of similarities between the old *El* of the Fathers and the religion of Yahwism the two forms of religion easily assimilated into one religion, equating *El* and Moses' *Yahweh* as one deity. J. C. de Moor contended that the Israelites in the Late Bronze Age elevated their tribal manifestation of *Yahweh-El* as the supreme God in response to the rising fame of Baal over a weak *El* figure among the Canaanites.[148] Others believed that the assimilation was much later. M. Köchert argued against Alt's assertion that the *El* epithets were solely early, contending that the patriarchs' form of family religion was not unique or pre-Yahwistic; it was essentially the same popular religion practiced down to the seventh or sixth centuries that coexisted with national Yahwism.[149] K. van der Toon's study of premonarchic religion also concluded that "the God of the Fathers" religion was still remembered, if not exercised, into the eighth century and later was reconciled to national Yahwism.[150]

The popular reconstruction of later Israel's merging of the original El religion and rising Yahwism has its problems. (1) As for the proposed equation between Canaanite *El,* the proper name of the chief deity of the Canaanite pantheon, and the patriarchs' "God *[El]* of the Fathers," the similarities of language and character between the two deities do not require that they were accepted as one and the same by the patriarchs. *Elohim* and the singular forms *El* and *Eloah* were widely used in the Semitic world as the common name for "God, god(s), deity." We must not assume that the shared use of the name *El* by Abraham and his Canaanite neighbors meant the patriarchs adopted the same *El* deity of the Canaanites.[151] The Melchizedek incident, for example, cannot be promoted as evidence for the patriarchs' adoption of Canaanite *El,* since the text is not clear that Abraham frequented a Jerusalem cult site (if one existed), for Melchizedek came *out* of the city to meet Abraham (14:18–20). (2) It is better to look at the character and practices of patriarchal religion for comparative purposes than to rely on the ambiguous name *El.* The polytheism, idolatry, and cultic fertility practices of Canaanite religion (albeit later centered in Baal) make it doubtful that the patriarchs possessed a form of Canaanite *El*-reli-

---

[147] Y. Kaufmann, *The Religion of Israel from Its Beginnings to the Babylonian Exile*, trans. M. Greenberg (New York: Schocken, 1972 [1960]), 222.

[148] J. C. de Moor asserts that this was not "pure monotheism," but the "roots of biblical monotheism" can be traced to Israel's ancestor Jacob (35:1–4) (*The Rise of Yahwism: The Roots of Israelite Monotheism*, BETL 91, 2d ed. [Leuven: Peeters/Leuven University Press, 1997], 363–64).

[149] M. Köckert, *Vätergott und Väterverheissungen: Eine Auseinandersetzung mit Albrecht Alt und seinen Erben,* FRLANT 142 (Göttingen: Vandenhoeck & Ruprecht), 1988.

[150] K. van der Toorn, *Family Religion in Babylonia, Syria, and Israel: Continuity and Change in the Forms of Religious Life,* SHCANE 7 (Leiden: Brill, 1996), 236–65.

[151] See J. G. McConville, "Yahweh and the Gods in the Old Testament," *EuroJTh* 2 (1993): 107–17.

gion.[152] (3) Furthermore, as observed by R. W. L. Moberly, there is reason to question the tolerance that official Yahwism would have had toward Canaanite *El* religion, which such theories call for (see more at "Monotheism" below).[153] The practitioners of Yahwism had a high respect for the religion of the patriarchs, which would imply that the religion of Moses continued the essential beliefs of the Fathers, as the biblical text presents.

Rather than the common historical-critical explanation for the juxtaposition of *El* and *Yahweh* in Genesis, Wenham propounded that the authors and editors imposed the name *Yahweh* on the Genesis narratives.[154] The patriarchs did not know the name *Yahweh,* but the storytellers, since they postdated Sinai, knew God predominantly by the personal name *Yahweh.* The early (pre-Yahwistic) stories were told from the later Yahwistic perspective of the narrators of Genesis. Although they maintained certain historical distinctives of patriarchal religion (e.g., "the God of the Fathers"), the names *El* and *Yahweh* for God were historically blurred. This anachronism in effect showed that the patriarchs' religion was pre-Sinai, that is, "the Old Testament of the Old Testament," as Moberly coined it.[155] In Wenham's analysis of the distribution of the divine names, he observed that the narration has *Yahweh* often, but it appears sparingly in the direct speeches of Yahweh and in the reports of Yahweh's words. But it is difficult to explain on the view of anachronism how the storytellers did this so freely if it were already accepted that the patriarchs did not know the proper name *Yahweh,* as the biblical writers reputedly evidence (Exod 3:14–15[E]; 6:2–3[P]). If this were the case, the authors and editors left hopeless contradictions where the name occurs in direct speech (e.g., 15:2; 24:12; 28:16; 32:9), including divine speech (e.g., 15:7; 16:11; 18:14,19; 28:13). Moreover, the assumption that the name *Yahweh* was unknown to Moses prior to Exod 3:13 raises the obvious problem about how the knowledge of the name per se would win an audience with the Hebrew slaves if they did not know the name to begin with (Exod 3:13). Kitchen dubs the name *Yahweh* as the real "password" that was needed for Moses' credibility.[156]

An exegetical alternative to the common interpretation of Exod 6:2–3 avoids contradictions within the text and comports well with what we know

---

[152] As argued by H. H. Rowley, *Worship in Ancient Israel: Its Form and Meaning* (Philadelphia: Fortress, 1967), 9–21; J. C. de Moor observed that the adoption of some Canaanite beliefs occurred but not uncritically, rejecting the ideas of magical powers associated with *El,* rising of spirits, and the sexuality of *El* and his wives ("El, the Creator," in *The Bible World: Essays in Honor of Cyrus H. Gordon* [New York: Ktav, 1980], 171–87, esp. 186).

[153] R. W. L. Moberly, *The Old Testament of the Old Testament: Patriarchal Narratives and Mosaic Yahwism* (Minneapolis: Fortress, 1992), 195–97.

[154] G. Wenham, "The Religion of the Patriarchs," *Essays on the Patriarchal Narratives,* 162–95.

[155] Moberly, *The Old Testament,* 53–78.

[156] Kitchen, *Reliability of the Old Testament,* 571.

from the ancient Near East regarding deities. The "revelation" of the name *Yahweh* at Sinai was new understanding given to Moses concerning the nature of Israel's God, not the disclosure of an unknown appellative.[157] The Hebrew slaves knew the name but did not know the significance of the name for their historical situation in Egypt. El Shaddai was known as the God of promise (e.g., 17:1; 28:3; 35:11,47; 48:3; 49:25), but now God will make known experientially Yahweh's attributes, not previously appreciated, when the people will realize the promises through deliverance from Egyptian bondage.[158] C. Seitz comments accordingly, "What that account [Exod 6] seeks to establish is that the God known as YHWH had appeared to the ancestors but was not known as he truly was until Exod 14 and the victory at the sea."[159] Moreover, Millard and Kitchen show that such an expansion of the significance of the name *Yahweh* is similar to the progression of divine names common in the ancient Near East (e.g., the roles of Aten and Amun-Re).[160] More came to be known or attributed to the deity. This was the case of the appellative *Yahweh* whose meaning ("I AM WHO I AM," Exod 3:14) provides new insight of Israel's need for a saviour (Exod 6).

In summary, we found the biblical portrait of continuity between the deity of the patriarchs and the God of Moses credible, and the common historical reconstruction resulting in two different deities unnecessary, if not untenable. Moreover, the name *Yahweh* was always known to the ancestors, thus avoiding an obvious contradiction in the text that both ancient and modern interpreters can readily observe.

---

[157] See J. A. Motyer, *The Revelation of the Divine Name* (London: Tyndale, 1959), 11–17. Alternatively, some interpret a rhetorical negative, i.e., "but by my name the LORD, did I not make myself known to them?"; see W. J. Martin, *Stylistic Criteria and the Analysis of the Pentateuch* (London: Tyndale, 1955), 17–19; G. R. Driver, "Affirmation by Exclamatory Negation," *JANES* 5 (1973): 109; and cf. F. I. Andersen, *The Sentence in Biblical Hebrew* (The Hague: Mouton, 1974), 102.

[158] A. P. Ross likens it to Isa 52:6: "Therefore, my people will know my name"; the Babylonian exiles knew the name *Yahweh* but now they will "know" (experience) liberation ("Did the Patriarchs Know the Name of the LORD?" in *Giving the Sense*, 337). Cf. the rhetorical function of *Shaddai* in Genesis and Exodus in W. Warning, "Terminological Patterns and the Divine Epithet *Shaddai*," *TynBul* 52 (2001): 149–53.

[159] C. Seitz, *Word Without End: The Old Testament Witness as Abiding Theological Witness* (Grand Rapids: Eerdmans/Cambridge, U.K., 1998), 245; Seitz demurs the old idea of conflicting sources, arguing that Exodus 3 and 6 cohere exegetically and theologically in their respect contexts, but he still retains a literary analysis that maintains different levels of tradition in the text.

[160] A. R. Millard, "Abraham, Akhenaten, Moses and Monotheism," in *He Swore an Oath*, 124 and Kitchen, *Reliability of the Old Testament*, 329.

(2) Monotheism

Was monotheism the religious tenet of Israel's earliest ancestors as the Bible implies? Or was it a later innovation? The influence of Wellhausen's developmental approach to reconstructing the history of Israel's religion can still be seen today. He argued that Israel's religion evolved from henotheism to monolatry (practical monotheism) and last to the "pure monotheism" of Deutero-Isaiah (exile). Opposition arose with W. F. Albright and others, who contended that monotheism was the invention of the Mosaic period, which stood in stark opposition to the polytheism of the nations. In Albright's view, Canaanite *El* was the same deity as the patriarchal deity *El Shaddai,* and at the Mosaic introduction of the name *Yahweh* the god *El* and *Yahweh* were accepted in the biblical tradition as the same deity who was identified as the God of Israel from the inception of creation. Thus *Yahweh* and *El* were accepted as the same deity.[161]

The trend since the 1970s toward giving priority to archaeological evidence over the biblical witness due to the skepticism of the biblical portrait's reliability led to a new understanding of Israel's religion, although it showed some superficial similarity to Wellhausen's developmentalism. Israel's religion and culture were indigenous to Canaan, including the Canaanite pantheon, headed by Canaanite El and his various consorts. Early in Israel's history, Yahweh was considered a member of El's pantheon as was Baal and the goddess Asherah. Thus El and Yahweh were historically two different deities and Baal was legitimate among the Israelites. Asherah was the consort of Yahweh as she was for El and Baal.[162] Remnants of this early form of "polytheistic Yahwism" can be seen in the Bible (e.g., 49:18,24–25; Deut 32:8–9; Ps 82:6). At the rise of the monarchy, the nation elevated Yahweh, and in the ninth century or afterward a "Yahweh alone movement"[163] played a major factor in forming Israel's national identity. Some scholars of this stripe argued that the idea of "Yahweh alone" reached back to earlier times (Moses), and, at

---

[161] Among those who believe that *Yahweh* and *El* were the same deity are Kaufmann, *The Religion of Israel;* Albright, *Yahweh and the Gods of Canaan;* Cross, *Canaanite Myth;* de Moor, *The Rise of Yahwism;* and W. H. C. Propp, "Monotheism and 'Moses': The Problem of Early Israelite Religion," *UF* 31 (Münster: 2000 Ugarit-Verlag, 1999): 37–75.

[162] Cf. "Yahweh and his Asherah" in the texts of Kuntillet 'Ajrud and Khirbet el-Qom. For a discussion of idols representing Yahweh, see R. S. Hendel, "Aniconism and Anthropomorphism in Ancient Israel," in *The Image and the Book: Iconic Cults, Aniconism, and the Rise of Book Religion in Israel and the Ancient Near East* (Leuven: Peeters, 1997), 212–18.

[163] The view of Morton Smith, *Palestinian Parties and Politics That Shaped the Old Testament* (New York: Columbia University Press, 1971) and B. Lang, "The Yahweh-Alone-Movement and the Making of Jewish Monotheism," in *Monotheism and the Prophetic Ministry: An Essay in Biblical History and Sociology* (Sheffield: Almond Press, 1983), 13–59.

the other end of the spectrum, others assigned it to the Persian period.[164] During the exilic and postexilic periods, the polytheism (whose vestiges alone can be recognized) was muted, either by erasing certain polytheistic elements or by reducing the hierarchy of gods to a divine counsel of angels (e.g., 6:1– 4). The characteristics of El, the original chief deity of Israel, were absorbed by Yahweh. Thus increasingly Yahweh became the prominent deity and eventually the sole deity. Monotheism, according to Mark Smith, was a rhetorical device that contributed to the formation of postexilic Israel's identity, separating them from the religions of the ancient Near East. Thus Smith concluded, monotheism in Israel was not the result of a contrast to polytheism or a stage in the religion's development but rather the result of a cultural dialogue within Israel's exilic and postexilic community. The exclusivity of Yahwistic monolatry was expressed in absolute language (monotheism) to reinforce Israel's sole loyalty to Yahweh and to identify the insiders.[165]

The objections to this proposal center on unsubstantiated assumptions of a common culture between Israel and Canaan, which led to the notion of a shared religion of polytheism.[166] The chief hurdle to this theory is the term *ʾel,* which in the Hebrew Bible can be either the deity's personal name El or the generic term "deity, god." Thus *ʾel* cannot always be confidently differentiated from Yahweh in the text. Also, that the imagery and symbols of Canaanite deities occur in the Bible does not mean that Israel worshiped these deities; one can conclude that the same symbols can be used for different entities. Further assumptions include that (1) the biblical texts underwent a substantial Deuteronomistic purging of polytheism, (2) the development of Israel's religion must be only in the direction from polytheism to the worship of a sole deity, and (3) that all references to "Asherah" in the monarchy are allusions to Yahweh and feminine language used of Israel's God indicates the assimilation of Asherah and Yahweh.

On the positive side, there are reasons for sustaining the traditional view that monotheism was accepted by the forebears of the Israelites from the beginning.

---

[164] Among those who contend that Israel's preexilic religion was a "subset" of Canaanite polytheism are R. Gnuse, *No Other Gods: Emergent Monotheism in Israel,* JSOTSup 241 (Sheffield: Sheffield Academic Press, 1997); Mark Smith, *The Early History of God: Yahweh and the Other Deities in Ancient Israel,* 2d ed. (Grand Rapids: Eerdmans, 2002); *The Origins of Biblical Monotheism: Israel's Polytheistic Backgrounds and the Ugaritic Texts* (Oxford: Oxford University Press, 2001); J. Day, *Yahweh and the Gods and Goddesses of Canaan,* JSOTSup 265 (Sheffield: Sheffield Academic Press, 2002); and E. Greenstein, "The God of Israel and the Gods of Canaan: How Different Were They?" in *Proceedings of the Twelfth World Congress of Jewish Studies Jerusalem, July 29–August 5, 1997, Division A: The Bible and Its World* (Jerusalem: World Union of Jewish Studies, 1999), 47–58.

[165] Smith, *Origins of Biblical Monotheism,* 154.

[166] We rely on R. S. Hess's review of "The Early History of God: Yahweh and the Other Deities in Ancient Israel," *Themelios* 18 (1992): 27.

As for the scholarly assumption that Exod 6:2–3 distinguishes historically between El Shaddai and Yahweh, it begs the question of why the putative Priestly author (exilic) would have introduced a contradiction to 4:26b, which many scholars presume was known to him. The scholarly rebuttal requires that 4:26b is a late exilic or postexilic addition. Moreover, Millard has shown that the monotheism of Pharaoh Akhenaten (Amenhotep IV) in the fourteenth century indicates that the idea of monotheism could have been experienced in the second millennium.[167] The deity Aten, the sun disk, became the sole deity venerated by Akhenaten. Neither the name nor the identity of Aten was newly introduced by the king; the name had a rich, complex prehistory. Millard shows that this feature can be demonstrated conclusively in the case of the north Arabian deity Ruda (for the seventh century down to the Roman period). The same could be posited for the name and meaning of *Yahweh*. The name could well have been known to Israel's ancestors and was perpetuated across the centuries. As the name and deity Aten took on new significance at the reign of Akhenaten, the name *Yahweh* had fuller meaning at the revelation given Moses. Kitchen builds on Millard's argument by showing that "monotheistic tendencies" in Egypt could be found earlier with the rise of Amun as the chief deity (e.g., The Cairo Hymn to Amun, ca. 1500–1400). Moreover, the patriarchs did not revere any deity other than El (at least monolatry), although they came into contact with widely received deities (Baal and Asherah).[168] Propp also observes that in Israel, unlike in Egypt, Mesopotamia, and Syria, there is no obvious evidence of polytheism: "Again, if the biblical authors were polytheists, where are their myths, god lists and prayers?"[169] It is best to understand that the allusions to other deities in Israel (e.g., Kuntillet 'Ajrud) were "what *was* but not what *ought* to be."

(3) El Names of God

The compound names of God *(El)* in Genesis are *El Elyon* (14:18–20,22), *El Roi* (16:13), *El Shaddai* (17:1; 28:3; 35:11; 43:14) and *Shaddai* alone (49:25), *El Olam* (21:33), and *El Bethel* (31:13; 35:7). Jacob named his altar at Shechem "El Elohe Israel," meaning "*El* (God), the God of Israel" (33:20). Here, clearly *El* is a proper name, referring to the one true God. Outside of Genesis is the compound *El Berit* (= *Baal Berit*, Judg 9:4,46), where it refers to the Canaanite deity Baal. The traditional renderings of these names use "God" for *El* and the take compound word as its appellative. Thus *El Elyon* is "God Most High" and so forth. The appellatives *Elyon* (e.g., Num 24:16) and *Shaddai* (e.g., 49:25; Num 24:4,16) can also stand by themselves.

---

[167] Millard, "Abraham, Akhenaten," 119–29.

[168] Kitchen, *Reliability of the Old Testament,* 330–33.

[169] Propp, "Monotheism and 'Moses,'" 522.

El Elyon ("God Most High") was the name of God known to Melchizedek who was king-priest of Salem (14:18–20; see comments there). Most likely "Salem" was the premonarchic name of Jerusalem (Ps 76:2[3]), but it is not said in Genesis that *Elyon* was tied to a Canaanite sanctuary at Jerusalem. *Elyon*, however, had a royal association by virtue of Melchizedek and David (2 Sam 23:1; Ps 110:4).[170] Melchizedek identified *Elyon* as "Creator of heaven and earth." As a Canaanite king Melchizedek acknowledged the God of the patriarch as the one true God by using the *El*-language that he knew.[171] "Creator of the earth" *(qnh ʿrṣ)* was an epithet used for Canaanite *El*.[172] Abraham accepted the language of the priest and further identified *Elyon* as *Yahweh* (14:22; cf. 2 Sam 22:14=Pss 18:14; 21:8; 47:2). The identity of *El Elyon* as *Yahweh* was presupposed in Melchizedek's blessing (vv. 19–20) but was clarified by Abraham when speaking to the king of Sodom (v. 22). This is shown by the allusion to "hand" in the blessing (v. 20) by the patriarch (v. 22). For Abraham the significance of the name *El Elyon* was the sovereign lordship of his God over creation and also the nations, as shown by the defeated kings of the east (cf. Deut 32:8–9).

El Roi ("the God of seeing" or "the God who sees me") was Hagar's name for God, who appeared to her in the wilderness near a spring and assured a future for her son (16:13). The precise meaning of the appellative is uncertain (see comments on 16:13). This divine encounter resulted in the naming of the nearby well "Beer Lahai Roi" (16:14), meaning "the well of the Living (God) who sees me." Her spontaneity in naming God reflects the currency of the divine name El, which the narration equates with Yahweh.

El Shaddai ("God Almighty") is the most puzzling of the *El* compounds, for its etymology remains elusive. Among the many proposals for *Shaddai (šdy)* is Akk. *šadû(m),* meaning "mountain, range of mountains" (i.e., "the one of the mountain," "mountain dweller"), which agrees with the common idea of ancient Near Eastern deities attached to particular mountains.[173] More fruitful for our understanding is the distribution of *Shaddai* in the Old Testament. In Genesis it is usually found in the context of God's revelation of covenant promises made to Abraham (17:1), which was remembered by Isaac (28:3) and reiterated to Jacob by God at Bethel (35:11). Jacob appealed to the name in the setting of prayer and blessing (43:14; 48:3). In his patriarchal blessing (49:25), *Shaddai* occurs alone, but in parallel with *El*, wherein Jacob identified the patriarchal

---

[170] M. Rose, "Names of God in the OT," *ABD* 4.1004.

[171] Sarna notes that from the biblical viewpoint, Melchizedek was a non-Israelite who maintained "the original monotheism of the human race in the face of otherwise universal degeneration into paganism" (*Genesis,* 109).

[172] *KAI,* 26A III, 18; see Cross, *Canaanite Myth,* 16.

[173] *HALOT* 4.1421. M. Weippert lists as many as eight different recommendations ("*šadday* [divine name]," *TLOT* 3.1304–10).

deity. It was this revered name *Shaddai* that was chosen as the chief appellative for the God of the patriarchs at Sinai (Exod 6:3). *Shaddai* was likely an ancient name for God, occurring in early poetry (49:25; Num 24:4; Ps 68:14[15]) and is most common in Job, where it may be truly archaic or perhaps archaistic, indicating a patriarchal setting. The English translation "Almighty" reflects the Greek *pantokrator*(Vg., *omnipotens*) found in the Apocrypha and New Testament, meaning "all power, might."[174]

El Olam ("Eternal God") occurs only in the account of Abraham's treaty with the Philistine king Abimelech at Beersheba (21:33). *El Olam* is equated by the narration with *Yahweh,* whom the patriarch worships in memorializing the event by planting a tamarisk tree. Perhaps the author included "Eternal God" in this context of treaty with the Philistine since the epithet *Olam* ("ancient, eternal") was used for Canaanite *El.*[175] *El* here, however, probably is a proper name for a deity, meaning in this construction "God."[176]

El Bethel, meaning "the God of Bethel," is the name assigned by Jacob to Bethel (Luz), where he established an altar upon his return from Aram (35:7). At that second visit, Jacob recalled the theophany of God in his dream at his departure from his father's house (28:10–22). *El Bethel* also suggested the inherent play in the name *Bethel* = "house of God *[El]*" (28:17). Jacob had also called the sacred site *Beth Elohim,* "house of God *[Elohim]*" (28:22). In both passages the God of Bethel is identified as *Yahweh,* in the words of the Lord in the dream (28:13) and by the patriarch (28:21). Also the patriarchal linkage of God and Abraham is in the foreground. As for the other occurrence of *El Bethel* (31:3), it too is a reflex of chap. 28's dream theophany.

(4) Features of Patriarchal Religion

The essential religious beliefs of the patriarchs and those of Moses' Israel were held in common, but each had different emphases. For the patriarchs their religion was primarily informal and personal, not defined by a designated cultic site. It was also relational, not devoted to maintaining exclusivistic cultic forms (except circumcision). A. Pagalou's study concluded that patriarchal worship and religious practices were consistent with their alien lifestyle and fundamental belief in a family God.[177] We do not want to draw too strong a disjuncture, however, for the Mosaic community as depicted in the Pentateuch assumed that the Fathers' faith was prototypical of their own religious understanding and

---

[174] B. Lillie, "Almighty," *ABD* 1.160.

[175] For the epithet *'l d' 'lm* ("El, the Ancient One" or "El, Lord of Eternity"), see Cross, *Canaanite Myth,* 19.

[176] Sarna observes that Hebrew does not usually permit a proper name in construct with a following noun (*Genesis,* 150).

[177] A. Pagolu, *The Religion of the Patriarchs,* JSOTSup 277 (Sheffield: Sheffield Academic Press, 1998).

experience. Still, patriarchal practices differed in remarkable ways from later Israelite prescriptions, such as the prohibition against founding sacred pillars (28:18; 35:14) and trees (21:33). The patriarchs did not observe sabbath or dietary laws, and the only priest in Genesis is the Canaanite Melchizedek. The occurrences of only one vow made to God (28:10–22) and only one act of purification ritual (35:1–5) distinguish the patriarchal practice from Mosaic law, which provides extensive regulations for vows (e.g., Lev 27; Num 30; Deut 23) and purification procedures (e.g., Lev 12:1–8; 14:49–53; Num 8:5–22; 19:11–19). Also Jacob buried foreign gods (35:1–5), which was common in the ancient Near East, whereas Moses required that they be destroyed (Deut 7:5,25; 12:3).[178]

The following features are not exhaustive, for the Genesis narratives only present a partial picture of how the Fathers worshiped God.

PERSONAL. In addition to the name *El Shaddai,* the patriarchs acknowledged God by the personal appellative *Yahweh,* the God of Israel, who had chosen and blessed the patriarch and his descendants. The recurring phrases "the God of my/your/his father(s)" indicated the clan relationship of God and Abraham's family. The "God of Nahor" reflected this same kind of clan relationship (31:53; cf. 46:1–3). Repeatedly, the divine promises are couched in the circumstances of patriarch and family. This feature distinguished patriarchal religion from their Canaanite contemporaries who focused on religious sites. For example, *El Shaddai* is not identified by a toponym (e.g., *El Bethel*). Canaanite shrines tended to localize the gods, but the God of the family abided with them in whatever place they sojourned. It was therefore the habit of the patriarchs to erect altars and pillars at the various sites where they resided. Patriarchal building of altars usually occurred outside settled communities, thus independent of prominent local shrines. Some places, such as Beersheba and Bethel, held special importance, but shrines were not central to their religion, as we find Jerusalem and Bethel were in later Israel. The building of altars usually occurred outside of communities unrelated to shrines. There is no indication in Genesis of an exclusive site as the place to meet with God, as was the case with the tabernacle in the Mosaic era (e.g., Deut 12:11).

RELATIONAL. Cultic form was essential to Mosaic religion with its tabernacle, distinctive priesthood, and sacrificial requirements. Religions in the ancient Near East typically demonstrated a highly organized system of cultic life. Patriarchal practice had no sanctuary, no official priesthood, and no cultic laws requiring sacrifice or festival. Relationship more than formal religious duties (excepting circumcision) characterized patriarchal religion (cf. 15:1; 17:1–2), especially God's linkage with the clan who superintended the life of the tribe. The religious response of the patriarchs was extemporaneous, not

---

[178] Ibid., 234.

imposed by the cult.[179] Mosaic practice was not void of relationship, including the vital human relationships, for the Sinai covenant presupposed the salvific bonding of God and a redeemed people (Exod 20:1), but Israel's relationship was precariously preserved by maintaining explicit cultic law (e.g., Lev 26; Deut 28).

Patriarchal clans identified themselves in relationship to the patriarch and his God. Thus genealogical relationships were critical to the religious life of the patriarchal tribes (e.g., 31:42; 32:9; 49:25). The relationship between God and patriarch, once established, could only be entered into by a relationship with the clan, either by birth or servitude. Both the natural children and the alien slave underwent circumcision. It was unthinkable that tribal intermarriage was permissible without the foreign members submitting to covenant sign (Shechemites, chap. 34). Although foreigners were not repugnant to the patriarchs, as was the attitude of later Israel (e.g., Exod 34:10–16), they did not adopt the religious life of Canaan's populations (e.g., polytheism, idolatry). R. L. Cohn contends that the boundary markers between the Fathers and foreigners (e.g., Egyptians, Philistines, Canaanites) were not framed by their religious differences in Genesis but by their marital (endogamy) requirements and by their detached territorial holdings.[180] They resisted amalgamation into local groups on the basis of marriage and economic interdependence, which would diminish their familial integrity and clan identity. The later enmity against the Canaanite religion during the settlement period (e.g., Deut 7:1–2) resulted from the political threat the Canaanites posed, which always included religious conformity. Cohn, however, wrongly thinks that the deity of the patriarchs and the natives was the same. We think, rather, that familial purity and economic independence were worthy goals only because of the undergirding religious identity that was required of them. A striking evidence of religious exclusivism is Jacob's demand that his family rid themselves of "foreign gods" and submit to purification ritual so that they might worship the God of Bethel (35:1–5). That "the terror of God fell on the towns" makes better sense if the deity of Jacob was distinct from Canaanite gods. Cohn was right when observing that the promissory blessings meant the patriarchs would be by definition "outsiders" who were not to be swallowed up by the "insiders." For religious reasons, marrying within the same family (endogamy) was the custom of the patriarchs (e.g., Rebekah and Rachel). Esau's marriage to Hittite women gravely distressed Isaac and Rebekah (26:34–35; 27:46), and they ensured that Jacob would not marry a Canaanite woman by dispatching him to Rebekah's family in Aram (28:1–2). Aversion to foreign entanglements was later endorsed by law

---

[179] Pagolu, *Religion of the Patriarchs,* 85.

[180] R. L. Cohn, "Negotiating (with) the Natives: Ancestors and Identity in Genesis," *HTR* 96 (2003): 147–66.

in Israel (Exod 34:15–16; Deut 7:2–4). When the patriarchs entered into treaty with foreigners, they gave priority to their own God and religious practice (21:22–23). Theirs was not a problem of religious syncretism as we find it among the Israelites during the settlement period.[181]

REVELATION.   God revealed himself to each of the three patriarchs (e.g., 17:1; 26:23; 28:13); no such theophany occurred for Joseph or his brothers.[182] Each revelation was personal and reiterated God's promises of blessing for the family. Divine appearances were many and diverse, often in dreams (e.g., 20:3; 31:11; 37:20; cf. Heb 1:1). At times the Lord was said only to have spoken (22:1), and at others he manifested himself as a man (18:1,16–17,33; 32:24,28,30). Pagan rulers, such as pharaoh (41:1,5,25), received God's message, including a foreboding warning (Abimelech, 20:3–7). For the Egyptian slave Hagar the appearance of the "angel of the LORD" (16:7–12; cf. the angel of God, 21:17–19) conveyed a message of hope and deliverance. Two angels accompanied the Lord and were instrumental in saving Lot (chaps. 18–19). Night revelations characterized the Jacob and Joseph stories (28:10; 31:24; 41:1,5; 46:2). And divine announcements prepared the way for the births of Isaac and Jacob (18:10; 25:23). Unlike the era of Moses during which he was the primary vehicle of divine revelation (cf. Num 12:6–8), often at the tent of meeting, revelations reported in Genesis involved diverse persons and places.

WORSHIP AND PRAYER.   Patriarchal worship involved individual acts of worship, contrasting with the common corporate character of Israel's religious expressions (Israel's worship also included individual acts, e.g., the psalmist).[183] Animal sacrifice was offered presumedly upon privately erected altars, usually in response to theophanies, migrations, and covenant rites (e.g., 12:7–8; 13:4,18; 22:9,13; 26:25; 31:54; 33:20; 35:7; 46:1). Animals and birds were ritually severed by Abraham in ratifying the covenant with God (15:9–10). Human sacrifice was not practiced by Abraham, substituting instead a ram, but his willingness to sacrifice his beloved son demonstrated the patriarch's loyalty to God (22:12–13). Circumcision on the eighth day of the newborn male, the mark of covenant identity in later Israel (Lev 12:3), was inaugurated by the patriarchs as the sign of covenant bond (17:11; 21:4). The custom of tithing by Israel (e.g., Lev 27:30; Num 18:21–26; Deut 12:6) was typified by Abraham's

---

[181] Ibid.

[182] W. L. Humphreys observes that God as a "character" appears differently in the progression of the book: he is ideal sovereign in chap. 1, then appears as a complicated unpredictable figure in chaps. 2–36, and last, in the Joseph narrative (chaps. 37–50), we learn of God fundamentally through the eyes of the human characters who understand him to be a quiet force shaping future events (*The Character of God in the Book of Genesis: A Narrative Appraisal* [Louisville: Westminster John Knox, 2001]). This interpretation is extreme at places, but it shows the general trend that reinforces the point here, i.e., that God is less *obviously* involved in the affairs of the ancestors.

[183] Rowley, "Worship in the Patriarchal Age," 24.

gift to the priest Melchizedek (14:20b; cf. Heb 7:9–10) and the tithe vowed by Jacob (28:20–22; 31:13). The record of only two instances of tithing in Genesis implies that the practice was unregulated and reserved to honor exceptional events, whereas in Israel the law of the tithe was a cardinal element in its religious activities.

Typically, prayers in the ancient Near East and also Israel were spoken in a cultic setting, often pertaining to absolution, and national and personal deliverance from enemies and sickness. Patriarchal prayers, however, were informal, noncultic, and conversational, often intercessory (e.g., 18:22–32; 25:21). They could petition God for the healing of infertility (e.g., 20:17), the birth of children (e.g., 30:17,22), rescue from danger (e.g., 32:9–13), and offer thanksgiving for divine guidance (24:26–27). Patriarchal blessings also differed because they were spoken in a family setting, not bound to cultic activity, invoking God for procreation, prosperity, and land (e.g., 24:60; 28:3–4; 48:15–16,20; 49:1–28).

As for the planting of the tamarisk tree *(ʾešel)* by Abraham, it paralleled the religious act of building an altar for worship (21:33).[184] In addition to 21:33, the three passages in the patriarchal stories where the phrase "called on the name of the LORD" appears all pertain to the building of an altar for worship (12:8; 13:4; 26:25).[185] Stone pillars *(maṣṣēbôt)* commemorated divine visitations (28:18,22; 31:13; 35:14) or memorialized a treaty or tomb (31:45,51–52; 35:14,20). Although Abraham and Isaac established altars in response to theophanies, Jacob additionally raised up a sacred pillar to commemorate the appearance of God (35:7,14). The upraised pillar was anointed with oil and a drink offering in an act of worship (28:18; 35:14), but there is no textual support for the idea that the stone contained the deity or that the stone itself was worshiped. Trees and pillars, as we saw above, occur in cultic contexts (e.g., 21:33; 28:18,22), but they were banned for religious purposes in later Israel because of their association with Canaanite fertility cults (Exod 23:24; 34:13; Lev 26:1; Deut 7:5; 12:2; 16:21–22; cf. Mic 5:12).

MORALITY. The marital practices of the Fathers also show that their customs preceded the time of Moses. Abraham married his half-sister (20:12), and Jacob married sisters (29:21–30); such practices were condemned in the Torah (Lev 18:9,11,18: 20:17). Intermarriage with foreigners, as by Judah, Simeon, and Joseph, was prohibited (Exod 34:16; Deut 7:3); and friendly relations with nearby nations (e.g., Amorites, Philistines, 14:13; 15:16; 21:22–34) were also unlawful (Deut 7:1–2,16; 20:17).

---

[184] N. M. Sarna, "Genesis 21:33: A Study in the Development of a Biblical Text and the Rabbinic Transformation," in *From Ancient Israel to Modern Judaism: Essays in Honor of Marvin Fox* (Atlanta: Scholars, 1989), 1.69–75, cited in Wenham, *Genesis 16–50*, 94. On the meaning of the Hb. אֶשֶׁל ("tamarisk" or "field"?) see comments on 21:33.

[185] Pagolu, *The Religion of the Patriarchs*, 109.

Moberly observed that unlike the Mosaic law and the divine call upon the prophets, the Lord did not impose specific moral stipulations in the promissory blessings for the patriarchs. The exception was Abraham, who faced the crisis of faith and obedience in his call and blessing (15:6; 17:1; 18:19; 22:16,18; 26:5).[186] This disparity does not suggest that the patriarchs had no conventional moral standards. The text assumes there were pre-Sinai obligations that Abraham obeyed: "My [God's] requirements, my commands, my decrees and my laws" (26:5; cf. 18:19). J. K. Bruckner has contended that the "oughts" and "ought nots" stated or implied in the Genesis narratives have creation as their theological context, indicating that law was operational from the beginning of human history.[187] In the narratives we find ample correspondences between the ethics of the patriarchs and the ethical imperatives imposed on Israel (e.g., adultery, 20:1–18; Exod 20:14,17). Yet there were significant differences too, such as marriage practices. There was no moral vacuum among the patriarchs; rather, the divergence in explicitly stated obligations lies in the contrasting nature of the patriarchal and Sinai covenants. The Sinaitic covenant is bilateral and specifies obligations upon its adherents (Ten Commandments), whereas the Abrahamic is a royal charter indicating a divine grant without reference to specific obligations (see vol. 1A, p. 62, n. 62). Patriarchal covenant focused on God's beneficence on future generations rather than present conduct. Genesis shows that the moral conduct of the patriarchs had serious consequences for reward and punishment, but their moral failures did not abrogate the covenant. Israel's later compliance with Mosaic stipulations, however, was required or the divine contract was severed.

There is no moral ambiguity in the Genesis narratives. The transgressions committed by the Fathers are admitted or inferred, such as Jacob's deceitful doings, but God's grace superseded the outcome of their sins. As the apostle Paul commented, "Where sin increased, grace increased all the more" (Rom 5:20). Joseph reflected this in his understanding of the sins of his brothers, which resulted in God's good purposes of their salvation (50:20; also 45:4–11). As for his betrayal of his father, Jacob succeeded in obtaining the patriarchal blessing, but it was at a high cost to him personally and the family. By the hard experience in Laban's household, Jacob underwent a transformation, and by the Lord's grace the patriarch proved to be an appropriate progenitor of Israel's families.

Embedded in the stories are many judgments that condemned immorality by showing the harmful consequences of sin. Chief among them is the destruction of Sodom and Gomorrah for their wickedness (chaps. 18–19). As the incestu-

---

[186] Moberly, *The Old Testament*, 97–98.

[187] J. K. Bruckner, *Implied Law in the Abraham Narrative: A Literary and Theological Analysis,* JSOTSup 335 (Sheffield: Sheffield Academic Press, 2001).

ous father of the Ammonites and Moabites, the historic enemies of Israel, Lot's behavior had far-reaching consequences. Reuben, the eldest son of Jacob, lost the privilege of primogeniture because of his immoral act with Bilhah, the concubine of his father (35:22; 49:4). The murderous rampage of Simeon and Levi (chap. 34) resulted in their rejection (49:5–7). It is usually left to the participants themselves to render judgments on moral failures. Pagan kings critique Abraham and Isaac for their deceitful behavior, showing greater moral sensitivity than even the progenitors of Israel (12:18–19; 20:9–10; 26:10). Judah remarked on his sordid treatment of Tamar, "She is more righteous than I" (38:26), to which the narrator added, "He did not sleep with her again." This episode also showed that God was not indifferent to patriarchal conduct, for the narrator attributed the deaths of Judah's sons, Er and Onan, to the Lord directly (38:6,10). Recognition of accountability for their sins is found among the patriarchs, such as Joseph's brothers (42:21–22,28; 44:16). Laban knew better than to harm Jacob, for the Lord forewarned of dire results if he dared (31:24,29). And we can conclude our discussion on the high moral tone of young Joseph's retort to the seductive advances of Potiphar's wife, knowing that he must answer to God for his conduct, "How then could I do such a wicked thing and sin against God?" (39:9).

CHRISTIAN WORSHIP AND PRACTICE.   For the Christian reader of the Old Testament, patriarchal religion has a greater affinity than Mosaic formality. Patriarchal religion was spontaneous and personal, as we find in the Christian gospel, but it also involved relationship with one's family clan, as we find the Christian in terms of relationship with the church. Patriarchal worship did not observe one site, and prescribed ritual did not dominate. Likewise, Christian liberty in worship as to place and ritual comes closer to the Fathers.

The ethical practices of the patriarchs cannot serve as a model for Christian readers, but they were never intended to be models. The church valued the faith pilgrimage of the Fathers (Rom 4; Heb 11) and explained their moral deficiencies as regrettable sins not to be glossed over. Genesis, as we have already said (vol. 1A, pp. 42–54), is a pentateuchal product, formed in the shadow of Sinai's revelation. Wenham rightly concluded that the ancestors' moral improprieties were a disappointment to the Israelite reader but not surprising in light of Israel's own experience in the wilderness.[188] Genesis's heroes were commissioned and forgiven, but they also received the fruit of their choices. For Moses' Israel this was familiar ground, and for the Christian audience the call to holy living and the forgiving grace of our Lord have their first evidence in the lives of the earliest of saints.

---

[188] Wenham, "The Face at the Bottom of the Well," in *He Swore an Oath*, 185–209, esp. 205–7.

3. Theme and Motifs

Together, the theme and motifs of the patriarchal stories enable an interlacing of the narratives and reveal their theological emphases.[189] By theme we refer to the overarching idea that holds the stories together, and by motifs we mean the recurring key words or ideas that appear throughout the patriarchal corpus.

(1) Theme

Genesis concerns God's promissory blessings upon Israel's ancestors that have their *partial* realization in the lives of the patriarchs and the rise of the nation Israel (see vol. 1A, pp. 54–60).[190] Genesis 12:1–3 exhibits the three elements of the promise around which the theme of the Pentateuch is built: descendents (seed), relationship (blessing), and land. As for the patriarchal narratives, these divine promises are repeated for Abraham (12:7; 13:15–17; 15:7–21; 17:4–8; 22:16–18), Isaac (26:2–4), and Jacob (28:13–14; 35:9–12; 46:1–4). These promises are not offered in a theophany to Joseph or any of his brothers. Judah is designated as the family successor to the promises but only by inferences (see comments on chap. 38; 49:8–12) and not, in any case, in the same sense as Isaac and Jacob. Judah's brothers are treated as inclusive recipients of the promise (see vol. 1A, p. 26). This is demonstrated in Jacob's blessing (49:28) and in God's reiteration of the land promise to Moses for all Israel, Jacob's twelve sons (Exod 6:6–8).

Throughout the patriarchal stories, the promises are of first concern; even in the Joseph narrative, where they are not as readily seen, the tension of the story is the survival of the family and the perpetuation of the blessing. Moreover, the book ends with Jacob's sons in Egypt, not Canaan, just as the Pentateuch concludes with the burial of Moses and with Israel not yet in the "Promised Land." Whereas Genesis 1–11 concerns universal matters and Exodus–Deuteronomy focuses on the fate of a nation, the patriarchal accounts revolve around a single family. The Abrahamic clan forms a bridge between the universal setting and the particularistic context of the nation. "The ancestral narratives are of decisive importance for Israel's faith and understanding; they provide ballast for life in a world that kept this community endlessly off balance and in jeopardy."[191]

---

[189] For more on the theology of the patriarchal narratives, see P. R. House, *Old Testament Theology* (Downers Grove: InterVarsity, 1998).

[190] See D. J. A. Clines, *The Theme of the Pentateuch,* JSOTSup 10, 2d ed. (Sheffield: University of Sheffield Press, 1997); T. W. Mann, "'All the Families of the Earth': The Theological Unity of Genesis," *Int* 45 (1991): 34–53.

[191] W. Brueggemann, *An Introduction to the Old Testament: The Canon and Christian Imagination* (Louisville: Westminster John Knox, 2003), 47.

The image of a lone, little-known family struggling to survive in uncertain environs and maintain loyalty to its God would appear to have little prospect of influence and consequence. Yet the lives of the patriarchs had international proportions when viewed from the standpoint of the whole of Genesis and Pentateuch. The blessing intended for all humanity was cradled in the arms of the mothers of Israel as the successors to the primeval promises (1:26–28; 3:15; 9:1–3). The peoples who met the patriarchs recognized by the patriarchs' testimony that God blessed them and those favorably related to them (e.g., 21:22–24; 24:31,50; 26:26–29; 30:27; 41:39).[192] And, from the perspective of later Israel, the vicissitudes of their forefathers cast the future for the nation. Only the uninformed person reads with indifference the successes and failures of the Fathers. This is all the more the case for the Christian audience since its cherished Founder, our Lord Jesus, had his life and message rooted in the ancient promises (e.g., Matt 1:1; Acts 7; Rom 4; Gal 3–4). But while the reader may grimace with each blunder by the patriarchs and wince at each threat to the family, the tension is always surmounted by the realization that God will somehow and in timely fashion graciously propel the family, hence the promises, forward.

In the Abraham narrative (11:27–25:11) the chief tension is the question of "seed." Will Abraham trust God for an offspring? This does not let up even with the birth of Isaac, for the story keeps before us the potential threat of rival Ishmael. Once Ishmael is dispatched, the narrative retains its tension by the test of faith put to Father Abraham. Chapters 12 and 22 are literary bookends that establish Abraham's credentials, his call to Canaan, and his love for God as shown by his offering of Isaac (22:15–18). For the account's continuing interest in offspring, the story includes the lengthy chapter on obtaining an appropriate wife (Rebekah) for Isaac (chap. 24), and the matter ends with Abraham's sons by Keturah safely exiled to the east (25:1–6).

Intertwined with the question of "seed" is the second issue of "land," for a burgeoning nation must secure for itself territorial sovereignty to thrive (e.g., 15:7–21). The gift of the land assumed that the Lord God owned the land and could dispose of it as he pleased (cf. Lev 25:23; also Exod 19:5; Lev 20:22–24; Num 36:7). The present occupants of the land will be removed because of their sin (15:16; Lev 18:25), and the patriarch's descendants will receive the land (12:6–7; 13:15,17; 15:7,18–21; 17:8; 24:7; 26:3–4; 28:13; 35:12; 48:4) because of the oath made to the Fathers (e.g., Exod 6:4,8; Deut 1:8; 4:31; 11:9,21; 26:3,15). Abraham did not possess the land in his lifetime but obtained portions of it, such as a well and its adjacent

---

[192] M. D. Carroll R. explains the church's missiological imperative in terms of the patriarchs' calling ("Blessing the Nations: Toward a Biblical Theology of Mission from Genesis," *BBR* 10 [2000]: 17–34).

property by cultivation (21:25–30; cf. 26:19–32) and a cave with its field by acquisition (23:9–20; cf. 33:19; 48:21–22). The building of altars, securing land usage, and the purchase of properties show symbolically Abraham's claim to the land and point to the future possession of the land that his descendants will someday enjoy.[193]

Regarding the Jacob section (25:19–35:29), the issue of "seed" is a narrative tension among the rival brothers Jacob and Esau, but this is mitigated by the early announcement to Rebekah of its outcome (25:23). Surpassing the problem of "seed," which after all was no problem for prodigious Jacob and his wives, was the promise of "land." Jacob's self-imposed exile at the advice of Rebekah led him to the site of Abraham's departure (Haran). Will Jacob languish in Haran under the thumb of Laban or return to Canaan to enjoy the divine promise? Jacob sojourned twenty years in Paddan Aram (31:38,41), and he escaped from Laban's household only by human deception and sovereign protection. But once out of Laban's sight, he still faced brother Esau's vengeful wrath. Before his departure from Canaan, the Lord had promised Jacob at Bethel, "I will bring you back to this land" (28:15). That remembered promise was accomplished, and the patriarch made peace with Esau, whereupon Jacob bought a parcel of land at Shechem and erected an altar (33:18–20). Another theophany at Bethel assured him of future nations and of the promised land that had been the promise to Abraham and Isaac (35:11–13). The final verse of the narrative brings an end to the struggle: "Jacob lived in the land where his father had stayed, the land of Canaan" (37:1). Esau's descendants had taken up residence at Seir in Edom (36:9,31). All seemed safely in place for Jacob's sons to realize their destiny.

For Jacob, however, the permanent possession of the land was elusive. In the Joseph story (37:2–50:26) famine forced the aging patriarch to look to Egypt for sustenance, and the ensuing events took the family to Goshen under the protective care of Joseph, who had risen from Hebrew slave to pharaoh's second-in-command. Joseph had named one of his sons "Ephraim," saying, "It is because God has made me fruitful *in the land* of my suffering" (41:52, italics mine). Jacob had found the same fruitfulness in Paddan Aram outside the land of Canaan, but Joseph had no intention of returning. It was only later, after his reconciliation with his brothers, that he looked to the land of his fathers (50:24–

---

[193] For a literary study of land ownership and transference, see B. Jayaraj, "Land Ownership in the Pentateuch: A Thematic Study of Genesis 12 to Deuteronomy 34" (Ph.D. diss., University of Sheffield, 1989). Jayaraj argues that land utilization and land possession by the patriarchs in Genesis are *not* symbolic indicators of the transference of the land; the patriarchs have the assurance of the land promise only, making the actual transference occur when the Israelites settle the land. But the land promise at 15:8 by the use of the perfect נָתַתִּי ("I give") indicates the grant to Abraham's descendants is immediate (cf. 23:11; also 1:29; 9:3; 20:16); Westermann views the perfect form of the verb here as the enactment of a legal agreement (cf. 20:16; *Genesis 12–36,* 229).

25). But Jacob had never lost heart that the land of Canaan would belong to his descendants. Jacob insisted that Joseph bury him in the tomb of Abraham (47:29–31; 49:29–32). Before going to Egypt, the aged man had worshiped the Lord a last time at Beersheba, and there God had appeared again and swore anew, "I will surely bring you back again. And Joseph's own hand will close your eyes" (46:4). It was Jacob who claimed as his own the sons of Joseph, Manasseh and Ephraim, and envisioned their descendants as copossessors of Canaan's land (48:3–6).

Thus Genesis ends with Jacob (=Israel) buried in Machpelah's cave (49:29; 50:4–14), anticipating the return of his progeny from Egypt to the land of his birth. The promissory blessing of land yet awaited them when their slim number of seventy (46:27; Exod 1:5) would achieve the multitudes that were to come.

(2) Motifs

The following motifs are not exhaustive but are central to the narrative theology of the patriarchal accounts.

SIBLING RIVALRY.[194] Sibling struggle dominates the patriarchal narratives, becoming increasingly more important in each narrative, and it is found in early Genesis as well (Cain vs. Abel/Seth; Shem/Japheth vs. Ham[Canaan]). There is no overt controversy between Abraham and his brothers, Nahor and Haran, but this rivalry is found between later generations. Lot, the son of the deceased Haran (11:27–28), was the beneficiary of Abraham's successes, and strife occurred between their herdsmen over grazing rights (chap. 13). Abraham's concessions to Lot (13:8–9) and his rescue of his nephew (14:16) were met with the Lord's reaffirmation of Abraham's bright future (13:14–17; 15:1–7). Jacob and Laban, although not siblings, represented their paternal ancestors Abraham and Nahor (31:53); their dispute over ownership ended in an uneasy treaty (31:43–53). In both cases the Abrahamic clan prospered despite the rivalry, showing God's blessing on the appointed lineage.

The tension between firstborn Ishmael and younger Isaac is seen in the story as much between their mothers (Sarah and her slave girl Hagar) as it is among the boys. The single recorded incident was Ishmael "mocking" the child Isaac (21:9). "Mocking" is of the same root word as "laughter" *(ṣḥq),* which describes the joy of Sarah and the naming of "Isaac" (21:3,6). Sarah viewed Ishmael's "laughter" as a threatening derision, which resulted in her expulsion of the rival (21:14–21). The "hostility" that characterized Ishmael's descen-

---

[194] For studies on this topic, see R. Syrén, *The Forsaken First-Born: A Study of a Recurrent Motif in the Patriarchal Narratives,* JSOTSup 133 (Sheffield: Sheffield Academic Press, 1993) and R. C. Heard, *Dynamics of Diselection: Ambiguity in Genesis 12–36 and Ethnic Boundaries in Post-Exilic Judah,* SemeiaSt 39 (Atlanta: Society of Biblical Literature, 2001).

dants (16:12; 25:18) was directed against the clan of Abraham only in the purchase of Joseph for a slave by Ishmaelite merchants (37:25). They were also joined by Midianite (and perhaps Medanite) traders in disposing of Joseph in Egypt (37:28,36). These merchants, like the Ishmaelites, were descendants of Abraham by Keturah, who also had been expelled a safe distance from Isaac (25:1–4). These potential rivals were of no immediate threat to the Abrahamic family since they dwelt a considerable distance from Canaan (25:4,18).

Central to the Jacob story is the fraternal dispute over the inherited blessing between Jacob and Esau. Unlike the former rivalries, this one occurred between the sons of one mother, Rebekah. Jostling babies during her pregnancy portended the struggle that would define their lives (25:21–23). As with the Isaac-Ishmael discord, God's election of the younger son superseded the custom of primogeniture. This came about, however, through the trickery of Rebekah, who had convinced Jacob to deceive his father in order to obtain the blessing (27:5–10). This underlying motif of family strife in the Jacob stories is shown again in the anguish experienced by Laban and Rachel, who also deceived her father by confiscating his "foreign gods" (31:34–35). The Jacob-Esau confrontation at Jacob's return to Canaan was happily resolved by the humble gestures of Jacob toward his sibling, and Esau returned to Seir leaving Jacob to live securely in Canaan (33:16–20; 36:9; 37:1). Although no conflict occurred in patriarchal times, the attention in Genesis to Esau's future generation, the Edomites and their rulers (chap. 36), reflected the trouble Israel experienced in their wilderness passage (Num 20:14–21; cp. Num 24:18; Deut 23:7).

Competition between Joseph and his brothers is the driving motif of the Joseph stories. Conflict between Joseph as the "Dreamer" and his siblings resulted in his slavery in Egypt but ultimately his rise to Pharaoh's court. Conversely, in Egypt the brothers suffered at the hands of Joseph's chicanery. By ironic twist the Dreamer's vision that he would rule over the brothers (chap. 37), for which his brothers had hated him (37:8), came to pass in Egypt. But whereas the rivalry between Cain and Abel meant murder and between Jacob and Esau meant exile, the strife among the sons of Jacob ended in their survival as a family under the benevolent hegemony of one of their own. Reuben, the eldest son and presumedly the successor to the promises, had the most reason to be threatened by Jacob's love for Joseph; yet he interceded in Joseph's behalf to save him from the hands of their irate brothers (37:19–21). Joseph's testing of the brothers in Egypt was designed to learn surreptitiously about his brother, Benjamin, also born of Rachel, as to how he had been treated by the others. When Judah stepped up to defend Benjamin in the face of the boy's incarceration (44:18–34), Joseph knew that the jealousy of the brothers that had landed him in Egypt was no more among the chastened sons. From the brothers' perspective, the revelation of Joseph and subsequent reconciliation (chap. 45) were an uneasy peace that they feared would be forgotten after the death of their father. Joseph assured them, however, that no vengeance would be exacted against them; rather, he saw the hand of God in these events, and he promised perpetual care for the brothers and their families (50:15–21). Here Joseph encapsulated the theological significance of the sibling rivalries that had been a part of his family's history from its beginnings. The conflict that had been the sin of the family, bringing about so much pain, was graciously guided by God toward higher purposes. By the Egyptian sojourn, the appointed family, despite its failures, was preserved; and it could await the realization of Joseph's final words, "God will surely come to your aid" (50:25).

DECEPTION. Related to the motif of sibling rivalry is the recurring idea of deception, particularly in the Jacob and Joseph stories. The idea of deception first occurred in the garden when the serpent tricked the woman into eating the forbidden fruit. Jacob's forefathers, Abraham and Isaac, established a family proclivity toward wily behavior in dealing with their neighbors (12:10–20; chap. 20; 26:6–11). Also the hermit Lot, nephew of Abraham, was led by his childless daughters into drunkenness and incest (19:31–37). Both Abraham and Isaac lied regarding their wives, hoping to escape harm at the hands of unscrupulous men. Although embarrassed once found out, the patriarchs actually gained from their duplicity; but their advancement came by God's hand despite them, not as a reward for their behavior. Their slippery words not only punished the innocent but also jeopardized the patriarchs' wives and the promise of an elect lineage. Lest the reader think their scandalous deeds went unanswered, however, the tricksters themselves were later duped, and in regard to the promissory blessing too. Rebekah reciprocated her husband's earlier deed by advising Jacob to steal the patriarchal blessing from Isaac's preferred son, Esau, by hoodwinking his blind father (chap. 27). Abraham too contemplated the loss of his cherished son when the Lord "tested" Abraham at Moriah (22:1).

Jacob's career from the womb to his last days involved some feature of double-dealing. Although he deceived his father Isaac, brother Esau, and uncle Laban (25:29–34; 27:1–29,35; 31:20; 33:14–17), he experienced far more trouble than he dished out. He was snookered by Laban in Paddan Aram for Rachel's hand, receiving Leah instead, requiring him to double his tenure of servitude to marry Rachel (29:21–30). Later, his greatest anguish came at the hands of his own sons, who faked Joseph's death and lied about his fate (37:31–36). Moreover, Joseph's charade against his brothers in Egypt necessarily involved the old man's anguish over young Benjamin (42:36–38; 43:11–14). And Jacob's sons Simeon and Levi also tormented him when they murdered the Shechemites through deceit, wrongly using the sacred rite of circumcision and hence threatening Jacob's status in the region (34:13,30). Simeon and his brothers themselves were later the victims of deception (42:24). The women of Jacob's house also used deceptive means. Rachel repaid her brother Laban by stealing his "household gods" and hiding them (31:19,34–35), and Tamar disguised herself as a harlot in order to obtain a child by Judah (38:13–15).

In the Joseph account, trickery is central to the occasion and resolution of the plot. As with the Jacob-Esau deceptions, sibling rivalry fueled the deception by Joseph's brothers against their father when they sold Joseph into foreign hands (37:12–36). In Potiphar's house Joseph was the victim of another malevolent plan that put him in Pharaoh's prison (39:7–20), but "the LORD was with him [Joseph]" in prison (39:21a; also 39:2), and he ultimately prospered despite the ordeal. When famine in Canaan forced Jacob's sons to seek food in Egypt, Joseph, who had risen to power, deceived them through Egyptian disguise and trumped up charges of sabotage and theft, threatening to enslave young Benjamin (chaps. 42–44). His brothers interpreted their troubles as their just due from the hand of God for mistreatment of young Joseph (42:28; 44:16).

By this generational practice of deception by and among the patriarchs, the author showed how the instigators despite their self-indulgent actions did not suspend God's goal of blessing the elect family of Abraham. Also the stories showed that the culprit was the recipient of the same treatment and often more severely. Although the narration did not comment explicitly on the patriarchs' actions, the pattern of "the deceiver also deceived" and the pain that resulted from it warned against the sin of self-interest. God's sovereign purposes, however, overcame human interference—whether it was a fearful husband (Abraham, Isaac), a meddlesome mother (Rebekah), ambitious men (Laban, Jacob), or quarreling, hotheaded siblings (Joseph's brothers).

ALIENATION/SEPARATION. Estrangement and detachment occurred in the primeval stories in the expulsion of Adam and Eve from Eden (3:23–24) and the further banishment of Cain to the "land of Nod, east of Eden" (4:16). The genealogical lines of Eve's sons showed the separation between the elect Sethite clan and the rejected Cainites (4:17–24; 4:25–5:32). Also the dispersion from Shinar engendered the diverse map of Nations (10:1–32; 11:1–9), which reflected the division among Noah's three sons (9:24–27).

The patriarchal narratives of Abraham, Jacob, and Joseph, however, are *rooted* in the motif of alienation and separation. Their three accounts involve a separation from their father's household, and this motif becomes increasingly important to each succeeding story. Their respective plots also share in sibling tension which in the Jacob and Joseph stories precipitates the patriarch's separation from the family. In the case of Abraham, the family tension was less pronounced; nevertheless, it was discord with his nephew Lot, representing the Haran branch of the Paddan Aram home, that ended in Abraham's completed separation (chap. 13; see more below). The outcome of the family rift in all three narratives was the enrichment of each patriarch. Abraham became increasingly powerful while Lot lost all his possessions (Sodom), and Jacob and Joseph overcame familial obstacles to achieve autonomy.

Reconciliation is also a feature of the patriarchal accounts. Jacob and Joseph reconciled with their brothers and returned to their homeland; Jacob and Joseph when dying in Egypt made provision for their final interment in Canaan (47:30; 49:29; 50:24–25). For Abraham reconciliation to Terah's household occurred by proxy through Isaac's marriage to Rebekah (chap. 24), granddaughter of Nahor (by Milcah). Subsequently, Jacob, at his mother's insistence (28:2), took the daughters of his uncle Laban in Aram as wives.

Abraham identified himself as "an alien *(gēr)* and a stranger" in the land of Canaan (23:4; cf. 17:8), and his progeny would also one day be "strangers" *(gēr)* in Egypt (15:13; cf. 47:4; Deut 23:7). The word "alien" *(gēr)* and its verbal cognate "sojourn" *(gûr)* indicated a foreigner who took up residence for a temporary or permanent time, as in Elimelech's residency in Moab (Ruth 1:1).[195] Isaac and Jacob (and Esau) also were described as aliens sojourning in Canaan (28:4; 35:27; 37:1; 36:7). Later, during Israel's occupancy of Canaan, the alien, by adopting Israel's Yahwistic faith and by establishing permanent residency in the land became a protected member of the community (e.g., Exod 12:19,49; 22:21[20]; 23:9; Lev 19:10,33–34).

Abraham's alien status was the consequence of the divine call to separate from his countrymen as well as from his father's house (12:1). This separation took three stages before its completion. His father Terah had begun the migration of Abraham's clan by departing southern Ur for the Upper Mesopotamian site, Haran (11:31). Abraham's subsequent move from Haran to Canaan (12:4) separated him from Terah and brother Nahor's family, but Abraham's nephew Lot, representing brother Haran's offspring, accompanied Abraham to Canaan. Later the quarrel between Abraham's and Lot's herdsmen resulted in Abraham parting from Lot, which completed the separation from his father's household of Nahor and Haran (chap. 13). Jacob's alienation in Aram occurred by his self-imposed exile from Esau in Canaan, but for Joseph his Egyptian sojourn was imposed by his brothers.

In Genesis the narrowing effect of familial separations resulted in differentiating the Abraham branch from his kinsmen. The genealogies of Genesis exhibit a complex set of biological relationships that show interdependence between and within groups but also differentiation within groups.[196] By leaving the Nahor family behind in Haran, "Abram the Hebrew" (14:13) was distinguished from Nahor's descendants, Bethuel and Laban, who were identified as "Aramean" (25:20; 28:5; 31:20,24; with 22:20–23). Also Lot's descendants Ammon and Moab were distinctive from Abraham's patriarchal line (19:30–38). The term "Hebrew," however, was initially a social designation that only later took on ethnic significance (see

---

[195] For discussion of the term(s), see D. Kellermann, "גּוּר *(gûr)*," *TDOT* 2.439–49.

[196] F. Crüsemann, "Human Solidarity and Ethnic Identity," in *Ethnicity and the Bible* (Leiden: Brill, 1996), 57–76.

comments on 14:13). Usually when the term "Hebrew(s)" appears in the Old Testament, it is used by foreigners or the biblical narrator to identify the people of the Israelite (Hebrew) people (e.g., 39:14,17; 41:12; 43:32; Exod 1:15; 2:6–7; 1 Sam 4:6) and their God as "the LORD God of the Hebrews" (e.g., Exod 3:18). Joseph could, however, already identify Canaan's homeland as "the land of the Hebrews" (40:15).

Alienation and separation also occurred within the Abraham line itself so as to distinguish the elect branch of the promised seed. As noted already fraternal rivalry resulted in defining patriarchal succession. Hagar and Ishmael were expelled as a potential threat to Isaac's favored place, and Ishmael's descendants became twelve tribal chiefs of Arab peoples (21:8–21; 25:12–18; cf. 17:20). It was this same motivation that meant the expulsion of Abraham's sons by his wife Keturah and his concubines (25:1–6). Esau, the father of the Edomites, voluntarily abandoned Canaan to Jacob, averting tribal strife (33:16; 36:6–8; cp. Lot and Abraham, chap. 13).

Theologically, this motif was integral to the covenant made with Israel's ancestors. Inherently, the covenant commission meant the alien status of the Hebrew family (17:8), and Israel's fathers were long remembered as strangers to their promised land (Exod 6:4). Israel itself was only a tenant, for the land belonged to the Lord (Lev 25:3). It was, however, Israel's four-hundred-year sojourn in Egypt (15:13; Acts 7:6; 13:17) that explained the special protections guaranteed for the resident alien under Mosaic law (e.g., Exod 22:21[20]; 23:9; Lev 19:34; Deut 10:19). Moreover, the Lord loved the stranger and exhorted the Hebrews to do the same (Deut 10:18–19).

For the Christian reader, we are reminded of the alien status of Gentiles in the church who received full rights as community members through the blood of Christ, despite their once-unfavorable place (Eph 2:11–21, esp. v. 19).[197] In a metaphorical sense, the Christian community also viewed itself as an alien population. Christians have a heavenly citizenship and are "aliens" in this world; therefore they must abstain from the vices of this temporary residence (1 Pet 1:1,17; 2:11). The writer to the Hebrews marveled at the faith of Abraham, who with his sons were pilgrims in Canaan, never receiving the inherited promise of land; yet Abraham's faith in the promise stood steadfast as he expected to receive a final permanent dwelling with God (Heb 11:9–10).[198]

---

[197] The LXX's παροικειν, "to sojourn, live as an alien," and its cognates often translate גּוּר/גֵּר ("sojourn"/"alien") and תוֹשָׁב ("stranger"); the Gk. term was continued in the NT (Luke 24:18; Acts 7:6,29; 13:17; Eph 2:19; Heb 11:9; 1 Pet 1:17; 2:11).

[198] For a helpful discussion of Abraham's faith, see F. F. Bruce, *The Epistle to the Hebrews,* NICNT (Grand Rapids: Eerdmans, 1964), 296–97.

———————————— *OUTLINE OF GENESIS 11:27–50:26* ————————————

VII. Father Abraham (11:27–25:11)
    1. Abram's Beginnings (11:27–32)
    2. The Promissory Call and Abram's Obedience (12:1–9)
    3. Abram and Sarai in Egypt: Blessing Begins (12:10–13:1)
    4. Abram and Lot Part: Promises Recalled (13:2–18)
    5. Abram Rescues Lot: Abram's Faithfulness (14:1–24)
    6. Covenant Promises Confirmed (15:1–21)
    7. Abram's Firstborn Son, Ishmael (16:1–16)
    8. Covenant Sign of Circumcision (17:1–27)
    9. Divine Judgment and Mercy (18:1–19:38)
    10. Abraham and Sarah in Gerar: Promises Preserved (20:1–18)
    11. Abraham's Promised Son, Isaac (21:1–21)
    12. Treaty with Abimelech (21:22–34)
    13. Abraham's Test (22:1–19)
    14. Nahor's Family (22:20–24)
    15. Sarah's Burial Site (23:1–20)
    16. A Wife for Isaac (24:1–67)
    17. Abraham's Death and Burial (25:1–11)
VIII. Ishmael's Family Line (25:12–18)
    1. Ishmael, Son of Abraham (25:12)
    2. Ishmael's Sons (25:13–16)
    3. Ishmael's Life, Death, and Territories (25:17–18)
IX. Isaac's Family: Jacob and Esau (25:19–35:29)
    1. Struggle at Birth and Birthright (25:19–34)
    2. Isaac's Deception and Strife with the Philistines (26:1–35)
    3. Stolen Blessing and Flight to Paddan Aram (27:1–28:9)
    4. Promise of Blessing at Bethel (28:10–22)
    5. Laban Deceives Jacob (29:1–30)
    6. Birth of Jacob's Children (29:31–30:24)
    7. Birth of Jacob's Herds (30:25–43)
    8. Jacob Deceives Laban (31:1–55[32:1])
    9. Struggle for Blessing at Peniel (32:1–32[2–33])
    10. Restored Gift and Return to Shechem (33:1–20)
    11. Dinah, Deception, and Strife with the Hivites (34:1–31)
    12. Blessing and Struggle at Birth (35:1–29)
    Appendix: Family Line and Death of Isaac (35:22b–29)
X. Esau's Family (36:1–8)
    1. Title (36:1)

VII. FATHER ABRAHAM (11:27–25:11)
    1. Abram's Beginnings (11:27–32)
        (1) Introduction: Terah (11:27a)
        (2) Terah's Family (11:27b–30)
        (3) Terah's Life and Death (11:31–32)
    2. The Promissory Call and Abram's Obedience (12:1–9)
        (1) The Command and Oath (12:1–3)
        (2) Abram's Obedience (12:4–9)
    3. Abram and Sarai in Egypt: Blessing Begins (12:10–13:1)
        (1) Abram Instructs Sarai (12:10–13)
        (2) Pharaoh Abducts Sarai (12:14–17)
        (3) Pharaoh Expels Abram (12:18–13:1)
    4. Abram and Lot Part: Promises Recalled (13:2–18)
        (1) The Quarrel (13:2–7)
        (2) The Promise (13:8–17)
        (3) Abram Worships (13:18)
    5. Abram Rescues Lot: Abram's Faithfulness (14:1–24)
        (1) The War of the Kings (14:1–12)
        (2) Abram Meets the Kings (14:13–24)
    6. Covenant Promises Confirmed (15:1–21)
        (1) The Word of the Lord in a Vision (15:1–6)
        (2) Covenant Promise and Prophecy (15:7–21)
    7. Abram's Firstborn Son, Ishmael (16:1–16)
        (1) Hagar's Flight (16:1–6)
        (2) Promise of a Son (16:7–14)
        (3) Birth of Ishmael (16:15–16)
    8. Covenant Sign of Circumcision (17:1–27)
        (1) El Shaddai Appears to Abram (17:1–3a)
        (2) Abraham: Father of Many Nations (17:3b–8)
        (3) Covenant of Circumcision (17:9–14)
        (4) Sarah: Mother of Nations (17:15–18)
        (5) Promise of Isaac (17:19–22)
        (6) Circumcision of Abraham's Household (17:23–27)
    9. Divine Judgment and Mercy (18:1–19:38)
        (1) Abraham's Visitors (18:1–15)
        (2) Destruction of Sodom and Gomorrah (18:16–19:29)
            Abraham Pleads for Sodom and Gomorrah (18:16–33)
            Angels Rescue Lot (19:1–29)

VII. FATHER ABRAHAM (11:27–25:11)

By the Abraham narrative, the author of Genesis reveals how God's promissory blessing at creation intended for all peoples (1:28; 9:1,7) will be acquired through Terah's son, Abram (12:1–3,7; 13:15–17; 15:7–21; 17:4–8,15–16; 18:18; 22:16–18; also Isaac, 26:3–4; Jacob, 28:13–14; 35:9–12; 46:3–4; cf. Josh 24:2–3; Neh 9:7; Ps 105:9; Acts 7:2–8). In the sequence of the eleven *tōlĕdōt* ("generations") headings in the Book of Genesis, "This is the account *(tōlĕdōt)* of Terah" (11:27) is the sixth, making the Abraham narrative the center unit of the book and creating five pre-Abrahamic and five post-Abrahamic *(tôlĕdōt)* sections (see vol. 1A, pp. 27–28). The appointment of the patriarch as the father of a new nation was God's gracious response to the troubled nations that had scattered from the Tower of Babel (10:1–11:9). The arrangement of the Shemite genealogy (11:10–26) following the Tower of Babel episode (11:1–9) completed the pattern of blessing-sin-grace that characterizes the Genesis stories to this point (see vol. 1A, p. 60). The list of descendants born to the lineage of Shem ends with Terah and his three sons (11:26), pointing toward the elect seed whom God calls to advance the divine blessing (see vol. 1A, pp. 428, 487).

Abraham's history tells of one family's experiences resulting from the patriarch's answer to God's call for the purpose of mediating the divine blessing for all families (12:1–3). This narrowing of scope from the human family in 1:1–11:26 to the Hebrew family in 11:27–50:26 is anticipated in the two Shemite genealogies (10:21–31; 11:10–26), which transition early Genesis to the Abraham story. The genealogies evidence a selection process involving Peleg versus Joktan (10:25; 11:16–19). Divine selection of one brother over another was the determinative factor in the direction of patriarchal history, showing how God's sovereign ways kept the blessing a possibility. Shem's line highlighted his descendant Eber *('ēber),* whose name was possibly appropriated by the Hebrews *('ibrî;* see vol. 1A, p. 460). Eber fathered Peleg and Joktan (10:21,25). Of these two branches, Peleg headed the appointed household that provided for the birth of Abram and his brothers (see vol.1A, pp. 459, 487–88). By the introduction of Abram, the connection between the elect line of Shem (9:26) and the fathers of Israel was accomplished.

COMPOSITION. A brief comment is in order on the Abraham corpus as a whole.[1] The Abraham narrative (11:27–25:11) is not a seamless composition since there are indications that it possesses diverse material, for example, genealogies and itineraries. From the end of the nineteenth century the common means of explaining the juxtaposition of the various narratives and other units has been a complicated and protracted literary process. A series of parallel literary documents—the Yahwist (J), Elohist (E), and Priestly (P), ranging from the tenth to the fifth centuries—were sequentially brought together in a unilinear fashion.

---

[1] Ours is a mere sampling; see G. Wenham, "Pondering the Pentateuch: The Search for a New Paradigm," in *The Face of Old Testament Studies: A Survey of Contemporary Approaches* (Grand Rapids: Baker, 1999), 116–44; for a defense of the traditional source approach, see E. W. Nicholson, *The Pentateuch in the Twentieth Century: The Legacy of Julius Wellhausen* (Oxford: Clarendon, 1998).

These were the same majority documents that constituted Genesis–Numbers (and for some scholars even in Joshua). H. Gunkel, for example, believed that the majority of the "legend-cycle" (JE) of Abraham's story was the work of the Yahwist.[2] The only pure Elohist contributions were chap. 20 (Gerar), 21:9–21 (Ishmael), and 22:1–19 (Isaac's sacrifice). To this from various hands were added other independent Abraham legends. The Priestly source, in addition to its bits and pieces here and there, is most obvious in chaps. 17 (circumcision) and 23 (Machpelah), the former having its parallel in chap. 15 (JE) but the latter without parallel. Genesis 14 was not from the customary sources but was an independent addition of the late Jewish period.

Various modifications that followed did not unseat the general theory's reign and were accepted as inevitable refinements. This consensus position experienced fissures, however, in the 1970s when scholars claimed that "the emperor had no clothes." The drumbeat continues to the present (see vol. 1A, pp. 68–75). Among the present trends pertinent to the Abraham corpus are the further erosion of the Elohist's role, the prominence of the Yahwist, a significant Deuteronomic revision, and as a consequence of the aforementioned changes a new way of explaining the process. In place of continuous parallel documents providing duplicate accounts of Israel's religious history, some scholars proposed a basic Abraham narrative that underwent supplementations. Among the chief voices was J. van Seters, who argued that the succeeding sources were directly dependent on the prior one(s).[3] On the basis of his analysis of the three wife-sister stories (20:1–10; 20:1–18; 26:1–11), he posited that there were three stages in the growth of the Abraham tradition. The Yahwist was an exilic author who drew on an early pre-Yahwistic *written* tradition (preexilic) of Abraham stories (12:10–20; 16:1–12; 18:1a,10–14; 21:2,6–7) to which had been added the Abraham-Abimelech collection (20:1–17; 21:25–26,28–31a). To this preexisting material, the exilic Yahwist supplemented his own compositions to produce the majority of chaps. 12–26. The next supplement was the priestly writer's version of the covenant (chap. 17), which was dependent on the earlier account (chap. 15), and the independent story of Sarah's burial (chap. 23). Last, the war of the kings in chap. 14 was joined. What is especially important is the Yahwist was no longer conceived of as a parallel literary source deriving from the early monarchy but an exilic author who produced the main narrative.

Another prominent figure in the new direction was R. Rendtorff, who argued that the patriarchal stories of Joseph, Jacob, Isaac, and Abraham were originally "independent narrative complexes" that were bound by the "promise addresses," in particular the promise of international blessing, to form the larger patriarchal unit (chaps. 12–50).[4] The longer chain or complex of Abraham stories was added first to the Jacob stories and next the Isaac stories. The patriarchal unit and those

---

[2] H. Gunkel, *Genesis,* trans. M. E. Biddle (Macon: Mercer University Press, 1997 [German 3d ed.]), 158–61, 257–58.

[3] J. van Seters, *Abraham in History and Tradition* (New Haven: Yale University Press, 1975).

[4] R. Rendtorff, *The Problem of the Process of Transmission of the Pentateuch,* trans. J. J. Scullion, JSOTSup 89 (Sheffield: JSOT Press, 1990 [German 1977]).

of the Pentateuch (e.g., the primeval story, Joseph, exodus) came together by the assistance of a Deuteronomic layer and finally a Priestly layer. The Abraham story possesses obvious groups of narratives, Abraham-Lot (chaps. 13; 18–19) and Abraham-Abimelech (chaps. 20–21). It differs from the other patriarchal complexes by its many layers of independent traditions that show no relationship to the context (e.g., 12:10–20; and chaps. 14; 16; 17; 23). At the opposite end of the spectrum, other narratives reflect an awareness of the Abraham story as a whole, including 12:1–8 and chap. 24. Chapter 15 shows familiarity with the themes if not the composition.

It is beyond the scope of this commentary to engage in a thorough analysis of the compositional history of the patriarchal stories. Briefly stated, we believe that most of the component parts can be shown to have been authored for their present context; we have attempted to demonstrate this in the commentary sections. Moreover, pre-Genesis reconstructions are not satisfying due largely to the absence of data or a credible interpretation of the data. The so-called pre-Genesis traditions whose history scholars confidently delineate (e.g., wife-sister stories) are at the same time said to be well "integrated" in their present context,[5] making one question the necessity of positing a complex oral and/or written history for them. Although Rendtorff argued for the independence of many Abraham narratives, he observed: "On the other hand, the reader gets the impression of an internal coherence which runs through the whole Abraham tradition and makes it appear to be a relatively self-contained unit."[6] We find increasing evidence along rhetorical lines (see "Structure" below) that the narrative's diverse parts fit suitably (though less so at some points) in the present arrangement as though penned for their context by an author responsible for the whole. Repetitions and differences are not certain indicators of sources or layers that can be confidently distinguished. T. D. Alexander's study concluded that the "existence of the heir plot [Isaac] suggests that its components were skillfully selected and combined to form a unified composition. However we explain the process of compilation, it is necessary to affirm that the final form of the narrative did not come about by chance; rather it displays the hallmarks of having been produced by a very competent writer."[7] Alexander contended that J was the final author/compiler of the Abraham corpus, although by J he did not mean the classic Yahwist source. G. Wenham, too, reasoned that J was the final editor who drew on earlier materials (such as the P sections, which he assigned to the second millennium) in the formation of Genesis.[8] The basic narrative J also underwent various supplementations. Thus Wenham viewed Genesis as the result of basically two major components (P/J).

Accompanying the redefinition of the Yahwist has been the trend of dating the

---

[5] See D. Carr, *Reading the Fractures of Genesis* (Louisville: Westminster, 1996), 23–40, 196–202.

[6] Rendtorff, *Problem of the Process,* 49.

[7] T. D. Alexander, *Abraham in the Negev: A Source-Critical Investigation of Genesis 20:1–22:19* (Carlisle: Paternoster, 1997), 127.

[8] Wenham, *Genesis 1–15,* xxxviii–xlii.

final composition to the exilic/postexilic periods (e.g., Van Seters, Whybray). Wenham, however, believed that the rhetorical purpose of the book best fit the era of David-Solomon when the nation was established and unified under Davidic rule and when Israel dominated the Arameans, Ammonites, Moabites, and Edomites.[9] Alexander recently relied on the role of Genesis in the framework of Genesis to Kings for assessing the date of the book.[10] He agrees that the emphasis on the promise of a royal seed in Genesis corresponds to the establishment of the Davidic dynasty as a beginning fulfillment, but the prominence of Joseph in Genesis does not harmonize well with the hegemony of David during the monarchy. Although Genesis contains earlier traditions, it was not completed until the exilic period in concert with the assembling of the Genesis-Kings history. For Alexander the fact that the exilic author/compiler retained the old stories that would not easily suit an exilic milieu (e.g., the reconciliation of Esau) indicated that the author maintained the old accounts because of his belief in their authentic memories of the past.

We cannot in this commentary format address thoroughly the factors that constitute the debate of the date of the Genesis corpus. We will speak to the vital dilemma scholars face when explaining the dual emphases of Joseph (Ephraim and Manasseh) and Judah in Genesis (e.g., 48:1–20; 49:10). Presumably, the final narrative (Jacob-Joseph in Egypt, chaps. 37–50) reflects the setting for the latest compositional stage. According to critical assessments, the struggle for legitimacy as to who will rule over Israel, that is, the Joseph tribes or the Judah tribe, fits best the monarchic or exilic/postexilic concerns for the institution or in the case of the sixth century the restoration of the nation. We have said, however, that the Mosaic setting of the second millennium is the proper setting for the book (see vol. 1A, pp. 76–81). For example, the religious and social practices of the patriarchs do not correspond with Mosaic tradition, which was normative in the later periods, and the hospitable relationships of the patriarchs with their neighbors do not match the political enmity that characterized Israel in the first millennium. How do the motifs of descendants and future nations in Genesis fit the earlier period? Genesis is the literary prelude of the Pentateuch, which in the whole anticipates the settlement of Israel, the emergence of a ruling house, and ultimately an authorized site for Israel's worship (e.g., Gen 17:6; 35:11; 49:10; Deut 12:5; 17:14–20). Although Genesis shows incidental updating (e.g., "Dan," 14:14; "Israelite king," 36:31), we find no compelling reason to reconstruct a major compositional layer from the monarchy or later periods. The prominence given the Joseph and Judah tribes in Genesis should not surprise the historian when we remember that the wilderness era in the Pentateuchal corpus already describes the ascendancy of these northern and southern tribes in population,

---

[9] G. Wenham, *Story as Torah: Reading Old Testament Narrative Ethically* (Grand Rapids: Baker, 2005), 41–43.

[10] T. D. Alexander, *From Paradise to the Promised Land: An Introduction to the Pentateuch*, 2d ed. (Carlisle Cumbria, UK: Paternoster/Grand Rapids: Baker, 2002), 83–94; "Authorship of the Pentateuch," in *Dictionary of the Old Testament: Pentateuch* (Downers Grove: InterVarsity, 2003), 61–72, esp. 66–67.

material wealth, and role.[11] Genesis presents a proleptic perspective on Israel's history, often employing patriarchal figures and events as early guides to what will occur in the life of the nation. The idea that Genesis is historically anachronistic actually undercuts the purpose of the author, whose book gives projections that the early wilderness community recognized as beginning to come to pass. We conclude that the Abraham corpus is essentially a unified corpus that fits naturally with the logical integration of the parts of Genesis as a whole, well suited for a mid-second millennium date.

STRUCTURE.   Abraham's narratives constitute a unified story that spans the patriarch's adult life. The boundaries of the story are defined by the *tôlĕdōt* beginning at 11:27 and the concluding report on Abraham's death and burial at 25:1–11. Although the story has some chronological interest, expressed usually by occasional references to the ages of Abraham (12:4; 16:16; 17:1,24; 25:7) and Sarah (17:17; 23:1) and once of Ishmael (17:24), its plot development is tied to the progression of Abraham's faith in the promise of an heir. The author is not interested in world history primarily; he explains the history of Israel's salvation, appealing to world history when it aids in his theological purposes. Attention to the theme of the promise of an heir and Abraham's faithful response explains why the author selected some episodes to detail and not others. For example, the events in the period from Abraham's call at Haran to the birth of Ishmael (chaps. 12–16) occurred over eleven years (12:4; 16:16), whereas no events were included during the first thirteen years of Ishmael's life until the covenant of circumcision (17:1,24).

The Abraham narrative as a whole (11:27–25:11) possesses matching episodes that form a chiastic arrangement, though not a perfect one.[12] Several scholars have observed that the feature of correspondences among the episodes is essential to the progression of the story.[13] In the outline below, the chief components of the whole become clear.

---

[11] E.g., Caleb of Judah and Joshua of Ephraim held special prominence. Judah was the largest tribe (Num 26:19–20) and held the lead position in the marching arrangement (Num 2:3–4,9). Joseph's tribes received a double tract of land, land that was especially rich in value (Deut 33:13–17; Josh 13; 16–17); Manasseh had the greatest percentage growth in the desert sojourn (Num 26:28–34), and the rights to land inheritance received special attention (Zelophehad's daughters, Num 27:1–11; 36:1–12). In passing we note that the decline of Ephraim's population (Num 26:35–37) shows that the second census must have predated the monarchic period when Ephraim was the most influential tribe in the north (e.g., Jer 31:9; Hos 13:1). See R. D. Cole, *Numbers,* NAC (Nashville: Broadman & Holman, 2000), 456–57.

[12] By gathering episodes into large blocks, Cassuto (also Rendsburg) and Westermann "improve" on the chiasmus (see following note).

[13] U. Cassuto, *A Commentary on the Book of Genesis: Part II. From Noah to Abraham,* trans. I. Abrahams (Jerusalem: Magnes, 1964), 294–96, followed by G. Rendsburg, *The Redaction of Genesis* (Winona Lake: Eisenbrauns, 1986), 28–29; C. Westermann, *Genesis 12–36: A Commentary,* trans. J. Scullion (Minneapolis: Augsburg, 1985[1981]), 129; G. W. Coats, *Genesis: With an Introduction to Narrative Literature,* FOTL 1 (Grand Rapids: Eerdmans, 1984), 100; T. D. Alexander, *A Literary Analysis of the Abraham Narrative in Genesis* (Belfast: Ph.D. diss., The Queen's University of Belfast, 1982), 24, 26, followed by G. Wenham, *Genesis 1–15,* WBC (Waco: Word, 1987), 263.

A 11:27–32 Genealogy of Terah
   B 12:1–9 Call and first test of Abram (land)
      C 12:10–13:1 Abduction of Sarai (Egypt)
         D 13:2–14:24 Abram and Lot
            E 15:1–21 Covenant ceremony
               F 16:1–16 Flight of Hagar and birth of Ishmael
            E′ 17:1–27 Covenant sign
         D′ 18:1–19:38 Abraham and Lot
      C′ 21:1–18 Abduction of Sarah (Gerar)
               F′ 21:1–21 Birth of Isaac and expulsion of Hagar/Ishmael
                  G′ 21:22–34 Abraham–Abimelech covenant
   B′ 22:1–19 Second "test" of Abraham (seed)
A′ 22:20–24 Genealogy of Nahor

The Abraham narrative as a whole is bordered by two genealogies (A/A′), both pertaining to Abraham's family connections, which envelop the theme of a promised heir to the childless Sarah.

Two "bookends" in the faith journey of Abraham stand out in the story: the call and first act of obedience (12:1–9,B) and the test of Abraham (22:1–19,B′). The common language shared by the two episodes (see comments) indicates these two events must be read with both in mind. Divine promise of an heir and reference to a settlement in the land begin 12:1–3 and reappear at the close of 22:16–19. The intervening episodes present the halting progress of the patriarch's faith and obedience to the divine word (12:4; 15:6; 22:16–18). The divine promises occur repeatedly, reassuring Abram of their future reality. Although both promises of land (13:14–17; 15:7,8–21) and progeny (15:4–6; 17:1–16; 18:10–17; 21:11–13) are reissued, each is emphasized at different points in Abraham's career. The patriarch's greatest obstacle is the provision of a son by his wife Sarah. Complicating the plot is a series of separations by the patriarch, especially involving Lot (chaps. 13–14; 18–19) and Ishmael (16:1–16; 21:1–21), who function as foils for Abraham and Isaac. The covenant promises are formally ratified by God in a ceremonial rite of sacrifice: a smoking firepot passes between the divided parts of slaughtered animals (15:17–18). This covenant oath made to Abraham and his offspring was confirmed through the custom of male circumcision (17:10). Genesis 22:1–19 presents his love for God as the crowning expression of his obedient faith; the trial of Abraham concludes with the heavenly voice (22:15–18) reiterating the triad of promises given at Haran (12:1–3). After the Mount Moriah test (22:1–19), the brief genealogical explanation of Rebekah's familial connection with the Abraham clan by her birth in the family of Nahor anticipates her role as wife to Isaac and matriarch of the promised seed (22:20–24).

The final three episodes (chaps. 23–25) prepare the way for Father Abraham's successor, Isaac. Sarah's death precipitated two preparatory events: (1)

the purchase of a burial plot for the Abraham family, his first legal claim to Canaan's soil (chap. 23), and (2) the marriage of Isaac and Rebekah, who took Sarah's place as matriarch (chap. 24). The final step for Isaac's full succession is the endowment of gifts for and separation of Abraham's other sons by a collateral line (Keturah); this left Isaac as the sole beneficiary of the family fortune after the death and burial of the patriarch (25:1–11). The completion of the transition is affirmed by the concluding verse of the Abraham story, "After Abraham's death, God blessed his son Isaac" (25:11).

Excursus: Abraham's Career and Legacy

ABRAHAM'S CAREER. Genesis does not present a biography in the usual sense of the word, and therefore our reconstruction of his career as derived from the bits and pieces of his story is limited. Named initially as "Abram," he was one of three sons born to Terah. Whether or not he was the firstborn is not known with certainty (see vol. 1A, p. 499, n. 34), although his name is listed first (11:26). The patriarchal account begins with the Terah clan located in Ur in southern Mesopotamia (11:28; cf. 15:7; Neh 9:7; Acts 7:3–4). Abram's brother Haran fathered a son (Lot) and two daughters (Milcah and Iscah), but Haran died in Ur. While in Ur, Abram married Sarai, and his brother Nahor married his niece Milcah, daughter of Haran. The Terah group (minus the Nahor branch) moved northwest about six hundred miles to the upper Mesopotamian site, Ha(r)ran (*ḥārān;*not the personal name Haran [*ḥārān*, see vol.1A, p. 500).[14] Haran later became the homestead of the Nahor branch (24:10) whose family provided wives for Abraham's son Isaac (Rebekah) and grandson Jacob (Leah, Rachel). At seventy-five Abram left Haran and arrived in Canaan, responding to the Lord's call (12:4). The childless couple, Sarai and Abram, were joined by his nephew Lot on their journey. They visited Shechem, Bethel, and Ai, where Abram erected altars to the Lord, and they proceeded south to the Negev (12:4–9). Famine forced Abram and family to Egypt, where the patriarch out of fear for his life convinced Sarai to tell Egyptian authorities that she was his sister. Their deception of Pharaoh resulted in their expulsion but only after the king had enriched them with possessions (12:10–20).

Upon their return to Canaan, a dispute among the herdsmen of Lot and Abram over grazing rights ended in the two taking up separate residences, Lot at Sodom in the luscious plain of Jordan and Abram at Mamre near Hebron, where again he built an altar of worship (chap. 13). Sometime afterward a coalition of five southern kings, including the king of Sodom, revolted against an eastern suzerain to whom they had paid tribute for thirteen years. The war that ensued ended in Sodom's defeat and the capture of Lot, his family, and possessions. When Abram received news of Lot's captors, he gathered an army, defeated Lot's captors at Dan, and recovered his relative and possessions. The priest-king Melchizedek of Salem met Abram returning from battle and blessed the patriarch, who in turn

---

[14] חָרָן is the Hb. spelling for the Akk. name *Harrānu*(Y. Kobayashi, "Haran," *ABD* 3.58); the REB distinguishes the site name by the spelling "Harran."

gave Melchizedek a tenth of the captured booty. Abram, however, refused to keep any of the spoil for himself and rejected the king of Sodom's reward; rather, he declared his dependence on the Lord for his prosperity (chap. 14).

Sometime following this battle, the Lord came to the patriarch in a night vision and assured Abram of future prosperity. The Lord ratified the divine covenant by directing the patriarch to prepare a ceremonial slaying of animals (chap. 15). After ten years in Canaan, however, Sarai remained barren. Consequently, she gave her Egyptian servant Hagar to Abram, who was already eighty-five years of age; Hagar bore to him a son, his firstborn Ishmael (chap. 16). Thirteen years later the Lord appeared again to Abram and called him to enter into a covenant of circumcision. He promised to make him "a father of many nations" and his wife "the mother of nations." The Lord renamed the couple "Abraham" and "Sarah," reinforcing his promise of future progeny. The patriarch believed God and circumcised his entire household, beginning with himself and the teenager Ishmael (chap. 17).

Soon afterward the Lord and his angels appeared at the tent of Abraham as three "men." After Abraham extended hospitality to them, the Lord made the startling announcement that Sarah would indeed bear a son in a year's time. Also he revealed to Abraham that the "outcry" at Sodom and Gomorrah required an inquiry to determine the extent of their wickedness. Fearing the worst, Abraham appealed to the Lord to deliver the cities because of the righteous few who lived in Sodom, meaning Lot and his family. Two angels entered Sodom, rescued Lot and his family, except for his disobedient wife, and destroyed the cities by a fiery conflagration (chaps. 18–19).

Early in the intervening year before the birth of Sarah's son, Abraham migrated to the Philistine city of Gerar in the Negev. Fearing for his life, as he had among the Egyptians, he lied again concerning Sarah, placing the promised seed in jeopardy. King Abimelech of Gerar took Sarah as his wife, but the Lord prevented their cohabitation and forewarned Abimelech by a dream. As a consequence he returned Sarah and presented gifts to Abraham compensating for the offense. The patriarch mediated again before God (as regarding Sodom) for the royal household, and the Lord answered, renewing the Philistines' ability to give birth (chap. 20).

Just as the Lord had predicted at Mamre, in a year's time Sarah at the old age of ninety bore Isaac, the son of promise. Some two or three years afterward, Sarah heard Ishmael ridiculing the child Isaac as the favored son. This incident incited Sarah to urge Abraham to send Ishmael and his mother Hagar away. Reluctantly, the old man agreed and dismissed them with provisions to the wilderness. They failed, however, to find refuge, and as their water ran out they approached death. At the prayer of Hagar, the Lord interceded by providing water and assured her that Ishmael would survive to father a prestigious nation (21:1–21). During this time a dispute arose between the Philistines and Abraham over water rights. Abimelech and his general Phicol entered into a treaty with Abraham, ensuring future amicable relations. The patriarch memorialized the event by planting a tamarisk tree and worshiping the Lord as his "Eternal God" (21:22–34).

Years later the Lord tested Abraham's loyalty by instructing him to offer up Isaac as a burnt offering. In following the Lord's commands completely, the aged father journeyed with Isaac from Beersheba to Mount Moriah, where he erected an altar for sacrifice. As he raised the knife to slay the boy, the angel of the Lord intercepted the patriarch and provided for him a ram as a substitute offering. The Lord acknowledged Abraham's faithfulness and declared again the divine promises (22:1–19).

Sarah died in Hebron at 127 years old, and Abraham purchased a cave for a burial plot in Machpelah from a Hittite named Ephron. This acquisition became the first property formally owned by Abraham in Canaan, serving as the family's traditional cemetery site (chap. 23). Abraham was ten years Sarah's senior, and with Isaac thirty-seven years old, he took steps to obtain a wife for him. He directed a trusted servant, perhaps Eliezer of Damascus (cp. 15:2), to obtain a wife for Isaac from his brother Nahor's family in Aram. The Lord answered the servant's prayer and revealed to him the chosen bride, the granddaughter of Nahor, named Rebekah. Rebekah received her brother Laban's approval to return with the servant and marry Isaac, where she comforted him in the tent of his mother, Sarah (chap. 24).

Little is known about the last thirty-five years of Abraham's life. He fathered six sons by a second wife, Keturah, whose children became the progenitors of new people groups. To protect Isaac's inheritance, Abraham provided gifts for his sons born to his concubine(s) and sent them away. Also, at 160 years old, the patriarch probably knew his grandsons Jacob and Esau, who were born to Rebekah. At the age of 175 years old, after having entered Canaan one hundred years earlier, Abraham died and was buried with Sarah at Machpelah by his sons Isaac and Ishmael (25:1–11).

ABRAHAM'S LEGACY. Abraham is honored as the father of the three "religions of the Book"—Judaism, Christianity, and Islam. For Jews he is the patriarch of Jewish religion and the Jewish nation; for Christians he is the ancestor of Jesus Christ and spiritual progenitor of all who have faith in Jesus as Savior; and for Muslims he is the ideal true monotheist and ancestor of the last and greatest prophet, Muhammad.

Muhammad looked to Abraham as the model for all true observers of Islam. Similar to Jewish tradition, Abraham in the Islamic Qur'an (book of divine revelations) opposed the idolatry of his contemporaries, including his father (*Surah* 6.74–82; 19:42–48; 21:52–68). Muhammad's monotheistic revolution among the Meccan idolaters therefore had its precedence in Abraham's actions. For Muslims their religion revived the only true and legitimate religion (Islam), which had been distorted by the Jews and Christians. In the Qur'an, God deemed Islam as the "religion of Abraham" and established Abraham and his sons as "models" of religion for all generations (*Surah* 2.124; 21.73). The Qur'an depicts the patriarch as the prototype Muslim who practiced four of the five religious pillars in Islam (except the fast of Ramadan): he rejected idolatry, obeyed God's will, made pilgrimage to Mecca, and offered sacrifice to God (*Surah* 37.99–109).[15] God commanded Abraham to dedicate himself to God: "When the LORD said unto him, 'Resign thyself *unto me*' (i.e., become a Muslim), he answered, 'I have resigned myself (as a Muslim) unto the LORD of all creatures'" (*Surah* 2.131).[16] According to Islam, although Jews and Christians also appealed to Abraham as their spiritual father, Abraham's religion (Islam) antedated both, for he lived before Moses' Torah and preceded Jesus' gospel.

The Qur'an's Abraham shows dependence on Genesis and later Jewish legends concerning him, but Muhammad expanded the roles of the patriarch and his firstborn, Ishmael. Sacred books were attributed to the patriarch (*Surah* 87.19; 53.37). He was a prophet (*Surah* 19.42–51), and Muhammad as his descendant through the line of Ishmael was God's last and greatest prophet. Abraham and Ishmael, who fathered the Arab peoples (*Surah* 2.132–36), prayed that God would someday send a prophet who would lead their people (i.e., Muslims). Islamic tradition interpreted the coming of Muhammad as heaven's answer to their prayer (*Surah* 2.129). Also in the Qur'an, Abraham and Ishmael were divinely directed to pilgrimage to Mecca, where they founded and purified the holy sanctuary Ka'ba. Muslims face toward the Ka'ba daily to offer their prayers to God. This holiest of mosques established by Abraham in the Islamic version is reminiscent of the Jewish association (*Jub.* 22.23–24) of Abraham's sacrifice of Isaac at Mount Moriah (Gen 22:2) and the building of Solomon's temple at that site (2 Chr 3:1). Abraham was for Muhammad the foundational figure for the exclusivistic claims of Islam as the only true religion.

Among Jews and Christians, however, Abraham is remembered above all as the father of the Jewish people (e.g., *4 Mac* 6:16–21; 17:5, 24; *1 Esdr* 9:55; Luke 3:8; John 8:39,53; Acts 3:25; 7:2; Rom 4:1; 11:11; 2 Cor 11:22; Jas 2:21), in accordance with the Old Testament (Deut 6:10; Josh 24:3; 2 Chr 20:7; Ps 105:6; Isa 51:2; 63:6; Mic 7:2). Within the biblical tradition, the close association of Abraham and the Lord's covenant resulted in the very identity of the nation with the patriarch. For example, in the history of Israel's monarchy, Abraham and his covenant as a royal grant (Gen 15; 17) prefigured King David's kingdom and covenant election by God (2 Sam 7). Abraham's journey from Ur to the Canaan homeland and Moses' exodus provided Isaiah's message of hope to the Babylonian exiles for another exodus. As the children of Abraham, they too would experience the new Exodus (Isa 51:2).[17]

The rabbis expanded this rudimentary typology of patriarch and nation by looking to Abraham's life and deeds as a model for Jewish religious life. *Genesis Rabbah* (ca. A.D. 400) honors Abraham as the pivotal character in world history who perfectly kept the Torah even before it came to Moses at Sinai. *Jubilees* shows Abraham observing the Mosaic feasts and sacrificial laws perfectly (15.1–2; 16.20; 22.1–20). The rabbis connected the details of the patriarch's experi-

---

[15] K. Kuschel, *Abraham: Sign of Hope for Jews, Christians, and Muslims* (New York: Continuum, 1995), 154–56.

[16] For this translation see G. Sale, trans., *The Koran* (London: F. Warn, n.d.); also see *Interpretation of the Meanings of the Noble Qur'an in the English Language*, 4th rev. ed. (Riyadh: Maktaba Dar-us-Salam, 1994).

[17] M. Fishbane, *Biblical Interpretation in Ancient Israel* (Oxford: Oxford University Press, 1985), 374–76.

ences and the later history of Israel (e.g., *Gen. Rab.* 40.6; 42.4; 61.7).[18] Jewish hope for a blessed future was already secured by God's election and covenant with Abraham (*Pss. Sol.* 9.15–19; *T. Levi* 15.4).

Since Abraham was the model of righteousness, Jews identified him with the final abode of the pious (e.g., *4 Mac* 13:16; *Sir* 44:18–21; *T. Abr.* 4.6; 10.14; *Pr Man* 8; *Jub.* 23.10; Matt 8:11; Luke 13:28; 16:23). The rite of circumcision practiced by the Jews to this day includes the declaration "entry into the covenant of Abraham our father" (see CD 12:11).[19] Jewish literature commonly appealed to Abraham and other heroes of the faith to inspire the Jews to adhere to tradition and resist the increasing hellenization of the day. It was said that Abraham endured ten trials and remained stalwart despite his afflictions (cp. Gen 22:1). The example of Abraham's loyalty encouraged obedience to Jewish law despite opposition by prohellenistic forces (*Jub.* 17.17–18; 19:8; 23.10; *1 Mac* 2.64–68; *Jdt* 8.25–26; *As. Mos.* 3.8–10; 4.5).

Abraham's role as prophet (Gen 20:7) in conjunction with the night vision in Gen 15:17–21 encouraged Jewish speculative thought about his mediatorial role. He alone of his generation learned from God "the end of the times" (*4 Ezra* 3:13) and "this world and the world to come" (*Gen. Rab.* 42.12). In the *Apocalypse of Abraham* (ca. A.D. 100) he is translated into heaven, where he received seven visions (15.5), and in *Pseudo-Philo* (ca. A.D. 100) Abraham received a divine vision of Canaan and other matters (23.5–7). Jewish depiction of Abraham as seer may have stood behind Jesus' remarks concerning Abraham's foreknowledge of his own day (John 8:56). Abraham's special status as mediator in behalf of Lot (18:16–33) in which the patriarch was uniquely taken into divine confidence elevated him above all others as the "friend" of God (2 Chr 20:7; Isa 41:8; Jas 2:23; *Apoc. Abr.* 9.6; 10.5; *T. Abr.* 1.6; 2.6).

Philo of Alexandria viewed the patriarch as the model of a truly free man who had escaped pantheistic materialism and the passions and senses of the body. This allegorical reading of Abraham by Philo created a hellenistic Abraham. By keeping the Mosaic law Abraham observed the higher law of nature, which was the prototype of the Mosaic law of the Jews. The patriarch's faith was extolled as the model of faith in God, for Abraham had reasoned that beyond the visible, physical realm was the God of first cause. Abraham's circumcision was not only the literal mark of the Jewish covenant but also indicative of his putting aside pleasures and senses of the body (*Abr* 88,92,268–69,275–76).[20]

As among Jews, the Christian church acknowledged Abraham's honored place as the recipient of God's promises (Luke 1:73; Acts 3:25; 7:2,8,17; Rom 4:13,16; Gal 3:16,18; Heb 6:13; 11:17). The New Testament's allusion to the burning bush revelation (Exod 3:6,15–16; 4:5) identified the Lord as the covenant God, "the God of Abraham, the God of Isaac, and the God of Jacob" (Matt 22:32 pars.; also Acts 3:13; 7:32). The Christian church pointed to Jesus Christ as the

---

[18] See J. Neusner, ed., *Genesis and Judaism,* BJS 108 (Atlanta: Scholars Press, 1985).

[19] I. M. Ta-Shma, "Abraham," *EncJud,* 2.116.

[20] See G. W. Hansen, *Abraham in Galatians,* JSNTSup 29 (Sheffield: JSOT Press, 1989), 189–92.

promised seed of Abraham through whom salvation could be received. Jesus was descended from Abraham and hence qualified as a legitimate heir to the covenant promises of old (Matt 1:1; Luke 3:34). Although the genealogical descent of the Hebrews from Abraham remained important (Luke 13:16; 19:9; Rom 4:1,9,12–13,16; 11:1; 2 Cor 11:22; Heb 2:16; 7:5), spiritual descent superseded any physical claims to the patriarch (Matt 3:9 pars; John 8:39–40). The faith that Abraham had exhibited in the living Lord (Gen 15:6) was the same faith of all who believed in Jesus Christ, whether Jew or Gentile (Rom 4:1–16; Gal 3:1,6–9,14). By faith Gentiles too entered into the promises and were heirs to those promises (Gal 3:6–29). The promissory blessing was realized in the "one" seed, Jesus Christ, who as the representative of the many achieved salvation for all those of faith (Gal 3:16).

Paul showed that the salvation promised in the covenant to Abraham came by faith and not by observing Mosaic tradition, including the sign of the Jews—male circumcision. Even Abraham who was considered the epitome of righteousness did not escape sin. He was indebted to God for his own deeds of sin (Rom 4:1–8). Dependence on individual merit as the means of salvation not only fails but it also makes salvation through faith promised by the covenant null and void. Paul argues in Rom 4:9–12 that Abraham was declared righteous (Gen 15:6) before his circumcision (Gen 17:24). Moreover, only by faith is the ancient promise of many heirs made possible. The Gentiles too are heirs of the promises, since the promise of many descendants preceded circumcision (Rom 4:13–25).[21] This inclusion of foreigners in the household of Abraham found its precedent in the inclusion of foreigners in the covenant of circumcision. Abraham and Sarah were promised that they would birth "many nations" (17:4–6,16); but these "nations" must have included peoples who were not descended from their union, which would have included only Israel's twelve tribes and Esau's sons, the Edomites. Rather, the covenant of circumcision was both for those born in his house as well as foreigners whom he had bought.[22] Hence, Abraham fathered all who submitted to the covenant, whether born in his house or foreign born (17:12–13).

To show that the Gentiles had no cause to undergo circumcision Paul appealed also to the example of Abraham's sons, Ishmael and Isaac (Gal 4:21–31). Both Ishmael and Isaac experienced circumcision according to Genesis, but the apostle pointed to the circumstances of their respective births, which antedated their circumcision. Each child's birth was indicative of a covenant: Ishmael, the son of the slave woman Hagar, and Isaac, the son who came by God's grace. Ishmael represented the old Sinai covenant with its demands; the opponents of Paul therefore were like Hagar, the Egyptian slave. By imposing the requirements of the law, hence enslaving the Gentiles, the Judaizers were producing children of slavery. Isaac, Abraham's son through God's grace, represented the New Covenant.

According to the New Testament writers, the two "bookends" in Abraham's life of obedience were carried out by faith: answering the divine call to search out

---

[21] See F. Thielman, *Paul and the Law* (Downers Grove: InterVarsity, 1994), 130–34, 184–87.

[22] T. D. Alexander, "Abraham Reassessed Theologically," in *He Swore an Oath* (Cambridge: Tyndale, 1993), 17.

a new land (Heb 11:8) and offering up Isaac (Heb 11:17; Jas 2:21). The confirming act of faith was the sacrifice of the promissory son, which in James's eyes demonstrates that works are the outgrowth of believing faith (Jas 2:21,23). The writer to the Hebrews explained, "Abraham reasoned that God could raise the dead, and figuratively speaking, he did receive Isaac back from death" (Heb 11:19). In effect Abraham did carry out the deed of sacrifice, and the return of the boy by God was in essence a resurrection from the dead. This act of obedience illustrates according to James that *faith works* (Jas 2:22).

Both Paul and James appealed to the same verse in Genesis to make his point: "Abram believed the LORD, and he credited it to him as righteousness" (15:6). For Paul this verse showed that faith was antecedent to Abraham's circumcision, which became the hallmark of later Jewish identity. But James came to the discussion of faith from a different perspective. He understood the offering of Isaac as a fulfillment of Abraham's faith (Jas 2:22). James made no mention of circumcision or any specific Jewish rite in speaking of confirming works. Thus the sacrifice episode was the carrying out of Abraham's utter confidence in the Lord's promise of an heir, which had its beginning more than twenty-five years earlier.[23]

As for the relationship between faith and obedience, Abraham's acts of obedience presumed an already-existing relationship of trust in the Lord. This was the case with Noah, whose righteousness also resulted in deliverance (Gen 7:1), but the flood narrative implies a prior relationship between Noah and the Lord. Further, the salvation of Israel at the Red Sea came before the giving of the law (Exod 19:3–6; 20:1). The covenant-law of Moses was revealed to a *redeemed* people; the law was not the basis of Israel's salvation but the consequence, a constitution whereby the people lived in the presence of their God. In the same way, Abraham's trusting relationship with God preceded Abraham's obedience to the divine call, and his offering of Isaac exhibited this trusting relationship with God.

CONCLUSION. As the "father of many nations" Abraham gives his believing seed a unity that transcends the diversity of the human family—gender, race, nationalism, and generations. Diversity is good and of God, but diversity falls under the shadow of the arching unity provided by Abraham's seed, our Lord Jesus Christ. Also, the divine charge to our father Abraham to be a blessing to the families of the nations helps us understand the mission of Christ in the world, which is our mission too as the church.[24] As the "light unto the Gentiles" we are to busy ourselves in adding brothers and sisters to the household of faith. Finally, Christians can best discover what they are to emulate of Abraham in the words of the writer to the Hebrews, "By faith Abraham . . . obeyed" (Heb 11:8).

1. Abram's Beginnings (11:27–32)

This introductory paragraph identifies the family members of the Terah clan and explains their relationships when Terah lived in Ur and Haran. This gene-

---

[23] K. Richardson, *James,* NAC (Nashville: Broadman & Holman, 1996), 140.

[24] See M. D. Carroll R., "Blessing the Nations: Toward a Biblical Theology of Mission from Genesis," *BBR* 10 (2000): 17–34.

alogical information is matched by the concluding genealogy in 25:1–11 but also by the Nahor genealogy in 22:20–24, which rounds out the chiasmus of 11:27–22:24 (see "Structure" in the introduction to the Abraham section). The passage functions in two ways in the context of the Abraham story: it transitions the primeval history to the patriarchal history by the father figure of Terah, and it establishes the chief thematic interest of the Abraham narrative, the birth of an heir. The passage concerns more than a local family genealogy and travel itinerary, however, for by its allusions to chaps. 10–11, if not all of chaps. 1–11, it provides the international context for interpreting Abraham's life.

COMPOSITION. Typically, scholars have attributed this passage to two sources, the Yahwist (J) in vv. 28–30 and the Priestly writer (P) in vv. 27,31–32. The basis for the division is the appearance of P's vocabulary and the kind of genealogical and chronological details that usually are assigned to P. Clearly, vv. 28–30 anticipate the call of Abraham (12:1–3) and the travel to follow (12:4–9). It functions on a broader scale too by introducing the tension of Sarai's barrenness, which is the central concern of the Abraham corpus. Carr rightly observes that the author of 11:28–30 and 12:1–8 was the one responsible for compiling the Abraham story as a whole in its present arrangement.[25] But peeling away vv. 27,31–32 is unnecessary since the paragraph as it stands is a coherent, self-contained unit. Westermann observed that without v. 27b ("Terah became the father of . . ."), vv. 28–30 have no obvious beginning.[26] Moreover, v. 31 ("Lot, son of Haran") assumes v. 28 ("Haran") and anticipates Lot's role in chaps. 12 and 13, which are commonly assigned to the Yahwist. Apart from the superscription (v. 27a), it is difficult to justify the isolation of two underlying sources, other than on the presuppositions that P possesses distinctive vocabulary (e.g., "land," "became the father of") and that P alone could have contributed the genealogical and chronological information.

STRUCTURE. The word "Terah" as father at v. 27 and "Terah" in his death notice at v. 32 form an inclusio and establish the boundaries of the paragraph. The passage blends some features of the linear form of genealogy, which distinguished the elect line of the Fathers in early Genesis (5:1–32; 11:10–26; see vol. 1A, pp. 296–99, 487–91), with the narrative style that dominates the patriarchal accounts. The nonelect sons of Terah are dispensed with first (see vol. 1A, pp. 34–35), leaving the focus on Abram and Sarai: (1) Haran's family (vv. 27–28); (2) Nahor's family (vv. 29–30); and (3) each one's relationship to Abram (vv. 31–32).

(1) Introduction: Terah (11:27a)

27This is the account of Terah.

---

[25] Carr, *Reading the Fractures of Genesis,* 204.
[26] Westermann, *Genesis 12–36,* 134.

"This is the account *[tôlĕdōt]* of Terah" (11:27a) introduces the seventh *(tōlĕdōt)* section of the book (11:27–25:11), providing the transition from early Genesis to the ancestors of Israel.

(2) Terah's Family (11:27b–30)

Terah became the father of Abram, Nahor and Haran. And Haran became the father of Lot. [28]While his father Terah was still alive, Haran died in Ur of the Chaldeans, in the land of his birth. [29]Abram and Nahor both married. The name of Abram's wife was Sarai, and the name of Nahor's wife was Milcah; she was the daughter of Haran, the father of both Milcah and Iscah. [30]Now Sarai was barren; she had no children.

11:27b–28 Terah was seventy when he became a father (v. 26). Although Haran's age when he fathered Lot is not recorded, the narrative gives the impression that he was a young parent. Haran also had two daughters, Milcah and Iscah (v. 29). In the Shem genealogy (11:10–26) their grandfather Nahor was the youngest to become a parent, at twenty-nine (v. 24). This family history of early procreation serves as a foil for Abram and Sarai, who were childless. Although no offspring is mentioned for Nahor-Milcah, there is no statement about Milcah's barrenness as there is for Sarai (v. 30). Later, Abram learns that Milcah bore eight sons to Nahor in Aram, and Nahor's concubine Reumah bore four sons (22:20–24). At age sixty-five Sarai would have been late in giving birth to a child (12:4; 17:17). Mention of her barrenness is a proleptic clue that Abram was the chosen descendant in Terah's household who would inherit the blessing. Barrenness was a distinguishing feature of the elect line, beginning with Abram (Sarai) and Isaac (Rebekah) and continuing with Jacob, who faced this trial with his favored wife, Rachel.

Lot is the only male descendant, however, from the Terah group at this point. He became a companion for Abram in his early travels (12:4; 13:5). As to whether Abram viewed him as a potential heir by adoption is not explicitly stated, as it is with Abram's servant Eliezer (15:2). Lot is identified in relation to Terah, not Abram (v. 31). Nevertheless, maintaining amicable relations with Lot is too important to Abram to jeopardize (13:8). Silence in the passage regarding how Haran died creates a mystery in the narrative and leaves the possibility that Lot too might meet the same fate prematurely. It is a devastating and unexpected sorrow for a father to outlive his son (cf. 37:34–35). The prospects of Terah's house for the future, which at first seemed so promising by the birth of three sons, became precarious in the next generation.

Reference to "Ur of the Chaldeans"[27] (11:28) identifies the native land of Haran but not necessarily of Terah and his sons Abram and Nahor. In fact, the

---

[27] Hb. "Chaldeans" כַּשְׂדִּים is *kaldu* (Akk.) in Assyrian texts, and the Gk. has καλδαιοι; the original *sd* has undergone a change to *ld* (see R. S. Hess, "Chaldea," *ABD* 1.886–87).

inclusion of this information for Haran may suggest the ancestral home was elsewhere (for this discussion see comments on 12:1). "Ur of the Chaldeans" occurs three times in Genesis (11:28,31; 15:7) and once elsewhere (Neh 9:7). Stephen identified the place of God's revelation to Abram as "Mesopotamia"[28] from which he departed: "So he left the land of the Chaldeans and settled in Haran" (Acts 7:3–4). The "land *[chōra]* of the Chaldeans" rather than "Ur of the Chaldeans" is the Septuagint translation, as reflected in Stephen's sermon, which can be explained as either a textual slip due to the prior phrase "land of his birth" or the ancient translator's uncertainty about the identity of the site. J. W. Wevers proposes that due to the apposition of "land of his birth," the translator interpreted "Ur" as a region.[29]

"Chaldeans" in Genesis probably is an explanatory addition, identifying Abram's city in the region of Chaldea in southern Babylonia. The Chaldeans as a people group are first known from Assyrian texts of the ninth century. They were of West-Semitic stock and perhaps were related to the Arameans, though this connection is unclear. A grandson of Nahor was named "Aram," and one of Nahor's eight sons by Milcah was "Kesed" (22:22), a name related phonetically to the Hebrew spelling for Chaldeans *(kaśdîm)*. The Chaldean ruler Nabopolassar (625–605), father of the Babylonian monarch Nebuchadnezzar, launched the rise of the Neo-Babylonian empire in the seventh–sixth centuries.

The ancient Sumerian city Ur (fourth millennium) is the site traditionally identified as Terah's residence.[30] C. L. Wooley's excavations (1922–1934) of the city (Tell Muqqayyar), located on the Euphrates in southern Iraq, yielded substantial information about the city's history and life.[31] It played an important political and cultural role in the ancient Near East during the latter half of the third millennium. Ur's ascendancy occurred with the flowering of the Third Dynasty of Ur founded by Ur-Nammu (ca. 2100), who is remembered for his law code and great ziggurat (see vol. 1A, p. 476). Both Ur and Haran honored the moon god Nannar (= Akk. god Sin), which probably was one of many dei-

---

[28] Μεσοποταμία, "Mesopotamia," is the Gk. translation of the Hb. אֲרַם נַהֲרַיִם (Gen 24:10; Deut 23:4[5]; Judg 3:8; 1 Chr 19:6; Ps 60:1[2]). EVs have the transliterated Hb. "Aram Naharaim" (NIV, NRSV [except Deut 23:4[5]; 1 Chr 19:6]) or the transliterated Greek "Mesopotamia" (AV, RSV, NASB).

[29] J. W. Wevers, *Notes on the Greek Text of Genesis,* Septuagint and Cognate Studies 35 (Atlanta: Scholars Press, 1993), 158.

[30] This identification has been challenged; alternative proposals have identified patriarchal Ur with north Mesopotamian sites, the cities Urfa (near Haran) in north Syria and Ura in Armenia (Hittite). See C. H. Gordon, "Abraham of Ur," in *Hebrew and Semitic Studies Presented to G. R. Driver* (Oxford: Clarendon, 1963), 77–84; "Where Is Abraham's Ur?" *BARev* 3 (1977): 20–21; and V. P. Hamilton, *The Book of Genesis Chapters 1–17,* NICOT (Grand Rapids: Eerdmans, 1990), 364–65.

[31] P. R. S. Mooney and C. L. Wooley, *"Ur of the Chaldees": A Revised and Updated Edition of Sir Leonard Wooley's Excavations at Ur* (Ithaca: Cornell University Press, 1982); Jean-Cl. Margueron, "Ur," *ABD* 6.766–67.

ties worshiped by Abram's ancestors (Josh 24:2) (see vol. 1A, pp. 498–99).

11:29–30 Endogamy, that is, marriage within a family group, prevailed among the patriarchs. Sarai was Abram's half-sister, having the same father (Terah) but a different mother (20:12).[32] Milcah married her uncle Nahor, brother of her father Haran (v. 29).[33] The parallel descriptions of Abram and Nahor's wives heightens the additional information given to Milcah's family connections. Silence about Sarai's kinships preserves the surprise outcome of Abraham's deceit of Abimelech (20:12). Sarai and Milcah share in possessing regal titles for names; "Sarai" probably means "princess,"[34] and the name "Milcah" is related to the Hebrew words "king" *(melek)* and "queen" *(malkâ).*[35] This may hint that the two wives were blood relations but the passage is concerned only with Milcah's family associations. As for Sarai's family connections at this point in the story, she is the outsider who is yet to be a contributor.

Milcah was the daughter of Haran, thus the niece of Nahor (her husband) and Abram and the granddaughter of Terah. The sister of Milcah, Iscah, is otherwise unknown; the sisters' names end in the rhyming sound *kâ* (cp. Adah, Zillah, 4:19). Lot was Milcah's brother. Milcah's linkage with the Abraham branch is reinforced by her granddaughter Rebekah, born to Milcah's son Bethuel, who marries Isaac. Rebekah's marriage in the Abraham line of Terah reunited the two branches of Terah's descendants. The Aramean connection of the Nahor clan with Abraham is also achieved through Milcah's grandson, Laban, whose daughters, Leah and Rachel, marry their Hebrew cousin, Jacob. By these two women, "who together built up the house of Israel" (Ruth 4:11), the Hebrew people can trace their ancestry to their prepatriarchal roots in Terah.

Sarai's condition explains the attention given to the women of Terah's family. Not only at this point does Sarai have no beginnings, she also has no continuation through a child. The message is thunderous: the woman is a "weak link," we would say, in the chain of blessing. Her barren state dominates the Abraham story since the divine promises involve a numerous host of progeny

---

[32] In contrast to later prohibitions (Lev 18:9,18; 20:17; Deut 27:22).

[33] Lev 18 and 20 have no prohibition against uncle-niece marriage, although nephew-aunt is banned (18:14; 20:20); the former may have been more acceptable since the male instigator was the higher generation (J. E. Miller, personal communication).

[34] *HALOT* 3.1354.

[35] N. H. Sarna, however, observes that the name Sarai means "queen," if related to Akk. *šarratu;* the term commonly refers to the female consort of the moon god Sin, the principle deity of Ur (בְּרֵאשִׁית *Genesis,* JPST [Philadelphia: Jewish Publication Society, 1989], 87). Milcah, a variant form of *malkâ* ("queen") comes from Akk. *malkatu (HALOT* 2.592), the title for the goddess Ishtar, daughter of Sin. The names indicate possible connections to Haran, which like Ur was a center of the moon-god cult.

for Abram (12:2a; 15:4–5; 17:1–2; 18:10). Here "she had no children"[36] (11:30) underscores at the start the need for God's help (17:17; 18:11–12; 21:1,7; Rom 4:19; Heb 11:11). This redundancy in the text occurs only for Sarai's barrenness unlike Rebekah (25:21) and Rachel (29:31), where "barren" alone occurs.

There is one other significance to be drawn from this short introduction to the Terah clan. The renaming of "Sarai" to "Sarah" will be instrumental in conveying her role as the mother of "nations" and the ancestress of "kings of peoples" (17:15–16). Despite her dim prospects, Sarai emerges by God's gracious intervention to achieve the regal stature that her name "princess" conveys. She becomes the matriarch of all Israel (Isa 51:2).

(3) Terah's Life and Death (11:31–32)

[31]Terah took his son Abram, his grandson Lot son of Haran, and his daughter-in-law Sarai, the wife of his son Abram, and together they set out from Ur of the Chaldeans to go to Canaan. But when they came to Haran, they settled there. [32]Terah lived 205 years, and he died in Haran.

11:31–32   The last two verses of this transitional paragraph prepare for the independence of Abram from his "father's household" (12:1). This is shown first by the geographical movements of the clan members and second by the death notice of Terah. Although the intent of Terah was "to go to Canaan" from Ur, the family "settled" in Haran (v. 31). This phrase "settled there [Haran]" indicates a sustained residency on Terah's part (e.g., 26:17; Ruth 1:4; 2 Sam 15:29; 2 Chr 28:18). Terah's movement raises a number of questions left unanswered by the passage. Why did he depart from Ur for Canaan, and why did he take such a circuitous route to Haran, where he remained? There is no explanation given for their departure. Also Haran, en route from Ur, assuming Ur was in the south, would be unnecessarily far to the north if traveling to Canaan. Perhaps the commercial and cultural connections between Ur and Haran explain Terah's residence in Haran if he abandoned plans early to go to Canaan. Or Haran may have been the clan's original homeland (see comments on 12:1).

More important, the language "settled there" echoes the Babel account (11:2,8–9), where the residents of Shinar refused to "fill" the earth in accord with the divine mandate (1:28; 9:1). This is not to say that Terah's migration was part of the scattering of peoples from Babel. Rather, the language "settled there" is chosen by the author to cast a shadow on Terah's decision to dwell in Haran, and it provides the negative contrast for Abram's faithful answer to the call (12:4). This is one of many ways the faith of Abram and his role in accom-

---

[36] The last word וָלָד (rather than יֶלֶד), "children," is a rare form, occurring elsewhere only as a *kĕthîb* reading in 2 Sam 6:23 in a similar context, describing the barrenness of Michal (cp. Judg 13:2; Isa 54:1; BDB 409; Westermann, *Genesis 12–36*, 139).

plishing the mandate to "fill" the earth are distinguished from those of his Shemite heritage (11:10–26).[37]

Until this point, however, Abram remained under his father's authority. "Took" *(lāqaḥ)* indicates Terah's authority (v. 31), as it later appears to define Abram's position (12:5). This same term "took" is translated "married," in the sense of to "take in marriage" (v. 29). The parallel occurrences of "took" in vv. 29 and 31 suggest that Abram has two allegiances, his wife and his father. Family ties to the Terah clan, however, must be loosened if Abram will enter into God's promises (12:1).

Lot, we have observed, accompanied his grandfather Terah as the lone representative of Terah's deceased son, Haran. Lot's future, tied as it was initially to the prosperity of Abram, turned shamefully from bad to worse, from living in Sodom to his incestuous relations with his daughters, who birthed the Ammonites and Moabites (chap. 19). With the union of Boaz and Ruth the Moabite, the schism between the Abram and Lot families is repaired (Ruth 4). It will be Milcah, the sister of Lot, however, who reconciles the Haran branch by giving birth to Bethuel, making her eventually the maternal grandmother (Rebekah) and great-grandmother (Leah, Rachel) of Israel.

Both ancient and modern interpretations have included Nahor and Milcah among the traveling members of the Terah caravan, so as to involve all three branches. The Samaritan Pentateuch includes Nahor and Milcah by name in v. 31. U. Cassuto retains the MT but interprets it to include the Nahor branch. Nahor and Milcah among all the family members are the ones who "set out," understanding the phrase "with them" to refer to the specific group of Abram, Sarai, and Lot (cp. 12:5).[38] This interpretation of the language, however, has been shown to be forced.[39] No mention is given in the story of the Nahor migration to Haran, which surely occurred (24:10). This is striking since the Nahor-Milcah family provides wives for the Abram group in Canaan. The author's silence about Nahor's movements may be attributed to Nahor's absence in Canaan, whereas Lot is named since he and Abram continue a relationship in Canaan. It is not until after the death of Sarah some sixty years later when Abraham dispatches his servant to retrieve a wife for Isaac that the Aram group is reintroduced (chap. 24). Moreover, the Nahor branch became so identified with north Mesopotamia that Haran could be cited as "the town of Nahor" (24:10).

---

[37] J. Sailhamer notes that the theme of "separation" (cp. 10:5,32) reinforces the author's purpose, connecting "blessing" and the command to "fill the earth" ("Genesis," EBC [Grand Rapids: Zondervan, 1990], 111).

[38] U. Cassuto, *A Commentary on the Book of Genesis. Part II. From Noah to Abraham, Genesis VI:9–XI:32,* trans. I. Abrahams (Jerusalem: Magnes, 1964), 280–81.

[39] J. A. Emerton, "When Did Terah Die (Genesis 11:32)?" in *Language, Theology, and the Bible: Essays in Honor of James Barr* (Oxford: Clarendon, 1994), 178–79.

"And together they set out" (11:31) in the NIV is the best that can be done to make sense of the MT in context. The Hebrew phrase "and they went out with them" is contextually difficult since "with them" has the same antecedent as the subject of the verb, that is, Terah, Abram, Lot, and Sarai. Since the subject of the previous clause is "Terah [took]," the ancient versions continue the same sense, "and he [Terah] brought them out."[40] This variant reading reinforces what we observed earlier in the verse but is not necessary to make the point: Terah leads the group out of Ur, and Abram is in tow.

Our passage presents the human perspective on the migration of Abram. The divine perspective is heard from later in Canaan: "I am the LORD who brought you out of Ur of the Chaldeans" (15:7). Both descriptions use the same verb *(yāṣāʾ)* and the same form *(hiphil* stem) if we read with the variant "he brought them out" (also Neh 9:7). Although it was Terah who "took" Abram, the Lord God who had appeared to Abram at Ur (Acts 7:4) had initiated their travel plans.

The death of Terah (v. 32), as the case with Noah's obituary (9:29), signals the end of an era (see vol. 1A, p. 491). As for the chronological questions concerning the age of the patriarch's death,[41] we have already spoken to them (vol. 1A, p. 499, n. 34). This notice closes out the role of Terah in the account, although he lived another sixty years. The same feature occurs for Abraham, who lived another fifteen years after the birth of Esau and Jacob (25:5,7,11 with 25:26). The transition is made complete with the announcement of Terah's death, whether the remark of his passing and Abram's move to Canaan reflects real time or is proleptic (12:4).

2. The Promissory Call and Abram's Obedience (12:1–9)

The divine call of Abram (vv. 1–3) is central to the patriarchal narratives, for it entails the triad of divine promises that explain the thematic development of the remainder of the book and the whole of the Pentateuch (see commentary Introduction and vol. 1A, pp. 54–60). Recurring thematic forms and motifs in chaps. 1–11 are bunched together in the promissory call: land/country, bless/curse, seed, nation/family, and name. All that had preceded in the panorama of creation and divine grace toward human life take their place as prelude to this first divine word announced to Abram. Although the promises are repeated elsewhere in the patriarchal narratives, they are only offered in whole at 12:1–3. The many promises of the passage cohere into three strands: land, seed, and

---

[40] For the MT's אֹתָם וַיֵּצְאוּ the SP, LXX, and Vg. reflect the *hiphil* sg., וַיֹּצֵא אֹתָם, "and (Terah) brought them out" (cf. NJB, NAB). Syr. reads the *qal* sg., "And he (Terah) went out with them" (so GNB).

[41] SP has 145 years; Stephen comments that Abraham left Haran "after the death of (Terah)" (Acts 7:4). The MT's 205 years means that Terah lived sixty more years.

blessing. The divine oath is like an avalanche of blessing cascading in wave after wave on the patriarch and his children yet to come.

But the blessing so bountifully promised is preceded by a word of command, "Leave . . ." (v. la).[42] His answer to the command is not by word but by deed: "So Abram left" (v. 4a). Emboldened by his faith in the sure word of the Lord, the patriarch embarked on the divine scheme. Abram's obedience is described in vv. 4–9 by the itinerary of his travels in Canaan. Through his vagabond journeys, traveling from north to south and leaving behind altars erected to the Lord, he symbolized what would become reality for his descendants— possession of the land and worship of Israel's God.

This promissory call is the first recorded speech since God's word of judgment at the Tower of Babel, resulting in the creation of the nations (11:5–6,9). This new word to Abram counters the old since it provides for the redemptive plan of "all peoples" (v. 3). By making his descendants a "great nation" (v. 2) who will be a "blessing" (v. 2), the Lord will bring salvation to the scattered nations. As the two parts of an hourglass are joined by a slender neck, the role of this one man connects the universal setting of chaps. 1–11 and the worldwide vista of the promissory call.[43] The language of the call evokes the Table of Nations as the theological setting for its interpretation. In the Table's refrain (10:5,20,31–32) are "lands" *('arṣôt)*, "families" *(mišpĕḥôt)*, and "nations" *(gôyîm);* also the Table has the recurring verb *yālad,* translated "father of" and "born" (10:8,13,15,21,24,25,26). These four terms appear in 12:1–3: "country" *('ereṣ,* v. 1), "peoples" *(mišpĕḥôt,* v. 3), "nation" *(gôy,* v. 2), and "people" *(môledet,* v. 1), which is related to *yālad.* Although the call is directed to the individual Abram, it is intended ultimately for the salvation of the world's peoples (see vol. 1A, p. 430). In addition the term "bless" *(bārak)* and its derivatives, which are the thematic glue of the entire book, dominate the oath, occurring five times (see vol. 1A, pp. 48–51). The promise of blessing(s) corresponds to the fivefold appearance of "curse" in the earlier telling of universal history (chaps. 1–11; see vol. 1A, p. 51).

The promissory call looks ahead to the travelogue of Abram's faith that ends at Mount Moriah, where, upon hearing the Lord's command again, he offers his son as sacrifice (22:1–19). The command at 22:2, lit., "Go yourself unto the land of Moriah," recalls the beginning, lit., "Go yourself from your land" (12:1).[44] As we observed earlier, these two commands are the "bookends" in the narration of the patriarch's obedient walk. Abram is called upon to leave both his past and his future in placing his trust in God.

The literary structure of the promissory oath focuses on the pledge God

---

[42] Other parallels from the patriarchal narratives where the command to depart is linked with a promise include 26:1–3; 46:1–5; cf. 32:10 (Westermann, *Genesis 12–36,* 147).

[43] See K. A. Mathews, "The Table of Nations: The 'Also Peoples,'" *SBJT* 5 (2001): 42–56.

[44] לֶךְ־לְךָ מֵאַרְצְךָ (12:1) and וְלֶךְ־לְךָ אֶל־אֶרֶץ הַמֹּרִיָּה (22:2), *Gen. Rab.* 39.9.

makes to the patriarch (see below).[45] The term "covenant" *(bĕrît)* in conjunction with Abram does not occur until the ceremonial affirmation of the covenant, where the customary language of formalizing a covenant is found (15:18). We will address the relationship of the four "covenant" passages (12:1–3; chaps. 15; 17; 22:16–18) in more detail at chap. 17, but here we can summarize the connections. The promissory nature of the call in 12:1–3 sets forth the provisions of the covenant that are authenticated by the ritual of animal sacrifice (chap. 15) and by the sign of circumcision (chap. 17). In the giving of the covenant of circumcision, the expression "establish *[hāqîm]* my covenant" (17:7,19,21) may refer to a preexisting agreement, as it does in this case (see, e.g., 26:3 and discussion in vol. 1A, pp. 367–68). After the successful testing of Abraham, the Lord repeats the provisions but in the form of a sworn oath: "I swear *[nišbaʿtî]* by myself" (22:16a). Both expressions, covenant and sworn oath, describe the divine promise made to Abram.[46]

No obligations are placed upon Abram to maintain the promises (as for Israel at Sinai); he must only respond to the Lord's command to "leave," an act of loyalty. There is at work here the assumption of an existing relationship.[47] The commitment rests with the Lord to "show" the patriarch the land that awaits him. In relating the promises of vv. 2–3, God is the initiator and consummator. Abram is dependent on the Lord to achieve the promises; he only has the divine word to rely on. Abram is the passive recipient of the divine will. His status in the arrangement between the two parties is illustrated when the covenant is formally ratified (15:8–15). Abram is a witness to the covenant ceremony, not a participant (15:17); only the Lord (symbolized by the firepot) passes through the animal parts. Circumcision (17:11–13) and the offering of Isaac (22:16–18) are not covenant prerequisites for Abram to enter into covenant; rather these are obedient steps of faith, which assume an existing commitment already made by God (12:1–3; 15:6,18; cf. Jas 2:20–24).

COMPOSITION. The standard explanation for 12:1–9 is a combination of the Priestly writer (P) in vv. 4b–5 and the Yahwist (J) elsewhere. The distinction of P is based on the assumption that the age of the patriarch and the travel itinerary (to "Canaan") are priestly features (cf. 36:6–7, P). The travel to Canaan is a contin-

---

[45] M. Weinfeld notes that the covenant God makes with Abraham follows the treaty pattern of royal grants common in the ANE, where gifts are bestowed upon individuals who excelled in loyally serving their masters ("The Covenant of Grant in the Old Testament and Ancient Near East" *JAOS* 90 [1970]: 185).

[46] For the language "covenant," see, e.g., Exod 2:24; Lev 26:42; 2 Kgs 13:23; 1 Chr 16:15–16/ /Ps 105:8–9; Acts 3:28; 7:8; also *2 Mac* 1:1 (LXX 1:2); *Sir* 44:19 (LXX 44:20). For sworn "oath" see, e.g., Gen 26:3,50:24; Exod 6:8; 32:13; Deut 1:8; Luke 1:73. Ps 105:7 has both covenant (Abraham) and oath (Isaac).

[47] See vol. 1A, pp. 62, 367–38; for a clarification of the terms and issues, see B. K. Waltke, "The Phenomenon of Conditionality within Unconditional Covenants," in *Israel's Apostasy and Restoration* (Grand Rapids: Baker, 1988), 127–30.

uation of P's account of Terah (11:31). This means that the P and J sources duplicate the mention of "Lot" in 12:4 (J) and 12:5 (P). Also, the destination of Canaan
was known to Abraham in P but unknown in J's account ("to the land I will show
you," 12:1).[48] Van Seters is correct to explain the travel itinerary in 11:31–12:9
as told in progressive stages, which explains why the passage provides the travel
stage of Abraham after that of Terah.[49] The mention of the divine appearance at
"Ur of the Chaldees" in 15:7 is not typically assigned to P (attributed to J or Deuteronomistic). The position of 12:1–3 makes perfect sense. The conclusion in
11:32 rounds off the Terah stage, and the call in vv. 1–3 gives the motive for
Abraham's continuation. The mention of "Lot" twice is not evidence of two parallel sources, making the redactor negligent in his work, nor is it a mere repetition
without purpose. The first occasion, "and Lot went with him" (v. 4a), uses *hālak*
("went"), which corresponds with the admonition to Abraham and his obedient
response in vv. 1,4a. The language indicates that Lot recognized the wisdom of
affiliating himself with Abraham. This connection anticipates the tension in chap.
13 and the necessary separation that follows. Separation is common and essential
to the plot and theology of the Abraham narrative as a whole. The second mention of Lot has the formulaic language "he [Abram] took *(lāqaḥ)* . . ." (v. 5),
which echoes Terah's patriarchal role (11:31), showing that Abram supplants
Terah as the new head of this traveling assembly whose members are named specifically (Sarai, Lot) in the verse. The precise identities of the travelers are important to the author's purposes; thus he mentions Lot the second time to show him
under the auspices of Abram's new patriarchy.

STRUCTURE.   The passage consists of two parts, vv. 1–3 and vv. 4–9 (or vv.
1–4a and 4b–9). Each part begins with the word *hālak* ("go, walk"): "Leave
. . ." (v. 1) and "So Abram left . . ." (v. 4). Genesis 12:1–3 consists of a command followed by seven clauses that entail the promises of the divine oath (vv.
2–3). There are two imperatives around which the promises cluster into two
groups. The first command ("Leave," v. 1a) is followed by the first group of
three promises (v. 2). These three employ a first-person verbal form (cohortative) conveying the Lord's resolve to bless the patriarch and his family: (1) "I
will make you into a great nation"; (2) "and I will bless you"; and (3) "I will
make your name great" (v. 2abc).[50]

The second group of three promises pertain to Abram's mediation of the
blessing for the world of nations (v. 3). The second imperative *(weheyēh)*,[51]
which is itself a promise, transitions the passage from Abram as the recipient

---

[48] Carr, *Reading the Fractures of Genesis,* 104–5.

[49] J. van Seters, *Prologue to History: The Yahwist as Historian in Genesis* (Louisville: Westminster John Knox, 1992), 202–3.

[50] GKC § 108d; *IBHS* §34.6.

[51] וְהְיֵה בְּרָכָה (lit. "be a blessing," v. 2d) is preceded by the cohortative וַאֲגַדְּלָה ("I will make
. . . great"); by this sequence of verbs the imperative expresses expected certainty or intension
(GKC § 110i). The use of the imperative instead of an imperfective verbal form heightens the certainty of the promise (*IBHS* §34.4c).

of blessing (v. 2) to his mediation of blessing: "and you will be a blessing" (v. 2d). The three promises in this second cluster consist of two more first-person verbal forms (cohortatives)[52] in arrangement and a third-person verb (perfect with *waw*): (1) "I will bless those who bless you"; and (2) "and whoever curses you I will curse"; and (3) "all peoples on earth will be blessed through you." The third-person perfective verb (v. 3c) presents the final promise and is the ultimate goal of the previously stated intentions toward Abram.[53] The promises of vv. 2–3 entail seven parts, perhaps a feature suggesting completion.[54]

v. 1   "Leave *(lēk)* . . .
v. 2a   (1)   so that I will make you a great nation
   2b   (2)   and I will bless you;
   2c   (3)   I will make your name great
   2d   (4)   so that you will be *[wehĕyēh]* a blessing (author's translation).
v. 3a   (5)   I will bless those who bless you,
   3b   (6)   and whoever curses you I will curse;
   3c   (7)   and all peoples on earth will be blessed through you."

After the calling of Abram, the account describes his act of obedience by detailing the patriarch's departure (v. 4), the members of the traveling party (v. 5), and his itinerary in Canaan, where he erected altars of worship (vv. 6–9).

(1) The Command and Oath (12:1–3)

¹The LORD had said to Abram, "Leave your country, your people and your father's household and go to the land I will show you.
   ²"I will make you into a great nation
   and I will bless you;
   I will make your name great,
   and you will be a blessing.
   ³I will bless those who bless you,
   and whoever curses you I will curse;
   and all peoples on earth
   will be blessed through you."

12:1   The call of Abram at Haran was preceded by the migration of the Terah clan from Ur (11:31–32), but the content of the message received at Ur

---

[52] The imperfective form אָאֹר ("I will curse") has cohortative force (*IBHS* §34.1d) since it matches the cohortative וַאֲבָרְכָה ("I will bless") in the chiasmus.

[53] וְנִבְרְכוּ ("so that . . . will be blessed") is the *niphal* perfective form with *wāw* consecutive; when preceded by an imperfect, as in this case (אָאֹר, "I will curse"), or a volitional form, as in the previous cohortative (וַאֲבָרְכָה, "I will bless"), the perfect may express the consequence of the foregoing situation (*IBHS* §32.21c; §32.2.2).

[54] Cassuto, *Genesis Part Two*, 312 (*Gen. Rab.* 17.4).

is not reported in 15:7, where the passage only recounts that the Lord "brought [Abram] out of Ur." Stephen's sermon reports that God "appeared" to Abraham before he lived in Haran, showing that the Lord supervised the journey of Abraham, from the beginning at Ur to his final destination in Canaan (Acts 7:2–4). Abraham fulfilled his calling in two stages. This relationship of the call in 12:1–3 and the theophany at Ur in 15:7 has been explained in different ways. (1) By translating 12:1 as "the LORD *had* said . . ." (italics mine; e.g., NIV, AV, NKJV), 12:1–3 is reciting the original call received at Ur. Although the grammar permits this translation,[55] it is not necessary. The literary context of 12:1–3 is Haran, not Ur, which may indicate that the narrative possesses a topical arrangement.[56] The author provides the details of the call as the narrative commences Abraham's career in Canaan. (2) Alternatively, some commentators posit that the calling occurred twice. Either explanation permits Stephen's interpretation of the call and move of Abraham.

The language of the call in 12:1–3 possesses many poetic characteristics, such as parallelisms, rhyme, and chiasmus. The most prominent feature is the repetition of the pronoun "you/your" *(kā)*, referring to Abram, and the first-person verbs, "I will . . .," referring to God. By juxtaposition the interplay between second and first persons shows Abram as the recipient and the Lord as the Promisor. The Hebrew also has the alliteration *lēk lĕkā,* lit., "Go yourself" (12:1a), where the imperative is made emphatic by a reflexive pronoun.[57] The following three phrases identify the spheres of influence in his life that Abram must leave behind, from the broad to the specific: from *[min]* "your country" *[ʾereṣ],* from "your people" *[môledet],* and from *[min]* "your father's household" *[bêt ʾāb].*[58] The alliterative "from" *[min]* heads each phrase (absent NIV), reinforcing the command of separation required of Abram by God.

Although the patriarch does not dishonor his heritage (e.g., Abram turns to his kinsmen for Isaac's wife, 24:4), it will be of no aid to him in answering God's command. The solace of country and family must give way to a higher allegiance. This is the requirement of those who enter the kingdom, as Jesus taught, "Anyone who loves his father or mother more than me is not worthy of me" (Matt 10:37). All is placed in the Lord's hands who will "show" him the land of destiny, Canaan. The land "I will show you" (12:1b) is the only road map that Abram can follow. Abram can depart and cohabit with his wife, but it is the Lord who will make of this alien and childless couple a "great nation." If the nations are to enjoy the promised blessing (1:28; 9:1) through

---

[55] *IBHS* §33.2.3

[56] Ross, *Creation and Blessing,* 258.

[57] *IBHS* §16.4g. Contra the position of T. Muroaka, who argues instead that the construction of verbs of motion followed by the preposition *lamed* with a pronominal suffix denotes movement toward a center ("On the So-called Dativus Ethicus in Hebrew," *JTS* 29 [1978]: 495–98).

[58] See also the parallels in 22:2 with reference to Isaac.

the founding of a new nation (Israel), there must be the possession of a land and the birth of a people. In the Abraham story the land is obtained in part, although possession is tentative, but it is especially the promise of offspring that proves most elusive.

"From your country" (NIV, AV, NASB, NRSV), lit., "from your land *['ereṣ]*," is used as in the Table of Nations, where "lands" *['arṣôt]* indicates particular places inhabited by specific peoples. "Your people *(môledet)*" refers to Abram's "relatives" (NASB, GNB; or "kindred," AV, NRSV, NJB). Both terms occur again in tandem when the Lord instructs Jacob to return from Aram (32:9; also Jethro, Num 10:30). "Your land" and "your relatives" can be taken as a hendiadys, "the land of your kinsfolk" (NAB), which would resemble the more frequent bound construction "the land of your relatives" (*'ereṣ môladtekā*, 31:13; also 11:28; 24:7; Ruth 2:11; Jer 22:10; 46:16; Ezek 23:15).

Since the geographical setting for 12:1–3 is the city Haran (11:31–32), the call of Abram ("Leave your country, your people," 12:1) indicates that his homeland is Aram; that Aram is the birthplace of the patriarch appears confirmed by Abram's instructions to his servant to seek out a wife for Isaac in the land of his relatives (24:4,7). If we assume that the Terah family were pastoralists, they would have resided near urban centers. The need for open pastures would have required travel, a feature of pastoralists in the early second millennium. K. A. Kitchen observed, "Thus a Terah might have had family origins around Harran and Nakhur, followed the common 'drift' southeastward, in his case to Ur, and then returned north with his family."[59] Aram as the original setting for the Terah group would help explain the association of several of their personal and place names in the upper Mesopotamian region (see vol. 1A, p. 498). In such a view the conflict with those passages (11:31–32; 15:7; Neh 9:7; Acts 7:2–4) that attribute Abram's origins to Ur is only an apparent problem. The Terah group first migrated south to Ur, at which time his son Haran was born (11:28); the movement back to Aram (11:31–32) was a return to the clan's original homestead. That the two cities Ur and Haran had commercial and religious connections may explain their travels between the two centers.[60] But this reconstruction may assume too much for the term *môledet* ("people," 12:1) when it occurs in conjunction with "land" *('ereṣ)*. The word *môledet* is flexible in range, including birth, progeny, and family (e.g., 43:7; 48:6; Ruth 1:11; Ezek 16:4; 23:15; Esth 2:10,20; 8:6). In which case, reference to a person's family land (as in 11:28; 12:1; 24:4,7) may only require that relatives are presently settled in that location.[61] That the expression of *môledet* and *'ereṣ* can mean birthplace, however, is attested by Jacob's experience (31:13; 32:9). A general

---

[59] K. A. Kitchen, *On the Reliability of the Old Testament* (Grand Rapids: Eerdmans, 2003), 318.

[60] S. Spero, "Was Abram Born in Ur of the Chaldees?" *JBQ* 24 (1996): 156–59.

[61] Cassuto, *Genesis Part II*, 274–75; Sarna, *Genesis,* 358, n. 2; G. Wenham, *Genesis 16–50,* WBC (Dallas: Word, 1995), 272.

picture of migratory activity may have been the author's only intent, so as to depict Abram's family from earliest times as sojourners. The promise of a permanent land for the Abram family would be both different and welcomed. By reporting the Ur migration, the author establishes the Tower of Babel (11:1–9) as the wider literary context for the patriarch's calling, not just Aram. The exit from southern Mesopotamia furthermore provides for a typology of the Hebrew exiles who are "called" again and delivered from Chaldea (Isa 49:22; 41:8; 51:2; Ezek 33:24; Mic 7:20).[62]

The next sphere, "your father's household," refers to Terah's household. When instructing his servant to find a wife for Isaac, Abram remembers his calling with the same language of 12:1. He refers to Aram Nahanaim, meaning Mesopotamia, as "my country" (*ʾarṣî;* 24:4,7) and to Nahor's family as "my own relatives" (*môladtî;* 24:4) and "my father's house" (*bêt ʾābî;* 24:7). Ruth's migration to Judah illustrates the separation Abram is called to do, when Boaz comments, "You [Ruth] left your father [*ʾābîk*] and mother [*ʾimmēk*] and the land of your birth [NIV "your homeland"; *ʾereṣ môladtēk*]" (Ruth 2:11).

Although Abram antedated the typical kinship structure of Israel's twelve tribes, the Hebrew tradition casts some light on the trifold levels of separation experienced by the patriarch: land, relatives, father's house. Three kinship units constituted Israelite social and economic life: (1) the tribe (*šēbeṭ/maṭṭeh*), which was the largest unit and yet least relevant to a person's daily life; (2) the clan (*mišpaḥat*), providing both kinship and geographic identity, which had an intermediate role between tribe and family; and (3) the family, the father's household (*bēt ʾāb*), which was the smallest unit and the most important to the identity of the individual (e.g., Josh 7:16–18).[63] A number of fathers' households made up a clan, and related clans together constituted one of Israel's tribes (e.g., Exod 6:14; Num 1:2; 3:20–24).[64] The father of a household was head over his wives, unmarried daughters (Num 30:3–5), his sons and their dependents (Gen 38:8), and other members, such as slaves and laborers. Married daughters were assimilated into their husband's household system (Gen 38:11; Lev 18:10; Deut 25:5–10). Sons divided their father's patrimony upon his death (Judg 11:2) or remained together (Deut 25:5; Judg 9:5). They formed their own families and were counted as heads of households (1 Chr 7:2; 24:6; Ezra 10:16). So strong was the identity of a person with his father's household that an individual's behavior had implications for the entire family (Josh 2:18; 1 Sam 17:25; 2 Sam 14:9; 24:17).

Abram cut the strongest family bond by leaving his father's domain, which provided his own household's socioeconomic viability. He trusted the veracity

---

[62] Sailhamer, "Genesis," 110.

[63] C. J. H. Wright, "Family," *ABD* 2.761–69.

[64] The phrase בֵּית אָב ("father's household") may also refer at places to higher levels, such as tribes (e.g., Num 17:21[17:6]); Josh 22:14); H. Ringgren, "אָב *ʾābh,*" *TDOT* 1.9.

of God's promised generosity and received more than he would have had he remained in Haran. Ironically, Abram's household, through Jacob at Haran, receives its original due and more from the reluctant Laban of Nahor's family (31:1), whose sisters (and their concubines) birth the twelve tribes of Israel.

12:2 After the promise of a land, the second promise is a numerous population base, a "nation" *(gôy)*. A nation is generally characterized as a political unit with common land, language, and government. This is the most startling promise, for Abram at seventy-five years has no children, and Sarai is "barren" (v. 30). It is God alone who "opens" and "closes" the womb (e.g., 20:18; 29:31; 30:22; 1 Sam 1:5–6; cp. 15:3; 16:2; 17:16; 18:14; 21:1). Abram's industry could have obtained for himself a land, wealth, and fame, but in the acquisition of children by Sarai he was helpless without God. The couple's vain attempts at a substitute successor (15:2–3; 16:2) admit their impotence to achieve the promise. This promise speaks of Abram ("you") and not directly of Sarai bearing a child, contributing to the ambiguity of the situation. On the face of it, the promise did not require Sarai's pregnancy. But it becomes increasingly clear that the Lord meant that the childless couple together would enter into this promise (15:4; 17:19,21). As the years of heartache pass, the idea of conceiving a child for Sarai at age ninety becomes a lamentable source of laughter (17:17; 18:11–12), but the arrival of Isaac fulfills God's assurances (18:14; 21:1–3). Isaiah's prophecy remembers the fulfillment of the promise: "When I (the LORD) called him (Abram) he was but one, and I blessed him and made him many" (51:2b).

The author of Genesis repeatedly explains the origins of "nation(s)," using the term twenty-seven times in the book.[65] Although the Table of Nations contains as many as seventy-two peoples, Genesis focuses on the birth of the nations that come from Abram and his descendants. Scattered throughout the book are allusions to the promissory language "I will make you into a great nation" (12:2; see 18:18), including references to Ishmael (17:20; 21:18) and Jacob (46:3). God proclaims to the three patriarchs the promise of numerous seed and nationhood,[66] and the book narrates how the oath is (partially) realized through the multiplying numbers of their offspring. As a result of the promise made to Abram (21:13; cp. 26:5), the nonelect sons of the family, Ishmael and Esau, also father populous tribes;[67] the inclusion of tribal lists naming chiefs and kings demonstrates the fulfilling of God's word to Abram (25:13–15; 36:9–43).

---

[65] For גּוֹי and גּוֹיִם, see 10:5(2x),20,31,32(2x); 12:2; 14:1,9; 15:4; 17:4,5,6,16,20; 18:18(2x); 20:4; 21:13,18; 22:18; 25:23; 26:4; 35:11(2x); 46:3; 48:19.

[66] Abraham (12:2; 17:4–6,16,20; 18:18; 21:13; 22:18), Isaac (26:4), and Jacob (25:23; 35:11). also, Jacob's blessing of Joseph's sons, Ephraim and Manasseh, promises nations (48:19).

[67] Ishmael (16:10; 17:20; 21:13,18) and Esau (25:23); also Abram's sons by Keturah form people groups (25:1–4).

Abram himself did not realize the promise of a burgeoning nation (cp. Heb 11:13), yet he trusted the Lord's revelation in a night vision that his descendants would become a powerful nation (15:5–6,12–21; Deut 1:10–11; Acts 7:17). The setting for such an emerging nation was established by Jacob's descent into Egypt, also through a night vision to Jacob, the Lord confirmed the promise of a "great nation" (46:3–4). Israel's historic confession, drawing on the language of the Abrahamic promise, memorialized the transformation of Jacob's insignificant number in Egypt: "My father was a wandering Aramean, and he went down into Egypt with a few people and lived there and became a great nation [gôy gādôl], powerful and numerous" (Deut 26:5). The promise of greatness also means a vigorous and distinguished people (Gen 18:18,20; Deut 4:6–8).[68]

Moses, therefore, inherited the "nation" that was destined to realize the mediatorial role of Father Abraham as a "kingdom of priests and a holy nation [gôy]" (Exod 19:5–6). Moses, who was the preeminent leader of the nation, was cast as a second Abraham (cp. Noah, vol. 1A, pp. 351–52). The idolatrous and rebellious treachery of the Exodus generation risked their annihilation on at least two occasions; the Lord was prepared to start anew, making Moses the new Abraham by proffering the old promise: "Then I will make you [Moses] into a great nation" (Exod 32:10; Num 14:12; Deut 9:14). But the mediation of Moses, as Abram had interceded for others (18:23–32; 20:17), resulted in their preservation, based on Moses' appeal to the patriarchal promise (Exod 32:13–14; Num 14:15–20; Deut 9:19–20,25–29). Jacob makes a similar prayer on his own behalf (32:9,12).

Following the promises of land and descendants, the Lord announces he will enrich Abram materially: "I will bless you." "Bless" *(bārak)* in Genesis describes primarily two benefits: progeny and material wealth (see vol. 1A, pp. 55–56, 158 and nn. 165–166). Here "bless" indicates material wealth for Abram, since the promise of a populous nation had already been made. This is the understanding of "blessing" given to Isaac's remarkable agricultural success; both the narrator and Isaac's neighbors attribute it to the Lord who "blessed him" (26:12,29; cf. 32:9). Wealth was measured by numerous and robust livestock, precious metals, such as gold and silver, and human labor, slave and alien.

Abram began his Canaan experience with possessions (12:5), and he obtained so much livestock from Pharaoh (12:16,20; cf. 20:14) that it became a source of friction among the herdsmen of Abram and Lot (13:2,6). The prominence of Abram is apparent by the large contingency of retainers (318) in his household (14:14) and by the testimony of local chieftains who entered into treaty with the Hebrew (21:22–23). In an effort to persuade Rebekah to leave her homeland to marry Isaac, the servant of Abraham's household reports on

---

[68] Sarna, *Genesis,* 89, 358.

Abraham's wealth (24:35). Isaac, too, was envied for his wealth by his neighbors the Philistines (26:12–15,28–29), and Jacob's immense acquisitions also resulted in a schism with Laban during his sojourn in Aram (30:27,29–30,43; 31:1,16–18). His own account of God's blessing testifies to his exceptional rise to wealth: "I had only my staff when I crossed this Jordan, but now I have become two groups" (32:10). As in the case with Abram (12:16,20), Jacob's household benefits from Pharaoh's prosperity, gained through Joseph's wise administration of the king's holdings (47:11–12,27). The number and wealth of the Hebrew people later in Egypt threatened their hosts, but this time their riches resulted in genocide for their children (Exod 1:6–7,15–22; cp. Gen 47:27).

The third promise, "I will make your name great," pledges that Abram's influence will be widespread, even across generations. "Name" *(šēm)* is another lexical item that brings the Babel story forward. The ambition of the city-builders was "so that we may make a name for ourselves" (11:4; see vol. 1A, pp. 482, 485–86). The Lord, however, had given the postdiluvian world the lineage of "Shem" *(šēm)* from whom would come Abraham (see vol. 1A, pp. 490–91). Whereas chaps. 1–11 depict the folly of human efforts to obtain wisdom (3:5) and fame ("name," 6:4 ["renown," NIV]) by unlawful means, the patriarch receives a "name" by divine grant. Although this promise speaks to Abram's stature in his own time, it also anticipates the change in Abram's name to "Abraham," which is conferred by God who will make him a father of future nations and kings (17:5–6; see vol. 1A, p. 500 for the linguistic significance of the patriarch's name). The naming of "Abraham" best explains the promise of 12:2; Abraham will be revered as "father" by a host of peoples whom he will influence throughout the centuries. The telling reality of this promise is that Judaism, Christianity, and Islam "look to Abraham" (Isa 51:2) as their spiritual progenitor (see Introduction to the Abraham section).

This promise also is proleptic of the divine oath given to David, which shares in the language of 12:2 (2 Sam 7:9).[69] The seed promised to Abram finds its future reality in the monarchic ideal through David's house. Psalm 72 portrays the glory of Israel's king and his kingdom, including echoes of 12:3 (and 22:18): "May his name endure forever; may it continue as long as the sun. / All nations will be blessed through him, and they will call him blessed" (Ps 72:17). The oath made to David includes this comparison of the king's fame, "like the names of the greatest men of the earth" (2 Sam 7:9b). But David's greatness was cast in the language and shadow of his ancestor Abraham, for whom there was no comparable measure, not until One greater than their "father Abraham"

---

[69] Except for Gen 12:2 and 2 Sam 7:9, only the name of God is characterized by the adjective "great." Gen 12:2 is simply וַאֲגַדְּלָה שְׁמֶךָ, lit., "I will magnify [make great] your name"; whereas 2 Sam 7:9 reads וְעָשִׂתִי לְךָ שֵׁם גָּדוֹל, lit., "and I will make for you a great name" (the parallel at 1 Chr 17:8 omits גָּדוֹל, "great").

came to his people (John 8:53; cp. 4:12). The Abrahamic and Davidic covenants also are the same in literary form, the royal grant. In both covenants the Lord as a mighty king bestows a gift upon his subjects (see vol. 1A, p. 368). Together, the divine charters given to these prototypes provide the hope for the coming of the messianic Savior (e.g., Matt 1:1; Luke 1:68–75).

The fourth promise, "so that you will be a blessing" (v. 2d; author's translation),[70] transitions the focus of the promises from the individual Abram and his descendants (vv. 1–2c) to all families who are influenced by him (v. 3). The statement is nonspecific, focusing attention at this point only on the mediator of the blessing, namely, Abram. The promise here is sufficiently broad to permit a blessing for any who invoke blessing in the name of Abram (cf. 48:40)[71] or for any who benefit from a relationship with the patriarchal family (e.g., Laban and Potiphar).[72] Verse 3 clarifies how and to what extent this blessing is realized by others.

12:3 The final triad of promises explains how Abram will achieve a blessing for others. Promises five and six are expressed explicitly as the actions of the Lord ("I will"). Although the precise meaning of the last promise is disputed (see below), the verse in context indicates that the Lord, not Abram, is the dispenser of blessing for the nations. Abram has no exclusive claim on God's blessing; rather, God has exclusive claim on Abram and on all those who submit to his God.

The fifth and sixth promises are parallel expressions—two sides of the same coin. The structure is a chiasmus *(abba):* "I will bless those who bless you//the one who curses you I will curse" (v. 3ab). "Bless" *(bārak)* and "curse" *(ʾārar)* are integral motifs in Genesis (see vol. 1A, pp. 54–56). In chaps. 1–11 "curse" is the consequence of unlawful behavior; now "curse" is explained by how a people mistreats Abram, the appointed heir of the blessing. Later events in the lives of the patriarchs illustrate this promise. Pharaoh and Abimelech suffer because of Abram and Sarai (12:17; 20:17–18); Laban learns to temper his anger against son-in-law Jacob (31:29); and both Potiphar and Pharaoh benefit from the Lord's blessing on Joseph (39:2–6; 47:5–15).

The chiastic arrangement of the two promises, however, shows imbalance at three points that many commentators have considered significant. First, unlike the clause concerning divine "curse" (v. 3b), the promise of blessing (v. 3a) is

---

[70] The syntax as a purpose clause has been analyzed under "Structure" above (cp. 45:18; Exod 3:10; 1 Kgs 1:12); for discussion of the syntactical options, see W. Yarchin, "Imperative and Promise in Genesis 12:1–3," *Studia biblica et theologica* 10 (1980): 167–88.

[71] Zech 8:13 has the similar construction וִהְיִיתֶם בְּרָכָה ("and you will be a blessing"), which involves an invocation; when viewed from the example of 48:40, where patriarchal names are mentioned, the idea in 12:2d may be a blessing formula in which Abram's name appears (Wenham, *Genesis 1–15,* 276).

[72] Westermann, *Genesis 12–36,* 150.

marked syntactically (cohortative with *waw*) as the purpose of the call, continuing the nuance of the previous clauses in v. 2.[73] From this observation, P. D. Miller concluded that God's command (v. 1) is not intended to bring about curse, only to bless; curse is subservient to the intent of blessing, included as a promise of protection for Abram.[74] But the chiastic construction implies that the second half matches the force of the first half. The purpose of calling Abram is to bless, for blessing dominates the call, but curse is also purposeful since the call assumes that opposition is the reality Abram faces.

Second, the plural "*those* who bless you" versus the matching phrase in the singular "*whoever* curses you" is thought by some to distinguish the two groups by number (italics mine); the one who curses Abram is the exception, thus the singular in number.[75] However, this is only a poetic effect, a morphological parallelism, observed in Hebrew verse indicating equivalency.[76]

Third, the two occurrences of the word translated "curse" are two different Hebrew words. "Whoever curses" renders the *(piel)* participle of *qll,* which in the basic stem *(qal)* means "to be small, insignificant." The *piel* stem carries a declarative sense, "to declare insignificant, to ridicule" (e.g., Exod 21:17). The second occurrence of "curse" is the common word in Genesis for curse *('ārar)*[77] Some derive from this difference that the severity of the two "curses" is different. Those who dare to treat Abram "lightly" *(qll)* will receive the greater weight of God's "curse *('ārar)*" But the parallel effect of the language supersedes any lexical difference in nuance; this is seen later by the repetition of the promises made to Jacob where *'ārar* ("curse") occurs instead of *qll* ("curse"; 27:29; see fuller discussion in vol. 1A, pp. 394–95).

The final, seventh promise reveals the inclusive character of the promissory blessing, "all peoples on earth." How this blessing is received involves Abram, although the precise way this is achieved is ambiguous in the language. The precise nuance of the verb *(nibrĕkû, niphal)* is disputed; the verb permits the passive ("will be blessed") or reflexive voice ("will bless themselves"). Divergence among the Genesis parallels of the promise has complicated the matter too, since the same verbal form as 12:3 appears in 18:18 and 28:14, but a different form of the verb occurs in 22:18 and 26:4 *(hithbārăkû, hithpael).* These two verbal forms overlap in semantic range (both can be pas-

---

[73] אָאֹר וּמְקַלֶּלְךָ מְבָרְכֶיךָ וַאֲבָרֲכָה (v. 3ab); the verb אָאֹר ("I will curse") does not have the conjunctive *waw.*

[74] P. D. Miller, "Syntax and Theology in Genesis XII 3a," *VT* 34 (1984): 472–76.

[75] NJB, NAB, REB, GNB, and HCSB translate both clauses as plural; NIV, AV, NRSV, NASB, and NJPS maintain the singular, e.g., "I will curse him who curses you" (NKJV).

[76] A. Berlin, *The Dynamics of Biblical Parallelism* (Bloomington: Indiana University Press, 1985), 32, 49.

[77] EVs commonly translate both words in 12:3 the same, "curse."

sive or reflexive), permitting the interchange of the two forms.[78]

(1) Traditionally, interpreters have understood the verb as passive, "will be blessed through you" (e.g., LXX, *Tg. Onq.*, Vg., *Sir* 4:21, Gal 3:8; Rev 3:25, NIV, AV, NASB, NRSV). By this translation, Abram is the vehicle of the divine gift for the nations. This suggests that a specific plan is envisioned for the blessing upon the nations.[79] (2) The reflexive meaning, "will bless themselves by you," has been argued by others (e.g., Rashi, Skinner,[80] Westermann, RSV, NJB, NEB, REB, NJPS) partly on the basis of the *hithpael* in Ps 72:17b ("And let *men* bless themselves *[yithbārĕkû]* by him," NASB, also RSV). In this case, the patriarch is a motivating example of faith, not the exclusive conduit; the promise therefore describes future nations who call for blessing in the name of Abram (as in 48:20: "By you Israel will invoke blessings, saying, 'God make you like Ephraim and like Manasseh,' " NRSV; also see under v. 2's discussion the similarity of language with Zech 8:13). (3) A third possibility has received support recently: taken in the middle voice, the verb is rendered "shall find blessing in you" (NAB).[81] This translation focuses attention on the discovery of blessing, not the means (agent).[82]

What the three interpretations have in common is the involvement of Abram. The passive translation probably suits the context of the passage best, since God is the source ("I will" [6x]) and Abram in our analysis is the channel ("you will be a blessing," v. 2d). It also is consistent with the idea of a divine plan, which the tenor of the entire book conveys by the motif of an exclusive family (chosen). As for the example of Ps 72:17b above, it can be contextually understood in the passive (e.g., AV, NIV, NRSV) and therefore cannot be determinative for Genesis.

Also significant is how the construction of this last verbal clause ("will be blessed," v. 3c) differs from the previous promises, which are first-person verbs (cohortatives); this final promise is introduced by the perfective form.[83] The construction indicates a purpose clause, as the previous promises, but its different expression distinguishes the final clause as the ultimate goal of the command, "Leave . . . so that all peoples on earth will be blessed through you" (author's translation). The passage transitions from Abram the man to Abram the means for blessing. Verse 3 explains the blessing promised for others, and the promises move to the chief end, worldwide blessing.

---

[78] Also 2 Sam 10:6 and 1 Chr 19:6; see *IBHS* §23.4h; §23.6.4.

[79] See Hamilton, *Genesis Chapters 1–17*, 374–75, for more discussion.

[80] J. Skinner, *A Critical and Exegetical Commentary on Genesis*, ICC, 2d ed. (Edinburgh: T&T Clark, 1910), 244–45.

[81] Wenham sees a progression of thought in the passage: Abram is blessed (passive), people use Abram's name for a blessing (reflexive), and all families find blessing in Abram (middle) (*Genesis 1–15*, 277–78).

[82] For the significance of the middle voice, see *IBHS* §23.2.2ab.

[83] וְנִבְרְכוּ "so that . . . will be blessed."

The revelation at Sinai to Moses repeats the promises and applies them to Israel (Exod 3:6–9,14–17; 6:2–8) as a priestly "nation" (Exod 19:6). For the psalmists, blessing upon restored Israel brings salvation to the nations (Pss 67; 98). In particular the Davidic offspring is the means whereby the Lord will enrich the nations (e.g., Ps 72:17; Isa 11:10–12; 55:3–5; Amos 9:11–12). The apostles also take up the promises and identify Jesus Christ as the Savior who obtains the blessing for those who believe. Peter appropriates the promise of universal blessing as found in 22:18 and 26:4 (alluding to 12:3), which read "through your offspring," referring to Abraham's descendants as the resource of blessing. Peter urges his fellow Jews to repent so that they will receive the fulfillment of the ancient promise (Acts 3:25–26). Paul also views the promise of blessing fulfilled in Jesus Christ, but he applies it to the Gentiles (Gal 3:28). He conflates the Greek of 12:3 and 26:4, where in the latter verse the LXX reads "all the nations" *(panta ta ethnē)*, suiting the apostle's application to the Gentiles.[84] Peter too moderated 22:18, LXX (26:4, LXX) for his Jewish audience by translating "all [the] peoples" *(pasai ai patriai;*Acts 3:25).[85] The apostles considered the church to be the recipients of the promises made to Abram, the Jew first and then the Gentile (Rom 1:16; 2:9–10)[86]; the Lord announced by 12:3 the "gospel" to the awaiting world of peoples (Gal 3:28).

(2) Abram's Obedience (12:4–9)

[4]So Abram left, as the LORD had told him; and Lot went with him. Abram was seventy-five years old when he set out from Haran. [5]He took his wife Sarai, his nephew Lot, all the possessions they had accumulated and the people they had acquired in Haran, and they set out for the land of Canaan, and they arrived there.

[6]Abram traveled through the land as far as the site of the great tree of Moreh at Shechem. At that time the Canaanites were in the land. [7]The LORD appeared to Abram and said, "To your offspring I will give this land." So he built an altar there to the LORD, who had appeared to him.

[8]From there he went on toward the hills east of Bethel and pitched his tent, with Bethel on the west and Ai on the east. There he built an altar to the LORD and called on the name of the LORD. [9]Then Abram set out and continued toward the Negev.

12:4–5 "So Abram left, as the LORD had told him" reports the first step of obedient faith; similar language commends Noah (6:22; 7:9,16) and Moses (Exod 39:43; 40:16) for their compliance. Two parenthetical statements reflect the chief obstacles to the patriarch's faith that he must overcome (vv. 4c,5b). First, his age at seventy-five years establishes the timeline that measures his

---

[84] 12:3, LXX differs by πᾶσαι αἱ φυλαὶ τῆς γῆς.
[85] 22:18, LXX and 26:4, LXX, πάντα τὰ ἐθνη τῆς γῆς.
[86] Bruce, *Book of the Acts,* 93–94.

twenty-five-year wait for the gift of an heir (v. 4a). Second, Canaanites inhabited the land Abram hoped to receive (v. 5b). He trusted, however, that the Lord by some unrevealed means would enable his descendants to dispossess Canaan's inhabitants.

12:6–7 Upon Abram's entry into Canaan, the Lord confirms the promises and in doing so recognizes Abram's act of obedience. First, he appears to Abram at Shechem, his first residence in the land (v. 7b). This theophany reassured Abram of the Lord's presence; the patriarch responded by building an altar, the first of many (v. 7b; cp. Jacob, 28:10–19; 35:1; 48:3 and Moses, Exod 3:2,12,16).[87] Second, the Lord reassured Abram by reiterating the two signal promises: children and land (v. 7a).

12:8–9 Abram's travelogue involved these locations: Shechem (oak of Moreh), Bethel/Ai, and the Negev. Both Jacob and later Israel make their claim to the land at these same sites (for the typological significance of this account, see vol. 1A, pp. 52–53). Shechem is situated at the strategic pass between Mount Gerizim and Mount Ebal in central Palestine, about forty-one miles north of Jerusalem. Excavations at the ancient site (usually equated with modern Tell Balatah) have been extensive (see comments on 33:18–20).[88] Shechem became an important religious and political center for later Israel (e.g., Josh 24; 1 Kgs 12:1–19,25). Its association with the patriarchs Jacob (33:19; 34:2–26; John 4:6) and Joseph (49:22; Josh 24:32; Acts 7:16) made it a historic place among the Hebrew people. The "oak of Moreh" occurs once more in the Old Testament where the plural, "oaks of Moreh," is associated with Ebal and Gerizim (Deut 11:30). Other references to "the oak" at Shechem include the burial of idols by Jacob (35:4) and the establishment of a testimonial pillar by Joshua (Josh 24:26; see Abimelech, Judg 9:6,37).[89]

From Shechem Abram traveled south, where he set up camp on the mountain located between Bethel and Ai, also situated in central Palestine. He revisited the place when retracing his steps from Egypt (13:3).[90] The appearance of the Lord to Jacob at Bethel (formerly Luz) underscores its importance (28:19; 31:13; 25:1–16). Bethel remained an important religious site (Judg 20:18,26–28; 1 Kgs 12:29; Hos 12:4), second only to Jerusalem, until the destruction of its sanctuary by Josiah (2 Kgs 23:15). Despite some opposition, the identity of Bethel with Tell Beitin and Ai with Et-Tell remains the popular opinion of mod-

---

[87] Y. Gitay views Abram's response as appropriate. "Canaan is not merely another new settlement," he writes, "but rather a sacred space" ("Geography and Theology in the Biblical Narrative: The Question of Genesis 2–12," in *Prophets and Paradigms: Essays in Honor of Gene M.Tucker,* JSOTSup 229 [Sheffield: Sheffield Academic Press, 1996], 209).

[88] L. Toombs, "Shechem," *HBD* 935–37; "Shechem," *ABD* 5.1174–86.

[89] For more discussion see M. Hunt, "Moreh," *ABD* 4.904.

[90] On the meaning of calling "upon the name of the LORD" [v. 8], see vol. 1A, pp. 292–94 and Introduction, "Religion of the Patriarchs."

ern scholars.[91] At this point in our knowledge, it is best to delay a conclusive identification of Ai until more information is available.[92]

Abram continued southward "toward the Negev" (v. 8); the Hebrew construction indicates he repeated the pattern of journeying by stages, where he built altars to the Lord.[93] The Negev is the region south of Judah where Abram and Isaac resided for brief periods (13:1,3; 20:1; 24:62).[94] "Negev" in Hebrew means "dry, south country." The wilderness generation lived in this area during its period of punishment (Num 13:17,22,29; 21:1; 33:40; Deut 1:7).

Excursus: The Patriarchs' Wealth

Although the wealth accumulated by the patriarchs and Israel's kings (e.g., 1 Kgs 10:23) attests to the Lord's blessing, it is reductionistic to think that the promise of material prosperity for Abraham (and later Israel, e.g., Deut 8:18) is intended for all generations who share in Abraham's covenant. A theology making riches the norm for the Christian experience fails to give sufficient weight to the whole biblical witness and misconstrues the significance of the biblical author's reporting on the wealth of the Fathers and kings. Genesis casts the patriarchs' wealth as unusual, not the norm.[95] In the Old Testament the Pentateuch's legal sections and the Hebrew prophets present the most extensive critique of wealth and poverty, followed by the wisdom literature and Psalms. The history writers purpose to show from selected events in the nation's experience the rise and fall of Israel from the perspectives of the moral corruption and religious apostasy of its leadership. Accounts regarding the material status of Israel's leaders are but part of the total portrayal presented.[96] When we consider that the patriarch Job also enjoyed wealth as a consequence of divine blessing, riches are best viewed as a trait of the Fathers that showed God's favor toward them. Moreover, in the case of Abram and the later exodus generation out of Egypt, their acquisitions established them as a people and nation that could survive and even influence how the nations viewed Israel's God.

A theology of wealth and poverty can only be derived from Genesis inferentially. The book cannot be seized as a model for individual or community wealth today. Genesis shows that the accumulation of possessions can be good as a part of God's creation, which he as Owner (Ps 50:10; 1 Tim 4:3–5) graciously

---

[91] On the excavations see H. Brodsky, "Bethel," *ABD* 1.710–12 and J. Calloway, "Ai," *ABD* 1.125–30; for an opposing view see D. Livingston, "The Last Word on Bethel and Ai," *BARev* 15 (1989): 11; "Further Considerations on the Location of Bethel at el-Bireh," *PEQ* 126 (1994): 154–59.

[92] See D. Howard, *Joshua,* NAC (Nashville: Broadman & Holman, 1998), 178–80.

[93] The infinitive absolutes וְנָסוֹעַ הָלוֹךְ describe the action of the main verb וַיִּסַּע ("he set out"; *IBHS* §35.3.2c); so NRSV renders "And Abram journeyed on by stages" (also NAB, NJPS; see NJB, GNB).

[94] For the environment and history, see S. Rose et al., "Negev," *ABD* 4.1061–68.

[95] Observed by Paul R. House (personal communication).

[96] J. Pleins, "Poor, Poverty," *ABD* 5.402–14; also the discussions in S. Mott, "Wealth," *HBD* 1122 and D. Adie, "Wealth, Christian View of," *EDT* 1159–63.

bestows for human benefit (cp. 1 Tim 6:17). Wealth is received from the hand of God by both covenant and noncovenant people in Genesis, both by the upright and the unrighteous. Wealth is therefore not merited by the recipient since ultimately it is the Lord who dispenses gifts by a variety of means. Job's experience alone sufficiently overturns the mistaken idea that righteous people prosper and the unrighteous languish in poverty due to their sin. In the biblical view wealth has no inherent moral value, either good or evil. The ethic of material possessions pertains to how wealth is obtained, managed, and shared (e.g., Deut 15:10–11; Prov 11:25; 23:4; 28:20,22; Luke 3:11; 2 Cor 9:11–12). The virtual identification of the rich with wickedness in the Hebrew prophets (Isa 53:9; Luke 16:19–31) was the historical reality of oppression that the prophets vociferously decried (e.g., Amos 2:6–7; 5:12). Yet the prophets did not decry wealth as an immoral entity by itself to be resisted; rather, they spoke against the wickedness of their day wherever it manifested itself, for God's judgment would fall upon the "great" and "small" house (Amos 6:11). Poverty also cannot always be equated with the morally oppressed since it may be the consequence of personal liability, such as laziness (Prov 10:4; 20:13), sensuality (Prov 21:17), or unfortunate circumstances, such as drought and war.

The Genesis portrayal of wealth is consistent with the scriptural view that wealth, in little or much, serves a higher purpose, not an end in itself. Prosperity enabled philanthropy, as seen in Abram's generosity toward Lot (13:8-17) and Jacob toward Esau (33:10–11). As we noted already, the wealth exhibited by Abram and by Israel (Exod 11:2–3; 12:35–36) enabled the people to become a viable nation. Abram's enrichment is explained within the call itself, "so that you will be a blessing" (v. 2d, NRSV). In the case of Israel, its wealth contributed to the building of the ornate tabernacle in the wilderness (Exod 25:1–8). As Carroll explains, "A nation thus shaped by faithfulness and benevolence would be a witness to the world of divine blessing" (see Deut 4:7–8; 15:6).[97] When taken up by Christian writers, the promises are commonly interpreted as prototypical of spiritual blessings that are known by the believer both in this age and fully realized in the eschaton (e.g., Eph 1:18; 2:7; 3:16–21). When the promises are cited, the apostles relate them to the salvation accomplished by Abraham's offspring, Jesus Christ, who inaugurates the Kingdom and hence realizes the covenant promises for all who believe, Jew and Gentile (e.g., Acts 3:13; 25; Rom 4:16–25; Gal 3:6–18; 4:21–31; Heb 11:10,13–16; Jas 2:21–23). Although there are relatively few references in the Old Testament to the promises made to Abraham,[98] enough is said to see the spiritual substratum that the covenant presumes and which the early church advances (e.g., spiritual circumcision, Gen 17:11; Deut 10:16; 30:6; Jer 4:4; 9:25; Col 2:11). The preeminence of the spiritual dimension is recognized by the prophets, for the Father of Israel is not Abraham but the Lord God who has redeemed them (Isa 63:16: Mal 2:10; Luke 3:8; cp. Isa 29:22). For the

---

[97] M. D. Carroll R., "Wealth and Poverty," in *Dictionary of the Old Testament: Pentateuch* (Downers Grove: InterVarsity, 2003), 884.

[98] Outside the Pentateuch, e.g., Abraham is mentioned in twenty-three verses, only seven of which occur in the prophets (Isa 29:22; 41:8; 51:2; 63:16; Jer 33:26; Ezek 33:24; Mic 7:20).

early church, which had experienced devastating poverty (in Jerusalem), the pre-eminence of God's provisions was spiritual, not material. Even the verse often quoted by Christians today, Phil 4:19, "And my God will meet all your needs according to his glorious riches in Christ Jesus," pertains first to the spiritual resources that sustain the Christian in difficulty (see "needs," 4:11–13).

3. Abram and Sarai in Egypt: Blessing Begins (12:10–13:1)

The events of Abram's sojourn in Egypt, set between the promises of bless-ing (12:1–3,7) and the acquisition of riches (13:2), show God is bringing to pass the promises. This account joins the previous episode where the Lord appears to Abram in Canaan (12:4–9), confirming that both inside and outside Canaan the Lord blesses him. However, whereas 12:4–9 tracks Abram's fidelity to God, the episode in Egypt does not commend his actions. The narrative does not convey the impression that Abram is awarded with riches for his conduct; neither does it explicitly condemn him. The author leaves it to Pharaoh to chide the patriarch for his deceit (vv. 18–19). The blessing depends on God's call, not Abram's conduct.

Where conduct does come into play is Pharaoh's mistreatment of the patri-archal family, though in ignorance. The kidnapping of Sarai illustrates the promise of blessing or curse upon the nations (12:3).[99] Despite Pharaoh's igno-rance of Sarai's marital status, the Lord counted her mistreatment against him by inflicting plague (v. 17). We will show that the author wants us to read the three "wife-sister" episodes (12:10–13:1; 20:1–18; 26:1–13) in concert (see below), which may suggest that Abram had some intercessory role in behalf of Pharaoh as he did for Abimelech (20:17–18; so for Lot, 18:16–33; see com-ments on 47:7).

On the surface, the sole reason for this episode is famine (12:10), but the lex-ical ties between this story of famine-turned-riches and the Lot conflict to fol-low (13:2) imply that the Egyptian episode created the occasion for the family's riches. Verse 10 has "the famine was severe" *(kābēd hārāʿāb),*which in Hebrew is similar to 13:2, "become very wealthy" *(kābēd mĕʾōd).* The Lord used the famine to initiate the series of events that resulted in the blessing of the patri-arch's house, despite the patriarch's fear and deception of Egypt's king. From the mouth of Pharaoh, Abram hears again the command the Lord had first spo-ken to him, "Go" *(lēk;* v. 19; 12:1). Abram himself later confesses that any blessing he would receive comes only by God's provision (14:23). Another irony at work may be the repetition of "very" *(mĕʾōd)* at 12:14 (Sarai was "very beautiful") and 13:2 (Abraham became "very wealthy"). By virtue of Sarai's

---

[99] G. W. Coats, "A Threat to the Host," in *Saga, Legend, Fable, Tale, Novella: Narrative Forms in Old Testament Literature,* JSOTSup 35 (Sheffield: JSOT Press, 1985), 71–81; M. Biddle, "The 'Endangered Ancestress' and Blessing for the Nations," *JBL* 109 (1990): 599–611.

beauty, not Abram's ability, the family was enriched. Reportedly, the passage insists that the events turn on account of Sarai (vv. 13,16,17), though she is mute throughout the story.

Abram's encounter with Pharaoh foreshadows the last years of Jacob, who with his sons take up residence in Egypt where they are enriched by the court and thereby avoid famine (45:16–20; 47:1–12). Abram's experience in Egypt also offered a typology for the Israelites who were enslaved and freed only after the infliction of grievous plagues, the tenth touching Pharaoh's house through the death of his son. Such a correspondence between father and descendants is underlying the prediction of the Egyptian sojourn in 15:13–14. As with Abram, the Hebrews emerged after their ordeal with many possessions so that it was Egypt that was "plundered" (Exod 3:21–22; 11:2–3; 12:35–36). The second "exodus" from Babylon (Ezra 1:6) may also echo the enrichment of its members by their neighbors. Thus "the past is not allowed to remain in the past" whose lessons continue to instruct God's people.[100]

Also elements in the narrative hearken back to the garden episode of chaps. 2–3. Although there are substantive differences in the two stories, similarities in plot and shared vocabulary suggest that the reader is to compare the two. Both accounts involve the backdrop of food (plenty or famine), depend on the idea of deception, and portray the wife in a critical role. Following the discovery of the deception, there is the interrogation of the parties (by God/Pharaoh), admission of the deed (by Adam/Abram), and expulsion of the parties (from Eden/Egypt). Also the subsequent stories tell of family schism (Cain-Abel/Lot-Abram). Important shared lexical items are lit., "What is this you have done *['āśîtā]* to me?" (12:18; 3:13); "Why didn't you not tell *[higgadtā]* me?" (12:18) and "Who told *[higgîd]* you?" (3:11); "I know *[yādaʿtî]"* (12:11) and "God knows" *(yôdēaʿ)* and "like God knowing" *(yōdĕʿê)* (3:5); "you will live *[yĕḥayyû]"* (12:12) and "the mother of all the living *[ḥāy]"* (3:20); "I will be treated well [good] *[yîṭab]"* / "he treated Abram well [good] *[hêṭîb]"* (12:13,16) and "good *[ṭôb]* and evil" / "good *[ṭôb]* for food" (3:5–6); "for your sake" *(baʿăbûrēk)* / "for her sake *(baʿăbûrāh)"* (12:13,16) and "because of you *(baʿăbûrekā)"* (3:17); the officers "saw" *(wayyirʾû)* her/she "was taken" *(wattuqqaḥ)* (12:15) and the woman "saw" *(wattēreʾ)* and "took" *(wattiqqaḥ)* (3:6); and lit., "they sent him away" *(wayšallĕḥû ʾōtô,* 12:20) and lit., "[the LORD God] sent him away *[wayšallĕḥēhû]"* (3:23).

The significance of reading the two events together is the remarkable difference in the outcomes. Adam and Eve lose the plenty of the garden by complying with the tempter's deception. This result is reversed in the Abram incident: Abram and Sarai emerge from Egypt wealthy because Pharaoh fell for the

---

[100] Sailhamer shows striking parallels between the narratives of Abram's sojourn (12:10–13:4) and Israel's ("Genesis," 116–17).

deception. The reversal, of course, does not suggest that God condones Abram's behavior, rather that the Lord will bless Abram and Sarai even though they jeopardized the blessing as did Adam and Eve.

WIFE-SISTER EPISODES. This story is the first of the three celebrated "wife-sister" accounts (12:1–13:1; 20:1–18; 26:1–13) in the patriarchal history. The first and second appear in the Abraham narrative and relate the abduction of Sarai by foreign hosts: Pharaoh in Egypt (12:10–13:1) and King Abimelech in Gerar (20:1–18). The third is the (threat of) abduction of Rebekah by the king of the Philistines in Gerar, also named Abimelech (26:1–13). The three stories possess similarities (e.g., 20:1–18 and 26:13 are set in Gerar), and it is contended that they share in this basic plot: (1) a problem arises; (2) a plan is devised; (3) the plan is carried out but with some complications; (4) an outside intervention occurs; and (5) good or bad consequences follow.[101]

How to explain the relationship of the three episodes is a special topic among scholars. Typically, source critics attribute the triplet to two parallel but independent literary documents: the Yahwist (J) presented 12:10–13:1 (Abram in Egypt) and 26:1–13 (Isaac in Gerar), and the Elohist (E) produced 20:1–18 (Abraham in Gerar).[102] The E account was a compositional variant of the same Abram story provided by the Yahwist in 12:10–13:1. Form and tradition critics departed from this opinion, observing that 20:1–18 is neither a true parallel nor independent of 12:10–13:1 but rather a moralistic adaptation of the story answering the question of "guilt" (20:9) raised in the former Abram story. The Isaac-Rebekah incident (26:1–13) reflects both stories, achieving a parallel between Isaac and his father.[103] R. de Hoop proposes the trilogy is a political allegory critiquing David, who like Abimelech and Pharaoh "took" Bathsheba (2 Sam 11:4) but unlike them murdered her husband (Uriah). De Hoop considers the wife-sister motif a pro-Solomonic account to legitimize his reign.[104] Although the precise relationship of the stories varies among form and tradition critics, they hold in common that (1) the stories were not originally reporting three separate events and (2) were not authored by the same person. T. L. Thompson challenges the notion that the three stories can yield a hypothetical original and can be or should be related developmentally. Although they share the same motifs, they are treated differently in their Genesis context. They are not self-contained units but integral to their respective narratives. What they possess in common is actually their Genesis

---

[101] For this analysis, see van Seters, *Abraham in History*, 168.

[102] E.g., E. A. Speiser, *Genesis: A New Translation with Introduction and Commentary*, AB (Garden City: Doubleday, 1964), xxxi–xxxii, 150–52.

[103] van Seters, *Abraham in History*, 183; for other form studies, see K. Koch, *The Growth of the Biblical Tradition*, trans. S. Cupitt (New York: Scribners, 1969), 111–32; Westermann, *Genesis 12–36*, 318–20, 412; Coats, "A Threat to the Host," 71–81, esp. 79; Biddle, "The 'Endangered Ancestress' and Blessing for the Nations," 599–611, esp. 611; and Carr, *Reading the Fractures of Genesis*, 200–201.

[104] R. de Hoop, "The Use of the Past to Address the Present: The Wife-Sister-Incidents (Gen 12,10–20; 20,1–18; 26,1–16)," in *Studies in the Book of Genesis: Literature, Redaction and History*, BETL 155 (Leuven: Leuven University Press/Sterling, Va.: Uitgeverij Peeters, 2001), 359–69.

connections. The three stories are contemporaneous, perhaps showing an awareness of the other but certainly not an interdependence whether oral or written.[105]

Along with the traditional source explanation described above, E. A. Speiser proposed that the wife-sister stories possessed a somewhat garbled rendition of an underlying Hurrian marriage custom (at Nuzi) in which a husband at the time of his marriage also adopted the bride as his "sister."[106] Although the proposal of a Hurrian connection with the practice of the patriarchs has been strongly resisted,[107] J. K. Hoffmeier has ventured another social custom, the diplomatic marriage, as a possible explanation. Diplomatic marriage involved a monarch's desire to form a friendly alliance with another king by giving his daughter in marriage. Hoffmeier suggests this may explain the literary connection between the wife-sister stories and the treaties at Beersheba that accompany them. Since the patriarchs had no daughters to achieve a diplomatic marriage, by a ruse they substituted their wives as sisters for the purpose of enacting a treaty.[108] Although Hoffmeier's proposal may result in viewing the accounts as three separate occurrences of diplomatic marriage, the suggestion of diplomatic marriage does not adequately explain why the patriarchs took the drastic step of substituting a wife when alternatively they could have proffered concubines or, if necessary, by deception presented a concubine as a princess. If Hoffmeier's solution is correct, however, the actions of the patriarchs were especially despicable since the pagan kings themselves did not practice wife swapping and repudiated adultery (see comments on 20:8–10).

T. D. Alexander's literary analysis of the wife-sister accounts led him to agree that the three accounts are separate events, but he relied on the firmer exegetical ground of explaining the stories contextually in their present arrangement. After comparing the three accounts in their details and their structural arrangements, he found that the trio are best explained as independent stories that came from one author.[109] They were composed by the author, who modified them during their incorporation into Genesis; they thus prove to be complimentary stories addressing the wife-sister motif and not literary duplicates or variants of the same episode. Genesis 20:1–18 and 26:1–13 presuppose 12:10–13:1, avoiding unnecessary duplication of earlier details and expanding on different aspects of the motif. For example, the dialogue with the king in 20:8–16 gives a detailed explanation of Abram's rationale for the deception, whereas the motif of deception is only briefly treated in chaps. 12 and 26. The author invites the reader to

---

[105] T. L. Thompson, *The Origin Tradition of Ancient Israel: I. The Literary Formation of Genesis and Exodus 1–23,* JSOTSup 55 (Sheffield: Sheffield Academic Press, 1987), 51–59.

[106] Speiser, *Genesis,* 91–94; "The Wife-Sister Motif in the Patriarchal Narratives," in *Biblical and Other Studies* (Cambridge: Harvard University Press, 1963), 15–28.

[107] E.g., S. Greengus, "Sisterhood Adoption at Nuzi and the 'Wife-Sister' in Genesis," *HUCA* 46 (1975): 5–31.

[108] J. K. Hoffmeier, "The Wives Tales of Genesis 12, 20 & 26 and the Covenants at BeerSheba," *TynBul* 43 (1992): 81–99.

[109] Alexander, *Abraham in the Negev,* 32–51 (cf. chart, p. 42), which relies on his earlier works, *A Literary Analysis,* 134–59, and "Are the Wife/Sister Incidents of Genesis Literary Compositional Variants?" *VT* 42 (1992): 145–53.

consider the three incidents together as they are found in the Genesis plot.

That Abraham and Isaac repeated the gimmick is not surprising in light of Abram's admission, "Everywhere we go, say of me, 'He is my brother'" (20:13). As for the mysteries of Sarai's aging and beauty (sixty-five years and ninety years [12:4; 17:17]) in chaps. 12 and 20 and of the continued potency of the elderly Abraham (e.g., Keturah's children, 25:1–4 [with 18:11–12; 21:7]), these elements along with some chronological problems in the stories are usually attributed to the existence of different sources (P's chronology) and the fictive nature of the accounts. The rabbis explained the apparent difficulties of their aging by ascribing to them the effects of the miracle of rejuvenation, which included her youthful appearance and his virility.[110] Alternatively, the longevity of the patriarchs (Sarai, 127 years [23:1]; Abraham, 175 years [25:7]) may explain her attractiveness even at sixty-five years (see comments on 12:11–13).[111] It should be remembered also that 20:2 does not say that Abimelech took Sarah because of her beauty. Some other motivation for her abduction, such as the king's interest in forming a treaty with the Hebrews, may be the explanation (see comments on 20:2).

STRUCTURE.   The arrangement of this pericope is bounded by the descent of Abram into Egypt, "Abram went down" (12:10), and his return, "Abram went up" (13:1). Sandwiched between are the speeches of Abram and Pharaoh in a chiastic order within the pericope. Sarai's viewpoint is not reported.

A Descent of Abram and Sarai (12:10)
   B Abram instructs Sarai (12:11–13)
      C Pharaoh kidnaps Sarai and the Lord intervenes (12:14–17)
   B′ Pharaoh instructs Abram and his men (12:18–20)
A′ Ascent of Abram (13:1)

The final verse (13:1) reiterates the outcome of the prior events by "his wife and everything he had" (12:20). As a bridge it anticipates the Lot pericope (13:2) by referring for the first time to Lot's presence: "and Lot went with him" (13:1).

(1) Abram Instructs Sarai (12:10–13)

[10]Now there was a famine in the land, and Abram went down to Egypt to live there for a while because the famine was severe. [11]As he was about to enter Egypt, he said to his wife Sarai, "I know what a beautiful woman you are. [12]When the Egyptians see you, they will say, 'This is his wife.' Then they will kill me but will let you live. [13]Say you are my sister, so that I will be treated well for your sake and my life will be spared because of you."

---

[110] For a contemporary defense of this position, see J. Ronning, "The Naming of Isaac: The Role of the Wife/Sister Episodes in the Redaction of Genesis," *WTJ* 53 (1991): 1–27.

[111] D. Kidner, *Genesis,* TOTC (Chicago: InterVarsity, 1967), 116–17.

12:10 Famine forced the migrations of the three patriarchs Abraham, Isaac, and Jacob (12:10; 26:1; 42:5; 47:11–13). Both Abraham and Jacob went to Egypt, where they could survive the droughts of Canaan. Egypt's Nile and, through irrigation, the Tigris-Euphrates valley provided a stable agricultural environment compared to Canaan, which was totally dependent on rainfall. Famine was not exceptional in the history of the ancient Near East, including the river valleys. In the cases of Abram and Jacob the famine in Canaan was sufficiently "severe" to travel outside the land (12:10; 47:13), whereas Isaac journeyed locally to Gerar, where the Lord prohibited him from descending to Egypt (26:1–2).[112] Although famine is associated with divine curse (e.g., Deut 28:23–24; Amos 4:6–8) or at least divine absence (Ruth 1:1,6), there is no hint of divine disapproval of the patriarchs or any objection to their leaving Canaan. In the case of Jacob, it is specifically condoned by the Lord (46:3–4).

"To live there for a while" translates the term *gûr,* meaning "sojourn," which usually describes a temporary residence. However, the same language describes the ten-year sojourn of Naomi's family in Moab (Ruth 1:1,4). Abraham later identified himself as an "alien *[gēr]* and a stranger" (23:4; cp. 17:8) as did Isaac and Jacob (28:4; 35:27).[113] The importance of the stranger in patriarchal history is illustrated best in chaps. 18–20, where the custom of hospitality plays a central role. A "sojourner" *(gēr)* is a person who lives among a population with whom he usually has no family affiliation (but cp. 32:4) and does not have full citizenship rights. Later, special protections are afforded for aliens living among Israel on the basis that Israel once had been sojourners in Egypt (e.g., Deut 16:9–12; Gen 15:13).[114]

12:11–13 When reading the incident together with Abram's later confession to Abimelech (20:11–13), we discover the full rationale and the premeditated plan of the deception. Abram fears two things: (1) Sarai's beauty will draw the attention of powerful men (12:11–12), and (2) since these men do not abide by the ethic of Abram's God, they will murder him and take her for a wife (20:11). By a ruse Sarai presented herself as his sister (12:13) and, accordingly, acknowledged Abram as "my brother" (20:13). The genius of the ruse was its half-truth. Abram could claim the truth—"she really is my sister" (20:12)—since they had the same father, and at the same time he avoids reference to her as wife (12:12). But the folly of Abram's plan was its consequences. Although he would save his life, he jeopardized his future by

---

[112] W. H. Shea, "Famine," *ABD* 2.769–73.

[113] For discussion of the motif "alienation," see the commentary Introduction.

[114] D. Kellermann, "גּוּר *(gûr)*" *TDOT* 2.439–49; and J. Spencer, "Sojourner," *ABD* 6.103–4.

placing at risk Sarai, the mother of the promised son.[115] Moreover, others suffered because of the deception, bringing guilt on themselves unknowingly (12:17–18; 20:9; 26:10).

That Abram's fears were probably well founded may be seen in David's abduction of Bathsheba and the murder of her husband, Uriah. How long Abram thought such a story could go undetected we cannot know. Sarai is essential to the success of the plot, but as for culpability, Sarai is little more than a pawn in the caper and bears no guilt. The guilt lies with the men (see more below); in both 12:10–13:1 and 20:1–18 she has no dialogue. We have no idea what she thinks of this matter, but we may surmise that her silence meant compliance with her husband's wishes. Generally, Hebrew narrative does not describe the physical features of the characters unless it is necessary for the plot. Modern readers stumble before the description of Sarai as a "beautiful woman"[116] at sixty-five years old (v. 11).[117] This reflects the significant cultural gap between our day and the time of the patriarchs, when beauty was measured by one's eyes and form (e.g., 29:17). In the Gerar incident (20:1–18), it is not clear whether her beauty is assumed as the reason for the king's interest or if Abimelech's interest was her eminent status as Abraham's relative.

(2) Pharaoh Abducts Sarai (12:14–17)

[14]When Abram came to Egypt, the Egyptians saw that she was a very beautiful woman. [15]And when Pharaoh's officials saw her, they praised her to Pharaoh, and she was taken into his palace. [16]He treated Abram well for her sake, and Abram acquired sheep and cattle, male and female donkeys, menservants and maidservants, and camels.

[17]But the LORD inflicted serious diseases on Pharaoh and his household because of Abram's wife Sarai.

12:14–17 Verse 14 accentuates Sarai's beauty, "very" *(mĕʾōd)* beautiful," explaining why Pharaoh's officials picked her out readily. Her acquisition into the royal harem is suggested by her residence in the "palace" (v. 15). Abduction of beautiful women may have been common as the reward of warfare; Israel's law set boundaries on the practice, requiring marriage (Deut 21:10–14).

---

[115] Coats rightly observes that 12:10–13:1 nowhere mentions the heir promise; but given the context of 12:1–3 and of 20:1–18, which prepares the way for the Isaac birth (21:1–7), the threat to an heir is an unstated implication of taking Sarai into the royal harem ("A Threat to the Host," 71–81).

[116] "Beautiful" translates יְפַת מַרְאֶה, lit., "beautiful (in) appearance"; this phrase describes Rachel (29:17) and Tamar (2 Sam 14:27), and טוֹבַת מַרְאֶה, lit., "good (in) appearance," describes Rebekah (26:7). Rachel is also depicted as יְפַת תֹּאַר, lit., "beautiful (in) form" (29:17) as was Abigail (1 Sam 25:3) and Esther (2:7; and Deut 21:11); the same language describes the handsome Joseph (39:6), whose description imitates Rachel's.

[117] Cp. 12:4 with 17:17.

Verse 16 is a brief but important digression in the story line. As for the gifts offered Abram, the language of bridal gift (*mōhar;* see comments on 34:12) does not occur, but compensation may have been the motivation for the gifts, not merely favor toward Abram.[118] The animals and human servants listed are typically associated with wealthy persons (e.g., Job 1:3).

The NIV's translation of v. 17, "But the LORD inflicted" highlights the contrast between Abram's welfare and that of Pharaoh. "Diseases" translates the Hebrew for "plagues,"[119] which is the same word describing the ten plagues against Pharaoh (Exod 11:1). The term refers to skin disease in Mosaic legislation (Lev 13), and the verbal form describes the leprous judgment by the Lord against Uzziah (2 Kgs 15:5). "His house" probably refers to the members of his royal court, including his harem, as with King Abimelech (20:7,17).

(3) Pharaoh Expels Abram (12:18–13:1)

[18]**So Pharaoh summoned Abram. "What have you done to me?" he said. "Why didn't you tell me she was your wife?** [19]**Why did you say, 'She is my sister,' so that I took her to be my wife? Now then, here is your wife. Take her and go!"** [20]**Then Pharaoh gave orders about Abram to his men, and they sent him on his way, with his wife and everything he had.**

[1]**So Abram went up from Egypt to the Negev, with his wife and everything he had, and Lot went with him.**

12:18–20 Unlike the parallel wife-sister stories (20:7; 26:8), this brief account does not explain how Pharaoh discovered the ruse. His three successive questions demonstrate indignant anger against Abram, describing his behavior as an offense against him personally (vv. 18–19). Again, due to the terseness of this account no place is given to Abram's response, and Pharaoh immediately follows his interrogation with the presentation of Sarai, lit., "behold [*hinnê*] your wife." Pharaoh insists on his departure, whereas Abimelech, probably impressed with Abram's status as a prophet (20:7), welcomes him to live in Gerar (20:15). The dismissal is not left to Abram's timing; Pharaoh ensures his expulsion by assigning "men," a different term than "officials" (v. 15), to escort him and Sarai with "everything he had."

13:1 The closing verse to the Egypt pericope reports Abram's return to the Negev, repeating 12:20 by the phrase "everything he had" *(kol ʾăšer lô).* The phrase signifies the wealth he had accumulated to this point (cf. Jacob, 31:21; 46:1; Potiphar, 39:6). Also, the same Hebrew describes Abram's wealth, which will be Isaac's inheritance (24:36; 25:5; also see 24:2). For the second time (12:5), the narrative reports Lot's presence with Abram, preparing the reader

---

[118] For the reference to "camels," see the commentary Introduction.

[119] The verb and its cognate accusative noun, נְגָעִים . . . וַיְנַגַּע, lit., "and (the LORD) plagued . . . plagues."

for the Abram-Lot stories to follow. Mention of Lot last after Abram's possessions may hint at the separation to come.[120]

4. Abram and Lot Part: Promises Recalled (13:2–18)

Chapter 13 is the first account in a trilogy of Abram-Lot stories (13:2–18; 14:1–24; 18:16–19:38). Lot, the son of Abram's brother Haran (11:27), provides in the Abraham section (11:27–25:11) a contrast for the patriarch and his heirs. Lot is passive and foolish. He initiates only scant actions (13:11; 18:3; 19:6–8,18–20,30), and even among these are the wrong decisions of selecting Sodom and of offering his daughters to the Sodomites.[121] This lead episode in the trilogy contributes significantly to the central theme of the patriarchal promises and, in particular, the emphasis on the promise of an heir in the Abraham narratives (11:27–25:11).[122] Genesis uses such opposites to distinguish the appointed lineage from its rival in the patriarchal narratives, for example, Isaac/Ishmael and Jacob/Esau. The Abram-Lot tension is a forerunner to the struggles among sibling rivals that are integral to the later patriarchal narratives (cf. Cain-Abel, chap. 4). Chapter 13 near the front of the patriarchal corpus is important to the whole by showing proleptically the difference between the selected and nonselected lines. As for the later history of Israel, the tension between the herdsmen of the two patriarchs (v. 7) is the first of perpetual conflicts between their descendants, Israel and Moab/Ammon (see comments on 19:36–38).

The Lot episodes come short of explicitly stating the inclusion or exclusion of Lot as potential heir, but they present a pattern of events that shows his illegitimacy. Abram advises their parting, so it is not the parting per se that forfeits the blessing but the circumstances of the parting by Lot, who exhibited poor judgment. Chapter 13 indicates his disregard for the promissory land. Lot ignored Canaan for the deceptively attractive "cities of the plain" (v. 12; 19:29); that the "cities of the plain" sat outside "Canaan" is clear from v. 12, a verse that draws a line between the two men. The geographical feature that is key to the underlying message of the story is highlighted by the recurring word *yāšab* ("stayed/lived," vv. 6[2x],7,12,18; also 19:1,25,29,30). This is apparent by the author's attention to the moral character of the place the nephew selected (vv. 10,13). Abram on the other hand "called on the name of the LORD" (v. 4) and resided in the land of Canaan (v. 18). Lot's action is reminiscent of the folly

---

[120] Sarna, *Genesis*, 97.

[121] L. A. Turner, "Lot as Jekyll and Hyde: A Reading of Genesis 18–19," in *The Bible in Three Dimensions: Essays in Celebration of Forty Years of Biblical Studies in the University of Sheffield*, JSOTSup 87 (Sheffield: JSOT Press, 1990), 97.

[122] L. Helyer, "The Separation of Abram and Lot: Its Significance in the Patriarchal Narratives," *JSOT* 26 (1983): 77–88.

of Esau, who treated lightly the promises (25:34) and eventually lost the inheritance due to deception (27:35). The geographical dislocation of Esau outside Canaan contributes also to the portrayal of his disqualification (36:43–37:1). That such geographical dislocations signal the rejection of potential heirs is further supported in the Abraham story by Ishmael's expulsion and settlement in the desert (21:10,20–21; 25:18) and the removal of Abraham's concubine sons, who migrate east (25:6). Genesis often signals ominous events by the geographical direction "east" (e.g., 3:24; 4:16; 11:2; see vol. 1A, p. 257); Lot's choice of the cities in the "east" portends an unpromising consequence (v. 11).

Together, the three Abram-Lot episodes demonstrate the benevolence of Abram toward his nephew, resulting in Lot's deliverance from servitude (chap. 14) and death (chaps. 18–19). Likewise, Israel later tolerates Lot's descendants, the Moabites and Ammonites (19:37–38), heeding God's instructions (Deut 2:9,19,37) to avoid hostilities against them (yet persistent belligerence against Israel [Num 22–25] results in intolerance [Deut 23:3–8(4–9)]). By granting Lot first option on the coveted Canaan, the patriarch resisted any proprietary jealousy, leaving his future in the hands of the Lord.[123] The spiritual disparity between Lot and Abram is implied by the description of Lot's choice of the Jordan plain in vv. 10–13; lexical allusions recall Eve's attraction to the forbidden (3:6) and the prohibited actions of the sons of God (6:1–2; see vol. 1A, pp. 331–32). In Lot's case he chose the "forbidden" cities, but Abram waited on the Lord to present him Canaan.

This lead story of the trilogy explains why Abram and Lot part, describing their wealth in livestock and the ensuing quarrel of their herdsmen over grazing rights. The narrative infers that the overflow of blessing for Abram in Egypt has benefited Lot according to the promises, "You will be a blessing" (12:2d) and "I will bless those who bless you" (12:3c). Lot's decision in chap. 13 shows that separation from the patriarch leads to the forfeiture of continued blessing and results in the opposite outcome (19:30–38).[124] Even so, Lot's descendants (Moabites and Ammonites) receive a land grant from the Lord (Deut 2:9,19). The separation of Lot, who was born to Abram's brother Haran, completes Abram's departure from his "father's household" (12:1a). Their separation may also be taken as an echo of the scattered nations (10:32; 11:8–9) whose dispersal ironically resulted in humanity encompassing the earth as the Lord had commanded, preparing them for the blessing envisioned (1:28; 9:1,7; 12:3d; see vol. 1A, pp. 429, 473–74). "Let's part company" (13:9) and the "spreading" of the nations (10:5,32) translate the same term *(pārad)*. As the scattering was

---

[123] W. Vogels compares Abram's surrender of the land to the sacrifice of his son Isaac (chap. 22), relinquishing by faith both land and descendant to God ("Abraham et l'offrande de la terre [Gen 13]," *SR* 4 [1974–75]: 51–57).

[124] G. W. Coats, "Lot: A Foil in the Abraham Saga," in *Understanding the Word: Essays in Honor of Bernhard W. Anderson,* JSOTSup 37 (Sheffield: JSOT Press, 1985), 113–32, esp. 117.

a step toward all peoples receiving the blessing, the parting of Abram and Lot contributed to identifying the conduit of blessing.

> COMPOSITION.   As to the origin of this account, chap. 13 is essential to understanding the whole of the Abram-Lot narratives; it also has many points of contact with widely distributed parts of the Abraham section (e.g., v. 2 with 12:16; v. 7 with 12:6; 15:19–21; v. 10 with 19:29), making it unlikely that it was penned independently of the Abraham corpus.[125] Typically, scholars have relegated vv. 14–18 to a late addition on the basis that these verses contribute nothing vital to the story.[126] That vv. 14–18 and vv. 9–12 share many lexical items opposes this standard proposal (e.g., "separate," vv. 9,11,14).[127] Moreover, the land promise (vv. 14–17) made to Abram's descendants is the point of the story. Without it the denouement in chap. 13 is unsatisfying, making the episode a mere family roust. The geography of the promise provides the metaphor by which the author shows that Lot's separation resulted in loss of blessing. The progression in his habitation—from fertile plain (chap. 13) to city (chaps. 14; 19) and to cave (19:30–38)—when coupled with the reader's knowledge of Lot's notorious descendants (Moab, Ammon) powerfully illustrates the potential for blessing or curse. By reiterating the promises of land and descendants at the close, the story sustains the narrative's suspense about the question of an heir.

STRUCTURE.   "[Now] Abram had become very wealthy" (v. 2) provides the backdrop for the story's quarrel among the herdsmen and the parting of Abram and Lot.[128] Earlier we saw that by employing the same Hebrew term *kābēd* (lit., "heavy") in 12:10 ("severe") and in 13:2 ("wealthy"), the author suggests that the two accounts (12:10–13:1; 13:2–18) be read together.[129] Verse 18 closes the story by describing the outcome in terms of Abram's final arrival in Canaan (Hebron), where he builds an altar of worship. Geography, as we have said, is the chapter's metaphor for appraising the men's respective place as to the promises. The account begins with the same geographical and cultic interests regarding Abram as at the end (vv. 3–5,18), tracing the movements of Abram from Egypt to Canaan and identifying the places of altar building.

The makeup of the narrative is two narrative-dialogue complements, with the dialogue responding to the problem presented in the passage. The two narrative sections describe the schism: (1) the herdsmen quarrel in vv. 2–7, and (2) Lot selects and departs for the cities of the plain in vv. 10–13. Each of the two narrative sections concludes similarly, giving supplementary information about the inhabitants of Canaan and Sodom (vv. 7,13). The first narrative consists of

---

[125] Wenham, *Genesis 1–15*, 295.

[126] E.g., Westermann, *Genesis 12–36*, 172, 178.

[127] Wenham, *Genesis 1–15*, 295, lists five parallel terms between vv. 9–12 and vv. 14–15,18.

[128] The initial-episode use of *waw* introduces the account, "Now *[waw]* Abram . . ." (e.g., NASB, NRSV).

[129] Gen 12:10 and 13:2 are parallel boundary markers, each beginning its respective episode.

two parts: (1) vv. 2–5 report the men's wealth and itinerary; and (2) vv. 6–7 describe the "quarreling" *(rîb)*. In the corresponding dialogue, Abram desires an end to the "quarreling" *(mĕrîbā)* and offers Lot a separate parcel (vv. 8–9). The second narrative describes (1) Lot's selection ("lifted up *[nāśā᾽]* his eyes," v. 10) of Sodom and (2) the consequent parting of the two groups (vv. 11–13). In the next dialogue, the Lord directs Abram to "lift up" *(nāśā᾽)* his eyes, and he assures him possession of the land for his descendants (vv. 14–17).

vv. 2–7	Abram's and Lot's herdsmen
vv. 2–5	Abram's and Lot's wealth and itinerary
vv. 6–7	The herdsmen dispute ("quarreling," *rîb*)
vv. 8–9	Abram: proffer to Lot ("quarreling," *mĕrîbā*)
vv. 10–13	Lot chooses the Jordan plain ("lifted *[nāśā᾽]* his eyes")
vv. 14–17	The Lord: promise to Abram ("lift up *[nāśā᾽]* your eyes")
v. 18	Abram worships the Lord at Hebron

(1) The Quarrel (13:2–7)

²Abram had become very wealthy in livestock and in silver and gold.

³From the Negev he went from place to place until he came to Bethel, to the place between Bethel and Ai where his tent had been earlier ⁴and where he had first built an altar. There Abram called on the name of the LORD.

⁵Now Lot, who was moving about with Abram, also had flocks and herds and tents. ⁶But the land could not support them while they stayed together, for their possessions were so great that they were not able to stay together. ⁷And quarreling arose between Abram's herdsmen and the herdsmen of Lot. The Canaanites and Perizzites were also living in the land at that time.

13:2–5 Reference to the livestock of Abram and Lot in vv. 2 and 5 respectively form the boundaries of this unit. Verse 2 describes Abram's wealth in terms of livestock and precious metals (cf. 24:22,35,53). Abram received the livestock from Pharaoh (12:16), and it is reasonable to assume the same for the silver and gold since King Abimelech gave silver to Abram for the similar offense against Sarah (20:16). Abram's "livestock" *(miqneh)* included domesticated "sheep and cattle" (12:16), which required bountiful grass and water; with the "flocks and herds" (v. 5) belonging to Lot's company the land could not supply sufficient grazing.

Abram retraced his steps from the Negev to Bethel and Ai where he again worshiped the Lord (vv. 3–4), presumably at or near the altar he first erected there (12:8–9). Twice the narrative states that his return trip mirrored his earlier travels (vv. 3–4). That Abram should take such care indicated his desire to recover his experience with God; the fact that the old altar remained suggests the permanency of the promises.[130] The patriarch's newfound wealth did not

---

¹³⁰ Wenham, *Genesis 1–15*, 296.

distract him from his worship of the Lord; his generosity toward Lot (vv. 8–9) and his later confession of trust in the Lord's provision (14:22–24) may reflect Abram's renewed faith as a consequence of the Egyptian sojourn. It was for the purpose of worship that the Lord delivered Israel from Egypt (Exod 3:12; Acts 7:7). Verse 4 is reminiscent of the beginnings of formal worship at 4:26; the repetition of "called on the name of the LORD" and the echo of the Hebrew word "earlier" (v. 3)[131] indicates for the author that there was a continuum between the roots of authentic worship and the practice of Abram.

Verse 5 explains that the collective wealth of the men made travel together impossible. The narrative continues to define Lot in terms of his relationship with his uncle. The narration never loses sight of why Lot prospers. Lot's wealth included livestock, "flocks and herds" (v. 5), which probably involved the "sheep and cattle" (12:16) obtained in Egypt. The mention of Lot's "tents" may be equivalent to the "menservants and maidservants" (12:16) noted in Abram's household, indicating Lot also accumulated servants. Abram later retrieved the many "women and the other people" of Lot's household who were taken captive by eastern kings (14:16). Reference to "tents" also anticipates the forthcoming division, resulting in Lot's "tents" near Sodom (v. 12) and Abram's at Hebron (v. 18; also vv. 3,12; 12:8). We later discover that Lot became a city-dweller (19:1,11–12).

13:6–7 "But the land could not support them" (v. 6) states explicitly that the vegetation required for so many herds could not be found in one grazing area. Twice v. 6 describes the nature of their companionship by "stayed together" *(lāšebet yaḥdāw)*, the same language used of Esau and Jacob's relationship before parting (36:7). "Together" *(yaḥdāw)* also describes in a poignant way the companionship of Abraham and his son Isaac at Moriah (22:6,8,19).

"Quarreling" or "strife," meaning a verbal wrangle among parties, appropriately translates the word *rîb* (e.g., Prov 15:18) rather than the technical meaning "lawsuit" (e.g., Exod 23:2–3,6; Deut 17:8). The related verb "quarreled" describes the water dispute between Isaac and King Abimelech (26:20,21,22; cp. Judg 8:1) and Israel's grumbling against Moses in the desert over the absence of water (e.g., Exod 17:2,7; Num 20:3,13). The synonymous term for "quarreling" *(mĕrîbâ)* in v. 8 was appropriated for naming the "waters of Meribah" in the desert; the word occurs again only for Israel's complaints against Moses over the need for water (Exod 17:7; Num 20:13,24; 27:14; Deut 32:51; 33:8; Pss 81:7; 95:8; 106:32). This led Sarna to suggest that the term's appearance here implies Lot's "base ingratitude."[132] The Philistines envied

---

[131] בַּתְּחִלָּה, lit., "at the beginning" ("earlier," NIV), and הוּחַל, "began," are related terms (4:26); for more on the typological significance of Abram's worship, see vol. 1A, pp. 292–93, 391.
[132] Sarna, *Genesis,* 98.

Isaac's wealth (26:13–14), and the same attitude may have been held by Lot's herdsmen. The tension between the herdsmen is the first of many struggles between the descendants of Lot and Abram (19:30–38).

Dispute over water and grazing rights may have been common for the patriarchs since they practiced a dimorphic lifestyle, involving both sedentary and migratory patterns (e.g., Isaac and Abimelech, 26:12–22). This helps explain the added comment regarding the Canaanites and the Perizzites "living in the land at that time" (v. 7). More important, the presence of such people groups in the land enhances Abram's offer since suitable grazing land would have been sought after by competing herdsmen. And, further, the promise of the land to Abram in vv. 14–17 requires Abram to believe that someday the Lord will dispossess the inhabitants of Canaan (see 15:16–21). The Lord reassures Moses concerning the fulfillment of this promise (Exod 3:8,17; 23:23; 33:2; 34:11), which is realized in the era of the conquest (Josh 3:10; 12:8; 24:11). For more on the Canaanites and Perizzites, see comments at 15:16–21.

(2) The Promise (13:8–17)

⁸So Abram said to Lot, "Let's not have any quarreling between you and me, or between your herdsmen and mine, for we are brothers. ⁹Is not the whole land before you? Let's part company. If you go to the left, I'll go to the right; if you go to the right, I'll go to the left."

¹⁰Lot looked up and saw that the whole plain of the Jordan was well watered, like the garden of the LORD, like the land of Egypt, toward Zoar. (This was before the LORD destroyed Sodom and Gomorrah.) ¹¹So Lot chose for himself the whole plain of the Jordan and set out toward the east. The two men parted company: ¹²Abram lived in the land of Canaan, while Lot lived among the cities of the plain and pitched his tents near Sodom. ¹³Now the men of Sodom were wicked and were sinning greatly against the LORD.

¹⁴The LORD said to Abram after Lot had parted from him, "Lift up your eyes from where you are and look north and south, east and west. ¹⁵All the land that you see I will give to you and your offspring forever. ¹⁶I will make your offspring like the dust of the earth, so that if anyone could count the dust, then your offspring could be counted. ¹⁷Go, walk through the length and breadth of the land, for I am giving it to you."

13:8–9 Abram appeals to their relationship as "brothers," that is, relatives, for a peaceful resolution (v. 8). In the hostile environs of rival people groups, Abram recognizes the importance of peaceful relations with his nephew. As it turns out, Lot benefits immediately by Abram's good will who rescues him from the eastern kings, where the same language "brother" ("relative," NIV) recurs (14:14,16). Abram's rhetorical question in v. 9, "Is not the whole land before you?" appears disingenuous since the land was largely held by Canaanites. The question, however, reflects Abram's early confidence in the Lord's promise of possession. Abram spoke proleptically as if the land were his to distribute to whomever he chose. The language of "left and right" is the language of decision (v. 9; 24:29). Lot has first option, and Abram kindly accepts whatever Lot rejects. The orientation here is one facing east, hence to the north ("left") and to the south ("right").

13:10 Lot's decision is told in a foreboding manner with lexical allusions to the infamous choices of Eve in the garden (3:6) and the "sons of God" (6:2). Shared terms between vv. 10–11 and these two earlier stories include: "eyes" (*ʿayin;* 13:10; 3:6–7); "saw" *(rāʾâ;* 13:10; 3:6; 6:2); "watered" *(šāqâ;* 13:10; 2:6,10); "destroyed" *(šaḥēt;* 13:10; 6:13 *passim);* "garden" *(gan;* 13:10; 2:8 *passim);* "you enter" ("toward," NIV; 13:10) and "went to" *(bôʾ;* 6:4); "chose" *(bāḥar;* 13:11; 6:2); "whole/all" the plain (13:11) and "from all" *(kol)* they chose (6:2). The direction "toward the east" *(miqqedem)* in v. 11 renews the motif of expulsion in the accounts of the garden (3:24), Cain-Abel (4:16), and the Tower of Babel (11:2; see comments on 25:5–6).

Verse 10 expresses the chief irony of the lead story: the lush land Lot chooses will be consumed by fire (19:12–29). The "plain of the Jordan" is likened to the well-watered "garden of the LORD" and "like the land of Egypt" (v. 10), whose beauty attracted Lot but also distracted him from the wickedness that lurked there. The clause sequence of v. 10 in the Hebrew points up the region's momentary facade: reference to the plain's destruction falls between the two descriptions of its former beauty: lit., "well watered . . . before the LORD destroyed . . . like the garden of the LORD, like the land of Egypt."

The narration enhances the beauty of the plain so as to explain Lot's infatuation and, also, to provide a visual contrast with the later report of the outcome: the "whole plain" *(kol kikkar),*[133] that is, "all *[kol]* of it" (absent in NIV) was well irrigated; the "garden of the LORD" (Eden) stamped it as idyllic (e.g., 2:8; Isa 51:3; Ezek 36:35; see vol. 1A, pp. 200–201); the "land of Egypt," the "bread basket" of the ancient Near East, deemed it rich in resources. Its surpassing beauty contrasts with the region's scorched residue of "all *[kol]* the land of the plain" (19:28) after the destruction. Lot "saw" *(rāʾâ)* the beauty of the "whole plain,"[134] and later, from another prominent vista, Abraham "saw" *(rāʾâ)* the plain's tower of smoke witnessing to the aftermath of the destruction (19:28). Verse 10 forebodes the sad turn in the career of Abram's nephew and testifies to the catastrophic extent of the fiery deluge to come.

---

[133] כִּכָּר, usually translated "plain," is etymologically related to the idea of "circle"; the location of the "plain" and its cities is uncertain (see discussion below); the before-and-after pictures of the plain in chaps. 13 and 19 mention the plain in its entirety (כֹּל, "all"; vv. 10,11; 19:25,29) for emphatic purposes, both its beauty and its complete annihilation; the full identification, "plain of the Jordan," occurs but four times (vv. 10,11; 1 Kgs 7:46; 2 Chr 4:17); often the description is simply "the plain" (e.g., v. 12; 19:17,28,29; Deut 34:3).

[134] Lot's view of the "whole plain" from his location between Ai/Bethel (v. 3) is a clue in the debate over the identity of the plain (see below).

13:11–13 Continued references to site locations contrasts Lot's abode outside Canaan versus that of Abram inside. Abram lives in the "land," whereas Lot resides "among the cities"; Abram dwells in Canaan, and Lot lives on the periphery of Canaan (v. 12). The same geographical metaphor distinguishes the chosen and rejected members of the Abraham lineage (Isaac/Ishmael, 16:21; 25:11,18; Jacob/Esau, 36:8–9,40; 37:1).

The geographical entities by themselves convey the message of judgment, for the cities Sodom and Gomorrah became proverbial types for societal evil and divine destruction (see below). The infamy of the male populace marked them forever as "wicked" *(rāʿîm)* and "great sinners" *(ḥaṭṭāʾîm mĕʾōd'* v. 13); the former term recalls the "wickedness/evil" *(rāʿǎraʿ)* of prediluvian times (6:5; also 8:21).[135] The story of Sodom's destruction (chap. 19) echoes the flood account (see comments on chap. 19) indicating that Sodom and Gomorrah's sins deserved the same catastrophic response from God. "Great sinners" ("were sinning greatly," NIV) is a unique Hebrew phrase, which may infer that Sodom's sin was exceptional in human memory,[136] as we would say, "one of a kind." "Sinners" *(ḥaṭṭāʾîm)* as a term designating class is opposite the category of "the righteous" *(ṣaddîq); sinners* are corrupting influences on society whose sins are violations against humanity, although relationally, as here, they are viewed as opponents of God (cf. 18:20).[137] Specific mention of Sodom's sin as "against the LORD"[138] only adds to the dire prospects of the cities' future. Identifying Sodom's populace as "sinners" calls for the reader by implication to identify "the righteous," who must be Abram's group, including Lot. It is the polarization between sinners and the righteous that motivates Abram's worries over the righteous in Sodom (18:23–25).

Sodom and Gomorrah were two of the five cities of the plain (14:2,8), which tradition (at least) identifies as a pentapolis (*Wis* 10:6). Of the five cities, Sodom is prominent in Genesis and continues as the chief interest of later authors.[139] Biblical authors often appropriated Sodom (and Gomorrah) as a prototype of

---

[135] The EVs render the word group רַע inconsistently by "wicked" or "evil"; the term for "wicked" in 18:23,25 is רָשָׁע.

[136] Wenham, *Genesis 1–15,* 298.

[137] R. Covin, "Sin, Sinners (OT)," *ABD* 6.37.

[138] חטא ("to sin") plus ל ("against") is often personal, against a human (e.g., 20:9; Judg 11:27) or against the Lord (e.g., Exod 10:16; Deut 14:1); חטא plus ב means opposition, usually more physical (e.g., 42:22). G. H. Livingston, "חָטָא *(ḥāṭāʾ)," TWOT* 1.277.

[139] The identity of the cities known as "the cities of the plain" (v. 12; 19:29; cf. 19:25) is inferential since they are not listed as such; the five kings of Sodom, Gomorrah, Admah, Zeboiim, and Zoar (Bela) are allied in 14:2,8; four of the five cities are listed in the Table of Nations (10:19), omitting Zoar, perhaps because it was the sole city spared (cp. Deut 29:22); "Admah" and "Zeboiim" are paired alone in Hos 11:8; in the twenty-three occurrences of "Gomorrah" in the Bible, it is always paired with Sodom, whereas "Sodom" as the lead city may stand alone (e.g., Isa 3:9; Lam 4:6; Ezek 16:46; Matt 11:23–24; Rev 11:8).

Gentile wickedness because of its scandalous sins and calamitous end.[140] Sodom's offenses exceeded sexual transgressions, including social evils against the alien *(gēr),* widow, and orphan (e.g., Exod 22:21–22).[141] Lot and his two guests were "aliens" *(gēr,* 19:9) in Sodom, whose citizens violated their customary right of protection as strangers. Ezekiel decried Sodom's sexual sins but also its shameless treatment of the disadvantaged (Ezek 16:49–50); its notorious pride had its origin in Sodom's once-idyllic existence (13:10). In the biblical corpus and also among later Jewish and Christian interpreters, these cities of corruption served as a standard of depravity[142] and a measure for the suddenness and severity of judgment a people might face.[143] Mention of "Zoar" too anticipates the trouble awaiting Lot. Formerly called "Bela" (14:2,8), the naming of Zoar is tied directly to Lot's flight from destruction (19:21–22).

As for the cities' locations, they are a perpetual subject of scholarly intrigue. Proposals from both antiquity and the present have resulted in three principal theories, including sites north and southeast of the Dead Sea as well as the southern basin under the Sea; but the southern locations, especially the southeastern plain of the Dead Sea, have generated more support based on literary and archaeological analysis.[144] More information is required before scholars will achieve a consensus on their identification.

13:14–17   The responses of Lot and of the Lord to Abram's offer are contrasted in this paragraph. Lot "parted" for his possessions (v. 14 with v. 9) after he had "lifted his eyes" ("looked," NIV; v. 10), but the Lord instructs the patriarch to "lift up your eyes" (v. 14) so as to see the vista of the whole land that will someday belong to his descendants. The magnimity of God's grant involves all the land that the patriarch can see (v. 15), all that he can walk (v. 17), and all the progeny that he could ever count (v. 16).

Verses 15–17 form a chiastic structure.[145]

A I will give (the land) to you (v. 15)
   B your offspring (v. 15)

---

[140] See W. Fields, *Sodom and Gomorrah: History and Motif in Biblical Narrative,* JSOTSup 231 (Sheffield: Sheffield Academic Press, 1997), 155–84.

[141] Cp. the "cry" of the disadvantaged heard by God (Exod 22:23) and the same imagery of "outcry" in Sodom (18:20–21).

[142] E.g., Deut 32:32; Isa 1:9–10; 13:19–22; Jer 23:14; Ezek 16:46–56; Jude 7; Rev 11:8; *3 Mac* 2:5.

[143] E.g., Deut 29:22–23; Lam 4:6 with Num 16:35 and Hos 11:6,8; Job 18:15; Isa 1:7; 13:19 with Rom 9:29; Jer 49:18; 50:40; Amos 4:11; Zeph 2:9; Matt 10:15; 11:23–24; Luke 10:12; 17:29; 2 Pet 2:6; *4 Esdr* 2:8; *Jub.* 16:5,6; 20:5; *T. Levi* 14:6; *T. Naph.* 3:4; 4:1; *T. Benj.* 9:1.

[144] B. MacDonald, *"East of the Jordan": Territories and Sites of the Hebrew Scriptures,* ASOR Books 6 (Boston: ASOR, 2000), 45–61.

[145] Wenham, *Genesis 1–15,* 295.

C dust of the earth (v. 16)
C′ dust of the earth (v. 16)
B′ your offspring (v. 16)
A′ I am giving it to you (v. 17)

Verses 15 and 17 explain that the Lord himself ("I will give," "I am giving") grants this land to Abram and his "seed" ("offspring," NIV), and it is the Lord ("I will make," v. 16) who will multiply his progeny. The land moreover is a permanent possession ("forever," v. 15; 17:8) as is the covenant of circumcision (17:7,13,19). The covenants made with Noah and David, both also divine grants, consist of perpetual provisions (9:12,16; 2 Sam 7:16; 22:51; Ps 89:4,36–37). His future seed is likened to the innumerable "dust *('āpār)* of the earth" (v. 16; also 28:14), tying together the promises of land and progeny. Similar language, "sand *[ḥôl]* on the seashore" and the countless "stars" (15:5; 26:4), describes Abram's prolific offspring (22:17; 32:12).[146] The Lord further instructs Abram to survey the land by traversing its "length" and "breadth" in a sign of ownership (v. 17).[147] How this will occur is not explained: the land is in the hands of Canaanites, and Sarai remains barren. Abram neither has the land in hand nor a descendant to whom he may bequeath it, yet he continues to wait on God.

(3) Abram Worships (13:18)

[18]So Abram moved his tents and went to live near the great trees of Mamre at Hebron, where he built an altar to the LORD.

13:18 Abram's response entailed his taking up residence at Hebron, by the "great trees of Mamre," and the building of an altar for worship. By the rapid-fire description in the Hebrew, "Abram pitched his tent, entered, and settled," the narrative conveys the patriarch's immediate compliance and assurance that the promises will take place.

The author mentions "Mamre" and "Hebron" for the first time, introducing an important cluster of sites in patriarchal history. Hebron is located in the south central mountains of Judah, the highest city in Palestine (3,040 ft.), about nineteen miles south southwest of Jerusalem. Mamre is about two miles north of Hebron (Ar. *el-Khalil,* "the friend"). Mention of a city "gate" in 23:10,18 indicates the site was an urban center at the time (cf. Num 13:22). The well-

---

[146] Elsewhere the "sand" imagery describes populations (1 Kgs 4:20; Isa 10:22; 48:19; Hos 1:10), innumerable armies (Josh 11:4; Judg 7:12; 1 Sam 13:5; 2 Sam 17:11), captives (Hab 1:9), grain (Gen 41:49), and wisdom (1 Kgs 4:29).

[147] הִתְהַלֵּךְ, "walk," in the *hithpael* stem means "to move about" (see *IBHS* §26.1.2b–2d). Sarna (*Genesis,* 100) agrees with the rabbis that Abram's walk symbolized his claim of legal ownership and points to a similar practice by the kings of the Egyptians and Hittites who took a ceremonial walk periodically to claim their territory anew; cp. Deut 11:24; Josh 11:3.

watered and fertile region supported almost uninterrupted occupations from the fourth millennium to modern times. Hebron-Mamre was the primary settlement of Abram and Isaac (e.g., 18:1; 35:27; 37:14); it was especially important as the burial site for the patriarchal family in the cave of Machpelah near Mamre (23:2,19; 25:9; 49:31; 50:13).[148] Hebron's former name, Kiriath Arba (see comments on 23:2), was attributed to the forefather of the Anakites, Arba (Josh 14:15; 15:13). Mamre too was associated with a person, an Amorite by the same name, allied with Abram (and others) who joined the patriarch in pursuing the eastern kings (14:13,24). After the era of the patriarchs, the city continued to be important to Moses' Israel and was remembered for its antiquity (Num 13:22[23]; for the conquest, Josh 10:36–37; 11:21; 12:3; 14:13–15; 15:13–14; Judg 1:10,20). Hebron's citizens were the first to acknowledge David as king from which he reigned over Judah for seven and a half years (2 Sam 2:4; 5:3); the association of David with this famed patriarchal site contributed to his image as the royal successor to the promise (2 Sam 7:9; Ps 89:3–4[4–5]; Gen 12:2).

5. Abram Rescues Lot: Abram's Faithfulness (14:1–24)

The war of the kings sets the scene for this second account in the trilogy of Abram-Lot stories (chaps. 13; 14; 18–19). Lot contrasts Abram in two ways in this episode: first, he is the passive, impotent figure compared to the courageous champion Abram; second, Lot is incompetent as leader of a household who fails to maintain his possessions compared to Abram, who devises a successful plan to reclaim them. In the context of chap. 13, the abduction shows implicitly that separation from Abram meant forfeiting the divine protection provided by the favored patriarch (cp. 21:22).

COMPOSITION. This chapter has been the subject of extensive scholarly speculation because it presents a unique episode in Abram's life and contains special interpretive problems.[149] We addressed the troubling literary and historical issues in the commentary Introduction. We concluded that the chapter is a cohesive literary unit, not a patchwork of disparate narratives, which fits suitably in the present context of chaps. 13 and 15.

STRUCTURE. The episode consists of two sections: the war of the kings

---

[148] Today, over the traditional site of Machpelah is the mosque known as *Haram el-Khalil*, meaning "the enclosure of the friend (of God)," an allusion to Abraham (2 Chr 20:7; Isa 41:8; Jas 2:23); no extensive excavation of the cave or within Hebron itself has been undertaken. The site showed remains from the Chalcolithic to the Islamic eras. A. Ofer, "Hebron," *NEAEHL* 2.606–9; P. Hammond, "Hebron," *OEANE* 3.13–14.

[149] Hamilton observes that this is the only portrayal of Abram as a warrior and the only chapter in chaps. 12–22 in which no divine voice speaks and no explicit reference to the promises is found (*Genesis Chapters 1–17*, 399).

(vv. 1–12) and Abram's encounter with the kings (vv. 13–24). Verses 1–12 provide an extensive narrative, possessing no dialogue, which delineate the two warring factions (vv. 1–4), the battle itinerary of the eastern kings (vv. 5–7), and their defeat of Sodom and Gomorrah (vv. 8–11). Verse 12 tells of Lot's capture, transitioning the narrative of the war (vv. 1–11) and the subsequent account of Abram's rescue of Lot (vv. 13–24). This verse anticipates how Abram intercepts "Lot and his possessions," described in v. 16. The second half of the chapter falls into two parts: Abram's pursuit and recovery of Lot, which involves his engagement of Kedorlaomer (vv. 13–16) and his encounter with the king of Sodom (vv. 17–24), and the embedded account of Abram and Melchizedek (vv. 18–20). The encounters of Abram with the king of Sodom and the priest-king Melchizedek provide a contrast between the spiritual character of the two kings that will result in accenting Abram's devotion to the Lord.

vv. 1–12 The war of the kings
    vv. 1–4 The identity of the kings
    vv. 5–7 The campaign of the eastern kings
    vv. 8–11 Defeat of Sodom and Gomorrah
    v. 12 Capture of Lot
vv. 13–24 Abram encounters the kings
    vv. 13–16 Defeat of the eastern kings and rescue of Lot
    vv. 17–24 Kings of Sodom and Salem

(1) The War of the Kings (14:1–12)

[1]At this time Amraphel king of Shinar, Arioch king of Ellasar, Kedorlaomer king of Elam and Tidal king of Goiim [2]went to war against Bera king of Sodom, Birsha king of Gomorrah, Shinab king of Admah, Shemeber king of Zeboiim, and the king of Bela (that is, Zoar). [3]All these latter kings joined forces in the Valley of Siddim (the Salt Sea). [4]For twelve years they had been subject to Kedorlaomer, but in the thirteenth year they rebelled.

[5]In the fourteenth year, Kedorlaomer and the kings allied with him went out and defeated the Rephaites in Ashteroth Karnaim, the Zuzites in Ham, the Emites in Shaveh Kiriathaim [6]and the Horites in the hill country of Seir, as far as El Paran near the desert. [7]Then they turned back and went to En Mishpat (that is, Kadesh), and they conquered the whole territory of the Amalekites, as well as the Amorites who were living in Hazazon Tamar.

[8]Then the king of Sodom, the king of Gomorrah, the king of Admah, the king of Zeboiim and the king of Bela (that is, Zoar) marched out and drew up their battle lines in the Valley of Siddim [9]against Kedorlaomer king of Elam, Tidal king of Goiim, Amraphel king of Shinar and Arioch king of Ellasar—four kings against five. [10]Now the Valley of Siddim was full of tar pits, and when the kings of Sodom and Gomorrah fled, some of the men fell into them and the rest fled to the hills. [11]The four kings seized all the goods of Sodom and Gomorrah and all their

food; then they went away. ¹²They also carried off Abram's nephew Lot and his possessions, since he was living in Sodom.

The narrative describes the conflict between two warring coalitions of kings, providing a detailed account of persons and places. The outcome of the war is the defeat of Sodom involving the capture of Lot, which establishes the military setting for the growing stature of Abram as a formidable figure in the region.

14:1–4 The eastern alliance consisted of four kings, led by Kedorlaomer, king of Elam (v. 1), who had received tribute from the western kings for twelve years (v. 4). "Elam," known as the son of Shem (10:22), designates a region in ancient Persia (modern southwest Iran) whose capital was Susa. In the thirteenth year the western kings refused to pay their annual tribute. Kedorlaomer's three confederates were Amraphel, king of Shinar (= Babylonia), Arioch, king of Ellasar, and Tidal, king of Goiim. None of the kings can be positively identified from independent sources, and the place names Ellasar and Goiim (meaning "peoples"?) are also unknown. Nevertheless, the names and events ring authentic, fitting best in the first half of the second millennium. Kitchen proposes an eastern ethnography for the names of the eastern coalition: "Kedorlaomer" is Elamite (Kutir + deity); "Tidal" is Hittite (Tudkhalia); "Amraphel" may be Semitic; "Arioch" has parallels at Mari (Arriwuk/Arriyuk) and Nuzi (Ariukki).[150] The listing of the western kings omits the name of "the king of Bela," which was the former name of the city "Zoar" (vv. 2,8). Zoar, one of the "cities of the plain" (13:10,12), was at the southern tip of the Valley of Jericho (19:22–23,30; Deut 34:3). "Bela" is the personal name of a king of Edom (see comments on 36:32) and the name of one of Benjamin's sons (46:21).

14:5–7 Kedorlaomer and his allies responded to the rebellious kings in a year's time. Description of their itinerary and impressive victories over the inhabitants in the region heightens the narrative's excitement as the foreboding army of Kedorlaomer makes its way toward Sodom. Abram's political importance is enhanced by the success of the eastern king against the west, since he in turn will later fall to Abram's militia (v. 15).

The catalogue of the six places defeated by the eastern kings progresses generally from a north to south direction along the King's Highway (Num 20:17; 21:22) in transjordan. (1) Ashtaroth Karnaim in Bashan, where the Rephaites resided, corresponds to Tell Ashtarah in south Syria, near Karnaim (= Tell Sa'd).[151] Ashtaroth and Edrei were the cities of Og, king of Bashan, who was the last of the Rephaites (Deut 1:4; 3:11,13). (2) The exact location of the second site Ham, the habitation of the Zuzites (= Zamzummim, Deut 2:20?), is unknown but can be placed between Bashan and

---

[150] K. A. Kitchen, *On the Reliability of the Old Testament* (Grand Rapids: Eerdmans/Cambridge, UK, 2003), 320.

[151] J. Day, "Ashtaroth," *ABD* 1.491 and "Ashtaroth-Karnaim," *ABD* 1.491.

Moab's Shaveh Kiriathaim (= "plain of Kiriathaim"). (3) This latter site was the home of the Emites; it probably names the "plain" near Kiriathaim, a town in Moab (Num 32:37; Josh 13:19; Jer 48:1,23; Ezek 25:9) whose exact location remains disputed.[152] The Rephaites, Zuzites, and the Emites were later treated as one group (Deut 2:11,20). Like the infamous Anakites (Num 13:28,33; Deut 1:28; see vol 1A, p. 336), they were remembered as the giants of Canaan (Deut 2:10–11). (4) The Horites inhabited the southern region of Seir (= Edom; cf. comments on 36:8) "as far as El Paran" (v. 6), which is Elath on the Gulf of Aqabah.[153] Also "the desert of Paran" is associated with the rejected son Ishmael (21:21). As for the relationship of the Horites with Edom, see the comments at 36:2–3,20–21,29–30. (5) By turning northwest to En Mishpat, the former name of Kadesh, Kedorlaomer engaged the Amalekites where he thoroughly routed the "whole territory" (v. 7). Kadesh (Kadesh Barnea) is near Tell 'Ain el-Qudeirat in north Sinai.[154] Its location is in the "Desert of Paran" (Num 13:26), on the western border of Edom (Num 20:16). Kadesh played an important role in the wilderness generation as the place where the Israelites refused to enter Canaan and consequently were condemned to wander in the desert for forty years (Num 13:14). The Amalekites were also a desert people the Israelites confronted (Exod 17:8–16; Num 13:29; 14:41–45). They were a notorious enemy of Israel (Exod 17:8; Deut 25:17; 1 Sam 15:2). The origin of the Amalekites is traced to Amalek, son of Eliphaz and grandson of Esau (36:11–12), who was renowned as an Edomite chief (36:15–16). So little is known about the Amalekites since they are not named in sources outside the biblical account that it is presumptuous of scholars to dismiss Gen 14:7 as a fictitious anachronism. Reference to Amalekites in this region may have been an updating by the author for his contemporary audience or used for an earlier people (e.g., Exod 17:14; Num 24:20) whose history later intertwined with the Edomites.[155] (6) The last people conquered by the eastern kings en route to Sodom were the Amorites, who resided in Hazazon Tamar (v. 7), identified as En Gedi in 2 Chr 20:2. Kedorlaomer's victory over the Amorites helps explain the Amorite allies who joined Abram's pursuit of the eastern confederacy (14:13). En Gedi sits midway on the western shore of the Dead Sea, an oasis in the wilderness of Judah (Josh 15:62). It was David's refuge when fleeing from King Saul (1 Sam 23:29[24:1]; 24:1[24:2]). The Amorites were one of the six nations the Lord promised to give over to Abram's descendants (15:11,21; Exod 3:8,17); the transjordan

---

[152] For proposals, see G. Mattingly, "Kiriathaim," *ABD* 4.85.

[153] M. Astour, "El-Paran," *ABD* 2.423.

[154] D. Manor, "Kadesh-Barnea," *ABD* 4.1–3.

[155] G. Mattingly, "Amalek," *ABD* 1.169–71; J. A. Thompson, "Amalek, Amalekites," *ISBE* 1.104; and B. K. Waltke, *Genesis* (Grand Rapids: Zondervan, 2001), 485.

population was ruled by Sihon, who fell to Moses' armies (Num 21:21–31; Deut 1:4). For more on the Amorites, see 10:16 (vol.1A, p. 456).[156]

This report of Kedorlaomer's victories was not appropriated by the author for solely antiquarian interests. The wilderness Israelites traverse the route from Kadesh to Moab once conquered by these eastern kings (Num 20:22; 21:4,10–13; Deut 1:46–2:8);[157] the ancient peoples who fell to Kedorlaomer were later supplanted by Israel (Josh 12:4; 13:12) or Israel's relatives. The Edomites displaced the Horites (36:20–21,29–30; Deut 2:12,22), and Lot's children, the Moabites and Ammonites, supplanted the Emites (Deut 2:11) and the Zamzuzites (= Zuzites; Deut 2:20), respectively. If Father Abraham could defeat the invincible Kedorlaomer, the Israelites could take courage facing enemies in their own day.

14:8–12 The participants of the two factions occur again (vv. 8–9), showing the inequity of "four kings against five" (v. 9). Nevertheless, as in their earlier wars, the eastern confederation easily prevails over the hapless kings of Sodom and Gomorrah. The author explains how the battlefield itself, the "Valley of Siddim" (vv. 3,10),[158] assisted Kedorlaomer by its tar pits in which the kings of Sodom and Gomorrah fell when fleeing.[159] The "rest" (v. 10) who escaped to the nearby hills indicates the remaining three kings (so TEV). Their avenue of escape to the mountains later becomes Lot's when he escapes with his daughters from Sodom and Zoar (19:30).

By using parallel language in the Hebrew of vv. 11 and 12, the passage calls attention to the abduction of the person Lot, not just his possessions. The same Hebrew words begin and conclude the parallelism between the verses: "they took ["seized," NIV] all the possessions of Sodom and Gomorrah . . . and they went away" (v. 11), but "they took ["carried off," NIV] Lot and his possessions . . . and they went away" (absent in NIV; v. 12). The victors were satisfied with confiscating the "goods" and "food" of the cities, leaving the kings to their bitumen jails, but Lot and his dependants (v. 16) are taken captive. The reason given is in the final clause of v. 12, "now he was living in Sodom," hence NIV's "since."

Irony occurs at many points in the passage, and here the taking of Lot proves to be Kedorlaomer's undoing. If he had been satisfied with the goods, resisting

---

[156] Also K. Schoville, "Canaanites and Amorites," in *Peoples of the Old Testament World* (Grand Rapids: Baker, 1994), 157–82.

[157] Astour, "El-Paran," 423.

[158] For *śādad,* "draw furrows," as the etymology of "Siddim," see M. Astour, "Siddim, Valley of," *ABD* 6.15–16.

[159] The NIV's "some of the men" ("some" in NRSV, NKJV) is an explanatory addition indicating the kings' armies fell as well, but the passage concerns the actions of the kings, and the natural reading of the Hb. is that the kings "fled" (וַיָּנֻסוּ) followed by "fell" (וַיִּפְּלוּ) (so NASB, NAB, NJB). The NJPS has "threw themselves" into the pits.

the greed of dealing in human flesh, he may well have left unhindered. But as the account emphasizes, Lot was "Abram's nephew" (v. 12), which precipitated the report of Lot's capture coming to Abram (v. 13). As in chap. 13, which portrays the blessing Lot enjoyed in accord with the promises made to Abram (12:3), Kedorlaomer's mistreatment of Lot, which was tantamount to opposing Abram, results in his destruction (12:3, "curse").

(2) Abram Meets the Kings (14:13–24)

¹³**One who had escaped came and reported this to Abram the Hebrew. Now Abram was living near the great trees of Mamre the Amorite, a brother of Eshcol and Aner, all of whom were allied with Abram. ¹⁴When Abram heard that his relative had been taken captive, he called out the 318 trained men born in his household and went in pursuit as far as Dan. ¹⁵During the night Abram divided his men to attack them and he routed them, pursuing them as far as Hobah, north of Damascus. ¹⁶He recovered all the goods and brought back his relative Lot and his possessions, together with the women and the other people.**

¹⁷**After Abram returned from defeating Kedorlaomer and the kings allied with him, the king of Sodom came out to meet him in the Valley of Shaveh (that is, the King's Valley).**

¹⁸**Then Melchizedek king of Salem brought out bread and wine. He was priest of God Most High, ¹⁹and he blessed Abram, saying,**

"**Blessed be Abram by God Most High,**
   Creator of heaven and earth.
²⁰**And blessed be God Most High,**
   who delivered your enemies into your hand."

Then Abram gave him a tenth of everything.

²¹**The king of Sodom said to Abram, "Give me the people and keep the goods for yourself."**

²²**But Abram said to the king of Sodom, "I have raised my hand to the LORD, God Most High, Creator of heaven and earth, and have taken an oath ²³that I will accept nothing belonging to you, not even a thread or the thong of a sandal, so that you will never be able to say, 'I made Abram rich.' ²⁴I will accept nothing but what my men have eaten and the share that belongs to the men who went with me—to Aner, Eshcol and Mamre. Let them have their share."**

In this second half of the narrative, Abram surprises the armies of Kedorlaomer by ambush (vv. 13–16), and then upon his victorious return he meets the kings of Sodom and Salem (vv. 17–24). Verse 13 begins the first paragraph in Hebrew with "came" *(bô²),* while the second part (v. 17) begins with its antonym "came out" *(yāṣā²).*

Abram's meeting the two kings, Sodom and Salem, in the "Valley of the King" (v. 17) follows the war of the kings. Two contrasts occur in this section: first, the king of Sodom's welcome to Abram contrasts the beneficent action taken by the king of Salem, Melchizedek (vv. 17–20); second, the selfish request of the king of Sodom contrasts the unselfish response of Abram (vv.

146

21–24). The king of Sodom "came out" *(yāṣāʾ)* to meet Abram (v. 17), but Melchizedek "brought out" *(yāṣāʾ)*[160] food (v. 18) and offered a blessing (vv. 19–20). The first word spoken by the king of Salem is "blessed" *(bārûk),* but Sodom's king first says "give me" (v. 21). Here, the passage also shows the second contrast; whereas the king of Sodom bargains for a portion of the booty, Abram takes none of it for himself, providing a tenth for Melchizedek (v. 20) and the share belonging to his allies.[161]

14:13–16 Unlike Lot, who resided in Sodom, aligning himself with the notorious Sodomites (cf. 19:1,7), Abram lived safely away at Mamre, where he had entered a pact with neighbors who are introduced as "allied with Abram"[162] (v. 13). Reference to Abram as "the Hebrew" distinguishes him from the person Mamre "the Amorite." This is the first place in the Old Testament where "Hebrew" *(ʿibrî)* occurs, although "Eber" *(ʿēber)* whose name may be the source for the term, appears prominently in the Table of Nations (10:21,25) and Abram's genealogy (11:16; 1 Chr 1:18–19). Alternatively, "Hebrew" may have been related to *ʿ-b-r,* "to cross over (from the other side)," from which Eber may have been connected (cf. *ʿēber,* "the other side," Josh 24:3).[163] The ethnic designation "Hebrew" occurs sparingly in the Old Testament, usually spoken by non-Israelites, such as the Egyptians (e.g., 39:14,17; Exod 1:15–16,19) and the Philistines (e.g., 1 Sam 4:9; 13:3,19), to distinguish members of the nation of Israel. Joseph identified himself with his homeland, "the land of the Hebrews" (40:15). Jonah identifies himself as a "Hebrew" primarily in terms of his religious affiliation ("and I worship *Yahweh*"; 1:9); this is reminiscent of the appellative for *Yahweh* in Exodus who is frequently identified as "the God of the Hebrews" (Exod 3:18; 7:16; 9:1,13; 10:3). "Hebrew" as a language is equated with "Judahite," the language of Jerusalem's residents (2 Kgs 18:26; 2 Chr 32:18; Isa 36:11,13). Paul, too, used "Hebrew" as an ethnic or language designation (Phil 3:5). At times the term also had social implications, not solely ethnic usage (e.g., 1 Sam 13:3,6–7; 14:21; 29:3).

The names Mamre and his relatives, Eshcol and Aner, occur only as persons in vv. 13 and 24. All three names also appear elsewhere identifying places.[164]

---

[160] "Came out" is וַיֵּצֵא *(qal)* and "brought out" הוֹצִיא *(hiphil),* both from יָצָא.

[161] A. Ross observes the chiasmus, "Sodom–Melchizedek–Melchizedek–Sodom," which places the blessing (vv. 18–19) between the appearance of the king of Sodom (v. 17) and his proposition (v. 20); Abram could better resist the offer "after receiving the blessing of Melchizedek" (*Creation and Blessing* [Grand Rapids: Baker, 1988], 295). On chiasmus see also Wenham, *Genesis 1–15,* 315.

[162] בַּעֲלֵי בְרִית־אַבְרָם, lit., "lords [possessors] of the covenant of Abram" (*IBHS* §9.5.3b), a phrase occurring only once; cp. 49:23; Neh 6:18.

[163] For more on the etymology of "Hebrew," see 10:21 (vol. 1A, p. 460, n. 107).

[164] Some scholars interpret the persons as fictive personifications of clans or sanctuaries originally related to the region of Hebron; but such reconstructions of their original names for these sites are based on uncertain etymological considerations. See Y. Arbeitman, "Mamre," *ABD* 4.492–93.

Eshcol, meaning "cluster," is a valley near Hebron that impressed the Israelite spies by its robust clusters of grapes (Num 13:23–24; 32:9; Deut 1:24). Aner is a Levitical city west of the Jordan in Manasseh (1 Chr 6:70). Mamre has been identified as the modern Ramat el-Khalil, two miles north of Hebron. Mamre only appears in Genesis; it was a place where Abram encamped (see comments on 13:18; 18:1) and located just west of the patriarchs' burial site, the cave of Machpelah (23:17,19; 25:9; 35:27; 49:30; 50:13). Mamre may have taken its name from the Amorite ally of Abram.

Verse 14 confirms our earlier observation that the capture of his "relative" Lot, not the possessions, drew Abram into the battle. Abram's leading ("called out"[165]) as many as 318 men, all born to his own household, shows the patriarch's substantial wealth and power. Lot was fortunate to have such a benefactor who came to his rescue both here and later through his intercession before the Lord (chap. 18). Specific mention of "household" not only means that Abram's family was prolific but it accentuates the idea of family loyalty germane to the passage. "Trained men" translates ḥānîk (i.e., a household member or retainer),[166] which occurs only here in the Old Testament; it refers to "armed retainers" by Canaanite chieftains in second-millennium texts.[167]

Dan (Tel Dan) is located in the far north at the base of Mount Hermon. Its settlement period was virtually continuous from as early as 5000 B.C. down to the Christian era. The former name of Dan was "Laish," which is mentioned in eighteenth-century texts from Egypt and Mari; the Danites re-named the site after they dispossessed it (Josh 19:47; Judg 18:29).[168] The appearance of the later name "Dan" is a post-Mosaic updating of the place name for later readers.

Abram's scheme involved dividing his men and surprising the unsuspecting kings at night, probably from the rear (v. 15). Such night attacks gave smaller forces the advantage required for victory (Judg 7:9,15–16). Kedorlaomer fled beyond Damascus north as far as the settlement Hobah. Two suggested sites include the modern city Hoba (60 mi. northwest of Damascus) and the ancient region Ube, named in both the Egyptian Execration Texts (ca. 1850) and the Amarna Tablets (ca. thirteenth century), whose chief city (Tell el-Salihiye) sat ca. ten miles east of Damascus.[169] Damascus was the home of Eliezer, Abram's servant (15:2). The city was the capital of the Aramean state in the tenth–eighth centuries. The absence of extensive archaeological work in old Damascus pre-

---

[165] The MT has וַיָּרֶק from רִיק, meaning "empty, pour out" (42:35) or "withdraw" a sword from its sheath (Exod 15:9); here the sense is "lead out" (*DCH* 3.270). Most EVs convey the sense of SP's וַיָּדֶק from דוּק, "muster," which may also be reflected by LXX's ἠρίθμησεν ("he counted"; Vg. *numeravit*) and *Tg. Onq.* וְזָרֵיז ("he armed," Jastrow, 412; see *HALOT* 1.217; 3.1228).

[166] *HALOT* 1.333.

[167] V. Hamilton, "ḥānîk," *TWOT* 1.301.

[168] A. Biran, "Dan" *ABD* 2.12–17.

[169] H. Thompson, "Hobab," *ABD* 3.235 and (unsigned) "Hobah," *ISBE* 2.724.

vents firm conclusions about the age of the city. The etymology of "Damascus," even as to whether it is semitic, is disputed. Its earliest certain mention outside the Bible is the fifteenth century inscription in the temple walls in Karnak (Luxor), although the region of Damascus (Apu[m]) is mentioned earlier in the Execration Texts.[170]

The repetitious character of the Hebrew in v. 16 brings the expedition of Abram to a detailed conclusion: "recovered" and "brought back" *(šûb);* "the goods" and "possessions" *(rĕkuš);* and twice "also" *(gam;* absent in NIV). "All the goods" indicates the booty of the whole city, which included Lot's personal "possessions." "Women" and the "(other) people" refer to Lot's household and those living in Sodom, presumably those belonging to the king of Sodom (v. 21).

14:17 The king of Sodom had emerged from his tar pit, and he "came out" to welcome the return of Abram. Earlier the narrative describes the king of Sodom as the one who "came out" ("marched out," NIV) with his allies to engage Kedorlaomer in the "Valley of Siddim" (v. 8). Now humiliated he stands before the victor Abram in the "Valley of Shaveh." "Shaveh," meaning "plain," is explained in the text as the "King's Valley" (2 Sam 18:18), perhaps the small plain where the Kidron, Hinnom, and Tyropoeon valleys come together, east of Jerusalem.[171] This proximity to Jerusalem explains the sudden appearance of Melchizedek, the king of Salem (= Jerusalem).

14:18–20 Melchizedek is identified as "king of Salem" and "priest of God Most High *[El Elyon]"* (v. 18). His name, *Malkî-ṣedek,* means "king of righteousness" (Heb. 7:2);[172] the language "king of Salem," *melek šālēm,* means literally "king of peace" (Heb. 7:2). By this parallel language between his name and his city there is an association of "righteousness" and "peace" (Salem). These two characteristics are found together in the Old Testament (Ps 85:10; Isa 9:7; 32:17; 48:18; 60:17). Jerusalem is often also linked with *ṣedek* in the Old Testament (e.g., Isa 1:21,26; 33:5; 46:13; 61:3; Jer 31:23; 33:16; Ps 118:19; cf. the kings of Jerusalem, Adoni-Zedek, Josh 10:1; Zedekiah, 2 Kgs 24:17–18). "Salem" *(šālēm)* is widely recognized as an ancient name for Jerusalem *(yĕrûšālayim)* in Jewish tradition;[173] "Salem" appears in parallel with "Zion," referring to the temple at Jerusalem (Ps 76:2[3]). In the Old Testament

---

[170] W. Pitard, *Ancient Damascus* (Winona Lake: Eisenbrauns, 1987), 7–10; "Damascus," *ABD* 2.5–7 and A. Bowling, "Damascus," *ZPEB* 2.7–9. For more, see commentary Introduction, "Anachronisms"; also Deut 10:22, vol. 1A, pp. 461–62.

[171] M. Astour, "Shaveh, Valley of," *ABD* 5.1168.

[172] Also Philo, *Leg.* 3.79; Josephus, *Ant.* 1.180; *J.W.* 6.438; but *Tg. Ps-J.* does not recognize it as an appellative and translates the Hb. *(malkî-ṣedek),* adding the identification Shem: "And the righteous king, he is Shem the Great . . ."

[173] E.g., 1QapGen 22:13; all Tgs.; Josephus, *Ant.* 1.10.2[180–81]; 7.67[7.3.2]; *J.W.* 6.437 [6.10.1]; *Gen. Rab.* 43.6; for more detailed discussion, see below "Excursus: Melchizedek."

the name "Jebus," referring to the pre-Israelite inhabitants of the city, is used of
Jerusalem (e.g., Josh 15:8). The earliest mentions of Jerusalem outside the
Bible are Rusalimum in Egyptian Execration texts (ca. 1850) and Urusalim in
the Amarna texts (fourteenth century).[174]

"Priest" *(kōhēn)* in v. 18 is its first occurrence in the Bible. Patriarchal blessing involved the divine benefits of prosperity and progeny for Abram and his
family (e.g., 12:1–3; 22:16–18; 26:3–4); the patriarchs in turn conveyed the
blessing under the auspices of the Lord upon the succeeding generation (e.g.,
27:27–29; 28:1; 49:28). This incident, however, is the only priestly blessing in
Genesis. Later, the priests were the chief agents of blessing in Israel (e.g., Num
6:24–26; Deut 10:8); however, often a national leader (Exod 39:43; 2 Sam
6:18) or a family member (24:60; Ruth 2:19–20; 2 Sam 6:20) blessed others by
invoking the Lord. Invocations typically assumed that only the Lord could ultimately bestow blessing; a benedictory prayer petitioned God for prosperity and
well being. The expression "bread and wine" refers to daily but luxurious provisions (Judg 19:19; Eccl 10:19; also Lam 2:12). That they were refreshment
for returning warriors makes sense (e.g., Judg 8:5; 2 Sam 16:1–2).[175] Although
both elements were part of Israel's worship offered to God (e.g., Lev 2:4–16;
23:13; Num 28:14)[176] and later functioned symbolically at the Lord's table
(1 Cor 11:26), there is no overt cultic meaning attached to them here.[177]

The Hebrew in v. 19 is ambiguous (lit. "and he blessed him") as to who is
blessing whom, but the blessing itself is directed toward Abram (so the LXX's
"and he blessed Abram") and to Abram's God. In both lines (vv. 19,20) the
emphasis is on the identity and participation of God as Creator and Deliverer:

A   Blessed be Abram by *El Elyon*
   B   who is Creator of heaven and earth (v. 19)
A′ And blessed be *El Elyon*
   B′ who delivered your enemies into your hand (v. 20).

The expected formula "Blessed be P(ersonal) N(ame) by *Yahweh"* *(bārûk*
PN lyhwh; Judg 17:2; Ruth 2:20; 3:10; 1 Sam 15:13; 23:21; 2 Sam 2:5; Ps
115:15) differs here by the divine name *El Elyon* *(bārûk ʾabrām lĕʾēl ʿelyôn;*
v. 19a); here *El Elyon* functions as a personal name for God. (For the significance of the divine name *El Elyon,* see the commentary Introduction "El
Names of God.") This name is appropriate to the content of the benediction

---

[174] P. King, "Jerusalem," *ABD* 3.751.

[175] Hamilton, *Genesis Chapters 1–17,* 408.

[176] P. Bird, "Vine," *HBD* 1113.

[177] D. Elgavish contends that the victuals indicated a celebratory feast following a treaty
arrangement (cf. 26:30; 31:54; Deut 23:5–7), but in context there is no certain indication of a covenant here ("The Encounter of Abram and the Melchizedek King of Salem: A Covenant Establishing Ceremony," in *Studies in the Book of Genesis,* 495–508).

since Melchizedek recognizes Abram's God as universal Creator and Sovereign over all peoples (cp., Num 24:16; Deut 28:1; 32:8; 2 Sam 22:14; Pss 47:2[3]; 83:18[19]; 97:9; Lam 3:38).[178] Melchizedek's prayer also blesses *El Elyon (bārûk ʾēl ʿelyôn;* v. 20a) instead of the typical formula, which has the name *Yahweh (bārûk yhwh).* The psalmists praised the name of the Lord as *Elyon* (Pss 7:17[18]; 9:2[3]; 92:1[2]). "Blessed be *Yahweh*" is in prayers of invocation and liturgy (e.g., Gen 9:26; 1 Kgs 8:15,56; 1 Chr 16:36; Ps 28:6), praise for divine grace (24:27; Exod 18:10; Ruth 4:14; 1 Sam 25:32,39; 2 Sam 18:28; 1 Kgs 1:48; Ps 28:6), and in recognition of divine blessing on others (e.g., 24:31; 26:29). To bless God means to recognize God's goodness as shown in the bestowal of divine benefits to his subjects.[179]

El Elyon is "Creator" (*qōnēh;* NJB, NAB, NLT, NJPV; "Maker," NRSV) or "Possessor" (AV, NKJV, NASB) of "heaven and earth" (vv. 19,22). The verb *qānâ* usually means "acquire, get" in the sense of obtaining something or someone (e.g., 25:10; 39:1); metaphorically, it may be used of redeeming Israel (e.g., Exod 15:16). The Ugaritic verbs *qny, ʿśy,* and *kwn* used for describing creation and procreation also occur in Hebrew for creation (e.g., Deut 32:6, where all three occur).[180] The parallel phrase "Maker *[ʿōśēh]* of heaven and earth" occurs in a few psalms (Pss 115:15; 121:2; 124:8). Although disputed by some (preferring the sense of "master"), the evidence points to the meaning of "create, procreate" for *qānâ* in some Old Testament texts (e.g., Gen 4:1; Deut 32:6; Ps 139:13; Prov 8:22). Ugaritic *qny,* meaning "create," which is used of *El* for creation, the LXX translation *(hos ektisen,* "who created"), and the contexts of the Old Testament passages favor "Creator."[181] In either case, Melchizedek is claiming for Abram's God the exalted place of Lord of the universe.

Also, *El Elyon* is identified as the One who delivered up the armies of Kedorlaomer to Abram (v. 20a). The NJB renders the clause as causal, explaining the reason for the priest-king's exultation: "for putting your enemies into your clutches." "Delivered" *(miggēn)* is a rare term occurring three times but twice in the sense of military conquest (14:20; Hos 11:8; see Prov 4:9).[182] More common is the expression "to give into the hand" *(ntn bĕyād;* e.g., Josh 6:2),[183] that is, "to hand over," as in the parallel line in

---

[178] T. Fretheim, "אל," *NIDOTTE* 1.400–401.

[179] M. Brown, "ברך," *NIDOTTE* 1.764–65.

[180] J. C. de Moor contends that where the sense of *qny* is generation/procreation by El, it is used figuratively for creation; similarly, when the terminology of procreation is used of *Yahweh* in the Bible, it is metaphorical for creation ("El, the Creator," in *The Bible World: Essays in Honor of Cyrus H. Gordon* [New York: Ktav, 1980]).

[181] T. Cornelius and R. Van Leeuwen, "קנה," *NIDOTTE* 3.940–41; W. H. Schmidt, "קנה *qnh* to acquire," *TLOT* 3.1147–53.

[182] The related term מָגֵן *(māgēn),* meaning "shield," in 15:1 links the two chapters (see comments on 15:1).

[183] BDB 390.

Hos 11:8 (but interestingly *nātan* also occurs in Gen 14:20).[184] The NIV's "Then Abram gave him a tenth of everything" (v. 20b) supplies the subject "Abram" (so NRSV, NJB, NAB, GNB, NJPS, HCSB), although the Hebrew is indefinite, permitting the view that Melchizedek granted a tenth to Abram, "He [Melchizedek] gave him a tenth." It follows, however, that in the custom of presenting a tenth to the Levites (Num 18:21–28; Deut 14:28–29) and to kings in Israel (1 Sam 8:15–17), the most natural reading is for Abram to be the tither, as Jacob too swears to give a tenth to the Lord (28:22); finally, this is the interpretation given by the writer to the Hebrews (Heb 7:2–6).

Excursus: Melchizedek

Although the name "Melchizedek" occurs but twice in the Old Testament (14:18; Ps 110:4),[185] Jewish and Christian interpreters recognized the religious significance of this cryptic figure. By virtue of his blessing the patriarch and by Abram's deference toward him in presenting a tithe to the priest-king, this person held a superior position. What individual could be greater than Father Abraham? In addition, his priesthood antedated that of the Levitical order, apparently functioning independently of the traditional priesthood of Israel. Melchizedek, moreover, appears and disappears in the text without mention of his parentage, his priestly accession, or death. What was the nature of his priesthood? Since he worshiped the same God as Abram, how did Melchizedek also know of the Lord? And, as the king of "Salem" (= Jerusalem), which became the center of Israel's political and religious life, what was the relationship of his priesthood and the royal house of David? These and related mysteries provided interpreters opportunities for speculation, producing even heretical views (e.g., Melchizedekians) about his identity and role and the significance of his name as well as his city's name.[186]

From Qumran Cave Eleven, 11QMelch (or 11Q13) presents (ca. 100 B.C.–A.D. 100?) an eschatological exegesis of biblical texts in which Melchizedek is depicted as an angel or a superior heavenly being, perhaps the archangel Michael. Melchizedek as God's instrument makes atonement for the righteous and exacts judgment upon the wicked (Belial).[187] The majority of Jewish interpretations, however, maintained that he was a man but an especially anointed priest, even high priest before God Most High (Philo, *Abr* 235; *Tgs. Onq., Neof.*).

---

[184] M. Grisanti, "נתן," *NIDOTTE* 2.844.

[185] Also Heb 5:6,10; 6:20; 7:1,10–11,15,17.

[186] J. Kugel, *The Bible As It Was* (Cambridge: Belknap at Harvard University Press, 1997), 151–62. For the discussion of Melchizedek in the history of interpretation, see D. Hay, *Glory at the Right Hand: Psalm 110 in Early Christianity*, SBLMS 18 (Nashville: Abingdon, 1973); F. Horton, *The Melchizedek Tradition: A Critical Examination of the Sources to the Fifth Century A.D. and in the Epistle to the Hebrews* (Cambridge: Cambridge University Press, 1976); and M. McNamara, "Melchizedek Gen 14,17–20 in the Targums, in Rabbinic and Early Christian Literature," *Bib* 81 (2000): 1–31; and M. Astour, "Melchizedek (Person)," *ABD* 4.686.

[187] G. Brooke, "Melchizedek (11QMelch)," *ABD* 4.687–88.

Josephus asserted that he founded Jerusalem as its first king and priest (*Ant.* 1.10.2[180–81]; *J.W.* 6.437[6.10.1]). Philo too implied that Melchizedek possessed a unique priesthood having no antecedents (*Leg.* 3.25–26 [79–82]; *Congr.* 99). A significant variation from this tradition was the identification of "Salem" with the Samaritan city Shechem, meaning Melchizedek functioned as priest at the temple of Mount Gerizim (Pseudo-Eupolemus, *Praeparatio Evangelica* 9.17.5 [= *OTP* 880]; *Jub.* 30.1), perhaps a view that was related to the rendering of Gen 33:18 in the LXX (Syr., Vg.): "and Jacob came to Salem, a city of Shechem."[188]

Jewish identification of the priest-king as Noah's son, Shem, in the Palestinian targums of the Pentateuch (and rabbinics, e.g., *b. Ned.* 32b; *Pirqe R. El.* 8; *Gen. Rab.* 44.7) was the result of typical Jewish speculation on the paltry biblical evidence and traditions about Shem during the intertestamental period.[189] This opinion is mentioned without comment by some Christian interpreters (Ephrem the Syrian, Epiphanius, and Jerome).[190] According to the chronology of chap. 11, Shem would have been Abram's contemporary, and Gen 9:26, "Blessed be the Lord, the God of Shem," may have influenced this view as well. Melchizedek's priesthood was subordinated to Abraham by the rabbis who contended that his priesthood was not perpetuated by his descendants, since he erred in blessing Abraham before he did God (*b. Ned.* 32b), understanding Ps 110:4 as addressed to Abraham: "You [Abraham] are a priest forever, according to the utterance [= Gen 14:19b–20a] of Melchizedek." Alternatively, another rabbinic tradition explained that it was the name of God or Torah that Melchizedek passed on to the patriarch (*Gen. Rab.* 48.6–8). A rabbinic tradition related that Melchizedek transferred his priesthood to the patriarch, making Abraham a priest (*Gen. Rab.* 45.5; 55.6; *b. Ned.* 32b).

The church fathers too viewed Melchizedek as a man, though exceptions, such as Origen, can be found.[191] For Justin Martyr (*Dial. with Trypho* 19:3–4; 33) and Tertullian (*Adv. Jud.* 2), it was significant that the origin of his priesthood was neither of circumcision (i.e., Gentile) nor of observance of Jewish law; the Levitical order as descendants of Abraham required circumcision. Christ's priesthood, greater than that of the Zadokites, was a priesthood carried on by the church. Whereas the rabbis interpreted the bread and wine brought by the priest-king as symbolic of the temple shewbread and wine libations or, alternatively, of Torah (*Gen. Rab.*), the church fathers did not commonly view them as typological of Christian communion. Clement of Alexandria was one of the first to do so (*Strom.* 26).

Christian interpretation rests on Hebrews 5–7, which draws on Melchizedek as the point of contrast with the Levitical order. The writer to the Hebrews may

---

[188] Kugel, *The Bible As It Was,* 160; M. Astour, "Salem," *ABD* 5.905.

[189] R. Hayward, "'Shem, Melchizedek, and Concern with Christianity in the Pentateuchal Targumism," in *Targumic and Cognate Studies: Essays in Honor of Martin McNamara,* JSOTSup 230 (Sheffield: Sheffield Academic Press, 1996), 67–80.

[190] McNamara, "Melchizedek," 11–15.

[191] Horton, *Melchizedek,* 88–89.

well have assumed that his readers believed Melchizedek was the first priest and hence had no genealogical requirements.[192] Psalm 110:4 was addressed by God to David's "Lord" (v. 1), who was the Christ (Mark 12:35–37; Acts 2:34–36); hence, like that of Melchizedek, Jesus was appointed the head of a new order, having no predecessors (Heb 5:5–6,10), since he like Melchizedek did not come from Levi's succession. Melchizedek's priesthood antedated that of Levi (7:10), and Jesus came from Judah, which possessed no priestly succession (7:11–17). The writer to the Hebrews emphasized the superiority of the priestly order of Jesus to Levi by observing the greater priesthood of Melchizedek in contrast to Levi. Whereas for Levi his divine appointment was not formalized by oath, the priesthood of Melchizedek was confirmed by divine oath (7:20–21). Melchizedek's priesthood was perpetual *(diēnekes)* (7:3), for he had no priestly heritage and no successors (7:3); also Abraham, representing Levi, who resided in the patriarch's loins, presented a tithe to Melchizedek and was blessed by the priest-king's priesthood (7:1). Jesus too has an "eternal" *(aiōna)* priesthood (5:6; 6:20; 7:17,21,24,28).[193] Even the name of Melchizedek and his city implied, to the writer to the Hebrews, the superiority of the priest-king to that of Levi (7:2).

In returning to the Old Testament references to "Melchizedek," there remains for us to consider the modern critical reconstruction of how the figure Melchizedek functioned in the religious and political life of monarchic Israel. The conventional thought is as follows: Gen 14:18–20 and Ps 110:4, written in the Davidic era, created Melchizedek, who as the priest-king of Jerusalemite origin legitimized the pre-Israelite (Jebusite) priesthood of Zadok and the kingship of David's reign.[194] According to this view, there existed a Jebusite lineage of priests at Jerusalem's shrine to Canaanite *El* when David acquired the city; Zadok was the priest of the Jebusite cult whom David retained to assuage the new Canaanite populace in his realm. He joined with the priest Abiathar, who was clearly associated with Yahwism, as dual caretakers of the ark and its shrine. The biblical claims of an Aaronide heritage for Zadok are spurious (2 Sam 8:17; 1 Chr 6:1–8[5:27–34]; 6:50–53[35–38]; Ezra 7:2–5). The MT's 2 Sam 8:17 (1 Chr 18:27) is a corruption of an original reading which leaves Zadok without

---

[192] Ibid., 163; J. A. Fitzmyer creates theological havoc when he accepts too readily the OT critical opinion that the late insertion of vv. 18–20 omitted the original reference to Melchizedek's origin and it was actually Melchizedek who paid the tithe to the superior Abram; when set in Gen 14, the reverse came to be understood, and it was from this misunderstanding that the writer to the Hebrews built his argument ("Melchizedek in the MT, LXX, and the NT," *Bib* 81 [2000]: 63–69).

[193] Horton observes that the use of διηνεκές (7:3) for Melchizedek's "perpetual" order may be intentional so as to distinguish the "eternal" (αἰῶνα) priesthood of Jesus (although the former term is used as a synonym in Heb 10:14, referring to Jesus' eternal sacrifice) (*Melchizedek,* 161–62).

[194] The best known proponent is H. H. Rowley, "Zadok and Nehushtan," *JBL* 58 (1939): 113–41, and "Melchizedek and Zadok (Gen 14 and Ps 110)," in *Festschrift, Alfred Bartholet zum 80 Geburtstag* (Tübingen: Mohr, 1950), 161–72; also see others in G. Ramsey, "Zadok," *ABD* 6.1034–36.

a patrimony.[195] The name "Zadok" is reminiscent of the two kings associated with Jerusalem before David's time, Melchizedek ("My King is Zedek") and Adoni-Zedek ("My Lord is Zedek," Josh 10:1). Some scholars have proposed there was a cult deity at Jebus named Zedek (Ug. *Ṣaduq*).[196] To bolster David's claims on Jerusalem and its cult, "Zion theology" drew on Canaanite mythology of Zion as a holy site for the gods, making the city the epicenter of Israel's religion. Zion as the abode of *Yahweh* was the chief sacred space in the new nation, and David's lineage, whom the Lord elected (2 Sam 7:13–16; Pss 2:7; 89:26–27[27–28]; 110:1–3), was the legitimate line of rulers over Israel.[197] Zadok was designated the head of a line of high priests by David. Jerusalem and the Davidic house then were inviolable. Together, the religious and political arms of the nation were joined in the royal city of David; he wedded this originally Canaanite ideology of sacral kingship devoted to the Canaanite deity *El Elyon* with the traditional tribal religion of Yahwism. In this view the oracles of Ps 110:1,4 are addressed to David as a prophetic utterance announcing God's decree. Psalm 110:4 and the Melchizedek appearance in Genesis made David's priestly order have legitimacy, although not mentioned by Moses. Also his priesthood was historically related to the *El* worship at the new capital, Jerusalem.

This proposal of a Jebusite priesthood David appropriated and the syncretism of an emerging "Zion theology" based on Canaanite religious thought is unfounded.[198] There is no certain evidence of a Jebusite lineage of priest-kings,[199] and the idea of a "Zion theology" of Canaanite character in Israel cannot be demonstrated. The antecedent to Zion's special place in Israel's religion was the event of Sinai; the transition of Sinai's covenantal significance to Jerusalem was affected by the entry of the ark under David's auspices (2 Sam 6). The subsequent appointment of David's house (2 Sam 7) completed the transition. But there was never an orthodox doctrine of inviolability attached to Jerusalem, evidenced by the requirement of Israel's obedience to the Sinai covenant.[200] Also David's resistance to foreign religion makes it unlikely that he as a devout Yahwist would have accommodated a Canaanite cult. Hebron as Zadok's origin rather than Jebusite Jerusalem better suits the historical setting of David's rise from the south before his conquest of Jerusalem (1 Chr 12:28[29]).[201] Last, it is

---

[195] Reading instead "Zadok and Abiathar, son of Ahimelech, son of Ahitub were priests"; this reconstruction relies on 1 Sam 22:20; 23:6; 30:7 and assumes there was one Ahitub, not two men of the same name. See M. Rehm, "Levites and Priests," *ABD* 4.305–6.

[196] E.g., Rowley, "Zadok and Nehushtan," 130–31; and D. Schley, "Adoni-Zedek," *ABD* 1.75.

[197] J. Levenson, "Zion Traditions," *ABD* 6.1098–1102.

[198] See also the critique of this interpretation by F. M. Cross, *Canaanite Myth and Hebrew Epic* (Cambridge: Harvard University Press, 1973).

[199] Horton, *Melchizedek*, 39–45.

[200] G. McConville, "Jerusalem in the Old Testament," in *Jerusalem Past and Present in the Purposes of God* (Cambridge: Tyndale House, 1992), 21–51, esp. 25–27.

[201] J. Day assumes the syncretism of Canaanite *El* and David's religion, but he argues against a Jebusite setting for Zadok and proposes Hebron ("The Canaanite Inheritance of the Israelite Monarchy," in *King and Messiah in Israel and the Ancient Near East*, JSOTSup 270 [Sheffield: Sheffield Academic Press, 1998], 75–78).

curious that the Zadokites did not trace their line back to Melchizedek; in the face of the explanation for Zadok's Aaronide heritage in biblical genealogy (2 Sam 8:17; 1 Chr 6:1–8[5:27–34]; 6:50–53[6:35–38]; Ezra 7:2–5),[202] there is no compelling reason to rewrite monarchic history in such a sweeping way.

Moreover, there is ambiguous evidence regarding the nature of David's priesthood. David's kingship was sacral, that is, divinely appointed; but his designation as priest may not have been technically sacerdotal, authorizing him to carry out sacrifice. There was a consistent division between the offices of priest and king in orthodox Yahwism; it is wrong to assume that the kingship of David was of the same priestly character as the kings of the ancient Near East.[203] He and his sons' role may have been limited to the commissioning of sacrifice and the supervision of worship, such as in the transfer of the ark (2 Sam 6:12–18; also see 2 Sam 24:25) and the building of the temple (1 Chr 22:15; also 1 Kgs 5–7; 8:4–5; 62–64; 9:25).[204] If sacrifice were practiced by David, it would have been justified by David as the successor to Melchizedek (Ps 110:4). But it is clear that the Davidic house did not operate typically as priests for the nation, which was limited to the tribe of Levi (Deut 10:8–9) whose Aaronic clan alone performed the exclusive rites of sacrifice at the central altar (e.g., Num 3:1–10; Exod 28:1,41; 40:14–15; Lev 8:12; 16:32–34; Heb 5:1). The king was subject to the Mosaic law (Deut 17:17–20), which provided only for Aaronic priests; the kings of Israel who transgressed this provision were condemned (1 Sam 13:9–10; 14:33–35; 1 Kgs 12:31–33; 2 Kgs 16:12–18; 2 Chr 26:16–20).[205] D. W. Rooke expresses the difference between David's priesthood and the Aaronic priesthood also in terms of function but adds that David's priesthood was "ontological," that is, he was a priest in his being forever, as Son of God, not by virtue of priestly activity.[206] This difference is further reflected by the writer to the Hebrews, "no one from that tribe [Judah] has ever served at the altar"; in other words there was no divine appointment for Judah in Moses. In particular from the time of David onward, the Zadokite lineage of Aaron held sole claim to the altar. Psalm 110:4 is best interpreted as a future ideal king in whom would reside the offices of both king and priest, a feature known elsewhere in the ancient Near East but not experienced by Israel's kings[207] until the illegitimate claims of the Hasmonean rulers (*1 Mac* 14:41).

---

[202] E. Carpenter, "Zadok," *ISBE* 4.1169–70.

[203] H. L. Ellison, *The Centrality of the Messianic Idea for the Old Testament* (London: Tyndale, 1953), 9–11; M. J. Paul, "The Order of Melchizedek (Ps 110:4 and Heb 7:3)," *WTJ* 49 (1987): 195–211; "Melchizedek," *NIDOTTE* 4.934–36.

[204] See the disputed passage 2 Sam 8:18 regarding David's sons as "priests" (כֹּהֲנִים) or "royal advisors" (NIV) in R. Bergen, *1, 2 Samuel,* NAC (Nashville: Broadman & Holman, 1996), 252–53.

[205] The difficult passage Zech 6:13 has been wrongly interpreted as combining the royal and priestly functions in the priest Joshua; the language "between the two" (v. 13b) and the chiastic structure argues for two distinct persons, Zerubbabel and Joshua, of Zech 4:11,14. See E. Merrill, *Haggai, Zechariah, Malachi* (Chicago: Moody, 1994), 198–99.

[206] D. W. Rooke, "Kingship as Priesthood: The Relationship between the High Priest and the Monarchy," in *King and Messiah in Israel and the Ancient Near East,* 187–208.

[207] F. F. Bruce, *The Epistle to the Hebrews,* NICNT (Grand Rapids: Eerdmans, 1964), 96, n.33.

Psalm 110:1,4 is two oracles addressed to "my Lord" (*'adōnî*) that ultimately must be taken as referencing David's "Lord," not David himself by a court prophet as assumed by many commentators.[208] Psalm 110 is oriented toward the future, ideal king who will be priest as well, a role David's lineage could not fulfill until the coming of the Messiah, who unites the two functions. David's "Lord" (*'adōnî,* "my Lord") was the Messiah as understood by Jesus (Matt 22:41–46 pars.) and the apostles (Acts 2:34–35; 5:31; Rom 8:34; Heb 1:13; 10:12–13). If David is the recipient of the oracles, rather than the author of the psalm, then the argument of Jesus and his apostles founders.[209] This is true as well of the second oracle, which was said to be directed to Jesus Christ in the argument of the writer to the Hebrews (5:5–6; 7:14–17). It makes no difference if Melchizedek in fact had predecessors or successors, for the writer to the Hebrews argues typologically, not actually, on the basis of the silence of Genesis regarding his heritage and succession (Heb 7:3).[210] Chrysostom commented: "How you ask, is it possible for a person to have no father or mother, and lack beginning of days and end of life? You heard he [Melchizedek] was a type; well, neither marvel at this nor expect everything to be found in this type. You see, he would not be a type if he were likely to contain every feature that occurs in reality" (*Homilies on Genesis* 35.16).[211] It is unnecessary for Melchizedek and Jesus to share in all traits; thus the ancient interpretation that Melchizedek was the preincarnate Christ is not required. Melchizedek is a copy of the heavenly priesthood of Jesus, "like *[aphōmoiōmenos]* the Son of God" (Heb 7:3), not Jesus a type of Melchizedek.[212]

14:21–24 Abram answers the king of Sodom's offer, "take [*qaḥ,* NIV "keep"] the goods for yourself" (v. 21), by swearing an oath, signaled by an uplifted hand (v. 22), to never "take" (*'eqqaḥ;* NIV, "accept"; v. 23) anything belonging to the king. The solemn language "swear" (*šāba'*)or "oath" (*šěbû'â*) is not in the text (cp. 21:22–34), but the Hebrew implies an oath by the conditional clause "if" (*'im,* 2x; absent in NIV) and by invocation of God, who judges the person's fidelity to the oath.[213] The uplifted hand is a gesture toward heaven (Dan 12:7), as Abram swore before the "LORD, God Most High, Creator of heaven and earth" (v. 22). Abram's oath echoes the name of God used in Melchizedek's blessing (vv. 19–20) and adds the divine name *Yahweh,*[214] identifying Melchizedek's God as his own.

---

[208] E.g., A. A. Andersen, *The Book of Psalms, Psalms 73–150,* NCBC (Grand Rapids: Eerdmans, 1972), 2.767; L. C. Allen, *Psalms 101–150,* WBC (Waco: Word, 1983), 86–87.

[209] D. Bock, *Luke 9:51–24:53,* BECNT (Grand Rapids: Baker, 1996), 1635–36.

[210] M. J. Paul contends that Heb 7:3 argues, not from the silence of Gen 14 but on the basis that Melchizedek's parents were not the required ones for priestly heritage, even as the Jews did not count a Gentile to have a father, i.e., a legal father.

[211] *ACCS* 2.26.

[212] Bruce, *Hebrews,* 138; also "pattern/copy" (ὑπόδειγμα), Heb 8:5; 9:23.

[213] T. Cartledge, "שׁבע" *NIDOTTE* 4.32–34.

[214] Absent in 1QapGen, LXX, SP.

Abram's reference to a "thread" *(ḥûṭ)* and "sandal *[naʿal]* thong *[śĕrôkʾ]*" indicates the smallest item of least value belonging to the king (Judg 9:13; Isa 5:7; Amos 2:6; 8:6; Matt 3:11 pars.; Acts 13:25). By his oath the patriarch affirms his faith in the Lord who will bless him; he will not be indebted in any way to the foreign king for his success, lest he boast he "made Abram rich" (v. 23). "To make rich" (from *ʿāšar;* cf. Ezek 27:33) may be a Hebrew wordplay on "tenth" *(mǎʿăśēr)* indicating that his wealth is from the Lord alone, which he devotes to him. Wealth is attributed to the Lord in the Old Testament (e.g., 24:35; 31:16; Deut 8:18; 1 Sam 2:7; Prov 10:22; Eccl 5:19), but trust in riches leads to folly (Deut 8:17; Pss 49; 52:7; Prov 11:4; Eccl 5:10,13; also 1 Tim 6:17). Abram only accepts the provisions already eaten on the campaign by his retainers and the payment to his allies who had earned their part of the spoil (v. 24).

6. Covenant Promises Confirmed (15:1–21)

After Abram confessed his reliance on the Lord in response to the king of Sodom (14:22–24), the patriarch received a vision in which two divine speeches expand on the two earlier promises (12:1–3; 13:14–17) of (1) a son whose prodigious progeny (vv. 1–6) will (2) possess the land of Canaan (vv. 7–21). Abram receives righteousness through faith (v. 6), and divine oath and the rite of "covenant" *(bĕrît,* vv. 9,18) confirm the promises. The chapter moves from the oracle of the "word of the LORD" (v. 1) to a ritual slaughtering of animals, ratifying the covenant commitment (vv. 9–11,17–18). As for the significance of this chapter for the Abraham narrative as a whole, C. Westermann remarks on its importance: "Gen 15 not only stands at the center of the external structure of the Abraham narratives, but also is regarded in the history of exegesis right down to the present as the very heart of the Abraham story."[215] It provides a theological commentary on the promises foundational to the theme of the Abraham narrative. Also chap. 15 establishes the promises in a broad historical vista by relating them to the exodus and conquest (vv. 13–16). In its immediate context, the chapter depicts the patriarch as the recipient of a divine bequest, modeled on a royal gift, which follows on his encounter with the kings (chap. 14). After this revelation Abram begins to bear children (chaps. 16; 21), which inaugurates the fulfillment of the promises.

COMPOSITION. Critical scholars have puzzled over the source and date of the chapter, resulting in widely diverse solutions.[216] Due to the parallels (viewed

[215] Westermann, *Genesis 12–36,* 230.
[216] For a comprehensive review of the chapter's interpretation, see J. Ha, *Genesis 15: A Theological Compendium of Pentateuchal History,* BZAW 181 (Berlin: deGruyter, 1989); for a renewal of the source-tradition approach, see H. Mölle, *Genesis 15: eine Erzählung von den Anfängen Israels,* FB 62 (Würzburg: Echter, 1988).

as "doublets") between the two halves of the chapter (vv. 1–6; 7–21, see "Structure" below), early critical studies proposed that two independent, parallel documents (Yahwist/Elohist) were stitched together. The results of redaction and rhetorical studies, however, have supplanted this view, making it now commonplace to recognize the unity of the chapter.[217] Since chap. 15 differs from typical patriarchal narrative (chaps. 12–13; 16), the new view usually considers it a late, independent work (although admitting some connection occurred with chap. 14 in transmission).[218] The trend toward recognizing Deuteronomic language and themes in the chapter (e.g., *y-r-š*, "heir, possession," vv. 3,4,7–8) pushed the date down from the customary period of David-Solomon[219] to the seventh century or after to the exilic/early postexilic eras (e.g., "Ur of the Chaldees," v. 7).[220]

Chapter 15 fits in the flow of chaps. 13–14, as we have already shown (see Introduction, "Genesis 14," p. 44), making it unnecessary to view the chapter as independent. Shared motifs (land, descendants, blessing) and lexical allusions support the literary dependence of chaps. 14 and 15. Such lexical affinities include: *māgēn* ("shield," v. 1) and *miggēn* ("delivered," 14:20); *dān*, "judge" ("punish," NIV, v. 14) and the city *dān*, "Dan" (14:14); and *rĕkuš*, "possessions" (v. 14) and "possessions, goods" (14:16,21). The Lord is Abram's "shield" (v. 1) who "delivered" (14:14) him from the eastern kings and will deliver his descendants from Egyptian enslavement (15:14). Also, as the patriarch had overcome the kings at "Dan" (14:14) and obtained their "possessions" (14:16,21), he will "punish" the Egyptians and enrich Abram's descendants with "possessions" (15:14).[221]

---

[217] The seminal work was N. Lohfink, *Die Landverheissung als Eid: eine Studie zu Gen 15,* SBS 28 (Stuttgart: Verlag Katholisches Bibelwerk, 1967).

[218] Unlike the surrounding narratives, the core of the chapter is two speeches with only some narrative necessary to relate it to its context; also the content does not contribute to the ongoing subject of family relationships. Westermann, *Genesis 12–36,* 214; Coats, *Genesis,* 123.

[219] E.g., R. Clements proposed that the original cult legend regarding Abraham at Mamre was taken up (via the Calebites at Hebron) by the Yahwist of the Judean court who reshaped the promise of entitlement to the land as a divine validation for David's empire (*Abraham and David,* SBT 5 [London: SCM, 1967], 57–60).

[220] E.g., L. Perlitt, *Bundestheologie im Alten Testament,* WMANT 36 (Neukirchen-Vluyn: Neukirchner Verlag, 1969); E. Blum, *Die Komposition der Vätergeschichte,* WMANT 57 (Neukirchen-Vluyn: Neukirchener Verlag, 1984), 362–83; M. Anbar, "Genesis 15: A Conflation of Two Deuteronomic Narratives," *JBL* 101 (1982): 39–55; Van Seters, *Abraham in History,* 268–69; Westermann, *Genesis 12–36,* 317; E. Noort, "'Land' in the Deuteronomistic Tradition, Genesis 15: The Historical and Theological Necessity of a Diachronic Approach," in *Synchronic or Diachronic?* OtSt 34 (Leiden: Brill, 1995), 143–44; Carr, *Reading the Fractures of Genesis,* 165–66. The threats to populace and land from the seventh century to the exilic/early postexilic eras explain the need for the patriarchal story. With the demise of the nation and Deuteronomic covenant, which required obedience to the law for life in the land, the land promise was reinterpreted as an unconditional oath made to the patriarchs, who obtained righteousness through faith (v. 6; Deut 7); see Van Seters, *Abraham in History,* 269; Anbar, "Genesis 15," 54–55; Carr, *Reading the Fractures of Genesis,* 165. But threat to the land occurred in many different periods in Israel's history (J. G. McConville, *Grace in the End: A Study in Deuteronomic Theology* [Grand Rapids: Zondervan, 1993], 47).

[221] D. Sykes, "Patterns in Genesis" (Ph.D. diss., Yeshiva University, 1985), 68–70, cited in Carr, *Reading the Fractures of Genesis,* 164 and n. 32; also Sarna, *Genesis,* 112.

Additionally, the chapter does not require a first-millennium date. We cannot on the basis of Deuteronomic language and themes alone establish a date, for we do not know if chap. 15's Deuteronomic language is the result of or the source of Deuteronomic reflection.[222] Also, the priority of faith over cult in chap. 15 as the basis for righteousness (v. 6) does not demand a period when the cult's importance had diminished; the anticipation of Israel's disobedience, loss of land but assurance of return, and the tension between (Horeb) covenant and election are the theological constituents of Deuteronomy's literary and theological coherence (e.g., 9:4–6; 10:16; 29:22–29; 30:6,11–14). The assurance of the land resides in the promise made to the Fathers, which is realized by an imparted righteousness (Deut 29–30). There is no reason to insist that such an understanding of law and covenant must be a late theological development.[223] In the exile/postexilic eras the identity of the Jews was tied to the signs of Moses, for example, sabbath, circumcision, and food laws. Abraham in chap. 15 can hardly be the ideal Jew in the eyes of those returning to the land. This is shown in the later diaspora, when the rabbis, also without land or cult, depicted Abraham as the perfect law-keeper in order to idealize him *(Gen. Rab.)*. Finally, the covenant oath and animal rite (vv. 9–11,17) conform better to the land grant attested in the second millennium, which argues for an earlier date.[224]

STRUCTURE.   The chapter consists of two roughly parallel sections involving two visionary oracles (vv. 1–6; vv. 7–21); the narrator's theological declaration "Abram believed the LORD . . ." (v. 6) links the two parts. Chapter 15's narrative framework is the progression of the two divine announcements. Chapter 17 shares with chap. 15 a structure entailing two parallel panels built around five successive speeches by God (see comments on chap. 17).[225] The question of literary dependence between chaps. 15 and 17 will be taken up at chap. 17. Read together, the two chapters reveal a progression in the revelation of the covenant: the promises of land and descendants are clarified, the confirming rite of animal slaughter is carried out, and the covenant sign of circumcision is ordained.

Structural and thematic features, rather than the splicing of two literary sources, best explain the parallels and the (apparent) disjunctures between the

---

[222] Wenham, *Genesis 16–50,* 326.

[223] McConville, *Grace in the End,* esp. 46–47, 132–39.

[224] Weinfeld, "The Covenant of Grant," 184–203; D. McCarthy contends otherwise, observing that the ANE grant and treaty are not opposites but "lie along a continuum in which one leads over into the other," for both involve obligations of vassalage (*Treaty and Covenant,* AnBib 21A, 2d ed. [Rome: Biblical Institute, 1981], 87–88).

[225] S. E. McEvenue, *The Narrative Style of the Priestly Writer,* AnBib 50 (Rome: Biblical Institute, 1971), 149–55.

two halves.[226] Each panel begins with a divine self-declaration: "I am your shield" (v. 1), and "I am the LORD" (v. 7).[227] We infer from the parallel pattern between the two halves that v. 7 introduces a second theophany, matching the first ("vision," v. 1). Also divine promises introduce the two visions, the bequeath of "reward" (v. 1) and entitlement to "this land" (v. 7). The promised "reward" is a broad, vague reference, encompassing the descendants pledged in vv. 1–5 and the gift of land (v. 7) highlighted in vv. 7–21 (esp. vv. 18–21). The promise of "this land" (v. 7) clarifies the meaning of "reward" (v. 1). Another evidence of matching between the two sections is the answer, "to give you this land" (v. 7), to the initial question, "What can you give me?" (v. 2).[228] The themes of descendants (vv. 4–5) and land (v. 7) come together in the final divine message (vv. 18–21). The fulfillment of the first half requires the fulfillment of the second, for an innumerable posterity must have a great land; likewise the land promise presupposes the earlier oracle of descendants.

Exchanges between God and Abram precede the initiation of the covenant sacrifice (v. 9), at which point Abram becomes only a passive observer (vv. 9–21). The distribution of speeches reflects Abram's acquiescence: Abram speaks only once in each section (vv. 2–3,8), and the Lord speaks twice in the first vision (vv. 1,4–5) and four times in the second (vv. 7,9,13–16,18–21). Each patriarchal address requests confirmation of the Lord's intentions (vv. 2,8). The first sign is the display of the innumerable stars (v. 5) and the second the passing of the blazing torch between the animal parts (v. 17), sealing the covenant promises. God's divine speech (vv. 1,18–21), the renewed promise of seed (vv. 4,13), and the bestowal of land (vv. 7,18) envelope the account.

 I. vv. 1–6 Promise of a Son
  A v. 1 "Vision": "the word of the LORD came to him": "I am" and "reward"
   B vv. 2–3 Abram's question of the "Sovereign LORD" *(Adonay Yahweh)*
    C vv. 4–5 "the word of the LORD came to him": promise and
     sign of stars

 v. 6 Abram believes the Lord

 II. vv. 7–21 Prophecy of Land
  A′ v. 7 Vision (implied): "I am" and "this land"

---

[226] Ha, *Genesis 15,* 39–62 (esp. p. 61); although Ha partially succeeds at explaining duplicates and correctly observes some parallels between the two sections, his analysis of the macrostructure questionably "improves" the parallelism at places, e.g., moving v. 12 to head the second half (p. 61); also, by the dubious translation "usurper" (i.e., Eliezer) for בֶּן מֶשֶׁק (v. 2), he finds a parallel with the birds of prey (v. 11); but Eliezer does not have the power to impose his succession on Abram (pp. 19–21, 61; also. cp. 24:2).

[227] Typically, this kind of Hb. construction is verbless, requiring EVs to supply a verb.

[228] Ha, *Genesis 15,* 49.

B′ v. 8 Abram's question of the "Sovereign LORD" *(Adonay Yahweh)*
    D v. 9 "the LORD said to him": instructions for preparing
             covenant sacrifice
        E vv. 10–12 Abram obeys and falls asleep
   C′ vv. 13–17 "the LORD said to him": prophecy and sign of
             passing torch
         F vv. 18–21 "and the LORD . . . said": description of the land

(1) The Word of the Lord in a Vision (15:1–6)

**¹After this, the word of the LORD came to Abram in a vision:
"Do not be afraid, Abram.
I am your shield,
  your very great reward."
²But Abram said, "O Sovereign LORD, what can you give me since I remain
childless and the one who will inherit my estate is Eliezer of Damascus?" ³And
Abram said, "You have given me no children; so a servant in my household will
be my heir."
⁴Then the word of the LORD came to him: "This man will not be your heir,
but a son coming from your own body will be your heir." ⁵He took him outside
and said, "Look up at the heavens and count the stars—if indeed you can count
them." Then he said to him, "So shall your offspring be."
⁶Abram believed the LORD, and he credited it to him as righteousness.**

In this first section, two speeches declare the Lord's intentions toward
Abram (vv. 1,4–5). Interspersed are Abram's responses: first, one of question and compromise (vv. 2–3) and second, one of belief in the Lord's truthfulness (v. 6).

15:1 "After these things" (and variations) introduces a new episode or
stage in a narrative (22:1; 39:7; 40:1; 48:1; Josh 24:29; 1 Kgs 13:33; 17:17;
21:1; Ezra 7:1; Esth 2:1; 3:1); "these things" refers to the events of chap. 14,
particularly his confession of faith in Melchizedek's God (14:17–24). "The
word of the LORD" occurs only twice in Genesis, both in this story (vv. 1,4),
but it is widely found in the Old Testament (e.g., Exod 9:20–21; Deut 5:5; Isa
2:3). The phrase appears in the prevalent prophetic formula of introduction,
"the word of the LORD came" (e.g., Jer 1:2; Ezek 1:3; Jonah 1:1; Hag 1:1,3;
Zech 7:1; 11:1).²²⁹ Its appearance here presages Abram's identity as "prophet"
(20:7; cf. chap. 18; Luke 13:28).

The word translated "vision" *(maḥăzeh)* occurs only four times (v. 1; Num
24:4,16; Ezek 13:7) in contrast to the common nouns *ḥāzôn* (35x) and *ḥizzāyôn*

---

²²⁹ Either יְהוָה דְּבַר הָיָה or יְהוָה דְּבַר וַיְהִי. The expression יְהוָה דְּבַר, "the word of the
LORD," occurs in the sg. 24x and pl. 17x, according to F. Ames, "דבר," *NIDOTTE* 1.913–14; its
many variations include "hear the word of the LORD" (e.g., Isa 1:10; Hos 4:1; Amos 7:16); "the
beginning of the word of the LORD" (Hos 1:2); "the word of the LORD which came unto" (Joel 1:1;
Mic 1:1; Zeph 1:1); and "the burden (oracle) of the word of the LORD" (Zech 9:1; 12:1; Mal 1:1).

(9x).[230] Visions and dreams were common modes of revelatory speech to the patriarchs (e.g., 46:2) and prophets. The term "saw" (rāʾâ,;e.g., 1 Kgs 22:19; Isa 6:1; Ezek 1:1; Zech 1:8) or "envisioned" (ḥāzâ; Isa 1:1; Amos 1:1; Mic 1:1; Hab 1:1) often precedes a revelatory event and can introduce a prophetic collection of oracles.[231] The juxtaposition of "vision" (maḥăzeh) and "saying" (lēʾmōr; represented by quotation marks in EVs) in the Hebrew text points up that theophanies are in essence revelatory words spoken by God. Many times a theophany entails a physical phenomenon, such as a thunderstorm (e.g., Exod 19; Hab 3:8) or human form (e.g., 18:1–2; 28:13; 35:24,30; also Exod 33:23; Josh 5:13–14; Judg 6:12; 13:3,10; Isa 6:1; Jer 1:9; Ezek 1:5; Zech 1:8,13). Even in those cases, however, the specifics of a divine manifestation are rarely detailed (Ezek 1) so as to give priority to the message.

Theophanies involving a divine "appearance"[232] are frequent in the patriarchal narratives (12:7; 17:1; 18:1; 26:2,24; 35:1,7,9; 48:3; cf. Exod 3:16; 4:5; 6:3). The signature formula for prophetic revelation, "the word of the LORD," may here by itself indicate that an appearance accompanied the message. The theophanic revelation to Jacob (35:9–10) is characterized in this way in 1 Kgs 18:31.[233] The only visual representation mentioned in the chapter is the blazing smokepot (v. 17). The text does not explicitly state that Abram saw the firepot since he was in a sleeplike trance (v. 12); that the message was an audible voice can only be implied from the text (vv. 13,18). Theophanies usually involved a fearful response (e.g., 21:17; 28:17; Exod 3:6[234]); the oblique reference to "dreadful [ʾêmâ] darkness" may reflect this common response of fear (v. 12; cf. "dreadful [nôrāʾ]place," 28:17).

The message is expressed by a poetic tricolon. "Shield" (māgēn) may be the poetic glue connecting lines one and three. G. Rendsburg finds in the verse a case of janus parallelism; māgēn as "shield" parallels the prior line, and its consonants m-g-n, meaning "give" (14:20; Prov 4:9), parallel the subsequent line (i.e., reward).[235] The second and third lines can be synonymous (as NIV) in which "shield" is the cause (metonymy) for the "reward," that is, the Lord will bring about his reward (see NJB, NAB). The parallel line thus gaps the subject: "I am your shield//[I am] your very great reward." If interpreted as a synthetic parallelism, the third line adds to the thought of protection, "Your reward [will be] very great" (NIV note, NASB, NRSV, HCSB).

"Do not be afraid" (ʾal tîrāʾ) urges the desired effect, resulting from the

---

[230] J. Naude, "חזה," *NIDOTTE* 2.58–59.

[231] T. Fretheim observes that visions and dreams have the same validity as when the person is awake (e.g., 28:12–13 with 35:1,9; 48:3; 1 Kgs 3:5; 9:2 with 11:9; "Word of God," *ABD* 6.965).

[232] "Appeared" is typically וַיֵּרָא (niphal) from רָאָה ("to see").

[233] Anbar, "Genesis 15," 41.

[234] J. Niehaus, "Theophany, Theology of," *NIDOTTE* 4.1248–49.

[235] G. Rendsburg, "Notes on Genesis XV," *VT* 42 (1992): 266–68.

divine promise of reward in lines two and three. Fittingly, words of consolation are spoken first (also 21:17; 26:24; 46:3; cp. Matt 1:20; Luke 1:13,30; 2:10; Acts 18:9) since theophany usually elicits a fearful response (e.g., Exod 20:18). Elsewhere in the Old Testament there is an association of "fear not" and the survival of descendants (e.g., 21:27; 26:24; 35:17; 46:1–7; Jer 30:10–11; 46:27–28). That the same theophanic message to the childless Zechariah (Luke 1:13) appears to recall our passage (15:1) is one of several possible links between birth announcements in the Old and New Testaments.[236] This verse is the first of only three passages where the name "Abram" or "Abraham" occurs in direct address (15:1; 22:1,11). "Abram" in this context of a promised son anticipates when God calls out "Abraham" to rescue that son (22:1,11).

The Lord identifies himself in terms of his relationship to Abram ("your shield," "your . . . reward"); the security fostered by this relationship explains why Abram should take courage. A similar combination of "do not be afraid" and "I am with you" (e.g., 26:24; Isa 41:10) emphasizes divine guardianship.[237] As the echo of "who delivered" *(miggēn)* in 14:20, "shield" *(māgēn)* assures Abram that in the face of hostilities he can rest in the protection that grants him victory. The term *māgēn* is the most frequently used of several words in the Old Testament for shield; it is typically used metaphorically in the psalms (e.g., Ps 3:4; 7:11; 18:30) for God who defends his people (Deut 33:29).[238] The LXX captures the sense well, "I am covering you as a shield."[239]

"Reward" *(śākār)* often denotes a laborer's or servant's wages (e.g., 30:28,32–33; Deut 15:18). It may figuratively refer to reward for faithfulness (e.g, Num 18:31; Jer 31:16) and the victor's spoil (Isa 40:10–11; 62:11). Abram had refused the rightful booty of his victory (14:22–23), but the Lord confirms that what Abram has entrusted to him will be rewarded. The "reward" is not paid to him as compensation for his heroic deeds of chap. 14, or he would have received payment from the kings;[240] rather, the "reward" looks ahead to the gifts of descendants and land already promised. Psalm 127:3 identifies the inheritance of children as a "reward" given by the Lord. There is no sense that God is indebted to Abram;[241] rather, the Lord reassures Abram that his confidence in the divine promise is well placed.

15:2–3 Although God had enriched him already (13:2; 24:35), he prom-

---

[236] E. Conrad, "The Annunciation of Birth and the Birth of the Messiah," *CBQ* 47 (1985): 656–63.

[237] Anbar, "Genesis 15," 41.

[238] T. Longman, "מָגֵן," *NIDOTTE* 2.846–47.

[239] ἐγὼ ὑπερασπίζω σου; Wevers observes that the translator's present tense shows the Lord is a constant source of protection, whereas in the next half verse, the translator has the future ἔσται, "your reward shall be very great," showing that it is a promise (*Notes on the Greek Text,* 202).

[240] Ha, *Genesis 15,* 43.

[241] C. Van Dam, "שָׂכָר," *NIDOTTE* 3.1245.

ised to multiply Abram's assets. This prompts the patriarch to pursue with God the unfulfilled promise of a son and numerous descendants. His many possessions are of little consequence if there is no family heir. Cautiously, the patriarch addresses God and employs the name "Sovereign LORD" (*'ădōnay yahweh;* vv. 2,8). This divine name is rare in the Pentateuch (Deut 3:24; 9:26) but common among the prophets, especially Isaiah and Ezekiel. It provides a verbal link with the Davidic covenant in 2 Sam 7, where "Sovereign LORD" occurs seven times (vv. 18,19,20,22,28,29). Moses and others use the same form of address when making special appeal for deliverance (e.g., Deut 9:26; Josh 7:7; Judg 16:28).

Since there is no heir ("childless," v. 2), Abram contemplates designating the servant Eliezer of Damascus as his heir (on Arameans/Damascus, see comments on 14:15; Introduction: "Anachronisms," and 10:22, vol. 1A, pp. 461–62). "Childless" (*'ărîrî)*occurs in only four verses where, excepting 15:2, it is indicative of divine punishment (Lev 20:21–22; Jer 22:30). The absence of a fertility rite to reverse barrenness in the passage, as is found in Ugaritic texts, may reflect Abram's reliance on God's will.[242] He places the ultimate responsibility of Sarai's barrenness on the shoulders of the Lord (v. 3), who alone can remedy his problem.

Chapter 15 is the only place where Eliezer is referred to, at least by name (cp. comments on 24:2); this may be due to the wordplay between his name (*'ĕlî'ezer)* and "children" (*zera')* in v. 3 (and perhaps "childless," *'ărîrî).* The word "children" (*zr')* shares in the (inverted) consonants of "Eliezer" (*'zr),* implying that since God has yet to provide *zera',* then Abram must provide an "Eliezer" (i.e., heir) from his household. Although Abram may not have envisioned the adoption of Eliezer as his son in the strict sense, there is in and outside the Bible (Prov 17:2; Nuzi and Larsa texts) evidence for the practice of handing down an inheritance to a servant.[243]

The description of Eliezer as a household servant who was associated with Damascus (vv. 2–3) is another lexical reminder of Abram's defeat of Kedorlaomer (chap. 14). The parallel references to "my estate//my household" (*ben mešeq bêtî//ben bêtî)* in vv. 2b,3b recall the 318 servants recruited from the ranks of those "born in his household" (*yĕlîdê bêtô,* 14:14; 17:23). Also mention of "Damascus" (*dammeśeq)* and the sound play *mešeq* ("the one who will inherit," NIV) in v. 2 recall the extent of Abram's victorious pursuit beyond "Damascus" (14:15).[244]

The meaning of *mešeq* is obscure, making the translation of the phrase *ûben*

---

[242] V. Hamilton, "עֲרִירִי," *NIDOTTE* 3.534–35.

[243] See discussion in M. Selman, "Comparative Customs and the Patriarchal Age," in *Essays on the Patriarchal Narratives,* 114,136.

[244] Sailhamer also notes that 318 (14:14) is the numerical equivalent of the sum of the letters in the name "Eliezer" ("Genesis," 125, 131–32).

mešeq bêtî notoriously difficult ("the one who will inherit my estate," NIV).[245]
Further complicating the interpretation is the following phrase, "Eliezer of
Damascus" *(dammešeq 'ĕlî'ezer),* which is usually construed as a gloss
explaining *mešeq.*[246] The LXX transliterates *mešeq* as the personal name of Eliezer's slave-mother, "but the son of Masek, my domestic female slave"[247];
other witnesses interpreted *mešeq* as defining Eliezer's role as "cupbearer, provider, or manager" (e.g., Aquila, Theod., *Tgs. Onq, Ps.-J.,* Vg.).[248] Modern
scholars also have stumbled at the meaning of *ben mešeq;* among the major
proposals are: (1) "usurper" (from *šqq,* "to attack");[249] (2) an early name for
Damascus (thus, "one from *mešeq"* = Damascus), whose name is updated by
the following gloss; and (3) "servant or cupbearer" followed by the Aramaic
gloss, *dammešeq,* which means the same thing.[250]

The common translation of *mešeq* among EVs is "heir" (or its equivalent),
importing the sense of "possessor" from the equally-dubious term *mimšāq*
("place possessed," Zeph 2:9).[251] The translation "heir" derives ultimately
from the parallel description in v. 3:

"heir of my house *[ben mešeq bêtî]* who is Eliezer of Damascus" (v. 2)
"a son of my household as my heir *[ben bêtî yôrēš 'ōtî]*" (v. 3)[252]

At least we can say that the present form of the text possesses a wordplay
between *mešeq* ("heir") and *dammešeq* ("Damascus") which plays up that the
inheritance will go to an alien (cp. Jer 49:1).

15:4–5 The Lord answers by telling Abram in effect to wait on the birth of
his own child (v. 4); such is the substance of faith, waiting on God to "make
good" on his promises. Whatever dim expectation of Sarai's pregnancy there
may have been soon flickered and died. Therefore, since Sarai is not specifically named as the birth mother, the offer of Hagar the Egyptian servant after
waiting some time (16:1–4) seemed to comply with the vision. Later the Lord
appears again to inform Abram that the impossible, the pregnancy of the aging
Sarai, will yet happen (17:19).

---

[245] For more on the ancient witnesses, see Skinner, *Genesis,* 278–79.

[246] Even the construction דַּמֶּשֶׂק אֱלִיעֶזֶר ("Eliezer of Damascus") is unusual.

[247] ὁ δὲ υἱὸς Μασεκ τῆς οἰκογενοῦς μου οὗτος Δαμασκὸς Ελιεζερ. Wevers speculates
that the translator presents a female servant as an analogue to Sarai's handmaiden Hagar, who provides a son (*Notes on the Greek Text,* 203)

[248] The traditional reading was the alternative spelling *mašqeh,* "cupbearer," W. Propp, "Eliezer," *ABD* 2.462;

[249] Cp. *maššaq* (Isa 33:4), first proposed by L. A. Snijders, followed by Ha, *Genesis 15,* 19.

[250] For an overview of modern attempts, see Hamilton, *Genesis Chapters 1–17,* 420–22, and
Sarna, *Genesis,* 382–83.

[251] BDB 606.

[252] (v. 2b) וּבֶן מֶשֶׁק בֵּיתִי הוּא דַּמֶּשֶׂק אֱלִיעֶזֶר
(v. 3b) וְהִנֵּה בֶן בֵּיתִי יוֹרֵשׁ אֹתִי

Not only will Abram father a child, but he will be the patriarch of multitudes, as numerous as the stars (v. 5). Another possible wordplay occurs between vv. 4 and 5: "coming *[yēṣēʾ]* from your own body" (v. 4) and "took *[wayyôṣēʾ]* him outside" (v. 5). The Lord instructs him to view the night sky *(šāmayĕmâ),* which the patriarch has already acknowledged as the domain of *Yahweh El Elyon,* "Creator of heaven *[šāmayim]* and earth" (14:22). Now Abram must leave the future to the God he has confessed. It is simply not feasible that a person can "count" *(sāpar)* the stars, but God can number and name them (Ps 147:4; Isa 40:26). This visual demonstration of the stars corresponds to the impossible challenge to "count *[mānâ]* the dust" of the land (13:16). Repetition of the star metaphor occurs for Abram at Moriah (22:17) and for Isaac (26:4), recalled by Moses at Sinai (Exod 32:13) and declared fulfilled by Israel at Moab (Deut 1:10; 10:22; 28:62; Neh 9:23). This patriarchal promise is further extended to the founding of the Davidic monarchy (Jer 33:22; 1 Chr 27:23 with Exod 32:13).

15:6 The narration describes Abram's response as belief (trust) in the Lord. The Hebrew construction translated "believed" *(heʾĕmin + bĕ* prep.) means to place trust in someone with confidence (e.g., Exod 19:9; 1 Sam 27:12). The general idea is reliance, and the orientation of the person's trust is the future. The LXX renders the Hebrew by *episteusen,* "[Abram] believed." There is no exact equivalent in the Hebrew for Greek's *pistis* ("faith") and *pisteuō* ("believe"), but this verbal form *(hiphil)* of the word *ʾāman* comes closest.[253] Here Abram's trust is placed in the Lord *(bĕyhwh),* whom he believes will carry out his promise (cp. Exod 14:31; Jonah 3:5). The text emphasizes that Abram entrusted his future to what God would do for him as opposed to what he could do for himself to obtain the promises.

Recognition of Abram's faith at this point in the story, however, should not be taken as the initiation of his faith. Abram had already responded earlier to the call and promise of God's word (12:1–3). Just as the covenant ritual of chap. 15 does not initiate God's commitment but formally ratifies it, so the narration's affirmation of Abram's faith in v. 6 declares the faith Abram had exercised from the outset. The verbal construction "believed" (v. 6) and reference to a past event at Ur (v. 7) substantiate that Abram already exhibited faith. The syntax of the verb *wĕheʾĕmin* diverts from the typical pattern found in past tense narrative. The force of the construction conveys an ongoing faith repeated from the past.[254] The author is editorializing on the events reported, not including

---

[253] See the word group in R. Moberly, "אמן," *NIDOTTE* 1.427–33; A. Jepsen, "אָמַן," *TDOT* 1.292–323; O. Michel, "Faith πίστις," *NIDNTT* 1.593–605; and J. Healey, "Faith, Old Testament," *ABD* 2.744–49.

[254] וְהֶאֱמִן ("believed") is the perfect verb plus *wāw;* the preceding and following verbs in the passage are the customary form of an imperfect verb plus *wāw* consecutive. See GKC §112ss and Wenham, *Genesis 1–15,* 324, 329.

Abram's faith in the chain of events as a consequence of the theophanic message.[255] The point of the author is that Abram continued to believe in the Lord. In addition, reference to the Lord's appearance to Abram at Ur (v. 7) implies an antecedent relationship (cp. Acts 7:2–4).

As a consequence of Abram's belief, the Lord "credited *[ḥāšab]*it," that is, his faith, as "righteousness" *(ṣĕdāqâ).*[256] The term "credited" (*ḥāšab*, NIV, HCSB), also translated "reckoned" (NASB, NRSV, NJB, NJPS) or "counted" (ESV, NLT[2], JPSV), means "to assign . . . value"[257]; in this case the Lord assigns Abram's faith the value of righteousness. It is striking that in the semantic field of "counting, reckoning" vv. 5–6 include two of its terms: *sāpar,*"counting" the stars (2x, v. 5) and *ḥāšab,* "valuating" Abram's faith (v. 6). In the parallel metaphor of 13:16, a third term occurs, *mānâ,* "counting" the dust of the earth. The literary association of counting the stars explains the appearance of the counting term *ḥāšab,* "credited." Abram believed in the "counting" promises of 13:16 and 15:4–5 and conversely the Lord "counted" his faith.

The precise meanings of the terms in the word group *ṣ-d-q* ("to be righteous, just") is disputed since they have a broad range of nuances; generally, the word group is associated with behavior that conforms to a standard,[258] hence "right standing" *(ṣĕdāqâ;* e.g., Gen 38:26), or the adjudication of behavior, that is, to declare righteous (*hiṣdîq;* e.g., Deut 25:1). The person or deity whose behavior conforms to the standard is "in the right" (*ṣaddîq;* Exod 9:27; 2 Kgs 10:9; Isa 41:2). Thus the person who acts rightly is also one who is esteemed as righteous (e.g., Noah, 6:9; 7:1, see vol. 1A, pp. 357–58, 371). Genesis 18:22–33 illustrates the Lord's evaluation of wicked or righteous *(ṣĕdāqâ)* behavior among the inhabitants of Sodom and Gomorrah (cp. Deut 9:4–6). In the Old Testament the setting may be forensic, but more often the context concerns behavior that conforms to covenant,[259] although this standard is usually only implied. Whether implied or stated (e.g., the law), the standard was determined ultimately by the Lord (e.g., Pss 7:9; 9:8[9]), not custom alone and not solely relative to circumstances. Among the chief meanings of *ṣdq* is the idea of

---

[255] Westermann, *Genesis 12–36,* 213; Sailhamer, "Genesis," 132; and Ross, *Creation and Blessing,* 309.

[256] The indefinite subject of וַיַּחְשְׁבֶהָ ("and he credited it") can refer to "Abram" or "the LORD"; reading the verse as chiasmus indicates that the subject is the Lord: "He [Abram] believed the LORD//he (the LORD) counted . . ." The LXX's passive rendering ἐλογίσθη ("it was counted") clears up the ambiguity, referring to Abram's believing God (see Wevers, *Notes on the Greek Text,* 206).

[257] J. Hartley, "חשׁב," *NIDOTTE* 2.305–6.

[258] D. Reimer, "צדק," *NIDOTTE* 3.744–69.

[259] E. Achtemeier, "Righteousness in the OT," *IDB* 4.80–85; D. Hill, *Greek Words and Their Meanings: Studies in the Semantics of Soteriological Terms* (Cambridge: University Press, 1967); J. Ziesler, *The Meaning of Righteousness in Paul* (Cambridge: University Press, 1972); and J. J. Scullion, "Righteousness (OT)," *ABD* 5.724–36.

relational (covenant) loyalty shown either by God (e.g., Ps 118:1–5,19,29) or human beings (e.g., 1 Sam 24:17; Hab 2:4). Related to this concept is the idea of salvation or victory, which is achieved by the Lord in behalf of the psalmist (e.g., Ps 71:2,15) or Israel (e.g., Isa 51:5–6) because the Lord is acting in faithfulness to his covenant pledge of deliverance. But the righteousness that Abram receives is not due to conformity to a covenant standard. Rather, this righteousness is extrinsic to Abram and is solely bequeathed by God's gracious declaration.[260]

For the New Testament interpretation of this verse (Rom 4:3; Gal 3:6; Jas 2:23), see the following excursus.

Excursus: Faith and Obedience

In the chronology of events in Genesis 15, there is no meritorious conduct that can be attributed to Abram. Only after the divine promise (vv. 4–5) does he carry out the Lord's instructions regarding the sacrifice (v. 10). The Lord had graciously bestowed a covenant (12:1–3; 13:15–16; 15:18) that promised a family for the patriarch in the face of all contradictory fact. Abram can do nothing to enter into the promise; he can only rely on the Lord. This benevolence is not the reaction of God to Abram's faith as though it obtained the covenant; instead, Abram believed that God would indeed give him the family of descendants as promised. Treatment of Abram's faith in 15:6 as an "act" like that of conformity to the law or a heroic deed is unfounded.[261] In those passages where $\bar{s}\bar{e}d\bar{a}q\hat{a}$ + $l\bar{e}$ occur (Deut 6:25; 24:13; Ps 106:30–31), there is reference to specific actions undertaken, whereas 15:6 stands alone, having no attachment to a specific action taken by Abram. To say that Abram's affirmation in response to God's promise constitutes a meritorious deed of the same order confuses the matter.

According to Jewish tradition, Abraham was found faithful in undergoing ten divine tests that secured for him the covenant (e.g., *Jub.* 19:2–3,8; *m. 'Abot* 5:3). Abraham's "faithfulness" (Gk. *pistos*) in these deeds and his exemplary conduct were emphasized as the explanation for his reward (e.g., *4 Ezra* 9:7; 13:23; *Sir* 44:19–21; *Wis* 10:5; *Jub.* 6:19; 23:10; *2 Bar.* 57:2; *Mek.*, Exod 14:15). First Maccabees 2:51–52 illustrates this persuasion, where Gen 15:6 and the offering of Isaac in Genesis 22 are viewed together: "Remember the deeds *[ta erga]* of the ancestors, which they did in their generations; and you will receive great honor and an everlasting name. Was not Abraham found faithful *[pistos]* when tested, and it was reckoned *[elogisthē]* to him as righteousness *[dikaiosunēn]?"* (NRSV).

The apostle James also connects the two passages (Gen 15:6; chap. 22), but for him Abraham's obedience is not the meritorious cause for the covenant. Rather, James shows that the patriarch's works corroborate his saving faith (2:21–24). Genesis 15:6 is also significant in the apostle Paul's soteriology (Rom

---

[260] See D. A. Carson, "The Vindication of Imputation: On Fields of Discourse and Semantic Fields," in *Justification: What's at Stake in the Current Debates* (Downers Grove: InterVarsity, 2004), 46–78.

[261] Contra Reimer, "צדק," 753–54, 768.

4:3; Gal 3:6). By appealing to Abraham's faith, the apostle proves in Romans that Abraham is the spiritual progenitor of both Jews and Gentiles (4:1–25). The righteousness of God (3:21–26), that is, acceptance by God, comes by a faith response, not works.[262] He illustrates this by explaining how the free gift of righteousness (Rom 5:17) was received through Abraham's faith *(pistis)*, not earned by human works *(ergon;* 4:1–5). Paul quotes Gen 15:6 (LXX) in 4:3 as evidence that the patriarch himself received justification by believing *(pisteuō),* not working *(ergazomai;* 4:4–5).

Whereas the Jewish emphasis centers on Abraham's faithfulness as the means of entrance into the covenant community, Paul argues that Abraham was among "the wicked" *(ton asebē;* 4:5), outside the covenant family, when he believed the Lord and was granted righteousness *(dikaiosunē;* 4:3,5).[263] Paul, however, would not have opposed the Jews, who contended that Abraham's works had their source in grace; for this reason Paul spoke of the "obedience of faith" (Rom 1:5; 16:26) by which he meant loyalty to the service of Christ that has its source in faith.[264] But righteousness is not obtained by human endeavors, whether it was by Jewish "works" of the law[265] or the human works of the Gentiles. It is faith in Jesus Christ whereby believers are credited *(elogisthē)* with righteousness before God.

(2) Covenant Promise and Prophecy (15:7–21)

[7]He also said to him, "I am the LORD, who brought you out of Ur of the Chaldeans to give you this land to take possession of it."

[8]But Abram said, "O Sovereign LORD, how can I know that I will gain possession of it?"

[9]So the LORD said to him, "Bring me a heifer, a goat and a ram, each three years old, along with a dove and a young pigeon."

[10]Abram brought all these to him, cut them in two and arranged the halves opposite each other; the birds, however, he did not cut in half. [11]Then birds of prey came down on the carcasses, but Abram drove them away.

[12]As the sun was setting, Abram fell into a deep sleep, and a thick and dreadful darkness came over him. [13]Then the LORD said to him, "Know for certain that your descendants will be strangers in a country not their own, and they will be enslaved and mistreated four hundred years. [14]But I will punish the nation they serve as slaves, and afterward they will come out with great possessions. [15]You, however, will go to your fathers in peace and be buried at a good old age. [16]In the fourth generation your descendants will come back here, for the sin of

---

[262] Ziesler, *Righteousness,* 184–85.

[263] T. Schreiner shows that Paul here views Abraham "godless" (ἀσεβῆ) before the call of 12:1–3, which is formally ratified in chap. 15 (*Romans,* ECNT [Grand Rapids: Baker, 1998], 216–17).

[264] I thank my colleague Frank Thielman for pointing this out; see J. Fitzmyer, *Romans,* AB (New York: Doubleday, 1993), 237–38.

[265] Fitzmyer (ibid., 372) contends that the apostle means "deeds (of the law)," i.e., Jewish law, whereas Schreiner (*Romans,* 218) argues that "works" in a fundamental sense is in view.

the Amorites has not yet reached its full measure." ¹⁷When the sun had set and darkness had fallen, a smoking firepot with a blazing torch appeared and passed between the pieces. ¹⁸On that day the LORD made a covenant with Abram and said, "To your descendants I give this land, from the river of Egypt to the great river, the Euphrates— ¹⁹the land of the Kenites, Kenizzites, Kadmonites, ²⁰Hittites, Perizzites, Rephaites, ²¹Amorites, Canaanites, Girgashites and Jebusites."

This second section consists of four divine speeches (vv. 7,9,13–16,18–21) involving the land and seed promises confirmed by a divine covenant. Interspersed between the speeches are Abram's two responses (vv. 8,10–12) and the covenant ceremony itself (v. 17).

15:7 The historical prologue to the covenant names the parties of the covenant and remembers God's beneficence toward Abram. This third occurrence of *yāṣā'* ("brought out") in the chapter recalls the two appearances of the verb in vv. 4–5 (*yēṣē'*, "coming," v. 4; "took [him] outside," *yôṣē'*, v. 5), disclosing the promise of a son and descendants. By this key wording the author ties the the two passages together: just as God had faithfully brought him to Canaan, he will also satisfy the promise of offspring. Reference to God's prior relationship with Abram at Ur shows that the ensuing covenant in chap. 15 assumed this event. (For the discussion of "Ur of the Chaldeans," see comments at 11:31.) This succinctly stated allusion to Abram's exodus prefigures the experience of Israel's return to the land. The similar wording of the divine self-identification ("I am") appears in Exod 20:2 (//Deut 5:6) pertaining to the nation's deliverance from Egyptian bondage (cf. Isa 41:8–10; 51:1–2).

15:8 Abram asks the Lord for confirmation of the land promise through tangible evidence of it (cp. v. 2).[266] The Lord responds by the presentation of a formal treaty with the passing of the torch (v. 17), and later he similarly answers Moses at the burning bush by a "sign" (Exod 3:11–12).

15:9 Three of the five animals requested for the ritual slaughter are ones typically prescribed for Israel's sacrificial rituals, but there are significant differences. Three times in v. 9 (in the Hb. text), once at each naming of the first three animals, the animal's age of "three years old" occurs, perhaps indicating the optimum age of value. Israel's practice, however, was the sacrifice of one-year-olds that were "without defect" (e.g., Exod 29:38; Lev 1:3; 9:3); also the term here for "young pigeon" *(gôzāl)* is not the customary word describing the bird in Israel's ritual *(ben/běnē yônâ, e.g., Lev 1:14; 12:6).*

The "heifer" *('eglâ)* was used only on special occasions: the appointment of David (1 Sam 16:2) and a purification rite pertaining to murder (Deut 21:1–9). It is the animal mentioned in the similar ceremony described in Jer 34:18–19.

---

[266] Similar Hb. constructions, calling for a sign, occur in 24:14; 42:33; Exod 7:17; 33:16 (Ha, *Genesis 15*, p. 49 and n. 19).

The animal was young but old enough to be producing milk, thus a "young cow" (Isa 7:21–22).[267] The "goat" (*ʿēz*) was a common animal that had diverse domestic uses (e.g., 27:9,16; 30:35; 32:14[15]; 38:20; 1 Sam 19:13). When appropriated for sacrifice, it was one of two permitted animals for the Passover (Exod 12:5) and was required for various sacrifices including the Day of Atonement (Lev 16:5).[268] Also the "ram" (*ʾayil*), a male sheep, was an important cultic animal (22:13), used in the ordination of the priests (Exod 29:1; Lev 8:18; 9:2) and other sacrifices including guilt offerings (Lev 5:15–18,25) and the Day of Atonement (Lev 16:3,5). The "turtledove" (*tōr,* "dove," NIV) was widely utilized in offerings (e.g., Lev 1:14; 5:7) and purification rites (Lev 12:6; 14:22; 15:14; cp. Luke 2:24), but the "young-pigeon" (*gôzāl*) is a rare term, occurring elsewhere only in Deut 32:11, where it is the young of a mother eagle.[269]

15:10–11 The repetition of the verb "take" (*lāqaḥ,* NIV "bring") from v. 9 describes Abram's prompt obedience (v. 10): "then he took [*wayyiqaḥ,* NIV "brought"] all these" (cp. 12:1,4). Abram "divided" in two the animals (*bātar,* NIV "cut in two"),[270] except the "birds" (*ṣippôr)* due to their size (Lev 1:17),[271] and he arranged their parts facing one another forming a passageway between the "pieces" (*beter,* NIV "halves"). No specific directions for the dissecting and pairing of parts are given, inferring that the patriarch's zeal outpaces the command.[272]

The word "pieces" (*beter*) appears in the similar ritual described in Jer 34:18–19. Often scholars appropriate the rite of Jeremiah 34 as the template for explaining the practice in Genesis 15.[273] Two wordplays describe the practice in Jeremiah. A calf was "cut" (*kārat,* v. 18) into pieces, formalizing a covenant that was "cut" ("made," NIV, i.e., "to cut a covenant," *kārat běrît*) between God and the leadership of Judah regarding the freeing of Hebrew slaves. Because they acted treacherously, the people are deemed "transgressors" (*hāʿōběrîm,* NIV "the men who have violated," v. 18) who had "walked between" (*hāʿōběrîm,* v. 18) the parts signifying acceptance of the sanctions of transgressing the covenant. The threat of death, like the gruesome results of the slaughtered calf, awaited them (v. 18). The Lord threatens that "the birds [*ʿôp]* of the air" will feast on the violaters' dead flesh (v. 20). This imprecatory aspect of the symbolic slaying has parallels with Assyrian and Aramaic vassal treaties

---

[267] D. Wright, "Heifer," *ABD* 3.114–15.

[268] J. Vancil, "Goat, Goatherd," *ABD* 2.1040–41.

[269] N. Kiuchi, "גּוֹזָל," *NIDOTTE* 1.834.

[270] As a verb it appears only here (2x); the noun occurs here and in Jer 34:18,19; Song 2:17.

[271] צִפּוֹר is used of "birds" in general (Gen 7:14) and is the bird in the ritual cleansing of the leper (Lev 14); for more see N. Kiuchi, "צִפּוֹר," *NIDOTTE* 3.837.

[272] Westermann, *Genesis 12–36,* 225, "The execution goes beyond the commission."

[273] E.g., ibid., 228–29.

of the first millennium. For this reason Genesis 15 is usually dated at the time of Jeremiah or later.

There are, however, significant differences between the practices in the patriarchal account and Jeremiah that make doubtful this conclusion. Although the Jeremiah passage involves the slaughter of a calf and mentions birds, the practice in chap. 15 calls for several animals. Also the description of the ritual cleaving in 15:10 uses the term *bātar* (NIV "cut in two") instead of Jeremiah's word *kārat* (NIV "made") occurring in the idiomatic expression "cut a covenant" (34:18). Also, importantly, the threat of curse for failure to observe the covenant is not explicit in chap. 15.[274] When read in light of Jeremiah 34's imprecatory character, it may be implied that God submits to his own self-imprecation by passing through the parts. It is difficult, however, to reconcile this idea of God theologically and impossible to explain how the imprecation could be carried out. More promising are the examples of second-millennium texts from Alalakh involving an oath by a superior that is confirmed by slaying a lamb or sheep.[275] If the Abram incident compares to these promissory oaths, Genesis describes a covenant pledge undertaken by God that is formally ratified by animal slaughter (cp. Exod 24:3–8).

There are still significant features of Genesis 15 that diverge from the oath rituals at Alalakh. The number and sort of animals and the halving procedure of chap. 15 have no parallel yet found in the ancient Near East. Although the rite of chap. 15 ostensibly affirms the covenant oath, the prophecy that follows (vv. 13–16) hints at an emblematic significance attached to the rite's peculiarities.[276] From hindsight we know that the prophecy previews Israel's Egyptian bondage, exodus, and conquest. Most agree that the smoking firepot and burning torch represent the Lord, a picture corresponding to the pillar of cloud and pillar of fire indicating the presence of God in the wilderness (e.g., Exod 13:21–22). The "birds of prey" Abram disperses indicate a threat against the slaughtered animals. "Birds of prey" (*ʿayiṭ*) differ from the general terms for "birds" (*ṣippôr*, v. 10; *ʿôp*, Jer 34:20) by their ravenous character (Isa 18:6; Jer 12:9) and are unclean.[277] In the context of the prophecy (vv. 13–16), the animal portions represent Abram's descendants, and the birds of prey are the nation

---

[274] McCarthy (*Treaty and Covenant,* 93–96, 255, n. 22), following E. Bickerman, agrees that the slaying of the animal is not necessarily imprecatory, although curse is found in Jer 34:18 and some first-millennium Assyrian treaties; the rite of animal slaughter expressed the power of the life force shared by the victim and the covenanter that is released by the shedding of the animal.

[275] G. Hasel, "The Meaning of the Animal Rite in Genesis 15," *JSOT* 19 (1981): 61–78; supported in the study of R. S. Hess, "The Slaughter of the Animals in Genesis 15," in *He Swore an Oath: Biblical Themes from Genesis 12–50* (Cambridge: Tyndale, 1993), 55–65.

[276] G. Wenham, "The Symbolism of the Animal Rite in Genesis 15: A Response to G. F. Hasel," *JSOT* 19 (1981): 61–78, *JSOT* 22 (1982): 134–37.

[277] Although the word הָעַיִט ("birds of prey") does not occur in the description of unclean birds (Lev 11:13–19; Deut 14:12–18), the birds are scavengers.

(Egypt) that enslaves them. The appearance of Abram as defender of the animal portions may refer to his obedient piety that confirmed his loyalty and ensured Israel's future (e.g., 22:16–18) or his intercessory function as prophet (e.g., 18:16–33; 20:7,17). Since Abram does not walk through the pieces, he is not under obligation to the Lord to realize the promises. By the passing of the firepot through the severed pieces, the Lord's presence with enslaved Israel symbolically ensures the preservation and deliverance of Abram's descendants.

15:12 The setting of the sun (v. 12) provides an ominous darkness for the prophecy and also a conducive setting for the brightness of the firepot and fiery torch (v. 17). Abram's trance is described as a "deep sleep" *(tardēmâ),* the same slumber that befell Adam (2:21). The term is associated with divine revelations in dreams and visions (Job 4:13; 33:15; Isa 29:10); here this visionary "deep sleep" is imposed by the Lord (cf. 2:21; 1 Sam 26:12).

Verse 12 presents a second night vision, counting the "day" of the covenant (v. 18) from sunset (vv. 1–5) to sunset (vv. 12–17).[278] The duplication of a night setting, however, may be for a rhetorical effect, retarding the narration by repeating the setting a second time and highlighting the prophecy and torch (vv. 12,17). The same rhetorical effect is achieved in the flood narrative (see vol. 1A, p. 355, n. 9). "Dreadful" *(ʾêmâ)* describes the "darkness" (v. 12), providing the appropriate atmosphere for the gloomy forecast of enslavement for his descendants (v. 14). The occurrence of "dreadful" befits the prophecy by anticipating the same reaction of the nations (vv. 16,19–21) to the approaching Israelites (e.g., Exod 15:16; 23:27; Josh 2:9).

15:13–14 The divine word, "Know for certain" *(yādōaʿ tēdaʿ;* v. 13), recalls Abram's earlier question, "How can I know *[ʾēdaʿ]* that I will gain possession of it?" (v. 8). By this prophecy, the Lord alleviates Abram's anxiety about the land. It describes in miniature the essential events in the life of his descendants Israel as depicted in the Pentateuch, anticipating the conquest of Canaan. A skeletal chronology provides the framework for understanding the relationship of the events foretold. Verse 13 prophesies the alien status ("strangers," *gēr)* of his descendants, who experience a four-hundred-year period of servitude in a foreign land.[279] Abram's own status as an "alien" in Canaan (23:4) who also resided at times outside the land (12:10–13:1; chap. 20) establishes a continuum between him and his offspring (see commentary Introduction: "Motifs Alienation/Separation"). Although it is not explained in the prophecy how the Hebrews become enslaved, the term "alien" expects a migration, such as the descent of Jacob (chaps. 37–50). The verbal form "sojourn" *(gûr)* describes Abram's descent into Egypt (12:10; cf. also 20:1;

[278] Ha, *Genesis 15,* 51, 55.
[279] On the question of 430 yrs. given in Exod 12:40–41, see commentary Introduction "Patriarchs in Historical Context."

21:34) and that of Jacob's residence at Goshen (47:4). The words "enslaved" *('bd)* and "mistreated" *('nh)* occur in the prologue to Exodus (1:11–14), describing his descendants' suffering.[280]

The discouraging future projected for his family, however, results in a surprising turnaround (v. 14). "But also the nation" begins the verse in the Hebrew text, contrasting Israel's victory over the oppressing nation with its servitude (v. 13). The first action is God's retribution ("I will punish") against the nation for its mistreatment of Abram's descendants (cf. "whoever curses you I will curse," 12:3). "And afterward" *(wĕ'aḥărê kēn)* introduces the next stage: the slaves are freed and enriched "with great possessions" *(birkuš).* Again there is an implied linkage between the patriarch's experience in Egypt (12:10–13:1) and that of his descendants. After the plague in Pharaoh's house, he expelled Abram, but he went away wealthy due to the gifts of the king (12:16,19–20). Israel will have the similar experience during the exodus after the ten plagues (Exod 3:21–22; 11:2–3; 12:35–36).

"Come out with many possessions" recalls the words "came out"/"set out" *(yāṣā')* and "possession" *(rĕkûš),* which describe Abram's departure for Canaan in 12:5. "Possessions" also appears in the description of Abram and Lot's wealth received from Pharaoh. Condemnation against Pharaoh for his mistreatment of Sarai (12:17) parallels Egypt's future enslavement of Israel (15:13). Abram can take comfort in knowing that in the same way the Lord provided for him personally in hostile Egypt, he will provide for the patriarch's descendants.

15:15–16 Verse 15 shifts attention back to Abram himself ("You, however"); unlike his posterity, he will experience a peaceful death in old age, presumably in the land of Canaan (25:8–9; cp. 2 Chr 34:28; also Deut 34:7; Judg 8:32; 1 Chr 29:28). The patriarchs all died in old age and in prosperity (Isaac, 35:29; Jacob, 43:27; 44:20; 49:33; Joseph, 50:22,26), which was an expression of divine favor (Ps 126:6); however, it is only said of Abram that he will die "in peace" *(bĕšālôm).*

After alleviating any concerns Abram may have had about his own safety, the Lord returns to the subject of Abram's offspring (v. 16). They will return to the land after the period of servitude in the "fourth generation." The Hebrew term *hēnnâ* occurs twice, translated "here" *(hēnnâ)* and "not yet" *('ad hēnnâ),* specifying place and time. Hebrew *dôr* ("generation") denotes a span of time, but not necessarily the same fixed number of years. The adult male population in Israel was counted at the age of twenty (e.g., Exod 38:26; Lev 27:3; Num 1:3; 14:29; 26:2; Ezra 3:28), yet forty years amounts to the wilderness "generation" (e.g., Num 32:13; 2 Kgs 10:30; 15:12; Ps 95:10).[281] The reference to

---

[280] Ha, *Genesis 15,* 125.
[281] D. N. Freedman and J. Lundbom, "רֹוד *dôr,*" *TDOT* 3.174.

"four hundred years" (v. 13) suggests that "generation" should also equate to a hundred years. This is supported by Abram's first generation (Isaac) who was born after a hundred years (21:5). "Fourth generation," however, may be only a stereotypical expression, conveying the idea of completeness; the duration of a father's life would not normally extend to four generations. The influence of a parent affected the "third and fourth generation" (e.g., Exod 20:5; Num 14:18), and four generations established a ruling dynasty (2 Kgs 10:30; 15:12).

The last clause of the verse explains why God was not giving them the land right away: the wickedness of the Amorites has not "reached its full measure" (v. 16b). "Amorites" fluctuates in meaning either designating the whole of Canaan's populations (v. 16; Amos 2:10) or one of many diverse groups inhabiting the land (v. 21; see vol. 1A, pp. 446, 456). The prophecy implies that the returning Hebrews will be instrumental in God dealing with the sin of the Amorites.[282] The reference to the "fourth generation" may be a double entendre; the notion of a completed exile converges with the idea of the Amorites' complete moral decay.[283] The extent of Amorite depravity is condemned in Mosaic legislation (Lev 18:24–25; 20:22–24; Deut 18:12; cf. 1 Kgs 14:24; 21:26; 2 Kgs 21:11) and illustrated by the violence and sensuality of their religious myths (e.g., Baal cycle from Ugarit). By delaying his judgment against the Amorites, the Lord expresses forbearance toward the nations. Retribution against their sins only at "its full measure" attests that judgment is neither capricious nor unwarranted (cf. 18:20–25). Nevertheless, divine temperance toward their iniquity reaches an appropriate point of intolerance.

15:17 The "smoking firepot with a blazing torch" symbolized the presence of God as it passed between the animal parts. Among the many different Hebrew words for oven/furnace is "firepot" *(tannûr)*, which was used for baking bread (Lev 26:26) and roasting grain for sacrifice (Lev 2:14; 7:9).[284] A metaphorical use of "furnace" *(tannûr)* depicts divine judgment against Israel's enemies (e.g., Isa 31:9; Ps 21:9[10]). "Smoke" *('āšān)* attends divine theophanies (e.g., Isa 6:4), functioning as a veil, and may also signify the Lord's wrath (2 Sam 22:9 = Ps 18:9). God's appearance at Sinai (Exod 19:18) brings together the four elements of 15:17: smoke *('āšān),* furnace *(kibšān),* fire *('ēš),* and lightning *(lappîd* at Exod 20:18). There is an unmistakable association between the events. A "torch" *(lappîd)* appears in prophetic descriptions of the awesome and eerie presence of God (cp. Ezek 1:13; Dan 10:6), and it pictures destruction (cp. Judg 15:5 with Zech 12:6).[285] The thunderclaps and lightning

---

[282] For a discussion of destruction in the conquest, see Howard, *Joshua,* 180–87.

[283] Sarna *(Genesis,* 115) observes that vv. 13–16 balance three stages of suffering (alienage, enslavement, and oppression) with three stages of divine redress (judgment, exodus, and settlement).

[284] For the terms for furnace, see I. Cornelius, "תַּנּוּר" *NIDOTTE* 4.313.

[285] W. Koopmans, "לַפִּיד," *NIDOTTE* 2.809.

(lappîd) with the thickly veiled smoke *('āšān)* at Sinai (Exod 20:18) created fear in the Israelites, who begged Moses to meet with God in their behalf (20:19). The same contrasting effects of awe and fear, that is, attraction and retraction, are symbolized by the flaming fire in 15:17. The covenant promises hold forth both blessing and curse (12:3; 27:29).

15:18–21 The final speech presents the dual promises of descendants and land as divine "covenant" explicitly for the first time (v. 18).[286] "Made a covenant" *(kārat běrît,*"to cut a covenant") is the technical expression for entering covenant relations (e.g., for the Pentateuch, 21:27,32; 26:28; 31:44; Exod 23:32; 24:8; 34:10,12,15,27; Deut 4:23; 5:2,3; 7:2; 9:9; 29:1,12,14,25[28:69; 29:11,13,24]; 31:16).[287] "On that day" (v. 18) heightens the solemnity of the covenant occasion (cp. 7:11; Exod 19:1); the same phrase elevates the act of covenant making *(kārat běrît)*in Josh 24:25; Hos 2:18[20]. "I give this land" reiterates the divine oath promised at Abram's traversing the land (12:7; 24:7).

The speech focuses on the land's perimeters and its occupants, defining in effect the nature of the promised "great reward" (v. 1) by the mention of the "great river" (v. 18) destined for Abram's descendants with "great possessions" (v. 14).[288] Two rivers form the southwestern (river of Egypt) and northeastern boundaries (Euphrates; v. 18). The "river *[nāhār]*of Egypt" occurs only once in the Old Testament (also *Jdt* 1:9). The name is not the expected designation for the Nile *(yě'ōr,* e.g., 41:1) and likely is synonymous with the "Wadi *[naḥal]* of Egypt," the familiar landmark for Canaan's southwestern border (e.g., Num 34:5; Josh 15:4,47; 1 Kgs 8:65; or just "Wadi," Ezek 47:19; 48:28). Neo-Assyrian inscriptions also mention the toponym "Wadi of Egypt." The wadi is usually identified with either the Wadi el 'Arish or the most eastern arm of the Nile delta (Pelusiac branch), the Shihor River (e.g., Josh 13:3; 1 Chr 13:5; Isa 23:3; Jer 2:18).[289] The Wadi of Egypt and the Euphrates mark the outer limits of the land of Canaan (Num 34:5; Deut 1:7; Josh 1:4; cp. 2 Kgs 24:7). The land mass demarcated in vv. 19–21 is probably the ideal standard (cf. Isa 27:12), a portrayal the author of Kings equated with the golden era of Solomon (1 Kgs 4:21[5:1]) though he did not fully dispossess the indigenous populations.[290]

---

[286] As to whether there is a contract in chap. 15 is disputed by many scholars; e.g., Westermann interprets בְּרִית in chap. 15 a solemn obligation/oath undertaken solely by God ("To your descendants I give this land"), not a covenant involving the mutual obligations of Abram and God as in chap.17 (*Genesis 12–36,* 113, 228–29).

[287] The source for the expression is usually attributed to the practice of cutting an animal in a symbolic rite associated with the making of a treaty, e.g., McCarthy, *Treaty and Covenant,* 91; for more on covenant formulations see vol. 1A, pp. 367–68 and M. Weinfeld, "בְּרִית *běrîth,*" *TDOT* 2.265–81.

[288] Ha, *Genesis 15,* 58.

[289] R. K. Harrison, "Brook of Egypt," *ISBE* 1.549–50; M. Görg, "Egypt, Brook of," *ABD* 2.231, believes Nahal Bezor better suits the Assyrian geographical references to the "Wadi of Egypt."

[290] Sarna, *Genesis,* 117.

Ten peoples inhabit the land (vv. 19–21). Since the number ten often symbolizes completeness, the ten nations named may be representative of the entire occupants. If so, both the extent of the land and its inhabitants are presented as the ideal gift to Abram's descendants.[291] The appellative "seven nations" (Deut 7:1; Acts 13:19), whom the Lord expels from Canaan (cp. seven nations in Josh 3:10; 24:11), are among these ten named (except the Hivites). There are as many as twenty-seven lists of the pre-Israelite nations in the Old Testament, ranging from two (13:7; 34:30; Josh 5:1; Judg 1:4–5) to twelve in number (10:15–18a; 1 Chr 1:13–18), with the predominant number of six nations (11x; Exod 3:8,17; 23:23; 33:2; 34:11; Deut 20:17; Josh 9:1; 11:3; 12:8; Judg 3:5; Neh 9:8; cp. Ezra 9:1).[292] Genesis 15 is the only ten-name configuration and the only one including the Kenites, Kenizzites, and Kadmonites, people groups in the Negev who probably assimilated with Judah. Also distinctive to this listing is the inclusion of the Rephaites (see comments on 14:5).[293]

The Kenites are mentioned elsewhere (e.g., Num 24:21–22; Judg 4:11; 1 Sam 15:6, 1 Chr 2:55), but the "Kenizzites" (v. 19) in its plural form occurs only here. The singular "Kenizzite" identifies Caleb's ancestry (Num 32:12; Josh 14:6,14). The name "Kenaz" appears first in 36:11 (1 Chr 1:36) as the grandson of Esau, who was head of an Edomite clan (36:15,42; 1 Chr 1:36,53). "Kenaz" also names Caleb's younger brother and the father of Othniel (Josh 15:17; Judg 1:13; 3:9,11; 1 Chr 4:13) and the grandson of Caleb (1 Chr 4:15). Little can be known about this group except what can be derived circumstantially from the tribes of the Edomites, Calebites, and Othnielites.[294] One proposal is that the Kenizzites migrated from Edom to the Negev, where they assimilated among the Judahites.[295] Even less is certain about the "Kadmonites" *(qadmōnî),* occurring only in this passage, whose name is related to *qedem,* "east." At most, we can surmise that due to their association in the list with the southern tribes, Kenites and Kenizzites, the Kadmonites may have resided in the Negev.[296]

Commonly, critical scholars attribute vv. 18–21 to the tenth-century Yahwist

---

[291] Rendsburg ("Notes," 268–70) finds additional significance to the arrangement of the nations: the "Amorites" in the seventh position reflects the importance they play in the Abraham story (on the seventh place, see vol. 1A, pp. 282, 303), and the "Jebusites" in the last position in the lists of pre-Israelite nations witnesses to the possession of Jerusalem by David, drawing the conquest to a close (also Sarna, *Genesis,* 117).

[292] T. Ishida, "The Structure and Historical Implications of the Lists of Pre-Israelite Nations," *Bib* 60 (1979): 461–90.

[293] For more on the specific groups, see vol. 1A, Kenites (pp. 260–61), Hittites (p. 455; also comments on 23:3), Amorites (p. 456), Canaanites (pp. 445–46), Girgashites (p. 456), and Jebusites (pp. 455–56).

[294] J. K. Kuntz, "Kenaz," *ABD* 4.16–17.

[295] E. C. Hostetter, "Kenaz," *EDB* 763.

[296] S. Reed, "Kadmonites," *ABD* 4.4

(J source) who described the boundaries of monarchic Israel, pointing to the Davidic-Solomonic era (1 Kgs 4:21[5:1]).[297] Others note that Israel's kings did not truly possess the land as described, and on the basis of Deuteronomic parallels with the seven ethnic groups of chap. 15 (e.g., Exod 3:8; Deut 7:1; 20:17; Josh 3:10), they date the list to the seventh century or the exile.[298] The peculiarities of the list and the passage's idealized future involving dispossession of all the land's inhabitants, however, make assigning a date unpredictable. That the ten-name list omitted the Philistines, Ammonites, and Moabites, peoples confronted by Israel, and that the three desert peoples later became apart of Judah argue that the list is pre-Israelite.[299]

7. Abram's Firstborn Son, Ishmael (16:1–16)

Like a roller coaster, the "ups and downs" of Abram's faith are staggering. After the remarkable commendation of his trust in the word of the Lord (15:6) and the reiteration of the divine promises sealed by covenant (15:7–21), the patriarch becomes a pawn in an unseemly plot hatched by Sarai to obtain an heir. Giving a concubine slave to a husband by a barren wife is attested elsewhere in the ancient Near East for remedying childlessness.[300] Although the passage does not overtly condemn Abram for his concession to Sarai, the allusion to the Garden (16:2b; 3:17), in which the Lord condemns Adam for his complicity with his wife (see v. 2 below), shows that Abram and Sarai are repeating "Eden's" sin of doubting the word of the Lord. The outcome is the birth of Ishmael, whose descendants will prove to be a threat to Sarai's own son's (Isaac) lineage (21:9–10; 37:25–28; Judg 8:24; Ps 83:6). The son of the slave will not be submissive, and his achievements will vindicate Hagar.[301] Possibly, another irony occurs if the slave Hagar were a gift from Pharaoh when the couple entered Egypt (12:16).[302]

"Hagar" occurs twelve times in Genesis (16:1,3,4,8,15[2x],16; 21:9,14, 17[2x]; 25:12) and twice as typology in Paul's argument against the Judaizers at Galatia (Gal 4:24–25).[303] The Genesis narratives (chaps. 16; 21) present an ambiguous view of Hagar-Ishmael: they are rivals to Sarai and Isaac, but they

---

[297] Clements, *Abraham and David,* 21 and n. 25.

[298] Van Seters, *Abraham in History,* 266; also disputed is whether the three desert tribes made up the original list to which the Yahwist added the traditional seven nations (Clements) or oppositely that the three Negev tribes were secondary (Van Seters).

[299] Lohfink, *Landverheissung,* 73, noted in Wenham, *Genesis 1–15,* 333–34.

[300] T. Frymer-Kensky, "Patriarchal Family Relationships and Near Eastern Law," *BA* 44 (1981): 209–14.

[301] Van Seters, *Abraham in History,* 193.

[302] One rabbinic tradition proposed that Hagar was the daughter of Pharaoh (*Gen. Rab.* 45.1).

[303] See K. A. Mathews, "Hagar," in *New Dictionary of Biblical Theology* (Leicester/Downers Grove: InterVarsity, 2000), 531–32.

are also blessed by the Lord by virtue of their relationship to Abram (16:10; 21:13,18). Ishmael as the firstborn and the first to be circumcised (17:23) and the honor of the double theophany to Hagar (16:7–12; 21:17–18) show their inclusion. The Lord "sees" and "hears" them, as the names "El Roi" ("the God who sees," 16:13; 21:9) and "Ishmael" ("God has heard," 16:11; 21:17) indicate. Yet Hagar is the "Egyptian handmaiden" (16:1,3; 21:9; 25:12) who unites her son to an Egyptian wife (21:21); twice she is located in the desert, where finally the mother and son live (16:7; 21:14,20–21; 25:12–18). Sarah, however, is in the "tent" of her husband (18:6,9–10), and in her "tent" Isaac resides with his bride (24:67). R. Syrén observes that the Lord ordains "also-sons" whose descendants are "also-peoples"; these additional lines of progeny (e.g., Ishmael, Esau) actually confirm the divine election of the appointed branch.[304] The theology of the marginal peoples shows an apparent ambiguity in evaluating foreigners: they are outside the covenant yet have a place if they submit to it. Israel's general sympathy toward outsiders was motivated by the outsider status the Fathers and enslaved Israel experienced.

Hagar and Ishmael typify in reverse Israel's experience of Egyptian hostility (16:6; Exod 1:11–12), expulsion (21:10; Exod 12:39), and flight (16:16; Exod 14:5). Hagar and Moses share in a pattern of events: oppression (Exod 2:11–15a), flight in the desert where theophany occurs (Exod 2:15b; 3:2), return and expulsion when miraculous deliverance occurs (Exod 10:11; 11:1; 15:22–27).[305] The historical irony in Hagar's revenge is the Egyptian enslavement of Sarai's descendants (cp. 15:13; 16:6). Also Hagar's son, who taunts Isaac, foreshadows the Egyptian purge of the Hebrew children (15:13; 21:10; Exod 1:16).[306]

The apostle Paul appropriated the image of Hagar as outcast to counter the Jewish agitators who insisted on circumcision (Gal 4:21–31). Whereas Philo had extolled Hagar as a converted proselyte (*Abr.* 247–53; also *Gen. Rab.* 61.4), the apostle centered on her status as slave whose children were born in slavery.[307] She was the old covenant, to be equated with Mount Sinai and earthly

---

[304] R. Syrén, *The Forsaken First-born: A Study of a Recurrent Motif in the Patriarchal Narratives*, JSOTSup 133 (Sheffield: Sheffield Academic Press, 1993), 144.

[305] T. B. Dozeman, "The Wilderness and Salvation History in the Hagar Story," *JBL* 117 (1998): 23–43. It is also tempting on the basis of parallels between the Hagar narratives and Mosaic legislation pertaining to foreigners to see a relationship (as P. Hughes, "Seeing Hagar Seeing God: *Leitwort* and Petite Narratives in Genesis 16:1–16," *Didaskalia* 8 [1997]: 43–59); but the Mosaic texts attribute the favorable treatment of aliens to the memory of Israel's own foreign status in Egypt, not Isaac's mother (e.g., Exod 22:21–24[20:23]; Deut 23:8[7]).

[306] *Gen. Rab.* 45.9 interprets Hagar-Ishmael as prefiguring Jewish oppression under Babylon and Rome.

[307] P. Borgen, "Some Hebrew and Pagan Features in Philo's and Paul's Interpretation of Hagar and Ishmael," in *New Testament and Hellenistic Judaism* (Peabody, Mass.: Hendrickson, 1997), 151–64.

Jerusalem, and Sarah in contrast represented the new covenant and the heavenly Jerusalem. The association of Hagar-Ishmael with the Sinai wilderness (21:21) and Arabian tribal descendants (24:12–16; *Bar* 3.23) explains the identification of Hagar as Sinai. Those of the covenant of flesh were indeed circumcised, as was Ishmael; but they remained enslaved to the law outside the promise, as too was Ishmael living outside the land.[308]

COMPOSITION.   Source critics recognize one primary compositional source underlying the chapter, the Yahwist (J source). Exceptions to the J attribution, however, are vv. 1,3b,15–16, due to their "P-like" features. There is no compelling reason, however, to segregate these verses. Verse 1 introduces the problem of Sarai's barrenness, which establishes the reason for the events of the story.[309] Verses 15–16 hardly seem foreign to the foundational account since they provide the story's outcome and also function structurally as the matching inclusio to v. 1. Verse 3 is more difficult but can be explained as integral to the story; first, its omission compromises the symmetry of the parallel panels in vv. 2–6[310]; second, the verse evidences a unity by the arrangement in the Hebrew sentence of the word pair "took" *(lāqaḥ)* and "gave" *(nātan;*cf. 30:9; also 3:6; Ruth 4:13);[311] and third, the chronological reference "ten years" and the phrase "land of Canaan," both usually assigned to P, are not dependable for distinguishing P from other sources.[312]

Although we disagree with the idea of a J source, we agree that the chapter exhibits a literary coherence. The two focal sections (vv. 1–6,7–14) show an interdependence that indicates one original composition. At the lexical level there are key terms shared between the two units: "(maid)servant" *(šipḥâ;* vv. 1–3,5–6,8) and "mistress" *(gĕbîrâ/gĕberet;* vv. 4,8–9). Also "in your hands" *(bĕyādēk),* "mistreated" *(ʾinnâ, piel),* and "fled" *(bāraḥ)* in v. 6 are found again in vv. 8–9 but in reverse order in the Hebrew: "running away" *(bāraḥ),* "submit" *(hithʿannâ, hithpael),* and "her hand" (absent NIV, *yādēhâ).* The discourse in the second section presupposes the account of vv. 1–6, and v. 1 anticipates the second, which provides the resolution to the problem. Verses 15 and 16 transparently rely on the earlier two sections: the chronological interest of the chapter (v. 3) is revisited with the age of the patriarch (v. 16); and the name of the child in the prophecy (v. 11) is repeated in both summary verses (vv. 15–16).

A special problem is the relationship between the two Hagar/Ishmael episodes (16:1–16; 21:8–21). They are commonly explained as a literary "doublet," that is, two independent stories recalling the same event.[313] Source critics tradi-

---

[308] For more see T. George, *Galatians,* NAC (Nashville: Broadman & Holman, 1994), 332–48.

[309] Van Seters, *Abraham in History,* 193.

[310] Wenham, *Genesis 16–50,* 5.

[311] L. Roersma, "The First-Born of Abraham: An Analysis of the Poetic Structure of Gen. 16," in *Verse in Ancient Near Eastern Prose,* AOAT 42 (Neukirchen-Vluyn: Neukirchener Verlag, 1993), 223–24.

[312] Alexander, *Abraham in the Negev,* 58–59.

[313] E.g., Speiser proposes an "underlying tradition" drawn on by two written sources (*Genesis,* 156–57).

tionally assigned chap. 16 to the Yahwist (J source; with P in vv. 1a,3,15–16) and 21:8–21 to the Elohist (E source); a redactor modified the two accounts to accommodate the chronology and theological theme of the Abraham narrative.[314] Behind the stories is a common tradition recalling the struggle between the rival wives of Abraham. Although there are differences between the two stories, the similarities in plot and characters point to the same underlying event.

Others have questioned this source analysis by contending for the essential literary unity of each episode and, importantly, by demonstrating that chap. 21 assumes a knowledge of and literary dependence on the prior narrative (chap. 16). Although Van Seters concluded that chap. 21 is a literary variant that consciously made use of chap.16, we agree that it is not an independent account arising from an oral tradition.[315] T. D. Alexander's analysis explored eight significant differences and concluded that the stories are too dissimilar to be explained as modified reports of one event.[316] For example, the driving force in the plot of each story is the motive for Hagar's departure: in chap. 16 Hagar flees the abusive Sarai (v. 6), but in chap. 21 Sarai demands that Abram expel the slavegirl and her rival son (v. 14). The two stories recount two separate events but which the author has crafted with both stories in mind. The potential threat Ishmael might have for Isaac's inheritance (21:9–10) is only understandable if the reader knows the episodes of chaps. 16–17. Also 21:6,17 alludes to the wordplay on Ishmael's name ("God heard") in 16:11; the author resists including the pun again in chap. 21 because it is assumed from 16:11 (and the author marginalizes Ishmael by omitting his name, referring to him as "son of Hagar"). Also Hagar's expulsion (chap. 21) resolves the ambiguity of Ishmael's status as heir to Abraham found in chaps. 16–17.[317]

STRUCTURE.   Chapter 16 consists of two major sections followed by a closing summary of the chapter: after an introduction (v. 1), vv. 2–6 describe the occasion for Hagar's flight; vv. 7–14 concern the divine promise regarding the future of her son, Ishmael; and vv. 15–16 present a summary (v. 15) and a conclusion (v. 16). The problem of Sarai's barrenness (v. 1) forms an inclusio with the concluding notice that Hagar gave a child to Abram (vv. 15–16). The intervening narrative explains how this remarkable outcome came about.

v. 1 Introduction: Sarai bears no child to Abram
   vv. 2–6 Sarai provides Hagar

---

[314] S. E. McEvenue reconstructs three parallel accounts (P/J/E sources) and differentiates the literary features of each ("A Comparison of Narrative Styles in the Hagar Stories," *Semeia* 3 [1975]: 64–80).

[315] Van Seters, *Abraham in History,* 192–202.

[316] Alexander, *Abraham in the Negev,* 52–69: (1) the stories begin at different points; (2) the cause for the tension between Hagar and Sarah differs; (3) Abraham's role differs in each event; (4) Hagar's character differs significantly; (5) Hagar's departures are dissimilar; (6) the well functions differently; (7) the names "Ishmael" and "Beer-lahai-roi" are important to chap. 16 but absent in chap. 21; and (8) the conclusion of each episode differs.

[317] Alexander, *Abraham in the Negev,* 68; *A Literary Analysis,* 133.

vv. 7–14 the "angel of the LORD" promises Hagar a son
vv. 15–16 Conclusion: Hagar bears Ishmael to Abram

The first section (vv. 1–6) begins with a description of the problem confronting Sarai and Abram (v. 1; 11:30); as the introduction to the entire episode, v. 1 in effect rewinds the script to 15:2 where Abram expressed his worries over the absence of a child. This Sarai-Hagar episode gives the woman's perspective on the matter, after ten years in Canaan without a child (v. 3). In contrast to the doings of Abram and Sarai, their son Isaac prays when Rebekah is barren (25:21). Prayer is also involved in remedying the barrenness of King Abimelech's household (20:17; cp. 24:12–15,45). Sarai's proposal of substituting Hagar gave the mistress only temporary comfort, for soon the pregnancy of the slave-made-wife created a bitter rivalry. Like cascading waters, one problem's apparent solution commenced another problem and in turn another.

Verses 2–6 entail two parallel panels, a prominent feature also in chaps. 15 and 17. In both parts Sarai complains about her state (A//A'), and Abram complies with her interests (B//B'). Sarai continues as the key instigator taking a course of action which redresses her complaints (C//C').

v. 1   Introduction: Sarai's barrenness and her slave Hagar
  A v. 2a Sarai to Abram: Complaint and substitute plan
    B v. 2b Compliance of Abram
      C vv. 3–4 Sarai provided Hagar who then despised her mistress
  A' v. 5 Sarai to Abram: Complaint and invocation to the Lord
    B' v. 6a Abram to Sarai: Compliance of Abram
      C' v. 6b Sarai oppressed Hagar who then fled her mistress

Repetition of the words "wife" (*'iššâ*, vv. 1,3[2x]) and "maidservant" (*šipḥâ*, vv. 1,2,3,5,6; also v. 8) in this section plays up the narrative tension between the rival women. Twice Sarai is identified as "Abram's wife" (vv. 1,3), and Hagar is usually named Sarai's "maidservant" (v. 1), "her maidservant" (v. 3), "my maidservant" (vv. 2,5), and "your maidservant" (v. 6). Verse 3b, however, calls her Abram's "wife," which is typical language for taking a concubine wife (e.g., 30:4,9 with 35:22). Their rivalry is amplified in the same verse by the terse juxtaposition of the language: "her husband [to be] his wife" (v. 3b).[318] Abram restores order to the household when he declares that Hagar is Sarai's "servant [*šipḥâ*] in [her] hand" (v. 6a). Her prominence, however, was never truly eclipsed as the narrative shows by referring to Sarai as "her [Hagar's] mistress" (v. 4b; also vv. 8[2x],9). Sarai took advantage of her power over the foreign woman, though we are spared the details, and the result was a complicating problem: a runaway slave who carried in her womb the only child of the patriarch.

---

[318]אִשָּׁה לּוֹ לְאִשָּׁה, "her husband to him for a wife."

Unit two (vv. 7–14) situates Hagar in the desert at the spring near Shur (v. 7), and it concludes similarly by a geographical reference to the naming of the well (v. 14). The structure is a chiasmus, making the angel's second and third speeches the center legs of the unit.[319] The recurring reference to the "angel of the LORD" (vv. 9,10,11), first found in the introduction (v. 7), punctuates the theophanic nature of the message, which entails the denouement of the episode. Three acts of naming are also prominent: "Ishmael" (v. 11; cf. v. 15), "El Roi" ("the God who sees me," NIV [v. 13]), and "Beer Lahai Roi" (v. 14). These popular etymologies tie the names to the significance of the event. The only true dialogue is limited to v. 8; the speeches of the angel dominate (vv. 9–12). The embedded poetic verse in vv. 11–12 detail the promise of the child and his future career. By naming the Lord the woman shows an unexpected faith (v. 13), and its authenticity is suggested by the notoriety of the well's name (v. 14).

A   v. 7 Hagar at well in the wilderness at Shur
  B   v. 8 Angel: Inquiry about Hagar's flight and Hagar's reply
    C   v. 9 Angel: Instruction to return to her mistress
    C′ v. 10 Angel: Promise of innumerable descendants
  B′ vv. 11–13 Angel: Prophecy announces son Ishmael and Hagar's
                     reaction
A′ v. 14 Hagar names the well "Beer Lahai Roi"

(1) Hagar's Flight (16:1–6)

¹Now Sarai, Abram's wife, had borne him no children. But she had an Egyptian maidservant named Hagar; ²so she said to Abram, "The LORD has kept me from having children. Go, sleep with my maidservant; perhaps I can build a family through her."

Abram agreed to what Sarai said. ³So after Abram had been living in Canaan ten years, Sarai his wife took her Egyptian maidservant Hagar and gave her to her husband to be his wife. ⁴He slept with Hagar, and she conceived.

When she knew she was pregnant, she began to despise her mistress. ⁵Then Sarai said to Abram, "You are responsible for the wrong I am suffering. I put my servant in your arms, and now that she knows she is pregnant, she despises me. May the LORD judge between you and me."

⁶"Your servant is in your hands," Abram said. "Do with her whatever you think best." Then Sarai mistreated Hagar; so she fled from her.

16:1 Verse 1 introduces the three human participants in this episode, defining each one's social status in the household. The account begins with the perspective of Sarai (vv. 1–6); she is the instigator of the action in the account. The attention of the narrative will shift to Hagar's condition in the second half

---

[319] Wenham, *Genesis 16–50*, 4.

(vv. 7–14). In both cases the women are distraught over their position in the household: Sarai is embarrassed by her barrenness, and Hagar faces the life of an outcast. "Sarai" and "Hagar" occur at the beginning and end of the verse; they are contrasted throughout the passage, Hagar functioning as a foil for Sarai. Hagar is a young slave woman and fertile; Sarai is old, free, and barren.

The terms "wife" (*ʾiššâ*) and "maidservant" (*šipḥâ*) also contrast the status of the women. Sarai has the prestigious role of "wife" to Abram, but Hagar is subordinate to Sarai and hence under her authority. Hagar may have been among the servants obtained in Egypt (12:6) or a part of the marriage dowry received by Sarai (cf. Bilhah, 29:29; 30:3; Zilpah, 29:24; 30:9). "Maidservant" (*šipḥâ*) is not a common slave but the personal servant of the "mistress" (*gĕbîrâ/gĕberet*, vv. 4, 8–9) of the house (cf. Ps 123:2; Prov 30:23; Isa 24:2).[320] Abram confirms Sarai's power over the young woman to do as she pleases (v. 6).

Moreover, Hagar is an "Egyptian," mentioned twice in the passage (vv. 1, 3; also 21:21), who as a foreign-born slave had little significance in the eyes of the household. Two lexical echoes of 15:13 point up the struggle between the two women and the two nations they typify: the name "Hagar" (*hāgār*) as a wordplay on *gēr*, "stranger," and the recurrence of "mistreated" (*ʿinnâ*, v. 6). Though the future oppression is reversed, the tug-of-war between the women anticipates Egypt's affliction against Abram's descendants (15:13–16,18). Also Joseph's experience in Egypt, where he was sold into slavery by Ishmaelites (37:12; 39:1–2) and imprisoned at the fault of (presumably) an Egyptian woman (39:14–20), foreshadows Israel's bondage.

16:2–4 In her first complaint Sarai attributes her barrenness to the Lord who has "kept" (*ʿāṣar*) her from pregnancy (v. 2); the same term occurs in 20:18, where the Lord "had closed up" the wombs of Abimelech's household. She reasons that future descendants will be gained by the surrogate Hagar. To "build *[bānâ]* a family" is the Hebrew idiom for establishing a physical progeny (e.g., 30:3; Ruth 4:11); although this was the woman's role, it was recognized that the Lord alone grants a family (30:2; Ps 127:1).[321]

Sarai never speaks directly to Hagar or speaks her name; Hagar is a tool to relieve Sarai's embarrassment. Yet Sarai never claims Ishmael as her son (cp. Rachel, 30:6; Leah, 30:20).[322] Ancient Near Eastern custom provided for the substitution of a slave for the purpose of bearing a child in the case of a barren mistress. If the wife could not produce children, the husband might marry

---

[320] A. Jepsen, "Amah and Schipchah," *VT* 8 (1958): 293–97, referenced in Westermann, *Genesis 12–36*, 238.

[321] D. Fouts, "בנה," *NIDOTTE* 1.678–79.

[322] P. Trible, "The Other Woman: A Literary and Theological Study of the Hagar Narratives," in *Understanding the Word: Essays in Honor of Bernhard W. Anderson*, JSOTSup 37 (Sheffield: University of Sheffield, 1985), 221–46.

another; perhaps the offer of a substitute circumvented the acquisition of a second wife.[323] That barrenness was grounds for a divorce after a ten-year period is a rabbinic explanation for Sarai's actions (*Gen. Rab.* 45.3).

Employing the language of chap. 3, vv. 2–3 describe Abram's agreement to Sarai's plan and her presentation of the slave girl. Abram's misguided compliance ("agreed to," v. 2, *šěmaʿ* ... *lěqôl*) is cast in the same terms as Adam's obedience to his wife (3:17). That Sarai "took" *(lāqaḥ)* her and "gave" *(nātan)* Hagar "to her husband" (v. 3) portrays the matriarch as another Eve (3:6). Reference to Abram's residence in Canaan for "ten years" (v. 3; 12:4) without a child indicates that patience for Sarai had run its course. The wait, however, had only begun, for it would be another fifteen years before Isaac was born to Sarai (17:17; 18:14) in Abram's "old age" (21:2). Perhaps dwelling in the land for a period of "ten years" signaled the end of her chance at the normal means of having a child (cp. 18:11; Ruth 1:4).

Rachel and Leah also presented their handmaidens *(šipḥâ)* to Jacob for wives *(ʾiššâ;* 30:4,7; 37:2). Concubinage involved a husband who added secondary wives, usually for purposes of procreation.[324] Concubines held an inferior status to the primary wife. They are portrayed in the Bible as a servant to the husband's primary wife but above the status of a slave *(ʿāmâ, šipḥâ).*[325] The language "concubine" *(pilegeš)* is not required to name surrogate wives; although identified as a "wife," Hagar (v. 3) and later Keturah (25:1) are not designated "concubines" in Genesis except by inference (25:6; also 1 Chr 1:32 for Keturah). Bilhah is Jacob's "concubine" (35:22), but Zilpah is not so named, though both are called his "wives" (37:2). Multiple wives were wrong according to God's will (2:24) and posed a threat to the stability of a family (29:30–31; 30:8; 35:22; Exod 21:7–11; Deut 21:15–17; cf. Deut 17:17; 1 Kgs 11:3–8), which is sadly illustrated by the strife in Abram's house (16:4,6; 21:9–10).

Abram's intimacy may have been limited to one occasion (so *Gen. Rab.* 45.4) but which resulted in pregnancy, in contrast to Sarah's perpetual barrenness. Hagar's pregnancy failed to bring delight to Sarai, however; the Egyptian "began to despise her mistress" (v. 4b). Although a surrogate wife bore the master's child, the slave woman did not displace the status of the barren wife.[326] Sarai reads Hagar's action as a threat against her place in the household. She later perceives another threat against her newborn by the actions of the slave woman's son Ishmael (21:9–10). Hebrew *qālal (qal;* "despise") means to consider someone lightly (cp. 1 Sam 6:22); NJPV renders the word

---

[323] Frymer-Kensky, "Patriarchal Family Relationships," 211–12.

[324] On concubinage see N. Steinberg, *Kinship and Marriage in Genesis* (Minneapolis: Fortress, 1993), 61–65; the sociological term "polycoity" describes this form of marriage.

[325] V. Hamilton, "פִּלֶגֶשׁ," *NIDOTTE* 3.618–19.

[326] Frymer-Kensky, "Patriarchal Family Relationships," 211.

"was lowered in her [Hagar's] esteem" (i.e., "contempt," NRSV). The term echoes the related word *qallēl (piel)* "curse" in 12:3 (see comments there; also 8:21). The effect of this literary association with 12:3 aligns Hagar with anyone who would oppose Abram's family.

16:5–6a In a second complaint Sarai considers herself wronged by Hagar, and she blames the matter on Abram (e.g., NIV, NAB, NJB, NJPV, NLT, HCSB; cf. Rachel, 30:2). Some EVs, however, construe her words as an invocation: "May the wrong done to me be upon you" (NASB; also AV, NKJV, NRSV; cp. Jer 51:35).[327] The underlying point is the same: in Sarai's mind Abram is culpable for her pain, and she appeals to the Lord to "judge" *(šāpaṭ)* between them (v. 5b; cf. 18:5). Yet she admits that she gave the slave-woman to Abram, although he apparently did not request her. Her reaction would be illogical since the pregnancy achieved Sarai's purpose, but the slave's demeaning of her provoked regret and a cry for vindication. The term rendered "wrong" *(ḥāmās)* often occurs in passages pertaining to malicious liars and betrayal (e.g., Ps 27:12; Mic 6:12; Zeph 1:9; 1 Chr 12:17) and even is used of physical violence (e.g., 6:11; 49:5; Judg 9:24). Sarai's complaint is like Job's outcry for justice, but Job views his offense due to God's hand *(ḥāmās, Job 19:7)*. Hagar's harm against Sarai is proleptic of the angel's prophecy (v. 12), which portrays her son Ishmael as a hostile neighbor—in this case, like mother like son. By describing Hagar "in your [Abram's] arms," which literally is "in your [Abram's] midst/lap/breast" *(bĕḥêqekā)*, Sarai pictures the intimacy ("embrace," NRSV) they enjoyed at her expense.

Abram plays on the complaint of Sarai by his retort, "Your servant [Hagar] is in your hands" (v. 6); putting Hagar "in your [Sarai's] hands" *(bĕyādēk)* rectifies the charge "in your arms" (v. 5). By issuing the decree Abram clarified Sarai's place as chief matron in the household. "Hands" also anticipates the characterization of Ishmael, whose "hand" opposes everyone and in turn their "hand" opposes him (v. 12). The submission of Hagar reestablishes the Hebrews' priority over the Ishmaelites, which is ordained by the Lord, "humble yourself under her hand" (v. 9, "submit to her," NIV). Abram, however, does not give her to Sarai to do whatever she pleases; rather, she is to treat Hagar as she sees "best" *(ḥaṭṭôb,* "the good"). Abram directs his wife to treat the handmaiden in the right way. Here, too, is a possible allusion to the Garden's prohibited "tree of good and evil" (2:17) from which Adam ate when he obeyed his wife (3:17). "In your eyes" ("think," NIV) replays "eyes" in v. 4: "She [Hagar] began to despise her mistress in her eyes" (absent NIV). Perhaps it is another allusion to Eve, who viewed the attractive fruit as "pleasing to the eyes" (3:6).

16:6b Sarai's choice was no better than Eve's because Sarai "mistreated"

---

[327] חֲמָסִי עָלֶיךָ (lit., "my wrong upon you").

(ʿinnâ) the Egyptian woman (cf. ʿinnâ at 31:50). The specific form of the affliction cannot be ascertained, since the word group (ʿnh) is widely used for subjugation and oppression, even despair (e.g., 15:13; 34:2; Exod 22:22–23[22–
23]; Judg 16:5,6,19; 1 Sam 1:11). Mosaic law provided for fair treatment of
foreigners (Exod 22:21[20]; 23:9; Lev 19:33; Deut 23:7[8]),[328] and equitable
consideration for a slave was characteristic of the upright (Job 31:3). By fleeing, Hagar took a desperate measure, for her survival depended on the protection of a family clan (cf. 21:14–19).

(2) Promise of a Son (16:7–14)

⁷The angel of the LORD found Hagar near a spring in the desert; it was the
spring that is beside the road to Shur. ⁸And he said, "Hagar, servant of Sarai,
where have you come from, and where are you going?"

"I'm running away from my mistress Sarai," she answered.

⁹Then the angel of the LORD told her, "Go back to your mistress and submit
to her." ¹⁰The angel added, "I will so increase your descendants that they will be
too numerous to count."

¹¹The angel of the LORD also said to her:

"You are now with child
  and you will have a son.
You shall name him Ishmael,
  for the LORD has heard of your misery.
¹²He will be a wild donkey of a man;
  his hand will be against everyone
  and everyone's hand against him,
  and he will live in hostility
  toward all his brothers."

¹³She gave this name to the LORD who spoke to her: "You are the God who
sees me," for she said, "I have now seen the One who sees me." ¹⁴That is why the
well was called Beer Lahai Roi; it is still there, between Kadesh and Bered.

16:7 The second half of the narrative (vv. 7–14) describes Hagar's
encounter with "the angel of the LORD" on the way to Shur. Shur was a wilderness region in northwest Sinai, situated between southwest Canaan and the
northeast border of Egypt; it was near the border of Egypt through which the
Israelites traveled (Exod 15:22//Num 33:8, Etham=Shur) and where Ishmaelites (see comments on 25:18) and Amalekites at times resided (1 Sam 15:7;
27:8). Shur may also be the name of a specific site as well as the region. Others
relate Shur (meaning "wall") to the wall of forts along the eastern Delta constructed to defend against foreign incursions.[329] The region was a temporary

---

[328] P. Wagner, "ענה," *NIDOTTE* 3.449–52.

[329] D. Seely, "Shur, Wilderness of," *ABD* 5.1230; also N. Na'aman, "The Shihor of Egypt and
Shur That Is Before Egypt," *Tel Aviv* 7 (1980): 95–109. *Tgs. Onq.* and *Ps.-J.* have *haqra'* (Hagar)
for Shur.

homestead for Abraham (20:1). Hagar as an Egyptian may have hoped to return home by way of Shur when she was met by the angel. While Sarai, who was barren, resided in a fertile land, Hagar, who was fertile, finds herself in a barren land.[330]

This passage is the first reference to "the angel of the LORD" *(mal'ak Yahweh)* in the Old Testament, where it occurs forty-eight times. In Genesis the theophanic name occurs six times, four in chap. 16 (vv. 7,9,10,11) and twice in the offering of Isaac (22:11,15). The precise relationship between the "angel of the LORD" and God is puzzling. The angel is equated with the Lord in some texts and yet appears distinctive in others (e.g., 22:15–16; Exod 3:2–4 with Acts 7:30–32; Num 22:22,31,35,38; Judg 6:11–18; 13:21–22; Zech 3:1,5–7; 12:8; cf. also Exod 33:1–3,5,14). Chapter 16 illustrates the ambiguity of the angel's identity. He speaks in first person as God himself (v. 10), and both the narrator and Hagar's speech identify the angel as the Lord God (v. 13). He also is identified as the Lord when he calls from heaven to rescue young Isaac (22:11,15). The solitary term "angels" describes two of the three "visitors" to Abraham (18:1 with 19:1,15), although all three are "men" (18:1; 19:5,10,12,16). It is clear, however, that one of the three "men" who engaged Abraham is the Lord (18:12,17,20,22,26,33); the two angels who go ahead to Sodom identify themselves as messengers of the Lord (19:13). Another distinction occurs between the two visiting angels when one speaks as the Lord (19:18,21,24–25), unless we are to believe that the Lord has rejoined the angels at Sodom.

The parallel title "the angel of God" *(mal'ak 'ĕlōhîm)* occurs in 21:17, who also speaks from heaven to Hagar; in giving the promise of descendants, the angel's language is authoritative like that of divine promises made earlier by God to Abraham: "I will make him [Ishmael] into a great nation" (21:18). The "angel of God" identifies himself as the "God of Bethel" and instructs Jacob to return home (31:11–13; cp. 31:2), as the angel does Hagar (v. 9). Although the term "angel" does not occur, the "man" whom Jacob wrestles at Peniel is God, seen "face to face," and later was interpreted by Hosea as an angel (32:24,30 with Hos 12:3–4[4–5]). Jacob probably has this incident in mind when he equates God and the "angel" who rescued him (48:15–16). In this last case, "angel" by itself can refer to the theophanic messenger. The plural "angels of God," however, are the host of the Lord who protect Jacob like a second encampment (32:1–2[2–3]). As in the theophany at Bethel in Jacob's dream (28:12–13), they are distinct from the Lord. Later Abraham referred to a guardian angel, identified as "his [God's] angel," by which he may have meant the "angel of the LORD" (24:7,40).

Some interpreters think the "angel of the LORD" was simply an angelic mes-

---

[330] Pointed out to me by Dr. Sheri Klouda.

senger or a hypostasis of God; others find that in some passages the interspersing of the Lord and his "angel" convey a theological tension or narrative ambiguity that provides for emphasis either on God's presence or his distance.[331] Traditionally, Christian interpreters ascribed to the appearance of the angel a Christophany, the preincarnate divine Son of God.[332] Exodus 23:20–23 implies that the angel who bears the divine Name has the power to forgive sin, a distinctive feature of deity. It is also striking that "the angel of the LORD" (definite article) is not mentioned in the New Testament. The appellative "angel of the LORD" may not be a technical reference for the divine Logos, but it is clear that the angel is deity in many Old Testament passages, including this Hagar incident.

16:8–10   Verses 8–12 report the angel's dialogue with Hagar; "angel of the LORD said" *(wayyōmer)* begins vv. 9–11 (v. 8 has "he," referring to the angel [v. 7a]).[333] The two foci of the angel's message are the status of Hagar in Abram's house (vv. 8–10) and the future of her son (vv. 11–12). The inquiries put to her by the angel (v. 8) introduce the conversation concerning Hagar's social status, implying that her prospects of flight are dim. He addresses Hagar as the "servant *[šipḥâ]* of Sarai" (v. 8) and instructs her to return to her "mistress" *(gĕbîrâ;* v. 9), a subordinate position Hagar herself admits to (v. 9). Hagar is further directed to "submit" to Sarai; again "hand," lit., "humble yourself under her hand" (v. 9b), appears, conveying confirmation of Abram's concession to Sarai (v. 6). "Humble yourself" *(hith'annî, hithpael;* "submit," NIV) is the term describing Sarai's oppression of Hagar that led to her flight *(tĕ'annehā, piel;* "mistreated," NIV, v. 6). The angel therefore in effect is instructing her to return to the oppressive life that a slave must endure. The motivation for her return is the grand future that Abram's patronage can provide (v. 10). The promise of innumerable offspring both elevates Hagar's place and also ensures her future provision (17:20). The language of the promise is like that made to Abram and his legitimate line of successors (e.g., 13:16; 15:5; 17:2; 22:17; 26:4,24; 28:3; 35:11; 48:4). It is striking that Hagar is the first woman to receive a birth annunciation and the first woman to receive promises from the Lord. By remaining submissive in Abram's household, she and her son will someday enjoy the benefit of the patriarchal blessing (12:3; 17:20). Ishmael receives a derivative blessing because of his relationship to Abram, as

---

[331] C. Newsom, "Angels," *ABD* 1.250; S. White agrees that the later editor used the angel figure rhetorically as a euphemism to emphasize divine transcendence ("Angel of the LORD: Messenger or Euphemism," *TynBul* 50 [1992]: 299–305).

[332] G. Funderburk, "Angel," *ZPEB* 1.162–63.

[333] Form critics commonly perceive the threefold repetition as redactional activity (Westermann, *Genesis 12–36,* 242); Alexander, however, shows that any omission of vv. 9–12 creates additional literary problems, and they are likely original, thus the repetition of the phrase is probably a rhetorical device for emphasis (cf. 15:2,3; 17:3,9,15; 21:6,7; *Abraham in the Negev,* 60–61).

is the case for Isaac's future blessing, "for the sake of my [the LORD's] servant Abraham" (26:24).

16:11–12 The embedded poetry of vv. 11–12 distinguishes this speech. The angel announces the pregnancy of Hagar, instructs her to name the child, and describes the hostility he and his descendants will manifest toward others. Similarly, God announces the birth of Isaac and directs Abram to name the child (17:19; 18:10; 21:3; cp. Judg 13:3–7; Isa 7:14; 8:3; Hos 1:4,6,9; Luke 1:13,31–33). Verse 11 contains a quatrain (so NIV). The first couplet entails the annunciation and specifies that the child will be a "son" (v. 11ab). The angel's acknowledgment of her pregnancy is not new information (v. 11a; cp. v. 4), but its mention recalls the circumstances of her plight. What is new to her is the gender of the child (v. 11b); the son promised to Abram appeared to be provided and her role as surrogate successful.

The second couplet of v. 11 involves the naming of the child and the name's etymology (v. 11cd). A birth announcement often included the name of the child followed by an explanation of the name (e.g., 17:19; 1 Chr 4:9; Isa 8:3–4; Hos 1:4; Matt 1:21; Luke 1:13,31).[334] Here the angel instructs the woman to name the child, which was not unusual (e.g., 4:1; 29:32; 30:24; Exod 2:10; 1 Sam 4:21; 11:1). "Ishmael" means "El [God] hears" *(yišmā'ē'l)*, commemorating the Lord who "heard" *(šāma')* her "affliction" *('onî,* "misery," NIV, v. 11cd). "Affliction" is a metonymy meaning her cries of affliction. The Hebrew term *'onî* ("misery," NIV) recalls Hagar's trials in vv. 6 and 9, which have the related verb *'nh* ("mistreated"/"submit"). Verse 11 points forward also by the similar play on Ishmael's name in 21:17, where both the mother and child bemoan their thirst (21:15–18). Moreover, "affliction" is associated in Genesis with both maternal rivalry (Leah, 29:32; Hannah, 1 Sam 1:11) and the land of Egypt (41:52). The oppression Hagar experiences, as we have said, will be reversed against the Hebrews, who later suffer by the Egyptians (15:13, *'innê;* Exod 3:7, *'onî*) and whose cries are also "heard" *(šama')* by the Lord (Exod 2:24).

Verse 12 also contains a quatrain; it describes Hagar's child by four features. (1) "A wild donkey of a man" *(pere' 'ādām)* indicates a lifestyle outside accepted social conventions (Hos 8:9) and also anticipates his desert residence (Job 24:5; 39:5–8). The image of a wild donkey could also convey Jerusalem's willfulness (Jer 2:24). (2) His independence is described further by his hostile behavior toward "everyone," (3) eliciting a corresponding response, "everyone's hand against him." (4) The final colon explains the extent of his violence, aimed against "all his brothers," hence breaking the bonds of family loyalty.

---

[334] R. Neff, based on his doctoral dissertation, isolates what he contends is a conventional form of birth announcements in 16:11–12; 17:19; 1 Kgs 13:2; Isa 7:14–17; and 1 Chr 22:9–10: (1) announcement of birth introduced by הִנֵּה ("behold"), (2) the name, and (3) the description of the child's destiny ("The Annunciation in the Birth Narrative of Ishmael," *BR* 17 [1972]: 51–60).

The fulfillment occurs in 25:18, where the similar phrase describes the practice of Ishmael's descendants. Taken together, each part of v. 12 intensifies the picture of Ishmael as antagonist whose hostilities are indiscriminate and without restraint. Hostility toward one's "brother" characterized the nonelect line in Genesis, beginning with Cain (4:8,23–24); Esau, like Ishmael, is portrayed as a wild belligerent (27:39–40).

16:13–14 Hagar learns that the Lord both "hears" (v. 11) and "sees" (v. 13) her sorrow. To memorialize the event Hagar acknowledges the Lord by giving the name, lit., "You are El-roi" (ʾattâ ʾēl rŏʾî ;v. 13a), meaning either "a God of seeing" (ESV) or "the God who sees me" (NIV). The former translation follows the Hebrew MT, vocalizing rŏʾî as the noun "seeing."[335] The second translation revocalizes rŏʾî as a participle and first person suffix; this vocalization is also in v. 13b, "who sees me" (rŏʾî), and in the name of the well "Beer Lahai Roi" in v. 14. Ancient versions (LXX, Vg.[336]) and some EVs (AV, NIV) read the Hebrew in this alternative way. One difficulty with the latter interpretation is that the narrative does not expressly say the woman "saw" the Lord's angel (cp. 21:19) or the angel "appeared" (cp. 17:1; 18:1). Yet her explanation for the name that follows provides for a visual manifestation (v. 13b).

Hagar's explanation also has been variously construed, some interpreting it as a mere acknowledgment of having seen the Lord (NIV, NLT), others reading it as a rhetorical question expressing wonder at surviving the theophany, that is, "Have I even remained alive here after seeing him?" (NASB; also NRSV, NJB, GNB, NJPS; cp. 32:30[31]; Exod 33:20; Judg 6:22; 13:22; Isa 6:5).[337] The Hebrew is very difficult and either rendering is defensible.[338] The inclusion of "Lahai" (laḥay), meaning "the Living (One)," for the name of the well (v. 14a) may be a reflection of what is subtly implied by v. 13b—she remained alive.[339] T. H. Booij defends the MT and proposes a translation that takes into consideration the potential dual senses of the name El rŏʾî in v. 13a (see above). He understands the word ḥălōm as "hither," referring to the wilderness, and the meaning of rʾh ("see") as "looking for" in the sense of searching for (e.g., 18:21; Exod 4:18): "Would I have gone here [i.e., wilderness] indeed looking

---

[335] אַתָּה אֶל רָאִי, see BDB 909; some EVs (ASV, NAB, RSV, NASB, HCSB) maintain the MT, e.g., "Thou art a God of seeing" (RSV); and NJB, REB, NRSV, NJPS opt for the transliteration "El-roi."

[336] σὺ ὁ θεὸς ὁ ἐπιδών με; *Tu Deus qui vidisti me.*

[337] The LXX has ὅτι εἶπεν καὶ γὰρ ἐνώπιον εἶδον ὀφθέντα μοι, "For even in person (face to face) I have seen the One appearing to me," i.e., in the form of his angel (see Wevers, *Notes on the Greek Text,* 226).

[338] הֲגַם הֲלֹם רָאִיתִי אַחֲרֵי רֹאִי, lit., "have I indeed here (or hither) seen after the One who sees me?"

[339] Cp. the explicit connection in the emendation רֹאִי אַחֲרֵי וָאֵחִי רָאִיתִי אֱלֹהִים הֲגַם (see BHS), proposed by Wellhausen: "Did I really see God, yet remain alive after my seeing him?" (quoted in Westermann, *Genesis 12–36,* 248).

for him that looks after me?" Captured here is both the search for God ("God of seeing") and God's caring for her ("God who sees me").[340] Perhaps the notion of "seeing" *(rʾh)* also plays on Hagar's original misdoing who "saw" *(rʾh,* NIV "knew") that she was pregnant and consequently despised Sarai (v. 4). Hagar marvels at the grace of the One who took pity on her, although she was a person of low standing (cp. Hannah's prayer, 1 Sam 2:8).

The site became known as Beer Lahai Roi, "the well of the Living (One) who sees me" (v. 14). The watering place sat between Kadesh and Bered in the Negev, where Isaac periodically resided (24:62; 25:11).

(3) Birth of Ishmael (16:15–16)

15So Hagar bore Abram a son, and Abram gave the name Ishmael to the son she had borne. 16Abram was eighty-six years old when Hagar bore him Ishmael.

16:15–16 Lit., "Hagar bore" and "Hagar had borne Ishmael" form an inclusio to v. 15, but also the final mention of "Hagar" in v. 16b creates an inclusio with v. 15: lit., "and so Hagar bore to Abram a son" (v. 15a) and "when Hagar bore Ishmael to Abram" (v. 16b). Mention that the child came from Abram three times in vv. 15–16 conveys the ambiguity of Ishmael's place in the household. As a child of the slave woman, claims on inheritance are not automatic (25:4–6; 27:32–41), but as the firstborn of Abram his position would be promising. That both Hagar and Abram name the child does not present a conflict of traditions (vv. 11,15); by naming the boy Ishmael as the angel had directed Hagar (v. 11), Abram signals acknowledgment of the child as his own and acceptance of the Lord's plan for Ishmael as revealed. Notices of the age of Abram, who was eighty-six at Ishmael's birth, track chronologically the improbable reality of the promised son (12:4; 17:1,17,24; 18:11–14; 21:5). Continued attention to the ebbing sands of time makes the birth of a son to the elderly couple only increasingly unlikely, magnifying the miracle of the child Isaac.

8. Covenant Sign of Circumcision (17:1–27)

Thirteen years after the birth of Ishmael (16:16; 17:1,24), the Lord appeared to Abram again, reiterating the promises of descendants and land (12:1–3; 13:14–17; 15:1,4–5,18–21) and instructing him in the sign and seal of covenant circumcision. The theophanic message addressed the same question of an heir both Abram and Sarai had raised. Abram had proposed the substitute Eliezer (15:3), and Sarai had provided the surrogate wife, Hagar (16:2), whose son Ishmael Abram hoped would be accepted (17:18). The

---

[340] T. H. Booij, "Hagar's Words in Genesis XVI 13B," *VT* 30 (1980): 1–7.

Lord, however, would accomplish his better plan through Isaac, the heir to be born to Abram's wife (vv. 16,19,21). The covenant promises in chap. 17 echo what had already been announced to Abram but with the new emphasis on the covenant's perpetuity (vv. 7,8,13,19; cp. 13:15) and the new feature of the "sign" of circumcision (v. 11). Circumcision of the male's foreskin as a sign and seal is especially fitting for the covenant's orientation toward future generations (vv. 7–10,19). The Lord provides also new assurances to Abram by conferring the names "Abraham" and "Sarah," attributing promissory significance to the couple's status as progenitors of new "nations" (*gôyim,* vv. 4–5,15–16; cp. 12:2).[341] Even Ishmael, the nonelect son, will father "a great nation *[gôy]*" by divine promise (v. 20). Ishmael, although he too is circumcised (v. 23), does not inherit the covenant (v. 21), and, while he receives "blessing" (v. 20), it is not in perpetuity.

COMPOSITION. Chapter 17 is commonly treated as a literary unity coming from the Priestly writer (P) because of its legislation of circumcision and the chapter's "P-like" vocabulary (e.g., *"El Shaddai,"* "confirm" *[hēqîm]* a covenant). The chapter, as we noted above, mirrors the Noahic covenant in significant features (9:8–17), which source critics also universally consider priestly (P). The date of the chapter is exilic, answering the exiles' need for assurance that there would yet be kings and a land for them. Typically, scholars interpreted chaps. 15 (E/J sources) and 17 (P source) as parallel traditions ("doublets"), recognizing that chap. 17 especially emphasizes the promise of numerous descendants.[342] Yet other voices explain chap. 17 as a free composition relying on a complex compilation of earlier sources rather than a true doublet to chap. 15's covenant account. McEvenue believes that 17:1–8 relies directly on chap. 15 and 17:15–22 rests on 18:1–16,33, the Yahwist's account of the promise of an heir. Chapter 17 is the priestly reinterpretation of both passages, transforming the simple oath and promise into an eternal covenant legislating circumcision.[343]

Not only is chap. 17 usually accepted as a late advancement over the earlier stories, many believe the chapter exhibits an original independence of its present context.[344] Among the arguments Carr puts forward are these: the appearance of *El Shaddai* indicates that the story comes from a literary layer in which the patriarchs do not know the name *Yahweh* (unlike 15:7); mention is made of the promises of children and land, but chap. 17 appears unaware of the same promises in prior stories (e.g., 15:4–5,7–18); the announcement of the birth, mention of Sarah's old age, and the surprise of Abraham (17:15–21) recur in 18:10–14, but

---

[341] O. Eissfeldt reasons that the renamings indicate a "high honour" whose descendants will have a "glorious future" ("Renaming in the Old Testament," in *Words and Meanings: Essays Presented to David Winton Thomas* [Cambridge: Cambridge University Press, 1968], 73).

[342] E.g., Coats, *Genesis,* 135–36.

[343] McEvenue, *The Narrative Style of the Priestly Writer,* 145–55; Van Seters also points to the correlations between 17:15–21 and 18:10–14 and dates the chapter after his exilic Yahwist in the restoration period (*Abraham in History,* 284).

[344] Carr, *Reading the Fractures of Genesis,* 82–85.

this time it is Sarah's laughter, not Abraham's; and finally the author of chap. 17, if aware of the present context, would not have "replayed" the events but would have modified them in his new composition.

We will show below that the author of chap. 17 is fully aware of the Abraham events, but not to the extent of direct literary dependence. Alexander has demonstrated that the proposed correlations between chap. 17 and chaps. 15 and 18 are not sufficiently clear to support a literary indebtedness.[345] The passages selected for comparison from chaps. 15 and 18 are limited to a few verses from each rather than the whole of the respective accounts. If the author of chap. 17 wants to adapt (or even "correct") the account of the patriarchal oath, it is striking that he avoids any mention of the animal slaughter (vv. 9–10), a subject that ordinarily was important to priests and a long-lost cultic practice probably desired by the exiles. Also it is difficult to see how such a tightly ordered structure as found in chap. 17 (see "Structure" below) could be achieved if the author embedded portions of two other pericopes without significant modifications. Moreover, the repetitions of chap. 17 with chaps. 15 and 18 are better explained on different rhetorical and exegetical grounds. Repetition of the promises, for example, is a common feature of the Abraham narrative as a whole, and there is no reason to insist that chap. 17 crossreferences earlier notices of the promises. Also the use of divine names (e.g., *El Shaddai*) for discerning different sources or redactional layers is now recognized by many critics as unreliable. Finally, the appeal to P's unique vocabulary is equally problematic as a criterion since the same words may appear in non-P passages. As we will show below (see "Covenant") the Noahic covenant (chaps. 6–9, see vol. 1A, pp. 352–56) and chap. 17 share remarkably the same terms; this is not the result of the same source (P), however, but the consequence of sharing the same subject matter of covenant and the use of the same basic covenant framework of a royal grant.

Chapter 17's episode is not unfamiliar with the events of chaps. 15–18, calling into question the popular view of an independent source.[346] The author of chap. 17 is fully aware of the Abraham complex of stories, especially chap. 15. It fits comfortably in the horizon of the promissory theme in the Abraham story, presupposing the promises of chaps. 12–13 and 15–16. Abraham's proposal of Ishmael as heir (17:18) makes sense only in light of the events in chaps. 15 and 16; further, the divine predictions respecting Isaac and his rival Ishmael (17:19–21) echo the same concerns raised by Abram and Sarai in 15:2–4 and chap. 16, pertaining to substitute heirs and a future for the outcast Ishmael. Chronological notices in 16:16 and 17:1 provide a smooth transition between the chapters. The promise of "many nations" (17:4–5) is presaged by the prediction of Ishmael's

---

[345] Alexander, *A Literary Analysis,* 170–82.

[346] Wenham finds that assigning chap. 17 to an independent source is suspect since the chapter shows an integral relationship with the predominantly Yahwist (J) material of chaps. 15–18 (*Genesis 16–50,* 18–19). According to Wenham, if one concedes that chap. 17 is from the independent P source, then it must antedate J due to its J-like redaction.

prodigious future (16:10; 17:20).[347] Also chap. 17 anticipates the additional revelation in chap. 18 by the prediction of the heir born to Sarah in a year's time
(17:21; 18:10,14); in turn 18:9–15 presumes the names "Abraham" and "Sarah"
(17:5,15). Sarah, as did Abraham, laughs at the impossibility of God's announcement (17:17; 18:12), but the differences in their respective exegetical functions
make it unlikely that the two occasions are the result of a borrowing. Chapters 17
and 18 also share interest in what the covenant meant for the destinies of Abraham's rejected relatives, Ishmael (17:20) and Lot (18:16–33). Both narratives
introduce and conclude their theophanic revelation by "appeared" (*wayyērāʾ;*
17:1; 18:1) and "finished speaking" (*kālâ dibbēr;* 17:22; 18:33).

Finally, there is similarity in the narrative structures occurring in chap. 17 and
chaps. 15–16 and 18–19; chap. 17 has parallel units or panels as found in chaps.
15–16 and is also chiastic in arrangement as found in 16:7–14 and chaps. 18–19
(see commentary there). Taken together, the evidence points to chap. 17 as an
original part of the complex of Abraham stories concerning Ishmael and Isaac
created by the same author. Chapter 17 is not a literary doublet of chap. 15,
although the two are related. We will now examine how best to explain exegetically and theologically the continuity and discontinuity the two chapters exhibit.

COVENANT. The "covenant of circumcision" (Acts 7:8) is a subsequent
stage in the revelation of the covenant made with Abram (15:18, "made a covenant," *kārat bĕrît*) and formally ratified by animal rite (15:17). Some scholars
prefer to characterize chap. 17 as a "confirmation" or "reaffirmation" of the initial covenant. In this view too, however, many admit that the covenant of chap. 17
evidences some development or clarification of chap. 15.[348] Although there is a
difference in these two interpretations, we do not want to overdraw them. What
they hold in common is more important, namely, that there is one covenant in
view, not two covenants. The idea of "covenant" is central to chap. 17; the term
bĕrît occurs thirteen times in nine verses (vv. 2,4,7,9,10,11,13,14,19). The patriarchal promises of heir, numerous descendants, land, nations, and blessing all
appear in this one chapter. Chapter 17, at the center of the Abraham narrative
(chaps. 12–22), emphasizes the transformation of barrenness to fruitfulness at the
personal, community, and national levels.[349] Unlike the covenant in chap. 15,
which had no requirements, chap. 17 includes two demands: (1) to live uprightly
before the Lord (v. 2) and (2) to practice circumcision faithfully (vv. 9–11).
These obligations, however, did not constitute a covenant relationship but presupposed one already in place. As J. A. Motyer observed, "Circumcision involves
the idea of consecration to God but not as its essence."[350] That the covenant is

---

[347] T. L. Thompson recognizes the present unity of chaps. 15–17 (but attributes it unnecessarily
to a redactor) whose theme is the "displacement" of Ishmael; chap. 17 is a "bridge" narrative that
looks ahead showing that God's promises are for the entire world and not Israel alone (*The Origin
Tradition,* 87–91).

[348] For a thorough review of the nuances of these approaches, see P. R. Williamson, *Abraham,
Israel and the Nations: The Patriarchal Promise and Its Covenantal Development in Genesis,*
JSOTSup 315 (Sheffield: Sheffield Academic Press, 2000).

[349] W. Brueggemann, "Expository Articles: Genesis 17:1–22," *Int* 45 (1991): 55–59.

[350] J. A. Motyer, "Circumcision," *NBD* 234.

fundamentally a spiritual relationship, founded and maintained by God's elective grace, is apparent by the continuation of the covenant despite the repeated failures of the patriarch and his successors to observe a blameless life, for example, the wife-sister ploy (chaps. 20,26) and the circumcision ploy (chap. 34).

The differences between the accounts of the covenant in chaps. 15 and 17 oppose the idea that chap. 17 is a priestly retread (P) of chap. 15's oath (E/J). These dissimilarities, however, do not indicate two separate covenants.[351] The Abraham narrative describes the giving of the same covenant in successive narrative stages,[352] thereby maintaining the story's tension and heightening the Genesis theology of divine provision expressed through human instrumentation (12:1–3; 13:14–17; 15:4–21; 17:1–22; 18:3–15; 21:1–7,10; 22:15–18). The differences in the settings and purposes of the stages explain the progressive character of the giving of the covenant. Chapters 12 and 22 form the introduction and conclusion to the narrative account of the covenant giving, requiring the patriarch at both points to act upon the divine word (12:2; 22:2). The call of Abraham entails the promises of the covenant (12:1–3; Acts 7:3; Heb 11:8–10), which are formally presented in the animal rite of 15:7–21. The covenant rite in chap. 15 answers Abraham's perplexity over an heir (15:4–5), reaffirming the promises made in 12:1–2c about the man and his progeny. Chapter 17 establishes the sign and seal of the covenant (Rom 4:3,11) and, as in 12:1, calls upon Abraham to obey the Lord's demands (17:1b–2; Acts 7:8), which he also fulfills (12:4; 17:3a,23–24). Chapter 17 also answers Abraham's question of an heir (chap. 15) but from the perspective of Ishmael's birth (chap. 16). The orientation of the covenant in chap. 17 is the promises pertaining to blessing for the nations, as in 12:2d–3c; the author achieves this by emphasizing Abraham's prodigious future, that is, circumcision, the new names "Abraham" and "Sarah." Finally, chap. 22 attaches to the covenant a divine oath (22:16; Heb 6:13–14,17), which follows the climactic act of obedience (22:2,10–12; Heb 11:17; Jas 2:21). The intervals between the announcement of the promises, the ratification, the giving of the sign, and the offering of Isaac are due to the theological explanation of the development of Abraham's faith. We recognize the same characterization of Jacob and of Jacob's sons, who undergo a progressive moral and spiritual transformation. The series of trials to Abraham's faith create the foils for the progressive revelations of God's promissory covenant. The tension of an heir in chaps. 12–14 are partially alleviated in the night vision of chap. 15; the interference of Sarai in

---

[351] That two related but different covenants existed has been proposed by T. D. Alexander, "Abraham Re-Assessed Theologically," in *He Swore an Oath: Biblical Themes from Genesis 12–50* (Cambridge: Tyndale, 1993), 7–28, and fully examined by Williamson, *Abraham, Israel and the Nations.* Alexander explores the constituent differences between chaps. 15 and 17, concluding that the former is an unconditional covenant and the latter a conditional one. The "covenant of circumcision" is announced in chap. 17 but is not established until 22:15–18 by divine oath after Abraham meets the requirements. Each covenant reflects a feature first promised in 12:1–3: chap. 15 focuses on the promises of nationhood (land, seed), and chap. 17 focuses on the promise of international blessing.

[352] E.g., D. Kidner, *Genesis,* TOTC (Downers Grove: InterVarsity, 1967), 128; and Wenham, *Genesis 16–50,* 16–17.

chap. 16 by the birth of Ishmael receives the divine demand for obedience and the clarification of the identity of the appointed heir in chap. 17. Moreover, the broadened horizon of "many nations" and "kings" featured in chap. 17 has its faith challenge in the issue of God's justice and righteousness, as well as Abraham's conduct (18:18–19), in chaps. 18–21. Chapter 22 provides the occasion for Abraham to express his faith through obedience, which receives the final confirmation of divine oath. The oath repeats the essential elements of nationhood (descendants, land) and international blessing (22:15–18). Theologically, this progression from faith to obedience is not an acrimonious pairing of opposites, as the apostle James shows in his interpretation of Abraham's offering of Isaac (Jas 2:21–24). A progression also is seen in the Noahic covenant in which the promissory announcement (6:18) is followed by obedience (6:22; 7:5,9,16) and, last, the sign of covenant (9:1–17).

The apostle Paul treats the covenant chapters in Genesis as one covenant when he contends on the basis of the life of Abraham that salvation is received by faith alone (Rom 4:1–25). The chronological arrangement of the Genesis narrative in which Abraham's circumcision (17:24) follows his faith (15:6) demonstrates that the rite was a "sign" *(sēmeion)* of faith, that is, a "confirmation" or "seal" *(sphragida),* confirming the righteousness he had already received while he was still "uncircumcised" *(en tē akrobystia;* Rom 4:11).[353] In his letter to the Galatians, he argued that Gentile Christians as imitators of Abraham's faith were genuine heirs of the promises through Christ (Gal 3:6–5:12). He appealed to the example of Abraham, without maintaining the order of chaps. 15 and 17. Paul avoided the covenant of circumcision of chap. 17, relying on chaps. 12; 15; 18; and 22 and on the Hagar-Sarah episodes of chaps. 16 and 21. F. Thielman observes how the covenant of circumcision taken alone, with its insistence on ritual observance and by its nature as eternal, could be appropriated by his opponents to make their case.[354] By the way the apostle treats chap. 17 in both passages, that is, the chronological argument in Romans and its omission in Galatians, he viewed chap. 17's circumcision as secondary to the promissory essence of the covenant.

The covenant of circumcision shares important features with the Noahic covenant (6:18; 9:8–17): the covenants are patterned after a royal land grant; covenant "signs" *(ʾôt)* are established (9:12–13,17; 17:11); the covenants are "everlasting" *(ʿôlām;* 9:12,16; 17:7–8,13,19); and they share covenant vocabulary, "establish a covenant" *(hēqîm bĕrît* and variations; 6:18; 9:9,11,17; 17:7,19,21; Exod 6:4),[355] "give a covenant" *(nātan bĕrît;* 9:12; 17:2; Num 25:12), and a covenant "between me and you (pl.)" *(bênî ûbênêkem;* 9:12,15; 17:10,11; Exod 31:13; see vol. 1A, pp. 367–68, 407–12). The Noahic grant, however, is made with all creation (9:9,12,13,16,17), while the covenant of circumcision pertains to Abram and his future generations (17:7,8,9,10), for example,

---

[353] T. Schreiner, *Romans,* ECNT (Grand Rapids: Baker, 1998), 224–25.

[354] F. Thielman, *Paul and the Law* (Downers Grove: InterVarsity, 1994), 121–22.

[355] Also the language of the Sinai covenant at Lev 26:9 and Deut 8:18; for discussion of covenant-making terms, see M. Weinfeld, "בְּרִית *bᵉrîth," TDOT* 2.260.

"between me and the earth" (9:13) versus "between me and you (sg.)" (i.e., Abram; 17:2,17).

Circumcision functions as a "sign" like the rainbow for the Noahic covenant and the Sabbath for the Mosaic covenant, all reminders of God's gracious promises.[356] The rainbow is a reminder to God (9:15–16), whereas circumcision and Sabbath are reminders to both God and Israel, indicating that Israel belongs to the Lord. Also circumcision and Sabbath involve community obligations which when practiced distinguish the community as members of the covenant. Failure to observe these rites resulted in expulsion (17:4) or death (Exod 4:24–26; 31:14). Circumcision signified that the community members were fit for God's purposes (e.g., 17:7–11; Josh 5:2–9); the metaphorical use of the rite, such as "circumcision of the heart," indicated spiritual readiness (e.g., Deut 10:16; 30:6; Jer 4:4; 9:25–26; Col 2:11).

Circumcision was not unique to the Hebrews; the Egyptians and some west Semitic groups employed circumcision (Jer 9:25–26), predominantly as a puberty rite or marriage rite.[357] Apparently, some of Israel's immediate neighbors did not practice the rite (e.g., Shechemites, Gen 34; Philistines, Judg 14:3; 15:18; 1 Sam 17:26,36).[358] The term "uncircumcised" ('ārēl) when used metaphorically as a slur ridiculed Israel's enemies, who were considered wicked ("unclean," Isa 52:1; cp. Ezek 28:10; 31:18; 32:17–32).[359] For the Hebrews circumcision above all possessed spiritual significance, which distinguished them as the people of God. Salvation at the Passover event in Egypt required the sign of circumcision (Exod 12:44,48). Circumcision by itself, however, had no probative value (Gal 5:6; 1 Cor 7:19) since it could be exercised by the unrighteous (Gen 34:15; Lev 26:41; Jer 9:25–26). Its practice upon infants on the eighth day (17:12; Lev 12:3, Luke 1:59; 2:21; Phil 3:5) reflected the covenant's attention to the whole household who inherited the promises by virtue of relationship to Abraham.[360] This relationship, although initiated by divine call and promise, demanded moral accountability (17:1,9).

When later Judaism faced the threat of an encroaching hellenization (second century B.C.), circumcision created a stir between the hellenized Jews and the orthodox. Although they agreed that spiritual circumcision was necessary, they differed over the requirement of ritual circumcision to be considered "Jewish" (e.g., *Jub.* 1:23–25; 15:25–34; *Jdt* 14:10; Esth 8:17, LXX; Josephus, *Ant.* 12.241; 20.38–48; 139,145; *1 Mac* 1:15; 2:46; Philo, *Migr.* 92; *QE* 2.2). The sectarian Qumran community differentiated itself from the "apostate Jews" in Jerusalem

---

[356] F. Helfmeyer, "אוֹת *ʾôth,*" *TDOT* 1.181–83.

[357] J. Sasson, "Circumcision in the Ancient Near East," *JBL* 85 (1966): 473–76; R. Hall contends that it was also a magical rite to avert evil ("Circumcision," *ABD* 1.1026).

[358] The Philistines as Indo-European did not adopt the practice of the west Semites (L. Allen, "עָרֵל," *NIDOTTE* 3.557).

[359] J. Oswalt, *Isaiah 40–66,* NICOT (Grand Rapids: Eerdmans, 1998), 360–61; and D. Block, *The Book of Ezekiel Chapters 25–48,* NICOT (Grand Rapids: Eerdmans, 1998), 99, 218.

[360] Sarna observes that "the eighth day is particularly significant because the newborn has completed a seven day unit of time corresponding to the process of creation" (*Genesis,* 125).

(who were also circumcised) by insisting they were the truly circumcised of heart (e.g., CD 16:4–6; 1QS 5:5).[361] The church faced a similar debate over the requirement of circumcision for the acceptance of the Gentiles (e.g., Acts 10:45; 11:2; 15:1–5; Gal 2:12; 5:11–12; 6:12; Phil 3:2; Titus 1:10). The apostle Paul addressed this early schism repeatedly and argued that circumcision was permissible, even expedient at times (Acts 16:3), but was not required of the Gentiles (e.g., Acts 15:2,28–29; 21:21; 1 Cor 7:18; Col 3:11). Spiritual circumcision alone was required for salvation, and physical circumcision when promoted as a requirement was to be repudiated (e.g., Rom 2:28–29; 3:30; 4:9–12; 1 Cor 2:11; 3:11; Gal 6:15; Phil 3:2–3). Circumcision, in fact, could be a liability, for it only had value to those who completely obeyed the Mosaic law in every other respect (e.g., Rom 2:25–26; 3:1–2; Gal 5:2–3; 6:13).

STRUCTURE. Abraham's "ninety-nine years" introduces and concludes the chapter (vv. 1a,24a). The theophanic revelation dominates the passage (vv. 1b–22), consisting of three parts: the promises are announced (vv. 1b–8) and explained (vv. 15–22), with instructions concerning the "sign" of the covenant (vv. 9–14) sandwiched in between. The chapter is more of a theological treatise than the typical Abraham story; the terse responses of Abraham (vv. 3a,17–18) take a minor place, giving the interchange the visage of a dialogue. After the divine pronouncements, a brief narrative reports Abraham's immediate compliance by undergoing circumcision (v. 23). The lengthy and repetitive divine speeches are met by the author with the directness of a single statement. The final verses give the ages of Abraham and Ishmael and a summary of the chapter's events (vv. 24–27).

v. 1a Introduction: Abram "ninety-nine"
vv. 1b–22 Covenant revealed
    vv. 1b–8 Covenant promises announced
    vv. 9–14 Sign of circumcision prescribed
    vv. 15–22 Covenant promises explained
v. 23 Circumcision inaugurated
vv. 24–27 Conclusion: Abraham "ninety-nine"

The major unit (vv. 1b–22) can be further analyzed in terms of the five divine speeches and Abraham's two responses. The speeches show counterbalancing themes: speeches one-two (vv. 1c–8) address the general promise of many progeny, and speeches four-five (vv. 15–16,19–21) move to the specific concern in an individual heir. The center speech (vv. 9–14) contains the instruction on circumcision.[362] Although only circumcision is specifically identified as a memorial "sign" (v. 11), each section of the covenant revelation contains its own reminder: the name "Abraham" for the first part (vv. 1b–8), circumcision

---

[361] For a review of interpretation among the Jews, see Hall, "Circumcision," *ABD* 1.1027–29.
[362] Van Seters, *Abraham in History,* 286.

for the second (vv. 9–14), and "Sarah" for the third part (vv. 15–22).[363]

    v. 1b The Lord appears
      vv. 1c–2 Lord: self-identification *("El Shaddai")* and preamble
        v. 3a Abram's response: collapses
          vv. 3b–8 Lord: "Abraham's" name, divine promise
            vv. 9–14 Lord: "Sign" of circumcision and obligations
          vv. 15–16 Lord: "Sarah's" name, divine promise
        vv. 17–18 Abraham's response: collapses, laughs, and offers Ishmael
      vv. 19–21 Lord's rebuttal: future for Isaac and Ishmael
    v. 22 The Lord ascends

    S. E. McEvenue observed a chiasmus in vv. 1–25 (yet not perfectly symmetrical) and two panels of parallel elements (cp. 15:1–6,7–21; 16:2–6).[364] In both the chiasmus and the parallel panels, circumcision is the structural focus. Below is the chapter's twin panels:

A Yahweh's intention to make an oath about progeny (1–2)
B   Abraham falls on his face (3a)
C   Abraham father of nations (4b–6)
D   God will carry out his oath forever (7)
E   The sign of the oath (9–14)

A1 God's intention to bless Sarah with progeny (16)
B1   Abraham falls on his face (17–18)
C1   Sarah mother of son, Isaac (19)
D1   God will carry out his oath forever (19b, 21a)
E1   The sign of the oath (23–27)

(1) El Shaddai Appears to Abram (17:1–3a)

[1]When Abram was ninety-nine years old, the LORD appeared to him and said, "I am God Almighty; walk before me and be blameless. [2]I will confirm my covenant between me and you and will greatly increase your numbers."
[3]Abram fell facedown,

17:1a This brief introduction and the conclusion of the episode (vv. 24–26) provide essential information for the reader. At "ninety-nine" Abram had been in the land for twenty-four years (12:4), and it was thirteen years since Ishmael's birth (16:16). Verse 24 repeats his age but uses the name "Abraham"; it also describes the new sign of circumcision. "Abram" may have had questions in his heart about an heir at the start, but by the end of the theophany

---

[363] Sailhamer, "Genesis," 138.
[364] His structural display fails to account for vv. 3b,18,23 in the chiasmus; see McEvenue, *The Narrative Style of the Priestly Writer,* 158–59, also followed by Wenham, *Genesis 16–50,* 17–18.

"Abraham" readily undergoes the pain of the knife. The whole episode occurs over one day, according to the notice "that very/same day" (vv. 23,26).

17:1b–3a Identification of the covenant parties typically begins such documents (e.g., 15:1; Exod 20:1). As in the night vision (15:1b,7), the Lord identifies himself (v. 1b); here he is *El Shaddai* (EVs "God Almighty"). Although its etymology is obscure, the epithet conveys in context the majesty and power of the divine person (e.g., Exod 6:3; Num 24:4,16; Job 11:7). *Shaddai* is associated in Genesis with the divine promise of children and nations (28:3; 35:11; 43:14; 48:3; 49:25; cp. Ruth 1:20; Ps 22:10).[365]

Two obligations, "walk before me . . . be blameless," are demanded followed by two outcomes: "[so that] I will confirm [lit., "give," *wĕʾettĕnâ*] my covenant . . . and (so that) I will greatly increase your number" (v. 2).[366] The commands require a spiritual preparation for receiving the covenant sign. The two Hebrew imperatives of the sentence echo the call to obedience in 12:1–3; "Go [*lek,* "leave," NIV] . . . and you will be a blessing [*wehĕyēh bĕrākâ]"* (12:1a,2d). Abram responded by departing (12:4), and because he obeyed the divine word, he is now in the place to receive this further word: "Go [*hitallēk,* "walk," NIV] . . . and be blameless" (*wehĕyēh tāmîm;* 17:1b).[367] Such moral conduct distinguished Noah in his day (6:9; 7:1; see on these terms vol. 1A, pp. 356–57). The exhortations call for Abram to take a course of action, as in 12:1 and 22:2. The requirements may be a generic obedience, but in the context of the chapter, the only action specifically called for is circumcision, which the passage notes he expediently fulfilled (vv. 23,26).[368]

Abram's gripping response of falling facedown expressed his awe at the theophany (vv. 3a,17). This is the demeanor of respect toward a superior (e.g., 37:10; 42:6; 44:14; 48:12; 2 Sam 9:6; 1 Kgs 18:7); also it is the action accompanying profound pleading before the Lord in a moment of crisis (e.g., Num 16:4,22; Josh 7:6; cp. the reaction of Moses to theophany, Exod 34:8). Such reaction in the presence of the Lord is recorded only of Abram and his servant (24:52) among the patriarchs (cp. the greeting, 18:2; 19:1).

(2) Abraham: Father of Many Nations (17:3b–8)

and God said to him, 4"As for me, this is my covenant with you: You will be the father of many nations. 5No longer will you be called Abram; your name will be Abraham, for I have made you a father of many nations. 6I will make you very

---

[365] For more on *Shaddai,* see commentary Introduction, "*El* Names of God."

[366] The sequence of the imperatives הִתְהַלֵּךְ . . . וֶהְיֵה (v. 1) followed by the cohortatives וְאֶתְּנָה . . . וְאַרְבֶּה (v. 2) indicates purpose/result ("so that"; *IBHS* §34.6a).

[367] The two imperatives can be taken as sequential, הִתְהַלֵּךְ לְפָנַי וֶהְיֵה תָמִים, "walk before me so that you will be blameless."

[368] Sarna notes that *Gen. Rab.* 46.1 states that all Abram lacked in holiness was the removal of the "blemish" of the foreskin (*Genesis,* 123).

fruitful; I will make nations of you, and kings will come from you. ⁷I will establish my covenant as an everlasting covenant between me and you and your descendants after you for the generations to come, to be your God and the God of your descendants after you. ⁸The whole land of Canaan, where you are now an alien, I will give as an everlasting possession to you and your descendants after you; and I will be their God."

17:3b–6 Verses 4–8 describe the covenant as divine in origin and character ("As for me" and "my covenant," v. 4); the subsequent paragraph (vv. 9–14) shifts attention to the obligations of Abram ("you," v. 9). The covenant possesses four features.

1. God will make Abram the "father of many nations" (*'ab hămôn gôyim,* vv. 4b,5b). This feature is central as shown by the parallel repetition of the promise, forming an inclusion around the change in the patriarch's name (v. 5a). By a sound play on the words "father" (*'ab*) and "many" *(hămôn),* the Lord provides Abram *('abrām)* the signal name "Abraham" (*'abrāhām,* v. 5; on "Abraham," see vol. 1A, p. 500). The giving of a new name may mark a special event (32:27–29; 35:10; cp. 41:45; Dan 1:7). "For I have made you a father of many nations" (v. 5b) expresses a future promise as though already realized.[369]

2. The Lord will grant him numerous progeny (*mĕ'ōd mĕ'ōd* = "exceedingly," v. 6). "Fruitful" *(pārâ)* is the common metaphor for physical descendants, here echoing the creation ordinance (1:22,28) and the Noahic covenant (8:17; 9:1,7); the imagery of fecundity depicts future multitudes, constituting new nations (e.g., 17:20; 28:3; 35:11; 41:52; 48:4; Lev 26:9; Ps 105:24). The beginning fulfillment of the blessing is the population explosion experienced by the Hebrews in Egypt, precipitating their oppression and expulsion (47:27; Exod 1:7). Reference to "kings" among Abraham's descendants indicates that autonomous nations will result (17:16; 35:11); Abraham, though not a king himself, is the ancestor of multiple royal houses. Genesis shows the progressive realization of this promise by including genealogical lists of Ishmael's tribal rulers (17:16; 25:12–17) and Edom's kings (36:9–43); allusion to future rulers in Jacob's household is the blessing of Judah's "scepter" (49:10; cf. 36:31).

17:7–8 3. This covenant is multigenerational, even an "everlasting" *('ôlām)* covenant for Abraham's "generations *[dōrōt]* to come" (v. 7). The verse, as with the covenant stipulations cited in vv. 4–8, progresses from the person Abraham to his collective offspring: "between me and you (sg.) and your seed ("descendants," NIV) after you." "Seed" *(zeraʿ)* refers to an individual (i.e., Abraham) and, as collective singular, to his posterity (see vol. 1A, p. 246). Echoes of the Noahic and Sinaitic covenants resound in this promise: the Noahic covenant with "between" *(bên,* 9:12–13,15–17) and "generations to come" *(dōrōt 'ôlām,* 9:12) and "everlasting covenant" *(bĕrît 'ôlām,* 9:16); the Sinai

---

[369] On the sense of the perfective form נְתַתִּיךָ ("I have made"), see note at 17:20.

covenant by "to be your God and the God of your people after you" (Deut 26:17; the similar Lev 11:45; 22:33; 25:38; Num 15:41; also "my people," also Exod 6:7; Lev 26:12). Unlike the Noahic, which is universal ("every living creature," 9:10a,12b,15a,16b), the Abrahamic is ultimately restricted to a particular branch of his descendants, only through Isaac (21:12), not the children of Hagar and Keturah. Genesis shows a narrowing of the appointed line, involving the election of the younger son (i.e., Jacob; see Rom 9:6–8; Heb 11:17–19).

A puzzling question for Christian readers is the meaning of an "everlasting" (ʿôlām) covenant, since circumcision ceased as a required practice among Christian converts. Circumcision was a "sign," not the essence of the covenant; the covenant depended ultimately on the spiritual allegiance of the parties. This spiritual dimension was inherent in the covenant as the expulsion of certain circumcised but disqualified members in Abraham's household shows (e.g., Ishmael); spiritual circumcision was the test required of all those who would enjoy the favor of the Lord (Deut 10:16; 30:6; Jer 4:4; Col 2:11). Hence the eternal nature of the covenant describes the spiritual regeneration of the believer.

4. The final promise combines the key elements of descendants and land. In anticipation of Israel's possession of Canaan, the promise entails the language of the settlement period: the land (ʾereṣ) is defined by three qualifiers: "your sojournings" (měgureykā, "alien," NIV); "all . . . Canaan"; "an everlasting possession" (ʾăḥuzzâ). The land promise is expressed in terms of covenant relationship, "I will be their God." That the promise is multigenerational is evidenced by its virtual repetition to Jacob (28:3–4). Ishmael in contrast to Isaac would not share in the "inheritance" (21:10; Gal 4:30), neither does Jacob's twin Esau (25:33–34; 27:37; Heb 12:16). This particular "inheritance" was understood in the New Testament as including the spiritual possession of eternal life (Rom 9:4–13; Heb 11:8; 1 Pet 1:4). Historically, Abraham's generations came into their possession under Joshua and the subsequent monarchy; their status as "aliens" (gērîm) was transformed by their dispossession of the Canaanites (21:23; Exod 6:3–4; 22:21; Lev 19:34). Theologically, the promise of "inheritance" (ʾăḥuzzâ) was the divine gift reserved for Abraham's offspring (Exod 32:13; Deut 4:21; 12:10; Josh 11:23; 23:4; Isa 61:7), tenants upon the good land (Lev 25:23). The church expanded the land grant to include the whole earth (Rom 4:3; Matt 5:5 with Ps 37:9) and interpreted it as the inheritance of eternal life (Heb 11:8; 1 Pet 1:4).

(3) Covenant of Circumcision (17:9–14)

⁹Then God said to Abraham, "As for you, you must keep my covenant, you and your descendants after you for the generations to come. ¹⁰This is my covenant with you and your descendants after you, the covenant you are to keep: Every male among you shall be circumcised. ¹¹You are to undergo circumcision, and it will be the sign of the covenant between me and you. ¹²For the generations

to come every male among you who is eight days old must be circumcised, including those born in your household or bought with money from a foreigner—those who are not your offspring. [13]Whether born in your household or bought with your money, they must be circumcised. My covenant in your flesh is to be an everlasting covenant. [14]Any uncircumcised male, who has not been circumcised in the flesh, will be cut off from his people; he has broken my covenant."

17:9–11 The third divine speech details the obligation of the covenant which involves the practice of the covenant's sign. The individual Abraham is emphasized at the start, "as for you" (*'attâ;* v. 9). "You [sg.] must keep" is expressed in the form of apodictic law, requiring observance of covenant obligations (e.g., Exod 23:15; Deut 19:19; 28:9). In v. 10 the shift to the plural pronoun "you are to keep" refers to future generations (Deut 6:17; 8:1). Throughout the second speech, an emphasis on future generations and the plural "you" reflects the association of the sign with procreation. "This is my covenant" identifies the covenant as the Lord's (v. 10), and it involves "every male." Verse 11 further clarifies the relationship between the covenant and the sign, specifying the nature of the rite. Circumcision (from *mûl*) involved the removal of the loose foreskin (*'orlâ*), which permanently exposed the gland of the penis.[370] Except for the extreme practice of the hellenized Jews, who underwent a surgical reattachment of the foreskin, the rite resulted in a permanent mark.

17:12–14 More specifics follow in v. 12: the male infant at eight days was circumcised (21:4; Acts 7:8; Luke 11:59; 2:21; Phil 3:5), thus adapting the practice of a puberty or marriage rite to religious ceremony. In the cult seven days of uncleanness were counted for the new mother, followed by the infant's circumcision on the eighth day and the thirty-three days of purification of the mother (Lev 12:2–4). The eighth held special meaning as the day of atonement or dedication to the Lord (e.g., Exod 22:30; Lev 9:1; 14:10,23; 15:14,29; 22:27; 23:39; Num 6:10; Ezek 43:27). The provision here refers to all male children born as "offspring" to the head of the household (v. 12), including Ishmael though born by a concubine. In addition, all others who either were born into the household by Hebrew parents of slavery or by those of foreign descent (vv. 12–13,23,27; cp. 14:14) must undergo circumcision. Such inclusion was based on the subservient relationship of the parent and child to the Hebrew household (cp. Exod 12:43–44; Ezek 44:9); by this mark in the body the slave identifies with the master's covenant with God.[371]

Verse 13 reiterates the inclusive and everlasting nature of the covenant. "In

---

[370] Egyptian circumcision was "a dorsal incision upon the foreskin which liberated the glans penis" (Sasson, "Circumcision," 474).

[371] Westermann observes that the inclusive nature of the obligation results in a unified household (*Genesis 12–36*, 266). Brueggemann comments, "The most striking dimension of this sacramental institution is the 'born' and the 'bought' are both included (vv. 12–13)" ("Genesis 17," 57).

your flesh" indicates the permanency of the mark and hence the perpetuity of the covenant. The phrase "in the flesh of his foreskin" in vv. 14,24–25 (absent in the NIV; see EVs; also Lev 12:3) suggests that "flesh" in v. 13 also refers to the male penis (cf. Lev 15:2–3; Ezek 16:16; 23:20).[372] No special concessions were made for any (adult) person who refused to undergo the custom; the severe threat of expulsion motivated any squeamish offender to reconsider (v. 14). Such excommunication symbolically meant the person's death in the eyes of the community (e.g., Exod 12:15,19; Lev 7:20–21,27; Num 15:30; 19:13,20; for its meaning of physical execution, e.g., Exod 21:14; Lev 20:3,5; 1 Sam 28:9; or death in war, Judg 21:5–6). Breach of this custom was more than a repudiation of the community, for the culprit in doing so rejected the Lord himself, that is, "broken my covenant." The language "to break [*prr*]covenant" describes Israel's apostasy (Isa 24:5; Jer 11:10; 33:21; Hos 6:7; 8:1; cp. Mal 2:11,14).

(4) Sarah: Mother of Nations (17:15–18)

[15]God also said to Abraham, "As for Sarai your wife, you are no longer to call her Sarai; her name will be Sarah. [16]I will bless her and will surely give you a son by her. I will bless her so that she will be the mother of nations; kings of peoples will come from her."

[17]Abraham fell facedown; he laughed and said to himself, "Will a son be born to a man a hundred years old? Will Sarah bear a child at the age of ninety?" [18]And Abraham said to God, "If only Ishmael might live under your blessing!"

17:15–16 The fourth speech names Abraham's wife "Sarah" (v. 15) and blesses her with the promise of a numerous progeny, even "nations" and "kings" (v. 16). This announcement exceeds that made to Abraham, as the man's reaction shows (v. 17; 18:12). Specifically, the Lord promises she will have a "son," in contradiction to her doubts (16:2). "Sarah" is an alternate form of the older "Sarai," meaning "princess" (see comments on 11:29); she as the lawful wife becomes the mother of all Israel (Isa 51:2; cp. typology, 1 Pet 3:6). In the context of patriarchialism, the husband is charged with the task of renaming his wife (cp. 3:20); no explanation of the etymology is given, only implied by the association of "princess" with the later word "kings" in the blessing (v. 16). Remarkably, the Lord announces blessing directly upon the woman, usually reserved in Genesis for the male progenitors (including Ishmael, v. 20; 12:2; 22:17; 26:24; cp. Luke 1:42).

17:17–18 Abraham's reaction consisted of the range of human response; initially, he collapses in reverential awe, laughs, reasons, and then urgently pleas. His laughter (*ṣāḥaq*) is shared later by Sarah at the annunciation of Isaac (18:12), which explained the meaning of the name "Isaac" (*yiṣḥāq;* 21:6).

---

[372] Sarna, *Genesis,* 125.

Abraham reasons that their elderly state prevents her pregnancy; again Sarah echoes the same inner dialogue of doubt (18:12). Abraham presents to the Lord a counterproposal by pleading for Ishmael's acceptance ("if only," *lû*, v. 18).[373] The NIV's translation "under your blessing" clarifies the literal "before you" (i.e., God).[374] Abraham's request is not neglected by the Lord ("I have heard you"), for the boy also receives a blessing (v. 20; 21:12–13).

(5) Promise of Isaac (17:19–22)

[19]Then God said, "Yes, but your wife Sarah will bear you a son, and you will call him Isaac. I will establish my covenant with him as an everlasting covenant for his descendants after him. [20]And as for Ishmael, I have heard you: I will surely bless him; I will make him fruitful and will greatly increase his numbers. He will be the father of twelve rulers, and I will make him into a great nation. [21]But my covenant I will establish with Isaac, whom Sarah will bear to you by this time next year." [22]When he had finished speaking with Abraham, God went up from him.

17:19–21 The fifth divine speech answers Abraham's concerns regarding the viability of a son born to Sarah and the future of Ishmael. The reality of a son born to Sarah is forcefully confirmed by God in vv. 19 and 21. (1) The Hebrew *ʾăbāl* can have an asseverative meaning ("yes, indeed," AV), but here the nuance is adversative ("no, but," NASB, NRSV or "no," HCSB; "nevertheless," NAB, NJPS). The NIV's translation "yes, but" retains both, with "yes" anticipating the blessing for Ishmael (v. 20) yet mitigated by the priority given to Isaac. (2) The participle "will bear you" *(yōledet)* is the imminent sense, "about to bear you a son"; in other words, the reality of the fulfillment can be expressed on a time line, "next year" (v. 21). (3) The annunciation includes a specific name for the child, "Isaac," which corresponds to the annunciation of his first son Ishmael (see comments on 16:11). The sound play of the name "Isaac" ("he laughs") in response to Abraham's inner laughter indicated the divine intent to answer the patriarch's wonder. (4) The Lord confirms his promise ("I will establish," *wahăqimōtî*), repeating the promissory language given to Abraham (vv. 7,19; cf. v. 2). The birth announcements of Ishmael (16:11–12) and Isaac (v. 19) present a striking contrast in the destinies of the two sons. Ishmael will become the father of a great people, but he and his offspring will be outsiders, whereas Isaac will assume his father's inheritance.

Ishmael is also the concern of the Lord; he ensures the troubled father that the boy will have a prominent future (v. 20). "I have heard you" is another play on the name "Ishmael" ("God hears"). The perfective use of "bless" *(bēraktî)* indicates the action is viewed by the speaker as completed in a future setting:

---

[373] For לוּ in a wish clause see *IBHS* §40.2.2d.

[374] NJPS "your favor" and REB "your special favour."

"I will bless him."[375] "Make fruitful" *(pārâ)* and "greatly increase" *(hirbêtî . . . bim'ōd mĕ'ōd)* recall prepatriarchal procreation (1:22,28; 9:1,7) and combine the promissory language of vv. 2 and 6 made to Abraham in chiastic order: "increase" (v. 2), "fruitful" (v. 6), "fruitful" (v. 20), "increase" (v. 20). Twelve "rulers" *(nĕśî'im)* for Ishmael are cited in 25:16; the number twelve corresponds to Jacob's household (35:22; 49:28). The term "ruler" is quite broad in usage, referring to any leader or chief, especially used of the leaders of later Israel (Num 1:16; 17:2); Abraham is designated as *nāśî'* ("prince," 23:6) as was "Shechem (34:2). It may also be used of kings *(melek;* 1 Kgs 11:34; Ezek 37:24–25).[376] As a result Ishmael produces "a great nation" (also 21:18) as in the divine promises to Abraham (12:2; 18:18) and Jacob (46:3; cp. Exod 32:10; Deut 26:5).

The adversative "but" of v. 21 contrasts the two sons of Abraham and their respective blessings. "My covenant" *(bĕrîtî)* heads the sentence, differentiating the covenant promises made to Isaac from those made to Ishmael. In the process of highlighting the qualifications of Isaac, the mother again is identified as Sarah. The prediction of his birth in one years is repeated to Abraham by the visitors (18:10,14) and is fulfilled exactly (21:1–2).

17:22 "God went up" indicates a visible ascension; it is the language of theophany (35:13; cp. 18:33; Exod 21:18).

(6) Circumcision of Abraham's Household (17:23–27)

23On that very day Abraham took his son Ishmael and all those born in his household or bought with his money, every male in his household, and circumcised them, as God told him. **24**Abraham was ninety-nine years old when he was circumcised, **25**and his son Ishmael was thirteen; **26**Abraham and his son Ishmael were both circumcised on that same day. **27**And every male in Abraham's household, including those born in his household or bought from a foreigner, was circumcised with him.

17:23 Abraham's obedience was immediate; "on that very day" (vv. 23,26) he carried out the circumcision in exact accord with divine direction ("as God told him"; cp. 12:4). The narrative description (vv. 23,27) of their circumcision corresponds to the earlier language of instruction (vv. 10–14). The paragraph repeatedly points to the inclusiveness of the rite, "all, every" (v. 23, *kol* [3x]; v. 27). The significance of the event is also pointed up by the twice-used phrase "on that very day" (vv. 23,27), a chronological remark used of other momentous occasions (7:13; Exod 12:17,41,51; Lev 23:21, 28–30; Deut 32:48; Josh 5:11; Ezek 24:2; 40:1).

---

[375] *IBHS* §30.5.1e identifies this use as "accidental perfective" where the speaker "vividly and dramatically represents a future situation both as complete and as independent" (cf. 17:5).

[376] K. Aitken, "נָשִׂיא," *NIDOTTE* 3.171–72.

17:24–27 The final verses (vv. 24–27) reiterate that Abraham himself performed the circumcision on his household, perhaps self-inflicted first (see v. 14),[377] then Ishmael, and all other males. The reports of Abraham's and Ishmael's circumcisions are parallel descriptions indicating solidarity between father and son (vv. 24,25).[378] Reference to their ages at ninety-nine and thirteen show further the extent of Abraham's obedience, which involved personal pain and vulnerability. Moreover, the same formulaic description of their circumcisions reinforces the entire unity of Abraham's household under the covenant.

Abraham's prompt action signaled a faith that indeed a child will be born to Sarah, as preposterous as it was to ponder (18:10–12). The writers of the New Testament recognized that Abraham believed that the Lord would intervene and provide a son from the aged couple (Rom 4:17–19; Heb 11:11–12).

9. Divine Judgment and Mercy (18:1–19:38)

The Lord appears again to Abraham (12:7; 15:1; 17:1) repeating the promise of a son, but here the annunciation concerns Sarah's response, whom the Lord seeks out by name (18:9).[379] Abraham and Sarah had each undertaken a plan for obtaining an alternative heir (15:2–3; 16:2), and by Sarah's laughter they now share the same response at the thought of a child born in their old age (17:17; 18:12). The annunciation of Isaac (18:1–15), however, forms the backdrop for an announcement of a different kind, the destruction of the cities Sodom/Gomorrah (18:16–19:29). This center narrative consists of two parts (see below) concerning the fundamental question of divine justice. (1) Abraham dialogues with the Lord regarding the just treatment of the innocent, entreating the Lord to spare the cities for the sake of the righteous (18:16–33). (2) The cataclysm that befalls the cities and the preservation of Lot match the former section by describing the divine decision (19:1–29). After the destruction, the story concludes with the births of Lot's sons by incest, Moab and Ben-Ammi (19:30–38).[380] The whole, therefore, is enclosed by narratives devoted to the birth of future heirs, providing a sharp contrast between the moral heritage of each one's beginnings.

---

[377] Verse 14 anticipates cases where an uncircumcised adult resists the procedure: if a father neglected to circumcise his child for whatever reason, the boy is responsible for his own circumcision upon reaching adulthood (Sarna, *Genesis,* 126).

[378] The NIV at v. 25 omits the second half of the Hb. verse, i.e., "when [Ishmael] was circumcised in the flesh of his foreskin" (NASB, NRSV, HCSB).

[379] Chap. 15 presents the perspective of Abraham, and chap. 16 depicts the involvement of Sarah; chap. 17 and 18:1–15 reflect the similar shift from focus on Abraham to the reaction of Sarah. Also both chaps. 15 and 17 possess formal covenant rites, followed in each case by the role of the matriarch in chaps. 16 and 18.

[380] R. Letellier divides the account into five sections, each initiated with a verb of motion (18:1–15,16–33; 19:1–23,24–29,30–38; *Day in Mamre Night in Sodom: Abraham and Lot in Genesis 18–19,* BIS 10 [Leiden: Brill, 1995], 44–45).

A 18:1–15 Visitors' announcement of Isaac's birth
  B 18:16–19:29 Destruction of Sodom and deliverance of Lot
A′ 19:30–38 Births of Lot's sons Moab and Ben-Ammi

COMPOSITION. Although scholars differ over whether chaps. 18–19 consist of redactional layers drawing on unrelated traditions (e.g., Wellhausen, von Rad, Westermann) or constitute the composition of one author (e.g., Van Seters, Alexander), all today recognize the remarkable unity of the chapters and the striking literary artistry they exhibit. Most attribute chaps. 18–19 to one source (Yahwist) with possibly two later additions (18:17–19,22–33); also 19:29 is assigned to the Priestly (P) writer, due to the appearance of *Elohim* and P's propensity to summarize. The final product dates to the seventh–sixth centuries or postexile when the issue of God's just dealings with the nations (cf. 18:23–33) among the prophets and exiles was of greater importance (e.g., Jer 5:1; Ezek 14:22–23; 18:5–32; 22:30; Zeph 1:12).

Regardless of methodological stripe, scholars have repeatedly observed the rich complexity of parallel language, theme, and motifs between the two chapters (see "Structure" below). On this basis Van Seters argued that a single author (his exilic Yahwist) combined two themes in creating his free composition: (1) the birth announcement of Isaac (18:1a,10–14) and (2) the primary contribution of divine visitors (18:1b–9,15–19:38).[381] Although we do not concur with his exilic date for the author, Van Seters convincingly demonstrates that the (almost) seamless integration of the various parts of the two chapters are best explained by a single hand than the unlikely chance that several oral traditions came together across centuries by redactional efforts. He further shows that 18:17–19,22–33 are in fact necessary to make sense of their contexts and evidence reasoned progression in the narrative flow.

As for Van Seters' proposal of two disparate themes for the conceptional background of the story, Alexander finds that vv. 10–14 fit well with vv. 9 and 14, rendering it unnecessary to posit a distinctive theme. Moreover, the absence of the actual birth and naming of Isaac (not until 21:1–3) warns that the author is not following the expected formula, since annunciation typically includes the name of the child (e.g., 16:11; 17:19; 1 Kgs 13:2; Isa 7:14–17; 1 Chr 22:9–10; Matt 1:21; Luke 1:13–17,31–33).[382] Van Seters recognizes this problem and offers that 21:2 originally followed 18:10–14; the author displaced the verse in order to suit his purpose of including the intervening stories. This appears to be special pleading, however, since on the one hand Van Seters appeals to a posited theme that close examination does not confirm. Alexander questions whether the proposal of an annunciation form is here and suggests that the author more likely created a unique work. Also the parallels between chaps. 18 and 19, especially 18:1–8 and 19:1–3, justify the conclusion that 18:1–15 as a unit is the original introduction to the remaining 18:16–19:29. Finally, on the assignment of 19:29 to P, Wenham observes that "God *(Elohim)* remembered" rather than *Yahweh* is

[381] Van Seters, *Abraham in History,* 203, 209–21.
[382] Alexander, *A Literary Analysis,* 202–3.

not necessarily a source different from its context's. As in chap. 19 elsewhere, 19:29 is a conscious authorial match with the flood account, "God [*Elohim*] remembered Noah" (8:1a).[383]

R. Letellier has presented the most compelling case for the unity of chaps. 18–19.[384] After presenting his reasoning for demarcating the story from chaps. 17 and 20, he argues that textual clues prove that chaps. 18–19 possess external and internal unity. For indicators of external unity he includes (1) the continuity of the characters, (2) the interest in time of day for the events, (3) the notice given to the places where the events occur, and (4) the logical movement from problem to resolution. On this last point Letellier admits that 18:1–15 does not appear at first to contribute to the tension of the Sodom story, but he finds that the resemblances in setting, vocabulary, and narration between 18:1–15 and chap. 19 (esp. vv. 1–3) must lead to the conclusion that chaps. 18–19 are "a deliberate literary composition."[385] Relying on the observations of Licht,[386] he demonstrates how the narrative's four movements in the two chapters interface, one episode naturally leading to another at spacial and thematic levels.

Movement 1 located at Mamre (18:1–15), Movement 2 situated midway between Mamre and Sodom (18:16–33), and Movement 3 at Sodom (19:1–29) describe the journey of the heavenly visitors. Movement 2 also provides the theological reflection on Sodom leading to Movement 3's cataclysm, and Movement 4 gives the final outcome of Lot (19:30–38). Also, by employing methods of semiotics, Letellier believes that chaps. 18–19 contain correspondences at the "deep structural" level: the sequence of (1) visitors, (2) hospitality, and (3) reward (i.e., a promised son//rescue from Sodom) expresses the deep meaning of each chapter.[387]

A good case also can be made for accepting 19:30–38 as the original conclusion to the Sodom-Gomorrah pericope. The final paragraph of the passage (19:30–38) presupposes the Sodom-Gomorrah narrative (19:1–29) to explain why Lot became a recluse and why his daughters, once betrothed to Sodomite men, took desperate steps to ensure children. Lot's departure from Zoar out of fear appears true to form in light of the preceding cataclysm. Also the absence of his wife is not perplexing since her fate previously was explained (19:26). In anticipation of their central role in 19:30–38, Lot's "daughters" are repeatedly mentioned in the prior narrative (vv. 8,12,14,15,16) as is their betrothal status whose consummation remained unfulfilled (19:8,12,14). Another literary link with the former narrative is the play on the word "know" (*yādaʿ*). The Sodomites desire to "know" (*yādaʿ*, "have sex," NIV) the guests (v. 5), but Lot offers his daughters who have not "known" (*yādaʿ*, "slept with," NIV) a man (v. 8); and Lot

---

[383] Wenham also observes that Amos's (4:11) allusion to 19:29 is consistent with an early date for the verse (*Genesis 15–50*, 45).

[384] Letellier, *Day in Mamre*, 30–70.

[385] Ibid., 41.

[386] J. Licht, *Storytelling in the Bible* (Jerusalem: Magnes Press/Hebrew University, 1978), 132.

[387] The category "reward" would be better termed "grace," indicating divine mercy, not reward for service rendered.

does not "know" (*yādaʿ*, "was not aware," NIV) he has committed incest (vv. 33,35). The irony of this outcome can hardly be missed. Also the angels preserve (*ḥāyâ*) the life of Lot (v. 19), and the daughters "preserve" (*ḥāyâ*) his posterity (vv. 32,34). Finally, as the preceding narrative (18:16–19:29) echoes the Noah story, Lot's drunkenness and sexual misconduct remind the reader of Noah's family shame also after destruction (9:20–27).

The moral standing of Abraham's future covenant household ("right and just," 18:19) versus the wickedness of Lot's world (Sodom, 19:7,9) and, concomitantly, the moral question of God's justice (18:25; also 20:4) cooperate with the larger narrative theme of promise to hold the pericope together (13:13; 18:23,25; 19:7). Such theological consideration hardly requires an exilic date, however, since such speculations on divine justice appear as early as the second millennium in the ancient Near East (e.g., *Ludlul bel nemeqi*, ca. 1500; and the Babylonian Theodicy, ca. 1000). Although we cannot date Job definitively, at least we know that the story's setting is patriarchal, suggesting an acquaintance with such questions raised from earliest times.

Also to chaps. 18–19 we can add the following episode of Abraham's encounter with Abimelech, king of Gerar, who unwittingly echoes Abraham by raising the issue of divine justice (e.g., "innocent nation," 20:4). R. Alter proposes that 18:16–20:18 forms a bridge, not an interruption, between the birth announcement of the covenant son (17:19–21; 18:1–15) and its fulfillment in Isaac's birth (21:1–3).[388] The intervening episodes of 18:16–20:18 present a morally perilous world that could derail the promises, but the Lord's saving grace ensures that they will be achieved. Although chap. 20 is not as closely linked to chaps. 18–19 as they exhibit between themselves, its author is fully aware of the prior story (see comments on chap. 20).

We conclude, therefore, that chaps. 18–19 are a literary whole whose origin can be attributed to one author. That the composition was of the second millennium corresponds well with the setting depicted in the account.

STRUCTURE. Earlier we commented that chaps. 17 (see comments there) and 18–19 evidence a compositional interdependence, indicating a common author drafted them. Each unit, for example, adapts the Noah narrative: (1) chap. 17 employs the same literary form of covenant and shares many covenant terms (9:8–17; for details see vol. 1A, pp. 367–68); (2) chaps. 18–19 contain identical language and the similar plot of a survivor (see vol. 1A, pp. 363, n. 21). Also each of the three narratives—the Noah story, the covenant of circumcision, and the Sodom and Gomorrah account—possess a chiastic structure (see vol. 1A, pp. 352–53 and comments on chap. 17). G. Wenham's analysis of the chiasmus in 18:16–19:29 is cited below.[389]

---

[388] R. Alter, "Sodom as Nexus: The Web of Design in Biblical Narrative," in *The Book and the Text: The Bible and Literary Theory* (Cambridge, Mass.: Basil Blackwell, 1990), 146–60 = *Tikkun* 1 (1986): 30–38.

[389] Wenham, *Genesis 16–50*, 41.

1. Abraham's visitors look toward Sodom (18:16)
  2. Divine reflections on Abraham and Sodom (18:17–21)
    3. Abraham pleads for Sodom (18:22–33)
      4. Angels arrive in Sodom (19:1–3)
        5. Assault on Lot and his visitors (19:4–11)
          6. Destruction of Sodom announced (19:12–13)
        7. Lot's sons-in-law reject his appeal (19:14)
      8. Departure from Sodom (19:15–16)
    9. Lot pleads for Zoar (19:17–22)
  10. Sodom and Gomorrah destroyed (19:23–26)
11. Abraham looks toward Sodom (19:27–28)
Summary (19:29)

Moreover, prior chapters featured parallel literary panels (15:1–6,7–21; 16:2–4,5–6; 17:1–14,16–27). This literary device of imitation between parts of a composition is accepted by all for chaps. 18–19. Although most studies have focused on parallel language in chaps. 18–19 (see examples 1–9 charted below),[390] Letellier expands the levels of correlation to similar settings, motifs, and actions. The correspondences often involve inversion (10–13) or completion of preceding actions (14–16).[391] On this basis he demonstrates how this literary device reinforces the narrative movement from the initial actions in chap. 18 to their denouement in chap. 19. A representative sampling of the parallels here is sufficient to make the point:

1.   [Abraham] was sitting at the entrance to his tent (18:1)
    Lot was sitting in the gateway of the city (19:1)
2.   When he saw them, he hurried toward them (18:2)
    When he saw them, he got up to meet them (19:1)
3.   and bowed low to the ground (18:2)
    and bowed down with his face to the ground (19:1)
4.   please do not pass your servant by (18:3)
    please turn aside to your servant's house (19:2)
5.   Where is your wife, Sarah? (18:9)
    Where are the men . . .? (19:5)
6.   Sarah laughed (ṣāḥaq, qal, 18:12,13,15)
    his sons-in-law thought he was joking (ṣāḥaq, piel, 19:14)
7.   the outcry against Sodom/Gomorrah is so great (rābab, 18:20)
    (their) outcry . . . is so great (gādal, 19:13)
8.   sweep away (sāpâ, 18:23–24)
    swept away (sāpâ, niphal, 19:17)

---

[390] Ibid., 43–44.
[391] Letellier, *Day in Mamre*, 64–66.

9. I will spare *(nāśāʾ)* the whole place (18:26)
    I will grant *(nāśāʾ)* this request (19:21)
10. the Lord promises a son (18:10)
    Lot offers his daughters (19:8)
11. Abraham will be the father of great nations (18:18)
    Lot is asked if he has sons-in-law, sons, and daughters (19:12)
12. Abraham pleads for the few righteous (18:23–32)
    Lot pleads for himself (19:18–20)
13. Abraham and Sarah live in tent (18:6,9,10)
    Lot and his daughters dwell in cave (19:30–38)
14. "Shall I hide from Abraham what I am about to do?"(18:17)
    "because we are going to destroy this place" (19:13)
15. The Lord promises mercy to the few righteous (18:26–32)
    Lot receives mercy (19:16,21–23,29)
16. The Lord will judge the guilty (18:21b,26–32)
    The Lord destroys the cities and Lot's wife (19:24–26)

MOTIFS.   Lot and his family, as in chaps. 13–14, provide a contrast to Abraham that enhances his stature as the standard bearer for blessing. In chap. 13 Abraham was the generous kinsman and in chap. 14 the impressive warrior who rescues his nephew; here Abraham is the generous host (18:1–15) and the confidant of the Lord whose intercessory pleas (18:16–33) contribute to Lot's rescue again. Lot cannot save his guests, not even himself (19:29); the Sodomites rebuff his feeble actions (cp. Judg 19:23–25). Ironically, it is his guests who must save themselves and deliver him from the city's citizens (cp. Judg 19:25–26). The similarities between chaps. 18 and 19 (see above) point up the dissimilarities of the two men: Abraham hosts the visitors in safety at his tent (18:1), whereas Lot welcomes the angels to his house (19:1–2), who are put at jeopardy among the Sodomites; the visitors gladly comply with Abraham's request to dine (18:5b), but the angels reluctantly agree to Lot's histrionic insistence (19:2b–3a; cp. Judg 13:16); Abraham's meal "in the heat of the day" (18:1) includes the delicacies of the fattened calf and curds, but the arrival of the angels "in the evening" (19:1) catches Lot unprepared, and he offers only a meal of unleavened bread (19:3);[392] and Abraham and Sarah scurry about to serve the guests, with Abraham attending to the seated men (18:8c); but Lot is not prepared, and his wife is not mentioned (19:3). Another striking contrast is their respective roles as progenitors of new nations. Lot generates two nations (19:30–38) but ignorantly, whereas Abraham is deliberately and honorably the "father of many nations" (17:5). Chapters 18–19 depict Lot as less competent and virtuous than Abraham, who is the sagacious leader of his clan.

---

[392] The preparation of an animal may imply a figure of sacrifice, and its absence suggests Lot was less diligent; see Judg 13:16,19.

Lot himself is besmirched by Sodom's evil when he offers his daughters in lieu of the guests (19:7) and foolishly ignores the angels' efforts to rescue him (19:16). Our predominantly negative interpretation of Lot's actions, however, must be balanced by Lot's positive features.[393] According to Jewish and Christian traditions, Lot was a "righteous man" (*Wis* 10:6; 19:17; *1 Clem* 11:1) who could be compared favorably with Noah, Abraham, and others (*Wis* 10:4–13). The apostle Peter appealed to his audience to hold fast to their faith despite the oppression they endured as had the examples of Noah, "the preacher of righteousness," and Lot, "the righteous man" (2 Pet 2:5–8). In what sense might we count Lot "righteous," given the narrative's generally negative portrayal when compared to Abraham? When Lot is compared to his Sodomite neighbors, he can be regarded a strikingly moral man. He followed rigorously the custom of hospitality toward strangers, despite the intense pressure of the threat of death. Moreover, although having committed incest, the passage makes it clear that he was a victim, which mitigates somewhat his culpability. Early Christian interpreters pointed to Lot's generosity toward the angels and commended him for resisting the wickedness of his fellow citizens as features worthy of Christian imitation (e.g., Chrysostom, *Homilies on Genesis* 43.10–12; Ambrose, *Flight from the World* 9.55–56).[394] Both Noah and Lot, whose lives ended disgracefully (drunkenness), nevertheless stood out as admirable people when set against the background of their wicked times. Commenting on Lot's sin against his daughters, Calvin remarked, "Yet such are commonly the works of holy men: since nothing proceeds from them so excellent, as not to be in some respect defective."[395]

The promise to "bless" or "curse" the nations, dictated by their treatment of Abraham's family (12:3ab), is manifested in the story by the mixed results of mercy toward Lot and judgment against the Sodomites. Abraham's plea for the "righteous" implies Lot is centrally in mind (18:22–33; 19:29), although his appeal involves the whole of the city. God's mercy toward Abraham has secured Lot's deliverance (19:29). Coats observes that the Lot-Sodom stories prove that Lot missed out on the blessing of God when he chose to separate from Abraham.[396] But this interpretation must be moderated. Divine grant of land to the Moabites and Ammonites (Deut 2:9,19; as with the Ishmaelites and

---

[393] T. D. Alexander, "Lot's Hospitality: A Clue to His Righteousness," *JBL* 104 (1985): 289–300; P. Tonson, "Mercy without Covenant: A Literary Analysis of Genesis 19," *JSOT* 95 (2001): 95–116; and T. R. Schreiner, *1, 2 Peter, Jude,* NAC (Nashville: Broadman & Holman, 2003), 341–42.

[394] *ACCS* 2.74–78; for an overview of early Jewish and Christian interpretations, see J. A. Loader, *A Tale of Two Cities: Sodom and Gomorrah in the Old Testament, Early Jewish and Early Christian Traditions* (Kampen: J. H. Kok, 1990).

[395] Calvin, *Comm.,* 1.500.

[396] Coats, "Lot: A Foil in the Abraham Saga," 128–29.

Edomites, Deut 2:5) shows that Lot was included in the benefits of the patriarchal promises by virtue of his positive connection to Abraham. Some Jewish
interpreters described Lot's virtues and achievements as derived in some way
from his association with Abraham (*Gen. Rab.* 50 and Rashi). An illustration of
curse against the enemies of Abraham is Sodom's mistreatment of Lot and his
guests. The extent of the Sodomites' moral blindness is sharpened in the narrative by their hostilities toward Lot, who begged them to repent of their evil
(19:7,9). His own sons-in-law, presumably Sodomites, epitomize opposition
when they snub Lot's warning as a tall story (19:14).

The Genesis motif of the chosen offspring versus the forsaken child is continued by showing the disqualification of Lot and his lineage who came by
drunken incest (Lev 18:6; Deut 23:2–3[3–4]). The typecasting of Noah and Lot
as survivors whose drunkenness leads to family disgrace is reinforced by the
many parallels the flood and Sodom narratives of destruction possess (see vol.
1A, p. 363, n. 21; cf. Luke 17:28–29; 2 Pet 2:5–8). It is typical of Genesis to
conclude its accounts of the forsaken offspring by giving a genealogical record
(e.g., Cain, Ishmael, Esau); here Lot's family account ends with the episode of
his children by incest, the Moabites and Ammonites.

(1) Abraham's Visitors (18:1–15)

[1]The LORD appeared to Abraham near the great trees of Mamre while he
was sitting at the entrance to his tent in the heat of the day. [2]Abraham looked up
and saw three men standing nearby. When he saw them, he hurried from the
entrance of his tent to meet them and bowed low to the ground.

[3]He said, "If I have found favor in your eyes, my lord, do not pass your servant by. [4]Let a little water be brought, and then you may all wash your feet and
rest under this tree. [5]Let me get you something to eat, so you can be refreshed and
then go on your way—now that you have come to your servant."

"Very well," they answered, "do as you say."

[6]So Abraham hurried into the tent to Sarah. "Quick," he said, "get three
seahs of fine flour and knead it and bake some bread."

[7]Then he ran to the herd and selected a choice, tender calf and gave it to a
servant, who hurried to prepare it. [8]He then brought some curds and milk and
the calf that had been prepared, and set these before them. While they ate, he
stood near them under a tree.

[9]"Where is your wife Sarah?" they asked him.

"There, in the tent," he said.

[10]Then the LORD said, "I will surely return to you about this time next year,
and Sarah your wife will have a son."

Now Sarah was listening at the entrance to the tent, which was behind him.
[11]Abraham and Sarah were already old and well advanced in years, and Sarah
was past the age of childbearing. [12]So Sarah laughed to herself as she thought,
"After I am worn out and my master is old, will I now have this pleasure?"

[13]Then the LORD said to Abraham, "Why did Sarah laugh and say, 'Will I

really have a child, now that I am old?' ¹⁴Is anything too hard for the LORD? I will return to you at the appointed time next year and Sarah will have a son."

¹⁵Sarah was afraid, so she lied and said, "I did not laugh."

But he said, "Yes, you did laugh."

"The LORD appeared to Abraham" (v. 1a) functions as a heading for the whole pericope, since theophany characterizes chaps. 18–19 (except the epilogue, 19:30–38). Divine-human dialogue pervades chaps. 18–19; each episode is occasioned by the visitors, who encounter Abraham and his relative Lot (18:1; 19:1). The introductory episode of 18:1–15 elevates Abraham and Sarah as the appointed couple for future blessing; Abraham is the perfect host (18:1b–8), and Sarah is the subject of divine announcement (18:9–15). The contrast at Sodom provided by Lot and his wife starkly shows the contrary outcome of Lot's disgrace to that of Abraham and Sarah's. The prologue also prepares for the private dialogue in 18:16–33 that portrays Abraham as intercessory prophet (cf. 20:7,17).

18:1a   Introduction to the theophany
18:1b–8   Abraham the host
    18:1b–2 Abraham hosts the three visitors
    18:3–5   Abraham's dialogue with the visitors
    18:6–8   Abraham and Sarah prepare the meal
18:9–15   Annunciation of Isaac's birth
    18:9–10a   The Lord reveals Sarah will give birth
    18:10b–15 The Lord dialogues with Abraham and Sarah

18:1–2 This is the last place where the language "appeared" describes theophany to Abraham (12:7; 17:1; 18:1; cp. 26:2,24). In this case the theophany involves "three men" (v. 2), the only place in Scripture where such a trio of heavenly guests occurs. This alone underscores the magnitude of the two announcements that follow: Isaac's birth and the destruction of Sodom/Gomorrah. The "men" included the Lord (v. 22) and two angels (19:1; see comments at 16:7). Reference to "Mamre" recalls earlier events in the lives of Abraham and Lot: their parting (13:18) and the elder's rescue of Lot from eastern kings (14:13,24). "[Abraham] looked up and saw" (lit., "lifted his eyes and saw," v. 2) often signals an important imminent event (24:63; 43:29; Josh 5:13; Judg 19:17). Again, from Mamre the patriarch will show the same paternal concern for his nephew. Abraham "in the heat of the day" (v. 2) took refuge from the sun at the door of his tent; the sudden appearance of travelers standing "before him" ("nearby," NIV) suggests immediately that these guests were extraordinary. His haste in offering the courtesies of hospitality exhibited the same generous spirit he had shown in the past (Lot, 13:8–9).

18:3–5 Abraham respectfully addresses one of the three men who evidently stood out from among the others, as indicated by the singular "my lord" (*'ădōnāy*) and singular verb "do not pass . . . by" (v. 3). His continued entreaty shifts, however, to the plural in number (vv. 4–5), referencing all three visitors. His request is delicately expressed, beginning his remarks with the honorific title "my Lord" (*'ădōnāy*) in the Hebrew sentence (as reflected in NASB, NRSV),[397] and the particle *nā'*, "please," occurs twice (see NASB). His plea is predicated on the visitors' "favor" (*ḥēn*) toward him (6:8, vol. 1A, pp. 345–46); "if I have found favor in your eyes" prefaces an entreaty made by a subordinate person (e.g., 30:27; 33:10; 47:29; Exod 33:13; 34:9; Judg 6:17; 1 Sam 27:5).

The custom of hospitality is illustrated by the visitors in chaps. 18–19 and the encounter of Abraham's servant with Rebekah's household (chap. 24). Stunning examples of breaches in hospitality include the wicked behavior of the Sodomites toward the visitors (chap. 19) and the Gibeahites toward the Levite and his concubine (Judg 19; cf. Luke 7:44–46). In the New Testament, hospitality was a common setting for Jesus' instruction about the kingdom (e.g., Matt 22:1–14; Mark 2:15–22; Luke 19:1–10) and was regulated in the Christian community (e.g., Rom 15:7; 1 Tim 3:2; 2 John 2:9; 3:9; Heb 13:2). Provision and protection for guests characterized a good host, including care of their animals (24:19,32; 43:24; Judg 19:21). The host provided water for refreshment (24:14; Judg 4:19) and the washing of soiled feet (v. 4; e.g., 19:2; 24:32; 43:24; Judg 19:21; 1 Sam 25:41; John 13:5; 1 Tim 5:10); a meal followed (v. 5; e.g., 19:3; 24:33; 43:16; Exod 2:19–20), and overnight accommodations were provided for pilgrims (e.g., 19:2–3; Judg 19:6–20).

18:6–8 Abraham busily set his house in action, drawing on Sarah to bake bread and instructing a servant to prepare a lavish meal of meat, curds, and milk (e.g., Deut 32:14; Judg 5:25; 6:18–19; Ezek 34:3). The tornado of activity ("hurried," vv. 6,7; "quick," v. 6; "ran," v. 7) reinforces the picture of Abraham as the extraordinary host. The passage specifies that Abraham stands alertly nearby under one of the trees observing their meal (v. 8); the depiction of theophany often includes the imagery of trees (e.g. 12:6–7; 21:33; Judg 6:11,19; Ps 29:9).[398] Mention of the "great trees [oaks] of Mamre" in v. 1 (13:18; 14:13) refers to the same site where Abraham had formally worshiped the Lord (13:18).

18:9–10a Collectively, the trio ("they," pl.) asked Abraham of Sarah's whereabouts (v. 9); a theophanic messenger also queried Hagar about her travels (16:8; cf. 3:9; 4:9). His response is terse in the Hebrew, *hinnê bā'ōhel*, "behold, in the tent," including perhaps a gesture toward it. The spokesman is the Lord, if v. 13 is our guide, who dialogues with Abraham and Sarah in vv.

---

[397] The particle אָ֫, traditionally rendered "I pray" or "please" (e.g., NASB), occurs twice in v. 3 (GKC §105b, n. 1); that the particle is a special form of address, however, is suspect; see T. Lambdin, *Introduction to Biblical Hebrew* (New York: Scribners, 1971), 170 and *IBHS* §34.7a.

[398] The "oak" is a typical setting for ancient worship; see, e.g., for false worship Judg 9:6,37; Isa 1:29; 57:5; Hos 4:13.

10–15.[399] "I will surely return" translates the emphatic Hebrew construction *(šôb ʾāšûb);* the certainty of the promise is further enhanced by a specific time-table, "this time next year" *(kāʿēt ḥayyâ,* "at the time of reviving" = spring; cp. 2 Kgs 4:16–17)[400] and by the particle *hinnê,* "and behold [a son]" (v. 10a).

18:10b–15 The miraculous nature of the announcement is underscored by the Lord's amazing discernment of Sarah's private thoughts (vv. 12–15). Sarah's position in the tent, "behind him" (v. 10b), and her internal monologue, "to herself" (v. 12a), indicate that by unusual means the visitor knew her heart, not having seen a facial expression or heard a chuckle. Such exceptional perception gave credibility to the visitor's unlikely prediction of a child. The domestic intrigue of Abraham's household involving rival siblings is intimated in Sarah's actions in this passage by the lexical hints "listening" *(šāmaʿ;* v. 10b) and "laughed" *(ṣāḥaq;* vv. 12–13), wordplays on Ishmael's name (16:11) and on Isaac's (21:6). Sarah will later defend her son by urging Ishmael's expulsion, at which time the Lord directs Abraham, "Listen *[šĕmaʿ]* to your wife" (21:12; cp. 3:17). Isaac's wife Rebekah, after "listening" (27:5), takes action to ensure that Jacob receives the firstborn rights in her household.

A normal biological conception was humanly ruled out due to Sarah's post-menopausal age. The passage captures the impossibility of her pregnancy by three successive descriptions: the couple is "old" *(zĕqēnîm);* "advanced in years," lit., "coming with days" *(baʾîm bayyāmîm);* and she is "past the age of childbearing," lit., "as the way of women had ceased for Sarah" *(ḥādal lihyôt lĕśārâ ʾōraḥ kannāšîm)* "Old" and "advanced in years" later describe the aged patriarch in his last days (24:1; also Joshua, 13:1; 23:1–2) and David (1 Kgs 1:1; so Jesse, 1 Sam 7:12). The Hebrew euphemism for menstruation occurs again in the description of Rachel's ruse (31:35).

Sarah's bitter amusement over the announcement (v. 12; cf. 17:17) reflects from her viewpoint the audacity of the man's claims; her inner thoughts poignantly confirmed that the couple had not engaged in sexual relations for years. "Pleasure" *(ʿednâ)* is used here for sexual delight ("enjoyment," NJPS) and elsewhere of luxuries, delicacies (ms. pl., 2 Sam 1:24; Jer 51:34; Ps 36:9).

Undeterred by Sarah's secret doubts, the divine spokesman continues his speech with Abraham, reiterating the promise (vv. 13–14). His two questions of Abraham are rhetorical, requiring no response from the patriarch.[401] Since the Lord can accomplish such a feat, Sarah's skepticism is unfounded.[402] The Hebrew for "hard" or "difficult" *(pālāʾ,* v. 14) means "wonderful" (NAB) in the

---

[399] The NIV's "then the LORD said" in v. 10a is an interpretation of the ambiguous Hb., וַיֹּאמֶר, "then he said."

[400] BDB 312.

[401] The NJB translates, "Nothing is impossible for Yahweh."

[402] "Why [לָמָּה] did Sarah laugh?" inquires after the basis of her laughter (T. Nakarai, "LMH and MDUʿ in TANAK," *HS* 23 [1982]: 47).

sense of extraordinary (e.g., Jer 32:17,27).[403] The works of the Lord are exceptional by human standards, evoking amazement by his people (e.g., Ps 118:2–3). God's knowledge of future events as well as the human heart was "too wonderful" (*pĕlî'â, qere* reading) to comprehend (Ps 139:6).

Sarah's interjection, "I did not laugh" (v. 15), shows that she, not Abraham, was the intended recipient of the man's statement. His unusual knowledge startled her, and she was "afraid" *(yārē'â)* of the man's response (v. 15). It was out of fear too that Abraham lied to Pharaoh and Abimelech concerning his wife (12:13,19; 20:11 with Isaac's explanation, 26:7). The divine rejoinder is emphatic (asseverative use of *kî*): "Oh, yes *[kî]* you did laugh" (NRSV); the definitive tone of his answer ended the matter.

(2) Destruction of Sodom and Gomorrah (18:16–19:29)

[16]When the men got up to leave, they looked down toward Sodom, and Abraham walked along with them to see them on their way. [17]Then the LORD said, "Shall I hide from Abraham what I am about to do? [18]Abraham will surely become a great and powerful nation, and all nations on earth will be blessed through him. [19]For I have chosen him, so that he will direct his children and his household after him to keep the way of the LORD by doing what is right and just, so that the LORD will bring about for Abraham what he has promised him."

[20]Then the LORD said, "The outcry against Sodom and Gomorrah is so great and their sin so grievous [21]that I will go down and see if what they have done is as bad as the outcry that has reached me. If not, I will know."

[22]The men turned away and went toward Sodom, but Abraham remained standing before the LORD. [23]Then Abraham approached him and said: "Will you sweep away the righteous with the wicked? [24]What if there are fifty righteous people in the city? Will you really sweep it away and not spare the place for the sake of the fifty righteous people in it? [25]Far be it from you to do such a thing—to kill the righteous with the wicked, treating the righteous and the wicked alike. Far be it from you! Will not the Judge of all the earth do right?"

[26]The LORD said, "If I find fifty righteous people in the city of Sodom, I will spare the whole place for their sake."

[27]Then Abraham spoke up again: "Now that I have been so bold as to speak to the Lord, though I am nothing but dust and ashes, [28]what if the number of the righteous is five less than fifty? Will you destroy the whole city because of five people?"

"If I find forty-five there," he said, "I will not destroy it."

[29]Once again he spoke to him, "What if only forty are found there?"

He said, "For the sake of forty, I will not do it."

[30]Then he said, "May the Lord not be angry, but let me speak. What if only thirty can be found there?"

---

[403] The term often describes salvific acts, e.g., Exod. 3:20; Ps 9:1[2]; P. Kruger, "פלא," *NIDOTTE* 3.616.

He answered, "I will not do it if I find thirty there."

³¹Abraham said, "Now that I have been so bold as to speak to the Lord, what if only twenty can be found there?"

He said, "For the sake of twenty, I will not destroy it."

³²Then he said, "May the Lord not be angry, but let me speak just once more. What if only ten can be found there?"

He answered, "For the sake of ten, I will not destroy it."

³³When the LORD had finished speaking with Abraham, he left, and Abraham returned home.

¹The two angels arrived at Sodom in the evening, and Lot was sitting in the gateway of the city. When he saw them, he got up to meet them and bowed down with his face to the ground. ²"My lords," he said, "please turn aside to your servant's house. You can wash your feet and spend the night and then go on your way early in the morning."

"No," they answered, "we will spend the night in the square."

³But he insisted so strongly that they did go with him and entered his house. He prepared a meal for them, baking bread without yeast, and they ate. ⁴Before they had gone to bed, all the men from every part of the city of Sodom—both young and old—surrounded the house. ⁵They called to Lot, "Where are the men who came to you tonight? Bring them out to us so that we can have sex with them."

⁶Lot went outside to meet them and shut the door behind him ⁷and said, "No, my friends. Don't do this wicked thing. ⁸Look, I have two daughters who have never slept with a man. Let me bring them out to you, and you can do what you like with them. But don't do anything to these men, for they have come under the protection of my roof."

⁹"Get out of our way," they replied. And they said, "This fellow came here as an alien, and now he wants to play the judge! We'll treat you worse than them." They kept bringing pressure on Lot and moved forward to break down the door.

¹⁰But the men inside reached out and pulled Lot back into the house and shut the door. ¹¹Then they struck the men who were at the door of the house, young and old, with blindness so that they could not find the door.

¹²The two men said to Lot, "Do you have anyone else here—sons-in-law, sons or daughters, or anyone else in the city who belongs to you? Get them out of here, ¹³because we are going to destroy this place. The outcry to the LORD against its people is so great that he has sent us to destroy it."

¹⁴So Lot went out and spoke to his sons-in-law, who were pledged to marry his daughters. He said, "Hurry and get out of this place, because the LORD is about to destroy the city!" But his sons-in-law thought he was joking.

¹⁵With the coming of dawn, the angels urged Lot, saying, "Hurry! Take your wife and your two daughters who are here, or you will be swept away when the city is punished."

¹⁶When he hesitated, the men grasped his hand and the hands of his wife and of his two daughters and led them safely out of the city, for the LORD was merciful to them. ¹⁷As soon as they had brought them out, one of them said, "Flee for your lives! Don't look back, and don't stop anywhere in the plain! Flee to the

mountains or you will be swept away!"

18But Lot said to them, "No, my lords, please! **19**Your servant has found favor in your eyes, and you have shown great kindness to me in sparing my life. But I can't flee to the mountains; this disaster will overtake me, and I'll die. **20**Look, here is a town near enough to run to, and it is small. Let me flee to it—it is very small, isn't it? Then my life will be spared."

21He said to him, "Very well, I will grant this request too; I will not overthrow the town you speak of. **22**But flee there quickly, because I cannot do anything until you reach it." (That is why the town was called Zoar.)

23By the time Lot reached Zoar, the sun had risen over the land. **24**Then the LORD rained down burning sulfur on Sodom and Gomorrah—from the LORD out of the heavens. **25**Thus he overthrew those cities and the entire plain, including all those living in the cities—and also the vegetation in the land. **26**But Lot's wife looked back, and she became a pillar of salt.

27Early the next morning Abraham got up and returned to the place where he had stood before the LORD. **28**He looked down toward Sodom and Gomorrah, toward all the land of the plain, and he saw dense smoke rising from the land, like smoke from a furnace.

29So when God destroyed the cities of the plain, he remembered Abraham, and he brought Lot out of the catastrophe that overthrew the cities where Lot had lived.

The message regarding the future son of Sarah and Abraham turns to a new but related subject, the survival of Lot. This section consists of two parts: the dialogue between Abraham and the Lord (18:16–33) and the destruction of Sodom and Gomorrah (19:1–29). The visitors who "looked down" *(šāqap)* toward Sodom (18:16) and Abraham who from the same spot "looked down" *(šāqap)* toward Sodom (19:28) frame the episodes, leaving 19:29 to summarize the outcome. The two units are held together by the query of covenant virtue and divine justice, with Sodom and the fate of Lot's family providing the contrast for Abraham and his legacy.

ABRAHAM PLEADS FOR SODOM AND GOMORRAH (18:16–33). The boundaries of this subsection are the actions of Abraham, who "walked along" *(hālak)* with the departing visitors (v. 16) and then "returned" *(šûb)* to his tent (v. 33). Both the beginning and ending describe the departure of the theophanic visitors: the trio "got up to leave" *(qûm)* Abraham's campsite (v. 16), with the Lord pausing to speak with Abraham, and then the Lord too "left" *(hālak)* Abraham (v. 33). The departure of the "LORD" in v. 33 forms an inclusio with v. 1 when the "LORD" first appeared. Between the movements of Abraham (vv. 17–32) are the divine reflection on covenant uprightness and the resulting dialogue of the Lord and Abraham, who, after learning of Sodom's probable demise, contends for the preservation of the city.

18:16 Abraham accompanies *(hālak)* the visitors
18:17–32 Abraham and the Lord reflect on divine justice

18:33 Abraham returns *(šûb)* to his place

The main unit divides into two parts, encompassing the Lord's viewpoint (vv. 17–21) and Abraham's viewpoint (vv. 22–32):

18:17–21   The Lord reflects on righteousness
    18:17–19   Abraham's covenant morality
    18:20–21   Sodom's injustice
18:22–32   Abraham's intercession for the righteous of Sodom
    18:22   Abraham remains with the Lord
    18:23–32   Abraham and the Lord negotiate

18:16   By detailing Abraham's accompaniment of the departing guests, the narrative completes its portrait of the perfect host. "Looked down" translates *šāqap,* which also describes the stance of Abraham toward Sodom (18:28); the term occurs elsewhere in morally dubious settings (e.g., 26:8) and describes the lofty perch of the Lord, who executes his judgment (e.g., Exod 14:24; Deut 26:15; Pss 14:2=53:2[3]; 102:19[20]; Lam 3:50).

18:17–18   The rationale for the divine disclosure to follow (vv. 20–21) is presented first.[404] The contemplative character of vv. 17–19 indicates the divine deliberativeness of involving Abraham (e.g., 1:26; 2:18; 6:7; 11:6–7);[405] his inclusion is reminiscent of the divine council (e.g., Job 1:6; Ps 89:7[8]) and prophetic circle of the Lord (e.g., 1 Kgs 22:14–28; Isa 40:1–2). Revelation is God's prerogative, which often occurred by dreams and visions (e.g., 15:1; 20:3; 28:12; 31:10–11,24; 46:2; Num 12:6; 1 Sam 3:1; and the prophets). The "face to face" encounter Moses experienced was distinctive (Num 12:8; Deut 34:10), "as a man speaks with his friend" (Exod 33:11); with Moses there was no angelic intermediary (e.g., 16:7; 21:17; 22:15; 32:30; Judg 6:22). There is also no parallel for Abraham's experience in which he *repeatedly* negotiates with the Lord, although human request and divine compliance was not unheard of (e.g., Exod 32:11–14; Amos 7:3,6). Abraham encountered the Lord like a "friend" (2 Chr 20:7), and thus he was a fitting prototype for the prophet, Moses.

The first reason for Abraham's status as confidant is tied directly to the divine call and promise of 12:2–3 (22:18; 26:4; 27:29,33; 28:14); the man will father "a great and powerful nation" (v. 18), language reminiscent of the progenitors Ishmael (17:20), Isaac (21:18; 26:16), and Jacob (46:3; cp. also

---

[404] Vv. 17–19, introduced by a *wāw* disjunctive, "Now the LORD (had) said" (וַיהֹוָה אָמָר; v. 17), provide supplementary information; the pluperfect "had said" (NJPS) brings out the antecedent tenor of the verse (*IBHS* §30.2.5b).

[405] The interrogative sentence, "Shall I hide . . . will be blessed?" (NASB), includes vv. 17–18 (NRSV, NJB, NJPS), with v. 18 as a subordinate, explanatory clause (with *wāw* disjunctive): "since Abraham [וְאַבְרָהָם] will surely become a great and mighty nation?" (NASB; *IBHS* §39.2.3b).

Moses, Exod 32:10; Israel, Num 14:12; Deut 26:5).[406] Assurance of the promise is affirmed both by the divine encounter itself and by the syntactical highlighting of the divine word, "Abraham will surely become *[hāyô yihyeh]* a great and powerful nation" (v. 18).[407]

18:19   Verse 19 (*kî,* "for") presents the second rationale for the revelation to Abraham; the divine election of the man ("chosen," *yāda',* lit. "known") will result ("so that," *lĕma'an*) in a people characterized by righteousness *(ṣĕdāqâ)* and justice *(mišpāṭ),* which in turn results ("so that," *lĕma'an*) in the Lord fulfilling his promise of worldwide blessing (v. 18). The ideas of election, promissory blessing, and righteousness come together in v. 19. The Lord chose Abraham for the purpose of blessing all nations (cp. Jer 4:2); this appointment also included the intermediary step of creating a righteous people whose conduct would be a beacon for the nations. "Election means election to an ethical agenda in the midst of a corrupt world of Sodoms."[408] Ultimately, however, the agenda is wholly God's to accomplish, for Israel did not live up to its calling, and the realization of the promises were achieved by divine grace (Deut 7:7; 9:4–6; 30:1–6).

The verse possesses covenant terminology, including "commanded" (*ṣiwwâ,* "directed," NIV), "keep" *(šāmar),* "righteousness" *(ṣĕdāqâ),* "justice" *(mišpāṭ),* and "spoken" *(dibber,* "promised," NIV). Exceptional to the Deuteronomic language of covenant is the term for "chosen," which translates *yāda'* ("to know"), rather than the common Deuteronomic word *bāḥar* ("to choose").[409] *Yāda'* conveys the idea of election with the nuance of familiarity, intimacy (e.g., Jer 1:5; Amos 3:2; Hos 13:5).[410] This sense of election fits the passage's setting of personal confidence; it also has a literary function with v. 21, where "know" reappears in the context of divine discovery (e.g., 20:6–7; 22:12). It is Abraham's expectation of what God will decide about Sodom that leads him to argue preemptively for clemency.

The consequence of Abraham's election includes his instructions to his household to observe the "way of the LORD" *(derek yhwh).* "Way" in its metaphorical sense conveys the idea of a lifestyle or pilgrimage.[411] The "way of the LORD" indicates a life whose conduct conforms to the prescriptions of the Lord. The "way" in Deuteronomic language is observance of the stipulations of the covenant, showing loyalty to the Lord (e.g., Deut 8:6; 9:12; Judg 2:22; 2 Kgs 21:22) by achieving "the requirements *(mišpāṭ)* of their God" (Jer 5:4,5; also Ezek 18:25,29; 33:17,20). In the case of Abraham the prescriptions are

---

[406] See the royal language of 17:6,16; 35:11.

[407] Typical for emphasis is the infinitive absolute construction הָיוֹ יִהְיֶה.

[408] C. J. H. Wright, "Ethics," *NIDOTTE* 4.590.

[409] בָּחַר occurs thirty-one times in Deuteronomy alone.

[410] T. Fretheim, "יָדַע," *NIDOTTE* 2.411; hence, "I have singled him out" (NJB, NAB, NJPS).

[411] K. Koch, "דֶּרֶךְ *derekh*," *TDOT* 3.282–93; E. Merrill, "דֶּרֶךְ," *NIDOTTE* 1.989–93.

expressed in ethical terms alone, meaning right behavior toward others: "by doing what is right and just" (v. 19b). Wisdom observed that the individual who chooses the way of the Lord enjoys the blessing of salvation (e.g., Ps 1:6; Prov 10:29). Conversely, the morally wicked travels the road resulting in destruction (e.g., Isa 35:8; Ps 37:34; Prov 11:5), but the prophets hold out hope for those who repent and reverse their "way" (e.g., Isa 55:7; Jer 36:3). The Sodom incident exemplifies the two different ways traveled by Abraham's family and by the Sodomites.

"Right and just" *(ṣĕdāqâ ûmišpāṭ)* are popular forensic terms, but here their meaning is the carrying out of ethical demands (e.g., Ps 33:5); it is a matter of "doing" what is right (e.g., Prov 1:3; 21:3; Jer 23:5; Ezek 18:21,27), especially social justice (e.g., Deut 16:19; Isa 1:17; Jer 22:3; Ezek 45:9; Amos 5:24).[412] It is incumbent upon Israel's rulers to ensure social equity (e.g., Ps 72:1–2; 1 Kgs 10:9; 2 Chr 9:8), for the Lord rules his people with moral integrity and fidelity *(ḥesed;* e.g., Pss 33:5; 89:14; Jer 9:24). "Justice" *(mišpāṭ)* is achieved by upright *(ṣĕdāqâ)* conduct (e.g., Ps 106:3), truth *(ʾĕmet;* e.g., Zech 7:9), and equity *(mêšārîm;* e.g., Ps 48:1[2]).[413] Particularly helpful for our understanding is Isa 5:7, where the prophet condemns the social injustice of his day; the Lord looks for "righteousness" *(ṣĕdāqâ)* but hears only the "cries" *(ṣĕʿāqâ)* of the oppressed.[414] The same Hebrew wordplay in 18:19,21 contrasts Abraham's "right" *(ṣĕdāqâ)* conduct and the "outcry" *(ṣĕʿāqâ)* of Sodom.

18:20–21 The Lord answers his own question of v. 17 by "tipping off" Abraham as to what is about to happen. Verse 20 presents the reason (i.e., complaint against Sodom-Gomorrah) why the Lord chooses the action of v. 21 (investigation); his probing is so that he might "know" (v. 22b) if the severity of Sodom-Gomorrah's sin is as grave as the "outcry" expresses.[415] By examining the situation, the Lord acts justly, not capriciously, in the determination he makes. Although the Lord does not state explicitly the foregone conclusion that the sin of Sodom deserves judgment, Abraham takes the Lord's investigation of Sodom as in effect a "search-and-destroy" mission. If the outcry has reached heaven, surely it had been heard by Abraham at nearby Mamre! The magnitude of their iniquity was probably known to the whole region since Sodom held the prominent place among allied cities (13:12;

---

[412] D. Ranier, "צדק," *NIDOTTE* 3.763–64.

[413] R. Schultz, "שפט," *NIDOTTE* 4.214.

[414] Isa 5:7 may allude to 18:19–22 by its two wordplays צְעָקָה/צְדָקָה ("right"/"outcry") and מִשְׁפָּט/מִשְׂפָּח ("bloodshed"/"just"); on its paronomasia, see J. Oswalt, *The Book of Isaiah Chapters 1–39*, NICOT (Grand Rapids: Eerdmans, 1986), 154 and n. 22.

[415] V. 20 can be the protasis with כִּי *(IBHS* §38.2d) and v. 21 the apodosis, as in NIV (also AV, NKJV, RSV, NAB, NJB); alternatively, כִּי can be emphatic here *(IBHS* §39.3.4e; GKC §148d), understanding v. 20 as exclamatory: "How great is the outcry . . . and how very great their sin!" (NRSV; also NASB, NJPS, REB).

14:2,8; also 10:19; Deut 29:23; Hos 11:8).

The Hebrew words translated "outcry," za'ăqâ (v. 20) and șĕ'āqâ (v. 21; 19:13),[416] may describe the woeful cry of victims who suffer injustice (e.g., Ps 9:12[13]; Job 34:28; Isa 5:7)[417] or express grief over distressful circumstances (e.g., Esau's loss, 27:34). Cries of lament may also be petitions for deliverance from oppressors (e.g., Deut 26:7; Judg 10:12) or for help (e.g., 41:55; Neh 9:9; Hab 1:2). The prophets likened the social injustices committed in Israel/Judah to the infamous cities Sodom-Gomorrah (Isa 1:9,10; Ezek 16:49; cp. Amos 4:11; 2 Pet 2:8), indicating that the outcries were related to social offenses.[418] From Sodom-Gomorrah the outcry is overheard by the Lord ("has reached me," v. 21), if not directed to him (cp. 19:13). Commonly, the terms translating "outcry" appear in those settings where the Lord is invoked, especially the suffering cries and appeals of his people under oppression (e.g., Exod 3:7,9; Num 20:16; 1 Sam 9:16).[419] Verses 20–21 recall the innocent blood of Abel that "cries out" (șō'ăqîm, 4:10) for vengeance (more below). It appears that the sin at Sodom-Gomorrah was social injustice, and the cries were either the result of the victims' pain or their pleas for vengeance.[420]

The Hebrew wordplay of za'ăqat with the term șĕ'āqâ ("right") brings the contrast between Abraham and Sodom into sharp relief. Ironically, the same term "outcry" in the Old Testament describes the cries of culprits themselves who suffer devastation at the hands of God or nations (e.g., Exod 12:30; Isa 14:31; Jer 18:22; 48:3–4; Zeph 1:10). It is the Lord who as "Judge of all the earth" (18:25) adjudicates the complaint and ultimately vindicates the oppressed. In the case of Sodom-Gomorrah, the exceptionally deplorable makeup of their sins subjects them to the prospects of total annihilation, prompting Abraham to query about the righteous whom he feared would be indiscriminately consumed with the guilty. The fury of Sodom's sin is described as "great" (rābbâ) and "grievous" (lit., "very heavy," kābĕdâ mĕ'ōd); the former recalls the gravity of the sin in Noah's day (6:5, lit., "great [rābbâ] was the evil of humanity"), and the latter description looks back to the setting of the Abram-Lot episode when Abram left Egypt (13:1, "very wealthy," kābĕdâ mĕ'ōd). Verse 20 then brings together the destruction motif of the flood and the occasion for Lot's errant choice of the deceptively attrac-

---

[416] זעק (v. 20a) and צעק (v. 21a; 19:13) are bi-forms, e.g., the refrain in Ps 107 has צעק in vv. 6,28 and זעק in vv. 13,19; A. H. Konkel, "זעק," NIDOTTE 1.1131.

[417] These injustices include, among others, murder, servitude, material oppression, and sexual violation (e.g., Exod 22:23[22]; Deut 22:24,27; Judg 6:7; 2 Kgs 8:5; Neh 5:6; Lam 2:18).

[418] C. J. H. Wright, An Eye for an Eye: The Place of Old Testament Ethics Today (Downers Grove: InterVarsity, 1983), 106–7.

[419] A. H. Konkel, "צעק," NIDOTTE 3.827–30, esp. 829.

[420] זעקת סדם, as an objective genitive (GKC §128h, §135m), "outcry against Sodom" (e.g., NIV; HCSB; NRSV; NJB; NAB; NKJV) or "outcry over Sodom" (REB).

tive cities of the plain (13:10,12,13).

"I will go down and see" (v. 21)[421] expresses anthropomorphically the divine inquiry."[422] Verse 21's language is reminiscent of the Tower of Babel narrative: "the LORD came down to see" (11:5) and "let us go down" (11:7). In each case the nefarious actions of the Babelites and Sodomites prompted the divine investigation. Sodom-Gomorrah were a microcosm of wickedness, which had once flourished in the days of Noah and which characterized the notorious Babel (see vol. 1A, pp. 468–76). The purpose of the present inquiry is to learn if the outcry against the cities[423] is an accurate picture ("as bad as the outcry"[424]) of what "they have done,"[425] language that echoes the first murder (4:10; cp. its links elsewhere, 3:13–14; 12:18; 20:9; 21:26; 26:10). By the Lord's descent, he will discover ("know") the extent of the violence among the cities' inhabitants.[426] "Know" in Exod 3:9 conveys the sympathetic hearing of God for the exploited Hebrews in Egypt. It is because the Lord is the upright "Judge of all the earth" (v. 25) that retribution is the appropriate response to human wickedness.

18:22 This verse provides the clearest identity of the three visitors: the two men (i.e., "angels," 19:1) are the entourage for the divine member, the Lord, who has been the spokesman all along. His dialogue with Abraham exhibits the exceptional condescension of God who appears as a man, hears out a man (Abraham), and then ultimately saves a man (Lot). The depiction of Abraham "standing *[ʿōmēd]* before the LORD"[427] as at a bar of justice is appropriate for the juridical appeal of the patriarch to follow (v. 25; cp. Deut 19:17;

---

[421] Cohortatives of resolve, אֵרֲדָה־נָּא וְאֶרְאֶה (*IBHS* §34.7b; GKC §108b); cp. 32:21; Exod 3:3.

[422] The voluntary concessions of the Lord to Abraham in this chapter probably contributed to the rabbinic *tiqqune sopherim* in v. 22, which elevates Abraham over the Lord by reversing their positions: "The LORD stood before Abraham" (C. McCarthy, *The Tiqqune Sopherim and other Theological Corrections of the Masoretic Text of the Old Testament,* OBO 36 [Freiburg: Universitätsverlag/Göttingen:Vandenhoeck & Ruprecht, 1981], 70–76).

[423] Lit., "its [sg.] outcry," referring collectively to both cities ("their outcry," EVs) or, alternatively, to the lead city, Sodom.

[424] הַכְּצַעֲקָתָהּ is a unique form, lit., "the according to its outcry" (*IBHS* §19.7d n. 32), article הַ plus preposition כְּ plus feminine singular noun צְעָקָה plus third feminine singular suffix הּ; the suffix is an objective genitive, "against it, concerning it" (GKC §135m). Perhaps the trauma of the subject matter in v. 21 is reflected by the unusual language; see also note below.

[425] It is not clear if the NIV renders כָּלָה (n.f.), "completely, altogether" (cp. EVs); the unusual use of the term adverbially here (also Exod 11:1) has encouraged the emendation כֻּלֹּה, "all of it," or כֻּלָּם, "all of them," (BDB 478 and *BHS*). But כָּלָה may be a double entendre, since its typical usage describes annihilation (by God; e.g., Isa 10:23), thus anticipating the verdict to come.

[426] יָדַע ("to know") in the sense of discovery is frequent (e.g., 20:6; 24:14; 42:33,34; Judg 6:37; Ps 56:9), as in God's "discovery" of Abraham's loyalty (22:12).

[427] The LXX reads ἑστηκὼς (ἵστημι), "standing," עֹמֵד; also the Gk. root describing Paul before tribunals (e.g., Acts 22:30; 25:10; also περίστημι, Acts 27:24).

1 Kgs 3:16). The same language, "standing before them" (v. 8; "stood near them," NIV), captures Abraham's humility before the trio of visitors, where the sense of the term is his service as host (cp. 1 Sam 16:22). In our verse, the patriarch stands in waiting at the presence of a superior (before God, e.g., Lev 9:5; Deut 4:10; before royal figures, e.g., Exod 9:10).[428]

Genesis 18:23–32 consists of a unique dialogue in Scripture between the Lord and a petitioner. Moses and Amos petitioned the Lord in behalf of Israel (Exod 32:11–14; Amos 7:1–6), but here the intercession is in behalf of the wicked foreigners. Abraham's role as an intermediary of blessing for others (12:3) is illustrated here and by his prayer for Abimelech's house (20:7,17). Jonah, on the other hand, could not abide the sufferance of God toward Nineveh. Abraham shows remarkable compassion, for in Jonah's case the Ninevites repented, but there is no repentance demanded of the cities of the plain.

Although Abraham launches into a lengthy disputation (vv. 22–25) and sustains his intercession for five more speeches, there is no feverish haggling here; the deference Abraham shows and the Lord's amicable agreement hardly make for a torrid debate. The passage ends with the Lord literally having the last word (v. 32), and the diminishing length of Abraham's speeches suggests that he is wearing down. One might think of the same trend observed among Job's friends who finally run out of words. Abraham is vigilant, perhaps reminding Christian readers of Jesus' parable of the friend in need (Luke 11:5–8). But the parable depends on the friend's genuine perseverance in the face of refusal; in Abraham's experience, however, the Lord's response is always compliance.

He rested his argument upon the twin pillars of divine justice and divine mercy. Abraham was at a moral impasse: if the cities are destroyed, the innocent suffer, in which case the justice of God becomes suspect; or if the cities are spared, the guilty escape their just deserts, again impugning the integrity of God. His prayer, therefore, was that the mercy of God would deliver the city, to which God agrees "for the sake" of the righteous (v. 26). But was there no end to the mercy of God? Was there a point at which unlimited mercy became a shallow sentimentalism, obviating the justice of God against the wicked?

The most striking feature of the moral enigma the story presents is the unexpected outcome in chap. 19; neither one of the two reasoned scenarios described above comes to pass. The innocent is spared, and the guilty appear consumed. Yet Lot's request for the exemption of Zoar from destruction (19:21) is answered, showing that God does preserve the guilty on the account of the innocent Lot (18:26). The outcome shows that the Lord's actions cannot be reduced to a simple juridical formula or precedent or that the Lord simply

---

[428] E. Martens, "עמד," *NIDOTTE* 3.432.

agreed to the patriarch's intercessions.[429] Both patriarchal figures, Abraham and Job, reflected openly on the justice of the Lord (as well as the psalmist) but ceased after hearing from the Lord (in each one's own way), recognizing that they had no legitimate vantage point from which to govern the moral universe (e.g., Job 40:8; 42:1–7; Ps 73). Chapters 18–19 show that the Lord is truly free in his judgment and that his judgment is inscrutable. If Abraham is to father a heritage that adheres to the "way of the LORD by doing what is right and just" (v. 19), the question of the righteousness of God's conduct is fundamental. The dialogue says more about the nature of God's justice than the intercessory character of Abraham (see comments on 19:29).

18:23–25 The rhetorical questions of vv. 23–25 assume the affirmation made by Abraham himself: "far be it from you!" (vv. 25,27). The beginning point of his plea is the assumption that the Lord indeed is righteous and can be counted on accordingly (v. 19). If the Lord's righteousness were truly uncertain in Abraham's mind, then the discussion that follows has no ground. It is because the Lord acts justly that Abraham is perplexed at the threat of the innocent's annihilation with the guilty; justice in the patriarch's view required discrimination between the righteous and the wicked (cf. Mal 3:18).

Functioning as antonyms in this context, "sweep away" (*sāpâ,* vv. 23–24) and "spare" (*nāśā'*, vv. 24,26) reappear in the passage so as to reinforce the two polar options in which Abraham couches the question of God's justice. "Sweep" (*sāpâ)*is the same term that describes Sodom's imminent demise (19:15,17) and elsewhere describes divine judgment against Israel (Num 16:26, 1 Sam 12:25; Isa 7:20). "Spare" (lit., "lift up, bear," *nāśā'*) can have the meaning of bearing or taking away guilt, that is, "forgive" (NRSV, NJPS),[430] but here it is a figure (metonymy) where the cause (bearing sin) is put for the effect, that is, "spare" (NASB, NJB, NAB, GNB, NLT). As here, the term "righteous" *(ṣaddîq)* is often contrasted with the "wicked" *(rāśāʿ)*in Psalms and Proverbs. The precise meaning of the term *ṣaddîq* is uncertain, as shown by the diversity of rendering among the versions in vv. 23–32.[431] "Righteous," which is the traditional translation (e.g., AV, ASV), conveys the idea of conformity to God's moral law, whereas "innocent" suggests juridical acquittal, a clearing of wrong behavior and hence the recognition of a person acting right. The juridical slanguage in this passage ("Judge," v. 25) is useful since God alone makes the determination. Yet the issue is not one of guilt or innocence before God but ethical behavior

---

[429] N. MacDonald ("Listening to Abraham—Listening to Yhwh: Divine Justice and Mercy in Genesis 18:16–33," *CBQ* 66 [2004]: 25–43) argues that Abraham's concern was judicial, whereas the Lord sought to teach him about the mercy of God as the "way of the LORD" (18:19).

[430] BDB 671; "pardon," REB.

[431] "Righteous/wicked" (AV, NIV, NASB, NRSV, HCSB); "upright/guilty" (NJB); "innocent/guilty" (NAB, NJPS, NLT); "innocent/wicked" (REB).

toward others, living in accord with the "way of the LORD" (v. 19).[432] Since the Lord himself is "righteous" *(ṣaddîq)*, both in his person (e.g., Ps 11:7) and in his ways (e.g., Ps 145:17; Dan 9:14), it is he who can evaluate human behavior as to whether the Sodomites acted properly, that is, "rightness."

Abraham proposes that upon examination if "fifty righteous" are found in Sodom, this should merit exempting the whole of the city from destruction (v. 24). This is the first of repeated proposals made by the patriarch in descending order from fifty to ten "righteous" (v. 32a), which are proffered on the same basis. The numbers of righteous reduce by five's, from fifty to forty (vv. 24,28a,29a) and then ten's from forty to ten (vv. 30a,31a,32a). Interspersed are the Lord's speeches, like a refrain, repeating the equivalent number in each case. This give-and-take arrangement, which in this case means Abraham "takes" and the Lord "gives," exhibits the Lord's grace and also Abraham's compassion for the recalcitrant city. In the later case of Nineveh, the prophet Jonah recoils at the city's deliverance, whereas the Lord seizes the occasion of the populace's repentance to preserve them (Jonah 4:11). The Lord does not require any "arm twisting" by Abraham to act benevolently; the tactic by Abraham only further exposes the compassionate heart God has for the "whole place" (v. 26), including the wicked. But God's grace has its end too; this is shown by the outcome of the matter, for the requisite number from Abraham's perspective, even the minimum of ten, could not be discovered—such were the deplorable conditions among the cities of the plain (cf. 15:16).

Abraham answers his own question in v. 25: no, it was incredulous that the Lord of justice would act unfairly toward the "righteous" *(ṣaddîq;* cp. Deut 32:4) by treating them as he does the "wicked" *(rāšāʿ)*. Abraham does not offer an apology for the wicked or refute their just deserts of destruction; rather, he contends that the Lord, if he is to be true to what is fair, must discriminate between the righteous and the wicked. Abraham's passion is indicated by the repeated interjection "far be it *[ḥālilâ]* from you" and by the rhetorical exclamation "Judge of all the earth." "Far be it" conveys repulsion at the thought of breaching an oath or a code of conduct (e.g., 44:7,17; 1 Sam 14:45).[433] By such an exclamation, the person calls upon the Lord implicitly or explicitly ("the LORD forbid," e.g., 1 Sam 24:6; 1 Kgs 21:3) to censure him if he fails. In this verse the patriarch appeals to the Lord to censure himself, if he "kill[s] the righteous"! In the same vein, Elihu defends the integrity of God by the exclamation "Far be it *[ḥālilâ]* from God *[El]* to do evil *[mērešaʿ]*, from the Almighty *[Shaddai]* to do wrong *[mēʿāwel]*" (Job 34:10).

The appellative for the Lord, "Judge of all the earth," occurs only here in Scripture (cp. 16:5; Ps 7:8[9]); the variant but similar expressions "the LORD/

---

[432] D. Reimer, "צדק," *NIDOTTE* 3.750–51.
[433] D. O'Kennedy, "חלל," *NIDOTTE* 2.150.

God of all the earth" (Josh 3:11,13; Ps 97:5; Mic 4:13; Zech 4:14; Isa 54:5 [God]) and "O Judge of the earth" (Ps 94:2) appear sparingly. The idea, however, of the sovereign Lord as ultimate adjudicator of all things is common and is typically the basis of the pious's plea for vindication (e.g., Ps 97:1–2,8–9; also 1 Sam 24:15[16]; Pss 7:11[12]; 9:8[9]; Isa 2:4; Joel 3:12).

18:26–32 The Lord's response is affirmative each time to Abraham's successive proposals, except his silence at the last. The potential efficacy of the "righteous" ("their sake") extends to the "whole place," which may include the whole region, but its immediate importance is the inclusion of the "wicked" (v. 26). Still fearing that the number is too many for the infamous cities, Abraham ventures forth cautiously and humbly with even more charitable scenarios (vv. 27–28a). The patriarch admits he stands precariously out of line by speaking in this way, "though [he is] nothing but dust and ashes" (v. 27).[434] Here the man knows his place, as he did as host awaiting the need of his visitors (v. 8). His contrition is reminiscent of another righteous man, Job, who regretted his outspokenness (42:6). Abraham pushes forward yet with a bolder request but carefully (v. 30).[435] Finally, he concludes with an added caution, "just once more," he begs to speak (v. 32).[436] We can only speculate about why the patriarch stops his plea at ten. Some suggest that ten is the smallest natural limit or social entity (cf. Ruth 4:2).[437] It may be that Abraham has learned that the number is unimportant, for God is merciful and will discriminate between the wicked and the righteous.

18:33 Since Abraham's initial plea (vv. 23–25), the Lord had responded six times (vv. 26,28b,29b,30b,31b,32b), but then he ceased (cp. 17:22). By the abrupt end, the narrative tension is retained, but more importantly the matter remains solely in the mysterious will of the "Judge of all the earth" (v. 25).

ANGELS RESCUE LOT (19:1–29). Four stages occur in this story, each introduced by a temporal reference (vv. 1–14; 15–22; 23–26; 27–29). The concluding verse (v. 29) presents the most significant information of the account for the Abraham narrative as a whole: the Lord honored his promise to Abraham, a picture of the hope that "all peoples" will be blessed (12:3c).

vv. 1–14   Visitors arrive in Sodom and announce its destruction
            "in the evening" (v. 1)
vv. 15–22   Visitors spare Lot

---

[434] "Dust and ashes" is a rare phrase, occurring once more in Job 42:6; "dust" may indicate lowliness (e.g., 1 Sam 2:8; Ps 72:9; Eccl 3:20) and mourning (e.g., Josh 7:6), and ashes signify mourning or repentance (e.g., 2 Sam 13:19; Esth 4:1; Job 2:8); for the rituals of sackcloth and ashes signifying humility, e.g., Isa 58:5, and sackcloth and dust for humility, e.g., Neh 9:1, and for mourning, e.g., Job 16:15; Lam 2;10; Jonah 3:6.

[435] V. 30 possesses the jussive, אַל־נָא יִחַר, "don't be angry," which is followed by the cohortative וַאֲדַבְּרָה, "and let me speak."

[436] NAB, NJPS, "this last time."

[437] Westermann, *Genesis 12–36,* 292, and Sarna, *Genesis,* 134.

"with the coming of dawn" (v. 15)
vv. 23–26   The Lord destroys the cities
             "the sun had risen" (v. 23)
vv. 27–29   Abraham witnesses the aftermath
             "early the next morning" (v. 27)

Each of the four stages is recounted in fewer words, with less dialogue, and hence increasing the pace of the story. The beginning stage (vv. 1–14) is cinematically detailed, recalling at a snail's pace the arrival and assault against the angels; this convincing portrayal ends in an understandable announcement of destruction. The next stage (vv. 15–22) has its protracted dialogue too, picturing a befuddled Lot, who is saved only because of the insistence of the angels. The final two paragraphs have no dialogue and pointedly describe the destruction (vv. 23–26) and the aftermath (vv. 27–29). Much of the pericope's language and motifs recall chap. 18, especially the petition of Abraham (vv. 16–33; see the chiasmus and parallel panels of chaps. 18 and 19 and comments there). We have noted already two prominent motifs shared by these two chapters: (1) the issue of divine justice and (2) the destruction by divine deluge (i.e., the flood imagery). The commentary below will note points of contact between the related episodes.

The custom of hospitality gives the two narratives their common plot line. Chapter 19 especially is occupied with Lot and his two guests as strangers (*gēr,* "alien," NIV) to Sodom. W. Fields has explored the biblical motif of "the stranger in your gates" (Exod 20:10; Deut 5:14; 16:4; 24:14; 31:12), identifying chap. 19 as the literary archetype for the pattern; he has found the same motif and its submotifs in two other exemplary narratives, the Ephraimite at Gibeah (Judg 19) and Rahab at Jericho (Josh 2).[438] Before we continue with chap. 19, we must remember the special place of the alien *(gēr)* in biblical law. The alien, widow, and orphan constituted the disadvantaged in society; Israelite law provided special protections for these members by promoting generous treatment (e.g., Lev 19:10; Num 9:14; Deut 1:16). The rationale for benevolent treatment was historical and theological; at one time Israel was a stranger in Egypt (e.g., Exod 22:21[20]; Lev 19:34), and God takes special inventory of the state of the disadvantaged (e.g., Exod 22:23[22]; Deut 10:18; 24:15). Thus right treatment of the disadvantaged was a badge of righteousness (e.g., Deut 26:13; Job 31:32). Mistreatment of the alien, on the other hand, was shameful and merited the sternest rebuke by society.[439] By showing the mistreatment of

---

[438] W. Fields, *Sodom and Gomorrah: History and Motif in Biblical Narrative,* JSOTSup 231 (Sheffield: Sheffield Academic Press, 1997).

[439] L. Bechtel comments that Lot's invitation to the strangers was a boundary violation, risking the community to spies, but the Sodomites respond by their own boundary violation when they threaten the strangers with rape ("Boundary Issues in Genesis 19.1–38," in *Escaping Eden: New Feminist Perspectives on the Bible* [Sheffield: Sheffield Academic Press, 1998], 22–40).

the angelic guests and also the alien Lot, the author paints a convincing portrait of the depravity of the Sodomites. In effect "the author holds them up to the mirror of the Torah, and they are found wanting."[440] That Lot did not conspire with the men of the city against his guests indicates that he was not part of the depraved community.[441] Lot functions as a foil for both Abraham and the men of Sodom. Abraham's conduct is superior to Lot's, but when viewed against the wicked Sodomites, Lot is "a righteous man" (e.g., 2 Pet 2:7–8; see "Motifs" in the introduction to 18:1–19:38). The thought of Lot as "a righteous man" confounds the contemporary reader, for his action against his daughters says otherwise. But the author of Genesis would have us evaluate Lot in terms of his conduct toward the traveling strangers. Lot commits a grievous sin by subjecting his two daughters to sexual predators, but we miss the author's chief point if we read Lot's checkered character solely in terms of his mistreatment of his daughters (see comments on 19:8).

As Fields notes, chap. 19 involves many reversals and incongruities that present a confused picture at Sodom; the world of Sodom is turned upside down.[442] Typically, a city was safer for travelers at night than the open country, and also a sojourner preferred a person's house over the city square (cf. 24:23,31). At Sodom this is turned around; at night the city is a place of danger, and the angels prefer the open square over residing with Lot. As travelers the angels' conduct differs from the expected; in the story of the Levite and concubine they arrive at the city square of Gibeah, waiting for someone to take them in (Judg 19:15–20). Among other surprises of the story is the figure of Lot himself. He is at the "gateway" when the story begins (v. 1), which implies that he is an integrated citizen of Sodom, if not a leader. But Lot in fact is disdained as an outsider and physically attacked by the men of the city (v. 9). Lot's rejection by his future sons-in-law, who were most likely themselves Sodomites, accentuates the little regard the community had for him (v. 14).

The surprising resistance of his sons-in-law leads us to reflect on the twists in the outcome of those who were saved. Although Zoar was among the doomed cities of the region, it is abruptly spared at the behest of Lot. Moreover, Lot and the members of his household resist the deliverance afforded them, even his wife failing to let go fully of Sodom. Lot's attempt to defend his guests presents him positively, but his sanctioning of the rape of his daughters sounds more "Sodomite" than "Israelite." These and other incongruities in the story with the vile events themselves contribute to the overall sense that the city was especially deviant.

Genesis 19:1–14 describes the events of one night, from the visit of the

---

[440] Ibid., 41.

[441] Turner effectively shows that Genesis presents Lot as a complex character who is righteous but who progressively degenerates by wicked decisions ("Lot as Jekyll and Hyde," 85–101).

[442] Fields, *Sodom and Gomorrah,* 86–115.

angels at Lot's house, where they announce to Lot the end of Sodom, and he repeats the message to his betrothed sons-in-law, who brush aside his warning. The motif of hospitality informs the arrangement of the section: the perspective on the events are told from "inside" or "outside" Lot's house. "Inside" the house where the angels are found is safety, whereas "outside" the house the Sodomites rage with lustful appetites.

vv. 1–5   The angels "entered" the house, and the Sodomites
             "surrounded" the house
vv. 6–11   Lot went "outside" the house, but the angels brought
             him back "inside" the house
vv. 12–13   From inside the angels warn Lot to "get (his family)
             out of the place"
v. 14   Lot "went out" and exhorted his sons-in-law to "get out
             of this place"

Irony pervades the discourse, for attachment to Lot's household results in both jeopardy and preservation. Those inside the house are threatened, including the daughters by their own father(!), but only those inside will finally be preserved (except Lot's wife). The sons-in-law are a microcosm of the Sodomite men; in both cases Lot "went out(side)" the house to meet them (vv. 7,14), and in both cases they reject Lot's admonitions (vv. 9,14). For the Sodomites, this is their final opportunity to avert disaster, but they would not have anyone "play the judge" (v. 9), an eerie echo of the erstwhile appellative, "Judge of all the earth" (18:25). The sons-in-law too neglect their chance (v. 14).

19:1–3 In the introduction to chaps. 18–19, we already commented on the contrast between Abraham and Lot, including their treatment of the visitors. Unlike the suddenness of the visitors' appearance before Abraham, hinting at their otherworldly origin (see comments on 18:2), the angels are received simply as common travelers without any detection by Lot. Not until the angels blind the Sodomites do they show their supernatural character (vv. 10–11). Verse 1 begins the description of the angels' visit with the term "entered" ("arrived"), which translates *bôʾ*, a word that also can mean sexual relations (e.g., 6:4; 16:2,4). It appears repeatedly (vv. 3,5,8,9,10) and perhaps is a double entendre, contributing to the sexual content of the story. Additional terms used for sexual relations appear: "lie down" (*šākab*, v. 4, "gone to bed," NIV), "to know" (*yādaʿ*, vv. 5,7,8, "have sex," NIV) and possibly "draw near" (*nāgaš*, v. 9[2x], "get out" and "moved forward," NIV; cf. Exod 19:15).

The description of Lot "sitting in the gateway" (*yōšēb bĕšaʿar;* v. 1) may, like other terms in the passage, have a double meaning in view. "Sitting" translates the root term *yāšab,* which often means "to live, reside" (e.g., 19:25,29,30); it is reminiscent of chap. 13, where the same word is integral to describing Lot's choice to "live" *(yāšab)* in Sodom (13:6[2x],7,12[2x],18). The imagery of the city gate adds to the picture of Lot's urban profile versus Abraham's tents, where he was "sitting" when the visitors appeared (see comments on 18:1; 13:12). The word "gateway" *(ša'ar)* also may imply Lot's social status; the city gate was the traditional location for civil decisions (e.g., Job 34:20). Perhaps his position at the gate infers that Lot had an influential role in the community. We later discover, however, that Lot is spurned as an alien *(gēr,* v. 9), and at least in moral matters he showed no influence on his neighbors at all. Yet another significance to the "gateway" is its possible relation to the imagery of "door" as a protective boundary (see comments on v. 6); as another incongruity in the account, the gate should indicate safety within the city, but Lot cannot provide that safety, for the city is perilous to strangers.

Lot showed proper deference to his guests, bowing in humility (v. 1) and addressing them respectively as "my lords" (v. 2). "Your servant's house" (v. 2) is the first of many appearances of "house" and is integral to vv. 1–14 (for the features of hospitality, see comments on 18:3–5). Chapter 18 depicts Abraham's hospitality as exceeding that of Lot in a number of ways (see intro. chaps. 18–19), for example, Abraham when seeing the travelers "ran" ("hurried," NIV) to greet them (18:2). When the two hospitality accounts are compared, Lot does not say, as does Abraham, "If I have found favor in your eyes" (18:3) when he invites them to lodge; this omission and the angels' initial refusal to spend the night indicate that Lot does not meet with the angels' approval.[443] It is only later that Lot's rescue can be interpreted as a show of "favor" (v. 19). The refusal to Lot's invitation is worded strongly, lit., "no, indeed" *(lō' kî)* or "no, but"[444] (cp. 1 Sam 8:19); the Hebrew construction also emphasizes "in the [city] square," as opposed to Lot's "house,"[445] which under normal circumstances would have been preferable.

"But he [Lot] insisted" describes his equally strong response to the reluctant visitors (v. 3). "Insisted" translates *pāṣar,* which anticipates the heated reaction of the Sodomites who "pressure" *(pāṣar)* Lot (v. 9). As one of many lexical plays in the chapter, the repetition of *pāṣar* expresses another irony: Lot's insistence at playing host results in jeopardizing his guests and himself. Another early signal that Lot struggles to provide properly for his guest is the nature of the evening "meal" *(mišteh).* The supper consists of unleavened cakes *(maṣṣôt),* which by themselves fall short of the typical *mišteh,* a "banquet" or "feast" of luxurious food and drink (e.g., 21:8; 26:30; 29:22; 40:20; 1 Sam 25:36). "Bread without yeast" *(maṣṣâ)* was bread made in haste (e.g., 1 Sam

---

[443] Bechtel ("Boundary Issues," 26–27) contends rather that the initial refusal is proper etiquette in a shame/honor society (cf. 33:6–11; Judg 19:7; 2 Kgs 2:17); but this is not the response of the visitors to Abraham (18:5).

[444] GKC §152c.

[445] GKC §142g.

28:24), which, as the bread of Passover, Israel memorialized in its Passover celebration and Feast of Unleavened Bread (e.g., Exod 12:8; 23:15). Unleavened bread was one of the items on Gideon's menu for his heavenly guest (Judg 6:19), but his meal included the tender meat of a young goat. Our verse is the only passage where *mišteh* and *maṣṣâ* occur together; they provide another incongruity in the passage by the offer of an inferior meal to honored guests.

19:4–5 Sleep usually follows the evening meal, but "before they had gone to bed" the Sodomite men disturbed the household (v. 4). The pack who "surrounded" the house is inclusive, involving men from every sector of the city and each age group. The merism "both young and son," that is, everybody (also v. 11), shows that their homosexual practices had become generational. The NIV's translation "every part [lit., "end"] of the city" accents the inclusiveness of the crowd. Alternatively, the Hebrew term *qāṣeh,* which means "end, extremity," can refer to the population directly, that is, "to the last man" (NRSV; cf. Num 22:41). The point is the same in either case: Sodom's sexual immorality was pervasive. They first "surrounded" *(sbb)* the house before addressing those inside, showing their hostile intentions from the beginning (e.g., Judg 16:2; Ps 22:16[17][446]); the wicked men of Gibeah took the same tactic (Judg 19:22; 20:5).

The crowd says what must be taken as a rhetorical question, "Where are the men?" (v. 5), since they do not wait for a reply but demand, "Bring them out!" News of strangers in town has spread, and the men very well know where they can find the visitors. They make no pretense about their business; they openly make known their intentions to assault the visitors sexually.[447] Sodom's blatant shamelessness especially caught the attention of the prophet Ezekiel (16:49–50).

19:6–8 Verses 6–11 describe Lot's failed attempts at dissuading the mob (vv. 6–9) and his rescue at the last moment from their angry grasp (vv. 10–11). Verse 6 details the emergence of Lot from his house. Reference to his shutting the "door" initiates an important key word in the telling of the episode (vv. 6,9,10,11[448]); the angels take the same action in saving the man (v. 10). Figuratively, "door" conveys multiple meanings. The door is in effect the boundary between the saved and the condemned; it is symbolic of the line between the righteous and the wicked (cf. comments on 13:13), the civil and the vulgar.

---

[446] L. Allen, "סבב," *NIDOTTE* 3.219.

[447] For the view that "to know" (יָדַע) is not sexual, see M. Morschauser, "'Hospitality,' Hostiles and Hostages: On the Legal Background to Genesis 19.1–9," *JSOT* 27 (2003): 461–85.

[448] Two different Hb. words occur in the passage that have both been traditionally rendered "door" (AV, also NIV, NRSV): פֶּתַח, meaning "doorway" or "entrance" (vv. 6,11), in the sense of an open access, and דֶּלֶת, the "door" itself (vv. 6,9,10; A. Baumann, "דֶּלֶת *deleth*," *TDOT* 3.231); this distinction, however, is now maintained in many recent EVs (NASB, NAB, NJB, NJPS, NLT), and it becomes important in v. 11 (see below).

Also related to the fundamental idea of protective boundary, "door" may represent protected virginity (cf. the "young sister," Song 8:9).[449] The "door" guards the sexual innocence of the angels and the purity of Lot's daughters.

Verses 7–8 portray Lot's reasoning with the intruders; he undertakes three tactics. First, he makes an urgent plea, "Don't do this wicked thing [*rāʿaʿ]*" (v. 7; cp. Judg 19:23).[450] Hebrew *rāʿaʿ*("do wicked") is related to the term *raʿ* (nom.), which recalls the description of the flood generation (6:5; 8:21) and Lot's choice of Sodom (13:13). How we understand Lot's address, "my friends" (*ʾaḥḥay*, lit., "my brothers"), is important for evaluating Lot's character. Hebrew *ʾaḥḥay* may be no more than a polite form of speech (e.g., 29:4)[451] or a reference to civic camaraderie (cp. a political treaty, 1 Kgs 19:13; Amos 1:9). In this latter case, Lot believes he is one with the Sodomite population, which is the basis of his appeal; this is striking when we recall Abraham's entreaty to Lot for peaceful relations by reason of their kinship (13:8; cp. 14:14,16, *ʾāḥ,* "relative," NIV). If so, another irony may be intended: Lot, whose relationship with Abraham meant blessing but whom he left behind, took up with a people who treated him as anything but a brother (v. 9). On the positive side, Lot's opposition to the men shows that he should not be counted among the wicked.

Second, Lot offers his virgin daughters in lieu of the two strangers (v. 8a); he makes the swap more lucrative by pointing out the sexual innocence of the women. Virgins were more valuable. "Do to them as you please" (v. 8b) means he places them under their power (cp. 16:16). That he does not directly invite them to rape the women is suggested by comparing the Levite's surrender in Judg 19:34: "You can use them and do to them whatever you wish." When we remember the outcome of the Levite's concubine in the hands of a brutal city gang (Judg 19:25–26), we can only conclude that Lot jeopardized the lives of his daughters, even any hope for a heritage—all for the sake of the strangers. By a bizarre twist, however, it is his daughters who finally take advantage of Lot, sexually abusing their father by which he gains male heirs after all (vv. 36–38).

Third, Lot contends that if they carry out such contemptible behavior it would be an appalling breach of hospitality (v. 8c). Hospitality requires "protection" (*ṣēl,* lit., "shade," e.g., Num 14:9), and at Lot's invitation the strangers had received sanctuary "under [his] roof." To violate this custom would (and did) brand the city lawless.

That Lot sanctions the rape of his daughters indicates a moral compass gone awry; he places hospitality above the protection of his own children. It is difficult to conceive of such a custom that would put a guest's well-being over fam-

---

[449] D. Garrett, *Proverbs, Ecclesiastes, Song of Songs,* NAC (Nashville: Broadman, 1993), 428.

[450] Samuel's same plea made to Israel adds another word important to chaps. 18–19, "swept away" (סָפָה, 1 Sam 12:25).

[451] H. Ringgren, "אָח *ʾāch*," *TDOT* 1.191.

ily. Such treatment by a father was despicable in the eyes of Israel; forcing a daughter into prostitution is specifically forbidden in Mosaic law (Lev 19:29). Yet offense against aliens was also grievous in the Mosaic tradition (e.g., Exod 22:21[20]; Lev 19:33–34; Deut 10:19). Lot is caught in a web of the most vile of circumstances, and he opts for a way out that can never salvage any good. He surely offends his own sense of right behavior while attempting to save face with the strangers. For a moment it is Sodom that has taken up residence in Lot's soul.

19:9 Like bullies, the men respond to Lot's refusal by attacking him, first verbally and then physically. The first recorded word from their mouths is the command to move aside (*nāgaš,* "get out," NIV), for Lot himself was the sole barricade; there is a play on the Hebrew here between the dialogue and the narrative report where the same term, *nāgaš* ("moved forward," NIV), describes their aggression. Since Lot would not voluntarily move aside, they would move him aside. The Sodomites ridicule Lot as a "know-it-all," so to speak, a self-righteous "carpet bagger" who as a foreigner thought himself a judge of their behavior. Their vitriolic rebuff includes two ideas important to the whole of the Lot-Sodom narratives. He is an "alien" in their midst (lit., "the one coming to sojourn," *hā'eḥād bā' lāgûr*[452] who "wants to play the judge!"[453]

We have mentioned above the importance of the motif "alien" (*gēr*) for interpreting Sodom's crimes. By Lot defending the traditional rights of his guests, he was also in effect defending himself as an outsider. This was not lost on the Sodomites, whose envy against Lot may have fueled their hatred in concert with their aggression against the newcomers. His admonition, however, was not skewed by virtue of his alien status, nor was he a silly comic (v. 14); rather, his warning was the same conclusion drawn by the "Judge of all the earth" (18:25). Hebrew *šāpaṭ,* commonly translated "judge," may also mean "rule"[454]; if taken in this sense, they are ridiculing Lot, who though an alien has taken charge ("already he acts the ruler!" NJPS). Attendant to this notion of "judge" are the categories of "wicked" and "righteous" (18:23,25); another play is in the recurrence of the word *rā'a',* "do wicked, evil" (NIV, "treat . . . worse"), in their response. Lot had deemed their plans "wicked" (*rā'a',* v. 7), and their rejoinder was "we'll treat you worse *[rā'a']* than them."[455]

19:10–11 The men, not satisfied with mockery, charge forward, pressing Lot so fiercely that the door buckled (v. 9b). At this the two heavenly witnesses

---

[452] לָגוּר, "to sojourn," is the infinitive form, related to the noun גֵּר, "alien."

[453] וַיִּשְׁפֹּט שָׁפוֹט, lit., "he judged judging," expresses intensity by the cognate infinitive absolute, "and he would play the judge!" (NRSV).

[454] R. Schultz, "שׁפט," *NIDOTTE* 4.215.

[455] אַל . . . תָּרֵעוּ, the *hiphil* jussive verb, "No . . . Don't do this wicked thing" (v. 7), has its counter in the response, נָרַע, the *hiphil* imperfect, lit., "we will harm [you]"; the nom. הָרָעָה, "this disaster" (19:19), aptly describes their just deserts.

had heard and seen enough (vv. 10–11). The visitors first yanked Lot inside, shutting the door, and then struck the thugs with blindness. "Young and old" is another reference to the inclusiveness of the culprits (vv. 8,11); none repented among them, for all those who approached the house also suffered the consequences. "Door" in v. 11 is actually the "entryway" *(petaḥ)*, indicating that blindness[456] hindered them from finding the portal that would have given them access to the door itself. This blindness was not punitive but defensive, perhaps temporary yet long enough for Lot to escape (cf. 2 Kgs 6:18,20). Their dramatic intervention prepared Lot for accepting the unbelievable message of the two envoys.

19:12–14 Verses 12–13 take place in the safety of the house, where the angels inquire about family members elsewhere, mentioning first "sons-in-law" whom in fact Lot will search out (v. 14); Lot's defense of the angels accrues consideration by the angels for his family (cp. Noah, 7:1; Rahab, Josh 2:12–14,18–19; 6:22–23,25). They announce the impending destruction of the "place," referring to Sodom and its allied cities. "Outcry" (v. 13) recalls the allegations (18:20–21) that had prompted Abraham's intervention for the righteous (18:22–32). The angels' admission, "the LORD has sent us to destroy it" (v. 13), indicates the earlier allegations are proven true, and, consequently, the judgment is in force.[457] The angels are the agents of God's destruction and thus of sparing (vv. 14,24–25 show it is the Lord who destroys).

The final verse of this subunit depicts Lot's response to the benevolent concession of the messengers (v. 14). The scene shifts outside, where he forewarns his sons-in-law of the coming destruction, using almost verbatim the alarming words of the angels. We must assume that the groping crowd has disbanded and Lot promptly encounters his sons-in-law. True to the depiction of the Sodomites, the sons-in-law scorn Lot and appear as blind to the inevitable as their fellow citizens are actually blind. The sons-in-law are unmoved by the stunning events at Lot's house and thus rate more dim-witted than the recalcitrant members of the mob. Perhaps their disregard for Lot's warning as a joke speaks also to the narrative's general picture of Lot as a confused, inept person who falls to his own short-sighted ambition and finally to the deceit of treacherous daughters. "Joking" translates *měṣaḥēq*, which recalls Abraham's and Sarah's laughter *(ṣāḥaq)* at the prospects of bearing "Isaac" *(yiṣḥāq;*

---

[456] סַנְוֵר, "blindness," occurs elsewhere only in 2 Kgs 6:18 (2x); the significance of this rare term versus the common term עִוֵּר, if any, is difficult. *HALOT* 2.760–61, has נוּר, "bright" plus *sa* preformative, meaning "dazzling, deception," thus "a blinding light" (NJB, NAB, NJPS). Both passages have blindness thwarting aggression.

[457] Fields (*Sodom and Gomorrah*, 76) points to the resumptive language of 18:22 (עָמַד) and 19:27 (עָמַד) and proposes that the two scenes, Abraham's intercession (18:23–33) and the investigation of the angels (19:1–26), were at about the same time, understanding that the visit of the angels carried out the inquiry of the Lord and found Sodom deserving of destruction.

17:19,21; 18:12; 21:3). The prediction of destruction is too fantastic for the sons-in-law to take seriously.

19:15–17 At last the night passes and the angels "at the coming of dawn" (v. 15) prepare for the destruction of the cities by ushering Lot and his family out of danger. Safety now lies "out[side] of the city" (v. 16). The prominent idea in vv. 15–22 is the urgency of Lot's flight to safety. The first and final verses are commands, "Hurry! Take . . ." (*qûm qaḥ;* v. 15) and "quickly flee . . ." (*mahēr himmālēṭ;* v. 22). A contest of wills dominates the passage; verbal forms expressing desire/will occur eight times. The tone of the passage can be captured in the words of Lot, "No, my lords, please!" (v. 18). It will take all morning to get Lot out of town to nearby Zoar. Twice the angels strongly exhort Lot to flee, but he is uncooperative. First, he hesitates, but they force him to move (v. 16); and second, he stops abruptly, bargaining to divert to Zoar, one of the cities scheduled for annihilation (vv. 20–21). Moreover, the angel admits (in frustration?) that Lot's reluctance hinders the completion of his assignment.

"Flee" *(mālēṭ)* appears five times (vv. 17[2x],19,20,22) and "run, flee" *(nûs)* once (v. 20). The two often occur in parallel (e.g., 1 Sam 19:10); the former describes slipping away successfully from danger and the latter open flight from danger.[458] Hebrew *mālaṭ* is a sound play on the name of Lot *(lôt);* the humor of the play is that Lot is anything but quick to leave.

"Or you will be swept away *[sāpâ]*" occurring twice (vv. 15,17) forms the boundaries of vv. 15–17. This word recalls Abraham's concern for the righteous *(sāpâ,* 18:23,24). Time has run out; only those immediately in the house can be saved (v. 15). The listing of the family members twice (vv. 15,16), absent the sons-in-law, indicates that they are doomed; further, the list anticipates the demise of Lot's wife, who until now has not been mentioned.

The story leaves it to us to explain why Lot "hesitated" *(māhah),* that is, he delayed (v. 16; Exod 12:39; Hab 2:3). He appears to be paralyzed with fear, which corresponds with his own explanation later for diverting to Zoar (v. 19). The angels, however, don't hesitate. On account of the Lord's pity on Lot,[459] they seized and "put" them *(nûaḥ,* hiphil; "led [them safely]," NIV) outside "ground zero"! "Put" *(nûaḥ),* that is, cause to rest *(hiphil),* is the chief lexical sound play in the survivor's story of Noah *(nōaḥ;* see vol. 1A, pp. 316–17 and n. 64). There is a childlike feature in this depiction of the Lot family, led by hand to safety (cp. Hos 11:3).

Of the two angels, one functions as the spokesman.[460] Verse 17 alone con-

---

[458] R. L. Hubbard, "מלט," *NIDOTTE* 2.950–54; J. Lund, "נוס," *NIDOTTE* 3.61–62.

[459] עָלָיו, lit., "upon him,"; the sg. suffix can be collective referring to the group ("them," NIV), but Lot is the point of reference in the verse, e.g., "his hand," "his wife's hand," "his two daughters' hands."

[460] The MT has וַיֹּאמֶר, lit., "and he said," whereas the LXX, Syr., Vg. have the plural ("they said") to conform to the plural "they" in v. 17a and "lords" in v. 18; but the singular verbs and pronouns dominate the dialogue between the angel and Lot in vv. 18–21.

tains four exhortations in chiastic arrangement: "flee . . . don't look back . . . don't stop . . . flee." The outer two elements (v. 17a,17d) indicate that their "lives" depend on reaching the "mountains"; the inner two parts (v. 17b,17c) warn that death is lingering in the "plain." To "look back" is tantamount to "stopping" in the "plain," short of the mountain's safety. By looking back, Lot's wife not only disobeyed the angel but also failed to separate herself completely from Sodom's hold on her. The "mountains" were typically sanctuaries of isolation, providing safety from human contact (e.g., Josh 2:16,22; 6:2; Judg 20:47; 1 Sam 22:1; fig., Ps 11:1). In this case the mountains were actually outside the area targeted for total annihilation.

19:18–20 Lot, however, refuses and makes a counterproposal (v. 18), the same kind of reaction Lot makes to the Sodomites (v. 6). His chief concern is "life" (vv. 18,20) and "death" (v. 19); since he cannot make it to the mountains before the disaster strikes, he proposes sanctuary in the small nearby town of Zoar (vv. 20–22). His "bargaining" with the lead angel (cf. v. 17 note) recalls the pleas of Abraham with his guest (18:22–33); lexical ties between Lot's appeal to the angels in vv. 18–19 and Abraham's initial encounter with the three visitors (18:3) bring both events together. The angels in both settings graciously concede to the pleas of the patriarch and his nephew. The point of the allusion to Abraham is to remind us that Abraham's intercession has been honored, even for the reluctant Lot. In what way Lot expected the calamity to "overtake" him (v. 19) is unstated; perhaps this adds to the depiction of Lot, who is slow, at times resistant, versus Abraham, who is immediately responsive in his demeanor (18:2,6,7).

Another basis for Lot's request is the insignificance of the town Zoar. The name "Zoar" (*ṣôʿar*, v. 22) is derived from the size of the city, "small" (*miṣʿār*, v. 20).[461] Lot argues his case by interjecting the rhetorical question (lit.), "Is it not small?" His contention is that the angels can spare the little town for his sake, and they can still achieve their main objective. This reasoning reminds us again of Abraham before the Lord; justice, he contends, requires sparing the wicked for the sake of a few. Ironically, this is what occurs at Zoar; although a member of the wicked cities, the angels spare it because of Lot. Such allusions promote the prophetic image of Abraham.

19:21–22 The story pictures the angels as graciously tolerant of the difficult Lot (v. 21). "Grant" (*nāśāʾ*) is another reminder of the Lord's pledge to "spare" (*nāśāʾ*) the righteous (18:26).[462] He promises not to "overthrow"

---

[461] צער (*ṣʿr*) means "to be insignificant" (BDB), i.e., small; מִצְעָר (n.m.), "small thing" (2 Chr 24:24; Job 8:7; Ps 42:7). Zoar was also a refuge for fleeing Moabites (Isa 15:5; Jer 48:34). Ancient and modern testimony converge on the modern site es-Safi for Zoar, located on the south bank of the wadi el Hesa (Zered), south of the Dead Sea in ancient Edom (M. Astour, "Zoar," *ABD* 6.1107).

[462] "I will grant this request" translates נָשָׂאתִי פָנֶיךָ, lit., "I will lift up your face," meaning favor, acceptance (see vol. 1A, pp. 269–70); cp. נָשָׂא at 18:26, meaning "spare."

(hāpak) Zoar; the term often describes the destruction of the wicked (e.g., Prov 12:7). As the primary term in the passage describing the destruction of the cities (vv. 21,25,29[2x]),[463] it became the preferred word by later authors when recalling God's judgment against Sodom (e.g., Deut 29:23[22]; Jer 20:16; Lam 4:6; Hos 11:8; Amos 4:11).[464]

The final speech in the passage is the angel's strongest exhortation to Lot, "But flee there quickly" (v. 22a), lit., "quickly flee there" *(mahēr himmālēṭ šāmmâ);* "quickly" at the head of the clause prompts the memory of Abraham and his household's swift responses to the visitors *(māhar,* 18:6[2x],7). If Lot continued dawdling, the angel could not destroy the wicked. The divine time-table for destruction is temporarily suspended for the outworking of divine grace. The verse ends with an explanatory note regarding the name "Zoar." The author employs a common etiological formula for the naming of sites.[465] This remark is a geographical reference point for the ancient reader, giving concrete expression to the story's report of the catastrophe. The charred remains of the plain eventually diminished from sight, either by the wild or by the sea, but Zoar remained as a testimonial both to the epic proportions of God's retribution (Sodom) and of his forbearance (Lot).

19:23–26 Verses 23–24 report the time and nature of the destruction, and vv. 25–26 narrate the extent of the destruction, including the end of Lot's wife. The destruction occurs only after Lot arrives safely in Zoar, as promised by the angel (v. 21). It is about one full day since the visitors first arrived at Abraham's tent (19:1). The culprits sinned in the cover of night, but their punishment is displayed in the light of day.

The author calls on the description of Noah's flood to describe this deluge by fire at Sodom (v. 24); "rained down" *(himṭîr)* and "from the heavens" repeat the language of the flood account *(mamṭîr,* "send rain," 7:4; "from the sky," 8:2; also 7:11,19). Twice v. 24 attributes the fiery destruction to the Lord's initiative. This heaven's rain cannot be explained solely as a natural phenomenon, such as earthquake; it was exceptional, never again repeated, providing the parade illustration of the fiery eschatological judgment against the wicked (e.g., 2 Pet 2:6–9). The twin calamities of Noah and Lot illustrate Jesus' teaching on the suddenness of the coming of the Son of Man (Luke 17:26–30). The Sodomites carried on their usual activities, "eating and drink-ing, buying and selling, planting and building," on the day of their destruc-tion, unaware of the imminent end. The Son of Man's appearance will likewise surprise the unexpecting world.

---

[463] Verb הפך occurs three times (vv. 21,25,29) and the noun הֲפֵכָה (v. 29), "overthrow" ("catastrophe," NIV).

[464] R. Chisholm, "הפך," *NIDOTTE* 1.1049.

[465] But 19:22 differs by referring to the site as "the town" (הָעִיר), which elsewhere is "the place/this place" (הַמָּקוֹם, 33:17; הַמָּקוֹם הַהוּא, Josh 7:26; 2 Sam 5:20).

"Burning sulfur" translates *goprît wā'ēš*, lit., "sulfur and fire," as a hendiadys.[466] "Sulfur" represented divine judgment against the wicked in later writings (Ps 11:6; Isa 30:33; 34:9; Ezek 38:22). Also the conflagration may have involved the natural pits of bitumen known in the area (14:10). This reversal of the region's vegetation spoils what originally had attracted Lot; now all is lost, including his possessions (cp. Deut 29:23[22]).

Verse 26 reports that Lot also lost his wife; by looking back she evidenced her affections for her life at Sodom. Lot's wife may have been a Sodomite; there is no mention of her prior to chap. 19, unless we are to assume she was among the "women" (14:16) rescued by Abram. In any case, the woman is nameless, no more than a prop in the story whose tragic end became a dreaded lesson (Luke 17:32). The description "looked back" is the same language in the angel's prohibition (v. 17). The feature of "salt" in the Dead Sea area (cf. "salt sea," 14:3) and its sterile effects on arable land may explain the casting of her figure in the mineral. Her physical translation into an edifice of salt, probably to be understood as a coating of salt, testified to the consequence of disobedience and was an appalling reminder of the events at Sodom (Luke 17:28–29,32).

19:27–29 These verses bring the narrative account back full circle to the initial revelation made to Abraham concerning Sodom (18:16–33). The words "stood" (*'āmad*, v. 27) and "looked down" (*šāqap*, v. 28) recall the prelude to the catastrophe he now witnesses (18:16,22). After another night had passed, the clear skies of the "morning" (v. 27) enabled Abraham from Mamre (Hebron; 18:1) to see the rising smoke of the conflagration (cp. Josh 8:20; Judg 20:38, Isa 9:18[17]).[467] "Like smoke from a furnace" (v. 28) refers to the intense concentration of the smoke; "furnace" *(kibšān)* is a kiln requiring extreme heat for baking pottery. Smoke often distinguishes divine theophany (e.g., 15:17; Isa 6:4); "smoke from a furnace" depicts the blaze at Sinai (Exod 19:18). Burning smoke also demonstrates divine anger and judgment (e.g., 2 Sam 22:9//Ps 18:9; cp. Rev 9:2).

Verse 29 presents a summary of the chapter's events. The verse includes an explanation for Lot's deliverance, attributing his salvation to God's covenant relationship with Abraham. "Remembered" *(zākar),* another allusion to the flood (8:1), is typical covenant terminology, indicating loyalty (e.g., Exod 2:24; 6:5; 32:13; Pss 105:42; 106:45). Wenham observes that "God remembered Lot" would be the true parallel to "God remembered Noah" (8:1) since

---

[466]גָּפְרִית is traditionally translated "brimstone" (e.g., AV, NKJV, NASB, RSV).

[467]קִיטֹר, "smoke," is uncommon (v. 28[2x]; Pss 119:83; 148:8); it is related to קְטֹרֶת, the "smoke" of sacrifice (e.g., Isa 1:13) and incense (e.g., Exod 25:6), and קָטַר, "to make sacrifices smoke" (BDB 882). עָשָׁן, "smoke," is the preferred term for burning cities (e.g., Josh 8:20,21), used figuratively for destruction (e.g., Isa 9:17).

the Lord delivers Noah and Lot.[468] "God remembered" identifies the prior covenant obligation (12:3) as the basis for the divine intervention, not the righteousness of Lot. Although the mention of Abraham brings to mind the appeal of the patriarch (18:16–33), "God remembered" directly refers to the privileged position of Abraham. The divine motivation for the initial disclosure to Abraham is his election ("For I have chosen him," 18:19), which then prompted his intercession for the cities. That God's benevolence toward Lot arose from his commitment to Abraham thus begins and ends the Sodom segment (18:17–19; 19:29). In a final jibe at Lot's failure, against the background of God's favor toward Abraham, the author mentions again that the destroyed cities are those "where Lot had lived *[yāšab]*." The word *yāšab* is the key word of chap. 13, the episode of separation (esp. v. 12).

(3) Births of Lot's Sons (19:30–38)

30Lot and his two daughters left Zoar and settled in the mountains, for he was afraid to stay in Zoar. He and his two daughters lived in a cave. 31One day the older daughter said to the younger, "Our father is old, and there is no man around here to lie with us, as is the custom all over the earth. 32Let's get our father to drink wine and then lie with him and preserve our family line through our father."

33That night they got their father to drink wine, and the older daughter went in and lay with him. He was not aware of it when she lay down or when she got up.

34The next day the older daughter said to the younger, "Last night I lay with my father. Let's get him to drink wine again tonight, and you go in and lie with him so we can preserve our family line through our father." 35So they got their father to drink wine that night also, and the younger daughter went and lay with him. Again he was not aware of it when she lay down or when she got up.

36So both of Lot's daughters became pregnant by their father. 37The older daughter had a son, and she named him Moab; he is the father of the Moabites of today. 38The younger daughter also had a son, and she named him Ben-Ammi; he is the father of the Ammonites of today.

This account of Lot's incest is the last word on Lot; he is not mentioned again in the Old Testament except in the phrase "descendants of Lot" (Deut 2:9,19; Ps 83:8[9]). Those scholars who attribute this story originally to an unrelated source understate its dependence on the prior Lot-Sodom narratives (see comments below). If the account had ended with Lot in Zoar (v. 23), as is the case at the close of the previous section (v. 29), the reader would be both

---

[468] Wenham also mentions that Lot's salvation is the consequence of the patriarch's intercession; yet, although "remembered" may indicate answered prayer (e.g., 30:22; 1 Sam 1:19), here the passage does not correlate Lot's salvation with the efficacy of Abraham's appeal (*Genesis 16–50*, 59).

dissatisfied and deceived. The prior story only brings a satisfying conclusion to what happened to Lot at Sodom, and it does not answer what became of Lot and his family afterward. If anything, 18:16–19:29 leaves the reader wanting to know more about Lot's end and his heritage. When the Sodom narrative is set in the broad framework of the Abraham promises and later Israel, its outcome grows in importance since Lot and his heritage are potential rivals to the promises (for it would appear that Moab/Ammon would be assured a future, Deut 2:9,19,37). What became of his heritage is the only way the author can bring closure regarding this branch of the family.

The story without this final episode also would mislead the reader. Lot did not remain in Zoar for long, and though his despicable career had been told effectively in the Sodom setting, the shameful last episode shows that the scandal at Sodom was only half of what could be told about this disgraced member of the family. Also it is difficult to imagine that this sordid story of the ancestors of the Moabites and Ammonites would have been widely popular among these peoples; it has been suggested that the story honors the unusual efforts of the daughters to guarantee the survival of Lot, the famous figure of the region,[469] but their efforts are not honorable but decadent, and Lot is no hero but a dope. It also is wrong to relegate the story to an anti-Moabite/Ammonite piece of propaganda. The account certainly could be used for such political purposes, but the story says much more than political commentary, speaking to the weightier matter of God's promises.

The pericope consists of (1) a brief introduction, offering background information (v. 30), (2) two essentially parallel paragraphs describing the incestuous plot of the elder daughter and then the younger (vv. 31–33,34–35), and (3) a final paragraph reporting on the sons born to Lot (vv. 36–39). The two corresponding panels are charted here:

31a	"Older daughter said"		34a	"Older daughter said"
31b	Problem: No spouse			
32a	Plan: "Let's get our father" to drink		34b	Plan: "Let's get [him] to drink wine again"
32b	"Lie with him"		34c	"you go and lie with him"
32c	"preserve our family line"		34d	"preserve our family line"
33a	Report: "older daughter went in and lay with him"		35a	Report: "younger daughter went and lay with him"
33b	"He was not aware"		35b	"He was not aware"

19:30 This verse reaches back to the prior episode, where we find Lot hunkered down at Zoar; but Lot was "afraid" (v. 30) and moved again "to the mountains," which was the initial directive of the angel anyway (v. 17). Perhaps he feared that the populace of Zoar would receive another divine

---

[469] E.g., B. Vawter, *On Genesis: A New Reading* (Garden City: Doubleday, 1977), 242–43.

inquiry, and he thus left, fearing a "second Sodom." His final abode was anything but a lush plain, only a "cave" fit for the life of a recluse. The scornful jibe in v. 29 (see above) is continued in v. 30 by the recurring use of *yāšab* [3x]; "settled," "stay," lived," NIV).

19:31–35 Lot's age and reclusive life meant the end of the family line without male heirs; the daughters were deprived of husbands and children, the customary role of women. To address the problem, the elder, lit., "first-born," daughter out of desperation hatches a plot with her sister to have sons by their father. The repeated references to the older daughter as "first-born" probably explains her acute motivation for hatching a plan (vv. 31,33,34,37; cf. 29:26). The intent to "preserve our family line" (vv. 32,34) was honorable, but the means of incest was deplorable (e.g., Lev 18:6–18; cp. Tamar 38:13–26). That it was so understood by the daughters themselves explains why they had to trick their father through drink. By this humiliation of Lot, we remember the survivor Noah, whose son disgraced him when the patriarch lay drunk (9:21–24). At least Noah "knew" ("found out," 9:24) his deception, whereas Lot is never said to have learned.[470] By adding that Lot was "unaware" (vv. 33,35), the author wants it clearly understood that the hapless man was sexually exploited.

19:36–38 Verse 36 is not redundant; it states specifically that the two women became pregnant and bore sons "by their father" (*mē'ăbî hen*, v. 36). This prelude to the report of their birth and naming (vv. 37–38) helps explain the significance of their names, Moab and Ben-Ammi. "She named him" (vv. 37,38) is a popular formula for naming a son who is the eponymous ancestor of a group (e.g., 29:32,33; 30:8,18; 35:18; also used in naming Moses, Exod 2:10). "Moab" was apparently derived from the combination of *min* ("from") plus *'āb* ("father"), which becomes *mē'āb*, "from [my] father" (v. 37); *mē'āb* is a reflection of the previous *mē'ăbî hen* (v. 36), meaning lit., "from their father."[471] "Ben-Ammi," born to the younger daughter (v. 38), is "son of my [paternal] kinsmen" or singular "kinsman."[472] By the embedded term "father" (*'āb*) in "Moab" and "kin" (*'ām*) in "Ben-Ammi," the names of these half-brothers provide detractors a jibe at the tawdry roots of their descendants. Their clans perpetuated the double entendre by the patronymics *mô'āb*, "Moabites,"[473] and *běnê*

---

[470] Turner, "Lot as Jekyll and Hyde," 98.

[471] The LXX supplies the explanation: λέγουσα ἐκ τοῦ πατρός μου, "saying (he is) from my father"; for modern proposals of the etymology, see J. M. Miller, "Moab," *ABD* 4.882.

[472] עַם can be used as a singular or a collective singular, hence the ambiguity of the name; R. O'Connell, "עַם," *NIDOTTE* 3.430.

[473] מוֹאָב ("Moab") is the proper noun for both people and land; מוֹאָבִי/הַמּוֹאָבִיָּה are adjectival forms for the people, e.g., "the Moabite" (Deut 23:4[3])/"the Moabitess" (Ruth 1:22; BDB 555).

'ammôn, "Ammonites."[474]

Remembered forever as the offspring of Lot, the "descendants of Lot" (Deut 2:9,19; Ps 83:8[9]) whose land was a gift from the Lord were granted special concessions by the invading Israelites. Yet their incestuous origins could not be overlooked in regulating the holy "assembly of the LORD" (Deut 23:2–3[3–4]). The long history of Israel's relations with these transjordan nations involved continued hostilities even down to the time of the Maccabees (e.g., 36:35; Num 22–25 with Micah 6:5; Judg 3:13,29; chaps. 10–11; 1 Sam 11:2; 2 Sam 10; 2 Kgs 3; 25:25; Neh 2:10,19; 4:3,7; *1 Mac* 5:6), but Israel was required initially to spare them by virtue of their ancestral relationship (Deut 2:9,19–21,37).[475] The psalmist and Hebrew prophets decried the mistreatment of Israel by Lot's descendants (Ps 83:5–8[6–9]; Amos 1:13–2:3; Isa 15:1–16:14; Jer 48:1–49:6; Ezek 25:2–11). Their historical association with the odious cities of Sodom and Gomorrah provided Zephaniah the subject of his satirical diatribe (Zeph 2:8–9). Yet the prophets envision an era of restoration when the Lord will favor anew the descendants of Lot (Jer 48:7; 49:6). Historically, the union of Ruth the Moabitess and Judah's descendant Boaz reconciled the alienated families of Lot and Abraham, providing for Israel's greatest king (Ruth 4:13,18–22; for the Ruth connection with Judah-Tamar via Perez, see comments on chap. 38).

Lot's incest discredited his heritage, which was contrary to Israel's legitimate and miraculous patrimony (18:1–15). Abraham, like Lot, was "old" (v. 31) and Sarah beyond childbearing years (18:11), but the Lord did not find it "too hard" to give them a son (18:14). Lot's choice of the plain (13:10–12) resulted in the loss of his possessions (13:5; 14:12,16) and a tarnished legacy (vv. 36–38).

10. Abraham and Sarah in Gerar: Promises Preserved (20:1–18)

Abraham's sojourn in Gerar results in the second abduction of Sarah by a foreign king (cf. Pharaoh, 12:10–13:1). The episode provides for the

---

[474] "Ammonites" is always עַמּוֹן בְּנֵי, "sons of Ammon," (except possibly 1 Sam 11:11; Ps 83:8) and עַמּוֹנִי, "Ammonite," is the Gentilic, e.g., Deut 23:3[4] (BDB 769–70). D. I. Block has shown that בְּנֵי, "sons," in עַמּוֹן בְּנֵי ("Bene-ammon") is part of the nation's name, unlike יִשְׂרָאֵל בְּנֵי, "the sons of Israel"; cf. בִּנְיָמִין ("Benjamin"), 35:18 (*"Bny 'mwn:* The Sons of Ammon," *AUSS* 22 [1984]: 197–212). Block considers the LXX translator confused, reading "Ammon" by itself but explaining the name as "Ben-Ammon": Αμμαν υἱὸς τοῦ γένους μου, "Amman (the) son of my family." Wevers rather suggests that the translator intentionally followed the pattern of v. 37 (Moab/Moabites; *Notes on the Greek Text,* 286).

[475] For a survey of the transjordan nations, including Edom, see the respective articles in A. Hoerth et al., eds., *Peoples of the Old Testament World* (Grand Rapids: Baker, 1994); and B. MacDonald, "*'East of the Jordan': Territories and Sites of the Hebrew Scriptures,* ASOR Books 6 (Boston: ASOR, 2000).

Abraham narrative another example of how the Lord interceded on the patriarch's behalf, rescuing Sarah so that the divine plan might be accomplished. Although there is no direct reference to the promise of an heir, allusion to Abraham's call (v. 1) and Sarah's barrenness (vv. 17–18) set the event in the framework of the Abraham narrative as a whole. "Moved on [nāsaʿ] from there" and "stayed" (gûr) in v. 1 look back to the migration of Abraham (cf. 12:4,9–10; 21:34); the penalty of barrenness for Abimelech's household brings to mind the chief narrative issue, Sarah's barrenness (11:30; 17:17–19; 18:10–12). As the prelude to the birth of Isaac in chap. 21, Sarah's abduction into a royal harem contributes to the thematic tension of the promised heir (18:1–15). The author reports specifically that the woman was not even touched by the king (v. 6a), making it certain that Abimelech was not the father of Sarah's child (cp. Matt 1:25). Also the context of Abraham's relationship with the nations (here the Philistines) shows that the birth of Isaac involves a vista greater than Israel alone (12:3).

COMPOSITION.   Two problems face the interpreter regarding the relationship of this chapter to the Abraham narrative. First, traditionally, source critics assigned chap. 20 to the Elohist (E) (except v. 18 to the Yahwist [J]) who handed down an independent version of the "wife-sister" tradition (12:10–13:1; 20:1–18; 26:1–13). The use of *Elohim* and the appearance of supposed E vocabulary led to this early opinion. Suspicion about the cogency of such criteria for discerning a distinctive E document resulted in offering another explanation. Many now view it as an adaptation or expansion of the J account of Abram in Egypt (12:10–13:1). In our earlier discussion (see "Wife-Sister Episodes" at 12:10–13:1) we concluded that the three stories are not duplicates from parallel sources but three originally independent narratives by one author who consciously penned each within the larger patriarchal framework so as to provide three complementary pictures of three similar events in the lives of the patriarchs. T. D. Alexander observed that the three stories when compared show a resistance to imitation. Each episode emphasizes different aspects of the motif, avoiding unnecessary redundancy. In the present story the author dwells on two features that are passed over quickly in the other two accounts: (1) the foreign ruler's discovery of the deception (vv. 3–7; 12:17; 26:8) and (2) the confrontation between Abraham and the ruler (vv. 8–16; 12:18–19; 26:9–10).[476] We learn that the wife-sister deception was a recurring tactic employed by the patriarch wherever he went (v. 13); this helps explain why more than one such event appears in the patriarchal narratives. The elaborate recounting of Abimelech's dream by which he learns of the ruse is more important to the immediate context, with its question of justice, than in the other two wife-sister episodes (12:17; 26:8). Further, we discover the patriarch's own justification for the ploy: he reveals that Sarah is actually a half-sister, the daughter of his father by another mother (v. 12). We also learn, through the

---

[476] Alexander, *Abraham in the Negev,* 42; id., *A Literary Analysis,* 157–58; id., "Are the Wife/Sister Incidents of Genesis Compositional Literary Variants?" *VT* 42 (1992): 145–53.

eyes of her husband, why Sarah cooperated in the scheme; he believed that his life was in her hands, and her compliance was his sole hope to escape harm (v. 13; cp. 12:12–13).

The second question for the interpreter pertains to the relationship of chap. 20 to the present context of Genesis. Many view 20:1–18 as the beginning of an independent narrative tradition regarding Abraham and Gerar that concluded with the treaty at Beersheba (21:22–34).[477] The redactor interspersed the Abraham-at-Gerar narrative (20:1–18; 21:22–34) in the promised heir narrative in which the birth of Isaac (21:1–7) originally followed on 18:1–15. The abrupt transition after 20:17–18 to Isaac's birth (21:1–7) led scholars to regard it an interruption in the Abraham-at-Gerar account. T. L. Thompson contends that the chapter had no original relationship to any earlier Abraham narrative; the year's interim before the birth of Isaac (18:10,14) provided the redactor opportunity to include the Gerar episode. The difficulty in this line of argument is the linkage chap. 20 evidences with the Abraham narrative and the immediate context of chaps. 18–19 and 21. That the same scholars admit there is some faint connection of chap. 20 with the context does not deter them since they deem any linkage to be the work of the redactor. Yet the chapter shows structurally a coherent scheme, including an embedded chiastic structure (see below) whose plot progresses naturally from problem to resolution. Also it is unlikely that half of an original Abraham-in-Gerar account (21:22–34) could be peeled away without significantly impairing the former half (20:1–18).

Also 20:1–18 is not loosely connected with its context. We mentioned above how the chapter contributes to the Abraham narrative as a whole, and it is clear that the author of chap. 20 knows of chaps. 18–19 as they now appear. The pericope continues the Sodom story of chaps. 18–19 by a geographical backreference and by addressing many of the same motifs. "From there" (v. 1a) references the geographical setting of earlier events including chaps. 18–19 at Mamre (Hebron; 18:1; 19:27; also 13:18; 14:13). The motif of a traveling alien *(gēr)* that dominates chaps. 18–19 is reintroduced by Abraham's movement, who "stayed" *(gûr,* "sojourned")* in Gerar (v. 1b). The name "Gerar" *(gĕrār)* as a soundalike to *gēr* may have contributed to the author's placement of the episode. Both the Sodom and Gerar stories concern the mistreatment of sojourners by sexual offenses. Another important subtext in chaps. 18–19 is the question of divine justice toward the "righteous" and "wicked" (18:23–32; 19:7); the same issue regarding the fate of an "innocent" *(ṣaddîq)* nation (v. 4) is central to the dream scene (vv. 3–7). Both stories address the subject of divine justice in the setting of a private dialogue between God and Abraham (chap. 18) or Abimelech (chap. 20). The motif of anxiety over "life"/"death" (19:19,20) and to "preserve" one's legacy (19:32,34) reappears in the dream sequence when the Lord declares Abimelech a "dead" man (v. 3) whose life and legacy can only be spared by the prophet Abra-

---

[477] Van Seters, *Abraham in History,* 185; Thompson, *The Origin Tradition,* 57, 96–97; Coats *(Genesis,* 149, 155) observes the parallel between 20:1–18; 21:22–34 and Isaac's encounter with the Philistines (26:1–17; 26:17–33) as part of the narrative tradition pertaining to the king of Gerar (pp. 189, 193).

ham (vv. 3,7,17). The intercessory role of Abraham (18:23–32; 19:29) develops in the Gerar story too where he as "prophet" (v. 7) prays successfully for the healing of the royal harem (vv. 17–18). Abraham's alarm that there is "no fear *[yirat]* of God" at Gerar (v. 11) and the fear of the king's advisors (v. 8) reminds us of Lot's fear at residing in Zoar (19:30). "This place" (v. 11) also recalls the destruction of Sodom ("this place," 19:13,14; also "place" 18:24,26; cp. 26:7). Both Lot and King Abimelech are unaware of their crimes and are duped by women (19:33,35; 20:5). Another link with the Lot-Sodom narratives is the offer of land to Abraham as partial compensation for the offense (v. 15; 13:9). By these connections, chap. 20 continues the author's occupation with the threats (Pharaoh, Abimelech) and possible rivals (Lot, Ishmael) to the legitimate heir born to the elderly man and his wife.

As for the connection of chap. 20 with the birth of Isaac (21:1–7), the common feature is the healing of the barren women at Gerar (20:17–18) and the immediate pregnancy of Sarah (21:1–2). The juxtaposition of Sarah's pregnancy with the outcome of Abraham's prayer for the Gerarites may suggest that the patriarch's intercession included Sarah. Isaac also prayed in behalf of Rebekah, resulting in her pregnancy (25:21). We already noted that 18:16–19:38 and chap. 20 form a bridge between the announcement and fulfillment of Isaac's birth by showing how the Lord preserves the promise in the context of foreign hostilities. This motif is continued in 21:8–21 when Sarah requires the expulsion of Hagar and Ishmael. By the intervening narratives the author shows that the blessing for Abraham's descendants also extends to the nations; the consequences of those who opposed the chosen family (Sodomites, Ishmaelites) and those who treated the family kindly (Philistines) illustrate the centrality of the Abraham family but also the scope of the blessing or curse for all peoples (12:3).

STRUCTURE. The structure of the chapter consists of four units. The introduction in vv. 1–2 provide the background for making sense of the scenes to follow: (1) Abraham sojourns in Gerar (v. 1) and (2) the deception and abduction of Sarah (v. 2). The second and third units are the two key scenes: (1) one in the night, the dream segment (vv. 3–7), and (2) one in the morning, the encounter segment (vv. 8–16). The outcome is reported in the final two verses (vv. 18–19), confirming Abraham as prophetic mediator whose prayer results in God healing the Abimelech household.

vv. 1–2	Introduction: deception and abduction
vv. 3–7	God-Abimelech encounter ("night" dream)
v. 3	Divine sentence of death
vv. 4–5	Abimelech's plea for justice
vv. 6–7	Divine instructions
vv. 8–16	Abraham-Abimelech encounter ("morning")
v. 8	Abimelech reports the dream to this court
vv. 9–10	Abimelech interrogates Abraham
vv. 11–13	Abraham defends his behavior

vv. 14–16   Abimelech compensates Abraham and Sarah
vv. 17–18   Conclusion: prayer and restoration

The dream sequence (vv. 3–7) shows a tight chiastic structure:[478]

A   v. 3   you are as good as dead
  B   v. 3   the woman you have taken
    C   v. 4   Abimelech had not gone near her
      D   v. 4   will you destroy an innocent nation?
        E   v. 5   with a clear conscience
          F   v. 6   God said to him in a dream
        E′   v. 6   with a clear conscience
      D′   v. 6   I have kept you from sinning
    C′   v. 6   I did not let you touch her
  B′   v. 7   return the man's wife
A′   v. 7   you will live . . . if you do not . . . you and all yours will die

In this arrangement the central leg (F, v. 6a) repeats the term "dream" (v. 3) so as to highlight the cause for the reversal in Abimelech's conduct and, for that matter, the reversal of the whole story. We are reminded of the dream in which the Lord forewarns Laban not to harm Jacob (31:24).

(1) God Warns Abimelech in a Dream (20:1–7)

[1]Now Abraham moved on from there into the region of the Negev and lived between Kadesh and Shur. For a while he stayed in Gerar, [2]and there Abraham said of his wife Sarah, "She is my sister." Then Abimelech king of Gerar sent for Sarah and took her.

[3]But God came to Abimelech in a dream one night and said to him, "You are as good as dead because of the woman you have taken; she is a married woman."

[4]Now Abimelech had not gone near her, so he said, "Lord, will you destroy an innocent nation? [5]Did he not say to me, 'She is my sister,' and didn't she also say, 'He is my brother'? I have done this with a clear conscience and clean hands."

[6]Then God said to him in the dream, "Yes, I know you did this with a clear conscience, and so I have kept you from sinning against me. That is why I did not let you touch her. [7]Now return the man's wife, for he is a prophet, and he will pray for you and you will live. But if you do not return her, you may be sure that you and all yours will die."

After the backdrop is painted in vv. 1–2, the pericope describes in detail the encounter of God with the Philistine king in a dream (vv. 3–7). This nocturnal revelation, to a foreigner no less, points out that God gives nations opportunity

---

[478] Alexander, *Abraham in the Negev,* 39 and *A Literary Analysis,* 150; Alexander proposes parallel panels between vv. 8–13 and vv. 14–17a but admits it is "less obvious."

to repent (Jonah 3:10).[479] Abimelech's reversal contrasts with the recalcitrance of the wicked Sodomites, whose depravity is incorrigible. Here is another case where the treatment of the Abraham household results in agreement with the earlier promises regarding the nations (12:3; 18:18; 22:18). The irony of the story is that Abraham occasions both curse and blessing for the Philistine: curse for obtaining Sarah, resulting in a barren household, and blessing by the intercession of the patriarch, eliciting the healing of the court's women. The implication is that the king's family will be prodigious. The preservation of Sarah and the blessing on the Gerarites illustrate again the surpassing grace of God, who ensures that the promises will come to pass.

20:1–2 Abraham moved again, for whatever reason, into the region of the Negev (v. 1). "Moved" *(nāsaʿ)* is the same term in 12:9, which describes his first itinerary toward Egypt (12:10–13:1). As 12:9 indicates, such migrations characterized the man's habits. An important feature of the Abraham narrative as a whole is his vagabond life as an alien *(gēr)*. "He stayed" *(wayyāgor)* employs the common related term "sojourned" *(gûr)*, and the name "Gerar" *(gĕrār)* itself reiterates the sound of the action. We have learned how a traveler can be molested by wicked men (Sodom); another kind of hostility threatens the survival of Abraham's family.

Abraham journeys "between Kadesh and Shur" (v. 1), the region where earlier Hagar had fled (16:7,14). The modern identification of Gerar is uncertain. Tell Haror (Tell Abu Hureirah), located on the north bank of Nahal Gerar about nine miles southeast of Gaza (cf. 10:19) and fifteen miles northwest of Beersheba on the way from Gaza to the Beersheba valley, has been suggested as the most likely candidate.[480] There is agreement that it was located in the western Negev near Gaza. Gerar marks the southern boundary of Canaan in 10:19.

"Abimelech" ("my father is king") is identified as "king" of Gerar (v. 2); the name occurs later in chap. 26, when Isaac attempts the same deception. Like the name Pharaoh, "Abimelech" may be the throne name for the Gerarites (see comments on 26:1). That Abraham repeated his wife-sister deception suggests that wife stealing was a common threat. The abduction of Sarah is reported briefly without reason (v. 2). The prior Egyptian incident credits Sarah's beauty for her abduction (12:14–16) as does Rebekah's in the later Isaac-Abimelech episode (26:1–13), but the silence of the passage on this crucial count may indicate that another consideration, such as forging an economic relationship with the Abraham clan, was the king's motive. The chronology requires that Sarah

---

[479] Milgrom observes that God appears to non-Israelites but three times in the Scriptures, forewarning them of interference (20:3; 31:24; Num 22:9; *Numbers,* 187).

[480] The possibility that Tell Jemmeh (ca. six miles south of Gaza) is biblical Gerar has been largely dismissed. E. Oren, "Gerar," *ABD* 2.989–91; "Haror, Tell," *OEANE* 2.474–76; "Haror, Tell," *NEAEHL* 2.580–84. On the question of Philistine anachronism in Genesis, see the commentary Introduction.

was ninety years old (17:17), and furthermore she describes herself as "worn out" (18:11–13).

20:3 God confronts Abimelech in a dream and announces his imminent death (v. 3).[481] The reason for the death sentence is stated clearly: the man took for himself a "married woman."[482] His death and its cause form an inclusio with "you will die" in v. 7, where the Lord will grant him a way of escape. Hebrew *lāqaḥ,* "has taken," is a play on the idea of marriage, for the word is a common idiom meaning "to marry" (e.g., 11:29). Mosaic legislation required the death penalty for adultery, both the man and the woman (Lev 20:10; Deut 22:22). It is termed a "great sin" ("guilt," NIV v. 9) and treated as a sin against God (v. 6; Ps 51:4[6]). Since Abimelech did not challenge the morality of the charge, only his innocence of the crime, we may deduce that adultery in the Philistine's eyes was illegitimate. Ancient Near Eastern law codes outlawed adultery which sanctioned execution of the offenders. In Hittite law the adulterer who can prove his ignorance of the woman's marital status at the time of the offense is acquitted.[483] Abimelech makes this argument in his defense (v. 5), but ignorance alone doesn't absolve the man in God's eyes; there must be a return of the woman and a mediation by her husband (v. 7). Kidnapping also was an offense in Israelite law, meriting the ultimate penalty (Exod 21:16; Deut 24:7).

As to the duration of the time between the seizure of Sarah and the dream, the passage is not clear. A fairly short period is required since the annunciation of Isaac (17:21; 18:10,14) permits one year, which entails her pregnancy by Abraham. The sense of the passage is that the dream occurred soon after the abduction. The failure of the king to consummate the marriage with Sarah probably is the result of a fatal disease impacting his sexual function (vv. 7,17–18). Anyway, it is the Lord's intervention alone that in fact saved him from committing adultery (v. 6); in effect, he was saved from himself!

20:4–5 Abimelech contends on the basis of his ignorance that he has been judged too harshly (vv. 4–5). This, he believes, is a mitigating factor and that he acted with a clear conscience. The couple themselves misled him, and hence he behaved in good faith. The narrative prelude to Abimelech's rejoinder explains that he "had not gone near her" (v. 4). "Gone near" translates *qārab* ("approach"), which is used to describe illicit sexual relations in Hebrew law (e.g., Lev 18:6,14,19; 20:16). The author bolsters the king's defense by stating categorically that no sexual offense had occurred. It is enough for God, however, that the man took the woman, and thus she must be returned unharmed (v. 7).

---

[481] "You are about to die" (author's translation) translates the participle מֵת (future instans).

[482] בְּעֻלַת בָּעַל, lit., "married (to) a husband" is the feminine passive participle, בְּעוּלָה, "married" (Deut 22:22; Isa 54:1; 62:4) in construct with בַּעַל, "husband, lord"; the exact phrase occurs again only in Deut 22:22.

[483] E. Goodfriend, "Adultery," *ABD* 1.84.

Abimelech sets his rebuttal in the broad context of divine justice (v. 4). His question is rhetorical; he assumes that this "Lord" would not condemn him if he knew the facts, for God acts justly toward an "innocent" ("righteous," *ṣaddîq*) nation. The king's appeal to the unspecified "Lord" *('ădōnāy)* corresponds with the typical polytheism of the ancient Near East. He did not know initially which of the gods confronted him. He will continue to refer to him in terms of God's paternal relationship to Abraham (21:22–23). Abimelech's appeal to divine justice recalls Abraham's same concern for the "righteous" *(ṣaddîq)* at Sodom (18:23–32). The Philistine believes that by extension whatever befalls him, as king, will harm the Gerarites. The appearance of "nation" *(gôy)* is a reflex of the promissory blessing recited in 18:18 ("nations," cf. 22:18). The patriarchal promises make Abraham and his legacy an important factor in the future blessing of "all peoples" (12:3). In microcosm the treatment of Abraham and Sarah by the Philistine presages the divine blessing that Abraham as mediator will afford the peoples of the world. In this case, Abraham mediates divine healing which enables the king's wives to bear children; in Genesis, blessing typically means a numerous offspring (e.g., 17:20; 22:12; 26:24; 28:3; cp. 1 Sam 2:20).

With respect to the crime of adultery, Abimelech explains that he acted without malice, "with a clear conscience and clean hands" (v. 5). The former expression is literally "with a perfect heart," meaning an upright conduct;[484] "perfect" *(tom)* indicates wholeness, integrity (cf. 6:9), and "heart" *(lēbāb)* often represents the human intellect (e.g., 6:5; 8:21). "Clean hands" *(niqyōn kappay)* means behavior that is free from guilt (e.g., Pss 26:6; 73:13[485]); the word group *nāqâ* conveys innocence, acquittal (e.g., Ps 24:4; Hos 8:5; cp. "cleanness," Amos 4:6).[486]

20:6 In the chiastic arrangement of the passage (see above), "then God said . . ." (v. 6a) turns the direction of vv. 1–7. Now God counters the defense of the king; in effect, God answers: "I know all this; in fact, I am the one who kept you from committing an irreparable transgression. You are a dead man anyway, unless you return the woman immediately!" His speech begins "I also," *gam 'ānōkî* ("yes, I," NIV, v. 6a), a direct rebuttal to Abimelech's charge, "Will you destroy a nation though *[gam]* innocent?" (v. 4b). God knows as well as Abimelech the circumstances of the abduction.[487] The second rebuttal has the same "I also," *gam 'ānōkî* ("so I," NIV, v. 6b); God himself was the one restraining *(ḥāśak)* Abimelech's sexual appetite so that he did not permit the king even to "touch" *(nāgaʿ)* Sarah. Hebrew *ḥāśak* ("keep in check") describes

---

[484] תָּם לֵבָב occurs 5x in 20:5,6; 1 Kgs 9:4; Pss 78:72; 101:2; it contrasts with "all the heart" and "whole heart" which indicate devotion (A. Luc, "לֵב," *NIDOTTE* 2.750–51).

[485] J. Olivier, "נקה," *NIDOTTE* 3.152–54.

[486] "I acted in complete innocence!" (NLT).

[487] BDB 169.

divine interference in the evil actions of humans (e.g., 1 Sam 25:39).[488] The word "touch" recalls the plagues *(nāgaʿ/negaʿ)* suffered in Pharaoh's house for his crime (12:17); the king at Gerar in Isaac's day decrees that no one shall "touch" *(nāgaʿ)* Rebekah or he will die (26:11). The inference of the divine speech is that the Philistine's "clear conscience" occurred only by the gracious intervention of God. The protection granted the woman clarifies for us in chap. 21 that Abraham is the father of her child, as the Visitor foretold (18:1–15).

20:7 Since Abimelech did not compromise Sarah sexually, there remains the possibility of forgiveness through restitution and intercession (v. 7). The king must return Sarah to her lawful husband, who as a "prophet" may "pray" for the condemned man. We observed above the intercessory function of the chosen family for the sake of the world; the Lot-Sodom narratives (chaps. 13–14; 18–19) illustrate the role of Abraham in international matters. Here the divine revelation to the Philistine confirms that Abraham is a "prophet" *(nābîʾ),* the first occasion of the word in Scripture. Abraham is considered a prophet by virtue of his mediatorial role; he is not the founder or model of the prophetic institution of Israel (cf. Moses, Deut 18).[489] However, he is the first in Scripture to intercede with God on behalf of others (18:22–32). That God does not "hide" what he will do (18:19) invites Abraham, like the prophets, to learn the plans of God for the purpose of intercession.[490] Abimelech's salvation ironically lies with the husband whom he offended; the "nation" *(gôy)* cannot survive apart from the benevolence of this chosen mediator of God.

No malady is named to explain the sentence of death, though we observed that "touch" may be an allusion to the "serious diseases" suffered by Pharaoh for the same offense (12:17). Verses 17–18 report that the king and his household are healed, but it is ambiguous as to what ailed him. That Abraham's intercession means that Abimelech "shall live" and that "God healed" him suggests he suffered a fatal illness. "For he is a prophet" explains to the king why his mediation can save him, but more is involved here. The passage assumes that as a chosen prophet Abraham enjoyed special protection that the king had unwittingly transgressed. Opposition to God's prophets resulted in divine retribution for a nation (e.g., Jer 11:21–22; Amos 2:12–13; 7:16–17). This is the psalmist's interpretation, which remembered this incident when he praised God for his protective mercies on the Fathers (105:12–15//1 Chr 16:22).[491]

The alternative to returning Sarah is expressed judicially: "You and all yours will die" *(môt tāmût;* v. 7b). The language of the verse is reminiscent of the Garden prohibition (2:17) and has the familiar ring of the Mosaic penalty for

---

[488] E. Martens, "חשׂך," *NIDOTTE* 2.301–2.

[489] P. Verhoef, "Prophecy," *NIDOTTE* 4.1067–78.

[490] MacDonald, "Listening to Abraham," 39.

[491] The psalm's vocabulary "oppress" (יכח) and "touch" (נגע) allude to our narrative: "vindicated," יכח, v. 16; "touch," נגע, v. 6.

capital crimes, "put to death" *(môt yûmāt;* e.g., Exod 21:16; cf. Abimelech's decree, 26:11). "All yours" in the Hebrew *(kol ʾăšer lāk)* is a subtle echo of Abraham's wealth, which was obtained under similar circumstances (12:20; 13:1; 25:5); here it primarily refers to Abimelech's royal lineage. As it turns out, the Philistine's household only experiences temporary barrenness (vv. 17–18), and he parts with a portion of his land and a payment of restitution to Abraham (vv. 14–16).

(2) Abimelech Encounters Abraham (20:8–16)

[8]Early the next morning Abimelech summoned all his officials, and when he told them all that had happened, they were very much afraid. [9]Then Abimelech called Abraham in and said, "What have you done to us? How have I wronged you that you have brought such great guilt upon me and my kingdom? You have done things to me that should not be done." [10]And Abimelech asked Abraham, "What was your reason for doing this?"

[11]Abraham replied, "I said to myself, 'There is surely no fear of God in this place, and they will kill me because of my wife.' [12]Besides, she really is my sister, the daughter of my father though not of my mother; and she became my wife. [13]And when God had me wander from my father's household, I said to her, 'This is how you can show your love to me: Everywhere we go, say of me, "He is my brother."'"

[14]Then Abimelech brought sheep and cattle and male and female slaves and gave them to Abraham, and he returned Sarah his wife to him. [15]And Abimelech said, "My land is before you; live wherever you like."

[16]To Sarah he said, "I am giving your brother a thousand shekels of silver. This is to cover the offense against you before all who are with you; you are completely vindicated."

The circumstances of the dreadful dream prompts the king to act immediately "the next morning" (v. 8). The interview and action taken by Abimelech occur in one day. Verse 8 provides the courtly background in which the interrogation will proceed. The dialogue consists of two speeches by the king (vv. 9–10,14–16) and the intervening explanation given by Abraham (vv. 11–13). Abimelech's first speech entails a rebuke of the patriarch's behavior, chiding him repeatedly by using words related to the key term, "done" *(ʿāśâ,* 5x). The overall sense of his complaint is that the king is the true victim; he clings, it appears, to his initial defense that ultimately he was the one wronged until he eventually concedes some fault. Overall Abimelech's behavior is much more conciliatory than Pharaoh's rancorous reaction, which resulted in immediate expulsion without a hearing. He is morally troubled by the offense he may have committed and also shows concern for the welfare of his people.[492] Abraham's apology consists of two arguments: (1) he was afraid of being murdered, and

---

[492] Wenham, *Genesis 16–50,* 72.

(2) Sarah was indeed his (half-)sister (vv. 11–13). The second speech of Abimelech is not a rebuttal to Abraham's defense; rather, he puts to rights his transgression against the husband and wife (vv. 14–16).

20:8–10   The king assembles his "officials" ("servants") in an emergency session first thing in the morning. Verse 8 presents the setting of Gerar's welfare for the summoning of Abraham; the fate of a city hangs on this one man. The ancient world believed dreams were a common means of divine visitation; Abimelech's remarkable account of his dream justified the citizens' unimaginable fear (cf. Jonah 1:10). Perhaps the literary linkage of chap. 20 with the context of the Sodom episode (chaps. 18–19) implies that the fear generated by Sodom's catastrophe still lingered (19:30) in the region. Wenham remarks that the fearful reaction of the men contradicted Abraham's self-justification for the deception (v. 11).[493]

"What have you done *['āśâ]* to us?" is the first question put to the patriarch (v. 9a); the question is rhetorical since all parties know the details of the ruse. The question is reminiscent of the offense exposed by the Lord in the Garden (3:13,14). The same reproach is made against the trickster in 12:18 and 26:10. The state brought the charge against Abraham, for his actions jeopardized the nation ("to us"). Although the chicanery duped the king personally, the Philistine keeps the wider implications of the ruse always before Abraham ("my kingdom," v. 9b). Abimelech cannot understand such depth of deceitfulness without cause; he unrelentlessly demands an explanation from the culprit whose scheming he insists he did not deserve. The king points up this inequity by the related terms *ḥāṭāʾ,* "wronged," and *ḥăṭāʾâ,* "guilt." In other words, what crime *(ḥāṭāʾ)* did the king commit against Abraham that elicited the fraud that resulted in their crime *(ḥăṭāʾâ)* against him?

This perplexity permeates the speech, ending on the same note in v. 10, "What was your reason . . .?" The king's fury is understandable since such conduct was reprehensible even in his own eyes. Moreover, he is at a serious disadvantage in dealing with a man whom he knows God has sheltered. Adultery is named a "great sin"/"great crime" in ancient Near Eastern texts, reflecting the severity of the offense in the eyes of society.[494] Is there yet a more subtle reason for his boldness of speech? One cannot help but think, however, that the rebuke has a divine cast to it; just as God choreographed Abimelech's repentance, does the king speak unwittingly the words of divine correction to Abraham?

20:11–13   The impotent excuses the patriarch presents casts him in an even more distasteful light. Abraham answers the king's chiding with a critique of his own for Gerar (v. 11). He did not expect to find a high code of ethical conduct as the rule of the city (cp. 12:12; 26:7). "Fear of God" *(yirʾat ʾĕlōhîm)*

---

[493] Ibid.
[494] See Goodfriend, "Adultery," 82 and bibliography.

means in this context conformity to a moral code of behavior (e.g., Exod 20:20), not the absence of religion.[495] "The fear of God" characterizes rulers who act justly (42:18; 2 Sam 23:3; 2 Chr 26:5; Neh 5:15); Abraham is aiming his rebuttal at the king. The patriarch reasons that murder is preferred by such despots to risking the "great sin" of adultery (v. 18). The psalmist's exposé of the person who has no "fear of God" *(pahad 'ĕlōhîm;* Ps 36:1–4; Rom 3:18) includes nocturnal planning of sinful deeds (v. 4). In the case of Abimelech, any such bedtime plots were interrupted by his dream!

His second rebuttal hinges on a technicality, one that provides a moral loophole absolving Abraham in his own eyes of the wrong leveled at him: Sarah "really" is his sister, the daughter of the same father but by a different mother, hence a half-sister (v. 12). Hebrew *wĕgam 'omnâ,* "and also truly," (v. 12, "Besides . . . really," NIV) is the second emphatic adverb in his speech (cf. "surely," *raq* v. 11),[496] pressing his point all the more. Marriage within the family (endogamy) characterizes the practices of the patriarchs. For example, Nahor married his niece Milcah; Isaac married Rebekah, his second cousin; and Jacob married sisters, Leah and Rachel, who were his cousins. The early practical effect of endogamy is preservation of the family's religious tradition (chap. 24). Mosaic legislation, however, repudiated certain forms of endogamy, such as a man's marriage to his sister and marriages to sisters (Lev 18:9,11,18; Deut 27:22). From Israel's later perspective, the marriage of Abraham to his sister was unlawful (see discussion in commentary Introduction, "Morality"). The passage does not mention the name of either wife of their father Terah, emphasizing solely their common father.

The final word of his defense is the necessity of his modus operandi; the couple had employed this ruse before successfully (v. 13). The Egyptian incident (12:10–13:1) is testimony to Abraham's track record. The two passages taken together suggest that Abraham employed the hoax for the first time in Egypt, and having met with moderate success continued to use the ploy when necessary. Mention of his "father's household" involves his status as a *gēr* ("alien") who was especially subject to exploitation by immoral men (chaps. 18–19). That God caused his wandering "from my father's household" is a reminder of the patriarch's call at Haran (12:1–3), where he left behind the security of family and property.[497] The pronoun of *"my* father's household" could as easily be *"our* father's household," for it anticipates the crux of their subterfuge (italics mine). Abimelech's polytheism may explain why the patriarch uses the plural verb "wander" *(hit'û)* with God *(Elohim)* rather than the customary singular. If this is not a simple grammatical accommodation, Abra-

---

[495] M. Van Pelt and W. Kaiser Jr., "ירא," *NIDOTTE* 2.533.

[496] רַק (v. 11) is restrictive, "only," but also can have an asseverative force (BDB 956; *IBHS* §39.3.5a); אָמְנָה occurs 2x (Josh 7:20).

[497] "Wander" תעה describes Hagar's desert existence (21:14; cf. Ps 107:4,40).

ham reaches an all-time religious low by granting such a concession to the pagan king. From the patriarch's confession to Abimelech, we learn that his persuasion of Sarah (12:17) included the inducement of spousal loyalty: "you can show your love to me." "Love" translates the word *ḥesed* which here means to help out a troubled party; relational loyalty is assumed in a family environment.[498] Although the force of law was not operable in this case, the power of custom encouraged Sarah's concession (cf. 1 Pet 3:6).

20:14–16 Although Abimelech pays reparations to Abraham and Sarah for his crime, this is not an absolution of Abraham's complicity in the matter.[499] The king compensates the couple in three ways: (1) to Abraham he delivers livestock and servants and returns Sarah (v. 14); (2) to Abraham he offers land (v. 15); and (3) speaking to Sarah, he announces a gift of silver to "her brother" (v. 16). The first provision recalls the items of restitution made by Pharaoh (12:16), but more importantly the king returns the woman as demanded by God (v. 7). The second reward of land is the opposite response of Pharaoh who expelled the couple (12:19–20); Abimelech sees an advantage in forming a friendly relationship with this "prophet" of God (21:22–32). After Abraham received a portion of land in the Gerar area, the patriarch acquired a well which was his first formal possession in Canaan (21:30–31). The third element of restitution involved a hefty payment of silver (v. 16). Relatively speaking, the figure of one thousand shekels is remarkably generous; four hundred shekels purchased the Machpelah cave (23:15–16), one hundred shekels a piece of land at Shechem (33:1), and a mere twenty shekels the purchase of a slave (37:28).

This payment is accompanied by a direct public apology to the woman in which Abimelech makes it clear that she was not defiled. In addressing her the king speaks of Abraham as "your brother" (v. 16), which may be an additional sign of concession to Abraham's defense or, perhaps, even a final jibe at the heartless ruse they carried out. "Cover the eyes" (*kĕsût ʿênayim,* "cover the offense," NIV) and "vindicated" *(nōkāḥat)* work together but differently in conveying the exoneration of Sarah. "Cover" *(kāsâ)* essentially means to conceal (e.g., clothing, Job 24:7); here, the metaphorical sense is that the forfeiture of silver hides the woman's shame wrongly brought by the king's actions (on the relationship of cover and shame, see e.g., Pss 44:15[16]; 69:7[8]); Ezek 16:8; Jer 51:51). Precisely the origin and meaning of the phrase "cover the eyes" are unknown. Here, the phrase applies to those who accompany Sarah, prohibiting them from disparaging looks, for their eyes are deprived from seeing her shame.[500] This public vindication becomes increasingly important to the Abra-

---

[498] D. Baer and R. Gordon, "חֶסֶד," *NIDOTTE* 2.211–12.

[499] Westermann, *Genesis 12–36,* 324–25.

[500] Theologically, God "covers" a person's sin by mercies and love (e.g., Ps 32:5; Prov 10:12); in the tabernacle, the burning incense "conceals" the holy ark consequently protecting the eyes of the high priest as well (Lev 16:13). W. Domeris, "כָּסָה," *NIDOTTE* 2.674–78.

ham family with the birth of Isaac (chap. 21).

The second absolution, "acquit, vindicate" *(yākaḥ),* typically describes a dispute between parties in a formal legal proceeding (e.g., Job 23:7) or an informal quarrel which may result in legal action (e.g., Abraham-Abimelech, 21:25; Jacob-Laban, 31:36–37).[501] Abimelech interprets his own action for us: his payment is an admission that Sarah had a legitimate basis for a complaint and by its deposit with her husband the king declares her clear of any culpability. In other words, the king settles his debt with the couple out of court. The recurring term *kol* translated "all" and "completely" promotes her full exculpation. This royal groveling must have left a profound impact on its witnesses, elevating the international stature of Abraham in the presence of both parties.

(3) God Heals Abimelech (20:17–18)

[17]Then Abraham prayed to God, and God healed Abimelech, his wife and his slave girls so they could have children again, [18]for the LORD had closed up every womb in Abimelech's household because of Abraham's wife Sarah.

20:17–18   The narrative's conclusion adds to the weight of Abraham's religious and political impact on the region. The name "Abraham" forms an inclusio for the conclusion (vv. 17a,18b). The inversion in the two verses makes it clear that on account of Abimelech's mistreatment of Sarah the Philistines experienced barrenness, which was reversed as a consequence of Abimelech's new benevolence toward the man. The author does not fail to establish, however, that the healing occurs at the grace of God; he, not Abraham, performs the restoration, even as he, not Abraham, had closed the wombs of the Gerarite women. The divine condemnation in the king's dream, "you are about to die" (v. 3, NRSV), has an unexpected twist when we learn that the penalty is so to speak the "death" of his kingdom by virtue of a barren harem. This is not to say that God does not threaten the king with an immediate personal death (e.g., 38:7), but the penalty of infertility extends beyond him to the whole of his realm. Philistine infertility also contributes in two additional ways to the account: (1) the penalty, including Abimelech's own wife, corresponds with the nature of the crime, since the abduction imperiled Sarah's sexual and maternal reputation; and (2) the penalty confirms that neither Sarah nor anyone else could be pregnant.

Abraham's prayer for Abimelech fulfills the provision of restoration in the king's dream (vv. 7,17). This is the first place in Genesis where the specific act of prayer is named; "call upon" has described the patriarch's worship and indicates a broad sphere of worshipful acts (e.g., 4:26; 12:8;

---

[501] J. Hartley, "יכח," *NIDOTTE* 2.441–45.

26:25). "Prayed" translates the common term *pālal* (always *hithpael*) from which is derived *tĕpillâ*, the popular word for "prayer." The mother of Samuel "prayed" similarly for the reversal of infertility (1 Sam 1:10). The same word describes the intercessory salvation of Israel by Moses in the wilderness (Num 11:2; 21:7; Deut 9:26) and of Aaron (Deut 9:20). The synonym "entreat" *('ātar)* describes Isaac's successful plea for Rebekah's conception (25:21; also Moses "entreats" for Israel (Exod 8:30[26]; 10:18). There are other occasions where prayer is in view in Genesis, though not described with the formal terms for "prayer" (e.g., 24:12,15; 32:9).

"God healed" the women of Abimelech's household, including the queen (v. 17). The word "healed" *(rāpā')* usually describes recovery from disease and physical malady (e.g., the Philistine sores, 1 Sam 5:6). Infertility is treated in the Old Testament as a physical disease. It is counted a curse against the Israelites for covenant disobedience (e.g., Exod 15:26; Deut 7:12–15) and, oppositely, the fruitful womb is divine blessing (e.g., Deut 30:9).[502] The author describes the outcome of the healing in but one Hebrew word,[503] focusing attention on the mediation by Abraham (v. 17) and the cause for the infertility (v. 18). The clause may read as purpose, "so they could have children again" (NIV) or as result, "so that they bore children" (NRSV). The final verse (v. 18) explains the malady and the necessity of Abraham's mediation: the Lord (*Yahweh*) "had closed up every womb" (v. 18a; cf. 1 Sam 1:5–6; for the "opened" womb, see 29:31; 30:22). The Hebrew construction accentuates the certainty of the infertility, which is best translated "had closed fast" (NASB, NRSV, NJPS) or "tightly closed" (NAB).[504] Only God could reverse their hopeless condition (see comments on 11:30; 12:2). The narrative ends recalling the cause for the penalty of infertility, "on account of Sarah, the wife of Abraham" (v. 18b; cp. 12:17). The term "closed up" *('āṣar)* occurs but one other place in Genesis, describing the infertile Sarah in 16:2 ("has kept me"). Two walls of protection therefore are in view in this chapter: the king could not engage in sexual relations, and the women could not conceive. This ensured that the child Isaac was indeed of Abraham and Sarah. From beginning to end the story concerns protecting Sarah's sexual honor, for as the "wife of Abraham," her miraculous conception testifies to the veracity of God's promise to husband and wife (17:16–19; 18:1–15).

---

[502] A. Kam-Yau Chan et al., "רפא," *NIDOTTE* 3.1163.

[503] וַיֵּלְדוּ, lit., "and they bore (children)."

[504] עָצֹר עָצַר lit., "closing he closed"; the cognate infinitive absolute typically emphasizes the force of the verbal action (*IBHS* §35.3.1b,d); see S. Rickert, "The Struct [*sic*] Patterns of the Paranomastic and Co-ordinated Infinitives Absolute in Genesis," *JNSL* 7 (1979): 69–83, cited in *IBHS* §35.3.a, n. 17.

11. Abraham's Promised Son: The Birth of Isaac (21:1–21)

Anticipation becomes reality in the nativity of Isaac. Since Abraham and Sarah's entrance into Canaan some twenty-five years earlier (12:4), the couple has looked to this day. Inheritance is the controlling motif of the Abraham narrative, and it finds its denouement in the birth of Isaac. The infant's rival is expelled, leaving Isaac's right to inheritance uncontested. The advent of Isaac, however, offers only a temporary sigh of relief for the reader; the denouement is after all an illusory end to the narrative tension. The arrival of Isaac only prepares the way for the final test of Abraham's faith—the climactic Akedah (sacrifice of Isaac) at Mount Moriah (chap. 22).

The birth of Ishmael and the promised succession of Isaac in 16:1–18:15 furnish the background for the anticipated clash between the competing wives created by Isaac's entrance; the expulsion of Hagar's son, already hinted at in the earlier narratives (16:12; 17:18–20), resolves the conflict. In typical fashion the author writes off the rival line before exploring the story of the chosen successor. It is not enough for the author to report only the fact of expulsion (v. 14); what became of Ishmael must be explained since he as the "offspring" ("seed," v. 13) of Abraham is also a recipient of divine promise (16:10–11). The miraculous salvation of Ishmael in the desert affirms that "God was with the boy" (v. 20), assuring his prosperity as pledged.

The conflict over inheritance is told in the simple terms of two mothers who protect their young. Sarah controls the first scene that is set in Abraham's camp (vv. 1–13). Hagar is mentioned only in the third person and in a disparaging way by Sarah: she is "that slave woman" (*hā'āmâ hazzō't*, v. 10[2x]). Sarah vents her antipathy by the juxtaposition of "*her* [Hagar's] son" with "*my* [Sarah's] son" (v. 10; italics mine). She refuses to acknowledge that the son of the Egyptian is in fact "your [Abraham's] son"! Ishmael's relationship to his father is only heard in the narration's "his son" (v. 11) and the Lord's "your offspring" (v. 13). The Lord does not speak directly to Hagar in this scene. He only refers to Hagar in the third person or in terms of her role, using the same word "maidservant" (*'āmâ*, vv. 12–13) but softening the expression by adding "*your* [Abraham's] maidservant" (italics mine); also the promise of blessing for Ishmael mitigates the story's somewhat dispassionate attitude toward Hagar.

The subsequent scene shifts to the rival mother and her son in the desert (vv. 14–21). The passage repeatedly mentions location of the events (vv. 14,15,17,20,21), attaching special importance to the metaphorical significance of where they occurred (see comments on chap. 16). Hagar's maternal instincts of protection are no less intense than Sarah's (cf. "his mother," v. 21). In a striking reversal from the first scene, Hagar is addressed by name by the "angel of God" (v. 17), who comforts and assures her that Ishmael will have a promising future (v. 18). The final depiction of Hagar in this chapter is the last we see of her in Genesis. She provides for Ishmael's future by obtaining an Egyptian wife (v. 21; 25:12); this event is the counterscene to Abraham's search among his relations for an appropriate wife for Isaac (chap. 24).

Also this episode tells the story of two sons. Although neither one has a word of dialogue, they hold special narrative interest as the question of inheritance remains the central theme. Repeatedly, the narrative's syntax has references to the boys (e.g., "his son") at the end of clauses, and the alternation of references to the two boys in vv. 8–14 (Isaac, vv. 8,10,12; Ishmael vv. 9,11,13) reinforces the story's contrast between the patriarch's two sons.[505] The passage cautiously marginalizes Ishmael, while retaining his importance for future developments (25:9; 28:9; 36:3; 37:25–36; 39:1). The name "Ishmael" does not occur in the whole of the pericope, suggesting that he has lost status in the household that he once held as the sole heir of the patriarch. We only know him in this passage by his roles: "son" *(ben),* both Hagar's (vv. 10,13) and Abraham's (vv. 9,11); "child" *(yeled,* "son," NIV; vv. 14,15,16); "boy" *(na'ar,* vv. 12,17[2x],18,19,20); and "seed" *(zera',* "offspring," NIV; v. 13). Echoes of "Ishmael" *(yišmā'ē'l)* also occur in the word "hear" *(šama',* vv. 6,12,17). The name "Isaac," however, is the preferred means of reference wherever the infant is mentioned: his name occurs six times (vv. 3,4,5,8,10,12) and is the source of wordplay three times ("laughter, laugh," v. 6[2x]; "mocking," v. 9).

The narrative's shift in describing Ishmael, from "child" *(yeled)* to "boy" *(na'ar),* shows his transition in the chapter from adolescence to manhood.[506] The seeds of aggression ("mocking," v. 9) evolve into his profession as a skilled hunter who is at home in the hostile wilderness (cf. 16:12). The word *yeled* typically means an "infant" or "young child" (e.g., Exod 2:3; Ruth 4:16; but not always, cf. Ruth 1:5). Though a teenager (ca. fourteen yrs. old, 17:25), Ishmael is a *yeled* in the poignant depictions of the boy in the care of his mother (vv. 14,15,16). But he is a *na'ar* ("boy") when God rescues him (vv. 12,17[2x],18,19,20a), and he eventually becomes hunter and husband (vv. 20b,21). Isaac grows, too, though only from infancy to toddler (v. 8); he is cast as a vulnerable child who is in the smothering care of his parents (vv. 5,7,10b).[507] Both sons are identified as Abraham's "seed" ("offspring," NIV; vv.

---

[505] L. Lyke, "Where Does 'the Boy' Belong? Compositional Strategy in Genesis 21:14," *CBQ* 56 (1994): 637–48. "Isaac" (vv. 3,8), "Isaac his son" (v. 5), "a son in his old age" (v. 7), "with my son Isaac" (v. 10), "his son" (v. 11), "seed" (vv. 12,13), "the boy" (vv. 14,19); also the wordplays on Isaac's name, "laugh with me" (v. 6) and "mocking" (v. 9) occur at the end of the sentence. Lyke suggests that the strategy of delaying reference to the sons imitates the wait Abraham experienced in obtaining them (p. 644). For another suggestion see comments on 21:14.

[506] The term for Isaac, as an infant, is always *yeled* in chap. 21 (vv. 2,3,5,8); at an older age he is *na'ar* in 22:5,12.

[507] Isaac leaps in the Abraham narrative from toddler (chap. 21) to teenager (chap. 22) to young husband (chap. 24) to father (chap. 25); in the Akedah he is regularly identified as "my son," and in marriage he chooses to live in the tent of his deceased mother (24:67).

12,13); the language "seed" by double entendre recalls the patriarchal blessing
in the form of a prodigious lineage and nationhood (e.g., 12:2; 15:5; 16:10;
17:20; 18:18; 22:18). This dual use of "seed" for Abraham's sons repeats the
narrative tension concerning the identity of the promised heir. As on the occasion of instituting the sign of circumcision (17:21), the passage by reciting the
word of God makes it clear that Isaac alone receives the inheritance of his father
(v. 12). Later the narrative's inclusion of Ishmael's genealogy of twelve tribes
(25:12–18) also confirms the efficacy of the divine promise.

COMPOSITION.   Customarily, critics carve chap. 21 into three distinct units
that are generally believed to be self-contained: vv. 1–7 describe the birth of
Isaac, vv. 8–21 tell of Hagar's expulsion, and vv. 22–34 report the treaty at Beersheba. We will discuss the Beersheba episode in the next unit of the commentary.
Source critics earlier interpreted vv. 1–7 as a combination of two or three
sources, but with the vanishing of the Elohist (E) source, source critics usually
delegated vv. 1a,2a,6–7 to the Yahwist (J) and vv. 1b,2b–5 to the Priestly (P).
Westermann, however, finds vv. 1–2 are a unit probably common to both J and P
sources, resulting in vv. 1–2,6–7=J and vv. 3–5=P. Westermann concludes that
the allusions in vv. 1–7 to earlier narratives indicate that the passage is the creation of the redactor, who combined two different reports of Isaac's birth as the
grand finale to satisfy both annunciation accounts in chaps. 17 (P) and 18:1–15
(J).[508] Chapter 20 is interpreted as an interruption to this conclusion, but in our
comments at chap. 20 we found that 21:1–7 has many literary allusions to chap.
20, making it difficult to view the two as originally unrelated. The postponement
of the birth episode (21:1–7) by the intervening threat of Sarah's abduction
(chap. 20) provides narrative tension and theologically reaffirms that the child
was a miracle achieved by God. Also the birth of Isaac and the rivalry with Ishmael (21:1–21) appear between two Abimelech episodes (chap. 20; 21:22–34),
imputing a broader significance to Isaac's birth. Moreover, within vv. 1–7 as they
stand there is a logical progression in events, leaving little reason to insist on a
hybrid of sources. The repetition in v. 1 ("he had said"//"he had promised") is a
parallelism emphasizing the fulfillment of the divine word, not the evidence of
two different sources (see comments on 21:1). Finally, the repetition of the birth
and naming of Isaac in vv. 2–3 is the result of adhering to set formulas rather than
the consequence of two sources.[509]
    Critics typically isolate vv. 8–21 as a separate narrative, duplicating Hagar's
flight in 16:1–16 (for the relationship of these two events, see "Composition" at
chap. 16). This places an impossible burden, however, on vv. 8–9 to introduce the
story; vv. 1–7 achieve an adequate introduction by identifying the newborn child,
presupposed in v. 8. Also if the naming of Isaac (v. 3) and its wordplays (v. 6[2x])
are clipped from the story, the wordplay "mocking" in v. 9 loses its effect. We
find that vv. 8–13 (see above) as a commemorative setting for the child Isaac nat-

[508] Westermann, *Genesis 12–36,* 331, 333.
[509] Alexander, *Abraham in the Negev,* 62–65.

urally follows the birth narrative (vv. 1–7). That the chapter was an original unity
is the more likely option.

STRUCTURE. The narrative consists of two settings: (1) the household of
Abraham, where the birth and celebratory banquet occur (vv. 1–13), and (2)
the wilderness of Beersheba, where Hagar and her child roam (vv. 14–21).
The first setting actually depicts in tandem two points in Isaac's early years
that the author effectively melds into one: the birth and circumcision (vv. 1–
7) and the weaning of the child (vv. 8–13). Verses 6–7 provide the transition
for the two events. Not only does the advent of the child tie the two passages
together, but the wordplays on Isaac's name also relate the two events (ṣḥq,
"laughter," v. 6[2x]; mṣḥq, "mocking," v. 9). Also the rhetorical question in
v. 7 ("who would have said . . .") may be a double entendre, for the question
if meant literally to be answered would point to Hagar's ridicule of Sarah
(16:4–5). This question then transitions to the same dynamic (ridicule) at the
feast when Ishmael mocks her son (v. 9). The mistreatment of Isaac leads to
Sarah's second speech (vv. 8–10); in a remarkably different tone than her
former speech, she angrily demands the expulsion of Hagar and her son. The
third and final speech of the first setting is the divine confirmation of God's
plan for Abraham's two boys (vv. 11–13).

> vv. 1–7   Birth and exultation over Isaac
> vv. 1–4   Naming and circumcision
> vv. 5–7   Laughter in old age
> vv. 8–13   Banquet celebration and provision for Isaac
> vv. 8–9   Ishmael mocks the child
> v. 10   Sarah demands expulsion
> vv. 11–13   God reassures a future for both sons

The second setting in the desert (vv. 14–21) contributes to the outsider
motif introduced by Hagar's flight into the wilderness (see comments on
chap. 16). The desert scene shows two reversals: (1) the wilderness, though
life-threatening initially, becomes home to Ishmael; (2) and, though the
rejected son, he receives the divine pledge of a celebrated posterity. By
reporting on the outcome of the elder son, vv. 14–19 continue the theme of
inheritance. Deliverance and promise supersede the imminent death of the
lad. Hagar refuses to see (rā'â) her son die (vv. 14–16), but the "angel of
God" intercedes, showing (rā'â) her the well of salvation (vv. 17–19). The
biographical notice of vv. 20–21, telling what became of the elder child who
lives apart, corresponds to the introductory vv. 1–4 regarding Isaac's honored
position in the household.

vv. 14–19   Expulsion and deliverance of Hagar and Ishmael
   vv. 14–15   Abraham expels them to the desert
   vv. 16–19   God delivers the boy in the desert
vv. 20–21   Desert life and marriage of Ishmael

(1) The Nativity of Isaac (21:1–13)

[1]Now the LORD was gracious to Sarah as he had said, and the LORD did for Sarah what he had promised. [2]Sarah became pregnant and bore a son to Abraham in his old age, at the very time God had promised him. [3]Abraham gave the name Isaac to the son Sarah bore him. [4]When his son Isaac was eight days old, Abraham circumcised him, as God commanded him. [5]Abraham was a hundred years old when his son Isaac was born to him.

[6]Sarah said, "God has brought me laughter, and everyone who hears about this will laugh with me." [7]And she added, "Who would have said to Abraham that Sarah would nurse children? Yet I have borne him a son in his old age."

[8]The child grew and was weaned, and on the day Isaac was weaned Abraham held a great feast. [9]But Sarah saw that the son whom Hagar the Egyptian had borne to Abraham was mocking, [10]and she said to Abraham, "Get rid of that slave woman and her son, for that slave woman's son will never share in the inheritance with my son Isaac."

[11]The matter distressed Abraham greatly because it concerned his son. [12]But God said to him, "Do not be so distressed about the boy and your maidservant. Listen to whatever Sarah tells you, because it is through Isaac that your offspring will be reckoned. [13]I will make the son of the maidservant into a nation also, because he is your offspring."

The setting is Abraham's household where the mirth (*ṣḥq,* v. 6[2x]) of the early days of Isaac's *(yṣḥq)* birth and circumcision are recalled (vv. 1–7). The jubilation turns threatening, however, when at the banquet celebrating the child's weaning the elder Ishmael makes sport (*mṣḥq,* v. 9) of the child; the result is Sarah's demand for Ishmael's expulsion, but the Lord reassures the despairing patriarch that both sons will prosper (vv. 8–13).

Verses 1–7 consist of a birth narrative (vv. 1–4) and the exultation of Sarah at the birth of her child in Abraham's old age (vv. 5–7). The introductory verses possess a chiastic structure (vv. 1–4), highlighting the fulfillment of the divine promise in chaps. 17–18:

   v. 1a   "as he had said" *('āmar)*
     v. 1b   "as he had promised" *(dibbēr)*
     v. 2b   "God had promised" *(dibbēr)*
   v. 4b   "as God commanded" *(ṣiwwâ)*

The exultation of Sarah (vv. 5–7) provides the literary bridge between the birth episode (vv. 1–4) and the banquet scene (vv. 8–13). The twice-mentioned age of the couple, forming the boundaries of the bridge (vv. 5,7), echoes the marvel of her pregnancy in the birth report: "[Sarah] bore a son to Abraham in his old age" (v. 2). Also her "laughter" *(ṣḥq,* v. 6) exhibits consonance with the celebratory nature of the banquet (v. 8); the laughter of joy, however, becomes hostile ridicule *(mṣḥq)* by the firstborn Ishmael (v. 9).

The banquet given by Abraham (v. 8) becomes unexpectedly a distressing event to the father when Ishmael ridicules the toddler; for Sarah it is the presage of a threat to her son's inheritance if the slave woman's child remains (vv. 9–10). Abraham is distressed over the prospects of losing his son, Ishmael, but the Lord comforts the old man by directing him to carry out Sarah's wishes, for as his "offspring" a promising future belongs to both boys, but to each in God's planned way (vv. 11–13).

21:1–2 Verses 1–2 describe the visitation ("was gracious to" is lit. "visited," *pāqad)* of the Lord, resulting in the miraculous pregnancy of Sarah who bears a son "to Abraham in his old age" (vv. 2,7). Verse 1 possesses parallel half-lines, emphasizing the faithfulness of the divine word revealed to Abraham and Sarah (17:16,19; 18:10,14):

> 1a   and the LORD—visited *(pāqad)*—Sarah—as he said *('āmar)*
> 1b   and [he] did *('āśâ)*—the LORD—for Sarah—as he promised *(dibbēr)*[510]

"Visited" (NIV "was gracious to") is a common metaphor conveying the intervention of God in nature and the affairs of humanity (e.g., Ruth 1:6). The "visitation" may be benevolent (e.g., 50:24–25; Ps 8:4) or punitive (e.g., Exod 20:5). A divine "visit" also explains the pregnancy of Hannah (1 Sam 2:21), the answer to Eli's invocation for blessing. The birth formula in our passage, "she conceived and gave birth,"[511] appears also in the Hannah narrative following "visited." The striking difference is the Genesis verses have the intervening fulfillment clauses, strengthening the idea of the prophecy's completion.

Not only was Sarah's pregnancy impossible by human resources alone, but the birth was at the "very time" promised. By the repetition of the word *lammô'ēd* in the annunciation promises (17:21; 18:14), the passage reiterates the accuracy of the Lord's dual predictions.

21:3–4 Verses 3–4 describe Abraham's obedient response at Isaac's birth: he names (17:16) and circumcises the child on the eighth day (17:10,12,19) precisely as the Lord had directed. The name "Isaac" is a typical west Semitic form: *yiṣḥāq,* derived from *ṣḥq,* means "he [i.e., child or

---

[510] The order of subject and verb in each half-line is for syntactic requirements. The episode-initial *wāw* requires the order of noun + verb: פָּקַד וַיהוָה ("now the LORD visited"); the typical past tense discourse order that follows is verb + noun: יְהוָה וַיַּעַשׂ ("and the LORD did").

[511] וַתַּהַר וַתֵּלֶד "[Sarah] became pregnant and bore . . ." (NIV); for this common introduction see e.g., 4:1,17; 30:17,23; 38:3; Isa 8:3; Hos 1:3,8.

father] laughs, smiles."[512] The name is appropriate for the joy a newborn brings parents. Sarah creates wordplays on the name by "laughter" *(ṣěḥōq)* and "will laugh" *(yiṣḥāq)* in her exuberance at his birth (v. 6). The description of the child's mistreatment by Ishmael, "mocking" *(měṣaḥēq*, v. 9; cf. *měṣaḥēq,* 26:8), is another play on its meaning. The name also recalls the reactions of the father (17:7) and mother (18:12), who snickered at the announcement of a forthcoming son by Sarah.

The Hebrew construction of v. 3 intensifies the identity of the birth mother. The expected word order in a naming formula is "*X* called the name of his son *PN*"; here, however, the formula is modified by an addition: lit., "Abraham called the name of his son *the one born to him whom Sarah bore to him* Isaac" (italics mine; cf. 17:21). The redundancy "bore to him" reinforces the significance of the birth mother. Although Abraham circumcises the infant in accord with the covenant (17:10–12), confirming the child as a covenant member (e.g., Ishmael, 17:23), Sarah as mother ensures that the boy is the covenant successor.

21:5–7 This paragraph ties together the explanation of Isaac's name and the elderly age of the parents. Dual references to the age of Abraham form the boundaries of the passage (vv. 5a,7b). Abraham, the narration clarifies, is a century of years (v. 5), and Sarah radiates with happiness at the thought she bears Isaac to her husband "in his old age" (v. 7b).

Sandwiched between the chronological notices is the explanation for the name Isaac (vv. 6–7a). Usually the person who names the child also provides the explanation, whether mother or father (4:24; 5:29). In this case the father announced the name (v. 3), and the mother supplied its significance. Moreover, customarily if an explanation occurs, it immediately follows the giving of the name, but here the narrative describing the circumcision of the boy (v. 4) and the age of the patriarch (v. 5) intervene. These modifications are made to point out the importance of each parent in the work of grace. Abraham's doubting laughter is transformed into obedient faith by his naming the child Isaac as the Lord has said (17:17,19). Verses 4–5 continue the narrative's attention to the father's obedience. Sarah's doubting laughter is transformed into a joyous faith (18:12–13). This privilege of declaration in vv. 6–7 is appropriately Sarah's, for she after all was the butt of the joke as the barren wife (16:4). The language of the birth report in vv. 3 and 5 are a literary reflex of the parallel episode of Ishmael's birth and naming (16:15–16). By the similarity in language, the passage points up the remarkable nature of the child's birth to parents in their elderly state.

Sarah's exuberance rightly attributes the child to God *(Elohim)*, who grants her "laughter" *(ṣěḥōq); here* she makes her point by a play, substituting "laugh-

---

[512]יִצְחָק, the imperfect verbal form third masculine singular; the common scholarly reconstruction of the name is the original hypocoristic *yiṣḥāq-ʾēl* (cp. "Ishmael," *yišmāʿ-ēʾl,* 16:10), thus "El smiles" or "El is favorable" (R. Martin-Achard, "Isaac," *ABD* 3.463).

ter" for the name *yiṣḥāq* ("Isaac," v. 6a). She improves on the play by juxtapos-
ing an allusion to Ishmael's name with the word *yiṣḥāq,* "he laughs" (v. 6b),
which is also the word "Isaac": "everyone who hears *[kol haššōmēaʿ]* will
laugh *[yiṣḥāq].*" "Who hears" contains the sound in "Ishmael," *yišmāʿēʾl* ("God
[El] hears," 16:11). This may be another jab at the rival mother and child, calling them to rejoice with her over the birth of the rightful heir. No one would
have predicted that Sarah could ever "nurse" (*yānaq,* v. 7; e.g., Exod 2:7,9;
1 Sam 1:23) a child.[513] Westermann suggests that Sarah has in mind the custom
of a father receiving news of his child's birth (Job 3:3; Jer 20:15).[514] In context
this may be another allusion to her chief detractor, Hagar, who "despise[d] her
mistress" (16:4).

21:8–10 Abraham hosted a "great feast" (Esth 2:18; "feast," e.g., 19:3;
26:30) at the weaning of the child (v. 8), which normally would have occurred
at two to three years of age (1 Sam 1:22–24; Hos 1:8). The festive banquet,
however, turned into a hostile setting when Hagar's son "was mocking"
(mĕṣaḥēq, piel) the child (v. 9; cf. 16:12; 37:27–28).[515] What actually occurred
is not certain since the Hebrew of v. 9 is open to different interpretations. Some
translations interpret *mĕṣaḥēq* as benign, not harmful (e.g., NRSV, "playing
with her son") since the term *ṣāḥaq* (21:6, *qal*) and its bi-form *(śāḥaq, piel)* can
refer to playful merriment (e.g., Zech 8:5; 2 Sam 6:5; Ps 104:26; Prov
8:30,31).[516] The verb *ṣāḥaq/śāḥaq* in the *piel* stem describes a wide range of
actions, including sexual caressing (26:8), entertainment (e.g., Exod 32:6; Judg
16:25,27*[qal];* Job 40:29), celebration (e.g., 1 Sam 18:7), contest in battle (e.g.,
2 Sam 2:14), and scorn (e.g., 19:14; 39:14,17; 1 Chr 30:10). The word in our
passage *(mĕṣaḥēq, piel),* however, usually conveys a harmful nuance, and
Sarah's stern and swift reaction agrees that some untoward behavior
occurred.[517] Exactly what Sarah witnessed is unstated. That Ishmael publicly
ridiculed the name of the toddler or the celebratory events surrounding his birth

---

[513] Sarna proposed that the rare Aramaic word, מֶלֵּל "[who] would have said" (v. 7) is a possible wordplay with מוּל, "circumcise" (*Genesis,* 146). The plural בָּנִים, "children," indicates the
abstract idea, not that Sarah was expected to bear more children.

[514] Westermann, *Genesis 12–36,* 334.

[515] The LXX (and Vg.) expresses the apparent object of the ptc., absent in the Hb.: παίζοντα
μετὰ Ισαακ τοῦ υἱοῦ αὐτῆς ("sporting with Isaac her son"), as in some EVs (NRSV, NJB, NAB,
REB, TEV); the rendering "was mocking" (NIV) assumes an unstated object, either Isaac or something pertaining to him, but an object is not required if the ptc. simply means "playing," i.e., "Sarah
saw that the son . . . was playing."

[516] E.g., Westermann (*Genesis 12–36,* 339) contends that for מְצַחֵק to mean "mocking" there
must be an object introduced by a preposition; also the notion that the wordplays on Isaac's name
is unsound because Ishmael is the subject and the wordplays derive from the *qal* stem of צחק
(v. 6). Ishmael's behavior is playful only, not ridicule, and thereby troubling Sarah, seeing that the
slave's son won favor in the eyes of the household.

[517] צחק in the *qal* may also indicate ridicule (e.g., Job 30:1; Pss 2:4; 59:8[9]; Hab 1:10).

fits well the negative nuance of the term and the obvious wordplay on the name "Isaac."[518] The apostle Paul, in reviving this historical memory (Gal 4:29), assumed the passage portrayed harmful behavior ("persecuted the son [Isaac]").

Expulsion of the slave and her son for teasing the child raises the question of the appropriateness of Sarah's reaction, especially if the Hebrew should be interpreted as mere children's play. That Sarah or Abraham was not always above inexcusable behavior is transparent from earlier episodes, but here the verse nuances the action of Ishmael as hostile. We have already noted the negative meaning of the prevalent use of *měṣaḥēq*. Also "Sarah saw" *(wattēreʾ)* recalls Hagar's taunt against Sarah when "[Hagar] saw she was pregnant" (NIV "knew," 16:4–5; cf. 3:6). Verse 9 mentions Ishmael's legitimate relationship to the patriarch ("borne to Abraham"), who as the firstborn could claim inheritance, but the boy's maternal lineage disqualified his seniority. Sarah's fear is the jeopardy Isaac may be in later, rather than the immediate offense of the teenager (v. 10). She saw the derision as an ominous foreshadowing of the strife that brothers, even more likely half-brothers, could experience (e.g., Jacob-Esau; Joseph-his brothers). Her entreaty is strongly worded: "get rid" *(gārēš)* describes the evictions of Adam (3:24) and Cain (4:14), the removal of Moses by Pharaoh (Exod 10:11), and the dispossession of Canaan's population (e.g., Exod 23:29–30; Josh 24; 18). In a demeaning way, she refers to Hagar as simply "that slave woman" and denies her son ("never"[519]) any possible claim on Abraham's inheritance. "With my son Isaac" is the mother's manner of asserting that Isaac alone is the genuine heir. By "inheritance" *(yrš),* alluding to 15:4, Sarah appeals to the divine word itself.[520]

21:11 Abraham is caught in the predicament that polygamists always experience: he ultimately must show preference for one child over another. The old man's love for his firstborn is the source of his anguish. Abraham's "distress" is his troubled state of mind as he frets over the repercussion of Sarah's directive.[521] The Lord had made it clear that Isaac was to receive the blessing (17:19), but the father's love had blinded him to the inevitability of losing his eldest. Although the word "firstborn" *(běkôr)* does not appear here, the idea

---

[518] On the basis of the word's context in the OT, the rabbis justified Ishmael's expulsion on the imagined grounds of illicit sexual practices, idolatry, or bloodshed (*Gen. Rab.* 53.11).

[519] לֹא יִירַשׁ, as to whether the syntax לֹא + imperfect verb is always an emphatic negation is uncertain (*IBHS* §34.2.1b, n. 6); here the context requires an absolute denial.

[520] Wenham, *Genesis 16–50,* 82.

[521] רָעַע (*qal* stem) ranges in intensity from a disheartened mood (e.g., Num 11:10; 1 Sam 1:8) to an anger that acts out (e.g., 48:17; Jonah 4:1), including evil actions (e.g., 38:10); the full idiom "to be displeasing in one's eyes" may describe human (e.g., 48:17; 1 Sam 8:6) or divine (e.g., 38:10; 2 Sam 11:27) aversion to a circumstance. D. W. Baker, "רָעַע," *NIDOTTE* 3.1156–57.

issues from the earliest times with the "firstborn" animal (4:4). The term also appears in Genesis for eldest sons (10:15; 22:21; 25:13; 35:23; 36:15; 38:6,7; 41:51; 43:33; 46:8; 49:3), most memorably Esau (27:19,32) and Manasseh (48:14,18; also "birthright," [bĕkōrâ] 25:31,32,33,34,36; 43:33). To ensure the proper distribution of possessions among rival sons, especially born by different wives, Mosaic law required a double portion for the eldest, regardless of the father's preference (Deut 21:15–17). Abraham, though not bound by Israelite law, reflects the custom of bequeathing gifts to secondary sons (Keturah's sons, 25:5–6). The absence of such gifts for Ishmael has been explained in relation to Hagar's status as a slave. Sarna observes that the code of Lipit-Ishtar provides for the freeing of a slave and her son in exchange for their surrender of any property claims.[522] Abraham provides only rations for their sojourn, trusting God to make good on his assurances for Ishmael (v. 14).

21:12–13 Apparently overnight (a dream?), God reveals to Abraham what he is to do and confirms his plan in store for each lad (cf. 16:10–12; 17:19–20). He offers first a word of comfort ("Do not be so distressed"[523]) and then instructs Abraham to follow Sarah's demand (v. 12a). The reason (kî, "because") the Lord gives for Abraham's concession is the place Isaac holds in the divine design of the Lord (v. 12b). Whereas Sarah's concern was on the immediacy of protecting Isaac's inheritance, the Lord's explanation provides for the innumerable future generations who will come by this single child. This explanation is not altogether new (17:19,21), but the passage adds that this son alone will bear the family name. "Reckoned" translates yiqqārē' (niphal), "will be called or named," which here indicates that Abraham's genealogy will be forever recited through the offspring of Isaac. The same term yiqqārē' appears in the transformed names of "Abram/Abraham" and "Jacob/Israel" (17:5; 35:10). The startling importance of the Lord's declaration was not lost on the New Testament authors, who appropriated this half-verse (v. 12b) to demonstrate the election of those who believe (Rom 9:7; Heb 11:18).

God quiets the patriarch's heart by repeating the promise of making the boy into a "nation" (gôy, v. 13b; "great nation," 17:20). "Also" (wĕgam, "and also") at the head of the Hebrew sentence connects the promise of v. 13 for Ishmael with the prior assurance made regarding Isaac. Both promises will be realized by the same reliable word. The basis for the promise made to Ishmael is the same for any people who will receive blessing, namely, on account of the promise that Abraham will father many offspring and peoples (e.g., 13:16; 15:5; 16:10; 17:5).

---

[522] Sarna, *Genesis*, 145–46.
[523] אַל יֵרַע בְּעֵינֶיךָ in the Hb. simply negates the same verbal form appearing in v. 11. The NIV's rendering "so" is an unwarranted nuance (cf. NASB, NRSV).

(2) The Expulsion of Hagar and Ishmael (21:14–21)

[14]Early the next morning Abraham took some food and a skin of water and gave them to Hagar. He set them on her shoulders and then sent her off with the boy. She went on her way and wandered in the desert of Beersheba.
[15]When the water in the skin was gone, she put the boy under one of the bushes. [16]Then she went off and sat down nearby, about a bowshot away, for she thought, "I cannot watch the boy die." And as she sat there nearby, she began to sob.
[17]God heard the boy crying, and the angel of God called to Hagar from heaven and said to her, "What is the matter, Hagar? Do not be afraid; God has heard the boy crying as he lies there. [18]Lift the boy up and take him by the hand, for I will make him into a great nation."
[19]Then God opened her eyes and she saw a well of water. So she went and filled the skin with water and gave the boy a drink.
[20]God was with the boy as he grew up. He lived in the desert and became an archer. [21]While he was living in the Desert of Paran, his mother got a wife for him from Egypt.

The second setting of the pericope is the wilderness expulsion of Hagar and her son. The section consists of two units: (1) the first is the expulsion and salvation of the slave woman and son (vv. 14–19), and (2) the second is the settlement of Ishmael in the desert (vv. 20–21). Verses 14–19 recount in two paragraphs their destitute condition in the wilderness (vv. 14–16) and the appearance of the "angel of God," who reveals a well of water (vv. 17–19). References to the "skin of water" (vv. 14,15,19) help hold the two paragraphs together. Water is a useful metaphor for signifying the sustaining provision of God. The water Abraham supplied for their sojourn is depleted, and the boy is dying; but God reveals a well, and Hagar refills the skin for the revival of her son. God's tidings of a prodigious future is affirmed by the sign of newly revealed waters. Thus the author can say "God was with the boy" (v. 20). By the movement from Abraham's care to the supervision of God, we witness the "weaning" of Ishmael to his new life apart from his father. The final verse captures the completed transition to Ishmael's autonomy in the desert, where he establishes the home of a new nation (vv. 20–21).

21:14–16 Abraham dismisses Hagar and Ishmael only after the Lord confirms the plan of Sarah (vv. 12–13). Abraham responded immediately, however ("the next morning," v. 14; cf. 20:8; 22:3). The picture is sadly poignant as the father sends away his elder son. Twice the passage tells that he is "distressed" (vv. 11,12). At one time Abraham hoped that Ishmael would be his heir (17:18); he is surely not indifferent to the plight of the mother and son any more than he is at offering his son Isaac at Moriah. In both cases the author depicts the father as dutifully carrying out the Lord's directions, relying on God to fulfil his promises. The narration's inclusion of the name "Hagar" also softens the portrayal of the father who attempts, although insufficiently, to equip them for the desert.

The Hebrew of v. 14 is difficult and subject to two different interpretations of Ishmael's age.[524] Either (1) Abraham places both the provisions *and* the child on Hagar's shoulders, hence indicating Ishmael is an infant (e.g., NRSV, NJPS, NJB, NAB, REB), or (2) he places only the provisions on her shoulders and gives over the boy, permitting Ishmael to be older (e.g., NIV, NLT, ASV, HCSB, NASB, NKJV). The former reading creates a contradiction with the earlier depiction of Ishmael, who is a teenager (17:25; 16:16 with 21:5). This contradiction is usually explained as the result of two conflicting sources (E—21:6–21; P—16:16; 17:25). The redactor attempted to harmonize his sources by the "clumsy" dislocation of the phrase "and with the child."[525] The ancient versions, however, support the MT as the original reading.[526] The author's awkward Hebrew has created two positive effects: (1) the troubled language captures the anguish of the moment, and (2) mention of "the boy" is delayed in the sentence so as to suggest that the transference of the boy from Abraham's hand to hers is undertaken at the last possible moment.[527] When we recognize that this "syntax of delay" is a feature of the passage,[528] it is best to accept the MT text, translating "the boy" as the second object of "gave," thus "and [he] *gave her* the boy" (NASB).[529]

"Sent her off" (*piel* of *šālaḥ*) is another subtle nuance of compassion (e.g.,

---

[524] For a discussion of the issues, see Lyke, "Where Does 'the Boy' Belong?" 637–48. The problem is the syntactical relationship of וְאֶת הַיֶּלֶד, "and [with] the child," in the sentence: the issues are (1) אֵת can be taken as a preposition ("with") or direct object marker, and (2) הַיֶּלֶד וְאֵת can be read either with the prior verbs שָׂם, "set, place," or וַיִּתֵּן, "gave," or the following verb וַיְשַׁלְּחֶהָ, "and he sent her away." *BHS* (as in some Gk. texts, but not the Syr. as *BHS* says) recommends an emendation, transposing the phrase to read, ". . . and he gave [the food and water] to Hagar, and he placed the child on her shoulder." Since the ancient versions appear to follow the MT's arrangement, however, this clever emendation is "too convenient" to adopt. If "child" is the object of the prior verb שָׂם, the construction also makes the child an infant, ". . . and he gave [the food and water] to Hagar, placing [them] and the child on her shoulder." If, however, the phrase is the object of וַיִּתֵּן, the translation permits an older Ishmael, ". . . and he gave [the food and water] to Hagar, putting [them] on her shoulder, and the child [to Hagar]" (Wenham, *Genesis 16–50*, 77–78). The NIV interprets the phrase as prepositional phrase and with the following verb וַיְשַׁלְּחֶהָ, thus also permitting the boy to be older.

[525] Westermann, *Genesis 12–36*, 341.

[526] The LXX has the same word order as the MT; it reads "the child" as the object of "placed," thus, "and placed the child on her shoulder." See Wevers, *Notes on the Greek Text*, 305.

[527] Wenham, *Genesis 16–50*, 78, 84.

[528] Lyke presents a convincing case for the authenticity of the MT text, and he effectively proves that the author's practice of placing references to the two sons at the end of key clauses (vv. 8–14) achieved a comparison between the two sons in 21:14 and 22:3; but he failed to draw this obvious conclusion, preferring to accept the critic's view of 21:14 inferring an infant Ishmael ("Genesis 21:14," 647).

[529] The ASV, NASB, NKJV interpret the phrase as the second object of "gave," e.g., "and gave *them* to Hagar, putting *them* on her shoulder, and *gave her* the boy" (NASB). The AV and ESV are so literal as to be as ambiguous as the Hebrew text. The NIV translates a prepositional phrase with the following verb, "he sent her off with the boy."

18:16; 24:56,59; 25:6; Deut 15:13; 24:1); the verb is not necessarily as harsh as Sarah's demand, "get rid" *(gārēš)*. The father does what he can for them; his hands are tied by the will of God. Abraham learns that (due to his own mistake, 16:4) the divine purpose at times can be an unpleasant task. The slave woman has no court of appeal; she must accept the destiny presented her without resistance. Hagar "wandered" *(tā'â, qal)* in the region of "Beersheba" (v. 14b; see comments on 21:31–32). "Wandered" indicates she is isolated, having no home for a refuge; this is the same description of Abraham's vagabond existence brought about by God (20:13, *hit'û, hiphil)*. Early mention of "Beersheba" may be ironic since the name refers to the site's "well" *(bĕ'ēr);* she does not discover a well, however, until it is supernaturally revealed (v. 19).

Once their water is gone, the end appears certain. Hagar "sent" (*piel of šālaḥ,* "put," NIV) the boy to take cover from the sun under a bush (v. 15), and also she distances herself from his misery about the distance of a "bowshot" (v. 16). This narrative detail may be another hint that the child will be saved, allaying the tension of the account; for the "bow" is the equipment of Ishmael's later vocation of archer (v. 20). Hagar hopes to be blind ("cannot watch," *ra'â)* to the suffering of her son; her distance also implies that she is deaf to his cries, which only God can hear (v. 17a). The MT suggests that Hagar's cries drown out those of her son, but the LXX reads at v. 16b Ishmael, not Hagar, "cried aloud and wept."[530] This latter interpretation fits nicely with v. 17 ("God heard the boy crying"), but the immediate context of vv. 14–16 focuses on Hagar's actions.

21:17–19 God initiates the rescue of the boy and his mother (16:7): "God heard" (*šāma';* v. 17a) and "God opened" (*pāqaḥ;* v. 19a; on the relationship between theophany and fear, see comments on 15:1). That God "heard" (v. 17a) and "has heard" (v. 17b) recalls the earlier pun on the name "Ishmael" (16:11). The "angel of God" speaks "from heaven" (cf. 22:11,15), indicating the supreme authority of God; in chap. 16 the messenger is the "angel of the LORD," who comforts Hagar (see comments on 16:7). Both episodes begin with the divine messenger querying Hagar about her condition (v. 17; 16:8). God's question to Hagar is rhetorical; he fully knows her dilemma and announces he will come to the boy's aid. Hagar cannot hear Ishmael, but the Lord can. "From the place where he is" reiterates the child's location is in the desert. The desert is the ultimate abode of the Ishmaelites (vv. 20–21). By the Lord hearing the child in the wilderness, the narrative shows that God's grace extends to outsiders.

The angel instructs the helpless mother not to abandon the boy any longer but to "take him by the hand" (v. 18, lit., "make strong your hand in his") so as to save him; he will not die but will flourish as "a great nation" *(gôy,* 17:20). This language honors Ishmael as the son of Abraham; it is reminiscent of 12:2;

---

[530] ἀναβοῆσαν δὲ τὸ παιδίον ἔκλαυσεν, "and the child cried out and wept."

18:18 and quite similar to the divine promise made to Jacob when entering Egypt (45:3).[531] It nevertheless falls short of the grander promises made to Abraham and his chosen line, who will enjoy an eternal relationship with God, inherit the land, and be a blessing for all peoples (12:2–3; 17:7–8; 18:18; 22:16–18).[532]

God reveals to the woman a well, which previously was available but unseen by her (v. 19). This surprise is like the unexpected ram provided for the sacrifice of Isaac (22:13–14). Hagar needs no further instruction from the angel; the narrative by a string of verbs describes her rapid reaction at seeing the water.

21:20–21 The passage shows that it was the Lord, in accord with his promises to the boy's parents (vv. 13,19), who enabled Ishmael to reach adulthood and eventually sire a tribal confederation (v. 20). The comparable phrase "God [or the LORD] was with him" explains the success achieved by his servants (e.g., 39:3,21; Deut 32:12; 1 Sam 18:14; 2 Kgs 18:7; 1 Chr 9:20; 2 Chr 1:1). "As he grew up" (*gādal*, cf. v. 8) also appears in descriptions of divine superintendence (cf. Judg 13:24; 1 Sam 2:21; 3:19; also Exod 2:10–11). Ishmael's adoption of the bow as his trade was a practical necessity since killing game in the wild required a skilled archer (25:27 with 27:3); also it was a needed weapon against hostilities, a life he would always know (16:12).

Ishmael's travels included the broad region of "Paran" (v. 21; "El Paran," 14:6), which was the territory later traveled by the Israelite refugees (e.g., Num 12:12,16; 13:3,26; Deut 1:1). Hagar's earlier flight into the desert was toward Shur (16:7), the same location of Abraham's travels (20:1), and it is the area settled by Ishmael's descendants (25:18). The association of Paran in this passage with an appearance of the angel recalls the theophany of God before Israel from Paran (e.g., Deut 33:2; Hab 3:3).[533] Since Paran is located between the southern boundary of Canaan and north of Sinai,[534] its proximity to Egypt made an Egyptian wife easily available for Ishmael. Perhaps Hagar obtained an Egyptian slave from traveling merchants (cp. Joseph, 37:28). The picture of Ishmael as the rejected son is complete: he is the son of a slave woman, married to an Egyptian, lives outside normal social bounds, and is remembered for his hostilities.

---

[531] 21:18 כִּי־לְגוֹי גָּדוֹל אֲשִׂימֶנּוּ, "for—unto a nation—great—I will make him,"

46:3 כִּי־לְגוֹי גָּדוֹל אֲשִׂימְךָ שָׁם, "for—unto a nation—great—I will make you—there."

[532] von Rad observes that the disparity in blessing between the chosen and rejected lines is more decisive between Jacob (27:28–29) and Esau (27:39–40; *Genesis*, 234).

[533] Dozeman notes the similarities between the geographical locations mentioned in chaps. 16; 21 and the wilderness itinerary of Israel in the Pentateuch, contending for a theological geography that presents a God who meets his people in the desert, where they undergo personal transformation and form community ("The Wilderness and Salvation History," 35–41).

[534] V. Hamilton, "Paran," *ABD* 5.162.

12. Treaty with Abimelech (21:22–34)

"At that time" introduces this episode, pointing to the events encompassing the birth of Isaac (chaps. 20–21). This treaty account does not mention an heir, but it serves an important role in the Abraham narrative at large and the theme of an heir in particular. The two episodes regarding Abraham-Abimelech form bookends (20:1–18; 21:22–34) for the narratives describing the birth of the heir (21:1–13) and the expulsion of his chief rival (21:14–21). By enveloping these two critical accounts with the Abimelech incidents, the author accomplishes theological and literary advantages. We will examine these contextual advantages under the discussion of the origin of 21:22–34.

COMPOSITION.   In our earlier discussion at 20:1–18, we explored the original relationship between the two Abraham-Abimelech accounts (see comments on 20:1–18). Scholars view the two accounts as part of the same document (Elohist [E] or Yahwist/Elohist [JE])[535] or an originally independent "Abraham in Gerar" story, which the redactor integrated into the Abraham narrative as a whole.[536] We found, however, that 20:1–18 was not a literary variant of an original wife-sister event but rather an independent account told in light of Abraham's sojourn in Egypt (12:10–13:1). Also the narrative possessed close associations with the motifs and language of chaps. 18–19 and 21:1–21, evidencing common authorship with its literary environment. Now we turn to the role and relationship of the second Abraham-Abimelech narrative (21:22–34). The narrative is fully aware of the preceding events, both the near context and the Abraham narrative at large.

First, the identity of Abimelech in 21:22 presupposes 20:1, which introduces the episode of Sarah's abduction. That the king is tentative about Abraham's good faith (v. 22) is the result of the wife-sister deception he suffered by the patriarch (20:8–13). The mention of Abraham's sojourn (*gûr*, "stayed," NIV) in Gerar in the conclusion (v. 34) recalls his initial travel to Gerar, "he stayed *[gûr]* in Gerar" (20:1b). The geographical references at the beginning and end create an envelope construction marking out chaps. 20 and 21. The treaty narrative suits its present context by providing a pause in the plot between the early events of Isaac (21:1–13,14–21) and the crowning Akedah (sacrifice of Isaac) incident (22:1–19). By 21:22–34 completing the Abraham-Abimelech involvement (20:1–18), the narrative is freed to center on the sacrifice of Isaac as the sole interest.

Also the "alien" subtext that is prominent in chaps. 18–20 continues in the treaty narrative commenting on the patriarch's powerful status even though he is an alien to the region (vv. 23,34). As at Sodom and Gerar, the natives mistreat the alien, and some compensation is in order. In this case their crime is the seizure of the patriarch's well (vv. 25,30). The treaty episode shows, however, that the patriarch's fortunes as an alien are reversed: Abimelech approaches the Hebrew out of

[535] Coats, *Genesis,* 155.
[536] Thompson, *The Origin Tradition,* 94–96; Carr, *Reading the Fractures of Genesis,* 202.

diplomatic deference, and Abraham presents him livestock for the treaty ceremony (v. 27), which reverses Abimelech's earlier gesture toward him (20:14). By this generosity and the additional gift of seven lambs to secure the well uncontested (v. 30), Abraham proves himself a wealthy, formidable chieftain. Now the king views the alien as under the protection of God who prospers in everything by divine favor; the narrative concludes by depicting Abraham as a welcomed visitor who remains in friendly relations (v. 34). The idea of the protected alien also echoes the expulsion of Hagar (21:14–21); both episodes mention "Beersheba" as an important site in their survival (21:14,31–33), and both acknowledge the presence of God protecting them in their ventures (21:20,22).

Second, the treaty narrative advances the Abraham narrative as a whole, including its theme of an heir. Although the promise of descendants is not directly mentioned, the foreign setting and political implications of the treaty elevates the significance of the heir by broadening the context of Isaac's birth and the potential loss of his sacrifice. The treaty episode shows the realization of other promissory features. The king's acknowledgment of Abraham's divine favor (v. 22b) recalls the bless/curse provision regarding the nations' relationship to Abraham (e.g., 12:3; 18:18; cf. 22:18). As in the war of the kings (chap.14), Abraham's stature is magnified as an international power in the region. Both chaps. 14 and 21 end with an expression of worship to *El Elyon* (14:20) and *El Olam* (21:33), divine names known also to Canaan's populations. Abraham's importance in each case draws attention to his God and the goodwill the patriarch enjoys. Also the formal recognition of Abraham's well (v. 30) by the indigenous Philistine suggests to the reader proleptically the possession of the land by his descendants. The portrait of Abraham in this episode therefore contains the pieces that profile the central elements of the blessing, except the all-important heir. There is personal greatness, blessing for others, and land, but without an heir the picture is incomplete. This prepares us for the Akedah, the culminating episode in the Abraham narrative.

Within the narrative itself the high incidence of repetitions (e.g., two oaths) has led many scholars to propose that two written sources or at least two oral traditions lie behind the present form of the text.[537] This is supported by the double etiology of Beersheba attributed to the passage; the name can mean "well of oath," as suggested by vv. 23,24,31, or "well of seven," as indicated by vv. 28,29,30. That the passage possesses two treaties resting on two separate traditions is only an illusion as a result of the rhetorical features of the narrative (see "Structure" below). There is only one treaty ratified (v. 27) and only one specific explanation for the name Beersheba (v. 31). The negotiations, however, consist of two related stages: first, the parties agree in principle to form a treaty (vv. 23–

---

[537] E.g., Van Seters assigns vv. 22–24,27,31b–34 to his exilic Yahwist and vv. 25–26,28–31a to his second pre-Yahwist ("Elohist"; *Abraham in History,* 184–86); Westermann has vv. 22–24,27,31b–32 (J) and vv. 24–26,28–31a (E), with vv. 33–34 as a late redaction (*Genesis 12–36,* 346–47); von Rad prefers two oral traditions used by the Elohist (*Genesis,* 234–37). Among those who view the chapter as substantially a unity are Speiser, *Genesis,* 160, Coats, *Genesis,* 155–56, and Alexander, *Abraham in the Negev,* 70–76.

24); second, the complicating factor of a stolen well is introduced (vv. 25–26). Both parties are sufficiently satisfied to proceed, and each matter in turn, first the ritual of treaty and then the gift of seven lambs, is formally presented (vv. 27–30). Two resulting events are additional commemorations of the treaty: (1) the name "Beersheba" and (2) the planting of the tamarisk tree (v. 33).

A brief word is in order regarding the relationship of 21:22–32 and the second Beersheba treaty between Isaac and Abimelech (26:26–31; on the literary character of chap. 26 see comments there). The similarities between the two passages (e.g., two etiologies for the name Beersheba, 21:31; 26:33) have led scholars to posit that we have two versions of the same event,[538] whether the two narratives are the result of a common oral tradition[539] or the result of a literary composition.[540] Yet, as Van Seters and Wenham have shown, chap. 26 is fully aware of the basic outline of the Abraham story at large and is constructed so as to show parallels (where possible) between the experiences of the two patriarchs, Abraham and Isaac.[541] As we saw in the case of the wife-sister trilogy (see comments on chap. 12), the Beersheba treaty narratives are not a true doublet, but chap. 26 is an independent composition that relies on the reader's knowledge of the earlier Abraham events. The same author is responsible for both chaps. 21 and 26, showing that the son as successor is retracing his father's steps.

STRUCTURE. The literary arrangement of the passage displayed below is not always obvious, but there are structural repetitions that indicate a combination of two rhetorical devices popular in Genesis, a chiasmus and embedded panels (see comments on chaps. 15,17,18–19).

A Introduction: "at that time" (v. 22a)
  B Abimelech: God is with you (v. 22b)
    C Swear an oath to me (v. 23)

D1 Abraham: I swear (v. 24)	D4 Abraham brings livestock for oath (v. 27)
D2 Abraham's complaint (v. 25)	D5 Abraham sets aside seven lambs (v. 28)
D3 Abimelech: I didn't know (v. 26)	D6 Abimelech: What are these about? (v. 29)

    C′ Abraham: Accept these seven lambs (v. 30)
      [Name Beersheba (vv. 31–32)]
  B′ Abraham's God, *El Olam* (v. 33)
A′ Double Conclusion: (1) "for a long time"
                  (2) "stayed" *(gûr)* with 20:1

The boundaries (A,A′) are the temporal references, "at that time" (v. 22a) and "for a long time" (v. 34b); both are vague, probably referring to the general

---

[538] E.g., Speiser, *Genesis,* 203.

[539] Coats, *Genesis,* 156.

[540] Van Seters, *Abraham in History,* 191; and Westermann, *Genesis 12–36,* 346, although he views 26:26–31 as the source for building J's composition in 21:22–24,27,31a,32 (later supplemented by E, vv. 25–26,28–30,31b).

[541] Van Seters, *Abraham in History,* 188–91 and Wenham, *Genesis 16–50,* 187–88.

period of chaps. 20–21 when Abraham sojourned in Gerar. Verse 34 functions as a double conclusion, forming a boundary with "stayed" *(gûr)* in 20:1. This indicates that chaps. 20–21 tell related episodes within the framework of the Philistine sojourn: (1) the abduction of Sarah (20:1–18); (2) the birth and celebration of Isaac (21:1–13); (3) the expulsion of Hagar and Ishmael (21:14–21); and (4) the treaty with Abimelech (21:22–34). The abduction account ends with the healing of the Philistine wombs, and the subsequent story relates the fruition of Sarah's womb.[542] The birth of Isaac then is naturally followed by consequences. Both the expulsion and treaty episodes occur in the vicinity of Beersheba, where Abraham obtains his first possession. Chapters 20–21 provide incidents that expound on the core issues of the patriarchal promises, such as offspring, land, and blessing/curse for the nations. The overreaching theological idea is Abraham's God, who protects and provides for the man in accord with the divine promises. These four episodes propel the story to the brink when Abraham confronts his greatest test (chap. 22).

Abimelech declares that God favors Abraham (B), and for this reason he seeks a treaty with him (C). The matching legs identify this God as *El Olam* (B′) and present Abraham's own request of Abimelech to accept his offering (C′). The parallel panels (D,D′) consist of three matching parts: (1) the patriarch swears an oath (D1) and confirms it with the presentation of livestock (D4); (2) Abraham complains about a stolen well (D2) and later sets aside lambs as evidence of ownership (D5); and (3) Abimelech confesses ignorance of the seizure (D3) and later is ignorant of the meaning of the seven lambs (D6). Verses 31–32 have no apparent parallel in the structure; they supply information about the geographical implications of the bartered agreement.

Other evidence of rhetorical patterning is the frequency of "sevens" and the play on the Hebrew word "seven" *(šebaʿ),* involving "swear" *(šbʿ)* and "Beersheba" *(bĕʾēr šābaʿ)*[543] "Abraham" and "Abimelech" each occur seven times; the subject of v. 33, "he [Abraham] planted," is left unidentified by the author to avoid exceeding the seven count. "Seven ewe lambs," "swear," and "Beer-sheba," all possessing the same letters of the word "seven," *š-b-ʿ,* each appear three times.

(1) Abimelech Requests a Treaty (21:22–26)

²²At that time Abimelech and Phicol the commander of his forces said to Abraham, "God is with you in everything you do. ²³Now swear to me here before God that you will not deal falsely with me or my children or my descendants. Show to me and the country where you are living as an alien the same kindness I have shown to you."

---

[542] Sarna, *Genesis,* 145.
[543] Ibid., 148.

²⁴Abraham said, "I swear it."

²⁵Then Abraham complained to Abimelech about a well of water that Abimelech's servants had seized. ²⁶But Abimelech said, "I don't know who has done this. You did not tell me, and I heard about it only today."

21:22–26 "At that time" generally refers to the prior events of chaps. 20–21. Abimelech's general Phicol accompanies him to entreat the patriarch to form a treaty, a nonaggression pact.[544] The name "Phicol" recurs under similar circumstances when Abimelech meets Isaac over sixty years later (25:26; 26:26,32); as in the case with Abimelech, the name Phicol may be a title or family name. The mention of the general reflects the author's interest in the rising political stature of the patriarch. His presence signalled the potential hostilities that could result if a peaceful settlement failed. That the king had provided Abraham open access to his territory (20:15) probably created the tension that called for a preemptive treaty (cf. 26:20). The king's admission that God favored the patriarch follows from his dream experience (20:6–7). The circumstances of the ruse probably motivated the Philistine to form an alliance, binding Abraham to deal forthrightly with him (v. 23). The idea of divine presence ("God is with you") echoes the recent description of God's supervision of the boy Ishmael (v. 20), guaranteeing success (also, Isaac [26:28] and Joseph [39:2,3,21,23]).

Abimelech's request indicates his fear of Abraham's potential to supplant his future dynasty and kingdom (v. 23). Mention of honesty ("[not] deal falsely," *šāqar*), "kindness" *(ḥesed)*, and Abraham's "alien" *(gûr)* status recall their earlier dealings in chap. 20. It follows from Abraham's own confession (20:13) that he can't be trusted; yet Abimelech recognizes the expediency of acting benevolently toward the patriarch. Prudence dictates that he secure goodwill with him by a formal pact. He bargains for fair play in the same vein he treated Abraham, referring to his public repentance and compensation for his offense (20:14–16). Abraham's gift of livestock to seal the deal (v. 27) recalls the same language describing the Philistine's reparation (20:14), indicating a spirit of reciprocity.

Since the king seeks open relations, the patriarch puts the proposal to the test by charging his servants with commandeering his well (vv. 25–26). "Complained" *(yākaḥ, hiphil)* is another reflex of the earlier confrontation, where Abimelech declares Sarah "vindicated" *(yākaḥ, niphal* [see comments on 20:16]). If its syntax is the frequentative use of the verb,[545] the sense is repeated censure, not merely mentioning the problem. "Seized" *(gzl)* may indicate an unlawful confiscation of goods (e.g., Lev 6:4[5:23]; Job 24:2) or the abduction of persons (e.g., Jacob's wives, 31:31). Here the sense is that the herdsmen control access to the well by congregating their flocks nearby (but cp. 26:15). Water

---

⁵⁴⁴ The LXX includes from 26:26, καὶ Οχοζαθ ὁ νυμφαγωγὸς αὐτοῦ, "and Oxozath his friend" (see 26:26).

⁵⁴⁵ GKC §112rr; וְהוֹכִחַ *(wāw* + perfect) is unexpected *(BHK* וַיּוֹכַח follows SP).

was valuable since it was rare, as the Isaac-Abimelech episode shows (chap. 26), and it was essential to pastoralists in this semiarid region. In such a mixed economy in Palestine, where pastoral migration and village agriculture often coincided, friction between urban environs and roaming visitors would be understandable.[546] It is a good test of their relationship to learn whether the vital resource could be negotiated fairly. Abraham's claim to the water probably relies on two factors: (1) he dug the well (v. 30), and (2) Abimelech has invited the man to reside in the area (20:15), which naturally requires the use of local pasturage and water. Abraham capitalizes on the king's own entreaty that relies on his fair treatment of Abraham in the past. From the perspective of Abimelech's servants, the well probably was on the margins of Philistine control ("returned to the land of the Philistines," v. 32), confusing somewhat the proprietary picture (but cp. 26:14,16,18).

If Abimelech were aware of the offense, it would show him an untrustworthy party because any deal would be disingenuous. The king answers by appealing to ignorance (as in 20:5), and he shifts some blame to Abraham, who has not notified him. Abimelech implies also that if he had known of the problem he would not have proposed the treaty ("today").

(2) Abraham Makes a Treaty (21:27–30)

[27]So Abraham brought sheep and cattle and gave them to Abimelech, and the two men made a treaty. [28]Abraham set apart seven ewe lambs from the flock, [29]and Abimelech asked Abraham, "What is the meaning of these seven ewe lambs you have set apart by themselves?"

[30]He replied, "Accept these seven lambs from my hand as a witness that I dug this well."

21:27–30 Abraham initiates the covenant ritual by submitting voluntarily sheep and cattle,[547] which probably are slain by both men (e.g., 15:10). This is a classic example of a bilateral covenant involving mutual obligations by the two parties. Exactly what is expected of the two parties is not stated; from v. 23 we may infer that the treaty at least provided for principled and peaceful relations. "Made a treaty" is the typical covenant formula, "cut a covenant" (*kārat běrît*, v. 27; see comments on 15:18; and vol. 1A, pp. 367–38). Following the rite, Abraham presents to Abimelech a distinct group of animals, "seven ewe lambs" (*kibśâ*, vv. 28,29,30), which involve a formal agreement regarding the well. The lamb was a popular animal among pastoralists; the female lamb was common in tabernacle ritual (e.g., Lev 14:10; Num 6:14). It was vital to propa-

---

[546] Matthews, "Wells in Gerar," 119–21.

[547] Sarna observes that if Abraham's animals are reciprocating Abimelech's earlier gesture (20:14), the absence of slaves shows perhaps the patriarch's resistance to trading human flesh (*Genesis*, 149).

gating the herd, and the generous number of seven (cp. 2 Sam 12:3–4,6) reflects the importance of the well for Abraham's prosperity.

That the offer of seven lambs is exceptional is indicated by Abimelech's puzzlement over their significance (v. 29). There is no such reservation by the king regarding the animals for the earlier covenant formality. D. J. McCarthy concluded that the gift put Abimelech on the defensive, since McCarthy thinks the patriarch by making the gift placed Abimelech under obligation.[548] Already Abimelech acknowledged the favored position of Abraham with God, indicating that the king seeks only security, not specific demands. By accepting the animals as a "witness" (*ʿēdâ;* v. 30), Abimelech would be accepting the version of Abraham's account of events. Commonly, agreements in the ancient Near East entailed witnesses; biblical covenants usually point to concrete objects, such as heaven and earth (e.g., Deut 4:26) and an erected pillar (Josh 24:27). The lambs and Laban's pillar (31:52), for example, are memorials to which parties can make appeal.[549] That the patriarch provides the animals displays his wealth and strength of bargaining position.

(3) Abraham Worships (21:31–34)

[31]**So that place was called Beersheba, because the two men swore an oath there.**
[32]**After the treaty had been made at Beersheba, Abimelech and Phicol the commander of his forces returned to the land of the Philistines.** [33]**Abraham planted a tamarisk tree in Beersheba, and there he called upon the name of the LORD, the Eternal God.** [34]**And Abraham stayed in the land of the Philistines for a long time.**

21:31–32 The naming formula (v. 31) involving the word "place" *(māqôm)* is attested also in 33:17; Josh 7:26; 2 Sam 5:20.[550] "Beersheba" means "well *[bĕʾēr]* of oath *[šĕbūʿâ]*" or "well of seven *[šebaʿ]*." The ambiguity of the word *šebaʿ* is useful to the account since both a covenant-oath and the gift of seven animals play memorable roles in the event. If the dependent clause of the verse is causal ("because," *kî*), then the meaning "oath" for "Beersheba" has priority.[551] The same name of the site is remembered later by Isaac under similar circumstances (26:33). Beersheba is located in the northern Negev and was a landmark for distinguishing the southern boundary of Israel in the formula "from Dan to Beersheba" (e.g., Judg 20:1; 1 Kgs 4:27; cp. Amos 8:14).[552] The place is especially important as the major residence of the Fathers (22:19; 26:33;

---

[548] D. J. McCarthy shows where the superior party presents a gift (1 Sam 18:3–4; 2 Kgs 20:12; "Three Covenants in Genesis," *CBQ* 26 [1964]: 182–83).

[549] R. Chisholm, "עוד," *NIDOTTE* 3.336–38.

[550] Unlike 21:31, these examples have שֵׁם הַמָּקוֹם, "the name of the place."

[551] Alternatively, here the conjunction כִּי can be temporal, "when."

[552] The reverse, "Beersheba to Dan," occurs in 1 Chr 21:2; 2 Chr 30:5.

28:10; 46:1,5).[553] The mutuality of the covenant is mentioned again by stating that both men (*šĕnêhem*, "two of them") strike the deal (v. 31; cf. v. 27b). Afterward the visiting party of Abimelech and Phicol "returned to the land of the Philistines" (v. 32); this suggests that Beersheba was not within Philistine control.

21:33–34 The final two verses provide a fitting end to chaps. 20–21. Moreover, the planting of the memorial tamarisk tree (*ʾešel*) where the patriarch worships ("called upon the name") recalls his early practice upon entering the land (12:6–8; cf. 13:18; 18:1).[554] By this echo of the patriarch's custom, the narrative prepares us for the chief act of worship to follow (sacrifice of Isaac). The tamarisk is a tree of the sandy Negev (also 1 Sam 22:6; 31:13); botanists have identified it as the leafless tamarisk tree (*Tamarix aphylla*), an evergreen whose numerous branches possess very small leaves. The tree is deciduous, however, providing good shade and extending from twenty to thirty feet in height.[555] Trees especially held symbolic religious significance in the ancient Near East indicating fecundity; the representations of flora in the tabernacle and Solomon's temple symbolized the divine Giver of fecundity. Abraham's gesture of planting the tree expressed his devotion to and recognition of God as the source of his prosperity.

The identity of the Lord (*Yahweh*) is the *El*-name, *El Olam* ("the Eternal God").[556] The association of the divine name at Beersheba is not simply the result of adopting a local Canaanite name for God as Abraham's own deity; rather, the significance "Eternal" (*ʿôlām*) lies with the far-reaching events of the Negev sojourn, especially chaps. 20–21 (see comments there). The Lord has promised Abraham a covenant relationship of eternal order with his descendants (e.g., 17:7–8), and the chosen line of descent is revealed in the birth of Isaac

---

[553] The precise identity of the ancient tell is disputed, most scholars attributing it to Tell es-Sabaʿ just east of the modern city of Beersheba. The absence of MB age remains during the patriarchal period and the site's well being dated to the Iron I settlement have led scholars to doubt the accuracy of the biblical account. Some attribute biblical Beersheba to the nearby Tell Bir es-Sebaʿ and identify Tell Beersheba with the biblical site Sheba (Josh 19:2); another view is that the two cities bore the same name, resulting in confusion for scholars today. In any case, the biblical description of Beersheba requires that the reference is only to an area that had a well and a place of worship, not necessarily a walled city in Abraham's day (26:33 may be a later editorial remark). See Z. Herzog, "Beersheba," *OEANE* 1.287–89; D. Manor, "Beer-sheba," *ABD* 1.641–45; and J. Bimson, "Archaeological Data and the Patriarchs," *Essays on the Patriarchal Narratives*, 75–76.

[554] אֵשֶׁל, usually translated tamarisk tree (e.g., NIV, NASB, NRSV), is translated "field" or "garden" in the versions (e.g., LXX, ἄρουραν, which means a "tilled field" or used of an Egyptian measurement of land [100 cubits square] [LSJ 245]). Hamilton follows the Gk., translating a plot of land (cp. v. 34; *Genesis Chapters 18–50*, 93–94); J. Barr suggests that the versions avoided "tree" because of the word's similarity to אֲשֵׁרָה, the idolatrous "Asherah" ("Seeing the Wood for the Trees? An Enigmatic Translation," *JSS* 13 [1968]: 11–20).

[555] M. Zohary, *Plants of the Bible* (Cambridge: Cambridge University Press, 1982), 115, and I. Jacob and W. Jacob, "Flora," *ABD* 2.806.

[556] See the commentary Introduction, "El Names of God."

(21:1–7,12). Now the Lord establishes Abraham in the eyes of the native populations as a leading chieftain in the land whose deity presides over him wherever he travels (v. 23). This attention on Abraham's deity as the Eternal One, whose will for the man and the nations cannot be thwarted, provides the striking setting for the challenge to the patriarch's understanding of God in the episode to come (chap. 22).

Verse 34 rounds out the Abimelech-Abraham episodes in chaps. 20–21 (cf. 20:1–2). The patriarch survives the troubles of the region as an alien and enjoys a prosperity that God alone can provide. In the climactic moment of the binding of Isaac, the patriarch will discover again divine provision (22:8,14).

13. Abraham's Test (22:1–19)

Chapter 22 is known in Jewish tradition as the Akedah *('ăqedâ),* "the binding [of Isaac]," taken from the word "bound" *(wayya'ăqōd)* in v. 9 (see Excursus: "The Sacrifice of Isaac"). It is the final test of the man's faith, the closing bookend to his discovery of God's sufficiency to achieve the promises made at Haran.[557] This remarkable episode brings together the foregoing events in the Abraham narrative by means of allusion. Among the striking connections between 12:1–9 and 22:1–19 are the twin commands, lit., "Go by yourself *[lek lĕkā]* from your country . . . to the land I will show you" (12:1) and lit., "go by yourself *[lek lĕkā]* to the land of Moriah . . . I will tell you about" (22:2). Both episodes share in many features: (1) the patriarch is commanded to separate from family, "[from] your country, your people and your father's household" (12:1), and "take your son, your only son, Isaac (22:2)"; (2) he faithfully carries out the divine instructions, which ends in promise of blessing and in the patriarch's worship ("built an altar," 12:7; 22:9).[558]

There are many allusions in this chapter to the promises issued in previous events (e.g., 12:2–3; 13:14–16; 15:4–5; 16:10; 17:2,5–6,16,20; 18:18; 21:18). By such a preponderance of back references, the author effectively brings forward all that has preceded. The impact is the elevation of this single event so as to make all of the past promises hang on Moriah's test. The call at Haran requires the patriarch to leave his former circles of security; the orientation of the promises is toward the future, emphasizing the birth of an heir. Now the Lord requires Abraham to relinquish the future by offering Isaac as a sacrifice. Similar to Job's trial, the patriarch chooses the Giver over the gift, relying on the Lord to make good on his promise. The Haran incident describes Abraham's immediate obedience to the command "Leave" (12:1) by the verbal

---

[557] According to Jewish tradition, Abraham experienced ten trials including the Akedah (*Pirqe 'Abot* 5:4; *Midrash Tehellini* 18:25; *Pirqe R. El.* 26; *'Abot R. Nat.* 33:2); *Gen. Rab.* 56.11 mentions this incident as "this last trial," spoken by God, who in effect swears never to test the man again.

[558] Sarna observes the similar-sounding Moreh (12:6) and Moriah (22:2; *Genesis*, 150).

echo, "So Abram left" (12:4). In the matching story, the author captures the same allegiance by Abraham's departure for Moriah "early the next morning" (v. 3); also his voluntary attitude is reflected by the repeated dialogue, "Here I am" (vv. 1,7,11). Repetition of the family connection, "son," "only son," and "father," heightens the pathos of the story.[559] Isaac is in fact not the "only son," but he is the "only son" who remains the potential heir; the patriarch expelled Ishmael, his firstborn, and now he faces sacrificing his "only" son.

That God "tests" *(nissâ)* his people is not exceptional; it is a means for revealing their obedience (e.g., Exod 15:25; 16:4; Judg 2:22), producing fear so as to engender piety (Exod 20:20; Ps 26:2), discovering their authenticity (Deut 8:2; 13:3[4]; 2 Chr 32:31), and producing their well-being (Deut 8:16).[560] In the present case, what is revealed is that the patriarch "fears" the Lord (v. 12). The object of the test is Abraham's proper response, which entails obedience and trust. There is a sure verbal linkage involving "test" and "fear," where the two words occur together in only two passages: Abraham's experience at Moriah (22:1,12) and Abraham's descendants at another mount, Sinai (Exod 20:20). Abraham's obedience is viewed as the archetype of God's expectations for Israel's loyalty to the Ten Words (Ten Commandments).[561] R. W. L. Moberly identifies Abraham's "fear of the Lord" as the Hebrew equivalent to what Christians mean when they refer to "faith." He parallels the Akedah to Matthew's portrayal of Jesus, who undergoes testing and responds obediently, refusing to seize power for his self-interests (cf. Phil 2:1–13).[562] What Jesus refused from Satan at the beginning he receives ("all authority") from God after his supreme act of obedience (Matt 28:18). Abraham, too, resisted the human impulse to withhold his son for his own advantage, expressing a submissive spirit.

The anthropomorphic portrayal of God ("Now I know," v. 12) preserves the narrative tension of the account; by the test the Lord takes the road of "discovery" that leads to the climax of Abraham's obedience (vv. 11–12). The chilling description of the command, the march up the mountain, and the raised knife have their denouement in the angel's intervention. The test is not born out of the necessity of divine knowledge but the requirement of human

---

[559] "Your son" (vv. 2,12,16); "my son" (vv. 7,8); "your only son" (vv. 2,12,16); "his son" (vv. 3,6,9,10,13); "Isaac" (vv. 2,3,6,7[2x],9); "his father" (v. 7); and "my father" (v. 7).

[560] T. Brensinger, "נסה," *NIDOTTE* 3.112.

[561] R. W. L. Moberly includes Abraham's sacrifice at Moriah as another archetype for Israel's worship in the temple (2 Chr 3:1), thus associating Abraham's act with Israel's two key figures, Moses and David ("Christ as the Key to Scripture: Genesis 22 Reconsidered," *He Swore an Oath*, 154–61). That the story of Balaam's donkey (Num 22:22–35) was cast by its author in the shadow of the Akedah was first proposed by the rabbis (*Gen. Rab.* 55.8; *Num. Rab.* 20.12) and more recently explored by J. Safren, "Balaam and Abraham," *VT* 38 (1988): 105–113.

[562] R. W. L. Moberly, *The Bible, Theology, and Faith: A Study of Abraham and Jesus* (Cambridge: Cambridge University Press, 2000).

faith's achievement. By presenting the challenge, the man could express his faith in a concrete way; now potential faith is realized, securing for the patriarch the promises God has all along ensured would come to pass (cf. Jas 2:21–23). Moreover, as Moberly observes, the phrase "now I know" conveyed a "deepened relationship" as God's response to the obedient choice of Abraham, showing the Lord's concern for Abraham.[563]

Nevertheless, the test has a double meaning, for the outcome of the matter reveals as much about God as it does about Abraham. Throughout the Abraham narrative, we learn about the Lord's gracious election and preservation of Israel's father. This episode, however, appears discordant with what we know of Israel's deity. Legal texts condemn child sacrifice (Deut 12:31; 18:10), especially the practice associated with the worship of Molech (Lev 18:21; 20:2–5). Later the practice appears in the Southern Kingdom (2 Kgs 16:3; 21:6) but is eliminated by Josiah (2 Kgs 23:10) and condemned by the prophets (e.g., Jer 7:31–32; Ezek 16:20–21).[564] The conflict between orthodox Yahwism and the Akedah, however, is only apparent; the author alerts the reader that the story is a "test" (v. 1), and thus it must be evaluated provisionally. This divine request for human sacrifice is unique in Israel's experience; the special circumstance of Abraham's role as the father of the covenant requires a test without parallel. The rabbis argued that the testing of Abraham was not devious since God tests only those who can withstand, that is, the righteous (Ps 11:5). Similarly, God's integrity is not questioned for his trying of Israel, and the test of Abraham is on the same level, for it is a prototype of later Israel's trials (*Gen. Rab.* 55.1–3). Christian tradition, however, focuses on the fulfillment of the promises (Heb 11:17–19; Jas 2:21–23) since Isaac alone could fulfill the promises, as God himself stated (21:12), making it certain that the boy would somehow survive. Hence, the issue lay with the Lord, not Abraham, for he left it to God to resolve the theological and moral problems he himself created.[565]

COMPOSITION. We have already observed that 22:1–19 fits in the Abraham narrative with numerous echoes of the preceding accounts. It also shares many features with the preceding expulsion narrative (21:12–19), indicating 22:1–19 originally was composed in concert with the Hagar-Ishmael episode. Both narratives contain a similar plot development and many striking correlations; for example, God requires the dismissal of Abraham's sons (21:12–13; 22:2), both sons almost die (21:16; 22:20), the angel calls from heaven (21:17; 22:11), and Hagar sees the well and Abraham sees the substitute ram (21:19; 22:13). Further, there are parallels in chap. 22 with the first Hagar-Ishmael episode in chap. 16,

---

[563] Ibid., 106–7.

[564] G. Heider, "Molech," *ABD* 4.895–98.

[565] F. F. Bruce, *The Epistle to the Hebrews* (Grand Rapids: Eerdmans, 1964), 311.

for example, the keyword "see/provide" (*rāʾâ*, 16:13–14; 22:8,14).[566] The significance of such connections shows the author's abiding interest in the inheritance theme as played out by the two sons; the verbal affinities among the three
narratives (chaps. 16,21,22) heighten the tension of what is at stake in the death
of Isaac.

The composition of the pericope according to source critics consists of two
sources; vv. 1–14,19 are attributed to the Elohist and vv. 15–18 to the Yahwist or
to the work of the later redactor.[567] Earlier critics also contended for a prior oral
form of an etiological story lying behind vv. 1b–14, concerning child sacrifice at
a cultic location (v. 14).[568] Westermann rejects this older view since chap. 22
does not make foremost child sacrifice or the cult; rather, all parts of the story
focus on the theme of divine test.[569] Both Westermann and Van Seters acknowledge that it is impractical to try to divide the narrative into such layers. The criteria for distinguishing the Elohist (E) as a separate source, the "shrinking" source
among critics (see vol. 1A, p. 75), are at best suspect.[570] The occurrences of the
name *Elohim*, for example, are no longer viewed as a reliable indicator of E. Conversely, the appearances of *Yahweh* in this E document create a dilemma (vv.
11,14[2x]). The convenience of attributing the occurrences of *Yahweh* to a redactor is an unsatisfactory explanation by E proponents, since the naming of the site
in v. 14 (using *Yahweh*) is integral to vv. 1–14. The name *Elohim* is best explained
as the result of the author's theological point, *Elohim* appearing in the early
verses that point up God's control over the human sacrifice. But for rhetorical
effect the name *Yahweh* occurs at the dramatic moment of the narrative. Moreover, Van Seters and others have shown that the chapter has a stronger relationship to the theme and language of the central source (his exilic Yahwist) of the
Abraham account than the proposed E connection.[571]

Finally, the promise section in vv. 15–18 is typically deemed secondary; it
possesses a different literary style and is anticlimactic to the plot as unfolded in
vv. 1–14,19.[572] Yet if vv. 15–18 are absent, the story fails to give an adequate
explanation for the purpose of the test; the nature of the event as a challenge to
Abraham's faith looks beyond the sacrifice itself to the larger question of the

---

[566] J. Lawlor ("The Test of Abraham, Genesis 22:1–19," *GTJ* 1 [1980]: 19–35) and Wenham
(*Genesis 16–50*, 99–100) detail many parallels between 22:1–19 and the Hagar-Ishmael stories
(chaps. 16; 21).

[567] E.g., von Rad, *Genesis*, 238, 242.

[568] E.g., Gunkel, including more recently G. W. Coats, "Abraham's Sacrifice of Faith: A Form-
Critical Study of Genesis 22," *Int* 27 (1973): 389–400, and Coats, *Genesis*, 159,161.

[569] Westermann, *Genesis 12–36*, 355.

[570] Alexander demonstrates the failure of the typical lines of evidence put forward for designating the E source in chap. 22 (*Abraham in the Negev*, 77–89).

[571] Van Seters, *Abraham in History*, 229–30.

[572] E.g., Westermann, *Genesis 12–36*, 354, 363; Carr includes 26:3b–5 (Isaac) as secondary
and related integrally to 22:15–18, which together redirect the nature of the promises found in 12:3
and 28:14 to a new emphasis on their provision as reward for Abraham's obedience at Moriah
(*Reading the Fractures of Genesis*, 153–59).

promise.[573] Also the striking verbal correlations of command *(bô')* and promise between 12:1–3 and 22:2,15–18 suggest that vv. 2 and 15–18 are the result of the same author, who has 12:1–3 in mind. The promise section is not a rehash of former promise oracles but expands and secures them, making vv. 15–18 the logical and most appropriate outcome of the chapter and the whole of the Abraham story.[574] The commentary on our passage in 26:3–5 shows that the event at Moriah involved the fulfilling of the promises.[575] Further, the essentially unified structure of the chapter (see below) comports well with the idea of one author.

STRUCTURE. The structure of 22:1–19 is particularly rich in complexity due to numerous repetitions within the narrative, giving the passage a coherence by following the story line of problem to denouement. The observation of repeated patterns has led scholars to propose chiastic structures and parallel panels in the chapter.[576] Although these studies exhibit differences in their results and practice diverse methods of analysis, some based more on content and others relying on words and clauses, they agree that the evidence of repetitions shows an artful design. This we believe is best explained as the creation of one author.

The narrative possesses three movements, each ending with the same clause, "and . . . went on together" (vv. 6b,8b,19a). Abraham's responses, "Here I am" (vv. 1b,7a,11b), appear in the three dialogues, each in one of the narrative movements.

v. 1a	Introduction—"tested"
vv. 1b–6	"Here I am" (*hinnēnî*, v. 1b)
	"the two of them went on together"
	(*wayyēlĕkû šĕnêhem yaḥdāw,* v. 6b)
vv. 7–8	"Here I am, my son" (*hinnennî bĕnî,* v. 7a; NIV "Yes, my son")
	"and the two of them went on together"
	(*wayyēlĕkû šĕnêhem yaḥdāw,* v. 8b)
vv. 9–19a	"Here I am" (*hinnēnî,* v. 11b)

---

[573] Coats ("Abraham's Sacrifice of Faith," 393–97) and Van Seters (*Abraham in History,* 239) argue for a unified work, contending that the promise motif in vv. 15–18 is essential to the story's theme of obedience, without which the test has no real consequences.

[574] Wenham, *Genesis 16–50,* 101–3; Wenham's "The Akedah: A Paradigm of Sacrifice," in *Pomegranates and Golden Bells: Studies in Biblical, Jewish, and Near Eastern Ritual, Law, and Literature in Honor of Jacob Milgrom* (Winona Lake: Eisenbrauns, 1995), 93–102, answers the arguments of R. W. L. Moberly, "The Earliest Commentary on the Akedah," *VT* 38 (1988): 302–23, and demonstrates on literary and theological grounds that vv. 15–18 are not secondary but "part of a comprehensive theological interpretation of the whole [Abraham] cycle" (p. 100).

[575] Alexander, *Abraham in the Negev,* 84–85.

[576] Y. Avishur reviews several studies in "The Sacrifice of Isaac (Genesis 22): The Structure of the Narrative, Its Link to Genesis 12 and Its Canaanite Background," in *Studies in Biblical Narrative* (Tel-Aviv-Jaffa: Archaeological Center Publication, 1999), 75–103, originally published in Hb. in *Studies in the Archaeology and History of Ancient Israel: In Honour of Moshe Dothan* (Haifa: Haifa University Press, 1993).

               "and they went on together" (NIV "set off")
               (*wayyēlĕkû yaḥdāw,* v. 19a)
v. 19b   Conclusion—"stayed in Beersheba"

The first movement begins with the initial dialogue of God and Abraham and continues with the description of Abraham and Isaac's approach to Mount Moriah (vv. 2–6). The second movement begins similarly with the dialogue of Isaac and Abraham and concludes with their continued trek up the mount (vv. 7–8). This center movement is the apex of the chiastic arrangement, encapsulating the narrative tension of the whole: the identity of the offering.[577] The third movement is the longest and most important, possessing a third dialogue between the angel of the Lord and Abraham and a protracted monologue by the angel, who speaks a second time (vv. 9–19a). This third movement includes two parallel panels (ABB'A'). It begins with the preparations and execution of the sacrifice (vv. 9–10, A), followed by the dialogue (vv. 11–12, B). The subsequent narration tells of the substitute ram and the naming of the place, "The LORD will provide" (vv. 13–14, B'). Again the angel speaks from heaven, announcing the favorable results of the test and the promissory reward of land, descendants, and blessing (vv. 15–18, A'). The movement closes by narrating the return of the party to Beersheba (v. 19a). The geographical references show the symmetry of the story: Beersheba-Moriah-Beersheba. The events and return in the final movement restore the father-son relationship as at the first.

Movement one:	From Beersheba to Moriah (vv. 1b–6)
Movement two:	Climb up Mount Moriah (vv. 7–8)
Movement three:	At Moriah and return to Beersheba (vv. 9–19a)
A	Execution of the Isaac sacrifice (vv. 9–10)
B	First call from heaven (vv. 11–12)
A'	Execution of the ram sacrifice (vv. 13–14)
B'	Second call from heaven (vv. 15–18)
	Return to Beersheba (v. 19a)

The direction of the story turns at the first heavenly dialogue in vv. 11–12. The repetition "Abraham, Abraham!" marks the reversal when the angel from heaven intervenes to arrest Abraham's hand. The second peak in the story is the second divine speech delivered from heaven, a monologue reiterating the promises substantiating Abraham's faith and future (vv. 15–18).

(1) The Test (22:1–6)

[1]Some time later God tested Abraham. He said to him, "Abraham!"
"Here I am," he replied.

---

[577] J. Doukhan, "The Center of the Aqedah: A Study of the Literary Structure of Genesis 22:1–19," *AUSS* 31 (1993): 17–28, but Doukhan underestimates the preeminent importance of the culminating promise in vv. 15–18, which is what makes the dialogue in vv. 7–8 of consequence.

²Then God said, "Take your son, your only son, Isaac, whom you love, and go
to the region of Moriah. Sacrifice him there as a burnt offering on one of the
mountains I will tell you about."
³Early the next morning Abraham got up and saddled his donkey. He took
with him two of his servants and his son Isaac. When he had cut enough wood for
the burnt offering, he set out for the place God had told him about. ⁴On the third
day Abraham looked up and saw the place in the distance. ⁵He said to his servants, "Stay here with the donkey while I and the boy go over there. We will worship and then we will come back to you."
⁶Abraham took the wood for the burnt offering and placed it on his son
Isaac, and he himself carried the fire and the knife. As the two of them went on
together,

The first movement in the story establishes the nature of the command to sacrifice Isaac as a test (vv. 1–2). The trek from Beersheba to the Moriah region
occurs across three days, resulting in the father and boy at the foot of the sacrificial mount (vv. 3–6). The passage emphasizes the obedience of Abraham and
the trusting compliance of his son, who is unaware of what will befall him.

22:1–2 "Some time later" (lit. "and it came about after these things")
points generally to the prior events at Gerar in chaps. 20–21 (cf. 15:1; 39:7;
40:1). The parallel phrase introduces the next episode in 22:20. The chronological notation distances the Moriah test from the expulsion of Hagar/Ishmael and
the Beersheba treaty with Abimelech (chap. 21). "For a long time" in 21:34
probably is inclusive of chaps. 20–21, but 22:1 indicates enough time has
elapsed for Isaac to have grown from a toddler (ca. two to three years old) in
21:8 to an adolescent in chap. 22. Isaac is old enough to endure a climb bearing
wood (v. 6) but is still considered a "boy" (na'ar, vv. 5,12). Although the author
does not concern himself with the extent of Isaac's knowledge and compliance,
it is apparent that Isaac must have dutifully conceded to his aged father's wishes.
That it is said God "tested" (nissâ) Abraham prepares the reader for the exceptional request to follow (see comments below). This reminds us of the patriarch
Job, whose devotion to God is called into question by Satan (Job 1:9); God's
response to Satan invites testing that results in remarkable suffering, including
the loss of Job's children. It is God who may test his people (e.g., Exod 16:4;
20:20), but they are castigated for trying him (e.g., Exod 17:2,7; Num 14:22;
Deut 6:16; Ps 106:15–16).[578] Reference to the man by name, "Abraham,"
recalls the promise of a legion of nations (17:5) and here prepares us for the last-
moment call from heaven, "Abraham, Abraham!" (v. 11).

The identity of the sacrifice is described with heart-rending precision, "your
son, your only son, Isaac, whom you love" (v. 2). Y. Avishur compares the gra-
dation of this three-phrase description of Isaac, from the general to the specific,

---

[578] The wilderness site Massah (מַסָּה), named for Israel's testing of the Lord (e.g., Exod 17:7;
Deut 6:16; 33:8; Ps 95:9), is derived from נָסָה (piel), "test."

with the first command to leave Haran, also three expressions: "Leave your country, your people and your father's household" (12:1).[579] "Your only son" translates *yĕḥîdĕkā*, lit., "your only one" (vv. 2,12,16); it is used of mourning an only son (e.g., Jer 6:26; Amos 8:10) and an only daughter (fem., *yĕḥîdâ*, Judg 11:34). It is equivalent to a person's life, which is irreplaceable (Pss 22:21; 35:17).[580] Ishmael is also his son, but Isaac alone remains the apparent heir, the "beloved." The similarities between the episodes of Ishmael's expulsion and Isaac's sacrifice (chaps. 21; 22) reinforce the comparison of the two sons. "Whom you love" is not to imply Abraham did not love Ishmael,[581] but his love is explicitly stated to emphasize the precious possession Isaac is in the eyes of the old man. The passage shows if anything that the expulsion of the elder lad made his heart fonder of the lone remaining boy. More important, it makes the test as severe as is thinkable; no test could be any more probing of the patriarch's loyalty, for even the taking of his own life would not pass the trial since the future promise lay with the boy.[582] Perhaps the mention of the name "Isaac" ("he laughs") by the Lord and repeatedly in the narrative (vv. 3,6,7,9) is designed to recall the joy of the boy's birth to the elderly couple (21:6–7).

The place for the sacrifice, however, is vaguely cited, "the land of Moriah" (v. 2). This uncertain destination is reminiscent of the first call at Haran; God alone knows the way ("I will tell you"; cf. 12:1). Moriah as "Mount Moriah" occurs only once more, but very importantly as the site for Solomon's temple (2 Chr 3:1); it is this association that generated the Jewish tradition that the temple mount was the place of Abraham's sacrifice (e.g., *Jub.* 18:13; *Gen. Rab.* 55.7).[583] Today the Muslim shrines El-Aqsa Mosque and Dome of the Rock occupy the traditional site of Mount Moriah.

Modern critics are skeptical of the authenticity of "Moriah" as the original site, suggesting rather that the original name was suppressed or lost and "Moriah" given to connect Abraham and the temple.[584] There are problems with the identification of Moriah and the temple site, such as the three-day journey, which appears too far from Beersheba, and the absence of the Chronicler's mention of the Abraham event. But there is no "Mount Moriah" in Genesis 22 that requires the equation with the temple mount which the critics have supposed for the text here. For this reason too the Chronicler made no attribution of the temple site with the Abraham sacrifice; Genesis only refers to a mountain

---

[579] Avishur, "The Sacrifice of Isaac," 93.

[580] BDB 402.

[581] Here is the first occasion in the Bible of the word group אָהֵב, "to love"; cf. comments on 24:67.

[582] Sarna, *Genesis,* 393.

[583] I. Kalmi, "The Land of Moriah, Mount Moriah, and the Site of Solomon's Temple in Biblical Historiography," *HTR* 83 (1990): 345–62.

[584] J. Davila, "Moriah," *ABD* 4.905.

range called Moriah ("on one of the mountains," v. 2), which permits both Genesis and the Chronicler to describe the sites accurately.

There are other problems with the name "Moriah." The ancient versions variously translate the word rather than recognize it as a place name.[585] This probably is due to the definite article with Moriah (ʾel ʾereṣ hammōrîyâ, lit., "to the land of the Moriah), which is uncommon for a proper name. The etymology of the name is troublesome too.[586] In the Genesis narrative, explanations for the name may occur, although only implicitly. The most obvious is the name assigned to the place in v. 14, "The LORD will provide" (Yahweh yirʾeh), which also is a subtle play on "see" (rāʾâ) in vv. 4,8; the idea of "see" reflects the versions and occurs again in 2 Chr 3:1 ("appeared," nirʾâ from rāʾâ).[587]

The exhortation, "Sacrifice him [haʿălēhû]... as a burnt offering [ʿōlâ]" (v. 2), is the language of tabernacle sacrifice (e.g., Exod 29:38–45; Lev 1:3–17; Num 15:1–10). In Jewish tradition the term "bound" (maʿăqidîn), an allusion to Genesis 22, first appears in m. Tamid (4:1) referring to the daily (tāmîd) offering of two lambs required in the tabernacle (Exod 29:38). "Burnt offering" first occurs in 8:20 (see comments) and thus long antedated the tabernacle system; both Noah and Abraham function prototypically for Moses' system (e.g., Exod 24:4–8). The "burnt offering" was fully consumed, producing an aroma that pleases the Lord (8:21; Lev 1:9).

22:3 "Early the next morning" (v. 3) occurs in settings of urgency in the Abraham narrative (19:27; 20:8; 21:14; also 28:18; 32:1; Exod 24:4). This remark indicates the patriarch's prompt obedience as in the prior divine instruction regarding Ishmael (21:14). The narration's "took" and "place God had told him about" (v. 3) correspond to the divine instructions of v. 2, evidencing Abraham's full submission. Unlike his earlier rebuttals to God, substituting Eliezer (15:2) or Ishmael (17:18; cf. 21:11), Abraham is utterly mute; his only words are absolute compliance and a confidence in the Lord's final provision. His testimony to the servants, "We will come back to you" (v. 5), conveys his reliance on God to make good on his prior promise, "Through Isaac . . . your offspring will be reckoned" (21:12). The provisions of servants, donkey, and prepared wood for the trip indicate Abraham's wealth, yet none of these can substitute for his most precious possession. The Hebrew construction of the sentence, "He took with him . . . his son Isaac," distinguishes the prized member of the reti-

---

[585] The LXX τὴν ὑψηλήν, "the high (land)," cp. 12:6, LXX (see Wevers, *Notes on the Greek Text,* 317); SP המוראה, Samaritan tg. ḥzjth, Symmachus τῆς ὀπτασίας, and Vg. *visionis,* perhaps render הַמֹּרְאָה ("vision"); Syr. has "the Amorites" = הָאֱמֹרִי (see BHS).

[586] See Hamilton, *Genesis Chapters 18–50,* 102–3.

[587] Other possibilities are môrāʾ-yah, "fear of Yahweh," influenced by "[you] fear [yĕrēʾ] God" (v. 12) and môrîyâ, "teacher," feminine for môreh from y-r-h, "to teach" ("Moreh," 12:6; Deut 11:30; Judg 7:1). See Sarna, *Genesis,* 391.

nue.[588] The two unidentified servants may suggest the rejected candidates Eliezer and Ishmael (so *Tg. Ps.-J.*), whose (symbolic) presence highlights the
gravity of the assignment.[589] Mention of wood is not because of the sparse
mountainside, as scholars sometimes surmise; rather it creates an irony in detailing the preparations made for sacrifice, pointing up the absence of the all-important sacrificial subject itself. In fact, unknown to the others, Abraham does bring
the sacrificial lamb (Isaac).

22:4–5 "On the third day" (v. 4) need not require three complete days
of travel; portions of days one and three may be intended (Jonah 3:3), or
three days may be a stereotypical expression for a journey (31:22; Josh
9:17; 1 Sam 30:1).[590] "Third day" also may signify a critical event (40:12–
13; Exod 19:15; Num 7:24; 29:20; 2 Kgs 20:5,8; Hos 6:2) or even the day
of annihilation (Lev 7:17–18; 19:6–7). "Looked up and saw" (v. 4) is one of
many parallel actions to Hagar in chap. 21 (v. 19); the expression also
recalls the earlier stories of Lot (13:10) and the three visitors at Mamre
(18:2). In our passage the expression "looked up" (lit., "lifted up his eyes")
occurs twice, tying together the events of discovery, both the mount and the
unexpected ram (vv. 4,13). Abraham's instructions to the servants reveal the
patriarch's ultimate trust in God's provision ("we will come back"); his
faith is therefore a testimonial to the servants as well as to the boy (cf. Heb
11:17–19).

By the narration's rhyming words *pōh* ("here") and *kōh* ("there") in v. 5, a
geographical contrast describes the two servants left behind and the pair who go
ahead to "the place" assigned for sacrifice. That Abraham's actions were
unusual is shown by the specific instructions required for the servants. If apparent to Isaac that the sacrificial beast is absent (v. 7), then it is apparent to the servants as well when Abraham divulges his purpose to "worship." The term
"worship" *(hištaḥăwâ)* already occurred in its nontheological sense, "bow
down, prostrate," in 18:2 and 19:1; of its 170 uses the word appears twenty-three
times in Genesis (e.g., 23:7,12; 24:26,48,52).[591]

22:6 Now Isaac becomes both the beast of burden, carrying the wood
(v. 6), and the sacrificial lamb. The passage continues its emphasis on Abra-

---

[588] Lit., "and he took his two servants with him *and Isaac his son*" (italics mine). B. Bandstra
comments that "with him" postpones and thereby marks the second object, "and Isaac his son"
("Word Order and Emphasis in Biblical Hebrew Narrative: Syntactic Observations on Genesis 22
from a Discourse Perspective," in *Linguistic and Biblical Hebrew* [Winona Lake: Eisenbrauns,
1992], 109–23, esp. 119). Lyke shows the similarity of syntax between 21:14 and 22:3, pointing
up the two sons, Ishmael and Isaac ("Genesis 21:14").

[589] J. Crenshaw, "Journey into Oblivion: A Structural Analysis of Gen 22:1–19," *Soundings* 58
(1975): 243–56, esp. 248.

[590] Bandstra observes that the absence of the conjunction *waw* beginning a new paragraph is
rare, here introducing significant new information in the action ("Word Order and Emphasis," 117).

[591] T. Fretheim, "חוה," *NIDOTTE* 2.42–44.

ham's complete obedience by repeating the language "took" *(lāqaḥ),* recalling
the initial directive "take *[lāqaḥ]* your son" (v. 2). The boy bearing the wood
portends the "burnt offering" *('ōlâ),* and Abraham taking the source of the
"fire" ("firestone," NJPS) and the knife identifies the offerer. The passage captures the poignant significance of Abraham's carrying the fire and knife by the
added depiction "in his (own) hands" ("himself," NIV). "Knife" *(ma'ăkelet)* is
a large tool used for dismemberment, including human victims (Judg 19:29; cf.
Prov 30:14).[592] Its appearance twice in vv. 6,10 may be a sound play on
"angel" *(mal'āk),* whose interception hinders the blade's purpose (v. 11).[593]
"As the two of them went on together" (vv. 6,8) presents another touching
depiction of the offerer and his gift to the Lord. The passage shows that there
was ample occasion across the three days and during the scaling of the mount
for Abraham to ponder retreat, but he steadfastly moved forward.

(2) Abraham and Isaac Together (22:7–8)

> [7]Isaac spoke up and said to his father Abraham, "Father?"
>
> "Yes, my son?" Abraham replied.
>
> "The fire and wood are here," Isaac said, "but where is the lamb for the
> burnt offering?"
>
> [8]Abraham answered, "God himself will provide the lamb for the burnt offer-
> ing, my son." And the two of them went on together.

At this acute point in the story, the boy speaks his only recorded words, raising the obvious question of a "lamb," which ironically bears on his own
unknown role (v. 7). "My father" ("father," NIV) and "my son" (v. 7) underscore the trust that such familial relations possess; Isaac's reliance is not misplaced. In a profound twist of outcome, his father's unreserved dependence on
God's promissory word, though it ostensibly means the loss of Isaac, assures
the boy's future blessing as pledged for Abraham's generations (cf. v. 17).

Abraham's answer is not evasion but his honest openness to God's operations (v. 8). "God" at the head of the clause emphasizes the source of the sacrifice. "Provide" *(r'h)* is the key word of the account, used in the offering of the
ram ("saw," v. 13) and the naming of the sacred site (v. 14[2x]). In Levitical
sacrifice the offerer himself provided the animal. Here, however, Abraham
reverses the means, showing that God's command made the matter his own
responsibility. Strikingly, the patriarch's words convey a theological profundity
that has its immediate reality in the unexpected ram (v. 13). The church fathers
viewed Abraham's answer a theological foreshadow of Christ's sacrifice. The
Christian reader today sees the additional irony that God supplies his own Son
for the sins of the world, whereas Abraham's son escapes unharmed.[594] The

---

[592] A. Tomasino, "מַאֲכֶלֶת," *NIDOTTE* 2.830–31.

[593] Sarna, *Genesis,* 152.

[594] That Paul had this specific allusion in mind at Rom 8:32 is doubtful; see the excursus below.

ambiguity of Abraham's intention by "my son" in the sentence enhances the already-cryptic nature of his answer. Grammatically, "my son" can be understood in two ways: Abraham's address to Isaac, which is the customary interpretation, or an appositional phrase defining the "burnt offering," meaning Abraham identifies Isaac as the offering. Such subtle allusions to the coming events of the chapter contribute to the mood of anticipation that characterizes chap. 22.[595] In the redemption of Israel's firstborn, the dedication of the child to the Lord signifies the relationship of the family to the Lord God (hence, also the entire nation) and the continuity of the family's generations consecrated to him alone (e.g., Exod 13:2,12–15; 34:1–20; Num 3:11–13).[596] The claim of the Lord on Abraham's son reflects his place as patron deity of the family and its generations. The redemption of Isaac by the substitute ram, as in later Israel's rite of the firstborn, provides for the life of the child who is consecrated unto the Lord.

(3) The Sacrifice to the Lord (22:9–19)

[9]**When they reached the place God had told him about, Abraham built an altar there and arranged the wood on it. He bound his son Isaac and laid him on the altar, on top of the wood.** [10]**Then he reached out his hand and took the knife to slay his son.** [11]**But the angel of the LORD called out to him from heaven, "Abraham! Abraham!"**

"Here I am," he replied.

[12]**"Do not lay a hand on the boy," he said. "Do not do anything to him. Now I know that you fear God, because you have not withheld from me your son, your only son."**

[13]**Abraham looked up and there in a thicket he saw a ram caught by its horns. He went over and took the ram and sacrificed it as a burnt offering instead of his son.** [14]**So Abraham called that place The LORD Will Provide. And to this day it is said, "On the mountain of the LORD it will be provided."**

[15]**The angel of the LORD called to Abraham from heaven a second time** [16]**and said, "I swear by myself, declares the LORD, that because you have done this and have not withheld your son, your only son,** [17]**I will surely bless you and make your descendants as numerous as the stars in the sky and as the sand on the seashore. Your descendants will take possession of the cities of their enemies,** [18]**and through your offspring all nations on earth will be blessed, because you have obeyed me."**

[19]**Then Abraham returned to his servants, and they set off together for Beersheba. And Abraham stayed in Beersheba.**

The arrangement of the final section consists of two sacrificial offerings, the Isaac offering (vv. 9–10) and ram offering (vv. 13–14), with two heavenly messages interspersed (vv. 11–12; 15–18). The final verse describes the party's

---

[595] Crenshaw, "Journey into Oblivion," 248, 251.
[596] C. J. H. Wright, "Family," *ABD* 2.765.

return and Abraham's residency in Beersheba (v. 19). The Isaac "offering" is a metaphorical picture of the boy's sacrifice. Although the Lord stops the patriarch short of killing Isaac literally (v. 11), the father's action is reckoned by God as in effect a burnt offering given (v. 12). After the ram sacrifice, the second message is the apex of the chapter, distinguished as an oath ("I swear by myself," v. 16), indicating the divine confirmation of the patriarchal promises. Christian readers will remember the baptism and transfiguration of Christ during which the heavenly voice confirms the sonship and ministry of Jesus (Matt 3:17 pars.; 17:5 pars.).

22:9–10 Reference to "the place" brings the reader to the appointed site for worship; "which God had told him about" reiterates the calculated obedience of the man (v. 9; cf. v. 3). This location is a divinely ordained, sacred space; that "the place" (vv 3,4,9,14) is the "mountain of the LORD" (v. 14) speaks prototypically of the Sinai setting (Num 10:33), where the tabernacle's "altar of burnt offering" is erected (Exod 40:29). "Mountain of God" is the common reference, however, to Sinai/Horeb (Exod 3:1; 4:27; 18:5; 24:13; 1 Kgs 19:8). The same language, "mountain of the LORD," describes Jerusalem's temple (Isa 2:3; 30:29; Mic 4:2; Zech 8:3). "The place" *(hammāqôm)* is a common designation for tabernacle (e.g., Exod 15:17; 23:20; Lev 4:24), noted in Deuteronomy as "the place the LORD God will choose" (e.g., Deut 12:5; 14:23; 15:20; 16:2; 17:8; 26:2; 31:11; for temple, e.g., 1 Chr 15:3; 28:11; esp. 2 Chr 3:1; Pss 26:8; 43:3; Isa 18:7; 60:13; Jer 7:13,14).

That Abraham built an altar fits his practice, recalling entry into the land at the start of his faith pilgrimage (12:7–8). This custom also foreshadows Moses, who erects an altar for burnt sacrifice (Exod 17:5; 24:4). In v. 9 the definite article, "the altar" *(hammizbēaḥ,* NIV "an altar"), may indicate an existing altar that is rebuilt by Abraham; but since the place appears unknown to Abraham, the article probably distinguishes this altar proleptically as the commemorated altar of Isaac's binding.

The almost matter-of-fact description of Abraham's preparation of the sacrifice is broken by the emotive identity of the sacrifice, "his son." Mention of the wood arranged on the altar not only gives a graphic picture for the reader but also contributes to the portrayal of Isaac as a willing victim who must have recognized at this point that he was the intended offering. "He bound" *(wayya'ăqōd)* translates the verb *'āqad,* which occurs only here in the Old Testament. Isaac, the stronger and swifter of the two, submits without struggle to the old man's binding to the altar.[597] Is it to ensure that the lad will not escape if his heart weakens in the face of the knife? Or is the binding rather Abraham's

---

[597] Wenham observes that binding is not a feature of the Levitical practice of the burnt offering, and, further, the victim is always slain before its parts are placed on the altar; the protracted ritual of binding Isaac means he cannot be slain unaware, and thus conveys again the boy's obedience to his father (*Genesis16–50,* 109).

assurance that the thrust of the knife will fall certain to kill mercifully the motionless victim? The delay required to bind Isaac may reflect the father's wish to postpone the painful end of the ordeal.

Verse 10 describes the patriarch's final steps in reaching for the knife; the two verses detailing the event are told in "slow motion" so the reader can experience with the father the anguish of the prolonged moment. That the author states clearly the purpose of the raised knife, "to slay his son," confirms the deliberateness of the man's action. There is no hesitation or any intercession, as in the dialogue over Sodom (18:23–26); the father fully concedes to the divine will (cf. Job 1:21; 2:10).

22:11–12 The "angel" speaks from heaven (v. 11) as in the deliverance of Hagar and Ishmael (21:17). The repetitive "Abraham, Abraham!" marks this as the turning point of the story; now that the test has accomplished its purpose, the story line reverses the threat to the boy. The fervency of the heavenly command is expressed by the emphatic "Abraham!" twice and the interruptive "do not lay a hand" (v. 12)[598]; the latter reverses the lethal action "he reached out his hand" (v. 10a). The urgency of the interdiction is magnified by its inclusiveness: do not do "anything" against the lad.

The angel's explanation "Now I know" (v. 12) is an admission that the ordeal was a test, a discovery of Abraham's depth of loyalty. The text reads the singular pronoun "you," referring to Abraham alone, indicating that despite what commendation might be inferred from Isaac's obedience, it is Abraham who is the object of the test. "Fear God" describes the man's obedience and trust motivated by his love of God (cf. Deut 10:12–13).[599] Job is "a man who fears God and shuns evil" (1:8; 2:3; cf. 1:1).[600] If Abraham is the model of faithfulness to *Yahweh* in Israel, Job represents the nations whose integrity is put to the test ("he is blameless and upright," 1:8; 2:3; cf. 1:1). The similar moral standard is expected of foreign rulers (20:5–6,11; 42:18; Deut 25:18).[601] The causal clause, "because you have not withheld from me," presents the test's evidence of the patriarch's devotion (cf. "because," vv. 16,18). It is not a theoretical matter; James capitalizes on this aspect of the event when he observes Abraham's "faith was made complete by what he did" (Jas 2:22). The term "withheld" *(ḥāśak)*[602] occurs twice, extolling the virtue of Abraham's obedience (vv. 12,16) that results in the

---

[598] The jussive form in אַל תִּשְׁלַח יָדְךָ, lit., "do not stretch forth your hand," indicates urgency, immediacy (*IBHS* §34.2.1b).

[599] M. van Pelt and W. C. Kaiser Jr., "ירא," *NIDOTTE* 2.529–30. The Hb. יְרֵא אֱלֹהִים is lit., "fearer of God" (GKC §116g).

[600] Rabbinic literature extensively debated whose righteousness triumphed, more often favoring Abraham over Job since the latter's challenge of God's ways was complaint (J. Weinberg, "Job Versus Abraham: The Quest for the Perfect God-Fearers in Rabbinic Tradition," in *The Book of Job*, BETL 114 (Leuven: Leuven University Press/Uitgeveri: Peeters, 1994), 281–86.

[601] Moberly, *The Bible, Theology, and Faith,* 84–88, 92–94.

[602] Cp. 20:6, where God "kept [חָשַׂךְ] you [Abimelech] from sinning."

repeated promise of many descendants (v. 17). By releasing his "only son" he gains a multitude of offspring, even as his name ("Abraham, Abraham!") conveys (cf. 17:5).

22:13–14 The death of the discovered ram "instead of [Abraham's] son" (v. 13) epitomizes the idea of substitutionary atonement, which characterized the Levitical system. Verses 13–14 mirror the earlier dialogue of father and son concerning the sacrificial victim (vv. 7–8). The timely presence of the entangled ram answers the boy's earlier perplexity, "Where is the lamb?" (v. 7). Abraham interprets the appearance of the animal according to his response in v. 8, "God will provide" *[ʾĕlōhîm yirʾeh],* in naming the place "The LORD will provide" *(yahweh yirʾeh,* v. 14). The opportune moment of the suddenly seen substitute implies the obvious—the Lord is responsible for the appearance of the surprising ram. Ancient versions (LXX, SP, Syr.) and a few medieval Hebrew manuscripts followed by many EVs (e.g., NIV [see NIV note], NRSV) read *ʾayil ʾeḥād,* "one ram," that is, "a ram" as opposed to *ʾayil ʾaḥar*(MT), which is traditionally translated "behind *him* a ram" (AV, NASB). Alternatively, translating *ʾaḥar* temporally, "a ram just caught,"[603] retains the MT reading and makes sense of the passage, indicating the immediacy of the snared animal. This is the point of the miracle, the sudden appearance of a sacrificial ram ("behold," *hinnê* ["there," NIV]) conveniently trapped at the perfect moment.[604]

The significance of the appellative *yahweh yirʾeh* for the name of the mountain also reflects the double sense of *rāʾâ*("provide/see") in "he saw" *(wayyarʾ)* (v. 13). The NJPS captures the double sense, "God will see to the sheep" (v. 8). The concluding phrase in v. 14, "it will be provided/seen" *(yērāʾeh),* refers to the animal promised in v. 8. The Greek reading (and *Tgs. Ps.-J., Neof.*), however, interprets the subject of "he saw" *(wayyarʾ)* as "the Lord": "On the mountain the LORD was seen."[605] In this case the naming of the site indicates a theophany occurred, as the Lord commonly "appeared" *(wayyērāʾeh)* to Abraham (12:7; 17:1; 18:1) and to Israel at Sinai ("the mountain"; e.g., Exod 3:1–2,16; Lev 9:4,6).[606]

22:15–16 That there is a "second" *(šēnît)* call from heaven (v. 15) emphasizes the importance of the event. The promise appears in a rare form of oath ("I swear by myself," v. 16), enhancing the pledge to follow (vv. 17–18). Although the Lord is said at many places in the Old Testament to undertake an oath (e.g., 1 Sam 3:14; Ps 89:3), this is the only place in Genesis that the Lord expresses

---

[603] Wenham, *Genesis 16–50,* 99; M. Pope ("The Timing of the Snagging of the Ram," *BA* 49 [1986]: 115–17) supports the temporal interpretation with biblical examples (e.g., Exod 11:5; Jer 25:26) and Ug. usage, explaining that "Abraham raised his eyes and saw the ram the instant it was snagged" (p. 116).

[604] Hamilton, *Genesis Chapters 18–50,* 113.

[605] ἐν τῷ ὄρει κύριος ὤφθη = בְּהַר יְהוָה יֵרָאֶה.

[606] Wenham, *Genesis 16–50,* 111.

the patriarchal oath under explicit obligation to his own character ("by myself"); other occasions of divine oath "by myself" in the first person are few and limited to the prophets (Isa 45:23; Jer 22:5; 49:13).[607] This oath was remembered as the basis for divine blessing of future generations (e.g., 26:3; Exod 33:1; Num 14:23; 32:11; Deut 1:35; 7:8; 10:11; 34:4; Josh 1:6; Judg 2:1; Jer 11:5). A second time the angel explains that the promise is confirmed by what Abraham accomplished ("you have done"), an amazing act of loyalty deserving of another heavenly mention. The development of the patriarchal promise, given in stages in the Abraham narrative from its inception in 12:1–3, reaches its terminal rendering in vv. 17–18.

22:17–18   As already noted, this culminating passage gathers descriptions of the Abraham promises from earlier narratives and expands upon them: (1) "I will surely bless you" adds "surely"[608] to the first occasion of the pledge in 12:2; (2) "the stars in the sky" recalls Abram's night vision (15:5) but here includes "and [I will surely] make your descendants as numerous"[609] (cf. also Hagar, 16:10; Eve, 3:16); (3) the motif of immeasurable "sand" *(ḥôl),* echoing the Abram-Lot separation (13:16, *'āpār,*"dust"), appears in conjunction with the stars only here in Genesis (cf. Jer 33:22; Heb 11:12); and (4) "possession of the cities [lit., gate[610]] of their enemies" (v. 17) is new to the promise, though it will appear in the familial blessing for Rebekah (24:60b). The blessing for Rebekah invoking the language of 22:17 ties together the promise of descendants through Isaac and the bride who would achieve it for the house of Abraham. In the life of Abraham, this provision reminds us of Abraham's defeat of the eastern bloc of kings (chap. 14) and the demise of the cities of the plain ("gate," 19:1, NIV "gateway").

Verse 18 ends the review of the promises by variations on the theme of blessing for all nations (12:3; 18:18; cf. 26:4; 28:14); it is also reminiscent of the meaning attached to the new names "Abraham" and "Sarah" in the covenant of circumcision (17:4–6,15–16), referring to their royal seed. The addition "through your seed" (*zera',* "offspring," NIV) in v. 18, not found in the earlier expressions (12:3; 18:18),[611] in context appropriately reflects the preservation of Isaac, the "offspring" of promise (21:12; cf. 26:4; 28:14). Blessing for "all nations [of the earth]" in Ps 72:17 and Jer 4:2 allude to 22:18/26:4 when the psalmist describes the idealized king who fulfills the promise, and Jeremiah acknowledges that only a repentant Israel can accomplish it. Hebrew *zera'*

---

[607] The third person "has sworn by himself" is in Jer 51:14; Amos 6:8; cf. also Ps 110:4; Isa 14:24; 62:8; Amos 4:2; 8:7.

[608] כִּי בָרֵךְ אֲבָרֶכְךָ, "I will surely bless," has the emphatic infinitive absolute.

[609] וְהַרְבָּה אַרְבֶּה, lit., "and I will surely make [your descendants] numerous."

[610] The term "gate" is rightly rendered "city" or "cities" since it is a synecdoche, meaning the gate of the city, which was the key possession upon a victor entering a captured city.

[611] The pronouns in 12:3 ("through you") and 18:18 ("through him") refer to Abraham.

("offspring") may refer to an individual or a collective group, requiring the context to indicate which is in view. As we suggested at 3:15, the ambiguity of the term *zera*ʿ serves the author's intent to bring both an individual and a nation in the purview of the promise (vol. 1A, p. 246). The same potential ambiguity appears in vv. 17 and 18; the former verse appears to demand the plural sense (as NIV "their enemies"),[612] whereas v. 18 permits an individual in view, though we would expect to interpret "offspring" in the same sense as v. 17. The parallel phrase to v. 17 in 24:60b assumes "thousands" of descendants and also is best understood as plural (EVs, "their enemies"). The semantic flexibility of "offspring" permits the promise to refer to both an individual (David) and a group (Israel).[613]

This feature explains how the early church could define the promise's fulfillment in terms of both ancient Israel's royal house and the messianic person Jesus Christ. The New Testament alludes to elements of 22:17–18 when acknowledging the patriarch's spiritual role for the Christian believer (e.g., Heb 11:12). The writer to the Hebrews (6:13–14) reminds his readers that the promise of salvation is irrefutable, for the Lord confirmed it swearing an oath by himself, for "there was no one greater for him to swear by" (6:13). Peter quotes 22:18 (perhaps conflating 12:3) in Acts 3:25 in showing the Jewish leaders that Christ is the fulfillment of the Abrahamic promise of blessing intended for all families (*patria;* cf. Gal 3:6–9,16), beginning first with the Jews (Acts 3:26; Rom 1:16; 2:9–10; see comments on 12:3).

The last words of the angel befittingly repeat the astonishing achievement of the patriarch, "because you have obeyed me" (v. 18b; cf. Adam, 3:17). Obedience is critical to the success of Abraham's descendants in establishing Canaan as their homeland (e.g., Exod 19:5; Deut 11:13). In Abraham Israel has its example, as does the church, who is the "father of us all" (Rom 4:16).

22:19 Verse 19 provides a double conclusion. "They set off together" (v. 19a) closely reflects the earlier expression, "the two of them went on together" (vv. 6,8), thus ending the third movement of vv. 9–19a. Verse 19b's reference to Abraham's stay at Beersheba is a second conclusion, ending the whole pericope as the comment in 21:34 concludes the former episode. Geographically, the trip to Moriah is an excursion; theologically, the matter of ultimate trust is finally settled, and the patriarch's spiritual sojourn nears its end.

---

[612] וְיִרַשׁ זַרְעֲךָ אֵת שַׁעַר אֹיְבָיו (v. 17b), lit., "and may your seed possess the gate of his enemies"; the ambiguity of number for "seed" is demonstrated in the AV ("his enemies") and the NKJV ("their enemies").

[613] The mixed response by T. D. Alexander ("Further Observations on the Term 'Seed' in Genesis," *TynBul* 48 [1997]: 363–67) to the proposal by J. Collins ("A Syntactical Note [Genesis 3:15]; Is the Woman's Seed Singular or Plural?" *TynBul* 48 [1997]: 139–48) that syntactic observances can adequately distinguish when "seed" is singular or plural only further demonstrates the uncertainty of the lexeme's meaning apart from a clear context.

The narration's mention of Abraham, not Isaac, returning (v. 19a) opened the way for Jewish speculation about Isaac's fate. The focus on Abraham alone, however, is in accord with vv. 15–18. Moreover, the language "they set off together" presupposes the parallel in vv. 6,8 ("went on together") in which the boy Isaac is specifically noted ("two of them").

Excursus: The Sacrifice of Isaac

The (almost) sacrifice of Isaac was significant for Jewish and Christian interpreters, though far more for Judaism than the New Testament. Some Jewish sources mention the "blood of Isaac" and "the ashes of Isaac" whose sacrifice achieved forgiveness and deliverance for future Israel in its time of trials. Such extrabiblical additions regarding Isaac's death and (implied?) resurrection have similarities to the Christian doctrine of atonement. Romans 8:32 is considered by many scholars as the chief allusion to Gen 22: "He who did not spare his own Son, but gave him up for us all." An important question for Christian interpreters today is to explain to what degree, if any, Jewish and Christian circles influenced each other regarding their respective views on the concept of a vicarious expiation by the shedding of blood.

EARLY JEWISH INTERPRETATIONS. The Akedah (Gen 22:1–19)[614] was a subject appearing in the entire range of Jewish sources, from early targums and rabbinic midrash to medieval commentators.[615] Jewish sources offer diverse and growing traditions, not a uniform interpretation developed unilinearly. It is not our purpose here to propose a chronological framework for the developments mentioned below, only to cite the main ideas. Exegetical mysteries in the episode, which are unique in the Torah, and pressing community needs were the seedbed for the elaborate retellings of the Akedah.[616] An example of an exegetical mystery was the absence of Isaac's name in Gen 22:19. The rabbis asked and attempted to answer, "Where did Isaac go?" (*Gen. Rab.* 56.11). In *Tg. Neof.* 22:19 it is explained that the angels took him to the "schoolhouse of Shem," presumably to learn Torah (so *Gen. Rab.* 56.11). Among Jewish community needs we can point to Roman oppression and the cessation of sacrifice at the destruction of the

---

[614] The term "Akedah" or "Aqedah" is used by scholars to refer to a specific facet or all of the Jewish developments of the doctrine; e.g., P. Davies and B. Chilton use the term for the vicarious atoning feature alone that becomes clearly evidenced in the post-Christian era ("The Akedah: A Revised Tradition History," *CBQ* 40 [1978]: 514–46). We use "Akedah" only as a synonym for the biblical text (22:1–19).

[615] See esp. S. Spiegel, *The Last Trial, On the Legends and Lore of the Command to Abraham to Offer Isaac as a Sacrifice: The Akedah,* trans. J. Goldin (Woodstock, Vt.: Jewish Lights, 1993 [original Hebrew *Me-agadot ha-akedah,* 1950]); and J. Swetnam, *Jesus and Isaac: A Study of the Epistle to the Hebrews in the Light of the Aqedah,* AB 94 (Rome: Biblical Institute Press, 1981). For recent symposium papers, see F. Manns, ed., *The Sacrifice of Isaac in the Three Monotheistic Religions,* SBF Analecta 41 (Jerusalem: Franciscan Printing Press, 1995).

[616] A. F. Segal, "The Akedah: Some Reconsiderations," *Geschichte–Tradition–Reflexion: Festschrift für Martin Hegel zum 70, Geburtstag* Bd. 1 (Tübingen: Mohr, 1996), 99–116.

temple in A.D. 70, making the martyrdom of Isaac a powerful message of encouragement to the besieged Jews (*4 Mac* 13:9–12; 16:18–20; *L.A.B.* 32:2–3).

1. In regard to Isaac, a fundamental shift occurred from the passive Isaac of Genesis to the mature, active, and virtuous volunteer, the perfect offering. Isaac's sacrifice became the idealized sacrifice, which was especially related to the New Year's feast or alternatively the Passover sacrifice. The preamble in *Tg. Ps-J.* records a debate between Isaac and Ishmael, each claiming to be the rightful heir based on their merits. At hearing Isaac's boast that he would yield all his members to God, the Lord proceeds with the test (also *Gen. Rab.* 55.4; *b. Sanh.* 89b). This voluntary spirit by Isaac is enhanced by his mature age of thirty-seven years (*Tg. Ps-J.*; also, e.g., *Gen. Rab.* 55.4),[617] by Abraham informing him in advance that he is the sacrifice (*Tg. Neof.* 22:8; also *Gen. Rab.* 56.2–3), and by the heavenly voice confirming his heroism (*Tg. Neof.*).[618] Josephus (*Ant.* 1.13.4[232]) depicts him receiving the news of his fate "with joy," whereupon "he rushed to the altar and his doom."[619] Later midrash (ca. fourth century) even portrays him binding himself (*Sifre Deut* 32).[620] Other explanations ascribed God's action to Satan's idea, as in biblical Job (1:9–11; *Jub.* 17:16; *b. Sanh.* 89a) or the envy of the angels (*L.A.B.* 32:1–2; *Gen. Rab.* 55.4). Also a rabbinic tradition cited Isaac's remarkable righteousness (*Gen. Rab.* 55.2, quoting Ps 11:5), showing another similarity to Job (1:8).

2. Another important discussion was the relationship of the Akedah event and the salvation Israel experienced as a chosen nation.[621] The Palestinian targums include a prayer by Abraham, calling upon God to forgive and save future generations (Gen 21:12) by remembering "the binding of their father Isaac" (*Tg. Neof.* 22:14; also *Ps-J.*). Pseudo-Philo depicts Isaac announcing that his sacrifice would be more effective for future generations than all other sacrifices (*L.A.B.* 32:2–4). Rabbinic midrash especially linked the merit of Isaac's binding for the salvation and deliverance of Israel throughout its history (e.g., *Gen. Rab.* 55.8; 56.10; *Lev. Rab.* 29.9).[622]

3. The claim by medieval sources that Isaac was actually killed and resurrected from the ashes of the altar (e.g., *Pirqe R. El.* 31:3[623]) has earlier anteced-

---

[617] Twenty-five years in Josephus, *Ant.* 13.2[227].

[618] "The one who slaughters does not hesitate, and he who is being slaughtered stretches out his neck" (22:10).

[619] L. Feldman shows how Josephus tailored his account to minimize the more objectionable parts to a pagan audience ("Josephus as a Biblical Interpreter: The *'Aqedah*," *JQR* 75 [1985]: 212–52).

[620] Others, however, depicted Isaac as subject to temptation who must be tied down, lest he disobey (*Gen. Rab.* 56.8).

[621] E.g., *Tg. Cant.* 1:13; *Tg. Est II* 5:1; and *Tg. 1 Chr* 21:15 specifically attribute Israel's deliverance to the efficacy of the Akedah.

[622] *Gen. Rab* 56.1, e.g., demonstrates the tie of the Akedah with Israel's salvation history through the motif "third day" (e.g., Exod 19:6; Hos 16:2); *Gen. Rab.* 56.2 links the word "worship" (חוה, "prostrate") used by Abraham (22:5) and future occasions of "worship" (e.g., Exod 4:13) that secured Israel's deliverance, indicating that by his prostration Israel received its future benefits.

[623] For citations see Spiegel, *The Last Trial*, 38–44.

ents, though how early is disputed. *Mek. R. Ishmael* (*Pisha* 7:78–82; 11:85–96), reflecting material from the second century A.D., mentions the "blood of the binding of Isaac" when commenting on the biblical Passover: "And when I see the blood, I will pass over you" (Exod 12:13). This midrash by the term ("see" *rāʾâ*) interprets the deliverance of the Hebrews from the Passover plague (Exod 12:13) and from the plagues against Jerusalem at the temple location (1 Chr 21:15) in terms of Abraham's naming of the site (22:14).

> ". . . and when I see the blood" (Exod 12:13):
> "When I see the blood of the binding of Isaac."
> Thus it is said, "And Abraham called the name of that place, 'the Lord will
>   see' (Gen 22:14); "And as he was about to destroy, the Lord beheld and
>   regretted" (1 Chr 21:15).
> What did he see? He saw the blood of the binding of Isaac, as it is said,
>   "God will see to a lamb for himself" (22:8).
> "I will pass over you"[624]

Although rabbinic references to the blood of Isaac are rare,[625] some think his death is implied in the Palestinian targums' retelling and in the tribute to his martyrdom in *4 Maccabees*.[626] Pseudo-Philo's *Biblical Antiquities* (*L.A.B.* 18:5–6) mentions the merit of "his blood," and as though deliberately reacting to the idea of death, Philo remarks that the act was not actually carried out but was perfect as if completed (*Abr.* 177). Later, *Gen. Rab.* 56.7 insists that not one harmful thing occurred, no blemish happened, and the medieval commentator Ibn Ezra specifically rejected the idea of Isaac's actual death and resurrection. With this mixed testimony among Jewish sources, the question arises as to how early and pervasive the doctrine of Isaac's blood atonement was and what was its relationship to Christian soteriology. Before speaking to these issues, we will consider the Christian interpretation of Gen 22 first.

EARLY CHRISTIAN INTERPRETATIONS. The Akedah influenced New Testament writers, but not in the same way or extent. Uniformly in the Gospels and Acts, Isaac is treated as a historical figure. He appears as a historical figure in Jas 2:21 and Heb 11:17–19, but in Hebrews his survival is termed a *parabola,* a "figure" (v. 19) of resurrection. The writer to the Hebrews recognized that Abraham believed the boy would return (22:5), which can only mean that Abraham trusted the Lord to raise him from the dead to fulfill his promise (21:12). This God did

---

[624] *Pisha* 7.8–9a. For translation see J. Neusner, *Mekhilta according to Rabbi Ishmael* (Atlanta: Scholars Press, 1988), 45.

[625] C. T. R. Hayward ("The Sacrifice of Isaac and Jewish Polemic against Christianity," *CBQ* 52 [1990]: 292–306) lists only five rabbinic sources: *Mek. de R. Ishmael, Pisha* 7:78–82; 11:85–96, *Mek. de R. Simeon b. Yohai,* 4–5, *Tanḥ. Wayyera* 23, *Yal. Shimʿoni,* and *'Abot R. Nat.* (p. 295, n. 14).

[626] E.g., R. Daly, "The Soteriological Significance of the Sacrifice of Isaac," *CBQ* 39 (1977): 45–75; F. Manns contends that the two essential elements of the targumic Akedah, namely, the self-oblation of Isaac and its meritorious effect of forgiveness for Israel (arising from the exegesis of Gen 22 and Isa 53), existed in pre-Christian times, and the virtual sacrifice of Isaac was presupposed in targumic theology ("The Targum of Genesis 22," *The Sacrifice of Isaac,* 69–80).

when the angel halted the knife, for the lad was as good as dead in the mind of his father—as well as in the reckoning of God (22:12,16). In both Hebrews and James the mention of Isaac is overshadowed by the faith and obedience of his father, though in Heb 11:20 Isaac does receive a brief commendation for his faith in blessing his sons. Paul mentioned Isaac collaterally as a historical illustration buttressing his argument in Rom 9:7,10 regarding Israel's election. Galatians 4:28 includes Isaac as a type in his *allēgoroumena* ("speaking figuratively," v. 24) of the two covenants represented by Hagar and Sarah (vv. 24–31). Through this survey it is important to observe that there is no *explicit* reference to an Isaac-Christ typology.

The most likely Pauline allusion to the Akedah proposed by commentators is Rom 8:32. "He who did not spare *[epheisato]* his own son" has the same verb used in Gen 22:12,16, LXX, "You have not spared *[epheisō]* your beloved son."[627] Yet the verb occurs in the similar expression of 2 Sam 18:5, LXX, "Spare *[pheisasthe]* for my sake the young man Absalom." Moreover, the root verb "spare, withhold" *(pheidomai)* is very common in the LXX, occurring ninety-five times (10x in the NT, including Rom 11:21). If Paul were intent on echoing the Akedah, he could have made an explicit reference (as in Gal 4:28) or repeated the LXX's translation *agapētos* ("beloved") for the passage's common term *yāḥîd*, "only" (22:2,12,16), especially with the passage's emphasis on the father's love.[628] Rather, Rom 8:32 has "his own *[tou idiou]* Son." Hebrews 11:17 also avoids this language, preferring "his one and only *[monogenē]* son." It is not self-evident that the apostle had the Akedah specifically in mind.

The church fathers, however, often read the Akedah episode typologically as the redemptive story of Christ's crucifixion, including the Greek, Latin, and Syrian branches of the church.[629] The first explicit reference to Isaac's sacrifice as a type of Christ's atonement was the *Letter of Barnabas* 7.3. Melito of Sardis (second century) is the earliest known to have related the wood borne by Isaac to the cross shouldered by our Lord (also, e.g., Irenaeus, *Haer.* 4.5.4; Tertullian, *Marc.* 3.18.2; *Adv. Jud.* 10.6; Ephrem the Syrian, *Hymns Nat.* 8.13; *Virg.* 8.16; *Comm. on Gen.* 20.3). Melito designates Isaac a *tupos*, a "type" of Christ (*Frag.* 9). He makes much of the astonishing deed of the father and his son who "carried with fortitude the model *[tupos]* of the Lord."[630] And for Melito the sacrificed ram

---

[627] Many other NT references are said by ancient and modern commentators to have Gen 22 in mind, such as Matt 3:17 pars.; 17:5 par.; John 1:29; 3:16; 19:17; and Rom 4:16–25.

[628] If one appeals to ἀγαπητός ("beloved"), a better case, though still unconvincing, can be made for Matt 3:17 pars. and 17:5 par., where the term occurs; see A. F. Segal, "The Sacrifice of Isaac in Early Judaism and Christianity," in *The Other Judaisms of Late Antiquity*, BJS 127 (Atlanta: Scholars Press, 1987), 109–30, esp. 125–26, originally published as "'He Who Did Not Spare His Only Son . . .' (Romans 8:32) Jesus, Paul, and the Sacrifice of Isaac," in *From Jesus to Paul: Studies in Honour of F. W. Beare* (Waterloo, Ontario: Wilfrid Laurier Press, 1984), 169–84.

[629] For a convenient survey see M. C. Paczkowski, "The Sacrifice of Isaac in Early Patristic Exegesis" and L. Cignelli, "The Sacrifice of Isaac in Patristic Exegesis," *The Sacrifice of Isaac*, 99–121, 123–26, who rely largely on J. Daniélou, *Sacramentum futuri. Études sur les origines de la typologie biblique* (Paris, 1950).

[630] For the text and translation, see S. G. Hall, *Melito of Sardis, On Pascha and Fragments* (Oxford: Clarendon, 1979).

also represented the Lord who was the "lamb" (*Frag.* 10); moreover, the ram "caught in a Sabek-tree[631] . . . displayed the cross" (*Frag.* 11). Augustine too pointed to the wood and the horned ram caught in the thicket as the cross of Christ and his crown of thorns (*City of God* 16.32). Even the otherwise reticent Chrysostom draws parallels between Gen 22 and the crucifixion (John 8:56; Rom 8:32), indicating that both the ram and Isaac foreshadowed the Savior (*Hom. Gen.* 47).

CHRISTIAN AND RABBINIC EXEGESIS. The relationship between the Jewish Akedah interpreted as expiatory and Paul's doctrine of forgiveness of sin by faith in the atoning blood of Christ has been an important topic among scholars.[632] A popular view is that Paul was indebted to contemporary Jewish notions about the Akedah (perhaps in conjunction with Isaiah 53), which informed his own development of the atoning death of Christ. Just as Isaac's "death" conveyed forgiveness and deliverance for future generations, the Passover death of Christ achieved salvation for the world (Rom 5:9; 1 Cor 5:7). Abraham represented God, and Isaac became the Christ. H. J. Schoeps summed it up this way: "Through the Aqeda the son of the promise became the Son of God."[633] The opposite view contends that the rabbinic interpretation of Isaac's blood as a doctrine of vicarious atonement was actually a post-Christian development, initiated by the Tannaim (first–second centuries A.D.) at the collapse of the temple (A.D. 70) and developed further by the Amoraim authorities (ca. A.D. 200–500) in reaction to Christian soteriology by offering its own version of expiation, drawing on features of the Christian Passover/resurrection account.[634] Somewhere between these two opinions is this middle of the road view: the Jewish Akedah antedated

---

[631] ἐν φυτῷ σαβεκ is interpreted as a "tree" rather than bush, thus better signifying the cross; the Jewish targums also have "tree."

[632] A monograph devoted to this subject is J. Levenson, *The Death and Resurrection of the Beloved Son, The Transformation of Child Sacrifice in Judaism and Christianity* (New Haven: Yale University Press, 1993), who argues that the Jewish and Christian communities transformed in different ways God's demand for child sacrifice, Israel's firstborn (Exod 22:28b): in the first case, ritual and narrative (Akedah) substituted for the beloved son, and in the second case, with the rejection of Torah, the apostle Paul espoused that the death of Jesus Christ alone was an adequate substitute. M. Perez Fernandez believes that Paul only uses the typology of the "beloved" (יָחִיד; 22:2,12,16), showing that Jesus is the one true heir (Gal 3:16,20; Rom 9:10), not a prefigure of a son's obedient, vicarious suffering ("The Aqedah in Paul," *The Sacrifice of Isaac,* 81–91).

[633] H. J. Schoeps, *Paul: The Theology of the Apostle in the Light of Religious History,* trans. H. Knight (Philadelphia: Westminster, 1961), 148; also see the influential study of G. Vermes, "Redemption and Genesis xxii—the Binding of Isaac and the Sacrifice of Jesus," in *Scripture and Tradition in Judaism: Haggadic Studies,* 2d rev. ed. (Leiden: Brill, 1983), 193–227, who boldly opined "That the Pauline doctrine of Redemption is basically a Christian version of the Akedah calls for little demonstration" (p. 219); R. Le Déaut, *La Nuit Pascale,* AnBib 22 (Rome: Pontifical Biblical Institute, 1963), 131–212; and R. Daly, "The Soteriological Significance of the Sacrifice of Isaac," *CBQ* 39 (1977): 45–75.

[634] P. Davies and B. Chilton, "The Aqedah: A Revised Tradition History," *CBQ* 40 (1978): 514–46; Chilton, "Isaac and the Second Night: A Consideration," *Bib* 61 (1980): 78–82; id., "Recent Discussion of the Aqedah," in *Targumic Approaches to the Gospels* (Lanham: University Press of America, 1986), 39–49.

the first century A.D. and included the expiatory interpretation of Isaac's sacrifice, but it did not originate in relation to the Christian paschal story and was not the source of Paul's development of blood atonement. Rather, a common body of tradition regarding the Akedah was the source of the Jewish and Christian versions, each view formed to meet the respective theological needs.[635] Two encumbrances hinder the interpreter when considering this question. First, the date of the material contained in the Palestinian targums as to whether it is pre- or post-Christian remains disputed. G. Vermes contends, however, that a Qumran fragment (4Q225[636]) dating in the pre-Christian era assures that the Jewish Akedah was current in the first Christian century.[637] Yet the broken text, although it contains elements of the Jewish Akedah, does not make any reference to the highly disputed points: the Passover, the lamb sacrifice, or Isaac's blood and ashes. Second, that there was clearly a pre-Christian view of the Akedah as a vicarious shedding of Isaac's blood is simply not demonstrable.[638] The Qumran evidence does not solve the second interpretive hurdle either. Moreover, one cannot assume that Paul's soteriology relied on an Isaac-Christ typology, since it also cannot be substantiated. P. Stuhlmacher shows that Paul's view of the atonement (e.g., Rom 3:25–26) is best explained conceptually in light of Leviticus 16, not a current theology of martyrdom.[639] Whether or not one dates the inception of the Jewish doctrine of expiation in relation to the Akedah as pre-Christian, the similarities between the Jewish and Christian traditions are superficial and do not require that the "blood of Isaac" was conceptually related to Paul's soteriology.[640] H. Maccoby rightly concludes, "It is clear, however, that even though a story did exist about the sacrifice, or partial sacrifice, of Isaac, this was of no central significance in Judaism, and therefore cannot really be compared to the Christian concept of the Crucifixion."[641] There is a fundamental theological dif-

---

[635] Segal, "The Sacrifice of Isaac," 130; R. Haywood, "The Present State of Research into the Targumic Account of the Sacrifice of Isaac," *JJS* 32 (1981): 127–50; id., "The Sacrifice of Isaac and Jewish Polemic against Christianity," *CBQ* 52 (1990): 292–306.

[636] For translation and discussion, see F. García Martínez, "The Sacrifice of Isaac in 4Q255," in *The Sacrifice of Isaac: The Aqedah (Genesis 22) and Its Interpretations* (Leiden: Brill, 2002), 44–57.

[637] Vermes ("New Light on the Sacrifice of Isaac from 4Q225," *JJS* 49 [1996]: 140–46) reports the original editors date the fragment in the Herodian period (ca. 30 B.C.–A.D. 20). Of the twelve elements listed by Vermes that he believes constitute the Jewish Akedah archetype, 4Q225 possessed six (e.g., the presence of angels), three of which were uncertain. Vermes' argument for the coexistence of the Jewish Akedah and Christian soteriology relies on a primal "pre-Christian skeleton of the targumic-midrashic representation of the sacrifice of Isaac" (found in 4Q225, *Jubilees*, Josephus, Pseudo-Philo, and *4 Mac*) that assumes an expiatory aspect.

[638] J. A. Fitzmyer, *Romans,* AB (New York: Doubleday, 1992), 531.

[639] P. Stuhlmacher, *Reconciliation, Law, and Righteousness: Essays in Biblical Theology*, trans. E. Kalin (Philadelphia: Fortress, 1986), 94–109.

[640] If anything, the appearance of similarity may have motivated the rabbinic restriction on the "blood of Isaac" observed in the midrashic sources, so Haywood, "The Sacrifice of Isaac," 303.

[641] H. Maccoby, *Early Rabbinic Writings* (Cambridge: Cambridge University Press, 1988), 149.

ference between the substitutionary doctrine of Christ's atonement and the developed Jewish Akedah, so that a simple exchange of Abraham for God and Isaac for Christ is not a satisfactory explanation for Paul's soteriology.

14. Nahor's Family (22:20–24)

[20]**Some time later Abraham was told, "Milcah is also a mother; she has borne sons to your brother Nahor:** [21]**Uz the firstborn, Buz his brother, Kemuel (the father of Aram),** [22]**Kesed, Hazo, Pildash, Jidlaph and Bethuel."** [23]**Bethuel became the father of Rebekah. Milcah bore these eight sons to Abraham's brother Nahor.** [24]**His concubine, whose name was Reumah, also had sons: Tebah, Gaham, Tahash and Maacah.**

The inclusion of Nahor's family lineage, the brother of Abraham (11:26), is the start of the narrative's epilogue (22:20–25:11). With the question of Abraham's faithfulness and the identity of the heir settled (22:1–19), the epilogue transitions Abraham's story to the Jacob narrative (25:19–35:29) by establishing the union of Isaac and Rebekah who parent Jacob and his brother (25:21–26). Before taking up the next patriarchal account, the author includes the Ishmael genealogy (*tôlĕdōt,* 25:12–18) so as to close out the former episodes of fraternal rivalry.

EPILOGUE.   The extended section we are considering here (22:20–25:11) possesses essential genealogical information (22:20–24; 25:1–11), reporting the status of the Terah family lines. As the epilogue to the entire Abraham narrative, it corresponds to the genealogical prologue in 11:27–31 that previews the three family lines of Terah. In effect the genealogy of Nahor in 22:20–24 reestablishes the identity of the Terah groups under the *tôlĕdōt* of Terah (11:27) and thereby ties again the patriarchal accounts to their primeval ancestry (11:24).[642] The borders of the episode itself consist also of genealogies, the prominent fraternal lines of Terah's clan: Nahor and his wife and concubine (22:20–24) and Abraham and his wife and concubines (25:1–11). That the author had this genealogical symmetry in mind may be seen by the juxtaposition of fraternal lines immediately following the Terah *tôlĕdōt.* The two *tôlĕdōt* of Ishmael (25:12–18) and Isaac (25:19–20) provide for the next stage in the patriarchal accounts, leaving the story of the Terah patriarchy behind. The author is interested in the promises via Abraham, not Nahor, and Isaac, not Ishmael.

The same beginning phrase, "some time later," in vv. 1 and 20 shows a formal connection between the Moriah incident (vv. 1–19) and the genealogy of Nahor (vv. 20–24). Reporting the productivity of the Nahor clan after the promise of blessing for "all nations" (v. 18) implies that the Nahor history is part of the beginning fulfillment; also, noting "Rebekah" in the genealogy (v. 23) refers to

---

[642] Thompson, *The Origin Tradition,* 99.

the future matriarch by whom blessing will occur for Abraham's family and, ultimately, all nations. If the events of 22:1–19 show inferentially the maturing of Isaac, who comes to succeed his father, the following chaps. 23–24 may also be said to depict his new independence from his deceased mother (cf. 24:67).

Attention on Nahor's descendants recalls the Aramean (v. 21) branch of the Terah clan who remained in Haran (11:28–31). The author brings forward the history of the Nahor family because of its importance for the Abraham-Isaac group; it anticipates chap. 24, which narrates the betrothal of Rebekah as Isaac's wife from the Nahor clan in Aram (24:10,15,24,47). The genealogical connection between Rebekah, the granddaughter of Nahor, and Abraham's branch explains the commissioning of his servant in 24:3–4 (see comments). The practice of endogamy (marriage within a family group) is common among the patriarchs, and the Nahor genealogy provides a precise accounting of the family tree. By such genealogical accounting, the inheritance of the promise is shown to be passed down within the family.

COMPOSITION.   Commonly, source critics attribute this genealogy to the Yahwist (J) since it does not bear the linguistic features normally cited as priestly (P), and also the genealogy clearly anticipates the Yahwist's account in chap. 24. We have addressed already the unfounded claims that the genealogies and their supplements on the basis of language and form can be confidently attributed to different sources (vol. 1A, pp. 435–36, nn. 22,27,28). Additionally, the location of 22:20–24 in the present arrangement leads many to believe the text has suffered some displacement. Westermann proposed that the Abraham cycle began with the genealogy of 11:27–32 and closed out with 21:1–7 (birth of Isaac) followed by the genealogies in 22:20–24 and 25:1–18, listing the children born by Milcah and Sarah (11:29) as well as their concubines to Nahor and Abraham. Genesis 21:8–24:67, excepting 22:20–24, supplements the original narrative.[643] The Nahor-Milcah genealogy, however, is an appropriate fit in the present narrative arrangement since it provides a buffer between the narrative's high point of 22:1–19 and the low point describing Sarah's death (chap. 23). And as an interlude 22:20–24 easily transitions to Sarah's death by the genealogy's mention of Milcah.[644] (For more on the role of chap. 23, see the commentary *ad loc.*). Moreover, Westermann's reconstruction and those of the same sort are in effect substituting their own notion of what constitutes a proper end to the story. The present symmetry of the canonical narrative, understanding 22:20–25:11 as the epilogue to the whole, makes literary sense; as an epilogue it does not diminish the force of the outcome to the main tension in 22:1–19, but it provides information the narrative requires in order to ensure the reader that the promises were passed down to Isaac as required. The motif of marriage and offspring so essen-

---

[643] Westermann, *Genesis 12–36,* 366–67; Van Seters proposes perhaps 25:1–6 (Keturah's children) originally was part of a complex of genealogies including 22:20–24, which preceded chap. 24 (assuming chap. 23 is a late supplement) followed by 25:11 (*Abraham in History,* 248).

[644] Alexander, *A Literary Analysis,* 62.

tial to the thematic thread of the whole links 11:29 and 22:20–24 and chap. 24, making it unnecessary to view chap. 24 as a supplement.[645] The question of the authenticity of the Hebrew-Aramean connection was considered in the Introduction to the commentary. Scholars deem the Genesis portrayal of the Hebrews and Arameans' common ancestry must be in a late period (ca. seventh–sixth centuries) when national hostilities had subsided. Genealogies are typically interpreted as snapshots of political relationships between peoples current at the time of their composition. The nature of biblical genealogies creates difficulties for social scientists since they include a variety of means for designating ancestral connections, such as geographical sites, persons, and tribal groups (see vol. 1A, pp. 432, 438). For example, "Canaan" is treated as a person in 9:18,20–27 but as a people group in the Table of Nations (10:6,15–19). Furthermore, the critical assumption is that such genealogies possess fictional eponymous ancestors though in some cases an authentic underlying historical basis. If such a method of dating is applied, since the Genesis author did not shrink from reporting the Aramean connection, one can equally argue that the list is truly archaic, reflecting a time long before David's conflicts (2 Sam 8:5).[646] If anything, the passing inclusion of "Aram" in the genealogy (v. 21), named after the heritage of the Arameans (see vol. 1A, 462), suggests that the list antedated the heyday of this northeast political power.

STRUCTURE.   The passage consists of two genealogical units, naming the sons born to Nahor by his wife (vv. 20–23) and his concubine (v. 24). The beginning sentence is a narrative transition (v. 20a) establishing the connection of the passage to the foregoing Abraham episodes. Verses 20b–23 present the "eight sons" born by Milcah to Nahor. "Milcah has borne" (v. 20b) and "Milcah bore" (v. 23b) form the boundaries distinguishing this unit. Verse 24 identifies four sons born by the concubine Reumah, making a total of twelve sons born to Nahor. The feature of twelve offspring parallels the number born to Ishmael (17:20; 25:16), Jacob (35:22; 49:28), and Esau (36:2–4,20–21). As in this case, Jacob's wives produced eight sons and their maidservants four sons (35:24–26). The genealogy is segmented (branched) in form, naming more than one person per generation (see vol. 1A, pp. 280, 295–96, 431–32, 487), but the depth of the genealogy is only one tier, with the important exception of Rebekah. Because of her importance in the life of the patriarchs, Rebekah is the only person appearing in the second tier and the only daughter mentioned at all. "Aram" too is mentioned as part of the next generation but as an aside, not in the second tier. The name Aram also holds importance for the author since the name by itself points up the future residence of the patriarch Jacob, where he produces the twelve ancestors of Israel (Aram Naharaim and Paddan Aram,

---

[645] Carr (*Reading the Fractures of Genesis,* 110, 198–99) makes this point relying in part on J. Emerton's finding that the passages are inseparable ("The Source Analysis of Genesis XI 27–32," *VT* [1992]: 41–42).

[646] Sarna, *Genesis,* 155: "The genealogical lists are of undoubted antiquity."

e.g., 24:10; 25:20; 28:2; 35:9).

Milcah, the daughter of Haran, marries her uncle Nahor, thereby uniting two of the three branches of Terah's family (see comments on 11:29–30). Since Rebekah is a descendant of Nahor-Milcah, her marriage to Isaac reunites all three branches. The Hebrew tribes recognize their indebtedness to the Aramean clan of Nahor, where their father Jacob resided and gained his sons, in the confession "My father was a wandering Aramean" (Deut 26:5).

22:20–23 Abraham is informed of his brother's impressive lineage. Mention of Milcah as "also a mother" (v. 20) must have Sarah in mind (see comments on 11:29). The point is that the Terah family, despite its slow beginnings, shows a number of descendants. Set against the genealogy of Milcah, the birth of Sarah's child Isaac is a unique work of divine grace. Although not stated specifically, the tenor of the patriarchal accounts implies that God too is overseeing the burgeoning house of Nahor with its twelve members. The Israelites can look back to two direct lines from Terah that produced their twelve tribal ancestors: the Abraham line provided the paternal ancestry (Isaac, Jacob), and the Nahor line provided the maternal ancestry (Rebekah, Leah, Rachel).

Uz (v. 21), distinguished as the honored "firstborn," bears the same name as the Shemite son of Aram (10:23) and the descendant of Esau (36:28–29), as well as the place of Job's residence (1:1); the significant differences between the three genealogies in Genesis show that they are different persons/tribes (see comments on 10:23). All that is known of *Buz* as a place name probably is an Arabian site due to its mention with Sedan and Tema in Arabia (Jer 25:23; cf. Elihu's association, Job 32:2,6). Esarhaddon lists campaigns in 677 B.C. against the Arabian places Bazu and Hazu, similar in name to the related descendants Buz and Hazo.[647] *Kemuel,* also the name of (unrelated) persons instanced in Num 34:24 and 1 Chr 27:17, is an unknown entity. *Aram* here is not the same as the descendant of Shem (see comments on 10:22); his very name, however, shows Aramean connections, appropriate for the Nahor clan.

Kesed (v. 22) shows a phonetic association with the "Chaldeans" (*kaśdîm;* see comments on 11:28); perhaps this figure is the ancestor of the Chaldeans, a tribe of southern Mesopotamia whose roots therefore would be Aramean. Nothing is known of *Hazo, Pildash,* and *Jidlaph,* cited only here. *Bethuel* (v. 23), the father of Rebekah and Laban, is repeatedly distinguished as an actual person, not a tribe (24:15,24,47,50; 25:20; 28:2,5); his name may mean "dweller in God" or is equivalent to *mĕtû'ēl,* "man of God."[648] He is specifically identified as an "Aramean" in 25:20, noting his residence in Paddan Aram.

The quoted report made to Abraham probably concludes with v. 22, leaving vv. 23–24 to the author's addition (note quote marks in EVs), if not v. 20. This means Abraham does not necessarily know of Rebekah before his ser-

---

[647] E. A. Knauf, "Buz (Place)," *ABD* 1.794.
[648] E. Hostetter, "Bethuel (Place)," *ABD* 1.715.

vant discovers her (chap. 24).[649] The meaning of the name "Rebekah" is uncertain; suggestions include *rbq*, "to tie a loop over an animal," *marbēq*, "a stall" (1 Sam 28:24), a bi-form of *biqrâ* (cf. Ar. *baqaraṯ*, "cow,"[650] or a wordplay on *bāqār*, "cattle,"[651] or *bĕrākâ*, "blessing" (cf. 24:60–66; 27:1–17).[652]

22:24 As a concubine *Reumah* is reminiscent of Hagar's role and the concubines of Jacob, Bilhah, and Zilpah, who contributed to the households of the patriarchs. Reumah's etymology is unknown, perhaps Ug. *re'um* ("wild ox"; cf. Hb. *rĕ'ēm*, "wild bull"),[653] or Ug. *rimt* ("coral"; cf. Hb. *rā'môt*, "corals"),[654] or Akk. *rāmu* ("to love"); her four sons, *Tebah, Gaham, Tahash,* and *Maacah,* are associated with sites in Aram and northern Transjordan.[655]

15. Sarah's Burial Site (23:1–20)

The death and burial of Sarah at Hebron is another transitional event (cf. 24:67) in the epilogue of the Abraham narrative (22:20–25:11) preparing the reader for the succession of Isaac-Rebekah. The occasion of her death required the purchase of a family burial plot. The notion of burial indicates permanency. That Abraham secures a family plot in Canaan rather than returning to Haran conveys the man's commitment to the land promised him. Ancient peoples cherished their ancestral burial ground; burial in the ancestral grave indicated honor and continuity with the family. Later, while in Egypt, Jacob and Joseph insist that their remains rest in Canaan according to their faith in the divine promises (49:29–32; 50:24–25).

Abraham's trust that his descendants will ultimately possess the land continues to demonstrate the faith proven by the offering of Isaac (chap. 22). That the land motif is central to this account is shown by the repetition of the location (Canaan) in the beginning and end of the narrative (vv. 2,19). The covenant promise of blessing for the nations is also reflected in chap. 23, although not in the explicit promissory form (12:2–3; 18:18; 22:18), by the recognition of Abraham's stature and the Hittites' evident regard for him (v. 6). The passage indicates his potential influence of blessing for others (cf. Abimelech's treaty, 21:22–23). The Hittites concede to Abraham's wishes and welcome him by offering him a burial site in their land.

---

[649] Wenham, *Genesis 16–50,* 120.

[650] *HALOT* 3.1182.

[651] A. Beck, "Rebekah," *ABD* 5.629.

[652] Wenham, *Genesis 16–50,* 120–21; also Akk. *rabāku,* "to be soft, springy."

[653] Sarna, *Genesis,* 156.

[654] *HALOT* 3.1162.

[655] E. Hostetter, "Reumah," *ABD* 5.694.

COMPOSITION. According to the dominant opinion among critical reconstructions, chap. 23 is a structural unity, a single work by the Priestly writer (P) that originally stood independent of its Yahwist (J) environment (22:20–24; 24:1–67).[656] Its present location awkwardly interrupts the flow of 22:20–24 and 24:1–67, which cohere around the ancestress Rebekah. Originally it followed on the birth of Isaac (21:1b–5) and preceded the burial of Abraham (25:7–11) in the priestly work.[657] The theological purpose of the narrative, however, is disputed among these same scholars, if indeed there was one at all. This "secular" account possesses no reference to the promises, nor does it tie the purchase of the cave to divine involvement, making no mention of deity.[658]

That the chapter should be assigned to the Priestly work, an author different from 22:20–24 and 24:1–67, has its impediments. There is an immediate admission by these same proponents that chap. 23 is not of the same literary kind as one expects of P (e.g., chap. 17). T. D. Alexander's literary analysis joins others such as R. Rendtorff who show the illegitimacy of relying on the traditional arguments for distinguishing the P work.[659] The chapter is no interruption, not an afterthought that motivated the editor to add on more to the main course in chaps. 12–22. Reporting the death of Sarah follows appropriately on the Nahor genealogy (22:20–24) since the genealogy alludes to Sarah by the description of her sister Milcah (11:29) as "*also* a mother" (22:20; italics mine). The status of the Abraham-Sarah family in chaps. 21–22 and 23, including the proleptic reference to Rebekah in 22:20–24, prepare for the reunification of the Terah families in chap. 24, for after the death of Sarah, Abraham initiates the search for a wife for Isaac (cf. 24:67). Also the mention of "Mamre" at Hebron (vv. 2,17,19) recalls the setting of prior events (13:18; 14:13,24; 18:1).

The chapter fits in the thematic development of the Abraham story. It reflects the same concerns of land and family succession that permeate chaps. 12–22. That the narrative would give concluding information about the family matriarch's death and the ancestral burial place is not surprising. It is difficult to imagine the absence of Machpelah in the original Abraham account since it played a central role in the life of his descendants (25:9–10; 49:29–32; 50:13), and the relationship of the Abraham clan to the Hittites reappears (26:34; 27:46; 36:2). This is especially the case when we consider the literary contribution to the patriarchal narratives as a whole. T. L. Thompson, though assuming the independence of chap. 23, considers it an important link that "creates the narrative unity" of the patriarchal materials, progressing from the purchase of the cave to the resting place of Jacob in chap. 49.[660] Since the chapter is related to the immediate con

---

[656] Van Seters presents the common arguments, including chap. 23's chronological framework, P-like vocabulary, repetitious style, and mention of Machpelah elsewhere in P passages (e.g., 25:9; [35:29]; 49:30; and 50:13; *Abraham in History,* 293).

[657] Coats, *Genesis,* 98,165; Westermann, *Genesis 12–36,* 371.

[658] נְשִׂיא אֱלֹהִים may be an exception ("a prince of God"), but "a mighty prince" is also possible (see comments on 23:6).

[659] Alexander, *A Literary Analysis,* 192–200, and Rendtorff, *Problem,* 128–30.

[660] Thompson, *The Origin Tradition,* 99–100.

text and also fits in the strategy of the scope of the patriarchal accounts as a whole, it is reasonable to consider it part of the original literary work of the Abraham account.

As for the theological contribution of the chapter, the episode reminds us of the Abimelech incident in 21:22–34, where the patriarch, viewed favorably by the local chieftain, discusses property rights and enters into league at Beersheba. In this incident, too, its theological message is not explicitly related to the divine promise, but no one would deem it "secular," since the Philistine king acknowledges Abraham as a person approved by God (21:22–23), and tellingly the chapter concludes by Abraham's worship of the Lord (21:33). The absence of explicit references to deity in chap. 23 makes it no less theological in importance than 21:22–34. Both events confirm the beginning fulfillment of the promises of land and blessing among the nations. By the exuberant recognition of the patriarch by the Hittites (23:6), the passage implies that the burial purchase has the same theological value for the author as does the Beersheba incident. Moreover, Abraham's refusal to receive the land without payment (23:13) reminds us of his refusal to receive a reward from the king of Sodom (14:21–24), though in that case with indignation. Although the settings of chaps. 14 and 23 differ significantly, the reason for the refusal of both offers lies in the same proposition that the patriarch has no indebtedness to the indigenous populations, sustaining his claim to God's favor for his successes (e.g., 14:22–23; 21:22; 24:1,35).

A related question to the identity of source is the date of the underlying legal tradition in chap. 23. Scholars have attempted to locate the era of the legal transactions reflected in the Abraham-Hittite incident by noting comparable legal terms and forms attested in the ancient Near East.[661] Parallels have been found among diverse legal transactions, including Hittite and Akkadian records of the second millennium and the neo-Babylonian "dialogue documents" of the first millennium.[662] Because chap. 23 is not the document of record itself but a narrative account of the transaction,[663] it is difficult to be definitive especially since the legal traditions in the ancient Near East shared much in common. It is enough to say that the transaction reported in chap. 23 is consistent with the general pat-

---

[661] E.g., cp. the technical language "full price" (מָלֵא כֶּסֶף בְּ, v. 9) with the common Akk. legal term *ana šīmi-šú gamrūti* ("for its full price") and its comparable expressions; also Akk. *maḫirat illaku,* "the rate that is current," parallels "the weight current among the merchants" (עֹבֵר לַסֹּחֵר, lit., "passes by the merchant," v. 16).

[662] M. R. Lehman claimed Hittite origin for the legal background to chap. 23 ("Abraham's Purchase of Machpelah and Hittite Law," *BASOR* 128 [1953]: 15–18), but G. M. Tucker exposed the weakness of Lehman's view, contending that the legal details are closer to neo-Babylonian patterns, though some features may go back to ancient legal traditions ("The Legal Background of Genesis 23," *JBL* 85 [1966]: 77–84). R. Westbrook relates the tripartite transactions in Akk. recovered from Ugarit (ca. 1200) to Gen 23 in which Abraham, Ephron, and the Hittites are the three parties, corresponding to two individuals involved in the property transfer and the Ugaritic king, who as legal authority permits the transaction to take place ("Purchase of the Cave of Machpelah," *Israel Law Review* 6 [1971]: 29–38). For more see Van Seters, *Abraham in History,* 98–100 and, more recently, Wenham, *Genesis 12–36,* 125.

[663] Tucker notes this factor in the discussion ("The Legal Background," 84).

tern known of deeds and transference of property at many different periods, but it possesses variations that preclude us from conclusively establishing the legal heritage of origin. Wenham rightly concludes that there is nothing in chap. 23 requiring a custom known only in the first millennium and no necessity (as shown above) to attribute the chapter to a source (P) different from the primary source of the Abraham story as a whole.[664]

STRUCTURE. The structure of the story is straightforward: vv. 1–2 present the introduction regarding Sarah's age and death at Hebron; vv. 3–18 describe the transaction between the Hittites and the patriarch for the burial parcel; and vv. 19–20 present the concluding details of Sarah's burial at Hebron, summarizing the Hittite deal. The central section (vv. 3–18) consists of three movements, each initiated by the same word *wayyāqom,* translated "rose" (vv. 3,7) or "was deeded" (v. 17). (1) The first movement (vv. 3–6) entails the initial round of negotiations in which Abraham requests a burial site, addressing the "Hittites," who reply agreeably. (2) The second movement (vv. 7–16) possesses two additional rounds of speeches, each introduced by the parallel phrase "bowed down before the people of the land" (vv. 7,12). The first round of speeches (vv. 7–11), addressed to the "people of the land," specifies and expands Abraham's initial request by naming and including the field of Ephron with the burial cave. Ephron interjects his response, remarkably exceeding the patriarch's request by donating the field to Abraham at no cost. The second round of speeches (vv. 12–16) begins with the patriarch's address, this time to "Ephron" himself, who accepts his insistence at paying full price and negotiates the terms of the Machpelah cave and field. (3) The last movement (vv. 17–18) narrates the completed negotiation.

vv. 1–2   Sarah's death at Hebron
vv. 3–18   Purchase of Machpelah for Sarah's burial
   vv. 3–6   Movement 1: Abraham requests a burial site (*wayyāqom,* "rose")
   vv. 7–16   Movement 2: Abraham transacts a burial site (*wayyāqom,* "rose")
      vv. 7–11   Round 1: Abraham chooses Ephron's field ("bowed down before the people of the land," v. 7)
      vv. 12–16   Round 2: Abraham and Ephron come to terms ("bowed down before the people of the land," v. 12)
   vv. 17–18   Movement 3: Machpelah "deeded" over *(wayyāqom)*
vv. 19–20 Sarah's burial at Hebron

Although the death and burial of Sarah are succinctly reported in vv. 1–2,19, the whole of the chapter is "by origin a unity"[665] since the purchase of Machpelah in vv. 3–18,20 is made understandably significant only by the matriarch's

---

[664] Wenham, *Genesis 16–50,* 125.

[665] Westermann views vv. 3–18,20 an elaboration on the death-burial report (*Genesis 12–36,* 371).

death and burial. Chapter 23 has a straightforward plot line held together by a number of lexical repetitions (as seen above). The recurring ideas of the Hittite burial site and the politeness sustained in the negotiations dominate the passage: "bury my/your dead" and "listen to us/me" interchange within the three dialogue sections (vv. 3–6,7–11,12–16):

v. 4 "bury my dead" ("listen to me")	v. 6 "listen to us . . . Bury your dead"
v. 8 "bury my dead . . . listen to me"	v. 11 "Listen to me . . . Bury your dead"
v. 13 "Listen to me . . . bury my dead"	v. 15 "Listen to me . . . Bury your dead"

Also important, the chapter repeatedly names the parties involved, detailing the successive stages in the negotiations. Although the specific meaning of each stage eludes us, it appears that Abraham fulfilled an established protocol. In the first round Abraham approached the "Hittites" (vv. 3,5), perhaps bureaucratic representatives of the people; in the second round he appeared before "the people of the land" (v. 7) including "Ephron," who is among them (v. 10), probably referring to a wider group of local citizens; in the third round he appeared again before "the people of the land" but addresses "Ephron" directly (v. 12). Twice the passage reports the setting, "in the hearing of all the Hittites who had come to the gate of his [Ephron's] city" (vv. 10,18). After Abraham specifies the field of Ephron as his choice (vv. 8–9), the scene evidently shifted to the town nearest the property whose chief residents witnessed the deal. The authenticity of the contract was beyond dispute and was indelibly marked in the memory of the community.

(1) Sarah's Death at Hebron (23:1–2)

[1]Sarah lived to be a hundred and twenty-seven years old. [2]She died at Kiriath Arba (that is, Hebron) in the land of Canaan, and Abraham went to mourn for Sarah and to weep over her.

23:1–2 The duration of 127 years for Sarah's life (v. 1) indicates she lived a long life blessed by God (cf. 24:36; 15:15; 25:8; Ps 90:10; Moses, Deut 34:7; Job, Job 42:16–17).[666] This chronological note puts the event thirty-seven years since the birth of Isaac (17:17), making Abraham 137 years old (17:17), and sixty-two years since entering Canaan (12:4). The location of her death is "Kiriath Arba" (v. 2), which is further defined as Hebron (e.g., 35:27; Judg 1:10) in the territory of Canaan (on Hebron, see comments on 13:18). The importance of the geographical notice is the reference to Canaan as the patriarch's residence and burial (v. 19; 25:9), reminiscent of the promises made to Abraham (12:5; 17:8). Mention of "Mamre" in v. 19 further identifies the site of burial as Hebron, which is the south Canaan home where many important

---

[666] The NIV follows the LXX, Vg. in which the last clause, "the years of the life of Sarah" (MT, see AV, NASB, NRSV), is omitted, probably judged a dittograph of v. 1a.

patriarchal activities concerning the promises occurred. "Kiriath Arba" means "city of four" *(qiryat 'arba'),*which may originally have referred to a group of four related cities (Aner, Eshcol, Mamre, and Hebron, see comments on 14:14).[667]

Abraham expresses the customary mourning over the deceased (cf. 37:34–35). Mourning rites in the ancient Near East and in the Bible include many of the same expressions of sorrow, for example, loud weeping, tearing clothes, sitting in dirt, wearing sackcloth, and shaving the head.[668] The passage describes the patriarch's audible cries at the side *(bô', "entered")* of Sarah's body. The terms "mourn" *(sāpad)* and "weep" *(bākâ)* are common in the vocabulary of grief over the dead or other disasters. *Sāpad* and its related noun *mispēd* ("mourning") involve crying out, exclamations of grief that may be a ritual lament (e.g., Jer 22:18; 34:5; 1 Kgs 13:30; Amos 5:16), although not the cries of a formal poetic lament *(qînâ).*[669] "Weep" *(bākâ)* is very common for a wide range of emotions, including joy (e.g., 29:11), but it usually expresses the grief of a person over the dead (e.g., 35:8) or troubling situations (e.g., 1 Sam 1:7–8; Ps 137:1). The term is associated at times with "tears" *(dim'â,* e.g., Isa 16:9); it is related to the verbal expressions of wailing. It occurs often in describing lament over the dead (e.g., 2 Sam 1:11; Isa 15:2–5).[670]

(2) The Purchase of the Burial Site (23:3–18)

³**Then Abraham rose from beside his dead wife and spoke to the Hittites. He said, ⁴"I am an alien and a stranger among you. Sell me some property for a burial site here so I can bury my dead."**

⁵**The Hittites replied to Abraham, ⁶"Sir, listen to us. You are a mighty prince among us. Bury your dead in the choicest of our tombs. None of us will refuse you his tomb for burying your dead."**

⁷**Then Abraham rose and bowed down before the people of the land, the Hittites. ⁸He said to them, "If you are willing to let me bury my dead, then listen to me and intercede with Ephron son of Zohar on my behalf ⁹so he will sell me the cave of Machpelah, which belongs to him and is at the end of his field. Ask him to sell it to me for the full price as a burial site among you."**

¹⁰**Ephron the Hittite was sitting among his people and he replied to Abraham in the hearing of all the Hittites who had come to the gate of his city. ¹¹"No, my lord," he said. "Listen to me; I give you the field, and I give you the cave that is in it. I give it to you in the presence of my people. Bury your dead."**

¹²**Again Abraham bowed down before the people of the land ¹³and he said to Ephron in their hearing, "Listen to me, if you will. I will pay the price of the field.**

---

[667] V. Hamilton, "Kiriath-Arba," *ABD* 4.84.

[668] For a detailed discussion, see X. H. T. Pham, *Mourning in the Ancient Near East and the Hebrew Bible,* JSOTSup 302 (Sheffield: Sheffield Academic Press, 1999).

[669] R. W. L. Moberly, "Lament," *NIDOTTE* 4.869–70.

[670] V. Hamp, "בָּכָה; *bākhāh*," *TDOT* 2.116–18.

Accept it from me so I can bury my dead there."

[14]Ephron answered Abraham, [15]"Listen to me, my lord; the land is worth four hundred shekels of silver, but what is that between me and you? Bury your dead."

[16]Abraham agreed to Ephron's terms and weighed out for him the price he had named in the hearing of the Hittites: four hundred shekels of silver, according to the weight current among the merchants.

[17]So Ephron's field in Machpelah near Mamre—both the field and the cave in it, and all the trees within the borders of the field—was deeded [18]to Abraham as his property in the presence of all the Hittites who had come to the gate of the city.

The interchange between the patriarch and the Hittites is a lively encounter that shows Abraham's elevated place in the eyes of his neighbors. As in the Abimelech treaty, the patriarch though an "alien" *(gēr)* is well received by the Hittites and is deemed a "mighty prince" (v. 6). The possession of Hittite property is reminiscent of the prophecy in 15:18–20 depicting Abraham's descendants receiving the land of the indigenous Canaanite populations, including the Hittites. By burying his wife within Hittite borders, the patriarch testifies to his faith in the divine word. This central unit consists of three dialogue parts (vv. 3–6; vv. 7–11; vv. 12–16) and ends in a completed transaction (vv. 17–18).

23:3–4 After an appropriate period of mourning, the patriarch "rose from beside his dead wife"[671] to seek property for a burial site from the Hittites. The term "Hittites" appears first in the Table of Nations (10:15, vol. 1A, p. 455) and is listed among the pre-Israelite inhabitants of Canaan (15:20), but their notoriety in the patriarchal accounts is the sale of land for the ancestral burial site at Hebron (25:9–10; 49:29–32). Later, intermarriage with Hittite women by Esau (26:34; 27:46: 36:2) distinguishes him from Jacob, whose wives are from the Terah-Nahor lineage residing in Aram (29:12,14). The presence of Hittites *(bĕnê ḥēt,* "sons of Heth") in the Hebron region, however, is puzzling to historians since the Hittites are not known to have resided in the southern area of Canaan. The problem is created by the term "Hittite," which can refer to at least three and possibly four different groups.[672] The Hittite empire of Anatolia (modern Turkey), probably an Indo-European people, experienced destruction in ca. 1200. The remnants migrated to northwest Syria, where they assimilated with existing Hittite vassal states forming the Neo-Hittite kingdoms (e.g., Carchemish, Aleppo, Hamath), although the entire promised land (from Lebanon

---

[671] Mourning rites involved the bereaved seated on the ground, e.g., Isa 3:26; 47:1; Jer 48:17–18; Job 2:8,13; Lam 2:10; sitting on the ground is a visible sign of emotional trauma (e.g., Ezek 26:16; Dan 10:15).

[672] H. A. Hoffner names the native Hattians, the immigrant Anatolian Hittites, the Neo-Hittite states of Syria, and the Semitic pre-Israelite "Hittites" in south Canaan ("The Hittites and Hurrians," in *Peoples of Old Testament Times* [Oxford: Clarendon, 1973], 197–200).

and the Euphrates to the Great Sea) was identified at one time as the "land of the Hittites" (Josh 1:4; cf. Judg 1:26). Aramean culture, however, eventually took over these states, and the term "Hittite" lost any remaining ethnic distinction. If the Hittites identified with Hebron, were possibly migrants from Anatolia or Syria, then we have a case of anachronism. Since the Hittites named in the Pentateuch, however, all have Semitic names (e.g., Ephron) and appear to fit in with the social practices of their Canaanite neighbors, it is reasonable to conclude that the Hittites of the Pentateuch were a separate group, not related directly to either the Anatolian or Syrian Hittites. The influence of Hittite culture (vocabulary, social and religious practices) in the Old Testament can be explained as the result of centuries of contact between Israel and those northern states that more directly exhibited Hittite influence.[673] Until more information becomes available, the origin of the pre-Israelite "Hittites" remains uncertain.

Abraham begins negotiations by citing his social status, "an alien *[gēr]* and a stranger *[tôšāb]*" (v. 4), which explains his landless condition. The foreigner motif essential to the Abraham story reappears (cf. comments on chaps. 18–19). "Stranger" *(tôšāb)*, also translated "settler, sojourner," is a nominal form from "dwell" *(yāšab)*. The terms "alien" and "stranger" appear as synonyms in many contexts (e.g., Lev 25:35; Ps 39:12[13]; 1 Chr 29:15); here the nouns may form a hendiadys, "a resident alien" (NAB, NJPS). The Levitical code distinguishes the two groups, suggesting that the stranger *(tôšāb)* has less status than the alien in some social and religious activities (Lev 22:10; 25:6; cf. Exod 12:45).[674]

Abraham makes the unassuming admission he is a "stranger" *(tôšāb),* indicating that he had no land, even for his dead. His request for land within Hittite holdings may be exceptional, and to win a hearing he presents himself unpretentiously as no threat. He specifies that his need for the property is as a sepulcher, not a homestead. Perhaps this explains in part the congeniality of the Hittite response (v. 6). "Property for a burial site" *(ʾăḥuzzat qeber,* vv. 4,9,20) indicates a tomb for the dead (49:30; 50:13). By itself *ʾăḥuzzâ* means "a landed possession" (36:43; 47:11; Lev 25:10), and its appearance here may allude to the earlier promise of a permanent "possession" for Abraham (17:8; cf. 48:4) though he remains "now an alien" *(māgôr,* "sojourning," 17:8). The man has no land of his own, but by acquiring Hittite property he demonstrates his reliance on the prior promise of the Lord (cp. Jer 32:6–15). Someday the one man will become a multitude, and his parcel of Hittite land will become a small part of a vast possession.

23:5–6 Abraham's requests are answered by the Hittites collectively (vv.

[673] Ibid., 221; id., "Hittites," *Peoples of the Old Testament World,* 152–54.
[674] A. H. Konkel, "תּוֹשָׁב" *NIDOTTE* 4.284–85.

5–6) and by Ephron individually (v. 11) in the same amicable mood.[675] The passage shows a delicately polite interchange between the parties by the recurring courteous address "listen to us/me" (vv. 6,8,11,13,15) and the prostrate or seated postures of the two chief participants (vv. 7,10,12). Special deference is shown Abraham by respectful address, "my lord" ("sir," NIV, vv. 6,11,15) and the commendation "You are a mighty prince" (v. 6). The Hebrew *'ĕlōhîm,* "mighty," may be a superlative adjective (e.g., AV, NIV, NASB, NRSV, REB),[676] or the customary divine name, "You are a prince of God" (NJB) or "an/the elect of God" (NAB, NJPS). Either rendering makes good sense in the passage (cf. comments on 30:8).[677] The Philistine Abimelech recognized that Abraham was a special recipient of divine favor (21:21). As a consequence of his stature, the Hittites exceed his request by granting any selection of "the choicest of our tombs" (v. 6) and assuring him that no one will refuse. R. Westbrook, however, proposes that the generosity of the Hittites and Ephron is self-serving, since a gift or partial payment can be easily rescinded whereas ownership based on a fully paid purchase must be conceded.[678]

23:7–9 Abraham bows before the Hittites (v. 7), taking a position of humility (18:2; Ruth 2:10) before proceeding with his specific request. This is the only place in Genesis where Abraham bows before inhabitants of Canaan. Reference to the Hittites as "the people of the land" may be a double entendre, however, meaning ostensibly the local inhabitants but also indicating that they are one of many populations in Canaan (v. 2) whose land will ultimately fall to Abraham's descendants (15:20). The patriarch was already prepared to name a parcel (v. 8), seeking land as well as a burial tomb as first promised (v. 9; cf. v. 6).[679] "Machpelah," based on its descriptions in vv. 17,19 and 25:9; 49:30;

---

[675] The MT has לֹו לֵאמֹר (v. 5), lit., "saying *to him* [Abraham]" (italics mine; not in NIV; see AV, NASB); SP, LXX have the homophone לֹא, "no," at vv. 5,11,14 as in MT's v. 11, "*No,* my lord" (italics mine); and *BHS* (also BDB 530) proposes לֻו, "*O that* you would hear me, sir!" (italics mine) at vv. 5,11,14 as in the MT's v. 13 ("if only you will"; cf. also 17:18; 30:34). These alternative readings to the MT are secondary, easing the redundant reference to Abraham in vv. 5,14 and at the same time heightening resistance (לֹא, as in v. 11) or courtesy (לֻו, as in v. 13) during the negotiations.

[676] *IBHS* §14.5b.

[677] D. W. Thomas concludes that there is no purely secular superlative when *'ĕlōhîm* occurs; it indicates that the person or object is superlative by reason of a relationship to God in some sense ("A Consideration of Some Unusual Ways of Expressing the Superlative in Hebrew," *VT* 3 [1953]: 215–16). In this way he deems "mighty prince" as a description of a person whose authority derives from God, thus making the prince exceptional.

[678] Westbrook, "Purchase of the Cave," 312–33.

[679] On the name "Zohar" cf. comments on 46:10.

50:13, likely named a plot of land entailing a field and cave.[680] By acquiring only the portion "at the end of his [Ephron's] field" (v. 9), the Hittite retains the territorial integrity of his land holding, and Abraham limits potential intrusion.[681] Moreover, by offering "full price" (lit., "full silver") the patriarch reflects both his wealth and his good faith in negotiating with Ephron, who can hardly refuse in light of the generosity already expressed by the Hittite council (v. 6). The mention of "full price" appears again only in the bartering between King David and Araunah for his threshing floor (1 Chr 21:22,24; cf. 2 Sam 24:22–23). Lest there be any ambiguity about ownership in the future, the patriarch makes the deal in the customary aboveboard manner.

23:10–11   Apparently, a delegation of Hittites and Abraham journey to Ephron's residence ("his city," v. 10) to make the proposal. The narrative describes the typical setting at the city gate for civil transactions (e.g., Deut 25:7; Ruth 4:1). Reference to Ephron's "sitting" *(yōšēb)* at the gate indicates his prominence (e.g., Job 29:7–8; Prov 31:23). Twice the narrative identifies the witnesses to the agreement, "all the Hittites who had come to the gate of his/ the city" (vv. 10,18), referring to the citizens.[682] The mention of "all the Hittites" reflects the idea of public awareness of the transaction; an arrangement with the alien Abraham draws a large gathering. That Abraham as "an alien and a stranger" (v. 4; 17:8; 21:23) appears at the Hittite town of Ephron recalls the motif of hospitality (18:1; 19:1). Earlier episodes depict local authorities abusing traveling strangers (12:15; 19:9; 20:2). The treatment in this case is favorable toward Abraham, again demonstrating the exceptional standing of the patriarch in the eyes of the nations.

The response of Ephron can be taken as a remarkable act of gratuity or a bargaining ploy. He respectfully demurs the idea of purchase and offers the cave and its field as a gift (v. 11). Three times the term "give" *(nātan)* appears, enhancing the generosity that Ephron's offer entails. This repetition matches the threefold occurrence of "give" *(nātan,* "sell, pay" NIV) spoken by Abraham (vv. 4,9,13). If this were a true counterproposal, Ephron may have wanted to

---

[680] The LXX (and Vg. *speluncam duplicem*) interprets the Hb. as a common noun instead of an appellative, translating τὸ σπήλαιον τὸ διπλοῦν, "double cave," perhaps understanding הַמַּכְפֵּלָה (Machpelah) from כָּפַל, "double, double over" (BDB 495). Today tradition identifies the Hebron cave with the tomb housed by the Arab mosque *Haram el-Khalil,* formerly a Byzantine church before the Arab conquest, making this traditional site sacred to Jews, Christians, and Arabs (Sarna, *Genesis,* 159).

[681] Westermann, *Genesis 12–36,* 374, "allowing the possibility that it (the burial plot) may be detached."

[682] The opposite occurs in 34:24, "all that went out of the gate of his city." Although "going out" (יָצָא) and "coming in" (בּוֹא) may be used of community leaders (e.g., Deut 32:1; 1 Kgs 3:17; 15:17; Jer 17:19; Amos 5:3), the expression does not require that these were elders (cf. Ruth 4:9–11); see G. Evans, "'Coming' and 'Going' at the City Gate—A Discussion of Professor Speiser's Paper," *BASOR* 150 (1958): 28–33.

curry favor with Abraham or his fellow Hittites. The passage is very conscious of the presence of his people ("his city," v. 10; "my people," v. 11). If understood this way, the shine of Hittite hospitality is dulled somewhat. N. MacDonald, however, regards the negotiations as a form of haggling. He comments on the practice: "Extravagant language and behavior often accompany the haggle: friendliness and expressions of affections may give way to ridicule and oaths. In the Middle East, the buyer may be addressed with kinship language and offered the item as a 'gift.' However, haggling is usually perceived as a practice that is socially negative; this is true of customers, traders, and anthropologists. For this reason, the practice usually requires a degree of social distance."[683] If so, Ephron's behavior is not benevolent but self-serving. Abraham's compliance kept the negotiations a positive experience and averted the detrimental effects that haggling can produce.

23:12–13 Abraham bows again (v. 12), expressing gratitude and humility before negotiating further (v. 13). To ensure a family burial for future generations ("so that I can bury my dead there," v. 13), Abraham prefers a formal business arrangement involving a purchase price in the presence of witnesses. He readily accepts, however, the offer of the "field" (v. 13), thereby securing his initial goal of property (v. 9).

23:14–16 Ephron concedes to the Hebrew's wish and sets the price at "four hundred shekels of silver" (v. 15). Whether the price is reasonable (cp. 20:16) or exorbitant (cp. Jer 32:7) is uncertain.[684] Ephron presents the price as irrefutable by minimizing the expense against the significance of the land deal. When Ephron exclaims "what is that between you and me," he indicates that their newly formed relationship supersedes any advantage gained by Abraham squabbling over the price. Further, Ephron's conclusion, "bury your dead," repeats the language in the Hittites' initial offer, "Bury your dead in the choicest of our tombs" (v. 6), suggesting that the price should not stand in the way of his goal. The language exhibits the interplay between the two passages by the inversion of terms: "bury your dead" (*qĕbōr ʾet mētekā,* v. 6) and "your dead bury" (*wĕʾet mĕtĕkā qĕbōr,* v. 15)

Verse 16 describes Abraham's acceptance of the price with no reservation (cp. 21:25). That the transaction is legitimate and permanent is the point of the verse; it describes Abraham counting out the purchase price in the eyes of numerous witnesses, adding that the silver met the proper standard (cf. Jer 32:9–10). Silver coinage was a much later development; thus the transaction price involved the measurement of a shekel by weight. Variance in scales

---

[683] MacDonald, "Listening to Abraham," 31 (esp. 30–31 and n. 22).

[684] Speiser considers the price exorbitant since Omri paid six thousand shekels for the entirety of Samaria (1 Kgs 16:24), but, as Speiser himself observes, the weight of the shekels often varied among centers; thus such comparisons, especially since the Omri period is much later, is speculative (*Genesis,* 171).

required agreement on the accepted ratio (e.g., "sanctuary shekel," Exod 30:13; cf. 2 Sam 14:26; Prov 20:10,23); in this case the measure was the one "current among the merchants" (cf. Amos 8:5; Mic 6:11).

23:17–18 These verses record the pertinent information of the transaction, including the property's location, the parties involved, and witnesses. The parcel sold by Ephron includes the field at Machpelah with its accompanying cave and trees (v. 17). The congregated Hittites at the gate witness the transfer of "property" *(miqnâ)* rights (v. 18), ensuring that the transaction is legitimate. The detailed, exacting language of the transferal reflects a formal recording of a deed, although no mention is made of a "written document" *(sēper miqnâ,* Jer 32:11,14,16). "Deeded" translates *qûm* at vv. 17,20,[685] used in a commercial sense, meaning "to transfer property obligated to someone" (e.g., Lev 25:30; 27:19).[686]

(3) The Burial of Sarah (23:19–20)

¹⁹Afterward Abraham buried his wife Sarah in the cave in the field of Machpelah near Mamre (which is at Hebron) in the land of Canaan. ²⁰So the field and the cave in it were deeded to Abraham by the Hittites as a burial site.

23:19–20 The author repeats the specifications of the burial site (v. 19) and ends the account with the transfer of the deeded property (v. 20) so as to confirm Abraham's possession of the land beyond dispute. Verse 19 forms an inclusio with v. 2, providing the denouement for the chapter. Mention of "Mamre" and "Canaan" again at the close reflects the author's intention at demonstrating the beginning fulfillment of the land promise. Verse 20 repeats the essentials of vv. 17–18 and adds that the property formerly belonged to the Hittites.

16. A Wife for Isaac (24:1–67)

This lively story of the search for Isaac's bride can be taken at first blush as a lovely romance but absent theological importance. Since the Abraham narratives as a whole are not typically verbose, the length of the chapter as the longest in the book implies otherwise. As a part of the epilogue (22:20–25:11) to the Abraham story, its value lies in transitioning to the heirs of the promise, Isaac-Rebekah. Also the story affords the revisiting of the central theme and important motifs of the Abraham story. In addition to the many allusions to the former accounts,[687] chap. 24 portrays a second "call" to leave Aram (Haran)

---

[685] The same term רְקִים ("rose") appears in vv. 3,7.

[686] *HALOT* 3.1087.

[687] E.g., v. 1 and 12:2; 18:11; 22:17. Wenham provides a wide range of references, linking chap. 24 with prior accounts *(Genesis 16–50,* 137); Van Seters concluded that "the chapter is not self-contained" *(Abraham in History,* 243).

and reside in Canaan.[688] Sarna points especially to v. 58 (cp. 12:1,4), where Rebekah unreservedly answers, "I will go" *(hālak).*[689] She is the "female Abraham"[690] who is challenged with a divine call to leave family and homeland on the testimony of the servant's answered prayer (vv. 40–48). The chapter affirms that the task and its success are the result of God's providential oversight both overtly and inferentially. The latter is evidenced by the ease in finding the woman and the absence of any serious obstruction to the servant's desires. All give assent to the mission and its divine direction (24:50). Yet it would be short-sighted to reduce the narrative to this one theological proposition. There are the human responses that contribute to the achievement of the divine assignment.[691] Even as Abraham answered the call to "go" *(hālak,* 12:1; 22:2) by choosing to depart *(hālak,* 12:4; 22:3), the persons involved in this decision must also make a choice (cf. the play on "take" and "go," 24:51,58,61). Typical Hebrew narrative assumes that the true protagonist of every account is God, whether or not explicitly stated, but the human dimension is real whose decisions are authentic choices. In this story the Lord achieves his purposes through the loyal but cagey servant, the ambitious Laban, and the respectful but independently minded Rebekah.

As another "Abraham," Rebekah's immigration to Canaan represents the Nahor branch of the Terah family (22:23) who remained outside the land, whereas Lot, a member of the Haran branch (11:27), travels with Abraham to Canaan (11:31; 12:4). Both the Lot and Rebekah accounts show that by virtue of their association with the Abraham family, they enjoy the blessing of prosperity (13:1–2,5; 24:1,35,53). Also Rebekah's move from Aram to the promised Canaan fits the pattern of the matriarchs of Israel; Sarai, of course, and later Jacob's wives, Leah and Rachel, depart Aram with their husband upon the call of God (12:1; 31:13). By proxy she also fulfills for Isaac the patriarchal role of departing one's homeland as an alien; Abraham and Jacob experience such alienation, but Isaac never leaves his land of birth (Gerar is the south boundary of Canaan, 10:19). He is specifically forbidden to leave for Egypt (26:1–2), unlike Abraham and Jacob.

For the survival and success of Jacob, Rebekah is instrumental in his escape from Esau. In Aram, Jacob finds refuge with her brother Laban, first mentioned in our account (24:29). Laban's family, including his sister, who is Rebekah,

---

[688] The term "go, went" *(h-l-k;* vv. 4,5,8,10,38,39,40,42,55,56,58,61,65) brings to mind the initial call and response of Abraham (12:1,4,5) as well as the Moriah test (22:2,3,5,6,8,13,19); cp. 24:7 in which Abraham links his call (12:1) to the task of his servant.

[689] Sarna, *Genesis,* 161.

[690] Wenham's term, *Genesis 16–50,* 138.

[691] E. J. van Wolde, "Telling and Retelling: The Words of the Servant in Genesis 24," in *Synchronic or Diachronic? A Debate on Method in Old Testament Exegesis* (Leiden: Brill, 1995), 227–44.

and his daughters Leah and Rachel, provides the wives of Israel's ancestors Isaac and Jacob. In both cases Laban benefits from the riches and blessing divinely bestowed by God upon the patriarchs. This Aram connection is another parade example of the blessing promised for the nations through Abraham's offspring (12:3).

The servant's sojourn to Aram is a reversal of Abraham's departure from the Terah family for Canaan (12:4). Expressing the acquisition of Isaac's wife in the vein of Abraham's trek further authenticates the call of God upon Rebekah as Sarah's successor. That the wives of the patriarchs come from outside Canaan recalls the patriarchs' alien status and contrasts the appointed lineage of Isaac and Jacob with the rivals Ishmael and Esau, who married locally (21:21; 26:34–35). The narratives of the two searches for wives, Rebekah and Rachel (chap. 29), reflect the two issues of family and territorial boundaries. Isaac and Jacob must marry within the family boundary (endogamy), but the search requires the search outside the land.[692] This tension in the respective stories is evident by Abraham's servant, who impatiently desires to return to Canaan (vv. 54–56) and by Jacob's intention to return as soon as possible (28:21; 30:25; 31:30).

COMPOSITION. That the chapter in its present form is a unified work by the Yahwist (J) has been widely supported in the last half-century.[693] Critics differ, however, about whether there was an underlying oral source adapted by the Yahwist or whether the chapter essentially was the Yahwist's own creation.[694] The proposal that an original story of betrothal was reshaped by a late theological hand so as to correlate the episode with the patriarchal theme of promise (e.g., vv.

[692] J. Cook, "Wells, Women, and Faith," *Proceedings of the Eastern Great Lakes Biblical Society* 15 (1997): 11–18.

[693] Although Wellhausen and early source critics contended for a unified chapter, those who followed argued for multiple sources (J,E), relying on perceived discrepancies (e.g., twice Laban goes to the well, vv. 29b,30b; e.g., Skinner, *Genesis,* 340); but these differences were minimized or explained away, making the now prominent view the old opinion of Wellhausen, e.g., Speiser, *Genesis,* 182; von Rad, *Genesis,* 253–54; Van Seters, *Abraham in History,* 240–42; Westermann, *Genesis 12–36,* 383; and Coats, *Genesis,* 167–70. It is interesting that although the same kinds of problems found in chap. 24 occur in other passages, leading these same critics to discern multiple sources, in this case they judged the problems as minor and assumed chap. 24 was a single work.

[694] The putative folktale varies: e.g., a story of an idealized, faithful servant who became an example (Roth, Coats), a family marriage tale modified into a guidance narrative (Westermann), or a bridal transfer story about a willing bride that became a theological epilogue to the Abraham narrative (Aitken); see, e.g., W. M. W. Roth, "The Wooing of Rebekah: A Tradition-Critical Study in Genesis 24," *CBQ* 34 (1972): 177–87; Coats, *Genesis,* 170; Westermann, *Genesis 12–36,* 383; and K. Aitken, "The Wooing of Rebekah: A Study in the Development of the Tradition," *JSOT* 30 (1984): 3–23. But Van Seters (*Abraham in History,* 246) departs from the notion of an oral folktale by contending for an original literary composition by his sixth-century Yahwist, who used a royal "messenger" form demonstrating Abraham's treatment by his relatives as a king (id., *Prologue to History,* 267).

33–36) underestimates the role of the promissory theme as the constituent building block of the chapter. This kind of form-tradition reconstruction typically assumes that a biblical story possesses an original simple plot line that is then elaborated upon in successive stages, culminating in the final, advanced theological formulation. There is no reason, however, why the theological meaning of the story could not have been original and the plot line could not have been complex. The similarities commonly cited between examples of the conventional plot (e.g., guidance narrative or search for a wife story) are so reductionistic as to be suspect for a useful indicator of such a "literary convention." What lies beneath these accounts is a prevailing social practice, not necessarily a story convention.

The explicit language of promissory blessing repeatedly echoed in chap. 24 (esp. 12:1–3,7; 22:17) is only one line of evidence showing dependence on the theme of call and promise that is central to the Abraham narrative. The motivation of the search, the parameters of the search, the divine authentication of the discovery, and the success or failure of the search are dependent on the call and promise given to Abraham. The call, blessing, and inheritance motifs are not addenda to the search, not even important ones, but are the essence of the search. The chapter only works because its author counts on the reader's knowledge of the Abraham account and the Isaac and Jacob events re-imaging Abraham (21:2; 25:5; 26:12–13,29; 29:1–14).

Further, it is apparent that the author has related the chapter to the whole of the Abraham story and knows also of the Isaac-Rebekah and Jacob-Laban narratives, indicating that the composition was conceived in light of the former.[695] There is no compelling reason, however, to date the chapter as late as the exile or even the monarchy.[696] The parallels between the Rebekah story and the accounts in chap. 29 and Exodus 2, where a wife is also obtained in a foreign land, suggest a betrothal custom that was known in an early period. The Ugaritic epic of King Keret depicts his search for a wife in a distant land. Its early date (ca. 1300) makes an early setting for chap. 24's composition plausible.[697]

STRUCTURE. This expansive chapter has three settings: (1) the Canaan context, where Abraham gives his servant the assignment to procure a wife from his father's family (vv. 2–9); (2) the Aram Naharaim setting, where the arrangement for Rebekah is negotiated successfully (vv. 10–61); and (3) the

---

[695] Although these intertextual relationships are admitted, they are usually attributed to a secondary editor whose purpose was to integrate disparate patriarchal stories into the epic account, e.g., Thompson, *The Origin Tradition*, 102; Van Seters, on the basis of chronological and other links, believes that the original arrangement was possibly 22:20–24; 25:1–6; 24:1–67; and 25:11 (*Abraham in History*, 248).

[696] E.g., A. Rofé, on lexical, syntactical, and theological grounds, contends for a postexilic (fifth century) date by a single author ("An Enquiry into the Betrothal of Rebekah," in *Die Hebräische Bibel und ihre zweifache Nachgeschichte: Festschrift für Rolf Rendtorff zum 65. Geburtstag* [Neukirchen: Neukirchener Verlag, 1990], 27–39).

[697] For discussion of the Keret epic and chap. 24, see S. B. Parker, "The Historical Composition of KRT and the Cult of El," *ZAW* 89 (1977): 161–75; Aitken, "The Wooing of Rebekah," 3–23; and Hamilton, *Genesis Chapters 18–50*, 163.

return to Canaan, where Isaac and Rebekah marry (vv. 62–67). The lengthy second section set in Aram Naharaim narrates two different backdrops: at the village well, the encounter of the servant and Rebekah (vv. 10–27), and at her mother's house, the appeal of the servant to Laban for Rebekah (vv. 28–61).

vv. 1–9   Abraham commissions the servant
             v. 1   Abraham blessed
             vv. 2–9   The servant swears an oath
vv. 10–61   The servant obtains Rebekah
             vv. 10–14   The servant's prayer
             vv. 15–27   Rebekah at the well
             vv. 28–33   Laban provides for the servant
             vv. 34–49   The servant reports answered prayer
             vv. 50–58   Rebekah agrees to return
             vv. 59–61   Laban blesses Rebekah
vv. 62–67   Isaac marries Rebekah

(1) Abraham Commissions the Servant (24:1–9)

¹Abraham was now old and well advanced in years, and the LORD had blessed him in every way. ²He said to the chief servant in his household, the one in charge of all that he had, "Put your hand under my thigh. ³I want you to swear by the LORD, the God of heaven and the God of earth, that you will not get a wife for my son from the daughters of the Canaanites, among whom I am living, ⁴but will go to my country and my own relatives and get a wife for my son Isaac."

⁵The servant asked him, "What if the woman is unwilling to come back with me to this land? Shall I then take your son back to the country you came from?"

⁶"Make sure that you do not take my son back there," Abraham said. ⁷"The LORD, the God of heaven, who brought me out of my father's household and my native land and who spoke to me and promised me on oath, saying, 'To your offspring I will give this land'—he will send his angel before you so that you can get a wife for my son from there. ⁸If the woman is unwilling to come back with you, then you will be released from this oath of mine. Only do not take my son back there." ⁹So the servant put his hand under the thigh of his master Abraham and swore an oath to him concerning this matter.

After the introduction gives the occasion of the commissioning (v. 1), two paragraphs of dialogue constitute this first section of the chapter (vv. 2–4; vv. 5–9). The sign of the oath, "put your/his hand under the thigh," forms the boundaries of the unit (vv. 2,9). Abraham in the first speech commissions his chief servant under oath (*šābaʿ*, v. 3) to seek a wife for Isaac (vv. 2–4); the charge appears twice, first negatively and then positively: "you will not get a wife for my son" (v. 3b) and "get a wife for my son" (v. 4b). Verse 5, spoken by the unnamed servant, provides the hinge verse connecting the two Abraham speeches. He raises the question, "Shall I then [certainly] take your son back?"

which leads to Abraham's second speech (vv. 6–8); the twofold prohibition, "do not take my son back," establishes the literary boundaries (vv. 6,8). The concluding verse (v. 9) describes the servant's acceptance of the charge (v. 2–3), back referencing the charge by repeating the key terms in the same order, "servant," "thigh," and "swear an oath" (*šābaʿ*, vv. 3,9). The symmetry evidenced in this first section is fitting for the last words spoken by Abraham, his final testament (cf. 49:29–33; 50:24–26). His speeches beautifully memorialize his call and his confidence in the Lord's promises but are turned outward as he prepares his household for his succession. As Wenham explains, "Abraham enters history through the divine promises (12:1–3,7); he passes out of history with this promise on his lips."[698]

ABRAHAM BLESSED (24:1). **24:1** The motivation for the dispatch of his servant to obtain a wife for Isaac is Abraham's anticipation of imminent succession. His aged condition and the accumulated wealth of his years make it prudent to secure for Isaac a wife whose offspring will perpetuate the inheritance. "Old and well advanced in years" describes the aged Joshua and David, who face the concluding events of their lives (Josh 13:1; 23:1; 1 Kgs 1:1). "Blessed" *(bārak)* indicates the man's prosperity (vv. 1,35; cp. 25:11); the Hebrew term *b-r-k* in various forms repeatedly appears in the story, reinforcing the idea of divine favor (vv.1,27,31,35,48,60).[699] Age and wealth are often signs of a blessed life (e.g., Job 42:12).

THE SERVANT SWEARS AN OATH (24:2–9). **24:2** The importance of the assignment is heightened by the stature of the servant Abraham selected; he is the senior administrator (*zāqēn*, "elder"; NIV, "chief") of the entire household (v. 2). Also the patriarch imposes an oath on the servant, requiring the sign of placing his hand on Abraham's thigh. The same rite occurs when aged Jacob implores Joseph to bury him in Canaan (47:29). The thigh indicates the procreative power and heritage of the patriarch's position as the source of the family.

24:3–4 The oath must be undertaken in the sight of the Lord, who will judge the efficacy of the servant's action. The unique creation appellative, "God of heaven and the God of earth" (v. 3), describing Abraham's deity does more than identify his God; its cosmic language adds further solemnity to the task. This divine title appears in a slightly modified form in the benediction of Melchizedek (14:19) and in the mention of Abraham's oath to God (14:22). In both chaps. 14 and 24, there is an association of the Creator and the election of Abraham, suggesting a cosmic significance for his calling. Also both passages show that Abraham's deity is not among the Canaanite deities, implying why no suppliant of the local gods can be chosen for Isaac's wife (v. 3b). Mosaic

---

[698] Wenham, *Genesis 16–50*, 140.
[699] Even the homonym *b-r-k,* "kneel," appears (v. 11).

legislation prohibits intermarriage with groups outside the covenant nation, leading to religious apostasy (e.g., Exod 34:15–16; Deut 7:3–4; cf. Judg 3:6; Ezra 9:2,12).

Only one family therefore can confidently qualify, the Nahor branch of his father's lineage (v. 4). "My country *['ereṣ]* and my own relatives *[môledet]*" (v. 4; also vv. 7,38,40,41) recall the divine commissioning of Abraham at Haran (12:1). "My son" is also a reminder of the promises, appearing five times (vv. 3,4,6,7,8; also vv. 37,38,40); the phrase occurs twice in the sacrifice of Isaac (22:7,8) and brings to mind the poignancy of "your son, your only beloved" (22:2,16; NIV "your only son"). The repetition further draws the contrast to the rejected son (Ishmael; cp. "my son," 21:10) whose wife was obtained from Egyptian stock by the mother Hagar (21:21). From the perspective of the patriarch's hope for the future, this assignment is the servant's most important one undertaken. The inner chiastic elements of the exhortation capture the task of the servant:

unto my land—unto my country—*you will go*
you will take—a wife for my son—Isaac

These same verbs but in opposite order echo 22:2: "Take your son . . . go to the region of Moriah." The unnamed servant has his own test to endure, but the patriarch assures him that the Lord's angel will superintend his journey (v. 5), perhaps reminiscent of the rescue by the angel of the Lord (22:11,15).

24:5 Because of the gravity of the matter, the servant seeks clarification so as to ensure carrying out his instructions exactly (v. 5). In the event of a contingency, the servant requests an exception to the prohibition. The emphatic rhetoric he employs, lit., "Should I certainly take back *[hāšēb 'āšîb]* your son?"[700] points up a possible complication anticipated by the servant. The servant here by his caution and foresight demonstrates why he had obtained high position in Abraham's eyes. On the face of it, there is good reason to suppose that the woman's family will require confirmation by meeting the suitor himself. Negotiations may only succeed by Isaac's personal presence.

24:6–8 "Watch yourself" (*hiššāmer lĕkā,* "make sure" NIV) accentuates the patriarch's warning against taking his son (v. 6).[701] He recalls his own successful sojourn to Canaan by the grace of the Lord and comforts the servant by promising the Lord's angel will lead the way (v. 7). The Lord's track record was sterling; he faithfully kept his oath by providing offspring and land.

The appellative "God of heaven" is more common in postexilic literature (e.g., 2 Chr 36:23; Ezra 5:11; Neh 1:4), leading many to cite it as evidence of a late composition. The expression, however, occurs in the preexilic prophet

---

[700] Infinitive absolute construction, הָשֵׁב אָשִׁיב.

[701] Cf. the same construction, e.g., in 31:24,29; esp. Exod 34:12; Deut 12:30, forewarning against foreign entanglements.

Jonah (1:9), but more importantly the name is likely selected as an allusion to heaven's rescue of Isaac and Ishmael (22:11,15; 21:17). Although in chap. 12 there is no mention of a guiding angel for Abraham's trek, his exhortation implies a parallel between his experience and the servant's journey, the reversal of Abraham's trail. "His angel" (24:7) may be taken as the "angel of the LORD" first met by Hagar in the wilderness (see comments on 16:7,9,11; cp. "angel of God," 21:17) who also rescued Isaac at Moriah (22:11,15). A guiding messenger was common in Israel's journey in the wilderness (Exod 14:19; 23:20,23; 32:34; 33:2; Num 20:16; 22:22).

Nevertheless, Abraham is not presumptuous; the woman (or her family, v. 41) may be unwilling, in which case the servant bears no responsibility ("released")[702] for failing to return her (v. 8). The only uncompromising obligation, however, remains. In the Hebrew the emphatic "only *[raq]* my son" occurs at the head of the prohibition (v. 8).[703]

24:9 With this one caveat now in mind, the servant submits to the oath and its signature ritual (v. 9).

(2) The Servant Obtains Rebekah (24:10–61)

[10]Then the servant took ten of his master's camels and left, taking with him all kinds of good things from his master. He set out for Aram Naharaim and made his way to the town of Nahor. [11]He had the camels kneel down near the well outside the town; it was toward evening, the time the women go out to draw water.

[12]Then he prayed, "O LORD, God of my master Abraham, give me success today, and show kindness to my master Abraham. [13]See, I am standing beside this spring, and the daughters of the townspeople are coming out to draw water. [14]May it be that when I say to a girl, 'Please let down your jar that I may have a drink,' and she says, 'Drink, and I'll water your camels too'—let her be the one you have chosen for your servant Isaac. By this I will know that you have shown kindness to my master."

[15]Before he had finished praying, Rebekah came out with her jar on her shoulder. She was the daughter of Bethuel son of Milcah, who was the wife of Abraham's brother Nahor. [16]The girl was very beautiful, a virgin; no man had ever lain with her. She went down to the spring, filled her jar and came up again.

[17]The servant hurried to meet her and said, "Please give me a little water from your jar."

[18]"Drink, my lord," she said, and quickly lowered the jar to her hands and gave him a drink.

[19]After she had given him a drink, she said, "I'll draw water for your camels

---

[702] נקה, "to be free from sworn obligation" *(niphal)*, 24:8,41 (*HALOT* 2.720), hence free from both the offense and punishment (cf. נקה + מן at 24:8,41 and Num 5:31; Judg 15:3; Ps 19:13[14]), G. Warmuth, "נקה *nāqâ*," *TDOT* 9.555–56.

[703] E.g., the strong prohibition employing רק, "only," at 19:8; cf. Exod 8:28–29[24–25]; Deut 12:16.

too, until they have finished drinking." [20]So she quickly emptied her jar into the trough, ran back to the well to draw more water, and drew enough for all his camels. [21]Without saying a word, the man watched her closely to learn whether or not the LORD had made his journey successful.

[22]When the camels had finished drinking, the man took out a gold nose ring weighing a beka and two gold bracelets weighing ten shekels. [23]Then he asked, "Whose daughter are you? Please tell me, is there room in your father's house for us to spend the night?"

[24]She answered him, "I am the daughter of Bethuel, the son that Milcah bore to Nahor." [25]And she added, "We have plenty of straw and fodder, as well as room for you to spend the night."

[26]Then the man bowed down and worshiped the LORD, [27]saying, "Praise be to the LORD, the God of my master Abraham, who has not abandoned his kindness and faithfulness to my master. As for me, the LORD has led me on the journey to the house of my master's relatives."

[28]The girl ran and told her mother's household about these things. [29]Now Rebekah had a brother named Laban, and he hurried out to the man at the spring. [30]As soon as he had seen the nose ring, and the bracelets on his sister's arms, and had heard Rebekah tell what the man said to her, he went out to the man and found him standing by the camels near the spring. [31]"Come, you who are blessed by the LORD," he said. "Why are you standing out here? I have prepared the house and a place for the camels."

[32]So the man went to the house, and the camels were unloaded. Straw and fodder were brought for the camels, and water for him and his men to wash their feet. [33]Then food was set before him, but he said, "I will not eat until I have told you what I have to say."

"Then tell us," [Laban] said.

[34]So he said, "I am Abraham's servant. [35]The LORD has blessed my master abundantly, and he has become wealthy. He has given him sheep and cattle, silver and gold, menservants and maidservants, and camels and donkeys. [36]My master's wife Sarah has borne him a son in her old age, and he has given him everything he owns. [37]And my master made me swear an oath, and said, 'You must not get a wife for my son from the daughters of the Canaanites, in whose land I live, [38]but go to my father's family and to my own clan, and get a wife for my son.'

[39]"Then I asked my master, 'What if the woman will not come back with me?'

[40]"He replied, 'The LORD, before whom I have walked, will send his angel with you and make your journey a success, so that you can get a wife for my son from my own clan and from my father's family. [41]Then, when you go to my clan, you will be released from my oath even if they refuse to give her to you—you will be released from my oath.'

[42]"When I came to the spring today, I said, 'O LORD, God of my master Abraham, if you will, please grant success to the journey on which I have come. [43]See, I am standing beside this spring; if a maiden comes out to draw water and I say to her, "Please let me drink a little water from your jar," [44]and if she says to me, "Drink, and I'll draw water for your camels too," let her be the one the LORD

has chosen for my master's son.'

⁴⁵"Before I finished praying in my heart, Rebekah came out, with her jar on her shoulder. She went down to the spring and drew water, and I said to her, 'Please give me a drink.'

⁴⁶"She quickly lowered her jar from her shoulder and said, 'Drink, and I'll water your camels too.' So I drank, and she watered the camels also.

⁴⁷"I asked her, 'Whose daughter are you?'

"She said, 'The daughter of Bethuel son of Nahor, whom Milcah bore to him.'

"Then I put the ring in her nose and the bracelets on her arms, ⁴⁸and I bowed down and worshiped the LORD. I praised the LORD, the God of my master Abraham, who had led me on the right road to get the granddaughter of my master's brother for his son. ⁴⁹Now if you will show kindness and faithfulness to my master, tell me; and if not, tell me, so I may know which way to turn."

⁵⁰Laban and Bethuel answered, "This is from the LORD; we can say nothing to you one way or the other. ⁵¹Here is Rebekah; take her and go, and let her become the wife of your master's son, as the LORD has directed."

⁵²When Abraham's servant heard what they said, he bowed down to the ground before the LORD. ⁵³Then the servant brought out gold and silver jewelry and articles of clothing and gave them to Rebekah; he also gave costly gifts to her brother and to her mother. ⁵⁴Then he and the men who were with him ate and drank and spent the night there.

When they got up the next morning, he said, "Send me on my way to my master."

⁵⁵But her brother and her mother replied, "Let the girl remain with us ten days or so; then you may go."

⁵⁶But he said to them, "Do not detain me, now that the LORD has granted success to my journey. Send me on my way so I may go to my master."

⁵⁷Then they said, "Let's call the girl and ask her about it." ⁵⁸So they called Rebekah and asked her, "Will you go with this man?"

"I will go," she said.

⁵⁹So they sent their sister Rebekah on her way, along with her nurse and Abraham's servant and his men. ⁶⁰And they blessed Rebekah and said to her,

"Our sister, may you increase
   to thousands upon thousands;
may your offspring possess
   the gates of their enemies."

⁶¹Then Rebekah and her maids got ready and mounted their camels and went back with the man. So the servant took Rebekah and left.

Critical to the development of this scene is the recurring testimony of the servant's answered prayer in discovering Rebekah (vv. 27,42–48). The result is the recognition by both parties that the betrothal is from God (v. 50).

The motif of alien *(gēr)* so important to the Abraham narrative as a whole (e.g., 12:10; 15:13; 19:9; 20:1; 21:23) reappears in this section, mentioned specifically by Abraham (24:4), but the alien depicted in this story is the servant who journeys to Aram. The passage repeatedly describes the hospitality of the Laban household toward the stranger, beginning with Rebekah at the well and continuing at her house. His prayer asks for a sign that will depend on the woman carrying out the custom of hospitality. The conclusion of the negotiations involves the question of waiting for a prolonged period of hospitality (ten days) to elapse before their departure (vv. 55–59; cf. Judg 19:1–10). The servant apparently believes he jeopardizes the mission by any delay, and Rebekah volunteers to depart immediately.

After the first scene at Abraham's household (vv. 1–9), the patriarch is no longer directly involved in the account, though he is constantly referred to by others. His servant dominates the second scene (vv. 10–61), whose speeches and actions serve to divide the passage into three units: the journey and prayer of the servant at Aram Naharaim (vv. 10–14), his encounters with Rebekah and Laban at the well and house (vv. 15–60), and his departure with the betrothed (v. 61). L. Teugels' study of characterization finds that the servant evolves into a complete representative of Abraham.[704] This occurs in two ways. First, although he appears in all scenes (except v. 67), he remains anonymous, highlighting his role as Abraham's proxy. Second, the titles "servant," "lord," and "blessed by the LORD" used of the servant mark a progression in his task. "Servant" (*ʿebed* [13x]) is his common title, but Rebekah (v. 18) addresses him as "lord" (*ʾădōnāy*). This title for Abraham ("master" [21x]; once for Isaac, v. 65) subtly identifies the servant with Abraham, for now he takes on the mantle of his master in her eyes. The appellative "you who are blessed by the LORD" (v. 31) is more appropriate for Abraham, for he is the one noted as blessed by God (vv. 24:1,35). For the Laban household who will never see Abraham or his son Isaac, the servant laden with gifts is the sole manifestation of their kinsman.

Rebekah is another protagonist in this section, but she recedes somewhat when Laban is introduced. Although the two men negotiate her future (v. 50), the woman has the final say in the decision and therefore retains her prominence in the account (vv. 57–58). The passive role of her father Bethuel is a puzzle for commentators, but this may have had a literary function, depicting both Laban and Rebekah as independent, aggressive persons (see comments on v. 50).

THE SERVANT'S PRAYER (24:10–14). The term "his/my master" (*ʾădōnāy*) marks the boundaries of this unit (vv. 10a,14b). The word "master" appears five times in the passage, all referring to Abraham (vv. 10[2x],12[2x],14). By the end of the chapter, Isaac is identified as the servant's "master" (v. 65). Here his prayer establishes the means whereby the servant will recognize divine guidance.

---

[704] L. Teugels, "The Anonymous Matchmaker: An Enquiry into the Characterization of the Servant of Abraham in Genesis 24," *JSOT* 65 (1995): 13–23.

24:10–11 These verses describe the journey of the servant to the town of Nahor, outfitted with ten camels bearing goods. The prominent idea of patriarchal blessing in the passage (vv. 1,35) is reinforced by the wealth shown by the train of ten camels.[705] "Aram Naharaim" literally means "Aram of the two rivers" (v. 10; Deut 23:4; Judg 3:8; 1 Chr 19:6; Ps 60:1). The region is the equivalent of the geographical name "Paddan Aram" (e.g., 25:20); the cities named in the region, known from Egyptian and Amarna texts, place the location at the upper bend of the Euphrates, perhaps in the Habur River triangle.[706] The city "Nahor" bears the family name of Abraham's brother and their grandfather (11:24, see Mesopotamia's Nahur, vol. 1A, p. 498). His arrival in town would naturally occur first at a place for watering his entourage, but in this case his mission especially requires him to appear where the potential bride likely would be found (v. 11). The picturesque description of kneeling camels at the well fits the mood of repose and prayer, but it also possesses by "kneel" *(bārak)* a sound play on the popular term "bless" *(bārak)* of the chapter. Indeed, the setting for blessing is ready. The cool of the "evening" explains the appearance of the women at the well whose daily task was to obtain water for the family.

24:12–14 In these verses the servant addresses the Lord as the deity of his master Abraham and intercedes in behalf of the patriarch ("show kindness," v. 12). The repeated term "kindness" *(ḥesed)* marks off the servant's prayer (vv. 12,14). By appealing to God's "kindness," the servant alludes to the divine promises and their provision for Abraham; he interprets his task as an extension of the promises, making his prayer a corollary to Abraham's faith in the Lord's adequacy. The Hebrew term translated "prayed" (NIV) is actually the nontechnical term "said" *('āmar),* often used of petition (e.g., 17:18; 32:9; 2 Sam 22:1) and intercession or thanksgiving (e.g., 24:26–27; Num 13:14; Amos 7:2,5). In his study of prayer in Israel, A. Pagolu observed that such ordinary terms introducing prayer reflected their conversational tone. The servant's prayer is like that of the patriarchs, whose prayers were noncultic, personal, and informal.[707]

The servant's request creates the means by which he can unerringly discern the woman "chosen" (v. 14) by the Lord. The servant seeks a woman for Isaac who demonstrates the revered quality of hospitality, including costly provisions for his many livestock (on this custom see comments on 18:3–5). The details "she went down" to obtain the water and "came up" indicate the added difficulty she faced in repeatedly drawing water for others (v. 16b).[708] The Abraham narrative earlier depicts the patriarch's mistreatment by local residents (chaps. 12,19,20) and idealizes him as the perfect host (chap. 18). By favorable

---

[705] On the question of camels in the patriarchal period, see commentary Introduction.

[706] W. Pitard, "Aram-Naharaim," *ABD* 1.341; W. S. LaSor, "Syria," *ISBE* 4.688.

[707] A. Pagolu, *The Religion of the Patriarchs,* JSOTSup 277 (Sheffield: Sheffield Academic Press, 1998), 99, 117–18.

[708] Wenham, *Genesis 16–50,* 144.

treatment of Abraham's servant, Rebekah's welcome contributes to the narrative's depiction of a "female Abraham" whose virtue matches that of the patriarch.

REBEKAH AT THE WELL (24:15–27).   The second subunit also ends in a prayer (v. 27); it is a spontaneous outburst of thanksgiving for the Lord's answer to the initial prayer, closing out the former subunit (v. 14). Two lexical links between the two prayers are "kindness" *(ḥesed)* and "master" (*ʾădōnāy;* vv. 14,27), but in the second prayer there are two additional nuances. The servant adds "faithfulness" to his tribute, for the Lord has proven trustworthy; and he mentions "relatives" of "my master," for God showed him the way to the right household (v. 27). Also, since this passage concerns the servant's discovery of Rebekah, the narrative begins by identifying Rebekah, the granddaughter of Abraham's brother Nahor, and reinforces her identity by Rebekah's answer to the servant's inquiry (vv. 15,24).

24:15   The narration implies that the Lord was setting the answer in motion before the servant's utterance was even completed. The deictic particle (*hinnê,* "behold"; not in NIV) and participle "coming out" ("came out," NIV) heightens the timeliness of her sudden appearance.[709] The author invites the reader to see the confluence of divine will and human activity achieve the providential purpose (cf. 22:13). By his later report we learn the servant's prayer was unspoken (v. 45).[710] Rebekah's name is assumed since she does not identify herself by name to the servant. Her identity as a descendant of Nahor-Milcah by their son Bethuel (22:23) provides the all-important genealogical criterion established by Abraham (v. 4).

24:16   Giving the physical profile of the "girl," who is "very beautiful" (v. 16), is uncommon in Hebrew narrative.[711] Her sexual innocence enhances her attractiveness as a potential bride. The sexual history of Rebekah is important since the nature of the promise concerns Isaac's future lineage. Sarna observes that the servant's prayer was "answered at once and in full," for he did not mention her beauty or chastity.[712] The NIV's rendering "virgin" for the word *bĕtûlâ* probably is best though the Hebrew word is not necessarily a technical term for virgin.[713] The alternate term "maiden" *(ʿalmâ)* is used also by the servant (v. 43) in reference to the women who come to draw water, the principle

---

[709] Cp. the surprise arrival of Boaz, וְהִנֵּה בֹעַז בָּא מִבֵּית לֶחֶם, lit., "and behold Boaz was coming from Bethlehem" (Ruth 2:4; cf. Gen 18:2).

[710] So as to harmonize the passages, SP, LXX, Vg. add אֶל־לִבּוֹ, "to his heart."

[711] But the physical appearance of the patriarchs' wives is mentioned when it contributes to the plot of the story (12:11,14; 26:7; 29:17; also 1 Sam 25:3; 2 Sam 11:2; 13:1; 14:27; 1 Kgs 1:3; Esth 2:2,3).

[712] Sarna, *Genesis,* 165.

[713] *DCH* 2.289 defines בְּתוּלָה as young, marriageable but not always a virgin; *HALOT* 1.167 has a "grown up girl" and inexperienced sexually but "married at a young age?" for Joel 1:8.

one of course being Rebekah in the servant's eyes. Rebekah then is defined by three different terms, "girl" (*nahărâ*, v. 14), "virgin" (*bĕtûlâ*, v. 16), and "maiden" (*'almâ*, v. 43). The word *'almâ* indicates a woman who is of potential childbearing status (Song 6:8; Isa 7:14).[714] If *bĕtûlâ* means a young woman of good reputation who is under the care of her father's household,[715] then Hebrew society would assume that the daughter is sexually pure (e.g., Exod 22:16–17[15–16]; Deut 22:13–21; 2 Sam 13:18), and thus the term in our passage indicates a virgin maiden. In Rebekah's case, however, the passage leaves no doubt by including the explicit explanation that no man has had sexual relations with her (cf. 19:18; Judg 21:12). Her spirited response to the servant's needs is conveyed in vv. 16,18–20 by eleven verbal forms given in a rapid fire "pizzicato-like series" and noted again in the servant's summary (vv. 45–46).[716]

24:17–18 The servant "ran" (*rûṣ*, "hurried" NIV) to intercept her as she withdrew from the well (v. 17). His action initiated the narrative chain of events where Rebekah "ran" (vv. 20,28) and Laban "ran" (v. 29). Later young Jacob's arrival in Aram initiates the same excitement by Rachel and Laban (*rûṣ*, 29:12,13). The point in chap. 24 appears related to the custom of hospitality, which reminds us of Abraham's same enthusiasm for entertaining his guests (*rûṣ*, 18:2,7). By this description Rebekah is again portrayed as another Abraham. The servant requests only a "little" water (v. 17b), and Rebekah complies graciously ("my lord") and cheerfully ("quickly lowered," v. 18). Again "quickly" (*mahēr*, vv. 18,20,46) is reminiscent of Abraham's model behavior (18:6,7). Even the action of lowering the vessel after she had already shouldered the heavy load does not escape mention by the author. Furthermore, the passage may suggest by noting her "hands" that Rebekah served the servant drink, rather than the servant taking the jar.

24:19–21 Another evidence of her generosity is her volunteering to care for the servant's animals, although he requested only water for himself (v. 19). She gave more than a "little" water, repeatedly drawing water until "all" the camels were fully satisfied (v. 20). Her exceptional assistance is studied (*šā'â*, "gazed"; NIV "watched her closely") by the servant, who is eager to learn if the Lord was answering his prayer (v. 21). The narration's expression "made his journey successful" (*ṣālaḥ darkô*, v. 21) twice more occurs in the servant's retelling (vv. 40,42), figuring in his calculated appeal to her household (v. 56). So as not to influence the outcome of the test, he waits at the well in "silence" (*ḥārēš*, "without saying a word," NIV). The impression left from the narrative

[714] J. Walton, "עֲלוּמִים," *NIDOTTE* 3.417.

[715] Id., "בְּתוּלָה," *NIDOTTE* 1.781–83; for different opinions see G. Wenham, "Betulah 'A Girl of Marriageable Age,'" *VT* 22 (1972): 326–48; M. Tsevat, "בְּתוּלָה *bᵉthûlāh*;בְּתוּלִים *bᵉthûlîm*," *TDOT* 2.341–43; and J. Schmitt, "Virgin," *ABD* 6.853–54.

[716] van Wolde, "Telling and Retelling," 236 and n. 18.

is that the man internally leaps with prayerful excitement but outwardly restrains his enthusiasm. He is hopeful but not presumptuous, not outpacing God's timing.

24:22–25 Her generosity is surpassed by the servant's gifts of gold jewelry (v. 22). The modern equivalents to the "beka" (half-shekel, Exod 38:26) and "shekel" cannot be determined definitely. The "nose ring"[717] was a sign of wealth and beauty (Prov 11:22; Isa 3:21; Ezek 16:12); a woman's nose was a physical feature valued for its elegance (Song 7:4[5]). The bracelets weighing ten shekels match the number of his camels. The narrative detail describing the golden gifts indicates the author's intent to show the wealth of the man. The woman already knew of the man's considerable station by the entourage of ten camels, but it could not have prepared her for this exorbitant gift. Laban is accordingly excited by the gifts (v. 30), and later he and his household benefit from the servant's conveyance of riches (v. 53). Although the reader knows Rebekah's family relationship (v. 15), the servant at this point does not and can only trust that she is related to Abraham (v. 4; but cf. comments on v. 47). He asks her identity for this reason next and then pursues the question of hospitality (v. 23).

Her relation as "the daughter of Bethuel" appears first in the Hebrew clause, although he has little to do with the events of the account (see comments on v. 50). So as to distinguish this "Bethuel" from others, she adds the identity of the prior generation, her grandparents Milcah and Nahor (vv. 24,48). Unknown to her at the time, it is actually the connection with the Nahor house that qualifies her as a member of Abraham's relatives (v. 4). The author assumes that both the reader (v. 15) and the servant understand the significance of her affiliation with the Nahor-Bethuel branch. True to her disposition thus far, Rebekah further offers to make provisions for the camels and the stranger (v. 25). The servant has yet to reveal his mission, delaying until he learns Rebekah's identity (v. 27), for anonymity is necessary if the sign is to be an unequivocal indicator of the divine will. If she knew of the man's connection with Abraham, her generosity toward this emissary would be more understandable.

24:26–27 The servant exhibits another mark of spiritual fervor when at the remarkable discovery of Rebekah he falls prostrate and praises the Lord (cf. vv. 48–49). He does not forget the Lord in the midst of his excitement, recognizing that God alone brought him to the very person required (vv. 4,7,14). "Bowed down" *(qādad)* and "worshiped" *(ḥāwâ)* translate a common tandem describing homage to God (e.g., Exod 4:31; Num 22:31) or an official (e.g., 43:28). "Praise" *(bārûk)* is another of many occasions that *bārak* ("bless") appears in the chapter (vv. 1,27,31,35,48,60; cf. *bārûk*, 9:26; 14:19,20). The servant's

---

[717] נֶזֶם, "ring," may indicate a nose (נִזְמֵי הָאָף, Isa 3:21) or ear (הַנְּזָמִים אֲשֶׁר בְּאָזְנֵיהֶם 35:4; also Exod 32:2–3) ornament; v. 47 clarifies that it was a nose ring.

exaltation of God recognizes his own humble place in the divine plan; his success comes only by virtue of his relationship to Abraham, "my master" (*ʾădōnî,* v. 27[2x]). It is the Lord's loyalty and reliability that are foremost in his exultation (cp. Ps 138:2). "Kindness" *(ḥesed)* and "faithfulness" *(ʾemet)* often occur together (e.g., Exod 34:6; Josh 2:14; 2 Sam 2:6; Ps 115:1; Prov 3:3), each depicting a strong relational commitment among humans or between God and humanity. The two terms are common in the narrative *(ḥesed,* vv. 12,14,27,49; *ʾemet,* vv. 27,48,49), assuming a prior commitment between God and Abraham.[718] It is God's ("his") loyalty to his promises that leads to the discovery of Rebekah (cp. Pss 25:10; 43:3; 57:3[4]; 89:14[15]).[719] The word "abandoned" *(ʿāzab)* conveys the opposite of fidelity *(ḥesed)* to a covenant bond (cp. 2:24; 28:15; Deut 29:25[24]; 31:16–17; Ruth 1:16; Isa 1:4; Jer 5:19). He is the "God of my master Abraham," indicating the covenant promises made to the patriarch. These promises extended beyond Abraham to future generations, and thus the servant rejoices that the Lord is trustworthy in guiding him to the wife and mother of new generations.[720] The servant testifies that it was the Lord who "led" *(nāḥâ)* him successfully (cf. v. 48). The servant may well be cast by the author in the image of Moses. In the song of victory Moses says similarly, "In your unfailing love *[ḥesed]* you will lead *[nāḥâ]* the people" (Exod 15:13), and the divine command to Moses, "go *[hālak],* lead *[nāḥâ]* the people . . . and my angel *[malʾākî]* will go before you *[lepāneykā]*" (Exod 32:34) recalls the servant's exultation (v. 27) and Abraham's promise of a guiding angel (v. 7).

LABAN PROVIDES FOR THE SERVANT (24:28–33). This section transitions the action from the well to the family's house, concomitantly shifting the focus from Rebekah to the brother Laban. Two parallel motifs appear in this short paragraph. The passage continues the idea of hospitality but centers it in the actions of Laban; the provisions made for the servant demonstrate that the welcome Laban exhibits is an extension of Rebekah's hospitality. As to who is actually carrying out the chores of hospitality is unclear from v. 32. The grammatical subject of the verbs describing the activities (see comments on v. 32) is ambiguous, providing for three possibilities: the servant, though this option in light of the hospitality already shown the man is unlikely; Laban himself; or by reading the subject as indefinite, thus a passive rendering, the servants of Laban are intended (cf. the passive *wayyûśam,* v. 33). The point of the ambiguity is to blend the activities of Laban and his servants so as to suggest that it is Laban himself who sees to this (cf. 18:3–8). The story also shows the family's exuberance by both Rebekah and Laban running *(rûṣ,* "ran" v. 28, "hurried out" v. 29, NIV) between the well and the house. They probably know little or nothing of

---

[718] D. Baer and R. Gordon, "חֶסֶד," *NIDOTTE* 2.213.

[719] בֵּית אֲחִי אֲדֹנִי, lit., "the house of the brothers ["relatives," NIV] of my master" (v. 27c); the versions reflect אֲחִי, "the brother of," referring specifically to Nahor (cf. v. 48; see *BHS* note).

[720] Ibid., 214 and A. Jepsen, "אָמַן" *ʾāman," TDOT* 1.313, 315.

what became of the adventurous Abraham, who left over a half-century earlier.[721] Unexpected news about Abraham generates the same excitement and
mystery we would experience at learning about distant cousins rediscovered.
Although accepting their generosity, the servant insists on fulfilling his mission
before enjoying the respite from his travels (v. 33). This leads to the discussion
of the second motif.

The second motif is the idea of retelling the story. The mentality of retelling
is not pedantic detail but a psychology of confirming the events as truthful (cf.
double dreams at comments on 41:32). From this point forward in the chapter
the passage repeatedly hearkens back to what is already known to the reader, in
many cases using the exact language. The words "told" *(nāgad)* and "tell"
(dibbēr), both verbs in the semantic range of reporting, form the limits of the
paragraph (vv. 28,33). Also Laban springs into action when he hears Rebekah
"tell" *(dibbĕrê,* lit., "the words of") of the events (v. 30). There is a chain of
telling: the events at the well are conveyed by Rebekah to Laban, and in turn
Laban welcomes the visitor to explain his mission. In agreement with the narrative's depiction of the faithful servant, he must tell his account and even force
a decision before he can receive his meal (v. 33).

24:28 Reference to the house as her "mother's" (v. 28; cf. Song 3:4; 8:2)
promotes the matriarchal role important to the ultimate goal of the servant,
finding a wife for Isaac. Milcah more than Bethuel is reminiscent of the early
days in Terah's family (11:29; 22:20,23). By Rebekah telling the "household
about these things" (v. 28b) occurring at the well, the author sets in motion his
practice of recalling earlier events (see comments on v. 34). In effect, telling the
"household" meant telling Laban, who takes the lead as spokesman.

24:29–30 "Now Rebekah had a brother . . ."[722] is providing supplementary information for the reader, not provided in the genealogy of Nahor-Milcah
(22:22–24). The relationship of Laban to Rebekah as her brother (v. 29; cf.
25:20) is important to the author since Laban is central to the account (vv.
50,55) and also to subsequent events in Jacob's life (27:43). Moreover, the idea
of "brother" *(ʾāḥ)* brings to mind the kinsman relationship between Abraham
and Nahor that generated the search in the Aram setting (vv. 4,15,48). Laban
does not wait for the man to approach; rather he races outside to greet him,
motivated at the sight of the gifts and by his sister's report (v. 30). Laban's
fondness for such riches is a characteristic that later motivates his mistreatment
of Jacob (29:25–27; 30:27–36; 31:2,6–8,28–29,38–42). Commentators often
point out the dislocation of v. 29b, which logically belongs after v. 30a in the
following arrangement: he saw . . . he heard (v. 30a) . . . he hurried (v. 29b) . . .

---

[721] 12:4; 17:17; 23:1 taken together indicate Abraham was in Canaan sixty-two years at the
death of Sarah.

[722] The *wāw* disjunctive distinguishes this clause, וּלְרִבְקָה אָח, lit., "now to Rebekah [was] a
brother."

then he came to the man (v. 30b).[723] This reconstruction fails to capture the rhetorical intentions of the author's arrangement. Verses 29b and 30b, both describing Laban's action, form an inclusion, highlighting the man's greed. He "hurried," it would seem, before he even heard the report because he saw the golden gifts. Also we have mentioned the chain effect of the narration, "the girl ran" (v. 28a) . . . "and he ran" (v. 29b, "hurried," NIV), which by displacing the latter clause would diminish the force of its juxtaposition. Moreover, the repetition describing Laban's response implies that he dashed so hurriedly that the man and his animals had no chance to leave. When Laban arrives at the spring, he finds the man and his entourage in the same place Rebekah had met him. The delineation that the servant was "standing" ('āmad; vv. 30,31) may be another intended allusion to Abraham, who was "standing" ('āmad, "stood," NIV) beside his three visitors (18:8; cf. 18:22; 19:27).

24:31 Relieved that the visitor is found, Laban praises the Lord and offers the servant the comforts of hospitality. We have already commented on the significance of Laban's address, "blessed by the LORD," but Laban's greeting also pertains to the recurring image of hospitality in the Abraham narrative. The language is reminiscent of the stranger motif (see comments on 19:1–29): "come" (bô'), "outside" (ḥûs, "out here," NIV), and "so the man came [bô'] into the house" ("went to," NIV; v. 32a).[724] The spacial significance of the traveler moving inward out of danger from outside the city, to the city square, and to the protective confines of the private home is what lies behind Laban's inquiry. Rhetorically, Laban is offering protection of the highest order for the visitor and his companions. "I [Laban] have prepared" should not be pressed literally at all points in the preparations since probably household servants are involved (cp. 18:5–8; see comments on v. 33). The root word translated "prepared" (piel, pānâ), meaning a clearing of the house (so NJB),[725] appears twice more in the chapter (in the qal stem), translated "turn" (v. 49) and "turn toward [evening]" (v. 63). Perhaps a play on the word occurs: by making room for the visitor (v. 31), the first step is taken toward the favorable outcome (vv. 49,63). Accommodations for ten camels and the accompanying servants (v. 32b) would have been enormous.

24:32–33 The Hebrew of v. 32 is unclear as to whether Laban is the one who unloads and feeds the camels and sets water before the visitor. The NIV (also NAB, REB, NJPS, HCSB) understands the verse as indefinite, rendering the verbs in the passive ("were unloaded," "were brought"),[726] whereas other

---

[723] See BHS note.
[724] Fields, Sodom and Gomorrah, 86–87.
[725] BDB 815.
[726] The third masculine singular forms occur without a specific subject named, וַיְפַתַּח and וַיִּתֶּן (lit., "and he unloaded . . . he gave").

versions assume the subject is Laban.[727] The same ambiguity occurs in v. 33, where the MT is passive ("was set"[728]), followed by most EVs, but the LXX has "he [i.e., Laban] set"[729] the food. The servant, consistent with his earlier sense of duty, resists gratifying his own needs until he settles the matter (v. 33; cf. v. 54). The members of the family are just as anxious to hear the news as he is to give it, and unhesitatingly Laban[730] complies ("speak on," *dabbēr,* ESV, NRSV).

THE SERVANT REPORTS ANSWERED PRAYER (24:34–49). The servant reviews for Laban his commission and journey, which essentially constituted the first half of the story: his beginning comments on Abraham's prosperity in vv. 34–36 are an explication of the brief narrative statement in v. 1; the mission and undertaking of the oath sworn to Abraham in vv. 37–41 retell vv. 2–9; the events at the well in vv. 42–48 detail again vv. 12–27. As in the Ugaritic myth *Keret,* where the king sets out to find a bride, chap. 24 presents a detailed repetition of the hero's journey. The servant repeats the crucial information, though not always slavishly, to emphasize the fortuitous hand of God in the servant's success. His testimony reshapes the account—sometimes curtailing, amplifying, or rearranging—so as to convince the family and Rebekah that it is God's will that she return with him, ending his recitation with a call to make their decision on the spot. There is a wordplay between Laban's initiating request, "Then tell *[nāgad]*us" (v. 33), and the servant's urgent counterrequest, seeking closure to the matter, "tell *[nāgad]*me . . . tell *[nāgad]*me" (v. 49). The response of Laban and Bethuel, "This is from the LORD" (v. 50), shows that the servant's case has won their support. Only the dullest of observers would miss the will of God in bringing the ambassador of Abraham to his relative's daughter. This was a match "made in heaven," as we sometimes say, and no one could resist it.

24:34–36 The servant begins by acknowledging his role as "servant" to his master Abraham, with "servant" *('ebed)* occurring in the emphatic position (v. 34). It is the mention of Abraham's name that opens the way for a serious hearing of his request. The servant is characteristically free to give credit to the Lord for the success of both his master and himself. He defines the blessing enjoyed by Abraham in terms of his material wealth (v. 35). This is not the time for modesty; the servant includes "abundantly" *(mĕ'ōd)* and "become great" *(gādal,* "wealthy," NIV) to prelude the detailed accounting of the master's possessions involving animals, precious metals, and servants. The language is reminiscent of the promise in 12:1–3, where "bless" *(bārak)* and "great" *(gādôl/*

---

[727] E.g., NASB, "Then Laban unloaded" (also RSV, NRSV, NJB).

[728] *Qere* reading וַיּוּשַׂם (*hoph.* or *qal* passive).

[729] LXX, καὶ παρέθηκεν (= וַיָּשֶׂם, *qal* impf.).

[730] Most EVs follow the MT, וַיֹּאמֶר, "he [Laban] said"; SP, LXX, Syr. have the plural וַיֹּאמְרוּ, "they said" (i.e., Laban and Bethuel, cf. v. 50), as does NAB.

gādal) also repeatedly occur; additionally, the catalog of possessions reflects the acquisitions from Egypt and Gerar (12:16; 13:2; 20:14–16). With the appearance of ten camels, servants, and the golden gifts, there was every incentive for Laban to believe the servant's report.

The issue of succession, however, is paramount in the servant's presentation. He alludes to the miracle of Isaac's birth (21:2,5) by mentioning Sarah's "old age"[731] (v. 36; cf. 18:13); this exceptional birth is another convincing evidence of God's provision. No mention is made of the complication with Ishmael, except perhaps obliquely in the reference to "maidservants" (v. 35); anyway, there is no longer a rival to Isaac since all has been bequeathed to Isaac, "everything he owns" (v. 36).[732] The notion of some commentators that the passage assumes the death of Abraham misses the literary function of the servant's tactic. He makes it clear from this remark that Isaac will soon obtain the inheritance, if not already practically in charge. At other places the servant speaks of Abraham as very much alive.

24:37–41 The servant quotes verbatim in some parts and summarizes in others the oath he swore in vv. 3–8. In doing so the Laban family hears the importance attached to obtaining a wife from the Terah clan versus that of the Canaanite populace. A conspicuous variation in the servant's retelling of Abraham's directive is "my father's house" and "my own clan," which supplant the general terms "my country" and "my own relatives" (v. 5). Although the servant's version restricts the search to Nahor's household, he is not merely offering a flattering embellishment or a sensationalizing of the precise discovery. In v. 7 Abraham makes use of "my father's household" when remembering his call at Haran (12:1). Since the story considers Rebekah another "Abraham," summoned by God to leave her household, it is not inconsistent with Abraham's sentiment for the servant to conflate Abraham's speeches in vv. 5,7 bringing to mind the first call. Because the Lord blessed Abraham's choice to leave his family, Rebekah and her relatives too can trust that God will honor her decision to leave.

Verse 39 recalls the one caveat the initial plan entailed: the woman may refuse (vv. 5,8). Although the servant avoids dwelling on this negative possibility, he does not dodge it altogether but broadens its implications by including the family in the responsibility of deciding (v. 49). Also he omits Abraham's refusal to grant Isaac's return, but this was a moot point by this stage in the negotiations (vv. 5–7). Moreover, it was the servant who first raised that possibility, not Abraham. Rather, Abraham confidently declared that this potential

---

[731] MT, זִקְנָתָהּ, "her old age"; alternatively, SP, LXX reflect זִקְנָתוֹ, "his [Abraham's] old age"; with Abraham as the subject of "he gave" (וַיִּתֶּן), the versions assured he was the prior referent (cf. 21:2,7). The MT's reading better suits the attention paid by the story on the matriarchal roles of Sarah and Milcah.

[732] כָּל־אֲשֶׁר־לוֹ, also 12:20; 25:5.

hindrance will be remedied by the Lord's guiding angel (v. 7). With this in mind, the servant then recalls the promised "angel" (v. 40), setting the principle of divine guidance in the broader context of Abraham's life-long piety (cf. 17:1), not solely the journey from Haran. The servant wishes to emphasize, however, the kinship of Abraham with the Aramean branch of the family. Repetitively and in chiastic order, the derivation of the patriarch is stated:

"to my father's family and to my own clan" (v. 38)
"from my own clan and from my father's family" (v. 40)

Twice he refers to the "oath" (v. 41[2x]; cp. v. 8) he undertook. By this he declares he has fully discharged his duty regardless of their final decision, and hence he infers he has no dire reason to deceive them. In effect he is saying he has done his duty, and now the responsibility lies with them. He is not satisfied with his explanation, for he next presents his most compelling proof.

24:42–48 The report skips any information pertaining to the journey itself (vv. 10–11), recounting only the crucial happenings at his arrival. By deliberately reciting his prayer and the events that followed (cf. vv. 13–27), he corroborates that the Lord answered his prayer, testifying irrefutably that the Lord led him precisely to Rebekah. The differences in his retelling are usually due to the different setting or to the curtailment of the details. Two substantive variations appear. First, he omitted his request for provisions for his entourage from her father's house (vv. 23,25). This probably was sparing himself and his audience unpleasant attention on his assertive behavior. At this point he does not want to run the risk of offending his audience by exhibiting a pushy attitude (but cf. v. 49). They will make the decision, and he will honor it. Another difference in his report is the order between presenting the gifts and his inquiry about Rebekah's identity: whereas the narration of the events has the gifts mentioned before Rebekah's identity (v. 22), his version switches the order, giving the jewelry after learning her identity (v. 47). The two passages, however, are not necessarily contradictory since the two descriptions differ in the verbs employed; in the narrative (v. 22) the passage says only "the man took" *(lāqaḥ)* the ornaments, but his report specifies that he "put" *(śîm)* the jewelry in her nose and on her arms. It is conceivable that he first produced the gifts, asked the identity of her father, and then upon learning the connection actually placed them on her. The connection between family identity and the gifts underscores the familial factor the servant emphasizes in the negotiations ("my father's family," vv. 38,40,48). Last, the servant concludes his report by alluding to the "faithfulness" *(ʾemet)* of God (v. 27); he repeats the word "right" *(ʾemet),* describing the "right way" the Lord led him to discover the girl (v. 48). The meaning of the wordplay is clear: God's fidelity to Abraham provided the map for the path leading to the virtual doorstep of the chosen maiden.

24:49 After this protracted telling, the servant addresses his appeal to

Laban and presumably Bethuel (see v. 50).[733] By "kindness" *(ḥesed)* and "faithfulness" *(ʾemet),* he echoes his earlier praise of the Lord at meeting Rebekah (v. 27). The servant is calling on them to act in good faith as has the Lord toward the servant. After his argument's *tour de force,* he puts pressure on the men to decide positively and without delay. He beseeches the men to decide now so that he can act accordingly, taking steps one way or the other (lit., "to the right or to the left"). Rebekah will yet have the final say (v. 58), but perhaps the servant must convince the elders first out of proper protocol (e.g., Num 30:4–6; Deut 22:16; Judg 14:3,10), or he may sense that Rebekah is willing and the men alone need a final push. If, however, they decline after hearing his testimony, the servant must concede and carry the news to his master as prearranged (v. 8).

REBEKAH AGREES TO RETURN (24:50–58). The movement in this paragraph is from the ruling authorities in the home, Laban and Bethuel, to the woman herself, Rebekah. The men first agree, observing that indeed this matter is of the Lord (vv. 50–51). Their acknowledgment, "from the LORD"[734] and "as the LORD has directed," work as bookends in their confession. Central to their affirmation is the tandem of key terms repeated in this chapter, "take *(lāqaḥ)* and go *[hālak]*" (v. 51), echoing both the call and test of Abraham (12:1,4; 22:2,3) and the servant's commission (24:4,7,10). The one possible "hitch" to the man's plans, however, still awaits him. The family announces that after ten days they will permit her to "go" *(hālak;* v. 55), but the servant begs leave to "go" *(hālak)* to his master immediately (v. 56). When the question is put to the woman, Will you "go?" *(hālak),* she ends the debate by speaking one word in the Hebrew, "I will go" *(hālak;* v. 58).

24:50–54a The leading men of the household respond first, confessing the overpowering testimony of the events. They cannot speak "bad or good" (v. 50, *raʿ ʾô-ṭôb,* "one way or the other," NIV; cf. 31:24,29; 2 Sam 13:22); by this figure of merism,[735] the men admit theirs is not the place to refuse in the face of God's will. Bethuel speaks only here in the chapter, but he does so at the most important point in the discussion (v. 50).[736] The chapter treats Bethuel in mixed fashion; he is the critical link tying Rebekah and Laban with the Nahor patrimony (vv. 15,24,47), but his role in the negotiations is vague. Laban and their mother are prominent (vv. 28,52,55), which suggests to some commentators that Bethuel's function has been curtailed in the transmission of the story

---

[733] Cf. the plural "you," אֶתְכֶם (v. 49).

[734] "This is from the LORD" was the basis for the rabbinic tradition that marriages are made in heaven (*b. Moʿed Qaṭ.* 18b ([118–19]), cited by M. Maher, *Targum Pseudo-Jonathan,* 86, n. 29.

[735] Merism consists of polar opposites indicating entirety, e.g., "day and night" (Ps 1:2).

[736] The singular verb וַיַּעַן, lit., "and he answered," is not unusual with a plural subject, as here, especially since Laban is the chief participant (e.g., Ruth 1:6–7).

or that the name here is an extraneous gloss.[737] It is not unusual for a brother to lead negotiations, however, such as we see in Jacob's sons dealing with the Shechemites (34:11–17) or with the disguised Joseph (e.g., 42:1–3). Generally in the ancient Near East the elder brother played a conspicuous role in the household and is known to have overseen marriage agreements for his sister.[738] From ancient Babylonian texts there are instances of brother and mother negotiating the sister's marriage. The author gives priority to Laban as the key figure because of his later importance in the Jacob account; second in priority is their mother Milcah (vv. 15,24,47,53,55), because she is the peer and foil of Sarah (11:29; 22:20,13), who though deceased remains important to the purpose of the story (v. 67). It is therefore understandable that Bethuel is not specifically named as one receiving gifts (v. 53), since he is not named a part of further negotiations (v. 55).

The men reiterate their acquiescence to God's will by entrusting Rebekah to the servant "as the LORD has directed" (v. 51). The verbless sentence accents their consent, lit., "Behold, Rebekah before you!"[739] In another sign of spontaneous gratitude, the servant collapses *(ḥāwâ)* before the Lord in worship (v. 52; also *ḥāwâ*, vv. 26,48). Only after acknowledging the Lord's grace, does he present Rebekah and the household with gifts (v. 53). Rebekah first receives unspecified articles of gold and silver as well as valuable clothing; the servant then generously extends "costly gifts" *(migdānōt)* to Laban and Milcah. The term *migdānâ* is used elsewhere of royal gifts, listed with gold and silver articles (2 Chr 21:3; 32:23; Ezra 1:62; Esth 1:6). The implication is that Abraham is like a royal person whose emissary provides token gifts (e.g., 2 Kgs 20:12; Esth 2:18; Prov 19:6). Only after the arrangement is sealed do the servant and his entourage eat (v. 54a).

24:54b–58 The literary tension is prolonged by a new request made by the servant. Whereas the servant's earlier request for Rebekah's hand met with unreserved assent, the second entreaty receives some hesitation. The paragraph repeats the two poles of their deliberation in intervals:

A "[and] send me on my way to my master" (v. 54b)
  B "then you [or "she"] may go" (v. 55b)
A′ "send me on my way so I may go to my master" (v. 56b)
  B′ "will you go with this man?" (v. 58b)

---

[737] E.g., Speiser, *Genesis,* 181–82; Westermann (*Genesis 12–36,* 388) assumes that Bethuel must be deceased, making "Bethuel" secondary. *BHS* (and *BHK*) recommends וּבֵיתוֹ, "and his household," instead of וּבְתוּאֵל, "and Bethuel" (cf. v. 28), but there are no versions supporting any textual variant.

[738] See Van Seters, *Abraham in History,* 77, and Selman, "Comparative Customs and the Patriarchal Age," 122, 138.

[739] הִנֵּה רִבְקָה לְפָנֶיךָ.

The interchange between the family and the servant establishes the stage for the sole remark of direct dialogue spoken by Rebekah in the household of Laban: "I will go" (v. 58b).

After the night's rest, the servant asks leave from their hospitality so that he can expedite the completion of his mission (v. 54b). Brother and mother, probably recognizing the finality of the girl's departure, answer by requiring about a ten-day farewell (v. 55).[740] Probably a visitor had a sense of obligation to appease a host, especially in this case asking the betrothed to leave abruptly. In the case of the Levite and concubine, they oblige her insistent father up to five days before departing (Judg 19:8–10; cf. *Tob* 8:20, fourteen days). Yet the anxious servant does not want to dawdle even for a few days, contending that the divine purpose of his mission must take precedence over family wants (v. 56). The divine will has made the normally mundane a pressing matter. This is vaguely reminiscent of the prophet who erred by staying with the old prophet in hostile territory, although the Lord forbade him, resulting in his death (1 Kgs 13:11–32). The decision is left in the hands of Rebekah (v. 57), who unhesitatingly agrees to go with the man (v. 58). The Hebrew verb may be a desiderative imperfect, "I want to go," expressing her strong wish.[741] Laban and his mother's request for the delay serves as a foil for Rebekah's better sense of the urgent moment.

LABAN BLESSES REBEKAH (24:59–61). This paragraph consists of an embedded poetic blessing (v. 60), bordered by the narrative descriptions of Rebekah's release (v. 59) and her departure (v. 61): "they sent Rebekah" (v. 59) and "and the servant took Rebekah" (v. 61). The word "sent" *(šālaḥ)* describes the compliance of the family by repeating the earlier petitions of the servant, "send me" *(šālaḥ,* vv. 54,56). The terms "took" *(lāqaḥ)* and "left" *(hālak)* repeat the tandem of key words in the chapter (vv. 4,10,38,40,51), bringing to denouement the plot of the story.

24:59 Again the prominence of Laban is made acute by reference to Rebekah as "their sister" (v. 59; "our sister," v. 60) as opposed to daughter.[742] The family bids her farewell, accompanied by her nurse *(mēneqet;* v. 59). The wet nurse of Rebekah, named Deborah (35:8), holds an honored position in the household. She probably accompanied Rebekah to provide some solace for the young girl so far away from her homeland. Deborah is a memento of the past

---

[740] עָשׂוֹר אוֹ יָמִים, lit., "days or ten"; יָמִים, however, can mean a "year" (Lev 25:29; Num 9:22), thus read as "one year or ten months" in Tgs., *Gen. Rab.* 60.12, and other Jewish authorities. The SP has "month," חֹדֶשׁ for "ten," meaning the odd option "a year or a month" or better "a few days or a month." Most EVs follow the more reasonable time period given in the LXX, ἡμέρας ὡσεὶ δέκα, "about ten days."

[741] *Qal* imperfect form, אֵלֵךְ.

[742] Alternatively, Wenham (*Genesis 16–50,* 150) suggests the term may mean "relative," as the comparable word "brother" functions at times (vv. 27,37).

kept by Rebekah (see comments on 35:8). The poignancy of the depiction suggests that the young woman's answer to duty eminently qualifies her as the wife of Isaac. Also mention of the wet nurse fits with the tenor of the blessing to follow, praying that Rebekah might issue numerous posterity.

24:60 The family invokes a blessing for Rebekah (cf. 31:55), praying for her descendants to be plentiful and triumphant (cp. Ruth 4:11–12). The words "bless" *(bārak)* and "ten thousands" *(rĕbābâ)* probably are sound plays on the name Rebekah *(ribqâ)*:

A Our sister,[743] may you become
   B thousands of ten thousands
   B′ may your offspring possess
A′ the gate of their enemies

"Thousands" *(ʾelep)* and "ten thousands" *(rĕbābâ)* are a common word pair (e.g., Deut 32:30; 33:17; 1 Sam 18:7; Ps 91:7; Mic 6:7). The superlative expression "thousands of ten thousands" magnifies the count even more.[744] Such numerous offspring will likely form mighty nations, leading to the second request of victory for her descendants. The nations that Rebekah will produce (25:23) will face incessant warfare, struggling for survival and supremacy, as the history of the region has proven. The blessing recalls the promises made to Sarah, who will be the mother of nations (17:16), and Hagar, whose offspring will be uncountable (16:10; 21:13). The coupling of numerous descendants and national sovereignty echoes the angel's promise to Abraham at Moriah. Laban's blessing repeats virtually the same wording found in the promise (see comments on 22:17).[745] By this and other inferences in the chapter, the author declares Rebekah the divinely chosen instrument who helps realize the promise made to Abraham and his descendants.

24:61 After the approval of her family, she and her "maids" *(naʿărōt)* set off with the servant. The caravan of camels increased according to the number of attendants Rebekah required. The woman's large entourage, including personal servants and beasts of burden, indicates that the Bethuel household also was prosperous (e.g., Exod 2:9; Esth 2:9).

(3) Isaac Marries Rebekah (24:62–67)

62Now Isaac had come from Beer Lahai Roi, for he was living in the Negev. 63He went out to the field one evening to meditate, and as he looked up, he saw camels approaching. 64Rebekah also looked up and saw Isaac. She got down from

---

[743] The plural pronoun "our" reflects the family's sense of solidarity; as *Tg. Ps.-J.* implies, the point may be that she will no longer be their "sister" but rather wife and mother.

[744] Cf. Num 10:36, רִבְבוֹת אַלְפֵי יִשְׂרָאֵל, "ten thousand thousands of Israel" (NRSV).

[745] Except 22:17b reads אֹיְבָיו, "his enemies," whereas 24:60b has שֹׂנְאָיו, lit., "those who hate him" (cf. Exod 20:5).

her camel [65]and asked the servant, "Who is that man in the field coming to meet
us?"

"He is my master," the servant answered. So she took her veil and covered
herself.

[66]Then the servant told Isaac all he had done. [67]Isaac brought her into the
tent of his mother Sarah, and he married Rebekah. So she became his wife, and
he loved her; and Isaac was comforted after his mother's death.

The account shifts suddenly to the new master, Isaac, who was living in the
Negev, perhaps overseeing his father's holdings. Although Isaac has no dialogue, he is the person who functions as the narrative glue. The passage begins
and ends with Isaac's location identified, indicating his transition from outside
the camp to inside the tent of his mother (vv. 62,67). The author transitions narrative interest from Abraham to Isaac and Sarah to Rebekah in this paragraph.
Abraham's name does not occur in this passage, leaving the stage to his successor. For the first time the narrative casts Isaac in a light independent of his
father; he is seen first apart from the Hebron home of the family. Ever the go-
between, the servant is the mediator between the betrothed parties. They do not
speak to each other. The servant answers her inquiry (v. 65), and he reports to
his new master (v. 66). The servant's attitude of deference toward the couple
shows the reader how to view the new first couple of the family. It is "out in the
field" (v. 63) before the retinue's arrival at the camp that the chance encounter
with Rebekah occurs (cf. Ruth 2:3–4). In light of the narrative's emphasis on
providence when Rebekah meets the servant at the well, the description of
Isaac's "meditation" implies that their encounter is also planned. From beginning to end the divine will superintends the selection of the bride.

24:62 The verse introduces a new scene in the episode, explaining
briefly Isaac's location during this time.[746] The repeated term *bô'* in this odd
construction, "had come" *(bā' mibbô'),*[747] suggests their later sexual consummation in marriage *(bô',* "brought," v. 67). The word *bô'* commonly expresses
sexual relations (e.g., 6:4; 38:2), as in the description of Abraham and Hagar
(16:2,4). The vocabulary of the verse reverberates with the language of the
Hagar story (chap. 16). "Beer Lahai Roi" is the name of the well designated
by Hagar where the angel encountered her, promising her child a great future
(see comments on 16:14); it also is where Isaac and Rebekah will live when
they succeed Abraham (25:11). Allusion to the events of Hagar's pregnancy
and her son's rejection contrasts the legitimacy of Isaac, who here possesses
the well, supplanting the firstborn Ishmael.

24:63–65 Verse 63 contributes to the book's picture of Isaac as a man of

---

[746]וְיִצְחָק בָּא מִבּוֹא is a disjunctive clause, "Now Isaac had come from . . ." (NIV).

[747]בָּא מִבּוֹא lit., "had come from coming"; SP, LXX have במדבר, "to the wilderness of" (see
BHS); BDB 98 tentatively suggests "as far as" for מִבּוֹא.

contemplation or prayer (25:21). "Meditate" is the traditional translation of the obscure term *lāśûaḥ*[748] (e.g., LXX, Vg.; also NIV, AV, NASB), believed derived from the well-attested root *śîaḥ* ("to meditate, talk, complain"). The targums *(Onq., Neof., Ps-J.)* and rabbinic tradition (e.g., *Gen. Rab.* 60:14) interpreted the term similarly, translating it "prayer." An alternative meaning, "complain, lament," has support from Isaac's consolation ("was comforted"[749]) over his mother's death (v. 67; cf. 23:1–2). In this case Isaac was distressed, lamenting the loss of his mother (although it had been three years). Others on the basis of Syriac and Arabic roots suggest "walking about, roving" (NRSV, NJB, NJPS, HCSB).[750] The passage can support this latter understanding where Rebekah describes his demeanor as someone "walking" *(haḥōlēk)* in the field (v. 65). Yet that Isaac was meditating at the moment of Rebekah's appearance also fits well with the providence-prayer motif of the chapter; the servant's prayer is answered at the exact moment, confirming to all that the discovery is of the Lord (24:15,45,50). The same sense of timely oversight is in Abraham's sight of the caught ram (22:13) and Hagar's discovery of the well at the right moment (21:19), both using similar language as here.[751] The author describes the "chance" moment where both bride and groom see each other at the same time (vv. 63–64), each "lifted up his/her eyes and saw" the other. At the excitement of the encounter, Rebekah dismounts her camel immediately, perhaps to better see the man or to express polite courtesy. As at the well when the servant acted before learning Rebekah's identity, she reacts at sighting the lone figure before asking his identity.

Apparently, Isaac is approaching the caravan from across the fields, "coming to meet us," she says (v. 65). When asked about the identity of the man, the servant refers to Isaac only as "my master," which has only been used of Abraham in this chapter (19x; cf. 18:12). The transition from the father as "master" to the son has already been anticipated (v. 36), even as Rebekah will supplant Sarah (v. 67). The proper decorum apparently for a betrothed woman of upper class was a veiled *(ṣaʿîp)* face (cp. Song 4:1,3; 6:7; Isa 47:2,

---

[748] לָשׂוּחַ is a hapax legomenon; G. Vall ("What Was Isaac Doing in the Field (Genesis XXIV 63)?" *VT* 44 [1994]: 513–23) has discovered as many as twelve proposals, and G. Rendsberg ("*LĀ ŚÛAH* in Genesis XXIV 63," *VT* 45 [1995]: 558–60) adds another.

[749] Vall compares the appearance of the same terms "comforted" (נָחַם) and "complain, lament" (שִׂיחַ) in Ps 77:3b–4; Job 7:11–13 ("What Was Isaac Doing?" 521).

[750] BDB 1002 proposes שׁוּט, "to rove about" (הִתְהַלֵּךְ, "walking to and fro," Job 1:7; 2:2); *HALOT* 3.1311 has שׂוּחַ, "walk, stroll, wander about." J. Kselman argues that the wandering of Isaac is a behavior of depression over his mother attested in ancient texts ("'Wandering About' and Depression: More Examples," *JNES* 61 (2002): 275–77.

[751] וַיִּשָּׂא עֵינָיו וַיַּרְא וְהִנֵּה, "and he [Isaac] lifted up his eyes and looked and behold" (v. 63); and וַיִּשָּׂא אַבְרָהָם אֶת עֵינָיו וַיַּרְא וְהִנֵּה, "and Abraham lifted up his eyes and looked and behold" (22:13); the two verbs, "lift" (נשׂא) and "saw" (ראה), appear again in the same context, though not in tandem (21:18–19).

ṣammâ).[752] This custom helps explain why beauty was defined by the eyes and form of a woman (e.g., 29:17; Prov 6:25; Song 1:15) as well as why Jacob failed to recognize Leah on their wedding night (see comments on 29:24–26; cf. Tamar, 38:13–14).

24:66 In another sign of Isaac's eminent position, the servant reports to him, not Abraham, the events of the journey. Earlier we rejected the idea that Abraham must be presumed dead; rather, the omission of the senior patriarch has a literary function, demonstrating the passage to the next generation. The servant surely would have given his report later to Abraham as well.

24:67 The final verse refers to Sarah "his mother" twice; in each place Rebekah fulfills the matriarch's role. In an unhappy way she will also imitate Sarah's childless condition (25:21; Rachel, 29:31). "Brought" *(bô)* and "tent" *(ʾōhel)* suggest sexual relations, which points up the significance of her role as child bearer and the irony of her barrenness. Mention of love ("loved," *ʾāhab)* in marriage is not always found in Hebrew story (e.g., Ruth 1:4); here it adds another poignant touch to the portrait of the couple's arranged marriage (cp. 29:18,20,30,32; 34:3).[753] The final brush stroke is the author's reference to the comfort she provides after the loss of Isaac's mother. "Comforted" *(nāḥam, niphal)* is used elsewhere in the context of grief over the deceased (e.g., 37:35; 38:12). This final verse shows that the objective of the search is now complete.

17. Abraham's Death and Burial (25:1–11)

The final section of the Abraham account brings to a close its central theme of an heir. "Blessed" *(bārak)* in 25:11 as the key word of the Abraham narrative back references the thematic thread of the patriarchal promise (e.g., 12:1–3; 22:17–18). The descendants of his second wife, Keturah, who have the least claim on Abraham's inheritance, are named and treated succinctly (vv. 2–4,6). Isaac and Ishmael, who are crucial to the theme of heir in the foregoing chapters, are mentioned next at the funeral of their father (v. 9). Isaac alone is twice designated the sole recipient of his father's possessions (vv. 5,11). If there is any doubt remaining after chap. 24, these concluding verses confirm Isaac's place as the appointed heir. It is only said of Isaac among Abraham's children

---

[752] See K. van der Toorn, "The Significance of the Veil in the Ancient Near East," in *Pomegranates and Golden Bells: Studies in Biblical, Jewish, and Near Eastern Ritual, Law, and Literature in Honor of Jacob Milgrom* (Winona Lake: Eisenbrauns, 1995), 327–39.

[753] S. Ackerman contends that when אֹהֵב and אַהֲבָה describe interpersonal relationships, the person expressing the love or who is said to love has the higher social status ("The Personal Is Political: Covenantal and Affectionate Love *[ʾĀHĒB, ʾAHĂBÂ]* in the Hebrew Bible," *VT* 70 [2002]: 437–58).

that "God [*ĕlōhîm*] blessed" him (v. 11; cf. 24:1,35);[754] this language is used rarely in Scripture, appearing in creation narratives (1:22,28; 2:3; 9:1).

The inclusion of Keturah's children does not diminish the miracle of Isaac's birth, as von Rad contends.[755] Rather, their birth testifies to the fulfilling of the promise that the patriarch will father many "nations" (17:5–7). This evidence of blessing (i.e., posterity) joins with the prior attention on the patriarch's wealth (24:1,35,53; 25:6); 25:1–6 further explains that "the LORD had blessed him [Abraham] in every way" (24:1). Gifts distributed to Abraham's sons by his concubine show that he acknowledges his sons, but their exile to the east eliminated them as rivals to Isaac; only Midian reappears in Genesis (36:25). Ishmael stands somewhere between the children of Keturah and the full privileges of Isaac. Ishmael's participation in the burial of his father and his impressive genealogy to follow (vv. 12–18) accord with divine promise (16:10; 17:26; 21:13,18).

COMPOSITION. Regarding the extent of this section, many commentators include the Ishmael genealogy (vv. 12–18) as the conclusion to the Abraham story; thus the two genealogies of the rejected lines (vv. 1–6,12–18) enclose the narration of his death and burial (vv. 7–11).[756] Critical scholars agree that the sources for vv. 1–18 are mixed, the Yahwist (J) in vv. 1–6 and Priestly (P) in vv. 7–18 (except vv. 11b,18 also J). Von Rad reflects the wide opinion that vv. 1–6 (Keturah) is a secondary addition when he says they "do not easily follow the narrative context by our standards."[757] Since it is contended that chap. 24 assumes the death of Abraham (24:36,65), vv. 7–11a (Abraham's funeral) are believed misplaced from chap. 23 (also P) and v. 11b (Isaac) follows naturally on chap. 24.[758]

Alexander's study exposes the weaknesses of the source-critical reconstructions, calling into question the criteria employed for determining the source division.[759] It is transparent that vv. 1–11 are familiar with earlier events in the Abraham narrative, but they are not necessarily a hodgepodge of earlier sources as critics usually claim. For example, they claim that mention of Machpelah (v. 9) must belong to P because of chap. 23 (P). Since the author of vv. 1–11

---

[754] וַיְבָרֶךְ אֱלֹהִים; for the phrase "the LORD blessed" and its variations, see 26:12; 39:5; Exod 20:11; Judg 13:24; 2 Sam 6:11; 1 Chr 13:14; Job 42:12.

[755] von Rad, *Genesis,* 261.

[756] Westermann, *Genesis 12–36,* 394–95.

[757] von Rad, *Genesis,* 261; Westermann (*Genesis 12–36,* 394–95) interprets vv. 1–18 as a composite of independent texts (see comments on 25:12–18), attributing the framework of vv. 1,5–6 to the last editor, which permitted his interpolation of the genealogy (vv. 2–4); Coats proposes that vv. 1–6, providing the conclusion to the Abraham account, possibly were related to 22:20–24 (Nahor genealogy; *Genesis,* 171).

[758] Skinner, *Genesis,* 349, 351; Westermann, *Genesis 12–36,* 394–95; Coats, *Genesis,* 172–73; Van Seters considers Sarah's death in chap. 23 also secondary, as do most commentators, since he thinks 24:63 assumes she is alive (*Prologue to History,* 266).

[759] Alexander, *A Literary Study,* 259–62.

knows of the Abraham story as a whole, it is best to attribute this ending to the same author who compiled the entire account.

First, regarding the parameters of the passage, the *tôlĕdōt* heading at 25:12 shows that Ishmael's genealogy is a new section (see vol. 1A, pp. 31–35), making vv. 1–11 the end of the Terah *tôlĕdōt* (11:27–25:11). Genealogy pertaining to Abraham both opens and closes his story (11:27–31; 25:1–6). Second, as already said above, vv. 1–11 offer a fitting conclusion to the whole of the Abraham account since they give the final outcome of the story's thematic focus on blessing and inheritance.

Third, vv. 1–11 reflect the immediate context of chaps. 23 and 24 in many ways, making the scholarly suggestions of their secondary nature and dislocation less attractive options. The idea that Abraham is already dead in chap. 24 since reference is made to Isaac's inheritance assumes too much (24:36). The passage itself makes it clear that Abraham commissions the servant (24:1), and he is treated by the servant as still alive. The whole of the chapter is generally proleptic, presenting what will become of the inheritance. The servant's mention of Isaac as "my master" (24:65) is appropriate since the persuasion of Rebekah relied largely on Isaac's future succession. Moreover, the expression has a literary function, contributing to the chapter's purpose of transitioning to the new generation. "Another wife" in 25:1 follows aptly on chaps. 23–24, which concern the wives of Abraham and Isaac. The acknowledgment of Isaac's inheritance (25:5) confirms the servant's testimony (24:36). "Gifts" *(mattānōt)* for Keturah's children (25:6) recall the "costly gifts" *(migdānōt,* 24:53) provided the Laban family. The memory of the Hittite origin of Machpelah (25:9–10) brings forward the whole of chap. 23. Mention of Beer Lahai Roi (25:11) back references the meeting place of Isaac and Rebekah (24:62), establishing the location of the Isaac story to follow (25:19) versus the desert tribes of Ishmael's lineage (25:18). In this vein also the well at Beer Lahai Roi, by virtue of its association with Hagar, a concubine wife, and her son Ishmael (16:14), provides for another statement on the prominence of Isaac, who has taken possession of the well.

Fourth, 25:1–11 is appropriately located just prior to the Ishmael and Isaac *tôlĕdōt's* (vv. 12,19) because it is forward looking. Since the passage speaks to the status of the rejected sons, the mention of Ishmael (v. 9), who has not been heard from since chap. 21, prompts the author to close out what became of Ishmael's family line in vv. 12–18. This feature of delineating the descendants of the rejected son is found also in chap. 36. The author reports the death and burial of Abraham (vv. 7–11) out of chronological order to prepare the way for the Isaac–Jacob succession. Abraham lives fifteen years after the births of Esau and Jacob, which would mean the death report belongs chronologically at the end of the birth narrative of the twins (25:26).[760] This dischronological account indicates that vv. 1–11 are placed topically so as to round out the former era and look ahead to the new generation.

---

[760] Speiser, *Genesis,* 190; Isaac marries at forty years old (25:20) and fathers at sixty (25:26), which makes Abraham 160 (21:5) at the twin's birth, fifteen years before his death at 175 (25:7).

Moreover, the arrangement of the narratives in 23:1–25:19 evidence a planned pattern that has its counterparts in the conclusions to the Jacob and Joseph cycles to follow. Wenham charts their six common features and parallel arrangements in narrating the transition and deaths of Abraham (23:1–25:19), Isaac (35:18–37:2), and Jacob (48:7–50:14). He rightly concludes that the similarities among the three endings point to an intended "editorial activity," not a "ragbag of traditions."[761]

As for the date and authenticity of the Keturah and Ishmael genealogies (25:1–18), we can address these items together. Van Seters points to evidence connecting the genealogical material with the Neo-Babylonian period. He concludes that they reflect the viewpoint of the sixth century when the author invented ancestral links between Israel and the Arameans and Arabs by means of "eponymous ancestors and mythical origins."[762] Yet the matter is not so simple since the genealogies have features that suggest early provenience. Notably, in the genealogy there is no use of the term "Arab" as an eponymous ancestor, and the inclusion of Midian as a kinsman of the Hebrews implies a period of peaceful relations between the two (e.g., Exod 18:1–12; Num 10:29).[763] The term "Arab" only first occurs in Assyrian records and in the Old Testament (Isa 13:20) during the ninth–eighth centuries. Also it is more likely that the genealogy antedates the rise of national Israel when Midian continually troubled Israel (Num 22:4,5; 25:6,17; 31:2–3,7–10; Josh 13:21; Judg 6:1–8:28; Isa 10:26; Hab 3:7).

STRUCTURE.   The passage consists of two units. Verses 1–6 report additional sons born to Keturah (vv. 1–4) and give the disposition of Abraham's wealth (vv. 5–6). Repetition of the name "Keturah" (vv. 1,4) forms the boundaries of vv. 1–4, enclosing the genealogy of her children (vv. 2–4). Verse 6 recounts the geographical migration of Abraham's sons by concubinage upon whom he bestows gifts. Verses 7–11 report his death, age, and burial (vv. 7–10), and, importantly, the divine authentication of Isaac's succession ends the narrative (v. 11).

vv. 1–6   Abraham's legacy
    vv. 1–4   Keturah's sons
    vv. 5–6   His bequest to Isaac and other sons
vv. 7–11   Abraham's death
    vv. 7–8   His age at death
    vv. 9–10 His burial at Machpelah
    v. 11   Confirmation of Isaac as heir

The term *ḥay*, "living, lived" (NIV) in vv. 6 and 7[2x][764] ties the two halves of the passage together. The former unit (vv. 1–6) concerns Abraham's last tes-

---

[761] Wenham, *Genesis 16–50,* 156.

[762] Van Seters, *Abraham in History,* 64.

[763] Sarna, *Genesis,* 171.

[764] שְׁנֵי־חַיֵּי אַבְרָהָם אֲשֶׁר־חַי, lit., "the years of Abraham's life which he lived . . ." (v. 7).

tament while "still living," and the second unit (vv. 7–11) summarizes his life, death, and burial. By addressing his legacy, the passage naturally refers to his total descendants. Each unit mentions the rejected sons in juxtaposition to the chosen heir. In the first unit the sons of Keturah are the foil for Isaac (vv. 2–4) and in the second unit Ishmael (v. 9) is the rejected son. No mention of Hagar occurs, though she may be inferred from the reference to "concubines" (25:6). Jewish tradition was not satisfied with an inference alone, choosing to identify Keturah as the Egyptian maid Hagar (*Tgs. Ps-J., Neof.* mg.; *Gen. Rab.* 61.4).

(1) Abraham's Inheritance (25:1–6)

[1]Abraham took another wife, whose name was Keturah. [2]She bore him Zimran, Jokshan, Medan, Midian, Ishbak and Shuah. [3]Jokshan was the father of Sheba and Dedan; the descendants of Dedan were the Asshurites, the Letushites and the Leummites. [4]The sons of Midian were Ephah, Epher, Hanoch, Abida and Eldaah. All these were descendants of Keturah.

[5]Abraham left everything he owned to Isaac. [6]But while he was still living, he gave gifts to the sons of his concubines and sent them away from his son Isaac to the land of the east.

At the end of the patriarch's life, the subject of inheritance is appropriately readdressed in the conclusion to his story. We already observed that the inclusion of Keturah's children enhances the narrative's exposition of divine blessing by the gift of many progeny. The form of genealogy for Keturah's six sons is segmented (vv. 2–4), meaning that more than one descendant per generation is reported (see vol. 1A, pp. 297–98). This is true, however, only of Jokshan and Midian (vv. 3–4), father of two and five sons respectively; the genealogy lists no descendants for the four remaining sons. The genealogy is three generations deep, or four when counting Abraham as the first (cf. comments on 25:13). The final generation consists of three peoples (via Jokshan-Dedan, v. 3), giving a total of sixteen descended from Keturah (1 Chr 1:32–33 adapts the genealogy with differences).

25:1 Although Keturah is prominent in the passage, the role of Sarah is also present by the inference "another" *(yāsap)* wife (24:67). Although designated here as a "wife" *('iššâ),* she is a concubine-wife (v. 6). The language "wife," "concubine," and "maidservant" are used of Jacob's concubine wives (cf. 30:4,9; 32:23; 35:22). This passage does not follow chronologically on the death of Sarah (see above), leaving it uncertain when Abraham took this concubine and produced children. The name *Keturah (qĕṭûrâ)* is related most likely to the word group meaning "smoke, incense" *(qṭr;* cf. *qĕṭôrâ,* "incense," Deut 33:10). This name and the tribes that are listed usually are related to the international spice trade centered in Arabia mentioned in Assyrian and biblical sources (e.g., 1 Kgs 10:2,20; Isa 60:6; Ezek 27:22). "Keturah" is not attested elsewhere, but there is no compelling reason to assume that she is a personification of the incense trade in Arabia.[765] A fictitious ancestor is not required to explain the geographical character of Old Testament genealogy. Real ancestry, as it is presented in the text, explains future trade associations between peoples as well or better.

25:2 *Zimran, Medan,* and *Ishbak* are not traceable, although we may assume based on their brothers that they are generally related to the region of Arabia (v. 2//1 Chr 1:32a). *Jokshan* is usually located in Arabia simply due to his children's locations, Sheba and Dedan (v. 3a). Jokshan should not be equated with Joktan of the Shemites in the Table of Nations, whose thirteen descendants are located in southwest Arabia (10:25,26,29; see vol. 1A, p. 464, n. 122). *Shuah* is the home of Bildad, one of Job's friends (Job 2:11) whose residences are also usually associated with Arabia. Shuah has been equated by E. A. Knauf, however, with the Euphrates site *Sūḫu* (Akk.) in northeast Syria, which was located on an important trade route in the first millennium,[766] but the context of Arabian sites for the genealogy questions this identification.[767] Another sibling, *Midian,* is the best known of the children born to Abraham and Keturah. Traditionally the region of the Midianites was northwest Arabia, the territory stretching along the eastern shore of the Gulf of Aqaba (Exod 2:15; 1 Kgs 11:8). The major oasis of that region is Bad'. Biblical references, however, show that they roamed far, including the southern Transjordan (Josh 13:21; Num 22:4–7; cf. comments on 36:35), the Arabah (1 Kgs 11:18), Egypt (37:25), and Syria (Num 22:4). They are also associated with the Ishmaelites (37:25–28,36; 39:1; Judg 8:24) who traded with Egypt, and they are counted among the "eastern peoples," including the Amalekites (Judg 6:3,33; 7:12; 8:10).[768] The exchange of the terms Midianites and Ishmaelites in Genesis can be accounted for on the basis of a later assimilation of the two peoples, related to one another as half-brothers by having the same father, Abraham.

25:3 *Sheba* and *Dedan* (v. 3a//1 Chr 1:32b), as the offspring of Jokshan in the Keturah genealogy, may be confused with the tribes bearing the same names who are identified as the sons of Raamah in the Hamitic lineage (10:7b). The Hamitic tribes were possibly located in northwest Arabia since Dedan (modern *al-'Ula*) was an important commercial center in the region. Also another "Sheba" is a descendant of Shem, whose father was the similar-sounding "Joktan" (10:26,28,29). The names Jokshan and Joktan cannot be equated, however, and the "Sheba" of Shemite lineage (10:28) probably was the famous southwest Arabian people. Ethnogeographical factors which may help account for similarities among these three genealogies are: different tribes possessed

---

[765] E. A. Knauf, "Keturah," *ABD* 4.31.

[766] Id., "Shuah," *ABD* 5.1225–26.

[767] F. Winnett, "The Arabian Genealogies in the Book of Genesis," in *Translating and Understanding the OT: Essays in the Honor of Herbert Gordon May* (Nashville: Abingdon, 1970), 193.

[768] T. V. Brisco, "Midian," *ISBE* 3.349–51.

the same names, migrations occurred between east Africa and southern Arabia, and the possible comingling of once-distinct but closely related peoples. As for the Keturah descendants, Sheba and Dedan can be differentiated from the Hamitic tribes of the same name by their relationship to Abraham (for more discussion, see vol. 1A, pp. 447–48, nn. 67, 68, 70–73).

The children of *Dedan* are three people groups, whose names are the only ones in the genealogy listed in the Hebrew plural form: the *Asshurites, Letushites,* and *Leummites.*[769] The same plural feature (Hb., *îm*) designates certain peoples in the Table of Nations (cp. 10:4,13–14; vol. 1A, p. 452). Asshur is a name occurring for different people groups (10:11,22; see vol. 1A, p. 461) and may well be related to the Asshur mentioned in v. 18 (see comments there). "Leummites" in Hebrew (*lĕʾōm/lĕʾummîm* [pl.]) means "clan, tribe, people" (Akk. *līmum;* Ug. *lʾim*) but here refers to a whole people group.[770] That these three unknown tribes were related to Dedan suggests they were subgroups of Dedan or located nearby in the same northwest Arabian region.[771] The targums and rabbinic interpretation, however, translated the names as vocations, "merchants, traders, and heads of peoples" (cf. *Ps.-J., Neof.; Gen. Rab.* 61.5).

25:4 The grandchildren of Abraham who descended through Midian are five. These five tribes or place names probably were located in Midian or nearby. *Ephah* is mentioned again in Isa 60:6, where it appears with Midian, referring to their spice trade by camel caravan. Scholars usually identify it with the Arabian tribe *Haiappa* named in Assyrian texts that place it in the area. The old identification of Ephah with the site Ruwafah (100 miles southeast of Badʿ)[772] has been recently challenged. Like Ephah, the remaining descendants —*Epher,*[773] *Hanoch,*[774] *Abida,*[775] and *Eldaah*[776]— are difficult to locate confidently, though most scholars assume they were in northwest Arabia associated with towns or oases along caravan routes.

---

[769] These three peoples are absent in 1 Chr 1:32–33; on these tribes see Winnett, "The Arabian Genealogies," 190–91. The LXX includes two more descendants, "Raguel," (= "Ruel," 36:4; = "Deuel," Num 1:14) and "Nabdeel" (= "Adbeel," 25:13; 1 Chr 1:29).

[770] A. Malamat, "A Recently Discovered Word for 'Clan' in Mari and Its Hebrew Cognate," in *Mari and the Bible,* SHCANE 12 (Leiden: Brill, 1998), 165–67.

[771] For more on Dedan, see D. Graf, "Dedan," *ABD* 2.121–23.

[772] J. Montgomery, *Arabia and the Bible* (Philadelphia: University of Pennsylvania, 1934), 43, and Winnett, "The Arabian Genealogies," 191–92; see E. A. Knauf, "Ephah," *ABD* 2.534, who questions this identification.

[773] See the suggestions of Knauf, "Epher," *ABD* 2.534–35; the name Epher also appears for Ezra's son (1 Chr 4:17) and a transjordan family of the Manasseh tribe (1 Chr 5:26).

[774] Hanoch is the same Hb. as Enoch (see vol. 1A, p. 285); it is far-fetched to associate this site with the city built by Cain (4:17) as by Winnett, "The Arabian Genealogies," 192 and others. Hanoch also was the name of a Reubenite tribe (e.g., 46:9; Exod 6:14).

[775] Abida is now usually associated with modern Badʿ, located in ancient Midian; see Winnett, "The Arabian Genealogies," 192 and M. Fretz, "Abida," *ABD* 1.14.

[776] Eldaah, meaning "God called" from Ar. *daʿâ* ("call"), has a form typical of personal names; its location is unknown (E. A. Knauf, "Eldaah," *ABD* 2.431).

25:5–6 As the designated heir (cf. 21:10,12), Isaac receives "everything [Abraham] owned" (v. 5); the sons by Abraham's concubine do not obtain a rival inheritance; rather they receive "gifts" (v. 6). The construction initiating v. 6, "but to the sons of his concubines,"[777] highlights the different manner Abraham provided for them. The plural "concubines" must include Hagar if it is a numerical plural, but the term is never used of Hagar in chaps. 16; 21, preferring "maidservant" (16:1) or "wife" (16:3) for her status as a concubine wife (cf. 30:4,9 with 35:22). Alternatively, it may be a plural indicating the abstract noun "concubinage," which could encompass Hagar and any others.[778] If she is in view, then it may be inferred that Abraham furnished them gifts as well as necessities at their departure (cf. 21:14).

According to Mosaic practice, the firstborn son received the "double share" of the father's estate so as to ensure the son's rights which otherwise could be jeopardized if the child were of an unloved wife (21:15–17; e.g., Leah and Rachel). That the patriarchal practice varies from the law indicates that it antedated Moses (cp. Esau/Jacob, 25:31–34; Manasseh/Ephraim, 48:8–22). The textual variant in v. 5 has "Isaac his son,"[779] which though not necessarily original shows an interpretation that accents his full status as Abraham's heir. Keturah's sons are related rhetorically in the story closer to their mother than father, whereas v. 6 has "his son Isaac." "All which belonged to him" (Abraham, v. 5) is a description of a person's estate (cf. 24:36).[780]

To guarantee Isaac's future position, Abraham dismissed all rival offspring to the east (v. 6). The imagery of the terms "sent" *(šālaḥ)* and "east *(qēdĕmâ, qedem)*[781] is reminiscent of the expulsion from Eden (3:23, 24; cp. Cain, 4:16). (On the significance of the spatial term "east," see vol. 1A, pp. 257, 478.) The same term "sent" describes the eviction of Hagar and her son (cf. 21:14).

(2) Abraham's Death (25:7–11)

[7]Altogether, Abraham lived a hundred and seventy-five years. [8]Then Abraham breathed his last and died at a good old age, an old man and full of years; and he was gathered to his people. [9]His sons Isaac and Ishmael buried him in the cave of Machpelah near Mamre, in the field of Ephron son of Zohar the Hittite, [10]the field Abraham had bought from the Hittites. There Abraham was buried with his wife Sarah. [11]After Abraham's death, God blessed his son Isaac, who then lived near Beer Lahai Roi.

The obituary consists of his age (v. 7), God's blessing on his life (v. 8), and his burial (vv. 9–10). Verse 11 closes out the Abraham narrative by stating the

---

[777] The *wāw* disjunctive occurs, וְלִבְנֵי הַפִּילַגְשִׁים; if the variant in v. 5 is followed (see note below), "his son" and "sons of" are chiastic.

[778] Speiser, *Genesis,* 187.

[779] SP, LXX, Syr. indicate בְּנוֹ, cp. v. 6.

[780] כָּל אֲשֶׁר לוֹ (e.g., 12:20; 24:36; 39:6 Job 1:10).

[781] The NIV omits "eastward" *(qēdĕmâ);* "eastward, to the land of the east" (NASB).

divine approval of Isaac's succession.

25:7–10   At 175 years (v. 7) Abraham lived a long period by traditional standards (Ps 90:10); he resided in Canaan for a century (12:4). Verse 8 entails the author's evaluation of the patriarch's life; his longevity signals divine blessing. The verse possesses stereotypical phrases describing death: "and he breathed his last" (v. 17; 35:29; 49:33; Job 14:10), including animals (7:21 "perished," NIV); "died at a good old age" (15:15; Judg 8:32; 1 Chr 29:28); "old and full of years"[782] (35:29; 1 Chr 23:1; 2 Chr 24:15; Job 42:17); and "gathered to his people" (v. 17; 35:29; 49:33; Num 20:24; Deut 32:50).[783] This last phrase means that the deceased joins his ancestors in the realm of the dead; the expression may be associated with the practice of family burial.[784] It is used of three patriarchs in Genesis and of Aaron and Moses. "A good old age" is the language of 15:15, where the Lord promises the patriarch long life, showing again that the divine word is trustworthy.

Verse 9 describes the burial by "his two sons," Isaac and Ishmael. Other than the Chronicler's genealogy (1 Chr 1:28), this is the only place where the names occur in tandem. The presence of Ishmael after so many years indicates the love shared by father and son (17:28; 21:11); although Isaac takes first place ("the beloved son," 22:2), the rejected son also benefits from Abraham's blessing (21:13). The repetition of details pertaining to the Machpelah burial site (vv. 9–10; chap. 23) gives again concrete expression to God's faithfulness and to Abraham's faith. The funeral service testifies to the (partial) fulfillment of promised descendants and land (cf. Matt 22:32 pars.). (On the name "Zohar," cf. comments on 46:10.)

25:11   The theme of inherited blessing that is central to the Abraham narrative appears in the final verse. The blessing, however, is not automatic, as the rivalry in the Jacob-Esau story shows. Unlike Isaac and Jacob's practice, Abraham did not formally invoke the blessing on Isaac (cf. 27:27–29; 28:1; 48:15,20; 49:28).[785] Our passage indicates that the Lord alone confers blessing. The language of blessing is reminiscent of 24:1 concerning Abraham, but only later can it be said as with his father that God blessed Isaac "in every way" (24:1). By this concluding verse, the author confirms that the transition of divine blessing to the new generation is complete. The blessing does not die with the favored patriarch; it is an eternal promise rooted in the will of God (13:15; 17:7–8,13,19).

---

[782] וְשָׂבֵעַ זָקֵן, "old and full" (v. 8); SP, LXX, Syr. add "days" filling out the regular formula זָקֵן וְשָׂבֵעַ יָמִים (35:29), "old and full of days" (NIV "years").

[783] Also "gathered to your people," Num 27:13; 31:2; Deut 32:50; "gathered to their fathers," Judg 2:10; "your fathers," and "to your grave," 2 Kgs 22:20//2 Chr 34:28; "gathered" alone, Num 20:26.

[784] For more see I. Cornelius et al., "אָסַף," NIDOTTE 1.470.

[785] Tg. Ps.-J. adds that Abraham refused to bless Isaac, fearing that Ishmael might hate Isaac (as Esau–Jacob); cf. also Gen. Rab. 61.6.

VIII. ISHMAEL'S FAMILY LINE (25:12–18)

The genealogy of Ishmael, Abraham's firstborn, provides the author of Genesis another opportunity to show God's faithfulness to his promises. The passage recalls the angel's assurance to a tormented Hagar (16:10–12; cf. 21:18) and the Lord's promise to a distressed Abraham (17:20b). Elsewhere too the author gives the lineage of the rejected son(s) before continuing with the appointed successor (e.g., Cain/Seth; Japheth and Ham/Shem). The pattern for the patriarchal narratives is similar (see vol. 1A, p. 39). The inclusion of the patriarchal lines of the rejected sons (Keturah's sons, Ishmael, Esau) achieves several ends: first, they round out the narratives of the key persons, completing the stories of Abraham and Jacob; second, they demonstrate that God honored the pledge of progeny (12:2), despite the sin and weakness of the human recipients; and third, the exclusion of the rejected offspring was not absolute, since the Lord also granted them benefits.

COMPOSITION.   The relationship of 25:12–18 to the Abraham narrative as a whole and the date of the genealogy have been already addressed at 25:1–11. As a new *tōlĕdōt* section, it transitions to the Isaac narrative by supplying the final record of Abraham's eldest son. As for what became of the chosen son, the Isaac *tôlĕdōt* begins at 25:19, initiating the extensive Jacob discourse (through 35:29). Isaac's family history, however, is reported in the form of narrative instead of genealogy.

The passage consists of genealogy bounded by a narrative frame. C. Westermann believes that the Priestly author (P) has adapted and inserted an independent source (vv. 13–16,18) in his framework of vv. 12 and 17, making v. 18 originally the continuation of v. 16.[1] G. Wenham concludes that the geneal-

---

[1] C. Westermann, *Genesis 12–36: A Commentary,* trans. J. Scullion (Minneapolis: Augsburg, 1985 [1981]), 395, 398–99.

ogy material (P-style) was indeed framed by a later author (J-style), but the same author as 16:12 (J).[2] Clearly, the passage knows the Hagar-Ishmael narratives (chaps. 16–17): v. 16 and 17:20 have "twelve rulers," and v. 18 shares the language of 16:12, "in hostility toward all their/his brothers." Whatever the original source, the passage suggests that the same author of chaps. 16 and 17 was responsible for appropriating and integrating the Ishmael genealogy to the Abraham narrative.

STRUCTURE.   The passage possesses a complex structure, involving two typical introductory statements (vv. 12–13a) and two corresponding conclusions (vv. 17–18). (1) "This is the account of [*tōlĕdōt*] . . ." is another instance of the book's eleven section headings (also Num 3:1; Ruth 4:18; see vol. 1A, pp. 31–35). The conclusion in v. 18 corresponds to the *tōlĕdōt* heading, for both verses pertain to the man and his posterity. (2) "These are the names of . . . ," appears in and outside Genesis, usually presenting a register of lineage.[3] The conclusion in v. 17, lit., "these are the years of the life of . . ." (RSV, NASB), complements the genealogical heading, "These are the names of" (v. 13a); the same pairing of phrases occurs in Exod 6:16,18. By the repetition of the rubric, "these are the names of," vv. 13 and 16 form an inclusion, marking the formal genealogy.

v. 12 The *tōlĕdōt* of Ishmael
v. 13a The "names" of his descendants
            vv. 13b–15 Nebaioth through Kedemah
            v. 16 The "names" of twelve tribal leaders
v. 17 Ishmael's life and death
v. 18 The territory of his descendants

1. Ishmael, Abraham's Son (25:12)

[12]This is the account of Abraham's son Ishmael, whom Sarah's maidservant, Hagar the Egyptian, bore to Abraham.

25:12   "This is the account of" (*tōlĕdōt*) is the key structural device in the Book of Genesis (see vol. 1A, pp. 27–28).[4] The same term, though not in the stereotyped formula, reappears in v. 13, lit., "according to their generations." The NIV's rendering "listed in the order of their birth" agrees with many translations and commentators due to the description "firstborn"

---

[2] G. Wenham, *Genesis 16–50*, WBC (Dallas: Word, 1994), 163.

[3] וְאֵלֶּה שְׁמוֹת, Gen 36:20; 40:8; Exod 1:1; 6:16; Num 1:5; 3:2,18; 27:1; 34:19; Josh 17:3; 2 Sam 5:14; 1 Chr 6:2; 14:4; Ezek 48:1; without *waw*, אֵלֶּה שְׁמוֹת, Gen 36:10; Num 3:3; 13:16; 34:17; 2 Sam 23:8.

[4] 1 Chr 1:29–31 parallel 25:13–15.

(v. 13). The same phrase, however, occurs in 10:32, meaning simply that the names listed entail a genealogy.

Ishmael is identified two ways in the *tōlĕdōt* heading. First, he is the "son of Abraham." "Abraham" appears twice in the verse, highlighting the connection of Ishmael with the patriarch and thus recalling the promise made on that basis (21:13). Second, he is the son of "Hagar the Egyptian," recalling the troubled life of his outcast mother who was oppressed and expelled by Sarah (16:6; 21:10). In both episodes the Lord's messenger announced that she and her son Ishmael would be the ancestors of numerous descendants (16:10; 21:18; cf. 17:20). By mentioning the mother of Ishmael, the passage clarifies that though a son he was not the legitimate recipient of the patriarch's inheritance, who by divine decree would be borne only by Sarah (17:18–19). So as to underscore his disqualifications, the title includes the disparaging identity of his mother. She was Egyptian, whose nation was hostile to the chosen lineage (e.g., 12:10–13:1; 15:13–14), and she was a slave "maidservant" *(šipḥâ)*, who had an inferior status in the household (see comments on 16:1). The author first introduced Hagar by this same social profile (16:1).

2. Ishmael's Sons (25:13–16)

The passage names Ishmael's descendants (vv. 13–15) and the twelve rulers, identifying their ethnic and territorial connections (v. 16).

(1) Names of the Sons (25:13–15)

[13]These are the names of the sons of Ishmael, listed in the order of their birth: Nebaioth the firstborn of Ishmael, Kedar, Adbeel, Mibsam, [14]Mishma, Dumah, Massa, [15]Hadad, Tema, Jetur, Naphish and Kedemah.

25:13a   On the significance of this second introduction, see "Structure."
25:13b   This segmented genealogy in vv. 13b–15 gives only one generation of descendants, listing twelve names (see vol. 1A, p. 298). Mention is not made of Ishmael's daughters Mahalath and Basemath (cp. 4:22), who married Esau (28:9; 36:3–4,10,13,17; on the problem of their identities, see comments on 26:34). The intermarriage of the Edomites and Ishmaelites further strengthened the two nations born to the outcast sons. Sarna suggested that members of the Keturah and Ishmael lines probably united since the prophets (Isa 60:6–7; Jer 25:23; Ezek 27:21–23) and Assyrian records show they are closely related.[5] Although the Keturah lineage in 25:2–4 contains more (three) generations than Ishmael's list (see comments at introduction to 25:1–6), she bore only six sons, half as many as Ishmael fathered, providing a foil for Hagar, whose lineage

---

[5] N. H. Sarna, בראשית *Genesis,* JPST (Philadelphia: Jewish Publication Society, 1989), 175.

received the advantage of divine promise (16:10; 21:18).

The Keturah tribes (vv. 2–4) resided generally in the Midian region and further south,[6] and the sons of Ishmael settled in the north(west) area of the Arabian peninsula whose influence was at its peak during the eighth to fourth centuries until the rise of the Nabateans (ca. 400 B.C.). For this reason the Ishmaelite genealogy has been customarily dated to the sixth century and later. The surprising importance in the genealogy attached to the Nebaioth ("firstborn") instead of the Kedarites, listed only second, who were the most powerful tribe, shows that the genealogy provides an authentic ancient memory.[7]

Nebaioth (Ar. **Nabayât;* Akk. *Nabaiātì*) has the distinguished position of "firstborn" (v. 13b//1 Chr 1:29; also 28:9; 36:3),[8] a feature occurring in many genealogies in Genesis (10:15; 22:21; 35:23; 36:15; 46:8; also Num 3:2; 26:5; 2 Sam 3:2; 1 Chr 1:13 *passim*). The tribe's location is surmised to have been centered at modern Ha'il on the basis of Assyrian and Arabic inscriptional references. The once popular idea that the Nebaioth were the ancestors of the Nabateans (Ar. *Nabaṭ*) has been found untenable.[9] *Kedar,* whose meaning in Hebrew *(qdr)* is "dark, black" (Song 1:5), was the most influential tribe during the first millennium until the Nabateans. The Nebaioth and Kedar are closely related in Isa 60:7. Although located in the region Jauf (= Jawf, "cavity" or "basin"), the Kedarites operated as far away as the eastern delta of Egypt, the southern Negev, and the Transjordan in the fifth century.[10] Due to its prominence in the incense trade, this tribe was often mentioned in Assyrian records and in prophetic judgment oracles (Isa 21:16–17; 42:11; 60:7; Jer 2:10; 49:28; Ezek 27:21).[11] That the Kedarites practiced a form of pastoral nomadism and sedentary life may be reflected by references to their "tents" (e.g., Song 1:5; Ps 120:5; Jer 49:28–29) and their "settlements" (Isa 42:11),

---

[6] J. A. Montgomery, *Arabia and the Bible* (1934; reprint, New York: Ktav, 1969), 46.

[7] F. V. Winnett dates the genealogy in the sixth century but admits that the prominence of Nebaioth is an ancient tradition ("The Arabian Genealogies in the Book of Genesis," in *Translating and Understanding the Old Testament: Essays in Honor of Herbert Gordon May* [Nashville: Abingdon, 1970], 194).

[8] E. A. Knauf ("Nebaioth," *ABD* 4.1053) explains the prominence given in Gen 25 to Nebaioth on the assumption that the biblical authors applied "Nebaioth" to the Kedarite clan Nabat, who became the dominant Nabateans (= Idumeans) in the fourth century (cf. Isa 60:7; also the association of the Edomites and Nebaioth in 28:9; 36:3). F. V. Winnett and W. L. Reed simply observe that the Hebrew and Arabic traditions believed that the Nebaioth were the oldest North Arabian people (*Ancient Records from North Arabia* [Toronto: University of Toronto Press, 1970], 100).

[9] Winnett and Reed, *Ancient Records from North Arabia,* 99–100.

[10] D. Graf, "Palestine in the Persian through Roman Periods," *OEANE* 4.223.

[11] A bowl inscription of the fifth century from Tell el-Maskhuta (in the eastern Nile Delta) identifies "Gashmu" (גשמו, "Geshem," NIV, Neh 6:6) as king of Kedar, a reference to Nehemiah's adversary, "Geshem the Arab" (Neh 2:19; 6:1–2,6); see J. Holladay, "Mashkuta, Tell el," *OEANE* 3.436; N. Williams, "Geshem," *ABD* 2.995.

the latter term mentioned in v. 16 (*ḥaṣĕrîm,* "settlements").[12] *Adbeel*[13] has been identified with the tribal (and personal) name *Idibaʾilu* whom Tiglath-Pileser conquered in the eighth century. *Mibsam,* meaning "spice" or "balm" (Hb., *bōśem,* Ar. *bašām;* cf. Basemath, 26:34),[14] appears again as a descendant of Simeon whose son was Mishma (1 Chr 4:25), the name of Mibsam's brother in 25:14.

25:14 *Mishma* is obscure (v. 14//1 Chr 1:30), but Winnette proposes a location near Jebel Mismaʾ, 160 miles east of the oasis city Tema.[15] Knauf proposes an identification with the tribe *Išammeʿ* by emending Hebrew *Mishma* to Arabic *Mušāmiʿ.*[16] *Dumah* (Hb. "silence," cf. Isa 21:11) is usually identified with the oasis Dumat al-Ghandal, known as al-Jauf today (see *Kedar* above). Dumah is an oasis town centrally located in the north Arabian peninsula; it was a key point in the incense trade, connecting both west to Palestine and northeast to Babylon.[17] It lies at the head of the Wadi Sirhan, about 250 miles northeast of Maʾan, at the northern edge of the Nafud. Its geographical importance is reflected by its occupation from as early as the paleolithic period.[18] This was the site known as *Adummatu* in Assyrian and Babylonian records, having great importance in the seventh century. Knauf identifies *Massa* (Hb. "burden, oracle," cf. Prov 30:1; 31:1) with the Arabian tribe Massaean, mentioned in Assyrian records with Tema (v. 15), and thus perhaps located nearby.[19] Tiglath-Pileser lists Massa with Adbeel (*Idibaʾilu,* v. 13), Tema, and Ephah (*Haiappa,* v. 4) among others whom he subdued.[20]

25:15 The name *Hadad* (spelled *ḥădad,*[21] v. 15//1 Chr 1:30) also appears for two Edomite kings (spelled *hădad*) in the line of Esau (36:35–36,39; 1 Chr 1:46–47,50–51) and for the Edomite ruler who opposed Solomon (1 Kgs 11:14–22,25; see comments on 36:35). The oasis town *Tema* (modern Taymaʾ) was located strategically in northwest Arabia where caravan routes converged, making it a major power (cf. Job 6:19; Isa 21:14; Jer 25:23). The archaeological remains include pottery from the second millennium. The Babylonian king

---

[12] A. Fulton and W. S. LaSor ("Kedar," *ISBE* 3.5) suggest that there were two groups of Kedarites, but it is better to view their lifestyle as pastoral dimorphism.

[13] The LXX reads "Nabdeel," Ναβδεηλ (metathesis of *beth/daleth;* also 1 Chr 1:29); cf. the addition Ραγουηλ καὶ Ναβδεηλ ("Raguel and Nabdeel") at 25:3, LXX.

[14] E. A. Knauf, "Mibsam," *ABD* 4.805.

[15] Winnett, "Arabian Genealogies in the Book of Genesis," 194.

[16] E. A. Knauf, "Mishma," *ABD* 4.871.

[17] K. A. Kitchen, "Dumah," *Baker Encyclopedia of Bible Places* (UK: InterVarsity/Grand Rapids: Baker, 1995), 102.

[18] J. Zarins, "Dumah," *ABD* 2.239–40.

[19] E. A. Knauf, "Massa," *ABD* 4.600; Winnett and Reed suggest somewhere between al-Jauf and Tema in the desert Nafud (*Ancient Records from North Arabia,* 101).

[20] Montgomery, *Arabia and the Bible,* 58–59.

[21] AV has "Hadar," חדד attested by Syr. and the Bomberg edition (see *BHS*).

Nabonidus fortified the city as his capital, residing in Arabia for ten years (ca. 552–42) and leaving Babylon to his son Belshazzar to administrate (cf. Dan 5:29). The tribe *Jetur* (//1 Chr 1:31) was in north Transjordan when it succumbed to the Israelites (1 Chr 5:18–19). There is an association of this tribe with the Hagrites who have been related by some scholars to Hagar and the Ishmaelites (1 Chr 5:10,19–21; Ps 83:6). Knauf explains the meaning of Jetur from the Arabic term *ẓwr* ("rock"; vb. "besiege"), thus "one who builds stone fences" or "the one who besieges."[22] They were the ancestors of the Ituraeans (Luke 3:1), who resided in the Biqaʿ valley (i.e., "valley of Lebanon," Josh 11:17; 12:7; cf. LXX, *Ietour/Iettour,* 25:15//1 Chr 1:31).

Naphish, meaning "precious" (Ar. *nafîs*),[23] appears with Jeter among those defeated by the transjordan Israelites (1 Chr 5:19). The similar name "Nephussim" identifies a family who returned from the Babylonian exile (Ezra 2:50 = Neh 7:52 [*Naphushesim,* NRSV]; *1 Esdr* 5:31 [*Nephisim,* NRSV]). *Kedemah* (Hb. *qēdĕmâ*) means "toward the east" in Hebrew (13:14; 28:14); the Arabic personal name *Qudamah* is reminiscent of this descendant's name.[24] The "Kadmonites" *(qadmōnî),* meaning "easterners," are listed among Canaan's inhabitants in 15:19. Jeremiah 49:28 associates the "people of the East" *(bĕnê qedem)* with the north Arabian tribe Kedar and Israelite Hazor. The land of the "eastern peoples" *(bĕnê qedem)* in 29:1 describes the region of Haran. Taken together, the terms identifying the "peoples of the east" were used broadly for different people groups who were in the general direction east of Canaan, including northwest Arabia.

(2) Twelve Rulers (25:16)

[16]**These were the sons of Ishmael, and these are the names of the twelve tribal rulers according to their settlements and camps.**

25:16 This verse reveals the ethnogeographical nature of the genealogy, providing both personal and tribal names according to their locations. "Settlements" translates *ḥaṣĕrîm,* referring to villages (e.g., Deut 2:23; cf. "Kedar," Isa 42:11); these were unwalled habitations (Lev 25:31) associated with nearby towns (*ʿārîm;* Josh 19:8; e.g., "their villages," Josh 13:23; Neh 11:30).[25] "Camps" (*ṭîrōt,* lit., "enclosures") may refer to settlements (1 Chr 6:24) or dwellings related to towns (*ʿārîm;* Num 31:10). They are also transient habitations; the term appears in poetic parallel with "tents" (Ps 69:25). Ezekiel 25:4 mentions "camps" and "tents" inhabited by "the people of the East." "Twelve tribal leaders" recalls the promised blessing in 17:20; Jacob

---

[22] E. A. Knauf, "Jetur," *ABD* 3.821–22.
[23] E. A. Knauf, "Naphish," *ABD* 4.1020.
[24] E. A. Knauf, "Kedemah," *ABD* 4.10.
[25] *DCH* 3.297.

too begets twelve descendants (35:22; 49:28). The term "leader" *(nāsî')* is broadly used, including tribal chief or prince (e.g., Num 1:16; 17:17,21), family clan leader (e.g., Josh 22:4; 1 Kgs 8:1; 2 Chr 1:2), king (e.g., 1 Kgs 11:34), and governor (e.g., Ezra 1:8).

3. Ishmael's Life, Death, and Territories (25:17–18)

[17]Altogether, Ishmael lived a hundred and thirty-seven years. He breathed his last and died, and he was gathered to his people. [18]His descendants settled in the area from Havilah to Shur, near the border of Egypt, as you go toward Asshur. And they lived in hostility toward all their brothers.

25:17 Ishmael died at 137 years, surviving Abraham by forty-eight years (16:16; 25:7; cp. 180 years for Isaac, 35:28). The description of Ishmael's death repeats fixed expressions commonly appearing in obituaries in Genesis (cf. comments on 25:7–8).

25:18 The location of the Ishmaelites originally was "from Havilah to Shur" (v. 18). From there their descendants must have diffused across northwest Arabia. The identification of Shur (see comments on 16:7) is defined in relation to Egypt, lit., "which is opposite (east) Egypt as you go toward Asshur." Although the exact location of Shur cannot be determined, the descriptions of military campaigns from Israel to Egypt (1 Sam 15:7; 27:8) suggest that the tract situated between the modern Suez Canal (west) and the Wadi el-Arish (east) probably was intended.[26] Havilah probably was in Arabia, not the same site mentioned in Eden (see 2:11; 10:7, vol. 1A, pp. 207, 447). "Asshur" does not refer to Assyria located in northern Mesopotamia, but probably a site in Sinai or Arabia is meant (cf. 25:3; Num 24:22,24). Two different peoples by this same name are mentioned in the Table of Nations (10:11,22; see vol. 1A, p. 461) and here may refer to yet another people group and location.

By using the language of 16:12b, v. 18 alludes to the angel's promise concerning Ishmael,[27] signaling its fulfilment (16:10–12). There are two translation problems occurring in v. 18b. First, the Hebrew of v. 18a has the plural verb, "they settled," referring to Ishmael's descendants, but v. 18b differs by employing the singular verb, "he lived."[28] Some EVs maintain the distinction (AV, NKJV, NASB, NRSV, HCSB), but others harmonize the two. The LXX and Vg. read the singular in both places, meaning Ishmael is the subject, whereas NIV has plural renderings, "his descendants settled" and "they lived." Although the latter can be interpreted as a collective singular in number, referring to the descendants as a group, the singular "he settled" (v. 18b) best suits the author's

---

[26] K. A. Kitchen, "Shur," *NBD*, 1099.

[27] 16:12, וְעַל פְּנֵי כָל אֶחָיו, and 25:18, עַל פְּנֵי כָל אֶחָיו, "hostility toward all his brothers."

[28] וַיִּשְׁכְּנוּ, "they settled," and נָפָל, lit., "he fell."

intention. When alluding to 16:12, he shows by the singular verb the fulfilment of the promises concerning the individual Ishmael, yet the ambiguity of the singular permits the secondary inference that the same character marked his descendants. Moreover, plural and singular verbs appearing together reflect the current view of solidarity between an ancestor and his tribal offspring.

The second problem is the final words of v. 18b, subject to two translations: the expression ʿal pĕnê may be either (1) "against the face," that is, hostility (e.g., NIV, NASB), or (2) "opposite, east of," that is, dwelt alongside of (e.g., NRSV, NJPS). Both make sense of the passage, but the former is preferred, for the allusion to 16:12 relies on its meaning whose context describes Ishmael's animus toward others ("his hand will be against everyone," 16:12). Also the unexpected verb nāpal ("lived," NIV) is a purposeful departure from 16:12, which employs yiškōn ("will live," NIV). The term nāpal, "fall [upon]," may indicate a climate of confrontation as it does in Judg 7:12, describing the incursions of foreign tribes.

—— IX. ISAAC'S FAMILY: JACOB AND ESAU (25:19–35:29) ——

The account of Jacob is subsumed under the *tôlĕdōt* heading of his father, Isaac (25:19). This formula follows the typical procedure of Genesis that names the patriarch's father at the head of a new *tôlĕdōt* section (vol. 1A, pp. 35–41). The formal boundaries of the Jacob narrative refer to Isaac's relationship to Abraham in life and death (25:19; 35:29). Embedded within the Jacob narrative is the Jacob-Esau conflict narrative that has as its background the deathbed of Isaac (27:1–2) and his death and burial by the twin brothers (35:28–29). By casting Isaac in the role of a "second Abraham," the author demonstrates the continuity of the family and its promised inheritance (chap. 26). The absence of a heading entitled "the *tôlĕdōt* of Abraham" is due to the brief treatment of Isaac whose career is important historically and thematically to the author but plays only a transitional role literarily. Isaac stands either in the shadow of his father Abraham or functions as background to his son Jacob. As the bridge between grandfather and grandson, Isaac interfaces the two chief figures in patriarchal Genesis—Father Abraham and the nation's namesake, "Jacob–Israel" (32:28–32; cf. the triplet "Abraham, Isaac, Jacob/Israel," e.g., Exod 32:13; 1 Kgs 18:36; Isa 41:8; 1 Chr 29:10). Thus, the Jacob story begins by paralleling the experience of his father Isaac with that of Abraham who both faced the hurdles of a childless family and an alien status (25:21; 26:1). As the legitimate purveyor of the Abraham blessing (26:3–4), he extends the blessing, albeit unknowingly, to his younger son, Jacob (27:33; 28:1). The absence of an Abraham *tôlĕdōt* heading also contributes to the author's theology. Abraham is more than an ancestor to Isaac and Jacob. He represents the whole of those who count themselves as descendants of covenant Israel. Abraham is not subject to the exclusive claims of any one person as father. He is the father of all Israel (Isa 51:2; Ezek 33:24; cf. John 8:39,53; Acts 7:2; Rom 4:1,12; Jas 2:21).

JACOB AND THE ABRAHAM AND JOSEPH NARRATIVES. The Jacob narrative continues the Abraham narrative in substantive ways but also departs from it. Jacob, like Abraham, receives revelatory promises and blessing (28:13–14; 35:9–12; 46:3–4) and repeatedly benefits from God's intervening protection (31:7,24,29,31,42; 32:11; 33:11), despite repeated moral lapses (27:35–36; 31:20,27; 34:13,30). But herein lies the major departure: the promises dominate the Abraham corpus, whereas in the Jacob story they are essential but not dominant in the unfolding of the account. The development of the promissory covenant as reported in the Abraham narrative is assumed in the Jacob narrative. The reappearing aspect of the promises is not an heir, as with the Abraham and Isaac stories, but the occupation of the land. Jacob at his own doing jeopardized his inheritance of the land when he fled in exile and returned under threat by his brother (27:41–45; 32:11). The promise of God at Bethel sustained his hope of reconciliation and motivated his daring return (28:4,20–21; 31:13; 35:1,7; 46:1–4). What occupies the Jacob narrative, however, is the metamorphosis of his character—from trickster to humbled servant—achieved against the background of serial conflicts. The concentric circles of the narrative's episodes (see Structure below) subtly enhance the turnaround in the man's character as portrayed in the account. The flight to Paddan Aram (27:1–28:9) and his return to Canaan (33:1–20), for example, are at the geographical level indicative of the moral change in the patriarch. He did not fully rid himself of the old Jacob, but he surely changed from the young man who had merited the meaning of his name Jacob ("Deceiver"). Conflict also appears in the Abraham story, but it is not as prominent as in Jacob's experience. Conflict is the constitutive motif for the Jacob narrative. T. L. Thompson observed that in Jacob's story are "conflict stories within conflict stories, placed one within the other like Russian Gigogne dolls."[1] The outer circle of conflict is the Jacob-Esau struggle, followed by the conflicts with foreigners by Isaac (chap. 26) and by Jacob's sons (chap. 34). Moving closer to the center is the Jacob-Laban tussle and the Leah-Rachel race for acceptance. Conflicts between two brothers and two sisters form the outer and the inner narrative perimeters of Jacob's strife. The climactic struggle is reserved for the trickster Jacob and the God of Bethel (28:20–22) that is resolved in the life and death struggle of Jacob and the "man" at Penu/iel (32:24–32).

Another departure from the Abraham story is the absence of a clear end to the career of Jacob at the close of his narrative (cp. 25:8–11). His death report appears only after his descent into Egypt at the invitation of Joseph (49:33) toward the close of the Joseph narrative. The death notice that ends the *tôlĕdōt* section is Isaac's death and burial (35:29). Jacob's survival provides for a significant overlap between the two stories, making Jacob the linking personality who maintains narrative attention beyond Jacob in Canaan to Jacob in Egypt. Joseph's story assumes and builds on the Jacob account, functioning as the second and concluding movement of the Jacob recital. The cross-references, parallels, and allusions between the two narratives show an interdependence that results in a Jacob-Joseph complex of stories.[2]

There are important differences, too, between the Jacob and Joseph stories

---

[1] T. L. Thompson, *The Origin Tradition of Ancient Israel: I. The Literary Formulation of Genesis and Exodus 1–23*, JSOTSup 55 (Sheffield: Sheffield Academic Press, 1987), 105.

[2] P. Miscall, "The Jacob and Joseph Stories as Analogies," *JSOT* 6 (1978): 28–40; D. M. Carr, *Reading the Fractures of Genesis: Historical and Literary Approaches* (Louisville: Westminster John Knox, 1996), 281–83; e.g., the blood and skin of a goat draw a parallel between Jacob's deception of blind Isaac (27:16–23) and the sons' deception of the elderly Jacob (37:31–32).

(see more at the Introduction to the Joseph narrative). The Joseph material does not rely on the Abraham account to the same extent, especially the promises of land and descendants. The identity of the patriarch's heir is clearly recognizable in the Abraham and Jacob narratives, but the successor to Jacob is only subtly identified at best, namely, Judah (see comments on chap. 38). Although a rivalry between Joseph and Judah has been argued by some, it is at best a rivalry that is underplayed, subservient to the pronounced narrative interest in the jealousy of the ten toward their father's love for Joseph (e.g., 37:3–11). Jacob grants a blessing for all his sons (49:28), and there is no struggle among the sons overtly for the blessing. The father Joseph is disturbed at the blessing of younger Ephraim, but there is no narrative development of the potential conflict between Ephraim and Manasseh (48:17–20). The identity of Israel's God was limited to the tripartite title, "the God of Abraham, Isaac, and Jacob." Neither Joseph nor Judah has the same stature as their trio of predecessors. None of the twelve sons was an outcast son, although Simeon and Levi were rebuffed; all twelve tribes were the beneficiaries who constituted Israel (e.g., Exod 3:6,15,16; 1 Kgs 18:36).

ESAU AND ISHMAEL.   A comparison between the Abraham and Jacob narratives encourages us to consider further the roles of the two "rejected" sons in the respective narratives, Ishmael and Esau. Roger Syrén observes, "The figure of Esau cries out for comparison with Ishmael."[3] The most obvious similarity is the literary function of the two figures as foils for the preferred sons Isaac and Jacob. Both are destined to live outside the land of promise (16:12; 27:39–40). These connections at the literary level have their parallel at the historical level, since the two lines of descent are intertwined through the marriage of Esau to one of Ishmael's daughters (Basemath, 36:3). In both cases, the narratives show that the father (Abraham/Isaac) prefers the elder son (Ishmael/Esau) and the mother (Sarah/Rebekah) favors the younger son (Isaac/Jacob). This comparison indicates that substantive differences also are between the outcast sons. The aforementioned analogy is not exact, because whereas Isaac and Ishmael have different mothers (Sarah/Hagar), Esau and Jacob are children of the same mother (Rebekah). B. Dicou observed that the three chief separations of the patriarchal narratives show differences too. Abraham and Lot are opposed as fathers (i.e., the Israelites versus the Ammonites, Moabites); Ishmael and Isaac are opposed as sons; but the separation of Jacob and Esau are as brothers.[4] The separation then was more profound since the relationship was more inherent. Other near but inexact comparisons abound. Hagar and

---

[3] R. Syrén, *The Forsaken First-Born: A Study of a Recurrent Motif in the Patriarchal Narratives*, JSOTSup 133 (Sheffield: Sheffield Academic Press, 1993), 68.

[4] B. Dicou, *Edom, Israel's Brother and Antagonist: The Role of Edom in Biblical Prophecy and Story*, JSOTSup 169 (Sheffield: Sheffield Academic Press, 1994), 135.

Rebekah receive prenatal announcements concerning their sons' future, but Hagar hears the promise of numerous offspring (16:11) and no such promise is overtly noted for Esau. The author and reader could presume this will be the case for Esau, too, since there has been a pattern of the "deselected son" establishing a prodigious lineage in Genesis (e.g., Cain, Joktan, Lot, Ishmael). The names "Ishmael" and "Esau" are important to the respective stories as well, although the name Ishmael has a divine origin and Esau's was a human invention. Furthermore, the sibling battles share similar outcomes, since a geographical separation results (cp. Cain, Lot). Ishmael, however, is expelled and Isaac remains with his father, whereas Esau remains and Jacob must leave his household. This brings us to another critical distinction in their careers. The hostility between Esau and Jacob is overt, even to the point of Esau contemplating murder, but the Ishmael threat to Isaac is subtle, albeit certain in the eyes of Sarah. Moreover, the Isaac/Ishmael reconciliation is correspondingly muted, but the reunion of Esau and Jacob plays a major part in the narrative structure of the Jacob story and the viewpoint of the author. The greater attention given to Esau by the author is due to the better example that the Esau and Jacob conflict provided him. Since they possessed the same mother, the selection of the younger Jacob served the author's theology of Israel's earliest history. The future of Israel was secured from the outset by virtue of God's commitment to their ancestor Jacob, even before his birth. The greater attention to the Esau/Edom story was also because of the historical involvement of the Israelites and Edomites as early as the wilderness period (e.g., Num 20) and the two nations shared a border (e.g., Num 34:3; Josh 15:1), contrary to the less frequent association of the Israelites with the bedouin descendants of Ishmael. Moreover, Genesis shows the relationship of the Israelites to that of the nations, the connections at their founding and the differences in their destinies.[5] Edom represented both features of Israel's relationship with the nations, since it was close to Israel in origin but painfully distant by Esau/Edom's status as the rejected brother (cf. Amos 1:11–12; 9:12; Jer 49:7–22; Ezek 35–36; Obadiah; Mal 1:2–5).

COMPOSITION.   Until the final quarter of the twentieth century, the scholarly consensus assigned to the Jacob story the standard Pentateuchal documents observed in the Abraham corpus—the Yahwist (J), Elohist (E), and Priestly (P) sources. These sources that once were independent compositions were patched together in pieces by a series of authors/redactors during a protracted period from the tenth to the fifth centuries. For M. Noth the J source provided the most complete continuous narrative that was recoverable from the extant text. The E source was also an independent narrative source, though this was less certain in Noth's

[5] Ibid., 134–36, 158–60.

mind, but the redaction of it left only remnants of the original E document. A subsequent redaction placed the JE composition in the framework provided by the P source.[6] As for the underlying oral/written traditions of the patriarchs, Gunkel and Noth believed that the Jacob tradition was the earliest of the three patriarchs. Noth distinguished between an "East Jordan Jacob" tradition (Jacob-Esau/Jacob-Laban) whose Jacob was essentially "worldly" and a "West Jordan Jacob" tradition whose Jacob was a cultic ancestor associated with Shechem and Bethel.[7] Although Noth's dichotomy of the Jacob traditions has been largely rejected by scholars, those who continue some form of source-tradition criticism still contend for a northern origin of the Jacob figure, perhaps originating at Bethel. After the Assyrian conquest and exile of the northern tribes, the Jacob figure expanded in importance to become the eponymous ancestor of all Israel, whose own exile had antecedents in Jacob's sojourn at Haran. The postexilic struggle between Israel and Edom explains the development and inclusion of the Jacob-Esau story.[8]

Growing doubts about the cogency of three parallel documents as conceived by source critics led to new models for reconstructing the patriarchal stories. Rhetorical discoveries, such as the unmistakable concentric patterning of the Jacob narrative and of other portions of Genesis (e.g., the flood and Babel accounts), led scholars to place more attention on the narratives as compositional wholes. For example, E. Blum, following the lead of R. Rendtorff, jettisoned the customary three-source approach to the Jacob narrative (chaps. 25–33), advocating a method centered on a succession of redaction expansions or layers to a nuclear story.[9] For Blum the nucleus was the Jacob-Esau rivalry (25:21–34; chap. 27), dated to the Davidic-Solomonic period, and the majority of the Jacob-Laban story (chaps. 29–31), ending in the treaty of Jacob and Laban (31:44–32:2a). To this kernel a succession of six redaction layers developed the Jacob corpus (chaps. 25–33), coming from the divided monarchy period, no later than the era of Josiah. To these were added the exilic and postexilic ("P") accretions (e.g., 27:46–28:9). The difference between Noth and Blum was that the old school believed the redactor drew on existing parallel documents to fill out the account, whereas Blum hypothesized that the evolution of the account relied on redaction layering.[10] This completed Jacob unit was the initial narrative around which the Abraham and Joseph units were added, creating the patriarchal corpus (chaps. 12–50). B. Dicou built on Blum's and J. Bartlett's opinions, although differing significantly by dating the Esau=Edom identity as the brother of Jacob in

---

[6] M. Noth, *A History of Pentateuchal Traditions* (Englewood Cliffs, N.J.: Prentice-Hall, 1972 [German 1948]), 228.

[7] Noth identified the Ephraimites migrating to transjordan as the purveyors of the Jacob traditions (*Pentateuchal Traditions*, 87–101, esp. 89–91).

[8] J. Strange, "Geography and Tradition in the Patriarchal Narratives," *SJOT* 11 (1997): 210–22.

[9] E. Blum, *Die Komposition der Vätergeschichte*, WMANT 57 (Neukirchen-Vluyn: Neukirchener Verlag, 1984); R. Rendtorff, *The Problem of the Process of Transmission in the Pentateuch*, JSOTSup 89 (Sheffield: JSOT, 1990 [German 1977]).

[10] See D. J. Wynn-Williams, *The State of the Pentateuch: A Comparison of the Approaches of M. Noth and E. Blum* (Berlin/New York: de Gruyter, 1997).

the sixth century, rather than the customary view that it occurred in the preexilic period (as early as David). Dicou followed Bartlett's view that the original connection of Esau was with Seir (chap. 27),[11] not initially Edom, to which was added in the seventh century the variant tradition of the twins' struggle over birthright, that is, Esau=Edom (chap. 25). The relocation of the Edomites to the west of the Arabah (Seir) into the sixth century fostered the link of the Israelites and Edomites as brother tribes. The hostility that arose between the nations came from the Babylonian destruction of Jerusalem which produced the tone of enmity that the Genesis stories took on and which the prophets exploited.

The old critical reconstruction of three parallel literary sources has been modified by recent trends in three significant ways.[12] First, scholars see less and less of the Elohist in the Jacob account.[13] Rather, the Yahwist is the primary author who took earlier traditions and gave them their promise-fulfillment perspective.[14] The former Elohist materials are now considered expansions of J's structure and material. Second, instead of early and extensive pasting together of numerous pieces of documents (sources), the Jacob narrative is a major composition in its own right, having its own developmental history.[15] Third, the composition in its final phases is dated late to the Persian period as opposed to the preexilic period that once dominated source critical thinking.[16]

---

[11] J. Bartlett, *Edom and the Edomites*, JSOTSup 77 (Sheffield: Sheffield Academic Press, 1999), 43–44, 177–79.

[12] E.g., the collected studies in J.-D. Macchi and T. Römer, eds., *Jacob: un Commentaire à plusieurs voix de Genèse 25–36: Mélanges offerts à Albert de Pury*, Le Monde de la Bible 44 (Geneva: Labor et Fides, 2001).

[13] E.g., G. W. Coats, *Genesis: With an Introduction to Narrative Literature*, FOTL 1 (Grand Rapids: Eerdmans, 1983), 22; C. Westermann, *Genesis 12–36: A Commentary* (Minneapolis: Augsburg, 1985), 571–72; and J. Van Seters, *Prologue to History: The Yahwist as Historian in Genesis* (Louisville: Westminster/John Knox, 1992), 205, 277–310, 328.

[14] Z. Weisman argues that the Jacob story is essentially by a *premonarchic* Elohist, for whose work the Yahwist merely provided a superstructure, connecting Jacob with the figures Abraham and Isaac; the Elohist's traditions reflect a pre-Yahwistic and pre-Sinaitic religion closer to Canaanite religious beliefs than those depicted in the Abraham and Isaac accounts ("The Interrelationship between J and E in Jacob's Narrative," *ZAW* 104 [1992]: 177–97).

[15] R. Rendtorff contends that the Jacob narrative is a coherent whole, structured around the three phases of Jacob's life ("The Future of Pentateuchal Criticism," *Henoch* 6 [1984]: 1–14). A. de Pury believes that the core of the Jacob cycle consists of an independent literary body, made up of earlier oral versions, coming from the eighth century and addressing Israel's relationship with Edom and Aram; the Yahwist harmonized the Jacob story with the Abraham narrative in the exilic era, and P further conformed it to the Abraham narrative in the postexilic period ("Le cycle de Jacob comme légende autonome des origines d'Israël," *Congress Volume, Leuven, 1989* [Leiden: Brill, 1991], 78–96). Also de Pury's "Situer le cycle de Jacob: Quelques réflexions, vingt-cinq ans plus tard," *Studies in the Book of Genesis: Literature, Redaction and History*, BETL 155 (Leuven: Leuven University Press, 2001), 213–41. de Pury, however, is especially noted for contending for the sources J and E in 28:10–22 (see *ad loc.*).

[16] E.g., Van Seters attributes the composition to his exilic Yahwist, observing that the story provided a paradigm of exile and return for Judah's exiles (*Prologue to History*, 300–306); S. L. McKenzie, "Jacob in the Prophets," *Jacob: un Commentaire à plusieurs voix de Genèse 25–36*, 339–57.

Exemplary of this new trend is D. Carr's *Reading the Fractures of Genesis* that posits an original core Jacob story written from a northern preexilic perspective (agreeing with Blum) that was taken up in a larger Jacob-Joseph complex. After the collapse of the Northern Kingdom, Judean authors gave this early complex of ancestral narratives a southern royal orientation, projecting the rise of the Davidic regime (e.g., chaps. 34; 38; and 49:1b–28). Abraham and Isaac stories and the primeval history supplemented this revised account, yielding the Genesis core (creation to Joseph) with its new perspective of promise and fulfillment. In this new context the Jacob-Joseph stories become the fulfillment of the promises to Abraham and Isaac.[17] For our comments regarding the failures of the old source and tradition-history approaches and also their new trends to present a convincing case, see vol. 1A, pp. 68–85 and the preface to this volume. Although the trend of positing coherent wholes for the patriarchal narratives is positive, it does not go far enough. We find at the macro and micro levels of the text that the unity of the composition can be demonstrated and can be satisfactorily explained as the result of essentially a single author as opposed to multiple hands across multiple centuries. We will consider in the commentary to follow the composition of each individual unit in the Jacob narrative.

STRUCTURE.   The Jacob narrative consists of two units. The major unit of the corpus is a symmetrical arrangement of matching elements ("legs"), creating an all-embracing literary chiasmus (see display). Although details differ among various structural analyses by scholars, there is wide agreement that the Jacob narrative possesses corresponding parts, exhibiting a reversal in the plot line.[18] Even after form and redaction critics excise what they deem as secondary accretions, the remaining rudimentary narrative by itself shows the same convention of structural inversion.[19] Within the chiastic structure of the whole are embedded inversions that make for a rich literary texture involving repetition, irony, and inclusio.

The second, short unit is a brief genealogical list of Jacob's twelve sons and the report of Isaac's death and burial (35:22b–29). This unit parallels

---

[17] To complete Carr's reconstruction, he finds a semideuteronomistic influence and other late additions that completed the non-P material. This non-P literary block and the priestly text (P) were two major literary bodies that lay before the priestly redactor of the postexilic era who gave organization to the whole and preserved the voices of the two precursory units.

[18] J. P. Fokkelman, *Narrative Art in Genesis: Specimens of Stylistic and Structural Analysis*, 2d ed. (Sheffield: JSOT Press, 1991 [1975]), 86–241; M. Fishbane, *Text and Texture: Close Readings of Selected Biblical Texts* (New York: Schocken, 1979), 40–62, revision of "Composition and Structure in the Jacob Cycle (25:19–35:22)," *JJS* 26 (1975): 15–38; J. Gammie, "Theological Interpretation by way of Literary and Traditional Analysis: Genesis 25–36," *Encounters with the Text: Form and History in the Hebrew Bible*, SemSup 8 (Philadelphia: Fortress: Scholars Press, 1979), 117–34; and G. Rendsburg, *The Redaction of Genesis* (Winona Lake: Eisenbrauns, 1986), 53–69; D. A. Dorsey, *The Literary Structure of the Old Testament: A Commentary on Genesis–Malachi* (Grand Rapids: Baker, 1999), 58.

[19] Coats, *Genesis*, 180 and Carr, *Reading the Fractures of Genesis*, 257.

the closing of the Abraham (25:1–10) and Joseph (49:3–50:14) cycles that include genealogical information and a patriarch's obituary.[20]

A 25:19–34 Struggle at Birth and Birthright
  B 26:1–35 Deception and Strife with the Philistines
    C 27:1–28:9 Stolen Blessing and Flight to Paddan Aram
      D 28:10–22 Promise of Blessing at Bethel
        E 29:1–30 Laban Deceives Jacob
          F 29:31–30:24 Birth of Children
          F' 30:25–43 Birth of Herds
        E' 31:1–55[32:1] Jacob Deceives Laban
      D' 32:1–32[2–33] Struggle for Blessing at Peniel
    C' 33:1–20 Restored Gift and Return to Shechem
  B' 34:1–31 Deception and Strife with the Hivites
A' 35:1–22a Blessing and Struggle at Birth
Appendix 35:22b–29

The shift in the narrative structure is the birth of Joseph by Jacob's barren wife Rachel (30:22–24).[21] Wenham observes that the phrase "God remembered Rachel" reminisces the flood account's pivotal verse, "God remembered Noah" (8:1), that signals the reversal of the floodwaters. After Joseph's birth the patriarch requests his rightful due from Laban so that he can depart for Canaan (30:25–26). From that point in the story, the intent is the return of Jacob and the realization of the divine promise at Bethel (28:15). The symmetrical arrangement of the passage contributes to the theology of the author, who shows that the events in the life of the patriarch exhibit method and purpose, resulting in the outcome ordained by the Lord.

The outside elements of A and A' are themselves reversed: (A) the uterine struggle of the twins and their barter for birthright are matched by (A') the blessing of Jacob and by Benjamin's difficult childbirth. The idea of "struggle" occurs in both elements, giving the whole a rhetorical symmetry.

The second correspondence of B and B' are typically assigned by scholars to redactors since the two elements do not show a direct connection to the flow of the story. Chapters 26 and 34, however, play tactical roles in the plan of the whole and are not afterthoughts. M. Fishbane rightly notes that the episodes describing Isaac's strife with the Philistines (chap. 26) and Jacob's strife (by his sons) with the Hivites (rape of Dinah, chap. 34) each provides a literary pause at two critical junctures in the flow of the narrative. The first breaks up the theft and promise of blessing (chaps. 25; 27),

---

[20] G. Wenham, *Genesis 16–50*, WBC (Dallas: Word, 1994), 462.
[21] Wenham analyzes the chiasmus as uneven in the number of its parts, making 30:22–24 the central leg of the composition (ibid., 170).

and the second matches it by intervening between the corresponding restitution to Esau and the realization of the promised blessing (chaps. 33; 35). The language and motifs shared by chaps. 26 and 34 indicate that the author cast the two narratives with both in mind so as to achieve symmetry for the whole.[22] In both events a "sister" is subject to potential or actual sexual relations with a foreigner (vv. 7,10; 34:2,14), and both accounts involve deception and strife with foreigners (vv. 7–11,20,27; 34:25–34), impinging on the Hebrew patriarchs' position in the community of nations (vv. 11,16,27–29; 34:30).

More than their literary function is the hermeneutical purpose the two episodes achieve; they establish a context for interpreting those critical events. They show that the events of Isaac and Jacob were not parochial; the family history impacted surrounding peoples in accord with the promise made to Abraham, Isaac, and Jacob that they will be a blessing to others (e.g., 12:3; 18:18; 22:18; 26:4; 28:14). Furthermore, the Isaac deception of Abimelech mimics the failure of Abraham, who also deceived the Philistine king (chap. 20). By this analogy (and others), the author shows that Isaac is the proper successor to his father's blessing. The deception of the Hivites by Jacob's sons exhibits the family trait that seems endemic to the appointed lineage. That it led to murder by Simeon and Levi testified to the depth of the family's moral decline. Chapters 26 and 34 exhibit the dark side of the patriarchs, but in each case the outcome benefits the patriarchs and the incidents prove the promise, "I will bless those who bless you, and whoever curses you I will curse" (12:3a).

The corresponding units of C and C′ and D and D′ pertain to the recurring idea of strife. First, Jacob and Esau vie for the inheritance of their father (C), and, second, Jacob wrestles the angel for blessing (D). The outcomes are both positive: the reconciliation of the brothers (C′) and the grant of the promised blessing (D′). In these episodes repeated geographical reminders, involving the departure and return of Jacob to Bethel, enhance the literary facet of reversal. The settings of D/D′ are the places Bethel and Peniel, whose names both commemorate the vital theophanic encounters experienced by Jacob. This pair of events encloses the Jacob-Laban narrative (E/E′ and F/F′) and thereby bridges the Jacob-Laban struggle and the outer circle of the Jacob-Esau struggle. J. Terino observed that the vertical stories of Jacob's encounters with God at Bethel and Peniel parallel the horizontal conflicts of Jacob-Esau.[23] The vertical events provide for the resolutions achieved at the horizontal level.

---

[22] Building on Fishbane's observations, Rendsburg provides many shared lexical correspondences (*The Redaction of Genesis*, 56–59).

[23] J. Torino, "A Text Linguistic Study of the Jacob Narrative," *VE* 18 (1988): 45–62.

Finally, the innermost legs of E/E' and F/F' entail the deception and strife between Jacob and Laban (E) and between the two wives, Leah and Rachel (F). By God's favor toward Jacob's wives (Laban's daughters) and their concubines, the patriarch builds a household (F), and the livestock of Laban furnish a bounty for Jacob (F').

1. Struggle at Birth and Birthright (25:19–34)

The introductory events in this first narrative anticipate the fraternal struggle that encompasses the whole of the Jacob narrative. The perimeters of the narrative involve the dominant idea of family inheritance: the heritage of the father Isaac (v. 19) to the barter for Esau's "birthright" (v. 34). Restating Isaac's relationship to Father Abraham at the outset brings to mind the former story of Isaac and Ishmael and their costly struggle affecting the family (v. 19). Within the megaframework of Genesis, vv. 19–26 transition the end of the Abraham-Isaac/Ishmael narrative to the beginning of the Jacob-Esau account.[24] As Abraham faced the problems created by fathering two sons, Isaac too must endure similar hardship, but this time not by his own doing. Although Esau bartering away his birthright for a pittance to a conniving opportunist is the struggle in the present story, the idea of rival brothers is *déjà vu*. The movement of vv. 19–34 comprises decades, from the time of Isaac's own young manhood ("forty," v. 20) to that of his grown sons. Isaac's prayer for children, its divine answer, and the oracle received by Rebekah testify to the piety of the couple. But their offspring do not exhibit the same measure of spiritual virtue. Three early events show the battle of wills that eventually fractures the family: the struggle in the womb, the tussle at birth, and the contentious sale of the birthright.

Early Jewish interpretation attributed to Jacob merit that won for him the appointment in the divine oracle, whereas Esau was regularly condemned for his impiety (e.g., *Tgs. Ps.-J.* and *Neof.; Gen. Rab.* 63.7–9; *Pirqe R. El.* 24 [177–78]). But even Jacob could lose the inheritance to his brother Esau if he could be enticed to break with the observance of the Torah (e.g., *Tgs. Ps.-J.* and *Neof.; Gen. Rab.* 67.7). Esau was said to have been, among other things, a murderer and an idolater (e.g., *Gen. Rab.* 63.11; *b. B. Bat.* 16b; *Tanḥ., Toledoth* 8(91).[25] Jacob, on the other hand, was a man "perfect in good work" *(Tg. Neof.)* and resided in the schoolhouse of Torah instruction (= "tents," 25:27). That Isaac preferred Esau was only because he had deceived his father, pretending to be a fastidious keeper of the tithe (e.g., *Gen. Rab.* 63.10). So troubled were some Jewish interpreters that the "younger" Jacob (25:23) had preference despite the

---

[24] Coats, *Genesis*, 184–85.

[25] Other references in M. Maher, *Targum Pseudo-Jonathan: Genesis: Translated, with Introduction and Notes* (Collegeville, Minn.: Liturgical Press/Michael Glazier, 1992), 90 n. 39.

law of primogeniture (25:31–34; cf. Deut 21:15–17) that they offered an elaborate midrash explaining that in truth Jacob was the first formed fetus within the womb (*Gen. Rab.* 63.8). He grasped the heel of Esau "by right," because Esau though formed second emerged first (see Rashi). One midrash tradition claims Esau sold to Jacob his share in the "World to Come" when they were yet in the womb and that Jacob was only suggesting that he receive from Esau his birthright in the same manner.[26] The early Church read the struggle in the womb as the conflict between good and evil by means of its typical allegorical method. The womb represents the Church, and the infants depict the struggles of the righteous and the wicked within the Church (e.g., Caesarius of Arles, *Sermon* 86.2; Augustine, *Gospel of John* II.10.2–3). This tension between opposing forces was internalized by Origen to refer to the spiritual battle that each person's soul undertakes (*Homilies on Genesis* 12.3). That the older served the younger was for Caesarius of Arles a picture of the elder people, the Jews, whose Scriptures prepared the way for the "younger" Christians (*Sermon* 86.3).[27] The prayer of Isaac and the barrenness of Rebekah provided Christian commentators ample opportunity to commend the patriarchs as examples of piety and patience.

If we learn anything from the author's perspective revealed in Genesis, however, it is that the vagaries of the struggles among the patriarchs' heirs for prominence (Isaac/Ishmael, Jacob/Esau, Joseph/brothers) and the differences in the historical solutions to these struggles point to a superintending Will that transcends the varying circumstances described in each case.[28] The will of the divine purpose is ultimately what counts, not the personalities, character, or intentions of the participants themselves. Yet, it is important to recall that with this sense of divine direction to which the text subtly alludes, the patriarchal narrative shows explicitly that human participation and accountability are involved in the outcome that proceeds. Franz Delitzsch observed, "Esau's forfeiture of these [firstborn] privileges is according to Romans ix. (comp. Mal. 1.2 sq.), a work of free Divine election, but not without being at the same time, as this narrative shows, the result of Esau's voluntary self-degradation."[29]

The surprising appointment of the younger over the older witnessed, in the eyes of the apostle Paul, to the grace of God (Rom 9:6–13; v. 12 quotes 25:23). That the salvation of God is not dependent on ethnic boundaries, too, was Paul's contention in Rom 2 and 9–11. When the Apostle answered the potential

---

[26] See B. Grossfeld, *The Targum Onqelos to Genesis: Translated, with a Critical Introduction, Apparatus, and Notes* (Wilmington: Michael Glazier, 1988), 97.

[27] *ACCS* 2.146–49.

[28] See R. C. Heard, *Dynamics of Diselection: Ambiguity in Genesis 12–36 and the Ethnic Boundaries in Post-Exilic Judah*, SBLSS 39 (Atlanta: SBL, 2001).

[29] F. Delitzsch, *A New Commentary on Genesis*, vol. 2 (reprint, 2001; Edinburgh: T&T Clark, 1888), 136–37.

charge that, if his thought were right, then God's promises made to Israel had failed (9:1–13), he pointed out that the grace extended to the Gentiles, despite God's historic covenant commitment to ethnic Israel, was consistent from the very beginning with the Scriptures' picture of God's mercies bestowed upon an unforeseen community. "The God of Israel's tradition, therefore, is paradoxically an untraditional God."[30] This was always the case, namely, that God's salvation was committed to those in and outside ethnic Israel who were people of faith because such mercies were not based in Israel's ethnicity. The calling of Jacob over Esau, since both had the same mother, showed that the salvation of Jews was never based on ethnic privilege but always and only on the mercies of God. That the Jews retained benefit (i.e., the recipients of God's revelation, Rom 9:4) was due to the historical reality of Israel's place in the covenant, but the "children of the promise" (Rom 9:8) were those Jews who were persons of faith. Only by this means could the Gentiles, too, be counted among the "children of the promise."[31] If it were not rooted in ethnic boundaries or personal good works, then on what basis were God's mercies bestowed? Paul's answer is the divine purpose and calling (9:11–12; 8:28–30).[32] We can derive from this the assurance that the salvation bestowed on Christians today is not predetermined by one's ethnicity. God's salvation is available to all persons—Jew and Gentile—and, to be sure, the heart of Christ's commission is that the Church harvests members of faith from all nations.

COMPOSITION.   Sources customarily attributed to this pericope are the Yahwist (J) and the Priestly (P) writer. The Priestly writer himself or a redactor created the first paragraph by wedding the J narrative (vv. 21–26a) and the Priestly framework (vv. 19–20,26b). The oracle (vv. 22–23) was an originally independent unit that the redactor's hand included, explaining the enmity between Israel and Edom. According to Westermann, the second paragraph (vv. 29–34), also independent in origin, was attached to expand on the sons' occupations as hunter and shepherd (v. 27), creating a parody on the hunter who succumbs to the wily shepherd. The connection between the latter story and the Jacob-Esau rivalry shows that their conflict was played out in the rise of civilization's livestock economy over the old economy of the hunter.[33]

After acknowledging the secondary nature of the P-style verses, Van Seters maintains that vv. 21–34 (excepting vv. 26b and 28) are a unified account, providing a folktale about the origins and relationship of the Edomites and Israelites. Carr views vv. 21–34 as the first of two introductions (with 27:1–45) to his "pre-promise" Jacob story that was unrelated to the Abraham narrative and its promise

---

[30] F. Thielman, "Unexpected Mercy: Echoes of a Biblical Motif in Romans 9–11," *SJT* 47 (1994): 169–81 (esp. 178).

[31] M. Cranford, "Election and Ethnicity: Paul's View of Israel in Romans 9,1–13," *JSNT* 50 (1993): 27–41.

[32] T. R. Schreiner, *Romans*, BECNT (Grand Rapsis: Baker, 1998), 499–500.

[33] Westermann, *Genesis 12–36*, 411, 417.

theme.[34] Originally, according to Van Seters, 25:21–34 followed on 25:11 (J) where the "blessing" motif appears, subsuming the old folk-tale in the Yahwist's narrative concerns.[35] Van Seters is right to challenge the sharp division between vv. 21–26 and vv. 27–34 proposed by Westermann. Shared interests between the two paragraphs (e.g., folk etymologies), especially the idea of rival peoples, are integral to the coherence of the narrative. J. Ska, too, acknowledged the general coherence of the composition, which he attributed to a post-P redactor.[36]

But Van Seters and Westermann both stumble when assuming that the underlying source was an original folktale about eponymous ancestors, unrelated to the patriarchal promises. G. von Rad notes that typically aetiologies involving ancestors show respect for the progenitor; the passage in this case, however, lampoons both Esau and Jacob. The origin of the passage is better explained as the labor of one author who tied together miniepisodes that anticipated the theme and elements in the Jacob narrative. The relationship of the two houses of Abraham's descendants, Israel and Edom, was important to the author of the patriarchal narratives since he establishes by such examples the pertinence of the national implications of the promises to Abraham and his descendants (e.g., 12:3; 22:18; 26:4; 27:29). The mention of such national eponyms in the patriarchal narratives cannot be interpreted apart from the promise theme. Westermann himself notes the parallel between the Abraham and Jacob introductions (11:27–12:9; 25:19–34), attributing them to the redactor who forged in each case a unity out of precursor parts. Wenham details correspondences between the two introductions, demonstrating the cohesion of each and the intentional match between them.[37] Thus, it is reasonable to expect that the same person authored both introductions and arranged them similarly to show continuity between the two patriarchs and the promises.

As for the P extraction of vv. 19–20 and v. 26b, the result leaves a story that has no suitable beginning. Van Seters solves this problem by placing the story after 25:11, but this proposed displacement is only necessary when one assumes that vv. 19–20 could not have originally begun the account. The significance of the answered prayer for the barren Rebekah in v. 22 is lost when the genealogical connection is stripped away. The genealogical notices of Isaac and Rebekah (vv. 19–20) echo the marriage arrangements in chap. 24 between Abraham's servant and the Laban-Bethuel household. The infertility of Rebekah recalls Abraham-Sarah but also jeopardizes the succession of Isaac's line through Rebekah. Also v. 26b fits the present arrangement nicely as the closing inclusio, matching the age of Isaac cited in v. 20. The pronoun "them" (v. 26b) requires the antecedents Esau and Jacob appearing in v. 26a. This chronological notice too is intrinsic to

[34] Carr, *Reading the Fractures of Genesis*, 257.

[35] Van Seters, *Prologue to History,* 281–83.

[36] J. L. Ska, "Genèse 25,19–34–Ouverture du cycle de Jacob," *Jacob: un Commentaire à plusieurs voix de Genèse 25–36*, 11–21.

[37] Wenham (*Genesis 16–50,* 173) lists eleven parallels, e.g., barren wives (v. 21; 11:30), the ages of the patriarchs (v. 26b; 12:4), and the wife/sister motif (26:1–11; 12:10–20).

the tension raised by barren Rebekah, since it shows the twenty-year wait for her pregnancy.

STRUCTURE.   Constructed as the preamble to the whole Jacob narrative, the passage contains three early conflicts, in which the younger supplants the elder son, preparing for the narrative's theme: the prenatal oracle (vv. 22–23), the birth (vv. 24–26), and the birthright (vv. 27–34).[38] The passage divides into three units, or four if the transitional vv. 27–28 are treated as a separate unit (see chart below). The first unit is the typical *tôlĕdōt* ("this is the account," NIV) introduction (v. 19), framed by the repetition of the name "Isaac" (v. 19). The boundaries of the second unit are the ages of Isaac at marriage and fatherhood (vv. 20,26b). This paragraph reports the prenatal and birth struggles of the twin boys that foreshadow their life-long clash (vv. 21–22; vv. 24–26a). Sandwiched between these verses that describe their struggles is the divine oracle (poetry) that foretells the ultimate outcome of the rivalry (v. 23). The oracle's message transcends the lives of the twins, looking well beyond to their descendants and the national hostilities that will ensue.

The transitional paragraph (vv. 27–28) links the birth account (v. 24–26) and the squabble over the elder's birthright (vv. 29–34). The mention of their diverse vocations as hunter and shepherd explains the circumstances of the sale, but also implies tension by their disparate lifestyles. Divided parental favor accentuates this discord, anticipating the parental involvement later in the account that fuels the smoldering feud.

The third unit consists of two rounds of dialogue embedded in a narrative inclusio. The inclusio of vv. 29a and 34a refer to the "stew" that occasions and concludes the haggling. The two dialogue exchanges cook up the swap of Esau's birthright for Jacob's stew (vv. 30–31; 32–33). Terino's analysis proposed a chiasmus in vv. 29–34a, identifying the focal element in v. 32b: "What good is the birthright to me?" The verdict by the author, "So Esau despised his birthright" (v. 34b), provides the answer.[39] The depiction of each man is unbecoming. The surly hunter Esau fails to kill game, making him subject to his brother's husbandry, and he compounds his downfall by devaluing his birthright. Jacob is the calculating opportunist who cheats the impulsive Esau in his weakened state. By this introductory episode the stage is set for the majority narrative's exposition of the brothers' dissension.

Part One   v. 19 Introduction: *tôlĕdōt* of Isaac

Part Two   vv. 20–26   Struggle between Esau and Jacob at Birth
              v. 20   Isaac marries Rebekah

---

[38] Thompson, *The Origin Tradition of Ancient Israel*, 104, 161.
[39] Terino, "A Text Linguistic Study of the Jacob Narrative," 52.

	vv. 21–22	Contention in the womb
	v. 23	Oracle concerning Rebekah's children
	vv. 24–26a	Battle at birth
v. 26b		Isaac becomes a father
Transition	vv. 27–28	Vocational and parental strife
Part Three	vv. 29–34	Struggle between Esau and Jacob for the Birthright
	v. 29	Jacob's stew and Esau's starvation
	vv. 30–31	Round one: the bargain proposed
	vv. 32–33	Round two: the bargain sealed by oath
	v. 34	Jacob's stew for Esau's birthright

(1) Introduction (25:19)

[19]This is the account of Abraham's son Isaac.

Abraham became the father of Isaac,

25:19 For the significance of the *tôlĕdōt* ("the account of") title, see the introduction to the Jacob section above and vol. 1A, pp. 31–35, 39. The title (v. 19a) imitates the Ishmael *tôlĕdōt* phrase exactly (v. 12a), reflecting the parallel claims of the brothers to the patriarchal heritage. Unlike the formal genealogies of the discredited sons Ishmael (25:12–18) and Esau (36:1,9) headed by the *tôlĕdōt* phrase, however, this *tôlĕdōt* heading begins a lengthy narrative, ending in 35:29. There is a brief genealogical reference provided in v. 20, which looks back (as in 11:27–29) to the roots of the once-barren matriarch (Rebekah) of the Aramean branch of the family.

The double mention of "Abraham" in the verse assumes the foregoing Abraham section (11:27–25:11), affirming the fulfillment of the promise in 21:12. The exact form of the term translated "became the father of"[40] *(hôlîd)* elsewhere occurs only in 11:27(2x) in Genesis. The mention of the father's identity, omitting reference to Sarah the mother, contrasts Ishmael's *tôlĕdōt* heading (25:12b) in which "Hagar" is named. The explanation of Ishmael's birth by Sarah's maid Hagar (v. 12b) and the description of Rebekah as "barren" in v. 21 offers a subtle reminder of the Sarah-Hagar struggle that led to the expulsion of the deselected son (21:9–14).

(2) Birth of Jacob and Esau (25:20–26)

[20]and Isaac was forty years old when he married Rebekah daughter of Bethuel the Aramean from Paddan Aram and sister of Laban the Aramean.

---

[40]הוֹלִיד ("became the father of") is the *hiphil* perfect; the forms that usually appear in chaps. 5; 11 are הוֹלִידוֹ, the infinitive construct plus the third masculine singular suffx, and וַיּוֹלֶד, the *hiphil* imperfect.

²¹Isaac prayed to the LORD on behalf of his wife, because she was barren. The LORD answered his prayer, and his wife Rebekah became pregnant. ²²The babies jostled each other within her, and she said, "Why is this happening to me?" So she went to inquire of the LORD.

²³The LORD said to her,

"Two nations are in your womb,

and two peoples from within you will be separated;

one people will be stronger than the other,

and the older will serve the younger."

²⁴When the time came for her to give birth, there were twin boys in her womb. ²⁵The first to come out was red, and his whole body was like a hairy garment; so they named him Esau. ²⁶After this, his brother came out, with his hand grasping Esau's heel; so he was named Jacob. Isaac was sixty years old when Rebekah gave birth to them.

The arrangement of the passage is a chiasmus, making the prophetic oracle the centerpiece (v. 23). The prenatal (v. 22) and birth (vv. 24–26a) struggles of the twins enclose it, identifying the ancestors of the anonymous "two nations" announced in the oracle. The marriage to barren Rebekah (v. 21) occasions the sequence of events that lead to the oracle (v. 23). The significance of the complex of events is succinctly stated at the conclusion in v. 26b: Rebekah gave Isaac successors. However, the disturbing prenatal behavior of the children and the mysterious oracle presage the trouble that Isaac and Rebekah must endure.

25:20 The introductory verse back-references the events of chap. 24 and the genealogy of the Nahor family in 22:20–24. The chronological and genealogical information supply a context for the infertility of the couple. Age forty at marriage means that only after a protracted wait of twenty years did Isaac become a father (v. 26b). The age for Rebekah is not given, unlike Sarah (17:17), since she was still of childbearing age.[41] The genealogy of Rebekah recalls the servant's search for a wife in Haran among Abraham's kinsmen, which exhibited the Lord's leadership of the servant and his answered prayers (chap. 24). Whereas the search for an appropriate mate met with no formidable obstacle, the bearing of a successor by Rebekah was not achieved so comfortably. Unlike his parents, who chose a substitute wife, Isaac turned to prayer, perhaps spurred on by the heartache his family had experienced by giving Hagar to Abraham (chap. 16).

Mention of Rebekah's Aramean connection prepares the reader for the flight of Jacob, establishing the background for the twenty-year sojourn of Jacob in "Paddan Aram" (28:2; 33:18; 35:9). The name "Paddan Aram" probably refers to the same site "Aram Naharaim" (see comments on 24:10), between the Habur and Euphrates rivers in upper northwest Mesopotamia, and occurs only

---

[41] Sarna, *Genesis,* 178.

in connection with Jacob's travels.[42] The precise meaning and location of Paddan Aram is uncertain, however.[43] Some define *paddān* as "field," pointing to a possible Arabic cognate and to the expression *śĕdēh 'ărām*, lit., "field of Aram" in Hos 12:12[13]. Others believe that *paddān* is the older name for the city Har(r)an, the city settled by Terah (11:31–32) and the residence of Laban that was the destination of Jacob (27:43; 28:10; 29:4). "Paddan" in this view is derived from Akk. *pad(d)ānu*, meaning "track, way," which is similar to Akk. *ḥarrănu* "road, street" a possible derivation of Har(r)an.

25:21–22 The barren condition of Rebekah parallels the Abraham-Sarah narratives (11:30; cf. Rachel, 29:31). In both cases, a message from the Lord follows, a promissory call (12:1–3) and a prophetic oracle (25:23). The absence of children contrasts with the success of the search for Rebekah and the hopeful expectation of children (24:60). The verb "prayed" *('ātar)* commonly concerns intercessory prayer for others. Isaac's intercession assumes that the Lord is responsible for human reproduction (e.g., 16:2; 29:32; 30:2). The narrative does not report that Rebekah prayed for herself as did Leah and Rachel (29:32; 30:22) and also Hannah (1 Sam 1:10).[44] The absence of any such petition focuses attention on intercessory prayer, likening Isaac to Abraham who prayed in behalf of the barren women of Abimelech's household (20:17). Rebekah's subsequent inquiry of the Lord (v. 22b) is the counterpart to Isaac's prayer. Isaac foreshadows Moses who offered intercessory prayers and constructed altars of worship (26:25; e.g., Exod 8:26; 17:15; cf. also David, e.g., 2 Sam 24:24–25). That the Lord "answered his prayer" repeats the same verb *'ātar*, forming a parallel between the two halves of the verse: "When Isaac prayed *['ātar]*. . . the Lord answered his prayer *['ātar]*"[45] This rhetorical feature underscores the effectiveness of the patriarch's intercession and the responsiveness of his God. The last clause of the verse presents the evidence that the prayer was realized. This terse report of pregnancy is striking since there was a significant waiting period of twenty years between marriage and conception.

"The babies jostled each one within her" (v. 22a) presupposes the presence of twins (or more). The birth of twins was considered an omen (38:27–30), and the sheer forcefulness of their movements prompted her worries. "Jostled" translates the root *rāṣaṣ*, meaning a violent collision, a crushing or breaking (e.g., Judg 9:53; Isa 36:6). The stem *(hithpoel)* of the verb indicates reciprocal

---

[42] 25:20; 28:2,5–7; 31:18; 33:18; 35:9, 26; 46:15; 48:7.

[43] *HALOT* 3.913; W. T. Pitard, "Paddan-Aram," *ABD* 5.55.

[44] A. Pagolu, *The Religion of the Patriarchs*, JSOTSup 277 (Sheffield: Sheffield Academic Press, 1998), 124–25.

[45] The difference lies in the verbal stems; the *qal* form means "to plead, supplicate," and the *niphal* (+ prep. *lamed*) indicates "to be pleaded with," i.e., answered prayer or accepted prayer (e.g., 2 Sam 21:14; 2 Chr 33:13,19; Ezra 8:23). The *niphal* usage with deity is often tolerative, "allowed himself to be entreated by him" (*IBHS* §23.4h).

blows occurred between the children. Rachel's perplexity is uttered in terse, syntactically difficult Hebrew: "if thus, why then/this (am) I?"[46] She interpreted the bizarre behavior of the children (cp. Luke 1:41) as an omen of animosity, and she pondered what this would mean for her and her children. In effect she is asking, "What good is my pregnancy?" "Will the children survive? Will I survive?"

That Rebekah sought out a prophet or cult functionary who could explain her condition is suggested by "she went to inquire *[dāraš]*." This expression commonly describes someone seeking divine direction, often through a cultic mediator (cp. Exod 18:15; 1 Sam 9:9; 28:7; 2 Kgs 3:11; Jer 21:2). The earlier verb describing Isaac's intercession, "prayed *(ʿātar)* to the Lord," may suggest a cultic setting, though it is rarely used in this way in Scripture (cf. 2 Sam 24:25).[47] In patriarchal society the patriarch himself offered sacrifices in worship or mediation (e.g., Job 1:5), though a priest such as Melchizedek was known (14:18). There is no evidence of cultic personnel or a dominant sanctuary during patriarchal times, making it more likely that Rebekah approached her husband who as mediator received and related the oracle of v. 23 (contrast Hannah, 1 Sam 1:10).

25:23 The verse consists of a quatrain. The first couplet entails a synonymous parallelism, announcing "two nations . . . two peoples" (v. 23ab) are in her womb. Here, the descendants are substituted for the two children who are the progenitors of Israel and Edom. These two peoples "will be separated" *(pārad),* recalling the migration of the peoples listed in the Table of Nations (10:5,32), but more importantly, echoing the parting between Abraham and Lot (13:9,11,14). It was by means of separations that resolutions came to the tensions between Isaac and Ishmael and Jacob and Esau. Syrén observed the irony of the term "separated," for the twins were locked together in the womb and dramatically at birth by the younger's grasp of Esau's heel.[48] Nevertheless, the divine purpose necessitated their ultimate separation (33:12–19).

The second couplet in the oracle explains that the parting involves the hostile usurpation of the elder brother by the younger and "stronger" brother (v. 23cd). The notion of the younger son holding sway over his senior was contrary to custom (29:26; 37:10–11; 43:33; Deut 21:15–17; Job 32:6), although in Genesis it was common for Israel's fathers (27:29,32–33; 38:27–30; 48:14–20; 49:8). That the "older"[49] will serve *(ʿābad)* the younger brother recalls the curse and blessing invoked by Noah (9:25–27), and it anticipates the blessing

---

[46] אִם־כֵּן לָמָּה זֶּה אָנֹכִי. Some EVs follow the Syr. reading that has "to live" *(BHS),* thus, "If it be this way, why do I live?" (NRSV); cf. 27:46.

[47] *HALOT* 2.905.

[48] Syrén, *First-Born,* 81–82.

[49] רַב, "older" (Akk. *rabû,* "great [one]") corresponds to גָּדֹול, 27:1,42; 44:12, who is the בְּכֹר, "firstborn" (v. 31).

stolen by Jacob at the expense of Esau (27:29,37,40). Ironically, it is Jacob who submits to his brother upon his return to Canaan (cf. "your/his servant," 32:4–5,19[5–6,20]; 33:3–5,14; cp. Num 20:21), for Edom is the stronger militarily (32:6[7]; 33:1; 36:31). That the oracle speaks of two "nations" shows that the prophecy and its fulfillment look beyond the brothers to their descendants. Edom's history reveals repeated submission to the Israelites (e.g., Exod 15:15; Num 24:18; 2 Sam 8:12–14; 1 Kgs 11:14–16; Isa 11:4; Amos 9:11–12; Obad 1:18).[50] Sibling rivalry and submission will occur also in the household of Jacob (e.g., 37:3–10; 42:6; 43:28; 44:23; 49:8).

25:24–26a These verses report the second conflict episode in the passage. Verse 24 confirms the first part of the oracle by announcing "twin boys" and by repeating the word "womb" *(beṭen)*, occurring in v. 23a. That the infants struggle at delivery corresponds to the oracle's prediction, "they will be separated." Unusual pregnancies or strange occurrences at birth may accompany a distinct event (e.g., 1 Sam 4:21) or signal an omen (e.g., 38:27–30). The description of the infant as strikingly "red" *(ʾadmônî)* and "hairy" *(śēʿār, v. 25)* is not derisive, for a ruddy complexion (*ʾadmônî* occurs only in 1 Sam 16:12; 17:42) and the growth of hair were valued (Num 6:5; 2 Sam 14:26; Song 5:11; 7:5; Isa 3:24; 7:20; Jer 7:29). Esau is distinguished especially by the hair over "his whole body," giving the appearance of a "garment" *(ʾadderet)*. This latter term is used of an outer covering, such as the prophet's mantle (e.g., 1 Kgs 19:13). The combination of the terms, "garment of hair" *(ʾadderet śēʿār)*, describes a prophet's dress (Zech 13:4; cp. Matt 3:4 par.).

In the typical manner of the patriarchal narratives, the names given to the twins hold special significance.[51] For Esau the passage produces three sound plays between his physical features and his two names, "Esau" and "Edom," associating the progenitor with his descendants, the Edomites, who settled in the mountain region of Seir (cf. 36:8–9). The child's natural reddish appearance presages later details recounting the loss of his birthright ("red," *ʾādōm*, v. 30) and the theft of the blessing through deception (*śāʿîr*, "hairy," 27:11,23). The

---

[50] Contra D. J. A. Clines, *What Does Eve Do to Help? And Other Readerly Questions to the Old Testament,* JSOTSup 34 (Sheffield: Sheffield Academic Press, 1990), 59–62, who with L. A. Turner (*Announcement of Plot in Genesis,* JSOTSup 96 [Sheffield: Sheffield Academic Press, 1990]) contends that the birth oracle and announcement of blessing by Isaac (27:29,37,40) mislead since in the narrative Esau does not submit to Jacob. But the narrative implies as much when Esau clearly relinquishes the land and perhaps his birthright too (cf. comments on 33:9).

[51] A standard naming formula is used: a form of the singular verb *qārāʾ + šĕmô + X,* "(he/she) called his name *X,*" appears in v. 26b for the naming of Jacob (e.g., 4:25; 5:29) and could refer to Isaac as naming the boy, but the indefinite plural subject of the plural verb, וַיִּקְרְאוּ, lit., "they called" (= "was called") appears for Esau (v. 25b). The LXX, Syr., and Vg. read the singular form at v. 25b in harmony with v. 26, whereas SP and Tgs. achieve agreement by the plural at v. 26b (see *BHS*). Both the third singular masculine and plural masculine may express an indefinite subject (GKC §144d–g).

child's "red" *('admônî)* skin (i.e., reddish) anticipates the sale of his birthright involving Jacob's "red" *('ādōm)* stew that precipitated the endowment of Esau's nickname "Edom" *('ĕdōm)* (cf. v. 30 below).[52] The author does not attempt to relate a precise derivation of "Esau," which remains unknown to us. He creates a sound play of the name "Esau" *('ēśāw)* and of the noun "hair" *(śē'ār)* by a reversal of the letters *ś* and *'* (v. 25b). Also the word "hair" *(śē'ār)* implies the name "Seir" *(śē'îr),*[53] historically, the chief location of Edomite possession (Deut 2:5; cf. comments on 32:3[4]).

"Jacob" *(ya'ăqōb),* meaning "he grasps the heel" in the present context, that is, he supplants (Jer 9:4), is related to the noun "heel" *('āqēb),* playing on the baby's grasp of Esau's heel at birth (cf. the verb *'āqab,* "deceived," 27:36; Hos 12:3[4]).[54] The word "heel" can be used metaphorically, indicating a trusted friend's deception ("lifted up his heel against me," Ps 41:9[10]). The structure of the name "Jacob," *ya'ăqōb,* is built on the imperfect verb construction *(ya +* verbal root; e.g., Isaac, *yiṣḥāq),* which is a common morphological configuration known among West Semitic appellatives.[55] The name is widely attested in extrabiblical texts from the early second millennium in Mesopotamia (e.g., *ya'ăqub-il)* and from Semite names recounted in Egyptian texts. A positive nuance of *'āqab* is the idea of protection ("follow closely on the heel").[56] Historically, the name probably was expressed as a theophoric name equivalent to *y'qb–'l,* "may God *[El]* protect" or "God has protected" (cp. Akk. *ya[ḫ]qub-ila).*[57] In our passage the sound of the name "Jacob" is a play on the words "heel" *('āqēb)* and "deceived" *('āqab,* 27:36). The noun *'āqēb* (e.g., Ps 49:5[6]) and the adjective *'āqōb* (e.g., Jer 17:9) by semantic extension mean "deceiver" and "deceitful," respectively. "Grasp/seize" *('āḥaz + bet,* i.e., "to lay hold of") appears also with "heel" at Job 18:9, indicating entrapment. The sense of *'āḥaz* in our passage is a firm grip (e.g., Exod 4:4; Song 3:4), thus Jacob latches on to the heel of Esau in an attempt to supersede him. That the child attacks the

---

[52] "Blood" (דָּם) is also a play with "Edom," e.g., 2 Kgs 3:20–22; Isa 34:5–7; Joel 3:19[4:19]; cf. Isa 63:1–6.

[53] Sarna observes the possible association of the red sandstone and shaggy terrain of Seir with the twin etiologies of Esau/Edom *(Genesis,* 182).

[54] S. H. Smith contends that Jacob's "grasping of the heel" is euphemistic for grasping the genitals, indicating the seizure of procreative powers, and that the divine "touching of the hollow of his [Jacob's] thigh" (32:25[26]) refers to the genitals, meaning that his procreation was due solely to God's blessing ("'Heel' and 'Thigh': The Concept of Sexuality in the Jacob-Esau Narratives," *VT* 40 [1990]: 464–73). Although there is some lexical basis for *kap* ("hand") meaning penis, at most there is a *double entendre* suggesting procreation secondarily, for Jacob actually limps from the injury at the hip socket (32:31[32]).

[55] See A. R. Millard, "Jacob," *ISBE* 2.948.

[56] The *piel* of *'-q-b* means "restrain, hold back" (Job 37:4).

[57] *HALOT* 2.422; see M. Noth, *Die israelitischen Personennamen im Rahmen der gemeinsemitischen Namengebung,* BWANT 46 (Stuttgart: Kohlhammer, 1928), 177–78, 197.

"heel" conveys the ideas of deception, betrayal, and opportunism (e.g., 3:15; 49:17,19; Job 18:9; Ps 41:10). Esau acknowledged the appropriateness of Jacob's name for the schemer who stole his blessing (27:36). The prophet Hosea, too, pointed to Jacob's behavior but at his birth, as indicative of the defiance that Judah showed against the Lord (12:3a[4a]).

25:26b The chronological notation concludes vv. 20–26, confirming the faith of Isaac after twenty years and the faithfulness of the Lord's promise (v. 23; cp. 16:1–2). According to a literal chronological reconstruction, Abraham lived to see his grandsons (see comments at the introduction to 25:1–11). At sixty years old Isaac became a father, much younger than Abraham when he fathered Ishmael (eighty-six years; 16:16) and Isaac (one hundred years; 21:5). Since his death is recorded as a hundred and eighty years (35:28), we can reckon that the twins were a hundred and twenty years old at that time.

(3) The Bartered Birthright (25:27–34)

[27]The boys grew up, and Esau became a skillful hunter, a man of the open country, while Jacob was a quiet man, staying among the tents. [28]Isaac, who had a taste for wild game, loved Esau, but Rebekah loved Jacob.

[29]Once when Jacob was cooking some stew, Esau came in from the open country, famished. [30]He said to Jacob, "Quick, let me have some of that red stew! I'm famished!" (That is why he was also called Edom.)

[31]Jacob replied, "First sell me your birthright."

[32]"Look, I am about to die," Esau said. "What good is the birthright to me?"

[33]But Jacob said, "Swear to me first." So he swore an oath to him, selling his birthright to Jacob.

[34]Then Jacob gave Esau some bread and some lentil stew. He ate and drank, and then got up and left.

So Esau despised his birthright.

The shift in setting in v. 27 signals a new unit. Verses 27–28 transition the struggle at birth to the sale of the birthright, giving the occupation and the parental preference of each lad. This background explains the confrontation to follow between the hunter and tent dweller, also hinting at the exacerbation of their competition by their parents' favoritism. Jacob's "red stew" (v. 29) greets Esau, who returns from the fields empty-handed without a kill. The impatient Esau and coy Jacob dual through two dialogue interchanges (vv. 30–33), negotiating the "red stew" for Esau's birthright (v. 34).

25:27–28 The age of the twins cannot be determined from the term "boys" *(na'ar),* since it may refer to diverse ages, including an infant (Exod 2:6), a boy of fourteen years (21:12), and young man of seventeen (37:2). The word in some passages occurs opposite "old," forming a merism, and thus may be used broadly of young adulthood or younger (e.g., 19:4; Exod 10:9; Josh 6:21). The LXX preferred "young man" *(neaniskos)* over "boy" *(pais),* although the two terms can refer to the same person's age (Acts 20:9,12). The language reporting the boys' age and vocation also describes Ishmael's development into a bowman (21:20). Like Ishmael, his counterpart, Esau became a hunter (16:16; cp. Nimrod, 10:9) who was at home in the "open country" disassociated from mainstream society. His descendants settled outside Canaan in Edom (Mount Seir), bordering the Arabah, south and southeast of the Dead Sea. That he was a "skillful" (*yōdēaʿ*, "knowing") hunter yet unsuccessful in his hunt gives the first hint that Esau is a failure. The depiction of Esau is unflattering; he is impetuous and clumsy, certainly no match for the wily Jacob. He fits the caricature of the unrefined brute whose irreverence toward his birthright disqualified him. Hunting is permitted in Mosaic law (Lev 17:13), but it did not hold the esteem that non-Israelite cultures gave it. Jacob, however, stands opposite his elder in temperament and vocation.[58]

Whereas Esau was a hunter, Jacob was a "quiet *[tām]* man." The word *tām* elsewhere refers to a person who is "perfect, blameless" (Job 1:1,8; 8:20; Ps 37:37; Prov 29:10). Here it indicates the normal or ordinary man. By double entendre this description ironically shows that Jacob is hardly "blameless" in this transaction. The succession of Jacob is not grounded in the character of Jacob but in the sovereignty of the Lord. Jacob was not an outdoorsman but a tent dweller, meaning that his work kept him close to the family's settlement, perhaps involved in small animal husbandry. He was perceived as socialized (cf. 4:20), whereas Esau possessed the "sword," casting aside authority (27:40).[59]

The division between the parents' love for the boys (v. 28) further exhibits the contrast between the two sons and offers another omen of the struggle that will ensue (27:7–10). The syntax of the verse, "but Rebekah,"[60] heightens the contrast between the parents' affections. Each parent "loved" a different son. "Loved" *(ʾāhab)* translates the common term that expresses affection among family members. We should not conclude that the parent felt animosity toward the disfavored son; rather, "loved" means each showed a strong preference toward one (cf. 37:3–4).[61] Partiality for a child was a recurring feature of all three patriarchal households (e.g., 22:2; 25:28; 37:3–4; 44:20). Based on his love for Rachel, Jacob too will favor her sons Joseph and Benjamin, resulting in painful discord and separation (29:30; 37:3–4; 44:20). The passage is silent regarding Rebekah's reason for preferring Jacob since it is not germane to the plot (27:3–4). We can only surmise that his domestic leanings were more invit-

---

[58] The initial *waw* of the clause is disjunctive-adversative, "but Jacob . . ."

[59] Sarna, *Genesis,* 181.

[60] The clause is disjunctive-adversative, "but . . ."

[61] Often "love" (אָהֵב) is coupled with the antonym "hate" (שָׂנֵא), either indicating preference over against another person (e.g., 29:30–31; 37:4) or devotion versus enmity (e.g., Exod 20:5–6; Lev 19:17–18; Ps 45:7); see E. Jenni, "אָהֵב *ʾhb* to love," *TLOT* 1.47–48.

ing to her, or the oracle that pointed to Jacob as successor influenced her.[62] That Isaac based his preference on the tasty game obtained by Esau functions in the Jacob narrative two ways.[63] It anticipates the background for the account of the patriarch's blessing; Isaac "loved" ("liked," NIV) the game prepared by Esau (27:4,9,14). Also it shows the alignment of Isaac and Esau. Both men loved game, and both tied the elder's birthright and blessing to their appetites. The attitude of Isaac is not appreciably higher than that of Esau, who will only evidence a belated appreciation for his lost blessing (27:34).

25:29 This verse establishes the circumstances for the negotiations to follow. That Jacob was preparing "stew" *(nāzîd)* follows from the description of his life as a tent dweller. The nature of the stew as "lentil" *('ădāšîm)* is clarified in v. 34 (e.g., 2 Sam 17:28). "Stew" is the alternative to a meal including meat (cf. 2 Kgs 4:38–40). Esau's hunger is ironic, since he was deemed a "skillful" hunter (v. 27). "Famished" translates *'āyēp,* a term that refers to a weakened condition due to thirst or hunger (e.g., 2 Sam 17:29; Job 22:7). The word group *('-y-p)* may describe the depleted state of a traveler (Deut 25:18) or an embattled army (e.g., Judg 8:4; 2 Sam 14:28,31). Although under normal conditions he was equipped to defend himself, now Esau was vulnerable to the weaker but shrewder Jacob (cp. Ps 10:2).

25:30–31 The first dialogue exchange consists of Esau's request for food and Jacob's proposed terms. "Quick, let me have . . ." translates the root *lā'aṭ,* a hapax legomenon, meaning something like to devour, that is, "gulp down" (NAB, NJPS).[64] Esau identifies the stew by its color, "some of that red stew" *(min hā'ādōm hā'ādōm hazzeh)* or "red stuff" (NRSV).[65] He justifies his brusque request by his dire condition. The causal clause has the word "famished" in the lead position, so as to make the point forcefully. The parenthetical aside that connects the name "Edom" *('ĕdôm)* with the "red" *('ādōm)* concoction reinforces the linkage between the progenitor and his offspring. The play on the name is not complimentary, since it brings to mind Esau's ineptness in dealing with the artful Jacob. It also recalls the birth conflict where he was described there as "red" (v. 25). By the convergence of the wordplays, the author shows that these events by which Jacob gets the better of Esau proved the veracity of the oracle (v. 23). "Like father, like son," we say. The oafish progenitor will

---

[62] R. Clifford, explaining Rebekah's preference, believes that she alone knew of the oracle ("Genesis 25:19–34," *Int* 45 [1991]: 397–401).

[63] SP, LXX have צֵידוֹ, "his [Esau's] game" (v. 28), thus particularizing the prey that pleased Isaac.

[64] הַלְעִיטֵנִי, *hiphil* imperfect; BDB 542, "swallow greedily"; *HALOT* 2.533, "to allow to take a quick drink," but from לעט (see Ps 57:4[5], II להט, "to devour," Ar. *lahaṭa, HALOT* 2.521) related to Syr. *lu'āṭā,* "jaw," and Akk. *lu'āṭu,* "to swallow."

[65] The term "red" *('ādōm)* varies in color, including red, reddish brown, or pink, describing blood (2 Kgs 3:22), garments stained by grape juice (Isa 63:2), a cow (Num 19:2), a horse (Zech 1:8; 6:2), and skin (Song 5:10); *HALOT* 1.15; R. Alden, "אָדֹם," *NIDOTTE* 1. 262.

produce an outcast nation that succumbs to the favored Israelites (e.g., Exod 15:15; Num 24:18; Judg 5:4).

Jacob drove a hard bargain (v. 31). He demanded the immediate *(kayyôm,* "today"; NIV "first") disposition of Esau's "birthright" *(běkōrâ)* (v. 31), taking advantage of the moment (v. 31; cf. 1 Sam 2:16). Societies of the ancient Near East typically recognized the eldest son (primogeniture) by granting him privilege, which usually involved inheritance rights, over younger sons. In Israel the "firstborn" *(běkôr*[66]*)* offspring, whether animal or human, belonged to God (e.g., 4:4; Exod 13:13,15; Num 3:40–41), as did the firstfruits of the harvest (e.g., Exod 23:19; Lev 2:14). Israel itself was the firstborn of the Lord (Exod 4:22; see vol. 1A, pp. 267–68). Apparently, the firstborn son received special honor because he symbolized his father's power and potency (cf. 49:3; Deut 21:17). Precisely what the "birthright" consisted of for Esau and Jacob is unknown, although in Mosaic law the "right of the firstborn" *(mišpat habběkōrâ)* entailed a "double share" *(pî šěnayim)* of the father's bequest (Deut 21:17).[67] Whatever the right included, it must have been viewed as valuable to Jacob's ambitions. Moreover, that Rebekah went to such great lengths to plot the deception of her husband shows that the "blessing" also was of esteemed value. Diverse practices attested in the ancient Near East pertaining to the rights of inheritance and to the ratio of inheritance between siblings indicate there was no uniform custom governing the treatment of the firstborn and younger siblings.[68] It may have been among the patriarchs that the inheritance of the "firstborn" and the recipient of the patriarchal "blessing" were not necessarily the same. Since the provision in Deut 21:15–17 required fathers to bestow the double honor on the firstborn, it probably was a practice that the law intended to restrict. That the patriarchs gave preference for the younger sons (Isaac [21:10–13], Jacob [27:27–33], Ephraim [48:13–20]),[69] shows that they were not subject to the law imposed by Deuteronomy. The negotiations initiated by Jacob assumed that Esau had the right to sell it apart from parental approval. This comports with ancient texts that describe the selling and buying of inheritances.

The blessing was not automatically given to the firstborn, however; Reuben, for example, though the firstborn of Jacob, did not receive the favorable bless-

---

[66] Also פֶּטֶר רֶחֶם, "first opens the womb" (Num 3:12, apposition to בְּכוֹר, "firstborn").

[67] The precise meaning of פִּי שְׁנַיִם is disputed, meaning either double the amount received by the younger brothers or two-thirds of the total inheritance; see M. Tsevat, *"bᵉkhor," TDOT* 2.121–27; B. Beitzel, "The Right of the Firstborn *(Pî Šnayim)* in the Old Testament (Deut. 21:15–17)," in *A Tribute to Gleason Archer* (Chicago: Moody, 1986), 179–90.

[68] No special favor for the firstborn is legislated in the Lipit-Ishtar and Hammurapi Codes; see I. Mendelsohn, "On the Preferential Status of the Eldest Son," *BASOR* 156 (1959): 38–40.

[69] Circumstances varied among these. In Isaac's case it was at the insistence of Sarah and no less than God; for Jacob, Isaac was duped, and for Ephraim, Joseph acquiesced to Jacob's adoption of the boys and his selection.

ing reserved for the firstborn by virtue of his sexual indiscretion against Jacob (35:22; 49:3–4). Evidently, the Hebrew patriarch could declare more than one blessing to sons (27:36,38), and the "father's blessing" could designate the chief heir (49:26,28; cp. 1 Chr 5:1–2). The theme of blessing in the patriarchal narratives urges the reader to ponder what the outcome of the stolen birthright means for the blessing. Isaac's "blessing" *(bĕrākâ)* was not necessarily coextensive with the birthright, since Esau's birthright and the father's blessing are independent in Esau's mind (27:36). But 1 Chr 5:1–2 appears to equate the two in the case of Joseph. The sound play of "firstborn" *(bĕkōrâ)* and "blessing" *(bĕrākâ)* point ahead to the plot that shows how Jacob obtained both the rights of firstborn and the coveted blessing.[70] The customs pertaining to the inheritance of a father's estate by the elder son and the disposition of it are many and widespread in both the second and first millennia. What can be gained from knowing the ancient background of the custom is its grave importance for preserving family solidarity and heritage. No father casually considered the matter, and the range of discretion he could employ had its limitations.[71]

25:32–33 In Esau's estimation he is at the threshold of death, and the only remedy is the food that Jacob possesses. The EVs rightly render *hôlēk lāmût,* "about to die" (v. 32a).[72] Esau's rhetorical question justifies in his mind the sale of his inheritance (v. 32b). If he were this desperate, Jacob's opportunism was even more ruthless, but Esau's claim is probably exaggerated. The phrase recalls Abimelech's entreaty to Abraham, "Now *['attâ]* swear to me . . ." (21:23; cf. also 47:31; 1 Sam 24:22; 30:15). The content of Esau's oath and whether there were accompanying rituals to the oath are not reported in the passage (cp. 21:21–31). If Esau is the hot-blooded actor who is hoodwinked, then Jacob is cast as the cold, calculating cheat. Jacob's actions must be judged a violation of honest trade (Lev 25:14,17), a mark of wickedness (Job 22:7; Ps 146:7; Ezek 18:7,16; Prov 25:21). This trade was no bargain, for lentils were common, whereas the family birthright was unmatched.

25:34 After the deal was struck, the narration ends by recounting the exchange itself. The description of Esau's coming and going gives Esau's actions the connotation of decisiveness: "Esau came in *[bô']* from the open country" (v. 29), and "he . . . left *[hālak]*" (v. 34). Esau gorges himself and then hurries off indifferent. This casualness leads the author to offer his evaluation afterward (v. 34b). The language of v. 34 ("gave *[nātan]* . . . ate *['ākal]*") is reminiscent of the fruit given to the man by his wife in the garden (3:6): she "gave" *(nātan)* and her husband "ate" *('ākal).* Also the dense succession of

---

[70] Clifford, "Genesis 25:19–34," 400.

[71] M. J. Selman, "Comparative Customs and the Patriarchal Age," in *Essays on the Patriarchal Narratives* (Leicester: InterVarsity, 1980/Winona Lake: Eisenbrauns, 1983), 93–138 (esp. 135–36).

[72] הֹלֵךְ לָמוּת, lit., "going to die"; the participle indicates imminent future.

verbs narrating Esau's manner is similar to the verbal staccato describing the first couple's disobedience (3:6; see vol. 1A, p. 237). The soup is identified as "lentil" *(ʿădāšîm),* a legume that was useful for satisfying the hunger of advancing armies (2 Sam 17:28; 23:11). Along with the bread, the stew could provide sustenance for another day (cf. Ezek 4:9).

The conclusion to the episode provides a retrospective assessment of Esau's decision: he "despised *[bāzâ]* his birthright." The term *bāzâ* indicates "to undervalue"[73] and may indicate a range of intensity, from neglect to utter scorn for someone or something (cf. Num 15:31; 1 Sam 17:42; Prov 15:20; Mal 1:6). By this incident the author implies that Esau's decision regarding his religious heritage disqualified him to succeed his father. Yet the passage hardly commends Jacob's actions to the reader, leaving it to the man's name "Deceiver" to say the obvious; the absence of explicit condemnation may also be related rhetorically to Jacob as heir apparent.

2. Isaac's Deception and Strife with the Philistines (26:1–35)

After the sale of Esau's birthright to Jacob (25:29–34), the narrative describes Isaac's emergence as a burgeoning power in the region of the Negeb, the same region well traveled by his father. We observe in this chapter a transformation in Isaac that is akin to the more dramatic change in the characters of Jacob (33:11) and of Judah (44:43–44). Isaac "stumbles out of the gate," so to speak, when he lies to Abimelech about Rebekah (v. 7), mimicking his father's earlier two transgressions (12:13; 20:2). Kidner points out that "the repeated lapses emphasize (like Peter's three denials) the chronic weakness of God's chosen material."[74] Yet he rises to the occasions, too, when he trusts the Lord for his protection and needs in the face of the onslaught of trials that his riches enjoin against him. Isaac's achievement became a source of strident envy among the neighboring Gerarites (v. 14) but also an incentive to peaceful relations between the two competing peoples (vv. 28–29). Although the Jacob-Esau conflict is the focus of the larger Jacob narrative, the episode involving Isaac and the Philistines at Gerar is a necessary interim. The chapter in effect provides evidence sustaining the author's declaration, "God blessed his [Abraham's] son Isaac" (25:11). This proof that Isaac is the sole purveyor of Abraham's inheritance legitimizes the patriarchal "blessing" that Isaac bestows (although unwittingly) upon Jacob (chap. 27), who is the principal protagonist of the present narrative section. This is instrumental to the author's case since no recorded blessing is uttered by Abraham, unlike Isaac and Jacob, whose bequests play significantly in the

---

[73] M. A. Grisanti, "בזה," *NIDOTTE* 1.629.

[74] D. Kidner *Genesis: An Introduction and Commentary,* TOTC (Downers Grove: InterVarsity, 1967), 152.

Jacob and Joseph narratives, respectively (27:27–29; 48:15,20; 49:28). The events of chap. 26 serve the larger Jacob account by linking the Abraham blessing with that received by Jacob/Israel, the namesake of the nation.

There are three principal ways the author shows continuity with the past.

1. The chapter casts Isaac in the image of Abraham, his name occurring no less than seven times (vv. 3,5,15,18[2x],24[2x]). Both men experienced a famine that led to migration and conflict with a powerful foreign king regarding their wives, and both entered into a treaty with the Philistines, whose king bears the same name, Abimelech (12:10–13:1; 20:1–18; 21:22–34). Both men are closely associated with the site "Beersheba" where they dug wells, lived, and entered into treaty (vv. 23,33; 21:31–33; 22:19). Isaac largely obtained his powerful position by duplicating the work of Abraham, who had founded the wells restored by Isaac's men (vv. 15,18). By clear allusions to Abraham's prosperity, the author established that Isaac is the divinely approved successor (vv. 12–14; 13:2; 24:1,35).

2. The passage explicitly identifies the divine promises made to Isaac (descendants, land, and blessing) as those very ones previously conferred upon Abraham, whose obedience exhibited faithfulness to the word of the Lord (vv. 3–5,24; 12:1–3). Like his father, Isaac responded by obedience (v. 6) and by erecting an altar of worship (v. 25; 12:4,7–8). Isaac as the recipient of the promises realizes great wealth, as did Abraham (vv. 12–13; 24:1,35). Central to the episode is the author's fundamental thesis that God had graciously bestowed upon Abraham and his successors promissory blessings by whom all nations would ultimately experience blessing (v. 4). From beginning to end the chapter exhibits the relationship that Isaac (and family) sustains with foreigners (vv. 1–33; 34–35). The experience with Isaac, however, hardly proved to be a blessing for the king initially, since the presence of Isaac and Rebekah proved a threat to the Gerarites if "one of the men" seduced Rebekah (v. 10) and, moreover, since the Philistines suffered the burgeoning growth of Isaac's "hundredfold" harvest. Isaac, from the perspective of the king, was like a lightening rod that attracted grief.[75] By reactionary encounters with Isaac, King Abimelech's fortunes vacillate from unwitting threat (wife-sister deception) to hostility (expulsion and strife) and finally to the friendship (nonaggression pact) that accrues for him a stable affiliation with the stronger power of Isaac. Both explicitly and implicitly in the chapter, the author shows that Isaac's advancement resulted from divine benevolence, not human merit. Like his father, however, his record with the "nations" was flawed due to his fears of oppression.

---

[75] "The long and short of it is that Isaac has proved to be the very opposite of a 'blessing' to the foreigners of Gerar" (D. J. A. Clines, *What Does Eve Do to Help? And Other Readerly Questions to the Old Testament*, JSOTSup 94 [Sheffield: Sheffield Academic Press, 1990], 81).

3. Chapter 26 continues two essential motifs that characterize the patriarchs: the reversals of conflicts and the inventions of trickery. Two major conflicts occur: Isaac's conflict with Abimelech regarding Rebekah (vv. 1–11) and his conflict with the Philistines regarding water rights at Gerar (vv. 14–16,20–21,28–29). Even the final verses describing Esau's marriage to foreign wives may be taken as generating conflict with his parents (vv. 34–35; 27:46). Trickery is a staple feature of the Abraham legacy, and Isaac reenacts the ruse that his father had concocted. Isaac, who became "Abraham, Jr.," mimicked his father in failures as well as successes, showing that it was the Lord alone who guaranteed the covenant's outworking. The account of Isaac's deception fosters the idea of *lex talionis* in the patriarchal narratives. Repeatedly, the Jacob narrative shows that the trickster in turn becomes the tricked. Isaac too had his comeuppance when Rebekah and Jacob deceived him so as to gain the blessing (27:8–29).

COMPOSITION.   Traditional source critics usually assign the majority of this chapter to the Yahwist (J), excepting some later "Deuteronomic" additions (e.g., vv. 3b–5) and the final two verses from the Priestly (P) work (vv. 34–35).[76] The apparent interruption of this chapter in the Jacob-Esau story that flows from chap. 25 to chap. 27 has led Westermann, as with most historical critics, to consider chap. 26 an interpolation, not coming from J. Although assigning the majority of chap. 26 to the Yahwist, G. von Rad concluded that the absence of any reference to the sons and their rivalry shows that the redactor resisted integrating the Isaac story into its present context.[77] According to Westermann, the author set itineraries (vv. 17,22a,23,25b) involving older traditions about the wells (vv. 15,18,19–25,32–33) in the narrative framework about Isaac and Abimelech (vv. 12–17,26–31), producing a "self-contained" composition with "a definite literary plan."[78] The chapter, however, is not an independent work, Westermann says. The author provides vv. 1–11 (wife-sister deception) as the introduction to the whole by drawing on the Abraham accounts, chaps. 12:1–10; 20:1–18. As many form and redaction critics concluded, Westermann believes the Isaac materials were shaped to fit into the promise scheme of the patriarchal narratives (vv. 2a,3a,24). The expansion of the promises in vv. 2b,3b–5 is Deuteronomic in flavor, coming from the exilic era (cf. Deut 11:1), and the promise in v. 24 is also relatively late, making Isaac explicitly the recipient of the inherited promises of Abraham (vv. 3,5,15,18,24). The comparison with Abraham is also implicit, such as in the strife that Isaac's servants endured with the Philistines (v. 20) and the

---

[76] E.g., von Rad, *Genesis,* 270; Coats isolates in the J account a wife-sister story (vv. 1–16) and an itinerary narrative that includes a number of old etiologies pertaining to the naming of local wells (vv. 17–33; *Genesis,* 188–95).

[77] von Rad, *Genesis,* 270.

[78] Westermann, *Genesis 12–36,* 423–24; Rendtorff also views the story as originally independent, containing a collection of various Isaac stories but not a narrative borne out of well etiologies (*The Problem,* 45–48).

quarrel between the herdsmen of Lot and Abraham (13:7–8). Carr also views the promises in 22:15–18 and 26:3–5 as late revisions to their respective narratives, evidenced by their comportment with Deuteronomistic trends, that is, stress on obedience, opposition to foreigners, and stereotyped phrasing.[79]

As with Van Seters, Westermann views the composition as an imitation of Abraham, each beginning with a wife-sister story and revolving around strained relations with Abimelech and the Philistines. We concluded earlier, however, that the trio of "wife-sister stories" were three separate events that the same author reported, penning them so as to create a complementary telling of the episodes (see the introductions to 12:10–13:1; 20:1–18). But Van Seters differs from form-tradition critics like Westermann who believe the promise is a later addition.

Although he fails to recognize the early provenience of the account, Van Seters rightly argues that the promises (vv. 3–5,24–25) are an essential part of the whole narrative, indicating that the author of the promises and the narrative is the same.[80] Verses 1–11 and 12–33 possess the same motifs and exhibit structural counterparts that produce a unified work.[81] The individual episodes that make up each half assume the prior episode, so as to make the narrative an interrelated whole. The strife created by Isaac's deception of the Philistine king matches the strife with the Philistines over the possession of wells. The resolutions to both events involve retractions by Abimelech, whose edict (v. 11) and treaty (vv. 28–29), appearing in their respective parts, testify to the attainment of the theophanic promises, "I will be with you and will bless you" (v. 3) and "I am with you; I will bless you" (v. 24). The presentation of the promises by the same expressions in two places (vv. 4–5,24) reinforces the mutual dependence of the strife stories. The promise "I will be with you" (v. 3) speaks to the protection from hostility that Isaac will undergo, and the corresponding affirmation "I am with you" (v. 24) shows that the promise is being realized. The promise "I will bless you" (v. 3) and its counterpart in v. 24 point to an abundant progeny and corresponding wealth.

G. G. Nicol's analysis confirms our contention that 26:1–33 is a continuous narrative.[82] The narrative structure exhibits the same embedded pattern of promise-threat-resolution in each half of the chapter: the promise of progeny is threatened and resolved in vv. 7–11; the promise of land is threatened and resolved in vv. 12–16,17–23; and the promise of blessing for the nations is threatened throughout and finally resolved in the Abimelech-Isaac treaty (vv. 7–31). The promises foster the cohesion of the narrative plot, with the promise of blessing to

---

[79] Carr, *Reading the Fractures,* 153–59.

[80] Van Seters, *Prologue to History,* 268–69, who assigns chap. 26 to his exilic Yahwist.

[81] Wenham observes the following correspondences: promises (vv. 1–6//23–25), Isaac and Abimelech (vv. 7–11,12–17//26–31), and the naming of wells (vv. 18–22,32–33; *Genesis 16–50,* 185).

[82] G. G. Nicol, however, does not advocate the simpler notion of a single author using original materials, preferring rather to view the chapter's unity as the redaction of the promises and the earlier narrative ("The Narrative Structure and Interpretation of Genesis XXVI 1–33," *VT* 46 [1996]: 344).

the nations as the chief interest of the author, who depicts Abimelech's repentance (vv. 16,26–32). Moreover, Nicol observes that the chapter's plot reversals indicate a continuous narrative: the about-face of the Philistines toward Isaac; the inversion of Abimelech going to Isaac; and finally, the redirection of Isaac's expulsion from Gerar by the return of the Philistine retinue in peace. The plot motif of "famine-water" (vv. 1,32) rounds out the symmetry of vv. 1–33.

Also chap. 26 shows the same theological perspective toward the promises as we find them explained in the Abraham narratives, especially 13:14–17; 15:1,5; and 22:15–18. Both promise passages at 22:15–18 and 26:24–25 are geographically congruent by the patriarchs' common residence at Beersheba (22:19; 26:23), where also they made treaties with Abimelech (21:31–33; 26:33). As for the "Deuteronomic" language of v. 5, we do not find it necessary to suppose a later hand is responsible for the Deuteronomic features appearing in Genesis (e.g., chap. 15). There is a tendency among scholars to assign any passage that has some association with Deuteronomic language to a Deuteronomic redaction that is exilic in origin. That the language of Genesis influenced Deuteronomy—where it was modified, stylized, and became a hallmark of the book—is a sound alternative explanation.[83] Moreover, this tendency toward positing a pandeuteronomic redaction is often based on the slightest of verbal indications. In the case of v. 5, Wenham observes that many of its terms occur frequently in priestly texts in Leviticus and Numbers, not as commonly in Deuteronomy.[84] What the verse projects by its succession of legal terms is rhetorically a surface agreement with Deuteronomic phrasing.

Further, we already noted in our comments on the symmetry of the Jacob account that chap. 26 is not an afterthought, a weak attempt at salvaging a place in the patriarchal history for the Isaac figure. Rather, the events of chap. 26 play important theological and rhetorical functions (see introduction to the Jacob *tōlĕdōt* section). We also discover that the chapter is not as abrupt to the flow of chaps. 25 and 27 as is usually proposed. J. Blenkinsopp remarks that the subject matter of Isaac's tenure in the land is timely, since the land promise is critical to the content of the birthright and blessing over which Jacob and Esau contend.[85] Chapter 26 furthermore possesses many of the same ideas in its neighboring chapters: deception, strife, oath, meal, and blessing. The "famine" as background to Isaac's movements (v. 1) fittingly follows on the imagery of the personal famine of Esau, who exchanges his birthright for Jacob's pottage (25:30–32). Isaac's obedience by staying in the land at God's direction serves as a mild rebuke to Esau, who valued his stomach more than the birthright.

---

[83] E. W. Nicholson advocates this opposite direction of influence (though we cannot agree with his dating scheme) (*The Pentateuch in the Twentieth Century: The Legacy of Julius Wellhausen* [Oxford: Clarendon, 1988], 242–44).

[84] E.g., "my requirements" occurs once in Genesis (v. 5) and in Lev 18:30; 22:9; "his requirements" once in Deuteronomy (11:1); the noun מִשְׁמֶרֶת ("requirement") occurs thirty-five times in Exodus, Leviticus, and Numbers together (cp. Lev 8:35; Num 9:19). See Wenham, *Genesis 16–50*, 190.

[85] J. Blenkinsopp, *The Pentateuch* (New York: Doubleday, 1992), 104.

Wenham also presents a convincing case for the appropriateness of chaps. 26 and 34 in their present position in the Jacob cycle, showing that they are not interpolations in the schematic pattern.[86] He notes especially the striking similarities in the events' sequences between chap. 26 and the early experiences of Abraham in Canaan in chaps. 12–14 as well as remarkable correspondences between chap. 26 and the encounters of Abraham with Abimelech in chaps. 20–21. The peaceful transfer of the blessing to Isaac (vv. 3b–5) and the subsequent riches he obtained as a result of divine favor (vv. 12–14,28–29) provide a foil for the broader narrative, describing the struggle for the blessing by Jacob and Esau, and explains why the twins so coveted the blessing. The function of an interim in the scheme of the Jacob *tōlĕdōt* (see above), paralleling chap. 34's role, may explain the absence of Jacob and Esau in the account. Alternatively, the chapter may well reflect early events before the birth of the twins.[87] Such a dischronological telling of events better suits the Rebekah subterfuge since the presence of grown children would make the ruse against the Gerarites a formidable task.

The downfall of Esau in his parents' eyes at the conclusion (vv. 34–35) parallels the narrator's remarks in 25:34b that discredit Esau. The Isaac story then ends on the parental motif that is so instrumental to understanding chaps. 25 and 27. The mention of Esau's marriages outside the family to Hittite wives and the inclusion of "Rebekah" at the end of chap. 26 recall happier times when Abraham's servant sought a wife for Isaac from their kin (chap. 24). This too insinuates a rebuke of Esau's practices. The parents' response to Esau's marriages appropriately paves the way for chap. 27 that reports Jacob's exodus to Rebekah's household (27:43), where he should take a wife according to his father's practice (27:47–28:2).

We conclude that the source of the chapter's narrative is best explained as the composition of the same author who penned the Abraham narratives. For example, the author depicts both patriarchs as altar builders who "called on the name of the LORD" (12:7–8; 13:4; 21:33; 26:25).[88] That the composition must be an interpolation in a preexisting Jacob-Esau account misunderstands its place in the Jacob account as a whole and its appropriateness to its immediate literary context, connecting the early and later events in the Jacob-Esau narrative.

STRUCTURE.　The chapter consists of two major parts (vv. 1–11,12–33), both describing a conflict between Isaac and the Philistines, followed by a final, brief unit (vv. 34–35) describing Esau's marriage to Hittite wives. The first unit is the deception and conflict between Isaac and the Philistine king,

---

[86] Wenham, *Genesis 16–50*, 186–88.

[87] G. G. Nicol, "The Chronology of Genesis: Genesis XXVI 1–33 as 'Flashback,'" *VT* 46 (1996): 330–38; also Sarna, *Genesis*, 184.

[88] Carr lists the primary similarities between the patriarchal narratives, concluding that chap. 26 is formed to reflect the Abraham story as a whole: introductory famine (v. 1; 12:10); divine command to travel and promise (vv. 2–3; 12:1–3; 22:2; also 31:3,13; 46:3–4); followed by a wife-sister story (vv. 6–11; 12:10–13:1; 20:1–18); transferal of original blessing (vv. 12–14; 12:2–3,16; 20:14); Abimelech's discernment of divine blessing (v. 28; 21:22); and naming of Beersheba (vv. 26–33; 21:25–33; *Reading the Fractures of Genesis*, 198–99).

Abimelech, regarding Rebekah's relationship to Isaac (vv. 1–11). It provides the explanation for Isaac's departure and sojourn in Gerar (vv. 1–6) and describes Isaac's hoax (vv. 7–11). Twin references to "Gerar" form the borders of the first paragraph (vv. 1,6). Sandwiched between are the theophanic promises made to Isaac (vv. 2–5), whom the Lord instructs to remain in the land. Repeatedly the name of "Abraham" appears (vv. 1,3,5), emphatically identifying the promises made to Isaac as those made to his father. The second paragraph (vv. 7–11) is the third wife-sister account in the patriarchal narratives (cf. 12:10–13:1; 20:1–18). Isaac's fear that the men of the city might "kill" him (v. 7) and the royal sanction "shall surely be put to death" (v. 11) form the borders of the paragraph. The border statements exhibit irony: Isaac the outsider who fears for his life receives special protections provided by the ultimate insider, the king.

The second part involves another conflict with the Philistines that also eventuates in a benefit to Isaac, a treaty between the two quarrelling parties (vv. 12–33). The first and third paragraphs pertain to the Philistine dispute. The first paragraph describes the conflict over water rights due to Isaac's swelling numerical strength (vv. 12–23), and the third paragraph entails the treaty that Abimelech instigates with Isaac, securing amicable relations (vv. 26–33). The act of naming wells and the mention of "Beersheba" appear at the close of each paragraph (vv. 22–23,32–33), tying the two together. Sandwiched in between, as in the first unit above (vv. 2–5), is a theophany that engenders Isaac's worship (vv. 24–25).

The events of the final two verses also involve conflict (vv. 34–35). Esau marries Hittite wives from outside the family (exogamy), disappointing his parents.

(1) Journey and Deception in Gerar (26:1–11)

[1]Now there was a famine in the land—besides the earlier famine of Abraham's time—and Isaac went to Abimelech king of the Philistines in Gerar. [2]The LORD appeared to Isaac and said, "Do not go down to Egypt; live in the land where I tell you to live. [3]Stay in this land for a while, and I will be with you and will bless you. For to you and your descendants I will give all these lands and will confirm the oath I swore to your father Abraham. [4]I will make your descendants as numerous as the stars in the sky and will give them all these lands, and through your offspring all nations on earth will be blessed, [5]because Abraham obeyed me and kept my requirements, my commands, my decrees and my laws." [6]So Isaac stayed in Gerar.

[7]When the men of that place asked him about his wife, he said, "She is my sister," because he was afraid to say, "She is my wife." He thought, "The men of this place might kill me on account of Rebekah, because she is beautiful."

[8]When Isaac had been there a long time, Abimelech king of the Philistines looked down from a window and saw Isaac caressing his wife Rebekah. [9]So

Abimelech summoned Isaac and said, "She is really your wife! Why did you say, 'She is my sister'?"

Isaac answered him, "Because I thought I might lose my life on account of her."

¹⁰Then Abimelech said, "What is this you have done to us? One of the men might well have slept with your wife, and you would have brought guilt upon us."

¹¹So Abimelech gave orders to all the people: "Anyone who molests this man or his wife shall surely be put to death."

What the two boys vie for in the two bouts over the elder son's birthright (25:29–34) and blessing (27:1–40) is the subject of chap. 26, namely, the inheritance of the land (cp. 27:28,39). Possession of the land is the promise that is in jeopardy in the Jacob narrative as a whole. Jacob's exile and return to the land provide the thematic and structural symmetry of the entire narrative (see "Structure" above). Jacob must flee the land to escape the wrath of his brother, and he returns after twenty years in Paddan Aram to make his claim on the land that the Lord has promised him (28:13–14; 30:25; 31:3,13; 32:9–10[10–11]). In chap. 26 Isaac remains in the land, obeying the Lord's command even as his father did many years before (12:4); but in Abraham's case, the Lord directed him to depart his homeland for Canaan, whereas Isaac's directive is to remain in the land. Verses 1–11 introduce the events that recount Isaac's struggle to remain in the land despite opposition from the Philistines, ending in a peaceful coexistence (vv. 12–33).

THEOPHANY AT GERAR (26:1–6). The focal attention of the first paragraph (vv. 1–6) is the divine promise, linked explicitly with Abraham.⁸⁹

Famine and Departure for Gerar (26:1). **26:1** The words "famine" and "Abimelech" bring to mind the patriarch's sojourns in Egypt (12:10–13:1) and in Gerar (20:1–18). Verse 1 essentially repeats the narrative structure of 12:10a, departing only by referencing Abraham's experience. The term "famine" *(rā'āb)* occurs first in 12:10(2x) and not again until here. The author identifies this famine in terms of the "earlier famine" in his father's day. The author makes the point that for better or worse Isaac is following in his father's footsteps. The common route to Egypt took a traveler through the Philistine plain (Exod 13:17), where in our passage the Lord intercepts the emigrant at Gerar.⁹⁰

Abimelech is identified simply as "king of Gerar" in 20:1, but in chap. 26 this second "Abimelech" is named "king of the Philistines in Gerar." Typically, scholars point to the same name for the king in 20:1–18 and the Abraham-Abimelech treaty in 21:22–34 as indications that 26:1–11,26–31 are variants of

---

⁸⁹ On the location of Gerar, see comments on 20:1.

⁹⁰ For the difference in the description and identity of the Philistines in the patriarchal period and of the later Philistine pentapolis in Judges–Samuel, see the introduction, "Historicity and History: (4) Anachronisms."

the same Abraham-Abimelech tradition. The considerable differences between the two narratives, however, call into question this standard opinion (see the "Wife-Sister Motif" comments at 12:10–13:1). A better explanation avoids the unwieldy hypothesis of parallel documents. First, the name "Abimelech," meaning "my father is king," may be a throne name among the rulers at Gerar, as in Egypt's practice of "pharaoh." Second, the broader title "king of the Philistines" in v. 1 is not a literary variant but a rhetorical device that contributes to the chapter's emphasis on divine blessing for the nations (vv. 4,28–29). "King of Gerar" occurs only in 20:2, and the narrative depicts the king as a chieftain of a small city-state. The term "Philistines" occurs in 21:32,34, where it names "the land of the Philistines." In chap. 26, however, the appellative "Philistines" repeatedly occurs (vv. 1,8,14,15,18), and the influence of Abimelech's realm appears greater. The national implications of Isaac's duel with the king in chap. 26 appear to surpass the case of Abraham where the nationality of the Gerarites is unimportant. The author treats Isaac as though he is a rival king whose stature requires a formal treaty of peaceful relations.

Divine Promises (26:2–5). The promissory command in these verses gives weight to the events in the remainder of the chapter. The divine encounter is reminiscent of those experienced by Abraham, and the message repeats the promises sworn to Abraham, recalling his obedience at Mount Moriah (22:16–18). Obeying the exhortations (vv. 2–3a) is assumed by the promises that follow (vv. 3b–4). This pattern of command and promise imitates the call of Abraham at Haran and his test at Moriah (12:1–3; 22:2,16–18). Although Abraham appears to be "all in all" for the realization of the promises, Isaac too must do his part, responding dutifully to the command set before him. As the theology of our passage shows throughout, the divine purpose of the call assumes human responsibility and accountability in an obedient response.

26:2 "Appeared" *(wayyērāʾ,* vv. 2,24) provides the standard introduction to theophany (e.g., 12:7; 17:1; 18:1; 35:9; 46:29). There are three exhortations that Isaac must follow, each with its own special significance. First, "do not go down *[yārad]* to Egypt" (v. 2b) echoes when Abraham "went down *[yārad]* to Egypt" (12:10). Some interpreters may reckon that Abraham's descent into Egypt was evidence of a wavering faith, but there is no explicit condemnation in chap. 12 or in this passage. The emphasis of chap. 26 is the obedience of Isaac, resisting the inclusion of any negative intonation. By not escaping to Egypt, the patriarch must endure the famine, trusting that the Lord will deliver him. The second exhortation, "live in the land where I tell you" (v. 2c), is a clear allusion to Abraham's consummate act of faith at Moriah (22:2; cf. 12:2). Functionally for Isaac, this call to wait on the Lord's deliverance corresponds to Abraham's ultimate test (cf. v. 5; 22:18). The term "live" *(šākan)* essentially means to "settle, dwell," and it often describes the presence of God among his people by means of the tabernacle (e.g., Exod

25:8). Yet it also provides a possible lexical allusion to an earlier patriarchal promise, but this time concerning Ishmael, who "will live" opposing his kinsmen (16:10–12; 25:18). Although the word "live" does not inherently mean a long duration, the connotation here is permanent residence.

26:3 "Stay in this land" is the third and final exhortation. The nuance of permanency made implicit by the word "live" (v. 2c) may be further reinforced by the contrasting term "stay" *(gûr).*[91] The word *gûr* ("to sojourn, inhabit") is a favorite term in Genesis, specifying the alien status of the patriarchs as foreigners (cf. 35:27; 37:1; Exod 6:4). Its appearance here is another echo of Abraham's visits to Egypt (12:10) and Gerar (20:1). In this case the "land" refers to the region of Gerar. Since Gerar marked the southern boundary of Canaan (10:19), the location provided a telling place of decision when Isaac obeyed the Lord's directive. By chapter's end Isaac returns to Beersheba, the chief abode of the patriarchs in the Negev (v. 23; 22:19; 28:10; 46:1,5).

The Lord repeats the essential patriarchal promises, establishing protection and prosperity for Isaac. "I will be with you" expresses the inviolate divine presence (v. 3; 31:3; Exod 3:12; Josh 1:5; Judg 6:16; 1 Kgs 11:38). "[I] will bless you" repeats the promissory call in 12:2. In immediate proximity to this promise in 12:2 and 26:3 is reference to the resulting proliferation of the patriarch's offspring. It will indeed require a prodigious nation to secure the extensive territories promised. There is no good reason for Isaac to remain in a barren land, excepting his adamant trust that God will sustain his family and possessions. Although the land is presently settled by foreign nations, the day will come when Isaac's descendants will be its masters. The promise "for to you and your descendants I will give *[nātan]*" and its variations are formulaic in the divine promises (v. 3; cp. 13:15; 17:8; 28:4; 35:12), but this restatement places "to you and your descendants" prominently at the head of the clause.

"All these lands" (vv. 3–4) contrasts with the term "land" in the singular (vv. 1,2,3,12,22) that plays such an important topic in the chapter. "Lands" must include those areas possessed by any number of different neighboring groups. The language corresponds to the comprehensive description "all the land that you see" promised to Abraham during his strife with Lot (13:15). This allusion may be a subtle alert that Isaac's wealth will result in strife with his neighboring host. Finally, mention of the sworn oath *(haššĕbū'â 'ăšer nišba'tî)*undertaken by God himself (v. 3b) hearkens back to 22:16 *(nišba'tî,* "I swear").

26:4–5 This second mention of numerous descendants and inherited lands (v. 4) not only emphasizes these two important promises, but also repeats the two essential factors that make a people a great nation, providing the platform for the realization of the third promise, a blessing for the nations. "I will

---

[91] The NIV occasionally renders גּוּר ("reside as an alien") with the gloss "a while," differentiating the term from יָשַׁב, "to settle, live" (e.g., 12:10; 20:1; Ruth 1:1; 2 Kgs 8:1).

increase" *(rābâ;*vv. 4,24) is part of the standard promissory rhetoric (cf. 15:1; 17:2,20; also 1:22,28; 9:1,7); coupled with the metaphor of innumerable "stars" (v. 4), the language plainly relives the Moriah incident (22:17a). Occupation of "all these lands" (v. 4b) is equivalent to the language "cities of their enemies" heard at Moriah (22:17a; cp. 24:60). The identity of the peoples who are in mind may be those already named in 15:18–21, where the similar language "to your descendants I give this land" (v. 18) introduces a catalog of nations. The nations that Israel will dispossess are typically named in structured ethnographic lists (e.g., Exod 13:5,11; Deut 1:7; 11:24; Josh 3:10).

"Because Abraham obeyed my voice" ("obeyed me," NIV, v. 5) is virtually identical to 22:18, pointing to the sacrifice of Isaac as the event foremost in mind. The remaining statutory language of the verse resonates with the covenant of circumcision that required specific statutory compliance (17:7,9). The forensic terms amassed here regularly appear in Mosaic legislation. When occurring with the first person pronoun, that is, "my requirements" (v. 5), they often appear in the parenetic sections (e.g., Exod 16:28; Lev 22:9,31; Deut 5:29; 11:1,13). By employing covenant terminology, the author depicts the complete obedience of Abraham as the ideal for Israel in the land who must observe the provisions of the Sinaitic covenant (e.g., Lev 26:3; Deut 4:40; 30:16).

Dwelling in Gerar (26:6). **26:6** This brief verse shows that Isaac obeyed the Lord by not proceeding to Egypt. Here, "lived" translates the typical lexeme for settlement, *yāšab,* overlapping at times with the term *gûr* that stipulates alien status (see v. 3; cp. 20:1; 37:1; 47:4; Ruth 1:5). The duration of Isaac's residence in Gerar is unstated here (cp. 21:34), but v. 8 indicates an extended visit.

DECEPTION AT GERAR (26:7–11). The second paragraph furnishes an implied link with Abraham by Isaac's revival of Abraham's old tactic of deceiving his host (vv. 7–11). Westermann comments that v. 11 provides the explanation for Isaac's continuation in the land (v. 12).[92]

Fear and Discovery (26:7–8). **26:7–8** The fear of harm, as with his father, motivated Isaac to say that Rebekah was his sister (v. 9; cf. 12:13,19; 20:11–13). Unlike the former occasions, the king did not abduct Rebekah. The possibility, however, of a Gerarite abducting her was enough to worry the king, who took steps to ensure that neither she nor her husband was aggrieved. Since no abduction had occurred, the discovery of the ruse was slow in coming (v. 8). No divine revelation by plague (12:17–18) or dream (20:3) alerted the king; rather it was by his chance observation of Isaac exhibiting physical affection toward his wife: "Isaac caressing . . ." *(yiṣḥāq mĕṣaḥēq).* "Caressing" (NIV,

---

[92] Westermann, *Genesis 12–36,* 425.

HCSB, NASB[93]) translates *měṣaḥēq*, a wordplay with the name *yiṣḥāq*, "Isaac" (cf. 21:6,9), meaning "Isaak was Isaaking."[94] The term is used of toying with someone (Judg 16:25) or revelry (Exod 32:6). The term also has sexual connotations when Potiphar's wife charges Joseph with degrading her by sexual advances (39:14,17). The narrative spares us the details of what precisely the king observed that was unbefitting a brother's behavior toward his sister. On the basis of 39:14,17, the conduct probably was sexual in nature, perhaps what we moderns call "foreplay," but to what scope the passage conceals.

Abimelech's Edict (26:9–11). **26:9–10** The interrogation of the culprit by the king involves a blistering accusation. An impassioned exclamation initiates the charge, "behold!" preceded by the emphatic adverb "indeed" (*ʾak hinnê*,[95] NIV "really"). Abimelech continues to express his shock at the man's behavior, "Why did you say . . .?"[96] Since a man does not treat his sister in this personal way, his behavior toward Rebekah proved the king's indictment. Isaac's defense of his behavior assumed what Abraham specifically had retorted, "there is surely no fear of God in this place" (20:11).[97] The king's response, however, showed a keener sense of moral decency than his guest (v. 10).[98] Abimelech reveals his concern for the entire populace of the city ("us") by incurring punishment for such a deed. In the earlier Abraham incident, the Philistine king also contemplated that the action of one man could impact a whole nation (20:4). Abimelech's question, "What have you done to us?" recalls the response of Pharaoh to Abraham's deception (12:18) and reaches back to the Garden when the Lord interrogated the woman (3:13). Abimelech marveled that no offense had occurred since it would have been an easy matter (*kimʿaṭ,* lit., "like a little"; NIV "might well") for someone to do.[99] The consequent "guilt" (*ʾāšām)* Abimelech dreaded (v. 10b) was actually the penalty that such guilt would warrant against the nation (e.g., Lev 5:6; cp. Ezra 9:13). For the repugnance of this offense in the eyes of society, see "great guilt" (lit., "great sin") at comments on 20:9.

26:11 Abimelech provided a blanket protection for the couple that

---

[93] The EVs also have "sporting" (AV), "laughing with" (ESV), "fondling" (NRSV, NJPS, NLT, NJB, NAB), and "making love" (GNB).

[94] Wevers, *Notes on the Greek Text,* 402; the LXX has παίζοντα, from παίζω, meaning "dance, play, amusement" (cf. 21:9, LXX; 1 Chr 15:29, LXX; 1 Cor 10:7), which Wevers renders "playing around [with]."

[95] אַךְ expresses a forceful sense, e.g., 18:32, see *IBHS* §39.3.5d n. 93.

[96] אֵיךְ + perfect verb may express astonishment or indignation, "how!"; see GKC §148ab.

[97] "Because [כִּי] I thought . . ." (v. 9b); GKC §157b interprets כִּי as possibly asseverative, "indeed"; if so, then Isaac answers with the same vigor as Abimelech had questioned him.

[98] The mood is hypothetical: "might well have slept" (*IBHS* §30.5.4c; 32.2.3c); Sarna notes that the king's anxiety over the safety of the couple confirms indirectly the immorality of the community that Isaac had assumed (v. 9; *Genesis,* 184).

[99] כִּמְעַט, "nearly" (cf. Prov 5:14), *HALOT* 2.611; "almost," BDB 590.

imposed the ultimate punishment by issuing a decree to "all the people." "Anyone who molests" translates *nōgēaʿ* (cf. v. 29), derived from the common term "to strike, touch" (*nāgaʿ;* e.g., 32:25,33[26,32]). Proverbs 6:9 forewarns anyone who "touches" *(nōgēaʿ)* a married woman by sleeping with her. The appearance of the related term in 12:17 for the "disease" *(negaʿ)* endured by the Egyptians implies that plague was likely the punishment Abimelech feared (cf. Exod 11:1). The language calling for the death sentence exhibits a common formula for capital punishment in Mosaic tradition, "shall surely be put to death" *(môt yûmāt)* (e.g., Exod 21:12; cp. comments at 20:7). A close parallel to the language of the edict appears in Exod 19:2, threatening anyone who "touches" the holy mount unlawfully. As in the case of the Abimelech-Abraham incident, the Lord preserved the patriarch, but here there is no evidence of a night revelation (20:3). The king acted out of an inherent fear of divine retribution for offending his moral conscience.

(2) Conflict and Treaty (26:12–33)

[12]Isaac planted crops in that land and the same year reaped a hundredfold, because the LORD blessed him. [13]The man became rich, and his wealth continued to grow until he became very wealthy. [14]He had so many flocks and herds and servants that the Philistines envied him. [15]So all the wells that his father's servants had dug in the time of his father Abraham, the Philistines stopped up, filling them with earth.

[16]Then Abimelech said to Isaac, "Move away from us; you have become too powerful for us."

[17]So Isaac moved away from there and encamped in the Valley of Gerar and settled there. [18]Isaac reopened the wells that had been dug in the time of his father Abraham, which the Philistines had stopped up after Abraham died, and he gave them the same names his father had given them.

[19]Isaac's servants dug in the valley and discovered a well of fresh water there. [20]But the herdsmen of Gerar quarreled with Isaac's herdsmen and said, "The water is ours!" So he named the well Esek, because they disputed with him. [21]Then they dug another well, but they quarreled over that one also; so he named it Sitnah. [22]He moved on from there and dug another well, and no one quarreled over it. He named it Rehoboth, saying, "Now the LORD has given us room and we will flourish in the land."

[23]From there he went up to Beersheba. [24]That night the LORD appeared to him and said, "I am the God of your father Abraham. Do not be afraid, for I am with you; I will bless you and will increase the number of your descendants for the sake of my servant Abraham."

[25]Isaac built an altar there and called on the name of the LORD. There he pitched his tent, and there his servants dug a well.

[26]Meanwhile, Abimelech had come to him from Gerar, with Ahuzzath his personal adviser and Phicol the commander of his forces. [27]Isaac asked them, "Why have you come to me, since you were hostile to me and sent me away?"

[28]They answered, "We saw clearly that the LORD was with you; so we said, 'There ought to be a sworn agreement between us'—between us and you. Let us make a treaty with you [29]that you will do us no harm, just as we did not molest you but always treated you well and sent you away in peace. And now you are blessed by the LORD."

[30]Isaac then made a feast for them, and they ate and drank. [31]Early the next morning the men swore an oath to each other. Then Isaac sent them on their way, and they left him in peace.

[32]That day Isaac's servants came and told him about the well they had dug. They said, "We've found water!" [33]He called it Shibah, and to this day the name of the town has been Beersheba.

After establishing Isaac's credentials as the successor to the inherited promises in vv. 1–11, the narrative in vv. 12–33 describes the success the patriarch experienced as a result of God's blessing. As in the former narrative, this unit entails a conflict with the Philistines, but not as a result of Isaac's malfeasance. It is rather due to the fallout of God's fulfilling the promise of blessing (vv. 2–5). That Isaac's prosperity ensues in conflicts (vv. 12–23) matches the sequence of events in the Abraham narrative (12:10–13:18). The Lord reassures the patriarch by repeating the promises in a second epiphany. Isaac's response of worship parallels his father's actions (vv. 24–25; 12:7). Additional evidence that the Lord would fulfill his promises was the recognition of the man's welfare by the foreigner Abimelech and his desire for a treaty (vv. 26–33). The passage describes the migratory movements of Isaac's family in stages from Gerar, to the valley of Gerar, and continuing inland to Beersheba. The discovery and naming of wells that occupy the narrative interest serve to show the connection of Isaac with his father Abraham, evidence the blessing of God, and establish the patriarch's place as the legitimate heir. The second naming of the site Beersheba confirms that he walked in the steps of Abraham, who initially had named the town by its well (21:31).

CONFLICT OVER WELLS (26:12–23).   Isaac's wealth created tension with the Philistines and disputed ownership of local wells, which led to his migration to Beersheba.

Isaac's Prosperity (26:12–14).   **26:12–14**   The passage describes Isaac's wealth according to a plentiful harvest and numerous livestock (vv. 12,14). Most likely grain or barley was cultivated; barley though does better in dry environments.[100] Multiplying livestock and servants characterized the wealth of Abraham (12:16; 13:2; 24:35) and Jacob (30:43; 32:5,15; 36:7). Jacob's sons also obtained wealth in livestock holdings but not always by honorable means (34:28–29; 47:16–18). The notion of abundant crops, however, is exceptional when Genesis describes the wealth of the patriarchs. This feature

---

[100] D. Hopkins, "Cereals," *OEANE* 1.479–81.

of Isaac's wealth is in keeping with the chapter's emphasis on the land promise, but it also explains the tension that his farming created with his neighbors. The semiarid state of the region required a diversified economy for
survival, involving animal husbandry and dry farming. Migratory groups settled seasonally near more sedentary centers whose contacts produced at times
disputes over water rights and grazing tracts.[101] This explains the strain that
Isaac's arrival placed on the limited resources in the region.

Two aspects made the bumper crop remarkable: first, the return was a hundred times the seed invested, and it occurred immediately the first year. The
bounty proved that the Lord had "blessed" Isaac (v. 12; cf. 24:1,35; 25:11;
39:5), indicating the first step toward the fulfillment of the promises revealed
in vv. 3–4. So as to highlight the enrichment Isaac received, the passage
amplifies his increasing wealth by repeating the word group *g-d-l* (3x), meaning "to become great, grow," and by the intensifying modifiers "continued"
(hālôk)[102] and "very" *(mĕʾōd)*. That the mighty Philistines became envious
further heightens the immense wealth that the passage depicts. "Envied"
translates the term *qānāʾ* that also describes the animosity Jacob's sons exhibited toward their brother Joseph (37:11; cf. 30:1).

Isaac's Expulsion (26:15–16). **26:15–16** The action of the Philistines
threatened Isaac's herds by cutting off treasured water resources (v. 15; cp.
2 Kgs 3:25). The three most common means of obtaining water involved
springs, wells, and cisterns. In arid conditions probably the digging of dry
riverbeds to capture the remaining water level was the first means of establishing a well. The second earliest well in Israel was found in the Beersheba
region (fourth millennium), including in the area signs of early irrigation and
water storage. Cisterns usually involved lining the chamber hewn from natural rock with plaster, catching and retaining rainfall; otherwise, an excavated
pit was lined with layered rocks and plaster.[103] That they destroyed "all" of
the wells indicates the intensity of their ire. Twice the name "Abraham" as the
father of Isaac appears (v. 15; also v. 18), hinting at the parallel between the
two men but also showing that the son had valid claim to the water (21:25–
30). The offending party is the Philistine rascals, not Isaac in this case. The
means of stopping up the wells was filling the cavities with dirt. Since the
wells could be redug (v. 18), this could only slow down Isaac's progress and
discourage his herdsmen. Abimelech expelled Isaac because of his numerical
strength. The term rendered "powerful" *(ʿāṣam)* occurs only twice more in

---

[101] V. Matthews, "The Wells of Gerar," *BA* 49 (1986): 118–26.

[102] וַיֵּלֶךְ הָלוֹךְ וְגָדֵל, lit., "he progressed progressing and becoming great"; the infinitive
absolute הָלוֹךְ and adjective גָדֵל indicate repetition or continuation (cp. 2 Sam 5:10; see *IBHS*
§35.3.2c and n. 39), i.e., "he increased more and more."

[103] T. Tsuk, "Hydraulics," *OEANE* 3.130–32; "Hydrology," *OEANE* 3.132–33; and "Cisterns,"
OEANE 2.12–13.

the Pentateuch, referring to the frightening increase of Hebrew children born in Egypt (Exod 1:7,20).

Discovery of Wells (26:17–19). **26:17–19** Isaac consented to the demand of the king (v. 17). The same term "moved" *(hālak)* in the king's mandate (v. 16) describes Isaac's immediate response. "From there" *(miššām)* is a recurring term in the chapter, calling attention to the repeated migrations and discoveries by Isaac (vv. 8,17,19,22,23,25). "Encamped" *(ḥānâ)* commonly describes Israel's encampment in the wilderness (e.g., Exod 19:2), but it appears only twice in Genesis for the migrations of Isaac and Jacob (26:17; 33:18). Wenham proposes that the patriarch's migration is another prefigure of Israel's desert experience.[104] Despite Isaac's retreat to the "Valley of Gerar" (v. 17), the squabble over water rights between the two peoples remained. Isaac's men persisted in reclaiming the wells that had been excavated by Abraham (v. 18; 21:34). By reassigning to the wells the names given by Abraham, Isaac upheld his entitlement to them. Additionally, the never-ending need for water in the Negev led his servants to find a valuable subterranean source of "fresh water" (v. 19).

Conflict between Herdsmen (26:20–21). **26:20–21** A conflict immediately arose over the newly found spring (v. 20). The language "quarrel" *(r-y-b)* in vv. 20–21 recalls the similar problem between Lot and Abraham whose herdsmen quarreled (13:7; cf. Israel's "Meribah," Exod 17:7; Num 20:13). The Gerarites made their claim to the water, probably on the basis that it fell within or near their territory—at least close enough to alarm them. Isaac named the well "Esek," *(ʿēśek),* creating a wordplay on the word "dispute, contend" *(ʿāśak);* and a second well of contention, "Sitnah," meaning "accusation" (v. 21; cf. Ezra 4:6). The author points to these occasions as evidence for the ongoing struggle the patriarch faced in that region. These struggles forced the patriarch to backpedal, resting again at the point of his departure (Beersheba). As was the case in Abraham's experience, Isaac returned to the land of his family's sojourning but only after he had become enriched in another land. The precise locations of these two named wells are unknown, but on the basis of the general description in the passage, they most likely were nearby the course of the river Nahal Gerar.[105]

Naming Wells (26:22–23). **26:22–23** Isaac took another step toward establishing good relations with his neighbors by moving yet again (v. 22), abandoning the wells to the Philistines. "Moved" *(ʿātēq, hiphil)* also describes Abraham's itinerant movements (12:8). Isaac's generosity toward the Philistines is reminiscent of his father's benevolence toward Lot (13:8–9). The sign that he had relocated sufficiently far enough was the absence of any

---

[104] Wenham, *Genesis 16–50,* 191.

[105] A. F. Rainey, "Sitnah," *ISBE* 4.535. On Gerar see comments on 20:1.

challenge to the discovery of a new well. He named the well "Rehoboth," meaning "wide, broad, spacious" (cf. 10:11; 36:37; 1 Chr 1:48), commemorating the Lord's provision for his growing wealth (cf. 2 Sam 22:20//Ps 18:19[20]; Ps 31:8[9]). His explanation for the name involves the root term *rāḥab*, "to make spacious" (*hiph.*, causative). Traditionally, the site is identified with Ruheibe, on the northeast side of the Wadi Ruheibe, about eighteen miles southwest of Beersheba (cf. "Rehoboth on the river," 36:37). The Nabatean site (ca. first century B.C.) probably was named after the biblical name Rehoboth, believing it was the same location as Isaac's well. It possesses the largest well in the Negev and the site second in size to Halusa (Elousa) in the Negev.[106] "Flourish" translates *pārâ,* which is a standard term in the blessing formula, usually rendered "to be fruitful" (e.g., 1:22,28; 8:17; 9:1,7; 17:6,20; 28:3). Afterward Isaac's family ascended the hills of the northern Negev to the location Beersheba (v. 23; cf. 13:1).[107]

THEOPHANY AT BEERSHEBA (26:24–25). **26:24** Immediately upon Isaac's arrival, a night revelation affirmed the promises in vv. 3–4 anew. The emphasis of "that night" underscores the significance of his return to his father's homestead. The self-predication, "I am the God of your father Abraham," identifies the Lord with the revelation of the "Eternal God" *(El Olam)* at Beersheba (21:32; cf. 15:1; 17:1). It further provides the historical linkage of succession (cp. 28:13; Josh 24:3; *Yahweh,* Exod 3:6). This rendition of the promises omits reference to the nations, assuming it as in vv. 3–5. Here the emphasis is personal consolation. The Lord comforted the patriarch as he did Abraham in 15:1 (cf. 46:3), assuring him of divine protection in the land of promise. The pronoun "I" *(ʾānōkî)* in "for I am with you,"[108] occurs additionally to the divine self-predication so as to highlight the presence of the personal God. "With you" heads the clause with the same effect of pointing up the irrevocable relationship with God that the patriarchs relied on. After Isaac had returned to the land and the Lord had blessed him with great wealth, this promise of expanding population is the appropriate concluding word, completing the triad of promises (land, offspring, and blessing). The legacy of the promises received by Isaac is "for the sake of my servant Abraham" (cp. "David," 1 Kgs 11:32; 2 Kgs 20:6). That the blessing was achieved vicariously by the merit of Abraham misunderstands the point of this attribution. The efficacy of the blessing did not rely on the merit of Abraham but rather was on account of the divine commitment made to Abraham and his descendants. The honored title "my servant" occurs also for the distinguished leaders of Israel in the desert, Moses (Num 12:7,8; Josh 1:2,7; 2 Kgs 21:8; Mal 4:4), Caleb (Num 14:24), and Joshua

---

[106] Ibid., and D. Groh, "Rehovot," *OEANE* 4.420.

[107] On Beersheba see comments on 21:31–32 and 26:32–33.

[108] Verbless clause, best rendered in the present tense as most EVs, כִּי אִתְּךָ אָנֹכִי.

by the variant "the servant of the LORD" (Josh 24:29).[109]

26:25 Three actions by Isaac show his determination to remain in the land and the object of God's favor. He first erected an altar of worship, which passed on the tradition and worship of his father (12:7,8; 13:4,18; 22:9). Second, "pitching his tent" meant he established his residence in the vicinity (cf. 12:8; 33:19; 35:21; Judg 4:11). Third, his servants sought water for his new habitation, digging a well.

TREATY WITH ABIMELECH (26:26–33). After the assurance of God's promise (v. 24) and Isaac's response of worship (v. 25), King Abimelech sought a treaty with Isaac (vv. 26–29), which resulted in a covenant meal and oath (vv. 30–31). The final two verses describe the boon of a new well discovered (vv. 32–33).

Abimelech Proposes a Covenant (26:26–29). **26:26** Accompanying the king were two subordinates, his adviser Ahuzzath and the general of the army, Phicol. The latter name is known in 21:22,32 when he escorted Abimelech to win a treaty with Abraham. Attempts at explaining "Phicol" etymologically have focused on an Egyptian or Anatolian (Asia Minor) source, reflecting the consensus that the name is non-Semitic.[110] The title "the commander of his forces" *(śar ṣĕbāʾô)* also appears here, identifying the courtier's position. The same title occurs for commanders in Israel's early monarchy (1 Sam 14:50; 26:5; 2 Sam 10:18). That this Phicol was the same person is unlikely since the former event was sixty years earlier. Ahuzzath's identity is obscure. The name occurs only here,[111] and his title "personal adviser" is uncertain,[112] though the EVs commonly translate *mērēʿēhû* here, "his friend/ counselor/adviser." The term *mērēʿēhû* usually means "his friend," describing a companion (Judg 14:20; 15:6; 2 Sam 3:8; Job 6:14; Prov 19:7), but when identifying an official capacity it most likely indicates a counselor. That *mērēaʿ* is an office is suggested by the parallel title "commander" *(śar),* describing Phicol's post in the king's administration. David and Solomon had a designated *rēʾeh,* who served as "friend of the king," that is, counselor

---

[109] Also "my servant," עַבְדִּי, e.g., Job (1:8; 2:3; 42:7,8), esp. David (e.g., 2 Sam 3:18; 7:5,8; Ps 89:3,20; Jer 33:21,22,26), Isaiah (20:3), the servant Israel (e.g., Isa 41:8,9; 42:1; 49:3,6; 52:13), and Nebuchadnezzar (Jer 25:9).

[110] J. Ray reconstructed possible Anatolian cognates Πικωλδος or Πιγωλλος, though neither was as yet attested ("Two Etymologies: Ziklag and Phicol," *VT* 36 [1986]: 355–61).

[111] The LXX inserts Οχοζαθ ὁ νυμφαγωγὸς αὐτοῦ, "Ahuzzath his friend," at 21:22,32, harmonizing the two passages (see comments at 21:22).

[112] J. Safren, on the basis of linguistic and sociological comparisons to the *merḫûm* (< *rʿy,* "pasture"), who managed the king's grasslands at Mari, explains that Ahuzzath represented the interests of the Gerarite pastoralists in the negotiations ("Ahuzzath and the Pact of Beer-Sheba," *ZAW* 101 [1989]: 184–98). By emending מֵרֵעֵהוּ (MT) to read מַרְעֵהוּ (< רָעָה, *hiph.* participle, "he who lets pasture"), he posits that the title originally was מַרְעֶה, i.e., "supervisor of the royal pasturage" (p. 195).

(1 Kgs 4:5; 1 Chr 27:33; cp. "friend of David," 2 Sam 15:37; 16:16). Also the list of Solomon's administrative officials included Benaiah, who was over the "army" *(ṣābāʾ)*, a title paralleling Phicol's role, and Zabud, who was "friend of the king" (1 Kgs 4:4–5; cp. 1 Chr 27:33–34). By the twin powers standing alongside the king, the supplicants represented the whole of the nation.

26:27–29 Isaac expressed his dismay at the arrival of the Philistine king and entourage (v. 27). This immediately put the Philistines at a disadvantage, requiring them to defend their behavior. "Hostile" translates the common term usually rendered "to hate" *(śānēʾ;* e.g., NASB, NRSV; cp. Jephthah, Judg 11:7). Their response involves an inclusion: "the LORD was with you" and "you are blessed by the LORD" (vv. 28a,29b; on the former expression, see comments on 39:2). It became self-evident ("saw clearly," v. 28[113]) to the Philistines that their attempts at hindering Isaac's rise were futile, for they opposed a power greater than Isaac alone. Their cause was at crosspurposes with divine favor. They make a pitch for a "sworn agreement," crafting a nonaggression pact (v. 28). The customary language for covenant making, "cut a covenant" *(kārat bĕrît)*, is further invoked by the Philistines ("treaty," NIV), explaining the nature of the agreement. "Sworn agreement" translates *ʾālâ,* which also can mean "curse"; it often occurs in conjunction with a formal agreement that normally included sanctions against offenders of the agreement. Thus as a metonymy, *ʾālâ* here may indicate the agreement as a whole (e.g., 24:41; Deut 29:11–13,18–20; Ezek 16:59; 1QS 2:16).[114]

They admit that their motivation is the fear of a clash between the two peoples (v. 29). The justification for their proposal is the history of their friendly disposition toward Isaac, referring to the events of vv. 1–11 by the same term "molest" *(nāgaʿ,* vv. 11,29). Of course, they overstate the case when they allege they only practiced favorable treatment of the Isaac family. By Isaac's perplexity over their approach, the passage suggests that he had not interpreted their treatment so favorably. The Philistines cogently contended, however, that they had not harmed Isaac (and Rebekah) when the opportunity was theirs. Furthermore, they did not resort to violence against him when the king faced the pressures of Isaac's increasing consumption of available pasturage and water. If we are to read this incident in light of the similar occurrence with Abraham (20:6), their benevolence toward Isaac could as well be explained as the unseen hand of God's protective presence. The acknowledgment of Isaac as "blessed by the LORD" (v. 29; cp. 24:31) corroborates by a foreigner's voice what the author has already shown (cf. 21:22). In doing so Abimelech illustrates the necessary response of the nations to experience the blessing God has

---

[113] רָאוֹ רָאִינוּ, lit., "seeing we saw," i.e., "we saw manifestly," with the infinitive absolute construction, expressing the certainty of their observation (cp. טָרֹף טֹרַף, 37:33; *IBHS* §35.3.1).

[114] *DCH* 1.272; *HALOT* 1.51; and R. Gordon, "אלה," *NIDOTTE* 1.403–4.

offered by Abraham's descendants (12:2).[115]

Covenant Oath and Meal (26:30–31). **26:30–31** Typical of ancient treaties, a shared meal by the two participants, even between superior and inferior parties, confirmed a pact (v. 30; cp. 31:46,54; Exod 24:11; Deut 26:17).[116] Isaac provided the covenant meal as the host, exhibiting his good will (e.g., 18:5; 19:3; 24:31,54) and also perhaps his superiority (cp. 2 Sam 3:20). The members of the pact the next morning formally subscribed to a mutually sworn oath (cf. 21:31; 31:52–53), and the Philistines left "in peace" (v. 31; cp. 2 Sam 3:21).[117] That the same description of their amicable departure ("sent," *šālaḥ*) already appeared in their disputed treatment of Isaac (vv. 27,29) reinforces the passage's report of the new arrangement.

Naming the Well at Beersheba (26:32–33). **26:32–33** The discovery of a well on "that day" (v. 32) presents another indication of the Lord's grace extended to Isaac. The passage implies that the new well was not a coincidence but a signal of the Lord's blessing.[118] The man could now rest comfortably in the land, knowing that his neighbors had been pacified and that provisions abounded.

A second explanation occurs in this passage for the appellative "Beersheba" (v. 33), already named by Abraham under similar circumstances (see the introduction to 21:22–32). Isaac often named wells the same names given by his father (v. 18b). As in the first case, the name "Beersheba" presents a convenient dual reference to "sworn oath" and "seven" (see comments at 21:31–32). The designation of the well "Shibah" (v. 33) is also the cardinal number "seven" (e.g., 7:2). It further sounds similar to the word "to swear" (*šābaʿ*), commemorating the sworn oath entered that same day (vv. 3,31). There is no apparent reason for the number "seven" employed unless the author assumed that seven animals were likewise involved in some aspect of the agreement, presenting the event with 21:28–29 in mind. On Beersheba as a city, see comments at 21:31–32.

(3) Esau's Wives and Conflict (26:34–35)

³⁴When Esau was forty years old, he married Judith daughter of Beeri the Hittite, and also Basemath daughter of Elon the Hittite. ³⁵They were a source of grief to Isaac and Rebekah.

This final section presents another conflict pertaining to marriage, providing the closing inclusio to the beginning account of Isaac's wife-sister ploy (vv. 1–

---

[115] Wenham, *Genesis 16–50,* 193.

[116] See D. J. McCarthy, "Three Covenants in Genesis," *CBQ* 26 (1964): 179–89.

[117] Sarna mentions the legal language "covenant of peace," בְּרִיתִי שָׁלוֹם (Num 25:12; Isa 54:10; Ezek 34:25; 37:26; cp. Josh 9:15; *Genesis,* 188).

[118] The LXX's οὐχ εὕρομεν ὕδωρ, "we have not found water," translates לוֹ ("to him") as the negative לֹא ("not"), creating the opposite meaning.

11). This terse description of Esau's marriage could as easily function as the introduction to the following segment in chap. 27, forming also an inclusio with Rebekah's dissatisfaction with the wives of Esau (27:46). At both places the report of Esau's wives and his parents' aversion to foreign wives contrast the son with his father, who took a wife from within the extended family (endogamy). This brief notice provides compelling evidence that Esau's attitude toward his family's religious heritage is deficient. By performing this rhetorical function, the passage transitions the chapter from its concentration on Isaac and Rebekah to the sons' dispute and their parents' roles in the animosity that develops. Since Rebekah may well have planned for her sons to find wives from among her kindred in Aram, the marriage to Hittite women would have fortified her preference for Jacob. Strong prohibitions against marrying Canaanite women, showing indifference to their religion, occurred in Israelite custom (e.g., Deut 7:3–4; 1 Kgs 11:2; Ezra 9:12; Neh 13:25). That the sons of Jacob proposed intermarriage to the Shechemites (although with malicious intent) presumed their adoption of the covenant (34:9,17).

26:34 The age "forty" provides an immediate comparison of Esau's practice with Isaac, who took a wife at the same age (25:20) but by honoring his parents. The first polygamist was Lamech (4:19), who also was of a rejected lineage (Cain). Judith is only mentioned here, unlike Basemath, who is prominent in the genealogies of Esau (36:3,4,10,13,17). This may imply that Judith was barren, motivating him to take a second wife. If so, his situation recalls the same problem faced by Abraham and Sarah. Perhaps the author resisted including additional information on Judith since this similarity with Abraham and Isaac would distract from his interest in establishing the priority of Jacob (11:30; 25:21; 29:31).

Ironically, although Hittite by descent, the name "Judith" is the feminine form of the later gentilic *yĕhûdî* ("Judean, Jewish"), thus meaning a "Jewess or (female) Judean"[119] (cp. 2 Kgs 18:26). Her father's name "Beeri" ("my well, pit") also was a known Hebrew name, including the father of the prophet Hosea (1:1). "Beer(i)" recalls the naming of the well at Beersheba (v. 31; cp. Num 21:16–18). "Basemath" is related to the Hebrew word *bōśem/beśem,* meaning "spices, perfumes, balsam (shrub or oil)," a term that can have connotations of wealth or intimacy (e.g., 1 Kgs 10:10; Song 6:2).[120] This name also identifies the daughter of Solomon, married to Ahimaaz (1 Kgs 4:15). Basemath's father "Elon" (36:2), meaning "great tree" (e.g., 12:6; Deut 11:30; EV's may also

---

[119] Denominative verb יהד, "to be a Jew" or "declare oneself a Jew" (*hith.,* Esth 8:17; see *DCH* 4.115); cp. the feminine יהודית, "the language of Judah" (2 Kgs 18:26,28 pars.; Neh 13:24) and feminine יְהֻדִיָּה, "Judean (wife)" (1 Chr 4:18; see BDB 397; *HALOT* 2.394). On the wordplay of the name "Judah," see comments at 29:35; 49:8.

[120] R. Averbeck, "בֹּשֶׂם," *NIDOTTE* 1.774–75; E. A. Knauf finds the personal name in Minaean, Sabaic, and classical Arabic ("Basemath," *ABD* 1.623).

translate "oak/terebinth"), was yet another popular Hebrew appellative, including Zebulun's son (46:14; Num 26:26; Judg 12:11–12), a site in Danite territory (Josh 19:43), and a court officer (1 Kgs 4:9).

The narrative accounts naming Esau's wives in 26:34–35 and 28:9 vary in name and descent from the genealogical listing of his wives in 36:2–3, generating a host of speculative reconstructions from antiquity to the present. First, the two narrative passages show that Esau married (1) Judith, daughter of Beeri the Hittite, and (2) Basemath, daughter of Elon the Hittite (26:34), after which he hoped to mitigate his father's displeasure by marrying within the family, his cousin, namely, (3) Mahalath, the sister of Nebaioth (Ishmael's firstborn son, 25:13) and daughter of Ishmael (see comments at 28:9). Second, Esau's genealogy (36:2–3) also names three wives, but their names and lineages appear to reflect another tradition: (1) Adah, daughter of Elon the Hittite, (2) Oholibamah, daughter of Anah and granddaughter of Zibeon the Hivite (36:2), and (3) Basemath, daughter of Ishmael, sister of Nebaioth (36:3). The names "Judith," "Mahalath," and "Oholibamah" occur in only one of the two versions. "Basemath" is the only name to occur in both accounts, but each attributes to her a different ancestry (Elon the Hittite or Ishmael).[121]

Scholars often attribute the two groups of names to two different traditions that have been preserved by the Priestly writer or later redactor (see "Composition" at comments on 36:1–8). Three important factors that sometimes occurred in assigning names may help explain how the two sets of appellatives may give an accurate picture of the wives' names and derivations. A person could bear two names (e.g., Reuel/Jethro), and a person could undergo a name change (e.g., Jacob/Israel; Joseph/Zaphenath-Paneah). Also multiple persons could bear the same name (e.g., Anah, 36:20,24). In light of the foregoing, it is possible that the sets of names include reference to the same women under two different names and/or a fourth wife but with the same name.[122] Since the women named "Basemath" bear two different derivations (Hittite/Ishmaelite), it is reasonable to posit that they are two different people with the same name.[123] On the other hand, Mahalath (28:9) and Basemath (36:2) are both Ishmaelites. All in all, the problem remains unsolved until more information is discovered that bears on the solution.

---

[121] Hamilton observes that the ethnicity of the two groups has the same order, if the versions are followed: Judith and Adah (Hittite); Basemath and Oholibama (Hivite, if "Hivite" is read [SP, LXX] at 26:34 for Basemath); and Mahalath and Basemath (Ishmaelite; *Genesis Chapters 18–50*, 392).

[122] J. H. Abraham ("A Literary Solution to the Name Variations of Esau's Wives," *The Torah U-Maddah Journal* 7 [1997]: 1–14, similarly in "Esau's Wives," *JBQ* 25 [1997]: 251–59) offers an imaginative solution relying strongly on the literary context, arguing that the two sets of names refer to the same three wives. Some of his suggestions may point us in the right direction, but his argument is not completely satisfying.

[123] F. C. Fensham ponders whether "Basemath" ("perfume") is a nickname for two women, Mahalath and Adah ("Basemath," *NBD*[3], 124).

26:35 The chapter concludes by reporting the sorrowful reaction of the parents at the new Hittite members of the family. The absence of a specific grievance implies that Esau's parents were troubled by virtue of the women's foreign lineage (exogamy). The brief observation of their disappointment by the author cracks the door open for the later, torrid objection made by Rebekah (27:42). We may surmise that she was especially distressed that her family in Paddan Aram had been spurned, not unlike Esau's earlier show of disdain for the family's birthright (25:34b). This bitterness will prove to be her "cover story" to Isaac for expediting the escape of Jacob. The final reference to "Isaac and Rebekah" (v. 35) in the context of Esau's wives recalls the parents' mixed preferences for their sons (25:18). No mention is made of Jacob in chap. 26, but the mere notice of Esau brings to mind the overarching plot line of his sibling quarrels. Also this parental disappointment anticipates the sibling strife to follow in chap. 27 in which Rebekah by deception ensures that Jacob wins out and then dispatches him to Paddan Aram, seeking for him a proper wife (27:46; 28:5).

3. Stolen Blessing and Flight to Paddan Aram (27:1–28:9)

After the interim of Isaac's experience in Gerar (chap. 26), the text takes up again the rivalry between Jacob and Esau (25:29–34). The message of the present passage is the perseverance of God's commitment to the Abraham clan despite the moral lapse and strife that threatens the solidarity of the family. We hear from the parents and the sons, but not the Lord. The silence of God is striking, since we have been treated to repeated revelations in chaps. 25 and 26. As we often discover in the Old Testament, human responsibility is subsumed under the will of God's plan for the world. Rebekah and Jacob are coconspirators in a grossly offensive ruse that fractures the family for two decades and contributes to the disgrace of Jacob for all time (cf. Hos 11:12–12:3). The mother by any means hopes to change the course of Isaac's intention, duping her husband and wronging her sons. Some would say that she strove to realize the oracle that predicted the rise of the younger, but the narrative does not attribute this directly to her motivation. Rather, it simply observes that she favors Jacob, perhaps for the sake of the oracle, but the text suggests that it is more likely his temperament and vocation she values.

Isaac appears "blind" in more than one way; he is blind to the betrayal of his wife and Jacob, apparently unaware of the forces that will rip apart his family. Among the reasons offered for Isaac's blindness, some rabbinic interpreters believed that Isaac was sightless because he took bribes from Esau (game) and was indifferent to Esau's wickedness (*Gen. Rab.* 65.5–8,10). The text does suggest that Isaac's pleasure in eating game distracts him, contributing to his negligence. Also, in this episode Esau is not the cunning hunter that Isaac assumes but a duped victim who falls into the trap set by his mother and brother. Early Christian interpreters, as with early Jewish traditions, would not accept the portrait of a devious matriarch, especially since Romans 9 attributes the appointment of Jacob as premeditated by God. Either by allegorical or moralistic interpretations, the picture of Rebekah was rescued, as was the virtue of Jacob. Chrysostom commented approvingly of Rebekah's action as "a mother's affection, or rather God's design," and of Jacob's "circumspection in showing his mildness of manner" and elsewhere "the child's dutifulness and his respect for his father" (*Homilies on Genesis* 53.4–5).[124] Calvin showed greater sensitivity to the text and balance when he critiques Rebekah's "sport in a sacred matter with her wiles." But Calvin, too, praised her faith, for she volunteers to intercept the wrath of her husband, should her plot fail.[125]

The two terms in the parallel narratives (25:19–34; 27:1–28:9) that describe the coveted objects of the sons are "birthright" *(běkôrǎ)* and "blessing" *(běrākâ)*. The Hebrew words sound alike, producing a play so as to heighten the twin clashes between the brothers (25:31,32,33,34,36; 27:12,35,36,38,41). The terms appear together in Esau's complaint at Jacob's acts of cruelty (27:36). We have already noted at 25:29–34, however, that the "birthright" and the "blessing" are not always to be equated. "Birthright" pertains to the inheritance of the father's possessions, whereas the patriarch's "blessing" only projects what the offspring will obtain in life. Inheritance customs in Israel and the ancient Near East were not uniformly practiced. Although some legal instruction gave direction regarding the order of inheritance (e.g., Num 27:6–11; Deut 21:15–17; 25:5–10), it did not anticipate every situation. Primogeniture (exclusive inheritance by the firstborn) was not automatic, since there was an assumption of split inheritance in some biblical examples (e.g., Num 27:9–10; 34:13–29; Deut 21:15–17).[126] Distribution was usually the prerogative of the father, whose decision typically honored seniority but also included other sons, even daughters (e.g., Job 42:15). If Esau and Jacob acted in accordance with established or at least agreed practice, the right of the firstborn in their household could be disposed of by the elder (25:32–34), a decision that proved binding (27:36). Moreover, the patriarch's "blessing" may be divided among his sons (e.g., 49:28). The father commonly made the decision about what is the fitting division of property and what is the appropriate blessing, if any (27:34,37). He could even bestow a curse when called for (9:25; 27:12; 49:7). Evidently, the formal "blessing" of Isaac implied an oath that could not be withdrawn, even under fraudulent conditions (27:33). Because of these complicating factors, the narrative maintains a tension in the plot as Jacob and Esau

---

[124] *ACCS* 2.169.

[125] Calvin, *Comm.*, 2.84.

[126] See F. E. Greenspahn, "Primogeniture in Ancient Israel," in *Go to the Land I Will Show You: Studies in Honor of Dwight W. Young* (Winona Lake: Eisenbrauns, 1996), 69–79.

jockey for the lion's share of the inheritance. Although Esau wanted to kill Jacob out of angry vengeance, the collateral benefit would have been the elimination of the sole claimant, leaving all to Esau. As it turns out, by the generosity of the repentant Jacob (33:11), Esau stood to gain what he had lost.

COMPOSITION.   Commentators commonly consider 27:1–45(28:10) a unified narrative that is the work of the Yahwist (J) and 26:34–35; 27:46–28:9 a parallel account deriving from the Priestly source (P).[127] The J passage continues the theme of strife occurring in 25:27–34 (also J), whereas the P story in 27:46–28:9 follows on 26:34–35, pertaining to the marriages of the brothers. We will explore each of these two proposals.

1. Although some attempt was made to discern the Yahwist and the Elohist (E) sources in 27:1–45, the supposed inconsistencies in the account (e.g., vv. 18b–23 [J]; vv. 24–28 [E]) have been explained as evidence of accrued layers of tradition or rhetorical style, not true duplicates indicating parallel sources. Westermann, for example, finds that chap. 27 is essentially one piece, reflecting an oral tradition secular in nature that J took up and integrated into his Jacob-Esau story (cf. vv. 27b–29,39–40).[128]

No one doubts the association of 25:27–34 (if not 25:19–34), especially 25:28, with the supposed J story in 27:1–45. Usually critics consign chap. 26 to a secondary intrusion in the otherwise smooth narrative from chap. 25:34 to 27:1. Although we found that chap. 26 was not a secondary disruption (see comments at chap. 26), a relationship between the two incidents of betrayal in chaps. 25 and 27 is certain. The crosscurrents show that the two passages have some dependence. Among these is the explicit reference to Jacob's theft of the birthright (v. 36; 25:31–34). Other allusions include usurpation of the elder brother by deceit (vv. 35–37; 25:22–23,33–34), national destiny (vv, 29,40; 25:23), occupations of the brothers (vv. 3,5,7,9,19,25,30–33; 25:27), play on the name "Jacob" (v. 36; 25:26), parental preference (vv. 4,10; 25:28), and the hairy body of Esau (25:25; 27:11,23). The question remains as to what the relationship is between the passages. The two narratives were not originally one chronicle but two companion events penned in a manner to highlight the latter account. The events of the stolen blessing in chap. 27 make better sense once 25:19–34 is taken into consideration, and the birth and bartered birthright scenes presage the feud over the blessing. Read in this way, the prenatal oracle (25:23) establishes the pattern for the following struggles that demonstrate the oracle's fulfilling.

Yet the contrast in the character of Esau in chaps. 25 and 27 creates apparent problems for interpreters. Von Rad, following the proposal of Noth, believes that the two "Esaus" reflect separate traditions: the Esau of chaps. 27; 33 (east Jordan) is a simple hunter, not the eponymous ancestor of Edom, whereas in chap. 25 (Judean) he is the father of a nation. Westermann even contends for a third "Esau" in 25:29–34 (excising v. 30 as secondary) who represents the older economy of food gatherers in the changeover to the advanced economy of herdsmen

---

[127] E.g., Speiser, *Genesis*, 211, 215; von Rad, *Genesis*, 281–82; and Coats, *Genesis*, 199–200.
[128] Westermann, *Genesis 12–36*, 435–36.

as exhibited by Jacob. Van Seters takes a somewhat different tact, consistent with his thesis of an exilic author (Yahwist). The two narratives are not independent stories or the result of variant traditions; rather, the author of chap. 27 penned a parallel episode, depending on the available tradition of 25:21–34, which resulted in a new account and a new "Esau." The blessing of 27:29 is thought by Van Seters to be a literary imitation of a royal blessing form, not an ancient tribal saying as is customarily recommended.[129]

We find, however, that the details sufficiently differ between the two accounts to support two separate events and that the interplay between the two narratives is the result of a single author who cast them as twin episodes built on the same theme, each functioning in an introductory role. In the first case 25:21–34 establishes the overarching premise of the whole Jacob-Esau narrative: the actions of the brothers had national implications, elevating their importance in the eyes of Israel's readers. Before proceeding to chap. 27, we mention briefly how chap. 26 functions in between the episodes. In continuity with this broad outlook, the content of chap. 26 defines what was at stake in the struggle. First, the chapter's events authenticated the power of Isaac's blessing, coming as it did in the train of Abraham himself; and second, the Isaac account exhibited the wealth and international stature that the blessing would bring to its recipient. If Isaac's descendants were to be an international player in the future, there must be a grand homeland to sustain them.

Returning to chap. 27, we remember that it forms an inclusio with 25:21–34 but also looks forward like 25:21–34 when repeating the same motifs. It facilitates the account of strife between Jacob and Laban (chaps. 28–31) embedded in the concentric pattern of the Jacob-Esau narratives (chaps. 25–27; 32–35) as a whole. Since the Jacob-Laban affair is set outside Canaan in Paddan Aram (28:2,7; 33:18; cf. 25:20), the author further promotes the idea embodied in the divine oracle (25:23), that is, the actions of the sons and their destinies impact other peoples.

As for the different "Esaus" proposed for chaps. 25 and 27, the characterizations of Esau in the chapters show more in common than in their variance. The change is only the shaded nuances of the same essential features: he is still the hunter who is passive or negligent of the family's heritage; he is his father's favorite; the scheming Jacob snookers him ("these two times," 27:36); and he is the ancestor of a nation. The true difference in Esau is his new attitude toward the blessing that he cherishes, unlike his scorn for the birthright (25:34). The change in Esau is understandable when we remember the purpose of chap. 26. The topical arrangement of chaps. 25–27 sets the envied consequences of the blessing (26:14) between the two episodes, explaining why Esau had a change of heart toward the family tradition. But even then Esau is passive, not aggressively seeking the transference of the blessing; his aging father initiates the ritual bequest. Esau's spirited desire for the blessing comes only after he realizes what he lost to his twin, receiving the chilling antiblessing (vv. 37–41).

2. Source critics assign 26:34–35; 27:46–28:9 to P on the basis of its P-like

---

[129] Van Seters, *Prologue to History*, 283–88.

vocabulary and inclusion of chronological and genealogical notices. Typically, as we have said above, scholars view this passage as a parallel to the J version of Jacob's departure (27:1–45).[130] Esau's marriages in 26:34–35 introduce the P version of Jacob's flight, which attributes the division in the family to his Hittite wives (27:46–28:9). Jacob obeys his father and leaves for Paddan Aram to obtain a proper wife. The J account of 27:1–45 tells a different story altogether, contributing to J's broader Jacob-Esau conflict narrative. Here Jacob deceives his father and flees his homestead to escape his wronged brother. P's account presents a positive picture of Jacob's departure, for he seeks a proper marriage in contrast to Esau's practice (cp. *Gen. Rab.* 65.1–4; 67.4), whereas the J story (27:1–45; 28:10) explains the departure as the result of Jacob's infamous trickery.

Wenham contests the certainty that critics have exhibited when assigning 26:34–35; 27:46–28:9 to another source (P).[131] The chronological reference in 26:34 is the only reason that 26:34–35 is considered P, and consequently 28:9 by its reflex "in addition to the wives" must be of the same source. The many "P terms" found throughout 28:1–8 (e.g., "Canaanite women," vv. 1,6,8; "Paddan Aram," vv. 2,5,7) are the stronger evidence that the passage is from the priestly hand. Yet Wenham's analysis of the reputed P-terms shows that they are not reliable for distinguishing sources. The "promise vocabulary" in 28:1–5 (e.g., "you and your descendants") involving the quotation or allusion to the promises is the result of the genre, not a faithful indicator of source.

Carr considers the P account a correction to J's unflattering depiction of Jacob; by including both accounts, the final compilation produced a "fractured whole," requiring a new, third reading.[132] To make his point, Carr shows that P was aware of the earlier J by noting the shared points between the accounts (e.g., passing on the blessing, 27:29//28:3–4). Carr recognizes also that P made use of the account of Rebekah's betrothal (chap. 24). Two observations made by Carr himself can counter the idea of P correcting the earlier J version. First, the similarities in the two passages are real, but they can be more simply explained as the product of one author who is writing the events in concert. Second, Carr himself offers a satisfying interpretation of the extant text: the dismissal of Jacob for a wife is Rebekah's cover story, another ruse fostered against Isaac (27:46), enabling Jacob to escape Esau and retain Isaac's favor. Jacob then imitates Abraham, who sought an acceptable wife for Isaac (chap. 24). Carr's elaborate reconstruction is an example of critics making the putative redactor a redundant author.

If the P account were designed to depict Esau's marriages as the reason for disqualification, thereby exonerating Jacob of foul play, the author impaired his objective by depicting Esau as a repentant person attempting to absolve himself through marriage within the family to Ishmael's daughter (28:9). Moreover,

---

[130] E.g., Coats, *Genesis,* 199–204.

[131] Wenham, *Genesis 16–50,* 203–4.

[132] Carr, *Reading the Fractures of Genesis,* 85–88, 321; Thompson thinks he avoids the problems of separate parallel sources when he posits that the two versions are mere variations in the "manner of telling" a single tale, meaning that the editor retained both variants of the same story (*The Origin Tradition,* 105).

27:1–28:9 does not bear incompatible events whose telling obviously includes a corrective redaction. The author does not paint simplistic one-dimensional characters whose actions can be easily moralized. Both sons are culprits whose choices produced schism in the family, exhibiting again that divine favor is not the result of human merit but the consequence of God's prior commitment to Abraham (28:4; cf. 26:5).

Wenham observes that 28:1–9 presupposes the rivalry in 27:1–45, making subtle allusion to it but not repeating the specifics. Esau's changed behavior in 28:6,8 suggests a competition between the brothers for their father's approval. This is a clear continuation of the parental favoritism known in chap. 27. Also 28:5,9 reflects both Rebekah's directive in 27:43 and Isaac's in 28:2, meaning that the author must have known 27:41–45 when penning 28:1–9. When the instructions in 28:1–2 are favorably compared to 24:3–4 and the blessing of 28:3–4 likewise is compared to 26:2–5,24, the evidence points to the same author's hand. Taken together, this contends for recognizing 26:34–35; 28:1–9 as part of the same narrative stream begun as early as chap. 24 and continuing through chap. 28.

STRUCTURE.   The passage consists of two major units, 27:1–46 and 28:1–9. The persistent motifs are the moral lapses of the family members (intermarriage, treachery, sibling revenge) and Jacob's departure for Laban's house, the brother of Rebekah. We found that the narrative describing Esau's marriage to Hittite women (see comments at 26:34–35) provides the transition for the sibling rivalry narrated in chap. 27. Mention of Esau's age and of the parents' attitude toward Esau's marriages (26:34–35) sets up the subsequent scene, which begins with the notice of Isaac's aging, precipitating the summons (*qārā',* "called," NIV) of his favorite son, Esau, for the blessing (27:1). The similar pattern appears at 27:46 that transitions to Jacob's departure in chap. 28. The transition repeats Rebekah's disgust toward the Hittite wives (27:46), but Isaac this time summons (*qārā',* "called," NIV) Jacob, grants him the blessing (this time knowingly), and instructs him to avoid marrying a Canaanite woman (28:1).[133]

Chapter 27 consists of two parts: the deception and discovery (vv. 1–40) and the stratagem for Jacob's escape (vv. 41–46). Together there are five narrative frames, each involving extensive dialogue. (1) The first scene depicts Isaac from his deathbed instructing Esau to obtain his favorite game in preparation for the bestowal of the blessing (vv. 1–4). (2) Rebekah overhears her husband's intention, and she convinces Jacob to steal the blessing by an elaborate ruse (vv. 5–13). (3) Rebekah and Jacob effect the plan, obtaining the blessing from Isaac when Jacob deceives his blind father (vv. 14–29). (4) Isaac and Esau discover the subterfuge, and Isaac bequeaths an antiblessing upon Esau (vv. 30–40). (5)

---

[133] Alternatively, other commentators treat 26:33–28:9 as a single unit, exhibiting another example of concentric patterning in the Jacob narrative: marriage (26:34–35); stolen blessing (27:1–45); and marriage (27:46–28:9).

Esau resolves to kill his brother, but Rebekah plots to dispatch Jacob under the ploy of obtaining a wife from her brother's household (vv. 41–46).

Rebekah is the prime manipulator who controls the direction of the action, though she does not speak to Isaac directly until the final verse (v. 46). The same narrative feature appears in the account of Ruth, where Naomi and Boaz never speak directly to each other, always employing Ruth as their loyal mediator. Jacob and Isaac are mere tools who carry out her objectives. Rebekah is also "omniscient," overhearing Isaac's intention to bless Esau (v. 5) and learning by some unstated means his angry plan to murder Jacob (v. 42).[134] At each point she springs to action by ordering Jacob to follow her schemes (vv. 6,42). Isaac is suspicious but unaware, and Rebekah is all-aware. Jacob becomes aware of events by his mother's directions, and Esau is the least aware, subject to the desires of others.

The second narrative in 28:1–9 consists of two parts: (1) 28:1–5 entails Isaac's command to Jacob to seek a wife in Paddan Aram (vv. 1–2), his bestowal of a parting blessing (vv. 3–4), and the narration of Jacob's obedience (v. 5); (2) 28:6–9 pertains to Esau's response to the events of vv. 1–5. Verses 6–8 repeat the essence of vv. 1–5, forming the backdrop for Esau's marriage selection of Ishmael's daughter for a wife (v. 9). The parallel descriptions "he went" *(wayyēlek)* in vv. 5,9 exhibit the corresponding actions of the twins; Jacob followed his father's instructions, and Esau, having seen the favor Jacob enjoyed, sought another wife whose heritage was the lineage of Abraham.

(1) The Stolen Blessing (27:1–46)

[1]**When Isaac was old and his eyes were so weak that he could no longer see, he called for Esau his older son and said to him, "My son."**

"Here I am," he answered.

[2]**Isaac said, "I am now an old man and don't know the day of my death.** [3]**Now then, get your weapons—your quiver and bow—and go out to the open country to hunt some wild game for me.** [4]**Prepare me the kind of tasty food I like and bring it to me to eat, so that I may give you my blessing before I die."**

[5]**Now Rebekah was listening as Isaac spoke to his son Esau. When Esau left for the open country to hunt game and bring it back,** [6]**Rebekah said to her son Jacob, "Look, I overheard your father say to your brother Esau,** [7]**'Bring me some game and prepare me some tasty food to eat, so that I may give you my blessing in the presence of the LORD before I die.'** [8]**Now, my son, listen carefully and do what I tell you:** [9]**Go out to the flock and bring me two choice young goats, so I can prepare some tasty food for your father, just the way he likes it.** [10]**Then take it to your father to eat, so that he may give you his blessing before he dies."**

---

[134] Jewish interpretations attributed Rebekah's knowledge to the Holy Spirit and the gift of prophecy (e.g., *Tgs. Ps.-J.* at v. 5 and *Onq.* at v. 13; *Tanh.,* Toledoth 10(93); *Gen. Rab.* 67.9; see Maher, *Targum Pseudo-Jonathan,* 94, n. 3.

¹¹Jacob said to Rebekah his mother, "But my brother Esau is a hairy man, and I'm a man with smooth skin. ¹²What if my father touches me? I would appear to be tricking him and would bring down a curse on myself rather than a blessing."

¹³His mother said to him, "My son, let the curse fall on me. Just do what I say; go and get them for me."

¹⁴So he went and got them and brought them to his mother, and she prepared some tasty food, just the way his father liked it. ¹⁵Then Rebekah took the best clothes of Esau her older son, which she had in the house, and put them on her younger son Jacob. ¹⁶She also covered his hands and the smooth part of his neck with the goatskins. ¹⁷Then she handed to her son Jacob the tasty food and the bread she had made.

¹⁸He went to his father and said, "My father."

"Yes, my son," he answered. "Who is it?"

¹⁹Jacob said to his father, "I am Esau your firstborn. I have done as you told me. Please sit up and eat some of my game so that you may give me your blessing."

²⁰Isaac asked his son, "How did you find it so quickly, my son?"

"The LORD your God gave me success," he replied.

²¹Then Isaac said to Jacob, "Come near so I can touch you, my son, to know whether you really are my son Esau or not."

²²Jacob went close to his father Isaac, who touched him and said, "The voice is the voice of Jacob, but the hands are the hands of Esau." ²³He did not recognize him, for his hands were hairy like those of his brother Esau; so he blessed him. ²⁴"Are you really my son Esau?" he asked.

"I am," he replied.

²⁵Then he said, "My son, bring me some of your game to eat, so that I may give you my blessing."

Jacob brought it to him and he ate; and he brought some wine and he drank. ²⁶Then his father Isaac said to him, "Come here, my son, and kiss me."

²⁷So he went to him and kissed him. When Isaac caught the smell of his clothes, he blessed him and said,

> "Ah, the smell of my son
>   is like the smell of a field
>   that the LORD has blessed.
> ²⁸May God give you of heaven's dew
>   and of earth's richness—
>   an abundance of grain and new wine.
> ²⁹May nations serve you
>   and peoples bow down to you.
> Be lord over your brothers,
>   and may the sons of your mother bow down to you.
> May those who curse you be cursed
>   and those who bless you be blessed."

³⁰After Isaac finished blessing him and Jacob had scarcely left his father's presence, his brother Esau came in from hunting. ³¹He too prepared some tasty

food and brought it to his father. Then he said to him, "My father, sit up and eat some of my game, so that you may give me your blessing."

[32]His father Isaac asked him, "Who are you?"

"I am your son," he answered, "your firstborn, Esau."

[33]Isaac trembled violently and said, "Who was it, then, that hunted game and brought it to me? I ate it just before you came and I blessed him—and indeed he will be blessed!"

[34]When Esau heard his father's words, he burst out with a loud and bitter cry and said to his father, "Bless me—me too, my father!"

[35]But he said, "Your brother came deceitfully and took your blessing."

[36]Esau said, "Isn't he rightly named Jacob? He has deceived me these two times: He took my birthright, and now he's taken my blessing!" Then he asked, "Haven't you reserved any blessing for me?"

[37]Isaac answered Esau, "I have made him lord over you and have made all his relatives his servants, and I have sustained him with grain and new wine. So what can I possibly do for you, my son?"

[38]Esau said to his father, "Do you have only one blessing, my father? Bless me too, my father!" Then Esau wept aloud.

[39]His father Isaac answered him,

"Your dwelling will be
   away from the earth's richness,
   away from the dew of heaven above.
[40]You will live by the sword
   and you will serve your brother.
But when you grow restless,
   you will throw his yoke
   from off your neck."

[41]Esau held a grudge against Jacob because of the blessing his father had given him. He said to himself, "The days of mourning for my father are near; then I will kill my brother Jacob."

[42]When Rebekah was told what her older son Esau had said, she sent for her younger son Jacob and said to him, "Your brother Esau is consoling himself with the thought of killing you. [43]Now then, my son, do what I say: Flee at once to my brother Laban in Haran. [44]Stay with him for a while until your brother's fury subsides. [45]When your brother is no longer angry with you and forgets what you did to him, I'll send word for you to come back from there. Why should I lose both of you in one day?"

[46]Then Rebekah said to Isaac, "I'm disgusted with living because of these Hittite women. If Jacob takes a wife from among the women of this land, from Hittite women like these, my life will not be worth living."

The narrative describes the (1) stolen blessing of Esau (vv. 1–40) and (2) the reactions of Esau's anger and Rebekah's instructions to Jacob (vv. 41–46). It begins with Isaac's favor toward Esau, intending blessing (vv. 1–4), and concludes with Rebekah's disgust with the foreign women from whom Esau had taken wives, which is tantamount to her disfavor toward Esau (v. 46; cf. 26:34–35; 36:2).

ISAAC BLESSES JACOB (27:1–40). Isaac summons Esau for his blessing and requests from him some tasty game (vv. 1–4), but Rebekah intercepts her husband's intentions through a devious plot (vv. 5–13). Jacob carries out the deception when Esau is absent by acting as if he were the older brother, and sightless Isaac unwittingly bestows the blessing on Jacob (vv. 14–29). At Esau's return from the field, father and son realize they have been duped, and Isaac has only an antiblessing for Esau (vv. 30–40).

This unit begins and ends with Isaac and Esau in dialogue regarding the inheritance of the patriarchal blessing, revealing several ironic outcomes (vv. 1–4,30–40). In the first paragraph Isaac initiates the conferral of the blessing, and in the final paragraph it is Esau who seeks a blessing. Ironically, the blessing received is actually an antiblessing. Both paragraphs include parallel words of address: "my son" (v. 1) and "my father" (vv. 31,34,38[2x]), reflecting the poignancy of the event and also the nature of the deception both suffered. Jacob achieved his ploy by exploiting the trust innate between a father and his son. Also, these first and last scenes emphasize the identity of Esau as the firstborn son, the elder brother (vv. 1,32; also vv. 15,19,42), whose position was usurped with the unwitting aid of the sightless father. Since Genesis often shows the neglect of primogeniture, there was no benefit after all to Esau's position in the family. Isaac's fondness for wild game that gave Esau preferred status (v. 3; 25:28) surprisingly becomes the vehicle by which Jacob snatches the blessing. Esau as a compliant son obtains the cherished game upon command, but it wins him no prize; rather, it actually contributes to his undoing.

Sandwiched between these two segments (vv. 1–4,30–40) are two narrative segments that entail Rebekah's instruction to Jacob (vv. 5–13) and Jacob's (feigning Esau) dialogue with his father (vv. 5–13,14–29). Of the brothers, Jacob is the sole speaker in these dialogue sections, leaving Esau who is in the field without a voice. These two inner segments show how the turn of events described in the outer two segments occurred. The first inner segment (vv. 5–13) contains the plan, and the second (vv. 14–29) recounts its accomplishment. Rebekah presents her plan to simulate the wild game by preparing goat steaks, but Jacob sees that the plot is imperfect, for discovery is likely since the twins' bodies felt entirely different to the touch. Jacob probably knew by experience that his father would commonly use touch to compensate for his inept eyesight. Further, personal touch and a kiss usually accompanied parental blessing (e.g., v. 27; 31:55; 48:10). Rebekah replies that she will take full responsibility and Jacob must only obey her directions. Ironically, her interference results in the loss of her favorite child, who flees for his life. The second segment (vv. 14–29) narrates Rebekah's solution to Jacob's worries when she clothes Jacob in Esau's garments and covers his smooth skin with animal hair, so as to obstruct the perceptive touch and smell of her husband. Jacob carries out the plan fully, receiving the blessing, but the plot did not take into account the difference in Jacob's speech. He must lie twice, claiming that he is Esau his brother. Through the painstaking, drawn-out dialogue between deceitful Jacob and the suspicious Isaac, the author exposes the cold, calculating Jacob, whose quick-witted mind alters irrevocably the course of history.

Isaac Summons Esau (27:1–4). **27:1–4** The introduction gives the motive for Isaac's summoning of Esau. Isaac's "old" age dictated preparations for succession by declaring his blessing before death (vv. 1–2; cf. 24:1; 48:10,21–22; 49:28–29; Deut 33:1; 34:5,7). Old age typically is accompanied by poor vision, serving as a sign of approaching death (cf. 48:10; Deut 34:7; 1 Sam 3:2; 1 Kgs 14:4). Used as a figure of speech, the dimming of the eyes expresses one's physical or emotional weakness (e.g., Pss 6:7[8]; 31:9[10]; Job 17:7; Lam 5:17). Actually, Isaac lived for another twenty years or more (31:41; 35:28). The mention of his blindness, moreover, anticipates the events that unfold, for by this infirmity Jacob will exploit his father. Isaac's blindness functions at the metaphorical level for the man's spiritual condition when he preferred Esau for his tasty cuisine.[135]

Although Isaac chose Esau for the apparent advantage that a skilled hunter could bring to his table (25:28), the mention of Esau as "his older son" (v. 1) perhaps indicates that he intended to practice the custom of primogeniture. Twice Jacob (disguised as Esau) and Esau identify themselves by the term "the firstborn" (vv. 19,32). In light of the frequent disregard for primogeniture in Genesis, however, this recurring appellative in the chapter (vv. 1,15,42) in effect announces to the reader that the favor will go to the younger, heightening awareness of the sibling reversal that follows. "My son" appears eight times in direct address, used by Isaac (vv. 1,18,20,21, 25,26,37) and Rebekah (v. 13). In Genesis the same vocative use occurs in only three more verses (22:8; 43:29; 49:9). The first appearance is Abraham's address to the victim Isaac (22:8); this coupled with the exclamation "Here I am" in 22:1,11 and 27:1 suggests that the chapter alludes to Abraham's love for Isaac, the son who now is the father.

Isaac instructs Esau to achieve a simple task for a hunter in preparation for the formality of blessing (v. 3). Once before, the "bow" *(qešet)* was the weapon of an outcast son *(qaššāt,* "bowman," 21:20). The term *kĕlî* ("weapon") may refer to a broad range of utensils (e.g., 31:37), but it often describes instruments of killing, both for war and the hunt (e.g., 49:5; 1 Sam 8:12). There is no doubt that Esau had both the ability and the will to carry out his threat against Jacob at the opportune moment (v. 41). That Esau was a hunter was conveniently matched by his culinary ability to please his father (v. 4). The rendering "tasty food I like" (NIV, NRSV, v. 4) may obscure the stronger nuance of the term

---

[135] Sarna, *Genesis,* 190.

"love" *(ʾāhab),* traditionally found in the EVs (e.g., AV, RSV, NASB, HCSB). This strong affection for the feast that only Esau could provide explains why the old man sought it as his last paternal request. Isaac's zeal for the meal matched Esau's zest for the blessing. The pronoun "I" *(nepeš),* "so that I *[napšî]* may give you my blessing" (also vv. 19,25,31), expresses the strong desire of the father.[136] The traditional rendering "soul" may be misleading (AV, ESV, NASB; see vol. 1A, 197–99), and here *nepeš* indicates the whole person, rightly translated as the personal pronoun "I" (NIV, REB, NRSV).[137]

Rebekah Plots Deception (27:5–13).   **27:5–7**   Rebekah "was listening" *(šōmaʿat,* v. 5) reminds the reader of Sarah, who "was listening" *(šōmaʿat)* to the three visitors from the door of the tent (18:10). With Esau away in search for game, Rebekah was free to "pull the strings" of Jacob and Isaac undetected (v. 6). The narrator's reference to Jacob as "her son" (i.e., Rebekah's) points up the conflict in the family, for Esau is identified as "his son" (i.e., Isaac's) in vv. 1,5 (also vv. 20,31). Some cajoling will be required to enlist Jacob in her risky plot. She first establishes her veracity by claiming that she heard the father's intentions, demanding immediate action on their part (v. 7). Her reference to Esau as "your brother" (v. 7) is the first of thirteen times the term "brother" *(ʾāḥ)* appears in this chapter. Their fraternal jealousy is reminiscent of the Cain-Abel struggle that materialized in murder (4:2,8,9,10,11,21). The term "brothers" in the blessing formula (vv. 29,37) appears in blessing rituals that project the supremacy of the chosen successor over relatives (cp. 9:25,27; 37:10; 49:8). Rebekah's version of Isaac's words accurately retells the father's plan[138] but takes special liberty by including reference to the divine name, "in the presence of the LORD" (v. 7b). Though occurring but twice more in Genesis (10:9; 18:22), this expression appears about 144 times in the remainder of the Pentateuch, often referring to worship. This addition by Rebekah gives the matter more gravity and connotes its religious significance.

27:8–10   Rebekah appeals to Jacob to follow her instructions carefully (v. 8). Three times the same exhortation occurs, "obey me" *(šĕmaʿ bĕqōlî,* lit., "hear my voice"), each time coupled with the same personal address, "my son" (vv. 8,13,43).[139] The admonitions in vv. 8,13 form the boundaries of her instructions, and the final appearance in v. 43, ironically, reflects the outcome of her instructions, namely, the flight of Jacob to her brother Laban's household. The word "command" *(ṣāwâ* in the *piel)* in the expression "as I command

---

[136] *HALOT* 2.712, "my personal preference"; cf. Deut 6:5; 12:20; Prov 23:2; see e.g., Westermann, *Genesis 12–36,* 437; Wenham, *Genesis 16–50,* 206.

[137] Cf. NJPS, "my innermost," reflecting נֶפֶשׁ.

[138] The inversion of verbs creates a chiasmus in vv. 4,7: "prepare . . . bring . . . bring . . . prepare."

[139] Twice the exact language occurs in her overtures, וְעַתָּה בְנִי שְׁמַע בְּקֹלִי (vv. 8,43); cp. the same jargon used for counsel in Exod 18:19.

you" ("as I tell you," NIV) typically describes a superior's charge to another (e.g., 12:20; 18:19; 26:11; 28:1,6); the same phrase (but using the plural "you" for all Israel) often characterizes Moses' admonitions in Deuteronomy (e.g., 4:2; 11:13,22,27,28; 12:11; 13:1; 27:1,4; 28:14). Her directives for Jacob (v. 9), repeated in v. 13, entail another reference to the unexpected outcome of her meddling in the family's affairs: "go . . . bring" *(lek . . . qaḥ)* are the very instructions Isaac later gives Jacob upon his departure for Paddan Aram (28:2). The two "choice young goats" provided a tender delicacy to win his favor (e.g., 38:17; Judg 6:9; 13:15; 14:6; 15:1). The term "tasty" for the dish cherished ("likes,"[140] NIV) by Isaac occurs but twice more outside chap. 27, where Proverbs (23:3,6) warns against its enticements. Special importance was attached to a deathbed decision ("before he dies," v. 10), making the "blessing" the most consequential ex officio act of the aging patriarch (cp. 50:16; Deut 33:1; 1 Chr 22:5).

27:11–13 Jacob recognizes the risk that the plot involves. If it backfires by Isaac's discovery of the ploy, Jacob will subject himself to the worst of all fates—his father's curse. Such could be the case for anyone who misleads the blind (Lev 19:14; Deut 27:18) or dishonors his parents (Exod 21:15,17; Deut 21:18–19; 27:16). First, Jacob strongly demurs, introducing his objection with the interjection *hēn* ("behold, if"; "but," NIV). Modern vernacular would render the sense "hold on here!" Second, he explains himself by contrasting his smooth skin with the coarse, hairy quality of Esau's body. Mention of the elder brother's hairy skin recalls the twins' birth narrative (25:25), which brings to mind the birth oracle that forecasted the outcome of the present deception. "Smooth" *(ḥālāq)* provides a double entendre, for the word also can describe lying lips (Ps 12:3–4; Prov 5:3). The term "tricking"[141] is rare (v. 12), the root *(tā'a')* occurring but once more where it means "to mock at" (2 Chr 36:16, "scoffed," NIV). A patriarch might call down a curse against his son *('ārar,* 9:25), though the practice would be wholly unnatural. Here the word translated "curse" is *qĕlālâ* (cp. 8:21; 12:3), which is often paired with blessing *(bĕrākâ;* Deut 11:26,29; 30;1,19; Josh 8:34). That God may transform a curse into a blessing is known (Deut 23:5; Neh 13:2), but not the reverse. Jacob himself admits the obvious irony should the conspiracy fall through. Rebekah, however, vows to suffer the curse in his place should it occur, showing the extent to which she would go. Jewish tradition that strives to justify Jacob's actions especially attributes blame to Rebekah *(Gen. Rab.* 67.15). For the remainder of the verse, see our comments at v. 8.

Jacob Deceives Isaac (27:14–29). **27:14–17** The passage describes the steps that Rebekah takes to carry out the plan. In typical narrative fashion, v. 14

---

[140] The term is traditionally rendered "loves" (אָהֵב; cf. AV, RSV, NASB, HCSB).

[141] כְּמִתַעְתֵּעַ, a *pilpel* participle plus preposition, "make a mockery of," *HALOT* 4.1770.

describes the action in the language of the prior commands so as to show that the plot runs its course according to plan. By simulating the smell and touch of Esau (vv. 15–16), Jacob can avoid obvious detection. Rebekah is the primary actor, making Jacob little more than a puppet as she dresses him and pulls the strings that put him into action. There is no question that the deception would not have occurred if it had been left to Jacob alone. Perhaps receiving the divine oracle and experiencing the twin's bizarre births fueled Rebekah's obsession (25:23–24). She leaves nothing to chance or to providence when she prepares the player for his part. Only the "best clothes" available will do (v. 16), and she adds "bread" for a sop to the cuisine (v. 17).[142] Ironically, Esau's finest clothes fit the proceeding's solemnity, but Rebekah debases it by her foul use of the garments (cf. v. 27). Rebekah shows her resourcefulness when she makes use of the goats' skins as well as their meat.

27:18–23 Jacob's address, "my father," ironically recalls Isaac's own call to his father Abraham at Mount Moriah, where as a boy he trusted his father (v. 18; 22:7). Jacob, however, betrays his father's trust. Isaac's question shows that he is uncertain about the identity of the voice, knowing only that he is a son (v. 18; cp. v. 32). Jacob answers with a blatant lie, identifying himself as "Esau your firstborn" (v. 19). Jacob's mention of Esau's status as "firstborn" *(bĕkôr)* inadvertently amplified the enormity of his deceit, seeing that it defrauded his elder brother, and also recalled his former exploitation of Esau's "birthright" *(bĕkôrâ,* 25:29–34). His second lie, "I have done as you told me," adds to the infamy of his deed, for it plays up his allegiance in carrying out Isaac's instructions—though all the while he dishonors his father. By employing the first-person pronoun in his response, "my game," Jacob insidiously continues the charade.

Isaac's suspicions are aroused, leading him to ask Jacob how the feat was carried out so quickly (v. 20). Jacob's answer is blasphemous, attributing to God his success (cp. 24:12). By noting especially "your God,"[143] Jacob is subtly claiming divine confirmation of the impending blessing, tying the success of his hunt to the God of the patriarchal blessing. Ironically, though, the assertion is not too far off the mark in one sense: the will of God as revealed in the birth oracle (25:22–23) was achieved after all by the sinister actions of Rebekah and Jacob. Isaac must be certain of the son's identity before he grants the irrevocable blessing, seeking confirmation by touch and sound. For the sightless, touch and sound are as reliable as a seeing person's eyes. Isaac leaves no doubt about the reason for his inquisition, confessing the need to touch the man so that he might "really" know (v. 21). The repeated use of the word *nāgaš,* mean-

---

[142] Bread and betrayal are matched again at Jesus' "table of blessing" (John 13:26–30).

[143] יְהוָה אֱלֹהֶיךָ, "the LORD your God," as the popular identity of Israel's covenant God, occurs here for the first time (e.g., Exod 20:2); the appellative appears 212 times in Deuteronomy alone (e.g., Deut 10:12).

ing "approach," raises the tension of Jacob's disclosure: "Come near" and "went close" (vv. 21–22), "bring" and "brought" (v. 25), and "Come here" and "went" (vv. 26–27). After feeling Jacob's counterfeit skin, Isaac admitted that he stood confused; the voice was that of his younger son, but the rough, hairy skin was surely Esau's body. Wenham notes that Jacob's responses had been rather loquacious until his father recognized his voice, after which he limited himself to a one-word answer.[144] Verse 23 provides supplementary information,[145] explaining why the old man will eventually bless Jacob despite his misgivings. There is no need to assume that the passage contains two separate acts of blessing or a contradiction between two different traditions (vv. 23,27).

27:24–27a   Isaac's senses of touch and hearing are failing him, and he pleads again for a final, truthful reply (v. 24). His terse, pointed question and its matching answer show Jacob to be an outright liar, not just a savvy negotiator. Jacob affirms his false identity three times (vv. 19,20,24). Isaac cautiously proceeds, and Jacob provides both meat and drink (v. 25). The crime is rapidly described by sequential actions: "brought . . . ate . . . brought . . . drank" (v. 25b). Afterward Isaac seeks a kiss (v. 26) to which Jacob complies as a dutiful son (v. 27a). The poignancy of the parting kiss accents the despicable character of the son's treachery against his pitiable father (e.g., 31:55; 48:10; 50:1; 2 Sam 19:39). His betrayal with a kiss for personal gain was superseded in Scripture only by Judas's infamous kiss of Jesus for silver (Matt 26:48–49 par.). The kiss gave Isaac another opportunity to test his senses; his sense of smell told him that the son was the hunter, resulting in the offer of the blessing (vv. 27b–29).

27:27b–29   This poetic blessing consists of two invocations: the fruition of the land (vv. 27b–28) and the growth of a great nation (v. 29).[146] Although not stated in typical promissory terms (cf. 28:3–4), both the Abrahamic land and progeny promises are assumed and reflected here. In the first tricolon (v. 27a), Isaac showed his affinity for the field by remarking first on Esau's relationship with the fragrances of the wild (v. 27b; cf. 24:63). The odor of the hunter's clothes prompted this outburst of approval for Esau. The matching sounds of *rĕʾēh rēaḥ,* "see, the smell" (AV, NASB, RSV; "Ah, the smell," NIV, NRSV, HCSB), provide a reflex of the foregoing inquiry by Isaac, who used his power of scent for eyesight. Comparing his son and the smell of the field in the two cola brings

---

[144] Wenham, *Genesis 16–50,* 208.

[145] The *wāw* disjunctive (contrastive) introduces the clause, וְלֹא הִכִּירוֹ, "but he did not . . ." (NLT).

[146] S. Gevirtz, on the basis of conventional maledictions in the ANE concludes that vv. 28–29 include three traditional blessings: "agricultural fertility, political supremacy, and personal inviolability" (*Patterns in the Early Poetry of Israel,* Studies in Ancient Oriental Civilization 32 [Chicago: University of Chicago Press, 1963], 35–47). We understand v. 29 to pertain to Israel's future political supremacy too.

to the foreground Isaac's earlier misapprehension that Jacob's deception produced.[147] Ironically, the opening words of blessing entailed the lie that Jacob
had fabricated. In the third colon the antecedent of "that" (*'ăšer*) refers to the
"field" but also by double entendre may hint at the blessing upon Esau, who had
quickly made his catch (v. 20). The antiblessing formulation for Esau in vv. 39–
40 are opposite the benedictions that appear for Jacob in vv. 28–29.

The second tricolon (v. 28) describes the lush produce of cultivated field and
vine. Although vv. 28–29 consistently employ the singular pronoun (*kā*,
"you"), referring to the person, the intention is broader. The ancestor stands for
the whole of the nation that he (Jacob) produces, thus anticipating the nation of
Israel. The language "heaven's dew" and "earth's richness" (lit., "fatness")
draws on common word pairs in the Bible and the ancient Near East: "heaven"/
/"earth" (e.g., Gen 1:1; Isa 1:2) and "dew"//"fatness" (cf. parallel lines in Ps
133:2–3).[148] The pairing of "heaven" and "earth" expresses the entirety of
nature's abundance (merism). Moses appropriates this formulaic rhetoric of
fertility when blessing the tribe of Joseph and the whole of Israel (Deut
33:13,28). The conventional inclusion of agricultural blessing reflects the sentiment of a pastoral people whose agrarian life was prized (cf. Deut 7:13;
11:14; 33:28) and who sought defined borders, establishing a developed economy and social system. The order of the blessings in vv. 28–29 is logical: the
possession of a fruitful land prepares for the blessing of v. 29 that foresees a
flourishing nation that subjugates rivals, even brother nations.

Verse 29 contains three bicola, speaking of the rise of a powerful nation.
Westermann observes that often in formal blessing fertility and dominion
appear together (e.g., 24:60; 48:15–19).[149] We find that this is the divine pattern for blessing established at creation for the human family (1:28). The first
bicolon (29a//29b) speaks generally of nations, employing the rhyming word
pair "nations" (*'ammîm*) and "peoples" (*lĕ'ummîm;* Ps 67:4[5]; Prov 24:24;
Isa 17:12), whereas the second bicolon (29c//29d) refers specifically to sibling
states, "brothers//sons of your mother." The term "peoples" echoes the birth
oracle (25:23), indicating that the prophecy of the elder brother's submission is
here unwittingly formalized in Isaac's blessing. The terms "serve" (*'ābad)* and
"bow down" (*hāwâ)* are also paralleled (e.g., Deut 29:25; reversed in Ps 72:11).
"Bow down," appearing twice in the benediction (vv. 29b,29d), indicates subservience and showing honor (e.g., 18:2; Ruth 2:10). The term expresses worship when extended to God (e.g., Exod 4:31; 20:5). The idea of servitude,

---

[147] SP has שדה מלא, "full field," as does the LXX's ἀγροῦ πλήρους, "abounding field" (also
Vg. MSS; see *BHS*), heightening the pungency of the lush wild.

[148] For a discussion of the traditional expressions and their variations, see Y. Avishur, *Stylistic
Studies of Word-Pairs in Biblical and Ancient Semitic Literatures,* AOAT 210 (Kevelaer: Butzon &
Bercker/Neukirchen-Vluyn: Neukirchener Verlag, 1984), 260, 603–4, 608.

[149] Westermann, *Genesis 12–36,* 441.

including sibling submission, appears in formal, patriarchal blessings in Genesis (9:25–27; 49:8–10; cf. Deut 33:16).

The second bicolon in v. 29c//29d possesses another set of parallel verbs: "be (lord)" *(hāwâ)* and "bow down" *(ḥāwâ).* The parallel occurs only here,[150] and the word "lord" *(gĕbîr)* is rare,[151] occurring only in vv. 27,37 (cf. fem. *gĕbîrâ,* "mistress," 16:8–9; "queen[mother]," 1 Kgs 11:19; 15:13). The word pair "brothers" and "mother's sons" is well attested (e.g., 43:29; Deut 13:7; Judg 8:19; Pss 50:20; 69:8[9]; cf. Song 1:6). The allusion to a "mother's sons" refers to a full-blooded brother, strengthening the idea of kinship between Jacob and Esau. Jacob's blessing for the tribe Judah bears the stamp of this benediction, entailing the similar familial reference to a "father's sons" (49:8). Since Rebekah is not known to have had other sons, the plural "brothers" is a poetic convention—not to be taken literally in Jacob's case. It is especially appropriate to mention the sibling's "mother," for Rebekah instigates Jacob's succession. Or, alternatively, the word "brothers" *('āḥ)* here may be merely "relatives," which the word may often mean (e.g., 24:27; Prov 19:7; Ezek 11:15); in this latter case, the parallelism is synthetic, involving inclusive and particular references to relatives. As an unexpected outcome, however, it is Jacob and his sons who bow before his brother Esau (33:3,6–7; cp. Joseph's brothers, 37:7,9–10; 42:6; 43:26,28). If we rightly understand the importance of this twist in the plot, the author shows that parental blessing does not dictate the flow of history; rather the Lord brings out of this odd twist the ultimate predominance of Jacob, and that after some time (cp. the early Edomite kingdom, 36:31).

The final bicolon (vv. 29e,29f) presents its rendition of the "curse/bless" formula in 12:3. The word pair is common in Genesis but also elsewhere (e.g., Num 22:12; Prov 3:23; Jer 20:14). Its wording is identical to a Balaam oracle, except the order "curse/bless" is inverted (Num 24:9, as in 12:3; Judg 5:23–24; Mal 2:2). The promise to Abraham has national implication, as shown by the closing benediction: "all peoples on earth will be blessed through you" (12:3c). The "curse/bless" benediction by Isaac also has a national horizon in mind, as with the Balaam invocation. Although the person (Jacob) is included in the series of benedictions, the future nation that the patriarch fathers is in sight, conforming to the initial birth oracle ("two nations are in your womb," 25:23a).

Isaac and Esau Discover the Hoax (27:30–40). **27:30–33** Verse 30 describes the near breathtaking encounter of the brothers at Isaac's tent upon Esau's return from the hunt. Two observations preface the appearance of Esau. First, the blessing ceremony had been concluded; Esau was too late to expose

---

[150] Gevirtz shows the pattern of verbs in v. 29, "serve"//"bow down" (//) "be (lord)"//"bow down," in which the second element is attested (e.g., Isa 28:23; *Patterns,* 43–44).

[151] The related terms גֶּבֶר ("man") and גִּבּוֹר ("mighty man") are common.

the interloper and retain his claim. Second, Esau just missed catching his brother in the act! The text underscores this latter point by the emphatic adverb "indeed" (*'ak,* cf. comments at 26:9) and the redundant verbal construction "going out, he went out" (*yāṣō' yāṣā';* i.e., "had scarcely left," NIV).[152] The near miss probably saved Jacob's life, judging from Esau's subsequent, deadly intent (v. 41). Although left unstated in the text, the reader senses that the Lord's hand had accommodated this "coincidence." The narrative sadly describes the devoted son, who "also" *(gam)* prepared a feast but ironically for an already satiated Isaac. Esau's entreaty of his father to "sit up and eat" (v. 31) recalls Jacob's earlier appeal (v. 19) with two poignant exceptions. The request is more respectful, expressed in the Hebrew third person *(yāqūm/yō'kal),* and the familial language of "my father" and "his son's" game (NRSV; "my game," NIV) is fitting for the solemnity of the paternal event.

Isaac's alarm, "Who are you?" (v. 32), was asked once before when he queried Jacob (v. 18). Esau's anxious response places emphasis on his status in the household, lit., "I am your son, your firstborn, Esau" (v. 32), whereas Jacob stated his false identity at the start of his reply, "I am Esau, your firstborn" (v. 19). Upon realizing that he had been fooled, Isaac reacted viscerally (v. 33a). The language can hardly exaggerate his condition any more than it does, lit., "Isaac trembled a great trembling exceedingly" ("trembled violently," NIV).[153] The word "trembled" *(ḥārad)*conveys the physical shaking, manifesting a person's terror (e.g., 42:28; Exod 19:16; Amos 3:6). The immediate apprehension was the irrevocable nature of the blessing, "and indeed he will be blessed!" (v. 33b). Isaac's question of the culprit's identity is only rhetorical (v. 33); he charges Jacob with the deed, knowing now that the voice was indeed that of the younger son (v. 35).

27:34–35   Esau's reaction was as vociferous as that of his father. The language employed to describe Esau's outcry is the same syntactical pattern, lit., "he cried a great and exceedingly bitter cry" (v. 34).[154] "Cry" *(ṣ-ʿ-q)* is a person's wailing over a great loss (e.g., Exod 11:6; 12:30) or the scream of a person violated (e.g., 4:10; 19:13; Deut 22:24,27; Isa 5:7). The NJPS captures the tumultuous scene by "he burst into wild and bitter sobbing." Esau appealed for a blessing also, presumably a comparable one, but Isaac cannot bequeath a blessing of value since Jacob by treachery received the full endowment, constituting the sole power and wealth of the father (v. 35). "Your blessing" here means that the blessing given was the one intended for Esau as the firstborn.

---

[152] וַיְהִי אַךְ יָצֹא יָצָא, "and Jacob had hardly gone out" (NASB); "no sooner had Jacob left" (NJPS).

[153] The cognate accusative noun intensifies the action of the verb:
וַיֶּחֱרַד יִצְחָק חֲרָדָה גְּדֹלָה עַד־מְאֹד.

[154] It is another use of a cognate accusative noun, וּמְרָה עַד וַיִּצְעַק צְעָקָה גְּדֹלָה מְאֹד; the same "cry" (צְעָקָה) describes Edom's (Esau's) punishment (Jer 49:21).

Isaac's portrayal of Jacob's deed is especially appropriate: "deceitfully" *(mirmâ)* describes the treachery that Jacob himself will someday suffer *(rāmâ,* 29:25; cf. *mirmâ,* 34:13), and "took" *(lāqaḥ)* earlier repeatedly described Rebekah's preparations (vv. 9,13,14,15).[155] Sarna observed allusions to the purchase of the birthright (25:31–34) by the wordplays of "birthright" *(bĕkôrâ)* and "blessing" *(bĕrākâ)* and the polysemantic range of "take" *(lāqaḥ),* used both of "taking away" and of "buying" (e.g., 20:3).[156]

27:36–37 Esau's exasperation is directed at both brother and father, the former for his success at twice getting the better of him and the latter for his failure to act judiciously, especially since Jacob was a reputed trickster (v. 36). The second term, "deceived" *('āqab),* differs from the previous verse, providing for a wordplay on Jacob's name *(ya'ăqōb;* cf. 25:26; Jer 9:4[3]; Hos 12:3[4]). Esau obfuscates the bargain struck between the brothers for the right of the firstborn (25:29–34) when he equates it here with this dastardly episode. He conveniently forgets his own part in the earlier deal (25:34). Esau also shifts blame to his father by reproaching Isaac's lack of forethought given to the whole of the matter, making him the unwilling collaborator to this plot. Isaac should have known by the conniver's name alone to take due precautions. Isaac admits that nothing of consequence remains for another blessing (v. 37). When repeating the rhetoric of the formal blessing, he alludes to the patrimony already bestowed upon Jacob (v. 29). His supplications that Jacob might be the overlord of many peoples and the proprietor of fruitful harvests reflect the customary conditions of blessing in Genesis—procreation and material wealth.

27:38–40 Esau is pitiably resolute. He is willing to take even the crumbs. Surely his father can speak a second blessing, he pleads (v. 38). His final appeal ends in a mournful wailing, indicating Esau realizes how much he has lost.[157] The effect on the reader is ambivalence: Esau is the weak dimwit (cf. v. 40) but also the victim whose heart-wrenching sobs demonize Jacob as the cruel knave.

Ironically, the belated zeal of the older son achieves only an antiblessing (vv. 39–40). The poetic stanza consists of three lines, half the length of the benevolent blessing intended initially for him (vv. 28–29). The first line (a tricolon, v. 39b) possesses no divine invocation as in Jacob's case (v. 28a). S. Gevirtz observes that the language reverses the benedictory wording in vv.

---

[155] So as to rehabilitate Jacob's character, Jewish tradition contended that Jacob acted shrewdly, not deceitfully *(Tgs. Onq.* and *Ps.-J.; Gen. Rab.* 67.4); thus he receives, not "takes," the blessing.

[156] Sarna, *Genesis,* 194.

[157] The LXX includes κατανυχθέντος δὲ Ισαακ (see *BHS*), "and Isaac being grieved" (κατανυσσομαι, "pierced," fig. "sharp pain," cf. Acts 2:37 [LSJ 903]); cf. 34:7(LXX), κατενύχθησαν=וַיִּתְעַצְּבוּ, "they were filled with grief," describing the brothers' reaction to the rape of Dinah. Wevers prefers "stunned in silence," contrasting Isaac's reaction and Esau's cries *(Notes on the Greek Text,* 438).

28–29, perhaps suggesting that Isaac's intention was to express the opposite for the rejected son, Esau.[158] Verse 39 describes Esau's parched and fruitless land as his home,[159] opposite Jacob's land enriched by "dew" and "fatness" (v. 28b). The chiasmus of terms, "dew-fatness//fatness-dew" (vv. 29,39) heightens the effect of Esau's contrary state. His "dwelling" will be Edom's wilderness, east of the Arabah toward the desert, the archetype of the castaway and outsider (see comments at 21:20). The second line (bicolon, v. 40a) also defines his way of life by the word "live" *(ḥāyâ)*, that is, "remain alive." The means of survival in the wilderness was the bow (v. 3; 21:20), but the "sword" *(ḥereb)* usually was the instrument of war (e.g., 31:26; 48:22; Exod 15:9; esp. Num 20:18). The eighth-century prophet Amos condemned Edom "because he [Edom] pursued his brother with a sword" (Amos 1:11). Despite Esau's experience in warfare, Jacob will subjugate him (cf. Ezek 25:13), inverting the blessing pronounced for Jacob, whom his brothers will serve (v. 29; 9:25–27). The last line (a tricolon, v. 40b) depicts Esau as a domesticated animal that shows his true character as a wild, recalcitrant beast by breaking free from its yoke.[160] This portrayal recalls the same characterization of the outsider Ishmael, whose nature is the obstinate, desert donkey (16:12). This struggle for superiority, the master or the beast, will mark the history of the sedentary Hebrews and their bordering Edomite relatives (e.g., Num 20:18; 1 Sam 14:47; 1 Kgs 11:14–16; 2 Sam 8:12,14; 2 Kgs 8:20–22; Obad 1–9; Ps 137:7). Amos, however, depicts a future for a surviving Edom who finally submits to the hegemony of David (9:12). Genesis uses the word "chiefs" *('allûpîm)* only for Esau's descendants in the book (chap. 36), defining them also as "kings who reigned in Edom" (36:31; cf. 17:6,16; 35:11). It is striking that upon Jacob's return to Canaan he takes the posture of servant toward Esau so as to win his kindness (32:4,18; 33:3–5). The internecine strife that Isaac's picture portrays will be the life of Israel and Edom in the wilderness (e.g., Exod 15:15; Num 20:20–21). Balaam's blessing also depicts the ultimate domination of Israel over its kinsmen (Num 24:18; cf. 1 Sam 14:47; 2 Sam 8:12,14).[161]

---

[158] Gevirtz acknowledges, however, that the technique of inversion of the first wording in a subsequent recurrence is an attested pattern in the Bible and Ugaritic texts and therefore may not have special exegetical significance for our verse (*Patterns,* 40). See R. Clendenen, *Haggai, Malachi,* NAC (Broadman & Holman, 2004), 280, n. 140.

[159] The prep. מִן is likely separative, i.e., "away from" the rich, cultivated land (most EVs), not partitive, i.e., "some of." Cp. the expulsion of Cain, "from the ground" (4:12) and "from the land" (4:14).

[160] תָּרִיד, hiphil imper., uncertain derivation; for MT, BDB 923 has רוּד, "be restless," thus "grow restless" (NIV); HALOT 3.1194, "tear oneself loose," thus "break loose" (NRSV); among variants, SP has תִּדְאַר, "you shall be great/glorious"; LXX (Vg.) has καθέλῃς ("you shall break down") = תָּרִיד (see BHS); for a discussion of the problem see Hamilton, *Genesis Chapters 18–50,* 225, n. 19.

[161] On Edom and the Edomites, see comments at chap. 36.

ESAU'S ANGER (27:41–46). Esau's anger led him to plan the murder of Jacob (vv. 41–42), but as before Rebekah steps in to favor Jacob by warning him to flee (vv. 43–45). She complains to Isaac that the prospects of Jacob marrying a local Hittite daughter are too troubling to make life worth living (v. 46).

Esau Plans Murder (27:41). **27:41** Esau's anger fomented into a plan to murder his brother once his father had passed away. "Grudge" *(śāṭam)* is a deep-seated anger that results in violent retaliation (v. 41; cf. 49:23; Ps 55:3[4]). At the death of Jacob, the same term describes the "grudge" that Joseph's brothers fear he might hold against them (50:15). That Esau felt free to act only at the death of his father exhibited reverence for his father, a respect that Jacob does not yet possess (35:27–29). Or, less charitably, we might cynically conclude that Esau worries of potential recompense (as with Cain, 4:14).

Rebekah Instructs Jacob (27:42–45). **27:42–43** Esau's secret plan must have somehow leaked out, for Rebekah learned of it (v. 42). Rebekah's penchant for meddling and her maternal posture probably explain her fortuitous discovery. She reports that Esau is "consoling himself"[162] with the thought of revenge, biding his time (v. 42; cp. vv. 4–5). The Hebrew construction implies that the end of his consolation is nearing.[163] The tactic she takes is familiar, overhearing (?) Esau and instructing Jacob (cf. vv. 5–6). For the third time in this chapter she commands Jacob to follow her instructions (vv. 8,13,43). The word "flee" *(bāraḥ)* becomes the motto of Jacob's life (v. 43), for he will also flee Laban when deceiving him (31:20,22). It is therefore ironic that Rebekah advises him to escape to "my brother Laban in Haran" (v. 43), from whom he must escape to return to Canaan. Rebekah's "brother," though providing Jacob's two wives, will not be a lasting refuge for Jacob just as his own brother was a threat.[164]

27:44–45 Rebekah's plan for Jacob to reside "a while" ("a few days," NASB) became twenty years of hard labor in Haran (31:41). She expects Esau's anger to subside after a time, but she never does send for him (vv. 44b–45a). Moreover, she reasons aloud, "Why should I lose both of you in one day?" (v. 45b). Transparently, she has in mind the death of Jacob, but in what way could she lose "both"? If she has in mind Isaac, she anticipates the murder of Jacob on the day of Isaac's death.[165] Or she may have completely alienated Isaac by her complicity in his deception. More likely, we are to understand her remark in light of Cain's expulsion (or fear of retaliation) after the murder of Abel (4:14; cf. *Tg. Ps.-J.*).[166] Her plan never materializes, however, for it is not

---

[162] *Hithpael* participle, מִתְנַחֵם; cf. the *hithpael* at 37:35.

[163] Particle הִנֵּה + the participle מִתְנַחֵם indicates imminence.

[164] On the site Haran see 11:31 and comments on 25:20.

[165] Mentioned by Sarna, *Genesis,* 195.

[166] Jewish targums (*Ps.-J.; Neof.*) and midrash (e.g., *Tanḥ., Emor* 13[460]; *Gen. Rab.* 67.8; *Sefer Ha-Yashar* 29[82]) explained that Esau avoided Cain's mistake when he murdered Abel before Adam's death, enabling the birth of Seth. See Maher, *Targum Pseudo-Jonathan,* 97, n. 34.

Rebekah but God who beckons Jacob to return home (31:3,13), and it is not the subsiding of Esau's wrath but the anger of Laban and his sons that prompts Jacob to leave (31:1–2). Upon his return to Canaan, he reconciles with "his father Isaac" (35:27), but there is no mention of Rebekah except her burial (49:31). She does in a sense lose both her sons on that regretful day.

Rebekah's Complaint (27:46).   **27:46**   Rebekah seized an opportunity to concoct a cover story for Jacob, complaining to Isaac that Esau had taken foreign wives (v. 46).[167] This establishes the ostensible motivation for sending Jacob to Paddan Aram (28:2). We do not mean that Rebekah was altogether insincere, since her expectations were most likely to obtain wives for her sons from her native home where she herself volunteered to marry Isaac (24:58). The difference lies in the refusal of Abraham to dispatch Isaac, sending only his servant (24:6,8), whereas in this case the parents insist that Jacob sojourn to Aram and, as it happens, he goes alone. "I'm disgusted with living" *(qaṣtî bĕḥayyay)* expresses Rebekah's strong enmity against these outsiders, not merely a disappointment in Esau (cf. e.g., *qûṣ*, Exod 1:12; Lev 20:23; 1 Kgs 11:25; cp. Job 10:1). After obtaining the blessing for her son, it would be of little consequence in her eyes if Jacob married from the "women of this land." The women of Canaan are collectively ruled out as suitable for Jacob; on him rested the perpetuation of the family's heritage, requiring a wife from the family of Terah (11:29; 22:20.23; 24:15).

(2) The Search for a Wife (28:1–9)

[1]So Isaac called for Jacob and blessed him and commanded him: "Do not marry a Canaanite woman. [2]Go at once to Paddan Aram, to the house of your mother's father Bethuel. Take a wife for yourself there, from among the daughters of Laban, your mother's brother. [3]May God Almighty bless you and make you fruitful and increase your numbers until you become a community of peoples. [4]May he give you and your descendants the blessing given to Abraham, so that you may take possession of the land where you now live as an alien, the land God gave to Abraham." [5]Then Isaac sent Jacob on his way, and he went to Paddan Aram, to Laban son of Bethuel the Aramean, the brother of Rebekah, who was the mother of Jacob and Esau.

[6]Now Esau learned that Isaac had blessed Jacob and had sent him to Paddan Aram to take a wife from there, and that when he blessed him he commanded him, "Do not marry a Canaanite woman," [7]and that Jacob had obeyed his father and mother and had gone to Paddan Aram. [8]Esau then realized how displeasing the Canaanite women were to his father Isaac; [9]so he went to Ishmael and married Mahalath, the sister of Nebaioth and daughter of Ishmael son of Abraham, in addition to the wives he already had.

---

[167] The Hb. text repeats מִבְּנוֹת־חֵת כָּאֵלֶּה, "from Hittite women like these," stressing their foreign status, whereas the phrase is absent in the LXX, probably due to scribal error (Wevers, *Notes on the Greek Text,* 442).

This final unit concerns family inheritance, both the past and the future. It assumes the foregoing account of deception, especially vv. 1–2, which recall the events of 27:41–46. The future resides in the wives taken by the twin sons who will bear them children. For Jacob the narrative anticipates the lengthy sojourn and trials of Isaac's successor in Paddan Aram, where he obtains his wives from the family of Rebekah and Laban (vv. 1–5). The last paragraph depicts the wives that Esau chooses, reinforcing the picture of the elder as the rejected son despite his efforts for acceptance (vv. 6–9). The past is encapsulated in the reiteration of the historic blessing first given to Abraham and also by the genealogical connections that the Rebekah branch has in the Terah clan. The mere mention of "God Almighty" *(El Shaddai,* v. 3) brings forward the memory of the covenant of circumcision (17:1).

ISAAC SENDS JACOB FOR A WIFE (28:1–5). The borders of the first paragraph narrate Isaac's directions for his son Jacob (vv. 1–2,5). The last verse narrates the fulfillment of the command initiated at the start. Although Isaac comes center stage in this unit, Rebekah's shadow remains. The family branch in Aram is always expressed by their relationship to Rebekah, though they were kinsmen of Isaac's too. Between Isaac's directives is his recitation of the Abraham blessing, calling upon God to endow Jacob with the family inheritance of blessing, descendants, and land (vv. 3–4).

28:1–2 Isaac instructs Jacob to find a wife in Paddan Aram (cf. comments on 25:20). The language "called for Jacob" (v. 1) parallels the introduction in 27:1 when he solicited Esau for the blessing. This brings forward the contest reported in chap. 27; now he enjoins Jacob, who is the authentic recipient of the blessing. This is not, however, a competing version of the blessing already granted (27:27–29); rather it expresses the patriarchal blessing in its historic terms (vv. 3–4; e.g., 16:10; 17:2,6,20; 22:17; 26:4,24; 35:11; 48:4). The force of the interdiction against marrying Canaanite women is underscored by employing language typical of Mosaic legislation. "Commanded" *(ṣāwâ)* in all its word forms characterizes divine instruction to and by Moses (e.g., Deut 32:6). "Do not marry" (lit., "you must not take") is the apodictic form of the law (e.g., Deut 7:3). The same unqualified language occurs in Abraham's prohibition regarding a wife for Isaac (24:3,37). The verbatim repetition of the prohibition in v. 6 further intensifies its significance. Moreover, the similar wording, "from the women of Canaan" (36:2), to describe Esau's wives heightens the contrast between the sons.

"Go at once" translates the dual imperatives, "arise and go," indicating the urgency of the moment (cf. 43:8; 2 Sam 3:21). The exhortation is the reverse direction from that of God's instructions to Abram, who was to leave his homeland of Haran and his father's household (12:1). Upon his return to Canaan, Jacob will traverse the same route as that of his grandfather Abraham (12:6–7; 33:18; 35:1). The identification of the Haran branch involves tracing the genealogy through Rebekah's line, not Isaac's. Jacob's connection with the branch of Nahor is closer, of course, through the Bethuel lineage (11:29; 22:22–23; 24:24). "Your mother's father" (Bethuel) and "your mother's brother" (Laban) set the background for the events that follow in Paddan Aram (e.g., 29:5,14). In fact, Isaac's exhortation to go to Paddan Aram produces an unexpected outcome: Jacob marries both daughters of Laban. When we take this feature of the story into consideration, it is another reminder that neither parents, nor anyone or any institution, can control the future behavior of persons. On the meaning and location of Paddan Aram, see comments at 25:20.

28:3–4 The name "God Almighty" *(El Shaddai)* especially hearkens back to Abraham's experience (v. 3; cf. 17:1). By this name the God of the patriarchs was honored by later Israel (e.g., Exod 6:3). The fulfillment of Isaac's prayer here is realized by the divine theophany at Bethel when Jacob returns from Paddan Aram (35:11; 48:4). The rhyming combination of "be fruitful" *(pārâ)* and "increase" *(rābâ)* reflects creation's blessing (1:22,28; 8:17; 9:1,7) and the divine intention for the Abraham family (17:6,20), finding its partial achievement in the populous community of Israel (Exod 1:7; Lev 26:9). Although the blessing is for the individual Jacob ("you," singular), it transcends his generation to include the "community" *(qāhāl)* of Israel. As a special reference to assembled Israel, the word "community" commonly appears in the Pentateuch (e.g., Exod 12:6; Lev 16:17; Num 14:5; Deut 31:30) yet infrequently in Genesis (35:11; 48:4; 49:6).

The name "Abraham" forms the boundaries of v. 4. The exact phrase "the blessing of Abraham"[168] occurs only this once, referring here to the land promise. "You and your descendants" appeared also in the promises made to Abraham and Isaac (17:8; 26:3), and "possession" *(yāraš)* is a reflex of the Abraham narrative, occurring in his night vision (15:7; cf. *yāraš,* 22:17; 24:60). Reference to Jacob as "alien" like his grandfather (e.g., 17:8; 23:4), though Jacob was the second generation born in Canaan, reflects the group consciousness that premonarchic Israel maintained in anticipation of the possession of the land (e.g., Exod 6:4; 23:9).

28:5 The genealogy is similar to the wording in 25:20, but here it takes into account the story of the twins. Although repeated information, it is not the same, giving the reader a precise genealogical record of the matrilineal relationship afforded Jacob and his uncle Laban. Mention of the "Aramean" status of the Bethuel clan reinforces the tribal connection Jacob/Israel (cf. 25:20; 31:20,34) once had with the neighboring Arameans (cf. Deut 26:5).

ESAU TAKES A NEW WIFE (28:6–9).   The second paragraph describes Esau's reactions to the blessing and Jacob's departure (vv. 6,9). In between, the narrative provides Esau's interpretation of the prior events (vv. 7–8). Instead of

---

[168] Variants among the versions have "Abraham your father" or "Abraham my father," paralleling the formula in 28:13; 32:9.

opposing Jacob, this time Esau attempted to imitate him. Once he recognized how ill advised it was for him to have wed Hittite wives (cf. Deut 20:17–18), he obtained a wife from the family's relative, Ishmael. It gave the final stroke to the picture of the hapless Esau, who sealed his status as the rejected son by marrying into the family of the discarded Ishmael.

Esau Realizes His Mistake (28:6–8). **28:6–8** Verses 6–7 explain the action of Esau, who takes another wife (vv. 8–9). Verses 6 and 8 begin the same, "Then Esau saw that . . ." (NIV "learned/realized"), tying the verses together. The parallel expressions draw attention to the contrast that follows: in the first case, Isaac "had blessed *[bārak]* Jacob"; and in the second case, Esau's marriages were "displeasing" *(raʿ)* to Isaac.[169] Esau showed no interest in his mother's opinion, probably conceding her affections to Jacob. The reader is somewhat surprised (and evidently Esau too!) that Isaac was so troubled by Esau's actions. Although Isaac was the one who prohibited Jacob from marrying a Canaanite woman (v. 1), the narrative attributes the disapproval on the whole to Rebekah, not Isaac (27:46; 26:35). It was Rebekah who after all is prompting Isaac (and Jacob) at each turn. This narrative subtly exhibits the intellectual dullness of Esau, who fails to realize that as Rebekah thinks, so thinks Isaac. The extended verbosity of vv. 6–8, a replay of the just-narrated events, may also suggest how long it took Esau to put together the pieces of the parental puzzle. Only after observing the favor Isaac bestowed on his brother did Esau "realize" ("see") that his actions were counterproductive to courting his father's favor.

Esau Marries (28:9). **28:9** The identity of "Mahalath" *(māḥălat)* as the granddaughter of Abraham gives the marriage its special importance. The name, whose meaning is uncertain,[170] appears also for David's granddaughter (2 Chr 11:18; see the musical note, Pss 53:1; 88:1). The ancestry of this new wife via Ishmael[171] could be taken as more in keeping with his parents' desires, but still it was irregular for the practices of Abraham and Isaac. Whereas Jacob sought a wife from Laban's household, on his mother's side, Esau has married a member of Isaac's side of the family.[172] As to the response of his father, we can only guess. For the purposes of the author, the connection of Esau and Ishmael is a fitting end to this slice of the narrative, for it matches the actions of the two outcast sons who form an ancestral bond (36:3). The wilderness tribes that come from their family union historically opposed the descendants of Jacob in the land (cf. Ps 83:6[7]).[173]

---

[169] (v. 8) וַיַּרְא עֵשָׂו כִּי רָעוֹת//(v. 6) וַיַּרְא עֵשָׂו כִּי בֵרַךְ.

[170] KBL 513, מְחוֹלָה (?), "round dance"; cf. Ar. *miḥālun* (?), "cunning, intelligence" (Noth, *Personennamen,* 249).

[171] Ishmael is deceased, making "Ishmael" a metonymy indicating the Ishmaelites; on the detailed chronological reckoning, see Sarna, *Genesis,* 363, n. 3.

[172] L. Shering, "Mahalath," *ABD* 4.472.

[173] On the names and identities of Esau's wives, see comments on 26:34. On "Nebaioth" see comments on 25:13.

4. Promise of Blessing at Bethel (28:10–22)

From a "stone pillow" to a "stone pillar," this account tells how Jacob's lodging place at Bethel became the most celebrated place of worship among the patriarchal narratives. Jacob's life became indelibly marked by these events, so much so that they eventually superseded his infamous reputation for trickery (Hos 12:4). A. Ross notes the importance of our passage, showing "how a place became a shrine, a stone became an altar, and a fugitive became a pilgrim— God in His grace revealed Himself to Jacob in that place."[174] The narrative refers to both the past and future, making it an important link in the Jacob narrative as a whole. Chapter 28 begins with Jacob's submission to his father, reversing the steps of his ancestor Abraham from Haran to Canaan, and ends in a solemn vow that presages his return after twenty years in self-imposed exile.

By the events of 28:10–22, the author establishes Jacob's continuity with the patriarchal promises (vv. 13–15) and proclaims the Lord's perfect grace, despite Jacob's scandalous behavior (chap. 27). Also, following as it does the disturbing marriages of Esau (28:8–9), the passage infers that Jacob is not like his brother and may yet faithfully adhere to the family's moral heritage. Jacob learns from his future troubles in Haran that he must entrust himself to the Lord, believing that the Lord will guide and protect him in accord with his word (v. 15). In the Jacob narrative to follow (chaps. 29–31), the Lord exceeds his pledge to the descendant of Abraham, ensuring that Jacob not only survives and returns safely but also flourishes. This is reminiscent of Abraham and Isaac, who prospered during their sojourns abroad.

Jacob, who typically was keen on negotiating deals, proposes a vow with God (vv. 20–22; 31:13). This is the only occasion where a patriarch made a vow to God. Jacob leaves his land empty-handed, but he will return with unimaginable wealth, well empowered to fulfil his vow of a tenth part. Also upon his return Jacob wrestles the "man" at Peniel, exploiting his advantage for sure (32:26,28), but he has changed from the person who cheated Esau (33:3,8–11). The ensuing account of his journey in Paddan Aram depicts how the pauper becomes affluent and the trickster undergoes moral metamorphosis (chaps. 29–31). J. Walton observes that with Jacob's vow we discover that his dealings with God are "backward" when compared to Abraham: God tested Abraham, but here Jacob tested God; God instructed Abraham to leave his country before he entered into blessing, but Jacob imposes conditions on God before he vows to benefit the Lord.[175] This behavior by Jacob is what we expect of him, but the Lord is gracious to him and is willing to begin his work with the unworthy Jacob. Jacob will learn that he is totally dependent on the Lord's mercy, leaving

---

[174] A. Ross, "Jacob's Vision: The Founding of Bethel," *BSac* 142 (1985): 225–26 (224–37).

[175] J. H. Walton, *Genesis: The NIV Application Commentary* (Grand Rapids: Zondervan, 2001), 573–74.

behind in Paddan Aram his haughty spirit.

The passage echoes the *past* by recalling the events at "Beersheba" (v. 10), where his father Isaac resided (26:23,33), and by anticipating "Haran" as the planned refuge from Esau's wrath (27:43). The site "Bethel" (v. 19) evokes memories of the early journeys and worship of Abraham (12:8; 13:3–4). Jacob's dream recalls the "night" (vv. 11–12) vision Abraham experienced (15:12,17), and the appearance of the Lord (v. 13) points back to the comparable events in the lives of Abraham and Isaac, to whom the Lord had appeared (12:7; 17:1; 18:1; 26:2,24). The formulaic language identifying God (v. 13) recalls the epiphanies made to Jacob's ancestors (15:1,7; 17:1; 26:24). The promises of land and descendants (vv. 13–14) are at points the exact wording made to Abram in 13:15–16, where the "dust" of the earth is similarly an apt simile. The promise of blessing for all peoples (v. 14b) repeats the precise formula of 12:3 at most points, and it is with slight variations similar to the promise language in 18:18; 22:18; 26:4. The promise of divine guidance and protection (vv. 15,20) hearkens back to the travels of Isaac (26:3,24). A guiding angel provided for Abraham's servant, who traveled to the same city of Nahor also seeking a wife (24:7,40). The fear ("awesome," v. 17) that Jacob knew reflects the fear that typically his ancestors experienced (15:1; 26:24). Last, the vow with its promise of paying a "tenth" (v. 22) echoes Abram's loyalty to God when he met the priest-king Melchizedek (14:20).

Genesis 28:10–22 also looks to the *future* return from Paddan Aram, fulfilling the promises received at Bethel. The first step toward this fulfillment is the discovery of Rachel, where another "stone" captivates our attention (29:2–3,8–10). God appears in a matching theophany, directing Jacob to return from Paddan Aram, in which he identifies himself by recalling this initial revelation at Bethel (31:13). The Bethel experience explains Jacob's return (35:1,3,6–7), which culminates in another theophany and cultic act at Bethel (35:9–15). Our passage has its counterpart in the return trip when again Jacob sees the "angels of God," acknowledging the place as "the camp of God" ("Mahanaim," 32:2), and at night encounters God, naming the place "Peniel" (32:30–31) with the same awe he had sensed at Bethel. The presence of God, the "Fear of Isaac," affords Jacob protection against Laban (31:24,42). Moreover, the mention of Beersheba (28:10) points ahead to the place that Jacob worships upon his departure with his family to Egypt (46:1,5). The theophany at Bethel also serves as the foundational event that prompts Jacob's blessing upon Joseph's sons when in Egypt (48:3).

Early Jewish and Christian Interpretation.   The narrative of Jacob's ladder has held fascination for interpreters from antiquity to the present. Early Jewish interpretation found in this story opportunity for elevating the spiritual status of Jacob by casting him in the role of receiving exceptional revelations. So as to demonstrate God's oversight of Jacob and the validity of God's promises to the father of the nation, Jewish midrash included in the Palestinian targums at v. 10 the account of the "five miracles" that God performed in behalf of Jacob during his journey to and arrival at Haran. The description of the ascending and descending angels impressed Jewish imagination, which understood that the angels came down from heaven to view Jacob asleep on earth. Jewish interpretation tied this story to the midrash of Isa 49:3 ("Israel, in whom I will be glorified," NRSV), which explained that the image of Jacob/Israel was inscribed in heaven; therefore the angels came to sneak a peek at the earthly visage of the patriarch known to them from his heavenly likeness (e.g., *Tgs. Ps.-J.; Neof.; Gen. Rab.* 68.12, 78.3; *Pirqe R. El.* 35 [265]).[176] Christian interpretation, fueled by Jesus' allusion to the ladder event (John 1:50–51), rendered the story allegorically as a description of Jesus on earth. In John's Gospel the apostle by Jesus' teaching showed that the sanctuary of Bethel, "house of God," was now embodied in the incarnational Messiah.[177] Jacob's ladder is best understood as a type of Christ's mediatorial position, connecting heaven and earth. The greater revelation that Nathaniel (and the church) would receive was the salvation afforded by the crucifixion of the Son of Man: "When you have lifted up the Son of Man, then you will know that I am he" (John 8:28, ESV).[178] Christian allegorists built on this connection by identifying Jacob's "stone" as Christ (cf. "cornerstone," Eph 2:20; 1 Pet 2:6) and the ladder as his cross. Augustine recognized the anointed pillar erected by Jacob, which was not an idolatrous pillar for the patriarch, as the anointed Messiah (*Tractate in the Gospel of John* 7.23.2).[179] Luther, like many others before him, followed the interpretation of Augustine, equating the ladder with the "Son of Man" (John 1:51).[180]

COMPOSITION. The theophany at Bethel in 28:10–28 has taken on special importance in the study of the composition of the Pentateuch by the work of form-tradition critics, especially by E. Blum. Because of this factor, we will give more attention to the question of source for this pericope than we have in other units. Although for source critics 28:10–22 was not a signal passage for their theory of multiple, parallel written sources, early proponents of two parallel documents (Yahwist/Elohist) underlying the Jacob narrative found support in this narrative: vv. 11–12,17–22 were from the Elohist (E), and vv. 13–16 derived from the Yahwist (J). Verse 10 is the only extant introduction to the pericope, and its origin coming either from E or J was disputed. Among the arguments put forward for duplicate but parallel sources were these: the varied names of God *(Yahweh/*

---

[176] See Maher, *Targum Pseudo-Jonathan*, 100, n. 19.
[177] G. L. Borchert, *John 1–11*, NAC (Nashville: Broadman & Holman, 1996), 149.
[178] F. F. Bruce, *The Gospel of John* (Grand Rapids: Eerdmans, 1983), 62–63.
[179] *ACCS* 2.192.
[180] *LW* 5.217; Calvin, *Comm.,* 2.113: "If then we say that the ladder is a figure of Christ, the exposition will not be forced. For the similitude of a ladder well suits the Mediator, through whom ministering angels, righteousness and life, with all the graces of the Holy Spirit, descend to us step by step."

Elohim); the duplicate responses of Jacob to his dream (vv. 16//17); the duplicate etiologies for the sanctuary at Bethel (vv. 16//17); and the incongruity of the promises (vv. 13–15) treated also as conditions in Jacob's vow (vv. 20–22). The problems created by this reconstruction were quickly apparent. The passage as it stands does not evidence from the Yahwist a clear beginning or a conclusion. The E source relates an epiphany but no revelatory message. Also the divine names could be explained on other grounds, making the names an unreliable criterion. Wenham, agreeing with others, observes that *Yahweh* is the name for God in the passage, and *Elohim* is the appropriate generic name for the expressions "angels of God" (v. 12) and "house of God" (vv. 17,22).[181]

Most form-tradition critics propose an incremental growth of 28:10–22 by stages, involving an original dream etiology for the cultic center at Bethel (vv. 11–12,17–19) and the later additions of the promises (vv. 13–16) and Jacob's vow (vv. 20–22).[182] The addition of the promises (vv. 13–16) is widely accepted as the contribution of J (though variously identified), who took up an early Jacob legend at Bethel when creating the broader Jacob narrative. Westermann believes the vow in vv. 20–22 (as well as vv. 13b,14) is the third and final phase of development.[183] Carr argues for a similar pattern but views the vow (vv. 20–22) as the second stage, linking the cult etiology to the Jacob story that tells of Jacob's return (thus vv. 10–12,17–22). He finds that the promises in vv. 13–16 show awareness of the context in which they now appear, indicating that these verses were inserted as the final stage.[184] In a strange departure from all others, N. Wyatt isolated v. 19 as postexilic, positing that the "place" was originally Jerusalem, not Bethel.[185]

Rendtorff, who contended that the three patriarchal narratives were originally independent, emphasized the role of the guidance promise ("I will be with you") in the Jacob narrative. It occurs at the start in the theophany account at Bethel (28:15), again at the turning point when the Lord directs Jacob to return (31:3), and finally at the end of the narrative (46:2–4). In his analysis the promise to bless the nations, found in 28:14 (Jacob), 12:3; 22:18 (Abraham), and 26:4 (Isaac), provided for the union of the three stories of the patriarchs.[186] Blum went further by assigning 28:10–22 a larger role in his reconstruction of Genesis-Numbers.[187] He separates vv. 11–13a,16–19a as an original, independent cult legend regarding Jacob at Bethel. He supports this claim in part by the tight chiasmus he posits for

---

[181] Wenham, *Genesis 16–50,* 220.

[182] E.g., M. Rose contends for an original cosmological story of heaven and earth that became part of the Jacob tradition (vv. 12,20–21), to which the Yahwist redacted the theophany of *Yahweh* (vv. 13–15) ("Genèse 28,10–22: l'exégèse doit muer en herméneutique théologique," in *Jacob: un Commentaire à plusieurs voix de Genèse 25–36,* 77–86).

[183] Westermann, *Genesis 12–36,* 452–53.

[184] Carr, *Reading the Fractures of Genesis,* 205–8, 256–68.

[185] N. Wyatt, "Where Did Jacob Dream His Dream?" *SJOT* 2 (1990): 44–57.

[186] Rendtorff, *The Problem,* 71, 75–77.

[187] E. Blum, *Der Komposition der Vätersgeschichte,* WMANT 57 (Neukirchen-Vluyn: Neukirchen Verlag, 1984); see the discussion in McEvenue, "Return to Sources," and Nicholson, *Pentateuch.*

vv. 12–13a and vv. 16a–17b. Verses 13b–15,20–22 are by another author, dating in the period of Jeroboam in the tenth century, who supplies them to relate the Bethel legend to the wider Jacob story (25:19–34; chaps. 27–33). Despite these differences in detail, there is wide agreement that 28:10–22 was originally an independent unit. Following von Rad's observation, many understand that 28:10–22 was integrated into the present arrangement of the Jacob narrative, functioning as the bridge from the Jacob-Esau material (chaps. 25:19–34; 27:1–28:9) to the Jacob-Laban narratives (chaps. 29–31).[188] Jacob's return and encounter with God at Peniel in chap. 32 is the matching narrative that redirects the inner circle of Jacob-Laban stories to the outer Jacob-Esau composition (chaps. 32–35).

Van Seters disagreed with most critics by arguing that 28:10–22 was not originally free of the Abraham and Isaac stories. Verses 10,20–22 only make sense if the author assumes the divine promises made to Abraham. Also Jacob's destination to Haran has its motivation in the expectation provided by Rebekah's directions (27:43–45). In typical fashion for Van Seters, his exilic Yahwist as author can account for the multiple redactions scholars commonly propose. By adapting a former cult etiology (vv. 11–12,17–19a), the Yahwist authored the narrative for his exilic audience, presenting their ancestor Jacob as the model of a hoped for, future return and as the exemplar of personal piety for the individual exile.[189]

The contention of the present work is that there was one original author for the whole, but unlike Van Seters there is no clear reason to assume a preexisting cult etiology for the story's foundation. A single composer of the account is indicated by evidence that the etiology did not circulate independently of the promise (vv. 13–16) and vow (vv. 20–22). Key wording creates the unmistakable coherence of the narrative. The threefold appearance of "place" *(māqôm)* in v. 11 is balanced by its threefold recurrence in vv. 16,17,19. This technique of key wording appears also with *hinnê* (lit., "behold, see"), occurring twice in v. 12 and twice more in vv. 13,15. These examples of key wording cut across the dream etiology (vv. 11–12,17–19) and the promise sections (vv. 13–16), suggesting that the units evidence an inherent unity. Wenham also shows that the passage consists of two (somewhat) parallel panels, vv. 11–15 and 16–21, exhibiting matching vocabulary and content, for example, "stones, headrest" (vv. 11,18). Especially the vow (vv. 20–22) reflexes the promises (vv. 13–15),[190] demonstrating as Van Seters also concludes that the promises and the vow are likely one composition.[191] Moreover, key wording and geographical notices shared by the introduction (v. 10) and the concluding vow (vv. 20–22) produce an inclusio, recommending that the vow was more likely an original part of the pericope. Further, the repetition of "go, went" *(hālak)* occurs in vv. 10,15,20. Also mention of "my father's house" has a geographical significance as well as thematic, serving as the counterpart to "Beersheba" in v. 10.

We conclude that the rhetorical features of the passage suggest that it is as rea-

---

[188] von Rad, *Genesis,* 39.

[189] Van Seters, *Prologue to History,* 296–98.

[190] Wenham, *Genesis 16–50,* 219, 224.

[191] Van Seters, *Prologue to History,* 294.

sonable (see "Structure"), if not more likely, that the passage was a compositional unity from the start.

STRUCTURE.   Following the introduction in v. 10 are three distinct parts. The first unit is the dream sequence in vv. 11–15, dominating the author's interest. Verse 11 possesses the threefold appearance of "place" *(māqôm),* preparing for the naming "Bethel" in vv. 16–19. Because of the striking visual character of the dream, the repeated term *hinnê* (lit., "behold," cf. AV, NASB) occurs in vv. 12(2x),13,15, creating a vivid word picture. The narrative description in which the first three uses of *hinnê* plus participles appear enables the reader to visualize the animation of the dream as Jacob sees it unfold. The sustained recitation of the patriarchal promises in vv. 13–15 is crucial to the event, tying Jacob to his ancestors Abraham and Isaac.

Verses 16–19, as the second unit, recount Jacob's response to the dream theophany when he names the site "Bethel." This unit corresponds to v. 11 in the dream sequence by providing another threefold appearance of "place" *(māqôm,* vv. 16,17,19). The third unit of vv. 20–22 completes the story by recounting the vow Jacob undertakes. Although the term "place" is absent in this final section, reverence for the place is reflected by the vow that depends upon his "return" to that place (v. 21). The mention of "house" twice (vv. 21,22) also points back to the "house of God" in the naming sequence of Bethel (v. 17). The vow requests three provisions from God: (1) "If God will be with me . . ." (v. 20a); (2) "give me food . . . clothes" (v. 20b); and (3) "I return safely to my father's house" (v. 21a). The pledge made by Jacob constitutes three corresponding commitments: (1) "the LORD will be my God" (v. 21b); (2) recognition of "God's house" (v. 22a); and (3) "I will give you a tenth" (v. 22b).

Fokkelman observes two matching units in vv. 11–13 and 16–19, the former describing Jacob's dream and the latter his reaction.[192] The word group *n-ṣ-b* provides for three linking terms: "resting" *(mūṣṣāb),* "stood" *(niṣṣāb),* and "pillar" *(maṣṣēbâ).* Thus, at the place on the earth where the stairway "rested," by which the Lord "stood," Jacob raised the memorial "pillar." Repetition of the word group *r-ʾ-š* also creates another sequence: "under his head" *(měraʾăšōtāyw),* "its top" *(rōʾšô),* "under his head" *(měraʾăšōtāyw),* and "on top of it" *(rōʾšâ).* The "head" stone upon which Jacob dreams of the stairway whose "top" ("head") reaches to heaven is the "head" stone on whose "top" ("head") he pours oil. The pillar marks the site where Jacob has accessed symbolically the abode of God. Thus, Jacob's dream theophany is the pattern whereby he offers his first act of worship. This site is not yet a sanctuary in the material sense, which explains why Jacob does not build an altar until his return (35:1,3,7).

---

[192] Fokkelman, *Narrative Art in Genesis,* 71–73.

(1) Dream at Bethel (28:10–15)

[10]Jacob left Beersheba and set out for Haran. [11]When he reached a certain place, he stopped for the night because the sun had set. Taking one of the stones there, he put it under his head and lay down to sleep. [12]He had a dream in which he saw a stairway resting on the earth, with its top reaching to heaven, and the angels of God were ascending and descending on it. [13]There above it stood the LORD, and he said: "I am the LORD, the God of your father Abraham and the God of Isaac. I will give you and your descendants the land on which you are lying. [14]Your descendants will be like the dust of the earth, and you will spread out to the west and to the east, to the north and to the south. All peoples on earth will be blessed through you and your offspring. [15]I am with you and will watch over you wherever you go, and I will bring you back to this land. I will not leave you until I have done what I have promised you."

After the introduction (v. 10), this unit consists of three parts: the preparation for the dream theophany (v. 11), the dream of a celestial stairway (v. 12), and a divine message involving the promises (vv. 13–15). Verse 11 focuses on the earthly "place" (3x), but vv. 13–15 report the heavenly sight and sound, with the deictic (pointing) particle "behold" (*hinnê* [4x]) repeatedly introducing the events as exceptional. Verse 12 transitions the scene from earth to heaven as the stairway rests on the "earth" and reaches above to "heaven." "Stopped for the night" (v. 11) marks this unit as reporting one night, and "awoke from his sleep" (v. 16) initiates the new unit (vv. 16–19). The divine speech in vv. 13–15 is introduced by the appearance of the Lord in v. 13a and concludes with the guarantee of divine presence and protection (v. 15). Sandwiched between are the typical promissory blessings of land, descendants, and blessing for all peoples (vv. 13b–14).

ON TO HARAN (28:10). **28:10**   The background for this passage is the events at Beersheba in 26:23–28:9 (also 22:19). Wenham suggests that reference to "Haran" rather than Paddan Aram, as mentioned by Isaac (28:2,5; cp. 27:43), recollects the call and obedience of Abraham, who departed the town for Canaan (11:31–12:5).[193] The terse report of v. 10 promotes the idea that Jacob is straightway obeying the request of Isaac and the wishes of his mother Rebekah (27:43; 28:2; cf. 29:4).[194] On Beersheba and Haran, see 11:31; 21:14; 25:20 and vol. 1A, p. 500.

DIVINE PROMISE OF RETURN (28:11–15).   The remainder of this unit describes the dream theophany. Verses 11–12 detail Jacob's place of rest and his vision. Verses 13–15 recount the message of divine promise.

Jacob's Ladder (28:11–12).   **28:11**   Although unspecified in the text to

---

[193] Wenham, *Genesis 16–50,* 221.

[194] Jewish tradition in the Palestinian targums included in the account at this point the "five miracles" God achieved in behalf of Jacob during his journey.

this point, the word "place" possesses the definite article, "the place" (NIV "a certain place"), anticipating the importance that this night will have for Bethel (v. 19). The word "the place" appears three times in the verse for emphasis and definiteness (but absent twice in NIV). Because of the presence of God, this public space becomes the holy, "the house of God." By morning the ordinary stone will mark a hallowed place. Such is the deity that Jacob worships; the Lord takes the mundane and transforms it into the sacred by his inimitable presence. The occasion for Jacob's stopping at this "place" was nightfall. There is no mention or expectation that the site had a special religious history prior to Jacob's experience. On the contrary, he was surprised at the presence of God in that place, or he would not have treated the site indifferently (v. 16). This indicates that the author of the passage distinguishes Jacob's experience from the Canaanite sanctuary dedicated to the god Bethel (Jer 48:13), known to have predated the patriarchs.[195] The fall of night recalls the night theophany Abraham received at Mamre (Hebron; 15:12,17). More important, lodging in this place presages the nightlong struggle he will brave with the angel at Peniel upon his return (32:13,21–32[14,22–33]). As for the use of a stone for resting the head, rocks were abundant and helpful for the fatigued (Exod 17:12). The EVs typically understand the stone as a pillow "under the head" (*měra'ăšōtāyw*, lit., "head place") of Jacob. In support of this common view, the word appears in a description of crowns fallen "from your heads" (*mar'ăšôtêkem*, Jer 13:18). Our text's description, however, may indicate simply that "the stones of the place" were positioned nearby the head (cf. 1 Sam 19:13,16; 26:7,11,16; 1 Kgs 19:6). This appears to be the interpretation of the LXX (*pros kephalās autou,* "on the side of" or "at his head"[196]), which renders the Hebrew consistently at each Old Testament passage, including 28:11,18. If this is the proper interpretation, the stones provided a makeshift enclosure for his head.

28:12 The dream sequence is reminiscent of Babel, whose tower reached toward heaven (11:4). There, however, human ambition spurred on its construction (11:4,7). Jacob's stairway, mounted only by an angelic cast, is the means of a gracious revelation from heaven. The "stairway" *(sullām)* connecting earth and heaven signifies divine presence and mediation. The precise meaning of *sullām* is uncertain, although usually rendered "stairway" or "ladder." Modern commentators typically prefer "stairway,"[197] but the LXX and Vulgate appear to imply a "ladder," although this is equally

---

[195] See especially the appendix in Sarna, *Genesis,* 398–400.

[196] Wevers, *Notes on the Greek Text,* 449.

[197] Some scholars derived סֻלָּם from סלל, "to cast up, lift up, exalt," meaning סֻלָּם was an earthen ramp; others have connected it with Akk. *simmiltu* as a loanword (in which a metathesis occurs in the Hb.), defining Jacob's staircase as "stepped ramp, flight of steps" (*HALOT* 2.757–58). P. V. Mankowski disagrees, concluding that the two words were totally separate in origin (*Akkadian Loanwords in Biblical Hebrew,* HSS 47 [Winona Lake: Eisenbrauns, 2000], 114–18).

uncertain.[198] The argument that a common "ladder" was too narrow for the train of simultaneously moving angels presses for a literalness that we would not require of a surrealistic dream. As for a possible cultural background to explain a heavenly staircase, scholars cite either Egyptian or Akkadian parallels to explain the imagery, the latter being more likely.[199] There is no clear connection of the stairway, however, with the Babylonian ziggurat, which possessed a series of steps, although there is some resemblance (see vol. 1A, pp. 470–72). What the ziggurat and similar representations share in common with Jacob's dream is simply the common imagery of a designated meeting place between earth and the divine sphere.

In Genesis "angels" *(malʾākîm)* deliver divine communications, or they accompany a message delivered by the Lord (e.g., 16:7–11; 19:1,15; 21:17; 22:11,15; 31:11–13; 32:1[2]). Here the angels do not speak, and therefore Jacob's encounter is direct with God, like the epiphanies to Abraham and Isaac. The angels' presence enhances the impression of a divinely sponsored message. Their motion along the ladder contributes to the animation and power of the dream's image in Jacob's mind as well as suggests their mobility as messengers (e.g., Ps 103:20, more below at v. 13). A rabbinic interpretation (e.g., *Gen. Rab.* 88.12; Rashi) was that the angels who ascended and who descended the ladder were two distinct groups that accompanied Jacob in his travels for his protection in and outside the land, respectively (cf. v. 15). When we remember the guiding angel of Abraham's servant who also traveled to Haran in search of a wife for Isaac, the idea of a protecting angel fits well here (24:7,40).

The Promises (28:13–15).　**28:13**　The rendition of the promises in vv. 13–15 relies heavily on the previous formulations made to Abraham and Isaac (e.g., 12:3; 17:7–8; 18:18; 22:18; 26:4), especially 13:14–16, which records Abram's and Lot's movements at Bethel. Transparently, by such allusions the author demonstrates that the ancient promises continue with Jacob as the appointed successor, despite his questionable character and his absence from Canaan. The substance of the promises is not new, but their recitation by the divine voice is new to Jacob's ears. The Lord identifies himself to Jacob by his covenant relationship with his ancestors, Abraham and Isaac (cp. 26:24; Exod 3:15–16). That the expression "your father" (meaning "ancestor," e.g., Josh 24:3) is used of Abraham, not Isaac, recognizes him as the chief recipient of the promises and the derivation of the family blessing.

---

[198] C. Houtman contends that the LXX's (κλίμαξ) and Vg.'s *(scalam)* renderings suggest a ladder, giving rise to the popular notion of Jacob's "ladder" ("What Did Jacob See at Bethel?" *VT* 27 [1977]: 337–51); Houtman, as with some commentators, interpreted the noun as the "way" that provided entrance into the later sanctuary at Bethel, meaning that סֻלָּם in Jacob's dream referred to the rising hillside at Bethel that became the location of the high place.

[199] On this discussion see A. Millard, "The Celestial Ladder and the Gate of Heaven (Genesis xxviii, 12, 17)," *ExpTim* 78 (1966/67): 86–87.

The text at v. 13a permits two different interpretations of the Hebrew that describes the position of the Lord in the dream: either the Lord stands above the ladder or stands at the side of Jacob.[200] The LXX[201] and many EVs translate the Hebrew as "above it," referring to the ladder, meaning that the Lord stood at the top of the stairway (e.g., NIV, AV, RSV, NASB). By this understanding, the Lord positioned above the ladder casts a forceful figure, looming over the earth beneath (cp. Exod 17:9). Alternatively, the antecedent may be Jacob, meaning that the Lord stood "beside him" on the earth, presumably at the base of the ladder (e.g. NJB, NAB, REB, NRSV, NJPS, HCSB). A similar Hebrew expression describes the three visitors at Abraham's side, "standing near him" (18:2, NRSV; cp. 1 Sam 22:6); also the Lord is pictured beside an inanimate object in Amos's visions (7:7; 9:1). The pronoun ("it") in v. 12 clearly refers to the stairway. Moreover, the depiction of the Lord at the top of the stair with ascending and descending angels conforms to the traditional image of patrolling angels who come and go at God's bidding (cf. 1 Kgs 22:19–22; Job 1:6–8; 2:1–3; Zech 1:10; 6:5).[202]

Notice of Jacob's posture, "the land on which you are lying" (v. 13), occurs at the head of its clause, emphasizing the specific place again (cf. v. 11) and making the promise of land unambiguous. Sarna adds that Jacob's lying prostrate on the land corresponds to Abraham's walking tour of the land in 13:17, where the Lord too likened his seed to the "dust of the earth" (28:14).[203]

28:14–15 The dispersion of Jacob's descendants, that is, "spread" (*pāraṣ*),is a new feature of the promises (v. 14). It provides another echo of the Tower and the nations that disseminated from the Babelites (*pārad*, 10:5,32; *pûṣ*, 10:18; 11:4,8–9). The same term describes Jacob's attainment of numerous cattle (30:30,43). The promise of God's protective presence, "I am with you" (v. 15; cf. 31:3; 46:4; 48:21), recalls the same promise made to Isaac during his sojourn in Gerar (26:3,24). The same assurance of preservation accompanies other leaders in Israel's history (Exod 3:12; Josh 1:5; 3:7; Judg 6:16; 1 Kgs 11:38; Jer 1:8) and Israel itself (Isa 41:10; 43:2,5; Hag 1:13; 2:4). Hebrew *hinnê* ("behold," absent NIV) introduces this promise, drawing special attention, for example, "*Know* that I am with you" (NRSV, NAB, italics mine). That God especially guarded the patriarchs became evident to all who encountered them (e.g., 21:22; 39:3–4). Jacob will require the same haven from potential hostilities outside Canaan (31:29). "Wherever you go" shows that his travels cannot outdistance the safekeeping of God. The Lord by explicit command will set in motion Jacob's return to the land according to his promise (31:3,13; 32:9). "And I will not leave you" is another variation on the motif of

---

[200] עָלָיו, preposition + third masculine singular suffix.

[201] ἐπ' αὐτῆς (fem. singular), "upon it," referring to the κλίμαξ (fem. singular), "ladder."

[202] Wenham, *Genesis 16–50*, 222.

[203] Sarna, *Genesis*, 198.

God's care. "Leave you" translates *ʾāzab,* which often appears in contexts pertaining to covenant loyalty (e.g., 24:47, "abandon"; Deut 29:24; Josh 1:5; Hos 4:10). Although Jacob had received the blessing, he straightway abandoned the land and inheritance to his brother Esau.[204] It was Esau, not Jacob, who appeared to have gained the possessions of their father despite the stolen blessing. All that Jacob had to rely on was the word of the Lord, and he patiently waited for twenty years until the divine directive came to return. He found that to trust God's promises was sufficient, no matter how long the delay.

(2) Worship at Bethel (28:16–22)

[16]When Jacob awoke from his sleep, he thought, "Surely the LORD is in this place, and I was not aware of it." [17]He was afraid and said, "How awesome is this place! This is none other than the house of God; this is the gate of heaven."

[18]Early the next morning Jacob took the stone he had placed under his head and set it up as a pillar and poured oil on top of it. [19]He called that place Bethel, though the city used to be called Luz.

[20]Then Jacob made a vow, saying, "If God will be with me and will watch over me on this journey I am taking and will give me food to eat and clothes to wear [21]so that I return safely to my father's house, then the LORD will be my God [22]and this stone that I have set up as a pillar will be God's house, and of all that you give me I will give you a tenth."

Jacob makes two religious responses to the theophany. He first erects a cultic stone, marking the location of the dream and names the site "Bethel" (vv. 16–19). Second, he proposes a vow in which he makes three conditions, entailing provision and protection, and concludes with three promises of consecration to God (vv. 20–22).

THE PILLAR AND NAMING OF BETHEL (28:16–19). **28:16–17** Upon awakening, Jacob proclaims surprise that his chosen bedchamber was a holy place. "Surely" *(ʾāḵēn)* and "aware" *(yāḏaʿ,* "know") appear together in Exod 2:14, which also describes the fear of discovery. Since he had unwittingly encroached upon holy space, he is fearfully startled by his dream, awaking in the midst of the night. "Awesome" *(nôrāʾ)* is derived from *yārēʾ,* meaning "fear, awe." The expression commonly reflects the speaker's contemplation of the incomparability of God (e.g., Exod 15:11; 34:10; Ps 96:4). Jacob declares the obvious: the residence of God in that place means that it is a divine sanctuary, "the house of God." Westermann rightly observes that the "house of God" does not refer to the stone pillar but rather to the "place," anticipating the sanctuary that Jacob promises (cf. v. 22).[205] The parallel statement, "the gate of heaven," derives from the dream directly, for the ascent he witnessed furnished

---

[204] Luther, *LW* 5.201–2.
[205] Westermann, *Genesis 12–36,* 456.

the entryway into heaven from the place where he spent the night.[206] Bethel signified to Jacob the assurance of God's superintendence and imminence. As we mentioned at v. 12, the idea of a divine passageway to heaven from earth was familiar to the ancients. The name "Babylon" means "gate of the god(s)" *(bāb-ili; bāb-ilāni;*see vol. 1A, p. 469), indicating the entryway to the deity's presence or the place of divine judgment.[207]

28:18   "Early the next morning" indicates Jacob's first act was the establishment of a cultic "pillar" *(maṣṣēbâ),* corresponding to the practice of constructing altars by Abraham (12:7–8; 13:18) and Isaac (26:25). That this immediate response characterized the three patriarchs demonstrates the power of the spoken word (19:27; 21:14; 22:3). The raising of cultic stones (also 35:14), as well as establishing pillars for other purposes (31:45,51–52; 35:20), was Jacob's habit. As with his predecessors, he also set up altars in obeisance to God (33:20; 35:1,3,7).[208]

There is no evidence that Jacob believed the cultic pillars he erected were inhabited by a deity named *Bethel* or that he worshiped sacred stones. Here the pillar symbolized Jacob's dedication to the Lord as expressed in his vow (cf. 31:13). According to 31:13, the pouring *(yāṣaq)* of oil on the pillar equated to "anointing" *(māšaḥ)* the pillar, consecrating it to the Lord. In Israel's cult the pouring *(yāṣaq)* of oil appeared in rituals of sanctification, such as the grain offering (Lev 2:1,6; Num 5:15) and objects and personnel (e.g., the "anointing" *[mišḥâ]* oil, Exod 29:7; 40:9; Lev 8:10–12; 21:10; and anointing of kings, 1 Sam 10:1; 2 Kgs 9:3,6). The pillar may also have functioned secondarily as a witness to the vow entered by Jacob (cf. v. 22; 31:52–54; Exod 24:4; Josh 24:26–27; 1 Sam 6:18; 7:12).

28:19   The naming formula, "He called that place," is the same one describing Abraham's memorializing of Mount Moriah (22:14; cp. 32:3; Num 11:3,34; Josh 5:9). That the author included the former name of Bethel, "Luz," pointed up the validity of the report and importance attached to the new name (35:6; 48:3). The same formula is used of the city "Dan" (Judg 18:9). Since Jacob named the place "Bethel," the earlier references to Bethel in the Abraham account are most likely the result of updating the place name (12:8; 13:3). Further, the Abraham narrative does not require a city at this location in his day, though 28:19 suggests that the city Luz was at this site in Jacob's time. That the location of Abraham's altar lay "east of Bethel" (12:8; 13:3–4) does not neces-

---

[206] Houtman explores this extensively ("What Did Jacob See at Bethel?").

[207] See D. J. Wiseman, *Nebuchadrezzar and Babylon* (Oxford: Oxford University Press/The British Academy, 1985), 44. Akk. *bāb-ili* rendered the Sumerian ká.dengir.ra ki, i.e., "gate of god"; the Eng. name "Babylon" follows the Gk. transliteration (Βαβυλών) of the Akk. dual form *bāb-ilān,* "gate of the two gods."

[208] For a discussion of the illicit practice of erecting pillars (e.g., Lev 26:1; Exod 23:24), see the Introduction, "Religion of the Patriarchs: Features of Patriarchal Religion."

sarily contradict that Jacob erected his altar at Bethel (35:1,12,14). Despite allusions to Abraham's experience at Bethel (vv. 13–14; 35:11–12), there is no equation of the two locations in the text. "Bethel" means "house of God [El]" *(bêt ʾēl)*, playing on Jacob's recognition that he had been in God's presence *(bêt ʾelôhîm,* "house of God," vv. 17,22). The same expression "house of God" refers elsewhere to a sanctuary, including the Jerusalem temple (Judg 17:5; 2 Chr 34:9; Ps 42:5), but in our passage Jacob uses the term metonymically, not referring to a literal sanctuary structure. The city's later history of idolatry made Bethel notorious among the prophets; its pious name was the source of a jibe by at least one prophet ("Beth Aven," i.e., "house of wickedness," Hos 4:15; 5:8[?]; 10:5; cf. Amos 5:5–6).

JACOB'S VOW (28:20–22). Jacob's vow involves three petitions: (1) God's protective presence (v. 20a), divine provision (v. 20b), and Jacob's safe return (v. 21a). The last requirement is actually stating the result of the former two preconditions. Verses 21b–22 state three promises made to God: (1) devotion to the Lord God (v. 21b), (2) dedication of the site to God (v. 22a), and (3) the offering of a tithe (v. 22b).

28:20–21a Jacob is the only patriarch who makes a formal "vow" *(neder)* to God (v. 20a; 31:13). That God is "with" Jacob indicates protection and prosperity, usually expressed in conjunction with the land (e.g., 21:22; 24:40; 26:28; 48:21; cp. Exod 3:12; Deut 31:23). Jacob was asking no more than the fulfillment of God's self-imposed obligations delivered in the dream sequence (v. 15). Divine care is also a tenet in God's promise to Isaac (26:3,24). The word group *š-m-r* ("watch") often expresses oversight (e.g., 2:15; 3:24), as in this case; among its uses are a shepherd guiding flocks (e.g., 30:31; 1 Sam 17:20), a sentinel keeping watch (e.g., Josh 10:18; 1 Sam 19:11; 25:21), and a personal bodyguard (e.g., 1 Sam 26:15–16; 28:2). The priest's benediction echoes this provision: "The LORD bless and keep you" (Num 6:24). Also it typically means to "keep, obey, observe" stipulations (e.g., 17:9; 18:19; 26:5), especially popular in pentateuchal legislation (e.g., Exod 19:5; Lev 18:4; Deut 4:2). This first condition Jacob later testifies that God has met (31:3,5,22; 35:1,3). Mention of Jacob's "journey" *(derek)* recalls the guiding angel who assisted Abraham's servant on his way to Haran (24:27,48; as well as Israel, Exod 18:8; 23:20).

As for the gifts of food and clothes (v. 20b), these provisions are typical needs of a roaming alien (e.g., Deut 10:18; Josh 9:5,13) and are Israel's needs during its lengthy wilderness sojourn (Exod 3:22; Deut 8:4; 29:5; Neh 9:21). By returning to his father's house "safely" (lit., "in peace," *běšālôm*), Jacob means that he avoids physical harm (e.g., Lev 26:6), achieving his mission successfully (e.g., 26:29,31; 44:17; Exod 18:23; Josh 10:21). The realization of this prayer occurs when Jacob returns to Shechem "safely" *(šālēm,* 33:18). Jacob's journey to Haran and his prayerful concern over returning recall Abraham's servant who returned safely to his master's house with a new wife for young Isaac (chap. 24). As above, the Aaronic benediction when describing God's blessing includes "peace" for Israel (Num 6:26).

28:21b–22 Of the three promises, the first, "the LORD will be my God," seals the bond between Jacob and God, reminiscent of the divine pact with Abraham (17:7–8) and Israel (e.g., Exod 6:7; 29:45; Lev 11:45; Num 15:41; Deut 26:17; 29:13; 2 Sam 7:24; Jer 31:33). Westermann believes that this vow promises sacrificial worship in the future sanctuary mentioned next (cp. 2 Sam 15:7–9).[209] Jacob promises second to establish a shrine of worship, "God's house" (e.g., Judg 17:5; Ps 42:4[5]). The building of a sanctuary is appropriate to the visitation that God afforded him (v. 17), using the head-stone to mark the site (v. 22a). Finally, Jacob commits one tenth of his hold-ings to the Lord (v. 22b), which recalls Abraham's offering to Melchizedek (see comments on 14:20). That Jacob's promise is emphatically expressed, lit., "I will surely give you a tenth,"[210] reveals his eagerness for the Lord's favor. His vow can only be fulfilled, however, if the Lord grants him riches in the land where he seeks a wife.

5. Laban Deceives Jacob (29:1–30)

This passage introduces the account of Jacob's life in Paddan Aram, where he will remain for twenty years, obtaining family and wealth (29:1–31:55[32:1]). After his stirring experience at Bethel (28:10–22), the patriarch arrives safely at Haran, the ancestral home of Abraham. The vision of ascend-ing and descending angels (28:12) and the multiple allusions in chap. 29 to the journey of Abraham's servant to Haran imply that divine supervision also brought Jacob to this place (cf. 24:7,40; 31:11; 32:1[2]). That Jacob himself ultimately understood his travels in this way is shown by his testimony at the end of his life (48:15–16). The author conveys subtly the fulfilling of the prom-ise of God's guidance ("I am with you," 28:15) in our passage by the appear-ance of another "stone" (29:2,3,8,10). It was the "stone" pillar at Bethel that reminded the patriarch of God's presence (28:11,18,22). That Jacob alone moved the gigantic stone covering the well of the shepherds and at the timely moment he first saw Rachel (29:10) corroborates for the reader the continuing provision and protection of the Lord (28:15,20). Whereas Rebekah cared for the animals of Abraham's servant, confirming the divine guidance of the ser-vant (24:19–20,22), here the direction is reversed: the stranger sustains the thirsty flocks of Laban with inaccessible waters. This depiction foreshadows the role that Jacob plays in Laban's household. He becomes the omen of bless-ing that Laban strives to hold on to at all costs (e.g., 30:27–36).

---

[209] Westermann, *Genesis 12–36,* 459.

[210] עֲשֵׂר אֲעַשְּׂרֶנּוּ, the infinitive absolute + imperfect construction (absent NIV; cf. most EVs).

Also 29:1–30 introduces us to the strife that the households of Jacob and Laban experience, ending in a standoff by a mutual peace treaty (31:52). By this struggle the Lord establishes the prosperity of Jacob, while reforming this trickster by giving him "a dose of his own medicine." Jacob meets his match in Laban's cleverness; Jacob is "out-Jacobed" by his senior, though the Lord finally reverses Jacob's losses and plunders Laban's ill-gotten gains. Their dispute was over the "wages" *(maśkōret/śākār)* that Jacob earned by working in Laban's household. His wages are the subject of 29:15–30 and are central to the remainder of the Jacob-Laban narratives. Repeatedly, Jacob's "wages" are the source of Laban's cunning, which in the end comes back to haunt Laban *(maśkōret,* 29:15; 31:7; 31:41; *śākār,* 30:28,32,33; 31:8).[211] The same term characterized the Lord, who is Abraham's "reward" *(śākār,* 15:1), a lesson Jacob will learn. Jacob complained that "ten times" his uncle changed the basis for his wages (31:7,41). The women too are incensed at their father's mistreatment of their husband and at his refusal to give them an inheritance (31:14–16). There is no temptation to remain in Haran under the auspices of Laban, or as we say, "no love lost" between these family members. By the end of the Jacob-Laban story, the family looks to God to deliver them from Laban's hostilities (31:16,42,53). Jacob discovers during his Haran sojourn that the Lord is indeed with him and will be his source of deliverance when he faces his greatest peril yet to come—confrontation with Esau.

COMPOSITION.   Genesis 29:1–30 begins the Jacob-Laban narratives (29:1–31:55[32:1]) that describe their ongoing conflicts and, finally, Jacob's return to Bethel as the Lord had promised (28:15). Critics today assign the Jacob-Laban narratives on the whole to the Yahwist (J) source, and the same naturally is true of 29:1–30. However, vv. 24 and 29, reporting Laban's gifts of two servant girls, are taken by critics as stemming from the Priestly (P) document,[212] though not always.[213] Carr acknowledges that vv. 24,29 are secondary, creating links with the birth narratives that follow (29:31–30:24), but they are not necessarily Priestly in derivation.[214] As with almost all modern interpreters,[215] Coats acknowledges the essential unity of the Jacob-Laban narratives as a story of family strife set in the frame of the Jacob-Esau account of family strife. He argues that chaps. 29–31 are not "intrinsic" to its context, lacking the promises of posterity and land; the glue that holds the narratives together is the motif of strife, not promise.[216] Westermann agrees that the Jacob-Laban story is essentially a unified account and fits the context of the Jacob-Esau struggle secondarily, but it

---

[211] The word group *ś-k-r* also describes the "hiring" of Jacob by Leah (30:16,18); the שָׂכִיר is a "hired servant" (e.g., Exod 12:45).

[212] E.g., von Rad, *Genesis,* 292; Westermann, *Genesis 12–36,* 467.

[213] E.g., Speiser, *Genesis,* 226–27.

[214] Carr, *Reading the Fractures of Genesis,* 102, 263.

[215] E.g., Rendtorff, *The Problem,* 44–45, who attributes this observation especially to Gunkel.

[216] Coats, *Genesis,* 212, 221.

does so by virtue of the "flight-return" structure that it provides. He finds, however, that vv. 1–14 and vv. 15–30 were originally independent oral accounts, the former a classic example of the well and marriage motif (e.g., comments on 24:11–33; Exod 2:15–22) and the latter the widely known traditional story of the substitute bride. The Yahwist rendered the two into one whole that functions now as introduction to the Jacob-Laban narratives (chaps. 29–31).[217] Carr views the Jacob-Laban narratives, including 29:1–30, as part of his "prepromise Jacob narrative" that originally existed apart from the Abraham or Joseph cycles.[218]

We find, however, that the evidence of multiple layers of tradition put forward is not compelling and is subject to alternative explanations. Notices of the servant girls in vv. 24 and 29 are not secondary accretions for bridging purposes alone. Yes, they anticipate the birth narratives that follow, but they also expose the greed of Laban, a characteristic that makes his later actions consistent with his personality. Unlike his generosity toward his sister Rebekah at her marriage (24:59–61), encouraged no doubt by the servant's gifts to the family, Laban has no blessing and presents only one maiden. As for the two distinct oral traditions that Westermann sees behind vv. 1–14 and vv. 15–30, he admits that the fusion has been so artfully achieved that the passage appears to be a unified composition. One wonders why the elaborate reconstruction by Westermann is called for.

More important, there is ample evidence that chaps. 29–31 are native to the Jacob narratives. Thompson, for example, contends opposite the prevailing idea that chap. 29 is independent of the main Jacob story line. He sees so close a connection that he believes that 29:1 originally followed directly on 27:45, describing Jacob's flight from Esau. In his view 27:46–28:22 interrupts the natural flow.[219] Although we cannot abide Thompson's notion that 27:46–28:22 is a variant tradition of Jacob's flight that interrupts the story line (27:42–45), he is right when he finds that 29:1–30 continues the main thought of the Jacob-Esau narrative. Moreover, chaps. 29–31 have a narrative symmetry that suggests a self-sufficient story, but the narrative must have been penned with the broad Jacob account in mind as well as the Abraham episode of his servant's search for Rebekah. These allusions to the Jacob and Abraham stories are not incidental but essential to the narrative's makeup. Chapters 29–31, as Westermann observes, are constituent to the "flight-return" plot. These chapters also build on many of the same motifs in the Abraham and Jacob/Esau narratives, for example, the effect of endogamy, tying in Nahor-Bethuel-Laban (as in chap. 24),[220] and inheritance; strife within the family for ascendancy (Jacob/Laban and Leah/Rachel); the barren, favored wife (Sarah, Rebekah, Rachel); the subversion of the "older" by the "younger" (Isaac/Ishmael; Jacob/Esau; Rachel/Leah); inner-family deception (Jacob/Esau; Jacob/Laban); the acquisition of wealth from the host (Abraham/Pharaoh; Isaac/Abimelech; Jacob/Laban); and hospitality leading to

---

[217] Westermann, *Genesis 12–36,* 463–64.

[218] Carr, *Reading the Fractures of Genesis,* 257.

[219] Thompson, *The Origin Tradition of Ancient Israel,* 106.

[220] G. Yee describes Jacob's wives as his mother's brother's daughters, making them "matrilineal cross cousins" ("Leah," *ABD* 4.268).

expulsion (Abraham/Pharaoh; Isaac/Abimelech; Jacob/Laban). Wenham observes an explicit connection to the Jacob-Esau narrative by the shared phrase "a few days" in 29:20 and in 27:44 ("for a while," NIV).[221]

Another indication of chaps. 29–31's autonomy, according to Coats and others, is the absence of the promises pertaining to posterity and land, once the secondary additions are eliminated. His analysis of the "secondary" intrusions, however, is suspect. Wherever the allusions to the promises in chaps. 29–31 are specific (e.g., 31:13), these are deemed clearly secondary. When the allusions are subtle (e.g., 29:12), they are regarded as too general to show dependency. But must the promises be overtly stated in order to prove the underlying nexus of chaps. 29–31 with the Abraham and Jacob accounts? The tensions exhibited in the Haran episodes over inheritance, land, marriage, and children speak to the promises of posterity and land. In 30:22–30 we find the interplay of the three elements of the promises. The birth of Joseph by Rachel resolves the posterity crisis, prompts Jacob's return to the land, and forces Laban to admit that he has been blessed by Jacob's favored status before God. Removal of this passage would disembowel the plot line of the Jacob-Laban narratives. The significance of these and other plot actions are furnished by the promises known from the Abraham and Jacob theophanies.

STRUCTURE.   Verse 1 provides an introduction to the whole of the Jacob-Laban narrative (29:1–31:55[32:1]), as well as to 29:1–30. This introductory verse reports the arrival of Jacob in Haran, and v. 30 relates the outcome of his arrival, namely, his marriage to the beloved wife, Rachel. The term "saw" provides a connecting thread between our pericope and the subsequent narrative (29:31–30:24). Verse 2 and the beginning verse of the next narrative (29:31) start the same, "[Jacob] saw *[wayyar$^{\jmath}$]* a well" and "the LORD saw *[wayyar$^{\jmath}$]* that Leah was not loved." It was at the well first that "Jacob saw Rachel" (v. 10).

After the introduction, our passage consists of two units: (1) vv. 2–14 describe Jacob's various encounters at the well, meeting Rachel and afterward Laban; and (2) vv. 15–30 entail the bartering between Laban and Jacob, who works for the hand of Rachel, only to win her after Laban had defrauded him.[222] The first unit (vv. 2–14) possesses two subunits (vv. 2–10; 11–14). Mention of the "stone over the mouth of the well" in vv. 2 and 10 forms the boundaries for the first subunit. The remarkable strength demonstrated by Jacob infers the divine confirmation of Jacob's success, for it was upon seeing Rachel that he moved the rock.[223] This superhuman feat

---

[221] Wenham, *Genesis 16–50,* 228.

[222] Wenham proposes two distinct episodes, supporting his chiastic arrangement of the Jacob-Laban narratives: (A) Jacob enters Haran and marries (29:1–14); (B) Laban outmaneuvers Jacob (29:15–30); (C) birth of Jacob's children (29:31–35); (B′) Jacob outmaneuvers Laban (30:25–43); (A′) Jacob and family exit Haran (31:1–55[32:1]; *Genesis 16–50,* 228–29).

[223] Fokkelman, *Narrative Art in Genesis,* 124.

parallels the servant's amazing discovery of Rebekah and Laban at the well (24:12–15,27,40–50). Luther followed others who explained that the "Holy Spirit rushed upon the patriarch," and his strength resulted from the "impulse of the Holy Spirit."[224] The second subunit (vv. 11–14) possesses an embedded parallelism: Jacob kisses Rachel and declares their kinship (vv. 11–12)//Laban kisses Jacob and declares their kinship (vv. 13–14). Another possible allusion to the experience of Abraham's servant is the similar phrases, "Jacob told *[waysappēr]* him all these things" (v. 13) and "the servant told *[waysappēr]* Isaac all he had done" (24:66; cf. also 24:28).

The second unit (vv. 15–30) narrates the wages that Jacob accepts for his tenure of service and the subsequent hoax that Laban perpetrates upon his nephew. It also possesses two subunits (vv. 15–25; 26–30). The first subunit (vv. 15–25) begins with Laban's offer to pay Jacob for his "work" (v. 15) and ends with Jacob's outrage when he discovers that his "work" gained Leah, not Rachel (v. 25). The second subunit (vv. 26–30) recites Laban's explanation that the "younger" daughter cannot marry before the "older" (v. 26), forcing Jacob to renegotiate for Rachel, whom he at lasts receives (v. 30). The language of the second unit recalls Jacob's ruse, deceiving his brother for the prize of the firstborn: "relative" (*ʾāḥ*) and "brother" (*ʾāḥ*), for example, 27:11,41,43; 29:15; "older" (*gĕdōlâ/gādôl*) and "younger" (*qĕtōnnâ/qātān*), 27:1,15,42; 29:16,18;[225] and "firstborn" (27:19,32; 29:26 [= NIV's "older one"). Jacob tastes the same bitter fruit as had his brother: "Why have you deceived me *[rimmîtānî]?*" (29:25), and, "Isn't he rightly named Jacob *[yaʿăqōb]?* He has deceived me *[yaʿqĕbēnî]* these two times" (see comments at 27:36 for wordplay).

(1) *Jacob Arrives in Haran (29:1–14)*

¹Then Jacob continued on his journey and came to the land of the eastern peoples. ²There he saw a well in the field, with three flocks of sheep lying near it because the flocks were watered from that well. The stone over the mouth of the well was large. ³When all the flocks were gathered there, the shepherds would roll the stone away from the well's mouth and water the sheep. Then they would return the stone to its place over the mouth of the well.

⁴Jacob asked the shepherds, "My brothers, where are you from?"

"We're from Haran," they replied.

⁵He said to them, "Do you know Laban, Nahor's grandson?"

"Yes, we know him," they answered.

⁶Then Jacob asked them, "Is he well?"

"Yes, he is," they said, "and here comes his daughter Rachel with the sheep."

---

[224] *LW* 5.281.

[225] The Hb. words in 29:26, though also translated "younger" (הַצְּעִירָה) and "older" (lit., "firstborn," הַבְּכִירָה), are different from those in chap. 27.

⁷"Look," he said, "the sun is still high; it is not time for the flocks to be gathered. Water the sheep and take them back to pasture."

⁸"We can't," they replied, "until all the flocks are gathered and the stone has been rolled away from the mouth of the well. Then we will water the sheep."

⁹While he was still talking with them, Rachel came with her father's sheep, for she was a shepherdess. ¹⁰When Jacob saw Rachel daughter of Laban, his mother's brother, and Laban's sheep, he went over and rolled the stone away from the mouth of the well and watered his uncle's sheep. ¹¹Then Jacob kissed Rachel and began to weep aloud. ¹²He had told Rachel that he was a relative of her father and a son of Rebekah. So she ran and told her father.

¹³As soon as Laban heard the news about Jacob, his sister's son, he hurried to meet him. He embraced him and kissed him and brought him to his home, and there Jacob told him all these things. ¹⁴Then Laban said to him, "You are my own flesh and blood."

After Jacob had stayed with him for a whole month,

Jacob's departure for the "land of the eastern peoples" (v. 1) and notice of his destination at Laban's residence (v. 14b) mark the boundaries of this unit. Mention of the cover "stone" and "sheep" that the well sustained enclose vv. 2–10. Verses 2–3 and 9–10 are the author's observations, surrounding the dialogue between Jacob and the shepherds of three flocks (vv. 4–8). That both the narration and the dialogue explain why the shepherds delayed watering their sheep highlights the impediment that the massive stone was to the locals (vv. 3,8). This prepares for the unconventional action undertaken by Jacob, whose strength and brazenness distinguished him as a newcomer. Providing for Laban's flocks in this manner is an omen of the many achievements he will accomplish to Laban's benefit. Verses 11–14a focus on his kinship with Rachel and Laban and the warm hospitality they extend. The author is satisfied with summarizing the affectionate behavior of the three relatives, saving the sole dialogue for Laban's remark, "You are my own flesh and blood" (v. 14b). The author probably relied on the detailed dialogue recorded in chap. 24 between the servant and Rebekah and Laban at the well to give the reader a sense of what must have been said here. "Kissed" *(nāšak)* brackets vv. 11 and 13, describing the touching resumption of old family ties. Verses 11–13 capture the excitement of the Laban household at Jacob's appearance.

JACOB AT THE WELL (29:1–10). Jacob arrives at Haran and discovers local shepherds waiting for assistance to uncover the well (vv. 1–3). He inquires about their knowledge of Laban's identity and then comments on the shepherds' peculiar delay (vv. 4–8). He removes the covering of the well at the same moment that Rachel, Laban's daughter, arrives to water her flock (vv. 9–10).

The Stone Blocks the Well (29:1–3). **29:1** Although a condensed verse, it contains two intriguing expressions. "Jacob continued on his jour-

ney" translates a unique figure of speech, lit., "Jacob lifted up his feet"
(v. 1). Typically, the verb "lifted up" *(nāśāʾ)* appears with "eyes," meaning a
person lifted one's eyes to look (e.g., 13:10), or it expresses "lifting one's
voice," as when Jacob "lifted his voice and wept" (v. 11) at coming across
Rachel ("began to weep aloud," NIV; cf. 27:38). Perhaps the expression is a
play on v. 11's event, underscoring that Jacob's immediate discovery of
Rachel made auspicious beginning to his journey. The implication is that
the hand of God was directing Jacob's travels. The second expression,
"eastern peoples" *(bĕnê qedem)*, refers broadly to people groups east of
Canaan, including Transjordan, Syria, and north Arabia (Judg 7:12; 8:10;
1 Kgs 5:10; Job 1:3; Isa 11:14; Jer 49:28). The author's customary terms
describing Jacob's destination are "Haran" (27:43; 28:10; 29:4) and "Paddan Aram" (28:2,5–7; 31:18; 33:18; 35:9,26; 46:15; cf. "Paddan," 48:7, and
"Aram," Hos 12:12[13]). Here the geographical direction "eastern" is probably meant to convey a double meaning, as the word "east" *(qedem)* does
elsewhere in Genesis (cf. 2:8; 3:24; 4:14; 11:2), especially 25:6 (see comments), which reports on Abraham's rejected children (see also vol. 1A, pp.
257–58, 478). The Nahor clan left behind in Paddan Aram was not the
favored branch of the Terah family (11:31–12:3).

29:2–3 Verse 2 describes the scene at the well, and v. 3 explains the
importance of the scene. Twice the interjection *hinnê* ("behold, see"!) occurs,
adding vividness to the narrative setting (v. 2). The well "in the field"
(baśśādeh) indicates that it was outside the city of Haran, providing water for
outlying herds. That Rachel and Laban could make a quick dash to the house
implies that it was nearby (vv. 12–13). The "stone" (v. 3) provided a protective
covering, impeding theft by unwelcome migrants or unwanted animals. Abraham's servant discovered Rebekah at the town's well, drawing water as women
customarily did in the evening (24:11). Here, however, Rachel is a shepherdess,
watching her father's folds (v. 9). Mention of the "field" *(śādeh)* may echo the
first meeting of Jacob's parents, Rebekah and Isaac, which was in the "field"
(śādeh, 24:63,65).[226]

Encircling the well were three sheepfolds whose shepherds strangely
delayed drawing water for their animals. Twice, once in the narration and again
by the shepherds' dialogue (v. 8), the passage provides the local custom that
explains why the sheepfolds were gathered but were not drinking (v. 3). The
definite noun "the stone" and early mention that it was "large" even before the
explanation in v. 3 makes the stone prominent in the eye of the reader. Due to
the exceptional weight of the stone, shepherds who congregated at this watering hole delayed removing it (see vv. 9–10 below for an alternative interpretation). No one person or even a few could remove the barrier, making it

---

[226] For more on water resources in this semiarid environment, see comments on 26:15–16.

obligatory to wait until others arrived. As cooperating parties, the shepherds cared for their thirsty flocks and then departed at the same time, always returning the stone to its place. The narrative's picture provides the background for the remarkable achievement of Jacob, who moves it single-handedly. Another reason for our author's interest in the stone and Jacob's handling of it is the passage's reminiscence of the stone pillar at Bethel that memorialized God's promise of protection for Jacob's journey (28:18). This allusion to the stone pillar suggests further evidence that the Lord is present with Jacob as he promised.

Jacob and the Shepherds (29:4–8). **29:4–6** Jacob addresses the shepherds with a polite greeting, "my brothers" (v. 4; cf. 19:7; Judg 19:23), inquiring first about their residence. Their response, "We're from Haran," is fortuitous for his visit, encouraging him to inquire further, but he does not let on about his reason for travel. He follows by asking if they know Laban, "Nahor's grandson" (v. 5). This genealogical connection of Laban with Nahor furnishes the all-important link between Jacob's derivation and Laban's ancestor Nahor, Abraham's brother (22:20–23). It is this kinship that will form the basis of their treaty of peace (31:53). His last inquiry about Laban's welfare (*šālôm,* v. 6a; cp. 43:27–28; 2 Sam 18:29,32; 20:9; 2 Kgs 4:26; 9:31) tells him generally what he needed to know, for news about the Nahor branch of the family probably was known already in Canaan (cf. 22:20). That "peace" (*šālôm,* "well," NIV) was their reply prepares us for the strife that Jacob's visit will mean,[227] despite his prayer at Bethel for a peaceful return (*šālôm,* "safely," 28:21). Nevertheless, the echo of the Bethel revelation further confirms the efficacy of the promises. Just at that moment, they recognize the flock of Rachel approaching, evidently at some distance, and identify her as the "daughter" of Laban (v. 6b; cf. v. 9). The sudden arrival of Rachel recalls the same timely appearance of Rebekah, just as the servant beseeched God (24:15,45; cf. 22:13). The drama of her entrance is accentuated by the lively Hebrew construction, combining the particle "behold, see" *(hinnê)* and the participle "coming" *(bāʾâ;* cf. Ruth 2:4).

29:7–8 True to his character, Jacob proceeds arrogantly, questioning the shepherds' carefree behavior (v. 7). For all the criticism one might level at Jacob's conduct, he was no slacker in his labor ethic (31:6,38–41). Their reluctance to water the sheep and move on to new pasturage while there remained plenty of sunlight puzzled him. His comment bristles with boldness. "Look" *(hēn)* and "still" *(ʿôd)* head the sentence (v. 7), expressing forcefully his incredulity. Three successive verbal imperatives thunder a presumptuous attitude, "water . . . go . . . pasture!" (NASB, NRSV), matched by his brazen action of removing the stone by himself (v. 10). Their retort was emphatic, beginning with the negative *lōʾ* ("not"), answering, "We

---

[227] Westermann, *Genesis 12–36,* 465.

can't" (v. 8). Their explanation is truncated. They do not admit that no one of them can possibly move the stone, requiring them to work together. They only outline the odd custom (something Laban conveniently did not do; cf. v. 26). It was, however, because of this practice that Jacob meets Rachel immediately, for otherwise he might not have tarried at the well. After all, it was for Rachel and perhaps others that the shepherds waited. Whereas the presence of God's guidance is explicit in chap. 24, divine providence at work in Jacob's encounter with Rachel is implied.

Jacob Moves the Stone (29:9–10). **29:9–10** The three shepherds function as a foil for Jacob, who unlike them can provide water for Rachel's sheep by exhibiting amazing strength. An alternative explanation for the shepherds' inaction is not their inability but their laziness. Jacob's zeal at the well corresponds with his zeal for the family's birthright in contrast to Esau. Verse 9 nostalgically relives the divine coincidence that the servant of Abraham and Rebekah experienced in Haran at the well (24:15,45). Rachel approaches just as Jacob learned of their local custom, giving him the stage to demonstrate his chivalry. That women assisted in watering flocks was not exceptional. The daughters of Moses' father-in-law (Jethro) cared for their father's sheep, which also produced the moment for Moses' heroics, defending them against rival herdsmen (Exod 2:16–17). "Shepherdess" *(rō'â),* the feminine form of the usual term "shepherd" *(rō'eh),* occurs only here in the Old Testament. Perhaps Rachel's vocation later contributed to her demands for an inheritance from her father (31:14–16,19; cf. 31:1). Since Rachel as a shepherdess must have frequented the well, she must have been impressed by the exceptional feat of this stranger (v. 10). That Leah was not said to have worked their father's herds may imply a vocational contrast between the sisters, a contrast also between the rivals Jacob and Esau ("a man of the open country" *[śādeh],* 25:27; cf. 27:27).

Inspired by Rachel's presence, Jacob removed the stone by rolling it aside and then drew water for her animals (v. 10). The author repeats Rachel's derivation, "Laban's daughter" (v. 6), and provides three times the vital information of their kinship, lit., "Laban the brother of his [Jacob's] mother." No doubt, the discovery of her identity and the opportune moment of her appearance motivated Jacob to move the stone. Wenham observes that repeated references to the sheep as Laban's indicate that Jacob hoped to ingratiate himself to Laban first and Rachel second.[228] The piety of Abraham's servant starkly contrasts with the action and character of Jacob. When Abraham's servant had discovered Rebekah's identity, he worshiped the Lord (24:24,26), but here Jacob flexed his muscle, proving his capacity to serve Laban's house.

JACOB MEETS RACHEL AND LABAN (29:11–14). The passage records a chain reaction: Jacob informs Rachel of his identity (vv. 11–12a), and

---

[228] Wenham, *Genesis 16–50,* 231.

Rachel informs Laban (vv. 12b–14).

29:11–12   Overwhelmed by the euphoria of finding family, Jacob "kissed" Rachel and "began to weep" (v. 11; contrast Esau's motivation, 27:38). The combination of these terms describes the emotional events of family reunion or separation (33:4; 45:15; 50:1; Ruth 1:9,14; 1 Sam 20:41). Kissing a family member (e.g., 31:28) or dear friend (e.g., 1 Sam 20:41) was common, including traditional greetings (e.g., Exod 4:27; 18:7; 2 Sam 20:9).[229] That he kissed her before identifying himself fits the picture we have come to know of the audacious man.[230] After Jacob explained his familial connection by his mother Rebekah (v. 12), Rachel reacted to the news in the same manner as Rebekah did upon learning the identity of the servant (24:28; cf. Judg 13:10). "Ran" and "told" are the same terms describing Rebekah, who informed the whole of her household. That Rachel's response mimics Rebekah's gives a subtle authentication to Rachel as the mother of future Israel, the imprimatur that Leah does not have at this early point. Here it appears that Laban alone is the sole survivor of the Nahor-Bethuel clan group.

29:13–14   The chain of events continues with the response of Laban, whose enthusiasm resembles his previous behavior toward Abraham's servant. "Heard" and "ran" describe his reactions to the visitor (v. 13; cf. 24:29–30), adding an embrace and kiss, which were appropriate conduct when greeting family (cf. 33:4; 48:10). Laban's kiss proved to be as incongruous with his treatment of Jacob as the patriarch's own beguiling kiss of his father (27:27). That Abraham's servant had bestowed valuable presents (24:29–31,53; cf. 32:20–21) may have added to Laban's enthusiasm at hearing of Jacob's arrival. Jacob recounted "all these things" (v. 13), reciting the events at the well. The nondescript expression "all these things" invites the reader to recall the ignoble happenings that prefaced Jacob's arrival, details most likely omitted by Jacob. That he reported to Laban the events at the well is also reminiscent of Rebekah and the servant, who also informed Laban what had occurred at the well (24:28,30,33–48; cf. v. 66). The point in telling the Jacob-Rachel encounter similar to the servant-Rebekah meeting was to infer that the Lord had guided Jacob as he had Abraham's servant.

The sole dialogue in this opening section by Laban is his recognition of Jacob's kinship, "my own flesh and blood" (v. 14). This has been the emphasis of the author, who repeatedly defined the familial connections of Jacob and the Laban clan, intimating the providential character of Jacob's

---

[229] Kissing was also related to formal activities, such as blessing and anointing (e.g., 48:9–10; 1 Sam 10:1), royal reception (e.g., 2 Sam 14:33; 15:5), and obeisance (1 Kgs 19:18; Ps 2:12; Job 31:27; Hos 13:2).

[230] The NIV translates a pluperfect, "had told Rachel," meaning he identified himself and *then* kissed her.

journey. Also it is Jacob's relationship that complicates how Laban should approach paying Jacob's wages, for he is neither slave nor typical hired laborer. Laban's subtle ploys repeatedly take advantage of their kinship, raising the ire of his daughters (31:6–7,14–16,26–28,31,41,43). He does not treat Jacob as well as the Mosaic law calls for in dealing with the hired worker (Lev 19:13; Deut 24:14; cf. Lev 25:39–41). The NIV's rendering translates in modern idiom the literal Hebrew "my bone and my flesh" (cf. 2:23; Job 2:5). "Bone" and "flesh" describe kinship among members of a tribal unit (Judg 9:2; 2 Sam 5:1; 19:13–14). "My flesh" alone appears in juxtaposition with "brother" in 37:27 (NIV adds "blood"), defining the relationship of Joseph and his brothers (cf. "my brother," v. 15).

The final sentence of v. 14 adds to the idea of Jacob's acceptance.[231] He resided with Laban a month's time, forming an appropriate end to Jacob's trek. The penniless, homeless Jacob found refuge in his uncle's house at the goodwill of the Lord. Also this chronological notice transitions us to the subsequent paragraph that defines Jacob's wages. Some arrangement must be made with Jacob during the longevity of his stay, but paradoxically due to Laban's cunning a mere excursion became virtually an incarceration (cf. 27:44; 31:38,41–42).

(2) Jacob Marries Leah and Rachel (29:15–30)

[15]Laban said to him, "Just because you are a relative of mine, should you work for me for nothing? Tell me what your wages should be."
[16]Now Laban had two daughters; the name of the older was Leah, and the name of the younger was Rachel. [17]Leah had weak eyes, but Rachel was lovely in form, and beautiful. [18]Jacob was in love with Rachel and said, "I'll work for you seven years in return for your younger daughter Rachel."
[19]Laban said, "It's better that I give her to you than to some other man. Stay here with me." [20]So Jacob served seven years to get Rachel, but they seemed like only a few days to him because of his love for her.
[21]Then Jacob said to Laban, "Give me my wife. My time is completed, and I want to lie with her."
[22]So Laban brought together all the people of the place and gave a feast. [23]But when evening came, he took his daughter Leah and gave her to Jacob, and Jacob lay with her. [24]And Laban gave his servant girl Zilpah to his daughter as her maidservant.
[25]When morning came, there was Leah! So Jacob said to Laban, "What is this you have done to me? I served you for Rachel, didn't I? Why have you deceived me?"
[26]Laban replied, "It is not our custom here to give the younger daughter in marriage before the older one. [27]Finish this daughter's bridal week; then we will

---

[231] Many EVs interpret the final clause as a dependent temporal clause (v. 14), introducing the main action in v. 15 (NIV, NJB, NAB, REB, NJPS, HCSB).

give you the younger one also, in return for another seven years of work."
²⁸And Jacob did so. He finished the week with Leah, and then Laban gave him his daughter Rachel to be his wife. ²⁹Laban gave his servant girl Bilhah to his daughter Rachel as her maidservant. ³⁰Jacob lay with Rachel also, and he loved Rachel more than Leah. And he worked for Laban another seven years.

After establishing the background in vv. 1–14, the author turns to the more important matter: Jacob's marriages to the daughters of Laban. And that Jacob married the sisters by the guile of Laban establishes the strained relationship the two men will have throughout the course of the story. Moreover, our passage provides the cause for the rivalry that the sisters sustain, for Jacob "loved" Rachel (v. 30), a rivalry resulting beneficially to Jacob by the brood of sons born (chap. 30). The first half of this section pertains to the trickery of Laban, substituting Leah for the younger Rachel (vv. 15–27). The second half recounts the successful negotiations and marriage of Jacob to his cherished Rachel (vv. 28–30). This second half brings the whole section full circle, from the well scene where Jacob first meets Rachel in vv. 2–14 to the temporary denouement when he marries her in vv. 28–30. "Older" and "younger," referencing the daughters in both halves (vv. 16,26), brings to mind the overarching tension of Esau and Jacob. By this subtle allusion to Jacob's past, the author indicates that Jacob must taste the bitterness to which he had subjected his family. But it also shows God's hand continues at work, for by the surprising reversal of the younger supplanting the older, we recall the oracle concerning the sons (25:23). Thus, paradoxically, the strife Jacob encounters in Haran confirms his appointment as the Lord's successor to Isaac, whose adventures outside the land result in his advantage.

JACOB WORKS FOR RACHEL (29:15–27). The negotiation for Jacob's marriage to Rachel is settled (vv. 15–20), but Laban surreptitiously switches Leah for Rachel to maintain local protocol (vv. 21–27).

Jacob Loves Rachel (29:15–20). **29:15** Laban addresses the subject of "wages," offering to pay for the younger man's labors (v. 15). As we noted in the introduction to this narrative, "wages" is a recurring topic in the remainder of the Jacob-Laban account. The word group "work" ("serve," *ʿ-b-d*) is a key term in the Jacob-Laban narrative, which is the subject of their dispute (29:15,18,20,25,27[2x],30; 30:26[3x],29; 31:6,41). Commentators often note that "serve" echoes the strife involving Jacob's deception of his kinsman Esau (25:23; 27:29,40).[232] His show of generosity disarms Jacob, who gullibly believes his uncle's offer is well intentioned. Laban mentions their relationship first, referring to his familial obligation toward Jacob. His initial question is rhetorical, meaning Jacob should not be utilized without compensation lest he be a slave. Yet he cannot establish the standard of payment for Jacob since he

---

[232] Sarna, *Genesis,* 201.

is not merely a hired worker either. His second question invites Jacob to consider his dilemma.

29:16–17 The author digresses from the main narrative line in these two verses by supplying significant background information regarding Laban's daughters.[233] They are identified and distinguished according to their relative ages, their names, and their relative beauty. Elsewhere, when two daughters or wives are named, the language is "first" and "second" (4:19; Exod 1:15; Ruth 1:4; Job 42:14). Here the author refers to their place as "older" and "younger" (v. 16) since this plays into Laban's motive for deceiving Jacob (v. 26).

"Leah" *(lēʾâ),* if related to Akk. *littu, lītu,* meaning "cow" (cf. Arb. *laʾātu,* "wild cow"),[234] provides for an interesting difference with the name "Rachel" *(rāḥēl),* meaning "ewe" *(rāḥēl,* 31:38; 32:15; Isa 53:7; Song 6:6), which is an appropriate name in light of Rachel's vocation (v. 9). The description of Leah's eyes is uncertain.[235] The term *rakkôt (rak),* rendered "weak" in the NIV, may also be used of a "gentle" maiden (Deut 28:56; Isa 47:1; cf. *rakkôt,* "gentle words," Job 40:27). Some EVs interpret the description of Leah positively, meaning she had "tender" (AV), "delicate" (NKJV, HCSB), or "lovely" (NRSV, NJB, NAB) eyes. If so, the biblical author is describing the positive appeal of each woman, Leah's eyes and Rachel's form. The tenor of the passage, however, contrasts Leah and Rachel, first their order of birth and perhaps here their charm. This suggests that the term has the negative nuance of feeble, impotent (e.g., Deut 20:8; 2 Sam 3:39), meaning "dull-eyed" (REB). If so, the irony is that though lackluster in her appearance, Leah is the fertile one of the sisters. Alternatively, R. Gradwohl contends that if a contrast were intended in the passage, it would be between Leah's and Rachel's eyes or between Rachel's and Leah's loveliness.[236] But the author's description of the women followed immediately by the narration of Jacob's love for Rachel implies that her beauty captivated him, whereas Leah was not enticing (v. 18). Moreover, there is the same association of beautiful form *(yāpeh)* and love in Amnon's attraction to Tamar (2 Sam 13:1; cp. 1 Kgs 1:3–4, where the narration must clarify that the woman's beauty in this case did not result in sexual relations). Also if the name "Leah" *(lēʾâ)* invoked a sound play on the word "weary, impatient" *(lāʾâ),* there may be a subtle play with her name, reminding one of her lifeless eyes (v. 17). The term *lāʾâ* first occurs in 19:11, describing the blind Sodomites who "wearied *(lāʾâ)* themselves groping for the door" (RSV).

A woman's eyes were deemed an important feature of her charm due to the

---

[233] The *wāw* disjunctive of וּלְלָבָן שְׁתֵּי בָנוֹת initiates the parenthetical material, lit., "Now belonging to Laban were two daughters."

[234] *HALOT* 2.513.

[235] She named her first son "Reuben" (cf. comments on 29:32), a possible play on the idea of eyesight; see M. Seelenfreund and S. Schneider, "Leah's Eyes," *JBQ* 25 (1997): 18–22.

[236] R. Gradwohl, "Waren Leas Augen hässlich?" *VT* 49 (1999): 119–24.

wearing of the traditional veil, covering the face except the eyes and cheeks (Song 4:1; 6:7), including a betrothed woman (e.g., 24:65–67; Song 1:7 with 15; 4:1,3; 6:7; 38:13–14). The same association of the term of beauty "tender" (*rakkâ*) and a "veil" (*ṣammâ*) appears in the personification of the "Virgin Daughter of Babylon" (Isa 47:1–2). "But Rachel . . ."[237] (v. 17) provides the contrast to Leah. Her shapely figure *(tō'ar)* exhibited her beauty, lit., "beautiful of shape and beautiful of appearance." The NIV's "lovely" translates the word *yāpeh* ("beautiful"), a term that is used of both men and women (e.g., 12:11,14; 1 Sam 16:12) as well as animal stock (e.g., "sleek," 41:2). Joseph is described with the same expression (masculine gender) used of Rachel: "Now Joseph was well-built and handsome" (39:6).[238] The phrase "beautiful" or "lovely in form" *(yĕpat tō'ar)* by itself describes beautiful women (Deut 21:11; Esth 2:7), and "beautiful in appearance" *(yĕpat mar'eh)* is also used alone for characterizing attractive women, including Sarah (12:11,16; cf. 2 Sam 14:27; also David, 1 Sam 17:42).[239]

29:18–20 Jacob "loved" Rachel (v. 18a; cf. vv. 20,20), which explains his choice of the younger sister. The word "loved" *('āhab)* is broadly and typically used when describing the affection of a person for another person (or thing), including romantic (sexual) passion (e.g., 34:3; Judg 16:4,15; 1 Sam 1:5; 2 Sam 13:1,15; 1 Kgs 11:1–2; 2 Chr 11:21; Esth 2:17; Sol 1:3). Isaac had the same high regard for Rebekah (24:67). Since Jacob was penniless, he had no means to take a wife; but he could contract his labor as a hired worker, substituting labor for the traditional betrothal gift presented by the groom (*mōhar,* Exod 22:17[16]; cf. Deut 22:29). "Seven years" probably indicated a considerable period of time, which was a handsome offer that Laban would relish (cf. Exod 21:2; Deut 15:12,18), especially for the grueling nature of the work (31:38–40). Mosaic law required all debts cancelled at the end of seven years (Deut 15:1; 31:10).

Mention of Rachel as the "younger daughter" ironically intimates the problem that his choice created for Laban and thus for himself. Laban accepts the offer, explaining that she will marry someone, and it is better that she marry Jacob (v. 19). Laban probably has in mind that Jacob as a relative would be the preferred choice (endogamy), though he may have considered Jacob's love for her as well. Laban played up the notion of their kinship again (cf. vv. 14–15) so as to perpetuate the impression of goodwill. Jacob faithfully completed the season of seven years, for his desire for Rachel made them like "a few days" (v. 20; cf. 27:44). The author returns to the love that Jacob has, explaining why Jacob willingly locked himself into

---

[237] The *wāw* disjunctive functions adversatively, וְרָחֵל הָיְתָה.

[238] Similar Hb. describes Queen Esther (2:7); see next note.

[239] The synonym is טוֹבַת מַרְאֶה, lit., "good in appearance," which is used of Rebekah (24:21; 26:7), Bathsheba (2 Sam 11:2), and Vashti (Esth 1:11) and Esther (2:7).

the deal. Also, from the reader's perspective, knowing the extent of his ardor for the girl makes the deception more crushing for the suitor, creating sympathy for Jacob.

Laban Substitutes Leah (29:21–27). **29:21–22** Verse 21 contains Jacob's request for Rachel's hand, coming immediately at the conclusion of the allotted period. His brusque insistence, "Give me!" (imperative of *yāhab*), suggests a man's impatience and perhaps frustration.[240] No reply from Laban is recorded. Rather, he obfuscates by initiating the wedding festival. The feast, however, will celebrate Leah's marriage! The direct verbal answer to Jacob's demand comes too late for Jacob, when Laban explains the substitution of Leah wherein "give" *(nātan)* appears twice (vv. 26–27; cf. *yāhab*, 30:1). "I want to lie with her" indicates the consummation of the marriage and also contains another sad irony for Jacob, since it is the moment of ultimate deceit. Laban takes advantage of the traditional wedding festival, since the "feast" *(mišteh)* involved drinking wine (v. 22). A betrothal period probably required the wearing of a veil, even to the wedding night itself. K. van der Toorn proposes on the basis of ancient Near Eastern practice that a groom veiled his bride ceremonially to induct her into the family at the time of the bridal payment, confirming the arrangement. If this were the case in Laban's household, Rebekah and Leah probably wore veils into the bedchamber (cf. comments on 24:65–67; contrast comments on 38:13–14).[241] A "tipsy," unsuspecting Jacob may help explain how he slept with his bride unaware of her identity. Since for Jacob the work for Rachel was short-lived in his mind and heart ("a few days," v. 20),[242] the gaiety of his wedding night must have turned quickly into a demoralizing, new seven-year service.

29:23–24 Verse 23 describes Laban's sleight of hand that "night," utilizing terms of sexual innuendo: "took" *(lāqaḥ)*, "gave" (causative of *bô'*, lit., "caused [her] to go [to him]"), and "lay" *(qal* of *bô'*, lit., "he went [to her]") commonly refer to marriage and/or sexual relations. Once Jacob engages in sexual relations with the virgin Leah, the action is irrevocable, requiring Jacob to fulfil his honorable duty to the woman (cf. Exod 22:16; Deut 22:28–29). Verse 24's early mention of Leah's handmaiden Zilpah, who was Laban's bridal gift (cf. 24:59), is out of order in the sequence of events, since the bride's identity is not yet revealed. This verse presupposes, however, the events of v. 25. Reference to her handmaiden fits this point in the story, since eventually

---

[240] *IBHS* §40.2.5c notes that יְהַב is Aramaic and rarely occurs in Hebrew except for the imperative form as here, from which is the urgent exclamation, "Come on . . ."!

[241] K. van der Toorn, "The Significance of the Veil in the Ancient Near East," in *Pomegranates and Golden Bells: Studies in Biblical, Jewish, and Near Eastern Ritual, Law, and Literature in Honor of Jacob Milgrom* (Winona Lake: Eisenbrauns, 1995), 327–39 (esp. 330–36).

[242] Contrast v. 30, "another seven years," so Wenham, *Genesis 16–50*, 237.

by sexual relations with Leah and her surrogate Zilpah, Jacob will obtain eight sons, including his firstborn (v. 32; 30:9–21; 35:23,26). Zilpah became the prolific ancestress of sixteen sons (46:18). Also "servant girl" and "handmaiden," both rendering the term *šiphâ*, recalls Hagar and the dissension she and Sarah experienced (16:1–8; 25:12). Trouble is on the horizon!

29:25–27 The "morning" light makes possible Jacob's discovery of the ruse. The terse construction highlights the surprise, lit., "And, behold, she [was] Leah"! Jacob's complaint echoes the protests of Pharaoh and Abimelech when duped by Abraham and Isaac: "What have you done?" (12:18; 20:9; 26:10; cf. Exod 14:11; Jonah 1:10). God utters similar language when he censures the snake ("you have done this," 3:14) and condemns Cain ("What have you done?" 4:10). Jacob's outrage also reverberates Rebekah's warning concerning Esau's anger because of what "you [Jacob] did to him" (27:45). Jacob's indignation is a fitting answer to the crime he perpetrated against Esau. Jewish midrash wondered aloud how Leah would have justified her duplicity in the matter. She only followed his example, for when his father Isaac called out to him "Esau," he answered to it, and likewise during the night when Jacob called out "Rachel," she too answered to it (*Gen. Rab.* 70.19). Laban's deception though will have its payback too, for he will later have the same complaint concerning his nephew, "What have you done?" (31:26). Jacob's second question, "Why *[lammâ]* have you deceived me?" in effect answers what Laban has "done" to him. By this question, Jacob asks for an explanation of the purpose for the trick.[243] Laban, of course, viewed his deed resulting from a principled stance, in keeping with the customs of his people (see below). "Deceived" (*rāmâ*) translates one of several terms denoting fraud in Genesis (cp. others at 3:13; 27:36; 31:26). The exact form in our verse occurs again in 1 Sam 28:12, describing Saul's deception of the witch of Endor (cf. Josh 9:22). The verb *rāmâ* often describes personal betrayal by family (1 Sam 19:7), servants (2 Sam 19:26[27]), or friends (1 Chr 12:18; Prov 26:19; Lam 1:19).

Does Laban offer a puny excuse (v. 26), one no better than Abraham's or Isaac's vain attempt (20:12–13; 26:7–9), or does his explanation have some underlying merit (cf. 34:7; 2 Sam 13:12)? If the MT "we will give you" (v. 27) is correct,[244] his wording mitigates his culpability by the inclusive verbiage that refers to the community rather than the singular "I will give you." Jewish midrash, for example, imagines the dialogue of a meeting between Laban and the elders of the city who plot the deception (*Gen. Rab.* 70.19). By another twist of irony, "older one" translates *habbĕkîrâ* (fem.), lit., "the firstborn," which is the comparable term *bĕkôr* (masc.), referring to Esau in 27:19,32. Mention of

---

[243] T. Nakarai, "LMH and MDU in the TANAK," *HS* 23 (1982): 45–50.

[244] וְנִתְּנָה (MT, *Tgs. Onq.; Ps.-J.*), but the versions have the singular וְאֶתֵּן, SP, LXX, Syr., *Tg. Neof.*, Vg. (see *BHS*); or וְאֶתְּנָה, cp. Exod 24:12; 1 Kgs 13:7; 21:2; 2 Kgs 18:23; Isa 36:8.

the "bridal week," lit., "(the) seven" *(šĕbūaʿ),* refers to the festal events of the week-long celebration (e.g., Judg 14:12,17; *Tob* 11:18; *Add Esth* 2:18).

By his treachery, Laban achieves two favorable outcomes: first, he ensures that both daughters marry, for Jacob's love compels him to marry Rachel; and second, he ensures another seven years labor from his industrious nephew. Oddly, we can say that the man's avarice coupled with Jacob's passionate love for Rachel created the reckless marriage of the patriarch to two sisters, a practice to be forbidden in Mosaic law (Lev 18:18). Laban's counteroffer to Jacob is essentially the same as that which was agreed upon initially for Rachel, except here Jacob receives Rachel at the start instead of waiting until the conclusion of another seven years (v. 27). By this arrangement, Jacob would be assured of acquiring Rachel, removing the possibility of another crooked deal.

JACOB WEDS RACHEL (29:28–30). **29:28–29** The episode concludes by a summary description of the fulfillment of the agreement, in which Jacob received Rachel and labored for another seven years. Repetition of the similar language describing the first marriage to Leah (vv. 20,23–24) buttresses the impression of hardship that Jacob underwent, laboring twice as hard for the woman he loved. Also the persistent appearance of the word group "work" *(ʿ-b-d)* in vv. 27–30 and the double occurrence of "another seven years" in vv. 27,29 convey the same sentiment. The passage picks up the language of Jacob and makes known as above that Jacob did precisely as laid out by Laban (v. 28), astutely avoiding any further entrapment or miscalculation. The narrative description of Laban furnishing Bilhah for a servant to Rachel (v. 29) differs from the earlier account of Zilpah (v. 24). By placing "Rachel" toward the start of the clause (v. 29), the author infers her favored position over Leah. Since Rachel remained childless for years, the gift of a maiden proved to be more important to her than in the case for Leah. Bilhah bore two sons in Rachel's place (30:3–7; 35:25) and was the victim of Reuben's (firstborn) illicit relations (35:22; 49:4).

29:30 That Jacob "loved Rachel more than Leah"[245] (v. 30) was the soil that yields sibling jealousy (29:31,33; 30:1,15). Jacob's penchant for preferential treatment (cp. Isaac and Rebekah, 25:28) proved destructive for his household in unforeseen ways (cf. 37:3). The occurrence of "also" *(gam)* twice in v. 30 (MT) is commonly emended,[246] but its repetition may have a rhetorical function, implying that Jacob's true love became the "also wife" through Laban's duplicity. Rachel was only the second wife,[247] a fitting answer to Jacob's own treachery who usurped his firstborn brother, making him the "also son."

---

[245] *IBHS* §14.4e prefers a comparison of exclusion, "He loved Rachel *rather than* Leah."

[246] וַיָּבֹא גַּם אֶל־רָחֵל וַיֶּאֱהַב גַּם־אֶת־רָחֵל מִלֵּאָה, "and he went in also unto Rachel, and he loved also Rachel more than Leah"; גַּם² is absent in the LXX (cf. *BHS*) and most EVs; but see AV ("also" [2x]) and NASB, HCSB ("indeed").

[247] Westermann, *Genesis 12–36,* 468.

6. Birth of Jacob's Children (29:31–30:24)

G. W. Coats considers the present account a "digression" in the Jacob-Laban narrative,[248] providing a series of birth reports that is subsumed under the broader narrative of the conflict between Jacob and Laban (25:1–31:55[32:1]). This observation rightly sees that the birth reports serve the broader narrative purpose, but they should not be viewed as secondary to the main plot. The birth reports fulfill a strategic role in the narrative development of Jacob's sojourn in Paddan Aram. The Jacob-Laban events recount the exile of Jacob, whom the Lord blesses and returns to the land of his father, according to promise (28:10–22). Our chapter shows that the Lord blesses the patriarch with numerous offspring, compelling Jacob to obtain his own purse and land, presumably in his native homeland of Canaan. Hence, at the birth of Joseph (30:23–24), the orientation of the Jacob-Laban story turns us toward Jacob's return to Canaan. From this point forward, Jacob devises a way to extricate himself from the hardships imposed by Laban, generating an independent household who are positioned to receive Isaac's inheritance. That the children born in Paddan Aram number twelve (including Dinah) symbolizes the full house of Jacob-Israel, although he was yet to return to Canaan and father the twelfth tribe (cf. Benjamin, 35:17–18). By this series of twelve birth announcements, the author indicates that the fathers of Israel were born outside the land, as was their ancestor Abraham, and that the land awaited them to inhabit. This message resonates with the wilderness generation whom Moses brought to the edge of Canaan.

After the tug-of-war between Laban and Jacob over the marriage to his daughters Leah and Rachel (29:1–30), the Jacob narrative turns to the account of their children. Nonetheless, strife cannot escape any part of Jacob's life in Paddan Aram. The sisters rival one another for the affections of their husband, utilizing their power to conceive. Every stratagem is undertaken to gain the upper hand, including prayer, substitute wives, badgering, bartering, and superstition (mandrakes). The explanations for the names of the children reflect the sisters' ongoing conflict. The household by virtue of the children's names will always bear witness to the struggle that Jacob could not escape. Jacob himself contributed to the cause of the sibling battle, for he loved Rachel more (29:30), making it clear that he came by Leah solely at the insistence of her father (29:26). At the commencement of our passage (29:31,33), the background statement that "Leah was not loved" recalls for us the results of Laban's sham, explaining the strife that follows. As we noted in the introduction to the Jacob narrative as a whole, the author built the Jacob narrative by embedding three concentric accounts of family struggle: the sibling strife between Jacob and

---

[248] Coats, *Genesis,* 209.

Esau (27:1–28:9; 33:1–20), the Jacob-Laban disputes (29:1–31:55[32:1]), and the sibling struggle of Leah and Rachel (29:31–30:24). Jacob experiences contentions outside and inside his home, both publicly and privately.

Although the struggle motif is paramount, the events in our passage also evidence the provision that God promised Jacob at Bethel (28:13–15). As in the scenarios of other struggles, the Lord employs the disputation to bring about blessings for Jacob. Here the narrative does not explicitly mention the promises or the key word "blessing," yet the theological contribution of this passage to the overarching message of the Jacob story is sure. The Lord uses the competition of the women to obtain an assembly of offspring for the patriarch, producing eleven sons and one daughter. Despite the imprudence, if not immorality (Lev 18:18), of marrying sisters, God derives from their unions the primogenitors of the tribes of Israel. Leah births the fathers of significant tribal members for the life of Israel, including Levi and Judah, and Rachel bears Joseph, whose sons Ephraim and Manasseh populate vast allotments in the cisjordan and transjordan regions. Moreover, the superstition of the women ("mandrakes," 30:14–16) does not prevent the Lord from supplying children. Repeatedly, the naming of the children evidence the women's conviction that the Lord "saw" (29:31–32) and "heard" (29:33; 30:6,17,22) their prayers, granting them children. In most cases the children's names explicitly memorialized this reliance on the Lord (cp. comments on 16:11). From the narrative we see that this is the viewpoint of the author as well. It is remarkable that none of the children's names, however, exhibits a certain theophoric element (i.e. divine name *yah* or *'ēl*). This follows the nontheophoric character of the names of the three chief patriarchs themselves. Our passage as a whole nonetheless is another monument testifying to the grace of God extended to the patriarch.

Another way the passage contributes to the Jacob narrative is the question of inheritance that has played a large part in the Abraham and Jacob narratives. N. Steinberg suggests that this is the underlying fundamental struggle between the wives as they vie for power in behalf of their sons.[249] There is no explicit announcement of who succeeds Jacob as the chief recipient of the promises. This departs from the former sibling rivalries in which Isaac (21:12) and Jacob (25:23; 27:27–29) are so designated by divine authority. When we consider the matriarchal patterns of Sarah and Rebekah, we expect Joseph or Benjamin, the sons of the barren and preferred wife, Rachel, to succeed their father. Moreover, she fits the type casting of a wife discovered at the well exhibited by Rebekah (chap. 24). Yet Leah and Rachel (including the surrogates) have equal status as legitimate wives whose children can make their claim. By this genealogy of the sons, the passage implies the tension of inheritance that looms in the background, subsumed under the struggles of Jacob-Laban and the wives.

---

[249] N. Steinberg, *Kinship and Marriage in Genesis* (Minneapolis: Fortress, 1993), 102–4.

The subsequent accounts of Reuben's incest (35:22), Simeon's and Levi's crimes (chap. 34), and Judah's sin (chap. 38) coupled with Joseph's approval by his father appears to point in his direction (cf. 48:22; 49:6). Compared to the earlier narratives of Abraham and Jacob, the issue of inheritance does not have the same sustaining force in the Joseph account, though it is decidedly in the background. That Joseph was the appointed heir is further supported by the narrative interest in Joseph by the author, who devotes chapters to Joseph's jeopardy at the hands of his brothers and his servitude in Egypt from which he ascends to secure a future for the Jacob-Israel clan. Yet this is not the case, for we discover that Jacob's blessing includes all of the twelve sons-tribes (chap. 49). Nevertheless, there is one member whose history hints at his future dominion over his brothers, namely, Judah. This is implied in 49:8–12, where he is described in regal terms (cp. 27:29; 37:10; 49:8). Another tacit indication of Judah's succession is the circumstance of his children's births by Tamar, whose twins, Perez and Zerah, wrestle for primacy (38:28–30). This sibling conflict is the signature for patriarchal succession in the Book of Genesis.

COMPOSITION. Source critics found in our passage evidence for the Yahwist (J) source with some information derived from the Elohist (E).[250] Among other evidence, proponents point to the "clumsiness and redundancy"[251] of the explanations for the names Issachar, Zebulun, and Joseph. Coats finds that the absence of an explanation for the naming of Dinah in v. 21 shows that it is secondary, dependent on the narrative in chap. 34.[252] Although Westermann does not identify two "documents," he effectively divides the passage into two "layers." An older narrative story related the rivalry of the sisters (29:31–32 with 30:1–6; and 30:14–18 with vv. 22–24), and a later hand included the genealogical insertions (29:33–35; 30:4–13,19–24) and made some changes in the reason for the names (39:32b; 30:6b,17–18,22–24).[253] Van Seters follows his theory of an exilic Yahwist as author when he repudiates the division of the passage. He acknowledges that it is foreign to the present context, reflecting an earlier tradition about the origin of the tribes. The Yahwist integrated it into the Laban-Jacob narrative by continuing the narrative line of Jacob's love for Rachel and the idea of strife that permeates the context. This earlier tradition does not know the seven-year parameter of the Jacob-Laban story in which all twelve children are born nor Jacob's pastoral work.[254] Carr agrees with Van Seters that 29:31–30:24 is secondary to its context, but he views it as an integral part of the early, original "prepromise Jacob narrative."[255]

---

[250] Speiser characterizes the passage as a "complex patchwork" of J and E whose inconsistencies remained (*Genesis*, 232–33).

[251] von Rad believes, however, that the passage consists of numerous small pieces from J and E (*Genesis*, 293).

[252] Coats, *Genesis*, 216.

[253] Westermann, *Genesis 12–36*, 471–72.

[254] Van Seters, *Prologue to History*, 205–6, 278.

[255] Carr, *Reading the Fractures of Genesis*, 257, 263.

The naming of twelve children in our passage and the traditional configuration of Israel's twelve tribes has generated much discussion in the history of interpretation.[256] Variations in the twelve members listed and their order in the tribal lists of Israel (e.g., Gen 29–30; 49; Num 26; Deut 33) and the mixed picture for tribal associations in the time of settlement (e.g., Judg 5) reflect a complex picture of Israel's tribal formation. Here Benjamin is absent, whose birth occurs in Canaan (35:18); the appearance of Dinah is reckoned a later addition, rounding out the expected twelve constituents. Although Benjamin does not occur in this listing, Rachel's explanation for the name "Joseph" anticipates Benjamin's membership in the twelve sons (30:24; cf. 35:17).

M. Noth's reconstruction of a twelve-tribe amphictyony assumed, as did his predecessors, that each eponymous ancestor stood for a corresponding tribal entity whose sibling relations, reflected in genealogical tradition, portrayed (more or less) tribal histories (memories) and their social and political connections.[257] The genealogies of Jacob's sons-tribes in 29:31–30:24; 49:1–17; and Num 26:4–51 provided the starting point for Noth's famed reconstruction of premonarchic Israel, whose twelve tribes were an Israelite amphictyony, analogous to the Delphi league (sixth century B.C.) of twelve tribes with a central shrine. The six Leah tribes formed a six-member amphictyony (located in Judah) that was extended into twelve members when new tribes, beginning with the Rachel tribes of Joseph and Benjamin (Israel), arose in the land. Key to Noth's theory was his belief that the twelve-tribe system could only have occurred in the land, not in the wilderness as the Bible portrays. Although this theory became scholarship's orthodoxy for fifty years, formidable arguments opposing it have resulted in its rejection by most today.[258] Since the Galilean tribes Issachar and Zebulun, for example, cannot be satisfactorily explained in the theory that the Leah tribes were southern in origin, R. Frankel proposed a new division based on the later geographical and geopolitical context actually known to the author.[259] He divides the tribes into two groups, those six whose histories are mentioned as individuals in the narrative of Genesis (Leah's first four and Rachel's two sons) and the six

---

[256] Westermann, relying on Weippert's study, reports that the twelve tribes are mentioned twenty-eight times in the OT, including these Genesis references: 29:31–30:24; 35:16–20; 35:22–28; and 49:1–17 (*Genesis 12–36,* 472).

[257] Detailed discussion occurs in the 1930 publication *Das System der zwölf Stämme Israels,* which Noth summarized in *Geschichte Israel* (1958), i.e., *The History of Israel,* rev. trans. (New York: Harper & Row, 1960), 85–97. Sarna, e.g., reflects this approach to the genealogies of Jacob but contends that the social and political associations they portray reflect presettlement tribal realities (*Genesis,* 400–403).

[258] For a history of the opposition to Noth's theory, see T. L. Thompson, "Martin Noth and the History of Israel," in *The History of Israel's Traditions: The Heritage of Martin Noth,* JSOTSup 182 (Sheffield: Sheffield Academic Press, 1994), 81–90. Consult the bibliography in A. D. H. Mayes, "Amphictyony," *ABD* 1.212–16, who provides a convenient summary of weaknesses, and add C. H. J. de Geus, *The Tribes of Israel: An Investigation into Some of the Presuppositions of Martin Noth's Amphictyony Hypothesis,* SSN 18 (Assen and Amsterdam: Van Gorcum, 1976).

[259] R. Frankel, "The Matriarchal Groupings of the Tribal Eponyms: A Reappraisal," in *The World of Genesis,* JSOTSup 257 (Sheffield: Sheffield Academic Press, 1998), 121–25.

Galilean tribes whose locations are outlying (Leah's two younger sons and the concubines' four). When does this configuration best suit Palestine's geopolitical history? Frankel assigns it to the period after the Assyrian conquest and beyond.

In its place are a number of competing social-scientific explanations for the formation of Israel in the premonarchic period.[260] Since the collapse of Noth's paradigm for the formation of Israel's beginnings, however, the genealogies of Jacob's sons tend to be read as solely political allegory with little or no value for discovering the *real Israel*.[261] That the sons were individuals and also represented their respective descendants is apparent from the orientation of Jacob's and Moses' blessings (49:1–28; Deut 33). The common practice of Genesis using the figures of the patriarchs as a foreshadowing device explains the linkage between individual and tribe. Jacob's sons in chaps. 29–30 are individuals, as von Rad and others acknowledged.[262]

By the discussion of the literary structure shown below, it is transparent that the passage exhibits a coherent scheme that testifies to a unified whole. As Wenham remarks, the notion that the puns on the children's names could have existed independently of the context does not appear likely since the explanations rely on the narrative account of the sisters' strife.[263] That the mix of genealogy and narrative interlude was a known genre in the ancient Near East can be shown from before Babylonian times, such as the Sumerian King List (vol. 1A, p. 432), down to the classical Greek period, including Hesiod's Catalogue of Women.[264] There is no reason to divide the passage into different sources on the basis of genre. Moreover, the mention of Dinah, the only daughter included, does not require a late hand, since her name provides a rhetorical function in the present context. As Rebekah's appearance in the Nahor genealogy (22:20–24) prepares us for chap. 24, Dinah's name anticipates the Shechem events in chap. 34 that describe her rape. By identifying Dinah as the daughter of Leah, the fury of her full-blooded brothers, Simeon and Levi, is understandable (34:25). The absence of an etymology for Dinah intentionally diverges from the naming of the sons, a reflection of a daughter's inferior value in the competition. But more importantly, the mention of the name "Dinah" itself symbolizes strife, for she is the victim of conquest (34:2) that ultimately led to the clash that Jacob had with his sons and that of his Canaanite neighbors (34:30–31; 49:5–7).

When we consider 29:31–30:24 as a whole, it fits comfortably in the immediate context, bridging the two rounds of conflict between Jacob and Laban over

---

[260] See P. McNutt, *Reconstructing the Society of Ancient Israel* (London: SPCK/Louisville: Westminster John Knox, 1999) and N. Gottwald, *The Politics of Ancient Israel* (Louisville: Westminster John Knox, 2001).

[261] Gottwald, *Politics,* 37, who comments, "The progenitors are later Israel in nuce" (for bibliography see p. 267, n. 3).

[262] E.g., von Rad, *Genesis,* 297; Westermann, *Genesis 12–36,* 472; and Van Seters, *Prologue to History,* 205–7.

[263] Wenham, *Genesis 16–50,* 242.

[264] M. L. West, *The Hesiodic Catalogue of Women* (Clarendon/New York: Oxford University Press, 1985), whose work is frequently cited by Van Seters, *Prologue to History,* cf. esp. 89–90, 197–99.

"wages" (29:15; 30:28). Marriage to Rachel (29:18) prompted the first quarrel, and the birth of Rachel's first child (30:28) initiated the second round of conflict. The notion of wages appears in the midst of the genealogy by the sale of the mandrakes and the subsequent pun on "Issachar" (30:16–18). The pericope does not directly refer to the Jacob-Laban episodes, but its various allusions do not permit us to lose sight of them. Jacob's love for Rachel and its implications are the most obvious (29:31 with 29:17–18,30,32,33,34; 30:3,6,8,15,18,20,22–24). The preferential treatment of Esau and Jacob by their parents (25:28) that initiated the schism of the brothers is revisited by Jacob's preference over Leah.

We have mentioned repeatedly the strife that the sisters underwent, but there is also the strife that Jacob and Rachel experienced over the bitter absence of children (30:1–3). "Give me *[hābâ]* children" and "angry" *(ʿap)* echo the earlier tensions of Jacob-Esau and Jacob-Laban (30:1–2 with 27:45; 29:21). Jacob's retort to Rachel's complaint that he cannot usurp the will of God recalls Sarah's complaint of infertility to her husband in 16:1–2. Rachel's alternative of the slave Bilhah possesses the same language of Sarah's proposal: "sleep" *(bôʾ)*, "maidservant" *(šipḥâ)*, and "I can build *[bānâ]* a family through her *[mimennâ]"* (30:3 with 16:2). In effect we have the Sarah-Hagar strife revived.

The appropriateness of the passage in its immediate and broad contexts, the cohesive symmetry of the passage (see "Structure"), and the many verbal allusions to earlier passages lead us to conclude that 29:31–30:24 was authored for the present context.

STRUCTURE. References to Rachel's barrenness in 29:31 and the birth of her first son (Joseph) in 30:24 form the borders of the passage. Although the passage concerns the children born to Jacob as a whole, the important story line is the absence of children by Rachel, Jacob's beloved wife. By God's intervention, her tormented life will be graciously reversed (30:22). Four discreetly marked parts make up this unit. The term "saw" *(rāʾâ)* introduces the first three (29:31; 30:1,9), and "remembered" *(zākar)* prefaces the final, climactic unit (30:22). This latter term in Genesis when used of "God" as the subject expresses the deliverance of Noah and Abraham (i.e., Lot; see comments on 8:1; 19:29). Also the passage regularly plays on the word "hear" *(šāmaʿ)*, indicating that the Lord both sees and hears the prayers of the women (29:33; 30:6,17,22; cf. 16:11; 21:17).

Unlike the other subunits, the third and most extensive subunit (30:9–21) groups two genealogies under the same banner statement ("Leah saw"): Zilpah's children (30:9–14) and Leah's additional children (30:15–21). Verses 9 and 21 form an inclusion by demonstrating the turnaround in Leah's potency; she stops having children, supplies Zilpah, but at eating "mandrakes" she becomes fertile again (30:16). The juxtaposition of the superstitious "mandrakes" in v. 16 and the intervention of God in v. 17 ("God listened") provides the author's understanding of human activity and divine will. Despite the superstitions of the women, the Lord overlooks their ignorance and answers their desires.

The introductory verses (29:31; 30:1; 30:9; 30:22) to the four parts exhibit a chiasmus (ABB'A') in which the names of God appear in the outside legs: "the LORD saw" (A), "Rachel saw" (B), "Leah saw" (B'), "then God remembered" (A'). That references to the Lord's interventions envelope the whole of the section fosters the author's belief that Providence had ensured children in accord with the promises at Bethel (28:13–15). Also the structural arrangement possesses another inversion (ABB'A'), naming the legitimate mothers and their children outside and the concubine mothers and their children inside: Leah (A), Bilhah (B), Zilpah (B'), and Rachel (A'). When we consider the surrogate roles of Bilhah and Zilpah, we discover this arrangement: Leah, Rachel (Bilhah), Leah (Zilpah), and Rachel. The intervals of the opposing wives and their surrogates enhance the rivalry that the passage focuses on.

The birth and naming of the children follow two formulas (with minor variations). The birth formula is "PN_1 became pregnant and gave birth to a son" (29:32); contextual or grammatical requirements produce many but slight variations (29:33,34,35; 30:5,7,17,19,23; cf. 4:1,17; 16:4; 21:2; 38:3,4). The second formula is the naming formula. It typically involves wordplay between the child's name and the mother's (Leah, Rachel) explanation of the name, which may precede or follow the giving of the name (exception is Dinah). The wordplay occurs by the same or similar root appearing in the explanation of the name (see vol. 1A, p. 264, n. 251). The lawful wives also provide the names of those sons born to their handmaidens. The usual formula is "she named him PN_1" (29:32,33; 30:8,18; cf. 19:37,38; 35:18; Exod 2:10), which may appear with a slight grammatical variation (i.e., nontranslated object marker, 30:11,13,20,21,24; cf. 4:25; 38:4,5). Other formulations include "therefore he was named PN_1" (29:34; cf. 25:30; 27:36; 31:48) and "therefore she named him PN_1" (29:35; 30:6). In most cases the narration and/or the woman's explanation attribute the pregnancy to God.

(1) Leah's Children (29:31–35)

[31]When the LORD saw that Leah was not loved, he opened her womb, but Rachel was barren. [32]Leah became pregnant and gave birth to a son. She named him Reuben, for she said, "It is because the LORD has seen my misery. Surely my husband will love me now."

[33]She conceived again, and when she gave birth to a son she said, "Because the LORD heard that I am not loved, he gave me this one too." So she named him Simeon.

[34]Again she conceived, and when she gave birth to a son she said, "Now at last my husband will become attached to me, because I have borne him three sons." So he was named Levi.

[35]She conceived again, and when she gave birth to a son she said, "This time I will praise the LORD." So she named him Judah. Then she stopped having children.

This first subunit establishes the immediate context of the running battle between Leah and Rachel that pervades 29:31–30:24. Verse 31 provides an introduction to this paragraph but also for the whole of the pericope. Verses 32–35 identify each of Leah's initial group of four sons, including an explanatory pun on the sound of the name (not an actual linguistic etymology).[265]

INTRODUCTION (29:31).   **29:31**   In our discussion of the structure (see above), we observed the role of the opening words that distinguish the present paragraph, "the LORD saw" (v. 31a). This one phrase sets the theological tenor of the whole pericope by showing that the children are a divine provision (cf. 28:13–15). It also exhibits the Lord's compassion for the neglected wife, and her pregnancy spurs on the competition among the women, redounding to the number of Jacob's offspring. The contrast between the two women involves two interrelated levels: loved versus unloved and fertile versus infertile.[266] By the latter level the unloved hopes to become precious to her husband (v. 34).[267]

That a husband would prefer one wife above the other was so common that a future law was required for dividing the estate of the father (Deut 21:15–17; cf. 1 Sam 1:5–6). When we consider vv. 30–31 together, the verbiage "loved" and "not loved" are antonyms, describing the preference of Jacob (cf. also Deut 21:15). "Not loved" (NIV) or "unloved" (NJB, NAB, REB, NJPS, HCSB) translates śĕnûʾâ (also v. 33), whose word group (ś-n-ʾ) typically means "hate," as in describing Joseph's brothers who "hated" him (37:4–5,8). Thus the LXX *(miseō)* and some EVs translate the verse "Leah was hated" (e.g., AV, RSV). The severity of emotion reflected by this term may vary from sheer aversion to vehement animosity (e.g., 24:60; 26:27; Ps 25:19; Prov 19:7; 25:17).[268] Since "hate" is the semantic opposite of "love" (e.g., Ps 11:5; Eccl 3:8; Amos 5:15), śĕnûʾâ is one means of expressing the idea of "unloved" or "rejected" (e.g., Isa 54:6; Mal 1:2–3). The word śĕnûʾa in Deut 21:15,17 describes a husband's aversion to a second wife (e.g., rendered "disliked," NRSV; "unloved," NLT; the LXX again has *miseō*). It is difficult to saddle Jacob with the modern notion of hatred, but that he had resentment toward Leah may explain why no number of sons she bore could reconcile him to her. That Leah's firstborn, Reuben, would betray his father rather than bring him delight was one of the many ironies in their relationship. Here the sense of śĕnûʾa is that Leah is not the preferred wife. According to the sages, one of the four aberrant features that destabilizes the welfare of society is "an unloved *[śĕnûʾa]* woman who is married" (Prov 30:23).

LEAH'S SONS (29:32–35).   The beginning group of offspring is Leah's four

---

[265] For more on the tribal histories of Jacob's sons, see the patriarch's blessing in 49:1–28.
[266] By the *wāw* adversative ("but Rachel was barren") of וְרָחֵל עֲקָרָה the contrast is explicit.
[267] For the imagery of the "opened" and "closed" womb (v. 31; 30:22), see comments on 12:2; 20:18; for the word "barren" see comments on 11:30.
[268] A. H. Konkel, "שָׂנֵא," *NIDOTTE* 3.1256–60.

sons. For the birth and name formulae, consult the discussion above under the heading "Structure."

Reuben (29:32).   **29:32**   Leah's explanation for the name "Reuben" *(rěʾûbēn),* meaning "see, [a] son!" is a pun on "has seen" *(rāʾâ;*cp. the pun on "hears," Simeon, v. 33). The name also corresponds to the narration, "When the LORD saw *[rāʾāʾ]*" in v. 31a. Moreover, Reuben's name may be suggestive of Leah's eyes (29:17). The "misery" *(ʿonî)* that she has in mind must be her neglected state since she connects it with her husband's love. A mother's "misery" explains the naming of Ishmael (16:11) and the vow of Hannah (1 Sam 1:11). The word "misery" appears in the Pentateuch for diverse human hardships that the Lord "hears" or "sees," that is, resolves, especially Israel's servitude in Egypt (e.g., 31:42; 41:52; Exod 3:7,17; 4:31; Deut 26:7).[269]

That the result Leah cherishes is her husband's affections reflects the motivation of the women for securing their sons (v. 32c). For Leah the birth of Jacob's firstborn must procure her husband's love, at last![270] Commentators often attribute the last sentence to a second etymology (see, e.g., NAB, NJPS), giving the name "Reuben" two different explanations. In this case the latter half of "Reuben" *(rěʾûbēn)* is a pun on *yeʾěhābanî,* "[my husband] will love me." Source critics once regularly recognized this contribution as coming from the parallel Elohist account. However, the absence of the introductory clause "she said" indicates that the last sentence is a continuation of the pun, providing further elaboration, not a competing etymology.

Simeon (29:33).   **29:33**   The narration assumes for the birth of Simeon the same involvement of the Lord. Leah expresses it explicitly in her explanation of the child's name. "Simeon" *(šimʿôn)* plays on the word "heard" *(šāmaʿ;* cf. "Ishmael," 16:11). "Too" *(gam,* "also") clues us that what the Lord "heard" was her cries arising from her "misery" (v. 31). Thus the birth of her first son did not meet her objective. Perhaps a second son will garner Jacob's love! Leah was not the last misguided parent who hoped a pregnancy could repair a fractured marriage. Her explanation "not loved" *(śěnûʾâ)*[271] confirms from her perspective what the narration already noted (v. 30).[272]

Levi (29:34).   **29:34**   "Now at last" expresses Leah's frustration at failing to win her husband's love. Three sons are too great a blessing for him to deny her, she must think.[273] The historic patriarchs Adam, Noah, and Terah fathered three sons. For the other children, Leah and Rachel name their children, but this

---

[269] On Reuben see also comments on 30:14; 35:22; 37:21–22,29; 49:3–4.

[270] כִּי עַתָּה is asseverative, "surely now," heading the clause.

[271] The NRSV translates "I am hated," unlike "unloved" in v. 31, suggesting that Leah in her pain exaggerated her unwanted state.

[272] On Simeon see also comments at chap. 34; 42:24; 49:5–6.

[273] ". . . on the principle that a threefold cord is not easily broken" (Skinner, *Genesis,* 386).

is not the case for Levi ("he was named Levi"[274]). The naming of "Levi" *(lēwî)* plays on the sound of "become attached to" *(yillāweh* from *lwh),* meaning, "joined to,"[275] presumably to her husband (cp. the wordplay in Num 18:2,4). This verse includes the second of five times that Leah refers to Jacob as "my husband" (vv. 32,34; 30:15,18,20), insisting on what was perhaps not so clear to Rachel (30:15). Hosea's message exploited the nuance of "my husband," implying exclusive ownership (2:16[18]).[276]

Judah (29:35). **29:35** In naming her fourth child, Leah departs from her obsession with winning the love of Jacob. Rather, she exalts the Lord at the birth of Judah. "I will praise" *(ʾôdeh* from *yādaʿ)* leads to the name "Judah" *(yĕhûdâ),* meaning "he will be praised." Perhaps it is a shortened form of a name meaning "May Yahweh/El (God) be praised." The phrase "I will praise/ give thanks" appears often in the Psalter, always directed to Yahweh (e.g., Pss 7:18; 9:2; Isa 25:1; on the meaning "confess," cf., e.g., Lev 5:5; Ps 32:5). Iron-ically, that she ceased bearing children for a season may have been the result of birthing four sons. Jacob may well have withdrawn his sexual attention after obtaining sons (see comments on 30:14–16).[277]

(2) Bilhah's Children (30:1–8)

[1]When Rachel saw that she was not bearing Jacob any children, she became jealous of her sister. So she said to Jacob, "Give me children, or I'll die!"

[2]Jacob became angry with her and said, "Am I in the place of God, who has kept you from having children?"

[3]Then she said, "Here is Bilhah, my maidservant. Sleep with her so that she can bear children for me and that through her I too can build a family."

[4]So she gave him her servant Bilhah as a wife. Jacob slept with her, [5]and she became pregnant and bore him a son. [6]Then Rachel said, "God has vindicated me; he has listened to my plea and given me a son." Because of this she named him Dan.

[7]Rachel's servant Bilhah conceived again and bore Jacob a second son. [8]Then Rachel said, "I have had a great struggle with my sister, and I have won." So she named him Naphtali.

Verses 1–3 report the dispute between Rachel and Jacob regarding her bar-renness, resulting in Jacob producing two sons, Dan and Naphtali, by her

---

[274] The masculine verb of קָרָא־שְׁמוֹ לֵוִי, lit., "he [one] called his name Levi," is an indefinite construction and translated in the passive voice, "his name was called" (LXX[A] ἐκλήθη; NIV, NASB, NRSV, NJPS; HCSB; cp. 25:30; 27:36; 31:48; 50:11; Exod 15:23; Judg 15:9). SP, LXX (but cp. 50:11LXX), Syr., however, reflect the feminine verb קָרְאָה־שְׁמוֹ לֵוִי, "she [Leah] called his name Levi" (NJB, NAB, REB, GNB). Benjamin receives two names (35:18).

[275] *Niphal* stem, יִלָּוֶה; cf. the *niphal* use for a binding covenant, Jer 50:5; Zech 2:11.

[276] On Levi see also comments on chap. 34; 49:5–6.

[277] On the similar wordplay see 49:8. For more on Judah see comments on 37:26; 38; 43:8–9; 49:8–12.

maidservant Bilhah (vv. 4–8).

INTRODUCTION (30:1–3).   Rachel complains that she has no children (v. 1) and insists that Jacob sleep with her surrogate handmaiden (vv. 2–3).

30:1   "When Rachel saw" initiates the second subunit, naming Bilhah's children (v. 1). This may be an implied connection with "the LORD saw" in 29:31, reflecting the convergence of divine and human involvement in the birth of Jacob's children. Rachel's infertility combined with Leah's success exacerbated their rivalry. "Became jealous *(qānā᾽)* of her sister" describes Rachel's reaction; the same discontent explains Jacob's sons' fraternal discord (37:11; cf. also 26:14). Rachel's pointed demand, "Give me children" (v. 1), echoes Jacob's blunt request for Rachel's hand (29:21) wherein he makes it known he wishes to sleep with her. The irony is rich, for the wedding night's deceit threatened their love, which is now not enough in Rachel's eyes. That the woman is overwrought is shown by her preposterous demands of Jacob. Rachel's complaint is based perhaps on a subtle allusion to the prayers of Abraham and Isaac, whose intercessions resulted in restored fertility (20:17–18; 25:21). Her anger may have originated from her disappointment in Jacob's failure to mediate. The text does not present Jacob as a sympathetic husband (cp. Elkanah, 1 Sam 1:5). In contrast to Rachel's demeanor, Hannah herself prayed fervently and attracted the ear of God (1 Sam 1:10,20). Rachel's lament, "or I'll die!" recalls another matriarch's frenetic threat (cf. 27:46).

30:2   Jacob's response is indignation at her demand (cf. "was angry," 31:36). Jacob's rhetorical question expresses his frustration with Rachel, and it assumes that children come from the Lord alone. He cannot supplant the Lord's will any more than she can. Joseph expresses the same sentiment to his troubled brothers (50:19). "Kept from" translates *mānaʿ,* meaning "to withhold," which appears only here when used of a woman's infertility; perhaps it provides an allusion to Sarah's complaint (16:2; see 30:3 below), though there the synonym *ʿāṣar,* meaning "restrained, closed, shut" (16:2; 20:18; Isa 66:9), occurs.

30:3   Rachel takes matters into her own hands by supplying her maid Bilhah as a surrogate. The purpose of the surrogate is stated twice, namely, for providing a child and hence a legacy in Rachel's name. As in the case of Sarah-Hagar, the provision of a servant for an infertile wife was a custom practiced in the ancient Near East, making the children the acknowledged offspring of the wife.[278] Her plan recalls Sarah-Hagar in 16:2, using the same, sometimes exact, verbiage. "Maidservant" *(᾽āmâ)* is used of Hagar in 21:10–13 when Sarah demands the expulsion of the slave and her son. Will Bilhah's child also become a liability in Rachel's plan? "So that she can bear children for me" translates a cultural idiom, lit., "that she may bear upon my knees" (NRSV). Sarna notes that a person's knees symbolized the power of procre-

---

[278] Selman, "Comparative Customs and the Patriarchal Age," 137.

ation.[279] The REB must think that an actual rite is intended when it adds for clarification that the child will "be laid" upon Rachel's knees (cf. 48:12; 50:23; Job 3:12; Isa 66:12). Whether Rachel uses the phrase metaphorically or literally, the reference to "knees" indicated that Bilhah's child would be welcomed as one of her own, giving the child legitimacy.[280] The first person appears repeatedly in Rachel's request, emphasizing that the child will be acknowledged as hers. The final clause juxtaposes Rachel and Bilhah so as to add to the same effect, lit., "so that I can build, even I, from her."

BILHAH'S SONS (30:4–8). Bilhah bears Dan (vv. 4–6) and Naphtali (vv. 7–8) in behalf of Rachel.

Dan (30:4–6). **30:4–6** The common, formulaic language of vv. 4–5 recalls Sarah's servant Hagar (16:3–4) and the birth of Isaac (21:2;cf. 30:9,17,23; 38:3; 1 Sam 2:21; Isa 8:3; Hos 1:3,8), though there she mistreated her concubine.[281] Rachel, not Bilhah, named the child, for the child by surrogate was hers (v. 6). Mothers typically named their children (e.g., 4:1,25; 19:37–38; 38:4–5; Exod 2:10; Judg 13:24; 1 Sam 1:20; 1 Chr 4:9), though fathers often did also (e.g., 4:26; 5:3,29; 41:51–52; Exod 2:22; 1 Chr 7:23; Luke 1:13,60–63). Both parents provide a name for Benjamin (35:18).

"Dan" *(dān),* lit., "he (has) judged, vindicated (me)," is a phonetic play on "vindicated me" *(dānannî* from *dîn),* also rendered "judged" in EVs (e.g., AV, NRSV). The full name is Daniel, "God (El) has judged" or "God (El) is my judge" (cf. also Dinah, 30:21; Abidan, Num 1:11; Dannah, Josh 15:49). For the same wordplay see 49:16. In accord with Leah's explanations, Rachel attributed the child to the Lord's intervention ("heard," cf. 16:11; 21:17). Additionally, she interpreted the event as God's approval of furnishing a maidservant.[282]

Naphtali (30:7–8). **30:7–8** The narrative repeats the birth formula (cf. 29:33,34,35; 38:4; Hos 1:6), attributing a "second son" (cf. v. 12) to Jacob by Bilhah (v. 7). Rachel relates the child's name "Naphtali" *(naptālî)* to the word group *p-t-l,* "twist, struggle" (v. 8), the word appearing twice in the explanation. The noun "struggle" *(naptûlîm,* "struggles") appears only here, and the precise verbal form, "I have struggled" *(niptaltî* from *pātal),* occurs only here, although the root occurs elsewhere (e.g., 2 Sam 22:27; Job 5:13). By grammatical and syntactical means of emphasis, Rachel's explanation magnifies her clash with Leah:[283] (1) "Struggle" *(naptûlîm)* occurs at the head of the clause,

---

[279] Sarna, *Genesis,* 208.

[280] Selman observes parallels in Hurrian and Neo-Assyrian texts, showing that this language indicated family acceptance of the child, not adoption ("Comparative Customs and the Patriarchal Age," 136–37).

[281] On the subject of a concubine "wife," see comments on 16:3.

[282] For more on Dan see comments on 14:14; 49:16–17.

[283] The targums avoid the intensive struggles of the sisters by interpreting the Hb. *p-t-l* as *p-l-l,* "pray"; thus Rachel prayed fervently for a child as her sister had received (Grossfeld, *Targum Onkelos,* 109 n. 4.

and (2) the modifier *ʾelōhîm* is intensive *(naptûlê ʾelōhîm),* indicating "great" (NIV), "intensive" (NLT) or "mighty" struggles (ESV, NASB, NRSV; cf. comments on 23:6; Jonah 3:3).[284] The NAB, NJB, and NJPS interpret the adjectival force of *ʾelōhîm* as extraordinary, translating a "fateful" struggle.

Alternatively, however, *ʾelōhîm* may be interpreted as the divine name, that is, "in my wrestlings with God" (HCSB), or related in specialized sense with the divine. D. W. Thomas concluded that there is no true example in the Old Testament of a solely secular use of *ʾelōhîm;* the appearance of the divine name suggests that the person or thing is superior by virtue of some connection with God.[285] Speiser explains *ʾelōhîm* as a modifier but one that as a figure of speech means the struggle was exceptional ("numinous, celestial"), not in the mere sense of "mighty."[286] Wenham departs from most modern commentators and most EVs when he interprets it as a noun, the divine name "God," meaning Rachel viewed herself as wrestling with God, for the Lord had opened Leah's womb but not hers.[287] Her experience therefore would parallel Jacob's battle in which he "contended" *(śārâ)* with the angel of God (32:28[29]). (3) Finally, the noun and verb as cognate words underscore the idea of fierce brawling. Rachel considers her battle the "mother of all battles," as we might say. It is no wonder in her elation she proclaims, "I have won" (*yākōl,* "prevailed, endured"), as did Jacob prevail *(yākōl)* over God at Peniel (32:28[29]).[288]

(3) Zilpah's Children and Leah's Additional Children (30:9–21)

[9]When Leah saw that she had stopped having children, she took her maidservant Zilpah and gave her to Jacob as a wife. [10]Leah's servant Zilpah bore Jacob a son. [11]Then Leah said, "What good fortune!" So she named him Gad.

[12]Leah's servant Zilpah bore Jacob a second son. [13]Then Leah said, "How happy I am! The women will call me happy." So she named him Asher.

[14]During wheat harvest, Reuben went out into the fields and found some mandrake plants, which he brought to his mother Leah. Rachel said to Leah, "Please give me some of your son's mandrakes."

[15]But she said to her, "Wasn't it enough that you took away my husband? Will you take my son's mandrakes too?"

"Very well," Rachel said, "he can sleep with you tonight in return for your son's mandrakes."

[16]So when Jacob came in from the fields that evening, Leah went out to meet him. "You must sleep with me," she said. "I have hired you with my son's mandrakes." So he slept with her that night.

---

[284] *IBHS* §14.5b.

[285] D. W. Thomas, "A Consideration of Some Unusual Ways of Expressing the Superlative in Hebrew," *VT* 3 (1953): 218.

[286] Speiser, *Genesis,* 230, who cites Thomas; see vol. 1A, 135, n. 91.

[287] Wenham, *Genesis 16–50,* 245–46.

[288] On Naphtali see also comments on 49:21.

¹⁷God listened to Leah, and she became pregnant and bore Jacob a fifth son. ¹⁸Then Leah said, "God has rewarded me for giving my maidservant to my husband." So she named him Issachar.

¹⁹Leah conceived again and bore Jacob a sixth son. ²⁰Then Leah said, "God has presented me with a precious gift. This time my husband will treat me with honor, because I have borne him six sons." So she named him Zebulun.

²¹Some time later she gave birth to a daughter and named her Dinah.

Leah returns to the foreground by producing a bounty of new sons and a daughter. First, she supplies her handmaiden Zilpah, who gives two children (vv. 9–13). By exchanging mandrakes with Rachel for Jacob's sexual services, Leah provides three more children (vv. 14–21).

ZILPAH'S SONS (30:9–13). Leah followed the example of Rachel by conscripting her handmaiden, who produced Gad (vv. 9–11) and Asher (vv. 12–13).

Gad (30:9–11). **30:9–11** "Leah saw" (cf. 29:31) introduces the third and longest subunit of the pericope (vv. 9–21). Since she had stopped bearing children (29:35), Leah employed the same tactic as her younger sister as well as Sarah. The similarities in the language of vv. 4 and 9 (and 16:3) point up the parallel actions of the women. What is striking is that Leah had already borne sons, whereas Sarah and Rachel were childless, making their actions more understandable. Leah evidently would not permit Rachel the comfort of thinking she had triumphed (v. 8). By reporting Zilpah's first child (v. 10), the passage gives the counterpart to Bilhah (v. 5).[289] "Gad" *(gād,* v. 11) derives from Leah's exclamation, "What good fortune *(běgād)!*"[290] Brief but buoyant, the explanation for "Gad" does not have explicit religious significance, but the tenor of the general context provides for it. Perhaps the absence of any mention of God is due to the overtly pagan association of the name Gad and deity (cf. "Fortune," Isa 65:11; "Baal Gad," Josh 11:17).[291]

Asher (30:12–13). **30:12–13** Reference to a "second son" (v. 12) by Zilpah recalls the description of her counterpart Bilhah in v. 7. Leah's happiness at the second birth encouraged her to name the child "Asher" *('āšēr),* meaning "happy, blessed" (cp. *'ašrê,* "happy," Deut 33:29; Ps 1:1). As in the explanation of Bilhah's second child Naphtali ("struggle," v. 8), the sound play occurs twice in the naming of the child (v. 13): "How happy I am" *(bě'ošrî)* and "will call me happy" *('iššěrûnî*[292]*).* That Leah refers to the "women" ("daughters") indicates the community setting in which the prestige of children accrued for a

---

[289] The LXX goes further than the MT, conforming v. 10 to vv. 4–5 LXX.

[290] The LXX, Vg., and most EVs read the *kethîb,* בְּגָד (as does *BHS*); Syr., Tgs. follow the *qěrê,* בָּא גָד, "good fortune has come!" and AV, NKJV have "a troop cometh/comes" (cf. גְּדוּד, "troop, band").

[291] On Gad see comments on 49:19.

[292] אִשְּׁרוּנִי is a use of the perfect, according to *IBHS* §30.5.1e, in which "the speaker vividly and dramatically" indicates a future event that is viewed as complete and independent.

woman. The women of Bethlehem present just such a benediction for Naomi at the birth of Obed (Ruth 4:14–15). As with Gad, there is no mention of God in her explanation for the name, perhaps for the same reason. The name Asher has a sound association with the Assyrian deity Ashur or may be the masculine form of the Canaanite goddess Asherah (*ʾăšērâ*)[293]

LEAH'S CHILDREN AND THE MANDRAKES (30:14–21).   Rachel negotiates for Leah's mandrakes by permitting her to sleep with Jacob (vv. 14–16). Leah bore two more sons, Issachar (vv. 17–18) and Zebulun (vv. 19–20), and a daughter she named Dinah (v. 21).

Mandrakes (30:14–16).   **30:14–16** These verses introduce us to the additional children born by Leah. In the wheat fields her eldest son Reuben discovered wild mandrakes that became a bartering advantage for Leah in her battle for her husband's love. "Mandrakes" *(dûdāʾîm)* appears elsewhere in the Old Testament only in Song 7:13[14] (also *T. Iss.* 1:3–5), where it speaks of their exotic smell, as part of a scene depicting lovemaking (cp. *dōdîm,* "love," e.g., Prov 7:18; Song 1:2). The standard identification of the "mandrake" is *Mandragora officinarum L.,* part of the nightshade, potato, and tomato family.[294] M. Zohary questions whether the Hebrew *dûdāʾîm* of our passage is to be equated with the Mandragora, on the basis that the Mandragora does not grow in Mesopotamia, but he does not offer an alternative identification. The Greeks rendered *dûdāʾîm* as Mandragora,[295] and we know that the plant appears in Israel today. The Arabs called it the "devil's apples" and the Greeks nicknamed it "love apple"[296] because of its legendary reputation as an aphrodisiac. It was further believed that the mandrake could enhance a woman's fertility. The plant exhibits long, dark green leaves in a rosette pattern; from the center of the leaves are flower stalks that each produce a "purple, bluish, or greenish-white flower." During the spring the plant produces a yellow-red fruit, likened to a plum in size and shape. Moldenke and Moldenke describe their appearance like "yellow bird eggs in a shallow nest."[297] Especially interesting are its dark roots that resemble the lower torso of a human form, which probably contributed to the mysteries surrounding its magical, sensual powers. Although the mandrake grows wild in Palestine, the royalty and nobility of ancient Egypt cultivated it in gardens, perhaps near water ponds. During the eighteenth dynasty Mandragora plants and fruit often adorned artistic depictions of the royal family. K. Bosse-Griffiths concluded that the mandrakes contributed to the imagery of potency shared by the Egyp-

---

[293] On Asher see comments on 49:20.

[294] H. Moldenke and A. Moldenke, *Plants of the Bible* (Waltham, Mass.: Chronica Botanica, 1952), 137–39.

[295] μανδραγόρας, LXX (Gen 30:14–16; Song 7:14).

[296] Zohary, *Plants of the Bible,* 188–89.

[297] Moldenke and Moldenke, *Plants of the Bible,* 137.

tian king and queen who represented the whole of the people.[298]

That Reuben found the mandrakes at the time of harvest implies that he did not seek them but only happened to come upon them (v. 14). The description "brought" *(bôʾ)*, as a term used metaphorically for sexual relations (e.g., 29:23,30; 30:3–4), may be an early hint at their sexual significance. The same subtlety might be at work for the description of Jacob, who "came in" *(bôʾ)* from the fields (v. 16). The mention of Leah "his mother" (v. 14) explains why she, not another, received the plants. Since Leah uses the mandrakes in a scheme against Rachel, Jacob's favorite, J. Sasson contends that the mandrake incident is an early indication that Reuben will lose the inheritance of his father's blessing.[299] This subterfuge only has limited success, however, since Rachel's access to some of the mandrakes results in the birth of the favored Joseph.

Unlike the former demands of her husband (30:1), Rachel must temper her request for the mandrakes from Leah with diplomacy ("please give me," v. 14b).[300] She is rudely rebuffed, however, by Leah who charges her with taking away her husband (v. 15a). By this she means Rachel has stolen the affections of her husband since she must share him. Leah's follow-up question is also rhetorical. By taking the mandrakes, Rachel robs her of the means she has of winning his pleasure (v. 15b). Rachel changes her tactic by proposing a business arrangement. In some way left unexplained in the story, Rachel must have at least temporary control over the conjugal life of Jacob, for she permits a one-night rendezvous in exchange for some of Leah's mandrakes. Since the passage reports that Leah had stopped bearing children (29:34), the renewal of her productivity by the mandrakes suggests that some kind of sexual dysfunction on her part or Jacob's had interrupted their relations.

The passage describes the aggressiveness of Leah (v. 16), who like her father has made a deal for Jacob's services. She did not wait for his arrival at the house but went out *(yāṣāʾ)* to meet him. Jacob is a pawn in the hands of these two scheming women. Progressively, the Laban-Jacob account demonstrates Jacob's growing passiveness. Laban previously had abused his trust through deception, and now Jacob is put to use for Leah's purposes. His quiescence recalls the vulnerability Esau experienced at the hands of a once-cocky

---

[298] Among other exhibits, K. Bosse-Griffiths describes "The Little Golden Shrine of Tutʿankhamûn," on which is a scene where the king wears a collar possessing thirteen mandrake pendants, and he receives a fruit of the mandrake from the queen ("The Fruit of the Mandrake," in *Fontes Atque Pontes. Eine Festgabe für Hellmut Brunner*, AAT 5 [Wiesbaden: Harrassowitz, 1983], 62–74).

[299] J. Sasson, "Love's Roots: On the Redaction of Genesis 30:14–24," in *Love and Death in the Ancient Near East: Essays in Honor of Marvin H. Pope* (Guilford, Conn.: Four Quarters Publishing, 1987), 205–9.

[300] Traditionally, the Hb. נָא has been interpreted as a particle indicating request (thus rendered "please"); the function of the particle, however, is disputed (*IBHS* §34.7). Nevertheless, if based on the situation or context of the verse, the nuance "please" may be an appropriate inference.

Jacob. Leah makes her claim on Jacob on the basis of the terms created between the women. "I have hired you" translates the emphatic construction, lit., "I have surely hired you" (v. 16).[301] The word "hire" *(śākār)* describes the financial remuneration a person receives for a service or work (e.g., Deut 23:4[5]). Here the term recalls the motif of "wages" *(maśkōret,* 29:15) that pervades the whole of the Jacob-Laban narrative.

Issachar (30:17–18).   **30:17–18**   That "God listened to Leah" (v. 17; cf. 21:17; 30:22) clarifies that divine superintendence, not the mandrakes, ultimately realized her hopes. Verse 18 shows that this is the opinion of Leah as well. Reference to Issachar as Leah's "fifth son" (v. 17) distinguishes her natural children from the adopted two born by Zilpah, although the maid's sons had equal status. Her prodigious contribution to the house of Jacob-Israel testifies to the grace of God in the life of a woman who suffered the emotional neglect of her husband. The genealogies of the sons sometimes differentiate the children born by legitimate wives and those by concubinage (35:25–26; 46:18,25).

Leah interprets the pregnancy as God's approval for supplying a surrogate to Jacob (v. 18). This is surprising since she, not the surrogate wife, bore the present child. We surmise that she believed the gift of Zilpah, who bore two sons, was an unselfish gesture that the Lord honored. She makes allusion to the mandrakes by repeating the word "hire" *(śākār,* NIV "rewarded"), spoken of when claiming Jacob for the night (v. 16). The implication is that she believed the mandrakes were effective, contributing to her conception that very first night. "Issachar" *(yiśśākār)* is a pun on "my hire" *(śĕkārî,* "has rewarded me," NIV), memorializing the deal that the women arranged. Theologically, the author shows by the episode of Leah's mandrakes that the Lord uses flawed human instruments, even superstition, to achieve his purposes.[302]

Zebulun (30:19–20).   **30:19–20**   Leah's final son, the "sixth son" (v. 19), is the coup de grace, assuring her the esteem that she merits (v. 20). At some later point, Leah must have obtained sexual privileges with Jacob. Although the incident is not explained, perhaps the reader should assume it came about in the same or similar way negotiated between the women that resulted in the conception of Issachar. Again there appear to be two explanations for the naming of "Zebulun" (cf. Reuben, 29:32). The verb *zābad,* meaning "endowed" (NIV, "presented"), and the cognate noun *zebed,* "endowment" (NIV, "gift"), appear in the first explanation. These terms occur only here in the Old Testament. Leah acknowledges by the name "Zebulun" that the child was a gift from God, a divine "dowry" (NRSV). We would, however, on the basis of the first explanation expect a name such as "Zabad" *(zābād),* a popular name known of seven persons in the Old Testament (1 Chr 2:36–37; 7:21; 11:41; 2 Chr 24:26; Ezra

---

[301] Infinitive absolute and the perfect verb, שָׂכֹר שְׂכַרְתִּיךָ.
[302] On Issachar see comments on 49:14–15.

10:27,33,43). The theophoric names Zebadiah ("the Lord *[Yah]* has given," e.g., 1 Chr 8:15) and Zabdiel ("God [El] has given" or "God [El] is my gift," 1 Chr 27:2; Neh 11:14), with others could also be considered. But the women consistently avoid theophoric elements in their children's names, and the sound of Zebulun corresponds nicely to the initial sound of *zebed* ("gift"). Moreover, the second sentence provides for the letters *z-b-l* in the name "Zebulun" *(zĕbūlûn)*, a pun on "honor me" *(yizbĕlēnî,* "treat me with honor," NIV).[303] This verbal root *zābal,* "exalt, honor," also occurs only in this passage (cf. Zebul, Judg 9:28). It is not uncommon for the punning of a name to require a rare term in constructing the sound of wordplay.[304]

Y. Zakovich, while rejecting the notion that the two explanations derived from two parallel sources, is of the opinion that the latter explanation is from a late hand that exhibited another literary preference for creating name derivations.[305] In cases where double explanations occur, as in Zebulun and Joseph in our passage, as well as others (e.g., Isaac, Jerubbaal), he explains the second derivation as the second editor's attempt to conform the explanation more closely to the root letters of the name. For example, the root *z-b-l* correlates closer to the letters of Zebulun than does the first explanation of *z-b-d*. But this procedure is suspect on two fronts. If the name's former explanation was part of the established tradition, there would be no reason to compromise what had become accepted for solely literary precision. Also there is a simpler answer in viewing the two explanations as naturally complementary, thus not requiring the encumbrance of two sources or editorial layers. The notion of a "gift" for an esteemed person fits the nuance well of showing honor to someone (Prov 18:16). Leah probably reasoned that since God has shown her honor by the gift of a sixth son, then surely Jacob must give her the same consideration. On Zebulun see comments on 49:13.

Dinah (30:21).   **30:21**   Leah's last child is Dinah, whose entry in this genealogy is distinctive. She is the only daughter named (cf. 46:15), and her name has no accompanying explanation. Her role in the events of chap. 34 that lead to her brothers' disapproval by Jacob give her a storied place in Israel's ancestry (34:30–31; 49:5–7). Also her inclusion achieves the preferred count of twelve members that characterizes the genealogies of Israel's ancestors. The absence of an explanation for her name may be as simple as the patrilineal character of Israelite society, since she does not create a member tribe. The attachment of a folk etymology for a woman is rare (e.g., 3:20). "Dinah" *(dînâ),* like "Dan," is derived from *dîn* ("to judge"), thus meaning "judgment."

---

[303] The AV, ASV, NKJV have "will dwell with me," deriving יִזְבְּלֵנִי as a denominative verb from זְבֻל, "lofty abode" (see BDB 259). Cf. also the questionable emendation of יִזְבֻּל in *BHS* at 49:13.

[304] Y. Zakovitch, "A Study of Precise and Partial Derivations in Biblical Etymology," *JSOT* 15 (1980): 43, n. 3 (31–50).

[305] Ibid.

(4) Rachel's Child (30:22–24)

²²Then God remembered Rachel; he listened to her and opened her womb. ²³She became pregnant and gave birth to a son and said, "God has taken away my disgrace." ²⁴She named him Joseph, and said, "May the LORD add to me another son."

This passage forms the closing inclusio to the genealogy that began with reference to Rachel's infertility (29:31). After seven years of strife and disappointment, she at last produces a child by the goodness of God's intervention.

30:22 That the Lord "remembered" *(zākar)* Rachel signals a significant reversal in his dealings with her (cf. 8:1; 19:29; Exod 2:24; Pss 78:39; 106:45). His attentive ear implies that she continued her petitions for a child, resulting in his gracious answer (20:18; 29:31; 1 Sam 1:5–6).

30:23–24 After the standard birth report, the passage provides Rachel's commentary on the name "Joseph" *(yōsēp)*. As in the names Reuben and Zebulun, we have two interdependent explanations for the name. "God has taken away *['āsap]* my disgrace" (v. 23) entails the first sound play, referring to the past. The typical term used for "removing" an object is *sûr* (e.g., 30:32), but *'āsap* achieves the intention of remembering the occasion for his birth. "Disgrace" *(ḥerpâ)* refers to Rachel's social stigma of barrenness (cf. ḥerpâ, 34:14); the term may also imply holding a person up to public ridicule since it is often used in such settings (e.g., Job 16:10; Jer 24:9). Sarah's ordeal illustrates the public humiliation that a woman might undergo (16:3–4). The high expectations of marriage and bearing children (cf. ḥerpâ, Isa 4:1) often led to excessive schemes by desperate women, as Jacob himself experienced by Leah (cp. 19:30–38; 34:14–15).

The euphoria of a barren woman at last giving birth is well expressed in the prophet's song (Isa 54:1). Here Rachel's naming of Joseph expresses her abiding faith in the generosity of God, who will yet grant her another child. Joseph as the last born is the twelfth child in the present genealogy, but his name signifies that this position is temporary. The word "add" *(yōsēp)* in her explanation provides for the pun. Joseph's name points both to the present alleviation of her distress but more importantly ahead to the birth of Benjamin (35:18). That the genealogy ends by directing our attention ahead to another child coalesces with the impetus of Jacob's looking ahead to Canaan (30:25). It is upon his return to Canaan that the child Benjamin, for whom Rachel has trusted God, will be realized. At this point in the Jacob narrative, the account turns structurally and thematically toward home. By ending the genealogy with a future orientation, the whole of the unit is turned outward, building anticipation of more to come by the prefiguring provided by Joseph's name.³⁰⁶

---

³⁰⁶ On Jacob's inordinate blessing of Joseph, see comments on 49:22–26.

7. Birth of Jacob's Herds (30:25–43)

This episode details how Jacob advanced from "pauper to prince." The accounts of Jacob's addition of many children (29:31–30:24) and the addition of many herds (30:25–43) exhibit parallel examples of God's blessing. After the fruition of his family (29:31–30:24), Jacob was ready to depart for home (30:25–26). God had met the conditions of Jacob's vow at Bethel, providing him with the necessities of food and clothing (28:20). Yet the Lord would overwhelm Jacob with manifold blessings of material gain to match Jacob's prosperity by acquiring numerous children (30:43). God had provided the child Joseph, meaning "he will add" (v. 24), and would "add" another son (Benjamin, 35:18), but before his departure he will add to Jacob great wealth. Twice we are explicitly told by the participants themselves that "the LORD has blessed" Laban on account of Jacob's presence (vv. 27,30). This pattern of blessing offered to others due to the patriarch's involvement was true of Jacob's ancestors (e.g., 14:18,20; 21:13; 26:28–29; cp. 39:5). Jacob was confident that the Lord would enrich him, too, when he returned home to build his own household (v. 30). Although the divine name occurs explicitly only in vv. 27,30, the pattern of divine blessing that will unfold for Jacob is anticipated by Laban's admission (v. 27). The Lord will bless Jacob's household, but it is surprising that it will be at the expense of Laban's holdings. In addition to Laban's admission (v. 27), the passage implies by lexical hints that Jacob's prosperity is the handiwork of the Lord. These hints include terms that echo the promissory vision Jacob experienced at Bethel (e.g., "watch," 28:15,20; 30:31; "spread/prosperous," 28:14; 30:30,43),[307] indicating that God was fulfilling the promises. Also Jacob's superstitious employment of peeled branches to obtain his herds (vv. 37–39) matches the women's use of mandrakes, recalling the repeated references to the Lord's intervention in their affairs (29:31–33,35; 30:24). God did the same for Jacob's herds. Moreover, the language describing his wealth (v. 43) is reminiscent of the wealth of Abraham, whom the Lord had "blessed" (24:1,35; cp. 26:12–14), indicating that Jacob succeeded his ancestors as the recipient of divine favor.

Jacob's duel with the cunning Laban provides the tension of the narrative. Would Jacob ever free himself from his uncle's hold, enabling him to return home as the Lord had promised? The little "while" (27:44) he intended to stay in Aram had become a long fourteen years. Jacob maintained the urgency to return, like Abraham's servant (24:56), once his beloved Rachel had been secured; but would he eventually forget his father's house, as would Joseph (though for different reasons, 41:51)? It is by Jacob's reputed shrewdness that

---

[307] Cp. also the oracle given to Rebekah: the "large" (רַבּוֹת) flocks (v. 43) with the "older" (רַב) serving the younger (25:23) and the "strong" (הַקְּשֻׁרִים) animals (30:42) with the synonym "stronger" (יֶאֱמָץ) people (25:23).

he resourcefully combats the duplicity of Laban. Jacob wins the duel hands down and in the process sets the scene for his pressing departure (31:1–2).

The author shows through Jacob's bonanza of wealth that the Lord is faithful to his promises, protecting and providing for him. The Lord accomplishes this outside the land, as he had done with Abraham and Isaac, proving again that Canaan's borders did not circumscribe the God of Israel's fathers. In the same way, he enriched the Hebrew slaves at their departure from servitude in Egypt outside Canaan (Exod 12:36). By transforming poverty into wealth at the expense of the powerful, the Lord carried out his plan while undoing the unjust treatment of his appointed people. We recall the promise made to Abraham, "Whoever curses you I will curse" (12:3c). Our episode attests that neither superstitious beliefs nor human devices can bind or befuddle the Lord. God blessed Jacob despite his superstitious employment of visual aids, and the Lord routinely frustrated Laban's hostility at every turn.

COMPOSITION. That source critics at one time contended for two sources (Yahwist [J], Elohist [E]) has been supplanted by the majority view that the narrative comes from the Yahwist. G. von Rad sees problems in the details of the narrative, but the overall cohesive presentation of the narrative is too convincing to divide confidently into two distinct literary sources.[308] Westermann views the narrative as essentially a whole but supplemented by expansions, presenting technical details of interest to herdsmen in vv. 32–33,35,40.[309] This story, he proposes, originally arose from the circles of nomadic herdsmen and was employed by the Yahwist in his account of Jacob-Laban, explaining how the Lord enabled the weaker Jacob to escape the stronger and selfish Laban. Carr also recognizes the essential unity of the composition, following P. Volz and others whose studies prove the logical progression of the narrative (see below), but he designates vv. 32,35 as interpolations.[310] Wenham, however, observes that such detail of Jacob's breeding method accompanying a narrative involving deception should not be surprising.[311]

Another question pertaining to the origin of this account is its relationship to the dream theophany reported in 31:10–11 (Elohist). The present account offered by the Yahwist is said to be a distinct, more complicated account of Jacob's riches than the simpler recounting by the Elohist (31:10–11). Moreover, the Elohist attributes the action to the initiative of the Lord, not Jacob's odd devices.[312] Yet there is no contradiction here since the differences are the result of each narrative's genre and emphasis. The present account focuses on the human role, and the second account offers a symbolic picture that conveys the divine directive in

---

[308] von Rad, *Genesis,* 298–99.

[309] Westermann, *Genesis 12–36,* 480,485.

[310] Carr identifies 30:25–43 as part of the original "prepromise Jacob story" (*Reading the Fractures of Genesis,* 257).

[311] Wenham, *Genesis 16–50,* 254.

[312] E.g., Speiser, *Genesis,* 238; von Rad, *Genesis,* 302.

a dream (31:10–11). The dream account reveals that Jacob's plan to breed multi-colored animals was divinely purposed as the means for releasing Jacob from Laban's greedy clutches. The actual mating procedures carried out by Jacob appear to be his own, and to report them again is out of place in the context of chap. 31's recital of Jacob's dream.

We find that the passage exhibits a unified account that can be attributed to one author. As Westermann says, the strongest argument for the unity of the passage is the "well thought out structure."[313] As many scholars have found,[314] the progression in the story includes these four steps:

1. Jacob proposes his wages will be the black animals among the sheep and the variegated animals among the goats (vv. 32–33).
2. Laban accepts the proposal, separates out the designated animals from his herd for himself, and transfers them to the supervision of his sons (vv. 34–35).
3. Jacob employs visual aids to increase the variegated goats (vv. 36–39) and black sheep (v. 40) for himself.
4. Jacob crossbreeds the strongest specimens of his stock (vv. 41–42).

This does not deny the difficulties that arise in the text's description of Jacob's breeding methods, but we will show in the text's commentary below that the scheme of a late editor who supplements the passage is uncalled for.

STRUCTURE.   A back reference to Joseph's birth (v. 25a) and the concluding record of Jacob's wealth (v. 43) form the limits of this narrative. The passage moves the reader from the birth of Jacob's children to the birth of his herds. Initially, Jacob is penniless, but by the end of the passage he is immensely rich. He has labored fourteen years for Laban; now he will work for himself. The mention of "Joseph" (meaning "he will add," cf. vv. 23–24) points ahead to the addition of the child Benjamin (v. 24), but in this context the mention of "Joseph" has the second significance of additions to Jacob's estate.

Sandwiched in between the borders are two segments. The first presents the parties agreeing to terms in two rounds of dialogue (vv. 25b–34), and the second segment narrates their two actions, showing that Jacob outsmarts Laban (vv. 35–42). The negotiations contained in the first segment possess key words in the dialogue important to the Jacob-Laban narrative as a whole. "Served/worked" (ʿābad, vv. 26[3x],29) and "wages" (śākar, vv. 32,33) recall the dispute over Jacob's wages for Rachel (29:18–27). "Give (tĕnâ) me my wives" (v. 26) is an eerie echo of the same incident, "Give [hābâ] me my wife" (29:21). Jacob's wages, however, are surprising: "Don't give me anything!" (v. 31). He bargains only to claim those animals that are rare and not yet born. Laban readily agrees. Another key word is "blessed" (bārak), describing the Lord's favor toward Laban due to Jacob's presence (vv. 27,30).

---

[313] Westermann, *Genesis 12–36*, 480.

[314] E.g., Carr, *Reading the Fractures of Genesis*, 269–70.

This is another illustration of God's promise to channel blessing to the nations (e.g., 12:3c; 28:14c).

The second segment narrates two competing actions undertaken by Laban and Jacob (vv. 35–42). Laban, true to character, gains the upper hand by sequestering the rare animals so that they will not reproduce offspring, cheating Jacob of an opportunity for wages (vv. 35–36). The outcome is a pleasant reversal of Laban's trickery. Jacob's mysterious breeding practices obtain for him the superior and more numerous animals, leaving Laban with the inferior stock (vv. 37–42). The mating of the animals involved two stages. Verses 37–40 report the proliferation of the rare animals, and vv. 41–42 describe the selective breeding of the stronger animals. The conclusion to the pericope (v. 43) reports the unprecedented wealth that Jacob obtained despite Laban's best efforts.

(1) Jacob and Laban Agree to Terms (30:25–34)

[25]After Rachel gave birth to Joseph, Jacob said to Laban, "Send me on my way so I can go back to my own homeland. [26]Give me my wives and children, for whom I have served you, and I will be on my way. You know how much work I've done for you."

[27]But Laban said to him, "If I have found favor in your eyes, please stay. I have learned by divination that the LORD has blessed me because of you." [28]He added, "Name your wages, and I will pay them."

[29]Jacob said to him, "You know how I have worked for you and how your livestock has fared under my care. [30]The little you had before I came has increased greatly, and the LORD has blessed you wherever I have been. But now, when may I do something for my own household?"

[31]"What shall I give you?" he asked.

"Don't give me anything," Jacob replied. "But if you will do this one thing for me, I will go on tending your flocks and watching over them: [32]Let me go through all your flocks today and remove from them every speckled or spotted sheep, every dark-colored lamb and every spotted or speckled goat. They will be my wages. [33]And my honesty will testify for me in the future, whenever you check on the wages you have paid me. Any goat in my possession that is not speckled or spotted, or any lamb that is not dark-colored, will be considered stolen."

[34]"Agreed," said Laban. "Let it be as you have said."

After the opening clause establishes the context of Joseph's birth (v. 25a), this unit entails two rounds of debate between Jacob and Laban. In the first dialogue Jacob requests dismissal from service, but Laban ignores his request and offers him wages, to which Jacob objects (vv. 25b–30). The second round has Laban making a renewed offer of wages, to which Jacob structures a counterplan, and Laban immediately agrees (30:31–34).

JACOB SEEKS DISMISSAL (30:25–30). Jacob requests release to return to his "homeland" (v. 25) so that he can build up his own "household" (v. 30).

Jacob Requests Release (30:25–26).   **30:25a**   This temporal clause establishes the connection between the passage and the foregoing account of Jacob's children. Especially important to the setting is the recognition of completion that the birth of Joseph gives to Jacob's sense of call. He understands the need to return home to Canaan to make his claim in response to God's promises (28:13–15). He has waited for this moment for fourteen years, but he will yet be derailed by Laban's offer, making his stay six more years (31:38,41).

30:25b–26   Jacob's tenure is complete and he requests Laban's dismissal, understanding that the endowment of service for his daughters is paid in full. "Send me on my way" (*šallĕḥēnî*, v. 25b) expresses the desire of an underling for release from duty (1 Sam 30:29; 1 Kgs 11:21). The same language appears in Deuteronomy's description of the released servant who had sold himself into service (15:12–13,18). In the context of Genesis, "send me on my way" recalls Abraham's servant, who sought dismissal from Laban for the return trip with the betrothed Rebekah (24:54,56). Moreover, the exact verbiage appears in Jacob's struggle with the angel of the Lord, "Let me go" (*šallĕḥēnî,* 32:27). "My own homeland" translates lit., "my place and my land." "My place" contrasts with "our place" ("here," NIV, 29:26) and "his place" ("home," NIV, 31:55[32:1]), referring to Laban's homeland. This reflects Jacob's sense of alienation despite his many years in Paddan Aram. But what "place" does he have in mind? Might it be Bethel, the unique "place" (28:11,16–17,19) where he first received the promise of return? "My land" (*'arṣî*) may be an intentional echo of Abraham's instructions to the servant, "go to my country" (*'arṣî,* 24:4), which refers to Abraham's hometown Haran. But for Jacob, unlike Abraham, Paddan Aram was not his home; rather, it was Canaan where the promises awaited their fulfillment.

Jacob's request next mentions his wives and children specifically (v. 26). According to Mosaic law, a Hebrew slave who receives a wife from his master must upon gaining freedom relinquish her and her children to the master (Exod 21:4). This law was not applicable to Jacob since he was not a slave. Special protections in the law ensured the fair and privileged treatment of an impoverished Hebrew by a master (Lev 25:39–43). For a Hebrew slave who was released after serving his tenure, his master must provide a financial stake to enable the fellow Hebrew to live independently (Deut 15:12–18). Sarna observes that this kind of generosity from the greedy Laban could not be counted on (cp. 31:38–42).[315] Jacob, in any case, was neither a slave nor a common hireling but a family member whose wages fulfilled a groom's traditional marital dowry paid to the family. Jacob expects and appears only to want his family. Three times in v. 26, the word group "work/serve" (*ʿ-b-d)* appears. Jacob forcefully asserts that his debt is paid in full and there is no

---

[315] Sarna, *Genesis,* 211.

basis for dispute ("you know . . ."). Jacob believes his indignation is justified, for twice more he will declare earnestly his fruitful execution of the former agreement (30:29; 31:6).

Laban Makes Offer (30:27–28). **30:27** Verse 27 contains Laban's admitted motivation for his unqualified offer that follows, "Name your wages . . ." (v. 28). His response to Jacob's request included the contrary reactions of disregard and flattery. First, Laban bypasses his nephew's request, choosing to make a counteroffer. Second, he politely, almost submissively, acknowledges his reliance on Jacob. "If I have found favor in your eyes" typically introduces a request to a person in a superior or preferred position (e.g., 18:3; 33:10; 47:29; 50:4; Exod 33:13; 34:9; Judg 6:17; 1 Sam 27:5). Laban does not hide his anxiety at hearing Jacob's plans, since he no longer has leverage over Jacob's service.

The EVs differ in v. 27b, interpreting the apodosis either as the unspoken but understood request, "stay"/"tarry with me" (e.g., NIV, AV, NJB note, NASB, HCSB), or as the subsequent clause, "I have learned by divination . . ." (e.g., NRSV, NJPS). Since the clause "if I have found favor in your eyes" usually is followed by a specific request, the former interpretation (as NIV) is more likely. Perhaps the best rendering, however, reflects the broken syntax of the Hebrew sentence: "If I have found favor in your eyes—" dangles alone, absent an apodosis (e.g., NAB, REB).[316] Laban's fractured sentence structure indicates his alarm, hurriedly blurting out his adulation of Jacob, who stands eminently before God. He admits that Jacob leads what we might call a "charmed life." This is another occasion that an outside party admits or implies that prosperity results from a favorable relationship with the patriarchs (e.g., 21:22–23; 26:28–29; cf. also 14:19; 39:5,23), hence fulfilling the promise that all nations will be blessed through Abraham's family (12:3c; 18:18; 22:18; 26:4). This is confirmed according to Laban by "divination" *(nāḥaš),* although what means of augury he performed is not told. That he practiced divination should not be startling, however, since we know that Joseph had access to the paraphernalia of such sorcery (44:5,15). If so, here is another example of the many crossassociations between the Jacob and Joseph narratives. Yet one must hear everything that this huckster says cautiously, for we do not know if this is a fabrication. What is striking is Laban's casual connection of divination with the Lord, for divination was one of the sorcerer's arts strictly forbidden in the law (e.g., Lev 19:26; Deut 18:10). Another irregularity is the use of divination at all to discern the source of his prosperity. For this reason some interpreters prefer the rendering afforded by the Akk. word *naḥāšu,* "to become wealthy, prosper";[317] thus

---

[316] GKC §159dd (cf. 38:17; 50:15).

[317] J. J. Finkelstein, "An Old Babylonian Herding Contract and Genesis 31:38f," *JAOS* 88 (1968): 34, n. 19. Among commentators, e.g., Sarna, *Genesis,* 211, and Wenham, *Genesis 16–50,* 251, 255.

Laban admits, "I have become prosperous" (REB) on account of Jacob ("because of you," cp. *biglal,* 12:13; 39:5).

30:28 The passage has exposed a significant irony that exhibits the theological conviction of the author. He regularly testifies of Israel's God as one who transforms a destitute situation into a victory for the patriarchs. Here, although Jacob is penniless, by virtue of his presence in Laban's homestead, Laban's wealth is dependent on Jacob's labor. Therefore it is not surprising that the reference to Laban's divination, whether true or a prevarication, injects an overt admission of God's provision and blessing. Verse 28 contains the logical, second word of Laban (*wayyō'mer,* "he added," NIV): "Name your wages."[318] This open invitation (29:15), as well as the term "give" (*nātan,* 29:19,24,26,27,28,29), recalls when Jacob and Laban bargained for the hand of Rachel. It has now been fourteen years since Jacob became indebted to Laban. At last he is free, but why would he venture to trust Laban again? He doesn't. As we will see, Jacob devises a special means whereby he will outwit Laban for the final victory.

Jacob Refuses (30:29–30). **30:29** Jacob does not play his hand too soon. He first seizes on Laban's admission and plays it up by reiterating the gain that Laban received by his hard and competent labor. He repeats in effect his opening salvo in v. 26 but then enlarges on his claims in v. 30. He has Laban "over a barrel," and he will negotiate accordingly.

30:30 Jacob makes three points in his rejoinder. First, Laban has accumulated great wealth. Jacob may well have exaggerated when he contrasted how "little" Laban had before his arrival. The word "increased" *(pāraṣ)* appears again in v. 43 when the author reports that Jacob "increased" in possessions (cf. 28:14), but here Jacob strengthened his point by including "greatly" (*rōb,* "multitude, abundant"). Second, Jacob agrees with Laban's theological reading of the situation, and he amplifies on Laban's admission by asserting that "wherever" Jacob accompanied the herds there was increase in their numbers. Third, "but now" *(we'attâ)* brings his argument to a forceful close. By his rhetorical question, Jacob insists that he deserves the opportunity to enrich himself. Repeatedly, he hammers the first person "I, my," including the emphatic expression "also I" *(gam 'ānōkî)*. It is my turn, he protests![319]

LABAN ACCEPTS JACOB'S OFFER (30:31–34). At Laban's invitation (v. 31a), Jacob presents the terms of the arrangements (vv. 31b–33), and Laban immediately agrees (v. 34).

Laban Makes a Second Offer (30:31a). **30:31a** Verses 31–34 contain

---

[318] "Name" (NIV) translates the root בקנ, "to designate, appoint" (e.g., Num 1:17), occurring only here in Genesis.

[319] On the significance of "household" *(bayit),* see comments on 12:1; cp. 31:14,30,37,41.

the second round of dialogue. Laban essentially ignored Jacob's first reply, evading Jacob's reasoned response. "What *[mâ]* shall I give *[nātan]* you?" is another uncanny allusion to their initial contract, "Tell me what *[mâ]* your wages should be?" (29:15b). Not to be outdone, the conniving Laban will actually "give" *(nātan)* the animals specified in the agreement to his sons for safekeeping (30:35).

Jacob Counters (30:31b–34).   **30:31b**   Jacob answers Laban pointedly, lit., "not you will give me anything." Jacob does not want to be subservient to Laban as in their earlier arrangement. His resistance is reminiscent of Abraham's refusal to accept a gift from the king of Sodom (14:21,23). Although Jacob does not state overtly the rationale for his refusal, the literary allusion to Abraham-Sodom intimates that Jacob had the same motive. The language of Jacob's pledge, "I will go on *[šûb]* tending your flocks and watching *[šāmar]* over them," repeats the promissory and votive language stated at Bethel (28:15,20,21). By this allusion, Jacob declares that he will trust in the Lord alone to provide for him, as God had promised at Bethel (28:13–15) and had proven to Abraham (15:1).

30:32–33   Jacob proposes to separate all speckled and spotted "sheep" *(śeh)* from the flocks that he agrees to tend (v. 32).[320] The term *śeh* can refer to sheep and goats, probably meaning in this context "animals" (cf. Exod 12:5; Deut 14:4).[321] The narrative does not employ *śeh* after its initial appearance in v. 32. The animals are specified as dark "lambs" (i.e., sheep, *kĕśābîm*) and spotted and speckled "goats" *(ʿizzîm)* (v. 32). The typical appearance of sheep and goats was the opposite coloration, namely, white sheep and dark-hued (black or brown) goats. Presumably, the animals designated by Jacob were fewer to begin with, and, moreover, he intended to remove these uncommon ones from the flock. Once these animals were removed, Jacob would have no animals designated for him to own since he was left with only the white sheep and dark goats. He could only count on any future births of black sheep and variegated goats. Laban must have reasoned that these births would indeed be scarce, since Jacob had only the one-color animals for breeding.

Jacob's proviso in v. 32 does not contradict his stated refusal to take anything from Laban (v. 31), for the nature of his wages in effect ensured that

---

[320] The clause led by the imperfect form אֶעֱבֹר, "I will go through . . .," is followed by the *hiph.* infinitive absolute הָסֵר, rendered adverbially "by removing . . ." (v. 32). The LXX, Vg. (NAB, NJB), however, translate both clauses as imperatives: παρελθάτω . . . διαχώρισον, "Go . . . remove . . .," influenced probably by וַיָּסַר, "he removed" (cf. v. 35). Thus, in this interpretation, Jacob is exhorting Laban to cull the animals.

[321] The five Hb. terms describing the animals in the narrative create special translation problems that confuse readers, esp. vv. 32,37,40: צֹאן ("flock" or "small cattle" = "sheep and/or goats"); שֶׂה ("an individual animal" = "a sheep or a goat"); כֶּשֶׂב ("sheep," i.e., male or female, young or old); עֵז ("female-goat, doe"); and תַּיִשׁ ("male goat, buck"). See Speiser, *Genesis,* 236–37, and L. Lincoln, "Translating Hebrew and Greek Terms for Sheep and Goats," *BT* 47 (1996): 322–35.

Jacob will begin without any venture capital. He names the categories of animals that he might obtain in the future as his wages, not the specific animals rounded up initially. By referring to his "wages," therefore, he is speaking proleptically, assuming that he will gain a herd through breeding. This explains the reaction of Laban, who immediately removed the selected animals so as to prevent Jacob from claiming their offspring (vv. 35–36). Laban must have reasoned that the mating of the designated animals would result in a herd that Jacob could claim. Laban's caution, however, only accomplished what Jacob himself had recommended, and Jacob accepts Laban's action without protest. What Laban did not anticipate was the success Jacob could achieve through selected crossbreeding.

In the future any animals that were found among Jacob's personal herd that were not of the uncommon varieties must be considered stolen (v. 33). Jacob presumed that Laban would periodically inspect his flocks. By this openness, Jacob wanted to avert any unjust charges of fraud leveled against him. He anticipated trouble with Laban's family, and he was not far from the mark (cf. 31:1–2,29). With what Jacob knows of his own past, we conjecture that with tongue in cheek, Jacob swears on his honor that he will treat Laban fairly. "My honesty" translates the term *ṣĕdāqâ*, which can mean "righteousness" and "vindication" (cf. 15:6; 18:19). The word group *ṣ-d-q* often occurs in a judicial setting (2 Sam 15:4; cf. 44:16). In the present context the idea is Jacob's compliance to an agreed behavior.[322] The word "testify" (*'ānâ*, "answer") may also convey a forensic nuance (e.g., Deut 19:18; Isa 59:12).[323] The image lying behind Jacob's remark is a hearing wherein Jacob's integrity witnesses to his adherence to their bargain. Laban will not risk deception anyway, choosing to assort the animals himself (cp. v. 35).

Laban Accepts (30:34). **30:34** Such an arrangement could hardly be refused (cp. *kidbārekā*, "as you say," 47:30), although Laban had no intention of fulfilling whatever agreement Jacob had proposed. He at once deviated from it by segregating the animals himself. Jacob could legitimately complain that Laban "changed my wages ten times" across the six years (31:41).

(2) Jacob Outmaneuvers Laban (30:35–42)

[35]That same day he removed all the male goats that were streaked or spotted, and all the speckled or spotted female goats (all that had white on them) and all the dark-colored lambs, and he placed them in the care of his sons. [36]Then he put a three-day journey between himself and Jacob, while Jacob continued to tend the rest of Laban's flocks.

[37]Jacob, however, took fresh-cut branches from poplar, almond and plane

---

[322] D. Reimer, "צדק," *NIDOTTE* 3.747.

[323] With the prep. ב, the word means "to testify for someone," as in our passage, or more often "against someone" (e.g., 1 Sam 12:3; 2 Sam 1:16; BDB 773).

trees and made white stripes on them by peeling the bark and exposing the white inner wood of the branches. [38]Then he placed the peeled branches in all the watering troughs, so that they would be directly in front of the flocks when they came to drink. When the flocks were in heat and came to drink, [39]they mated in front of the branches. And they bore young that were streaked or speckled or spotted. [40]Jacob set apart the young of the flock by themselves, but made the rest face the streaked and dark-colored animals that belonged to Laban. Thus he made separate flocks for himself and did not put them with Laban's animals. [41]Whenever the stronger females were in heat, Jacob would place the branches in the troughs in front of the animals so they would mate near the branches, [42]but if the animals were weak, he would not place them there. So the weak animals went to Laban and the strong ones to Jacob.

After the negotiations are completed, each man takes action. Laban makes a preemptive strike, thinking that his precautions will ensure his victory (vv. 35–36). But Jacob outsmarts his elder by employing a plan of animal husbandry that created a numerous and stronger herd, leaving Laban's sons a few feeble animals (vv. 37–42). The narrative's oblique descriptions function rhetorically. The passage resists a uniform description of the animals and of Jacob's breeding procedures so as to demonstrate two important aspects of the account. First, the narrative reflects subtly what Jacob later accuses Laban of, "You changed my wages ten times" (31:41). Second, the perplexities of the passage enhance this point: it was God's gracious intervention that assured Jacob's prosperity, not his bewildering schemes. Neither Laban's actions nor Jacob's counteractions satisfactorily explain the result. Thus Jacob rightly realizes that God protected him from Laban's dishonesty (31:7).

LABAN CHEATS JACOB (30:35–36). **30:35–36** Laban wasted no time. The narrative pointedly asserts "that same day" (v. 35) he removed the animals designated by Jacob.[324] By placing them under the oversight of his sons, he prevented Jacob from tending the selected animals. This is the first of only two references to Laban's sons (vv. 35; 31:1), but their antagonism will weigh heavily in Jacob's decision to leave clandestinely. The author notes that "all" (*kol*, 3x) of the marked animals were removed. Both the variegated "male goats" *(tĕyāšîm)* and variegated "female goats" *(ʿizzîm)* were transferred, as well as all the dark sheep *(kĕśābîm),* seemingly foiling Jacob's plans of building a herd.

Further, Laban established a wide buffer zone of three days' travel between the herds tended by his sons and those by Jacob (v. 36; cf. Exod 3:18; 5:3; 8:23; Num 10:33; 33:8). This second step reduced the chances that stragglers would roam into Jacob's sector. This tactic, however, would backfire on him, since it freed Jacob from the oversight that might have hindered

---

[324] The identity of the subject, "he removed," is either Jacob or Laban, which we understand as "Laban" (also Rashi; among EVs, cf. NRSV, ESV, NAB, REB, NLT).

his schemes (31:20,22). By referring to the "rest" of Laban's herds, the passage indicates that the sons tended only the animals that their father had removed from Jacob's supervision. Jacob was stuck with a large number of the wrong specimens, but he remained true to his word by maintaining Laban's flocks despite his indiscreet behavior (v. 31).

JACOB OUTSMARTS LABAN (30:37–42). As an experienced herdsman, Jacob knew that he could yet outwit Laban. First, he produced stock that met the coloration standard (vv. 37–40), and second he crossbred the stronger type (vv. 41–42).

The Variegated Branches (30:37–40). **30:37–39** The procedure he followed involved a folk custom. He stripped the bark from newly cut branches of poplar, almond, and plane trees, exposing the underlying white shoot (v. 37). This gave the branches the multicolor appearance of alternating dark and white hues. By utilizing fresh branches, the bark was easier to strip and the healthy core yielded a brighter white. The types of trees that he selected were especially effective specimens for his purposes.[325] References to the "poplar" (*libneh,* v. 37) tree and the recurring color "white" (*lābān*[3x], vv. 35,37) provide wordplays on Laban's name, injecting humor at the thought of Laban's undoing by Jacob's superior cunning. This species of poplar was probably the white poplar *(Populus alba),* whose under leaves are especially white. Its branches are long and straight, providing pleasant shade (Hos 4:13). The almond tree is probably the *Amygdalus communis.* The Hebrew word translated "almond" *(lûz)* is a hapax legomenon,[326] and it may play on the former name of Bethel ("Luz," 28:19), where God originally met with Jacob. The "plane" *('ermôn)* tree *(Platanus orientalis)* also appears in Ezek 31:8, where mention is made of its imposing, wide branches. This tree typically sheds its bark in sheets, revealing a smooth interior bark of white or yellow color.

Jacob next placed the stripped branches in the water troughs where the "flocks" *(ṣō'n)* would view them at the time for mating (vv. 38–39).[327] Speiser shows that the term *ṣō'n,* which can refer to sheep or goats (as well as to both sheep and goats; cp. *bāqar,* Num 7.3,6), refers in these verses to the dark goats left by Laban (see v. 40 below). Ostensibly, this visual impetus resulted in the birth of variegated offspring. But how can this be explained, since the vision of stripped branches could not have had anything to do with the results? Ancient interpretations attributed the outcome to the miraculous. *Gen. Rab.* 73.10 explains that the proliferation of the designated sheep was due to "ministering angels" (cf. "looked up," 31:10) who transported animals

---

[325] For the discussion of three species, see Moldenke, *Plants of the Bible,* 35, 37, 180–82.

[326] שׁקד is the common word group meaning "almond" (e.g., Exod 25:33; Jer 1:1).

[327] The verb וַיֵּחַמְנָה, "when (the flocks) were in heat" (v. 38), with the *yod* preformative instead of *taw,* is a rare feminine plural form occurring only three times (1 Sam 6:12; Dan 8:22). See GKC §47k.

from Laban's flock to Jacob's. Chrysostom, too, concluded that the odd employment of the rods was not born of human logic "but with grace from on high inspiring [Jacob's] mind" (*Hom. Gen.* 57.7).[328]

We believe that Jacob's folk methods corresponded to Rachel and Leah's use of mandrakes in their competition for children (30:14–16). Although the women believed that the mandrakes somehow conveyed potency, they also understood that ultimately pregnancy was the result of God's gracious favor (e.g., 30:17–18,22–23). It was their prayers, not the mandrakes, that resulted in the birth of children. Some commentators object that Jacob actually believed his tactics would work. He employed this elaborate plan as a hoax to distract Laban's attention from the crossbreeding that he practiced. Yet the passage does not indicate that Jacob's plan involved "deceit" or "stealth," which are descriptions commonly used when narrating deceitful actions (e.g., 27:35–36; 29:25; 31:20,26–27; 34:13). Furthermore, it appears he attributes the idea to a divine revelation (31:10–13). Modern eugenics can explain technically how he succeeded by breeding animals that possessed the desired, recessive genes and further by selective breeding to multiply the stronger animals;[329] but Jacob's knowledge would have been dependent on learned experience as a seasoned herdsman, or possibly by divine instruction in his dream (31:10).[330] Whatever the precise explanation for his success, the passage shows that Jacob relied on the visual aids, as did the women on the mandrakes, but ultimately he credited God with the prosperity of his herds (31:10–13). The Lord tolerated Jacob's imaginative devices and transcended them. God was pleased to bless despite whatever erroneous notions Jacob may have had about animal husbandry.

30:40 Verse 40 creates a special problem by the confusing mention of the "young of the flock" and "streaked and dark-colored animals" from Laban's flocks. This does not appear to conform to Laban's transfer of the streaked goats and dark-colored sheep to his sons' safekeeping (vv. 35–36). The resolution is the recognition of two factors in v. 40. First, the verse pertains to the breeding of the young of the sheep *(kĕśābîm),* wherein he modified his procedure to the goats described in vv. 37–39. Second, v. 40 names two groups of goats: variegated and black "animals" (i.e., goats, *ṣōʼn).* Thus, Westermann explains that Jacob isolated the young white sheep and set them facing the speckled goats (from Jacob's own flock) and the dark

---

[328] *ACCS* 2.204.

[329] For this discussion see Hamilton, *Genesis Chapters 18–50,* 284.

[330] Luther attributes Jacob's knowledge of the rods to the patriarchs or divine inspiration, but he also attributes the outcome to "magic art" and "natural magic" (*LW* 5.380). Calvin, too, explained the event as the Lord's doing but also stated that the peeled rods seen by the mother had an effect on the unborn offspring (*Comm.* 2.155–56).

goats (from Laban's flock).[331] The combination of speckled and dark goats approximated the alternating colors of the peeled branches employed for the goats. Thus, Jacob derived the dark sheep that he could claim. That the passage exhibits difficulties probably is the result of the fluid arrangements that occurred across the six years that Jacob cared for the herds. That Jacob employed more than one method is clear from vv. 41–42, and it is understandable that he varied his earlier approach when dealing with the sheep.

Mating the Animals (30:41–42). **30:41–42** Verses 41–42 further describe how Jacob produced stronger animals for himself. He routinely selected the stronger females who mated near the multicolored branches, leaving the weaker ones for Laban's collection. By the weaker ones reproducing for Laban's herd, his stock gradually became few and puny.

(3) Jacob's Wealth (30:43)

43In this way the man grew exceedingly prosperous and came to own large flocks, and maidservants and menservants, and camels and donkeys.

30:43 As in the case of his father (26:13) and grandfather (12:16; 13:2; 24:35), Jacob became wealthy in animals and servants. By building massive herds of small cattle, he could trade and purchase servants and burden-bearing animals, such as camels and donkeys. The possession of camels shows that the man was exceptionally rich (e.g., 12:16; 24:10; 32:15; 37:25), since these animals were rare and costly (see Introduction for more on the question of camels in the patriarchal period). "Prosperous" *(pāraṣ)* is a link with the original promise made to Jacob ("spread," *pāraṣ,* 28:14), showing that the Lord had made good on his word. Also there is an ironic twist indicated by this word; it appeared earlier in v. 30 ("increased," *pāraṣ),* describing Laban's wealth by virtue of Jacob's efforts. Now, after retaining his nephew, Laban unexpectedly becomes the inferior of the two.

8. Jacob Deceives Laban (31:1–55[32:1])

The features of strife and deception that we have come to expect in Jacob's life again imprint this second story of flight (cf. Esau, 27:43). The overriding conflict between Jacob and Laban in the story is the patriarch's clandestine departure for Canaan. The narrative begins with the envy that Laban and his sons have for Jacob (vv. 1–2), and it ends with the peaceful resolution of a treaty (vv. 44–54), ensuring that Jacob's success would no longer be their nemesis. The ancillary conflict in the account is the divided household of Laban, whose daughters are coconspirators in Jacob's plot.

---

[331] Westermann, *Genesis 12–36,* 454.

The wives, who had struggled for the love of their husband (29:30–30:25), are now partners, repaying their father for mistreatment (vv. 14–16). This testimony by the daughters themselves disproved Laban's final, desperate charge that Jacob had abducted his daughters (vv. 26–28). His contest with Rachel and Leah ended in a traditional farewell kiss and blessing (v. 55[32:1]), providing an uneasy sense of reconciliation. The irony of course is Laban's show of concern for Rachel and Leah's welfare in his proposed peace agreement (v. 50), when it was Jacob who had their best interests in mind.

Deception also takes center stage in this episode. The second-most frequent verb in the narrative is the word "steal/deceive" *(gānab),* occurring eight times (vv. 19,20,26,27,30,32,39[2x]). It is one-sided, however, making Laban the victim of Jacob's and his daughters' duplicity. The instigators often provided a justification for their treatment of Laban (vv. 6–9,14–16,31,36–42). Moreover, they could claim that their departure had divine impetus (vv. 3,13), although there is no indication that their sneaky tactic had divine sanction. The likelihood of losing their hard-gained possessions to Laban and his sons prompted the collusion of Jacob and his wives in an underhanded plan. Laban had a track record of cheating that they could point to, convincing the reader that their fears, if not their actions, were right. Jacob and his family surreptitiously left when Laban was at his most vulnerable moment, away overseeing the shearing of his flocks (vv. 19–20). As had been characteristic of their relationship, Laban and Jacob eventually struck another deal, initiated again by the senior member (v. 44). Because of divine interference, Laban could not forcibly recover his daughters and Jacob's animals (vv. 7,29), but he could save face, establishing the rules of their relationship through a treaty arrangement (v. 52). There is no true denouement here in their relationship, however; it is more of a mutually accepted standstill between tired combatants.

Another act of deception recorded in the narrative is the embedded account of Rachel's theft of Laban's "household gods" *(tĕrāpîm).* The episode provides another opportunity for the author to show Laban's further mistreatment of Rachel and Leah, surpassing even the contemptible circumstances of their marriages. Laban had maliciously withheld the bridal gift, squandering it on himself (v. 15). In a twist of just deserts, Rachel stole his idols, which held in some undisclosed way great value for Laban (vv. 19,34). Again Laban suffered loss in the battle of wits, this time with his own daughter (vv. 34–35)! Rachel's deception exposed another struggle within the family that is not so obvious. The author asserts that Jacob was totally unaware of the theft (v. 32b), even vowing to put to death the culprit if the *tĕrāpîm* (or any items) were indeed discovered in his camp. The earlier tension between Rachel and Jacob over her childlessness (30:1–2) continues in this episode, although only inferentially, by Rachel withholding information from her husband. By her stealth, she not only repaid her father but also expressed surprising independence of her husband. She must have judged that Jacob would not have approved of her behavior if he had knowledge of the ploy. We find that the author does not condone her deception, but then he shows no sympathy for Laban either.

The intervention of God by means of Laban's dream contributes to the author's overall message, demonstrating again that divine benevolence and faithfulness provided for the prosperity and protection of the patriarchs (v. 24). The patriarchs typically exhibited the moral flaws of deception and strife, but God superseded their deficiencies, carrying forward the promises. The present episode joins a constellation of stories in the Jacob account, showing the efficacy of the divine Word despite the vicissitudes of human character and condition. This is one of many similarities in the Jacob narrative to Abraham's career (20:3). Both patriarchs obtained wives in Aram, albeit in Abraham's case for his son by means of his servant (chap. 24). The struggle between Jacob's wives recalls the Sarah-Hagar conflict (chap. 16). Also, in a foreigner's dream (20:3–7), the Lord intervened in behalf of Abraham's family, as in the case of Jacob (v. 29). These foreign excursions always involved serious threats to the patriarch but inevitably resulted in his enrichment. By drawing such similarities, there is an implied authentication of Jacob as the appointed successor to the patriarchal blessing. It would seem now that nothing could interfere in Jacob's plans. The happy conclusion of the story, however, sets up the greater challenge that he would soon face, the confrontation with Esau.

Another bond between Jacob and his grandfather Abraham was the return of Jacob to his homeland, retracing the original Abraham trek from Haran to the land of Canaan. The circumstances of Jacob's departure, however, severed the Aramean and Hebrew branches of the Terah family. That they eventually became two distinct peoples is suggested repeatedly in the narrative, especially by the naming of the stone heap in each one's native tongue (v. 47). The Arameans had supplied the Hebrew fathers their wives, but this would no longer be the case for Jacob's sons. By recounting the decision of Rachel and Leah to flee their father's household (vv. 14–16), the narrative confirms their loyalty to their husband's family and to his God. As for Jacob himself, he returned to the land a chastened man who after twenty years in exile had learned that his security ultimately rested with the Lord, not with his own cleverness.

COMPOSITION. Documentarians contended that the narrative was a composite text of three sources. Primarily, the narrative is indebted to the Elohist (E), evidenced by the common use of the divine name *Elohim* (or *El;* vv. 5,7,9,11, 16,24,29,42,50,53) and the inclusion of dream reports (vv. 10–14,24), features believed to be characteristic of the Elohist.[332] Furthermore, the passage alludes to the vow taken at Bethel, the house of God (*Elohim;* v. 13; 28:17–18,20–22). In addition to the Elohist, some parts of the chapter were credited to the Yahwist (J; e.g., vv. 1,3,49), and there was widespread agreement that v. 18(b) is a Priestly (P) addition. Scholars identified doublets in the narrative that involve differences, which they attributed to the varying perspectives of the Elohist and Yahwist documents. Speiser notes four differences: (1) the threat of Laban's sons in v. 1 (E) and the mood of Laban in v. 2 (J) give two motivations for Jacob's flight; (2) divine revelation (31:10–13, E) and Jacob's schemes (30:27–42, J) offer two explanations for the patriarch's prosperity; (3) Laban's concern for his daughters (v. 50, J) and the desire for a peace treaty with Jacob (v. 52, E) give two reasons for entering the pact; and (4) a pillar (v. 45, E) and a heap of stones (v. 46, J) are two witnesses to the treaty. Although Speiser observed the dominant presence of E in chap. 31 (with some inclusion of J), he did not venture to divide the text into these two sources because of their difficulty.

Speiser's sensitivity to the unity of the passage presaged the trend in Pentateuchal criticism of a dwindling role for the Elohist. The substantial change toward viewing chap. 31 as the narration of the Yahwist, even denying any evidence of the E source, is now common. Westermann characterized the chapter as "a well-knit, self-contained unit" authored by the Yahwist, who employed a number of preexisting traditions and whose work underwent two major expansions (vv. 4–16,43–54). Van Seters recognizes the dependence of chap. 31 on 28:10–22, which he already assigned to the Yahwist, showing that chap. 31 was largely the result of the same author.[333] Carr, too, contends that parallel sources cannot adequately explain the constitution of chap. 31 or the relationship of 31:4–13 and 30:25–43.[334] He (like Blum) believes that the author of the "prepromise Jacob story" took over early Jacob traditions about his trickery and redirected them, producing a moral Jacob who was the honorable ancestor of northern Israel. In Carr's reconstruction the promise passage of 31:3 was a later addition to the Jacob-Joseph compilation, when reorienting it to the broader patriarchal promise theme. Finally, the Priestly hand gave us 31:17–18 as part of his extensive revision of Genesis, adding here the return segment of P's particular explanation of Jacob's travel to Paddan Aram to find a wife (27:46–28:9).

We find that the overall unity of the chapter suggests best that it belongs to one author. That the denouement to the Jacob-Laban narrative occurs in chap. 31 argues for the same author as that of chaps. 29–30. The incidents of strife between Jacob and Laban and between Rachel and Leah have their resolve in chap. 31. The chapter, moreover, transitions from the Jacob-Laban account to the second half of the wider Jacob-Esau narrative, making it the necessary link in the whole. Also Rendtorff observed that the guidance motif contributes to the symmetry of the Jacob story as a whole, requiring 31:3 as essential to the plot of the

---

[332] E.g., Speiser, *Genesis,* 249; also see von Rad, *Genesis,* 305, who identifies the Elohist in vv. 2,4–18a,19,24,26,28–45,53–55 (with Yahwistic parts).

[333] Van Seters, *Prologue to History,* 295.

[334] Carr, *Reading the Fractures of Genesis,* 106, 211–13, 256–64.

wider composition.[335] The promise of divine guidance at the start (28:15), mid-point (31:3), and end (46:2–4) of the Jacob-Joseph story shows that chap. 31 is integral to the development of the whole and cannot be an independent composition. Also Van Seters rightly indicates that 31:3,13 alludes to 28:10–22, involving both the promise and the vow, making the many references in chap. 31 to divine appearances (vv. 24,29,42) and to the God of the fathers (vv. 5,29,42,53) additional inferences.[336] Most likely the chapter's author was the same figure who drafted the departure of Jacob (chap. 28) as well as the events of his return (chap. 31). As for the proposed doublets in the passage, there are plausible explanations based on a thorough exegesis that do not require parallel sources. We will examine these in the commentary below.

STRUCTURE.   The section begins with dissension between Laban's "sons" *(bānîm)* and Jacob (v. 1) and ends with amity between Laban and his "grandsons" *(bānîm)* and "daughters" *(bānôt; v. 55)*. That 31:1 and 31:55 [32:1] both refer to Laban and his children recommend that 31:55[32:1] is the conclusion of the section. For a satisfying closure to the engagement of Jacob and Laban, we would expect mention of Laban's return to his home, leaving Jacob at liberty. The author's interest in Laban comes to an end at this point. Reference to "Laban" occurs again only in passing when recalling earlier events (32:4[5]; 46:18,25). Moreover, the brief narrative of angels encamped at Mahanaim shows the signs of beginning a new episode at 32:1–2(2–3); see comments there).

The chapter consists of four scenes: (1) the decision to flee (vv. 1–16); (2) the flight and deceptions (vv. 17–21); (3) the overtaking of the fleeing party and the dispute (vv. 22–44); and (4) the peaceful settlement of the disputing parties (vv. 45–55). The four scenes are essentially a series of speeches that are connected by brief narratives. The most common verb in the chapter is "said/saying" *('āmar)*, appearing twenty-three times (vv. 1,3,5,8[2x],11[2x], 12,14,16,24,26,29[2x],31[2x],35,36,43,46,48,49,51). In the first unit Laban's sons speak among themselves disparagingly about Jacob (v. 1), but the Lord counters by encouraging Jacob with the directive to return home (v. 3). Jacob offers the longest speech of the unit, defending his decision to depart (vv. 4–13), and the women answer by granting consent (vv. 14–16). The second unit is a narrative bridge, absent any discourse (vv. 17–21). The third unit begins with a narrative prelude (vv. 22–25), establishing the background setting for the prolonged speeches of the disputing parties, first Laban (vv. 26–35) and second Jacob (vv. 36–42). Laban's answer is really no answer to Jacob's allegations; rather, he proposes a settlement (vv. 43–44). The fourth unit has a brief word from Jacob to his own group (v. 46), and Laban's speech dominates, presenting the stipulations of the covenant (vv. 48–53a).

[335] Rendtorff, *The Problem,* 75.
[336] Van Seters, *Prologue to History,* 295.

The first unit explains the motivation and decision of Jacob and his wives to return secretly to his father's house (vv. 1–16). Verses 1–3 give two motivations: Laban and his sons' objections to Jacob's new wealth and the divine directive to return. Verses 4–13 narrate Jacob's elaboration of these two motivations, explaining to Rachel and Leah the deceit he suffered by Laban and the dream he received from God instructing him to return. Verses 14–16 entail the response of the wives supporting both motivations: first, they too had suffered their father's abuse, and, second, they consented to follow God's command.

The second unit describes their clandestine departure (vv. 17–21). Two deceptions occur in this unit: first, Rachel "stole" *(gānab)* her father's *tĕrāpîm* ("household gods," NIV) and, second, Jacob secretly stole away *(gānab,* "deceived," NIV), that is, fleeing Paddan Aram with his family and possessions. The geographical movement is structurally important to the flow of the narrative, crossing west of the Euphrates from Paddan Aram to the hill country of Gilead.

The third unit is the dominant segment, providing the narrative tension of Laban overtaking Jacob (vv. 22–45). The two men present their allegations: first, Laban accused Jacob of harming him by stealing away secretly and by stealing his *tĕrāpîm* (vv. 26–35); second, Jacob countercharged Laban with duplicity in his wages (vv. 36–42). Laban's response is mixed, proposing a peace treaty but only after he sounds a sour note (vv. 43–44).

The fourth unit portrays the agreement that the men enter into (vv. 45–55). Two witnesses to their compact, a stone pillar and a stone heap (vv. 45–47), and two rituals, an oath and covenant meal, conclude it (vv. 53b–54). Sandwiched between is Laban's declaration of the treaty's contents (vv. 48–53a). The last verse provides closure to the ordeal, describing Laban's final farewell and peaceful withdrawal home (v. 55).

(1) Decision to Depart (31:1–16)

[1]Jacob heard that Laban's sons were saying, "Jacob has taken everything our father owned and has gained all this wealth from what belonged to our father." [2]And Jacob noticed that Laban's attitude toward him was not what it had been.

[3]Then the LORD said to Jacob, "Go back to the land of your fathers and to your relatives, and I will be with you."

[4]So Jacob sent word to Rachel and Leah to come out to the fields where his flocks were. [5]He said to them, "I see that your father's attitude toward me is not what it was before, but the God of my father has been with me. [6]You know that I've worked for your father with all my strength, [7]yet your father has cheated me by changing my wages ten times. However, God has not allowed him to harm me. [8]If he said, 'The speckled ones will be your wages,' then all the flocks gave birth to speckled young; and if he said, 'The streaked ones will be your wages,' then all the flocks bore streaked young. [9]So God has taken away your father's livestock

and has given them to me.

[10]"In breeding season I once had a dream in which I looked up and saw that the male goats mating with the flock were streaked, speckled or spotted. [11]The angel of God said to me in the dream, 'Jacob.' I answered, 'Here I am.' [12]And he said, 'Look up and see that all the male goats mating with the flock are streaked, speckled or spotted, for I have seen all that Laban has been doing to you. [13]I am the God of Bethel, where you anointed a pillar and where you made a vow to me. Now leave this land at once and go back to your native land.'"

[14]Then Rachel and Leah replied, "Do we still have any share in the inheritance of our father's estate? [15]Does he not regard us as foreigners? Not only has he sold us, but he has used up what was paid for us. [16]Surely all the wealth that God took away from our father belongs to us and our children. So do whatever God has told you."

This unit entails the introduction in vv. 1–3 and two speeches in vv. 4–16, the first by Jacob addressing Rachel and Leah (vv. 4–13) and the second the response of his wives (vv. 14–16). Jacob heard the angry voices of Laban's sons and next received the divine voice of God, who directed him to return to his father's house (vv. 1–3). These opening three verses furnish in microcosm the full explanation that Jacob gives Rachel and Leah, offering a defense for his decision to return (vv. 4–13). First, by his new demeanor their father had signaled resentment toward him, despite Jacob's devoted endeavors in their father's behalf. Second, God had shown Jacob the secret means of increasing his flocks and had given him the command to return to his father's land. The women answer Jacob's speech with their own, complaining likewise that their father had cheated them and concluding that Jacob must follow God's decree to depart (vv. 14–16).

The key word in this unit is the word "father(s)," occurring with various pronouns, "our father" (vv. 1,14,16), "your fathers" (v. 3), "your father" (vv. 5,6,7,9), and "my father" (v. 5). This recurring term establishes the interest of the passage, namely, the question of inheritance. The passage contrasts the inheritance owed Laban's sons and daughters and the inheritance that Jacob will obtain from his own father's house (Isaac). The sons protest that Jacob has swindled their father's possessions, and the daughters complain that their father robbed them of their dowry. But God instructs Jacob to return to the "land of *your fathers*" (v. 3; italics mine), indicating the promissory blessings made to Jacob's ancestors Abraham and Isaac. Jacob stands to gain far more in Canaan than even the vast possessions that he accrued in Paddan Aram (cf. 28:13–14). He is the recipient of God's immeasurable favor, who also protects him, for he promised Jacob, "I will be with you" (v. 3; cf. 26:3; 28:15).

Another important feature of this unit is the women's trust in Jacob's God. Paradoxically, it is Jacob's integrity that is essential to Rachel and Leah's acceptance of his claims to divine assistance. He makes his case for departing Paddan Aram surreptitiously. He proves that their husband's affluence came by divine order and hard work, not some sleight of hand. He must enlist the daughters of Laban as willing accomplices in his plan if it is to have a chance at success. By the women agreeing to flee with Jacob, leaving behind the proper estate due them, they cast their lot and that of their sons with Jacob, believing the veracity of Jacob's God. The daughters of Laban placed their trust in God's promises made to Jacob, as their husband had professed them. Whereas they could not rely on their father's word, they turn to their husband's God. This is another case of the "Ruth effect," where the foreign wife commits herself and future to the God of her adopted family. By abandoning their father's household, they are in effect "Arameans" no more, for they have sided with the God of Jacob, who establishes their posterity in the land of Canaan. Like Rebekah before them, who left her home in Paddan Aram for the unseen, they chose to flee to Abraham's land of Canaan.

DISSENSION AND DIVINE DIRECTIVE (31:1–3). After describing the prosperity Jacob enjoyed (30:43), the narrative addresses the obvious concern of the Laban household. The men of the house resented Jacob for his wealth, for in their view he had obtained it to their loss. The sons stood first in line to fall heir to their father's holdings, but the odd turn of events in the previous six years reversed the status of their brother-in-law, a male "Cinderella," whose work and "luck" meant rags to riches. Verses 1–2 give the human perspective of envy on Jacob's prosperity, and v. 3 gives the divine perspective, instructing Jacob to return and claim his own father's inheritance. This interspersing of the human-divine descriptions recalls chaps. 30 and 31; the human description of Jacob's breeding methods in chap. 30 precedes the divine perspective of his achievements in chap. 31.

31:1 Mention of Laban's "sons" (v. 1) provides for a comparison with Laban's daughters, who will also complain about inheritance but against their father (v. 14). That Jacob both "heard" (*šāmaʿ*, v. 1) and "saw" (*rāʾâ*, "noticed," v. 2) corroborates the danger Jacob fears for his sons. Also the verbs "heard" and "saw" repeat the etymologies of Jacob's first two sons, Reuben (29:32) and Simeon (29:33), calling to mind God's benevolent provision (29:25–30:24). "Has taken" *(lāqaḥ)* was their charge against Jacob, one that Esau had justly made *(lāqaḥ,* 27:36), but not a valid one in this present case. Jacob and his wives explained his acquisitions as the gift of God, not by thievery. The chiasmus of v. 1 exaggerates the idea of Laban's holdings, further embellished by the repetition of "all":

took-Jacob-all-which-belonged-to-our father//
from-which-belonged-to-our father-he gained-all-this wealth

As in the catalog of Jacob's holdings in the previous 30:43, the term "wealth" *(kābôd)* recalls the account of Abraham's riches *(kābēd,* 13:2). The language "this wealth" is a reference to 30:43, as though the sons had taken the same accounting of Jacob's possessions, as had the narrator.

31:2–3 Laban regretted the enlistment of Jacob, since his nephew had outwitted him. "Laban's attitude" (v. 2; cf. v. 5) renders the literal phrase "the face of Laban" *(pĕnê lābān),* which parallels the prior phrase "the words of the sons of Laban" *(dibrĕ bĕnê lābān,* v. 1). This repetition reinforces the obvious, namely, that Laban's feelings toward Jacob changed for the same reason the sons had complained. Unlike Laban's change of favor, God's attitude had not altered toward him. The passage indicates this contrast in two ways. First, "with him" (*ʿimmô,* "toward him," v. 2) parallels "with you" (*ʿimmāk,* v. 3), meaning that God's promise in v. 3 echoes the commitment first made at Bethel (28:15). Second, the phrase "face *[pānîm]* of Laban" (v. 2) creates a subtle wordplay anticipating the narration of Jacob's continued progress to Canaan, when he meets God "face to face" *(pānîm ʾel pānîm)* at Peniel (32:30) and encounters Esau, recognizing in him the "face of God" *(pĕnê ʾĕlōhîm,* 33:10). The Lord will exchange the anger of Laban for his favor, rescuing Jacob from Laban and Esau.

Verse 3 entails both a directive ("go back") and a promise ("I will be with you"). Verse 3 is not from a source differing from vv. 1–2 (J vs. E), as some scholars have proposed. As Van Seters points out, vv. 2–3 are introductory, anticipating Jacob's elaboration of these events in vv. 5–13.[337] Verse 3, we have noted, contrasts God's unchanged relationship and Laban's changed demeanor toward Jacob. The verse recalls the first appearance to Jacob at Bethel (28:13–16). Now is the time for God to make good on that promise, requiring Jacob to muster the courage to strike out on his own. "Land of your fathers" provides another contrast with Laban, who is the "father" of the Aramean clan (cp. "our/your father," vv. 1,5,6,7,9,14,16). Jacob's heritage lies in the land of Canaan, the land promised to his fathers; his destiny does not lie in the household of Laban.

JACOB'S DEFENSE (31:4–13). Jacob summoned his wives Rachel and Leah to hear his plan, seeking their endorsement (v. 4). His speech presents a well-reasoned and impassioned plea for their collaboration in his scheme. He first establishes that Laban's change of heart has created the crisis that Jacob must now address (vv. 5–7). The problem wholly lies with their father. His contention begins by deflecting any possible countercharge that Jacob's plight was the result of delinquency in his service to Laban. He makes it clear that he is the victim. He then accuses Laban with duplicity by varying the basis of his wages for his own advantage (vv. 8–10). Finally, and most important, he shows that God delivered him from Laban and directed him to return home (vv. 11–13). The author shows that God superseded the mischief of Laban: first, despite the harm intended, Jacob still prospered, and, second, the Lord

---

[337] Ibid.

had revealed the means of this prosperity through a dream.

Summons (31:4).   **31:4**   Mention of Rachel first is due to her prominence in the chapter. The absence of the concubine wives (Bilhah, Zilpah) is
because of Rachel and Leah's relationship with Laban as his daughters. As
legitimate wives, they had more at stake in the decision to return, and further
these two represented the whole of Jacob's heirs. The purpose in calling them
away to the "field" was for secrecy, but symbolically, the setting apart from
Laban's camp indicated the division that had begun between Laban and his
daughters. The women come into view on the side of their husband, unsym-
pathetic to their father's plight. In addition, mention of "*his* flocks" (italics
mine) as Jacob's reinforces that the animals are legitimately his possession,
not Laban's (cf. 30:43). The presence of the herds also represented the wealth
that had been the women's sore spot with their father.

Laban's Duplicity (31:5–7).   **31:5**   Jacob initiates his speech by reporting on the state of his relationship with their father, giving the reason for his
summons. His remarks repeat in effect what was narrated in v. 2. Jacob does
not include the grumbling of their brothers, probably because the seat of the
dispute rested with him and Laban. The viewpoint of the sons would be predictable, but what was the opinion of the daughters? Their father's cool disposition toward him contrasts with Jacob's "God of my father." "Toward me"
versus "with me" heightens the polarity. Jacob's acknowledgment of his heritage ("my father") recollects the promises, specifically the promise of divine
presence.

31:6–7   Verse 6 initiates the specific defense he employs.[338] Jacob begins
with what would be clear to them, stressing the pronoun "you know."[339] By
mentioning his hard work first, Jacob reveals the extent of Laban's inequity.
Repeated reference to "your father" (vv. 6–7), however, shows respectful deference to the women's family tie to Laban. Also "your father" parallels the
sons, who spoke of "our father" (v. 1), maintaining the passage's focus on
inheritance. "All *[kol]* my strength" is another emphatic element, amplifying
the argument of his case. "Worked" *('ābad)* has been a recurring term in the
Jacob-Laban narrative, showing that the present dispute is essentially a continuation of an ongoing grievance.

Verse 7 begins with the phrase "your father," creating a chiasmus with v. 6.
In this verse Jacob makes his charge definitively: Laban "cheated" *(tālal)*
him. The term "cheated" means deceived or fooled in the sense of failing to
follow up on a commitment (cf. Exod 8:29[25]; Jer 9:5[4]).[340] Here it
describes Laban's repeated change in Jacob's wages whenever the need

---

[338] Introduced by the *wāw* disjunctive, וְאַתֵּנָה יְדַעְתֶּן, "Now you know . . ."

[339] The pronoun provides focused attention on the subject (*IBHS* §16.2.3e).

[340] E. Carpenter and M. Grisanti, "תלל," *NIDOTTE* 4.299.

arose.[341] "Wages" *(maśkōret)* is another key word, hearkening back to the first travesty against Jacob (29:15). "Ten times" seems extreme, if held literally, and probably is a hyperbole here (cf. v. 41; 24:55), meaning many times, that is, "time after time" (NAB; e.g., Lev 26:26; Num 14:22; Amos 6:9; Zech 8:23). The two men had agreed on Jacob's wages (30:28,32–33), but Laban's words were empty promises. "However, God" (v. 7b) continues the contrast between Laban's and God's behavior toward Jacob. It reinforces his fundamental claim that the Lord showed his favor by rescuing him (cf. v. 5). "Has not allowed him" translates the literal text "did not give *[nātan]* him" (cp. v. 9), meaning that the Lord did not grant Laban the freedom to mistreat him (cp. Exod 12:23; Hos 5:4). That the Lord controls Jacob's welfare, protecting him against "harm" *(rā'a'),* anticipates the Lord's warning against Laban, not to say anything "good or bad *[ra']*" against him (v. 24).

Cheating Wages (31:8–9). **31:8–9** Jacob illustrates his charge by describing how Laban altered the basis of their agreement whenever Jacob met with some success (v. 8). It was to no avail, however, for Jacob explained that his prosperity did not abate under the new arrangements Laban made. How was this possible? Verse 9 indicates that Jacob attributed his success ultimately to God, not the wizardry of the variegated rods he employed (30:32–39). He implies that as God intervened in the matter of their possessions, he would secure their future apart from their father. Abraham's servant implied the same when describing his master's wealth as the consequence of divine favor (24:35–36). The verb "has taken away" *(nāṣal,* v. 9) differs from the typical term "has taken" *(lāqaḥ,* v. 1). The word *nāṣal* is a common word but usually indicates deliverance or salvation from physical harm (e.g., 32:11[12],30[31]; 37:21–22).[342] Here, by employing *nāṣal,* Jacob may be implying that as God had plucked the animals from Laban's clutches, he will deliver their family from injury. That God had delivered the animals proved his resourcefulness to rescue them (cf. v. 16). Since "has given" *(nātan)* echoes v. 7, where it occurs with "harm," its reappearance in v. 9 reinforces this notion of divine rescue.

Dream Theophany (31:10–13). **31:10–13** Jacob withheld the strongest justification for his plan to the last of his defense, that is, the report of his dream theophany. So as to confirm that he rightly attributed his success to God (v. 9), he related the dream in which the angel of God had spoken to him (presumably before the agreement with Laban in 30:31–36). We would

---

[341] GKC §112h identifies וְהֶחֱלִף (MT), "and he changed," as a frequentive (continuous or repeated action) use of the perfect; *IBHS* §32.3.b analyzes הֵתֶל בִּי וְהֶחֱלִף as a hendiadys (i.e., "two aspects of a complex situation")—"cheated me by changing," as in NIV, NJB, NJPS. SP has the imperfect plus *wāw* consecutive, וַיַּחֲלֹף as in v. 41 (see *BHS*).

[342] Sarna notes that נצל and נתן ("give") describe the transference of property in Aramaic legal documents (*Genesis,* 214, 365–66).

expect vv. 11–12, the speech of the angel ("Look up and see," v. 12), to appear in the narrative before v. 10 ("I looked up and saw") that describes his response to the angel's command. But Jacob is anxious to show that the success of his breeding was the result of God's benevolence, not his own genius or good luck; thus he mentions the contents of the vision twice (vv. 10,12). Moreover, the description of his action before relating the divine directive shows the man's fervent obedience. Verse 13 expands on what was first stated in a condensed form (v. 3).

Dreams were a medium of divine revelation that ancient peoples highly esteemed, playing a special role in the patriarchal accounts (cf. 20:3,6; 28:12; 31:24; 37:5–10,19–20; 40:5,8,9,16; 41:1–32; 42:9). The dream occurred at the propitious time of the breeding season. Jacob remarks that he "saw" variegated goats mating with the flock (vv. 10,12). Since he does not include any verbal instructions from God pertaining to breeding, the visual alone must have incited Jacob to employ his peculiar methods of peeled branches. This device was his doing, not a direct instruction from God. The Lord blessed his efforts, though unenlightened as they were.

What Jacob heard from the "angel of God" (cf. comments on 16:7; 21:17) is reminiscent of former revelations to the patriarchs. That he "looked up and saw" repeats the formulaic language introducing theophany (13:14; 18:2); it also is formulary for crucial encounters in the life of the patriarchs (22:4,13; 24:64; 33:1,5; 37:25; 43:29). The angel's call to Jacob and his response, "Here I am," reminds us of Abraham at Moriah (22:11). "Lift up your eyes" (v. 12; NIV "Look up") are the exact words heard by Abraham in the Lot incident (13:14). Most obvious, v. 13 rehearses the revelation to Jacob at Bethel, where he consecrated a pillar with oil and vowed allegiance to the Lord (28:18–22). "I am the God of Bethel"[343] self-identifies the Lord in terms of the theophany at Bethel, while on the contrary he identified himself initially in terms of family relationship (28:13). It is the promise of the land that is paramount in the revelation. The mentions of "pillar" and "vow" capture the author's focus on Jacob's expressions of worship at Bethel. That the resumptive use of the adverb *šām* ("there")[344] occurs twice in v. 13 strengthens awareness of the place of the initial revelation (cf. 28:11). The place Bethel became especially connected with the revelation that God gave the patriarch (e.g., 35:1,8,15; Hos 12:4).

Jacob bolsters his argument when repeating the message of the angel. First, God affirms Jacob's claim of mistreatment (v. 12b). Jacob states clearly

---

[343] אָנֹכִי הָאֵל בֵּית־אֵל; on the uncommon use of the definite article, see the explanation in GKC §127f.

[344] אֲשֶׁר מָשַׁחְתָּ שָּׁם, lit., "which you anointed there" ("where you anointed . . .," NIV) and אֲשֶׁר נָדַרְתָּ לִּי שָׁם נֶדֶר, lit., "which you vowed to me there" ("where you made a vow to me," NIV).

the connection (*kî*, "for") between Laban's misbehavior and the Lord's gracious intervention. "I have seen" indicates the Lord's supervision and sympathy for Jacob's plight, safekeeping him as he had first promised (28:20–21; cp. Exod 3:7,9). The Lord's description of Laban's wrongdoing is a general observation, but if a specific incident is in mind, it would refer to the fourteen years Jacob worked for his wives since the dream preceded the additional six years of breeding. Jacob complains to Laban that he changes his wages during the whole of the twenty-year service (31:38–42; cf. 31:4–9).

Second, by this divine authority, Jacob entreated his wives to join him in flight to Canaan (v. 13b with v. 3). The urgency of the divine directive is conveyed by "now" and three imperatives, "arise," "leave," and "go back." The former two are asyndetic interjections, lit., "arise, leave!" *(qûm ṣēʾ)*,[345] which the NIV, NRSV render "leave . . . at once." The relationship between the two exhortations to leave in vv. 3 and 13 is not clear. One explanation is that vv. 10–13 contain two dreams: the first is in the past (vv. 10–12), and the second is in the present (v. 13), referring to the same message recalled in v. 3.[346] An alternative explanation is that the exhortation in v. 13 takes into account the period of breeding, instructing Jacob to leave after he gained his flocks. The phrase "at once" in v. 13 is an inference only and not explicit in the Hebrew text. The last imperative, "go back *[šûb]* to your native land," echoes the promissory and votive language spoken at Bethel (28:15,21; cf. 32:9[10]). Reference to the "land of your birth" immediately connects the command with the ancestor's heritage of land, but the promises are not dependent on the land. They are dependent on God's faithful word. Whether Jacob is in or outside the land, the Lord is with him and provides for him.[347]

HIS WIVES CONSENT TO LEAVE (31:14–16). Rachel and Leah not only agree with their husband's decision but also add other reasons for departing their homeland.

31:14–15 "Rachel" appears first in the duo since she plays the prominent role in the narrative (v. 14). The women's rhetorical question complains that their father has not provided an inheritance for them. The terms "portion" (*ḥeleq*, "share" NIV), "inheritance" *(naḥălâ)*,[348] and "our father's house" (*bêt ʾābînû*, "estate" NIV) speak to the women's main concern. They admit that they (and their sons) have no future if they remain under their father's custody (cp. the hostilities in 2 Sam 20:1; 1 Kgs 12:16). The NLT reflects their sentiment

---

[345] GKC §120g. Cf. 19:14, קוּמוּ צְּאוּ, "hurry and get out!" (also Exod 12:31).

[346] G. C. Aalders, *Genesis,* BSC, trans. W. Heynen, 2 vols. (Grand Rapids: Regency/Zondervan, 1981), 2.129; Sarna, *Genesis,* 214.

[347] On the significance of "your native land," lit. "land of your birth" *(môledet),* in 31:3,13, see comments on 11:28; 12:1; 24:4,7; 32:9[10].

[348] The NIV translates חֵלֶק וְנַחֲלָה, lit., "a portion and an inheritance," as a hendiadys, "share in the inheritance" (cf. NAB, NJB, REB, NJPS).

well, "There's nothing for us here." "Portion" and "inheritance" when pertaining to tribal lands often appear in tandem, describing the omission of property for the priestly station (e.g., Num 18:20; Deut 18:1). Since women did not customarily inherit property (cf. Num 27:7–11), their accusation probably refers to the circumstances of their marriage.

They explain obliquely why they were cut off from their father's inheritance (v. 15). He regarded them as "foreigners" *(nokrî,* v. 15), aliens or outsiders, whom he debased by selling them and then squandering their bridal gift. Laban took advantage of their husband's circumstances, trading on his poverty. In some way uncertain to us, the women were to benefit monetarily from the work that Jacob did for Laban, substituting his work for payment of the bridal gift *(mōhar).* Not only were the daughters offended at the way Laban arranged their marriages, but he added injury by draining ("has used up," *yōʾkal gam ʾākôl,*[349] cf. "consumed," v. 40) "what was paid for us" (lit., "our silver/money," cf. 43:21–22).

31:16 They conclude by agreeing with Jacob that God had intervened in their state of affairs, delivering over *(nāṣal,* cf. v. 9) the stolen wealth to Jacob. Jacob and his wives each interpret the transference of property as just payment for the offense each suffered from Laban's deviousness. In their minds, their actions are the outworking of divine reparations. Jacob was anxious to show his wives that he received only what was legitimately earned. The women answer that they thereby received only what propriety called for. Mention of "our children" evidences the women's zeal for their own heirs, distinguishing their family from that of their father and brothers. The line in the sand is drawn, and their allegiance is solely to their husband and children.

(2) Jacob's and Rachel's Deceptions (31:17–21)

17Then Jacob put his children and his wives on camels, **18**and he drove all his livestock ahead of him, along with all the goods he had accumulated in Paddan Aram, to go to his father Isaac in the land of Canaan.

19When Laban had gone to shear his sheep, Rachel stole her father's household gods. **20**Moreover, Jacob deceived Laban the Aramean by not telling him he was running away. **21**So he fled with all he had, and crossing the River, he headed for the hill country of Gilead.

Verses 17–18 describe the preparations for their escape, and v. 21 sets forth the actual escape to Gilead. Between these accounts the passage tells the deceptions that Rachel and Jacob each committed against Laban (vv. 19–20). They repaid Laban's treachery wreaked upon them with treachery.

31:17–18 The text begins with "he arose" *(qûm,* v. 17; absent NIV),

---

[349] וַיֹּאכַל גַּם־אָכוֹל, "he has even used up . . ." (imperf. + adv. + infin. absol.; cf. *IBHS* §35.3.1f).

which corresponds to the divine command, "arise!" *(qûm)*, in Jacob's dream (cf. v. 13), indicating thereby his compliant response. In keeping with the passage's focus on inheritance, the verse mentions "his children" before Jacob's wives (v. 17). The detail of "camels" presages the deception Rachel achieved (v. 34). It also exhibits Jacob's wealth and provides another literary link to the historic discovery of Rebekah in Paddan Aram (24:61,64). Camels would provide a quicker getaway than by foot, meaning that Jacob arranged for the escape of the women and children at the very least.

Verse 18 elaborates on his vast possessions, noting Jacob's ("his") ownership of the herds (not Laban's, contra v. 43). The verse involves cumbersome but purposeful redundancy, creating the rhetorical effect of abundant belongings.[350] The repetition of "all" (*kol* [2x]) further conveys the idea of fulfillment. "All the goods he had accumulated" typically appears in those passages describing a person's migration, including Abram's move to Canaan (12:5; 36:6; 46:6). Two rhetorical contrasts in the verse heighten the effect of indicating a completed transference. (1) Geographically, the movement is away from Paddan Aram to the new residence of Canaan and hence new ownership. (2) "His father Isaac" closes the circle for Jacob, who departed his father's household in search of a wife (27:46–28:5) and now will return with wives and numerous possessions, transferring them from their father's house to "his" father's house. Whatever wealth Abraham may have forfeited upon leaving the family unit of Terah in Haran comes to his heirs in this most unimaginable way.

31:19 Verses 19–20 describe the "thefts" by Rachel and Jacob, employing the same word *gānab* ("to steal, steal away") in each description, translated "stole" (v. 19) and "deceived"[351] (v. 20). Verse 19 provides the supplementary but important information that Laban was away, overseeing the shearing of his animals.[352] This bit of information explains why Rachel and Jacob could achieve their deeds without detection. Biblical and extrabiblical sources indicate that shearing typically occurred in outlying areas and required considerable manpower (e.g., 38:12–13; 1 Sam 25:2; 2 Sam 13:23). The activity of shearing was in April-May (Deut 18:4), and it was a festive occasion involving family and friends.[353] This meant that Laban and his sons were preoccupied with the demands of their flocks, leaving their home and grounds vulnerable to mischief.

---

[350] The NIV does not show this as clearly as some EVs (e.g., AV, ESV, NASB, NRSV). Repetition of the phrase אֲשֶׁר רָכָשׁ, lit., "which he possessed" (2x), explains the error of the LXX, Syr., omitting the first occasion by homeoarcton (cf. *BHS*).

[351] וַיִּגְנֹב יַעֲקֹב אֶת לֵב לָבָן, lit., "Jacob stole the heart of Laban."

[352] The *wāw* disjunctive introduces v. 19, וְלָבָן הָלַךְ, "Now Laban had gone . . ." (e.g., NASB, NRSV).

[353] O. Borowski, "Sheep," *EDB* 1203.

Rachel seized this opportunity to steal Laban's "household gods" *(tĕrāpîm;* v. 19). The EVs translate the word *tĕrāpîm* in our passage in varied ways, for example, "images" (AV), "household gods" (NIV, ESV, REB, NRSV), and "household idols" (NJB, NAB, NASB, HCSB, NJPS). The LXX has "idols" *(eidōla),*[354] and the targums translate "images" *(ṣalmānayyā').* These renderings are derived from the context itself, where the *tĕrāpîm* are identified as "gods" *('ĕlōhîm,* 31:30,32). What we know about *tĕrāpîm,* however, is sketchy, despite its frequent occurrence in fifteen passages.[355] The etymology of the term remains disputed, giving us little insight.[356] From the Old Testament's usage we can summarize the following traits. First, description of *tĕrāpîm* in Michal's ruse (1 Sam 19:13–16) presents a figure that was human-like in (upper) torso and size. Yet, since Laban's *tĕrāpîm* could fit undetected in a camel's saddle (v. 34), we may surmise that *tĕrāpîm* constituted different sizes and perhaps shapes. Second, in addition to the equation of the *tĕrāpîm* with "gods" (vv. 30,32), the word occurs in lists of religious icons, especially with the "ephod," inferring that *tĕrāpîm* sometimes had a cultic function (e.g., Judg 17:5; 18:14,17–20; Hos 3:4; Zech 10:2). Third, *tĕrāpîm* is listed among various forms of divination (1 Sam 15:23; 2 Kgs 23:24; Ezek 21:21[26]; Zech 10:2). Finally, mention of *tĕrāpîm* in at least one domestic setting implies that they were household figurines of some sort (1 Sam 9:13,16; cf. Judg 18:18).

As to what their significance was, interpreters are divided. E. A. Speiser popularized the view held by many scholars that Laban's *tĕrāpîm* paralleled a Hurrian practice known from Nuzi documents (fifteenth century), where the possessor of the household gods identified the legal heir of the estate.[357] In this case *tĕrāpîm/'ĕlōhîm* parallels the Mesopotamian *ilāni,* "house gods." M. Heltzer's study of the inheritance texts from Emar (Syria, fourth–twelfth centuries) showed that the chief heir received the household gods exclusively, prohibiting the sharing or selling to any other claimant. Since one of Laban's

---

[354] Aquila has μορφώματα ("forms"), and Symmachus transliterates θεραφείν (φείμ) (= תְּרָפִין; Wevers, *Notes on the Greek Text,* 505); also θεραφιν in Judg 18:14 *passim;* 1 Sam 15:23; 2 Kgs 23:24.

[355] 1:19,34,35; Judg 17:5; 18:14,17,18,20; 1 Sam 15:23; 19:13,16; 2 Kgs 23:24; Ezek 21:21 [26]; Hos 3:4; Zech 10:2; though always occurring in the plural form, תְּרָפִים can refer to a single item (e.g., 1 Sam 19:13,16).

[356] H. A. Hoffner debunks the traditional Semitic proposals (*rp',* "heal," *rpy,* "languid, limp," *ptrym,* "interpreters"), favoring Hittite *tarpi-,* meaning "spirit, demon," concluding that the *tĕrāpîm* were objects of cultic inquiry ("Hittite *Tarpiš* and Hebrew *Terāphîm,*" *JNES* 27 [1968]: 61–68).

[357] Speiser, *Genesis,* 250; for the technical literature arguing this view, including Speiser's articles, see M. Greenberg, "Another Look at Rachel's Theft of the Teraphim," *JBL* 81 (1962): 239–48 and K. van der Toorn, "The Nature of the Biblical Teraphim in the Light of the Cuneiform Evidence," *CBQ* 52 (1990): 203–22.

sons (v. 1) was most likely the designated heir, the family gods could not have been transferred legitimately to Jacob, an alien, or to the daughters, who had no standing to inherit Laban's land.[358] The advantage of this interpretation is the context of our passage since the women recognized that they did not have an inheritance, making it understandable why Rachel stole the *tĕrāpîm* and why Laban searched for them so vigorously.[359] Yet the context also shows that the departure of the women and their children for distant Canaan would make a claim on Laban's inheritance moot. Greenberg long ago observed that the women and Jacob "appear to have had quite enough of Laban and family."[360] K. Spanier offers alternatively that possession of Laban's *tĕrāpîm* gave Rachel's son (Joseph) priority over Leah's children as head of the family.[361] This proposal would make more sense if the *tĕrāpîm* belonged to Jacob, since the issue was an inner-Jacob struggle for supremacy. More important, the struggle between the women reached its denouement with the birth of Joseph, ending the narrative interest in the sisters' dispute. The struggle in later years is among the brothers, not between their mothers. K. van der Toorn, drawing on extrabiblical parallels (Old Akk., Nuzi, and Emar documents), speculates that *tĕrāpîm* were possibly equivalent to the Mesopotamian *eṭemmū*, "the spirits of the dead (ancestors)."[362] He proposes that some biblical texts show that *tĕrāpîm* functioned as cultic ancestor figurines (cf. Deut 18:11 with 2 Kgs 23:24) that served the purpose of necromancy. The chief difficulties with his view are on the biblical side of the evidence, which van der Toorn himself acknowledges is inadequate to establish that *tĕrāpîm* signified ancestral spirits in Israel. Still others have explained *tĕrāpîm* as household gods that turned away evil or were part of a healing ritual.[363]

What we do know is that *tĕrāpîm* were associated with divination in some biblical settings. If mention of *tĕrāpîm* suggests divination in the Jacob-Laban narrative, it provides a literary parallel to Joseph's silver "cup" used for divination, also considered stolen (cf. comments on 44:5). That Laban practiced some form of divination is clear from 30:27. What was important to

---

[358] M. Heltzer, "New Light from Emar on Genesis 31: The Theft of the Teraphim," in *Und Mose schrieb dieses Lied auf: Studien zum Alten Testament und zum alten Orient; Festschrift für Oswald Loretz zur Vollendung seines 70. Lebensjahres mit Beiträgen von Freunden, Schülern, und Kollegen*, AOAT 20 (Münster: Ugarit-Verlag, 1998), 357–62.

[359] Calvin scathingly rebukes Rachel's action as the consequence of idolatrous infatuations, long practiced by her ancestors (Terah-Bethuel-Laban; *Comm.*, 169–70).

[360] Greenberg, "Another Look," 245.

[361] Greenberg first proposed that at Nuzi possessor of the household gods indicated the leader of the family, the *"paterfamilias"* (ibid.); see K. Spanier, "Rachel's Theft of the Teraphim: Her Struggle for Family Primacy," *VT* 42 (1992): 404–12.

[362] van der Toorn, "The Nature of the Biblical Teraphim," 203–22.

[363] See T. J. Lewis, "Teraphim תְּרָפִים," *DDD* 844–50, for a helpful discussion.

both stories is that the ruling head lost a valued article to theft. If we conjecture that Laban's *tĕrāpîm* were made of costly metal (cf. Judg 17:4), they would have been highly valued heirlooms. In this situation we can explain Rachel's theft of the *tĕrāpîm* for their inherent value, compensating for the bridal money that Laban had depleted.

31:20 The rare idiom "steal the heart" (*gānab lēb/gānab lĕbab,* vv. 20,26) means "deceive"; in v. 27 the term *gānab* occurs by itself, equating to the whole idiomatic expression (cf. *rāmâ,* "deceived," 29:25). Mention of Laban as "the Aramean" at this point in the story reinforces the identities of the two peoples in accord with the emphasis of the author (e.g., vv. 24,47; cf. 25:20; 28:5). The verse continues by explaining how Jacob deceived his father-in-law. He secretly fled, avoiding any possible interference from Laban (30:26). The term "to flee" *(bāraḥ)* occurs also in v. 21, recalling Jacob's hasty flight from the anger of Esau (27:43; 35:1,7; cf. Hagar's running away, 16:6,8; also Moses, Exod 2:15). Jacob's comings and goings were marked by fearful escapes. His life of deception entailed personal and family cost.

31:21 This verse forms an inclusion with vv. 17–18. It describes the episode directly, asserting again the disposition of his departure as "flight" *(bāraḥ),* not the customary parting of family members (cp. 24:56–61; Judg 19:3–10). Sarna observes that the verse's arrangement of the verbs "flee" and "arise" brings the narrative of Jacob's flight full circle, from his homeland and back.[364] At 27:43, when Jacob fled Esau's wrath, the Hebrew has "arise, flee" *(qûm bāraḥ),* which are reversed in the Hebrew text, describing Jacob's flight from Laban to his home, "he fled . . . arose" *(wayyibraḥ . . . wayyāqom).* His escape included his entire holdings, making for a slow journey. The route Jacob took becomes important in the narrative. By crossing the Euphrates ("River"), he moved beyond central Paddan Aram and arrived in the transjordan region Gilead (cf. vv. 25,47–48). Gilead stretched from its northern boundary of the Yarmuk River, lying alongside the eastern side of the Jordan valley, to the southern border of the Arnon River, an area approximating modern Jordan. The flow of the River Jabbok divides the region into northern and southern sectors, which was the momentous site of Jacob's crossing (32:22). Mention of the "hill country" suits the topography of the region that was mountainous and lushly forested. Such challenging terrain for the migration of herds would have impeded his progress significantly but provided a good hideout.

(3) *Jacob and Laban's Disputes (31:22–44)*

[22]On the third day Laban was told that Jacob had fled. [23]Taking his relatives with him, he pursued Jacob for seven days and caught up with him in the hill

---

[364] Sarna, *Genesis,* 217.

country of Gilead. [24]Then God came to Laban the Aramean in a dream at night and said to him, "Be careful not to say anything to Jacob, either good or bad."

[25]Jacob had pitched his tent in the hill country of Gilead when Laban overtook him, and Laban and his relatives camped there too. [26]Then Laban said to Jacob, "What have you done? You've deceived me, and you've carried off my daughters like captives in war. [27]Why did you run off secretly and deceive me? Why didn't you tell me, so I could send you away with joy and singing to the music of tambourines and harps? [28]You didn't even let me kiss my grandchildren and my daughters good-by. You have done a foolish thing. [29]I have the power to harm you; but last night the God of your father said to me, 'Be careful not to say anything to Jacob, either good or bad.' [30]Now you have gone off because you longed to return to your father's house. But why did you steal my gods?"

[31]Jacob answered Laban, "I was afraid, because I thought you would take your daughters away from me by force. [32]But if you find anyone who has your gods, he shall not live. In the presence of our relatives, see for yourself whether there is anything of yours here with me; and if so, take it." Now Jacob did not know that Rachel had stolen the gods.

[33]So Laban went into Jacob's tent and into Leah's tent and into the tent of the two maidservants, but he found nothing. After he came out of Leah's tent, he entered Rachel's tent. [34]Now Rachel had taken the household gods and put them inside her camel's saddle and was sitting on them. Laban searched through everything in the tent but found nothing.

[35]Rachel said to her father, "Don't be angry, my lord, that I cannot stand up in your presence; I'm having my period." So he searched but could not find the household gods.

[36]Jacob was angry and took Laban to task. "What is my crime?" he asked Laban. "What sin have I committed that you hunt me down? [37]Now that you have searched through all my goods, what have you found that belongs to your household? Put it here in front of your relatives and mine, and let them judge between the two of us.

[38]"I have been with you for twenty years now. Your sheep and goats have not miscarried, nor have I eaten rams from your flocks. [39]I did not bring you animals torn by wild beasts; I bore the loss myself. And you demanded payment from me for whatever was stolen by day or night. [40]This was my situation: The heat consumed me in the daytime and the cold at night, and sleep fled from my eyes. [41]It was like this for the twenty years I was in your household. I worked for you fourteen years for your two daughters and six years for your flocks, and you changed my wages ten times. [42]If the God of my father, the God of Abraham and the Fear of Isaac, had not been with me, you would surely have sent me away empty-handed. But God has seen my hardship and the toil of my hands, and last night he rebuked you."

[43]Laban answered Jacob, "The women are my daughters, the children are my children, and the flocks are my flocks. All you see is mine. Yet what can I do today about these daughters of mine, or about the children they have borne? [44]Come now, let's make a covenant, you and I, and let it serve as a witness between us."

This is the primary unit of the chapter, detailing the anxious encounter of the two men. Verses 22–25 establish the setting for the two rounds of dialogue in vv. 26–44 that dominate the unit. After rapidly marking off ten days (vv. 22–25), the narrative pace becomes deliberate, telling the elaborate arguments of the two antagonists.

1. Laban speaks first, bringing serious charges of deception and theft against Jacob (vv. 26–35). "You have done a foolish thing" (v. 28b) reflects the belittling tone of the elder's allegations. His first indictment was the covert manner of Jacob's getaway, preventing him from giving his family a proper good-bye (vv. 26–29). The more injurious charge was theft of Laban's "household gods" (v. 30). Jacob rebuts Laban's charges by justifying his actions against the first charge but denying the second, inviting Laban to scour the premises for the allegedly stolen property (vv. 31–32a).

A narrative interlude follows, recounting Laban's search (vv. 32b–35). The author heightens the narrative tension by depicting Laban's thoroughgoing inspection of each person's tent, making central the ruse that Rachel carries out. The author makes it clear, however, that Jacob was unaware of Rachel's burglary, absolving him of the charge.

2. After no fault was found against him, Jacob unleashed twenty years of anger, rehearsing in painful detail his ordeal at the unscrupulous hands of Laban. His bitter complaints end, charging that had God not rescued him Laban would have harmed him (vv. 36–42). In effect he utterly rejected Laban's phony expressions of devotion to his daughters. Laban completes the second round of speeches by a deferential offer, inviting Jacob to enter into a compact, but only after he had made a disingenuous claim of ownership (vv. 43–44). There was no true reconciliation between them, and the dual function of the pillar as both witness and boundary marker reflected their abiding suspicions (cf. v. 52).

LABAN CONFRONTS JACOB (31:22–25). After three days Laban learns of Jacob's treachery (v. 22), and he hotly pursues him all the way to Gilead, where both encamp (vv. 23,25). In a night dream God forewarns Laban against harming the patriarch (v. 24).

31:22–23 "Three" and "seven" days probably are formulaic expressions for relatively shorter and longer durations, not to be taken as ten actual days. Sarna observes that the distance from Haran to Gilead (ca. four hundred miles) far exceeds what a caravan would be expected to travel in such time, moving only about six miles a day.[365] By assembling a host of kinfolk, Laban's actions suggest that he had harm in mind, or at least intimidation, requiring God's intervention to deliver Jacob. "Pursued" *(rādap)* often describes trailing armies with hostile intentions (e.g., 14:14–15; Exod 14:9; Judg 8:12). Laban's later boast implied that Jacob's small band of servants was of no consequence

---

[365] Sarna, *Genesis*, 217.

(v. 29). This bravado even in the face of God's forewarning gives credence to Jacob's fears (vv. 31,42). One can only imagine what havoc Laban would have committed if the Lord had not restrained him.

31:24 The dream sequence is reminiscent of Abimelech's dream (20:3–7). The brevity of the divine message may be due to the author's assumption that the reader recalls the fuller message delivered to Abimelech. In the present situation, however, Laban has no room to raise objection, leaving him speechless. The dream is effective, for Laban refers to it as the sole restraint on his strength (v. 29). "Be careful" *(šāmar)* is a typical expression when exhorting a person to observe a command (e.g., 24:6; Exod 10:28). It is an echo of God's promise to Jacob at Bethel, "I will watch *[šāmar]* over you" (28:15; cf. v. 20). The prohibition entails the merism "good or bad," which could be understood as absolute silence (cp. 2 Sam 13:22). But if so, Laban transgresses the command, since not only is he wordy (producing one of the longest speeches in Genesis) but also threatening in his tone. More probable, "good or bad" is a figure of speech, warning Laban not to exceed his authority. Laban thinks, at least, that he properly submitted to the directive when he refrained from assaulting Jacob (cf. v. 29). The expression "good or bad" is used of making an assessment (Lev 27:12,14,33; Num 13:19) or taking an action that is called for by God (Num 24:13; Jer 42:6). The significance of the prohibition is that Laban must not overstep the protective hedge encircling Jacob that the message implies (cf. Job 1:10).

31:25 Verse 25 portrays the dramatic standoff of the two parties. The Hebrew verse first states that "Laban overtook *[nāśag]* him," amplifying the narrative tension that follows (cf. the combination of "pursue" *[rādap]* and "overtake" *[nāśag]* in Exod 14:9). Each company established its camp on opposing hills in the Gilead highlands. The passage repeats that kinsmen accompanied Laban (v. 23), contrasting the strength of his group with Jacob, who alone is mentioned. The implication is that Jacob was in a precarious position. Only Laban and the reader know that God had admonished Laban, but the question remains whether he will strictly adhere to it. At this point in the narrative, mention of Laban's "relatives" and the absence of such a reference for Jacob's kinfolk effectively distinguishes the Aramean band from Jacob and his "relatives" who are primarily to be found in Canaan (v. 3; cp. 24:4,27, where the division is insignificant). The narrative notes that Jacob did have "relatives" with whom Laban's clansmen were instrumental as witnesses to the men's dispute (vv. 32,37). At a much later time, the Israelites lose the Gilead region to the superior Aramean armies (2 Kgs 10:33; Amos 1:3).

LABAN'S ACCUSATIONS AND JACOB'S REBUTTAL (31:26–32). Laban takes the offensive by charging Jacob with deception and theft (vv. 26–30), but Jacob vehemently objects (vv. 31–32).

Charges of Deception and Theft (31:26–30). **31:26–28** Shamelessly,

Laban reproaches his son-in-law, twisting the facts and playing on the sympathies of his audience as a victimized benefactor. In a series of accusatory questions, Laban made two charges against Jacob: deception and theft. First, he accused Jacob of deceiving him by abducting his daughters and grandchildren (vv. 26–30a). "What have you done?" (v. 26a) implicates Jacob in a crime, which Laban sets about to detail. Ironically, at the discovery of Leah as his bride, Jacob put a similar question to Laban (29:25). This same censure introduced Abimelech's complaint concerning Abraham's ruse (20:9; cf. 4:10; Num 23:11; 1 Sam 13:11). Laban's allegation, however, was simply wrong. The women were collaborators in the plan (v. 16), not forced as "captives of war," as their father purported (for "captives," *šĕbûyôt*, cf. Deut 21:10–14; 1 Sam 30:2–5; "war" renders *ḥereb*, "sword," e.g., ESV, NASB, NRSV). The term "carried off" *(nāhag)* is especially fitting in Laban's diatribe, since it is the same word rendered "drove" in v. 18, describing the forced migration of Jacob's flocks. On the idiom translated "deceived" see v. 20.

Laban pretended to be incensed at the *manner* of Jacob's departure, namely, in secret, not at Jacob's wish to leave Paddan Aram (v. 27). "Secretly" (*ḥābā²*, "to hide, withdraw") appears twice more in Genesis, describing the covert actions of Adam and Eve in the garden (3:8,10). If he had only been given the chance, Laban complains, he would have provided a proper send-off (cf. 24:60). The guilt lay with Jacob in his estimation. What possible reason could there be for such disgraceful behavior? His father-in-law depicts a far-fetched picture of a heartwarming farewell, arrayed with joyful song and instrument. "Tambourines" *(tōp)* and "harps" (*kinnôr*, cf. 4:21) were often used in celebratory processionals (e.g., Exod 15:20; 1 Sam 10:5; 2 Sam 6:5). Moreover, he grumbles that Jacob's action denied him the opportunity to give a last kiss to his daughters and grandchildren (v. 28). This he later remedies at his own departure (v. 55). A farewell "kiss" *(nāšaq)* was practiced among family members and loyal friends (Ruth 1:9,14; 2 Sam 19:39; cf. Gen 50:1). Jacob's unwarranted behavior, according to Laban, merited the strongest rebuke, naming his action "foolish" (*sākal;* cf. 1 Sam 13:13; 2 Chr 16:9).

31:29 Laban threatened that he had the power to recover his daughters and flocks but admitted that God had impeded any such possibility. His braggadocio endeavored to convince his audience that Jacob was not the better man. The expression "to have power" or "to be powerless"[366] occurs in a context of captured family (Deut 28:32; Neh 5:5; cf. also Prov 3:27; Mic 2:1). By reference to plural "you" *('immākem),* Laban expressed his hold over the entirety of the family. He later rudely expressed the same sen-

---

[366] E.g., יֶשׁ־לְאֵל יָדִי, lit., "my hand has strength" (31:29), or negatively וְאֵין לְאֵל יָדֶךָ, lit., "your hand does not have strength" (Deut 28:32).

timent, claiming that all that Jacob had was in fact the result of his largesse (v. 43). But the power over Jacob's future rested with God, not Laban. It was God who transformed Laban's deceit into Jacob's prosperity (vv. 5–8). Laban himself confessed that God had tied his hands (vv. 24,29; cf. v. 7). "God of your father" indicates either a different deity (cf. v. 53; Josh 24:2) or is another notice in the narrative of the difference between Jacob and his relatives, the Arameans (i.e., "your father" vs. "our father"). Laban acknowledged that Jacob's deity was the historic benefactor of his ancestors with whom they had entered covenant.

31:30 The second indictment is the charge of stealing Laban's gods. Laban impugned Jacob's character further by pondering aloud why Jacob would want his gods if he had only wanted to escape with his goods, as he had claimed.[367] The REB's rendering understands Laban's remark as a mitigation of Jacob's guilt: "I expect that really you went away because you were homesick and pining for your father's house." If so, it is probably a feigned feeling of sympathy for Jacob's condition. Laban exaggerated here again to make his point. "You have gone off" and "longed to return" are syntactical constructions that emphasize the action undertaken.[368] Laban pressed that his homesickness was no excuse for taking his gods. In Laban's mind he had Jacob cornered. Jacob could not defend such an outrageous trespass. Yet, being wholly unaware of Rachel's part, he made a gaff in his argument by assuming that Jacob was the culprit.

Jacob's Rebuttal (31:31–32). **31:31** Jacob admitted to the first charge, but not the second. His rebuttal to the first was his fear at Laban's reaction to an announced departure. His father (Isaac) had deceived his host too, for fear of being killed (26:7; cf. 12:12; 20:11). "You would take" translates the root *gāzal,* meaning "to seize," as when Abimelech's servants captured Abraham's well (21:25; cf. Judg 21:23). The contexts in which this lexeme appears is often a violent robbery (e.g., Deut 28:31; Judg 9:25; Jer 22:3). The cognate noun *gĕzēlâ* indicates stolen property (e.g., Lev 5:23; Isa 3:14). Surely Jacob would have defended his family, putting his life at jeopardy in such a clash. Jacob spoke of the women as "your daughters" rather than "my wives," which would better explain the probability of this scenario.

31:32 The severity of the second charge deserved the most severe punishment (v. 32). Jacob is so confident of his party's innocence that he can invite a search, offering the harsh sentence of death against the culprit. He

---

[367] The relationship between the first and second clauses in this verse is variously rendered; NIV, NJB, NASB, HCSB, and NJPS understand a contrast ("but"), and other EVs interpret the initial clause as a concession, "Even though . . ." (NRSV; cf. also NAB)

[368] Infinitive absolute + perfect verb: הָלֹךְ הָלַכְתָּ, "you have indeed gone away" or "you had to go" (NRSV) and נִכְסֹף נִכְסַפְתָּה, lit., "you longed greatly" (ESV), i.e., "you yearned intensively (to return) . . ." (*IBHS* §35.3.1i).

made it a public matter, inviting the "relatives" to witness who was guilty, if any. Further, Jacob broadened the scope of discovery to include any stolen object. The same penalty, "shall not live" *(lō' yiḥyeh),* was named for a transgressor of religious law, meriting capital punishment (Exod 19:12–13), or of sorcery (Exod 22:18[17]), or of theft through exorbitant usury (Ezek 18:13). Certainly, any stolen object would be returned without resistance; "take it," he insisted! Jacob's brashness raised the stakes of the search, contributing to the narrative tension that ensues. The author clarifies that Jacob was unaware of Rachel's ruse (v. 19).[369] Perhaps she refrained from informing her husband because she knew he would sternly disapprove. By not knowing of his wife's guilt, however, Jacob jeopardized her life (cp. Saul's rash oath that imperiled Jonathan's life, 1 Sam 14:24–45). Only Rachel and the reader know the peril that awaits her. This confirms that Jacob was truly unaware of the theft, or he would not have made such a pledge.

RACHEL'S RUSE (31:33–35). The brief encounter between Rachel and Laban provides the secondary conflict between the daughters and their father. The episode lampoons Laban and his polytheism, showing the inferiority of his gods to the true God of Jacob. The story's tension builds incrementally as the search narrows finally on Rachel, who is sitting on the tiny idols. Laban, however, is no match for the superior wit of his daughter, just as his gods are no match for the Defender of Jacob's household. The narrative tension experiences a brief humorous release when the woman feigns her menstrual cycle, meaning that the gods are not only useless chattel but also cultically unclean. Yet poor Laban searched desperately for them as though they were of real value.

31:33–34 The author records in detail the search, which commands our attention, giving us a crystal clear picture of each anxious step (v. 33). He began with his chief suspect, Jacob's tent, moving on to the tents of Leah and the secondary wives. That he inspected the women's tents shows that Laban did not truly believe they were innocent parties to Jacob's scheme. The narrative's comment "but he found nothing" sets up the dramatic hunt in the last tent, namely, Rachel's.[370] The author first informs us that Rachel had concealed the *tĕrāpîm* inside her riding saddle on which she was seated (v. 34). Mention of the "camel" reinforces the author's disapproval of Laban's gods, since the Hebrews viewed the animal as unclean (Lev 11:4; Deut 14:7). The depiction of Laban's search inside the tent shows him at his most impotent moment. "Searched" translates the root *māšaš,* meaning "to feel," which is used of the blind "groping" in the dark (Deut 28:29; Job 5:14; 12:25). Sight-

---

[369] The sentence is disjunctive, וְלֹא־יָדַע יַעֲקֹב, "now Jacob did not know . . . ," providing supplemental information to the main narrative line.

[370] *Gen. Rab.* 74.9 (and Rashi) interprets "Jacob's tent" as Rachel's abode, meaning that he checked out her tent twice, i.e., first and last.

less Isaac had to "touch" *(māšaš)* his sons to confirm their identity (27:12,21,22). Laban fumbled around "through everything" *(kōl)*, leaving nothing undisturbed except the one hiding place. "But [he] found nothing" is the second of three times this phrase occurs, exaggerating the failed results of his search.

31:35   The author delays the telling of Rachel's fabrication that explains why Laban failed to discover the idols. Such disrespect of a daughter for her father caps off the author's belittlement of Laban. It was her payback for his violation of her wedding plans (29:25). Her lie is sugarcoated with her disarming plea, "Don't be angry, my lord." She explained that the pain of her menstrual cycle (lit., "the way of women") prevented her from showing proper respect by rising at his presence. Mosaic law declared a woman culticly unclean during the time of her monthly discharge (Lev 15:19), specifying that anything she sat on was defiled (Lev 15:25–26). Purification laws also declared that anyone who came into contact with her was unclean (Lev 15:19). This sentiment may explain why Laban accepted her explanation without further inspection. "Searched" *(ḥāpaś,* cf. 44:12) in this verse is the second of two terms describing Laban's investigation (cf. *māšaš,* vv. 34,37). "But [he] could not find" is the third and final occasion of this declaration. The repetition enhances the idea that Laban exhausted every means of discovery (save one!), providing Jacob greater justification for his outburst to follow (vv. 36–42).

JACOB'S COMPLAINTS AND LABAN'S OFFER (31:36–44).   Jacob's anger fuels his two-pronged response: first, he chastens Laban for his unwarranted accusations (vv. 36–37), and, second, he condemns Laban for the twenty years of mistreatment he suffered under his supervision (vv. 38–42).

Jacob's Anger (31:36–42).   **31:36–37**   "Jacob was angry" translates the root *ḥārâ* ("to burn, be furious"; "was incensed," NJPS), which also described Jacob's anger against Rachel (30:2) and later the brothers' anger against Shechem (34:7). That Rachel pled "don't be angry" *(ḥārâ)* in the prior verse implies a contrast between the justified anger of Jacob and the selfish hostility of Laban. Jacob in fact had not wronged Laban. Laban's anger therefore was wholly misdirected. Although the reality was that Rachel had stolen the *těrāpîm,* thus meriting some censure, Laban's crimes against Jacob far outweighed her misdeed. Even so, one could argue that her confiscation of the deities was in her mind just recompense for her father's misuse of the rightful bridal gift. The verb *rîb,* "took [Laban] to task," describes the public berating Jacob dispensed ("berated," ESV; "upbraided," NRSV, NAB; for the forensic nuance, cf. "brought charges," HCSB). The same term described the "quarrel" the herdsmen of Gerar had with Isaac's servants (26:20–22; cf. Exod 17:2; Deut 33:8). "My crime" *(pišʿî)* refers to a transgression among brothers in 50:17. It often appears parallel with "sin" *(ḥaṭṭāʾâ,* e.g., Exod 34:7; Ps 32:1;

ḥaṭṭāʾt, e.g., 50:17; Josh 24:19). Jacob challenged Laban to justify his harassment, "that you hunt *[dālaq]* me down." The psalmist's characterization of his enemy suits Laban also: "In his arrogance the wicked man hunts down *[dālaq]* the weak" (Ps 10:1). The word *dālaq* can mean to "set on fire" (Obad 18) or "burn" (Ps 7:14), thus "to pursue hotly" (NRSV, REB; cf. 1 Sam 17:53).

So as to expose Laban's charges as mindless ravings, Jacob defied him to make his case before their relatives (v. 37). He forcefully stated that the search was sufficiently thorough ("all," *kol*) and the concomitant absence of any shred of Laban's property ("of all *[kōl]* of your household goods," NRSV; "all" absent NIV) proved him thoroughly wrong. "Found" *(māṣāʾ)* recalls Jacob's invitation for the search (v. 32) and the narration's thrice-told conclusion, "he found nothing" (vv. 33,34,35). "Your relatives" and "my relatives" ("mine," NIV) is another indication in the narrative of the separation of Terah's extended family into two nations. In the absence of judges (Deut 25:1), the community (of relatives)—perhaps the elders (e.g., Num 16:2; Deut 19:12; 21:19)—served as the adjudicators between the men (cf. Num 35:24).

31:38–40 Verses 38–40 give testimony to the trying life that Jacob endured for twenty years as a herdsman under Laban's authority. He presents himself as a flawless shepherd whose track record proved his worth. If true, this made the charge against Laban more grievous. Despite Jacob's splendid care, Laban would have cheated him of his wages had it not been for God's preservation (vv. 41–42). Jacob's argument concentrated on the absence of any loss to Laban. Shepherds worked by consignment, expecting a return on the investment (cf. Ezek 34:10). Jacob claimed that Laban received more than was expected. First, there was no natural loss of young due to miscarriage (*šākal*, v. 38; Job 21:10; cf. "lose," 27:45), presumably because of Jacob's attentiveness. Or are we to understand that this was the benevolence of God, as suggested earlier in vv. 8–9? Second, Jacob did not pilfer any rams for himself. Third, he did not surrender for credit slaughtered animals due to a wild beast (v. 39). It was standard practice that a shepherd could prove his innocence of theft or mismanagement by presenting the remains of the victim, demonstrating an assault against the herd (cf. Exod 22:13[12]; Amos 3:12; Code of Hammurapi #266[371]). Brutalized livestock were devalued specimens (cf. Exod 22:30; Lev 7:24), and Jacob "bore the loss" (*ḥāṭāʾ*, "to sin, incur guilt," v. 39), meaning that he accepted responsibility for the outcome (cf. "bear the blame," 43:9; 44:32). He did not assess the animals against the number of animals on consignment. Jacob further explained that this practice was the result of Laban's hard-hearted policy, requiring compensation ("demanded payment"[372]) of him regardless of the circumstances ("stolen by day or night," v. 39). Finally, Jacob capped off his recitation of life

---

[371] *ANET* 177.

[372] מִיָּדִי תְּבַקְשֶׁנָּה, lit., "from my hand you sought it,"; cf. this idiom at, e.g., 43:9; 1 Sam 20:16; Ezek 3:18,20; 33:8; 34:10.

under Laban by depicting his day-to-day existence (v. 40).[373] He worked in the harshest elements of heat and cold (cf. Jer 36:30) and withstood sleep deprivation to carry out his tasks.[374]

31:41–42 Verse 41 provides a summary of Jacob's work record in the employment of Laban, elaborating on his defense made to Rachel and Leah (v. 7). His complaint entailed two inequities: first, the excessive duration of his work and, second, the recurring change in his wages. The combination of twenty years of servitude for the two women would be disproportionate according to Hebrew sabbatical law, in which a slave worked but six years before automatic release (Exod 21:2; Deut 15:12,18; Jer 34:14). That Jacob referred to the change in wages again (vv. 7,41) shows that he considered this injustice incontrovertible proof of injury. To bring the matter to a moving end (v. 42), he charged Laban with the worse kind of fraud against a worker, withholding his wages (Lev 19:13; Job 7:2; Mal 3:5). Jacob seized upon Laban's own boast (v. 29) to render him silent: God's mercy alone made the difference.

Jacob only escaped Laban's deviousness by God's intervention (v. 42).[375] "Fear of Isaac" *(paḥad yiṣḥāq)* in v. 42 and the similar appellative "Fear of his father Isaac" *(paḥad 'abîw yiṣḥāq)* in Jacob's oath in v. 53b are unique names for God (cf. "Mighty One of Jacob," *'ābîr ya'ăqōb*, 49:24). That the word *paḥad* in Hebrew often means emotional "terror" has raised suspicions about the appropriateness of this interpretation, since it is foreign to the patriarch's relationship with God.[376] Two popular alternatives for *paḥad yiṣḥāq* rely on the identification of *paḥad* as "thigh" (Arabic, Hebrew, Aramaic).[377] The tradi-

---

[373] הָיִיתִי, lit., "I was," another use of the frequentive perfect (cf. note at 31:7), meaning "this was how it was for me."

[374] וַתִּדַּד שְׁנָתִי, "my sleep fled," is also an idiom for insomnia in Esth 6:1, "the king could not sleep."

[375] לוּלֵי אֱלֹהֵי אָבִי ... הָיָה לִי, "If the God of my father . . . had not been with me" is a conditional clause contrary to fact (*IBHS* §38.2e).

[376] Tgs., e.g., read "the God whom Isaac feared" (cf. NLT, "the awe-inspiring God of my father, Isaac"). But the different word יָרֵא, "fear," indicates reverential fear, e.g., יִרְאַת אֱלֹהִים, "the fear of God" (2 Sam 23:3) and יִרְאַת יְהוָה, "the fear of the LORD" (Prov 1:7).

[377] For a summary of the prominent views, see M. Malul, "More on *paḥad yiṣḥāq* (Genesis xxxi 42, 53) and the Oath by the Thigh," *VT* 35 (1985): 192–200. W. F. Albright proposed that the original meaning "thigh" by semantic extension came to mean "kinsman," thus "the Kinsman of Isaac" (so NJB), emphasizing the divine patronage of Isaac. Or, as proposed by Koch and Malul, the word פַּחַד is a Aramaism, meaning "thigh," thus "the thigh of Jacob" (K. Koch, *"pāḥād jiṣḥaq—eine Gottes Bezeichnung?"* in *Werden und Wirken des Alten Testaments: Festschrift für Claus Westermann zum 70 Geburtstag* [Göttingen: Vandenhoeck & Ruprecht, 1980], 107–8). Koch contends the synonym יָרֵךְ ("thigh") is a euphemism for genitals in the oaths by Abraham's servant (24:2,9) and Joseph (47:29), both oaths concerning family solidarity. Here Jacob's reference to "thigh" is symbolic for descendants, meaning the posterity of Isaac. Malul suggests loss of family cohesion was at stake in v. 42, and Jacob's oath in v. 53b invoked ancestral spirits to oversee the perpetuity of family continuity. The problems with appealing to the oaths in 24:2,9; 47:29 as supporting evidence is that the first occasion in 31:42 does not involve an oath, and in the second occasion in v. 53b the oath is not a near-death occasion (as with Abraham and Jacob) but a peace pact.

tional view of "fear," however, is actually more appropriate to the context than has been admitted by many. In its present context (31:42), the name *paḥad yiṣḥāq* is in apposition to "the God of my father," a clear reference to vv. 5,29. The exact expression "the God of my father" appears twice in 32:9, where the passage alludes to the theophany of our chapter (31:3,13). Of the two occasions of "father" in this passage, the first refers to Abraham and the second to Isaac.

In our verse the same pattern appears, in which "the God of my father" is identified as the deity of Abraham first and as "the Fear of Isaac" second. In the prior Bethel theophany the reference to deity is connected with Isaac by the standard formula "the God of Isaac" (28:13; cf. Exod 3:6,15; 4:5). "Fear" probably is a metonymy, substituted for "God," in which the effect ("fear") is placed for the cause ("God"). The cryptic name refers to God as the One of Isaac, who brings about terror in the hearts of others. This interpretation corresponds to the impact that Laban's dream created, preserving Jacob from danger (vv. 24,29). The same divine intervention by dream saved Abraham from Philistine harm (20:6–8) and possibly Isaac as well (26:10–11). The word "fear" *(paḥad),* moreover, commonly describes the alarm that Israel's enemies at times exhibited (e.g., Exod 15:16; Deut 2:25; 11:25; Ps 105:38; Esth 8:17; cf. Ps 14:51).[378]

"God has seen" echoes the deliverance from childlessness that Leah experienced ("the LORD has seen," 29:32; cf. Hagar, 16:13; Israel, Exod 3:9,16). Jacob testified to the deliverance that God equally bestowed upon him (cf. the psalmist's plight, 35:22). The nature of the oppression he endured has just been recounted in detail. Our passage by the language "see" *(rāʾâ)* and "my affliction" *(ʿonyî)* shares in common the psalmist's praise for deliverance (31:7[8]; cf. 25:18; 119:153; Lam 1:9; cf. lament, Ps 9:13[14]). "Toil of my hands" *(yĕgîaʿ kappay)* refers to the common labor of the workman (Ps 128:2; Jer 3:24; Hag 1:11; cf. human creation, Job 10:3). That God had "rebuked" *(yākaḥ)* Laban answered Jacob's call for adjudication, proving that he was in the right *(yākaḥ,* "judge," v. 37; cf. *niph.,* "vindicated," 20:16).

Laban's Compromise (31:43–44). **31:43–44** Grudgingly, Laban offered a compromise, a peace treaty (cf. Josh 9:15). "All you see is mine" (v. 43) expressed his bitterness at Jacob's attainments. Herein laid the basis of the dispute: Laban believed that Jacob was indebted to him, since he had become rich at Laban's loss, but conversely Jacob believed that Laban owed him because of his unrequited labor. Laban's rhetorical question, "What can I do today about these . . .?" confessed that his hands were tied, liberating the women and their children to do as they pleased. In effect, Laban believed that Jacob had turned his family against him (vv. 26–28), but the

---

[378] Also the "fear of the LORD" produces fear in the people (1 Sam 11:7; 2 Chr 17:10; Isa 2:10,19,21).

dialogue with his wives (vv. 4–16) and Rachel's treachery (vv. 19,34–35) show the reader otherwise.

The typical covenant formulary, "(to) cut a covenant" *(kārat bĕrît)*, appears in Laban's proposal (v. 44; cf. 6:18, vol. 1A). The number of witnesses *('ēd)*, beginning with the "covenant" *(bĕrît)* itself (also the pillar and heap), that the men call for exhibits the depth of their suspicions (vv. 48,50,52).[379] That the agreement itself could serve as a witness is not exceptional (cf. Deut 31:26).[380] Laban's emphasis on two separate parties, "you and I" and "between you and me" (NIV "us"), prepares the reader for the narrative that follows, describing the treaty as a peace pact between the now two independent communities, the Arameans and Hebrews.

(4) Jacob and Laban's Agreement (31:45–55[32:1])

[45]So Jacob took a stone and set it up as a pillar. [46]He said to his relatives, "Gather some stones." So they took stones and piled them in a heap, and they ate there by the heap. [47]Laban called it Jegar Sahadutha, and Jacob called it Galeed.

[48]Laban said, "This heap is a witness between you and me today." That is why it was called Galeed. [49]It was also called Mizpah, because he said, "May the LORD keep watch between you and me when we are away from each other. [50]If you mistreat my daughters or if you take any wives besides my daughters, even though no one is with us, remember that God is a witness between you and me."

[51]Laban also said to Jacob, "Here is this heap, and here is this pillar I have set up between you and me. [52]This heap is a witness, and this pillar is a witness, that I will not go past this heap to your side to harm you and that you will not go past this heap and pillar to my side to harm me. [53]May the God of Abraham and the God of Nahor, the God of their father, judge between us."

So Jacob took an oath in the name of the Fear of his father Isaac. [54]He offered a sacrifice there in the hill country and invited his relatives to a meal. After they had eaten, they spent the night there.

[55]Early the next morning Laban kissed his grandchildren and his daughters and blessed them. Then he left and returned home.

This passage consists of four parts, describing the settlement entered by

---

[379] The disparity in gender between fem. בְּרִית ("covenant") and masc. וִהְיָה ("and let it be"; NIV, "let it serve") has prompted a variety of emendations, e.g., the insertion of "let us make a heap (גַּל, masc.)" (e.g., BHS, Westermann); the insertion of "God" (Rashi; e.g., NAB, "the LORD"); and cp. the LXX's addition in v. 44b, ὁ θεὸς μάρτυς ("God is witness"); the proposed Aramaism of עַד ("pact, treaty") for Hb. עֵד ("witness"), thus וְהָיָה עַד, "and let us make a pact," NJB (see F. O. Garcia-Treto, "Genesis 31:44 and 'Gilead,'" ZAW 79 [1967]: 13–17). The REB reads an indefinite construction, "and let there be a witness . . .," anticipating the "pillar" in v. 45, or "that there may be a witness," NJPS (see Hamilton, *Genesis Chapters 18–50*, 310–11, nn. 2–3).

[380] The textual difficulties in vv. 44–54 suggest to many commentators that the passage was textually disturbed. The LXX tends to read longer (e.g., vv. 44,46), reflecting the translators' attempts to smooth out the text. For discussion and proposals, see the standard commentaries, e.g., Skinner, Westermann, Hamilton.

the two parties and their peaceful parting. The narrative describes the construction and naming of a stone pillar and stone heap, serving as two witnesses to the compact (vv. 45–47). The focus of the passage is the following speech by Laban, who explains the stipulations of the agreement (vv. 48–53a). The narrative recounts Jacob's assumption of the covenant oath and provision of the community meal (vv. 53b–54). The concluding verse describes the farewell the next morning by Laban, who kissed his daughters and grandchildren good-bye (v. 55). The passage has been commonly divided between two literary sources (J and E) on the basis of the two features of the treaty, a marriage contract and a peace settlement. A better explanation lies in the rhetorical nature of the passage. The narrative explains the final parting of the Terah clans, highlighting the two different peoples, the Arameans and Hebrews, which the two men represent. Sarna notes that the passage possesses two features of most everything important in the treaty arrangement.[381] There are two stone markers as witnesses, each erected by two different parties (Jacob/his men); two names for the stone heap, one in two different languages; two place names; two conditions of the treaty (marriage/boundary); two meals; and two invocations of God by two names (the Lord/the God of their father) with one involving two ancestors (Abraham/Nahor).

STONE WITNESSES (31:45–47). **31:45–47** The narrative describes Jacob's response to Laban's offer. He established a stone pillar (v. 45), an activity especially associated with Jacob for cultic purposes (see comments on 28:18,22; 31:13; 35:14,20). In this case the pillar memorializes a treaty. Jacob next instructed "his relatives," presumably those of his own camp, to form a "heap" *(gal)* of stones (v. 46; cf. vv. 48,51,52). This is the only occasion in the Old Testament that a pile of stones functions as part of a treaty agreement (cp. "stone," Josh 24:25–27). Such a cairn may mark a burial site (Josh 7:26; 8:29; 2 Sam 18:17) or describe a defeated city's ruins (e.g., 2 Kgs 19:25).[382] The eating of a meal is a rite often associated with a covenant arrangement (cf. v. 54; 26:30–31; Exod 24:11). That the narrative specifically includes that they ate "there" *(šām)* anticipates the role of the heap as a boundary marker (v. 52).

The author provides the names given to the heap by the two parties in their different tongues (v. 47). "Jegar Sahadutha" *(yĕgar śāhădûtāʾ)*transliterates the Aramaic equivalent of the Hebrew name "Galeed" *(galʿēd)*, meaning "witness heap." Closely related to "Galeed" is the sound of the name "Gilead" *(gilʿād)*, designating the location of their treaty (vv. 21,23,25; cp. Beersheba; see comments on 21:31). The inclusion of both names for the same marker reinforces the narrative's emphasis on the two

---

[381] Sarna, *Genesis*, 221.
[382] גַּל may indicate in the case of water a "wave" or "billow" (e.g., Josh 38:11).

different peoples that Laban and Jacob represent, showing the parity of the participating members.

PEACE AGREEMENT (31:48–53a). These concluding verses of Laban's speech explain the second function of the heap and pillar as witnesses. They are boundary markers distinguishing the territories of the Arameans and the Hebrews. Twice "go past" *('ābar)* appears in his speech (v. 52), perhaps making a subtle allusion to the appellative "Hebrew" *('ibrî;* cf. comments on 14:13). Laban's appeal to the deity of the respective clans, "the God of Abraham and the God of Nahor" (v. 53a), perpetuates the passage's contrast between the two peoples.

31:48–49 Laban explained the purpose of the stones and the conditions of the treaty in vv. 48–50. He reiterated that the stones were a "witness," intensifying the solemnity of the treaty by adding the definiteness of "today" (v. 48). The agreement is a parity treaty formulated by equal parties.[383] The author supplies the connection of the event and the name of the heap, "Galeed." The name formula is best interpreted as an indefinite construction (e.g., 25:30; 29:34), translating the passive voice (NIV, NASB, NJPS, HCSB, NAB, REB).[384] Some EVs (e.g., NRSV, NJB), however, attribute the naming to Laban specifically, translating the active voice, "He [Laban] called it Galeed," which would appear to contradict v. 47.

Clearly, the narrative indicates that Laban gave the heap the alternate name "Mizpah" *(miṣpâ,* v. 49).[385] The word *miṣpâ* is also a common noun, meaning "watchtower" in 2 Chr 20:24; Isa 21:8. Laban related "Mizpah" to the word "keep watch" *(yiṣep)* from the root *ṣāpâ,* "to keep watch, guard" (v. 49; cf. 1 Sam 14:16, *haṣṣōpîm,* "the lookouts, watchmen"), conveying by the name a second function of the heap, a reminder that "the LORD" (Yahweh) himself will "judge" (cf. *šāpaṭ,* v. 53)[386] the fidelity of the parties. Since Laban cannot pass judgment on Jacob's actions far away in Canaan, he calls upon God to fill the role. That the deity served as the adjudicator of such treaties was commonly indicated in the text of ancient treaties (cf. Deut 28:20,22,45). Although the specific imprecations are not given, the mention of the deities implied divine retribution against the transgressor. "Mizpah" of

---

[383] For a typology of ancient treaties, see M. Barré, "Treaties in the ANE," *ABD* 6.654–55.

[384] עַל־כֵּן קָרָא־שְׁמוֹ גַּלְעֵד, lit., "therefore, he called its name Galeed."

[385] Yet the SP has המצבה ("the pillar") in lieu of the MT's הַמִּצְפָּה ("Mizpah"). The earlier mention of מַצֵּבָה ("a pillar") in v. 45 and the unexpected definite article of הַמִּצְפָּה ("the Mizpah") here may have led to an intentional change. Although the SP's text eliminates the obvious play of the name on יָצֶף ("keep watch"), the variant "pillar" indicates the nature of the stones established by Jacob (v. 45). The NRSV translates "and the pillar Mizpah." The LXX's rendering, καὶ ἡ ὅρασις ἥν εἶπεν ἐπίδοι ὁ θεὸς, "and the sight which, he said, May God behold . . .," preserves MT's wordplay (Wevers, *Notes on the Greek Text,* 524).

[386] Cf. the sound play of צָפָה, "to watch," and שָׁפַט, "to judge" (Hamilton, *Genesis Chapters 18–50,* 315).

Gilead was located north of the River Jabbok, not to be confused with the better-known city Mizpah of Benjamin (Tell en-Nasbeh) located at the boundary between Israel and Judah, eight miles northwest of Jerusalem (e.g., Judg 20; 1 Sam 7:16–17). The Gilead site was the hometown of Jephthah, where he entered an agreement with the leaders of Gilead (Judg 11:11,29,34).

31:50 Laban next referred to the conditions of the treaty (v. 50), mentioning again the threat of a divine witness (v. 49), although neither he nor his surrogate can oversee the arrangement. Speaking suddenly with the voice of a protective father ("my daughters," 2x), he maintained Rachel and Leah's permanent positions as Jacob's chief wives, knowing that their children stood to gain more. A common feature of marriage contracts included the provision that a husband would not take another wife. Laban may have reasoned that at least no other collateral line would benefit from what Jacob had obtained from him. Mosaic law redressed the typical problems of polygamy, including inheritance (Exod 21:10; Deut 21:15–17). The word "mistreat" (*'inneh, piel*)[387] also described Sarah's harm of Hagar in their struggle for preeminence (16:16; cf. Exod 22:22–23[21–22]). Although he personally could not administer retaliation, he reiterated that God himself was "witness" (*'ēd*), implying that any violation would be subject to no less than the severest denunciation. The imperative "remember" (*rě'ê*) translates *rā'â*, meaning "to see," which recalls the earlier references to the Lord's oversight (cf. 29:31,32; 31:42).[388] By mentioning that both pillar and God (Elohim) were witnesses, Laban indicated that the pillar was a token of God's oversight, not that the pillar was inhabited by the deity.[389] There is no evidence that Laban treated the pillar as an object of worship. That Laban continued to refer to God as Elohim rather than Yahweh may indicate that he did not worship the same God as the Abraham branch (cf. v. 53).

31:51–52 To strengthen his point, Laban forcefully states the obvious (twice the interjection *hinnê*, "behold!" occurs) at the outset of his speech

---

[387] J. Paradise suggests, on the basis of his interpretation of עֹנָה ("upkeep") in Exod 21:10 and various Akk. texts, that the idea of "general needs/support" best translates תְּעַנֶּה, interpreting it as a privative *piel;* thus Jacob was not to deprive the women of their livelihood or take new wives ("What Did Laban Demand of Jacob? A New Reading of Genesis 31:50 and Exodus 21:10," in *Tehillah le-Moshe: Biblical and Judaic Studies in Honor of Moshe Greenberg* [Winona Lake: Eisenbrauns, 1997], 91–98). The term "mistreat" is broad in usage, including physical abuse (e.g., Exod 1:11; Deut 22:24) but not necessarily here (as 16:16 shows), thus possibly referring to mental cruelty or mere neglect. See P. Wegner, "ענה," *NIDOTTE* 3.450. Rashi explains this "mistreatment" as sexual abstinence (also *Yoma* 77b).

[388] *HALOT* 3.1159 identifies it here as an exclamation, "See!" (cf. 27:27).

[389] Pagolu identifies the pillar as a legal stone, reminding persons of treaties and boundaries (also Exod 24:4; Josh 224:26–27); this function for the stones is known in extrabiblical examples from the third to the first millennium (*The Religion of the Patriarchs*, 147).

(v. 51). He next combines the two purposes of the pile of stones and pillar as witnesses and boundary markers (v. 52). The stone "witnesses" observed the regard of the two peoples' for their respective territories. By mentioning the term "witness" *('ēd/'ēdâ)* at the head of the construction in v. 52, Laban highlighted the importance of the parties' continued observance under the threat of divine retaliation. Laban appears most concerned about installing a defensive measure against any future encroachments by Jacob or his descendants. This was the same worry that prompted Abimelech's treaty with Isaac (26:29a). Laban did not trust Jacob any more now than before, making it prudent to plan for the worst. "Harm" *(rāʿâ)* alludes to the dream communiqué warning Laban not to "harm" *(rāʿ)* Jacob (v. 29). Laban had boasted of his superior power, but by this insurance he admitted that God's superintendence of Jacob's life put him at an insuperable disadvantage.

31:53a   In accord with the typical pattern of treaty between peoples, Laban invoked deity to observe their compliance to the stipulations of the covenant. Different interpretations of Laban's invocation have implications for understanding the nature of Laban's religion.[390] The plural number verb in the clause ". . . judge *(yišpĕṭû)* between us" may indicate that the deities of Abraham and Nahor are different gods. The SP and LXX reflect the single verb *(yišpōṭ)*, indicating that the deity is the same. The further expression, "the God [or gods] *[ʾĕlōhê]* of their father," recalls the two parties' common ancestor, Terah, who practiced polytheism (Josh 24:15, "the gods *[ʾĕlōhîm]* your forefathers served beyond the River"). A plural interpretation, "the gods of their father," is possible, referring to different deities (cf. "their ancestral deities," NAB, NJPS). Since the phrase is absent in the LXX,[391] some commentators and EVs (NJB, REB) consider the clause a gloss. That it suits, however, what we know of the author's desire in this chapter to show the final severing of the two clans argues for accepting it as original. That Jacob swears by his own father's God ("Fear of his father Isaac") implies a difference in the deities of the families. Some EVs indicate Laban's different religion by translating "the god of Nahor" (NJB, NAB, NJPS) or "the gods of Nahor" (HCSB), distinguishing his deity from the orthodox "God of Abraham."

The language "judge *[šāpaṭ]* between us" calls to mind Laban's earlier challenge of Jacob's integrity when Jacob summons their kinfolk to "judge" *(yākaḥ)* between them (v. 37). Sarah implored God to settle the strife she had with Abram (cf. *šāpaṭ,* 16:5; also 18:25).

---

[390] In the history of religious studies, A. Alt's popular theory of the patriarchs' "God of the Fathers" religion largely relied on v. 53's reference to the respective deities of the two fathers, Abraham and Nahor (see "Religion of the Patriarchs" in "Introduction").

[391] Wevers concludes that the omission is the LXX's avoidance of a tautology (*Notes on the Greek Text,* 526).

OATH AND COVENANT MEAL (31:53b–54). **31:53b–54** Jacob concurred with Laban's proposal, entering into a formal oath and confirming the agreement by a ritual sacrificial meal. A sworn oath and meal commonly accompanied a peace agreement (cf. 21:23–24,31; 26:31; Exod 24:11; 34:15; Deut 29:11,13). Jacob did so in the name of his God, "the Fear of Isaac" (cf. 31:42), a practice that was required by later law (Deut 6:13; 10:20; Isa 48:1). Jacob had imposed on Esau an oath in transacting the purchase of the elder's birthright (25:33). The sacrifice Jacob presented and the corresponding meal partaken by the covenant parties sealed the finality of the negotiations. That the kin of the two men ate of the meal fits the special interest the passage showed in the people groups represented by their respective camps and their roles as witnesses to the proceedings (vv. 23,25,32,37,46,54). That they spent the night indicates the irenic spirit of hospitality that characterized their parting (e.g., 19:2; 24:23; 26:30–31).

FAREWELL (31:55[32:1]). **31:55[32:1]** "Early the next morning" repeats 28:18, describing the morning after the historic revelation to Jacob at Bethel. It was the memory of that revelation that led to Jacob's departure from Paddan Aram and the tension with Laban that ensued (31:3,13). The peaceful arrangement with Laban showed the faithfulness of God, who protected Jacob and returned him to the land without loss. By kissing his children and grandchildren good-bye, Laban completed what Jacob's clandestine escape had prevented (v. 28). The substance of the parting blessing probably paralleled what Laban extended toward his departing sister, Rebekah, a generation earlier (24:60). The passage ends on the sure note that Laban left for "his own place" ("home," NIV), making the separation complete.

9. Struggle for Blessing at Peniel (32:1–32[2–33])

That Jacob had successfully freed himself from Laban (31:55[32:1])[392] prepared the way for his greatest challenge, facing his brother Esau, who had vowed to kill him (27:41). This account of Jacob's return corresponds to his Bethel revelation (28:10–22) in the structural arrangement of the Jacob narrative as a whole. Shared language employed by the author creates an envelope pattern, bringing to mind Jacob's first encounter with God at Bethel. Whereas the Bethel incident was one of promise, this encounter at Mahanaim/Peniel (vv. 2[3],30[31]) was one of fulfillment. When Jacob prays for deliverance from Esau (vv. 9,12[10,13]), he bases his appeal on the promises made at his first

---

[392] Throughout this chapter, the versification cited first is the traditional English followed by the Hebrew verse in brackets.

meeting with God at Bethel (28:13–15). As Jacob is at the precipice of receiving the promise of Canaan, he is not yet morally ready to carry out the blessing. Jacob must possess his own faith, obtaining the blessing through personal encounter, not by heredity alone. The present chapter's episodes depict the decisive transforming events in the life of Jacob. The antagonists in the patriarch's life have been first Esau, then Laban, and now again Esau. But the surprising antagonist that confounds us is the unknown assailant who injures Jacob in the night. By these disquieting episodes in his life, we witness the transformation of Israel's father and namesake. What has been called "the violent presence and darkness of Peniel"[393] proves to be the patriarch's greatest challenge, ending in the victorious yet humbled figure of the new Israel.

Life under the unfair treatment of Laban showed that Jacob must rely on the provision of God, not himself or another (31:9,11,42). That growing realization is the prelude to the change Jacob undergoes at Peniel, from a cocky trickster to a humble servant who acknowledges his indebtedness to God and to a human (Esau). The naming "Israel" is the chief signal of Jacob's conversion (v. 28[29]). That Jacob hoped to assuage Esau by gifts does not cancel the evidence of true repentance by Jacob. In the manner that the psalmists would later pray for rescue, Jacob lamented his unworthiness of God's pity, crying out for deliverance (vv. 9–12[10–13]). When he meets Esau, his conciliatory offer implies that he had mistreated his brother and owed him dearly (33:10–11). More importantly, as the former "Jacob," he had obtained his father's blessing by thievery; but in his tussle with God he sought the realization of the blessing, knowing that only God could grant it (cf. 28:13–15; 31:3,13).

In narrating this life-transforming experience, the author shows that ambiguity and mystery characterize such divine-human meetings.[394] Two celestial revelations form the boundaries of the chapter: a meeting with the angelic "camp of God" (vv. 1–2[2–3]) and a nocturnal wrestling with the "man," whom Jacob recognized as God (vv. 28,30[29,31]). The God of promise met him by surprise. Jacob's dual responses of naming the sites "Mahanaim" ("two camps") and "Peniel" ("the face of God [El]") commemorated the divine nature of these encounters for future generations. He turned to God in prayer, submissively confessing his dependence on God (vv. 9–12[10–13]), and he pled so tenaciously with the "man" to bestow the ancestral blessing that he risked "life and limb" (vv. 26,30[27,32]). G. von Rad likened Jacob's

---

[393] C. Burdon rightly observes the "agonistic" feature of the episode but is too pessimistic when he contends that Jacob's struggles with his brother and God have no closure in the narrative, calling the reader to "continued agonistic living" ("Jacob and the Dominion of Edom," *ExpTim* 109 [1998]: 360–63).

[394] See Fokkelman, *Narrative Art in Genesis*, 198–223; S. Geller, "The Struggle of the Jabbok: The Uses of Enigma in a Biblical Narrative," *JANES* 14 (1982): 37–60; and E. Curtis, "Structure, Style and Context as a Key to Interpreting Jacob's Encounter at Peniel," *JETS* 30 (1987): 129–37.

entreaty to the "unabashed pleading" in prayer that Jesus commended (Luke 11:8).[395] The initial gifts Jacob provided in preparation to meet Esau were not deception or the returned blessing, only the actions of wise counsel. Jacob did not relinquish Isaac's blessing. The early tactics Jacob took to rob Esau of birthright and blessing have no parallel here.

Complex literary devices of ambiguity, irony, and wordplays produce a multifarious text that conveys the profound theology of a man's encounter with the living God. The ambiguities begin with the encampment of angels, which Jacob identifies as the "camp of God," naming the site "Mahanaim," which means "two camps" (vv. 1–2[2–3]). The text does not indicate how he saw the angels (dream, vision?) or the purpose of the camp. Is the "camp of God" established to assist or harm Jacob? Were there two camps, and what were their identities? Is the second camp Jacob's own camp that he in turn divides into two (v. 7[8])? But might it be Laban's or Esau's? The chief mystery, however, is the identity of the "man," which remains uncertain until the end of the narrative (vv. 22–32[23–33]). Is this attacker a member of the angelic camp, or is this Esau? Gradually, the narrative shows that the assailant is greater than a mere man as the night melts into dawn.

If this is indeed God, why does he attack Jacob? And furthermore, why does a mere mortal appear to get the better of the divine combatant? The reader wonders who truly has prevailed. R. Barthes's structural analysis of the narrative exposes what we would deem the "meaning" of the embedded paradoxes of the story line.[396] It is by the impossibility of a man defeating God that God "brands" Jacob, signified by the change in name and physical limp. This inversion in the account, Barthes points out, parallels the prenatal struggle of the brothers in which the younger supersedes the older. Barthes finds that in the birth incident Jacob's action marks himself. He concludes that God in the Jabbok encounter substitutes for Esau, meaning that Jacob defeats Esau once again. We will discover that the interface between Esau and God is crucial to understanding the reconciliation of the brothers (33:10). By Esau accepting the gift of his brother, he is in effect distinguishing Jacob as the true successor, relinquishing any claim on the paternal blessing (33:11).

The author of the passage employed several wordplays in addition to the site names, Mahanaim ("two camps") and Peniel ("face of God"). The text especially by the shared sounds h and n connects the frequent terms "camp/group" (*maḥăneh,* vv. 2,7,8,10,21[3,8,9,11,22]; 33:8), "gift" (*minḥă,* vv. 14,19,20,21,22[15,19,21,22,23]; 33:8,10), and "favor" (*ḥēn,* v. 5[6]; 33:8,10; also "graciously given," *ḥānan,* 33:5,11). The phonetic links of *y-q-b* and *y-*

[395] G. von Rad, *Biblical Interpretations in Preaching,* trans. J. Steely (Nashville: Abingdon, 1977), 43.

[396] R. Barthes, "The Struggle with the Angel: Textual Analysis of Genesis 32–33," in *Structural Analysis and Biblical Exegesis,* PTMS 3 (Pittsburgh: Pickwick, 1974), 21–33.

b-q occur for the names "Jacob" *(yaʿăqōb)* and "Jabbok" *(yabbōq)* with the key action of the story, "wrestled" *(yēʾābēq,* v. 24[25]; cf. v. 26[27]). There is a further parallel created between Jacob's encounters with the mysterious "man" and with Esau, in which God "wrestled" *(ʾ-b-q)* with Jacob but Esau "embraced" *(ḥ-b-q)* him (33:4). God must fight with Jacob before Jacob can survive Esau, indicated by the reconciling embrace of his brother. The imagery of "face" *(pānîm)* in v. 30[31] and 33:10 reinforces this apparent connection between the two events (also the related terms *pĕnê/lipnê,* "before, ahead of," vv. 3,16,17,20,21[4,17,18,21,22]; 33:3,14,18). Also important is the term *ʿābar,* variously translated in this narrative as "crossed/go/went on/passed," conveying the idea of movement from and toward Canaan (vv. 10,16,21–23,31[11,17,22–24,32]; 33:3,14). Central to the narrative's historical perspective is the naming "Israel" *(yiśrāʾēl),* in which the sound *yśr* is reversed by *śry* in the explanation "you have struggled *[śārîtā]* with God and with men and have overcome" (v. 28[29]). A number of less important word connections also occur, for example, the mention of Edom and Seir (v. 3[4]) with the earlier descriptions of Esau (25:25,30; 27:11,23). Not only do these allusions bring to mind the schism between the brothers but also heightens the geographical interest of the Jacob narrative. The resolution finds its echo in the final concession of the land, Esau returning to Seir (33:16) and Jacob pressing on to Shechem in Canaan by way of Succoth (33:17–18).

The chief irony in the account is the physical disability Jacob received when struggling with the "man" (v. 25[26]). His dislocated hip created a limp that (presumably) marked the remainder of his life, the occasion for a dietary law that Israel practiced in observance of their ancestor's experience (vv. 31–32[32–33]). By this infirmity the narrative indicates both the victory and the defeat of Jacob when he encountered the divine. Neither Abraham nor Isaac had such a confrontation with the Lord God, making Jacob a remarkable ancestor to whom his descendants could look as their example (cf. Moses, Exod 4:24–26). The many literary and theological enigmas that occur in this Jabbok account point up the distinctiveness of the naming Israel (v. 28[29]) in contrast to Edom's naming (Esau, 25:30). Moreover, that Israel's namesake had contested the divine and had won communicated the importance of the nation's origin. Jacob was the idealized alien who lived much of his life outside Canaan, where God enriched him, despite the abuse suffered under his host (Laban). At the instruction of God, he hurried away only to be met by his enemy in the wilderness, but God granted him deliverance from Esau, ensuring his survival (33:4).

Finally, what is the purpose of this account? The significance of the passage lies primarily in Jacob's discovering the freedom and enduring grace of God.[397] The passage shows that God is free to bless whom he pleases. The

---

[397] F. Brossier, "Jacob à Penuel," *Monde de la Bible* 46 (1986): 39–40.

blessing Jacob so desires is not an automatic bestowal based on God's promises to his fathers, Abraham and Isaac. Nor is it a promise Jacob can achieve through his own strength or wit. Through the transforming grace of the Lord, this man undergoes a moral conversion that will render him an appropriate vessel of divine blessing. A. Ross comments, "Now crippled in his [Jacob's] natural strength he became bold in faith."[398] S. Geller finds that the narrative in the wider context of Israel's historical experience shows that the people's relationship with God involves the danger of the holy. There is risk for Jacob, who when seeking blessing comes close to death, expressing relief that "I saw God face to face, and yet my life was spared" (v. 30[31]).[399] At the national level, too, the event encourages Israel to remember the significance of its name, assuring the people that they will prevail over their adversaries in fulfillment of God's blessing. Jacob's entrance into the land (Mahanaim, Peniel, Succoth, Shechem, chaps. 32–33) when he became "Israel" forecasted the nation's occupation of Canaan.

COMPOSITION.   Source critics typically believed there were two literary sources (Yahwist [J] and Elohist [E]) that made up chap. 32. Gunkel, for example, attributed vv. 3–21[4–22] to two parallel accounts: the Yahwist in vv. 3–13a[4–14a] provided one version of Jacob's preparations to meet Esau (dividing the flock), and the Elohist related another explanation in vv. 13b–21[14b–22], describing the gifts that assuaged Esau's anger.[400] The account of Jacob's wrestling with the deity (vv. 22–32[23–33]) was a composite of J and E. As we have seen with earlier narratives, however, most commentators dismissed a role for E, preferring to assign the majority of chap. 32 to J (with additions).[401]

Nevertheless, viewing the passage as a complex literary growth, though of a different nature, still prevails. Thompson, for example, contends that there are three narrative variations of Jacob's return that have been preserved: (1) the defensive measure of dividing his camp into two parties (vv. 6–8[7–9]); (2) the diplomatic measure of dividing the flocks into serial presentations of gifts (vv. 3–5[4–6],13–21[14–22]); and (3) the forward measure of dividing the children into three maternal groupings, headed by Jacob himself (32:9–12[10–13],22–23[23–24]; 33:1–3). The resolution in 33:4–11 satisfies two of the variants: 33:4–7 corresponds to the narrative describing the maternal divisions, and 33:8–11 reflects the variant regarding the serial presentations of gifts. Jacob's conflict with the "man" was an independent tale that quite late became attached to the story of Jacob's return, equating Jacob and the nation Israel. The final verse's etiology of Israel's dietary prohibition was a means of concluding the episode (vv. 24–32[25–33]). Thompson assumes that the three means of dividing Jacob's camp in

---

[398] A. Ross, "Jacob at the Jabbok, Israel at Peniel: Part 2 of Studies in the Life of Jacob," *BSac* 142 (1985): 350.

[399] Geller, "The Struggle of the Jabbok," 55–57.

[400] Gunkel, *Genesis,* 345–47; and von Rad, *Genesis,* 317.

[401] E.g., Speiser, *Genesis,* 255.

the narrative are inherently contradictory. We find, however, that Jacob's taking both a defensive measure and a diplomatic measure does not require two narrative variations since they are compatible strategies. As for the grouping by children, at which Jacob takes the lead in 33:1–3, it is the result of the prior night's experience, emboldening him to meet his brother head-on.[402] The mention of "two groups" in vv. 7,10[8,11]) indicates the interdependence of the narratives of vv. 6–8[7–9] and 9–12[10–13].[403]

Westermann's analysis also exhibits the typical approach. He distinguishes two discreet narratives in 31:55–32:21[32:1–22] and 32:22–32[32:23–33], which J (minus additions) has constructed for the itinerary of Jacob's return.[404] He concludes that vv. 1b–2[2b–3], a secondary note attached to the itinerary, were originally independent material the Yahwist appropriated to show that God's army would defend the patriarch against his brother. C. Houtman contends on the analogy of the parallel encounter at Bethel (28:10–22) that originally there was an independent tradition of a sanctuary *(hieros logos)* at Mahanaim that subsequently lost its original function and was integrated into the present Jacob narrative.[405] The obvious difficulty with Houtman's suggestion is that there is no mention of a sanctuary at this location in the Old Testament.

For Westermann vv. 3–21[4–22] are a composite of different episodes, not a literary unity, that prepare for the telling of the twin brothers' encounter. The Yahwist relied on two oral stories in constructing vv. 3–7a[4–8a] and 13–21[14–22]. Verses 7b–8[8b–9] are an independent "old etiological note," explaining the name Mahanaim (lit., "two camps," v. 2[3]). The original prayer of deliverance (v. 11[12]) later expanded to include vv. 9–12[10–13]. Westermann joins the majority of commentators who identify many secondary accretions (vv. 25b[26b],27–28[28–29],30b[31b],32[33]) to J's second narrative of vv. 22–32[23–33]. Verses 25b[26b] and 32[33] are considered postexilic additions that are midrashic commentary on the dietary prohibition against eating the sinew of the hip. The naming of "Jacob-Israel" in vv. 27–28[28–29] is an addition that is reminiscent of the Priestly (P) material in chap. 17 and 35:10. It is typical of Israel's later tendency to idealize Jacob. The inclusion of the Peniel etiology in v. 30b[31b] was a later addition that sought to suppress the older "Jabbok/struggle" etiology, although the reason for this rejection is unknown. As with Gunkel, Westermann believed the original legend underlying J's version was a local story about the Jabbok ford in which a demon or monster opposes the crossing of a

---

[402] Hamilton remarks that Jacob moved "from rearguard to vanguard" (*Genesis Chapters 18–50*, 342–43).

[403] Thompson himself appeals to the phrase "two groups" as evidence that the redactor believed the two narratives belonged together (*The Origin Tradition*, 109–10). On the flimsy basis that the geography, "this Jordan" (v. 10[11]), conflicts with the earlier locale Jabbok (v. 3[4]), he posits two variant traditions. But see the note below.

[404] Westermann, *Genesis 12–36*, 452, 504–5.

[405] C. Houtman, "Jacob at Mahanaim: Some Remarks on Genesis xxxii 2–3," *VT* 28 (1978): 37–44. Coats agrees that an older, original *hieros logos* was a possibility (*Genesis*, 223–24); also W. Dietrich, "Jakobs Kampf am Jabbok (Gen 32,32–33)," in *Jacob: un Commentaire à plusieurs voix de Genèse 25–36*, 197–210.

traveler.[406] Because of the legendary origin of the story, the Yahwist avoided using Yahweh, preferring the general name "God" (El).[407] A nationalistic reading of the passage dominates modern interpretation. During the monarchic period the Yahwist adapted this Jacob tradition to show that Jacob=Israel could prevail over Edom (Esau) and Aram (Laban), since Jacob had prevailed over God and was the recipient of the blessing. And the work of P, who added to it, appropriated the story as a metaphor for Israel's return to the land from Babylonian exile.[408]

Carr likewise explains the core of the narrative as essentially one narrative composition, not two parallel sources, extending it to 33:20. The inclusion of two etymologies for Mahanaim (v. 2[3], E; vv. 7,8,10[8,9,11], J), for example, is not the result of two documents, as source critics had assumed, but the union of different etiological traditions that have been modified for the broader compositional purpose. We differ here with both source and tradition critics, for the Mahanaim event (vv. 1–2[2–3]) finds its human corollary by Jacob's imitative act (vv. 7,8,10[8,9,11]), not two different etiologies. Carr finds that 32:1–8[2–9] and 32:13[14]–33:20 are parallel halves of one continuous account, pointing to evidence that betrays a literary whole. Verse 5[6] anticipates the "gifts" in the second half of the story. Both halves involve the same wordplays on "camp"/"to encamp" *(maḥăneh/ḥānâ)*, "Mahanaim" *(maḥănayim)*, and "favor" *(ḥēn)*. Both halves are also presupposed in chap. 33, suggesting that the author had a continuous chap. 32 in mind.[409] Wenham also concludes that chaps. 32 and 33 are one compositional piece, the virtual conclusion to the Jacob accounts. He furnishes numerous examples of allusions in chaps. 32–33 to the content of the earlier Jacob-Esau and Jacob-Laban narratives (e.g., vv. 7–9[8–10] with 27:41–45).[410] We agree that the coherence within chap. 32 and its continuum in chap. 33 indicate one author and that the whole of the foregoing Jacob narratives was known at their composition.

Two special problems are the prayer by Jacob (vv. 9–12[10–13]) and the concluding note observing Israel's dietary prohibition (v. 32[33]). Carr goes off course, as does Westermann, when he insists that Jacob's prayer in vv. 9–12[10–13] is secondary. Carr believes it is a late semi-Deuteronomistic modification of the text.[411] He argues that the prayer interrupts the natural flow of the narrative that describes the division of Jacob's camp and his distribution of gifts for Esau (vv. 7–8[8–9],3–21[14–22]). Yet the prayer's mention of "two camps" ("groups," NIV) that infer his great wealth fits nicely in its context. Carr further says the piety of the prayer does not fit with the context's emphasis on the deception Jacob

---

[406] Gunkel, *Genesis*, 350–52; e.g., von Rad, *Genesis*, 321.

[407] Westermann, *Genesis 12–36*, 514–19.

[408] S. McKenzie, " 'You have Prevailed': The Function of Jacob's Encounter at Peniel in the Jacob Cycle," *ResQ* 23 (1980): 225–31.

[409] Carr, *Reading the Fractures of Genesis*, 256–57, 259, n.76, 270.

[410] Wenham, *Genesis 16–50*, 288–89.

[411] Carr notes, e.g., that the language "this Jordan" (v. 11[12]) is reminiscent of the Deuteronomist's typical geographical marker (e.g., 3:27; 31:2), although in the Genesis context Jacob is stationed at the Jabbok River (*Reading the Fractures of Genesis*, 168–69). But Sarna observes that the Jordan is "clearly visible" when standing at the Jabbok (*Genesis*, 225).

committed. Also the prayer resembles the royal prayers of the Deuteronomist (e.g., 2 Sam 7:18–29). T. Römer also views it as a late interpolation in the postexilic period, tying the Jacob cycle to Abraham and the conquest.[412] Van Seters shows, however, that vv. 9–12[10–13] are original to the Yahwist's account, finding support in 33:5,10,11, which also attribute Jacob's success to God's involvement.[413] Moreover, the theology of his prayer is not so distinctive as to suit only the royal prayers of the Deuteronomists (e.g., 19:19; Ps 31:22).[414] Since the prayer reflects its context, we find that it is at least as likely that it was native to the context. Another late addition commonly proposed by commentators is the dietary prohibition (v. 32[33]). No one can doubt that it is part of the narrative frame and can be no earlier than the author's own time ("to this day"), but that does not require a very late accretion. Wenham observes that the absence of the prohibition in Jewish law argues for an early rather than late origin of the practice.[415]

STRUCTURE.   The borders of this account are variously explained. Commentators disagree on both the beginning point (32:1[2] or 32:3[4]) and the conclusion (32:32[33]; or 33:17; or 33:20). We have contended that 31:55[32:1] closes the prior narrative as a fitting end to the Jacob-Laban narrative (see "Structure," introduction to 31:1). The surprising meeting of angels at Mahanaim in vv. 1–2[2–3] and the mysterious attack of the "man" at Peniel in vv. 22–32[23–33] create the boundaries of the narrative. Since chap. 32 describes the preparations for the encounter with Esau, the first sighting of Esau by Jacob in 33:1 ("looked up") alerts the reader to the new narrative, describing the meeting of the brothers. Alternatively, one can analyze chap. 33 as the conclusion to chap. 32's preparations, extending the account to 33:17 or 33:20.[416] There are shared vocabulary and imagery that support this possibility. The arrangement of the Jacob narrative at large (25:19–35:29), however, suggests that chaps. 32 and 33 are two distinctive narratives (see comments at introduction to the Jacob section). Chapter 33's account of the siblings' reconciliation corresponds well to the narrative of their conflict in 27:1–28:9 (see comments at chap. 33). Chapter 32's

---

[412] T. Römer, "Genèse 32,2–22: Préparations d'une rencontre," in *Jacob: un Commentaire à plusieurs voix de Genèse 25–36*, 181–96.

[413] Van Seters, *Prologue to History*, 296; but he distinguishes three pre-Yahwistic local folk etiologies of cult sites and place names in the Jacob story, 28:10–22 (Bethel), 32:1–2[2–3] (Mahanaim); and 32:21–31[22–32] (Peniel) (pp. 211, 279).

[414] Wenham, e.g., mentions that the thought of v. 11[12] is common to OT prayer at large (*Genesis 16–50*, 291).

[415] Ibid., 297.

[416] Coats explains that the two etiologies, 28:10–22 (Bethel) and 32:1–2[2–3] (Mahanaim), frame the entire Jacob-Laban story (29:1–31:55[32:1]; *Genesis*, 180, 223–31). The Jacob-Esau strife first introduced in 27:41–45 and its resolution in 32:3[4]–33:17 form the outer framework. Jacob's struggle in 32:24–32[25–33]) is an etiology of "Israel," providing a story within a story, telling how the struggle with God prepares for the reconciliation with Esau.

description of Jacob's encounters with the angels and the "man" when he receives God's blessing at his return to Canaan (Peniel) corresponds nicely to the blessing first promised at his departure from Canaan (Bethel) in 28:10–22.[417] This latter correspondence is especially evident by the common setting and vocabulary of 32:1–2[2–3] and 28:11–12, involving the "angels of God." It is not as evident in the description of Jacob's struggle with the "man" (vv. 22–32[23–33]), although the account shares in imagery with 28:10–22. Thompson considers vv. 24–32[25–33], for example, the natural balance and expansion of the theophany reported in 28:13–14.[418] In both narratives the divine encounters Jacob in the night, and only afterward at the dawning of day he realizes that the encounter was with God. The patriarch also each time makes a plea for divine favor. In the first occasion he appeals for God's provision and offers a loyalty oath (28:20–22), and in the present case he barters for a blessing (32:26[27],29[30]). In each instance also he memorializes the revelatory event by renaming the location. The correspondence of Bethel's promise of blessing (28:14) and of Peniel's act of blessing (32:29) shows that chap. 32 is best understood as a distinctive literary unit, the counterpart to the Bethel theophany (28:10–22).

Our passage consists of three units. Wordplays and segmentation of the passage by a recurring reference to "night" or "morning" contribute to distinguishing the threefold arrangement of the passage.[419] The mention of "night" and "morning" in the previous narrative (31:54–55[31:54–32:1]) alerts the reader to the series of chronological references to days and nights in this chapter. The events of the first unit (vv. 1–12[2–13]) appear to occur on one day, if we rightly infer this from 31:55. This unit describes two different groups of "messengers" (mal'ākîm), one heavenly and the other human. Verses 1–2[2–3] describe heavenly messengers sent from God who encounter Jacob along the way. He perceives that they constitute the "camp" (mahăneh) of God, therefore naming the site "Mahanaim" (mahănayim). Fokkelman observes that the dual form of the Hebrew name Mahanaim, meaning literally "two camps," introduces narrative ambiguity and tension that continues to the end of the narrative.[420] The word "camp" appears six times in the account, all in the first two units of the passage (vv. 2[3],7[8],8[9] twice,10[11],21[22]). This would provide for several possible identifications of the two camps (see

---

[417] E.g., Carr identifies these two narratives as parallel members of his prepromise story of Jacob's travels (Reading the Fractures of Genesis, 257).

[418] Thompson, The Origin Tradition, 111.

[419] Westermann proposes three parts: the camp of God (vv. 1–2[3–4]), the preparation to meet Esau (vv. 3–21[4–22]), and the wrestle with God (vv. 22–32[23–33]) (Genesis 12–36, 506); for vv. 3–21[4–22] Westermann (p. 504) places the prayer at the center (vv. 9–12[10–13]), framed by the two delegations to Esau (vv. 3–8[4–9]; vv. 13–21[14–22]).

[420] Fokkelman, Narrative Art in Genesis, 198.

comments on v. 2[3]). Verses 3–8[4–9] describe the second group of messengers in the narrative, human messengers whom Jacob dispatches to encounter Esau. After recounting the dire report related by the returning messengers to Jacob, the passage presents the prayer of the patriarch, who fearfully beseeches the Lord's deliverance from Esau (vv. 9–12[10–13]).

The second unit (vv. 13–21[14–22]) describes the "gift" *(minḥâ)* that Jacob sends ahead to appease Esau's anger. The word "gift" occurs four times in the passage, all in this second unit (vv. 13[14],18[19],20[21], 21[22]), creating a sound play on the term "camp" *(maḥăneh)*. The dual references to "gift" and "spent the night" in vv. 13[14] and 21[22] provide the perimeters of the unit. After the narrative details the generous gift (vv. 13–16[14–17]), the passage reports the first speech by Jacob in the account. He instructs his servants, whom he divides into several camps (NIV, "groups"), to deliver in succession his tidings to Esau and to extend a gift (vv. 17–20[18–21]). Rather than using the term "messenger" when describing Jacob's servants as in the first unit, this narrative unit employs the word "servant" (v. 16[17; 2x]). As in the former unit, Jacob speaks of himself as Esau's "servant" (vv. 18,20[19,21]; cp. also vv. 4,10[5,11]). The last verse of the unit (v. 21[22]) brings together a final time the key terms "gift" *(minḥâ)* and "camp" *(maḥăneh)*.

The third unit (vv. 22–32[23–33]) describes the struggle for blessing that Jacob achieves from the "man," whom Jacob eventually recognizes as God. Wordplay on Jacob's struggle at the Jabbok helps distinguish this unit from the former. "Jabbok" *(yabbōk, v. 22[23])* plays on "wrestled" *(yēʿăqōb, vv. 24–25[25–26])* and also "Jacob" *(yāʾăqōb)*. Reference to the night and day become more important in the telling of this final narrative unit. The divine-human wrestling match extends the whole "night" (v. 22[23]), ending at sunrise (v. 31[32]). It was the threat of "daybreak" (vv. 24[25],26[27]) that precipitated the man's desperate action at freeing himself, whereupon he conceded a blessing on Jacob. By the light of the advancing dawn, Jacob could recognize that the opponent in his nocturnal battle was God. As with the site where he encountered the camp of angels (Mahanaim, v. 2[3]), he christens the holy place with the new name, "Peniel," meaning "the face of God [El]" *(pĕnîʾēl)*, explaining that he had seen God "face to face" *(pānîm ʾel pānîm, v. 30[31])*. The final verse of the chapter (v. 32[33]) stands outside the narrative's events, providing corroboration (i.e., the custom of a dietary restriction) of the events reported.

(1) Messengers (32:1–12[2–13])

¹Jacob also went on his way, and the angels of God met him. ²When Jacob saw them, he said, "This is the camp of God!" So he named that place Mahanaim.

³Jacob sent messengers ahead of him to his brother Esau in the land of Seir, the country of Edom. ⁴He instructed them: "This is what you are to say to my master Esau: 'Your servant Jacob says, I have been staying with Laban and have

remained there till now. ⁵I have cattle and donkeys, sheep and goats, menservants and maidservants. Now I am sending this message to my lord, that I may find favor in your eyes.'"

⁶When the messengers returned to Jacob, they said, "We went to your brother Esau, and now he is coming to meet you, and four hundred men are with him."

⁷In great fear and distress Jacob divided the people who were with him into two groups, and the flocks and herds and camels as well. ⁸He thought, "If Esau comes and attacks one group, the group that is left may escape."

⁹Then Jacob prayed, "O God of my father Abraham, God of my father Isaac, O LORD, who said to me, 'Go back to your country and your relatives, and I will make you prosper,' ¹⁰I am unworthy of all the kindness and faithfulness you have shown your servant. I had only my staff when I crossed this Jordan, but now I have become two groups. ¹¹Save me, I pray, from the hand of my brother Esau, for I am afraid he will come and attack me, and also the mothers with their children. ¹²But you have said, 'I will surely make you prosper and will make your descendants like the sand of the sea, which cannot be counted.'"

After the peaceful resolution with his nemesis Laban, Jacob immediately faced the more daunting challenge of confronting his brother Esau. However, Jacob first unexpectedly meets a camp of angels ("messengers," NRSV), which he commemorates by naming the site Mahanaim ("two camps," vv. 1–2[2–3]). He then dispatched messengers to Seir, the land of Esau, announcing his return, but his prospect of a peaceful welcome soon appeared lost when he learned that Esau and a band of four hundred men were en route (vv. 3–7[4–8]). He took two steps to prepare. First, he planned for the worst by dividing his group into two, believing that one of the two camps might escape (vv. 7–8[8–9]). Second, perhaps prompted by the prior encounter with the angelic camp of God, he prayed for deliverance in accord with the promises of divine favor made to him and his fathers (vv. 9–12[10–13]). This prayer is located at the narrative center of the preparations that Jacob makes to meet Esau in vv. 3–21[4–22].[421]

MESSENGERS OF GOD (32:1–2[2–3]).   **32:1[2]**   The abrupt appearance of the "camp of God" (v. 2[3]) may well have reminded Jacob of God's protective presence, first promised at Bethel (28:15). "Jacob *also* went on his way" (italics mine, v. 1[2]) alludes to the prior verse (31:55[32:1]) that reports Laban had returned home (31:55[32:1]), freeing Jacob to continue on his journey peacefully. The geographical directions of the participants in the account highlight the motif of Jacob's inheritance in Canaan. He, too, is returning to his ancestral roots. Although Jacob and the reader anticipate a confrontation with Esau, the engagement with a camp of angels is surprising. His two heavenly encounters in this chapter (vv. 1–2[2–3],24[25]) ultimately

---

[421] Westermann observes that the prayer as the center (vv. 9–12[10–13]) is framed by the two delegations sent to Esau (vv. 3–8[4–9]; vv. 13–21[14–22]; *Genesis 12–36*, 504).

make the difference in Jacob's successful encounter with Esau. The unexpected character of this meeting contributes to the many intriguing ambiguities and mysteries of this chapter. The reader gathers that an encounter with God "face to face" cannot be told otherwise.

The description of meeting the angelic host points us back to Jacob's dream theophany in 28:10–12: "went/set out" *(hālak)*, "met/reached" *(pāgaʿ)*,[422] and "the angels of God" *(malʾăkê ʾĕlōhîm)*. This latter expression appears only in 28:12 and 32:1[2] in the whole of the Old Testament. In Jacob's departure from Canaan and in his return, the angels of God appeared to him, suggesting their accompaniment of the patriarch during the entirety of his travels. The absence of a verbal message from the angels in chap. 32 is another facet of the account that creates perplexity in the reader. At Bethel, too, the angels do not speak, but there the Lord delivers a message (28:12–13). In the first case Jacob "reached" *(pāgaʿ)* the sacred "place" *(māqôm)* of Bethel (28:11), but in the "place" *(māqôm)* of Mahanaim the angels "met" *(pāgaʿ)* the patriarch. It was they who were scouting the area for Jacob. Although outside the land of promise, he was not outside the hand of promise. Houtman observes that the word "camp" *(maḥăneh)* indicates a temporary, mobile settlement versus the permanency of the "house of God" *(bêt ʾĕlōhîm)* at Bethel. He finds that the "stairway" resting on earth in the Bethel dream conveys the same sense of a mobile residence.[423] Are the angels Jacob's unseen traveling companions (cf. 24:7; 48:16)?

32:2[3] Impressed by what he "saw," Jacob exclaimed that he had encountered the "camp of God" *(maḥănēh ʾĕlōhîm)*. This reaction parallels Jacob's exclamation at the vision of the Lord at Bethel, "This is none other than the house of God" *(bêt ʾĕlōhîm, 28:17)*. Taken together, the similarities of the two events suggest that his experience at Mahanaim was also a night vision. Also the naming formula of Mahanaim is almost verbatim the formula for naming "Bethel" in 28:19 (cp. 22:14). "Mahanaim" *(maḥănayim)* is the transliteration of the Hebrew dual form of *maḥăneh* ("camp"), thus meaning literally "two camps." The word *maḥăneh* ("group/camp") is a key lexical item in chaps. 32–33, appearing six of the seven times it occurs in all of Genesis (vv. 3,8,9,11,22[4,9,10,12,23]; 33:8; also 50:9).

What the "two camps" in the name Mahanaim refers to has always puzzled interpreters. Targumic and rabbinic sources speculated, for example, that the camp may have consisted of messengers from Laban's camp, or Esau's company, or angels dispatched to deliver Jacob from both antagonists.[424] Ostensi-

---

[422] The word צַבַ in 28:11 and 32:1[2] occurs but once more in Genesis (23:8) but appears forty-six times in the OT.

[423] Houtman, "Jacob at Mahanaim," 39.

[424] E.g., *Tgs. Neof.* and *Ps.-J.; Tanḥ (A) III* and *(B) III*. See B. Grossfeld, *Targum Neofiti I: An Exegetical Commentary to Genesis Including Full Rabbinic Parallels* (New York: Sepher-Hermon Press, 2000), 223.

bly, the "two camps" refer to the camps just mentioned in the text, namely, Laban and the angels. We remember that Laban and Jacob set up their respective camps in the hills of Gilead, and it was also there that Laban experienced a night dream (31:24–25), although an angel is not specifically mentioned (cp. 31:11; also 16:7; 21:17; 22:11,15). Another potential identification of the two camps is Jacob's company of messengers whom he sent to meet Esau (v. 3[4]) and Jacob's own camp (v. 21[22]). Yet that the ensuing narrative describes the partition of Jacob's encampment at the Jabbok into two groups makes this event the likely reference (v. 7[8]). Since the passage does not mention Mahanaim, however, we cannot be certain that the division into "two camps" (*šĕnê maḥănôt,* "two groups," NIV) corresponds to the dual term *maḥănayim.*

Often, *maḥăneh* refers to a military camp (e.g., Exod 14:24; Judg 7:9) or to Israel's encampment in the wilderness (e.g., Exod 16:13), and as just noted it is used for Jacob's partitioned groups, involving his family and animals. That the term "camp" is used of a military camp and the very same phrase, "camp of God," appears but once more and there in a military context (1 Chr 12:22[23]) may argue that the angel's camp has a military assignment. The expression "met" *(pāgaʿ + bĕ)* also typically indicates an attack (e.g., Judg 8:21), though not always (28:11). If the purpose of the camp was hostility, was it against or in behalf of Jacob? Since the passage intentionally echoes the Bethel revelation (see above), however, Houtman concludes that the encampment was peaceful in nature. But the encounter at Mahanaim we already noted omits any idea of a revelatory message like that at Bethel, making it more likely that the camp has another function, one of protection for the two assemblies of Jacob's family (see discussion v. 7[8] below). This would fit nicely with the Bethel revelation also, for it focused on the protection and provision of the patriarch in his sojourn.

The precise locations of Mahanaim and Peniel/Penuel are uncertain. R. Coughenour has made a case for identifying the twin mounds of Tell edh-Dhahab el-Gharbi (Mahanaim) and Tell edh-Dhahab esh-Sherqiyeh (Peni/uel) as the biblical sites.[425] According to the tribal lists in Joshua, Mahanaim was in the region of the tribe Gad, at the southern border of Manasseh (Josh 13:26,30) in transjordan Gilead (Josh 13:24,31; 2 Sam 2:8–9; 17:26–27). Its strategic location at a ford of the Jabbok (Nahr es-Zerqa; see comments on v. 22[23]), just east of the Jordan River, provided a good view of the area, making a secure position for stationing an army (2 Sam 2:8,12,29; 17:24) or establishing an administrative post (1 Kgs 4:14).

MESSENGERS FROM JACOB (32:3–8[4–9]).   By dispatching messengers

---

[425] R. Coughenour, who also posits that Mahanaim was valued for its iron ore during the monarchic period ("A Search for Mahanaim," *BASOR* 273 [1989]: 57–66). W. Zwickel argues that Peniel is best identified as Tell el-Hamme ("Penuel," *BN* 85 [1996]: 38–43).

for Esau's camp immediately following his vision, the passage infers that the vision of the heavenly messengers (vv. 1–2[2–3]) encouraged Jacob to initiate contact with Esau (vv. 3–5[4–6]). Yet the messengers' report of Esau's rapid approach with a retinue of four hundred men frightened Jacob, leading him to take defensive actions (vv. 6–8[7–9]).

The Message (32:3–5[4–6]). **32:3–5[4–6]** "Messengers" *(malʾākîm,* v. 3a[4a]) is an intentional reflex of "angels" *(malʾākîm)* in v. 1[2]. In the seventeen occurrences of *malʾāk* in Genesis, it always refers to angels, except here in vv. 3,6[4,7]. In the Pentateuch the term is typically used of angels but also is used of human messengers (Num 20:14; 21:21; 22:5; 24:12; Deut 2:26). The description of Esau in v. 3b[4b] is familiar to the reader, recalling Esau's appearance and his ruin in chaps. 25; 27. "Esau his brother" ("his brother Esau," NIV) identifies Esau twice when describing Jacob's theft of Esau's blessing (27:23,30). "Seir" *(śēʿîr)* recalls the term "hairy" *(śāʿîr,* 27:11,23; 25:25), bringing to mind the elaborate ruse of Rebekah and Jacob. Also "Edom" *(ʾĕdôm)* recalls the "red" stew *(ʾādōm)* that was instrumental in the loss of Esau's birthright (25:25,30).

By referring to Esau as "my master/lord" *(ʾădōnî;* vv. 4,5,18[5,6,19]) and to himself as "your servant" *(ʿabdekā,* 33:5), Jacob expresses submissiveness to Esau, paving the way for a possible settlement (cf. 44:9,16,33; 2 Sam 19:28).[426] The language "lord" and "servant" may be diplomatic courtesy (1 Kgs 20:9), but Jacob means more than extending formal pleasantries. His deference to Esau ironically reverses the roles that their father's original blessing had anticipated (see comments on 27:29; cp. 25:23; 27:40; 33:3,6–7). Jacob's message explains his twenty-year absence (vv. 4b–5[5b–6]). He describes himself as an alien in the household of Laban. The verb "staying" renders *gûr* ("to sojourn," v. 4b[5b]), indicating that he was only a temporary resident who has now returned to his homeland. Furthermore, he describes his immense wealth acquired during this absence, referring to herds and servants (as in 30:43). He then explains the purpose of his message, "that I may find favor *[ḥēn]* in your eyes" (v. 5[6]; cf. 33:8,10,15), an expression that typically features the request of a subordinate seeking acceptance (see vol. 1A, pp. 345–46, n. 161; 18:3). Although Jacob's message approaches his brother delicately, he does not forsake his claim to their father's blessing.[427] The picture of his enrichment that he paints is similar to Abraham and Isaac, who as sojourners also had gained great wealth (12:16; 24:35; 26:12–14). Particularly, the travel

---

[426] Speiser (*Genesis,* 254 n. 5), followed by Hamilton (*Genesis Chapters 18–50,* 318 n.1), observes on the basis of extrabiblical parallels that "to my master Esau" is part of the address spoken *by* the messengers (cf. REB, NJPS) rather than *to* the messengers, as in the MT (notice *athnach*); though an unnecessary departure from the MT, if correct, it would strengthen Jacob's sentiment (cf. 33:5).

[427] Westermann contends that Jacob gives up his privileges to Esau (*Genesis 12–36,* 407).

of Jacob, making the trek from Haran to Canaan, recalled the journey of Father Abraham (12:1–9).

Esau's Approach (32:6–8[7–9]).   **32:6–8[7–9]**   The narrative's silence regarding what transpired between the messengers and Esau heightens the suspense. The returning messengers delivered the dire news that Esau was already en route to Jacob's camp (v. 6[7]). The participle *hōlēk,* "he [Esau] is coming," conveys an alarmingly vivid picture of the man and his horde approaching rapidly. A party of four hundred men was considerable, proving that Esau too had done well during the twenty-year separation. Abraham collected three hundred and eighteen retainers to chase down the kings of the East (14:14); David's gang consisted of four hundred or six hundred confederates (1 Sam 22:2; 25:13; 27:2; 30:9). The contrast between Esau's army and Jacob's flocks suits the twin's occupations when we first met them (25:7), especially Isaac's picture of Esau (27:40). But unlike his brother, Jacob had invested in his family and herds, evidently leaving himself a smaller count of male servants whom he could have enlisted.

Although Jacob cannot be sure that Esau comes with malicious intentions, Jacob assumes the worst (cp. the ambiguity of the "camp of God," v. 2[3]). Jacob concedes that his company could not withstand the formidable Esau band when he takes a preemptive measure, dividing his number into "two groups" (v. 7[8]). The string of verbs in close order heightens the urgency of his reaction, lit., "Jacob was greatly afraid . . . distressed . . . divided." The NLT captures the moment well, "Jacob was terrified at the news." But he was not paralyzed with fear. He still had his wits. The author provides Jacob's reasoning for his plan (v. 8[9]). The mention of Jacob dividing "people" before dividing his herds implies that his first concern was his family (v. 7b[8b]). If Esau were unaware of the tactical move, his army would pursue one group, leaving half of Jacob's company to escape in another direction. Reference to the key word "camp" (*maḥăneh,* "group," NIV) in this verse reiterates the mention of "two groups" ("two camps") in the prior verse. This is a reflex of the (double?) camp of angels at Mahanaim (vv. 1–2[2–3]), suggesting that each of Jacob's groups was understood to be under the supervision of God's agents (cf. 31:11; 48:16). The same notion of a guiding messenger appears in Israel's escape and wilderness sojourn (e.g., Exod 14:19; 23:20,23; 32:34; 33:2; Num 20:16; Judg 2:1; cf. Zech 12:8). The psalmist celebrated the Lord's rescue by the same image: "The angel of the LORD encamps around those who fear him, and he delivers them" (Ps 34:7[8]).

Mention of "camels" (v. 7[8]) again reminds us of Jacob's hurried flight from Laban, utilizing them for his family (31:17; cf. 30:43; 32:15). Jacob clearly interprets the approach of Esau as dangerous (v. 8[9]), and he takes his cue from the vision of angels when he splits his camp into two. This would correspond to the source of his idea for breeding his variegated herds when under Laban's authority. Jacob testified that the notion came to him in a dream from God (31:10).

PRAYER OF JACOB (32:9–12[10–13]). Jacob confesses his dependence on God in the past (vv. 9–10[10–11]) and petitions for deliverance from Esau (vv. 11–12[12–13]).

Confession (32:9–10[10–11]). **32:9–10[10–11]** Jacob's fears prompt him to seek the Lord through prayer, expressed as a lament. Repeated use of divine epithets, "God of my father Abraham, God of my father Isaac, O LORD" (v. 9[10]), emphasizes the relationship Jacob had with God by virtue of the fathers.[428] This historic relationship of the Lord and Jacob's family was vital to the divine command to return home (28:13,21; 31:3,13). Jacob paraphrases the words of the command to return that were first heard in 31:3,13. The language "to go back/return" *(šûb)* further recalls the promise and vow made at Bethel pertaining to Jacob's protection and ultimate restoration to his homeland (28:15,21). "I will make you prosper" paraphrases the earlier promises of divine presence, "and I will be with you" (31:3; 28:15,20). By appealing to the promises of the past, Jacob entrusts his present challenge to the Lord.

He appears to sidestep his own culpability that had created the rift with Esau (chap. 27), but he implicates himself when discrediting his worthiness of God's charity (v. 10[11]). "I am unworthy of all . . ." translates, lit., "I am too small *[qāṭōnĕtî]* for all . . ." Saul and David expressed the same sentiment of unworthiness at their selection as king by God (1 Sam 9:21; 15:17; 2 Sam 7:19; cf. Solomon, 1 Kgs 3:7). Both Jacob and David were the younger/est sons *(qāṭōn;* 27:15,42; 1 Sam 16:11). Perhaps the mention of *qāṭōn,* meaning "to be small, inconsequential," confesses Jacob's secondary status as the younger *(qāṭān)* son who had illicitly robbed his elder's blessing (27:15,42; cf. 25:23). On "kindness and faithfulness" see comments on 24:27. The Hebrew plural of "kindness" *(ḥăsādîm)* expresses intensity. "Your servant" often expresses a supplicant's lowly station before God (e.g., 1 Sam 3:9; Ps 19:14; cf. Exod 4:10). That he had admitted his "servant" status to Esau (v. 4[5]) and now to God indicates his new attitude of submission to human and God.[429] Ironically, by this self-humiliation he will prevail over human and God (v. 28[29]). Jacob explains that the Lord fulfilled the pledge to enrich the patriarch (28:13–15), transforming his single staff into two mighty camps. The Hebrew word meaning "staff" *(maqqēl)* also describes the "branches" that Jacob employed when increasing his flocks (30:37–41). By referring to "this Jordan," Jacob recalls the poverty he suffered when leaving his homeland. Jacob hoped only for sustenance to survive (28:20–21), but God had graciously far exceeded the young man's wishes (31:9–13; 33:5,11).

---

[428] Pagolu, *The Religion of the Patriarchs,* 114.
[429] Fokkelman, *Narrative Art of Genesis,* 203.

Supplication (32:11–12[12–13]).   **32:11–12[12–13]**   Jacob's appeal for deliverance, "save *[nāṣal]* me . . . from the hand of" (v. 11[12]), is language reminiscent of the psalmists' laments (e.g., Pss 31:16; 59:1[2]; 143:9; cp. Judg 10:15). The word *nāṣal* is widely used of rescuing a victim, as when David snatched *(nāṣal)* a sheep from the jaws of a wild animal (1 Sam 17:35; cf. Amos 3:12). The repetition in the Hebrew, lit., "from the hand of my brother, from the hand of Esau," reinforces that he is held firmly in the grasp of Esau. Only God can save him now. Jacob's ingenuity can only take him so far. The explanation for his desperate appeal is familiar, for he was afraid for his family's abduction by Laban (31:31; cf. 32:8). Now, when facing the more formidable opponent Esau, he expected an all-out "attack" *(nākâ,* vv. 8,11), involving an armed conflict (e.g., *nākâ,* 14:5; 34:30; 36:35). That he feared Esau's unrequited revenge is shown by his fear of a massacre of the women and children.

His subsequent word of confidence (v. 12[13]) relied solely upon the Lord's former promise at Bethel of an expansive progeny (28:14; cf. 13:16; 15:5; 16:10), which must mean the preservation of his children. At both the beginning and end of his prayer, Jacob quotes God, "who said to me" and "you said to me" (vv. 9,12[10,13]), relying on the Lord's own promises.[430] Jacob has no other avenue of escape. Is it not God who has really cornered the slippery patriarch? That the Lord is the patriarch's true antagonist is evidenced by the repetition of the word in his prayer "save" *(nāṣal)* when Jacob admits that his life "was spared" *(nāṣal,* v. 30[31]). The answer to Jacob's prayer is rendered in the battle with the nocturnal assailant, only secondarily the confrontation with Esau. This may explain the ironic commentary by Jacob, who meets Esau, saying, "For to see your face is like seeing the face of God" (33:10).

(2) Jacob's Gift for Esau (32:13–21[14–22])

13He spent the night there, and from what he had with him he selected a gift for his brother Esau: 14two hundred female goats and twenty male goats, two hundred ewes and twenty rams, 15thirty female camels with their young, forty cows and ten bulls, and twenty female donkeys and ten male donkeys. 16He put them in the care of his servants, each herd by itself, and said to his servants, "Go ahead of me, and keep some space between the herds."

17He instructed the one in the lead: "When my brother Esau meets you and asks, 'To whom do you belong, and where are you going, and who owns all these animals in front of you?' 18then you are to say, 'They belong to your servant Jacob. They are a gift sent to my lord Esau, and he is coming behind us.'"

19He also instructed the second, the third and all the others who followed the herds: "You are to say the same thing to Esau when you meet him. 20And be sure to say, 'Your servant Jacob is coming behind us.'" For he thought, "I will pacify

---

430 Hamilton, *Genesis Chapters 18–50,* 323.

him with these gifts I am sending on ahead; later, when I see him, perhaps he will receive me." ²¹So Jacob's gifts went on ahead of him, but he himself spent the night in the camp.

The passage describes Jacob's next move, coupling his prayer with pragmatic diplomacy. "Spent the night" marks the boundaries of this unit (vv. 13,21[14,22]), indicating one day's events. Jacob removed from his herds an exceptionally generous gift (vv. 13–15[14–16]), instructing his servants to drive the animals ahead of him by intervals in designated groupings. The leader of each group when encountering Esau was to explain that the bounty was from Jacob (vv. 16–20[17–21]), producing a sequence of gifts that would incrementally soothe Esau's anger. Jacob himself remained behind, spending the night in the camp (v. 21[22]). Was this action that of a coward? Or was he a man of faith who waited on God to empower him?

GIFT OF ANIMALS (32:13–15[14–16]).   **32:13[14]**   This verse provides the topic of the unit, Jacob's gift of appeasement for Esau. A gift typically buys a hearing (e.g., 43:11; Prov 21:14) as when Nabal's wife placated David's anger (1 Sam 25:27–28). Jacob's gift is not the return of the patriarchal blessing but rather an olive branch, seeking the favor *(ḥēn)* of Esau (v. 5[6]; cp. 33:8,10,15). By Jacob extending this gift, he restores the benefits of the blessing once stolen (33:11), yet not disowning his chosen destiny. Since the word "gifts' is used for an offering of friendship or of a subordinate, Sarna observes that it is another ambiguity in the episode, one that Esau must decipher.[431] References to "there" (v. 13) and "camp" (v. 21) prepare us for the later importance of this site, Peniel (v. 29[30]). Mention of "gift" *(minḥâ)* and "brother" recalls Cain's murder of Abel (4:1–12; *minḥâ,* "offering," NIV; 4:3,4,5). This potential fratricide, however, is averted by Jacob's humility before God and his brother *(minḥâ* also plays an important role in the Joseph account, 43:11,15,25,26).

32:14–15[15–16]   The breadth and number of the animals selected evidences how lucrative Jacob's sojourn in Aram had been (cf. 30:43). All the animals included were valuable stock, especially the female and young that would provide prospective herds. The obvious omission of human servants (cf. v. 5[6]) probably reflected Jacob's fear that Esau might visit his reprisal upon the servants first.

INSTRUCTIONS TO THE SERVANTS (32:16–20[17–21]).   **32:16–18[17–19]** Jacob plans to inundate his brother with wave after wave of gifts. By sending these ahead of his own appearance, we surmise that Jacob hopes to soften his opponent's disposition (v. 16[17]). To the leader of each drove, Jacob provides both the questions and answers that his brother will likely raise (v. 17[18]). The anxious Jacob micromanages every detail. Esau would want to learn the identity of the master and the itinerary of the servant, so as to

---

[431] Sarna, *Genesis,* 225.

measure what he should do in response. The servants' charitable concessions to Esau, "your servant Jacob" and "my lord Esau," are calculated to flatter Esau, dissolving his anger. Further, by each servant announcing Jacob's nearing, Esau would have no reason to pursue him, encouraging Esau to wait passively for his brother's arrival (v. 18[19]). Ironically, as Fokkelmann observed, Jacob, who had previously always sought first place "before" (*lipnê*) others, even at birth (25:25–26), retreated to arrive "behind" (*'aḥărê*) in last place (vv. 18,19,20[19,20,21]).[432]

32:19–20[20–21]   The author leaves the precise number of droves to our conjecture, but the passage suggests many separate flocks, making the communication repeatedly offered (v. 19[20]). Especially important to Jacob were the expressions of humility and the reassurances of Jacob's arrival. We can imagine that the animals would congregate around Esau in mounting numbers across the long day. Jacob probably reasoned that the cumulative effect would be the disarming of the brother. Only then did Jacob believe he had a chance at reconciliation (v. 20[21]). "Pacify" (v. 20b[21b]) translates the common cultic term *kippēr,* meaning "to make an atonement, reconciliation" (e.g., Exod 29:33); here the term refers to human appeasement (Prov 16:14; 2 Sam 21:3). The expression "to cover his face" ("pacify," NIV) indicates that Esau cannot see Jacob's shame. Wenham suggests that the cultic terms Jacob used, including "gift" (*minḥâ,* cereal offering), "atonement" (*kippēr*), and "accepted" (*rāṣâ,*33:10), implies that Jacob makes peace with God by reconciling with Esau (cf. Matt 5:23–24; 18:15–35).[433] The Hebrew of v. 20[21] contains four appearances of the key word *pānîm* (lit., "face"). "When I see his face" ("him," NIV) anticipates his encounter with the "man" at Jabbok (32:31) and with Esau on the next day (33:10). "He will lift up my face" ("receive me," NIV) also recalls the Cain-Abel narrative, where the expression describes God's potential acceptance of a repentant Cain (see comments on 4:7). In Jacob's case he appeared to have been forgiven by God, but now he must learn what Esau's response will be. Will Esau be another Cain?

JACOB IN THE CAMP (32:21[22]).   **32:21[22]**   This verse provides an obvious summary but not a repetition of the foregoing. The new information provided here is Jacob's further delay by staying in the camp overnight. The language of the verse repeats two words key to the narrative: "his face" ("him," NIV) and "camp." The word "gift" *(minḥâ)* provides a play on "camp" *(maḥăneh).* Mention of "camp" again brings to mind Mahanaim, meaning "two groups/camps" (v. 2[3]). That Esau's camp was intended by the name Mahanaim does not appear likely since the word "camp" never appears with Esau in the narrative. Rather, as we said earlier, the place name anticipates Jacob's

---

[432] Ibid., 205–6.
[433] Wenham, *Genesis 16–50,* 292.

division of his two camps (v. 7[8]). "But he himself spent that night"[434] clarifies that Jacob was left alone in the camp. The identity of the mysterious attacker in the encounter to follow could only be taken by Jacob as the enemy.

(3) Jacob's Struggle for Blessing (32:22–32[23–33])

[22]That night Jacob got up and took his two wives, his two maidservants and his eleven sons and crossed the ford of the Jabbok. [23]After he had sent them across the stream, he sent over all his possessions. [24]So Jacob was left alone, and a man wrestled with him till daybreak. [25]When the man saw that he could not overpower him, he touched the socket of Jacob's hip so that his hip was wrenched as he wrestled with the man. [26]Then the man said, "Let me go, for it is daybreak."

But Jacob replied, "I will not let you go unless you bless me."

[27]The man asked him, "What is your name?"

"Jacob," he answered.

[28]Then the man said, "Your name will no longer be Jacob, but Israel, because you have struggled with God and with men and have overcome."

[29]Jacob said, "Please tell me your name."

But he replied, "Why do you ask my name?" Then he blessed him there.

[30]So Jacob called the place Peniel, saying, "It is because I saw God face to face, and yet my life was spared."

[31]The sun rose above him as he passed Peniel, and he was limping because of his hip. [32]Therefore to this day the Israelites do not eat the tendon attached to the socket of the hip, because the socket of Jacob's hip was touched near the tendon.

After the scene is set for the meeting with Esau, the narrative takes an unexpected diversion, recounting an enigmatic encounter with a "man," who proves to be God. The passage details the movements of the Jacob family across the Jabbok (vv. 22–23[23–24]) so as to establish that Jacob is alone and that the unidentified "man" he battled through the night was not of his own camp. "Wrestled" (ʾābaq) in vv. 24[25] and 25[26] form the boundaries of the narrative action, specifying the injury the patriarch sustained. The dialogue between the two combatants that follows centers on Jacob's request for blessing that he eventually wins from the stranger. That the "man" renames him "Israel" confirms what the reader already had suspected, namely, that the opponent was more than a "man" (vv. 26–29[27–30]). The naming of the site "Peniel" ("face of God [El]") and Jacob's explanation for it explicitly solves the riddle of the "man's" identity (vv. 31–32[32–33]). The final verse is the concluding etiology, exhibiting the enduring prominence of the event by the dietary tradition Israel had long maintained (v. 31[32]).

CROSSING THE JABBOK (32:22–23[23–24]). **32:22–23[23–24]** "That night" (v. 22[23]) alludes to the previous verse, suggesting that Jacob impro-

---

[434]וְהוּא לָן בַּלַּיְלָה־הַהוּא, the wāw is disjunctive, contrastive with the pronoun at the head of the clause, "but he [himself]."

vised on his strategy of sending ahead gifts. He arose in the same night, sending ahead his family and presumably any servants who would accompany his remaining possessions. The Jabbok River is Nahr es-Zerqa ("blue river"), a tributary that flows west, emptying into the Jordan about fifteen miles north of the Dead Sea. It provides the natural division of the region Gilead into two parts (Deut 3:12,16).[435] The term "crossed" (*'ābar*) that describes the migration of the family across the Jabbok (v. 22[23]) also describes the dispatching of Jacob's gifts (vv. 16,21[17,22]). He himself did not cross (permanently), not until after he encountered God when "he passed *['ābar]*Peniel" as a changed man (v. 31[32]). The recital of the family's members, including the concubines, further confirmed that Jacob was left to himself. The obvious omission of Dinah must be understood as the author's interest in Jacob as Israel, whose sons' descendants constituted the nation.[436] Why he chose to stay behind is unstated. Was he a coward, hiding behind his wives? When Jacob actually met Esau, however, he approached him "ahead" of his family (33:3; cp. 32:3[4],16[17],20[21], 21[22]; 33:14). Was this the result of his moral change? As in his earlier efforts at guarding his family (31:31; cp. the pledge, 33:50), he may have reasoned that by isolating himself he would draw away Esau's ire, hoping that the children and women would avoid the brunt of Esau's wrath. Or his family as the last wave might foster some sympathy in Esau before their confrontation. The delay, for whatever reason, led immediately to the attack that changed the course of his life and that of his descendants.

WRESTLING WITH THE "MAN" (32:24–25[25–26]). **32:24–25[25–26]** Verse 24[25] establishes that Jacob was the only one remaining behind,[437] contributing to the mystery of the unidentified assailant. The opponent is blandly identified only as "a man" (*'îs*). There is no explanation provided for the attack. The word "wrestled" (*wayyē'ābēk*) is a play on "Jabbok" (*yabbōk*, vv. 24,26[25,27]). As a play also on Jacob's name (*ya'ăqōb*), it is a prelude to the name change he receives by virtue of outdueling the "man." The passage heightens the name "Jacob," for it conveyed as much as anything the selfish character he exhibited until his transformation at the Jabbok. Mention of the "dawn" also prepares us for the closure of the nightlong struggle, showing that Jacob and the "man" possessed remarkable strength and endurance (cf. v. 26[27]). Moreover, mention of the dawn infuses the narrative with mystery, since the unidentified "man" wishes to remain anonymous. Physical strength characterized Jacob's life: at birth grasping the heel of Esau (25:26[27]), moving the stone to water Rachel's sheep (29:10), and working Laban's herds for twenty years in difficult conditions (31:38–40). Here he vigorously

---

[435] G. Mattingly, "Jabbok," *EDB* 664.

[436] Sarna, *Genesis*, 226.

[437] וַיִּוָּתֵר יַעֲקֹב לְבַדּוֹ, "Jacob remained behind by himself"; cp. 2:18: לֹא טוֹב הֱיוֹת הָאָדָם לְבַדּוֹ, "it is not good that the man is alone."

clinches the "man," who in what appears to be desperation injures the patriarch in a failed attempt to free himself. The irony is that Jacob's physical weakness will recall the transformation of his moral strength. An apparent victory for Jacob was threatened at the last moment when the "man" wounded Jacob by a blow *(nāgaʿ + bĕ)*to the hip *(yārēk)*,[438] dislocating the joint (v. 25[26]). The intensity of the strike required by the intruder to weaken Jacob cannot be determined from the text. The phraseology *(nāgaʿ + bĕ)*may indicate a mere "touch" (3:3; Exod 19:12) or an aggressive "strike" designed to harm (26:29; Ps 105:15; Ezek 17:10).[439]

The idea of the Lord attacking Jacob is puzzling to commentators, although it is reminiscent of Moses' experience in Exod 4:24–26, when Moses failed to circumcise his son. Gunkel argued that the original Jacob story had the patriarch delivering the blow against the god, but the redactor's addition in v. 32b[33b] reversed the direction, attributing the blow to the deity. For Gunkel, followed by many scholars, the oral tradition lying behind the Jacob story was a local cultic legend of a nocturnal battle in which the god who impedes the human's crossing is forced to bestow a gift on the triumphant human.[440] Gunkel shows from ancient sources that many cultures maintained a common legend in which a god, demon, or monster who guards a river opposes the migration of a human. Sarna shows convincingly, however, that the idea of a guarded river does not correspond to the Jacob incident. Jacob has no trouble passing back and forth across the river in the narrative, and it is he, not the god, who suffers the debilitating blow. These striking differences lead Sarna to reason that the Israelite author, whose monotheism prohibited the unqualified adoption of the tale, has purged the folktale version.[441] We would go further than Sarna, expressing the conclusion that his arguments should lead us. The passing of the river is incidental to the narrative's emphasis on the blessing Jacob obtains, transforming him into Jacob-Israel. The river is important only as part of the prototype that depicts the nation Israel's future inhabitation of Canaan. If there were a connection between the biblical account and ancient river legends, it is now so vague as to be undetectable and useless for interpretation.

NAMING AND BLESSING "JACOB-ISRAEL" (32:26–29[27–30]). Jacob

---

[438] Hamilton speculates that כַּף־יְרֵכוֹ, traditionally rendered "socket/hollow of the hip," may be the male scrotum, based on the use of יָרֵךְ (when meaning "thigh") as a euphemism for the male genitals (cf. 24:2,9; 46:26; 47:29; Exod 1:5; Judg 8:30; *Genesis Chapters 18–50*, 331). Although the male scrotum may not be an adequate translation, we think a double entendre of יָרֵךְ may be in view, alluding to Jacob's descendants. This would correspond to the promise of descendants, indicating that the Lord alone determines the destiny of the patriarch's future heirs.

[439] *TLOT* 2.668; *DCH* 5.608.

[440] Gunkel, *Genesis*, 349, 352; also von Rad, *Genesis*, 321, and Westermann, *Genesis 12–36*, 516–17.

[441] Sarna, *Genesis*, 403.

demands a blessing (v. 26[27]), and the stranger changes Jacob's name and blesses him (vv. 27–29[28–30]).

Command for a Blessing (32:26[27]). **32:26[27]** Jacob held fast, despite the "man's" trickery, who resorted to pleading for release. The light of dawn would reveal the identity of the stranger, evidently giving Jacob an advantage over the "man." Jacob seized his chance, knowing that the figure he encountered was his superior. Was this God's angel? This would be a reasonable deduction made by the patriarch, since he had encountered angels camping nearby (vv. 1–2[2–3]). Moreover, the "man's" reaction to the rising sun signaled that Jacob dealt with a superior being (cf. Exod 33:20,23; Judg 13:1–22). The author maintains the enigma of the "man's" identity until Jacob announces it (v. 30[31]). That Jacob believes the "man" can render him a blessing indicates that Jacob knows his identity. That the combatant was Esau appears unlikely since his brother had no blessing to bestow upon Jacob. The ambiguity of the "man's" identity contributes to the author's theology of God's hiddenness. He confronts Jacob in a personal way, but he resists full disclosure. As long as God maintains this veil, Jacob cannot truly rival God's power and position. And for the Christian interpreter, an even more remarkable exhibit of God's grace is the fuller disclosure in the condescension and incarnation of Jesus Christ (John 1:14,18; 2 Cor 3:13–18; Heb 1:3).

Since this is God's messenger, Jacob has his opportunity to obtain the blessing from God that had escaped him until now, for he had only received his father's blessing and that was given unwittingly. The earlier narratives have implied that Jacob is already the recipient of the Lord's blessing (30:27,30; cf. 35:9; 48:3), but it is explicitly stated for the first time that God "blessed him" (v. 29[30]). This experience provides Jacob (and his descendants) the confirmation of God's blessing. The precise nature of this blessing is unstated. We may surmise that Jacob sought the power only God could provide him to overcome his enemies. The difficulty with this understanding, however, is that Jacob had already overpowered the "man," leaving the impression that the blessing Jacob sought transcended the circumstances. He seeks from the Lord the assurance that his descendants will endure, creating the nation God had promised (28:13–14; 31:3,13). That the blessing is or is related to the name "Israel" fits textually since the name presumes the nation that his sons will furnish.

Name and Blessing (32:27–29[28–30]). **32:27–29[28–30]** By asking Jacob's name, the "man" indicated his superior position to Jacob. The change in name signaled God's favor toward the patriarch (cp. Abram and Sarai, 17:5,15). The dubious meaning of the name "Jacob" was suspicious at best. Historically, the name "Jacob," meaning "one who supplants" ("grabs the heel of"), was given for the seizure of his twin brother's heel at birth (see comments on 25:26). If there were any ambiguity about the disrepute of the name "Jacob," Esau rendered his verdict in no uncertain terms: "Isn't he rightly named Jacob *[ya'ăqōb]?* He has deceived me *[wayya'qĕbēnî]* these two times" (27:36). By the change in name to "Israel," the passage announces that Jacob's moral character is about to undergo a metamorphosis.

The phonological derivation of the name "Israel" is disputed, but it is of no importance to the interpretation of the text anyway.[442] The sound of the name provides the significance of "Israel" *(yiśrā'ēl)* in the passage, playing on the word "struggled" *(śārâ),* "for you have struggled *[śārîtā]* with God *['ĕlōhîm].*" The word *śārâ* occurs only here and in Hosea's interpretation of the event (12:3–4[4–5]).[443] If we follow the typical pattern of theophoric appellatives, "Israel" means "God *[El]* struggles" or "May God *[El]* struggle." The explanation of the name given by the "man," however, reverses this sense by saying that it was Jacob who had "struggled" successively "with God *[Elohim]* and with men" (32:28[29]; cf. Judg 9:9,13).[444] Even in the name "Israel," therefore, we meet another ambiguity in the narrative. The name "Israel" emphasizes that it was God who initiated the struggle, and the explanation that the "man" gives emphasizes the outcome. Both are true. There is no other person who could legitimately bear the name "Israel," and it is not used of another person in the Old Testament (cf. Matt 1:16). The victories over human rivals were recounted in the former episodes (chaps. 27–31), in which the patriarch triumphed over Esau and Laban, but had he indeed won the match with God? And, if so, in what sense?

Jacob, true to his competitive nature, reciprocated by seeking the name of his opponent (v. 29[30]). Could he claim a victory over the "man" without obtaining his name? That the "man" questioned the need of Jacob to know his name admits the advantage that it would have yielded to the patriarch. The similar scenario occurred when an angelic messenger visits Samson's parents, announcing the child's birth (Judg 13:17–18), but there the angel refuses the request for his name on the grounds that the parents would not understand its meaning anyway. Jacob does not pursue the matter further with the combatant, ending the dialogue abruptly. It is left to the narrator to present the outcome, simply reporting, "He blessed him there" (v. 29[30]). Jacob had received the inviolable blessing of his father but by deceit (27:23,27,33), which tarnished but did not annul its legitimacy. By mentioning "there" *(šām),* the passage prepares the reader for the importance of the place and its naming (Peniel/Penuel).

---

[442] Cf. *HALOT* 2.442: II שׂרה, "to rule, prove oneself" (Noth); Ar. *šariya,* "to shine" (Bauer); and Ar. *y/wšr,* "to heal" (Albright); see also שׂרר, "rule" (BDB 979) and ישׁר, "to be upright" (E. Jacob) in R. Coote, "The Meaning of the Name Israel," *HTR* 65 (1972): 137–46, who preferred "*El* [God] judges" from *śry* or *yśr* (cf. מִשְׂרָה, "dominion, rule," Isa 9:6–7[5–6]).

[443] Hos 12:4[5] has וַיָּשַׂר (MT) as from שׂוּר, but if repointed וַיִּשַׂר, from שׂרה.

[444] Westermann understands "with God and with men" as a totality (merism; *Genesis 12–36,* 518); *Gen. Rab.* 78.3 explains it as heavenly beings (the angel prince of Esau) and earthly beings (Esau; cf. 33:10).

NAMING "PENIEL" (32:30–31[31–32]). **32:30[31]** The naming of the site, "Peniel," follows a common naming formula in Genesis (v. 30[31]; cf. 22:14; 28:19; 32:2; 35:15). As Wenham notes, the name "Peniel" is preferable to the author of Genesis since it is closer in sound to the explanation "face to face" *(pānîm el pānîm)* than the variant "Penuel" (v. 32[33]).[445]

The appellative *pĕnî'ēl* means "the face of God *[El]*)," originated by Jacob because he survived this face-to-face *(pānîm el pānîm)* meeting with God. By this the reader learns from Jacob that the "man" was indeed deity, as we had come to expect from earlier hints. Hosea further interpreted the incident as an encounter with God's "angel" (12:4), which is consistent with theophany in the lives of the patriarchs (16:7; 19:1,15; 21:17; 22:11,15; 24:7; 28:12; 31:11; 32:1; 48:16). Much ancient Jewish and Christian speculation arose from this fascinating encounter of Jacob and the "man."[446] Targumic and rabbinic interpretations identified his assailant as an angel in the appearance of a man, not a theophany, and sometimes recognized the angel by name (Michael and Sariel).[447] That a man could wrestle and prevail over God created a theological tension in Jewish interpretation, resulting in the substitute of an angel (e.g., *Gen. Rab.* 78.1). Philo's allegorical reading transformed the wrestling's meaning into the human soul that prevails over the human passions and wickedness *(Leg.* 3.58.190). Augustine's *City of God* (16.39) represented the popular interpretation that the angel was a type of Christ. The blessing bestowed on Jacob was meant for his descendants, who would believe in Christ.[448] From Jacob's standpoint, what was most remarkable was that he had made demands on the divine combatant and had lived (cf. 16:13; Exod 33:20,23; Deut 5:24; Judg 13:22–23; John 1:18).[449] Jacob's power over the divine intruder was only apparent, however, for at the breaking of dawn his life was in jeopardy at any time the "man" wished to take it. The passive voice of the Hebrew verb, "was spared" *(niph., wattinnāṣēl)*, suggests that Jacob admitted that he lived only

---

[445] Wenham, *Genesis 16–50,* 297. On the location of Peniel (Penuel), see comments on v. 2[3] (cf. Judg 8:8–9,17; 1 Kgs 12:25); for the personal name Penuel, cf. 1 Chr 4:4; 8:25.

[446] W. Miller. *Mysterious Encounters at Mamre and Jabbok,* BJS 50 (Chico: Scholars Press, 1984), 112. Miller provides a study of the many early Jewish and Christian sources.

[447] E.g., *Tgs. Ps.-J.* and *Neof.; Gen. Rab.* 77.3; 78.3; *b. Ḥal. 92a; Tanḥ. (A)* II,VII; *Pirqe R. El.* 36; and *Yal. Genesis* 132, noted by Grossfeld, *Targum Neofiti I,* 225–26 and Miller, *Mysterious Encounters,* 112. Sarna follows the tradition that the "man" was Esau's guardian angel (so *Gen. Rab.* 77.3; 78.3; *Cant. Rab.* 3.5–6; Rashi; cf. 33:10; *Genesis,* 405); he adds that the angel impeded Jacob from entering Canaan, functioning prototypically of Israel's and Edom's long history of struggle.

[448] Miller, *Mysterious Encounters,* 122,30.

[449] Fear of death by a mortal at seeing God was related to seeing his "face." Abraham conversed with the Lord without fear, and the text does not mention the "face" of the Visitor (chap. 18). Moreover, the "face" that Moses viewed (e.g., Exod 33:11) must have been a different manifestation from the "face" (i.e., the glory) that he could not see (Exod 33:20,23; cf. Exod 3:6).

because God's grace preserved him. His survival was a presage of the face-to-face encounter with Esau that he also will survive (33:10).

32:31[32] Mention of the risen sun recalls the urgency of the "man's" release and the nightlong duration of the struggle (v. 31[32]). The word translated "limping" *(ṣōlēaʿ)* is the less common term used to describe the lame (Mic 4:6–7; Zeph 3:19; cf. *pissēaḥ,* e.g., Lev 21:18). By the text's juxtaposition of the "sun" and the limping Jacob, we have a visual reminder of the battle that resulted in Jacob's victory but at the cost of a painful injury. Fokkelman explains the significance of the imagery when he comments, "The old Adam has been shaken off, 'Jakob' stays behind on one bank of the river. A new man, steeled and marked, Israel, has developed and he continues the journey on the other bank."[450]

CONCLUSION (32:32[33]). **32:32[33]** The narrative concludes that the incident at Peniel explains the dietary practice of the Hebrews known in the author's own day. The prohibition against eating the "tendon" muscle *(nāšeh)* arises from its association with Jacob's struggle with God. By this observance, Israelites honored the Lord and their ancestor Jacob-Israel.

10. Restored Gift and Return to Shechem (33:1–20)

The Jacob-Esau conflict comes to a happy resolution in this final episode of their lifelong wrestling match. Jacob's exclamation, "For to see your face is like seeing the face of God" (v. 10), links his nocturnal struggle at Peniel (32:22–32[23–33]) and his reunion with Esau across the Jabbok. Jacob implies that the pugilistic encounter with God substituted for the fisticuffs Jacob feared would occur when meeting Esau. Jacob had received God's "grace" *(ḥānan,* vv. 5,11) and thus Esau's "favor" *(ḥēn,* vv. 8,10,15). Although the tug-of-war began physically in the womb (25:26), their battle as adults was one of wits and words by which Jacob the trickster gained advantage (chap. 27). Esau had sworn that he would get his revenge against his conniving brother (27:41), but after twenty years of separation the men had undergone change.

We do not learn from the text explicitly why Esau's hatred succumbed to a rekindled love for his brother. The passage, however, hints at what incited Jacob's change of heart. That his moral transformation occurred in conjunction with his brutal treatment by Laban and with the encounter by God is implied at several points in the account. First, whereas Jacob had sent his servants and family ahead in chap. 32, now he takes the lead, subjecting himself to danger first (v. 3). Second, he acknowledges that his prosperity in Paddan-Aram was the benevolent favor of God (vv. 5,11), refusing to boast in his

---

[450] Fokkelman, *Narrative Art in Genesis,* 222.

hard work and sleight of hand (30:37–43; 31:20,26,38–41). Third, he provided a gift that exhibited his repentance, alluding to the blessing he had stolen (vv. 10–11) and evidencing humble submission to the elder (cf. "my lord," vv. 8,13,14[2x],15; "your/his servant," vv. 5,14). His remorse over his actions indicated that the man had changed his moral condition.

Since this account provides the conclusion to the Jacob-Esau narrative, it is instructive that the chapter ends with Jacob back in the land and at worship (v. 20). The narrative tension created by the self-imposed exile of the patriarch finds satisfaction in his successful return as God had promised (28:13–15). His attention to worship at entering the land expresses symbolically his commitment to fulfilling the vow he made at Bethel (28:21–22). By Jacob's return and worship, the passage depicts "Abraham revived," pointing to Jacob as the successor to the promises whose trek from Paddan-Aram and arrival in Canaan led to the same act of worship (12:6–8). Jacob's testimony to Esau is that God has graciously sustained him during his journey, returning him and favoring him. Although the divine name occurs but three times in the chapter (*Elohim*, vv. 5,10,11, excepting v. 20), the author implies that the remarkable outcome, so vastly different from once expected, was the outcome of God's doing. The same God who wrestled with Jacob was the One who had superintended his days from the beginning promise at Bethel to the present moment (cf. 28:15,20; 31:3,5; 31:42; 33:10). Jacob exhibits a mood of peaceful resignation, accepting whatever God has in store for him (v. 11). He is not the grasping young man he once was whose avarice had torn his family asunder. His naming the altar "El Elohe Israel" (= *El*, the God of Israel), referring both to himself and his descendants, confirmed the patriarch's trust, who had pledged, "The LORD will be my God" (28:21; cf. Exod 15:2).

This pleasant account that recalls the high spiritual moment in the patriarch's life, however, paves the way for the troubled life Jacob must continue to endure. The trouble he had perpetrated upon his father and brother would have its further recompense by his own sons Levi and Simeon, whose dastardly murder of the Shechemites impugn his good reputation among his neighbors (34:30).[451] The mere mention of Shechem in 33:18–19 brings to mind the trials that yet await him. He suffers further consequences instigated by treacherous sons, including Reuben's incest (35:22; 49:4) and the kidnapping of Joseph (37:23–28). Chapter 33 then is a conclusion but one that has no end for Jacob's woes.

COMPOSITION. The compositional character of 33:1–20 is viewed widely today as the product of the Yahwist (J; vv. 1–17) and a secondary addition (vv. 18–20).[452] This was not always the case. Gunkel, for example, contended for a

---

[451] Cp. David's poor example before his sons Amnon and Absalom.

[452] Thompson is pessimistic when he says that 32:1–33:20 is "hardly to be seen as a unity" (*The Origin Tradition*, 109–11); see the earlier discussion of source at chap. 32.

Yahwist composition in vv. 1–17 with some details derived from the Elohist (E; cf. the name Elohim, vv. 5b,10b,11ab), but vv. 18–20 he attributed to E (except v. 18a to the Priestly source).[453] Speiser discerned the same division and sources as Gunkel, except he attributed all of vv. 1–17 to J.[454] Westermann also assigned vv. 1–17 to J, who penned it to satisfy the flight-return theme initiated in chap. 27, but Westermann differed by reckoning vv. 18–20 as originally independent, probably made up of several diverse pieces.[455] However, since the description "safely [šālēm] at the city of Shechem" in v. 18 alludes to the Bethel vow, "so that I return safely [běšālôm] to my father's house" (28:21), Carr assigns the unit vv. 18–20 to the same original Jacob composition. He further explains the naming of the altar "El Elohe Israel" (v. 20) as the reflex of the renaming "Israel" in 32:28[29], which he thereby understands as another indication of a shared compositional level.[456] E. Blum identifies the worship of "El" (v. 20) as an early tradition antedating the rise of Israel's Yahwism, and vv. 18–19 show priestly and even hexateuchal redactions (e.g., Shechem, Josh 24:32).[457] Wenham views vv. 18–20 as that of J (like vv. 1–17), noting that the language (e.g., camp, altars, and naming, 12:7–8; 26:17,20–22,25) and the role of the passage as a transition in the story (i.e., to the Shechem episode, chap. 34) suit well what is known of J's style.[458]

We agree that chap. 33 is best interpreted as a unity. That the narrative describing Jacob's meeting with Esau in chap. 33 depends on the events of chaps. 27–32 contends for interpreting the authorship of the whole complex of Jacob accounts as the same person. The birth oracle (25:21–26) requires a separation of the brothers ("two nations"), which the peaceful parting achieves (vv. 12–17).[459] At least we can say that the author of chap. 33 had the preceding Jacob composition in its entirety in mind.

STRUCTURE. The structure of the narrative is threefold. The centerpiece is a prolonged dialogue between the brothers (vv. 5–15), which consists of three rounds of speeches. Two narrative paragraphs frame the dialogue unit (vv. 1–4; 16–20), the first introducing the dialogue and the second describing the outcome. Repetition of language distinguishes the parts of the composition. The beginning narrative and dialogue units each begins with the same idiom: "[Jacob/Esau] lifted up his eyes and saw . . ." (vv. 1a,5a). In the first

---

[453] Gunkel, *Genesis,* 353–56; von Rad identified E in vv. 5,11 but the remainder to J (*Genesis,* 328), and Noth assigned vv. 4–5,8–11,19–20 to E (*Pentateuchal Traditions,* 25,29–30).

[454] Speiser, *Genesis,* 260–61.

[455] Westermann, *Genesis 12–36,* 527–29.

[456] Carr, *Reading the Fractures of Genesis,* 259–60; also Coats, *Genesis,* 232. That 35:1–7 was usually assigned to E and clearly presupposes 33:18, thus also assigned to E, Carr answers by recognizing the dependence of 35:1–7 on 28:10–22 and the parallel narratives describing the building of the altar at Shechem (33:20) and at Bethel (35:7).

[457] E. Blum, "Genesis 33,12–20: Die Wege trennen sich," in *Jacob: un Commentaire à plusieurs voix de Genèse 25–36,* 227–38.

[458] Wenham, *Genesis 16–50,* 289.

[459] Blum, "Genesis 33:12–20."

case Jacob sees Esau approaching (v. 1a), and the remainder of the unit describes their respective responses to their meeting (vv. 1b–4). The second use of the idiom initiates the dialogue unit (v. 5a), and the exchanges of Esau's inquiries and Jacob's answers complete the unit (vv. 5b–15). Additional repetitions of language provide for the cohesion of the two units. The repeated word "bowed" *(ḥāwâ)* in the two greetings by Jacob and by his family (vv. 3,6–7) encircles the description of Esau's welcoming embrace (vv. 4–5). Westermann observes that this arrangement heightens the natural contrast of the two men's reactions—the greeting of a servant who bows versus that of a superior who embraces.[460]

Fokkelmann's analysis proposed a chiasmus in vv. 9–11a, involving four matching pairs.[461] We have adapted it below by employing the NIV translations:

A "I already have plenty *[yeš lî rāb]*,my brother. Keep what you have for yourself." (v. 9)
　　B "if I have found favor *[ḥēn]* in your eyes" (v. 10a)
　　　　C "accept this gift *[minḥātî]* from me" (v. 10a)
　　　　　　D "for truly to see your face *[pāneykā]*" (v. 10b)
　　　　　　D′ "like seeing the face *[pĕnê]* of God" (v. 10b)
　　　　C′ "please accept the present *[birkātî]*" (v. 11a)
　　B′ "for God has been gracious to me *[ḥannanî]*" (v. 11a)
A′ "I have all I need" *(yeš lî kōl,* v. 11b)

The presence of key words already known from chap. 32 leads Fokkelmann to consider vv. 9–11 the core of the narrative: "favor/be gracious" *(ḥēn/ḥānan);* "gift/blessing" *(minḥâ/bĕrākâ);* and "face" *(pānâ).* The balanced arrangement underscores the parallel between Esau's acceptance of his brother and God's forgiveness of Jacob. The reconciliation Jacob experienced with God at Peniel receives its confirmation by Esau's acceptance of his brother's goodwill. The interchange of the verb "be gracious" *(ḥānan)* and its noun cognate "favor" *(ḥēn)* also exhibits this parallel: Jacob acknowledges God's "gracious" treatment (v. 5b), twice seeks Esau's "favor" (v. 8b,10b), acknowledges again that God has been "gracious" (v. 11a), and refers finally to Esau's "favor" (v. 15b).

The third unit (vv. 16–20) reports the geographical outcome of the episode, Esau to Seir (v. 16) and Jacob to Succoth and Shechem (vv. 17–19). That the parting of the two parties is essential is shown by the initial verb "[Esau] returned" ("started back," NIV, v. 16), which is a typical expression for a person's departing (cf. Laban "returned," 31:55[32:1]). The final verse

---

[460] Westermann, *Genesis 12–36,* 524.

[461] Fokkelman, *Narrative Art in Genesis,* 226.

(v. 20) combines the force of the geographical interest and the religious significance of Jacob's arrival by erecting an altar at Shechem (cf. "there," *šām*, vv. 19,20). That Jacob built shelters at Succoth but an altar at Shechem signals the importance attached to his arrival in Canaan, the land of his fathers (e.g., 28:21; 31:3). The chapter began with the threat of Esau's approach (v. 1) and ends with the naming of Jacob's altar that declares God's patronage (v. 20). Many lexical items shared by vv. 16–20 with the prior narrative units evidence the interdependence of the compositional parts: "Seir" (vv. 14,16), "journey/went" *(nāsâ,* vv. 12,17), "come/brought/arrived" *(bôʾ,* vv. 1,11,14,18[2x]), "ahead/face/before/sight of" *(pāneh/pĕnê,* vv. 3,10[2x], 14,18), and lit., "from the hand of . . ." *(mîyad,* "from," NIV, vv. 10,19), and finally the divine name "God" *(Elohim,* vv. 5,10,11,20).

Each of the three units shows that the twins reach a peaceful acceptance of their destinies. In the first unit (vv. 1–4) the actions of Jacob (bowing) and Esau (embracing) exhibit the striking change in their behavior from what we know of them at Jacob's departure (chap. 27). In the second unit (vv. 5–15) the dialogue ends in Esau's acceptance of Jacob's gift and Jacob's special request to travel unaccompanied. The final unit (vv. 16–20) describes the peaceful departure to their respective settlements, Seir and Shechem.

(1) Jacob and Esau Meet (33:1–4)

¹Jacob looked up and there was Esau, coming with his four hundred men; so he divided the children among Leah, Rachel and the two maidservants. ²He put the maidservants and their children in front, Leah and her children next, and Rachel and Joseph in the rear. ³He himself went on ahead and bowed down to the ground seven times as he approached his brother.

⁴But Esau ran to meet Jacob and embraced him; he threw his arms around his neck and kissed him. And they wept.

After twenty years of separation the brothers at last meet (v. 1a). The passage describes their different actions in poignant terms: one bows in humility, the other embraces in love. Verses 1b–3 narrate Jacob's caution and courage, and v. 4 depicts Esau's clemency.

JACOB SEES ESAU (33:1a). **33:1a** The construction in Hebrew depicts vividly for the reader's imagination the fast-approaching band.[462] Reference to "four hundred men" accompanying Esau recalls the messengers' initial report (32:6[7]). Whereas there Jacob had responded in fear, here he will place himself at the head of his entourage (v. 3).

JACOB PREPARES FOR ESAU (33:1b–2). **33:1b–2** In each situation, however, Jacob "divided" *(wayyaḥaṣ,* v. 1b; 32:7b[8b]) his company into

---

[462] For parallels to בָּא עֵשָׂו וְהִנֵּה עֵינָיו יַעֲקֹב וַיִּשָּׂא, "Jacob lifted his eyes and looked and behold Esau was coming," see, e.g., 18:2; 24:63.

groups as a defensive measure against an attack. Here he organizes three groups according to wife and children. The concubine wives and their children are at the front, making them more vulnerable than his preferred wives, Leah and Rachel. Of the two, Leah and her children are next, and last is Rachel with her lone child, Joseph. Jacob's preferential concern for Rachel and Joseph is consistent with the special love he had for Rachel (29:30), shielding Joseph and her at the back. Joseph is the only child of the twelve named by the author, anticipating the rivalry of the siblings created by Jacob's special affection for Rachel's child (37:3–4).

JACOB BOWS BEFORE ESAU (33:3). **33:3** So as to convey the moral change in Jacob's character, the author contrasts Jacob, who takes the lead, with his family that follows. Earlier his messengers and family had taken the lead, but now he escorts the troupe by going "ahead" (*ʿābar lipnêhem*, lit., "crossed ahead of them"; cf. 2 Kgs 4:31). "He himself" heads the clause, highlighting his new station.[463] Jacob's actions of "bowing" seven times, meaning "to prostrate oneself" (*ḥāwâ*, cf. vv. 6,7), is a remarkable reversal in our expectations, if measured by Isaac's blessing (27:29). Calvin contended that the patriarch was worshiping God, doing so before he came into the sight of Esau (also Tgs.; *Gen. Rab.* 78.8).[464] That Jacob humbles himself before Esau is consistent, however, within the context of Jacob's conciliatory expressions of lowliness, that is, "my master Esau" and "your servant Jacob" (32:4[5],18[19],20[21]). This concession should not be taken as a signal of reversing the blessing (cf. comments on 25:23) but rather the response of humility. Jacob fully admits that his success derived from God's grace alone, not by his superiority to Esau or any other (v. 10). That the narration includes the specific language "approached [*nāgaš*] his brother [*ʾāḥîw*]" provides another allusion to the paternal ritual (*nāgaš*, "come near/here," 27:21,22,25,26,27) and language of their father's blessing, "Be lord over your brothers [*ʾaḥêkā*]" (27:29). "Bowing" may be a mark of hospitality and service (e.g., 18:2; 19:1), humble entreaty (e.g., 23:7; 1 Kgs 1:16), or worship (e.g., 24:26; Deut 4:19). Here the excessive act of bowing seven times, indicating completion and wholeness, reinforces Jacob's voluntary posture as Esau's subordinate (e.g., 42:6; Ruth 2:10; 2 Sam 15:5; contrast Mordecai, Esth 3:2,5). Perhaps the act of prostration expresses a double meaning for the narrative, including an act of obeisance toward God, since Jacob admits that in Esau's face he recognizes the "face of God" (v. 10). Sibling submission often appears in formal, patriarchal blessings in Genesis (9:25–27; 49:8–10; cf. Deut 33:16). Joseph's dreams

---

[463] The *wāw* is adversative, וְהוּא עָבַר, "But he himself went on . . ." (cf. NASB).

[464] Calvin admits that Jacob showed proper deference but did so knowing that ultimately he would receive the promised birthright (*Comm.*, 206).

involving the submissive "bowing" of family members create the fraternal contention that dominates the account (37:7–10).

ESAU EMBRACES JACOB (33:4). **33:4** The verse piles up five verbs, virtually one after another, describing in quick order the surprising reaction of Esau. A similar description recounts Laban's enthusiastic reception of his nephew Jacob (29:13), but here the hatred that Esau once had for his brother makes this reaction dumbfounding. Outward emotions of embracing and kissing express strong family solidarity (e.g., 29:11,13; 45:15; 48:10; 2 Kgs 4:16). Perhaps a sound play between Esau "ran" *(wayyāroṣ)* and Jacob "divided" *(wayyaḥaṣ,* v. 1) heightens the disparity in Jacob's fears and Esau's kindness. Not only does Jacob undergo a change in heart but also Esau, whose hatred against his only brother had melted. What precipitated the change in Esau is even more oblique than the forces that transformed Jacob. We must surmise that there was some correlation between the nocturnal struggle of Jacob's assailant and the change Esau underwent the same night. That God had forewarned Abimelech and Laban against mischief by a dream may provide a clue (20:3–7; 31:24). The affection of Esau, however, betrays a genuine outpouring of forgiveness, not a begrudging admission as by Abimelech and Laban. As we already have noticed in chaps. 32 and 33, the author made use of vocabulary to echo the evil deed that fostered their schism; mention of Jacob's "neck" and Esau's "kiss[ed]" recalls the treachery (27:16,27,40). On the wordplay of "embraced" *(ḥ-b-q)* and "wrestled" *(ʾ-b-q),* see comments on 32:24[25]. Joseph, too, "threw his arms around his [father's] neck" (lit.) at their reunion (46:29).

(2) *Jacob and Esau Reconcile (33:5–15)*

⁵Then Esau looked up and saw the women and children. "Who are these with you?" he asked.

Jacob answered, "They are the children God has graciously given your servant."

⁶Then the maidservants and their children approached and bowed down. ⁷Next, Leah and her children came and bowed down. Last of all came Joseph and Rachel, and they too bowed down.

⁸Esau asked, "What do you mean by all these droves I met?"

"To find favor in your eyes, my lord," he said.

⁹But Esau said, "I already have plenty, my brother. Keep what you have for yourself."

¹⁰"No, please!" said Jacob. "If I have found favor in your eyes, accept this gift from me. For to see your face is like seeing the face of God, now that you have received me favorably. ¹¹Please accept the present that was brought to you, for God has been gracious to me and I have all I need." And because Jacob insisted, Esau accepted it.

¹²Then Esau said, "Let us be on our way; I'll accompany you."

¹³But Jacob said to him, "My lord knows that the children are tender and that I must care for the ewes and cows that are nursing their young. If they are driven hard just one day, all the animals will die. ¹⁴So let my lord go on ahead of his servant, while I move along slowly at the pace of the droves before me and that of the children, until I come to my lord in Seir."

¹⁵Esau said, "Then let me leave some of my men with you."

"But why do that?" Jacob asked. "Just let me find favor in the eyes of my lord."

Esau dominates this unit by controlling the dialogue with Jacob, making two inquiries and a proposal. Yet it is Jacob's crafted responses that provide insight into the purpose of the narrative. The unit begins with their renewed brotherhood but ends with their agreement to part (vv. 5,15). Esau "lifted up his eyes" ("looked up," NIV, v. 5) as had Jacob when they first met (v. 1). He first asks Jacob about the identity of his family members (vv. 5–7) and then the purpose of the groups of animals that Jacob had sent ahead by messengers (vv. 8–11; 32:13[14]). In both cases the Jacob clan responds submissively, the women and children bowing (vv. 6–7) and Jacob presenting the herds and flocks as gifts *(minḥâ),* even a "blessing" *(bĕrākâ,* vv. 10–11; cf. *minḥâ,* 43:11; 1 Sam 25:27; 2 Sam 11:8; 2 Kgs 5:15). Multiple references to Esau as "my lord" (vv. 8,13,14[2x],15) and Jacob's conciliatory expressions "his/my servant" (vv. 5,14) characterize the gentle tone of Jacob's responses. Only at the insistence of Jacob, Esau accepted the gifts and then generously offered to accompany Jacob's clan, thinking of protection. Jacob refused, however, explaining that the young, both children and flocks, required a slower pace and that Esau's offer was too charitable. He proposes alternatively a later meeting at Seir (vv. 12–15). To what degree the "give and take" between the two was social courtesy is difficult to assess.

ESAU'S FIRST INQUIRY (33:5–7).   **33:5**   To Esau's inquiry about the members of his company, Jacob elevates the discussion by attributing his success to God's favor *(ḥānan,* "to be gracious," also v. 11; as a wordplay, see introduction to chap. 32). Jacob's answer presupposes the birth narratives of his family (29:31–30:24), which include the etymologies acknowledging the children as a divine gift. That the children and their mothers will survive this encounter with Esau is the answer to Jacob's earnest prayer (32:11[12]). At this early yet heartening juncture in their meeting, Jacob studiously avoids the potentially offensive term "blessed" *(b-r-k;* but cf. comments on 33:11), which recalls the original conflict in their house (chap. 27).

33:6–7   In succession the two concubines and their children, Leah and her children, and last Joseph and Rachel bowed before Esau (cp. Jacob, v. 3). One means of distinguishing the concubines (Bilhah, Zilpah) from the legitimate wives (Leah, Rachel) is the feminine form of "bowed down" in v. 6 for the servants and the masculine form of the verb in v. 7 for Leah and

Rachel.[465] The order of the family members' approach to Esau recalls the manner in which Jacob divided the family (v. 2), but here v. 7 has the reverse order of "Joseph and Rachel," creating a chiasmus of the names Rachel-Joseph-Joseph-Rachel.[466] The text again points up especially Joseph by name (cp. v. 2), the sole offspring of Rachel at this time.[467]

ESAU'S SECOND INQUIRY (33:8–11). Esau pursues further the significance of the animals (vv. 8–9), and Jacob insists that Esau accept them as a sign of reconciliation (vv. 10–11).

Find Favor (33:8–9). **33:8–9** Judging from Jacob's response to Esau's question, Esau was requesting further explanation for the herds that Jacob had sent ahead. That the messengers had already offered some explanation (32:4–5[5–6]) does not necessarily indicate the present verse is a variant tradition, as some believe. Esau probably was requesting clarification for the purpose of the herds since the number of animals was excessively generous. Or, since Jacob's response did not differ from the earlier message, except by the deferential address "my lord" (cp. 32:6[7]), Esau may be initiating the customary show of refusal typical of negotiations. (On "to find favor" see vol. 1A, pp. 345–46, n. 161; see comments on 18:3) Esau courteously rejected the offer (cf. comments on 23:10–11), referring to Jacob only here as "my brother" (v. 9). He insisted that Jacob should retain his possessions. Esau's conciliatory spirit matches his earlier show of emotions, impressing the reader that Esau is not the archenemy Jacob had feared. If anything, his magnanimous attitude made Jacob's past wrongs appear more insidious. Some commentators believe Esau's surrender, "Keep what you have for yourself," implies his final abandonment of any claim on his birthright.[468]

Face of God (33:10–11). **33:10–11** The concept of "favor" forms an inclusio for v. 10: "I have found favor" (v. 10a) and "have received me favorably" (v. 10b). Jacob pressed forward ("No, please!"[469]), appealing to his brother on the grounds that Esau's acceptance reflected his own acceptance with God. That the patriarch viewed Esau as the counterpart to the "man" (chap. 32) by virtue of their shared visage ("face") alludes to the forgiveness he had received from God at Peniel. The sign of acceptance with God was Esau's reception of his "gift" *(minḥâ,* v. 10).[470] The acceptance of the gift

---

[465] וַתִּשְׁתַּחֲוֶיןָ (fem., v. 6) and וַיִּשְׁתַּחוּ (masc., v. 7).

[466] The LXX (Syr.) has "Rachel and Joseph," maintaining the sequence in v. 2.

[467] The attention on Joseph probably explains the masc. sg. perf. נִגַּשׁ ("approached") versus the previous fem. sg. imperf. וַתִּגַּשׁ ("approached") with Leah as its grammatical subject.

[468] E.g., *Gen. Rab.* 78.11 and Rashi; also Sarna, but he admits that Esau's rejection and Jacob's insistence may have been social decorum (cf. 23:11–16; *Genesis,* 230).

[469] אַל נָא conveys a negative entreaty (e.g., 13:18; 18:3; Num 10:31), an abbreviated jussive clause (GKC §152g; *IBHS* §39.3.3a n.59).

[470] *Gen. Rab.* 78.12 justifies Jacob's gift on the basis that he offers it to God, whose face is reflected by Esau (cf. Exod 23:15).

was appropriate since Jacob already had been accepted by God and now by Esau. For Jacob the transformation of his moral character would be incomplete if he did not also experience reconciliation at the human dimension (cf. Matt 5:23–24; 1 John 4:20). The implication of Jacob's plea is that he has "found favor" *(māṣā᾽ ḥēn)* with the Lord, a stature enjoyed by Noah and Moses (Gen 6:8; Exod 33:12; 34:9; cf. Luke 1:30). The occurrence of "to be favorable to" *(rāṣâ)* is striking since it appears only here in Genesis and is a cultic term, referring to the divine acceptance of sacrifice (e.g., Lev 1:4; 7:18; Ps 51:16; Jer 14:10,12; Hos 8:13; Mal 1:8,10,13). On other cultic terms in chap. 32, see comments on vv. 19–20[20–21].

"Accept" *(qaḥ)* and "accepted" *(wayyiqqāḥ)* create an inclusio in v. 11. Again, firmly but respectfully ("please accept,"[471] v. 11) Jacob presses further by referring to the immense wealth God had bestowed, leaving him no want. He echoes the prior exchange (vv. 9–10) in two ways when making this appeal. First, Jacob continues the comparison between Esau's acceptance and God's by referring to the favor the Lord had shown him. The term translated "has been gracious" *(ḥānan)* is cognate with "favor" *(ḥēn)*, reflecting Jacob's description of Esau's acceptance (v. 10); in other words, Jacob avows that he has received kindness from both Esau and God. Second, Jacob counters Esau's reason for declining the offer by improvising on Esau's own argument: Esau alleges, "I already have plenty" *(yeš lî rāb, v. 9)*, and Jacob answers, "I have all I need" *(yeš lî kōl, v. 11)*.

Another telling remark made in Jacob's argument is his choice of *birkātî* (lit., "my blessing") for describing this "present" (v. 11), which departs from the prevalent term *minḥātî* ("my gift"), occurring in v. 10 and in the prior narrative (32:13,18,20,21[14,19,21,22]). The word *běrākâ* may indicate generally a "gift" (e.g., Josh 15:19; 1 Sam 25:27; 2 Kgs 5:5) or a benefit (Isa 65:8).[472] The suggestion by some commentators that Jacob by this allusion to Esau's complaint (27:36) is returning the stolen "blessing," in the sense of invalidating his father's blessing, overstates Jacob's intention. Neither is it a "slip of the tongue," resulting from a guilty conscience. Structurally, *minḥātî* (v. 10) and *birkātî* are parallel terms in this context, the latter nuancing the former as a gesture of goodwill. Jacob understood very well from his own losses to Laban (31:6–8,31,41–42) that Esau had suffered injury by his crime, desiring to make amends through this offering. The author indicates that the reason for acceptance of the gift was due to Jacob's earnestness, "because Jacob insisted *[wayyipṣar]*," not that Esau made a claim on Jacob's possessions. The term rendered "insisted" *(ṣāpar)* indicates passionate persuasion

---

[471] For this phrase, קַח־נָא, cp. 2 Kgs 5:15.
[472] Rashi identifies the "blessing" as a salutation, a blessing of peace (e.g., Gen 47:7; 2 Kgs 18:31).

(19:3,19; 2 Kgs 5:16), at one point even a fervent stubbornness or presumption likened to rebellion (1 Sam 15:23). Abraham's displeasure at a stolen well illustrates the language of a complainant (23:25–26). We do not have claim and counterclaim here but congenial social conventions.

ESAU'S PROPOSAL AND JACOB'S COUNTERPROPOSAL (33:12–15). **33:12** Esau assumed that their restored brotherhood afforded at least traditional hospitality (e.g., 24:31–33), if not joint settlement (cp. 13:5–6). He offers to "accompany" his brother, probably meaning to assure safe passage. Esau's hortatory language, "Let us set out and let us travel" ("Let us be on our way," NIV), captures the new spirit that Esau has for his sibling. The rendering "accompany you" *(lenegdekā)* is possible since the preposition *neged* may indicate "in one's view or presence" (Ps 90:8; Isa 1:7); but it often means "in front of, before [you]" and can mean "lead the way" (NLT; cf. AV, ESV, NASB, HCSB), meaning Esau will lead the assembly.

33:13–14 Jacob resists the offer courteously ("my lord," v. 13), explaining that the children and young cattle would falter if driven at a strenuous pace. His description of the children as "tender" *(raq)* refers to their physical weakness and vulnerability (2 Sam 3:39; Prov 4:3). Likewise, a forced march would rob newborn animals of needed nutrition, resulting in the death of both mother and young. Jacob offers an alternative plan, suggesting that Esau's company move ahead and leave Jacob's herds to a leisurely pace en route to Seir. "I move along" *(ʾetnāhălâ)* expresses the tender care of a shepherd (e.g., 47:17; Exod 15:13; Ps 23:2; Isa 40:11). The language Jacob speaks recalls the flocks presented to Esau; first, "go on ahead" *(yaʿăbor . . . lipnê)* repeats Jacob's instructions (32:17[18]), and second, "droves" renders *mĕlāʾkâ,* the feminine form of *malʾāk* ("messenger," 32:4,7[5,8]; cf. v. 15 below). By making this counterproposal, Jacob can express a measure of humility ("my lord" [2x] and "his servant") and at the same time retain control over his liberal gift to Esau. On the significance of Seir, see comments on 14:6 and 36:8.

33:15 Esau accepts his explanation but follows with another offer, delegating some men, presumably, to guide and guard Jacob's company. Jacob declines again, rhetorically answering that this excessive care is unnecessary.[473] "Just let me find favor . . ." reflects the earlier acceptance already granted by Esau (32:5[6]; 33:8,10). The NAB captures the idea: "Please indulge me in this, my lord." Since the text does not record a rebuttal, we may assume that Jacob again found favor from his sibling.

(3) Jacob and Esau Part (33:16–20)

16So that day Esau started on his way back to Seir. **17**Jacob, however, went to Succoth, where he built a place for himself and made shelters for his livestock.

---

[473]לָמָּה זֶּה, "what is the purpose of this?" or "what is the need of this?"; see T. W. Nakarai, "LMH and MDUʿ in the TANAK," *HS* 23 (1982): 45–50.

That is why the place is called Succoth.

¹⁸After Jacob came from Paddan Aram, he arrived safely at the city of Shechem in Canaan and camped within sight of the city. ¹⁹For a hundred pieces of silver, he bought from the sons of Hamor, the father of Shechem, the plot of ground where he pitched his tent. ²⁰There he set up an altar and called it El Elohe Israel.

Verses 16–20 contain a plethora of geographical locations. Esau returns home to Seir where he remains, and Jacob continues his trek toward his father's home by moving to Succoth (vv. 16–17). He arrives at Shechem, purchases land, and erects an altar—fitly named for the God of his protection and provision (vv. 18–20).

ESAU RETURNS TO SEIR (33:16–17).   **33:16–17**   The tenor of the passage indicates that they parted on friendly terms, although the narrative description is succinct. Westermann notes that the brothers' parting spirit did not require a treaty (cp. Jacob-Laban, 31:51–53).[474] The disparate geographical routes taken by the two parties metaphorically convey the different destinies of the brothers. Esau's descendants will reside outside the land of promise, and Jacob's household moves closer to Canaan (Succoth) and ultimately to Shechem (v. 18).

Succoth ("shelters") is often identified with Tell Deir 'Alla, although the location is uncertain. Tell el-Ekhas (Arb. "booths"), located one and a half miles west of Deir 'Alla, has also been proposed by H. J. Franken, who excavated at Deir 'Alla.[475] Jacob's Succoth should not be confused with the place by the same name mentioned in the Exodus route (Exod 12:37). Succoth is "in the plain of the Jordan" near "Zarethan," a site also unknown (1 Kgs 7:46). Joshua 13:27 places it in the tribal inheritance of Gad and a former possession of Sihon king of Heshbon. The psalmist associates the site with Shechem, as in our Genesis passage (v. 18), when referring to the "Valley of Succoth" (Pss 60:6; 108:7). Tell Deir 'Alla sits prominently in the valley and is three miles east of the Jordan River and about two and a half miles north of the Jabbok (Nahr es-Zerqa).[476] If Deir 'Alla is the correct site, then Jacob moved north and west, the opposite trek of Esau, who returned south to Mount Seir.

Apart from providing a staging area for crossing the Jordan River, the importance of Succoth for Jacob was the building of temporary shelters for himself and his cattle. Although Jacob may have resided at Succoth for some time, it was not a permanent settlement, for he was not yet returned to the land of his fathers (31:3; cf. 12:6; 48:21; 49:29). A stop before the task of

[474] Westermann, *Genesis 12–36*, 527.

[475] See J. A. H. Seely, "Succoth," *ABD* 6.218 for discussion.

[476] H. J. Franken, "Tell Deir 'Alla," *OEANE* 2.137–38; T. Dothan, "Deir 'Alla, Tell," *EAEHL* 1.338–47.

crossing fits with Jacob's expressed concern for his children and sucklings (v. 13), suggesting that his resistance to Esau's accompaniment was authentic, not a Jacobean ploy. The text says he built a "place" *(bayit)* for himself, which is the typical term for "house." The word is broad in usage, however, and may indicate a temporary shelter (Ruth 2:7). The temporary "shelters" *(sūkkôt)* that housed his stock confirm the interim purpose of Jacob's *bayit.* Jacob commemorated the event by assigning the place name "Succoth" *(sūkkôt),* referring to the animal sheds. The word *sūkkâ* describes a covered booth or shelter that served temporary purposes (e.g., 2 Sam 11:11; Isa 1:8; Job 27:18; Jonah 4:5). The word is best known for naming the structures built during Israel's wilderness sojourn, whose provision they celebrated in the annual "Feast of Tabernacles/Booths" *(ḥag hassūkkôt; e.g.,* Lev 23:33–43).

As to why Jacob did not proceed to Seir is unstated in the text. It is a "gap" in the story that the author may want the reader to fill from the earlier struggle between Jacob and Laban. In the Jacob-Laban experience, the Lord specifically directed Jacob to leave Laban's house and return to the land of his father (31:3,13,30a; 32:9[10]), and perhaps we are to assume that the Lord directed Jacob again to Canaan, the land promised him twenty years earlier (cf. 28:13–22). The text has been candid heretofore about deception and obfuscation by Jacob, and its silence here implies that Jacob's action is not a violation of the peaceful intention agreed upon by the brothers. Later we learn at the instigation of Esau that the two brothers chose not to reside together because their cumulative wealth prohibited it (36:6–7; cf. Abraham and Lot, 13:6). That the exchange between the men is mere social convention is another possible explanation for Jacob's action.

JACOB BUILDS AN ALTAR AT SHECHEM (33:18–20). **33:18** Verse 18 describes the successful conclusion to Jacob's hurried and excited flight from Paddan-Aram, residing "safely" *(šālēm,* adjective) in Canaan near Shechem. The rendering of *šālēm* as the place name "Salem" has textual support (LXX, Syr., Vg.; cf. "Shalem," AV), but recent EVs prefer the adjective "in peace," meaning "safely" (as SP has *šlwm [šālôm],* "peacefully"). Thus Jacob's travels, despite the potential threats of Laban and Esau, ended without incident in Shechem. If interpreted as the place name "Salem," its relationship to "Shechem" can be explained in two ways. First, and less likely, "Salem" is a village in the area of Shechem, that is, "Salem, a city of Shechem." Second, "Salem, the city of Shechem," understands "Shechem" as a person, the son of Hamor (34:2), not the city.[477] The advantage of this interpretation is its accord with the customary use of a person with the construction "the city of . . ." (e.g., *ʿîr nāḥôr,* "the town of Nahor," 24:10; Num 21:26). Also it has been

---

[477] Wenham identifies שָׁלֵם as the modern city "Salim" located near Shechem (Tell Balaṭah; *Genesis 12–36,* 300).

argued that the adverbial expression *bĕšālôm* (cf. 26:29; 28:21), rather than the adjective *šālēm,* would be more appropriate if "safety" were intended. Yet the grammar of the adjective *šālēm* is not improbable, and there is no clear evidence that Salem existed as a near but distinct site from Shechem, making it preferable to adopt the popular interpretation "safely."[478] We add that the rendering "safely," over the place "Salem," is favored, since it functions as an echo of Jacob's prayer at Bethel (28:21, *bĕšālôm);* this is another example of the author's practice of recalling prior events through shared lexical items, demonstrating that the prayer has been answered. Also the plural form *šĕlēmîm* ("friendly") in the Dinah narrative (34:21) probably continues the irony begun in our verse by mention of "safely."[479] Jacob and his sons dwell near Shechem in safety, but this will prove to be a place of violence for the households of Jacob and Hamor (cf. 34:30). As for the common usage of the expression "the city of" with a personal name, the construction, though infrequently, may also be used with a place name (Josh 15:62; 2 Kgs 19:13; perhaps Deut 34:3). Moreover, vv. 17–18 focus on geographical entities, making the city Shechem suitable.

Several features of vv. 18–20 recall Abraham's arrival in Canaan from Haran. "Shechem" was Abraham's and Jacob's first place to reside in Canaan (12:6), where each "pitched his tent" (12:8) and established an "altar" (12:9). That it is identified as a "city" *(ʿîr)* in Jacob's day suggests that the site had become a town since the time of Abraham, which is not required in the Abraham narrative (12:6). Shechem (Tell Balaṭah) is some thirty-five to forty miles north of Jerusalem in the central hill country of cisjordan, at the eastern end of the narrow pass between Mount Ebal (north) and Mount Gerizim (south). Shechem was crucial to the infrastructure of the central highlands during the LB and Iron Ages, serving as a major crossroad for north-south and east-west highways. D. Dorsey proposed that as many as eleven roads during the Iron Age connected Shechem to the Jordan River.[480] Especially interesting for our purposes is one that runs from Shechem north turning southeast via the Wadi Fariʿa that reaches the Jordan just south of the fords at Adam (Tell ed-Damiya, cf. Josh 3:16) on the east side at the Jabbok. Perhaps Jacob took this route from Succoth, crossing the Jordan near Adam (as did his descendants under Joshua), and making his way along this natural route up to Shechem. For those interpreters who subscribe to the place Salim as his destination (see above), Dorsey discovered a

---

[478] J. A. Emerton, "The Site of Salem, the City of Melchizedek (Genesis XIV 18)," in *Studies in the Pentateuch,* VTSup 41 (Leiden: Brill, 1990), 45–71 (esp. 64–69).

[479] Observed by Sarna, who does not indicate a preference but who contends for interpreting Shechem as the person in chap. 34 (*Genesis,* 232).

[480] D. Dorsey, "Shechem and the Road Network of Central Samaria," *BASOR* 268 (1987): 57–70.

side road via Salim that links Shechem to the Wadi Fariʻa.

Our knowledge of Shechem (Tell Balaṭah) is extensive as a result of ancient references and numerous excavations and field surveys.[481] Egyptian texts of the nineteenth century B.C. refer to the city, and material evidence at Balaṭah points to occupation at the same period. The Egyptian texts indicate that Shechem referred to a city and to a region.[482] Shechem in biblical history had a checkered history as a religious and political center (e.g., 12:6; chap. 34; Josh 24; Judg 9; 1 Kgs 12:1,25). R. S. Hess observes, "Thus, the seemingly contradictory themes of lawlessness and a religious center dominate the biblical texts describing Shechem."[483] In the case of Jacob, we find it appropriate that the man of moral contradictions established himself at Shechem upon arriving in Canaan.

33:19 Verses 16–20 also are transitional, preparing the reader for the subsequent account of Dinah's rape by Shechem (chap. 34). That Jacob purchased land from the Hamorites (v. 19) is another similarity to his grandfather, who acquired a family burial site from the Hittite, Ephron, for the purchase price of four hundred shekels (23:16,20). Like Abraham's, the purchase probably was for a burial plot, as shown by Joseph's burial at Shechem (Josh 24:32; Acts 7:16[484]). Westermann suggests that the Abraham narrative is presupposed, implying that Jacob bought the field in the presence of the Hamorites.[485] The price of one hundred pieces of "silver" *(qĕśîṭâ)* paid by Jacob was probably modest. We say "probably" because the unit of measure *(qĕśîṭâ)* is uncertain, appearing only in Josh 24:32 and Job 42:11. The EVs typically render the term "silver" or "money." The LXX has "one hundred lambs" *(ekaton amnōn;* cp. *amnōn,* however, 31:7 LXX, where it refers to a counting unit[486]), but its use in Job 42:11 makes "lamb" unlikely. Suggestions for the term include some connection between the weight and a lamb, either the weight's cast or its value.[487]

33:20 The final verse brings the main narrative interest of the Jacob account to its conclusion. What will follow in chaps. 34–36, although impor-

---

[481] Including esp. the German E. Sellin (1913, 1926–27) and American G. E. Wright (1956–69); for a survey of its archaeological history, see E. F. Campbell, "Developments in the Excavation and Reexcavation of Shechem/Tell Balatah," in *Biblical Archaeology Today 1990* (Jerusalem: Israel Exploration Society, 1993), 598–605, and R. Tappy, "Shechem," *EDB,* 1200–3.

[482] E. F. Campbell, "Shechem Tell Balâtah," *EAEHL* 4.1345–54; J. D. Seger, "Shechem," *OEANE* 5.19–23.

[483] R. S. Hess, "Shechem," *NIDOTTE* 4.1215.

[484] An example of Stephen's telescoping events, since Jacob himself was buried in Machpelah (50:13; F. F. Bruce, *The Book of the Acts,* NICNT [Grand Rapids: Eerdmans, 1973 reprint], 149, n. 39).

[485] Westermann, *Genesis 12–36,* 528; Sarna, *Genesis,* 232.

[486] Wevers, *Notes on the Greek Text,* 556.

[487] J. Shepherd, "שׁקל‎," *NIDOTTE* 4.239.

tant, falls outside the itinerary motif of Jacob's departure and return that dominates the Jacob narrative as a whole. It is appropriate then as the last act in the Jacob-Esau conflict and the first act in Jacob's return that he should build an altar for worship. This expression of piety also characterized the travels of Abraham and Isaac (12:7–8; 13:18; 26:25). Jacob erected and named the altar "El Elohe Israel," meaning "El, the God of Israel." Jacob's naming of the altar is unique to the patriarchs and rare elsewhere, practiced by Moses and Gideon (Exod 17:15; Judg 6:24).[488] The narrative's portrayal of erecting Jacob's altar departs from the prevalent depictions, where an altar is "built" *(bānâ,* e.g., 8:20; 12:7–8; 13:18; 22:9; 26:25; 35:7; Exod 17:15; Judg 6:24). Here the passage prefers "set up" *(nāṣab),* drawing on the telling of the nocturnal theophany at Bethel. The ladder "resting" (28:12) on the earth and the Lord who "stood" above (28:13) translate the same root term *(nāṣab).* By this allusion the author reminds his readers of God's loyalty to the promise at Bethel. Hence, the title "Elohe Israel" that points back to the renaming of "Israel," the man (Jacob), and points forward collectively to his progeny, "Israel" the nation, trumpets the narrative's resolution to Jacob's wayward character and his sojourn vacating Canaan (to Paddan Aram).

11. Dinah, Deception, and Strife with the Hivites (34:1–31)

After recounting Jacob's reconciliation with Esau (chap. 33), the author includes a vignette concerning Jacob's stay at Shechem (33:18–19), the outcome of which compelled Jacob's departure for his original destination, Bethel (35:1–7). The episode initiates a disturbing moral decline exhibited by Jacob's sons in his later years (Reuben and Bilhah, 35:22; Joseph's brothers, chap. 37; Judah and Tamar, chap. 38). There is ostensibly nothing about chap. 34 that is commendable. The chapter begins with the moral outrage of Dinah's rape by the prince of Shechem but ends on an even lower standing when Jacob's sons, Simeon and Levi, murder the whole male populace of the city.

MESSAGE.   What message does such a sordid episode have in the Jacob-Joseph narratives? At this point forward, Genesis turns its attention to Jacob's sons, the progenitors of Israel's twelve tribes. After the tension of the Jacob-Esau struggle was alleviated in chap. 33's account of the twin's pacification, the author sets out to demonstrate the seedy character of Jacob's descendants,

---

[488] Westermann finds that the building of an altar instead of a "pillar," which was Jacob's practice (e.g., 28:18), and the needless purchase of a field to erect it shows that the passage is secondary, but this misses the point of Jacob's actions *(Genesis 12–36,* 529). He is imitating the pattern of Abraham in Canaan (12:7–8; 17–18).

raising the specter that the promises are again in peril. In the context of the Joseph narrative (chaps. 37–50), chap. 34 provides for the author's goal of demonstrating the surpassing grace of the Lord, whose redemptive purposes survive the moral failures of the nation's fathers. The purpose to bless the patriarchal family was not cancelled by the villainous behavior of Jacob's sons. We will discover in the Joseph narrative that the brothers' Egyptian descent was the divinely designated antidote to the brothers' evil behavior (42:28; 44:16; 45:5–9; 50:17–20). The brothers will undergo moral reclamation that results in the family's reconciliation (chaps. 42–44).

The matching episode to chap. 34 in the broad arrangement of the Jacob narrative is instructive here (for the chiastic construction, see "Structure" in the introduction to the Jacob narrative). Chapter 26 details Isaac's deception of King Abimelech at Gerar (Philistines), resulting in an amiable treaty though after bitter contention over water rights. The present episode tells how Jacob's sons Simeon and Levi answered conflict with another non-Israelite tribe (Hivites), contrasting remarkably with Isaac's history. We also recall Abraham's honorable dealing with the Hittites when he purchased the family's burial site at Machpelah (chap. 23). Jacob entered into a similar agreement with the Hivites (33:18–19), acquiring property where Joseph's mummified body was finally buried (Josh 24:32; Acts 7:16). This we assume occurred early in Jacob's arrival and explains why the Hivites trusted Jacob's sons in their negotiations (34:21).

Although both chaps. 26 and 34 involve deception and strife, the different moral tenor of the narratives points up the author's purpose. The incidents of deception invite us to compare the brothers to their ancestors' conduct. Although Isaac deceived the king of Gerar for self-preservation (like Abraham in 12:10–13:1; chap. 20), Simeon and Levi deceived their neighbors for vengeance, murdering the defenseless Hivites. The other sons joined in the violation by looting the dead, enslaving the women and children, and confiscating their possessions. The gravity of the sons' actions also distinguishes them from Jacob's past when he mistreated Esau (chap. 27) and tricked Laban (chap. 31). Of course, Jacob's struggles were against his own kinsmen and not the nations, but the resolutions to Jacob's offenses were morally superior to those of his sons' repugnant conduct. The disputes with Esau and Laban ended in peaceful agreements. Moreover, the sons of Jacob compare unfavorably to Esau, since they carried through the vengeance against Shechem that Esau had only initially hoped to do against Jacob (27:41). Jacob himself viewed Simeon and Levi as enemies because he believed their action placed the family in jeopardy (34:31; 49:5–7).

By such moral contrasts, chap. 34 indirectly casts doubt about the moral character of Jacob's apparent successors. Since Esau and Jacob underwent moral change, Simeon and Levi's treachery and unrepentant stance appear all the worse. They indignantly defy their father's reprimand. The brothers appear

more concerned about their sullied reputation than the welfare and wishes of
Dinah (contrast Laban and Bethuel, 24:55–58). Unlike the Isaac incident in
chap. 26, the present chapter possesses no prayers, no divine revelations, no
mention of promissory blessings, and no explicit mention of God. The brothers
profane the sole religious allusion (circumcision) in the account for nefarious
purposes by guilefully requiring it of the Hivites. Whereas the ritual of circumcision symbolized life and blessing for Abraham's seed and ultimately the
nations (chap. 17), the sons of Jacob employ it for revenge and death against the
nation(s). In effect chap. 34 exhibits again the jeopardy that the promises are
subject to, despite the return of Jacob to the land. The return of Jacob did not
guarantee the favorable outcome of those promises that God had purposed.

HISTORY OF INTERPRETATION.   Interpreters attempted to answer what the
moral disposition of the author is toward the events of the chapter. Is this story
about the rape of Dinah or the rape of the city of Shechem?[489] The chapter artfully provides for potentially conflicted interpretations of the brothers'
actions.[490] Is the treachery of Simeon and Levi condemned, or is it justified in
the eyes of the author? This complex picture of the brothers' character reminds
us of the Jacob/Israel ambiguity that the Jacob story creates. Jacob's zeal is commendable, but his conduct did not match the honor of his ardor. We have already
indicated above the interpretation we give to the brothers' actions. The passage
is not neutral, judging by the overt reference to their deception of the Hivites
(v. 13) and by the fiery rebuke from Jacob (v. 30).[491] But we should not take
from this that the passage absolves Shechem and the Hivites. There are no
heroes in this episode. Any mitigation of Shechem and Hamor's mistreatment
of Dinah by the author serve only to heighten our disgust at the sons. Like the
later remark of Judah regarding Tamar, "She is more righteous than I" (38:26),
we are not to take it that Shechem or the sons acted ethically any more than we
judge Tamar to have behaved appropriately.

---

[489] Coats entitles this chapter "The Rape of Shechem" (*Genesis,* 233).

[490] See, e.g., M. Caspi, "The Story of the Rape of Dinah: The Narrator and the Reader," *HS* 26
(1985): 25–45 and M. Sternberg, *The Poetics of Biblical Narrative* (Bloomington: Indiana University Press, 1987), 441–82. Sternberg argues that the narrator strives to balance the reader's competing views of the actions of Simeon and Levi. Since the heinous crime of the sons is so grave, the
narrator must moderate the reader's aversion by softening the brothers and hardening opinion
against the original perpetrators of the crime, Shechem and Hamor. By the final opposition between
the brothers and their father Jacob (vv. 30–31), the narrator's sympathies lean ultimately toward
the brothers, who are the ideologues. Their behavior driven by principle contrasts with the greedy
Shechem and Hamor, the disinterested pragmatist Jacob, and the predatory other brothers. Ross
reflects the ambiguity the narrative presents when he concludes that the "instincts" of the two
brothers are admirable, but their actions are repugnant (*Creation and Blessing,* 525).

[491] J. Kugel deems the silence of the narrative's author as a case of "studied neutrality"; he
observes that Jacob's opinion in 49:5–7 makes clear the immorality of the brothers (*The Bible as
It Was* [Cambridge: Belknap Press of Harvard University Press, 1997], 233).

The wide variance among interpretations, including ancient and modern analyses, reflects the many ambiguities appearing in the chapter, producing contradictions in the depictions of the characters. That no person comes across as purely good or wholly wicked is because the author treats the characters as they really were. They are not one-dimensional figures, cardboard images, but flesh-and-blood persons whose moral conduct fluctuates. No one escapes the author's ambivalence toward the participants in this gloomy account, not even Dinah. Did her hubris or curiosity or sensuality compromise her virtue when she "went out to visit the women of the land" (v. 1)? The conduct of the other participants is subjected to moral remonstrations, usually given obliquely by the author. Commentators have assigned varying degrees of culpability to the actions of the culprits. Shechem, the Hivite prince, attacks Dinah; but Hamor and Shechem show good faith in their negotiations with Jacob's family, and the author repeatedly reminds us of Shechem's "love" for her (vv. 3–4,8,11–12).

But even this analysis is too simple. Some question whether a rape actually occurred, preferring to render v. 2 as "have [sexual] intercourse with" (*'ānâ*) rather than violation.[492] From the contrary perspective, the question arises of whether Hamor and Shechem in fact negotiate in good faith. Since the Hivite leaders failed to represent fully their negotiations with Jacob's household when presenting their case to the townspeople of Shechem, they are suspect of deceitful bargaining in the view of some commentators. The characterization of the brothers also swings pendulously between condemnation and commendation. The protestations of Simeon and Levi against their father's inaction (v. 31) leaves room for interpreting the author's viewpoint as tolerating, if not advocating, the extermination policy of the brothers. That their action corresponded to Moses' rules for engaging the inhabitants of Canaan, including the Hivites (Deut 7:1–3), may suggest that the author judged them favorably. Jacob's apparent apathy ("kept quiet," v. 5), on the contrary, is not indifference but measured wisdom in dealing with outsiders, an attitude that the hardliners, Simeon and Levi, reproach, endangering the survival of the Jacob family.[493]

Jewish interpretation especially presented Simeon and Levi's action in a positive light, omitting references to their deceit and defending their behavior by exaggerating the moral depravity of the city's inhabitants and their culpability in Shechem's crime (e.g., *Jdt* 9:2–4; *Jub.* 30; *T. Levi* 4–6; *Migr.* 224; *Gen. Rab.* 80.2,8). Jewish retellings of the incident sought to deter intermar-

---

[492] E.g., L. Bechtel, "What If Dinah Is Not Raped?" *JSOT* 62 (1994): 19–36; T. Frymer-Kensky, "Virginity in the Bible," in *Gender and Law in the Hebrew Bible and the Ancient Near East,* JSOT 262 (Sheffield: Sheffield Academic Press, 1998), 79–96; and M. Gruber, "A Re-examination of the Charges Against Shechem Son of Hamor," *Beit Mikra* 157 (1999): 119–27 (Hebrew).

[493] E.g., A. Shapira contends that "silence" (*ḥ-r-š*) is best understood as the commendable discipline of contemplation (e.g., Gen 24:21; Exod 14:14; "Be Silent: An Immoral Behavior?" *Beit Mikra* 39 [1994]: 232–44 [Hebrew]).

riage with Gentiles and promote circumcision; they exonerated the brothers and conveniently omitted references to the misappropriation of circumcision that resulted in the slaughter of the Shechemites.[494] The targums, for example, substituted "with wisdom" for the MT's "deceitfully" in v. 13. Also, according to *Tgs. Ps.-J.* and *Neof.,* the brothers rationalize that the "uncircumcised" Hivites would not be able to boast that they treated a daughter of Jacob like a prostitute who had no defender (v. 31). Jewish traditions also attribute the brothers' war on the Hivites as a divine commission, "The judgment was ordered in heaven against [the Shechemites]" (*Jub.* 30.5). That they were foreigners probably disqualified Shechem in Jewish eyes from the provision in Deut 22:28–29 for marriage to a virgin and a monetary penalty (*Jdt* 9.2; *Jub.* 30.111–14; *Ant.* 1.337–38). Moreover, since the Hivite population was part of Canaan's evil society that must be exterminated (Deut 7:1–3), Simeon and Levi carried out the deed under the command of God (e.g., Theodotus, *Frag. 7; Jub.* 30.5–6; *T. Levi* 6.8–7.1; *Jos. Asen.* 23.14). Does the narrative itself somewhat diminish the villainy of Simeon and Levi? Repeatedly, the author notes the heinous nature of the crime that incited the brothers to deceit and murder (vv. 2,5,7,13,27). Moreover, Shechem and Hamor exhibit no remorse, ignoring the assault and reducing the marriage to an economic opportunity. By Shechem's attack on Jacob's daughter, the brothers interpreted the offense as an assault on the household of Jacob. From the later Israelite point of view, did their aggression presage Israel's extermination policy against a belligerent population in Canaan (e.g., Deut 7:2–3)?

Patristic and medieval Christian interpreters, however, denounced the deed of the brothers. In Tertullian's *An Answer to the Jews* (10), the scribes and Pharisees who oppressed Christ were the moral descendants of Simeon and Levi; Jacob's condemnation of the brothers who "hamstrung a bull" (49:6) referred allegorically to the Jews' crucifixion of Christ. As in a Jewish tradition (*Gen. Rab.* 80.1), many Christian interpreters assigned Dinah blame for the ensuing incident because of her curiosity and pride. For purposes of warning the clerical orders, interpreters, such as Bernard of Clairvaux *(On Humility and Pride),* utilized Dinah as an example of the evils of idleness and worldly lust. Her wandering among the women of the land (34:1) was allegorized as the soul (=Dinah) that falls into sin. Gregory the Great, for example, explained that Shechem indicated the devil who overcomes the wayward soul (=Dinah; *Pastoral Rule* xxiv [admonition 30]). Chrysostom appears to lay no blame on Dinah, using the chapter to decry youthful passions, especially noting that Shechem's lust resulted in his city's demise (*Homilies on Genesis* 59). The Reformer Luther,

---

[494] R. Pummer, "Genesis 34 in Jewish Writings of the Hellenistic and Roman Periods," *HTR* 75 (1982): 177–88; see J. Kugel, "The Story of Dinah in the Testament of Levi," *HTR* 85 (1992): 1–34, who explores various Jewish exegetical traditions concerning chap. 34 that occur in *T. Levi,* and his general treatment in the *Bible as It Was.*

too, had a gentler attitude toward Dinah, reckoning that she was still "a little girl" (twelve years or younger; cf. *Jub.* 30.2) and that her downfall was innocent curiosity.[495] The sin of the Hivites deserved death, and the Lord used the sons of Jacob to execute divine "secret" vengeance, though they too acted out of pride and sinned through their deceitful retaliation. Jacob condemned their act for its unjustness, and he endured their ridicule, trusting that God would deliver him. Through the example of the godly Jacob, the purpose of the narrative for Luther's audience was to teach patience when the trials of life confront them. Like the patristic commentators (as did the Jews, *4 Mac* 2.19–20) and Luther, Calvin treated Jacob favorably as a godly man. He was less sympathetic of Dinah than Luther. Calvin especially condemned the action of the brothers, pointing out that though the Hivites had sinned egregiously, the conciliatory overtures Shechem and Hamor made should have mitigated the brothers' rage. The sons' wickedness, however, showed Calvin's readers that the Lord condemned lust and wanton fornication.[496]

With the rise of historical criticism, the trend was to explain the chapter's ambiguities as the result of a redactor's wedding of two independent accounts or one main account supplemented by a later source. We will address this especially in the section to follow. Recently, chap. 34 has been a favorite subject of literary,[497] feminist,[498] and sociological studies.[499]

---

[495] Luther, *LW* 6.190. J. Schroeder comments that Luther's attitude differed from Bernard, who paralleled the sins of Dinah with Eve and ultimately Satan ("The Rape of Dinah: Luther's Interpretation of a Biblical Narrative," *Sixteenth Century Journal* 28 [1997]: 775–91); rather, Luther identified Shechem as the devil (*LW* 30.260 on 1 John).

[496] Calvin, *Comm.*, 227.

[497] E.g., Sternberg, *The Poetics of Biblical Narrative*, 441–82; D. Fewell and D. Gunn, "Tipping the Balance: Sternberg's Reader and the Rape of Dinah," *JBL* 110 (1991): 193–211; and Sternberg's fiery response, "Biblical Poetics and Sexual Politics: From Reading to Counter-Reading," *JBL* 111 (1992): 463–88; and the response to both in P. Noble, "'Balanced' Reading of the Rape of Dinah: Some Exegetical and Methodological Observations," *BibInt* 4 (1996): 173–204.

[498] See esp. R. Parry, "Feminist Hermeneutics and Evangelical Concerns: The Rape of Dinah as a Case Study," *TynBul* 53 (2002): 1–28. E.g., N. Graetz, "Dinah the Daughter," *A Feminist Companion to Genesis* (Sheffield: Sheffield Academic Press, 1993), 305–17; S. Scholz, "Through Whose Eyes? A 'Right' Reading of Genesis 34," in *Genesis: The Feminist Companion to the Bible (Second Series)* (Sheffield: Sheffield Academic Press, 1998), 150–71; id., "Was It Really Rape in Genesis 34? Biblical Scholarship as a Reflection of Cultural Assumptions" (in *Escaping Eden: New Feminist Perspectives on the Bible* [Washington Square, N.Y.: New York University Press/ Sheffield: Sheffield Academic Press, 1999], 182–98) provides a typology describing how modern interpretations moderate the severity of the rape (if one occurred at all) due to contemporary cultural attitudes toward rape.

[499] E.g., C. Bailey, "How Desert Culture Helps Us Understand the Bible: Bedouin Law Explains Reaction to Rape of Dinah," *BRev* 7 (1991): 14–21, 38; Bechtel argues that chap. 34 reflects a group oriented response involving the struggle between insiders and outsiders over tribal social boundaries ("What If Dinah Is Not Raped?" 19–36); Frymer-Kensky gives an anthropological view of chap. 34 in terms of family shame and honor ("Virginity in the Bible," 79–96).

Where the results of these studies have assisted our understanding, we will refer to them in the commentary remarks below.

COMPOSITION. As in our earlier discussions at chaps. 14 and 26, the extent of inquiry into the compositional history of chap. 34 requires us to give more attention to its debate. The two prominent concerns that interpreters must address are: (1) the question of narrative unity or multiple sources (or redaction layers) and (2) the question of whether the account is original or secondary, since for many interpreters it does not appear to fit in the flow of the plot (cf. 33:18–20 and 35:1–5).

1. Traditional documentarians, such as Gunkel, argued that the narrative was the redaction of two parallel sources, the Yahwist (J) and Elohist (E) accounts, due to reputed doublets and inconsistencies. Since each account's central character differed between Shechem and Hamor, they were respectively dubbed a "Shechem tradition" (J) and a "Hamor tradition" (E).[500] Some contended that the hand of the Priestly (P) account could be seen in the Hamor version, assigning parts or all of it to P. Others, such as Noth, contended for a supplement explanation, believing there were numerous additions to one original Shechem account (J).[501] Y. Zakovitch proposed that an original story that told of Shechem's love for Dinah, whose request for marriage was met with Simeon and Levi's treachery, was later supplemented. Aware of the similarities of the Shechem-Dinah story to the story of Amnon's attraction to and rape of Tamar in 2 Sam 13, a later redactor added the rape of Dinah, which he derived from the Amnon-Tamar episode to justify the brothers' intemperate reaction.[502] Van Seters contends for Priestly supplements to an existing narrative (vv. 5,7b,13b,27–29,31; cp. P at Num 31:9–11,32–41),[503] although critics dispute that P would have permitted such a story (concerning Levi). Van Seters finds the J version (exilic) disapproving of the brothers' deceit of Shechem, whereas the priestly embellishments represent the brothers' violent reaction as justified. In addressing the peculiarity of Shechem's psychological inconsistency, namely, the rape of Dinah followed by his love for her (vv. 2–3), the supplemental approach explains that abduction occurred in one layer and rape occurred in the other.

Source critics typically cite three prominent doublets. First, Hamor proposes marriage to Jacob and his sons in behalf of Shechem, involving intertribal marriage (Hamor version, vv. 4,6,8–10), but Shechem makes a simultaneous proposal offering a substantial dowry (Shechem version, vv. 11–12). Second, the negotiations phase involves different responses to the counterproposal of circumcision by Jacob's sons. Hamor accepts their answer and convinces the men of the city to observe the precondition to formulating a treaty with the Jacobites (Hamor

---

[500] Gunkel, *Genesis,* 357–59.

[501] Noth, *History of Pentateuchal Traditions,* 30, n. 99.

[502] Y. Zakovitch, "Assimilation in Biblical Narratives," in *Empirical Models for Biblical Criticism* (Philadelphia: University of Pennsylvania Press, 1985), 185–92.

[503] Van Seters, *Prologue to History,* 278; also Y. Amit, "Implicit Redaction and Latent Polemic in the Story of the Rape of Dinah," in *Texts, Temples, and Traditions: A Tribute to Menahem Haran* (Winona Lake: Eisenbrauns, 1996), 11–28 (Hebrew).

version, vv. 18a,20–24). Yet Shechem's response is his immediate submission to circumcision (Shechem version, v. 19). The obvious question, as the narrative stands, is why he would do this before the city's people had agreed to the terms. Third, the descriptions of the attack appear twofold. Simeon and Levi murder Shechem and Hamor, taking Dinah back with them (Shechem version, vv. 25a–26),[504] and the (other?) brothers kill the city's male population and loot the slain (Hamor version, vv. 25b,27–29).[505] The impression this analysis gives is that there are two accounts, one dealing with Shechem's household alone and the other pertaining to the whole of the Hivite city. Typically, the two stories were assigned to the presettlement or early settlement eras when the Hebrew tribes conquered Shechem (city) and when the tribes of Simeon and Levi had declined. The eponymous persons in the two stories represented historical tribes (e.g., Shechemites, Israelites), and the events portrayed distant memories of conflict and social change.[506]

Westermann departs from this popular opinion by attributing the final written account to an independent author during the exile when the Jews lived in proximity with the Gentiles; the author's exilic viewpoint presupposed the practice of Deut 7:1–5, prohibiting intermarriage on religious grounds. The author desired to interdict a rise in the marriage to non-Israelites that occurred during the exilic and postexilic eras. For Westermann the older, shorter Shechem account (a family narrative) was originally an oral tradition that possibly came from patriarchal times, telling of the offence against Dinah by Shechem that leads to deception and the murder of Shechem's household by Simeon and Levi. As a family tale, the characters must be individual persons, not tribal representatives. An original report from the settlement period pertaining to an agreement made by the Hivites and Israelites underlay the Hamor version that became a tribal narrative when it was integrated with the family narrative by the author.[507] Westermann likens the narrative to the independent composition of chap. 14 that also arose from a late period.

Against the multiple source or supplement views, a smaller number of scholars contended for a literary unity, relying on the logical progression of the chapter as a whole. [508] Speiser on the basis of the "smooth flow of the narrative" attrib-

---

[504] The final clause "killing every male" of v. 25b is often reassigned to v. 27.

[505] Gunkel believed that 49:5–7 contains an indirect reference even to a third variant, the oldest of the three versions in which the action by the brothers is strongly renounced (*Genesis,* 357–60). Skinner varied from the standard documentary opinion when he concluded that the two accounts were not part of the main J and E sources but were in the Yahwistic and Elohistic "schools," which were added to the main corpus by the JE redactor due to 33:19(E; *Genesis,* 417–22).

[506] E.g., von Rad, who cautiously adopts the two source opinion; his skepticism of the account's historical value extended even to whether the older Shechem account knew of the patriarch Jacob (*Genesis,* 330–35,).

[507] Westermann, *Genesis,* 535–37; Gunkel thought the opposite, i.e., the Shechem account was merged into the later Hamor recension (*Genesis,* 362).

[508] F. C. Fensham, however, argued for the likelihood of one author based on the similarities of the literary and cultural components of the biblical narrative and an Assyrian letter (ca. 1300) describing a tribe at Mari that betrays a nonaggression pact with a local village ("Genesis XXXIV and Mari," *JNSL* 4 [1975]: 87–90).

uted the chapter to one source, believing that it exhibits the impartiality typical of
the Yahwist's perspective (e.g., Shechem and Hamor are sympathetic figures).[509]
Coats also attributes the whole to J and proposes that there were probably earlier
forms of the tradition that depicted the fall of the offending tribes, Simeon and
Levi.[510] Wenham concludes that the coherence of the narrative argues for single
authorship, probably J.[511] Recently, R. Parry's study countered the literary
incongruities cited by proponents of a composite narrative, finding that there was
no compelling reason to ascribe the work to more than one author (or source).[512]

Explanations involving multiple sources or redaction layers do not best
explain the literary composition of chap. 34. The source critics' imaginations of
literary doublets in the chapter fade when the interpreter recognizes the functional purpose of repetition, creating literary cohesion and reinforcement of vital
motifs in the composition. The so-called double proposals of marriage by Hamor
(vv. 4,6,8–10) and Shechem (vv. 11–12) are neither the same proposals nor contradictory ones. They are coordinate, showing the divergent outlook of an elder
generation and a younger one. Fathers of a couple typically negotiate marriage
for their children, but sons also commonly contribute to the negotiations according to custom (cf. Laban and Bethuel, 24:49–50; Song 8:8; Judg 22:21). Chastity
of daughters in the household had a direct bearing on the honor of the family, for
which the father and sons were responsible to maintain. This explains why
Hamor refers to Dinah at one point as "your [pl.] daughter," when speaking to her
brothers (v. 8). What makes Shechem's entrance into the negotiations striking is
that the sons in our biblical examples are the brothers of the intended bride whose
charge is to protect their virgin sister. That Shechem speaks up for himself is consistent, however, with his rash passion for the girl that the narrator has already
indicated (vv. 2–3; cf. v. 19 also).

Also the narrative exhibits special interest in father-son relationships, as we
would expect at this point in the developing plot of Jacob and his strained relationship with his sons that becomes acute in the Joseph account (chaps. 37–50).
There is symmetry to the father-son motif in chap. 34; it begins with Shechem-
Hamor and ends with Jacob-Simeon/Levi. The affinity of the Hivite father for his
son is the literary foil for the schism that Jacob has with Simeon and Levi.
Observing protocol, Shechem first seeks Hamor's intervention, "Get *[qaḥ]* me
this girl as my wife" (cp. 24:51; Judg 14:1–3). Jacob does not answer the initial
inquiry, since his sons are not present. Hamor then engages the brothers upon
their return from the field, and, as we would expect of an elder, he takes the long
view of such a marriage, explaining the future, mutual benefits of a treaty sealed
through intermarriage (vv. 9–10). By Jacob's later remarks (v. 30; 49:5–7), we
judge that Jacob was not opposed to such an arrangement. Shechem, the anxious
suitor, entices Dinah's brothers by proposing an immediate payoff for them per-

[509] Speiser, *Genesis,* 266–67.

[510] Coats, *Genesis,* 234–35; although adhering to the two-source understanding, Gunkel
remarked that the redactor's additions to the two sources created a "passable unity" (*Genesis,* 362).

[511] Wenham, *Genesis 16–50,* 310.

[512] R. Parry, "Source Criticism and Genesis 34," *TynBul* 51 (2000): 121–38.

sonally, a generous dowry for the girl (vv. 11–12). The proposals of Hamor and Shechem are coordinate, and the responses of Jacob and Simeon/Levi are discordant. Jacob wants to establish favorable relations, and his sons seek vengeance.

Also the logical response of Jacob's sons to Hamor and Shechem (vv. 13–17) makes clear that the Hivite proposals are essentially two parts of one presentation. The chiasmus, when referring to the Hivite offer and the Jacobites' response (Hamor-Shechem//Shechem-Hamor), reinforces the reasoned progression of a unified narrative: Hamor speaks (vv. 8–10) and Shechem speaks (vv. 11–12) followed by the Jacobites' response to Shechem (v. 14) and then Hamor (vv. 15–18). The sons of Jacob answer the proposal in reverse order, beginning with Shechem ("to a man," v. 14) and then answering Hamor ("like us by circumcising all your males," v. 15), making their double refusal effectively one by virtue of the common rationale of their decision. Since they could not give Dinah to an uncircumcised husband (v. 14), they obviously on the same basis could not entertain tribal intermarriage, unless the whole Hivite male populace underwent the practice (vv. 15–17). It was the cogency of their counterresponse that made the ruse convincing (vv. 18–24), enabling the eventual rout of the entire city.

The two supposed descriptions of the attack (Shechem version, vv. 25a–26; Hamor version, vv. 25b,27–29), moreover, are not evidence of two sources but a fluid account moving again between the two poles of the story, the city at large and the chief individuals involved. Simeon and Levi exacted their revenge against the city, especially upon the offenders Shechem and Hamor personally, clarifying for the reader that Dinah was retrieved from Shechem's house (vv. 25–26). Then the narrative describes how the *other* sons of Jacob looted the slain and took captives (vv. 27–29). The transposition of the phrase "killing every male" (v. 25b) to v. 27 suggested by some commentators satisfies two problems for critics. First, it preserves the assumption of two different murderous attacks; the first was against Hamor and Shechem, and the second story pertained to the murder of the whole city. Second, it relieves the problem of how Simeon and Levi alone could have murdered the men of the entire city, according to v. 25 as it now stands. But Parry provides a helpful observation when he notes that by moving "killing every male," the passage loses the functional purpose of the description, which is to highlight the murder of the two chief Hivites. The description progresses from the general ("every male") in v. 25 to the inclusion of the specific persons ("Hamor and Shechem") in v. 26.[513] We can add that the effect of this also fronts Simeon and Levi, the two matching antagonists, who are distinguished from the other sons in vv. 27–29. As to the question of how two men could have murdered the whole city, one must remember that this was the purpose of the deception. Since the two brothers alone, even the whole of Jacob's sons, were greatly disadvantaged against the numerically superior Hivites, they devised a desperate scheme. The two could succeed only because their deception was a brilliantly conceived plan. The brothers had elevated their father's penchant for treachery to new heights, much to his chagrin. Additionally, we might consider that the two brothers had assistance from servants or even mercenaries.

---

[513] Ibid., 132.

If this were the case, the absence of such assistance stated in the narrative is reasonable, since the author wants attention focused on Simeon and Levi alone.

2. Typically scholars interpret chap. 34 as an independent composition, and some hold that the original conclusion to the episode is 35:5 or 35:1–7. Coats, for example, considered it "isolated in its context," appearing in its present position by virtue of the references to "Shechem" (33:18–20; 35:1–7).[514] Carr gives three indications that the chapter is an interpolation in the progression of the narrative. (1) The passage interferes in the natural flow of 33:20 to 35:1. (2) Jacob's children in 31:41; 33:1–8 are young, whereas in the present account they are adults. (3) The insertion of Dinah's birth is secondary (cp. 30:21; 32:22[32]), anticipating the Shechem-Dinah story that has been added.[515] Many scholars have recognized the symmetry of the Jacob narrative (see "Introduction" to the Jacob *tôlĕdōt* section). Coats observed that chap. 34 functions at a higher structural level in the JE narrative arrangement of the Jacob story, serving as the counterbalance to the earlier tale about a threat to the ancestress (Rebekah, chap. 26).[516] The purpose of the inclusion was to show that strife with Israel meant death to its neighbors. The crime against Dinah and the subsequent reprisal illustrate the promise, "I will curse those who curse you" (12:3; 27:29). Van Seters believed chap. 34 originally followed 29:30–30:24 and was concluded by 35:1–5. He assigned the narrative to his "pre-Yahwistic" source (as with chap. 38) that the exilic Yahwist fit into the Jacob narrative as part of the itinerary, describing his migration to Bethel.[517] J. Soggin holds to an even later date, after P, perhaps as late as the Hasmonean era when Gentiles were converted to Judaism.[518] Carr takes a mediating position, dating the addition sometime from the late eighth century to the exile and assigning it to a Judean redactor. It was part of the Judean editor's redactional strategy (with 30:21; 35:21–22a; 37:36–38:30; 49:1–28) that explained the disqualification of the older brothers and promoted Judah's succession.

Contrary to the viewpoint that chap. 34 is an interpolation, the chapter possesses obvious connections with the geographical setting found in chaps. 33 and 35. The prior narrative mentions the locale of Shechem (33:18–19), expecting the Shechem story that follows. That Dinah "went out to visit the women of the land" (34:1) flows out of the prior geographical notice, identifying the inhabitants she visited. Also the conclusion of 34:30, where Jacob fears "the people living in this land," prepares the way for his departure to Bethel (35:1). The attraction of Jacob's family to the nearby Canaanites (35:1), evidenced by Dinah's inquisitive eyes, helps explain Jacob's new zeal for ridding his family of foreign entanglements, such as their gods (35:2,4), before approaching the Lord at Bethel. Also the hostilities that chap. 34 portrays are the background for 35:5 that shows the

---

[514] Coats, *Genesis,* 233, as do most analyses, e.g., Thompson, *The Origin Tradition,* 112.

[515] Carr, *Reading the Fractures of Genesis,* 252.

[516] Coats, *Genesis,* 233–35.

[517] Van Seters, *Prologue to History,* 206, 296.

[518] J. A. Soggin, "Genesis Kapitel 34: Eros und Thanatos," in *History and Traditions of Early Israel: Studies Presented to Eduard Nielsen,* VTSup 50 (Leiden: Brill, 1993), 133–35.

opposite of what Jacob had dreaded, for the Lord indeed was with Jacob (35:3) despite the nefarious actions of his sons. One other connection is with the favored son Joseph, whose narrative refers to Shechem (37:13) and where he eventually comes to rest (Josh 24:32).

We can look again at Carr's three reasons (see above) for holding the dictum that chap. 34 is not original to the Jacob narrative.

1. He remarks that Jacob's itinerary from Shechem to Bethel (33:20; 35:1) is seamless, interrupted only by chap. 34's placement. As we commented earlier, however, the structure of the Jacob narrative at large (see "Structure" in the introduction to the Jacob narrative) assigns an important structural and thematic role for chap. 34. Carr recognizes this pattern but attributes it to a later redactor. It is reasonable that the original author of the Jacob narrative also penned chap. 34, deliberately paralleling the Isaac-Abimelech episode in Gerar (chap. 26). In both cases the accounts appear to intrude in the flow of the immediate narrative, but chaps. 26 and 34 have legitimate roles in the direction of the plot line, providing a wider national context for the family events that surround them (reverberating the promises, e.g., 12:3). Here the narrative shows the strained relationship that the Israelites continue to experience among their neighbors despite their longevity in the region. They are still aliens, as were their ancestors, always viewed as outsiders by the author of Genesis. The event at Shechem explains the change in Jacob's itinerary, since he complains that he is now malodorous to Canaan's inhabitants (v. 30). Further, the Simeon/Levi betrayal in juxtaposition with the narration of Jacob's return to Bethel (35:1–7), as the Lord had long ago promised (28:10–22), reminds the reader of why Jacob had fled in the first place and that his return to Bethel, as projected in his vision (chap. 28), must occur to bring the narrative tension of the itinerary to a full closure in chap. 35. Although there is acceptance of Jacob by Esau in chap. 33, the symmetry of the itinerary framework of the Jacob narrative requires satisfaction by the return to Bethel. Deception is the recurring motif of the itinerary, appearing again in chap. 34 when the brothers deceive the Hivites and to a lesser degree their father. This becomes more pronounced in the Joseph narrative involving sibling rivalry and deception, but in chap. 34 we have an early sign that Jacob's sons characteristically dishonor their father. The contrast between Simeon and Levi's overreaction to the abduction of Dinah and the peaceful outcomes of the threats to Abraham's and Isaac's wives (albeit there is no rape) points up the difference between the moral fiber of their respective generations.

2. In answer to Carr's observation that the chapter depicts the sons in their adulthood, though only youngsters in the previous accounts, Genesis at other places leaps ahead chronologically to significant events (e.g., the death of Sarah, 23:1; the advancement of Isaac to adulthood, chaps. 22 and 24). Besides, the sojourn at Shechem may well have lasted for years, which helps explain Jacob's anger (v. 30) since he would have built goodwill with his neighbors.

3. Finally, Carr notes that Dinah's birth (cp. 30:21; 32:22[32]), which he assumes is secondary, anticipates the Dinah account, suggesting that it too is an interpolation. But Wenham observes that the genealogical notation that anticipates the Dinah episode is a pattern already seen in the case of Rebekah (22:23;

chap. 24).[519] Inclusion of a daughter in such genealogies departs from the norm, showing a narrative plan is in mind, not an afterthought. As for the place of Dinah as a secondary insertion, chap. 34 is not a subscript to the direction of the Jacob narrative, for the chapter concerns not so much the rape of Dinah as it does the murder of the Hivites by Simeon and Levi. The incident maintains the narrative focus on Jacob and his relationship to his sons, displaying the moral degeneration of Jacob's sons. This is one of several episodes in the lives of the sons that reveal the spiritual deterioration of Jacob's successors. Further, as noted above, it fits well with the narrative's attention to family deception that has dominated the whole of the Jacob account to this point.

We conclude that chap. 34 is best understood as a unified account. It is not an interruption in the flow of the passage but part of the author's original strategy, giving structural balance to the whole. It contributes to the narrative transition in the latter chapters of the Jacob account that depicts the patriarch's older years when his sons stand soon to succeed him.

STRUCTURE.　　The structure of the narrative involves three movements.[520] This trifold narrative reminds us of the negotiations detailed in Abraham's purchase of the Machpelah cave from the Hittites in which the center unit is also the most significant (see comments on chap. 23). The first stage establishes the tension of the account (vv. 1–4); the second recounts the reactions of the parties, including the lengthy speeches of the negotiators (vv. 5–24); and the final movement describes the vicious outcome (vv. 25–31). The passage progresses from bad to worse, describing the molestation of Dinah to the subsequent murder of the Hivites. The same Hebrew root word, "went out" *(yāṣāʾ)*, is a key word contributing to the narrative's progress. When Dinah "went out" *(yāṣāʾ,* v. 1) to see the neighboring women, her fateful action set the events of the chapter in motion. The second movement describes Hamor, who "went out" *(yāṣāʾ,* v. 6) to reach an agreement with Jacob, and the Hivites, who "went out" *(yāṣāʾ,* v. 24) to the city gate, where they accepted the negotiated deal. Finally, the brothers, after murdering Shechem, retrieved their sister and "went out" (NIV "left") of the city (v. 26).

Many embedded speeches provide insight into the disposition of the participants in this tragic account of deceit and murder (*ʾ-m-r,* "to say" in its forms appears 9x; *d-b-r,* "to speak" in its forms 5x). They also create much of the ambiguity that characterizes the chapter. The center unit contains protracted speeches, which give the verbal jousting for the marriage of Shechem and Dinah (vv. 6–23). Especially Hamor and Shechem have extensive speeches, both to the sons of Jacob (vv. 8–12) and to the Hivites (vv. 21–24),

---

[519] Wenham, *Genesis 16–50,* 309.

[520] Among commentators analyzing four parts are Skinner, *Genesis,* 418–20 (vv. 1–12,13–17,18–24,25–31), Westermann, *Genesis 12–36,* 535 (vv. 1–3,4–24,25–29,30–31), and Wenham, *Genesis 16–50,* 307–8 (vv. 1–4,5–19,20–24,25–31).

revealing their forthrightness and naïveté. They function as the mediators of the deal, for the city's men do not hear directly from the brothers. The towns-people are props in the account as is Dinah who, although she is central to the topic of the chapter, does not speak a word in the whole of the account (contrast Rebekah, whose thought mattered to the plot, 24:58). We do not learn Dinah's opinion on any aspect of the horrid affair. The author does not necessarily exhibit indifference toward her by this omission; rather, his narrative focus examines the criminal actions of the men, the Hivites and the Jacobites. That Dinah's viewpoint was that of her family's is a sensible conclusion, since she probably possessed the Israelite view on the crime of rape ("defiled," "disgraceful," vv. 5,11,13,27; cf. 2 Sam 13:22).[521]

The foremost concern of her father and brothers, though for different reasons, was the reputation of Jacob's family among the nations (vv. 14,31). In the former narratives Jacob was never short on words, especially when it came to delicate negotiations. Although his name appears ten times in the narrative, he is conspicuously silent until the end when he rebukes his sons for jeopardizing his standing in the region (v. 30). Simeon and Levi, who are neither silent nor inactive, recoil at the public disgrace to which the house-hold has been subjected (v. 31). Jacob and his sons share in their hubris and its guilt. Only God's grace, not the moral perfections of the Jacobites, keeps alive the promises.

(1) Shechem Molests Dinah (34:1–4)

[1]Now Dinah, the daughter Leah had borne to Jacob, went out to visit the women of the land. [2]When Shechem son of Hamor the Hivite, the ruler of that area, saw her, he took her and violated her. [3]His heart was drawn to Dinah daughter of Jacob, and he loved the girl and spoke tenderly to her. [4]And Shechem said to his father Hamor, "Get me this girl as my wife."

This initial scene provides the occasion for the conflict the chapter reports. Verse 1 describes the action of Dinah (v. 1), who "sees" (*rāʾâ*, "visits," NIV) the local women, and vv. 2–3 describe Shechem's response when he "saw" *(rāʾâ)*Dinah, culminating in his request for her hand (v. 4).

DINAH VISITS THE HIVITES (34:1). **34:1** The fourteen occasions of the word "daughter" *(bat)* provide the central motif for the narrative account, eleven times describing the relationship of Dinah to her father's household. On three occasions "daughter(s)" refers to the intermarriage of the two tribes (vv. 9,16,21). Only here and 36:39 does the Bible introduce a woman by her mother's name.[522] The importance of Dinah as the "daughter of Leah" is her

---

[521] Cf. Tamar's feeling, 2 Sam 13:12–13; see Parry, "Feminist Hermeneutics and Evangelical Concerns," 19–22.

[522] Observed by Scholz, "Through Whose Eyes?" 164.

full-blood relationship to Simeon and Levi, also born by Leah (29:33–34; 35:23); this connection is emphasized by the author in v. 25 ("Dinah's brothers") so as to explain their particularly violent reaction to her molestation. Although Jacob was Dinah's father ("borne to Jacob"), Leah still played "second fiddle" to the preferred wife, Rachel. His reputation in the community was more important to Jacob, intending to make a success of his settlement. Perhaps he saw the advantage of a treaty for securing his place in the region (cf. Josh 24:32). The vengeful brothers ruined any plans along these lines. Since her other full-blooded brothers (Reuben, Issachar, and Zebulun) have no part in the murder, this suggests that Simeon and Levi responded recklessly. Hebrew law, for example, provides for a lenient response to a similar circumstance. The man who molests a betrothed virgin must marry her without possibility of divorce and pay a hefty penalty to the girl's father (Deut 22:28–29). Here, however, it must be admitted that the law concerns fellow Israelites, not non-Israelite offenders; that Deuteronomy as a whole resists inclusion of outsiders may explain why no mention of such a provision is made for an alien. The purpose of the rape, seduction, and slander laws (Exod 22:16–17[15–16]; Deut 22:13–29) was to maintain the integrity of marriage and family, protecting the honor and value of a daughter.[523] Thus the law dissuades unacceptable sexual relations, whether involving force or deception, by attaching a penalty fitting to the measure of injury against the offended parties. The problem with the response of Simeon and Levi was its excess.

That Dinah "went out" (*yāṣāʾ*, also v. 6) describes her intention to observe the habits of Canaanite women (cf. 41:45–46; Exod 2:11,13), leaving the protection of her father's settlement. Later her brother Judah also will stray from the fold (so to speak) by becoming entangled in a web of sexual mischief (38:1–2). Jewish interpretation charged Dinah with prostitution, blaming her for the incident and likening her to her mother Leah, who "went out" (30:16) to entice Jacob sexually (*Gen. Rab.* 80.1). Dinah's inquisitiveness toward foreigners, though she was certainly here the innocent party, functions as an early omen of the trouble to come in Jacob's household. The NIV's rendering "the women of the land" conceals the lexical importance of the Hebrew, lit., "the daughters of the land." This early mention of "daughters" reinforces the dominant repetition of Dinah's identity as the "daughter" of Jacob (vv. 3,5,7,8,19; cf. v. 17 also), and it anticipates the issue of intermarriage with the Hivites that his sons will exploit when exacting revenge (vv. 16,21). That such a marriage with "the daughters of the land" could have occurred with Jacob prompted Isaac and Rebekah to send him to Paddan Aram for a wife (27:46–28:2).

---

[523] See Frymer-Kensky, "Virginity in the Bible," 91–95 and V. Matthews, "Honor and Shame in Gender-Related Legal Situations in the Hebrew Bible," in *Gender and Law in the Hebrew Bible and the Ancient Near East*, JSOTSup 262 (Sheffield: Sheffield Academic Press, 1998), 97–112.

SHECHEM VIOLATES DINAH (34:2–3). **34:2** The language of v. 1 ("daughters") and v. 2 ("saw," "took") is reminiscent of another infamous Genesis account: the sons of God "saw" the daughters of men and "took" wives for themselves ("married," NIV, 6:2). In our verse, however, "took" is not meant metaphorically ("married"), since that is yet to be negotiated by the respective households. The language "and violated her" renders two verbs as a hendiadys, lit., "he lay [with] her *[wayyiškab ʾōtāh]* and humbled her" *(wayʿannehā)*." The NJPS also translates the verbs as one, "(he) lay with her by force." The HCSB offers the traditional interpretation of the act, "[he] raped her!" However, the precise meaning of the description "lay . . . humbled" is disputed. This description of the offense committed by Shechem has been traditionally interpreted as the rape of Dinah. The absence of a technical term meaning "rape" (forced sexual relations) in biblical Hebrew has left open the question as to whether the description in Shechem's case is rape or simply "sexual relations." If in this latter case Shechem's crime was not rape but his transgression of customary sexual behavior, his specific violation could be one of two possible breaches. First, his crime was the mere fact that as a foreigner (uncircumcised, v. 14) he engaged in sexual relations with an Israelite. Or second, he did not go through the proper procedure of betrothal, but having done so, he further offended Jacob's household by failure to admit his crime and to provide proper compensation for the offense. The result was a shaming of the woman and the household of Jacob.

L. Bechtel interprets *ʿnh* in the broad sense of "humiliation," that is, to shame a woman.[524] The remedy was the treaty offered by Hamor (v. 9) that would restore honor by creating the possibility of family bonding through marriage. She relies on the usage of *ʿnh* in four passages (Deut 22:23–24,25–27,28–29 and 2 Sam 13:11–14), arguing that the verb pattern (*ʿnh* follows *škb*) in Deut 22:23–24 and 22:28–29 compares most favorably with 34:2. In these two legal cases, there is no rape but a shaming of the woman because of improper sexual intercourse. When rape occurs in the remaining two passages, the description of the act includes the verb *ḥāzaq*, "seized" (Deut 22:25–27; 2 Sam 13:11–14). In the case of Deut 22:25–27, where a virgin is raped in the countryside, there is no shame for her action, thus the absence of *ʿnh* in the description. In the Samuel passage, however, Tamar's rape carries shame (*ʿnh*, v. 14; here *ʿnh* precedes *škb*) because she had sexual relations with a family member, thus a "disgrace" *(ḥerpâ)* that Tamar must bear (v. 13). We agree that the examination of *ʿnh* clarifies that the term cannot be automatically equated with rape. Each passage's context must give additional

---

[524] Bechtel, "What If Dinah Is Not Raped?" 19–36; Gruber argues also that Deut 21:14 and 22:24 show that עָנָה *(piel)* means "sexual intercourse," not a term for rape ("A Re-examination of the Charges Against Shechem Son of Hamor," 119–27 [Hebrew]).

clues to determine the nature of the sex act. We know the term *ʿnh* can mean rape in the sense of abuse, as in the case of the old man's virgin daughter and the Levite's concubine (cf. "use," Judg 19:24; "raped," 20:5). Also we question that Deut 22:28–29 does not describe molestation, since the man "seizes" *(tāpaś)* the victim. The description in 34:2 has the equivalent idea of taking by force in the description "[Shechem] took *[lāqaḥ]* her" (cp. "seized her," NRSV, NAB, NJB).

A related issue is the significance of the construction *wayyiškab ʾōtāh*, lit., "he lay [with] her" (v. 2), in which the verb *škb* takes the direct object marker *ʾeth*. This contrasts with *škb* followed by the prepositional phrase, *škb ʿimmāh*, "he lay with her" (e.g., Deut 22:23,25,28–29; cf. 19:32; 30:15). Neither construction can be said to function as a technical expression for permissible or unlawful sexual relations. The former construction may describe rape (e.g., 2 Sam 13:14), but not always, though it can be said that *škb* with the direct object *ʾeth* often bears an illicit connotation (e.g., 26:10; Lev 15:24; Num 5:13,19). Moreover, the alternative expression *škb ʿimmāh* ("lay with her") may describe a case of rape (Deut 22:25), and instances of *škb* followed by the preposition "with" *(ʿim)* describe typical and atypical sexual relations (e.g, 19:32; 30:15). We conclude that Dinah was raped.

The two verbs *ʿnh* and *škb* describing Shechem's action in 34:2 also depict (inverted order) Amnon's rape of his half-sister, Tamar (2 Sam 13:14). The succinct report of Shechem's assault, lit., "he saw . . . took . . . lay . . . humbled her," contrasts to the prolonged dialogue between the parties prior to the rape in the Amnon-Tamar narrative. The rape of Dinah, though the act is powerfully portrayed in v. 2 by the preponderance of verbs, is prelude to the narrative's main interest. What the narrative delves into is the outcome of the rape, detailing the discourse of the men, especially their negotiations and the deception fostered by Jacob's sons. Nevertheless, the description of the attack effectively shows that Dinah was not a willing partner in the incident.

Shechem's importance to the Hivite populace was his princely status, son of Hamor, the Hivite "ruler" *(nāśîʾ,* cf. 17:20; 23:6; 25:16). He held an esteemed position in the eyes of the community (vv. 19–20), which probably encouraged the Hivites' ready acceptance of his treaty proposal despite the painful, incapacitating circumcision. The later inhabitants of the city Shechem prided themselves on its founder, Hamor (Judg 9:28). The name "Hamor," meaning a male "donkey" *(ḥămôr)* in Hebrew, occurs nine times in the chapter, usually in conjunction with the name "Shechem." "Hamor" may be a pejorative name conferred by the Israelites,[525] but more likely the name

---

[525] C. M. Carmichael, *Women, Law, and the Genesis Traditions* (Edinburgh: Edinburgh University Press, 1979), 34, 62.

is honorable since the donkey was a valued animal.[526] Sarna remarks that the title "ruler" *(nāśî')* is appropriate for Hamor, as opposed to "king" *(melek)*, which usually refers to a city and its suburbs. Pre-Israelite Shechem was a city-state involving an extended region.[527] The "Hivites" were among the Canaanites who survived the conquest of the land and became the religious threat that Moses had forewarned (Deut 20:17–18; Judg 3:5). An ironic twist in history is that the Hivite population at Gibeon employed deception against the Israelites to secure a peace arrangement (Josh 9:7–13; 11:19) but became subject to the Israelites (Josh 9:21–23; 24:11; 1 Kgs 9:20–21). The incident with Dinah became the first of several notorious episodes at Shechem that involved treachery (Judg 9:30–49; Jer 41:4–8; Hos 6:9).

The Hivites are numbered among the "seven nations" occupying the land of Canaan (Deut 7:1; Acts 13:9; cf. also Josh 3:10; 24:11). They were the inhabitants of the prominent city Gibeon (Josh 9:7). The precise ethnic identity of the Hivite *(ḥiwwî)* is disputed, complicated by the term's relationship to the biblical Horite *(ḥōrî)* and the extrabiblical Hurrian *(ḥurru)*.[528]

34:3 That Shechem will precipitously seek an arrangement for Dinah's marriage is explained by the lustful passion that he had for her. His sexual tryst resulted in a greater determination to secure her; this is an obvious contrast with the Amnon episode, whose rape of Tamar led to his intense hatred for the victim (2 Sam 13:15). The verse displays the affectionate intensity of Shechem's love by its repetitious and vivid language. He "clung" *(dābaq,* "drawn to," NIV) to her, "loved" *('āhab)* her, and spoke to her "heart" *(lēb)*. This last expression indicates his attempt to comfort her (cf. Isa 40:2; Ruth 2:13) and perhaps woo her (cf. Hos 2:14[16]).[529] This description is similar to the passion that Solomon showed toward his many foreign wives whom he "loved *['āhab]*... and held fast *[dābaq]* to them in love *['ahăbâ]*," leading to his idolatrous downfall (1 Kgs 11:1–2).

SHECHEM ENLISTS HAMOR'S HELP (34:4). **34:4** Shechem requests Hamor to enter into mediation for Dinah's hand. That he refers to her as "this girl" and that her name never occurs in direct discourse in the chapter reflects

---

[526] E.g., the donkey was important to the practice of covenant-making, known to have been ratified through a rite at Mari in which the animal was slain. Some scholars believe the expression "the sons of the ass/Hamor" (33:19; Josh 24:32; Judg 9:28) possibly refers to the Shechemite citizens, meaning the "people of the covenant," thus suggesting that they were a coalition of diverse people (e.g., W. F. Albright, *Archaeology and the Religion of Israel,* 4th ed. [Baltimore: Johns Hopkins Press, 1953], 113). But the narrative treats Hamor and Shechem as individual persons, and it was common to name persons with animal names (see Kidner, *Genesis,* 173; K. A. Kitchen, "Hamor," NBD 443; and E. Hostetter, "Hamor," ABD 3.42–43).

[527] Sarna, *Genesis,* 233–34.

[528] For discussion see comments on 36:2 and on "Hivites" in the Table of Nations (10:17), see vol. 1A, pp. 456–57.

[529] E.g., NLT, "and he tried to win her affection."

her subordinate status in the eyes of the participants and the author's focus on the men's negotiations. She is a pawn in the hands of the men. The word for "girl" *(yaldâ),* occurring just twice more in the Old Testament (Joel 3:3[4:3]; Zech 8:4–5; cp. masculine *yeled,* e.g., "child," 21:8; also Joel 3:3[4:3]; "boy," 37:30), suggests that Dinah was young. Shechem's demand, "Get me . . . my wife," may sound brusque to modern ears, but it is the typical expression for marriage *(lāqaḥ ᾿iššâ,* "took a wife"; e.g., 11:29; 24:67; Judg 14:2; 1 Chr 7:15). It recalls Laban and Bethuel's agreement to give Rebekah in marriage (24:51). That a father sought a wife for his son was common (e.g., 38:6; cp. 21:21; Exod 21:7,9; Deut 22:16; 2 Sam 13:13).

(2) The Hivites Negotiate Marriage to Dinah (34:5–24)

5When Jacob heard that his daughter Dinah had been defiled, his sons were in the fields with his livestock; so he kept quiet about it until they came home.

6Then Shechem's father Hamor went out to talk with Jacob. 7Now Jacob's sons had come in from the fields as soon as they heard what had happened. They were filled with grief and fury, because Shechem had done a disgraceful thing in Israel by lying with Jacob's daughter—a thing that should not be done.

8But Hamor said to them, "My son Shechem has his heart set on your daughter. Please give her to him as his wife. 9Intermarry with us; give us your daughters and take our daughters for yourselves. 10You can settle among us; the land is open to you. Live in it, trade in it, and acquire property in it."

11Then Shechem said to Dinah's father and brothers, "Let me find favor in your eyes, and I will give you whatever you ask. 12Make the price for the bride and the gift I am to bring as great as you like, and I'll pay whatever you ask me. Only give me the girl as my wife."

13Because their sister Dinah had been defiled, Jacob's sons replied deceitfully as they spoke to Shechem and his father Hamor. 14They said to them, "We can't do such a thing; we can't give our sister to a man who is not circumcised. That would be a disgrace to us. 15We will give our consent to you on one condition only: that you become like us by circumcising all your males. 16Then we will give you our daughters and take your daughters for ourselves. We'll settle among you and become one people with you. 17But if you will not agree to be circumcised, we'll take our sister and go."

18Their proposal seemed good to Hamor and his son Shechem. 19The young man, who was the most honored of all his father's household, lost no time in doing what they said, because he was delighted with Jacob's daughter. 20So Hamor and his son Shechem went to the gate of their city to speak to their fellow townsmen. 21"These men are friendly toward us," they said. "Let them live in our land and trade in it; the land has plenty of room for them. We can marry their daughters and they can marry ours. 22But the men will consent to live with us as one people only on the condition that our males be circumcised, as they themselves are. 23Won't their livestock, their property and all their other animals become ours? So let us give our consent to them, and they will settle among us."

24All the men who went out of the city gate agreed with Hamor and his son Shechem, and every male in the city was circumcised.

This unit describes the negotiations that resulted from Shechem's plea to his father to pursue the hand of Dinah. There are four subunits that make up this lengthy unit (vv. 5,6–12,13–17,18–24). The passage moves the reader from the conspicuous silence of Jacob to the naïve agreement of the Hivites. The same verb, "heard/agreed" *(šāmaʿ),* begins and ends the unit (vv. 5,24; cf. vv. 7,17), first describing news of the scandal (v. 5) and last describing the unwitting compliance of the Hivites (v. 24). The contrast between Jacob's and his sons' reactions to Dinah's humiliation could not be starker in vv. 5 and 13–17. The recurring key term "defiled" *(ṭimmēʾ,* vv. 5,13; cf. v. 27) heightens the contrast. Jacob remained "silent" at hearing of Dinah's abuse (v. 5), but his sons deceitfully "spoke" (v. 13) because of Dinah's abuse. Sandwiched between their reactions is the proposal of Hamor and Shechem for marriage (vv. 6–12). They present two benefits to the Hebrew men as incentives: first, a treaty with the Hivites, presumably strengthening the tribes, that includes intermarriage and, second, a generous financial award for Dinah. Simeon and Levi's response is deceitful, requiring the Hivites to undergo circumcision before intermarriage could be granted. Here we discover a second contrast involving the brothers: the Hivites negotiated in good faith, whereas the brothers renegotiated treacherously (vv. 13–17). But a noticeable omission in Hamor's presentation, as well as Shechem's, of any admission of guilt in the way by which Shechem came to love Dinah shows their indifference to her plight, if not their outright duplicity. Finally, the unit describes the relating of the brothers' proposal by Hamor and Shechem to the men of the city and their agreement (vv. 18–24). Verses 18 and 24 repeat vital information, describing the favorable response of the leaders and then the total male populace. The irony is caustic: Shechem's sexual deceit is answered by the brothers' deceit involving marital relations. Furthermore, by the Hivites' attempt to enrich themselves through treaty, they endanger themselves and eventually lose all.

JACOB WAITS SILENTLY (34:5). **34:5** "In the fields" is where we would expect Jacob's sons to be. This is where we find them in the Joseph account, which also associates them with the city Shechem (37:7,13–16). Ironically, by Simeon and Levi's ploy, though Jacob's sons left their fields, they end up benefiting from the Shechemite incident, obtaining herds from the city and from "out in the fields" (v. 28). This may be a twist in the account to expose the greed Jacob's sons will exhibit when looting the dead, compromising any principled position they may have held (vv. 27–29). That God commanded and directed the insurgency of the Israelites against Canaanite strongholds (e.g., Deut 7:1–4) contrasts with this incident, where there is no divine directive for retaliation.

How Jacob heard about his daughter's molestation is not stated; the point is that the degradation was part of community gossip, a public disgrace, and it was this particularly that enraged Dinah's siblings (vv. 7,13–14,31). The word group "to be unclean, defile" (*t-m-ʾ*, vv. 5,13,27)[530] conveyed unmistakably the idea of cultic impurity for the reader familiar with Mosaic law (e.g., Lev 5:2–3). Forbidden sexual relations made offenders themselves morally unclean (e.g., Lev 18:20,23; Num 5:13–14,20,27–29) or others unclean (Ezek 18:6,11,15). The word also commonly describes "defilement" that impugns the whole of the camp (e.g., Num 5:3), resulting from transgression of sexual taboos (e.g., Lev 18:20,23; cf. the requirements of the camp, Deut 23:14). The former inhabitants of Canaan especially practiced sexual perversions, leading to their expulsion. The same fate awaited Israel if it chose the same aberrant path (e.g., Lev 18:24–30). That Dinah "had been defiled" meant that she was mistreated sexually, making her like an adulteress (cf. Deut 24:4).[531] We have already noted that such reproach impacts the whole of the Jacob household whose responsibility is to protect and maintain the honor of the family.

In the case of rape, Deuteronomy requires that the offender of a betrothed virgin receive death (Deut 22:25), but it provides for marriage and a financial penalty when the crime is against an unbetrothed virgin (Deut 22:28–29; also Exod 22:16–17[15–16]).[532] We do not know Dinah's marital status, but it appears that she is unpledged, making the actions of Hamor and Shechem therefore correspond roughly with the obligations of the law. The analogy may not be appropriate, since the law assumes the offender is Israelite.[533] The retaliation taken by the brothers is excessive, making them murderers in the eyes of their father and Canaanite society. From the brothers' perspective, however, Dinah's mistreatment amounted to treating her as a "prostitute" (*zônâ*), a most disgraceful state for a family's daughter (cf. Lev 19:29; Deut 22:21; a priest's daughter requires death, Lev 21:9). Prostitution is deemed

---

[530] The *piel* form in vv. 5,13,27 means "to defile," e.g., a woman (Ezek 18:6) or daughter-in-law (Ezek 22:11); it also describes "profaning" the name of Yahweh (Ezek 43:7–8), tabernacle (Lev 15:31), or land (Lev 18:28). For the wide range of usage of this word group, see R. Averbeck, "טָמֵא," *NIDOTTE* 2.365–76.

[531] See E. Merrill, *Deuteronomy,* NAC (Nashville: Broadman & Holman, 1994), 318.

[532] Middle Assyrian Laws #55–56 show parallels to Deut 22:23–27; the "ravisher" must pay a penalty to the offended father and must marry the daughter without possibility of divorce, if the father desires; or the father may take the monetary payment but refuse to give her to the offender. One interesting difference is if the "ravisher" is married, the offended father may take the offender's wife (*ANET* 185). The Laws of Eshnunna #26–28 call for the rapist's death for a betrothed virgin; parents must give their consent for a man to marry a daughter even if the woman has lived in the house for a year (*ANET* 162).

[533] Since Shechem was a foreigner, Fensham thinks death, not compensation, would be expected ("Genesis XXXIV," 88).

"to be unclean, defiled" *(ṭ-m-ʾ,* vv. 5,13,17) in the prophets (e.g., Ezek 23:7; Hos 5:3; 6:10; cf. Ps 106:39). The brothers believed that their actions were justified, even incumbent upon them and their father (v. 31).

That Jacob did not act until his sons arrived may be understandable if we remember that Laban, the brother of Rebekah, played an important role in the negotiations of her marriage (24:50–51). Moreover, Absalom advised the forsaken Tamar to remain quiet, freeing him to plot revenge (2 Sam 13:20). But negotiations for Dinah had not yet been initiated (v. 6), and Jacob's "absence" in the ensuing events provides striking contrasts with his counterpart, Hamor, the father of the suitor, and with the angry reaction of the sons of Jacob. Hamor is front and center in the account, but Jacob is virtually offstage until the end of the narrative when the matter had been concluded. Moreover, the sons of Jacob are enraged at what had occurred to their "sister" (vv. 13,14,27,31). That they were out in the fields implies that Jacob was responsible for Dinah in the camp, and he failed to provide the paternal/fraternal oversight that was customary. The narrative suggests by these differences between Jacob and the other participants' involvement that Jacob has lost the respect of the community and his household, revealing the ascendancy of his sons, as he helplessly stands by and witnesses concomitantly their growing moral corruption. Others, following Jewish interpretation of Jacob as a godly man, have understood Jacob's role in a favorable light. Luther and Calvin explained that his grief was so devastating that he could not share it with anyone until his sons arrived. As for Jacob's fear of Canaanite reprisals, Calvin contended that Jacob meant only to scare his sons into repentance.[534] Luther maintained that the patriarch was a godly man whose burden was increased by the wickedness of his sons.[535] Since Jacob's outrage does not surface until after the matter, when he complains about his personal (and family's) welfare (v. 31), it is difficult to interpret Jacob's silence so charitably.

HAMOR AND SHECHEM MAKE PROPOSAL (34:6–12). Hamor proposes intermarriage and points out the economic advantages of a peace pact (vv. 6–10). Shechem further pleads with the Jacobites, adding that he is willing to pay any price they require (vv. 1–12).

Hamor Offers a Treaty (34:6–11). **34:6** "Went out" *(yāṣāʾ)* indicates that Hamor left the city and entered Jacob's territorial boundaries, where he initiated the offer for Dinah. That he fails to address the sexual boundaries his son transgressed is an obvious omission that calls for comment. Hamor's active role, however, provides a foil for Dinah's silent father. "Went out" is repeated from the report of Dinah's questionable behavior (v. 1), showing the cause-effect relationship of her action and those that follow, resulting in the

---

[534] Calvin, *Comm.,* 219,ʼ229.

[535] Luther, *LW,* 6.218–19.

destruction of all those "who went out *[yāṣāʾ]* of his city gate" (v. 24, "in the city," NIV; cf. v. 20). Also the author may be giving a subtle appraisal of Hamor and Shechem's offer. That the Hivite men omitted any reference to the sexual attack may be chalked up to wise strategy, but the bottom line is that they do not offer compensation for the offense. From their negotiating position, no transgression has occurred and thus the offended family receives no satisfaction for the robbery of their daughter's honor. That Hamor "went out" *(yāṣāʾ)* as a clear allusion to Dinah's action (v. 1) implies that Hamor should be making amends by addressing the incident responsibly. In other words, the reason he "went out" was precipitated by the events that ensued when Dinah "went out."

34:7 Verse 7 provides the very important information that the brothers were silently enraged when Hamor and Shechem made their appeal (vv. 8–12). "Jacob's sons" and "Jacob's daughter" form an inclusion in v. 7, stressing Jacob's connection with the aggrieved parties. But Jacob himself appears only aggrieved after the retaliatory crime of his sons (v. 30). This passive demeanor of Jacob is unlike the earlier personality the reader has come to know. The Old Testament has other examples of fathers who in their aged years lose control over their sons' behavior (e.g., Eli, Samuel, David). "Now Jacob's sons had come . . ." initiates the sequence of retaliatory events, explaining the mood of the sons who assertively lead in the negotiations that follow. The temporal clause "as soon as they heard" is subject to two different interpretations. When they "heard" of the offense, they returned from the fields (NIV, NASB, NJPS, HCSB, NJB, REB), or when they "heard" of the offense, they became angry (LXX, NRSV, NAB). The variance may shed light on how the brothers learned of the crime and the sequence of events that occurred. Did they receive a message from their father or from some other quarter, whereupon they returned? Or did they return coincidentally at the time of Hamor's appeal, only learning of the rape at their return? If the Joseph case is parallel (37:12–13), the brothers received a messenger from their father and they immediately returned, perhaps hatching the plot along the way (37:18). This time lapse would explain the brothers' well-thought-out ruse and the emotional control they exhibited. The brothers must harness the volatile emotions of sadness (*yitʿaṣṣĕbû, hithpael;* cf. comments on 6:6) and rage *(yiḥar)* until the apt moment.

The similar duo of terms describe the brothers' reaction to Joseph upon learning of his identity: "do not be distressed *[tēʿāṣĕbû, niph.]* and do not be angry *[yiḥar]* with yourselves" (45:5). Our narrative repeatedly notes the reason for the brothers' fury; Shechem's act had committed a shameful crime, having consequences for their father's household. The formulaic expression "a disgraceful thing *[nĕbālâ]* in Israel" usually refers to grievous sexual misconduct (Deut 22:21; Judg 20:6,10; 2 Sam 13:12; Jer 29:23; but see Josh 7:15

pertaining to Achan's sin). "Disgraceful thing" *(něbālâ)* may also characterize sexual obscenity (e.g., Judg 19:23–24; Isa 9:16; or other reckless violations, cf. "Nabal," 1 Sam 25:25). In Deut 22:21 it describes the scandalous reputation of a promiscuous daughter who must be executed for her crime. Frymer-Kensky notes that Deut 22:21 seeks to restore order to the father's authority ("while still in her father's house") over the chastity of the daughter.[536] In the case of Dinah, Jacob should demand restitution for the fallen virgin. "A thing that should not be done" *(lō' yē'āśeh)* may describe a mere breach of etiquette or a deplorable transgression (e.g., 29:26; Jer 40:16). The protest of Tamar against her brother's ravenous intentions echoes the language of our passage, condemning his unlawful conduct: "Don't force me. Such a thing should not be done *['al ta'ăśēh]* in Israel! Don't do this wicked thing *[něbālâ]*' (2 Sam 13:12). That the brothers' repudiation of the rape mentions tribal "Israel" exhibits their sense of ethnic distinction from the Hivites, which becomes increasingly important in their plot to trap the unsuspecting foreigners. The mention of "Israel" does not mean necessarily that the author made a gaffe, introducing an anachronism, as Westermann has assumed.[537] Because the chapter portrays adult sons, indicating that considerable time has passed since Jacob received the new name "Israel" (32:28[29]; 35:10), the clan may have already begun to distinguish themselves from their neighbors by the appellative. Or the chapter's events effectively foreshadow future Israelite contact and conflict with the Canaanites during the settlement period.[538] The use of the tribal name "Israel" heightens the typological effect. On the common idiom "lie down" *(šākab),* meaning sexual relations, see, e.g., 19:32; 39:10,14; Exod 22:16[15]; 2 Sam 11:13.

34:8 Hamor approaches them all, referring to Dinah as "your [pl.] daughter" (v. 8), recognizing that the brothers take a paternal stance toward their sister (cf. 24:50; 2 Sam 13:20,32; Song 1:6). Hamor describes his son's love by a common word for desire ("set on," *ḥāšaq),* meaning a longing attachment for the girl. The same term describes God's elective love for Israel (e.g., Deut 7:7) and the psalmist's devotion to him (Ps 91:14). The EVs usually choose "his heart" to render what was traditionally translated "his soul" *(napšô,* AV, ASV, ESV; cf. Isa 38:17). The word *ḥāšaq* ("set on") appears in the law concerning captive women from whom a Hebrew man might select his wife (Deut 21:11). There are special provisions requiring equitable and benevolent treatment (Deut 21:10–17; cf. Gen 29:30; 1 Sam 1:4–5). By his

[536] Frymer-Kensky, "Virginity in the Bible," 94.
[537] Westermann, *Genesis 12–36,* 538.
[538] S. Geller submits that the sequence of events in Gen 33–35 typifies the future sequence of conquest-idolatry-covenant known from historical Israel's settlement and covenant religion ("The Sack of Shechem: The Use of Typology in Biblical Covenant Religion," *Prooftexts* 10 [1990]: 1–15).

comment Hamor hopes to convince the family that Shechem genuinely desires Dinah for a wife, presumably mitigating the severity of the crime.

34:9–10 Hamor demonstrates the solemn commitment that his son has for Dinah by offering a treaty arrangement involving intermarriage with the Jacob clan (v. 9). He welcomes Jacob's sons to settle in their territory, encouraging them to develop communities and commercial interest (v. 10; on "trade," cf. v. 21). "Acquire property" *(hēʾāḥăzû)* in the *niphal* stem typically refers to property rights (cf. 47:27; Josh 22:9,19). The Hebrews would enjoy full partnership with the Hivites. Hamor probably envisioned the Jacobites becoming fully assimilated into Shechemite society. This practice was specifically prohibited in the Mosaic period, due to the influence of pagan worship that inevitably followed ("intermarry," *ḥātan,* e.g., Deut 7:3–4; Josh 23:12–13; Ezra 9:14).[539] That the patriarchs formed nonaggression pacts with various people groups shows that their custom antedated this prohibition (e.g., Philistines, 21:27; 26:28). There is no evidence in these treaties, however, that intermarriage was the patriarchs' practice, and the special steps taken by Abraham and Isaac-Rebekah for their sons to acquire wives from Aramean relatives instead of local Canaanite women (24:3–4; 27:46–28:2) indicates that the sentiment of Jacob's sons opposing intermarriage reflected patriarchal custom. The patriarchal fear of such contact with foreigners was not xenophobia but a justified bulwark against corrupting religious influences (e.g., Judg 3:5–7). This makes the marriage of Judah to a Canaanite wife a disturbing deviation (38:2). The sons' concerns, however, are only secondary at best; theirs was a desire for revenge from the beginning, using their religious heritage as a sham.

Shechem Pleads (34:11–12). **34:11–12** After his elder speaks, Shechem steps forward and makes a second plea, enticing the brothers to name their price for Dinah. His zeal for the girl propels him to speak up before the brothers have opportunity to respond to Hamor's overture (cf. v. 19).[540] Whatever advantage he had by still possessing the girl in his house (v. 26), he forfeits by his boyish enthusiasm. Leaving nothing to chance, he sweetens the pot. (On the expression "find favor," v. 11, see vol. 1A, pp. 345–46.) The *mōhar* ("price for the bride," v. 12; cf. Exod 22:17[16]; 1 Sam 18:25) is the customary marriage transaction paid by the bridegroom to the parents, that is to Jacob in this case (cf. 24:53; 1 Sam 18:25). Although

---

[539] הִתְחַתֵּן *(hithpael),* "to become/make a son-in-law," is cognate with חָתָן, "son-in-law" (Gen 19:12,14) or "bridegroom" (Exod 4:25–26), חֹתֵן, "possessing a son-in-law = father-in-law" (Exod 3:1), and חֹתֶנֶת (fem.), "possessing a son-in-law = mother-in-law" (Deut 27:23; *HALOT* 1.364–65).

[540] Westermann contends that vv. 11–12 are a doublet, disrupting the Hamorite version of the negotiations; but he unnecessarily makes too much of the "interruption" when a simpler explanation for the text's travail suffices (*Genesis 12–36,* 539–40).

money accompanies marriage in Hebrew custom, it is not the purchase of a wife (contrast a female slave's purchase, Exod 21:7–11). Biblical law especially regulated the payment of the *mōhar* when an unlawful seduction occurred (Exod 22:16–17[15–16]). Shechem's offer of a "gift" *(mattān)* can be understood as an additional sum paid to the bride (Dinah) when entering into the agreement (cf. 24:53; 29:24,29; 1 Kgs 9:16),[541] or the two nouns may be a hendiadys here, "the *mōhar* gift." In any case, the impetuous offer made by the Hivite prince is excessively generous when he invites the family to name their own price. Deuteronomy 22:29 specifies a stiff payment of fifty shekels to an offended father in a similar instance.

THE BROTHERS DECEIVE HAMOR AND SHECHEM (34:13–17). The narration explains that the brothers' answer is disingenuous (v. 13). They agree to enter the pact on the condition of circumcision (vv. 14–17).

Their Cunning Plan (34:13). **34:13** The narrative informs us that the ensuing complaint of the brothers is a ruse (cf. "deceit[fully]," *mirmâ*, 27:35; Prov 26:24; Jer 9:8[7]). There is nothing admirable about their conduct. "Jacob's sons" refers to all the brothers at this point. Although Simeon and Levi alone murder the Hivites, the other brothers ruthlessly finish off the village by scavenging the remains and enslaving the survivors (vv. 25,27). The passage reiterates the reason for their treachery, planning revenge on account of Shechem's brutish attack (also v. 27).[542] Simeon and Levi later make this defense when answering Jacob's rebuke (v. 31). It sounds rather hollow when measured against the gravity of their retaliation. By characterizing their speech as deceptive, the author's stand toward the sons of Jacob is certain. He condemns their tactics and their reaction. The repeated reference by the author to the assault explains their reaction but does not attempt to justify it. The author does not build sympathy for the brothers; rather for him their conduct exhibits the consequences of illicit contact with the Canaanites. If the author intends us to measure their action against the moral code of the law, it was a vile transgression of murder through deceit (cf. v. 5 above; see, e.g., Deut 22:28–29; Exod 22:16–17[15–16]). The abusive treatment of Tamar by her half-brother Amnon after the rape (2 Sam 13:13–18) provides a noteworthy contrast with Shechem's conduct.

Covenant of Circumcision (34:14–17). **34:14–17** The brothers answer the proposals of Hamor and Shechem in reverse order. First, they explain that marriage to an uncircumcised husband (Shechem), meaning a person outside

---

[541] W. C. Kaiser Jr., "מָהַר (māhar)," *TWOT* 1.492.

[542] ὅτι ἐμίαναν Διναν τὴν ἀδελφὴν αὐτῶν (LXX), "because they had defiled Dinah," indicating that they are speaking to both Hamor and Shechem (Wevers, *Notes on the Greek Text,* 564). The NIV, NAB translate אֲשֶׁר טִמֵּא אֵת דִּינָה אֲחֹתָם as indefinite subject, "because their sister had been defiled" (Eng. passive voice), and others interpret the subject as third person, "because he (Shechem) had defiled/violated their sister Dinah" (e.g., NRSV, NJPS, HCSB, NJB, REB, NLT).

the family covenant with God (cf. 17:9–14; Exod 12:44,48; Judg 14:3; Ezek 44:9), would be a "disgrace" (v. 14). The word "disgrace" *(ḥerpâ)* is associated with public humiliation (e.g., Josh 5:9; Job 16:10), often describing the scorn suffered by the psalmist ([20x], e.g., 22:6[7]; 79:4). As to why this intermarriage would be humiliating to Israel in the eyes of their neighbors is unclear; if their reasoning has any authenticity, not just part of the ruse, their humiliation would be their own self-reproach ("to us") at compromising their tribal heritage. This interpretation of their remark fits the condition "that you [pl.] become like us" (v. 15).

Second, they answer Hamor's treaty offer (vv. 15–17). That theirs is an anxiety pertaining to tribal identity is shown by the recurring emphasis on every male submitting to circumcision so that they "become one people with you" (v. 16; cf. v. 22). The language "by circumcising all your males" *(lehimmōl lākem kol zākār)* echoes the provisions in the Abrahamic covenant of circumcision (17:10,12). Yet again their pious reservation may have been part of the elaborate ruse, not a true impediment. The term "consent" *('ût)* appears three of its four occurrences in this chapter (vv. 15,22,23; 2 Kgs 12:9), reinforcing the narrative's picture of the duped Hivites whose ready compliance means their doom. Jacob's sons spell out the result if they refuse their counteroffer, saying, "We'll take *[lāqaḥ]* our sister and go." Their choice of language may be a wordplay on the events leading to their decision. The term "take" *(lāqaḥ)* describes the rape ("took her," v. 2), Shechem's marriage demand ("get *[lāqaḥ]* me this girl," v. 4), and the intermarriage the Hivites have proposed ("take *[lāqaḥ]* our/your daughters," vv. 9,16). After hearing Shechem's incautious pleas, the brothers know that they can intimidate the lovesick suitor into their net.

HIVITES AGREE TO TERMS (34:18–24). This passage describes the acceptance of the plan by the city's leaders, Hamor and Shechem (vv. 18–19), and then by the townsmen themselves (vv. 20–24).

Shechem's Acceptance (34:18–19). **34:18–19** The matter "seemed good" (v. 18; cf. 41:37; Deut 1:23) to both men for their own reasons; Shechem would gain his wife and Hamor a business interest. That they were willing to undergo the painful operation shows how profitable the deal sounded to each. We learn of Shechem's impetuous response (v. 19) before hearing their appeal to the city (vv. 20–24). In modern terms the youth on a whim rushed down to the courthouse to obtain a marriage license without regard for the cost. The text's description of his deed, "doing what they said" (lit., "to do the thing," v. 19), suggests that he performed the circumcision on himself or submitted to it immediately. The statement, however, may only mean that he joined his father in going straightway to the city gate.

The verse describes, first, the zeal of Shechem, whose love for Dinah fuels his instant response, and, second, his prestige among the citizens. The language in v. 19 underscores Shechem's hasty reaction. "[He] did not delay [*ʾēḥar*] to do the thing" occurs at the start of the sentence ("lost no time in doing what they said," NIV), riveting our attention on his eagerness. It is reminiscent of the servant's insistence that he not be held up (24:56; cf. "remained," 32:5[6]). Here he is identified as "the young man" *(hannaʿar)*, recognizing he acted out of youthful passions. The term may also reflect the naïveté of Dinah, who was described as "the girl" *(hannaʿărā*, v. 3[2x]). That the terms *naʿar* and *naʿărâ* may refer to a servant without reference to age is possible (cf. 18:7), but it is likely that the character of the two, repeatedly identified as a "son" and "daughter" still under the watchcare of their households, indicates their youth (cf., e.g., 21:12; 22:12; 24:14; 43:8). The same terms are regularly used in Deuteronomy's instructions regarding treatment of a virgin (22:15–16,21,24–25,27,29). As to why Shechem acted even before he had learned the decision of the community, the text explicitly explains (*kî*, "because") that she pleased Shechem. "Delighted" *(ḥāpēṣ)* is extensively found in the Old Testament, including settings where matrimony is involved (e.g., "pleased," Deut 21:14; "want," Deut 25:7,8; "desires," Song 2:7).

Moreover, the narrative comments on Shechem's lofty esteem in the eyes of the community noted as "the most honored" of the royal household. This aside explains why the townspeople receive his recommendation readily.[543] Although Shechem has violated Israel's honor, the narrative presents him as a sympathetic character, albeit a simpleton. He is the "second Esau." Shechem's reputation and his commendable effort to remedy the circumstance are a foil for the dastardly character of the brothers, casting them in the account as morally impotent figures (cf. Ps 12:2[3]). Ironically, these two murderers (Simeon, Levi) will be the most despised in the memory of Jacob's house, alone receiving among their siblings their father's curse (49:7; cf. Deut 27:16,24).

Hamor and Shechem Persuade the Hivites (34:20–24). **34:20–21** The scene shifts to the city gate of Shechem, the location for civic and commercial affairs (e.g., 23:10; Deut 17:5; Ruth 4:1,11), where Hamor and Shechem appeal to its inhabitants to accept the condition of the Israelites (vv. 20–24). The father and son speak in one accord (lit., "they spoke to the men . . .," v. 20b). First, they disarm potential worries by reporting on the Israelites' harmless disposition (v. 21a). "Friendly" *(šĕlēmîm*, pl. adj.) is related to the word group *š-l-m*, whose semantic range is broad, indicating completion, peace, and well-being. The word *šālēm* describes here a peaceful relationship between parties, an arrangement that sometimes was ratified by mutual oath (e.g., *šālôm*, "peace," 26:29,31; Josh 9:15).[544] Second, the men show that the

---

[543] וְהוּא נִכְבָּד, "Now he was the most honored . . ." (NRSV), is disjunctive, functioning parenthetically in the main flow of the narrative line.

[544] Sarna suggests that the language refers to an existing nonaggression pact (*Genesis,* 237).

Hivites stand to gain from their relationship, especially by "trade" (*sāḥar,* vv. 10,21b; cf. 42:34).[545] The wealth that the Jacobites exhibited would give the Hivites an opulent, new market. The fecundity of the land is amply sufficient to support their herds ("plenty of room," *raḥăbat yādayim,* lit., "breadth of hands," v. 21b; cf. Judg 18:10; 1 Chr 4:40; Neh 7:4), noting thereby there was no jeopardy of their own flocks, and, more important, intermarriage would seal their mutual mercantile interests (v. 21c). That they did not unveil the details of their earlier negotiations with the brothers has often prompted commentators to impugn them with deceptive tactics. For example, Hamor and Shechem omit the personal reason (Dinah) for the treaty, and they do not admit that the Israelites also expect to receive financial advantages out of the arrangements. But the general picture the narrative gives us of the Shechemites is that they negotiate fairly while Jacob's sons do not. This suggests that the report of their presentation to the city is not meant to show them untrustworthy men. It may be that the author wants the reader to assume that the audience knows the essential elements of the prior negotiations and that a rehearsal of every feature would be unnecessary in telling the account.

34:22–23 After establishing the benefits, they continue that the sole hurdle to such a lucrative arrangement is the custom of male circumcision (v. 22; on "consent," see v. 15). Stated again in the text, the condition requires "every male" (*kol zākār,* "males") to undergo the rite (vv. 15,22, 24,25; cp. 17:10,12,23). Yet to avert any resistance, they remind the audience that they will profit, despite the painful inconvenience (v. 23). Hamor and Shechem paint the brightest picture of the transaction. At the head of the sentence[546] are the items that the Hivites will possess, including "all" *(kol)* their animals. The juxtaposition of "their" (i.e., Israelites) livestock and possessions and the claim that they will "become ours" (i.e., Hivites) buttress their appeal. In effect they present a win-win situation that can only be welcomed. They clinch their reasoned presentation by making this final appeal, "So let us give our consent . . ." (v. 23b).

34:24 The following narration of v. 24 underscores the men's ready, naïve assent; the first word of the verse reports that they "agreed" (*šāmar;* cf. v. 17; 23:16; 37:27; Jer 34:10), and it was unanimous, "all *[kol]* the men." That these were the men "who went out of the city gate" indicates that these

---

[545] סחר, here usually translated "to trade" in ancient texts (e.g. LXX, ἐμπορεύομαι, "to travel for business, to trade") and EVs, occurs more often in the participle form, סֹחֵר, where it means "merchant" (e.g., 23:16); but the precise nuance of the verbal forms is uncertain, and on etymological grounds Speiser (*Genesis,* 265) defined it "to move about freely" (cf. 42:34). It is not too great a stretch even if this is the case to imagine that such license to fraternize would involve merchandising.

[546] A *casus pendens* for emphasis (*IBHS* §16.3.3d).

were the adult men of the city (Job 29:7; cf. 23:18).[547] And "every *[kol]* male, all *[kol]* who went out of the gate of his city" ("and every male in the city," NIV) who had voiced agreement faithfully submitted to the procedure. The matter-of-fact way their disablement is reported reinforces the hasty nature of their decision. The narrative contrasts the naïve, trusting Hivites with the devious character of Simeon and Levi. Who could have imagined such a treachery? The repeated description of inclusion ("every male") explains why the brothers could carry out their heinous deed unimpeded against a numerous populace.

(3) Levi and Simeon Murder the Hivites (34:25–31)

[25]Three days later, while all of them were still in pain, two of Jacob's sons, Simeon and Levi, Dinah's brothers, took their swords and attacked the unsuspecting city, killing every male. [26]They put Hamor and his son Shechem to the sword and took Dinah from Shechem's house and left. [27]The sons of Jacob came upon the dead bodies and looted the city where their sister had been defiled. [28]They seized their flocks and herds and donkeys and everything else of theirs in the city and out in the fields. [29]They carried off all their wealth and all their women and children, taking as plunder everything in the houses.

[30]Then Jacob said to Simeon and Levi, "You have brought trouble on me by making me a stench to the Canaanites and Perizzites, the people living in this land. We are few in number, and if they join forces against me and attack me, I and my household will be destroyed."

[31]But they replied, "Should he have treated our sister like a prostitute?"

The account reports the actions of the sons of Jacob (vv. 25–29) and the reaction of Jacob (vv. 30–31). First, Simeon and Levi attack the city when the men were incapacitated, resulting in the rescue of Dinah (vv. 25–26) and the theft of the city's possessions (vv. 27–29). Second, when Jacob learned of it, he chided Simeon and Levi, fearing reprisals from Canaan's inhabitants (v. 30). Simeon and Levi answer their father indignantly, justifying their revenge on the basis of the exceptionally vile violation of their sister (v. 31). Recognition of the consanguine relationship of Simeon and Levi to their sister frames the unit: "Dinah's brothers" and "our sister" (vv. 25,31). Their birth relationship as children of the same mother (Leah) explains why they acted so ruthlessly, whereas the docile Jacob did not strenuously object to the marriage remedy. A wordplay on "took" *(lāqaḥ)* occurs in the description of their deed. They "took their swords" (v. 25), "took Dinah" (v. 26), and "took" (NIV, "seized") the city's plunder (v. 28). This was in retaliation to Shechem, who initially "took" (v. 2) their sister. The brothers' seizure of the women and herds creates another irony, since the Hivites agreed to circumcision so that they would enrich themselves by intermarriage

---

[547] I.e., "able-bodied men" (HCSB).

("take our/your/their daughters," *lāqaḥ*, vv. 9,16,21) with the Jacobites. By the treacherous ruse of the brothers, the Hivites gained nothing and lost all. A straightforward reading of the sequence of events follows. Simeon and Levi, independently of the other brothers, first slaughtered the male populace and second murdered Hamor and Shechem in their house, from which they liberated their sister. Upon retrieving her, they left the city, probably placing her under protective care in their household (cp. 2 Sam 13:20). The looting by the brothers ensued (vv. 27–29).

RETRIEVING DINAH (34:25–26). **34:25** As we just mentioned, the key word "took" is important to the author's telling. That Simeon and Levi "took" swords (v. 25) and "took" back their sister (v. 26) directly answers the crime of Shechem, who "took" Dinah (v. 2). The continuing description further echoes the narration of the rape in vv. 1–2: that they "left" *(yāṣā')* Shechem's house (v. 26) matches the description of Dinah, who "went out" *(yāṣā')* from her household to view the women of the land (v. 1). The intended effect of the wordplay is unmistakable. The brothers, who expressed no interest in solely commercial advantage (vv. 12,15), exact their revenge, acquiring their compensation in blood! This is the first place in the narrative that the two brothers are distinguished from the other sons of Jacob (v. 25). As to why the other brothers of Dinah born to their mother Leah (Reuben, Judah, Issachar, Zebulun) do not seem to have joined in the bloodbath is perplexing. Hamilton's observation that Levi's three clans were responsible for the cult (e.g., 46:11; Num 3:25–26,28,36–37; 4:4; 7:9) and were the chief defenders of orthodox Yahwism (e.g., golden calf, Exod 32:25–29; Phinehas, Num 25:7–8) may help explain the stronger reaction of Levi.[548] It is tempting to attribute the Levites' zeal to the fiery spirit of their ancestor, whose personality they embodied. Such an interpretation may be justified in view of the tendency of Genesis to show connections between the patriarchs' activities and their descendants. For example, the crime of Ham and Canaan is a good indication of what their descendants will be like (vol. 1A, p. 421). Also Jacob's blessing draws in part on his sons' character in projecting the future of their descendants (chap. 49). It is reasonable that the Levites reflected their ancestor's personality too. That this interpretation is old is shown, for example, by *Jub.* 30.18–20 that reports Levi's rise to the priesthood in the context of his purge of the Shechemites. Also *T. Levi* 4 and Theodotus's *On the Jews* (Frag. 4 and 6), according to J. Kugel's analysis, contrast Levi's zeal and the ritual laxity of Jacob and his firstborn Reuben. In this tradition Jacob and Reuben honestly offered circumcision to the Hivites for the purpose of intermarriage, but Levi opposed it from the start and intervened to avert it.[549]

---

[548] Hamilton notes the shared language אִישׁ חַרְבּוֹ ("each his sword") in 34:25 and Exod 32:27 (*Genesis Chapters 18–50,* 369, n. 14).

[549] Kugel, "Testament of Levi," 6–7 (on the translation of *T. Levi* 6.3–4, see H. C. Kee, "Testaments of the Twelve Patriarchs," *OTP* 1.790).

That they attacked on the "third day" was the optimum moment, according to Jewish tradition (e.g., targums; *y. Šabb.* 19.4; *Gen. Rab.* 80.9; *Pirqe R. El.* 29),[550] since the men's wounds were at their most tender, maximizing the vulnerability of the city's defense (v. 25; cp. Josh 5:8). The identity of the culprits is important in the account; they are described by name ("Simeon and Levi") and also by kinship, first in relation to their father Jacob and next to their sister Dinah. The weapon of choice was the "sword," a basic weapon of war; Israel's rules of future engagement against Canaanite strongholds provide for putting "to the sword" all the males of a city and the plundering of its people and resources (Deut 20:13–14; cf. 7:2). That the city is described as "unsuspecting" *(beṭaḥ)* further explains the success of the two brothers as well as reinforces the recurring emphasis on the depth of their treachery (cf. Judg 8:11; 18:7,10,27). The brothers breached accepted civic responsibility, as reflected in Prov 3:29: "Do not plot harm against your neighbor, who lives trustfully *[beṭaḥ]* near you" (cf. Amos 1:9). Simeon and Levi exacted their vengeance against "every male," thus including the innocent townspeople. Their vengeance far exceeded equitable retribution against the guilty party, Shechem. But that Dinah was still imprisoned and that the brothers were numerically disadvantaged have been put forward by some commentators as mitigating the heinous nature of their response.

34:26 The account especially specifies the murders of Hamor and Shechem. Their names are prominent at the head of the Hebrew sentence, underscoring Simeon and Levi's personal vindictiveness. "To the sword" translates *lĕpî ḥāreb,* lit., "the edge of the sword," an expression that often appears describing the annihilation of an entire city (e.g., Deut 13:15[16]; Josh 6:21; 1 Sam 22:19). It is the language of Deut 20:13, instructing the Israelites in warfare. That Simeon and Levi rescued Dinah from "the house of Shechem" indicates that she had been incarcerated, held against her will, all along. Although no charge of kidnapping occurs in the sons' rejoinder to their father (v. 31; cf. Exod 21:16), that she remained vulnerable to the prince's passions may have provoked their charge that Shechem treated Dinah as a "prostitute" (v. 31).

PLUNDERING THE CITY (34:27–29). **34:27–29** Now the narrative returns to the mistreatment of the general populace, stripping the dead *(ḥalālîm)* and plundering *(bāzaz)* the city (v. 27). Are we to read here "the other sons" (e.g., NRSV, NJPS, HCSB, NAB, NJB, REB, GNB) plundered or assume that Simeon and Levi are still in view?[551] That Jacob does not reprove any son other than Simeon and Levi contends for the latter under-

---

[550] Grossfeld, *Targum Onqelos to Genesis,* 121.

[551] The translators of NIV, NASB render the Hb. literally בְּנֵי יַעֲקֹב בָּאוּ, "the sons of Jacob came upon," thus not exhibiting clearly a particular interpretation.

standing (v. 30; 49:5–7). The language of the verse, however, implies a different subject. The nonsequential construction of the sentence[552] and the same expression "Jacob's sons" (vv. 7,13,25; lit., "the sons of Jacob"), which earlier referred to the whole of his sons, commend the interpretation "other sons." Gathering the victors' spoils in battle was common (e.g., Num 31:9; 1 Sam 31:8; 2 Sam 23:10; 2 Kgs 7:16; 2 Chr 20:24–25; Isa 23:13). Also *ḥālāl* often refers to the "dead" slain in battle or by murder (e.g., Num 19:16; Nah 3:3), but here it may also provide a sound play for a "defiled woman," a prostitute (*ḥalālâ*, Lev 21:7,14), which alludes to the defilement of Dinah. The last clause of v. 27 specifically recalls the defilement (*ṭimmē᾽, piel; see* v. 5 above) of Dinah, which most EVs understand as causal, "because *[᾽ăšer]* their sister was defiled" (e.g., NRSV).[553] The NASB also renders the clause as causal but interprets the syntax in the active voice, identifying the culprits: "because they [i.e., the men of the city] had defiled their sister."[554] In other words, the whole populace of the city is deemed accountable for its acquiescence to Shechem's deed. The seizure of the people's herds was inclusive, "and everything else" (v. 27), matching the thoroughness with which they carried out their revenge against the male inhabitants. The merism "in the city and out in the fields" indicates the whole of their holdings was subject to the brothers' pickings.

Specific mention of "flocks and herds and donkeys *[ḥămōrîm]*" (v. 28) as their prize at the head of the sentence underscores the excessive wealth the Jacobites acquired (cf. 12:16; 24:35; 30:43; 32:5[6]). Some irony may be attached indirectly to Hamor, whose English spelling is the transliteration of the Hebrew word "donkey" *(ḥămōr)*. Verse 29 tallies up the captured spoils, naming items typically confiscated by battlefield conquerors (cf. Num 31:9). "Wealth" *(ḥayil)* is best taken as the inanimate property, such as precious metals and clothing (cf. Ps 49:10[11]; Zeph 1:13), followed by mention of the women and children. The final phrase, "everything in the houses," again indicates the comprehensive character of their greed.

JACOB SCOLDS HIS SONS (34:30–31). **34:30–31** Jacob's foremost concern was the impression that his sons' actions would leave with Canaan's inhabitants (v. 30). But as von Rad explains, "His censure is more a peevish complaint."[555] That the possibility a coalition of armies would descend upon Jacob was not far-fetched is shown by punitive actions taken by an alliance, including Canaanites and Perizzites, against the Israelites, who had defeated

---

[552] The *wāw* consecutive pattern (sequential) would be expected if continuing the action performed by Simeon and Levi in vv. 25–26.

[553] The NIV interprets the clause as a relative clause (אֲשֶׁר), describing the place (הָעִיר) of the incident.

[554] אֲשֶׁר טִמְּאוּ אֲחוֹתָם. If the subject of the verb is indefinite, the English passive rendering is typical (e.g., HCSB).

[555] von Rad, *Genesis,* 334.

Jericho and Ai (Josh 9:1–2). Only by God's imposition of "terror" in the heart of the Canaanites did Jacob's clan escape retaliation (35:5). "You have brought trouble on me" translates the word *ʿākar*, best known by English readers for its wordplay with the "valley of Achor" (valley of trouble) where Achan was condemned (Josh 7:24–25; cf. Isa 65:10; Hos 2:15). The Achan incident illustrates how someone's transgression can bring "trouble" against himself and upon others (cf. 1 Kgs 18:17–18). The word for "stink" *(bāʾaš)* may describe the foul odor emanating from dead fish (Exod 7:18,21) and rotten bread (Exod 16:20). The expression "to make a stench" *(hibʾîš)* is used metaphorically, depicting an offensive behavior that results in ridding the "smell" by reprisal (e.g., Exod 5:21; 1 Sam 13:4; 27:12; 2 Sam 10:6; 16:21). Jacob feared the same eradication of his "household" as Simeon and Levi had exacted upon the Hivites, leaving him without descendants. His admission to a numerical inferiority realistically reflected how one clan would likely fall to a confederacy of peoples (thus Abram forms a coalition, 14:13–15). The word group "destroy" *(š-m-d)* usually refers to the annihilation of a group of people (e.g., 2 Sam 21:5).[556]

The brothers respond by a rhetorical question, angrily declaring that anyone who treated their sister in this fashion must answer for it (v. 31).[557] If Jacob is concerned for his appearance before the neighboring nations, they wonder aloud how he can permit this public disgrace. Frymer-Kensky suggests that Shechem's molestation of Dinah signaled that the clan is weak, unable to protect its women.[558] By offering them money for Dinah's hand, the brothers interpreted this as prostitution. Prostitution was prohibited in Israel and deemed contemptible by the community, both the cult prostitute and the common harlot (Lev 19:29; 21:9; Deut 23:17–19[18–20]; Prov 23:27–28; Amos 7:17). Shechem deserved in their eyes the strongest retaliation. That the penalty for Tamar's adulterous behavior was death shows the gravity of sexual infractions of this sort in the patriarchal period (38:24). Simeon and Levi lecture their father, contending that Jacob's refusal to defend the honor of the family meant that they must do so for "our sister." The implication is that Jacob has failed in his role to defend the honor of his daughter. That the sons have dishonored their father by their conduct may be suggested by 49:6, in which Jacob forswears he will not join his "honor/glory" *(kābôd)* with them (see comments on 49:7).[559] Their crime from Jacob's viewpoint shamed their father (cf. Noah and Ham, 9:24–25). This was in effect an attack on his patriarchal position; their conduct could be likened to the sin of Reuben, whose incest challenged the integrity of Jacob and his household. The cohesion of the family is crumbling, and Jacob is impotent to stop it.

---

[556] G. Hall, "שׁמד," *NIDOTTE* 4.151.

[557] Sarna reads their answer sympathetically, likening their rhetorical question to the compelling conclusion to Jonah (4:11; *Genesis*, 238).

[558] Frymer-Kensky, "Virginity in the Bible," 90.

[559] אַל־תֵּחַד כְּבֹדִי, lit., "let not my honor be joined [to their company]" (49:6).

12. Blessing and Struggle at Birth (35:1–29)

Against the backdrop of Jacob's fear of the nations (34:30), God encouraged the patriarch, instructing him to depart for Bethel (35:1). Calvin observed that "God chooses and assigns Beth-el, rather than any other place, for his [Jacob's] sanctuary; because the very sight of it would greatly avail to take away terror, when he would remember that there the glory of the Lord had been seen by him."[560] By remembering the past, Jacob would be ready to face the trials of the future. The formal conclusion to the "account *[tōlĕdōt]* of Abraham's son Isaac" (25:19), which entails the Jacob narrative proper (25:19–35:29), occurs with this chapter, describing the death and burial of Isaac (vv. 27–29). The following *tôlĕdōt* sections pertain to Esau (chap. 36) and primarily Jacob's sons, though Jacob continues as an important figure in the Joseph story (chaps. 37–50). Chapter 35 in the chiastic structure of the wider Jacob narrative (25:19–35:29) gives balance between the halves of the narrative. The idea of completion gives the diverse units of this chapter cohesion, which is organized around the itinerary of Jacob's movements from Shechem to Hebron.

Chapter 35 centers on events that bring closure to the past.

1. "God appeared to him [Jacob] *again* and blessed him [there]" (35:9; italics mine) is the essential message of this final chapter in the Jacob section. The author brings together the pinnacle events in Jacob's life, the theophanies at Bethel and Peniel. The word "again" refers to the dream vision at Bethel when the patriarch departed Canaan for Paddan Aram (28:10–22). "Again" could also have been brought to bear on "blessed," for God had already "blessed" Jacob at Peniel, where he wrestled the Lord (32:29[30]). The naming again of "Jacob/ Israel" and "Bethel" (vv. 10,15) reinforces the importance of these two pivotal moments in the patriarch's story, reminding us of the giving of the names in conjunction with the revelations at Bethel and Peniel (28:19; 32:28[29]). That God "blessed" Jacob (32:29[30]; 35:9; 48:3) directly links the patriarch with the forefathers Abraham (24:1) and Isaac (25:11) whom also the text explicitly says God "blessed."

2. Chapter 35 also reports the grueling delivery of Benjamin when Rachel dies giving birth at Bethlehem (35:16–20). By including this event, the author reminds us of Rebekah's pregnancy, which was disturbed by the prenatal struggle of Esau and Jacob (25:21–26), a sign and oracle that predicted the siblings' tussle for the paternal blessing of Isaac (chaps. 27–33). Jacob won his father's blessing through deceit, but that God himself is said to have "blessed" the patriarch (32:29[30]; 35:9) occurs only after Jacob's moral transformation (chaps. 32–33). By the retrospect contained in chap. 35, the author makes the ultimate declaration that God has fulfilled the oracle given

---

[560] Calvin, *Comm.*, 233.

at birth and the promises made at Bethel and Peniel.

3. The author also gives in chap. 35 a reflex of Jacob's sojourn under God's loving-kindness that safeguarded the patriarch. The recurring motif of divine guidance appears in the patriarch's speech to his family: "[God] has been with me wherever I have gone" (35:3; cf. 28:15; 31:3; 46:4). The births of Jacob and his son Benjamin by the matriarchs Rebekah (25:22) and Rachel (35:16b–17) also contribute to the motif of a completed itinerary. These were the most important women in the life of the patriarch; the two were close kin, aunt and niece, related by birth to Laban's household. Jacob's mother incited him to deceive his father, whereupon he received Isaac's blessing; she directed him to escape to Paddan Aram, just one step ahead of his vengeful brother, Esau (27:43–28:5). Rachel was also a source of love and difficulty in Jacob's life. He favored her, but his love for Rachel gave opportunity for the strife between the patriarch and her father Laban when he tricked Jacob into fourteen years of hard service (chaps. 28–29). The loss of Rebekah, with whom Jacob never appears again in the narrative, and the loss of Rachel mark the twenty-year exile of the patriarch.

4. Chapter 35 also reports four burials, signifying the end to the past era in expectation of the new generation represented by Jacob's twelve sons. The hiding of the foreign gods and rings under the oak at Shechem was a symbolic burial of the past, leaving behind the family's defilement (v. 4; 31:19; 34:29). The burials of Deborah (v. 8), Rachel (v. 19), and Isaac (v. 29) signaled closure to the past. Deborah, Rebekah's nurse, and Rachel represented Paddan Aram (chaps. 28–33), and Isaac represented the former generation that passed on to Jacob the promises of God (chap. 27).

5. The string of five locations in the chapter also indicated Jacob's exile had come to an end. The general movement southward, in this case from Shechem to Hebron, retraced the steps of Abraham, who had settled in the southernmost region of Canaan. Hebron especially was the focal point of the family. Isaac too resided at Hebron, and he dwelt in the southernmost town of Beersheba as one enters the Negev (26:23,33; 28:10; cf. 24:62). Shechem, with its stained memory of rape, deceit, and murder (chap. 34), was left behind (vv. 1–4); and Bethel, which symbolized the presence and promise of God, became their new destination. It was also a place of worship and vow (28:10–22). At Jacob's return to Bethel (v. 6), God fulfilled his promise to Jacob, and Jacob fulfilled his vow to the Lord (vv. 7,14; cf. 28:10–22; 31:3,13). God's revelation at Bethel "again" where he "blessed" the patriarch (v. 9) did not merely repeat the original promises; the message expanded on the promises and added to the significance of the name, "Israel" (vv. 10–12; cf. 28:4,13–15; 31:3,13; 32:12,28). At Ephrath-Bethlehem the death and burial of Rachel at the birth of Benjamin (vv. 17–20) recalled the striving among the wives of Jacob in Paddan Aram who together gave birth to the historic twelve tribes of Israel (chaps. 29–30). Finally,

the reunion at Hebron with Isaac fulfilled God's promise of return (v. 35; 28:21; 31:3,18,30). Now the torch was solely in the hand of Jacob, the man whom God had prepared for this time.

COMPOSITION. Source critics have long espoused a composite of sources in the chapter, attributing its various parts to the traditional sources of the Yahwist (J), Elohist (E), and Priestly writer (P). According to Gunkel, the chapter consists primarily of J and E material, with especially the E source dominant (vv. 1–5,6b–8,14,16–20). It is E's recollection that produced two separate revelations at Bethel in the Jacob narrative. J provided in chap. 35 the account of Reuben's sin (vv. 21–22a), and P's version of the first Bethel revelation (paralleling 28:10–22) appears in this chapter (vv. 6a,9–13a,15). Also P presents in vv. 22b–26 an alternative birth tradition to 35:16–20, placing Benjamin's birth in Paddan Aram (v. 26), and P concludes the Isaac *tôlĕdōt* section with the obituary of the patriarch (vv. 27–29). The primary basis of the source division is the vocabulary, which is believed to be distinctive of the three sources (e.g., Elohim, El Shaddai, Jacob//Israel, and pillar *[maṣṣēbâ]*), and the genealogical material (attributed to P).[561] Gunkel characterized the Bethel material (E, vv. 1–5,6b–14) as an incoherent "heap" that was the product of a redaction, not an old legend. Speiser remarked that the "converging" of the three sources (J, E, P) concerning Bethel, where two events occurred, produced a predictable amount of "duplication and confusion."

Westermann, on the other hand, pointedly differs with Gunkel's analysis, assessing P's passages as evidence of a "clearly conceived plan" that concluded the Jacob-Esau narrative to which the redactor added texts from J and his own construction in vv. 1–7 (using P's v. 6).[562] Coats, Van Seters, and Carr also reject the notion of a distinctive E contribution and generally agree on the identity of the P passages. Coats, for example, concludes that 35:1–7 is not a literary doublet of 28:10–22, prompting him to assign both passages to the same author (J).[563] J. Soggin argues on lexical grounds, however, that vv. 1–7 are Deuteronomic or Deuteronomistic in date, not an early purification ritual, concluding that the ritual fits the sixth century, resulting from a long process begun by the prophets who reestablished Yahwistic monotheism.[564] For Carr the non-P units, 35:1–8,16–20 (J), are part of the wider Jacob account (chaps. 32–35) that transformed the "pre-promise Jacob story" (chaps. 25,27–31) into a story about Jacob as a national ancestor. The later southern (Judean) editor of the Jacob-Joseph composite inserted the Reuben-Bilhah incident (vv. 21–22a) to comment negatively on Judah's older brother as in the case of Simeon and Levi in chap. 34. P's version

---

[561] Gunkel, *Genesis,* 365–71, 373; for specific verse variations see, e.g., Skinner, *Genesis,* 422–23; Speiser, *Genesis,* 269–75; and von Rad, *Genesis,* 335–42.

[562] Westermann, *Genesis 12–36,* 548–49.

[563] Coats, *Genesis,* 236.

[564] J. A. Soggin, "Jacob in Shechem and in Bethel (Genesis 35:1–7)," in *Sha'arei Talmon: Studies in the Bible, Qumran, and the Ancient Near East Presented to Shemaryahu Talmon* (Winona Lake: Eisenbrauns, 1992), 195–98.

of the first theophany at Bethel (vv. 9–15) did not just nuance the received Jacob story but straightforwardly contradicted the non-P representation in 28:10–22. The redactor who combined P and non-P materials preserved both versions, however, so as to create a literary balance in the Jacob narrative, but in doing so he assured that the P remembrance (35:9–15) had the final, prominent voice on the matter.[565]

In our view, that the chapter makes many allusions to the former narratives indicates that the essential whole of the Jacob narrative was before the author of chap. 35. The chapter exhibits organization and coherence. Since the motif of itinerary establishes the broad structure of the Jacob narrative as a whole, it is fitting that the final chapter should be arranged according to Jacob's itinerary in Canaan upon his return. In the account he moves in a southern direction, from Shechem to Bethel to Hebron; these sites are signal places in the history of the patriarchs and the establishment of the nation Israel.

The chapter also exhibits the same organizing principle that occurs for the Abraham and Joseph sections. Westermann and Wenham draw attention to the final verses detailing the death and burial of Isaac by his sons (vv. 28–29) as part of the framework of the Jacob narrative, which hearkens back to the narrative pattern observed in the Abraham conclusion and appears again in the Joseph finale (25:7–11; 49:33–50:26).[566] Carr, too, charts the genealogical frameworks that distinguish the three patriarchal narratives, and he includes the Adam *tôlĕdōt* section (chap. 5) as evidence of the same pattern.[567] Each narrative starts with the stereotypical expression *tôlĕdōt* ("generations") and concludes with the death and burial of the patriarch or his son.[568] The termination of the Jacob account imitates closely the Abraham narrative by use of stock vocabulary (see comments) and shared narrative imagery. The final scenes of both depict the sons of the patriarch burying their father (25:7–11; 35:28–29). The same locale, Hebron, is the burial site of Jacob by his sons, also reconciled, who go in procession from Egypt to the cave of Machpelah (49:29–33; 50:13). Further, the Hebron setting for the final unit (35:27–29) places Jacob squarely in the mainstream of patriarchal history and theology, for all three figures—Abraham, Isaac, and Jacob—are united in the land at the one place, Hebron. The burial account of Jacob in chaps. 49–50 emphasizes that he joined his fathers along with their wives in the same resting place.

Although the author ends the Jacob narrative in the manner of the Abraham and Joseph series, he includes other events leading to the burial of Isaac that pertain to the last days of Isaac and Jacob. He uses diverse materials, including gen-

---

[565] Carr, *Reading the Fractures of Genesis,* 226–27, 252–53, 257, 260, 298, 313, 316.

[566] Westermann, *Genesis 12–36,* 548; and Wenham, *Genesis 16–50,* 322.

[567] Carr, *Reading the Fractures of Genesis,* 94.

[568] Terah and Abraham (11:27–25:11), Isaac (25:19–35:29), and Jacob and Joseph (37:2–50:26). The pattern is not inflexible, either in its precise language or constituents; e.g., the Terah *tôlĕdōt* section records his death early in the narrative (11:32), ending it formerly by Abraham's burial (25:10–11), and the Jacob *tôlĕdōt* section closes with two funerals, the burial of Jacob and the mummifying of Joseph (50:13,26).

ealogical list, birth and death reports, and theophany pertaining to Jacob's return. Despite the assorted units, there is a discernible course of thought to the selection and placement of the events recalled. First, the arrival at Bethel, where the promise and vow in 28:10–22 are fulfilled, receives the prominent place (vv. 1–15). Second, the birth of the final descendant, Benjamin, completes the twelve-tribe nation (vv. 16–20). Third, the incestual shame committed by Reuben challenged his father's authority (vv. 21–22a). These three elements precede the genealogical listing of Jacob's descendants (vv. 22b–26), an appropriate prelude to the death notice of Jacob's father, Isaac (vv. 27–29).

The Bethel report in vv. 1–15 is not a literary duplication or alternative version as source critics customarily propose. It shares in and yet differs at significant points from 28:10–22, as we would expect, since it reports the fulfillment of the promise and vow first made at Bethel. The central idea in the initial Bethel theophany was the guidance of God and the return to Bethel. The Jacob story, despite the respite of Jacob and Esau's reconciliation (chap. 33), would have no true denouement unless the Bethel promise and vow were achieved. Verses 1–15 are essential to the cogency of the whole underlying scheme worked out by the author, showing that God guided the patriarch on his round-trip journey in accord with his promise. The reiteration of the naming "Israel" and "Bethel" (vv. 10,15), already found in the Jacob narratives (chaps. 28,32), does not duplicate but indicates additional significance now that the promise is fulfilled. Whereas the setting for the naming of "Bethel" and "Israel" initially concerned Jacob's personal return, their recurrence after his return concerns Jacob/Israel as a nation in the making. Thus the name "Israel" was not attached in this chapter to the nocturnal struggle at Peniel that symbolized Jacob's moral transformation and anticipated his confrontation with Esau (32:28[29],30[31]; 33:10); rather, "Israel" (v. 10) precedes the author's attention to the Abraham promise of "nations" and "kings" (v. 11), giving new impetus to the question of legitimate succession to Jacob. Jealousy among rival successors is the background for understanding the account of Joseph's sojourn in Egypt. Naming "the place El Bethel" (35:7), which projects the importance of Bethel as a cultic site, identifies the site where Jacob's national descendants will worship God (Judg 20:18,26; 21:2; 1 Sam 7:16; 10:3; 1 Kgs 12:29; 13:3–4; 2 Kgs 17:28). The term "place" *(māqôm)* may refer to holy spaces where theophanies occurred (Exod 3:5; Josh 5:15). "Where he [God] had talked with him" describes Bethel, which appears three times (vv. 13,14,15), underscoring the cultic function of the place. A special problem is the inclusion of Deborah's death and burial (v. 8). It fits in the present arrangement because of the connection with Bethel, but, more importantly, the chapter places Deborah in the company of Jacob's migration (v. 8). How Deborah, Rebekah's nurse, joined Jacob is not stated (from Paddan Aram?), but her presence recalls Abraham and Isaac, whose connection with Paddan Aram arose from the servant's attainment of Rebekah (24:59). Deborah then represented the past, and her presence in Jacob's circle meant that the past is revived in the return of Jacob. Similarly, the death of Rachel in conjunction with Benjamin's birth also recalls the past in Paddan Aram (vv. 16–20), which is now only a painful memory for Jacob. The burials of Deborah and Rachel meant the end of the Aramean era. At this point forward, the patriarchal story and the founding of the nation will be centered in the Canaan-Egypt orbit.

We find that the chapter's contents bridge the past, pertaining to Jacob's succession to Abraham and Isaac, and the future struggle among Jacob's sons. Geographically, the chapter moves the focal point from Paddan Aram to Canaan and readies us for the family's descent to Egypt. The units in this chapter fit together, exhibiting a premeditated inclusion and arrangement that no matter the precise origin of the parts have been effectively strung together, aware of the Abraham recital and anticipating the Joseph account.

STRUCTURE. The chapter consists of four units, arranged according to the patriarch's itinerary from Shechem to Hebron and points in between. The terminology of itinerary, including "moved, set out," (*n-s-ʿ*, vv. 5,16,21) and "came to, entered" (*b-w-ʾ*, vv. 6,16,27), mark the major units in the chapter. The first unit pertains to the command and preparations for Jacob's return to Bethel (vv. 1–4). The second unit describes Jacob's worship of God, who again appeared to the patriarch, reiterating the promises of descendants and land (vv. 5–15). In the third unit (vv. 16–20), Jacob moved on toward Hebron (farther south), but en route near Ephrath (Bethlehem) Rachel died when delivering Jacob's twelfth son, Benjamin. The fourth and final unit (vv. 21–29) reports the last events of the Jacob narrative in the region of Hebron, ending on the death and burial of Isaac.

The recurring ideas of death and burial provide the transition to the new focus on Jacob's sons in chaps. 37–50, after dispensing with the ancestral history of Esau (chap. 36). The burials of Deborah, Rebekah's nurse, Rachel, and Isaac (vv. 8,19–20,29) signal the end of an era. Deborah and Isaac represent the former generation, and Rachel indicates the end of Jacob's experience at Paddan Aram and rounds out the birth of the next generation. The term for the burial of the foreign gods is the different word *ṭāman,* customarily translated "hid" (but can mean "buried" at Job 40:13; Jer 43:9–10), indicating the putting away of the past. The chapter prepares for the future history of Jacob's sons by the reports of Benjamin's birth, the youngest son, the offence of the eldest son, Reuben, and the twelve-name genealogical record of Jacob's offspring.

(1) Preparing for Bethel (35:1–4)

[1]Then God said to Jacob, "Go up to Bethel and settle there, and build an altar there to God, who appeared to you when you were fleeing from your brother Esau."

[2]So Jacob said to his household and to all who were with him, "Get rid of the foreign gods you have with you, and purify yourselves and change your clothes. [3]Then come, let us go up to Bethel, where I will build an altar to God, who answered me in the day of my distress and who has been with me wherever I have gone." [4]So they gave Jacob all the foreign gods they had and the rings in their ears, and Jacob buried them under the oak at Shechem.

Two speeches dominate this opening unit: God directs Jacob to depart Shechem for Bethel, where he is to erect an altar (v. 1), and Jacob directs his household to yield their false cult objects and purify themselves so that they can carry out God's instructions (vv. 2–3). The final verse describes the family's obedience, after which Jacob buries their gods and earrings at Shechem (v. 4).

DIVINE INSTRUCTIONS (35:1). **35:1** Verse 1 contains four Hebrew imperatives—"arise, go up, settle, build."[569] The directive to return to Bethel specifically relates to the first theophany at Bethel (28:10–22), in accordance with the promise made to Jacob, "I will bring you back to this land" (28:15). The instruction, "Go up [qûm ʿălēh] to Bethel" (v. 1; cf. 2 Kgs 1:3), renews the command given at Paddan Aram: "Now leave [qûm ṣēʾ] this land . . ." (31:13; cf. 31:3). Jacob's original vow promised to establish Bethel as a place of worship, if the Lord returns him "safely to my father's house" (28:20–22). That divine promise is fulfilled when Jacob meets his father, Isaac, at Mamre (v. 27). His vow to worship the Lord coalesces with the instruction to erect an altar. Jacob will have this is mind when he commands spiritual preparations for the return to Bethel (vv. 2–3). The next imperative, "settle [šeb] there" recalls Abraham's itinerate stops in Canaan ("stayed," 20:1; 22:19), where he often built an altar of worship (13:18; cf. 12:6–9). The word "settle" may be a reflex of the same term occurring frequently in the prior narrative, describing the sons' notorious dealings with the Shechemites (34:10,16,21,22,23,30). Initially, permanent settlement at Shechem would have meant intermarriage with the Shechemites and likely the adoption of their ways (e.g., Deut 7:1–5); as it turned out, the Israelites left behind a trail of murder and plunder as they set out. The move to Bethel set a new tone of repentance for Jacob's family, for settlement in Bethel required purification and resulted in the worship of God. "Build an altar" is the final directive and is the goal of the former imperatives. It is the only occasion that the Lord specifically instructs a patriarch to construct an altar (cf. Exod 27:1; 2 Sam 24:18). There is no explicit mention of an altar in 28:10–22, but Jacob's vow provides for a place of worship, which would likely involve an altar (28:22).

The repeated use of "there" *(šām)* reinforces the importance of Bethel in Jacob's exile. The text ties the revelatory event ("the God who appeared to you"; cf. 12:7) to the threat of Esau's revenge. "Fleeing [bāraḥ] from your brother" recalls Rebekah's instruction to Jacob to "flee [bāraḥ] . . . to my brother Laban" (27:43). That Rebekah is mentioned in this chapter only in conjunction with her nurse's death (v. 8) implies that she was dead and, thus, the sweet reunion she and Jacob assumed would happen never came to pass. The promise at Bethel emphasized divine presence and protection for Jacob's jour-

---

[569] קוּם עֲלֵה . . . וְשֵׁב . . . וַעֲשֵׂה, "arise, go up . . . dwell . . . build"; NIV renders the first two "go up."

ney (28:20), and it is this feature of the promises that is uppermost in the recollection of that event (cf. "I will be with you," 31:3). "Esau" functions as an inclusio in the chapter (vv. 1,29), pointing to the initiation and termination of Jacob's travels. The ideas of rift and reconciliation bracket this final chapter (vv. 1,29), as they do for the broader Jacob narrative (chaps. 25; 35).

JACOB'S INSTRUCTIONS (35:2–3).   **35:2**   The patriarch's audience included his family ("his household") and others who were joined to his clan ("all who were with him," v. 2), such as slaves from Shechem (34:29) and Deborah (cp. circumcision, 17:12,23). Two commands make up the patriarch's instructions: first, to remove foreign cultic items and second, to purify themselves. These two commands especially suit God's requirements of Israel for worship. The first two commands of the Ten Commandments specifically forbade worship and image making of foreign gods (e.g., Exod 20:3–6,23), and purification was obligatory upon those who worshiped God (e.g., Exod 19:10; Num 8:15).

"Get rid of" *(sûr)* elsewhere in the Old Testament (e.g., 2 Kgs 18:4; 2 Chr 30:14) describes removing cult objects. The language presages the admonition of Joshua after the conquest of Canaanite cities (Josh 24:23). Purging the camp of foreign deities indicated spiritual renewal (Judg 10:16; 1 Sam 7:3–4; 2 Chr 33:15). The source of the "foreign gods" most likely was among the items confiscated from the murdered Shechemites. Although Jacob may not have had in mind specifically Laban's "household gods" taken by Rachel (31:19,32), the incident shows us other ways religious items could have come from outside the clan. The second exhortation, "purify yourselves" *(hiṭṭahărū),* derives from the cultic term *ṭ-h-r,* "to be clean, pure." Ceremonial purification was required to enter the presence of the Lord (e.g., Exod 19:10; 30:19–21), including entrance into the camp of Israel (Lev 16:26,28; Num 5:3), and purification rites often involved physical washing including garments (e.g., Lev 13:34; 14:8; Num 8:21). Purification may have been required because of the looting of the corpses at Shechem (34:29; cf. Num 31:19–20).[570] Jacob's third exhortation called for a change of clothes, which was a practice that preceded the supplicant's approach to the Lord (e.g., Lev 6:10–11; 2 Sam 12:20). The description of Dinah's rape as "defilement" (34:5,13,27; cf. 34:7; 2 Sam 13:12) and the murder and plundering of the corpses that followed would have rendered the camp of Jacob unclean. Murder, however, cannot be ritually expiated (cf. Num 35:33–34; cf. Ps 51:16–17[18–19]). Jacob treats the incident as an act of war whose soldiers can be cleansed through purification rites (cf. Num 31:19–20,24). The ashes of the red heifer cleansed those contaminated by touching corpses (Num 19:11–13,16–19), such as the looters of the Shechemites.

35:3   Jacob explains the purpose of the call for purification, imitating the

---

[570] This is the opinion of *Tg. Ps.-J.*

language of God's command in v. 1. "Who answered me in the day of my distress" is a new expression, referring to the Esau and Laban incidents, where also in each situation God's enduring presence is a significant promise made to the patriarch (28:15; 31:3). "Who has been with me wherever I have gone" is another testimonial to the faithfulness of God (cf. 31:5,7,42). "Distress" *(ṣārâ)* is a common term, indicating various and widespread troubles (e.g., Deut 31:17; 1 Kgs 1:29); it especially describes the psalmists' oppressions, who appealed for the Lord's help (e.g., Pss 22:11[12]; 77:2[3]; 86:7; 142:2[3]). Joseph's brothers, unlike God, refused to answer the pleas of Joseph in his distress (42:21).

LEAVING THEIR IDOLS (35:4). **35:4** The clan complied by surrendering their "gods" and earrings. That the rings also were part of the booty from Shechem is possible (34:29), for we find that the same item taken from captured Midianite booty was dedicated to the Lord (Num 31:50; cf. Judg 8:24). The added significance of the Shechemite rings may be the pagan representations they bore (*Tg. Ps.-J.; Gen. Rab.* 81.3) or their precious metal, which could be easily melted down for gain (Deut 7:25) or for shaping foreign gods, as in the case of Aaron's golden calf (Exod 32:2–4; also Judg 8:24–27). Alternatively, "the rings in their ears" could refer to the idols' earrings, which could be recycled for making images. That idols possessed earrings is widely attested in the ancient Near East.[571] Jacob buried the devoted items "under the oak *[ʾēlâ]* near Shechem"[572] (cf. "great tree," *[ʾēlôn]* at Shechem, Judg 9:6). The word "buried" renders *ṭāman,* meaning "to hide, conceal," the same term describing the concealment of Achan's stolen booty in his tent (Josh 7:21–22). Trees as symbols of fecundity provided a typical setting for Canaanite worship (e.g., Isa 57:5; Hos 4:13; Ezek 6:13). Legitimate worship also occurred in the shadow of trees, memorializing the place of God's provision (e.g., 12:6; 13:18; Judg 24:26). (See Deborah's burial under the oak, v. 8.) The importance of the oak for our passage is its association with the revelatory nature of God's presence and word (e.g., Judg 6:11; 1 Kgs 13:14). Sarna observed that Deut 7:5,25 calls for the destruction of pagan cult objects; their burial rather than demolition is unique, which may have been designed to desecrate the oak, excluding it as a proper place for worship of the Lord.[573] By abandoning their gods and rings at Shechem, Jacob closed the chapter at Shechem and looked ahead to the realization of the Bethel promise and vow.

---

[571] A. V. Hurowitz, "Who Lost an Earring? Genesis 35:4 Reconsidered," *CBQ* 62 (2001): 28–32.

[572] The LXX adds the gloss καὶ ἀπώλεσεν αὐτὰ ἕως τῆς σήμερον ἡμέρας, "and he destroyed them until this day" (cf. v. 20), meaning that the idols remain buried (Wevers, *Notes on the Greek Text,* 577–78).

[573] Sarna, *Genesis,* 240.

(2) Worshiping God at Bethel (35:5–15)

⁵Then they set out, and the terror of God fell upon the towns all around them so that no one pursued them.

⁶Jacob and all the people with him came to Luz (that is, Bethel) in the land of Canaan. ⁷There he built an altar, and he called the place El Bethel, because it was there that God revealed himself to him when he was fleeing from his brother.

⁸Now Deborah, Rebekah's nurse, died and was buried under the oak below Bethel. So it was named Allon Bacuth.

⁹After Jacob returned from Paddan Aram, God appeared to him again and blessed him. ¹⁰God said to him, "Your name is Jacob, but you will no longer be called Jacob; your name will be Israel." So he named him Israel.

¹¹And God said to him, "I am God Almighty; be fruitful and increase in number. A nation and a community of nations will come from you, and kings will come from your body. ¹²The land I gave to Abraham and Isaac I also give to you, and I will give this land to your descendants after you." ¹³Then God went up from him at the place where he had talked with him.

¹⁴Jacob set up a stone pillar at the place where God had talked with him, and he poured out a drink offering on it; he also poured oil on it. ¹⁵Jacob called the place where God had talked with him Bethel.

This extensive unit describes the purpose of the divine command to leave Shechem and move to Bethel. At Bethel the Lord will reinforce the promises made to the patriarch, who will worship the Lord through the establishment of an altar and erection of a pillar. En route to Bethel, the Israelites received the protection of the Lord (v. 5), arriving safely at Bethel, where Jacob built an altar and named the site "El Bethel" (vv. 6–7). A brief interlude describes the death and burial of Rebekah's nurse Deborah at Bethel (v. 8), symbolizing the end of Jacob's foreign sojourn. God appears to Jacob as at the first (28:10–22), recalling his name "Israel" (32:28[29]) and accentuating the ancient promises (vv. 9–13). The unit closes with another allusion to the first appearance at Bethel. The patriarch erects a pillar and offers again the name of the site "Bethel," commemorating the theophany (cf. Mic 7:20).

MOVE TO BETHEL (35:5).   **35:5**   "Then they set out" initiates the itinerary that will bring them to Bethel (v. 6) and ultimately to Hebron, where Jacob will reunite with his father (v. 27). This verse achieves two purposes in the narrative. First, it provides the response to Jacob's real concerns in 34:30. The fears of Jacob were not imaginary, but the Lord's purposes for Jacob's clan superseded any retaliatory plans made by the Canaanites. On the significance of "terror" *(ḥittâ)* as a foreshadowing event, see vol. 1A, p. 401. Second, this verse illustrates that the Lord was proving himself faithful to the promise of accompanying Jacob in his travels (cf. comments on v. 1). "Pursue" *(rādap)* is common for describing the hunting down of an enemy (e.g., 14:14–15; Josh 10:10). For examples of enemies pursuing Israel, see Exod 14:4,8,9,23; 15:9; Deut 1:44; 11:4; Jer 39:5; Amos 1:11.

ALTAR NAMED "EL BETHEL" (35:6–7). **35:6–7** Repeatedly, "Luz," the former name of Bethel, is recorded down to the conquest period (28:19; 48:3; Josh 16:2; 18:13; Judg 1:23,26). The significance of this reminder in Genesis is the unusual circumstances of its new naming, recalling the superintendence of God's presence during Israel's travels in Canaan. "There" *(šām)* occurs twice in v. 7, reinforcing the importance of the site. The religious significance of Bethel in Israel's history was a perpetual testimony to the benevolent relationship that God formed with Israel's ancestor Jacob. In accordance with God's directive (v. 1), the patriarch immediately built an altar upon arriving at Bethel. This act is one of many recorded by the narrative to associate the patriarch with Abraham. "He built an altar" is the exact wording describing the altars of Abraham (12:7–8; 13:18) and Isaac (26:25; cf. also 1 Sam 7:17). The importance of the name "Bethel" ("the house of God [El]") is paramount to the author, who gives it twice in the chapter (vv. 7,15). Here, however, the name is "El Bethel," meaning "the God of Bethel" (see "El Names of God" in the Introduction). The name assumes that the reader recalls the former naming of Bethel in 28:10–22. By the addition "El," Jacob emphasizes the presence of the deity, not exclusively the place. The word "place" *(māqôm)* often refers to holy centers, appearing repeatedly in our chapter (vv. 7,13,14,15; cf. 22:14; 28:17; Deut 12:11; 1 Kgs 8 *passim).* The term rendered "revealed himself" *(niglû*[574]) in this reflexive stem *(niphal)* means "to show oneself" (e.g., 1 Sam 14:8; 2 Sam 6:20),[575] which aptly fits the experience of a vision in 28:10–22. The word "appear" *(nir'eh)* is typically preferred to describe theophany, as in vv. 1,9. "Reveal" is especially appropriate for our passage, for it often describes the disclosure of God's will and word (e.g., Isa 40:5; 53:1).[576] Since *g-l-h* may describe a prophet's function (1 Sam 3:7,21; Isa 22:14), its usage may insinuate that Jacob was a prophet, as was his ancestor Abraham (20:7). When Jacob reiterates the connection of the theophany with his flight from Esau (v. 7b; cf. comments on v. 1), he recalls the defining moment in his life that eventually led full circle to his return to Bethel.

DEATH AND BURIAL OF DEBORAH (35:8). **35:8** Mention of Deborah's death and burial in the narrative, without giving the same attention to Rebekah's death, is surprising.[577] Rebekah's burial place at Machpelah is only noted in 49:31. The author includes Deborah's obituary to symbolize the end of the prior

---

[574] The word נִגְלוּ, "revealed himself," is grammatically plural; the ancient versions reflect the singular number נִגְלָה (ptc.), which usually appears with "God/Elohim" (הָאֱלֹהִים) as its subject. The plural may be due to the numerical congruity with Elohim, which is grammatically plural, or the plural may be an allusion to the angels who accompanied God (28:12–13).

[575] The word group "reveal" *(g-l-h)* occurs only once more in Genesis (9:21, *hith.).*

[576] H.-J. Zobel, "גָּלָה *gālāh," TDOT* 2.476–88.

[577] Waltke attributes the omission of Rebekah's death to her deception of Isaac and to Jacob's absence at the time of her death *(Genesis,* 473).

generation; she represents the older generation, as does Isaac (vv. 28–29).[578] Since she accompanied Rebekah from Haran (24:59) and Rebekah had promised to send for Jacob in Haran (27:45), Deborah's presence in Jacob's camp gives the promise of return, further confirming genealogical and geographical fulfillment. The association of Deborah's interment with the "oak" (*'allôn*) at Bethel also encouraged the inclusion of this burial in the passage (see "oak [*'ēlâ*]," at Shechem, v. 4). Her burial under a tree was not exceptional (cf. "tree" [*'ēlâ*],1 Chr 10:12; also 1 Sam 31:13), although in the patriarchal period a hewn cave for multiple burials was typical.[579] The name given to the site, "Allon Bacuth," means "oak of weeping." Burial sites continued to be honored by later generations, providing future descendants a psychology of identity with the land (47:29–30; 49:29–32; 50:25; Exod 13:19). The grievous mourning and raising of a special memorial evidenced the deep heartache Jacob must have felt toward the passing of the nursemaid who had attended him in his childhood.

THEOPHANY AND BLESSING (35:9–13).   The passage describes the divine promises (vv. 10–12), sandwiched between the notices of the theophany's appearance (v. 9) and ascension (v. 13).

Divine Appearance (35:9).   **35:9** By the word "again," the verse alludes to the first visit to Bethel, although in the prior narrative (28:10–22) the typical language "appeared" *(wayyērā')* does not occur (e.g., 12:7; 17:1; 18:1; 26:2,24). Mention of his return "from Paddan Aram" contributes to the narrative's emphasis on fulfillment (28:2). "And he blessed him" recalls the naming of Israel when the stranger first "blessed" him (32:29[30]); by this acknowledgment the author links Jacob with his ancestors (24:1; 25:11; cf. 48:3). This is appropriate for the reissuing of the name in v. 10. The substance of the "blessing" follows in vv. 10–12, which foretell the nation that he will father.

"Israel" and the Promises (35:10–12).   **35:10** This is the second divine speech in the narrative. The expansion of the promises in these verses confirms the approval of Jacob. Wenham offers that it parallels the Abraham narrative in which God declared the promises anew after the successful passing of the test (22:16–18).[580] The significance of the redundancy in v. 10 is to reinforce the message of the new name but with a different emphasis.[581] In the first naming, the context of chaps. 32–33 focused the reader on the patriarch's transformation, from "Jacob" the trickster to "Israel" the one blessed of God. Here the context highlights the national and royal importance of the name, shown by the new character of the promises in v. 11 and the first formal listing of his twelve tribal descendants (vv. 23–26).

---

[578] Sarna calculates her age at about 130 years (cp. 47:8; *Genesis,* 365, n. 10).

[579] For burial customs see E. Bloch-Smith, "Burials," *ABD* 1.785–89.

[580] Wenham, *Genesis 16–50,* 329.

[581] Sarna observes that the second naming in Canaan matches up with the first naming on the transjordan side (32:28[29]; *Genesis,* 242).

35:11 The self-identification "I am God Almighty *[El Shaddai]*" points back to the Abraham experience (17:1) but also brings forward the wording of Isaac's blessing upon Jacob (28:3). "Be fruitful and increase in number" echoes Isaac's prayer (28:2), but the new circumstances broaden the meaning. As a young man the prayer of Isaac invoked God's blessing for sons, which the Lord realized through the gift of twelve sons. But now Jacob is an old man, meaning that the call for procreation must refer to future generations who will create a nation. Wenham remarks that the chapter's events anticipate future events, such as the nation's wars of conquest, pertaining to Israel's purification and the supervision of collected booty (Num 31:20; Deut 7:25–26; Josh 7:21).[582] We earlier remarked that the treatment of the Shechemites by Simeon and Levi foreshadowed Israel's rules of engagement in Deut 7:1–5; 20:13–14 (see comments on 34:7,25–26). The sites noted in Jacob's route in chap. 35 from Shechem to Hebron, including his intervening stops, imply the future transition from the patriarchal era to Israel's twelve tribes and finally Israel's first kings, Saul (Benjamin) and David (Hebron).[583]

The language "fruitful and increase" is similar to the promises made to Abraham in 17:2,6 (cf. Ishmael, 17:20). "A nation *(gôy)* and a community *[qěhal]* of nations *[gôyim]*" is another reflex of his father's invocation ("a community *[qěhal]* of peoples," 28:3). The connection with Abraham is apparent here (17:4–6), who will be "a father of many nations *[gôyim]*." Another shift in perspective is indicated by the departure from the former expression "peoples" *('ammîm)* to the word "nation" *(gôy)*. The term "nation" indicates a nation-state with land, and the word "people" reflects the community bonding of a people group (see vol. 1A, p. 430). The term "nation" is fitting for the expansion of the promises by the inclusion of "kings," a feature of the Abrahamic version but not yet stated for Jacob (17:6,16). "Will come from you" and "will come from your body" are parallel lines that present only slight variations on the former language made to Abraham and Sarah. Moreover, the verse recalls the birth oracle given to Rebekah that announces that "two nations are in your womb" (25:23). In Jacob's case, "body" (i.e., "loins," *ḥălāṣayim*) is appropriate, referring to the strength of the man (e.g., 1 Kgs 8:19; Job 38:3). This is another passage in Genesis that anticipates the royal offspring promised to the nation Israel (cf. 36:31).

35:12 The land promise is reiterated, in which the repeated term "land" *('ereṣ)* in the Hebrew text forms an inclusio. Three appearances of the verb "gave/give" *(nātan)* emphasize the grace that God bestows upon Israel's fathers (cf. 17:8; 26:3–4). The promise is expressed from the historic perspective of Jacob's ancestors first ("to Abraham and Isaac") and of Jacob personally

---

[582] Wenham, *Genesis 16–50*, 330.

[583] T. Knopf, "Rachels Grab—Ein Tradition aus dem TNK," in *Dielheimer Blätter zum Alten Testament und seiner Rezeption in der Alten Kirche* 27 (1991): 73–127.

second ("to you"). That the promise extends to "your [Jacob's] descendants after you" is the exact language promised Abraham in the covenant of circumcision (17:7–8; cf. also 13:15; 26:3–4). The passage voices the same blessing invoked by Isaac (28:4). The promise then encompasses the past and the future, making Jacob essential in God's plan to transform the single family of Abraham into the nation Israel.

Divine Ascension (35:13). **35:13** The description of God's ascension is another narrative reflex of the covenant of circumcision "when God went up" from Abraham (17:22). In our passage, however, the "place" *(māqôm)* Bethel is accentuated. The term *māqôm* often refers to a worship site (see comments on v. 7; cf. 12:6; 22:14; 28:16–17; 32:2[3]; Exod 3:5; 20:24; Deut 12 *passim*; Ps 132:5).

PILLAR AND NAMING OF BETHEL (35:14–15). **35:14–15** Again the verse emphasizes the "place" *(māqôm)* of revelation (v. 14). The pillar and the subsequent two anointings recall the theophany and vow first made at Bethel (28:18,22; cf. 31:3). This present act of worship is the fulfillment of Jacob's vow. One difference in the two events is the inclusion of a "drink offering" *(nesek)* poured over the stone pillar. It is the only occasion of a drink offering in Genesis, although it was a common religious practice in antiquity (e.g., 2 Sam 23:16; Isa 57:6; Jer 44:17–19). Various sacrifices at the tabernacle, including the daily offerings and burnt and peace offerings (e.g., Exod 29:40–41; Num 15:5–10), and special designated occasions (e.g., firstfruits, Lev 23:13) required a drink offering, constituting "wine" (e.g., Exod 29:40–41; Num 15:5) or "fermented drink" *(šēkār,* "strong drink," Num 28:7). That Jacob vowed to present the Lord a tenth of his possessions (28:22) has no correlation with Jacob's actions at Bethel. Setting aside the gods and rings at Shechem (v. 4) may have been his voluntary tithe, or more likely the narrative does not report what the reader should assume, that is, the patriarch fulfilled this feature of his vow as well. Verse 15 again remarks on the "place" *(māqôm)* but reinforces that the "name" was "Bethel." The absence of an explanation for the name presupposes the reader knows its significance from the earlier account (28:17,19). Again the passage acknowledges the remarkable nature of the event; this was the very place that God announced the promises to the nation Israel's namesake.

(3) Birth and Death Near Bethlehem (35:16–20)

[16]Then they moved on from Bethel. While they were still some distance from Ephrath, Rachel began to give birth and had great difficulty. [17]And as she was having great difficulty in childbirth, the midwife said to her, "Don't be afraid, for you have another son." [18]As she breathed her last—for she was dying—she named her son Ben-Oni. But his father named him Benjamin. [19]So Rachel died and was buried on the way to Ephrath (that is, Bethle-

hem). **²⁰Over her tomb Jacob set up a pillar, and to this day that pillar marks Rachel's tomb.**

The second stage in the clan's journey was to continue south toward Hebron (v. 16b). "Rachel" forms the boundaries of the unit's topic (vv. 16b,20). Rachel's difficult labor and birth of her second son, Benjamin, results in her death (vv. 16b–18). Jacob erects a pillar to mark her burial site near Bethlehem (vv. 19–20).

MOVE TO EPHRATH (BETHLEHEM) (35:16–17). **35:16a** The text gives no reason for the departure from Bethel, but we may assume Jacob expected to "return safely to [his] father's house" in Hebron, according to the fulfillment of his vow (v. 27; cf. 28:22).

35:16b–17 The location of Benjamin's birth and Rachel's tomb are important to the narrative (vv. 16b,19). The site provided a reference point for future generations ("to this day," v. 20), indicating that the last son born to the patriarch occurred in the land. Even Rachel's burial in the land demonstrated that God's word had been truthful. Although Rachel had lived outside Canaan, her final place was permanently in the land of promise as the matriarch of Israel's tribes, Joseph and Benjamin. "Still some distance from Ephrath"⁵⁸⁴ gives a vague description of the locality. The identification of Ephrath(ah) with the town Bethlehem in Judah (v. 19; 48:7) places the tomb south of Jerusalem and north of Bethlehem (see also Ruth 4:11; 1 Chr 4:4; Mic 5:2[1]; cf. Ruth 1:2; 1 Sam 17:12; Matt 2:18). How far the tomb was from Bethel toward Bethlehem in relation to the trek taken by Jacob must be derived from elsewhere. The traditional site today is one mile north of Bethlehem,⁵⁸⁵ but we will see that this is unlikely the correct burial site. Another clue to its location is 1 Sam 10:2, placing it "at Zelzah on the border of Benjamin"; but this implies that the tomb was north of Jerusalem in Benjamin's territory. One explanation is that "Bethlehem" is an incorrect gloss (v. 19); the Samuel passage reflects the accurate location in Benjamin, which accords with Jer 31:15 that links Rachel's weeping with Ramah (= er-Ram [?], five miles north of Jerusalem, Josh 18:25).⁵⁸⁶ Some scholars find further confirmation that the location is north of Jerusalem in Ps 132:6 that parallels "Ephrathah" and "Jaar"; this latter site is probably the town Kiriath-jearim (cf. 1 Chr 2:50), which is eight miles northwest of Jerusalem on the border of Benjamin and Judah (Josh 18:15). But Sarna explains that 1 Chr 2:50–51 shows that the two towns Bethlehem and Kiriath-jearim were con-

---

⁵⁸⁴כִּבְרַת־הָאָרֶץ, "*kibrath* of the land," is uncertain (cf. 48:7); it also appears in 2 Kgs 5:19, where the phrase indicates a measure of distance (cf. Rashi).

⁵⁸⁵Eusebius (fourth century) and the Jewish *Guide to Jerusalem* (tenth century) are the earliest traditions placing the tomb near Bethlehem.

⁵⁸⁶L. M. Luker contends that a location near Ramah also accounts for the inclusion of the "Oak of Weeping" in 35:8 and the location of the "Weepers Place" [Bokim] noted in Judg 2:1,5 ("Rachel's Tomb," *ABD* 5.608–9).

nected with the common ancestor Ephrath, suggesting that the original Judahite clan Ephrath extended its influence to both locations.[587] Since Zilzah is thought necessary by the author in 1 Sam 10:2 to locate the tomb's vicinity, we may agree with B. K. Waltke's suggestion that "near Rachel's tomb" was not intended to be a precise designation. This unspecific description permits the location to be on the Benjamin-Judah border, just south of Jerusalem.[588] Moreover, the connection scholars make between Rachel's tomb and Ramah is taken for granted, but Jeremiah does not make this connection (31:15). Ramah is along the route taken by the exiles of Benjamin and Judah, whose deportation by the Babylonians evokes the wailing of Rachel's children (*Gen. Rab.* 82.10).

Her "difficulty" *(qāšâ)* pertained to her labor pains (cf. birth "pangs" *ṣîrîm,* 1 Sam 4:19; Isa 13:8; 21:3). The adjective *qāšeh* describes the "hard labor" of the Hebrew slaves (Exod 1:14; Deut 26:6). The severity of pain during a woman's labor was proverbial (e.g., Isa 42:14; Jer 30:6; Mic 4:10). The midwife encouraged Rachel by hailing the child as "another son" (v. 17). The midwife of Phinehas's dying wife offered similar comfort, "Don't despair [lit., be afraid]; you have given birth to a son" (1 Sam 4:20). By referring to Benjamin as "another son," the midwife in effect announces that Rachel's prayer when naming Joseph has been fulfilled (30:24).

BIRTH AND NAMING OF BENJAMIN (35:18). **35:18** Rachel's naming of the child "Ben-Oni" is her dying word. "Ben-Oni," meaning "son of my sorrow,"[589] would be a sad reminder of Rachel's adversity at the child's birth (cf. "Ichabod," 1 Sam 4:21). Although the wives of Jacob had always named his sons (chaps. 29–30), he preferred a name of confidence, "Benjamin," that is, "son of [my] right hand."[590] The "right hand" indicated the place of power and favor (e.g., 48:18; Exod 15:6; 1 Kgs 2:19); he later characterized Benjamin as

---

[587] Sarna, *Genesis,* 408.

[588] B. K. Waltke, "Rachel's Tomb," *ZPEB* 5.25–26.

[589] For אוֹנִי (from אָוֶן), "my sorrow," see Deut 26:14; cf. "mourners" Hos 9:4 (also Ezek 24:17,22, if emended; *DCH* 1.333). אוֹן, "strength, virility," has also been suggested, thus "son of my strength," corresponding to Jacob's naming "son of my right hand," indicating that the child depletes Rachel of her vitality or that the child possesses Rachel's strength (S. Schäfer-Bossert, "Den Männern die Macht und der Frau die Trauer? Ein kritischer Blick auf die Deutung von *'ôn*— oder: Wie nennt Rachel ihren Sohn?" *Feministische Hermeneutik und Erstes Testament* [1994]: 106–25). But the term אוֹן when applied to a parent's vigor refers to the father's "strength, virility" (49:3; Deut 21:17; Pss 78:51; 105:36).

[590] Alternative explanations have included "son of the south [יָמִים]" (Rashi) and "son of days [יָמִים]" (Rashban; *T. Benj.* 1.16); Delitzsch (*New Commentary on Genesis,* 232) rendered the name "son of prosperity" (i.e., the lucky right side), attributing the name to Jacob's period of prosperity or the completion of the "fortunate number of twelve (sons)" (cf. "son of fortune," Westermann, *Genesis 12–36,* 555). The Akk. parallel is the personal name *Bi-ni-ya-mi-na,* discovered at Mari; the tribal name "Yaminites" *(DUMU.MEŠ-yamina),* "sons of the right" (i.e., southerners), corresponds in name to the biblical Benjaminites (A. Malamat, *Mari and the Early Israelite Experience: The Schweich Lectures of the British Academy 1984* [Oxford: British Academy, 1989], 31, 35).

a ravenous wolf in 49:27. Benjamin held the distinction of being the only son of the twelve born in Canaan. From the Joseph narrative we learn that Joseph maintained Jacob's life-long favor, although Benjamin as Rachel's child held special value in the patriarch's eyes (42:4,38; 44:29). Benjamin was a source of pride and of anguish for his father, making both "Ben-Oni" and "Benjamin" prospective of the joy and pain that the boy would mean for Jacob. The attention on the birth of Benjamin that leads to Rachel's death contributes to the background for the sibling strife that characterized Jacob's sons. Her passing accentuated Jacob's protection of her two sons, Joseph and Benjamin, who were also Jacob's youngest. Not only did Leah's continued survival mean more influence, her sons were older and exhibited moral waywardness that threatened the younger boys.

DEATH AND BURIAL OF RACHEL (35:19–20).   **35:19–20**   On the location of the burial site, see comments on v. 17. Jacob made a practice of establishing a "pillar" *(maṣṣēbâ)* for religious and legal purposes (v. 14; also e.g., 28:18,22; 31:45). Rachel's tomb is mentioned again in Samuel's instructions to Saul (1 Sam 10:2; cf. Jer 31:15; Matt 2:18). That the site continued its prominence into the monarchic period extends the possible meaning of the time "until this day" (v. 20).

(4) Events Near and at Hebron (35:21–29)

21Israel moved on again and pitched his tent beyond Migdal Eder. 22While Israel was living in that region, Reuben went in and slept with his father's concubine Bilhah, and Israel heard of it.

Jacob had twelve sons:
23The sons of Leah:
> **Reuben the firstborn of Jacob,**
> **Simeon, Levi, Judah, Issachar and Zebulun.**

24The sons of Rachel:
> **Joseph and Benjamin.**

25The sons of Rachel's maidservant Bilhah:
> **Dan and Naphtali.**

26The sons of Leah's maidservant Zilpah:
> **Gad and Asher.**

These were the sons of Jacob, who were born to him in Paddan Aram.

27Jacob came home to his father Isaac in Mamre, near Kiriath Arba (that is, Hebron), where Abraham and Isaac had stayed. 28Isaac lived a hundred and eighty years. 29Then he breathed his last and died and was gathered to his people, old and full of years. And his sons Esau and Jacob buried him.

This unit describes the next two stages in Jacob's return to Canaan. His move to the vicinity of Migdal Eder (v. 21) was stamped by the incestuous act of Reuben, his firstborn (v. 22a). This startling impropriety by Jacob's eldest with Bilhah prompted the author to include a listing of his twelve sons, according to Jacob's wives (vv. 22b–26). The conclusion of Jacob's journey is his reunion with Isaac at Hebron (v. 27). The completion of the Jacob *tôlĕdōt* narrative, like the Abraham narrative (25:9–11), ends by recalling the burial of Isaac by his two sons, Jacob and Esau (vv. 28–29).

REUBEN'S INCEST (35:21–22a). **35:21** The location of Migdal Eder (lit., "tower of the flock") remains obscure, probably situated somewhere on the line between Bethlehem and Hebron. The same Hebrew *(migdal ʿēder)* appears in Mic 4:8, either in apposition to the city Jerusalem, "O (watch)tower of the flock" (e.g., NIV, NRSV, NASB) or as the proper name again "Migdal Eder" (cf. NAB). The proper translation may be "the tower of Eder" (e.g, NRSV, HCSB), which would imply that Eder was the name of a town known for this edifice. "Eder" *(ʿēder)* means "flock" or "herd" (e.g., 29:2). It was a popular name, designating a town at the far southern border of Judah's territory (Josh 15:21) and persons descended from Benjamin (1 Chr 8:15) and the Levite Mushi (1 Chr 23:23; 24:30). Because of the association of nearby Bethlehem with the messianic figure in Mic 5:1, *Tg. Mic* 4.8 and *Ps.-J.* at 35:21 identify Migdal Eder as the location for the appearance of the coming messiah.[591]

35:22a The prominence of the name "Israel" emphasizes the tribal implications of Reuben's crime against his father. Because of this insubordination, Reuben later received Jacob's condemnation (49:4), which had bearing on the future of his descendants (49:1). Although Genesis does not address Reuben's loss of birthright explicitly, the author of Chronicles explains the favored status of Joseph's sons, Ephraim and Manasseh, on this basis when referring to the transference of Reuben's privilege to Joseph, thus granting Joseph a double portion (48:5–20; 1 Chr 5:1–2; cf. Deut 21:15–17). The Chronicler's explanation for Reuben's loss is, however, derived from Genesis implicitly, which indicates that Reuben suffered Jacob's disfavor (49:3–4).[592] Luther observed the disso-

---

[591] Maher, *Targum Pseudo-Jonathan,* 121 n. 21.

[592] Transferal of the firstborn's blessing does not mean the recipient necessarily succeeds in his father's position; Gen 35:23 and 1 Chr 5:1–2 continue to refer to Reuben as the "firstborn" (also Num 1:20; 26:5; *Gen. Rab.* 82.11); this is possible because of the fluid use of the term "firstborn" (בְּכוֹר), which may refer to biological order and/or to a person's status in the father's eyes (e.g., Isaac and Joseph were not their father's biological firstborn, but they were the firstborn of the father's favored wife). Cf. N. Rubin, "The Social Significance of the Firstborn in Israel," *Beit Mikra* 33 (1987): 155–70 (Hb.) and G. Brin, "The Story of the Birthright of Jacob's Sons," *Tarbiz* 48 (1978): 1–8 (Hb.); Greenspahn (for more on the Genesis and Chronicles perspectives see comments on 48:5–22) contends unnecessarily that Genesis and Chronicles provide two competing explanations for the ascendancy of Joseph's sons (Ephraim and Manasseh), arguing that Genesis attributes their rise to Jacob's adoption (48:5–10) and Chronicles to Reuben's sin (*When Brothers Dwell Together,* 121–22). But the two viewpoints of the incidents are not irreconcilable; Genesis implies what the Chronicler later makes explicit, when we remember that the blessing for Joseph's sons by Jacob in 48:5–22 is followed by the critique of Reuben in 49:2–3. Moreover, the Chronicler's later perspective focuses on the historical realities of the prominence of Ephraim and Manasseh, which he notes was superseded by Judah, who never received the favor of firstborn in any sense.

nance between Reuben's and God's regard for Jacob; the firstborn's shaming of his father followed on the divine bestowal of the honored name "Israel."[593] The affront to Jacob/Israel was an affront to the God, who had favored Jacob. Geography continues its importance in the narrative; "that region" is the setting for this historic perversion of Israel's family. The identification of Bilhah as "his father's concubine" is central to understanding the nature of Reuben's transgression.[594] Earlier Bilhah was always identified in terms of her relation to Rachel as her "(maid)servant" (*šipḥâ*, 29:29; 30:3,4,7), but here the narrative mentions only Bilhah's relationship to Jacob. Levitical law reflected the customary boundaries established for proper sexual relations. The principle was the forbiddance of sexual relations with a "close relative" (Lev 18:6); this restriction included relations with a father's wife (Lev 18:8), which required the death penalty for the offenders (Lev 20:11). Also the text does not explain Reuben's motive. We surmise that it was a grasp for power, a symbolic action indicating his claim to his father's place. That this was a customary gesture of royal usurpation is attested in Israel's history (e.g., 2 Sam 12:8,11; 16:21–22 with 20:3; 1 Kgs 2:22; 20:3–7). Since Bilhah was the maidservant of Rachel (v. 25; 30:3–8), the favorite wife of Jacob, his affront was a pointed claim to Jacob's place. Moreover, retaliation in behalf of his mother Leah, the rejected wife, may have emboldened him to humble Bilhah.[595] Reuben's acquisition of the mandrakes for his mother Leah factored in the early struggle between the wives Leah and Rachel for ascendancy over the household (30:14–16). Although Bilhah was not Leah's sister, sexual relations with the one who played a surrogate role for Rachel may have implied another offense. The prohibition against sleeping with your mother's sister (Lev 18:13,18) stands out in the case of Jacob since he married sisters. That Jacob's marital polygamy impacted his sons may have extended beyond their characteristic sibling rivalry to the adoption of relaxed sexual boundaries. When we consider Jacob's apparent indifference toward the circumstances of Dinah's humiliation, one outcome might have been the unintended reinforcement of his children's libertine attitudes. That the author remarks that Jacob only "heard" of the crime and did not condemn it shows that

---

[593] Luther, *LW* 6.277.

[594] וַיִּשְׁכַּב ("he lay [with Bilhah]") is a common idiom for sexual intercourse (e.g., 30:16); *T. Reub.* 3.11–15 and *Jub.* 33.2 interpret 49:4 ("turbulent as the waters") as Reuben observing Bilhah bathing (cp. David/Bathsheba, 2 Sam 11:2), which precipitated his sin (see J. Kugel, "Reuben's Sin with Bilhah in the *Testament of Reuben*," in *Pomegranates and Golden Bells: Studies in Biblical, Jewish, and Near Eastern Ritual, Law, and Literature in Honor of Jacob Milgrom* (Winona Lake: Eisenbrauns, 1995), 525–54.

[595] G. Nicol remarks that Reuben's incest meant not only reversal of favor for him but also reversed Jacob's fortunes, who had rejected his mother, Leah (29:31–32); by the death of Rachel and the defilement of Bilhah, Rachel's servant, Jacob faced life without love ("Genesis xxix.32 and xxxv.22a: Reuben's Reversal," *JTS* 31 [1980]: 536–39).

the old man's authority had dwindled.[596] Further, Reuben may well have concluded that his brothers Simeon and Levi had strengthened their position in the household when they opposed their father.

APPENDIX: FAMILY LINE AND DEATH OF ISAAC (35:22b–29). **35:22b–26a** The listing of Jacob's twelve sons at this point in the narrative fits the context of the conclusion. The new focus will be on the sons' rivalry in the Joseph narrative. Listing the sons by their mother provides the background for the rivalry between the Rachel children, Joseph and Benjamin, and the other children, especially those born to Leah. Special recognition of Reuben as the firstborn corresponds with the narrative interest in the Bilhah incident just recorded. This privileged position was compromised, raising the question of who among the brothers will succeed Jacob. The list of twelve descendants also comes appropriately here since we have just learned that from Jacob will arise "kings" from his loins (v. 11). This contributes also to the issue of succession. Which of these sons will produce the royal seed that will realize the patriarchal promises?

Further, the mention of the sons of Jacob here demonstrates the faithfulness of God, who assured Jacob that he would produce numerous offspring (28:14; 32:12). That Jacob and his descendants reside in Canaan corresponds to the promise of land (28:13; 35:12). The number "twelve" indicates the national implications of Jacob's descendants correlating with the "twelve tribes of Israel" (49:28). The offspring of Jacob compares with the *tōlĕdōt* of Esau that follows, listing his descendants and providing the genealogy of Edomite kings and chiefs (36:31). The list of Jacob's sons, however, does not compare so favorably. The realization of the promises remains for future generations to claim for their fulfillment. The orientation of the text is toward the future and the necessity of continued faith by his offspring as they look to God's sustaining grace to make the promises a reality. There is not yet a nation, and the land remains under the control of the Canaanites. The sons' lack of integrity is troubling, and the prospects are uncertain. The narrative creates this tension that comes to a head when the brothers risk selling off one of their own (Joseph).

35:26b "Who were born to him in Paddan Aram" is not meant to be exact, since Benjamin obviously in this narrative was born in Canaan. That the sons were born outside the land and yet their futures were destined for life in the land would speak encouragingly to their descendants who were born outside the land too. The Mosaic audience had not known the land, but they could take heart that the land was theirs and awaited their arrival.

35:27 The importance of this reunion, though stated briefly, trumpets the completion of God's promise to bring Jacob back to his father's house

---

[596] The LXX has the comment, καὶ πονηρὸν ἐφάνη ἐναντίον αὐτοῦ, "and the thing appeared evil before him," completing the patriarch's reaction (Wevers, *Notes on the Greek Text*, 586); moreover, the addition equates the patriarch's reaction to a divine repudiation (cf. 38:7,10; 1 Chr 2:3; 21:7).

(28:15,21). The identification of the meeting site significantly associates Jacob with his ancestors, Abraham and Isaac, who also "had stayed" *(gûr)* at Hebron (Mamre; e.g., 13:18), though Isaac's residence had been at Beersheba when Jacob departed (e.g., 26:23; 28:10). The Hebrew word *gûr* typically describes the residence of the patriarchs as aliens (e.g., 12:10; 15:13; 20:1; 21:23,34; 23:4; 26:3). That the Hebrew includes the adverb "there" *(šām)* intensifies the moment of the event, since the family sepulcher was at Mamre (23:2,19; 25:9), the center of the family's heritage and claim on the land. That Isaac had moved to Hebron was anticipatory of his death to follow.

35:28–29 The description of Isaac's obituary consists of formulaic expressions. (On these stock expressions of the obituary, see comments on 25:7–8.) That he was buried in the family's tomb at Machpelah is assumed here and confirmed in 49:31. The mention of Isaac's death functions topically, closing out the Isaac *tôlĕdōt* section. Chronologically, Isaac lived twelve years beyond the sale of Joseph,[597] meaning that Isaac witnessed the pain Jacob experienced at the loss of his son. Isaac's 180 years exceeded Abraham by five years (25:7) and far more than his son Jacob (47:8). Although Isaac's place in the trilogy of patriarchs did not garner the same level of interest, he was essential to the survival of the family and the perpetuation of the promises: "It is through Isaac that your [Abraham's] offspring will be reckoned" (21:12; Rom 9:7; Heb 11:18; cp. Amos 7:9,16). His name was forever enshrined with his God, "the God of Abraham, the God of Isaac, and the God of Jacob" (e.g., Exod 3:15; Acts 3:13; cf. 50:24).

That the death notice echoed the obituary of Abraham is one of many efforts by the author to connect Jacob to Abraham and Isaac. Jacob and Esau conducted the funeral service (v. 29) as did Isaac and Ishmael for their father Abraham (25:9). The picture of serenity between the brothers contrasts with the power struggle among Jacob's sons that is the centerpiece of the Joseph narrative. At the death of the patriarch Isaac, Jacob takes his father's role in Canaan (37:1) according to Isaac's blessing and the promise made by God. The transition is complete, and the future stretches forward before the fractious sons of Jacob. Only the gracious purposes of God will ensure the survival of the family during this most perilous time (45:5–7; 50:19–20).

---

[597] The calculation is made by Rashi; see also Sarna, *Genesis,* 364, 368. Jacob was 120 years old when Isaac died (25:26; 35:28); since Jacob was 108 years old (41:46; 45:6,11; 47:9 show that Jacob was 91 [130 yrs. minus 39 yrs.] at Joseph's birth) when Joseph was sold at seventeen years old (37:2), the sale of Joseph was twelve years before Isaac's death (120 yrs. minus 108 yrs. = 12 yrs.). Rashi presents an alternative explanation for the age 108 years: Joseph was ruler at thirty years old (41:46), and Jacob arrived in Egypt nine years later (7 yrs. plenty [41:47] plus 2 yrs. famine [45:6,11]) at 130 years old (47:9; thus, Joseph was 39 yrs.); since Joseph was sold at seventeen years old, there was a twenty-two year period difference (39 yrs. minus 17 yrs. = 22 yrs.), meaning that Jacob was 108 years (130 yrs minus 22 yrs. = 108 yrs.) when Joseph was sold.

X. ESAU'S FAMILY (36:1–8)

"Do you have only one blessing, my father? Bless me too, my father!" (27:38). Although the blessing Esau received from his father was a dubious distinction (27:39–40), the narrative of Jacob-Esau shows that Esau prospered despite living outside the promised Canaan (33:9). The two *tōlĕdōt* sections (36:1–8; 36:9–37:1) affirm that Esau's lineage prospers, becoming a notable nation in its new homeland of Seir. We have already observed at the Ishmael section (25:12–18) that the inclusion of the genealogical records of the less-favored sons broadcasts weighty theological meaning. The birth oracle given to Rebekah and the blessing bestowed by Isaac indicate that Esau would be the progenitor of a great people, although subservient to his twin's descendants (25:23; 27:39–40; cf. Heb 11:20). The Esau *tōlĕdōt* sections show that the expectations of an Edomite nation were met. God had promised that Ishmael would produce a "great nation" (17:20; cf. 21:13,18). Genesis does not offer the same explicit promise to Esau, but the inclusion of his descendants and their ascendancy as rulers (36:9–43) imply that Edom's rise was also the consequence of God's blessing. That Esau dwelt securely in Seir (32:3[4]) implied that the Lord would establish his descendants in the land (36:30–31). The upsurge of the Edomites above the Israelites is indicated by the admission that kings "reigned in Edom before any Israelite king reigned" (26:31). What Genesis only implied, later history made explicit (e.g., Deut 2:5,12,22; Josh 24:4; Judg 5:4). God's blessing then reached outside the line of Jacob, for the promises made to their ancestor Abraham included the making of "many nations" (17:4–5). As in the case of the Table of Nations (10:1–32), the proliferation of Edomite tribes typified God's intention to bring salvation to the nations also (e.g., 12:3; 26:4; 28:14).

631

Another purpose for inclusion of the Esau family history was to emphasize the connections with but also the differences between Esau/Edom and Jacob/Israel.[1] The Edomites were of the same mother (Rebekah) as the Israelites, whereas Ishmael descended from Sarah's maid, Hagar. Among the foreign nations, the Edomites had a special relationship with Israel by virtue of their close blood ties and shared history. They were not in the patriarchal line of inheritance, but they were a collateral line, closer than their Ammonite and Moabite relatives (19:30–38). Concessions to the Edomites in Deuteronomic law reflected this linkage: "Do not abhor an Edomite, for he is your brother" (Deut 23:7). Whereas the third generation of the Edomite may enter the assembly, the Ammonites and Moabites were restricted to the tenth generation (Deut 23:3,8). Especially important was Israel's association of Yahweh's theophany with Edom's territory, including Seir, Paran, and Teman (Deut 33:2; Judg 5:4; Hab 3:3; cf. Sinai/Horeb, Judg 5:5; Ps 68:8[9],17[18]; Neh 9:13; Exod 19:20; 1 Kgs 19). What these sites and Sinai have in common is their southern region, and it is reasonable that at these wilderness sites in addition to Sinai the worship of Yahweh also occurred (cf. Jethro, the Midianite priest [Exod 3:1; 18:1]). Moreover, Edomite clans (Gen 36:9–43) show connections with Abraham (25:2,4) and Judah (see comments on 36:9–37:1 for details).[2] That the Israelites encountered the Edomites in their trek to Canaan and that Judah lay close to Edomite country made their history and geography singularly significant for Israel.

Structurally, the two Esau sections serve an important purpose in the scheme of the patriarchal narratives. The two sections of 36:1–8 and 36:9–37:1 are each introduced by the customary *tōlĕdōt* heading that marks a new section in Genesis (vol. 1A, pp. 35–41). That there are two *tōlĕdōt* headings for Esau makes his treatment in two consecutive sections exceptional in the book. The first section focuses on family and homeland, and the second centers on his offspring as a developing nation. These two sections are flanked by the major narrative *tōlĕdōt* sections of Isaac (25:19–35:29) and Jacob (37:2–50:26). The same sequential pattern in which the genealogical section of the less-favored son precedes the favored descendant appears for Ishmael and Esau (vol. 1A, pp. 28–29). Another feature shared by the *tōlĕdōt* sections of the rejected sons, Ishmael (25:12) and Esau, is that the content of each sec-

---

[1] J. Bartlett, *Edom and the Edomites,* JSOTSup 77 (Sheffield: Sheffield Academic Press, 1999), 86.

[2] See L. Axelsson, *The Lord Rose Up from Seir: Studies in the History and Traditions in the Negev and Southern Judah,* ConBOT 25, trans. F. Cryer (Lund: Almquist & Wiksell International, 1987), 56–59; but he draws a questionable conclusion when he proposes that in the southern regions both east and west of the Arabah (i.e., southern Negev and Edom) *Yahweh* was widely worshiped in pre-Israelite times and that these peoples brought their "mountain of god" traditions when assimilated into Israel's national history.

tion consists chiefly of genealogies and lists. The *tōlĕdōt* headings of the favored sons, Isaac and Jacob, introduce extensive narrative blocks that pertain chiefly to their descendants.

COMPOSITION. The various titles that appear in chap. 36 indicate that the content of the chapter involves the accumulation of diverse and distinct sources (cf. "Structure" below). Since the two Esau *tōlĕdōt* sections (36:1–8; 36:9–37:1) show interdependence and are usually discussed together, we will address both here. Source critics attributed the compilation of chap. 36 to the Priestly writer (P), although acknowledging that the majority of its contents had older origins. Gunkel, for example, assigned only vv. 1–5,6–8,40–43 to P per se and vv. 9–14,15–19,20–28,29–30 to an older hand. The list of Edomite kings in vv. 31–39 he assigned to yet another source.[3] It is somewhat embarrassing to source critics that the wives of Esau named in vv. 1–5 do not correspond in name or ethnicity to the wives already named by P in 26:34; 28:9. Thus P as an author must shrink in their eyes and become a compiler who does not care to modify his older sources.[4] Coats also identifies P (or a supplement to P) as the source of vv. 1–30, which relied on earlier traditions but which cannot be safely reconstructed; P himself produced vv. 40–43 to close out the compilation. The Edomite king list in vv. 31–39 is an independent unit, foreign to its present literary environment, which P added on the basis of the theme of the land of Edom.[5] Westermann agrees that P composed vv. 1–5, joining it to the end of the Esau account in vv. 6–8. The remainder of the chapter (vv. 9–43) was "an already existing unity from the royal archives" that P or a later redactor had extracted, making the task of separating out the underlying sources impossible.[6] R. Syrén interprets the wives' names of vv. 1–5, which differ from the narratives (26:34; 28:6), as a "secondary harmonization" with the names of vv. 9–14.[7] Bartlett believes that the lists of Esau's descendants in vv. 9–14 and Seir's descendants in vv. 20–28 are likely the earlier lists on which depend the others (except the king list [vv. 31–39], which is unrelated). He goes further than the data permit when he concludes that Esau was originally closer to the lineage of Seir than to Edom; for Bartlett the identification of Esau as the ancestor of Edom is a secondary assertion. He argues on the slim basis of two names shared in the Esau list in vv. 9–14 and the Seir list in vv. 20–28—Timna (vv. 12,22) and Oholibama (vv. 14,25). He also assumes that the editor confused the name "Anah," son of Seir, in vv. 20,25 and "Anah," the son of Zibeon, who discovered desert springs in v. 24. The editor erred in v. 14

---

[3] H. Gunkel, *Genesis*, trans. M. Biddle (Macon: Mercer University Press, 1997 [1910 third German ed.]), 375.

[4] E.g., E. A. Speiser, *Genesis: A New Translation with Introduction and Commentary,* AB (Garden City: Doubleday, 1964), 281.

[5] G. W. Coats, *Genesis with an Introduction to Narrative Literature,* FOTL (Grand Rapids: Eerdmans, 1983), 246–57.

[6] C. Westermann, *Genesis 12–36: A Commentary,* trans. J. Scullion (Minneapolis: Augsburg, 1985[1981]), 561.

[7] R. Syrén, *The Forsaken First-Born: A Study of a Recurrent Motif in the Patriarchal Narratives,* JSOTSup 133 (Sheffield: Sheffield Academic Press, 1993), 128.

when he named Oholibamah the daughter of Anah, the daughter of Zibeon.[8]

Yet, that the two lists include duplication of "sons" and "chiefs" only shows that the author uses the lists to demonstrate that the offspring of Esau and Seir developed into significant tribes. This parallels the experience of Jacob's sons, whose descendants form prosperous tribes. Also, that there is some repetition of names across generations is not a compelling reason to attribute the replication to a redactor's mistake since different persons in a shared lineage may bear the same appellation. Pertaining to the question of the wives' names and heritage, we prefer another explanation for the differences that does not require a speculative, complex process of editorial failures at adjusting contradictory sources (see comments on 26:34). Finally, there is growing recognition that vv. 9–43 show a logical scheme of presentation (see "Structure" below), implying that they are an indivisible unit. That v. 43 forms a natural inclusion with v. 1 indicates that the entire content was before the author when he designed the whole. The contrasting verse in 37:1 does more than contrast with v. 43 or v. 8; it provides a fitting contrast and end to the subject of the full chapter. The author penned the final verse to bridge the present passage to the following account of Jacob's descendants (37:2–50:24).

Generally, scholars doubt the historical value of the lists pertaining to Esau, except the catalogue of Edom's kings (vv. 31–39), which is often accepted as a reliable ancient source, perhaps derived from official Edomite records that had been relocated in Israel's palace archives.[9] Typically, earlier analyses found the historical setting for the compilation of Edomite kings and chiefdoms (territories) was the Davidic era when he subjugated Edom (2 Sam 8:13–14). Bartlett reflects a trend among scholars, however, that contends the earliest possible date of the core list was the eighth century. The archaeological record testifies that Edomite settlements did not prosper until the late eighth to sixth centuries.[10] The centralization of Edomite rule, furthermore, did not occur until the ninth century at the earliest, and "Bozrah" (modern Buceira) in the list was not an important urban center before the eighth century (v. 33; cf. Amos 1:12). Archaeological recoveries at Bozrah show an occupation period from the eighth to fifth centuries.[11]

Despite these indicators, there are reasons for understanding the list as premonarchic in origin, which was perhaps later updated (e.g., v. 31). That the list indicates that Edomite rule was not dynastic and that the succession of kings was evidently regional in character reminds us of the period of the Israelite judges.

---

[8] Bartlett, *Edom and the Edomites,* 86–87.

[9] E. A. Knauf, however, interprets the list of kings as originally of Aramean kings, not Edomites ("Genesis 36,1–43," in *Jacob: un Commentaire à plusieurs voix de Genèse 25–36: Mélanges offerts à Albert de Pury,* Le Monde de la Bible 44 [Geneva: Labor & Fides, 2001], 291–300).

[10] P. Bienkowski, "The Edomites: The Archaeological Evidence from Transjordan," in *You Shall Not Abhor an Edomite for He Is Your Brother: Edom and Seir in History and Tradition,* Archaeology and Biblical Studies 3 (Atlanta: Scholars Press, 1995), 41–92.

[11] E. A. Knauf finds the coexistence of Canaanite and Arabic names in the king list reflects the late Persian period, certainly no earlier than the end of the sixth century ("Alter und Herkunft der edomitischen Königsliste Gen 36:31–39," *ZAW* 97 [1985]: 245–53).

Moreover, the term "king" *(melek)* does not require a settled, centralized monarchy. Sarna observes that tribal "kings" in the ancient Near East ruled over limited regions and were not necessarily rulers of centralized city-states (e.g., the Assyrian King List names "17 kings living in tents"[12]; cf. "tents of Edom," Ps 83:6[7]). K. A. Kitchen adds that nonurban kings *(sheikhs)* ruled alongside sedentary kings in Babylonia in the early second millennium.[13] Biblical evidence also shows that "kings" were tribal chiefs (cf. Num 31:8, "kings" *[mĕlākîm]* with Josh 13:21, "chiefs" *[nĕśîʾîm]*).[14] First Kings 22:47 reflects this situation during the time of Jehoshaphat: "There was no king in Edom; a deputy was king" (NRSV). The point appears to be that Edom had no centralized monarchic dynasty (contrast David), but it did have a "king" in the sense of a local ruler (cp. 2 Kgs 8:20). The mention of "chiefs" *(ʾallûpîm)* and their territories (36:30) may reinforce this picture in vv. 31–39. Reference to "kings," therefore, does not require a developed urban culture with a centralized bureaucracy.

The special interest in Edomite history would have been as relevant to the wilderness and settlement periods as to the later monarchy and afterward. It was during the wilderness sojourn that Israel first had its contact with the Edomites (e.g., Exod 15:15; Num 20:14, "king of Edom"; 24:18) and it was during this era that the law established Israel's cultic practices pertaining to its neighbors such as the Edomites (Deut 23:7). The territorial holdings of the region were also important in the drawing up of the boundaries of Judah, making the Edomite history especially significant to the southern tribe during the settlement period (e.g., Num 34:3; Josh 15:1). That a gloss occurs in v. 31 from the monarchic period and that the list may have undergone some updating is reasonable, without requiring a late date for the substance of the list and its inclusion in Genesis.

STRUCTURE. The distinctive units that make up the two *tōlĕdōt* sections of Esau are marked by recurring superscriptions and colophons: "sons of" *(bĕnê),* "chiefs of" *(ʾallûpê),* and "kings" *(mĕlākîm).*[15]

36:1–8 "the account of *(tōlĕdōt)* Esau (that is, Edom)" (v. 1)
   vv. 2–5 "These were the sons of *(bĕnê)* Esau" (v. 5)
   vv. 6–8 "Esau (that is, Edom) settled in the hill country of Seir" (v. 8)

The boundaries of the present *tōlĕdōt* section begin and end with the verbatim phrase, "Esau is Edom" (vv. 1,8).[16] Sandwiched between are two units: (1) Esau's genealogy of five sons born by three wives (vv. 2–5) and (2) the description of the family's move to Seir (vv. 6–8). Each unit begins similarly:

---

[12] *ANET* 564.

[13] K. A. Kitchen, *On the Reliability of the Old Testament* (Grand Rapids: Eerdmans, 2003), 196–97.

[14] N. Sarna, בראשית *Genesis,* JPS Torah Commentary (Philadelphia: Jewish Publication Society, 1989), 409.

[15] For the specifics of the second *tōlĕdōt* structure, see comments on 36:9–37:1.

[16] The NIV (HCSB) inadvertently obscures the word order in v. 8, rendering the phrase first in the sentence instead of at the end (cf. ESV, NRSV, NASB).

Esau "took" *(lāqaḥ)* his wives from the women of Canaan" (v. 2), and he "took" *(lāqaḥ)* his wives and family to Seir (v. 6). Each unit also concludes with a reference to the residency of Esau: "(Sons) who were born to him in Canaan" (v. 5) and "settled in the hill country of Seir" (v. 8). The passage focuses on the migration of Esau from his indigenous home in Canaan to Seir, outside of Canaan. This geographical motif provides the contrast with Jacob and the favored line whose residence was in the promised land of Canaan. What is implied here is specifically stated in vv. 42–43. Especially important is the explanation for Esau's departure, stated twice in v. 7, echoing the language that described the separation of Abraham and Lot (13:6). The brothers enjoyed fruitful and peaceful relations, not the rancorous attitude that dominated their descendants.

The genealogy is built on the naming of the three wives of Esau.

Adah	Basemath	Oholibamah
↓	↓	↓
Eliphaz	Ruel	Jeush, Jalam, Korah

The genealogical form is a modified version of the segmented (branched) type (e.g., 10:1–32), providing a brief family history; the history gives the names of Esau's three wives and includes the genealogy of their five sons (contrast the linear form of genealogy in 5:1–32 and 11:10–26). The nature of ancient gene-alogies often involved more than biological descent; the family relationships described may reflect social and commercial dependencies between tribes (see vol. 1A, pp. 434, 438). This feature, however, does not necessarily mean that actual ancestral connections between the tribes did not exist. Although the names of women appear at times in patrilineal genealogies in Genesis (e.g., 4:19), the three wives of Esau are prominent in the identification of his descen-dants. The sons born to Esau are named according to their mothers. This gene-alogical feature also occurs in the listing of Jacob's sons in 35:23–26. What distinguishes the two lists is the identification of the women's ethnicity in Esau's case. Their foreign status recalls the disapproval Rebekah showed for Esau's intermarriage and which prompted the exile of Jacob (27:46–28:9). On the correlation of the genealogical information and the narrative reports of Esau's marriages (26:34; 28:9), see the explanation at 26:34.

Excursus: Edom and the Edomites

The ancestor of the Edomites was Esau, whose sons and grandsons became major clan chieftains (36:1–19).[17] The Edomites displaced the Horites (Deut 2:22) and established regional chiefdoms (36:31–43). Seir was the ancestor of Horite chiefs (36:20–30) whose name also specified the territory of their settle-

---

[17] For a helpful survey see K. Hoglund, "Edomites," in *Peoples of the Old Testament World* (Grand Rapids: Baker, 1994), 335–47.

ments. The attitude of Israel toward the Edomites compared to other rivals, such as the Ammonites and Moabites, was less adversarial. This was because the Edomites were close relatives, counted as "brothers" by the Israelites (e.g., Num 20:14). For this reason Deuteronomy made concessions for the Edomites who lived among the Israelites (Deut 2:4–5; 23:7–8; contrast 23:3). The reconciliation of Esau and Jacob (Gen 33) depicted the possibility of a peaceful coexistence between the neighboring peoples. Probably during the early period of Edom-Judah relations, the tensions were not as acerbic as the monarchic period, especially in the eighth–sixth centuries when Edom prospered and Judah declined, in which Edom played a major role, resulting in the Edomites becoming the hated symbol of Gentile oppression (e.g., Ps 137:7; *Sir* 50:25–26).[18] Israel during the wilderness sojourn already knew an entrenched, recalcitrant Edom, but the Lord affirmed by Balaam's vision that Jacob's future ruler would subjugate their kinsmen (Num 24:17–19). The psalmist in the same spirit prevailed upon the Lord to defeat the nations, including Edom and Ishmael, who had conspired against his people (Pss 83:3–6[4–7]; 137:7; cf. Ps 2:1–3). During the monarchy the Edomites succumbed to the army of David (2 Sam 8:13–14; 1 Kgs 11:15–16; cf. 1 Sam 14:47–48) and struggled to free itself from Hebrew rule with varying degrees of success (e.g., 1 Kgs 11:14; 2 Kgs 8:20–22; 14:7). The consolidation of the Edomite tribes into a centralized state occurred most likely in the ninth century, which it maintained during the subsequent two centuries under Assyrian hegemony. The prophets especially condemned the Edomites for their crimes against their neighbor and kinsman, Judah. The eighth-century prophet Amos condemned Edom's merciless treatment of Judah (1:11–12; cf. Isa 34:5–15), and Obadiah especially castigated its participation in and gloating over the demise of Judah at its fall (vv. 10–14; cf. Jer 49:7–22; Ezek 25:12–14; Lam 4:21–22).

Although Edom was subject to the Assyrian and Babylonian incursions, the nation not only survived but actually prospered for a season, taking advantage of Judah's decline by establishing Edomite settlements west of the Arabah in Judah's southern territory. This high tide for Edom came to a crashing end during Nabonidus's western campaign when Babylonia probably made it an imperial province (553 B.C.).[19] Some archaeological evidence suggests that Edomite holdings in Judah continued, however, under Babylonian and Persian rule, resulting by the mid-fourth century in the new regional identity, Idumea. The Jewish resurgency under the Hasmonean kings enabled the Jews to exact some revenge, compelling the Idumeans to convert to Jewish religion by John Hyrcanus (134–04 B.C.). But, ironically, the Idumeans can be said to have struck back with the rise of the hated Herod the Great, Rome's appointed king of the Jews, who himself

---

[18] N. Lapp, "'Who Is This That Comes from Edom?'" in *Scripture and Other Artifacts: Essays on the Bible and Archaeology in Honor of Philip J. King* (Louisville: Westminster John Knox, 1994), 216–29.

[19] P. Bienkowski, "New Evidence on Edom in the New-Babylonian and Persian Periods," in *The Land That I Will Show You: Essays on the History and Archaeology of the Ancient Near East in Honour of J. Maxwell Miller,* JSOTSup 343 (Sheffield: Sheffield Academic Press, 2001), 198–213.

was an Idumean (Matt 2:1–18; Luke 1:5). Meanwhile, the Nabateans saturated the former Edomite center to the east, establishing the city of Petra as its trading capital. Precisely what the relationship between the indigenous Edomite population and the migrating Nabateans was remains uncertain. History confirms that the prophetic anticipation of Edom's demise effectually took place. Although Amos's oracle probably was the first to condemn the Edomites, he was also the first prophet to predict explicitly the creation of redeemed Edomites who would submit to the Lord's revived reign of David (9:11–12). By God's grace expressed through Israel's blessing, Edom and the nations would some day "bear [the LORD's] name" (Amos 9:12; cf. Isa 43:7; Mal 1:11,14). Visitors from Idumea were among those who heard Jesus' preaching (Mark 3:8). Ultimately, this glorious transformation of Israel's historic enemy was realized spiritually through the conversion and incorporation of the Gentiles into the Christian church (Acts 15:15–18/Amos 9:11–12).

What we know about the Edomites outside of the Bible is minimal. Scarce epigraphic and archaeological remains are testimony to Ezekiel's prediction: "You will be desolate, O Mount Seir, you and all of Edom. Then they will know that I am the LORD." Our knowledge of Edom's geographical boundaries and its history, culture, and religion has substantial gaps. One of the major hindrances to our knowledge is scholarly indecisiveness regarding what exactly constitutes Edomite material culture, that is, what is "Edomite"?[20] Also the name "Edom" was variously applied, ethnographically, topographically, and to the political state.[21] Another hindrance is the unwarranted skepticism that scholars often have toward the usefulness of the biblical texts, especially the nonprophetic texts.[22] The nonprophetic texts are dated late in accord with the standard conclusions of historical-critical reconstruction, anywhere from the divided monarchy period to the exilic/postexilic periods. E. A. Knauf-Belleri remarks: "The dating of biblical references to Edom remains as controversial as anything in biblical studies. Suffice it to note that in the opinion of the present writer, hardly any OT reference to Edom predates the 7th century."[23] The archaeological record especially produces suspicion, since settlement and material evidence does not show substantial population in Edom (modern south Jordan) before the ninth century. Thus, that there were Edomite "kings," according to Genesis, and a significant Edomite army, according to Num 20:20, in premonarchic times appears untenable. Egyptian literary texts, however, suggest otherwise. According to texts from the thirteenth and twelfth centuries, the inhabitants of the southern transjordan area, known as

---

[20] P. Bienkowski and L. Sedman, "Busayra and Judah: Stylistic Parallels in the Material Culture," in *Studies in the Archaeology of the Iron Age in Israel and Jordan* (Sheffield: Sheffield Academic Press, 2001), 310–22.

[21] D. Edelman, "Edom: A Historical Geography," in *You Shall Not Abhor an Edomite for He Is Your Brother*, 1–11.

[22] E.g., B. MacDonald, "Early Edom: The Relations between the Literary and Archaeological Evidence," in *Scripture and Other Artifacts*, 230–46.

[23] E. A. Knauf-Belleri, "Edom: The Social and Economic History," in *You Shall Not Abhor an Edomite for He Is Your Brother*, 94.

the *Shōsu* (or *Shasu*) people, were sufficiently numerous to have gained Egyptian notice and subjugation. That there were temporary settlements in the EB and LB into the Iron I periods in the transjordan areas of Edom, Moab, and Gilead has been shown by archaeological remains.[24] Moreover, the nonsedentary lifestyle the inhabitants practiced would leave fewer remains compared to the settled towns and fortifications that archaeology relies on. As for the presence of "kings" *(mĕlākîm)* in Edom's early period (e.g., Gen 36:31; Num 20:14; Judg 11:17), we commented earlier that the term may well refer to regional tribal chieftains (*'allûpîm,* Exod 15:15), comparable to the Hebrew judges in premonarchic Canaan, as opposed to a unified political state that "king" typically indicates to modern readers.

Distinctive boundaries determined Edom's tableland (five thousand ft.), the heart of its original homeland.[25] To the north was the Brook Zered (Wadi el-Ḥasā), forming a border with Moab (Num 21:12; Deut 2:13–14), and to the west was the edge of the plateau overlooking the cavernous Wadi Arabah. The southern border is less clear, perhaps to Ras en-Naqb, and the eastern border was the desert fringe. Judah's position viewed Edom from the west, where they encountered the precipitous cliffs that rose dramatically from the Arabah, leading the Hebrew prophets to depict the Edomites as nestled birds: " 'Though you build your nest as high as the eagle's, from there I will bring you down,' declares the LORD" (Jer 49:16; cf. Obad 4). The relationship of the terms "Edom" and "Seir" is not always clear, perhaps because Seir was at one time a distinctive region within Edom (e.g., Ezek 35:15) and became functionally a synonym. As a synecdoche "Seir" could represent the whole land (Josh 24:4; Ezek 25:8; 2 Chr 20:10), as "Zion" did for Jerusalem or Judah. According to Egyptian sources, the people inhabiting Seir and Edom were named the same, the *Shōsu*. The biblical authors equated "Seir" with the nation Edom (e.g., 32:3[4]; Num 24:18; Judg 5:4). Edom's elevation accounts for the toponym "Mount Seir" *(har śēʿîr,* e.g., Deut 1:2; Ezek 35:2; not to be confused with the "Mount Seir" in Judah, Josh 15:10). That Seir *(śēʿîr,* meaning "hairy") referred to the region west of the Arabah is only suggestive (cf. Num 20:16; Deut 1:2,44–45). There is a remarkable similarity in some names of the clans of Esau and the Horites in chap. 36 and clan names of southern Judah (see the discussion of the individual names below). The location of Edom held strategic value in the trade routes extending from Arabia and from the Red Sea. The King's Highway provided the primary north-south corridor (Num 20:17; 21:22), and perhaps another traveling east-west existed (from Kadesh into Edom, Num 33:41–49; cf. Amos 1:6). The "Arabah road" proceeded from Elath and Ezion Geber into Judah (Deut 2:8), providing a route for the export of the ore deposits well known in the Arabah locale (Deut 8:9).

---

[24] Kitchen, *Reliability of the Old Testament,* 198–99; J. M. Miller, "Central Moab," *OEANE* 1.447–48; and J. Bartlett, "Edom," *OEANE* 2.189–91.

[25] For more on the topography and regions of Edom, see Bartlett, *Edom and the Edomites,* 33–54.

As for the religion of the Edomites, our knowledge is very sparse. That the chief deity was named Qos has been proposed from Edomite personal names; the storm deity Hadad is also another attested Edomite appellative (e.g., 36:35,39; 1 Kgs 11:14), possibly suggesting the deity was honored in Edom. Bartlett rightly recognizes that the biblical writers are not as strident in their criticism of Edom as other peoples whose gods were viewed as a threat to Israel's survival. The prophets nevertheless employed vitriolic language, but not against Edom's religious practices, rather against its opposition to Judah (e.g., Isa 34:5–11; Jer 49:7–20). We should not conclude from this, however, that Israel was tolerant of Edom's polytheism. Judah was subject also to the enticement of "the gods of Edom" (2 Chr 25:20).

1. Title (36:1)

¹This is the account of Esau (that is, Edom).

36:1 The title to the section is the *tōlĕdōt* catchphrase that introduces each of the new sections in the book of Genesis (vol. 1A, pp. 35–41). The identification of Esau as "Edom" emphasizes his status as progenitor of the nation (cf. also vv. 8,19,43; 25:30). The literary boundaries of the subsequent section in vv. 8,43 express this connection specifically: ". . . Esau the father of the Edomites." The names Esau and Edom are a word pair in Obad 1:8. The original significance of "Edom" *(ʾĕdôm)* was Esau's trade of his birthright for Jacob's "red stew" *(ʾădôm;* see comments on 25:30).

2. Esau's Wives and Sons (36:2–5)

The genealogical unit consists of two parts, the identification of Esau's three wives (vv. 2–3) and his five sons (vv. 4–5). "Canaan" (v. 2), naming the locale of the women and the birthplace of their sons (v. 5), brackets the passage. This is the "Canaan phase" of Edomite ancestry when the Esau clan resided in the land before their move to Seir. Unlike the ensuing history of the nations Israel and Edom, the two peoples originally lived peacefully. The subsequent unit will explain that the move to Seir was voluntary (vv. 6–8).

(1) Esau's Wives (36:2–3)

²Esau took his wives from the women of Canaan: Adah daughter of Elon the Hittite, and Oholibamah daughter of Anah and granddaughter of Zibeon the Hivite— ³also Basemath daughter of Ishmael and sister of Nebaioth.

36:2 Reference to Esau's wives from among "the women of Canaan" translates the same Hebrew phrase in 28:1,6 that describes the disapproval Isaac had toward Esau's marriage to foreign women (cp. Dinah's visit, 34:1; also 38:2). The Canaanite derivation of Esau's wives contrasts with the favored line of Abraham's descendants who practiced endogamy, taking their wives from their Aramean kinsmen.

The name of the first wife listed, *Adah,* is also the name of Lamech's wife (4:19; vol. 1A, p. 286); it is a common name in the ancient Near East.[26] On the meaning of the name *Elon the Hittite,* the father-in-law of Esau, see comments on 26:34. The second wife listed is *Oholibamah,* which also names an Edomite chief (v. 41; 1 Chr 1:52). The Hebrew means "the tent of the high place" *('ŏhŏlî* + *bāmâ)*[27] but its etymology remains uncertain.[28] *Anah,* whose meaning is unclear, is Esau's father-in-law (vv. 2,14,18,24,25; 1 Chr 1:40), probably named after his uncle, a son of Seir the Horite (vv. 20,29; 1 Chr 1:38,41). *Zibeon* ("hyena"[?]; cf. *ṣābûaʿ,* Jer 12:9) is a "Horite" *(ḥōrî)* chief (vv. 20–21,29–30; cf. also 1 Chr 1:38,40), but here he is called a "Hivite" *(ḥiwwî,* v. 2). Also the LXX at 34:2 and Josh 9:7 reads "Chorrite" *(Xorraios)* instead of the MT's "Hivite."[29] The precise identity and relationship of the Hivites and Horites is problematic (see vol. 1A, pp. 456–57). The convenient but doubtful resolution to the identity of Zibeon is to prefer "Horite" at 36:2, attributing "Hivite" in v. 2 to a simple textual corruption.[30] More likely the term "Horite" was extended to different people groups, or the Israelites adopted the Egyptian practice of using the term generally for the region.[31] On the relationship of the Horites and Edom, see v. 20 below.

36:3 Esau's third wife is *Basemath* (on the name see comments on 26:34), whose derivation (Ishmaelite) is technically not Canaanite (v. 2), but her mother's foreign descent (whether Egyptian or otherwise) probably is in the author's mind. Ishmael may have taken Canaanite wives in addition to his Egyptian wife (21:21). By Basemath's marriage to Esau the descendants of the rejected sons intermarry. *Nebaioth* was the firstborn of Ishmael (see comments on 25:13; cf. 28:9; 1 Chr 1:29).

---

[26] U. Hübner, "Adah," *ABD* 1.60.

[27] Cf. personal names with the word "tent": "Ohel" (1 Chr 3:20) "Oholah/Oholibah" (Ezek 23); "Oholiab" (Exod 31:6; 35:34; 36:1,2; 38:23).

[28] U. Hübner, "Oholibamah," *ABD* 5.10; if *'ōhel* ("tent") is its etymology, Hübner suggests "my (god's) tent (i.e., protection) is with them" or "my tent (i.e., protection) is (divine name)"; alternatively, if the Arabic word *('hl)* for "people, clan," then possibly "people of a (certain) god."

[29] All other versions, however, at 34:2 and Josh 9:7 have the MT's "Hivite"; J. W. Wevers believes that the Greek variant at 34:2 is a simple misreading of the similar Hb. הֹחֹרִי ("Horite") for הַחִוִּי ("Hivite"; *Notes on the Greek Text of Genesis,* SBLSCS 35 [Atlanta: Scholars Press, 1993], 557).

[30] Also the MT has "daughter (בַּת) of Zibeon" (e.g., AV, ESV), but the ancient versions have "son (בֵּן) of Zibeon" in agreement with v. 24 (e.g., NJB, NRSV); yet the MT may mean "granddaughter," referring to Oholibamah (e.g., NIV, NAB ["Oholibamah, granddaughter through Anah of Zibeon"], NLT, HCSB, NASB).

[31] F. W. Bush, "Horites," *ISBE* 2.756–57.

(2) Esau's Five sons (36:4–5)

⁴**Adah bore Eliphaz to Esau, Basemath bore Reuel, ⁵and Oholibamah bore Jeush, Jalam and Korah. These were the sons of Esau, who were born to him in Canaan.**

36:4 *Eliphaz* (perhaps "my God/*El* is pure gold"[32]), the son of Esau who became an important tribal chief (vv. 10–12,15–16; 1 Chr 1:35–36), was also the name of Job's friend (2:11), who was from Teman (Edom, cf. Jer 49:7). In Esau's genealogy "Teman" is the son of Eliphaz (vv. 11,15). *Reuel* ("friend of God/*El*" or "God/*El* is friend"), who became a tribal chief (vv. 10,13,17; 1 Chr 1:35,37), was a common person's name, naming Moses' father-in-law (Exod 2:15; Num 10:29), a Gadite (= "Deuel," Num 1:14), and a Benjamite (1 Chr 9:8).

36:5 Oholibamah bore three sons. *Jeush* became an Edomite chief (vv. 5,14[33],18; 1 Chr 1:35). The name may be derived from *ʿûš*, "to lend aid, come to help" (Joel 3:11[4:11]), meaning "may he (God?) help/protect."[34] It occurs also for Benjaminites (1 Chr 7:10; 8:39), a Levite (1 Chr 23:10–11), and the sons of Rehoboam and Mahalath (2 Chr 11:19). *Jalam* also became a major chieftain (vv. 5,14,18; 1 Chr 1:35; the AV has "Jaalam"). The meaning of the name is unclear (cf. *yāʿēl*, "ibrex" or "mountain goat," Ps 104:18[35]). *Korah* (*q-r-ḥ*, "bald"?), like his brothers, became a tribal head (vv. 5,14,16,18; 1 Chr 1:35); the name also designates a grandson of Esau, one of the sons of Eliphaz (v. 16). Further occurrences of the name "Korah" appear for Hebron's son (1 Chr 2:43) and the infamous Levite who rebelled in the desert (Num 16–17; for the "Korahites," descended from Kohath, see e.g., Exod 6:18,21; 1 Chr 6:22[7],37; 26:1; 2 Chr 20:19).

3. Esau's Move to Seir (36:6–8)

The references to "Esau" in vv. 6 and 8 bracket the unit. The passage describes Esau's travel itinerary: he "took [v. 6a] . . . moved [v. 6b] . . . settled [v. 8]." Verse 7 provides the explanation for his departure from Canaan and thus from the company of his brother.

---

[32] U. Hübner suggests **pūz*, meaning "God/El is the victor" or "God/El is pure/shinning" ("Eliphaz," *ABD* 2.471,)

[33] Read the *qěrê* spelling *yěʿûš* in vv. 5,14.

[34] D. F. Roberts, "Jeush," *ISBE* 2.1056; E. A. Knauf observes the name in the Samaria Ostraca; he equates the name with *Yagut*, a deity in classical Arabic and a personal name in Safaitic and Palmyrene ("Jeush," *ABD* 3.882).

[35] Also cp. *yāʿēl* + *am;* or from **ʿlm*, "to be strong" (from עֶלֶם, "young man"? *HALOT* 2.421,835; U. Hübner, "Jalam," *ABD* 3.616).

(1) Esau's Possessions (36:6–7)

6Esau took his wives and sons and daughters and all the members of his household, as well as his livestock and all his other animals and all the goods he had acquired in Canaan, and moved to a land some distance from his brother Jacob. 7Their possessions were too great for them to remain together; the land where they were staying could not support them both because of their livestock.

36:6 The description of Esau's migration includes stereotypical language (e.g., Abraham, 12:5; Jacob, 46:6). The inclusion of all his possessions and family is equivalent to our proverbial saying, Esau moved "lock, stock, and barrel." The point is a permanent new residence, meaning that Esau will forever be associated with Seir. What distinguishes v. 6 and the parallel language is the separation from his brother Jacob. This heightens the importance of the move, leaving Jacob alone to inherit Canaan. That the Hebrew reads literally "from the face of *[mippĕnê]* Jacob his brother" creates a double entendre, recalling the siblings' struggles and reconciliation (e.g., 25:6; 33:10). Jacob was the one who initially fled "from *[mippĕnê]* his brother" (35:7). That Esau voluntarily abandons Canaan corresponds to his disregard for his birthright in his youth (25:31–34). There is no mention in Genesis of Esau's daughters by name. On *nepeš* as "people" see comments on 12:5; 14:21; cf. 2:7.

36:7 This verse provides the explanation for Esau's departure. It is an echo of the parting by Abram and Lot (13:6). Like Abram and Lot, the brothers parted on peaceful terms. More importantly, when Lot moved away, the Lord promised Abram that his descendants would receive the whole of the land (13:14–17), which finds its partial fulfillment by Jacob's renewed residence in Canaan and Esau's vacancy. It is also significant that the rejected son achieves great wealth, suggesting that like Ishmael and Abraham before them (17:20; 21:13), the Lord ensured that Esau too received blessing by virtue of his descent from Isaac (27:38–40). The word "great" *(rāb),* describing Esau's wealth, recalls his own exclamation, "I already have plenty *[rāb],* my brother!" (33:9).

(2) Esau's Residence (36:8)

8So Esau (that is, Edom) settled in the hill country of Seir.

"Settled" *(wayyēšeb)* is the same Hebrew depiction of Jacob's residence in Canaan (37:1), language typically describing someone's new permanent residence (e.g., 13:18; 19:20; 20:1; 26:6,17). The contrast with Jacob is reinforced by the same term "stay" *(māgôr,* "sojourning") in v. 7 and 37:1. "The hill country of Seir" describes the original Horite possession in 14:6; 36:20,21,30, whom the Edomites dispossessed (Deut 2:5,12,22; Josh 24:4). On the wordplay of "Seir," see comments on 25:25; 32:3, and cf. v. 1 above for "Edom."

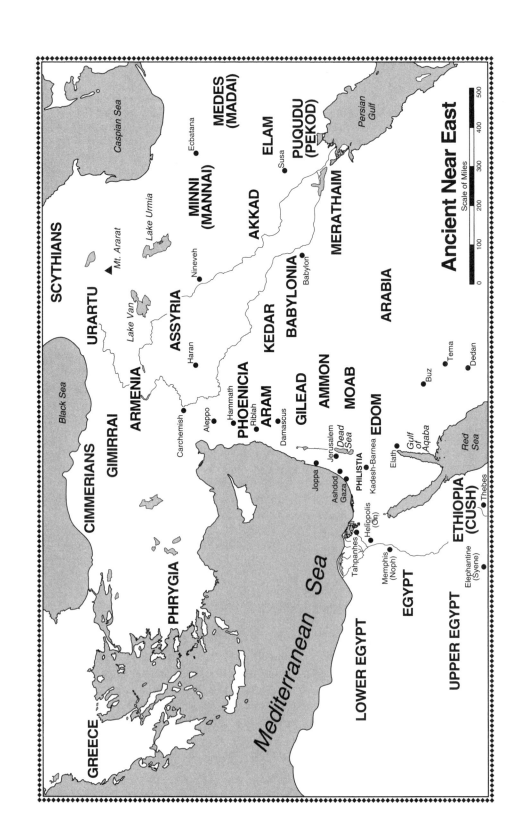

Ancient Near East

Scale of Miles

0   100   200   300   400   500

XI. ESAU, FATHER OF THE EDOMITES (36:9–37:1)

The second *tōlĕdōt* section pertaining to Esau's descendants focuses on Edom as a burgeoning people. The author's interest is the political development of the Edomite clans. He compares the Edomites with the history of Israel's kings, reporting that the Edomites possessed a series of rulers long before Israel's monarchy (v. 31). As we noted in the previous section, the descendants of Esau received the blessing of God by virtue of their father's descent from Abraham. The tribes of Jacob must wait for their ascendancy, relying on the Lord as their sole sovereign to establish them in the land. That there will be kings born to Jacob (35:11; cf. 17:6,16) and a "scepter" raised in Judah (49:10; Num 24:7) is a promise for which the Israelites must wait by faith. After Israel's settlement, when neighboring populations like the Edomites became a menace, in particular the Philistine lords, the people lost patience and requested a king (1 Sam 8:19–20; 14:47).

This second *tōlĕdōt* section provides a brief political history of Edom, including four lists of persons and places. The first list names the chiefdoms that emerged from Esau's family (vv. 10–19). Another listing recalls the dominion of the Horites (vv. 20–30), whom the Edomites ultimately displaced (Deut 2:12,22; cf. 14:6). A third catalog of eight Edomite kings and their cities confirm the political ascendancy of the Edomites (vv. 31–39). The final list pertains to the clans and territorial possessions that prominently made up Edomite settlements (vv. 40–43). By this catalog of rulers, cities, and territories, the author provided later Israel a snapshot of their kinsmen's control over the transjordan area that they circumvented en route to Canaan (Num 20:14–21; Judg 11:17–18). Against this background, the final verse of the section comments on Jacob's residency in Canaan (37:1). The Israelites, too, had a place in the world—the land of their father Jacob, where he settled according to promise (cf. 28:13; 35:12; Exod 6:3–4,8; Ps 105:10–11).[1]

COMPOSITION. The discussion of the sources that contribute to the present section is at 36:1–8.

STRUCTURE. The passage (36:3–37:1) consists of three units: descendants of Esau (vv. 10–19), descendants of Seir the Horite (vv. 20–30), and lists of the kings and chiefs of Edom (vv. 31–43). Within each unit there is the alternating pattern of a list of "sons" (vv. 10–14,20–28) or "kings" (vv. 31–39) followed by a list of "chiefs" (vv. 15–19,29–30,40–43). The beginning verse provides the title (v. 9), and the final verse of the section is transitional (37:1), creating a frame for the three units:

> 36:9–43 "the account of *[tōlĕdōt]* of Esau the father of the Edomites" (v. 9)
> vv. 10–14 "these are the names of the sons of *[bĕnê]* Esau" (v. 10)
> vv. 15–19 "the chiefs among *[ʾallûpê]* Esau's descendants" (v. 15)
>
> vv. 20–28 "the sons of *[bĕnê]* Seir the Horite" (v. 20)
> vv. 29–30 "the chiefs of *[ʾallûpê]* the Horites" (v. 29)
>
> vv. 31–39 "the kings *[mĕlākîm]* who reigned in Edom" (v. 31)
> vv. 40–43 "the names of the chiefs of *[ʾallûpê]* Esau" (v. 40)
> 37:1 "Jacob lived . . . in the land of Canaan"

The genealogies of Esau that give descendants and chiefs (vv. 10–19) are segmented (branched), providing a depth of three generations. The "sons of Esau" are named in vv. 10–14, and the "chiefs of the sons of Esau" appear in vv. 15–19 (see below). The conclusion in v. 19, however, links the two lists.[2] The birth of Amalek, Esau's grandson, by the concubine Timna indicates the illegitimacy of the Amalekite heritage (v. 12). When Amalek is not counted, the genealogy consists of nine grandsons and three sons (by Oholibamah), giving a total of twelve offspring born to Esau. By placing the three sons born to Oholibamah on the same tier as Esau's grandchildren and by omitting her grandchildren, the number twelve is achieved. Twelve corresponds to the number born to Ishmael and Jacob (25:12–16; 35:22–26). Although the lists of descendants and chiefs include the same names (except possibly one[3]), the purpose of each list differs and is to that degree not redundant information. The inclusion of

---

[1] For more on the purpose of this *tōlĕdōt* section, see the introduction to 36:1–8.

[2] Observed by B. K. Waltke, *Genesis: A Commentary* (Grand Rapids: Zondervan, 2001), 486.

[3] "Korah," grandson of Adah, is mentioned among the chiefs in v. 15 (absent in SP) but absent in the list of descendants in v. 11.

chiefs was to underline the stature of Esau's descendants; all his sons and grandsons became the heads of tribal clans, suggesting that theirs was a prestigious and prodigious heritage. As to which list depended on the other cannot be known; logically, the list of chiefs (vv. 15–19) must follow that of the son list (vv. 10–14).

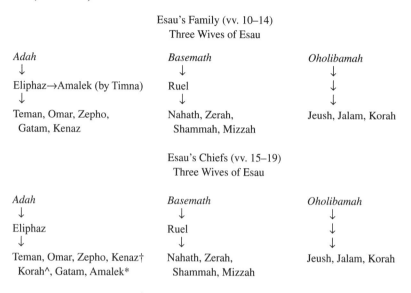

Esau's Family (vv. 10–14)
Three Wives of Esau

Adah	*Basemath*	*Oholibamah*
↓	↓	↓
Eliphaz→Amalek (by Timna)	Ruel	↓
↓	↓	↓
Teman, Omar, Zepho,	Nahath, Zerah,	Jeush, Jalam, Korah
Gatam, Kenaz	Shammah, Mizzah	

Esau's Chiefs (vv. 15–19)
Three Wives of Esau

Adah	*Basemath*	*Oholibamah*
↓	↓	↓
Eliphaz	Ruel	↓
↓	↓	↓
Teman, Omar, Zepho, Kenaz†	Nahath, Zerah,	Jeush, Jalam, Korah
Korah^, Gatam, Amalek*	Shammah, Mizzah	

†Kenaz and Gatam differ in position (v. 16; cp. v. 11)
^Korah, son of Eliphaz, grandson of Esau, is additional (v. 16).
*Amalek is listed on line (v. 16).

A major departure occurs in vv. 20–30 with the registers of the "the sons of Seir the Horite" (vv. 20–28) and "the Horite chiefs" (vv. 29–30). The motivation for inclusion of the Horite generations was Edom's history of intermarriage with the Horites (cf. 36:20,22,25) and the Edomite incursion that displaced the Horites who occupied the land (Deut 2:12,22). "Thus Gen 36 is moving backward from the conquerors (vv. 9–19) to the conquered (vv. 20–30)."[4] The citing of Seir's seven sons and their seven clans bracket the genealogy (vv. 20–21; vv. 29–30). The genealogy of descendants is segmented and contains three generations. Seven sons father twenty children, including the daughter Oholibamah. The mention of the "sons" becoming "chiefs" in the list of Horite descendants, "These sons of Seir in Edom were Horite chiefs" (v. 21; cp. v. 19), confirms that the purpose of giving two lists bearing the same names was to highlight the expansion of the descendants into powerful clans. By

---

[4] V. Hamilton, *The Book of Genesis Chapters 18–50,* NICOT (Grand Rapids: Eerdmans, 1995), 397.

showing that Edom's predecessors were a robust people, measured by their numerous chiefdoms, the author reinforces the prestige of the Edomites who dislocated them.

Seir's Family (vv. 20–28)

Lotan*	Shobal	Zibeon	Anah	Dishon°	Ezer	Dishan
↓	↓	↓	↓	↓	↓	↓
Hori	Alvan	Aiah	Dishon	Hemdan	Bilhan	Uz
Homam	Manahath	Anah^	Oholibamah*	Eshban	Zaavan	Aran
	Ebal			Ithran	Akan	
	Shepho			Keran		
	Onam					

*Timna was the sister of Lotan (vv. 12,22)
^Who discovered the hotsprings
*daughter of Anah
°Reading "Dishon" (1 Chr 1:41), not MT's "Dishan" (v. 26)

Horite Chiefs (vv. 29–30)

Lotan, Shobal, Zibeon, Anah, Dishon, Ezer, Dishan

The king list in vv. 31–39 signals another departure from the type of lists already cited. The author continues his interest in tracing the political history of the region, suggesting some development in the organization of Edom's populace. The list, however, is not of a single dynastic family; rather, it provides eight succeeding rulers who "reigned in Edom" before the Israelite monarchy (v. 31). Reference to the city from where the king reigned implies that they had a limited realm that was regional. Edomite kingship therefore compares more favorably to the appointment of Saul (versus David's dynasty) and the limited territories governed by Israel's provincial judges during the settlement period than to the great nation states that usually boasted dynastic succession. Such an impressive array of kings served to magnify David's triumph over Edom (1 Sam 8:13–14). One striking feature of this list is the presence of names that also were names of the noted deity Baal/Hadad.

Kings of Edom (vv. 31–39)

Bela, Jobab, Husham, Hadad, Samlah, Shaul, Baal-Hanan, Hadad

The final listing names the eleven "chiefs descended from Esau" from vv. 40–43. Similar language in vv. 40 and 43 frame the list; the phrase "the chiefs of Edom" (v. 43) parallels the heading in v. 40, "the chiefs [of] Esau." Although some of the names of the eleven chiefs occur in the sons and chiefs of Esau (vv. 9–19), this list includes new information, showing some independence from the earlier catalog. The present list names "settlements" (v. 43), making it likely that the names of descendants could also designate territories (e.g., "Judah" could refer to a person, a tribe, a territory, a nation).

Edomite Chiefs (vv. 40–43)

Timna, Alvah, Jetheth, Oholibamah, Elah, Pinon, Kenaz, Teman, Mibzar, Magdiel, Iram

Last, the author composed 37:1 as a transition, connecting the *tōlĕdôt* of Esau with the literary surrounding. The former narrative left off with Esau and Jacob burying their father in Hebron (35:27–29), and the following narrative recounts the story of Jacob's sons (37:2–50:26).

1. Title (36:9)

⁹This is the account of Esau the father of the Edomites in the hill country of Seir.

36:9 The title encapsulates the contents of the remainder of the section. The term "account" *(tōlĕdôt)* indicates that a genealogical record or history follows. The specifics of Esau as paterfamilias of the Edomites and their relationship to Seir the Horite and the land that bears his name occur. See "Structure" above for more.

2. The Sons and Chiefs of Esau (36:10–19)

This unit names Esau's five sons and ten grandsons (vv. 10–14), who became tribal chiefs (vv. 15–19). See the discussion above under "Structure" for more.

(1) Esau's Sons (36:10–14)

¹⁰These are the names of Esau's sons:
Eliphaz, the son of Esau's wife Adah, and Reuel, the son of Esau's wife Basemath.
¹¹The sons of Eliphaz:
Teman, Omar, Zepho, Gatam and Kenaz.
¹²Esau's son Eliphaz also had a concubine named Timna, who bore him Amalek. These were grandsons of Esau's wife Adah.
¹³The sons of Reuel:
Nahath, Zerah, Shammah and Mizzah. These were grandsons of Esau's wife Basemath.
¹⁴The sons of Esau's wife Oholibamah daughter of Anah and granddaughter of Zibeon, whom she bore to Esau:
Jeush, Jalam and Korah.

36:10   On the significance of these names, see comments on 26:34; 36:2–4.

36:11–12   Eliphaz, the son of Esau and Adah, fathered five sons (v. 11) and a sixth by his concubine Timna (v. 12). If the order of the descendants named is significant, *Teman* may be the eldest son of Eliphaz, the eldest son of Esau (v. 11//1 Chr 1:36; cf. v. 15). The term may derive from *y-m-n,* meaning "south" (*têmān,* e.g., Exod 26:18). The region Teman was noted for its wisdom (Jer 49:7) and was an important site in Edom (Jer 49:20; Obad 9). Although its precise location is uncertain, the term "Teman" may have originally referred to north Edom in the region of Bozrah (modern Buṣeirah; v. 33; cf. Amos 1:12; Ezek 25:13) and later came to refer to the southern areas and Edom at large.[5] The Edomite king Husham was located in the "land of the Temanites" (v. 34), and the name occurs again for an Edomite clan (v. 42). Job's friend, Eliphaz, was a Temanite (2:11), but the location of this Teman is disputed, either located in Edom or N. Arabia if equated with Tema (see comments on 25:15; cf. comments on 36:34). The prophet Habakkuk recognized the prestige of Teman when he employed it to refer to the place of God's theophany (3:3; cf. comments on 14:6; Deut 33:2). *Omar* is unknown (v. 11//1 Chr 1:36; cf. v. 15); it may mean "lamb" (Hb. *ʾimmēr;* cp. Akk. *emārum/imārum,* "donkey") or something like "eloquent"[6] derived from "to speak" (*ʾāmar*).[7] *Zepho* is also unknown (v. 11//1 Chr 1:36, "Zephi"; cf. v. 15), perhaps related to "see, behold" (*ṣ-p-y/h*) or "clean, pure" (*ṣpw/y*).[8] *Gatam* is unknown and its meaning obscure (v. 11//1 Chr 1:36; cf. v. 15). On the name *Kenaz,* see the Kenizzites at comments on 15:19. Timna was the concubine of Eliphaz and mother of *Amalek* (v. 12//1 Chr 1:36; cf. v. 40); she was the daughter of Seir the Horite, sister of Lotan (v. 22//1 Chr 1:39).[9] She provided a genealogical link between the families of Esau and Seir. The identification of Amalek's mother as a concubine wife disparaged his ancestry; his descendants were an especially troublesome foe for the Israelites (for more on Amalek, see comments on 14:7).

36:13   Ruel, the son of Esau and Basemath, fathers four sons. The meaning

---

[5] E. A. Knauf, "Teman," *ABD* 6.347–48; that Teman should be identified with modern Tawilan (north of Petra) is suspect, since the latter is a city and Teman appears to refer to a region (H. G. May, ed., *Oxford Bible Atlas,* 3d ed. [New York: Oxford University Press, 1984], 142; P. Bienkowski, "Tawilan," *NEAEHL* 4.1446–47).

[6] BDB 57.

[7] U. Hübner suggests an original theophoric name ("Omar," *ABD* 5.15); cp. e.g., אֲמַרְיָה(וּ), "Amariah," "*Yah(u)* has spoken" (e.g., 1 Chr 23:19).

[8] Ibid., "Zepho," *ABD* 6.1080.

[9] The straightforward reading of the parallel passage in 1 Chr 1:36 recommends that Timna is a son of Eliphaz, not a daughter (e.g., NASB, NRSV), but many EVs harmonize the two passages by a gloss (e.g., "*by* or *of* Timna," NIV, ESV, NKJV); since "Timna" is also a clan or regional name in 36:40, it is reasonable that Timna in Chronicles does not refer to a person (1 Chr 1:36,51). See D. S. Williams, "Timna," *ABD* 6.553.

of *Nahath* is unknown (v. 13//1 Chr 1:37; cf. v. 17).[10] The name describes a Levite, son of Zophai (1 Chr 6:26[11]; cf. 1 Chr 6:34[19]; 1 Sam 1:1), and a Levite supervisor (2 Chr 31:13). *Zerah,* which means "dawning, shining" *(zeraḥ)* in Hebrew (v. 13//1 Chr 1:37; cf. v. 17), also named an Edomite king (v. 33) and a Cushite ruler (2 Chr 14:9[8]). One of the twin sons born to Judah and Tamar received this name (38:30; 46:12; Matt 1:3). It is another name in this list identifying clans among the Israelite tribes of Simeon, Judah, and Levi (e.g., Num 26:13,20; 1 Chr 4:24; 6:21[6],41[26]). The etymology of *Shammah* (v. 13//1 Chr 1:37; cf. v. 17) has been explained by many proposals, including "to hear" (*šāmaʿ,* i.e., one heard of, fame?[11]) and "to keep" (*šāmar,* cp. e.g., "Shemariah"[12]), but remains speculative. The name occurs especially in the time of David, naming his brother (1 Sam 16:9; 17:13) and two mighty warriors among David's honored military (2 Sam 23:11,25). *Mizzah* is unknown (v. 13//1 Chr 1:37; cf. v. 17).

36:14 Esau-Oholibamah parented three sons. The pedigree of Oholibamah is important since she is descended from Seir the Horite (vv. 20,25). On the textual problem pertaining to her ancestry, see the footnote at comments on 36:2. For the names of her sons, see the comments at v. 5.

(2) Esau's Chiefs (36:15–19)

15These were the chiefs among Esau's descendants:
  The sons of Eliphaz the firstborn of Esau:
  Chiefs Teman, Omar, Zepho, Kenaz, **16**Korah, Gatam and Amalek. These were the chiefs descended from Eliphaz in Edom; they were grandsons of Adah.
17The sons of Esau's son Reuel:
  Chiefs Nahath, Zerah, Shammah and Mizzah. These were the chiefs descended from Reuel in Edom; they were grandsons of Esau's wife Basemath.
18The sons of Esau's wife Oholibamah:
  Chiefs Jeush, Jalam and Korah. These were the chiefs descended from Esau's wife Oholibamah daughter of Anah.
19These were the sons of Esau (that is, Edom), and these were their chiefs.

36:15–19 The repetition of "chiefs" and "sons of Esau" (NIV, "Esau's descendants") in vv. 15 and 19 frame the roster. The term "chief(s)" (*ʾallûp*) occurs forty-three times in the chapter, dominating the passage as the most frequent word. It typically refers to Edomite and Horite leaders, appearing in the

---

[10] U. Hübner mentions possibly related to Arabic **nḥt,* "clear, pure" ("Nahath," *ABD* 4.996).

[11] M. Noth, *Die israelitischen Personennamen im Rahmen der gemeinsemitischen Namengebung,* BWANT 46 (1928; reprint, Hildesheim: Georg Olms, 1966), 39, 185; and U. Hübner, "Shammah," *ABD* 5.1157.

[12] שְׁמַרְיָהוּ, "*Yahu* has kept, protected" (1 Chr 12:5[6]; *HALOT* 4.1554).

parallel passage (1 Chr 1:51–54) and once more in the Pentateuch (Exod 15:15). It may also distinguish Judah's leaders (Zech 12:5–6), including the incorporated Philistine leader (Zech 9:7). The term, traditionally rendered "chief" (e.g., LXX, Vg., AV), is also translated "clan" by some EVs (e.g., NAB, NRSV). The word probably is related to *'elep,* "tribe, clan, a thousand," thus "the chief of a thousand."[13] The word "chief" may designate a clan and tribal chief or name a regional chief (vv. 40–43).[14]

The same names in vv. 10–14 appear again in this list of Edomite chiefs, but there are three variations. (1) The rank of Kenaz and Gatam in the two lists differs: in the prior catalog Gatam in the fourth slot precedes Kenaz (v. 11), and in the present list Kenaz takes the fourth slot, followed by Korah and Gatam (vv. 15–16). (2) The addition of "Korah," grandson of Eliphaz (v. 16; cp. v. 11), who is the nephew of Korah, the son of Oholibamah (vv. 5,14,18), brings the number of Eliphaz's sons to seven. (3) The name Amalek appears on the same genealogical tier as his half-brothers (v. 16; cp. v. 12), giving Amalek a more favorable standing. These differences suggest that the two catalogs provided the author two different sources of information; the differences in this roster of chiefs probably reflect altered political circumstances among the Edomite tribes.

3. The Sons and Chiefs of Seir the Horite (36:20–30)

The frame for this unit is the repetition of the names of Seir's seven sons and seven clans (vv. 20–21; vv. 29–30). The number seven or a multiple of seven is a common feature of genealogies (see vol. 1A, pp. 282, n. 304). Sandwiched between is the genealogical record of the sons who produced nineteen sons and one daughter, Oholibamah (vv. 22–28). The final two verses tersely list the seven chiefs among the Horite clans (vv. 29–30).

(1) Seir's Sons (36:20–28)

[20]These were the sons of Seir the Horite, who were living in the region:
Lotan, Shobal, Zibeon, Anah, [21]Dishon, Ezer and Dishan. These sons of Seir in Edom were Horite chiefs.
[22]The sons of Lotan:
Hori and Homam. Timna was Lotan's sister.
[23]The sons of Shobal:
Alvan, Manahath, Ebal, Shepho and Onam.
[24]The sons of Zibeon:
Aiah and Anah. This is the Anah who discovered the hot springs in the desert while he was grazing the donkeys of his father Zibeon.

---

[13] *HALOT* 1.54.
[14] G. Johnston, "אַלּוּף," *NIDOTTE* 1.406–10.

[25]The children of Anah:
   Dishon and Oholibamah daughter of Anah.
[26]The sons of Dishon:
   Hemdan, Eshban, Ithran and Keran.
[27]The sons of Ezer:
   Bilhan, Zaavan and Akan.
[28]The sons of Dishan:
   Uz and Aran.

36:20–21 Mention that the seven sons of Seir lived in the land establishes their habitation before Esau's descendants dispossessed them (Deut 2:12,22). This chapter shows that the Edomites intermarried with Horite women, and Deuteronomy testifies that they routed the Horites.[15] The "Horites" are a little known people, mentioned only in the scattered references of the Old Testament (14:6; 36:20–30; Deut 2:12,22). Seir was the ancestor of the Horite clans, and Hori was a grandson (v. 22). Deuteronomy identifies them as the predecessors to the Edomites. Egyptian sources from the fifteenth century and following refer to the inhabitants of Seir and Edom as the *Shōsu,* who were particularly remembered as foreign mercenaries and brigands.[16] Scholars today question the former identification of the Horites with the Hurrians, best known in history as the non-Semitic people of Mittani who ascended to power in the fifteenth century B.C. This earlier identification by scholars is bolstered by the linguistic identity of *ḥōrî* and the cuneiform *ḥurru,* and by the Egyptian term "Hurru-land" naming Palestine in the fifteenth century. But the locations of Hurrian populations known in Canaan do not correspond to Horite possessions in the south and Transjordan. Moreover, the names of the Horites in vv. 20–30 include many Semitic names.[17] The etymology of "Horite" is uncertain, though often associated with *ḥōr,* meaning "hole, cave," thus "cave dweller" (cf. 1 Sam 14:11).

Lotan is unknown (v. 20//1 Chr 1:38; cf. vv. 22,29; 1 Chr 1:39), and its meaning is unclear, perhaps related to Hebrew *lôṭ,* meaning "covering, veil" (Isa 25:7; *lûṭ,* "to wrap, envelop," 1 Sam 21:10). *Shobal* (v. 20//1 Chr 1:38; cf. vv. 23,29; 1 Chr 1:40) is also the name of a Calebite and a Judahite (1 Chr 2:50,52; 4:1–2). The name may be related to Hebrew *šibbôlet,* "ear of grain" (41:5; Akk. *šubultu,* Ug. *šblt*).[18] On *Zibeon* and *Anah,* cf. v. 2. *Dishon* is the

---

[15] On the meaning of "Seir," see commentary on 36:2–3 and the excursus "Edom and the Edomites," at 36:1–8.

[16] J. Bartlett discusses the Egyptian evidence (*Edom and the Edomites,* JSOTSup 77 [Sheffield: Sheffield Academic Press, 1999], 77–82).

[17] F. W. Bush, "Horites," *ISBE* §2.756–57.

[18] E. A. Knauf notes that *sbl* occurs in Safaitic (third–second centuries B.C.), and the name "Shobal" appears in the geographical names Jebel Sôbala and Khirbet Sôbal ("Shobal," *ABD* 5.1224); D. J. Wiseman connects the Edomite and Judahite Shobal(s) as related persons ("Shobal," *NBD*[3], 1098).

son of Seir (v. 21//1 Chr 1:38; cf. v. 30) and the name of a grandson (vv. 25–26[MT has "Dishan"]//1 Chr 1:41). The name is the word for the wild goat "ibex" (Deut 14:5, LXX *pugargos*, "white rump antelope").[19] *Ezer (ʿēṣer* and its variants, *ʿēzer, ʿezer*) is a widely used name (v. 21//1 Chr 1:38; cf. vv. 27,30), referring to a Judahite (1 Chr 4:4), an Ephraimite (1 Chr 7:21), a Gadite leader who followed David (1 Chr 12:9[10]), a ruler of Mizpah (Neh 3:19), and a priest (Neh 12:42). Although the name sounds similar to the word for "restraint" *(ʿeṣer/ʿōṣer)*, the variant spellings of the name (noted above) mean "help" *(ʿēzer)*. *Dishan* is the last named son of Seir (v. 21//1 Chr 1:38; cf. vv. 28,30). The spelling is similar to his brother's (v. 21) and nephew's name (vv. 25–26), "Dishon," creating some textual confusion among the versions at v. 26.[20]

36:22–23 Lotan fathers two sons, Hori and Homan. *Hori* (v. 22//1 Chr 1:39) also names a Simeonite, one of the twelve spies (Num 13:5). On the significance of the name, see comments on v. 20. *Homam,* spelled here as "Heman," occurs only again in the Chronicler's account (1 Chr 1:39). On *Timna* see comments on v. 12. Shobal produces five sons (v. 23//1 Chr 1:40). *Alvan (ʿalwān)* appears only in 1 Chr 1:40, spelled "Alian" *(ʿalyān*, cf. e.g., NRSV) due to the scribal confusion of the similar Hebrew letters *wāw* (ו) and *yōd* (י). The meaning of *Manahath* (v. 23//1 Chr 1:40) probably is related to "rest" *(n-w-ḥ)*, for example, *mānôaḥ,* "resting place" (8:9), and personal name "Manoah" (1 Sam 13:2).[21] The "Menahathites" are a Caleb clan in 1 Chr 2:52,54 (v. 54 has "Menuhoth," cf. NASB, NRSV), which provides in chap. 36 another possible link between Edomite and Judahite heritage. *Ebal* (v. 23//1 Chr 1:40) is also the name of the son of Joktan in 1 Chr 1:22, which Gen 10:28 has as "Obal." The name of the Ephraimite site, Mount Ebal (e.g., Deut 11:29), may not be necessarily related. *Shepho* (v. 23) in the parallel passage is spelled "Shephi" (1 Chr 1:40), due to letter confusion of *wāw/yōd*. The last son is *Onam* (v. 23//1 Chr 1:40), which also identifies a Judahite (1 Chr 2:26,28). His name may be connected to "vigor, regenerative power" *(ʾôn,* e.g., 49:3).

36:24–25 Zibeon had two sons. *Aiah* (v. 24//1 Chr 1:40), meaning "kite" of the hawk family (e.g., Lev 11:4), also names the father of Saul's concubine, Rizpah (e.g., 2 Sam 3:7). For the name *Anah* (v. 24//1 Chr 1:40), who is here nephew of his namesake, see comments on v. 2. That Anah discovered water in the arid region of Edom was a memorable achievement, an indication of successful settlement. Moreover, the herd of donkeys shows the wealth the family had built, for the animal was typically affiliated with the powerful as an ideal beast for bearing goods (e.g., 30:43; 45:23; Judg 10:4; 2 Sam 16:1–2). The word

[19] LSJ 1550; D. H. Madvig, "Dishon," ZPEB 2.1422.
[20] Read "Dishon" with SP, Syr.; 1 Chr 1:41 (MT). On its meaning see "Dishon" above.
[21] HALOT 2.602; E. A. Knauf, "Manahath," ABD 4.493.

rendered "hot springs" or "springs" *(yēmim)* in EVs is a hapax legomenon whose meaning is uncertain.[22] Ancient versions (Syr., Vg.) and commentators related it to "seas" *(yāmmîm),* and Jewish midrash (e.g., *Gen. Rab.* 82.14) and *Tg. Ps-J.* explained it as "mules." Also *Tg. Onq.* has "mighty ones," thinking the Hebrew was related to *ʿēmîm* (cp. the Emites, "a people strong and numerous," Deut 2:10).[23] The LXX rendered it as a place name, *Iamin.*[24] Anah, brother of Zibeon and uncle of Anah, possessed two children, a son Dishon (whose uncle bore the same name, v. 21) and a daughter Oholibamah (v. 25//1 Chr 1:41 omits Oholibamah). For more on these names, see comments on vv. 2,21.

36:26–28 Dishon had four sons (v. 26//1 Chr 1:41a). *Hemdan* appears again in 1 Chr 1:41 but as "Hemran" due to the confusion of the letters *dalet* (ד=*d*) and *rēsh* (ר=*r*). The Hebrew means "desire" *(ḥemdâ,* e.g., 1 Sam 9:20).[25] *Eshban* and *Keran* (some EVs *Cheran*) are unknown. *Ithran* is also the name of an Asherite (1 Chr 7:37; = "Jether"? 7:38). Ezer had three sons (v. 27//1 Chr 1:42). *Bilhan* also names a Benjaminite (1 Chr 7:10). *Zaavan* is unknown. *Akan* occurs as "Jaakan" in Chronicles (cf. EVs). Two Edomite sites contain the name Bene Jaakan (Num 33:31–32) and Beeroth Bene Jaakan (Deut 10:6; NIV "Jaakanites").[26] Dishan produced two sons (v. 27//1 Chr 1:41b). *Uz* not only identifies a Horite clan but also names an Aramean tribe descended through Aram and the patriarchs Milcah and Nahor, Abraham's brother (10:23; 22:21; 1 Chr 1:17). Job's home was "in the land of Uz" (Job 1:1), whose location is disputed, though Edom is preferable.[27] On "Uz" see vol. 1A, p. 462. *Aran* is unknown, unless it is a variant of "Oren," a Judahite's name (1 Chr 2:25) meaning "fir, cedar tree" (Isa 44:4).[28]

(2) Seir's Horite Chiefs (36:29–30)

29These were the Horite chiefs:
Lotan, Shobal, Zibeon, Anah, 30Dishon, Ezer and Dishan. These were the Horite chiefs, according to their divisions, in the land of Seir.

---

[22] Some lexicographers derive the word from Ar. *wamiha,* "to be hot"; see the bibliography in *HALOT* 2.415; modern proposals include "marsh fish(es)" and "snake(s)," see *DCH* 4.229.

[23] Cf. discussion in B. Grossfeld, *The Targum Onqelos to Genesis* (Wilmington: Michael Glazier, 1988), 125, n. 2.

[24] For the diversity in the inner-LXX tradition, see J. W. Wevers, *Notes on the Greek Text of Genesis,* SBLSCS 35 (Atlanta: Scholars Press, 1993), 601.

[25] E. A. Knauf observes the name in Sabaic and Arabic ("Hemdan," *ABD* 3.137).

[26] V. H. Matthews, "Jaakan," *ABD* 3.591.

[27] J. Day, "How Could Job Be an Edomite?" in *The Book of Job,* BETL 114 (Leuvain: Leuven University Press, 1994), 392–99, who argues that even an exilic date for the authorship of Job does not preclude Edom for the model Job; E. A. Knauf, "Uz," *ABD* 6.771, notes the Arab tribe *ʾAuḍ* appearing in a North Arabian inscription.

[28] V. H. Matthews, "Aran," *ABD* 1.350–51.

36:29–30 The seven Horite descendants of Seir (vv. 20–21) are named again in these two verses, observing that they produced Horite clans.

4. The Kings of Edom (36:31–39)

[31]These were the kings who reigned in Edom before any Israelite king reigned:
[32]Bela son of Beor became king of Edom. His city was named Dinhabah.
[33]When Bela died, Jobab son of Zerah from Bozrah succeeded him as king.
[34]When Jobab died, Husham from the land of the Temanites succeeded him as king.
[35]When Husham died, Hadad son of Bedad, who defeated Midian in the country of Moab, succeeded him as king. His city was named Avith.
[36]When Hadad died, Samlah from Masrekah succeeded him as king.
[37]When Samlah died, Shaul from Rehoboth on the river succeeded him as king.
[38]When Shaul died, Baal-Hanan son of Acbor succeeded him as king.
[39]When Baal-Hanan son of Acbor died, Hadad succeeded him as king. His city was named Pau, and his wife's name was Mehetabel daughter of Matred, the daughter of Me-Zahab.

The unit consists of a superscription (v. 31) and list of eight Edomite kings and their cities (vv. 32–39). A recurring formula marks the succession of each new king: "*X* died *[wayyāmot]* and *Y* reigned as king *[wayyimlōk]* in his place" (vv. 33,34,35,36,37,38,39). Compare the same and variant expressions in the recital of Israel's kings (e.g., 1 Kgs 16:22; 2 Kgs 1:17; 13:24; 1 Chr 19:1).

36:31 This historical comment probably is a post-Mosaic explanation from the Davidic-Solomonic era, introducing a vague nexus between the royal histories of the two peoples. This addition implied that Isaac's blessing on Esau, "You will live by the sword and you will serve your brother" (27:40), was realized at the advent of Israel's monarchy. That Edom first possessed numerous kings who later became subject to the dynastic reign of David's house added prestige to the accomplishments of Judah's sole ruling family. This verse does not appear in the Chronicler's review (1 Chr 1:43–54).

36:32 The first of the eight kings was *Bela* (//1 Chr 1:43). Bela also was the name of Benjamin's firstborn/clan (e.g., 46:21; Num 26:38,40; 1 Chr 7:6–7; 8:1,3) and a Reubenite clan, located in transjordan (Moab; 1 Chr 5:8). It was also the ancient name of the city Zoar in the Negev (14:2,8). A number of LXX manuscripts have "Balak," probably a mistake influenced by "Balaam son of Beor" in Num 22:5,[29] and *Tg. Ps.-J.* has "Balaam," again influenced by the infamous "son of Beor."[30] As for the meaning and derivation of the name

---

[29] Wevers, *Notes on the Greek Text,* 604; cp. similarity of בלע (Bela) and בלעם (Balaam).

[30] M. Maher observes the similarity in the name Bela *(blʿ)* and the popular etymology of Balaam *(blʿ ʿm),* "he swallowed the people" (*Targum Pseudo-Jonathan: Genesis* [Collegeville, Minn.: Liturgical Press, 1992], 123, n. 9).

"Bela," it remains uncertain but has been related to *bl^c* (II), "to report, announce" *(piel)*, which Ar. *baluġa,* means "to be eloquent."[31] Among the Edomite toponyms in the king list are many that are obscure.[32] The identity of "Dinhabah," the town of Bela, is unknown.

36:33–35 *Jobab* (v. 33//1 Chr 1:44) appears for five different persons, including a Shemite (10:29), King of Madon (Josh 1:11), and two Benjaminites (1 Chr 8:9,18). On the name "Jobab" (10:29), see vol. 1A, p. 465. For "Zerah," see vv. 13,17. "Bozrah" is two sites in the Old Testament: Edom (v. 33//1 Chr 1:44; Isa 34:6; 63:1; Jer 49:13,22; Amos 1:12) and Moab (Jer 48:24). Bozrah (modern Buṣeirah) was the ancient capital of Edom (e.g., Isa 34:6), located twenty-eight miles north of Petra in modern Jordan.[33] The third king was *Husam* "from the land of the Temanites" (v. 34//1 Chr 1:45). Husam is not otherwise known; Arabic *ḥusām* means "sword."[34] On the significance of "Temanites," see above commentary on vv. 11–12. *Hadad (hădad)* is the name of the fourth (v. 35//1 Chr 1:46) and eighth kings (v. 39). The name also occurs for a descendant of Ishmael (but spelled *ḥădad,* 25:15; 1 Chr 1:30) and an opponent of Solomon (1 Kgs 11:14–22,25). As a personal name, it is attested for Edom and south and north Arabic dialects as well as classical Arabic.[35] The name is best known as the name of the Syrian male deity Hadad (Akk. *ḥaddu;* cf. "Hadad Rimmon," Zech 12:11; "Ben-Hadad," 1 Kgs 15:18), perhaps meaning "Thunderer" (Hb. *hêdād,* "a shout," Isa 16:9); in the Old Testament he is typically known by the Canaanite name Baal ("Lord/Owner").[36] The list distinguished this fourth ruler as the son of *Bedad* and remembered especially for his impressive victory over the Midianites in Moab (cf. comments on 25:2). In Arabic "Budaid" and various *bd* forms are known (cp. Hb. *b-d-d,* "separate, alone") and the Ugaritic personal name *bddn.* The city Avith remains unknown (*^căwît;* cp. LXX *Geththaim* and Ar. **Ghuwaith*).[37]

36:36–39 Hadad's successor was *Simlah* (cp. Hb. *śimlâ,* "outer garment"; Ar. *šamlah,* "cloak"[38]), whose city was Masrekah, a site unknown (v. 36//

---

[31] Noth, *Personnenamen,* 229 n. 7; *HALOT* 1.135; and E. A. Knauf, "Bela," *ABD* 1.653–54.

[32] A summary of the scholarly discussion of the sites' identities is B. MacDonald, *"East of the Jordan": Territories and Sites of the Hebrew Scriptures,* ASOR Books 6 (Boston: ASOR, 2000), 188–94.

[33] P. Bienkowski, "Buṣeira," *OEANE* 1.387–90; S. Hart and U. Hübner, "Bozrah," *ABD* 1.774–75 and Hübner, "Bozrah in Moab" and "Bozrah in Ḥaurān," *ABD* 1.775–76.

[34] E. A. Knauf, "Husham," *ABD* 3.339.

[35] Knauf explains the meaning of the name as "the one who smashes" ("Hadad," *ABD* 3.11–12).

[36] W. Maier, "Hadad (Deity)," *ABD* 3.11.

[37] E. A. Knauf, "Bedad," *ABD* 1.633 and "Hadad (Person)," *ABD* 3.11–12; Wevers, *Notes on the Greek Text,* 606; F.-M. Abel recommends Khirbet al-Gitte between modern Maʾân and el-Basṭa (south Jordan; MacDonald, "East of the Jordan," 189).

[38] E. A. Knauf, "Samlah," *ABD* 5.948.

1 Chr 1:47).[39] The sixth ruler was *Shaul* (v. 37//1 Chr 1:48). The name is best known for Israel's king, Saul (1 Sam 9:2). In the Bible, the name occurs for a Simeonite clan (e.g., 46:10; Exod 6:15) and a Levite (1 Chr 6:9). The name was used in Syrian and North Arabian epigraphy.[40] His ruling city was "Rehoboth on the river," usually understood as the Euphrates River when "river" *(nāhār)* occurs by itself (e.g., 31:21; cp. "Rehoboth on the Euphrates," NRSV; also ESV, NASB; "Rehoboth-on-the-River," HCSB). Additionally, two other places bear this name (10:11; 26:22). On the meaning of "Rehoboth" ("plazas"), see vol. 1A, p. 452. The identity of the site is disputed.[41] *Baal-Hanan* was the seventh ruler (v. 36//1 Chr 1:49), whose name means "Baal is gracious." Unlike the other Edomite kings, no city is ascribed to his rule. The name also occurred for a supervisor of trees in the time of David (1 Chr 27:28) and is attested as the name of the ruler of the Phoenician city Arvad (cf. 10:18) during the reign of Ashurbanipal.[42] Baal-Hanan was the son of "Acbor" (v. 38; also EVs, "Achbor"), a name also held by an official in Josiah's court (2 Kgs 22:12,14; Jer 26:22; 36:12); compare *ʿakbār,* meaning "mouse, rat" (e.g., Lev 11:29).[43] The last named king was *Hadad,*[44] who was distinguished from the earlier named "Hadad" (v. 35) by his place of rule (Pau) and by his wife's name (Mehetabel; v. 39//1 Chr 1:50). "Pau" (*pāʿû;* cf. *pāʿî,* 1 Chr 1:50[45]) is not identified confidently; ancient witnesses (Eusebius and Jerome) placed it in the Gebalene (= al-Jabal), which is in north Edom.[46] *Mehetabel* means "God/*El* benefits"[47] and appears again for the ancestor (ancestress?) of Shemaiah (Neh 6:10). Her mother was *Matrid* and her grandmother was *Me-Zahab.* "Matrid" may be related to the rare term *ṭārad,* "to run continuously" (Prov 19:13; 27:15). "Me-Zahab" in Hebrew is "waters of gold" and like Matrid occurs here (and parallel Chr). The unusual practice of naming two women in an ancestral line may have prompted the LXX's (Syr.) translation "son of [Me-Zahab]" (e.g., NAB). It may be that the women's names, if their meanings above are accurate, conveyed a greater splendor, that is, "continuous streams of gold."[48]

---

[39] Some suggest the location is in the vicinity of Jabal al-Mushraq, about twenty-two miles southwest of Maʾân (see MacDonald, *"East of the Jordan,"* 190).

[40] E. A. Knauf, "Shaul," *ABD* 5.1167.

[41] For the proposals see MacDonald, *"East of the Jordan,"* 191.

[42] E. A. Knauf, "Baal-Hanan," *ABD* 1.551–52.

[43] Noth, *Personnenamen,* 230; *HALOT* 2.823; and W. J. Beecher, "Achbor," *ISBE* §1.31.

[44] The MT has הֲדַר, "Hadar" ("ornament, honor") but see 1 Chr 1:50; Hb. MSS., SP, and Syr. have הֲדַד, "Hadad" *(BHS),* and LXX, Αραδ/Αδαδ υἱὸς Βαραδ, adds "son of Barad" (cp. v. 35).

[45] Cp. Vg. *Phau;* LXX's Φογωρ *(Phagōr)* probably reflects Hb. פְּעוֹר, "Peor" (e.g., Num 23:28; Deut 3:29; Wevers, *Notes on the Greek Text,* 607–8).

[46] U. Hübner, "Pau," *ABD* 5.186; according to *HALOT* 3.949, A. Musil *(Arabia Petraea)* identified it with the town Wadi Fāʾi.

[47] BDB 406.

[48] E. A. Knauf understands the name as a toponym (cp. "Dizahab," Deut 1:1), making "son of" (i.e., citizen of) preferable (cp. 2 Kgs 15:10; "Mezahab," *ABD* 4.804–5).

5. The Chiefs of Esau (36:40–43)

40These were the chiefs descended from Esau, by name, according to their clans and regions:
Timna, Alvah, Jetheth, **41**Oholibamah, Elah, Pinon, **42**Kenaz, Teman, Mibzar, **43**Magdiel and Iram. These were the chiefs of Edom, according to their settlements in the land they occupied.
This was Esau the father of the Edomites.

This unit consists of a superscription (v. 40a), identifying the sons of Esau as also Edomite chiefs, named according to their geographical identities. Eleven tribes are listed (vv. 40b–43a), followed by a colophon (v. 43b), noting the nature of the list by settlements and reaffirming their ancestral heritage of Esau.

36:40a "According to their clans" renders the same Hebrew colophon in the Table of Nations (10:5,20,31). Additionally, the list includes place names according to "regions."

36:40b For the name "Timna," see v. 12. *Alvah* and "Alvan," son of Shobal (v. 23), probably are derived from *ʿlw/**ʿly,* "to go up, ascend"; each has a variant name in the parallel list in Chronicles, "Aliah" (1 Chr 1:51) and "Alian" (1 Chr 1:40).[49] *Jetheth* (//1 Chr 1:51) is unknown.

36:41–43a For the name "Oholibamah," see v. 2. *Elah* (v. 41//1 Chr 1:52) also means "terebinth" (*ʾēlâ*).[50] It is speculated by some to refer to the seaport Eilat.[51] The name Elah is common, occurring for an Israelite king (e.g., 1 Kgs 16:6), the father of Hoshea (2 Kgs 15:30), a descendant of Caleb (1 Chr 4:15) and the son of Uzzi (1 Chr 9:8). *Pinon* appears only here (v. 41//1 Chr 1:52) but usually identified as the place "Punon" in the Wadi Arabah (Edom), which was a copper mining and smelting site (Num 33:42–43). The LXX's *Phinō(n)/Pheinōn* is modern Feinan. Rameses II (thirteenth century) equated *pwnw* (*Pûnô* or *Pônô*) as a region settled by *Shōsu* (see the excursus "Edom and the Edomites" in Section IX).[52] On the names "Kenaz" and "Teman" (v. 42//1 Chr 1:53), see comments on v. 11. *Mibzar* in Hebrew means "fortification" (v. 42//1 Chr 1:53); as a place name it may be *Mabsara* (Gk.) near Petra (Eusebius).[53] Others link it with "the fortified city" (*ʿîr mibṣār*) in Ps 108:10, possibly referring to Bozrah.[54] *Magdiel* (*meged* + *ʿēl*[55]), meaning "the gift of God/El,"

---

[49] The NIV harmonizes the two passages by repeating the spelling of Genesis; cf. the *kĕthîb,* עֲלְיָה ("Aliah") and the *qĕrê,* עַלְוָה ("Alvah") in 1 Chr 1:51.

[50] BDB 18; but Noth suggests the short form אֵל (*Personnenamen,* 38, 90). Cp. also אֵלָא, "Ela" (1 Kgs 4:18; see BDB 41; *HALOT* 1.51–52).

[51] BDB 18; U. Hübner, "Elah," *ABD* 2.423.

[52] R. Gribble, "Punon," *ZPEB* 4.957; E. A. Knauf relates *Paynân to Ar. *faynân,* "to have long, beautiful hair," referring to the region's grassy vegetation ("Punon," *ABD* 5.556–57).

[53] U. Hübner mentions the wadi *Ṣabra* (Ar.), southwest of Petra ("Mibzar," *ABD* 4.805–6).

[54] MacDonald, *"East of the Jordan,"* 191.

[55] *HALOT* 2.543.

(v. 43a//1 Chr 1:54a), is possibly a place name in the Gebalene too (Eusebius), but its identity is obscure.[56] The last named is *Iram* (v. 43a// 1 Chr 1:54a), which is not known.[57] The LXX has the equally mysterious *Zaphōn(ein)/ Zaphōim (Āram* in 1 Chr 1:54a).

36:43b The final colophon provides a conclusion for the immediate listing of Edomite chiefs (vv. 40–43) but also for the whole of the chapter. The mention of "chiefs" recalls the repeated expression in vv. 15,16,17,18,21,29,30 (cf. "the chiefs of Edom" 1 Chr 1:51,54b; Exod 15:15). "Edom" reflects the territorial interests of the list (vv. 1,8,9, 16,17,19,21,31) and appears here as a substitute for "Esau." "According to their settlements *[môšĕbōt]*" recalls the Table of Nations (10:30), which also includes place names. "In the land they occupied" recalls the promise made to Abraham and his descendants (17:8; see comments on 37:1); the word "occupied" translates the common term for land "possession" (*ʾăḥuzzâ,* cf. 48:4). By this language the author indicates that the Edomites received their land by divine commission, as did the Israelites. The final association of the Edomites, "this was Esau the father of Edomites," forms an inclusio with v. 9. Its recurrence also reinforces the contrast that names Jacob's inheritance in Canaan (37:1).

6. Jacob in Canaan (37:1)

[1]Jacob lived in the land where his father had stayed, the land of Canaan.

37:1 "Lived" *(yāšab)* is lexically related to the above term "settlements" *(môšĕbōt,* v. 43), heightening the contrast of their respective residence. Jacob's land is defined by two thematically important descriptions: (1) the land of his father's sojournings and (2) "the land of Canaan." "Had stayed" renders the noun "sojourning-place" *(māgôr;* also 36:7), which is cognate with "alien, sojourner" *(gēr* from *gûr).* The word group *(g-w-r)* often describes the outsider status of the patriarchs (e.g., 15:13) who received their land by promise. The same word *māgôr* defines the alien Abraham, thus here making another allusion to 17:8 (see above verse), and appears in Isaac's blessing of Jacob (28:4). A third allusion to the Abraham promise in 17:8 is mention of "Canaan," but there it is "the whole land of Canaan" that is bequeathed. Abraham and Jacob's descendants must wait for centuries until this promise finds its realization in David's monarchy. Nevertheless, Jacob for now remained entrenched in Canaan until news came from Egypt of his long-lost Joseph (45:25–26).

---

[56] U. Hübner, "Magdiel," *ABD* 4.464.

[57] U. Hübner commends **ʿair,* "male donkey" (Hb. *ʿîr,* e.g., Gen 49:11; "Iram," *ABD* 3.449).

XII. JACOB'S FAMILY: JOSEPH AND HIS BROTHERS (37:2–50:26)
  1. The Early Days of Joseph (37:2–36)
    (1) Title (37:2a)
    (2) Joseph the Dreamer (37:2b–11)
      Joseph's Coat of Favor (37:2b–4)
      Joseph's First Dream (37:5–8)
      Joseph's Second Dream (37:9–11)
    (3) The Deceivers (37:12–35)
      Joseph's Search for His Brothers at Shechem (37:12–17)
      The Deception and Selling of Joseph at Dothan (37:18–30)
        The Brothers Plot against Joseph (37:18–20)
        Reuben Plots to Rescue Joseph (37:21–22)
        The Seizure of Joseph (37:23–25)
        Judah Urges the Sale of Joseph (37:26–28)
        Reuben Mourns Joseph's "Death" (37:29–30)
      The Deception and Mourning of Jacob at Hebron (37:31–35)
    (4) Conclusion (37:36)
  2. Judah and Tamar (38:1–30)
    (1) Judah's Sons and Tamar (38:1–6)
      Judah Leaves His Brothers (38:1)
      Judah's Wife and Sons (38:2–5)
      Judah Obtains Tamar (38:6)
    (2) Tamar's Threat to Judah's Sons (38:7–11)
      The Lord Kills Er (38:7)
      The Lord Kills Onan (38:8–10)
      Judah Sends Tamar Away (38:11)
    (3) Tamar Deceives Judah (38:12–14)
    (4) Judah Impregnates Tamar (38:15–19)
      Judah Mistakes Tamar for a Harlot (38:15–16)
      Judah Gives a Pledge (38:17–19)
    (5) Tamar Steals Judah's Pledge (38:20–23)
    (6) Judah's Threat to Tamar (38:24–26)
    (7) Judah's Sons by Tamar (38:27–30)
  3. Joseph in Egypt (39:1–23)
    (1) Joseph Prospers in Potiphar's House (39:1–6a)
      The Lord Prospers Joseph (39:1–2)
      Potiphar Puts Joseph in Charge (39:3–6a)
    (2) Potiphar's Wife Seduces Joseph (39:6b–19)

XII. JACOB'S FAMILY: JOSEPH AND HIS BROTHERS (37:2–50:26)

The narrative describing the events of Joseph and his brothers is subsumed under the *tôlĕdōt* ("the account") heading of their father, Jacob (37:2). This was the pattern for the Abraham (11:27) and Jacob (25:19) narratives in which the father's name (Terah, Isaac) introduces the narrative interest in the son (cf. vol. 1A, pp. 35–41). This is plainly illustrated by the juxtaposition of "Jacob" and Joseph": "This is the account of Jacob. Joseph . . ." (37:2). The closing boundary of the Jacob *tôlĕdōt* is made obvious by the summary report of Joseph's last days (50:22–26). The dual references of "in Egypt" (50:22,26) form the boundaries of the final paragraph, concluding the account. Yet the phrase "in Egypt" achieves the equal effect of turning the narrative outward by looking ahead to the realization of the promises made to the Fathers and Joseph's deathbed instructions to return his bones to Canaan (50:24–25). Since the promises could only be fulfilled in Canaan, the Genesis narrative has no satisfying denouement, inducing the reader to discover what became of the Jacobites after the death of Joseph (Exod 1:8).

That the events in this section are appropriately headed by the rubric, "the account of Jacob," however, is not due to pattern alone. Unlike the former patriarchal *tôlĕdōt*, the father (Jacob) plays an important role in the episodes of the narrative, and although Joseph is the chief narrative interest, he is seldom viewed independently of his father and brothers (only chap. 39). For example, the narrative description of his rise in the Egyptian court (chaps. 40–41), in which neither Jacob nor the brothers appear, nevertheless alludes to his father's troubled household (41:51) and ends with the anticipation of his brothers' first visit (41:57). Moreover, Joseph in Egypt explains the migration of the Jacob clan, which gives the point of reference for the Egyptian sojourn of the nation and its exodus (Gen 15:13–16; Exod 1:1–8, "who did not know about Joseph," v. 8). The alternative renderings of *tôlĕdōt,* the "generations" or "family" of Jacob, is particularly fitting for chaps. 37–50, since they tell of Joseph *and* his brothers. Reuben and Judah, for example, are significant in the development of the events (37:21–30; 42:22,27; 44:14–34). Therefore, the heading permits the Judah-Tamar incident (chap. 38), which is not out of place. Moreover, this *tôlĕdōt* section includes the genealogical table of all twelve sons (46:8–27) and the tribal blessing for all "the sons of Jacob" (49:1–28).

That the *"tôlĕdōt* of Jacob" pertains to more than one son (Joseph) is shown by the author's attention on the fourth son born to Leah, Judah, whose role increasingly influences the outcome of the section. Judah's speech in 44:18–34 is not only the longest speech of any participant in chaps. 37–50 but also is structurally crucial to the contour of the plot (see "Structure"). Judah betters the firstborn son, Reuben, when his argument wins over the brothers to sell Joseph (37:26–27) and when he convinces Jacob to release Benjamin (43:11–14), which Reuben earlier could not accomplish (42:37–38). Although there is no mention of Joseph's family in the episode of the temptation offered by Potiphar's wife (chap. 39), the sexual debacle of Judah and Tamar in the prior chapter provides the foil for interpreting Joseph's moral superiority. Further, that Judah "left" (from *yārad,* "to go down," 38:1) his brothers parallels Joseph, who was "taken down" (*hoph.,* from *yārad,* 39:1).[1] Moreover, the deception perpetrated against Jacob results in his avowed sorrow, "In mourning will I go down to the grave to my son" (37:35), and Judah pleads that failure to return Benjamin "will bring [Jacob's] gray head down to the grave" (44:29,31). Also Judah emerges from the pack when he offers himself sacrificially for the brother Benjamin, confirming that the brother has indeed experienced a moral reclamation (44:33–45:1). Finally, he receives the coveted blessing that designates his future offspring as the ruler over his brothers (49:8–12),[2] presumably including the house of Joseph despite his elevated status in Egypt ("the prince among his brothers," 49:26; Deut 33:16).

JOSEPH AND THE PATRIARCHAL NARRATIVES.   A word is in order for how the Joseph narrative relates to the former accounts of the patriarchs. The Joseph section is well aware of the earlier Abraham and Jacob narratives, sharing in the theme of promissory blessings (e.g., 41:52; 46:1–4; 47:27; 48:15–16; 50:24)

---

[1] E.g., *Gen. Rab.* 85.2; see also R. Alter, *The Art of Biblical Narrative* (New York: Basic Books, 1981), 6.

[2] *Gen. Rab.* 85.1 observes the importance of chap. 38 for its messianic theme, for the Messiah was born to the offspring of Judah-Tamar.

and the motifs of sibling rivalry and deception (e.g., 37:3–8,31–32; 38:14,25; 42:25; 44:1–2).[3] That "all peoples on earth will be blessed" through the patriarchal family (12:3; 18:18; 22:18; 26:4; 28:14) is well illustrated by Joseph's provision of grain for "all the countries" (41:56–57; 47:13). That this final section should in so many ways draw on and imitate the lives of the earlier Fathers fits the overarching idea of promise and fulfillment, which binds the three patriarchal narratives together.[4] That the narrative brings an end to the patriarchal history is no better exemplified than the return of Jacob's remains to the ancestral burial cave in Canaan, where he joins his fathers, their wives, and his wife, Leah. The return for burial portrays a future vista, however, projecting the return of Jacob's offspring to their homeland. Thus Joseph's final instructions build on this imagery, which call for his return when the family comes again to the land of their ancestors. What is strikingly different in the Joseph narrative is that the account closes without the return of Joseph and his brothers to Canaan. Abraham and Jacob had both returned from their sojourns outside the land, but not so for Jacob's sons. The Joseph narrative with the three descents into Egypt functions like a hinge, remembering Abraham's descent into Egypt in the past but looking ahead to the Israelites' ascent as Abraham and Jacob (albeit his corpse) had known. This symmetry of shared experience created a sense of destiny for Israel, who could trust that God would deliver on his word. Yet that the final episode closes with Israel's families thoroughly ensconced in Egypt worked to the advantage of Genesis's recurring idea of expectancy and hope, by lacking full contentment and producing a hunger for the future work of God.

The linkage of the "*tôlĕdōt* of Jacob" (37:2–50:26) with the preceding narrative (25:19–37:1) is so obvious that one can speak confidently of the present section as the continuation of Jacob's history. The essential features of the two plots are congruous: family conflict due to parental favoritism leads to the separation of one brother who prospers in a foreign land for a period of twenty years, which eventually results in a sibling reunion who together oversee the burial of their father. There are unmistakably specific ties between the two accounts as well: for example, the skin of a goat provides for the deception of the father (27:16,21–23; 37:31–32); there is a search for a stolen item (Laban's *tĕrāphîm*, 31:19,34–35; Joseph's cup, 44:1–17); and the same verbiage spoken by Jacob and by Joseph, "Am I in the place of God?" (30:2; 50:19b).[5]

An important departure from the previous Abraham and Jacob *tôlĕdōt* is the

---

[3] E.g., the events of Abraham's sojourn in Egypt (12:10–13:4) presage the migration of Jacob's family to Egypt and the subsequent exodus (Gen 41:54b–Exod 12:4); see J. Sailhamer, "Genesis," *EBC* (Grand Rapids: Zondervan, 1991), 2:116–17.

[4] G. Wenham, *Genesis 16–50*, WBC (Dallas: Word, 1994), 358, 461.

[5] See P. Miscall, "The Jacob and Joseph Stories as Analogies," *JSOT* 6 (1978): 28–40; D. M. Carr, *Reading the Fractures of Genesis: Historical and Literary Approaches* (Louisville: Westminster John Knox, 1996), 281–82.

indirect manner in which God's involvement in the Joseph episodes is recognized by the text.[6] The former narratives rely on divine theophany as the means of revealing the agenda for the future direction of the promises (e.g., 12:7; 26:2; 28:13). Symbolic dreams in the Joseph narrative are the means by which God's will for the future is unveiled. The dreams of Joseph and those he interprets are potentially ambiguous, since they do not possess a revelation of God, whereas the four previous dreams in chaps. 12–36 are direct revelations (20:3; 28:12–13; 31:11; 31:24). When understood in the larger framework of the narrative, Joseph's dreams must be taken as coming from God, although in chap. 37 by itself it is not so certain. It is left later to Joseph's speech, which declares that dreams are from God (40:8; 41:16,25,28). Thus the reader should interpret 37:5–11 as of divine source, exhibiting the author's "subdued theology" of God's providence.[7] The divine origin is confirmed by the fulfillment of the dreams when the brothers bow before Joseph the Egyptian ruler (e.g., 42:6; 43:26,28).

The only direct encounter with God is the revelation to Jacob in 46:2–4, which echoes the theophany received by Isaac (26:24). The reason for this exception may well be that Isaac was prohibited from descending to Egypt (26:2), and a direct command to Jacob was required to assure him to continue down into Egypt. Moreover, it reinforces the dissidence between God's relationship with Jacob and that with Jacob's sons. Otherwise the narration only occasionally indicates God's presence (e.g., 39:3,21), implying that behind the events is the hand of God. The author prefers the participants themselves to propose the divine connection (e.g., 41:25,28,32,39; 42:28; 44:16; 45:5,9; 48:11; 50:20). Whereas the divine oracle given to Rebekah is private and reveals the outcome of the struggle from the beginning (25:23), Joseph's dreams of his ascent over his brothers and father (37:5–10) are made public and are subject to repudiation.[8] The narrator does not affirm that the dreams are from God, creating a narrative tension regarding how these dreams can possibly be fulfilled once Joseph is taken to Egypt. The motivations for Jacob's actions of deceit and later his reunion with Esau are much clearer than Joseph's reason for the harsh steps to try his brothers.

The relentless famine that ostensibly is the threat to the existence of the family is only the surface cause for fret. The era of God's "silence" in the patriarchal family coupled with the moral decline of the brothers, even to the depths of contemplating fratricide, signals that the greatest threat to the promises is the fractured family itself. The divine design of Joseph's descent that results in reconciliation and deliverance preserves the family and future promises for the

---

[6] See the discussion in W. L. Humphreys, *The Character of God in the Book of Genesis: A Narrative Appraisal* (Louisville: Westminster John Knox, 2001), 205–16.

[7] See L. Turner, *Announcements of Plot in Genesis*, JSOTSup 96 (Sheffield: JSOT Press, 1990), 145–46.

[8] See the discussion of Miscall, "The Jacob and Joseph Stories as Analogies," 33–34.

nation (e.g., 48:20–21; 50:20,25). Goshen's refuge and Egypt's segregation policy encouraged a renewed commitment and family interdependence (43:32; 46:34). That the book ends with Joseph counting himself as one in company with his brothers, not superior to them, depicts the sibling loyalty that the family has recovered (50:18–19; cf. 45:15).

INTERPRETATIONS OF JOSEPH THE MAN. Since the author's opinion is typically unstated, interpreters bear more responsibility for discerning the implied messages of the text. The history of the interpretation of Joseph's character reflects widely diverse judgments. One elevated Joseph to the ideal of morality and faith, and another interpretation regarded him a flawed, arrogant sibling who wronged his father and brothers.

Early Jewish Traditions. Early Jewish renderings tended to depict Joseph as the ideal figure (e.g., *Jubilees, Testament of Joseph*) who was innocent of wrongdoing in the family, maintained his sexual purity despite oppression, resisted disgracing his brothers, and fostered love from the Egyptian people despite the measures he took during his rule.[9] The depiction of Joseph by the early Hellenistic Jewish historian Artapanus in his *Peri Ioudaion* ("On the Jews," ca. second century B.C.), known from Eusebius's *Praeparatio Evangelica* (9.23), was only admiring of the Jews' ancestor, emphasizing Joseph's administrative skills and innovative land reforms. Joseph's intelligence enabled him to escape his brothers' attempt to murder him by convincing local Arabs to assist him to Egypt. Joseph was not a victim of his brothers or a slave in Egypt. The targums utilized Joseph's stellar moral behavior (chap. 39) as the centerpiece of their teaching from Joseph's life on religious values. *Tg. Ps.-J.* embellishes Joseph's youth, portraying him as a student of Midrash who faithfully observed Jewish laws. The brothers, on the other hand, are transgressors of the basic Noahic food laws, which was the accusation in Joseph's "bad" report (37:2; "for he had seen them eating flesh torn from a living animal, the ears and the tails" (*Tg. Ps.-J.* 37:2). The targums generally admit openly the harmful actions Joseph committed against his brothers during their testing. But he remained a valuable figure for religious instruction because he overcame these temptations and exhibited a righteous character. Philo of Alexandria, in a full treatment of the patriarch, portrayed Joseph positively, that is, the ideal statesman, in *On Joseph,* and negatively, that is, a type of bodily passion, in *On Dreams.*[10] In the former presentation Joseph is the ideal Jew and ideal politi-

[9] For the discussion of Jewish interpretation, see M. Niehoff, *The Figure of Joseph in Post-Biblical Jewish Literature,* AGJU 16 (Leiden: Brill, 1992) and S. Docherty, "Joseph the Patriarch: Representations of Joseph in Early Post-Biblical Literature," in *Borders, Boundaries, and the Bible,* JSOTSup 313 (Sheffield: Sheffield Academic Press, 2002), 194–216.

[10] See E. Hilgert, "The Dual Image of Joseph in Hebrew and Early Jewish Literature," *Journal of the Chicago Society of Biblical Research* 30 (1985): 5–21; the former characterization arises from the biblical story and the latter because of Joseph's identification with repugnant Egypt (allegorically = the body versus the higher soul).

cian who lives in the diaspora. His ascension over Egypt is due to his moral virtue in contrast to Egyptian licentiousness. Josephus in *Jewish Antiquities* addressed the career of Joseph, improving on the biblical account of his youth and painting a sympathetic figure among his brothers' villainy. Moreover, Joseph is a laudable figure among the Egyptians who serves the king well and who exercises humanitarian governance. The Palestinian Jewish viewpoint of Joseph reflected in *Genesis Rabbah* differed from the Hellenistic perceptions of Joseph. The treatment of Joseph is closer to a balanced appraisal, showing how his faults in his youth justified the divine response that he endures. His bad report on his brothers is a brutal castigation of their behavior. Joseph is not so accommodating to his Egyptian environment, requiring circumcision of the Egyptians. *Genesis Rabbah* (89.2) contended that he remained in prison two more years (41:1) because he trusted in man more than God. He is, of course, a morally esteemed figure, especially proven by his resistance to Potiphar's wife, which is given lengthy attention by the rabbis. He is not altogether innocent, however, for rabbinical tradition (e.g., *b. Soṭa* 36b) charged him with complicity and lusty intention, which he overcomes upon considering Jacob's admonition against fornication.[11] Nevertheless, the encounter is a designed "trial" imposed by Providence so as to exhibit how the righteous suffer in the irreligious world.

   Christian Traditions.   Christian allegorical interpretation regularly interpreted Joseph as a type of Christ, "the true Joseph." Ambrose in *On Joseph,* for example, explained that the bowing and rising sheaves in Joseph's dream revealed the resurrection of Christ and the eleven disciples. For the allegorists, most every facet of the story provided a revelation of the life of Christ and the church. The coming of Joseph to his brothers, the rejection, the stripping of the robe, sale to the Ishmaelites, the blood of the goat, the imprisonment that followed, the provision of food for the famished (of soul), the forgiveness of his brothers, the reception of his father and brothers at Goshen, the prophetic tribal blessing by Joseph—all spoke of Christ and his soteriological mission to Israel and the church. The Reformer Luther, based on *Wis* 10:13–14, went so far as to conclude that it was Christ ("Wisdom") who was with Joseph in the pit and prison. He likens Joseph's experience in Pharaoh's dungeon to death and resurrection: "And so the very saintly and good Joseph was crucified, died, was buried, and descended into hell during these two years."[12] The difficulties that the brothers and Jacob undergo at Joseph's hands are benevolently designed to test them and to elicit their confession for cleansing of sin. "Truly he [Joseph] was so holy that he could not have hated them [his brothers]. . . . He wearied

---

[11] J. Kugel, "The Case Against Joseph," in *Lingering over Words: Studies in Ancient Near Eastern Literature in Honor of William L. Moran* (Atlanta: Scholars Press, 1990), 271–87.
[12] Luther, *LW* 7.129.

them with so many tribulations, in order to arouse them in a confession of their sin and the healing of repentance" (Caesarius of Arles, *Sermon* 91.6).[13]

THE BIBLICAL CHARACTER. That Joseph resists the enticement of Potiphar's wife (39:9) and that he ultimately forgives his brothers (50:15–21) depict his virtues. The narrator informs us that "the LORD was with Joseph/ him" (39:2,3,21,23; cf. Judg 1:22), which is an indication of divine favor. He is instrumental in God's salvation for Jacob's family and the peoples of the world from an unprecedented famine: "You [brothers] intended to harm me, but God intended it for good to accomplish what is now being done, the saving of many lives" (50:20; cf. also 41:56–57; 42:18; 45:5,7; 47:25). Even Pharaoh recognizes him as a unique vessel of God's revelation: "Can we find anyone like this man, one in whom is the spirit of God?" (41:38). Sold into slavery, he is an innocent victim of his brothers and the Egyptians (37:28,36; 39:19–20). In his imprisonment Joseph defends his integrity, "For I was forcibly carried off from the land of the Hebrews, and even here I have done nothing to deserve being put in a dungeon" (40:14). Joseph's humility, "Am I in the place of God?" (50:19; cf. 41:16), can be taken as ironic, suggesting that he unwittingly is by proxy divine salvation. He champions the faith in the promises by requiring his brothers to return his bones to the land of Canaan (50:25), which was remembered by Moses (Exod 13:19; Deut 33:13–17). The biblical poets and prophets remember the house of Joseph sympathetically (e.g., Pss 77:15; 80:1; 105:17–22; Ezek 37:15–28; Obad 1:18; Zech 10:6). Steven's sermon (Acts 7:9–18) and the writer to the Hebrews (11:21–22) speak favorably of Joseph's place in salvation history.

On the other hand, the narrative's picture of Joseph is not univocally flattering.[14] Joseph's youthful ambitions can be understood as arrogance, at least this was the reaction of Jacob (37:10). "He brought their father a bad report about them" (37:2) is subject to the negative interpretation of a wily character. The most common evidence put forward of Joseph's duplicitous temperament is his tortuous deception of his father and brothers, including his outright favoritism toward his full brother, Benjamin. Some scholars have proposed that Joseph's mistreatment of his brothers arises from his youthful dreams.[15] The first dream is fulfilled in 42:3,6, but Joseph attempts to fulfill the second dream by a series of ruses to bring Benjamin and Jacob under his hegemony. When Joseph realizes fully that he has jeopardized his father's life through his own hubris (44:31), he breaks down and reconciles (45:1–3).

---

[13] M. Sheridan, ed., *Genesis 12–50,* ACCS 2 (Downers Grove: InterVarsity, 2002), 277.

[14] E.g., W. L. Humphreys, *Joseph and His Family: A Literary Study* (Columbia, S.C.: University of South Carolina Press, 1988), 91.

[15] E.g., J. S. Ackerman, "Joseph, Judah, and Jacob," in *Literary Interpretations of Biblical Narratives, Volume II* (Nashville: Abingdon, 1982), 85–113; Turner, *Announcement of Plot in Genesis,* 160–65.

M. A. O'Brien found that Judah's speech (44:18–34) in which he offers himself for the freedom of Benjamin reveals as much about Joseph's need for transformation as it evidences the change Judah and his brothers have already undergone. He contended that Joseph's hold on power over his brothers required placing his father's life in jeopardy (42:38; 44:29,31).[16] Moreover, his admission—"God has made me forget . . . my father's household" (41:51)—is potentially ambiguous, since Joseph may have interpreted his success as license to forsake the patriarchal promises. On this point, R. Pirson is highly cynical. Joseph neglected his family because of his ambition to achieve divine status in Egypt, a goal that Jacob would oppose and possibly jeopardize. In Pirson's view, Joseph would not have relented in his mistreatment of the brothers if Judah, the true hero of the story, had not skillfully manipulated Joseph into taking pity on their father.[17] Finally, the depiction of Joseph's lineage in later biblical tradition is not flattering, for the tribes of Ephraim and Manasseh represented the apostates in the north (e.g., Ps 78:67; Amos 5:6,15; 6:6). Y.-W. Fung, based on the study of Joseph's speeches alone, paints a stridently negative picture of Joseph (though Fung says he resists making a "value judgment").[18] According to Fung, Joseph views subservience as necessary for survival. He himself was victimized by enslavement, and God used this regrettable event as the means of preserving life through mass enslavement. Thus Joseph interprets his experience as divinely sanctioned, according to the current worldview of hierarchical dominance and servility (e.g., 44:18–34; 45:5–11 with vv. 25,28,32; 47:13–26; 50:18,20). W. L. Humphreys, agreeing with R. Alter's viewpoint, thinks the story is developed according to a psychological aim, "psychological unbalancing." The charge of spying and the subsequent trials are designed to break down the guilty parties psychologically. The motivation of Joseph's testing is unclear from the text; the motivation is complex and not fully known to the reader. Joseph as courtier (47:13–26) and as brother (chaps. 42–45) shows a harshness in his authority, but for the latter case "protracted and extreme measures, it can be argued, are needed to heal it [the family rift of chap. 37]."[19] M. Sternberg best captured Joseph's true motivation for his behavior in this paraphrase: "To reproduce the past, I [Joseph] will put the life of one of them

---

[16] M. O'Brien, "The Contribution of Judah's Speech, Genesis 44:18–34, to the Characterization of Joseph," *CBQ* 59 (1997): 429–47.

[17] R. Pirson, *The Lord of the Dreams: A Semantic and Literary Analysis of Genesis 37–50*, JSOTSup 355 (Sheffield: Sheffield Academic Press, 2002).

[18] Y.-W. Fung, *Victim and Victimizer: Joseph's Interpretation of His Destiny*, JSOTSup 308 (Sheffield: Sheffield Academic Press, 2000); Fung contends that the explanation for the conflicted interpretations of Joseph's character is that interpreters have taken into account his ambiguous behavior.

[19] Humphreys, *Joseph and His Family*, 43–44, 181 (quote).

[brothers] into the hands of the rest and plant temptation in their bags to equal or exceed the profit they hoped to make by selling me into slavery. Will they now opt for the brother or for the money?"[20]

CONCLUSION. The explanation for the mixed messages discerned by interpreters of Joseph's character is due to several factors. First, the nature of Hebrew narrative itself contributes to the complexity. A biblical narrative often includes variant viewpoints among the narrator, a character's own words or inner thoughts (41:50–52), and the comments of other characters. For example, the participants in the story differ in their evaluation of the silver returned in the brothers' sacks (43:12,17–23). We must also include their cumulative impression on the reader because it is common for a narrative to include disparate points of view.[21] Typically, the reader is not told directly what the narrator thinks and which characters' speeches are accurate or erroneous and truthful or duplicitous. For example, the reader does not hear Joseph's interpretation of his abduction until later moments in the story (40:15; 45:5; cf. the brothers' recollection, 42:21). On the other hand, the narrator may include the reader in knowledge that the characters themselves do not possess (e.g., 42:23). The omniscient narrator permits ambiguities and multiple possibilities to stand.[22] Second, the major characters in Hebrew narrative are not simple, one-dimensional characters; neither are they uniformly heroes or rogues. They are real, many-sided human personalities that evidence positives and negatives, both virtues and flaws. One of the draws to the Joseph narrative, valued by most readers through the centuries as exceptionally crafted literature, is its rich characterization of the leading roles, Joseph, Jacob, and Judah. The suspense that the narrative holds on the reader is possible because the actions of the characters are not always predictable. Moreover, the mental and emotional states of the participants, such as anger, love, fear, sorrow, and guilt, foster mystery at the personal level that seduces the reader to "feel" with the characters what they feel, or at least surmise what emotions are at work. Third, the theological perspective of the writer requires complexity of characterization. Common in biblical narrative, but particularly true of this one, is the author's juxtaposition of divine will and human contingency. At times the two do not mesh, leaving the reader insecure about which words and actions follow the divine script and which ones oppose it. A final factor worthy of our recognition is the impact of a "test" (*bāḥan*, 42:16) in the telling of these events. As in the case with chap. 22, a "test" by definition requires a measure of subterfuge. That a test is even necessary has been challenged, since reconciliation between Jacob and Esau

---

[20] M. Sternberg, *The Poetics of Biblical Narrative: Ideological Literature and the Drama of Reading* (Bloomington, Ind.: Indiana University Press, 1985), 293.

[21] E.g., chap. 37, see A. Berlin, *Poetics and Interpretation of Biblical Narrative*, Bible and Literature Series 9 (Sheffield: Almond Press, 1983), 48–52.

[22] See Alter, *The Art of Biblical Narrative*, 159.

occurred without the latter putting Jacob through a series of tests.[23] Yet this overlooks a key difference: there is no father and siblings in jeopardy in Esau's case, whereas Joseph's test had to take into account the state of Benjamin and Jacob about whom he had no independent information for twenty years. The test was designed to achieve full disclosure (cf. "Now I know . . .," 22:12), ostensibly to learn if they were spies, but finally to give occasion for their mutual revelations. It is difficult to imagine a test that could be as effective without the deception fostered by Joseph until the emotional speech of Judah's plea (44:33–34). Taken together, we find that Joseph's character exhibits a real person whose life is marred by faults but also laudable due to his shining moments. Sternberg observes that no one explanation can satisfy the character development and change that the narrative depicts: "Predictably enough, however, each line is wrong because all is right."[24] Joseph, too, undergoes transformation but of a different order than his brothers. His change involves a rekindled commitment to family and its spiritual heritage. He is no longer the "Egyptian" in their eyes but he is "Joseph" (45:3); he is their "brother" (45:4), who becomes one of them again. Moses undergoes a similar experience, but his is an awakening to his Hebrew heritage (Exod 2:11). Joseph picks up the discarded mantle of his heritage and looks confidently to a renewed future.

COMPOSITION. Modern interpretation of the compositional history of the Joseph narrative has undergone significant changes. Source criticism's atomizing of the text into three literary sources (J, E, P) dominated until the twentieth century.[25] Although the criterion of dividing sources on the basis of divine names (*Yahweh/Elohim*) was deemed ineffectual for the Joseph narrative, the names "Israel" (J) and "Jacob" (E and P) were used similarly for this purpose. Also doublets such as those in chap. 37 encouraged the splicing of the chapter into two versions; for example, the E account has Reuben as savior (37:22), who advises the casting of Joseph into a pit from which passing Midianite traders retrieved him (37:28a,36), and the J source promotes Judah (37:26–27) as the one who recommends selling him to traveling Ishmaelites (37:25,27,28b). Source scholars viewed such internal "contradictions" as best explained along traditional source lines.

This old viewpoint succumbed, however, to a growing recognition of a unified "Joseph novella," which was originally independent of the Abraham and Jacob

---

[23] Turner, *Announcements of Plot in Genesis,* 158–59.

[24] Sternberg, *Poetics of Biblical Narrative,* 286.

[25] E.g., F. Delitzsch, *A New Commentary on Genesis,* vol. 2, trans. S. Taylor (1888; reprint, Eugene, Ore.: Wipf & Stock, 2001); H. Gunkel, *Genesis,* trans. M. Biddle (Macon: Mercer University Press, 1997 [3d German ed.]); J. Skinner, *A Critical and Exegetical Commentary on Genesis,* ICC, 2d ed. (Edinburgh: T&T Clark, 1930); G. von Rad, *Genesis: A Commentary,* OTL, trans. J. Marks, rev. ed. (Philadelphia: Westminster, 1972 [9th German ed. 1972]; E. A. Speiser, *Genesis,* AB (Garden City: Doubleday, 1964); and more recently, L. Schmidt, *Literarische Studien zur Josephsgeschichte,* BZAW 167 (New York: de Gruyter, 1986).

stories.[26] The character of the Joseph narrative does not evidence a compilation of sagas, forming "cycles" of stories, like that of the Abraham and Jacob narratives. Although Gunkel worked with the traditional source categories, his emphasis on the unity of the composition (Novella) contributed to the rise of new explanations for the Joseph composition.[27] G. von Rad went further by identifying the Joseph story as a wisdom Novella, which reflected the wisdom ideals of the Hebrew sages during the time of Solomon's court.[28] M. Noth, too, recognized the independent nature of the Joseph story and contended that as a late work filled the gap created by the credo, "Jacob and his sons went down to Egypt" (Josh 24:4), explaining how this migration came about.[29] Questionable methodology used by source critics and alternative explications of the alleged doublets and inconsistencies motivated scholars as well to interpret the "Joseph story" as a unified composition that had undergone significant redaction. Typically, tradition critics correlate the transmission history to the socio-political realities in Israel's history, namely, a pro-David version of the Solomonic era, or a story of north Israelite provenance (Divided Monarchy) that was later shaped by a pro-Judean version of southern origin. D. Redford's proposal of a three-stage development for the Joseph narrative is one of many tradition history explanations offered by scholars. The original Joseph story was the "Reuben version," which was modified by a pro-"Judah-expansion," and finally underwent embellishments and add-ons (e.g., *tôlĕdōt* heading, 37:1–2; also 38; 46:8–27; 49) by the "Genesis Editor."[30] The "Reuben version" was the Hebrew adaptation of "the common motif of the boy who dreamed great things"; the second stage expands the story to give place to Jacob's family descent, and the final stage establishes

---

[26] Not all scholars, of course, as illustrated by H. Seebass, *Geschichtliche Zeit und theonome Tradition in der Joseph-Erzählung* (Gütersloh: Gütersloher Verlagshaus, 1978), who argued for two parallel sources; for a helpful analysis of diachronic studies of the Joseph corpus, see H. C. White, "Reuben and Judah: Duplicates or Complements?" in *Understanding the Word: Essays in Honor of Bernhard W. Anderson*, JSOTSup 37 (Sheffield: JSOT, 1985), 73–98.

[27] E.g., R. N. Whybray, "The Joseph Story and Pentateuchal Criticism," *VT* 18 (1968): 522–28.

[28] G. von Rad, "The Joseph Narrative and Ancient Wisdom," in *The Problem of the Hexateuch and Other Essays* (London: Oliver & Boyd, 1966), 292–300 (= "Josephsgeschichte und ältere Chokma," German original, 1953); this once-popular appraisal by von Rad has been discredited; e.g., M. Fox finds that the concept of wisdom in Joseph is not that of Wisdom literature but comparable to the pietistic wisdom of Daniel ("Wisdom in the Joseph Story," *VT* 51 [2002]: 26–41).

[29] M. Noth, *A History of Pentateuchal Traditions,* trans. B. W. Anderson (Englewood Cliffs, N.J.: Princeton-Hall, 1972 [German original 1948]), 208–13.

[30] D. Redford, *A Study of the Biblical Story of Joseph (Genesis 37–50),* VTSupp 20 (Leiden: Brill, 1970); see also J. Van Seters, *Prologue to History: The Yahwist as Historian in Genesis* (Louisville: Westminster/John Knox, 1992), who attributes to his exilic "Yahwist" the integration of the independent Joseph and Judah-Tamar stories into the Jacob account. Van Seters contends that the Yahwist integrated the separate Joseph narrative into his patriarchal history and made many additions in order to elevate Judah's place in the history, to include the Ephraim and Manasseh tribes, and to provide the link between the patriarchal traditions and the Egypt/Exodus story (p. 324). For a critique of "second edition hypotheses" (i.e., Redford) and tradition history, see G. W. Coats, *From Canaan to Egypt: Structural and Theological Context for the Joseph Story* (Washington, D.C.: Catholic Biblical Association, 1976), 69–79.

the story in the broad context of the patriarchal history.[31] The background and date of the composition are roughly the same, ca. 650–425 B.C. H.-C. Schmitt also differentiated three layers in the text but of a different order: the "Judah stratum" attempted to set the oldest (northern) Joseph traditions in the context of Judah's monarchy; the subsequent "Reuben stratum," composed at the end of the monarchy, embellished the firstborn's role and linked the story to the exodus; and the "Yahweh stratum," added during the exilic period, cast the tradition in the broader theology of blessing for the nations. This corpus was inherited and enhanced by the priestly writer.[32]

Others, however, viewed the original "Joseph story" as an unbroken composition, made up of chaps. 37; 39–45 (or to chap. 47).[33] G. W. Coats contended that the original Joseph story was a coherent narrative (probably by J) that included 37:1–47:27 (except Judah-Tamar, chap. 38 and 47:13–26).[34] The similar geographical descriptions of 37:1 and 47:27 form the boundaries that frame the story. Coats concluded that the major elements could not be eliminated "without seriously impairing the artistic quality of the story."[35] Because the theme of the original Joseph story was family strife, like that of the earlier patriarchal accounts of Abraham and Isaac, it served conveniently the redactor's aim of the broader narrative, closing out the last days of Jacob and the patriarchal history (47:28–50:14). The redactor set this story in the broader framework of Jacob's sons (chaps. 38; 47:28–50:26), to which were added brief priestly elements (e.g., 37:2a). Thus the "Joseph tradition" (the Joseph story and the additions) bridges the patriarchal stories and the exodus, showing how the reconciliation of the family can hold promise for a future united nation.

D. M. Carr, too, concluded that the Joseph narrative could not be explained in terms of parallel documents, but he did not view the story as independent of the Jacob tradition as tradition critics usually thought.[36] The originally independent Egyptian traditions regarding Joseph (chaps. 39 and 40–41) preexisted in some form around which the account of Joseph and his family was progressively built (chaps. 37; 42–50). This original Egyptian Joseph and the northern version of the Jacob story were variants of a common north Israelite hero myth, though the two diverge significantly in the way they develop the hero myth (trickster vs. family

---

[31] Redford, *Joseph,* 251.

[32] H.-C. Schmitt, *Die nichtpriesterliche Josephsgeschichte: Ein Beitrag zur neuesten Pentateuchkritik,* BZAW 154 (New York: de Gruyter, 1980). See also W. Dietrich, *Die Josephserzählung als Novelle und Geschichtsschreibung: Zugleich ein Beitrag zur Pentateuchkfrage,* BTS 14 (Neukirchen-Vluyn: Neukirchener Verlag, 1989), who argued for an independent (northern) story of Joseph (Divided Kingdom) that a Judean reviser expanded after the fall of the north so as to link the patriarchal and exodus traditions.

[33] E.g., C. Westermann, *Genesis 37–50, A Commentary,* trans. J. Scullion (Minneapolis: Augsburg, 1986 [1982 German]), 22–28.

[34] G. W. Coats, "Redactional Unity in Genesis 37–50," *JBL* 93 (1974): 15–21; *From Canaan to Egypt: Structural and Theological Context for the Joseph Story*; and *Genesis with an Introduction to Narrative Literature,* FOTL 1 (Grand Rapids: Eerdmans, 1983); and "Joseph, Son of Jacob," *ABD* 3.976–81.

[35] Coats, *From Canaan to Egypt,* 53–54.

[36] Carr, *Reading the Fractures of Genesis,* 271–89.

reconciliation). The graduated development of the Joseph tradition included a northern version of a combined Jacob-Joseph story (adding the Manasseh and Ephraim portions, 41:50–52; 48:1–2,8–14,17–20) that next underwent a Judean (southern) modification (e.g., chaps. 38,49), elevating Judah as the successor to Jacob. To this "prepromise" Jacob-Joseph-Judah story were joined the narratives of the Abraham and Isaac stories in a broader "proto-Genesis" rendition, linking the primeval and the patriarchal materials. In the case of the Joseph corpus, theological supplements were necessarily made by allusions to the earlier promises made to Abraham, Isaac, and Jacob (e.g., 46:2–4; 48:15–16,20–21). Carr finds that P's contributions in the Joseph section compared to the Abraham and Jacob sections are comparatively thin; here are the promise text 48:3–6, various Jacob migration reports (e.g., 45:19–21), and the death-bed scenes, burial, and death notices of Jacob and Joseph (e.g., 49:29–33; 50:12–13,22–23,26a).

Still others, although recognizing in chaps. 37–50 a wider Jacob *tôlĕdōt* level in which a narrower Joseph level occurs, contend for a unified composition for the whole of the Joseph narrative. J. A. Soggin, for example, contended that the story is a novel that was created in the late postexilic period to answer the crisis of faith that the Jews experienced at the continuing struggles of the Jews for independence. The message of the story was that God would yet transform their difficult times into blessing as he had with Joseph in Egypt (e.g., 45:4–8; 50:19–21).[37] H. C. White, after exposing the inherent contradictions of source and tradition-history reconstructions, shows by a sample study of chap. 37 (Reuben/Judah roles) how a literary theory of reading that takes into account the whole of the narrative can potentially resolve the problems imagined by critics.[38] The arrangement of chaps. 37–50 exhibits a well-ordered, balanced structure (see "Structure" below). Those studies that advocate a unified palistrophe structure recognize the same center—the unveiling of Joseph's identity (45:1–4)—at which point the Jacob *tôlĕdōt* framework reverses. R. Longacre's breakdown of the macrostructure describes chaps. 43–45 as "a long and action-packed" episode, which is the denouement of the Joseph narrative. The narrative's message as a whole is encapsulated at 45:5, ". . . it was to save lives that God sent me ahead of you."[39]

The Judah-Tamar story (chap. 38) and the blessing of Jacob (chap. 49) are not extraneous interruptions but exhibit important thematic and structural purposes.[40] The attention to Judah is not the evidence of a Judean version or revision

---

[37] J. A. Soggin, "Notes on the Joseph Story," in *Understanding Poets and Prophets: Essays in Honour of George Wishart Anderson*, JSOTSup 153 (Sheffield: Sheffield Academic Press, 1993), 336–49.

[38] White, "Reuben and Judah," 83–94.

[39] R. Longacre, *Joseph A Story of Divine Providence: A Text Theoretical and Textlinguistic Analysis of Genesis 37 and 39–40* (Winona Lake: Eisenbrauns, 1989), 28, 43, 51.

[40] See, e.g., U. Cassuto, "The Story of Tamar and Judah," in *Biblical and Oriental Studies. Volume I: Bible*, trans. I. Abrahams (1929; reprint, Jerusalem: Magnes, 1973), 29–40, who also answers the apparent chronological problems created by the placement of chap. 38; S. D. Matthewson, "An Exegetical Study of Genesis 38," *BSac* 146 (1989): 373–92; E. M. Menn, *Judah and Tamar [Genesis 38] in Ancient Jewish Exegesis*, JSJSup 52 (Leiden: Brill, 1997); and W. Warning, "Terminological Patterns and Genesis 38," *AUSS* 38 (2000): 293–305.

but is essential for the account's exposition of the brothers' moral contrition. A. J. Lambe concluded on the basis of the development of Judah's character "that ch. 38 is of vital importance to understanding Judah's role in the latter parts of the Joseph story."[41] The Judah-Tamar incident gives background information necessary for appreciating the transformation that Judah undergoes (44:18–34). He is the chief exemplar of repentance whom Jacob recognizes as worthy of the obligation of ruling and providing for his brothers (49:8–12). Moreover, Longacre notes that chap. 38 may serve a tactical purpose for the master storyteller; the literary pause in Joseph's fate provided by chap. 38 and the absence of Joseph create tension, paralleling the years of silence that Joseph was lost to the family. Verbal and motif associations of chap. 38 with the surrounding Joseph account (chaps. 37; 39) indicate the author's continuity of purpose. Among these are the recurring word "recognize" (*n-k-r*, 37:32–33; 38:25–26; 42:7–8) and the motif of the "deceiver-deceived," for Judah, who had tricked his father by a blood-stained robe, was himself deceived by a garment (37:31–33; 21; 38:14,19; see comments on chap. 38).[42] W. Warning's study of terms key to the structure of chap. 38 highlights a motif "that enables us to better understand the eminent role that Judah holds among his brothers in the last chapters of Genesis and that his (royal) descendants have held throughout the history of Israel."[43] P. Noble contends that the intertextual similarities of chap. 38 with the Jacob/Esau and Joseph/brothers accounts are not incidental and coincidental connections but are fundamentally central ("type-scene") to the manner the narratives are told. Such comparative elements in the plots of the three stories enrich the characterizations of the three protagonists—Jacob, Judah, and Joseph.[44] Humphreys, although viewing the episode as a later addition to the "Joseph novella," admits that the chapter reinforces and anticipates "certain themes (deceit, different reactions to death, retribution, and acknowledged unfairness) in the larger novella."[45] In other words, the chapter's motifs connect with the larger story and "thereby [. . .] shape perspectives for reading what is to come."[46]

As for the blessing of Jacob (chap. 49), Longacre has shown that its poetic structure distinguishes the episode as the "peak" episode in the Jacob *tôlĕdōt*.[47] The chapter is also important to the structural makeup of Genesis and functions as a "seam" binding together major narrative blocks of the Pentateuch (see vol. 1A, pp. 46–48). The chapter then is not secondary to the strategy of the author;

---

[41] A. J. Lambe, "Judah's Development: The Pattern of Departure-Transition-Return," *JSOT* 83 (1999): 53–68 (see p. 55).

[42] Others include יָרַד, "go down" (37:35; 38:1; 39:1); שָׁלַח "sent" (37:32; 38:25); the motifs of garments (37:3,23,31–33; 38:14,19; 39:12–18) and a goat (37:31; 38:17,20,23). See, e.g., *Gen. Rab.* 84–85; Cassuto, "The Story of Judah and Tamar," 30–31; and Alter, *The Art of Biblical Narrative*, 3–12.

[43] Warning, "Terminological Patterns and Genesis 38," 305.

[44] P. Noble, "Esau, Tamar, and Joseph: Criteria for Identifying Inner-biblical Allusions," *VT* 52 (2002): 219–52.

[45] Humphreys, *Joseph and His Family*, 205.

[46] Ibid., 37.

[47] Longacre, *Joseph*, 23.

the dual content elevating Judah and Joseph is consistent with the Joseph story whose protagonists are Joseph, Judah, and Jacob. It also maintains narrative tension, since it is not so obvious from chap. 49 that the house of Joseph will be willingly subservient to Judah. The eschatological character of the blessing forecasts the division that plays out along natural geographical lines, in which the sons of Joseph dominate the northern sphere of Israel and Judah to the south. Chapters 48–50 as a whole are troublesome to tradition critics, which they typically view as an assortment of embellishments and add-ons to the Joseph story from independent sources and from P's hand. G. Wenham's study of chaps. 48–50 has shown otherwise by noting the favorable comparison of the conclusions of the Joseph, Abraham (22:15–25:10), and Jacob (35:9–29) narratives. The double deathbed blessings (48:1–22; 49:1–32) are not out of place but have their precedent in the double blessings of Isaac in 27:1–28:5. For these and other reasons, Wenham concludes that chaps. 48–50 form a "coherent, well-organized unit."[48] Taken together, there is sufficient evidence to conclude that the Joseph narrative was originally the central part of the Jacob *tôlĕdōt* composition, evidencing interdependence. If the two levels are split, as tradition critics propose, then the Joseph level is reduced to a local family story with little historical significance for Israel, a conclusion that undermines altogether the present arrangement of the Jacob-Joseph-Judah account.

STRUCTURE. The Joseph narrative exhibits an extensive literary chiasmus (37:2–50:26), as we also found in the Jacob narrative (see "Structure," 25:19–35:22a).[49] The many reversals in the chiasmus create narrative structures of repetition and irony. The balance in the narrative is aesthetically pleasing to the reader and, more importantly, reflects the book's theological viewpoint of divine providence superintending the lives of the patriarchs, leading to unexpected outcomes. The literary pattern consists of two sets of seven corresponding units. (1) The first set of seven units develops the motif of rivalry between Joseph and his brothers, building the narrative tension up to the brothers' passing of a test slyly implemented by Joseph (A–G). (2) The second set of seven units works out the resolution to the rivalry, entailing the provision that Joseph makes for his father and brothers in Egypt (G'–A'). The evident cohesion of the Joseph account is complex, involving two narrative interests or "levels."[50] The dominant level in terms

---

[48] G. Wenham, *Genesis 16–50,* WBC (Dallas: Word, 1994), 462.

[49] See, e.g., G. Rendsburg, *The Redaction of Genesis* (Winona Lake: Eisenbrauns, 1986), 80; D. A. Dorsey, *The Literary Structure of the Old Testament: A Commentary on Genesis-Malachi* (Grand Rapids: Baker, 1999), 60; B. K. Waltke, *Genesis: A Commentary* (Grand Rapids: Zondervan, 2001), 21.

[50] See Longacre, *Joseph,* 22–23, whose analysis also identified fourteen episodes; he distinguished Joseph's rise to power (chap. 41) and reconciliation (chaps. 43–45) as the climax and denouement, respectively, of the Joseph plot, and he identified the blessing of the twelve tribes (chap. 49) as the narrative "peak" of the Jacob *tôlĕdōt* account.

of the narrative's character interest tells the story of Joseph's youthful dreams and their fulfillment, presenting his rise to power over his brothers and father. The second level, dealing with Jacob and his sons as a whole, provides for the book's broader interest in Israel's founding patriarchs. This is reflected in the story's heading "the account [*tôlĕdōt*] of Jacob" (37:2). The "*tôlĕdōt* of Jacob" is the last *tôlĕdōt* section of the book (37:2–50:26), completing the patriarchal accounts of Abraham, Isaac, and Jacob. This plot of all Jacob's sons is the frame in which the narrower Joseph narrative functions, contributing to the higher interest of Jacob's family descent to Egypt, where we find them at the close of the book. Thus both the wider and narrower narrative interests set up the Egyptian backdrop (Exod 1:1–8) for the exodus narrative that follows. This wider plot line recounts the factors that resulted in Jacob's migration and, in doing so, identifies Judah (not Joseph) as ultimately the future lord of his brothers.[51] The chief participants in the two plots, Joseph, Judah, and Jacob, join the two narrative interests into a single, coherent story line. It consists of two halves arranged in a "problem-resolution" framework, moving from the problem of family estrangement (A–G) to the family's reconciliation and anticipated future (G'–A'). The narrative exhibits shifting locations between Canaan and Egypt for the episodes until the final word of the story confirms their residence "in Egypt" (50:26; cf. Exod 1:1). But it is also proleptic, for the word Egypt "is itself a metonymic reference to his [Joseph's] uncertain promised future to follow in Canaan" (50:25).[52] The structure of the Joseph narrative appears below:

A 37:2–11 Joseph the Dreamer
  B 37:12–36 Jacob Mourns the "Death" of Joseph
    C 38:1–30 Judah and Tamar
      D 39:1–23 Joseph's Enslavement in Egypt
        E 40:1–41:57 Joseph, Savior of Egypt
          F 42:1–43:34 Journeys of Brothers to Egypt
            G 44:1–34 Joseph Tests the Brothers
            G' 45:1–28 Joseph Reveals His identity
          F' 46:1–27 Journey of Family to Egypt
        E' 46:28–47:12 Joseph, Savior of Family
      D' 47:13–31 Joseph's Enslavement of the Egyptians
    C' 48:1–49:28 Jacob Favors Joseph and Judah
  B' 49:29–50:14 Joseph Mourns the Death of Jacob
A' 50:15–26 Joseph the Provider

---

[51] Ackerman argues that Judah is the central character of the Joseph story ("Joseph, Judah, and Jacob," 85–113).

[52] H. C. White, *Narration and Discourse in the Book of Genesis* (Cambridge: University Press, 1991), 275.

The outside elements (A/A') exhibit the transition of Jacob's family from Canaan (37:1) to its residence in Egypt ("Joseph stayed in Egypt, along with all his father's family," 50:22). The means of movement between the two locations is the vehicle of Joseph's dreams (37:6–10) whose fulfillment result in his lordship, protecting and providing for his brothers' families ("I will provide for you and your children," 50:21). Units B/B' sound an obvious reversal, showing the brothers' rivalry for their father's love (37:4–8,20), in which Judah has a major role (37:26–27), and their joining together in the burial of their father (50:12–14). The entombment of Jacob's remains in Machpelah closes the geographical circle of the patriarch's journey.

Units C/C' especially address the fall and rise of Judah; these matching episodes particularly show the narrative's interest in Jacob's sons as a whole. That Judah is the designated leader of the tribes is evidenced subtly by the birth narrative of his twin sons by Tamar (38:27–30)[53] and explicitly by the blessing of Jacob ("your father's sons will bow down to you," 49:8; cf. "scepter," v. 10).

The subsequent pair of elements (D/D') exhibit a reversal of Joseph's fortunes from Egypt's slave in Potiphar's house (39:1,18,20) to Egypt's lord in Pharaoh's house ("May we find favor in the eyes of our lord; we will be in bondage to Pharaoh," 47:25). This turnabout is the narrative's consummate witness to God's superintendence of Joseph's destiny, and, although Jacob's family is absent in this episode, it portends the nation's future deliverance. In effect we have Israel (i.e., Joseph) in Egypt before "Jacob/Israel" descends into Egypt. Units E/E' return to the motif of dreams (prisoners', 40:8/Pharaoh's, 41:8) by which Joseph rises to power, preserving both Egypt (41:55–57) and Jacob's family (47:4–6) in the midst of famine. The three descents into Egypt, the first two by Jacob's sons (F) and the third by the whole clan (F'), intersect the two plots of the Joseph narrative. The descent of Jacob's sons to purchase food where they fall subject to Joseph's power advances the story of sibling rivalry ("Then [Joseph] remembered his dreams about them and said to them, 'You are spies!' " 42:9), and the final migration of Jacob's entire clan to Egypt establishes a residence where under Joseph's (and Pharaoh's) auspices they receive sustenance ("Israel's sons took their father Jacob and their children and their wives in the carts that Pharaoh had sent," 46:5). The final pairing of episodes (G/G') narrate the test of the brothers' character (Judah said, "Please let your servant remain here as my lord's slave in place of the boy, and let the boy return with his brothers," 44:33) and the disclosure of Joseph's identity ("I am Joseph . . . I am your brother Joseph," 45:3–4). The narrative interest in Jacob's family as a whole is not absent, however, for Joseph recognizes that God had

---

[53] See J. Goldin, "The Youngest Son or Where Does Genesis 38 Belong?" *JBL* 96 (1977): 27–44.

sent him to Egypt to deliver many peoples ("it was to save lives that God sent me," 45:5), especially Jacob's family, who under his supervision will have a new life in the safety of Goshen. So as to show his goodwill, Joseph with Pharaoh's permission provides his brothers with new clothes and sends them back to Jacob with cartloads of Egypt's best goods (45:21–23).

1. The Early Days of Joseph (37:2–36)

The title, "This is the account *[tôlĕdōt]* of Jacob" (37:2a), provides the heading for this final section of Genesis, narrating the account of Joseph and his brothers (37:2–50:26).[54] Unlike the section headings naming "Terah" and "Isaac" (11:27; 25:19), who each play a minor role in the Abraham and Jacob narratives respectively, in the present section Jacob is a significant participant. He is in mind from the first chapter to the last. The section is a sequel to the former Jacob narrative (25:19–35:29), which ends with two vignettes pertaining to Jacob's sons (35:16–20,21–22a) and a complete listing of the twelve sons by the four mothers (35:22b–26). The accounts of Rachel's death, the mother of Joseph and Benjamin, and the incest of Reuben with Leah's servant Bilhah hint at the competition between the sons of Rachel and Leah. Nevertheless, a hopeful prolepsis is found at the end when Esau and Jacob come together to bury their father Isaac (35:28–29). The same setting occurs at the end of the present narrative when Joseph and the brothers join in the burial processional of Jacob (50:7–14).

Chapter 37 introduces the whole of the Joseph account, establishing the main characters and the plot line of the story. Any remaining semblance of cohesion among the brothers soon dissipates. The account begins with Joseph in the company of his brothers (v. 2), but later he is in isolation (vv. 15–16) and finally is sold away into Egypt (vv. 26–28). That the family remains fractious is evidenced even in the final scene when Jacob resisted the comforting presence of his sons and daughters ("daughters-in-law"? cf. comments on v. 35). The remainder of the Joseph narrative (chaps. 38–50) recounts how the fracture undergoes healing through the reconciliation of the brothers, symbolized by the reversal of the enmity among the brothers who previously "could not speak a kind *[šĕlōm]* word to him" (37:4), when Joseph "reassured them [brothers] and spoke kindly to them" (50:21).[55]

The relationship between Judah and Joseph in the Joseph narrative best represents the schism and reconciliation the twelve brothers experience. The character, role, and relationship of the central figures Joseph, Jacob, and Judah are introduced in chap. 37, previewing the story's development of these primary

---

[54] On the significance of the designation *tôlĕdōt,* see vol. 1A, pp. 35–41.
[55] White sketches the narrative development of this central idea ("Reuben and Judah," 83–94).

personalities. Reuben, the eldest brother and the hopeful savior of the boy Joseph who is prominent in chap. 37, recedes for the most part in the remainder of the story because he is a literary foil for evaluating Judah and the brothers. Reuben is not a part of the group of conspiring brothers, and he fails to lead them in the nobler direction; Judah, representing the self-interested brothers, provides a compromise for ridding themselves of "that dreamer" without incurring bloodguilt (v. 19). The irony is that his measure proves to save the boy, which will in turn lead to the outcome forecasted by Joseph's dreams. Moreover, Judah unwittingly is the instigator of the steps that lead to reconciliation (43:8–14; 44:18–34).

COMPOSITION.   Westermann comments on the importance of chap. 37 for the standard source interpretation: "Source division found its strongest arguments in this chapter . . . ."[56] The duplicates in the chapter especially gave source critics sufficient reason for finding the traditional pentateuchal sources that they discovered in the Abraham and Jacob narratives. Gunkel, for example, concluded that two coherent stories could be discerned in the chapter which had been combined (Yahwist[J]/Elohist[E]) plus some additions (e.g., vv. 5b,8).[57] Although variations appeared, the same essential story of sibling rivalry and Joseph's sale to Egypt was told. The motivation for the brothers' jealousy was Joseph's coat (vv. 3–4 [J]) or his dreams (vv. 5–11 [E]); the interceding brother was Judah (vv. 21[the redactor changed "Judah" to "Reuben"],23,26 [J]) or Reuben (vv. 22,24,29–30 [E]); and the traveling merchants varied between the Ishmaelites (vv. 25–27,28a [J]) and the Midianites (vv. 28b,29,36 [E]). Verse 2's *tôlĕdōt* heading signals the priestly (P) source. The trend toward an essentially unified text, however, has overtaken the approaches of a divided text, whether sources or redaction layers (Reuben, Judah recensions). Critics continue to believe there is evidence of secondary accretions, such as P's heading (v. 2a) and perhaps a "Midianite" expansion, but the narrative flow shows no seams. Scholars acknowledge a basically consistent text with some minor additions.[58] Coats analyzes vv. 1–4 as the exposition and vv. 5–36 as the narrative complication.[59] In our opinion the conjectured repetitions are best explained on rhetorical grounds, not sources or redaction layers. The "repetition" of the brothers' anger against Joseph (vv. 3–11), for example, is not the evidence of two sources but the indication of a spiraling hatred that results in selling the brother off.[60] Our approach recognizes the unity of the passage, and the commentary remarks on the exegetical cogency of this opinion.

STRUCTURE.   The chapter possesses a logical progression, introducing, developing, and showing the fruit of the enmity Jacob's sons have for Joseph.

---

[56] Westermann, *Genesis 37–50,* 23.

[57] Gunkel, *Genesis,* 387–95.

[58] E.g., Carr concludes that there are some "minor, isolated additions" (*Reading the Fractures of Genesis,* 287).

[59] Coats, *Genesis,* 264, 271.

[60] Carr, *Reading the Fractures of Genesis,* 285.

The chapter consists of two interdependent units: (1) the first unit describes the favored son Joseph, whose dreams especially result in sibling hatred and jealousy (vv. 2b–11), and (2) the second unit recounts the outcomes, the deceptions of Joseph and Jacob by the brothers (vv. 12–36).

The first unit observes three times that the brothers "hated" *(śānā᾿)* Joseph (vv. 4,5,8) and provides three reasons for their escalating anger that results in their violent "jealousy" (v. 11). (1) Their father loved Joseph more and proved it by bestowing on him a special coat (vv. 2b–4). (2) The second source of their rising anger was his first dream (sheaves), presaging their subordination to his rule (vv. 5–8). The comment "they hated him all the more" in vv. 5,8 brackets the second part. (3) Finally, another dream (sun, moon, stars) audaciously broadens his future realm to include his father and mother (vv. 9–11), thus ending in "his brothers were jealous of him" (v. 11). Therefore the passage structurally reflects the mounting hatred that eventually spills over in hostility.

The second unit also consists of three parts. (1) Jacob dispatches Joseph to find his brothers, who are shepherding in Shechem (vv. 12–17); (2) the brothers plot against him and sell him to traveling Midianite merchants (vv. 18–30); and (3) the brothers dip Joseph's special coat in goat's blood, suggesting that he was mauled to death by a wild beast (vv. 31–36). This second unit builds on the geographical movements of Joseph that contribute to the motif of danger and estrangement in the chapter. Joseph's itinerary takes him from Hebron, the geographical center of the Abraham clan and residence of Jacob (cf. 35:27). That the brothers were near "Shechem" (37:12–14) signals trouble for the young man, for it was there that the deceitful, murderous actions of the brothers against the indigenous Hivites led to the censure by Jacob and presumably the flight of the family (34:30). Shechem is also remarkably far from Hebron, about sixty miles north of Hebron in the hill country of Canaan (Shechem is ca. forty-one miles north of Jerusalem). That the brothers move for better grazing to "Dothan" (37:17), situated about fourteen miles north of Shechem, takes Joseph further away from his father's protection. Moreover, Dothan was located near a major trade route, providing the brothers the temptation to sell off their nemesis. "Egypt," whose history indicated hostility toward the patriarchs (12:10–20; 21:9; 26:2) and their descendants (15:18), is his ultimate destination (37:25,28,36). The multiple settings of the chapter progress from the favor of Joseph's parental care to the slave's house of the Egyptian official Potiphar.

After the *tôlĕdōt* heading (v. 2a), the chapter entails the alternation of narration and dialogue, occurring in four locales. Accordingly, the chapter's structure can divide into four units, each containing embedded dialogue (Hebron, vv. 2b–11; Shechem, vv. 12–17; Dothan setting vv. 18–30; Hebron setting, vv. 31–35). The final verse has yet another setting, but there is no dialogue, only a brief report of Jacob's arrival in Egypt (v. 36), distinguishing it as the conclusion to the chapter.

(1) Title (37:2a)

²This is the account of Jacob.

The title is the standard *tôlĕdōt* introduction that announces the major sections of Genesis (see vol. 1A, pp. 35–41). Wenham correctly notes that 37:2–50:26 concerns all the sons of Jacob, although in the history of Israel the Judah and Joseph tribes figure prominently. The ancestors of Joseph's descendants (Ephraim and Manasseh) in the north and Judah in the south maintain the spotlight.

(2) Joseph the Dreamer (37:2b–11)

Joseph, a young man of seventeen, was tending the flocks with his brothers, the sons of Bilhah and the sons of Zilpah, his father's wives, and he brought their father a bad report about them.

³Now Israel loved Joseph more than any of his other sons, because he had been born to him in his old age; and he made a richly ornamented robe for him. ⁴When his brothers saw that their father loved him more than any of them, they hated him and could not speak a kind word to him.

⁵Joseph had a dream, and when he told it to his brothers, they hated him all the more. ⁶He said to them, "Listen to this dream I had: ⁷We were binding sheaves of grain out in the field when suddenly my sheaf rose and stood upright, while your sheaves gathered around mine and bowed down to it."

⁸His brothers said to him, "Do you intend to reign over us? Will you actually rule us?" And they hated him all the more because of his dream and what he had said.

⁹Then he had another dream, and he told it to his brothers. "Listen," he said, "I had another dream, and this time the sun and moon and eleven stars were bowing down to me."

¹⁰When he told his father as well as his brothers, his father rebuked him and said, "What is this dream you had? Will your mother and I and your brothers actually come and bow down to the ground before you?" ¹¹His brothers were jealous of him, but his father kept the matter in mind.

The passage introduces the sibling rivalry through the vehicle of dreams that establishes the commanding motif of the chapter and largely the remainder of the Joseph narrative section. Two competing narrative functions are introduced in vv. 2–11: the first is the family strife that eventually leads to Joseph's "death," and the second is the mystery of the dreams that foreshadow the ascent of Joseph over his brothers.[61] The two plots work together to create the narrative tension evidenced at the end of the chapter. The irony is that the sale of Joseph actualizes the dreams that the brothers meant to subvert.

---

[61] See H. C. White, "The Joseph Story: A Narrative Which 'Consumes' Its Content," *Semeia* 31 (1985): 49–69.

It is fair to say that no one in chap. 37 exhibits noble character, including Jacob, whose exaggerated favoritism aggravated the enmity that half-brothers exhibit. At least this was the pattern in the Abraham clan, one that Jacob evidently did not learn from his parents Isaac and Rebekah (25:28). The passage presents three motivations for the hatred that Joseph's older brothers had for him, culminating in their jealousy: the favored status of Joseph, evidenced by the father's gift of a splendid coat (vv. 2b–4), and the two dreams that symbolically foretell Joseph's ultimate rule over the household of Jacob (vv. 5–7; 8–11).

The critical building blocks in this introductory passage (vv. 2–11) are "sight" and "word." Verse 4 contains both ideas: "When his brothers saw . . . they . . . could not speak a kind word." By repeated use of the terms "saw" *(rā'â)* and "behold" *(hinnê)*, the author conveys in the chapter the importance of the visual dimension of the events. The brothers "saw" *(rā'â)* their father's love (i.e., the coat, v. 4), "saw" *(rā'â)* Joseph from afar (i.e., again, due to the coat, v. 18), "saw" (from *rā'â* and *hinnê)* a caravan of Ishmaelites (v. 25), and finally Reuben "saw" *(hinnê)* the empty cistern (v. 29). When coupled with the visually lifelike telling of the dreams by Joseph (vv. 6,9), the importance of sight is second only to the dimension of "word." Joseph delivers a "bad report" *(dibbâ*, v. 2b), the brothers "could not speak" *(dibbēr)* kindly to Joseph (v. 4), he "told" *(nāgad)* them the first dream (v. 5), they hated him because of "what he had said" *(dābār*, v. 8), he "told" *(sippēr)* the second dream (vv. 9,10), and finally Jacob "kept the matter *[dābār]* in mind" (v. 11). This last comment gives the ring of authenticity to the dreams, indicating that Jacob pondered their significance. The two ideas of "sight" and "word" occur together again, reversing the effects of v. 4, at the critical moment of reunion: "You can see [from *rā'â]* for yourselves . . . that it is really I who am speaking *[dibbēr]* to you" (45:12). Reversal of the spoken "word" especially marks the reunion of the brothers in Egypt: "Afterward his brothers talked *[dibbēr]* with him" (45:15), and "he . . . spoke *[dibbēr]* kindly to them" (50:21b).

JOSEPH'S COAT OF FAVOR (37:2b–4). **37:2b** The relationship between Joseph's place in the family as accounted in v. 2b and the favoritism and dreams that precipitated the brothers' hatred in vv. 3–11 is not clear. Read in isolation, the "bad report" (v. 2b) is not cause for the hatred that foments in the family.[62] It is when we set v. 2b in the wider narrative of vv. 3–11 that the "bad report" takes on the shading of favoritism that vv. 3–11 explicitly describe. A number of questions elicited by v. 2b remain unanswered. What was the content of the "bad report"? Did Joseph initiate this report, or was he an agent of Jacob, checking up on the brothers for his father? This ambiguity about Joseph's char-

---

[62] Westermann thinks the "bad report" is unrelated to the brothers' hatred (vv. 3–11; *Genesis 37–50*, 36).

acter is one that is maintained throughout the narrative until the end. Was he a pesky tattletale? Or was he an obedient son, carrying out his father's instructions (cf. v. 13)? Verse 2b provides this opaque glimpse into his personality— a tattletale or a dutiful son—which would depend on the differing perceptions by the brothers or by his father. But, it is certain, that at this point he is not such a troublemaker that his "report" engenders thoughts of murder. It is Jacob's own doing, the gift of the coat, that ignites any smoldering of resentment against Joseph.

The verse possesses parallel members, commenting on his status in the family.

A Joseph <u>seventeen years old</u>
  B was tending <u>with his brothers</u> the flock
A′ and he was a <u>young man</u>
  B′ <u>with the sons of Bilhah and the sons of Zilpah</u>, the wives of his father
    C and Joseph brought a bad report to their father.

Parts A and A′ indicate Joseph's youth, and B and B′ place him among his brothers. C′ makes it plain that trouble between Joseph and brothers is at hand. Despite an expected lower status as the youngest brother in the field (Benjamin may have been too young to be in the field, or at least his father kept him in the tents), he held a powerful position over his siblings by producing the report of their conduct to Jacob. As to whether he was given this assignment (cf. vv. 13–14) or took it upon himself (consider the voluntary report of his dreams) is uncertain. That the text provides Joseph's age also gives a chronological anchor for the remainder of his career in Egypt (41:46; 50:26).[63] The mere mention of Joseph's age as the youngest brother is an ominous sign of trouble to come, given the earlier narratives in Genesis (Isaac-Ishmael, Jacob-Esau). The contrast between his youth and his trusted position by their father (at least by vv. 13–14) portends the incongruities that characterize Joseph's life in Egypt: from slave in Potiphar's house to ruler in Pharaoh's court. In prison and palace it was Joseph's wisdom and ability that distinguished him, but the present passage implies that his elevation is the result of Jacob's love for his mother, which is alluded to again in v. 3.

Mention of the two concubine wives, Bilhah and Zilpah, brings forward the rivalry between Leah and Rachel (30:3,9) and thus the tension among their respective sons. That Joseph was shepherding with the sons of the secondary wives heightens the incongruity of his youth and influential voice with Jacob,

---

[63] The time period between the sale of Joseph (37:2a) and the family's final descent into Egypt (46:1–7) is twenty-two years (Joseph's thirteen yrs. in Egypt [37:2a; 41:46] + seven yrs. of plenty [41:46–49] + two yrs. of famine [45:6–7]). Joseph's death at one hundred ten years (50:22,26) meant he lived ninety-three years in Egypt.

but we are not to understand that Joseph was only among the sons of the secondary wives. The above parallel entails a general reference to all the sons ("his brothers," B), and the matching element ("sons of Bilhah . . . Zilpah," B′) specifies the secondary wives for purposes already mentioned. The construction "was tending" indicates the recurring practice of Joseph's role in the past, that is, "he often tended . . ." (NLT), or alternatively, he "was at one time [i.e., at just that time] tending the flocks"[64] with his brothers. The description "young man" *(naʿar)* translates a term that indicates a young male, used broadly in age, anywhere between infancy and young adulthood (e.g., 21:20; Exod 2:6; 2 Sam 14:21). The passage points up the psychological barrier the brothers face when hearing Joseph's dreams. The term *naʿar* may also refer to the subservient role of "servant" (e.g., 18:7; Exod 33:11; 1 Sam 14:1). This latter meaning has been suggested (i.e., "he was a helper to the sons of Bilhah . . .," NRSV), thus indicating his particularly lowly role, since he followed after the sons of the concubines.

The word rendered "report" *(dibbâ)* typically appears in a disparaging context (e.g., the spies, Num 13:32), suggesting that the report is denigrating. The nature of the "report" is described generally as "bad" *(rāʿâ,* i.e., "evil"). The word group *r-ʿ-h* is a recurring key word in Genesis (e.g., 6:5). It foreshadows Joseph's final "report" of his brothers' action, "You intended to harm *[rāʿâ]* me, but God intended it for good *[ṭôbâ]*" (50:20). God would transform Joseph's "bad report" concerning his brothers into a "good" outcome for the family and beyond. In the immediate scene, however, the "bad *[rāʿâ]* report" casts a shadow across Joseph's future, for the same term describes the purported "ferocious *[rāʿâ]* animal" (vv. 20,33) that devours him. That Joseph reported to "their father," not "his father," underscores the tension of favoritism that will dominate the whole of the Joseph narrative. Joseph is said to be in the company of his father (vv. 13–14) as well as his brothers, bringing to mind Jacob's own predilection to reside in the shadow of (his parents'?) tents (25:27).

37:3–4 Verse 3, "Now Israel loved Joseph . . .,"[65] provides background information for understanding the comment in v. 4. The narration echoes the divided love that Jacob and Esau received from their parents (25:28) and, more importantly, the preference Jacob had for Rachel (29:30). The names "Israel" and "Jacob" can be used interchangeably in the Joseph narrative when referring to the person (e.g., 37:3,13; 42:5), although "Jacob" occurs for the occasions that his human weakness is forefront.[66] "Jacob" heads one of the two patriarch's genealogies (35:22), and the fuller genealogy possesses

---

[64] *IBHS* §37.7.1b.

[65] וְיִשְׂרָאֵל אָהַב אֶת־יוֹסֵף is a disjunctive sentence.

[66] Wenham, *Genesis 16–50,* 351.

both (46:8). "Israel" also appears for the people (e.g., 47:27; 48:20). The appellatives are a common word pair (Jacob//Israel, e.g., Isa 44:1,5[67]) in the Old Testament, appearing already in Genesis (49:2,7; cp. 48:2). The appearance of both names, "Jacob" ("grasps the heel," "deceiver") and "Israel" ("struggler with God"), brings to mind the transformation of the patriarch and the destiny God had foretold (see comments on 25:26; 32:28[29]). That Jacob suffered betrayal and spiritual struggle before he underwent his change is the course that his sons must also endure. Jacob's partiality for Rachel and for her two sons doomed his family to the same strife he had experienced in his father's household. The reason for the preference alludes to the barrenness of Rachel until their older years. The similar language, "the child of his old age" (NRSV, 44:20), was applicable to Benjamin when Rachel died in childbirth (35:18);[68] the equivalent expression, "son in his old age," describes the miracle of Isaac's birth (21:2,7). By "old age" the text points ahead to the circumstance of Benjamin's favor, which becomes the subject of Joseph's test. This expression reinforces Jacob's affection for Rachel's children, who alone, due to her untimely death, remained of his first love. Moreover, like Sarah, who valued Isaac as the miracle child of answered prayer, Rachel's children received Jacob's special protection.

Jacob exacerbated the tension when he provided Joseph a "richly ornamented robe," distinguishing his son. This garment introduces the important literary idea of clothing in the Joseph narrative. The bestowal and removal of Joseph's attire signified change in his social standing.[69] The stripping of his garment by his brothers (v. 23) and the seizure of his cloak by Potiphar's wife (39:12–13) represented his descending status—from favored son to slave, from slave overseer to prisoner. The snatched garments were used in both cases to bolster false claims against Joseph. The clothing and accessories he received from Pharaoh, on the other hand, announced his superior role as courtier (41:42). The final reference to clothing is the reversal of chap. 37, when Joseph presents clothing to his brothers, especially favoring Benjamin (45:22). Sadly ironic, the brothers probably recognized Joseph from afar by the splendid coat (v. 18), which they produced as evidence of his death (vv. 23,31–33). The coat that had given Jacob pleasure became the symbol of his daily anguish. The precise meaning of the description of the garment *(kĕtōnet passîm)* remains uncertain; outside of this narrative it occurs only in 2 Sam

---

[67] Y. Avishur, *Stylistic Studies of Word-Pairs in Biblical and Ancient Semitic Literatures,* AOAT 210 (Kevelaer: Butzon & Bercker/Neukirchen-Vluyn: Neukirchener Verlag, 1984), 238.

[68] Since Benjamin was identified as the child of Jacob's old age (44:20), the targums attributed his love for Joseph to another reason: "a wise son" *(Tg. Onq.)* or "Joseph's features were like his own features" *(Tg. Ps.-J.;* cf. *Gen. Rab.* 84.8).

[69] See V. Matthews, "The Anthropology of Clothing in the Joseph Narrative, *JSOT* 65 (1995): 25–36.

13:18–19. The term *kĕtōnet* occurs eight times in the chapter (vv. 3,23[2x],31[2x],32[2x],33).[70] The *kĕtōnet* was an undergarment that corresponded to the Greek *chitōn* and Roman tunic, which was worn next to the body or over the loincloth by a man or woman (e.g., 2 Sam 13:18–19; Song 5:3). The *kĕtōnet* was half or full sleeved and could flow as low as the ankles. It was typically woolen but the priestly *kĕtōnet* was linen (e.g., Exod 28:39; Lev 16:4).[71] The traditional rendering of *kĕtōnet passîm*, "a coat of many colors" (AV, ASV; cf. "a robe of many colors," HCSB, or "a varicolored tunic," NASB), followed the Greek and Vulgate understandings.[72] The Greek term *poikilos* may also mean embroidered, hence "an ornamented" garment (NIV, NJPS).[73] The alternative interpretation is "a long robe with sleeves" (NRSV, REB; or "a long tunic," NAB), reading *pas* literally, the "flat" palm and/or sole of the foot. The LXX tradition also included this alternative interpretation.[74]

The text explains that it was the special coat that particularly angered them, taking it as proof of their father's special love (v. 4). That the passage says they "hated" *(śānēʾ)* Joseph is another reminder of the competition between his wives; the Hebrew term describes Leah as "unloved" *(śānēʾ, 29:31,33)*, which, however, prompted the divine bestowal of her children, much to the affliction of Rachel. Their intense dislike produced only contemptuous words for him; Jacob's household was tumultuous, absent common courtesy ("kind," "peaceably," *šālôm*). "There is no peace *[šālôm]*, says the LORD, for the wicked" (Isa 48:22; 57:21).

JOSEPH'S FIRST DREAM (37:5–8). **37:5** The twicefold reference to Joseph's "dream" and the comment "they hated him all the more" form the boundaries of this unit (vv. 5,8). The expression "more" *(wayyôsipû)* renders the verb "to add to," a probable play on Joseph's *(yôsēp)* name (cf. comments on 30:24). Whereas Rachel hoped Joseph's birth would portend an added son (i.e., Benjamin), for the brothers his dream only added to their disgust. We do

---

[70] The word and its alternate spelling *kuttōnet* occur 29x in the OT.

[71] D. Edwards, "Dress and Ornamentation," *ABD* 2.233–34.

[72] χιτῶνα ποικίλον, "a garment of varied kinds/colors"; Vg. *tunicam polymitam*.

[73] ποικίλο", "wrought in various colors, of woven or embroidered stuffs," (LSJ 1430); LXX ποικίλο" describes Jacob's stripped branches (e.g., 30:37), speckled animals (31:8), and an ornamented (רֹקְמָה, "variegated") garment (e.g., Ezek 16:10); also see Matt 4:24; 1 Pet 4:10. Cp. *Tg. Neof.*, "embroidered ornamented garment," *prgwd ṣyyr*, and *Tg. Ps.-J.*, "embroidered *(prgwd)* cloak," which rely on the Latin loan word *paragauda* "a tunic or garment with purple border" (see M. McNamara, *Targum Neofiti 1: Genesis: Translated, with Apparatus and Notes*, Aramaic Bible 1A [Collegeville, Mass.: Michael Glazier/Liturgical Press, 1992], 171, n. 5) or "laced border" (M. Maher, *Targum Pseudo-Jonathan, Genesis: Translated, with Introduction and Notes*, Aramaic Bible 1B [Collegeville, Mass.: Michael Glazier/Liturgical Press, 1992], 124, n. 8).

[74] Aq., ἀστράγαλον(ων),"a tunic down to the ankle(s)"; Sym. χειριδωτόν, "a tunic with sleeves"; see J. W. Wevers, *Notes on the Greek Text of Genesis*, SBLSCS 35 (Atlanta: Scholars Press, 1993), 614, n.7.

not know what motivated Joseph to share his dream, but transparently the double scene functions in the story as the presage of the narrative's outcome. As to how this dream would come to pass is the subject matter of the remaining story of Joseph's rise to power.

37:6–8 The picture of sheaves (v. 7) is striking because the brothers are shepherds (although cf. 26:12), but it makes sense when we remember the "heads of grain" in Pharaoh's dream (41:22) and Joseph's wisdom that filled the granaries of Egypt (41:48).[75] Moreover, it was famine in Canaan that occasioned the brothers' descent in Egypt, where the dream has its fulfillment (42:5). This imagery of the "bowed" *(ḥāwâ)* sheaves in the field presages the depiction of the subservient brothers who "bowed" before Joseph (42:6). The specific fulfillment involving all eleven brothers "bowed" occurs in the second descent when Benjamin accompanied them (43:26,28; cf. 44:14; 50:18). The language of the brothers' response exhibits their amazement at hearing Joseph's dream (v. 8).[76] The repeated ideas "reign" and "rule" and the adverbial constructions ("actually") reinforce their disapproval. Their anger arose from both his "dream" and "what he said." The mention of a dream is tantamount to claiming a divine decree, and the content of the dream is obviously offensive.

JOSEPH'S SECOND DREAM (37:9–11). **37:9** "Another dream" confirms the authenticity of the revelation (cf. 41:32). All of the dreams in the Joseph narrative occur in pairs. That there are two dreams exhibits the pattern of doubling often employed in the narrative. The second dream has obvious differences from the first, but the fundamental meaning, namely, that Joseph will rule over his family members, is essentially equivalent.[77] These two dreams are like Pharaoh's dual dreams, "one and the same" (41:25). The imagery of celestial bodies contrasts with the terrestrial representation in the former, producing the merism of earth and heaven as witnesses to the divine prediction (e.g., Deut 4:26; cf. Deut 19:15). It is not so obvious how the astral figures can signify the future Egyptian events, as we suggested for the agrarian scene above. Egyptian religion had its prominent sun god, Re, and ancient religion in general revered

---

[75] The language in vv. 7,9 vividly displays the dreams: הִנֵּה, "behold!" and participles מְאַלְּמִים ("were binding") and מִשְׁתַּחֲוִים ("were bowing"; cf. *IBHS* §37.6d); "almost choreographic," Westermann, *Genesis 37–50*, 38.

[76] The infinitive absolute construction in each clause intensifies the improbability (from their vantage point) of the verbal action, הֲמָלֹךְ תִּמְלֹךְ, "will you actually reign over us?" ("do you intend to reign" in the NIV) and מָשׁוֹל תִּמְשֹׁל, "will you actually rule us," *IBHS* §35.3.1g.

[77] R. Pirson argues that אַחֵר, meaning "different (dream)" (v. 9), indicates that Joseph dreams two different dreams; the second dream portrays a span of years, not family members, in which the sun, moon, and eleven stars refer to the thirteen years between his dreams (37:2) and his installation as second in command (41:46; "The Sun, the Moon, and Eleven Stars: An Interpretation of Joseph's Second Dream," in *Studies in the Book of Genesis: Literature, Redaction and History*, BETL 155 [Leuven: Leuven University Press, 2001], 561–68).

the sun, moon, and stars (cf. Jer 43:13; also Deut 17:3; 2 Kgs 23:5; Ezek 8:16). Since the heavenly bodies bow to Joseph, this would elevate him above creation (cf. Ps 148:3; Jer 8:2).

37:10–11 Unlike the first dream, Joseph reported his second to his father, probably because the dream directly referred to him ("sun"). Mention of the "moon," which Jacob appears to understand as Joseph's mother ("your mother and I") is problematic (v. 10b), since Rachel had died in childbirth (35:18–19) and Benjamin must be counted in the "eleven" stars. *Genesis Rabbah* (84.11) explained that the reference was to Rachel's handmaiden Bilhah, who reared Joseph as his mother.[78] Turner argued that the problem is inherently insoluble since if Rachel is alive there will be ten sons ("stars"), not eleven, meaning that the dream cannot be fulfilled. On the basis that the later dreams in the story are literally fulfilled, that is, the threes of the officers' dreams refer to three days (40:12,18,20–22) and the sevens in Pharaoh's dreams refer to seven years (41:26–27,53–54), Joseph's second dream requires the inclusion of Benjamin, Jacob, and Rachel. Thus Turner contended that Joseph designed his test to force the descent of Benjamin and Jacob, but the dream is not fulfilled—not only because of the impossibility of Rachel but also because Jacob never bows to his son (46:29). The message, Turner concluded, was that divine sovereignty does not predetermine the fulfillment of the dreams. Rather, because Joseph took matters into his own hands, the dream was not realized. Thus, theologically, the story shows that divine sovereignty can be thwarted by human hubris.[79] Most likely, however, we can be satisfied that the "sun" and "moon" were meant only to represent the family as a holistic unit, thus including the matriarch. Calvin remarked that the sun and moon "designate the head of the family on each side: thus, in this figure, Joseph sees himself reverenced by the whole house of his father."[80] As for the notion of a thwarted divine sovereignty, this insists on too narrow an understanding of sovereignty. The key theological texts (45:5; 50:20) do not deny human accountability, only that human endeavor, ill or good, does not frustrate the purposes of God. Divine sovereignty is not a rigid detailed blueprint that manipulates and straitjackets human behavior. Also the differences in the first and second dreams are not as substantive as Turner assumes. Since the dreams occur in pairs in Joseph's story, we should read them in tandem as of the same fabric, as we are instructed to for the two officials and for Pharaoh's double dreams (chaps. 40–41).

Jacob admonished his son for his impudence ("rebuked," *gāʿal;* e.g., Ruth 2:16; Jer 29:27). Jacob doubts the validity of the dream by the rhetorical question, "What is this dream you had?" (v. 10) since it would be

---

[78] Rashi contended that Jacob denied the validity of the dream (v. 10b) because Rachel's death prohibited its fulfillment.

[79] Turner, *Announcements of Plot in Genesis,* 159–69.

[80] Calvin, *Comm.,* 2.262.

unthinkable that he and his family would serve his son ("actually come"[81]).
The brothers were "jealous" (*qānā*, v. 11; cf. Rachel's jealousy, 30:1), but
Jacob pondered the incident (cp. Luke 2:19), for he knew firsthand that the
oracles of God foretold his own elevation (cf. "bow down" at comments on
27:29; also 25:23; 28:12–15).

(3) The Deceivers (37:12–35)

[12]Now his brothers had gone to graze their father's flocks near Shechem,
[13]and Israel said to Joseph, "As you know, your brothers are grazing the flocks
near Shechem. Come, I am going to send you to them."

"Very well," he replied.

[14]So he said to him, "Go and see if all is well with your brothers and with the
flocks, and bring word back to me." Then he sent him off from the Valley of
Hebron.

When Joseph arrived at Shechem, [15]a man found him wandering around in
the fields and asked him, "What are you looking for?"

[16]He replied, "I'm looking for my brothers. Can you tell me where they are
grazing their flocks?"

[17]"They have moved on from here," the man answered. "I heard them say,
'Let's go to Dothan.'"

So Joseph went after his brothers and found them near Dothan. [18]But they
saw him in the distance, and before he reached them, they plotted to kill him.

[19]"Here comes that dreamer!" they said to each other. [20]"Come now, let's kill
him and throw him into one of these cisterns and say that a ferocious animal
devoured him. Then we'll see what comes of his dreams."

[21]When Reuben heard this, he tried to rescue him from their hands. "Let's
not take his life," he said. [22]"Don't shed any blood. Throw him into this cistern
here in the desert, but don't lay a hand on him." Reuben said this to rescue him
from them and take him back to his father.

[23]So when Joseph came to his brothers, they stripped him of his robe—the
richly ornamented robe he was wearing— [24]and they took him and threw him
into the cistern. Now the cistern was empty; there was no water in it.

[25]As they sat down to eat their meal, they looked up and saw a caravan of
Ishmaelites coming from Gilead. Their camels were loaded with spices, balm and
myrrh, and they were on their way to take them down to Egypt.

[26]Judah said to his brothers, "What will we gain if we kill our brother and
cover up his blood? [27]Come, let's sell him to the Ishmaelites and not lay our
hands on him; after all, he is our brother, our own flesh and blood." His brothers
agreed.

[28]So when the Midianite merchants came by, his brothers pulled Joseph up
out of the cistern and sold him for twenty shekels of silver to the Ishmaelites, who
took him to Egypt.

[29]When Reuben returned to the cistern and saw that Joseph was not there, he

---

[81] Another infinitive absolute construction, הָבוֹא נָבוֹא.

tore his clothes. [30]He went back to his brothers and said, "The boy isn't there! Where can I turn now?"

[31]Then they got Joseph's robe, slaughtered a goat and dipped the robe in the blood. [32]They took the ornamented robe back to their father and said, "We found this. Examine it to see whether it is your son's robe."

[33]He recognized it and said, "It is my son's robe! Some ferocious animal has devoured him. Joseph has surely been torn to pieces."

[34]Then Jacob tore his clothes, put on sackcloth and mourned for his son many days. [35]All his sons and daughters came to comfort him, but he refused to be comforted. "No," he said, "in mourning will I go down to the grave to my son." So his father wept for him.

The focus of the narrative is deceit, the recurring feature of the Jacob and Joseph narratives. The occasion for the deceit is Jacob's inquiry into the circumstances of his sons, dispatching Joseph on a reconnaissance mission. As we mentioned earlier, this unit is built around the geographical settings: Joseph's journey from Hebron to Shechem (vv. 12–17), his brothers found at Dothan (vv. 18–20), and the return of the brothers to Hebron (vv. 31–35).

JOSEPH'S SEARCH FOR HIS BROTHERS AT SHECHEM (37:12–17). **37:12** Since Shechem was the site of Simeon and Levi's murder of the Hivites (34:25–31), it is surprising that the brothers would return to its pastures. This suggests that the times were peaceful toward their neighbors or an early indicator of the famine to come since the brothers appear to go afar in search of sufficient grazing. On the city Shechem, see comments on 12:6.

37:13–14 Despite the enmity for Joseph, Jacob sent his son into the hostile environment of the angry brothers. Jacob does not yet see his own flesh and blood as a threat to Joseph. Jacob's ignorance of the situation fits the Joseph narrative's motif of Jacob and the brothers as uninformed players in the story. Joseph's assignment probably was not exceptional, and there had been problems in this arrangement previously. That Joseph readily agreed indicates that he too was caught unaware of the brothers' intense hatred. "Very well" translates *hinnēnî*, meaning "here am I," indicating the son's compliance (v. 13; cf. 22:1,11; 27:1; 31:11; 46:1). Specific instructions follow in v. 14. He is to check on the welfare of his brothers and the condition of the flocks. That the father's instructions contained the term *šālōm* twice, "well" (v. 14, but once in the NIV) may be another unhappy omen, for the brothers could not speak peaceably *(šālōm)* to Joseph (v. 4). The separation from his father had begun; he had long been separated from his brothers in spirit.

37:15–17 The two occasions of the word "found" (from *māṣāʾ*) marks the boundaries of this episode (vv. 15,17). The "man" found Joseph and enabled Joseph in turn to find his brothers. Joseph roamed about, obviously befuddled by the absence of the brothers, but the "man" intervened. The picture of the roaming Joseph reinforces the young man's vulnerability and naivety. Fortunately, a "man" rescued him from his bewilderment. The unidentified "man" who informed Joseph that his brothers had moved on to Dothan reminds the reader of the "man" Jacob had wrestled (32:24–32). Jewish tradition considered him an angel in the form of a man.[82] For Calvin the inclusion of the "man" episode was to depict the diligence of Joseph in carrying out his duty and concomitantly reveals the heinous atrocity of the brothers' crime.[83] The word order in Joseph's response, lit., "my brothers I'm seeking" (v. 16), making familial relationship paramount in his thinking, reinforces the trust that he presumes and the brothers' transgressed. Since the "man" intercepted Joseph, overheard the private conversation of the brothers, and correctly directed Joseph to discover his brothers at Dothan, the passage conveys the theological orientation of the narrative as a whole. Whether the "man" is an angel or a human, the unseen hand of the Lord is apparent here. He is directing Joseph to discover his brothers so that the divine plan for the salvation of Jacob and many peoples (50:20) might be realized, although it meant a troubling time for the house of Jacob. Where are Joseph's custodial angels who like his father's might save him from his brothers, as they did with Jacob and Esau (32:1–2[2–3])? Luther answered, "In such danger we see the deepest silence of God and the angels . . . But behold how much good God draws forth from this."[84]

THE DECEPTION AND SELLING OF JOSEPH AT DOTHAN (37:18–30). Collectively, the brothers schemed to kill the approaching Joseph, saying, "Here comes *[bāʾ]* that dreamer" (vv. 18–20). But Reuben, secretly planning a rescue, broke ranks by directing them to hold the boy in a pit (vv. 21–22). When Joseph "came *[bāʾ]* to his brothers," they seized, stripped, and forced him into the pit, after which they saw a caravan of "coming" *(bāʾâ)* Ishmaelite traders (vv. 23–25). With Reuben absent, Judah convinced his coconspirators to sell Joseph to the merchants, and they "brought" *(yābîʾu,* from *bôʾ;* NIV "took"*)* Joseph to Egypt (vv. 26–28). At Reuben's return to the empty pit, he dejectedly exclaimed, "The boy isn't there! Where can I turn *[bāʾ]* now?" (v. 30).

The Brothers Plot against Joseph (37:18–20). **37:18–20** Joseph's coat probably betrayed his appearance from afar, prompting the brothers to plot his murder (lit., "kill him," v. 18) "before he reached them."[85] Little did Jacob realize when he bestowed the favored coat that it would lead to his son's affliction. "Plotted" (from *nākal*) occurs but three more times in the Old Testament (Num 25:18; Ps 105:25; Mal 1:14), indicating deceitful action. That the brothers talked among themselves ("to each other," v. 19) indicates that there was no leader in the pack but that a mob mentality prevailed. The sarcasm "dreamer,"

---

[82] E.g., *Tg. Neof.*; *Pirqe R. El.* 38; identified as "Gabriel" in *Tg. Ps.-J.*; Rashi points to Dan 9:21 as corroboration; three angels in *Gen. Rab.* 84.14.

[83] Calvin, *Comm.,* 264.

[84] *LW* 6.351–52.

[85] וּבְטֶרֶם יִקְרַב אֲלֵיהֶם, the imperfect preceded by בְּטֶרֶם indicates past time (*IBHS* §31.6.3c).

ba'al haḥălōmôt, lit., "the lord of dreams"[86] (v. 19), reveals the deep resentment they held for him and the root of their deviousness. The construction gives a forceful vividness to the depiction (lit., "behold, that dreamer is coming"[87]). Here the motifs of Joseph's distinctive clothing and his dreams introduced in chap. 37 are brought together (vv. 18–20,23).[88] The plan is simple: kill him, toss his body in the nearby pit, and then cover up the crime by attributing his death to the attack of a wild animal (v. 20). The plural exhortations "come now, let's kill him" suggests that the brothers have whipped themselves into a frenzy, willing to commit a crime that each individually otherwise would not have carried out. "Kill" renders the frequent term *hārag* (vv. 20,26), meaning "slay," that is, a violent killing, which customarily refers to the killing of humans (but also cattle, Isa 22:13) in diverse contexts, including murder (e.g., Exod 21:14), war (e.g., 1 Kgs 9:16), and criminal execution (e.g., Lev 20:15–16).[89] The word also described the earlier cases of fratricide in Genesis (4:8; 27:41–42; cf. also 34:25; 49:6). The purpose of the murder was explicitly admitted, namely, a preemptive step, eliminating any chance of the dreams coming to pass.

Reuben Plots to Rescue Joseph (37:21–22). **37:21–22** Reuben the eldest, however, intervened, arguing that the murder of Joseph was excessive. Nature could take its own course by abducting him and tossing him into a pit.[90] The text twice states that Reuben wanted to "rescue" *(nāṣal)* the lad, the word forming the boundaries of the two verses (vv. 21,22). The second occasion adds "and take him back to his father," suggesting that Reuben had his own plan for recovering him unharmed. As to why Reuben had this moment of conscience, we can only surmise that he labored under the guilt of injuring his father already (35:22), and perhaps he hoped to return to his good graces by appearing the hero. To his credit, for whatever reason, Reuben was the only brother who showed pity on Joseph and concern for their father Jacob (vv. 29–30), although Judah's greed at least kept his brothers from murder (vv. 26–27). Joseph only learned of his oldest brother's advocacy later in Egypt, which moved his emotions, triggering a trickle of tears (42:22–24). Reuben's verbiage is a solemn echo of 9:4–6 (see comments on 9:4–6; cf. Num 35:33), which calls for the sternest reprisal for murder. The brothers are the horrid "Cain's" of the Jacob family (4:9). The worded action "take *[nākâ]*" (v. 21) is a common term for

---

[86] *IBHS* §9.5.3b, בַּעַל הַחֲלֹמוֹת, "possessor of dreams"; the construction describes the nature or character of the person, hence a "dreamer" (cf. *HALOT* 1.143).

[87] הִנֵּה בַּעַל הַחֲלֹמוֹת הַלָּזֶה בָּא; cf. the deictic particle plus participle (*IBHS* §40.2.1; but *IBHS* takes this specific case as a ground clause, "[Since] that dreaming lord is here—come on, now, let's kill him," *IBHS* §40.2.1d). The demonstrative, הַלָּזֶה, occurs only once more (24:65).

[88] Observed by Westermann, *Genesis 37–50*, 40–41.

[89] H. Fuhs, "הָרַג *hāragh*," *TDOT* 3.447–57.

[90] Sarna observes that "in the desert" (בַּמִּדְבָּר) in v. 22 must refer to pastures ("wilderness," NRSV, NASB, NJPS, HCSB) since there is no desert in the Dothan region (*Genesis,* 259).

"striking" and appears in the legal description of murdering an innocent person (e.g., Exod 21:12; Lev 24:17,21; for the full expression, "take the life"[91]; cf. Deut 19:11). The parallel clause "don't lay a hand on him" recalls the binding of Isaac (22:12); the language describes physical harm (Job 1:12) and murder (e.g., 1 Sam 26:3).

The Seizure of Joseph (37:23–25). **37:23–24** The brothers heeded Reuben's plea by forcing Joseph into a nearby pit, probably one of those used for drawing water for the flocks. Again Joseph's attire has a significant place in the story; the text specifies that he wore the same special robe. Seizure of the robe was crucial to the success of the plot. "Stripped" (from *pāšaṭ,* v. 23) is another term in the passage that conveys violence, sometimes used to describe forceful removal of a garment from the frail or slain (e.g., 1 Chr 10:8–9; Mic 2:8). His incarceration in the pit provided a natural holding cell until the brothers could dispose of him (v. 24). A cistern was either a natural receptacle or one dug out to catch rainwater. Jeremiah's enemies, too, imprisoned the prophet in a cistern, expecting him to starve to death (Jer 38:9). If this were the plan of the brothers, it was a mere technicality that they did not shed blood in the murder of their sibling. The empty cistern explained why Joseph would not drown, but that it was in the wilderness left little possibility that he would be discovered and rescued. The dry pit may be an indicator also that water was scarce and famine loomed on the horizon.

37:25 That the brothers gathered to eat, presumably while Joseph languished without food or water, reveals how impervious they were to Joseph's plight. Jewish midrash recognized the irony of this picture: the brothers ate bread, while Joseph was left in the pit, when it would be Joseph who fed bread to the whole world (*Gen. Rab.* 84.17). Moreover, the scene is reversed in Joseph's house when the brothers next eat in Joseph's presence (43:33–34). The only sympathetic person was Reuben, and he was elsewhere (cf. v. 29). We learn later by the brothers' own admission that Joseph pled for deliverance, but they had no pity (42:41). The narrative's silence on Joseph's perspective reinforces the symbolic "death" portrayed in the chapter. The sudden appearance of the Ishmaelite traders can be taken as a gift, meaning that the ordeal in the pit was not prolonged. The language "looked up and saw" is a stock phrase that signals a significant event is in the making, not only before the participants' eyes but ours as well (e.g., 13:10; 18:2; 22:4; Exod 14:10). The location of Dothan near a major trading lane provided for the timely appearance for traders from Gilead (on Gilead see comments on 31:21). There is ample Egyptian evidence that the slave trade with Egypt from locations in Asia was a brisk one in the time of Joseph.[92]

---

[91] The language is a form of נכה ("to strike") plus נֶפֶשׁ ("life/soul"), meaning that the blow results in destroying the person's life-force.

[92] K. A. Kitchen names representative texts ("Genesis 12–50 in the Near Eastern World," in *He Swore an Oath: Biblical Themes from Genesis 12–50* [Cambridge: Tyndale, 1993], 77–79).

That the traders were "Ishmaelites" is striking, since the very name brings to memory the sibling struggle that reached back to the earliest days of the Abraham tribe. Moreover, the passage intimates that Ishmael's descendants had rapidly prospered in number and trade (cf. 17:20; Judg 8:24). They are also referred to as "Midianite traders" in vv. 28,36; the terms "Ishmaelites" and "Midianites" overlap referents, indicating the same group (cf. v. 36 with 39:1; also Judg 8:24).[93] The use of the dual names Ishmaelites and Midianites for the same caravan is not the evidence of two sources or literary growth, as critics typically claim.[94] "Midianite" might designate a group of different ethnic peoples, for "Midianites" are mentioned living in diverse areas, including northwest Arabia, Sinai, Canaan, and the Transjordan. They were part of the notable "eastern peoples" (e.g., Judg 26:3; cf. 29:1).[95] Another proposal is that "Ishmaelite" is the broad term and "Midianite" is the limited ethnic reference.[96] Longacre contended on a discourse basis that the dual terms referred to the same group; typical practice of "participant reference" in Hebrew narrative suggests that the "Midianites" is not the introduction of a new people. Longacre noted parallel events in the fabric of the narrative between Joseph's appearance at a distance (vv. 18–24) and the appearance of the Ishmaelites from afar (vv. 25–28). When first sighted the "Ishmaelites" were seen (v. 25) and then as they come nearby they are identified as "Midianites" (v. 28).[97] We can add that the narrative's return to the name "Ishmaelites" in v. 28b forms an inclusion with v. 25, creating a discrete paragraph that describes the caravan's role in the development of the story, with a movement from Gilead to Egypt (vv. 25–28).

Other than historiographical purposes, the author employs "Midianites," as he had Ishmaelites, to reinforce the motif of sibling rivalry that had now come to haunt the Jacobite clan. The author remembers that "Midian" was among the rejected sons of Abraham born to Keturah, who were expelled to the east (see comments on 25:2,4–6). Although there is no account of rivalry between Midian and Abraham's son Isaac, their respective offspring engaged in strife; the Midianites were instrumental in oppressing the wilderness Israelites (e.g., Num 25:17–18; 31:1–16). From this later perspective it would not be surprising to learn that Midianites had been involved in Joseph's sale and bondage. Ironi-

---

[93] See K. A. Kitchen, *Ancient Orient and Old Testament* (London: InterVarsity, 1966), 119, 123, who cites individuals and groups with double names; also id., "Joseph," *NBD* 657.

[94] E.g., Gunkel, *Genesis,* 387; Carr, *Reading the Fractures of Genesis,* 284–85; Redford (*Joseph,* 145–46), in his "Reuben version," has the Midianites retrieve (v. 28a), transport (v. 28c), and sell Joseph in Egypt (v. 36), and the "Judah version" has the Midianites sell him to the Ishmaelites (vv. 25,28b) who trade him in Egypt (39:1).

[95] G. Mattingly, "Midianites," *HBD* 634–35.

[96] Hamilton, *Genesis Chapters 18–50,* 423.

[97] Longacre, *Joseph,* 30–31, 155.

cally, the three spices that the Midianites transported were among the "best products of the land" (43:11) that Jacob will send as a gesture of goodwill to the "man" (Joseph) of Egypt.

Judah Urges the Sale of Joseph (37:26–28). **37:26–27** By a rhetorical question, Judah proposes that they make money from the disposal of Joseph. Murder and its cover-up will not pay as handsomely as a slave's price. "Profit" *(beṣaʿ)* often bears the negative connotation of greed or dishonest gain (e.g., Exod 18:21; Prov 15:27). This feature of the incident becomes the basis for Joseph's tests of Judah and his brothers. Will they be satisfied with the mistakenly returned silver and grain, or will they sacrifice themselves for their brothers Simeon and Benjamin (42:19–38; 44:1–34)? Ironically, whereas family solidarity should have meant protection,[98] Judah argues that kinship ("our own flesh and blood," lit., "our flesh"; cf. comments on 29:14) prevents them from murdering "[their] brother" (v. 27). Although he did not want to kill the boy, Judah's motivation was opposite that of Reuben, who hoped ultimately to return the boy (vv. 21–22).

37:28 The unusual trifold repetition of "Joseph" in the Hebrew text, "pulled and brought up Joseph . . . sold Joseph . . . and took Joseph," signals the importance of this verse for the episode.[99] "His brothers pulled Joseph up" (NIV) interprets the ambiguous subject of the action, lit., "they pulled Joseph up," which may refer to the Midianites (e.g., HCSB, NAB, REB) or to the brothers (e.g., NLT). Since the Midianites and Ishmaelites are best understood as identifying the same traveling band (see comments on v. 25), v. 28b shows that it must have been the brothers who brought him up and sold him. Joseph's accusation coincides well with this understanding (45:4–5). Otherwise the Midianites and Ishmaelites were two different groups, and the former sold Joseph to the Ishmaelites who went down into Egypt, but this would contradict the narrative at 37:36 and 39:1. The term "pulled" *(māšak)* also describes the retrieval of Jeremiah from his cistern jail, using ropes for the task (Jer 38:13; cf. Job 41:1; Jer 31:3; Hos 11:4). Canaanites, that is, "Asiatics" in Egyptian records, were common in Egypt, not only in the delta region north but at least as far south as Thebes (ca. three hundred miles). These "Asiatics" varied in role, including temple functionaries, household servants, and slaves. K. A. Kitchen comments, "Thus, many a young Semite (like a Joseph) might enter Egypt as a bought slave, as a slave sent as tribute, or as a prisoner-of-war (as in later times)."[100] The sale price of "twenty shekels of silver" was the typical price for a slave in the early second millennium (e.g., Laws of Hammurapi).[101] Votive offerings set twenty pieces of silver for

[98] E.g., Lev 19:17; 25:14–17; Deut 15:7–18; 25:5–10; Jer 34:14.
[99] Longacre, *Joseph*, 30.
[100] Kitchen, "Genesis 12–50 in the Near Eastern World," 79.
[101] Ibid., 79–80.

a young male of five to twenty years old (Lev 27:5). No doubt his youth and vigor would have brought a higher price for a slave in Egypt.

Reuben Mourns Joseph's "Death" (37:29–30). **37:29–30** Where and why Reuben had left his brothers, the text does not say. This may be one of several indications that Reuben had lost his moral authority, for neither his brothers here nor his father later accepted his leadership (42:37–38). That Reuben was absent, however, permitted Judah's scheme to transpire unhindered. This is an early indication of Judah's rising position among the brothers. Upon Reuben's return he first checked on Joseph's condition. Perhaps he intended to rescue Joseph at that very moment. When he discovered the empty pit, lit., "behold, there [was] no Joseph" *(wĕhinnêh ʾên yôsēp),* [102] he spontaneously tore his clothing. This act of grief anticipates two future outbreaks of sorrow: Jacob at learning of Joseph's death (v. 34) and the brothers' surprise at Benjamin's sudden peril (44:13). Such expressions characterized the distraught at hearing of death and disaster or the mournful at a funeral procession (e.g., 1 Sam 4:12; 2 Sam 3:31; 13:31; Job 1:20). Reuben assumed that Joseph was dead. Shocked at his discovery, Reuben exclaimed pointedly, "The boy isn't there!" *(hayyeled ʾênennû,* v. 30; cp. Enoch, "he was no more," *ʾênennû,* 5:24). The brothers describe to (the undisclosed) Joseph his "death" similarly, "one is no more" *(hāʾeḥād ʾênennû,* 42:13,32; cf. 42:36; cp. Judah's pleas with *ʾênennû,* 44:26,30,34). Reference to Joseph as a "boy" *(yeled)* may reflect Reuben's sense of responsibility as the eldest brother. His secret plan is foiled, and now he must face his father. He considers this turn of events as tantamount to his own demise, lit., "(as for) me, where (shall) I go?" Reuben later scolds his brothers by expressing a belated "I-told-you-so!" kind of reply (42:22). Reuben will fear the pain of a father's loss, too, when he offers up his own sons as security for taking Benjamin to Egypt (42:37).

THE DECEPTION AND MOURNING OF JACOB AT HEBRON (37:31–35). **37:31–33** The brothers' ruse was a believable scenario. The distinctive robe could not be mistaken. The cultic significance of "dipped" *(ṭābal,* v. 31) in blood may provide a double entendre in context, signifying the death of an innocent (e.g., Exod 12:22). The Hebrew in v. 32, lit., "they sent the ornamented robe and brought (it) to their father" is difficult. It may mean that the brothers sent the garment ahead by a messenger (cf. NRSV, NAB, NJB). If by a messenger, the text shows them to be cowards as well as liars. The brothers baldly lie, "we found this," but then leave it to their father to draw the obvious conclusion from the blood-soaked robe. They heartlessly spare themselves further prevarication. "Examine it" *(nākar,* v. 32) is a key word in the Joseph narrative, meaning "to recognize" (v. 33; 38:25–26), which describes the failure of the brothers to recognize Joseph but his ability to identify them (42:7–8). The

---

[102] With *IBHS* §40.2.1d, a ground clause, "Because Joseph was not in the pit."

center of power shifts from the brothers to that of Joseph. The term echoes Jacob's ruse against the blind and aged Isaac, "who did not recognize *[nākar]* him" (27:23). That they refer to Joseph as "your son" rather than "our brother" hints at what they strive to keep hidden from their father. Jacob knew the risks of a shepherd and a traveler in the wild (e.g., Lev 26:6; Ezek 14:15,25) since he had made a career of both. The severity of the torn garment led him to imagine that the attack was brutal; Joseph was "devoured" (*ʾākal,* i.e., "eaten") and "torn to pieces" (*ṭārōp ṭōrap,*[103] v. 33). Jacob convinced himself. Ironically, he had betrayed his own father Isaac, also at his brother's expense (Esau), by wearing a hunter's clothes and the skin of a goat (27:15–16,22–23,27). "Payday someday" had arrived!

37:34–35 As Westermann observed, "The brothers could do away with their preferred brother, but not with the love of the father for his son."[104] Jacob performed the traditional acts of mourning the dead (for tearing the clothes, see v. 29; cf. Jer 16:5–8). Scruffy "sackcloth" (*śak*) was worn (here, lit., "on his loins") by mourners to inflict on themselves biting discomfort (e.g., 2 Sam 3:31; Joel 1:8; cp. Ps 30:12). The term "sack" appears again when Joseph fosters his own scheme against the brothers (42:25,27,35). The term "mourn" (*ʾābal*) usually describes laments for the dead (also *ʾābēl,* v. 35), which are often accompanied by emotional and physical demonstrations, such as weeping, fasting, wearing mourning clothes, removal of cosmetics, heaping up dirt and ashes, and tearing of garments (e.g., 2 Sam 14:2; 19:1; Neh 1:4; Esth 4:3; Jer 6:26; Ezek 24:17). Professional mourners were a hired skill (e.g., 2 Sam 1:24; Amos 5:16). Those bereft of a son received the deepest sympathy and "comfort" (*nāḥam;* e.g., Job 42:11; 1 Chr 7:22; Jer 16:7). That Jacob refused his children's consolation was uncommon, revealing the intensity of his grief (cf. Isa 22:4), for his rejection of comforters meant the most aggravated anguish (e.g., Ps 69:20[21]). Mention of "daughters" (v. 35) may indicate that he has daughters in addition to Dinah or that the women are his daughters-in-law.[105] Typically, a period of mourning would be appointed (e.g., 27:41; 50:4; Deut 34:8), but in Jacob's mind no end to his sorrow is possible (e.g., Isa 51:19); therefore he believes he will die "in [the state of] mourning"[106] (v. 35), finding relief only in meeting his deceased son "in Sheol" (v. 35, "grave," NIV). But God had a better outcome for Jacob because "many days" (v. 34) proved to have an end—twenty-two years until they were reunited (cf. 41:46; 41:3; 45:6). Later at Jacob's death Joseph reciprocates by weeping (50:1). The term "sheol"

---

[103] The construction is another case of the infin. absolute, intensifying the certainty of the action: "Without a shadow of a doubt, he has been torn to pieces" (*IBHS* §35.3.1b).

[104] Westermann, *Genesis 37–50,* 44.

[105] Rashi, "for a person does not hesitate to call his son-in-law his son, or his daughter-in-law his daughter."

[106] *IBHS* §10.2.2d, n. 18.

(šĕ'ôl) is fluid in its usage,[107] referring here simply to the grave, the abode of the dead (also 42:38; 44:29,31; 1 Kgs 2:6,9). That Jacob anticipates meeting his son once again indicates that he expects some form of life after death (e.g., 2 Sam 12:23).

(4) Conclusion (37:36)

36Meanwhile, the Midianites sold Joseph in Egypt to Potiphar, one of Pharaoh's officials, the captain of the guard.

37:36 The final verse describes the specific destination of the enslaved brother. The summary information anticipates the continuing account of Joseph's sojourn, which reappears in 39:1 (excepting "Ishmaelites" for "Midianites,"[108] see v. 28). The prominence of Joseph's new master was afforded by Potiphar's elite connection with Pharaoh as his "captain of the guard" *(śar haṭṭabbāḥîm,* 39:1; 40:4; 41:10,12). The similar title *rab ṭabbāḥîm* identifies the Babylonian Nebuzaradan (2 Kgs 25:8; Jer 39:9) and Arioch (Aramaic *rab ṭabbāḥayyā',* Dan 2:14), who exercised "policing operations of a military nature."[109] He held the prestigious position of an "official" *(sārîs)* in the royal court (39:1; 40:2,7), which will play an important role in the disposition of Joseph by the angry husband (39:19–20). Despite the importance attached to Potiphar's role, the Joseph account usually casts Egyptian characters in an unfavorable light. The same literary property characterizes the books of Daniel and Esther in which the Jews live under Gentile rule. Potiphar, who is naive about his wife's wayward behavior and who is easily manipulated by her lies, contrasts with Joseph, who exhibited insight into human character and did not fall prey to her exploitation. Eventually, all the officers of Pharaoh's court will come under the hegemony of Joseph. The names "Potiphar" *(pôṭîpar)* and "Potiphera" *(pôṭîpera'),* Joseph's father-in-law (41:45,50; 46:20), are perhaps related etymologically; if so, the former is a shortened form of "Potiphera." There is general agreement that the Hebrew reflects Egyptian *Pa-di-Pre,* meaning "he whom Re has given."[110] On the significance of Egyptian names for dating the Joseph account, see the Introduction.

---

[107] R. L. Harris, "שְׁאוֹל *(shᵉ'ôl),*" *TWOT* 2.892–93; E. Merrill, "שְׁאוֹל," *NIDOTTE* 4.6–7.

[108] The MT's הַמְּדָנִים, "Medanites," in v. 36 is usually "corrected" in ancient and modern versions to read "Midianites" with v. 28; the ancestor of the Medanites, "Medan," was the brother of Midian (see comments on 25:2).

[109] Redford, *Joseph,* 56. Kitchen, "Joseph," *NBD* 658, agreeing with J. Vergote, *Joseph en Égypt: Genèse Chap. 37–50, à la lumière des études égyptologiques récentes* (Louvain: Publications Universitaires, 1959), contends for "butler"; cf. Gk. ἀρχιμαγείρῳ, "chief butler."

[110] Kitchen, "Genesis 12–50 in the Near Eastern World," 85–86; J. K. Hoffmeier, *Israel in Egypt: The Evidence for the Authenticity of the Exodus Traditions* (Oxford/New York: Oxford University Press, 1997), 84; Y. Muchiki, however, differed from the common view, understanding פּוֹטִיפַר ("Potiphar") as meaning "he whom the companion has given" *(Egyptian Proper Names and Loanwords in North-West Semitic,* SBLDS 173 [Atlanta: SBL, 1999], 221).

2. Judah and Tamar (38:1–30)

The Judah-Tamar episode imparts another insight into the troubled household of Jacob and the wayward character of his sons. Chapter 38 shows that the purposes of God for Jacob's family and, from a historical perspective, for the nation Israel, overcame human obstacles—the selfishness of evil sons (Er, Onan), the ignorance and sensuality of an old man (Judah), and the disgraceful actions of a desperate widow (Tamar)—to provide heirs for Judah, even a royal legacy by the child Perez. The tribal ancestor Judah is of special interest to the author of Genesis because of his importance to the Joseph story (37:26–27; 44:16–34) and to the history Jacob envisions for the Judah clan (49:8–12). At the level of the Joseph story, Judah exhibits the worst and best of the brothers as a whole, becoming the chief spokesman and leader of the band (cf. his impassioned plea for Benjamin and Jacob, 44:18–34). Chapter 38 shows him at his worse. The author forecasts that Judah is the progenitor of the royal tribe that rules over Israel. This is hinted by the uterine struggle of the twins born to Judah and Tamar (vv. 27–30) and made explicit in the blessing spoken by Jacob (49:8–12).

At the national level, Judah was the prominent tribe in the south as Joseph's sons (Manasseh, Ephraim) were the prominent tribes to the north. In both cases, Judah and Joseph's family histories show the providential practice of choosing the younger son for prominence. Judah was the fourth son born to Leah, but he surpassed his brothers, who had discredited themselves in Jacob's eyes (Reuben, Simeon and Levi). Joseph, though not the youngest of the twelve after the birth of Benjamin, held that position in name since he was the youngest born in Paddan-Aram. Also the sons of Judah and Joseph evidenced this providential feature. The peculiar birth story of the twins Perez and Zerah revived the celebrated struggle the twins Jacob and Esau experienced, which was previewed by a divine oracle that foretold the superiority of the younger child (25:23). Although no oracle precedes the birth of Tamar's twins, there is by implication the same assumption, for in all of Scripture only Rebekah and Tamar produce twins. The announcements of each mother's birth twins employ the exact same words, "There were twin boys in her womb" (25:24; 38:27). Joseph's sons, too, manifested this transposition in leadership by Ephraim's favor over the elder Manasseh in Jacob's blessing (48:13–20). Joseph's protestations reinforce the unexpected nature of his father's action, signaling the future importance of Joseph's house. This is confirmed in Jacob's deathbed blessing (49:22–26). That the chapter concerns the continuation of family inheritance is evidenced by the structure of the narrative in which the two birth narratives (vv. 1–5; 27–30) form an inclusion.

The placement of the Judah-Tamar event has a narrative function for the entire Joseph narrative (see "Structure" below), but its position between the sale of Joseph in chap. 37 and the Joseph-Potiphar's wife account in chap. 39 serves another important goal. By juxtaposition, chap. 38 calls for a contrast with the surrounding events of Joseph's Egyptian sojourn. The strongest contrast is the innocent behavior of Joseph versus the wickedness of Judah's household and the sensuality of Potiphar's wife. Moreover, the descent of Judah brings to the fore the fragmentation the brothers experienced during this period. Both Joseph and Judah, the chief protagonists of the Joseph narrative, live in isolation from their brothers and father. Both are in a foreign environment where they excel, marry native wives, and produce future Hebrew tribes. A significant contrast is the sordid episode of Tamar, who bore Judah's famous children by illicit means. Judah succumbed to the temptation of the harlot, unwittingly impregnating his son's wife, but Joseph resisted the seduction of Potiphar's wife. That Tamar should be interpreted sympathetically, a person victimized by the recalcitrant men of the household, may be intended when we compare her behavior with Potiphar's wife. The latter is interested only in the sensual experience with the handsome young Hebrew, but Tamar to her credit, at least as recognized by Judah (v. 26), sought to fulfill her maternal calling in behalf of her husband's family.

If, however, we read this episode as only a moral story warning against inflamed passions and against abrogating family duty, or as a folkloristic telling of Israel's chief ancestors, we lose the theological importance of the narrative for the Joseph story and for Genesis as a whole. The absence of God's intervention in the matter of Tamar and Judah (vv. 6–30), which is made explicit by the author only in the brief family portrait in vv. 1–5, should not deceive the reader. That the passage omits the viewpoint of God toward the culprits Tamar and Judah, if indeed they are to be interpreted as offenders, and the absence of God in the passage at bringing about the remarkable births of the twins, unlike the births of the earlier tribal ancestors (25:21; chaps. 29–30), produces a disconcerting silence for the reader. This demonstrated for the author that the working out of God's purpose is not always overt but may be covert and never thwarted by the vicissitudes of human life. As at many points in the Joseph narrative and prominently in the theology of the Ruth account,[111] chap. 38 implies that the hand of God is behind the events that transpire. After explicitly declaring divine involvement (vv. 1–5), the passage exhibits the hiddenness of God's involvement in the lives of Israel's fathers. This is shown by the historic outcome of the Judah-Tamar union, producing the ancestral lineage of the royal house through Perez (Ruth 4:18–22; 2 Chr 2:5–15; Matt 1:3–6; Luke 3:31–33). Strikingly, David's daughter was named Tamar, who also suffered at the hands of rival brothers and was relegated to a childless life (2 Sam 13:20). When we

---

[111] See R. M. Hals, *The Theology of the Book of Ruth* (Philadelphia: Fortress, 1969); D. Block, *Judges, Ruth* (Nashville: Broadman & Holman, 1999).

remember Ruth's marriage to Boaz, also in the lineage of David, we find a remarkable contrast between these two ancestresses of David. That such a comparison is called for is the allusion to Tamar's twins in the elders' invocation: "Through the offspring the LORD gives you [Boaz] by this young woman [Ruth], may your family be like that of Perez, whom Tamar bore to Judah" (Ruth 4:12). Both are childless widows who depended on family members to provide children, but whereas Tamar feigns the harlot, Ruth acts nobly when resisting the opportunity to entrap Boaz in an untoward way (3:7–14). We can reach further back when we remember that the ancestry of Ruth is Moabite, the child of Lot's incest (19:30–38). The women of David's ancestry exhibit the sordid and the splendid sides of humanity, both of which God employed to build the house of kings in Israel.

Excursus: Levirate Marriage

A brief comment on the subject of levirate marriage is in order here. It is another element significant to the chapter's emphasis on new generations. Levirate marriage is the marriage of a widow to her husband's brother. The Latin term for "brother-in-law" (Hb. *yābām*[112]) is *levir* (although the term does not occur in the Vulgate), so that the custom is identified as "levirate marriage." The word group *y-b-m*, which identifies these "in-law" relationships, describes the practice and the roles of the parties involved.[113] The legal formulation governing the convention is stipulated in Deut 25:5–10. Additionally, the Book of Ruth refers to the idea of levirate marriage (1:11–13). Also the Sadducean debate of Jesus' day concerning the resurrection of the dead alludes to levirate marriage (Matt 22:23–33 pars.).

The "widow" (*'almānâ*) was not only the survivor of her deceased husband but a woman whose economic life was threatened when she no longer had a male provider/protector.[114] A woman typically was dependent upon the male members of her household to provide for her sustenance—first her "father's house," including her father and brothers, and, second, upon marriage, her husband's household, including her husband, sons, and the male members of her husband's family (e.g., brothers and father). In the event a husband died childless, she was obligated to marry in her husband's household (Deut 25:5–10). In turn the husband's household was obligated to provide a male heir. The order of responsibil-

---

[112] The Hb. tractate *Yebam/Yebamot* addresses levirate law in rabbinic Judaism.

[113] The *piel* form of יָבַם (38:8; Deut 25:5[2x],7[2x]) describes the act of impregnating the widow, i.e., carrying out the duty of the יָבָם (Deut 25:5), "brother-in-law," i.e., the brother of the deceased; the "sister-in-law," i.e., the brother's widow, is יְבָמָה (Deut 25:7,9; Ruth 1:15). The word for "father-in-law," i.e., husband's father, is חָם (38:13,25; 1 Sam 4:19,21; contrast "wife's father, father-in-law," חֹתֵן, e.g., Exod 3:1), "mother-in-law," i.e., husband's mother, is חָמוֹת (e.g., Ruth 1:14; Mic 7:6), and "daughter-in-law" is כַּלָּה (e.g., 38:11,16,24; Ruth 1:6).

[114] See H. A. Hoffner, "אַלְמָנָה *'almānāh*" *TDOT* 1.287–91; M. D. Carroll R., "Widow," in *Dictionary of the Old Testament: Pentateuch* (Downers Grove: InterVarsity, 2003), 890–93; and J. Rook, "Making Widows: The Patriarchal Guardian at Work," *BTB* 27 (1997): 10–15.

ity usually was with the brother(s) of the deceased husband, and in ancient Near Eastern practice the father of the deceased husband (her father-in-law) was eligible.[115] The role of the male member of society not only cared for her general well-being but was the protector of the woman's sexuality (e.g., Lev 21:9; Deut 22:13–21; Song 1:6). Any sexual impropriety committed by the woman reflected on the good name of her father before marriage and on the household of her husband (whether dead or alive) after marriage. When Judah directs Tamar to live as a "widow," he is speaking of her chastity, for without a male protector (husband, son, brother, father-in-law) she had no automatic provision of a sexual partner in the family guaranteeing her a husband and eventually a child. By returning to her "father's house," Judah suspends his immediate supervision of Tamar, leaving it again to her father and male relatives to protect and provide (e.g., Lev 22:13; cf. as a brother, Absalom's care of Tamar, 2 Sam 13:20). But by living as a widow she cannot go outside the bounds of Judah's family to marry unless he releases her. If released she may seek out another husband or pursue a profession. If not, she must await the next eligible male, Shelah. Thus Judah's directive, coupled with his refusal to yield Shelah, meant a life-long barrenness. She evidently remained under his watch care since Judah exercised authority over her fate after the discovery of her pregnancy.

Scholars have thoroughly examined chap. 38 in light of the custom, although coming to differing opinions regarding the exact nature of the practice and the history of its development.[116] The relationship of chap. 38's description to the details of the Mosaic legislation and the marriage of Boaz and Ruth has generated the most discussion. The chief problems are hermeneutical and literary critical. First, the hermeneutical difficulty is the different genre in which the passages occur; the narratives of chap. 38 and the Book of Ruth are descriptions of specific instances, and the legislative genre of Deuteronomy is prescriptive, pertaining to its general practice. Second, neither the Judah-Tamar nor the Ruth-Boaz case falls squarely in line with the requirements of the Mosaic law. Moreover, scholars vary significantly in assigning dates to the biblical passages, creating diverse explanations for their relationships.

The legislative description of Deuteronomy involves "brothers who are living together" under the auspices of their father (Deut 25:5). If a brother dies without a male successor, the surviving brother, that is, the "brother-in-law" (yābām) of the widow, shall "take her and marry her and fulfill the duty of a brother-in-law to her" (25:5). The law bound the widow to undertake the family marriage, freed only if the male party refused. "Performing the duty of a brother-in-law" (piel, yibbēm) means engaging in sexual relations with the "sister-in-law" (yĕbāmâ) for the purpose of perpetuating "the name of the dead brother so that his name will not be blotted out from Israel" (Deut 25:6). The law's provisions are told largely from the perspective of the widow, who was obligated to marry the available male and who as a childless woman was the vulnerable party. That this dis-

---

[115] MAL §§30,31, *ANET* 182; HL §193, *ANET* 196.
[116] See the selected bibliographies in R. Kkalmin, "Levirate Law," *ABD* 4.296–97; and V. Hamilton, "Marriage (OT and ANE)," *ABD* 4.567–69.

advantage to the widow could result in suffering is aptly illustrated in the case of Tamar. The failures of Onan and Judah, each in a different way, to fulfill their duties toward Tamar created the circumstances that led to her deed. According to Deuteronomy, the brother-in-law who refused to carry out his familial obligation suffered public humiliation, and the woman was released from her obligation so that she could seek a husband outside the family whereby she could produce a son (25:7–10). It is significant that the legislation required marriage, expressed by the traditional idiom for wedlock, "to take" *(lāḥaq)*. Thus the law was not only concerned for the preservation of family longevity and inheritance but the well-being of the widow as well.

Neither the Judah-Tamar relations nor the Ruth-Boaz marriage matches the specified requirements of the Deuteronomic law, although they share in the general idea of family marriage. The difference among the three accounts (beyond the details) is the extent of affinity by the male relative to the widow. Boaz is the most distant, a relative not even known to Naomi initially (Ruth 1:11–13; 2:19–20). The Deuteronomic law specified the eligible males as "brothers [who] are living together," which was designed to limit the practice among the Hebrews. Judah as father-in-law of Tamar is in-between these two cases. That the Ruth-Boaz marriage did not conform precisely to Deuteronomy shows that the force of custom, not the force of law, encouraged the offer of Boaz to marry the Moabitess (versus the nearer kinsman, Ruth 4:6). The apparent familial distance between Boaz and Elimelech (Boaz is not the brother of Ruth's husband Mahlon or of Naomi's husband Elimelech) permitted his marriage to Ruth (and even that of the "nearer kinsman," Ruth 3:12–13). Also the verb "perform the duty of a brother-in-law" does not occur in Ruth, and Boaz is referred to as the family's "kinsman-redeemer" *(gōʾēl;* e.g., Ruth 2:20).[117] Ruth's marriage is, generally speaking, better described as a *gĕʾullâ* marriage ("redemption marriage"). The repeated references in chap. 38 to Judah as Tamar's father-in-law *(ḥām,* vv. 13,25) and to Tamar as his "daughter-in-law" *(kallâ,* vv. 11,16,24) reinforces the closeness of their marital affinity, apparently ruling out marriage. Although marriage to Shelah (cf. "wife," v. 14b), an eligible brother to Er and Onan, was promised by Judah and patiently expected by Tamar, there is no suggestion of marriage as a possibility by Tamar and Judah. This raises the question of how to characterize their relationship. Was it incest? Was it permissible, despite the deviation from the expected pattern of male order?

The notion of "in-law" marriage is not unique to Hebrew custom, found in Hittite and Assyrian cultures.[118] The Middle Assyrian Laws[119] and Hittite Laws[120] provided for a father-in-law marriage when a brother-in-law was unavailable. Ancient Near Eastern laws indicate there was a sequence of priority

---

[117] See T. Thompson and D. Thompson, "Some Legal Problems in the Book of Ruth," *VT* 18 (1969): 79–99.

[118] It is uncertain if the practice was known at Ugarit and Nuzi; see E. Kutsch, "יבם *ybm et,*" *TDOT* 5.369; V. Hamilton, "יבם," *NIDOTTE* 2.392–93.

[119] MAL §33, *ANET* 182.

[120] HL §193, *ANET* 196.

among eligible males when the matter was marriage, beginning with the deceased's brother to father and beyond. Though not certain,[121] Genesis 38 may reflect a similar customary order of obligation among sons, from the eldest to the youngest. Deuteronomy, however, has "brothers [who] are living together," giving no directions of required order. What the ancient Near Eastern laws held in common with the Hebrew practice was the desire to address family inheritance and secure a measure of social stability. It is striking, however, that the ancient Near Eastern examples do not address the role of the children born to the levir and widow, whereas in Hebrew law the child's perpetuation of the name of the deceased brother is the specifically stated purpose (Deut 25:6; also Gen 38:8).[122] Hebrew law especially provided for the well-being of the widow by obligating the family's male members or releasing her from obligation. The enticement that Tamar arranged comes closer to the father-in-law practice, though again we recall that Shelah, her brother-in-law, was eligible, and further, Tamar did not marry Judah. Moreover, such a sexual venture between father-in-law and daughter-in-law was deemed incestual according to Mosaic standards and demanded the sanction of death (Lev 18:15; 20:12). Levirate marriage clearly was an exception to the proscription in Lev 18:16, but the issue remains as to what degree the father-in-law provision known in the ancient Near East may mitigate the censure of Tamar's action. That Judah called for the burning of Tamar preceded the revelation that he as her father-in-law was the offender. The assumption of the accusers and of Judah was that Tamar had engaged in harlotry with a nameless man (38:24). Since the penalty of burning (cf. Lev 20:14; 21:9) imposed by Judah does not explicitly correspond to the punishment called for in the prohibition against intercourse with a daughter-in-law (Lev 18:15,29; 20:12), it is further difficult to judge if a case of incest should be charged against Judah and Tamar. Although Judah and Tamar escaped the sanction of death, as called for by Israelite law, it is probable that the liaison was considered illicit, since the text meticulously notes that Judah ceased any further sexual contact with her ("he did not sleep with her again," v. 26), indicating that she was not his wife by levirate marriage or otherwise. Levirate marriage involved taking a "wife" (v. 14b), and more than one child was possible ("firstborn," NIV "first son"; Deut 25:6).[123] Alternatively, G. P. Hugenberger contends that Judah's intercourse with Tamar, although unknowingly with his daughter-in-law, formed a legitimate marriage; sexual intercourse is what triggers levirate marriage. Judah, according to ancient Near Eastern law, stood in line after Shelah.[124] Judah accordingly withdraws his denunciation. For Hugenberger's view, the statement "he did not sleep with her

---

[121] F. E. Greenspahn argues that seniority was not an established right in the practice of Hebrew levirate marriage (*When Brothers Dwell Together: The Preeminence of Younger Siblings in the Hebrew Bible* [New York: Oxford University Press, 1994], 52–53).

[122] This observation was brought to my attention by Rebekah Josberger, "Levirate Marriage in Genesis 38 as Evaluated by Judah in Genesis 38:26" (Ph.D. seminar paper, April 2002).

[123] Kutsch, "יבם ybm," 371.

[124] G. P. Hugenberger, *Marriage as Covenant: A Study of Biblical Law and Ethics Governing Marriage Developed from the Perspective of Malachi* (Leiden: Brill, 1994), 250, 319.

again" presupposes marriage in which sexual relations would have been expected. As to whether Tamar viewed her union with Judah as legitimate or as an act of desperation cannot be ascertained; yet we can be confident that she knew that the idea would have been loathsome in Judah's eyes. A. J. Lambe believes that the contrast between the "evil" sons and "righteous" Tamar shows that the men thwarted the law of primogeniture whereas she promoted it.[125] Moreover, the contrast in the outcome illustrates that God's judgment against the sons was over and the justice in the case of Tamar was covertly worked out, "transformative and creative." God "can see into the hearts of humans," seeing the evil of Er and Onan. For Tamar justice is "progressive" and indirect, seen through the actions of Tamar.

The interpreter therefore faces the dilemma of understanding what precisely Judah had in mind when he declared, "[Tamar] is more righteous than I," although he offers the explanation, "since I wouldn't give her to my son Shelah" (v. 26).[126] There must be a logical connection between the declaration and the reason given for Judah's admission. In effect he is absolving Tamar based on his denial of a levirate marriage. But what was his view of Tamar's deed? Was it justified in his eyes? Or simply more tolerable than his behavior given the impossible circumstances she faced? The chief problem is the translation of the sentence, and even once understood, we have no certainty that Judah's perspective reflected the divine view, since his statement and some innuendoes are all we have. To this we can add any number of hypothetical questions, such as why did she not entrap Shelah, or did she intend to "marry" Judah, making the passage all the more oblique. Typically, EVs and commentators interpret the Hebrew phrase as a comparison: "more righteous than I."[127] Although Judah acknowledges his guilt, the statement can be taken as relative, that is, they are both righteous, but she more than Judah, or conversely, they are both guilty but she less than Judah.[128] An alternative interpretation produces a complete exoneration of Tamar: "She is righteous, not I"[129] (cf. 1 Sam 24:17[18]). The word *ṣādaq* in a judicial context can mean "innocent" (e.g., *ṣādaq*//*nāqî*, "innocent," Exod 23:7). The ambiguity the Hebrew permits is one of many narrative ambiguities in the story. That Tamar was perceived as a "harlot" (vv. 15,24) points up the ambiguity of Tamar's role and also the ambivalence of Judah's reaction to her. On the one hand, she is embraced and on the other she is condemned. She is perceived to be socially repugnant as a harlot but proves to be the heroine of the story.[130]

---

[125] A. J. Lambe, "Genesis 38: Structure and Literary Design," in *The World of Genesis: Person, Places, Perspectives*, JSOTSup 257 (Sheffield: Sheffield Academic Press, 1998), 106–8.

[126] Luther somewhat mitigates Judah's culpability by assigning to Judah the sin of fornication but to Tamar adultery and incest (*LW* 6.43–44). Nevertheless, Luther admits that Judah's crime was depriving Tamar of her right to bear children.

[127] צָֽדְקָה מִמֶּנִּי; comparative use of the preposition *min* of מִמֶּנִּי, i.e., "more . . . than. . . ."

[128] Calvin, for example, finds them both guilty, and Judah admits that he had no justification for his anger since he himself could have been accused by Tamar (*Comm.*, 288).

[129] See *IBHS* §14.4e, which considers the preposition *min* a "comparative of exclusion" (e.g., 29:30; Ps 52:3[5]), i.e., the subject alone bears the quality described.

[130] P. Bird, "The Harlot as Heroine: Narrative Art and Social Presupposition in Three OT Texts," *Semeia* 46 (1989): 124.

As in the case with the Ruth episode, the state of affairs Judah created produced a set of contingencies that Deut 25:5–10 does not address. In other words, the force of the levirate law as found in Deuteronomy was not applicable to the specific situation that Tamar was presented. Biblical law does not attempt to speak to every possible scenario, and human vulgarities typically produce unspecified conditions that must be correlated with the purpose of the legislation on a case-by-case basis. Therefore the force of custom, that is, maintaining her obligation to the family, motivated her to seek a child by the next best means, namely, by her father-in-law. Although irreverent in her actions, she sought what was "righteous" *(ṣādaq)* for the family and for herself. Judah's culpability, refusing to live up to his obligation, canceled the fiery judgment he had hastily pronounced against her. It is difficult, therefore, to condemn Tamar from afar when the patriarch's own words turned the light of scrutiny on himself.

TAMAR AND "SHRINE PROSTITUTION." The references to Tamar as *zônâ,* "prostitute" (v. 15) and *qĕdēšâ,* "shrine prostitute" (vv. 21–22) has produced extensive discussion.[131] The female *qĕdēšâ* has been generally thought to be the Hebrew equivalent to the religious prostitute of Canaanite and Babylonian worship, often rendered "temple prostitute" (NIV, NAB, NRSV, NASB, REB) or "cult prostitute" (NJPV); thus the masculine equivalent *qādēš* was, e.g., "male shrine prostitutes" (NIV) or "male temple prostitutes" (NRSV, NASB; 1 Kgs 14:24; 15:12; 22:26[47]; 2 Kgs 23:7). Male and female functionaries at Canaanite *(qdšm)* and Babylonian *(qadištu)* temples as *qĕdēšâ* in Deut 23:17–18[18–19] and Hos 4:14 has led interpreters to assume cult prostitution must be meant by *qādēš/qĕdēšâ.* Moreover, the terms *qādēš/qĕdēšâ* are named among various sinful practices of pagan worship that are purged and condemned (1 Kgs 14:23–24). The word *qĕdēšâ* occurs outside chap. 38 just twice more in Deut 23:17[18] and Hos 4:14. The word *zônâ* ("prostitute") occurs in the same context (2 Kgs 23:4–8; Hos 14:12–14). The identification of *qĕdēšâ* as cult prostitution relies in part on the basic etymology of *q-d-š,* meaning "one set apart," that is, a devoted one. Also Akk. *qadištu,* which has been thought to designate a "cult prostitute," appears to support this interpretation of the Hebrew *qĕdēšâ.* Ugaritic *qdšm* were male and female temple servants. That many assume Tamar was a Canaanitess, although her ethnicity is not given, probably contributes to the notion that *qĕdēšâ* means a shrine prostitute in chap. 38. Despite this evidence drawn from the biblical text and extrabiblical usage, there is no explicit evidence that *qādēš/qĕdēšâ* and their

---

[131] See the general remarks in K. van der Toorn, "Prostitution (Cultic)," *ABD* 5.510–13 and J. M. Sprinkle, "Sexuality, Sexual Ethics," in *Dictionary of the Old Testament: Pentateuch* (Downers Grove: InterVarsity, 2003), 749–50; for the ANE evidence, see M. I. Gruber, "Hebrew *QĔDĒŠĀH* and Her Canaanite and Akkadian Cognates," *UF* 18 (1986): 133–48; and J. G. Westenholz, "Tamar, *QĔDĒŠĀ, QADIŠTU,* and Sacred Prostitution in Mesopotamia," *HTR* 82 (1989): 245–65.

cognates described ritual sexual activities. Furthermore, opponents to this traditional interpretation point out that Ugaritic *qdšm* and Akk. *qadištu* identified varied roles, for example, midwifery and cultic chanter, but never specifically to cult prostitution. Finally, they argue that Hebrew *qādēš/qĕdēšâ* refer to illegitimate cultic functions but not cultic prostitution. J. Westenholz has concluded that the prevalent idea among scholars that sacred prostitution was common in the ancient Near East "is an amalgam of misconceptions, presupposition, and inaccuracies."[132] As to whether Tamar was understood by the townspeople to be a "shrine prostitute" is a defensible interpretation (vv. 21–22) but not a definite one.

EARLY JEWISH AND CHRISTIAN INTERPRETATIONS. Ancient interpreters faced two opposing considerations: first, the vaulted place of Judah as the ancestor of the messianic lineage of kings and second, his sullied reputation by the affair with Tamar. Early Jewish interpreters imaginatively recast the biblical account, exhibiting this conflict of viewpoints.[133] In the pseudepigraphic *Testament of Judah* (second–first century B.C.[134]), the patriarch is the paragon of a warrior king who overcomes animals and enemies but falls to the tyranny of his passions—first, to the Canaanite wife Bathshua and second, to his daughter-in-law Tamar. Nevertheless, the *Testament* moderated his weaknesses by attributing the problems of his household to the wicked manipulation of Bathshua (*T. Jud.* 10.1–11.5) and to the wily deception of Tamar during his drunken stupor. More importantly, Judah recognizes that the matter "was from the LORD" (*T. Jud.* 12.6), giving his actions the divine purpose of establishing the royal line. *Targums Neofiti* and *Pseudo–Jonathan,* on the other hand, preserve the dignity of the Jewish ancestor by attributing to Judah and Tamar honorable character. Their willingness to burn rather than compromise the sanctity of God merits absolution: "A voice went out from heaven and said, 'Both of you are innocent. From before the LORD is the decree.'" Tamar utters an extrabiblical prayer that accepts her death by burning should Judah not own up to the evidence of his crime, and Judah too, upon hearing her confession, risks his own burning for his deed by admitting publicly his culpability. They are like Daniel's three friends, who from the fire hallow God's "holy Name" (Dan 3). God brought about the events of Judah and Tamar, creating a divine purpose for their actions. The rabbinical commentary *Genesis Rabbah* reads chap. 38 especially in light of royal and messianic promises. Rabbinic interpreters recast Judah and Tamar as worthy ancestors of Israel's kings. It was not Judah's own lust that propelled him but an angel's instructions, ensuring that the royal seed might be born (*Gen. Rab.* 85.8). By an exegetical sleight of hand, Judah's confession

---

[132] Westenholz, "Tamar," 263.

[133] Especially see E. S. Menn, *Judah and Tamar (Genesis 38) in Ancient Jewish Exegesis: Studies in Literary Form and Hermeneutics,* JSJ 51 (Leiden: Brill, 1997).

[134] The Christian revision of this Hellenistic work dates to ca. the second century.

"she is more righteous than I *[mimmennî]*" (38:26) is transformed into an admission by God. The Hebrew *mimmennî* can also mean "from me," referring to God: "The Holy Spirit said, 'From me have these things come'" (*Gen. Rab.* 85.12). Judah and Tamar's roles are the result of divine purpose, not human immorality (so Rashi). The rabbis also depicted Tamar favorably by comparing her to the honored matriarch Rebekah (*Gen. Rab.* 85.7).

Early Christian interpreters also hoped to rehabilitate the images of the patriarch and Tamar. Tamar had no personal ambitions for marriage, but although a Gentile she desired the holy blessing that God had promised the Jews. Thus her prayer to receive her father-in-law's "treasure" was answered by God. Ephrem the Syrian (d. 373) comments, "The prayer of Tamar inclined him (Judah), contrary to his usual habit, [to go] to a harlot" (*Comm. on Genesis* 34.4).[135] Chrysostom (d. 407) also betters the couple's reputations: "She [Tamar] was carrying out the divine plan, and hence neither did she incur any blame, nor did Judah lay himself open to any charge" (*Hom. on Genesis* 62.5). Cyril of Alexandria (d. 444) diminished Judah's deed to a "slight fault" (*Glaphyra on Genesis* 6.2). Cyril reflected allegorical readings, using the union of Judah and Tamar as a type of Christ's incarnation or of the spiritual union of the Christian (*Glaphyra on Genesis* 6.1–2). Jerome (d. 420), as did others, viewed the twins as typological of two peoples, and "the hand tied with the scarlet ribbon already then speckled the conscience of the Jews with the passion of Christ" (*Letter* 123.12).

COMPOSITION.   For the discussion of the origin and placement of chap. 38, see the discussion (above) under "Composition" in the introduction to 37:2–50:26 (Joseph narrative).

STRUCTURE.   The structure of the chapter evidences a well-organized, coherent plot line that is bounded by two narratives concerning the sons of Judah (A/A'). In the first paragraph his wife gives birth to three sons, but the Lord strikes dead the eldest two, leaving the youngest, Shelah. The final paragraph describes the birth of Perez and Zerah, which restores the number of sons to three, suggesting thereby that the full complement of heirs has been reinstated (cf. Job's reinstatement, 42:12–13).[136] This is the chief narrative interest, describing the succession of Judah's heirs. In the structural arrangement (see below), the center "leg" (D) details the sexual union of Judah and Tamar, resulting in her pregnancy (vv. 15–19).[137] This segment, too, exhibits three witnesses

---

[135] *ACCS* 2.244–47.

[136] Menn observes the importance of triplets in chap. 38 (*Judah and Tamar,* 18).

[137] Alternatively, Lambe proposes that the direction of the plot turns on the death of Judah's wife (v. 12a), after which Judah makes a journey ("went up"), as in v. 1 ("went down"), that like the first leads to the birth children ("Genesis 38," 102–20); the developmental stages show parallel symmetry: Phase 1, Equilibrium (vv. 1–6); Phase 2, Descent (vv. 7–11); Phase 3, Disequilibrium (v. 12a); Phase 4, Ascent (vv. 12b–26); Phase 5, Equilibrium restored (vv. 27–30).

(seal, cord, staff), and it possesses the chief literary motifs of the story: Judah's heirs by Tamar's pregnancy, deception of Judah by her change of clothing, and Judah's ignorance of her true identity. The latter two motifs correspond to Judah's malicious trickery of Jacob by means of Joseph's garment and Jacob's ignorance.

> A Judah's Sons and Tamar (38:1–6)
>> B Tamar's Threat to Judah's Sons (38:7–11)
>>> C Tamar Deceives Judah (38:12–14)
>>>> D Judah Impregnates Tamar (38:15–19)
>>> C′ Tamar Steals Judah's Pledge (38:20–23)
>> B′ Judah's Threat to Tamar (38:24–26)
> A′ Judah's Sons by Tamar (38:27–30)

The semantically parallel elements B/B′ manifest the opposition of Judah and Tamar. In the first case Judah wrongly perceived that Tamar was the reason for his sons' demise, not knowing that their deaths were the result of God's punishment. In the matching unit, however, Judah by demanding her death is the real threat, since, ironically, he himself is the antagonist to his own twin sons that Tamar carries. These parallel segments reinforce the admission of Judah's culpability (v. 26) by highlighting his obstruction to the birth of his future generations. In both paragraphs Judah's progeny is in doubt.[138] Elements C/C′ describe Tamar's initiation and consummation of the elaborate ruse. Ironically, by bartering with Judah behind the veil of her false identity, she made off with the witnesses to Judah's identity.

(1) Judah's Sons and Tamar (38:1–6)

[1]At that time, Judah left his brothers and went down to stay with a man of Adullam named Hirah. [2]There Judah met the daughter of a Canaanite man named Shua. He married her and lay with her; [3]she became pregnant and gave birth to a son, who was named Er. [4]She conceived again and gave birth to a son and named him Onan. [5]She gave birth to still another son and named him Shelah. It was at Kezib that she gave birth to him.

[6]Judah got a wife for Er, his firstborn, and her name was Tamar.

The passage provides the family background for understanding the episode detailed in the chapter, introducing the major characters Judah and Tamar. Judah moved away from his brothers (v. 1), where he produced three sons by a Canaanite wife (vv. 2–5). Judah arranged for his eldest son Er to marry Tamar (v. 6). The primary narrative interest is the succession of Judah's family, which is jeopardized by the behavior of the men of the household.

JUDAH LEAVES HIS BROTHERS (38:1).   **38:1**   "At that time" correlates

---

[138] Lambe, "Genesis 38," 114.

with the previous incident and suggests that the present episode should be interpreted in light of it. That Judah "went down" (from *yārad*) is a veiled allusion to the descent of Joseph into Egypt (37:25,35; 39:1; cf. 12:10; 46:3–4), meaning that both sons have left their father's house, though under vastly different circumstances. Ironically, Joseph's case was instigated by Judah's brainstorm. Judah in the Joseph narrative is an active participant whose choices, for good or for ill, make ripples in the lives of others. Taken together, chaps. 37 and 38 show that Jacob's family was experiencing fragmentation, corrupted by hatred and licentiousness. Joseph's noble rejection of Potiphar's wife in chap. 39 provides a brief respite in the downward spiral and signals a hopeful reversal in the moral character of the family. Mention of "his brothers" (v. 1) rather than "his father" not only reflects the former incident but also anticipates the problem of inheritance in Judah's family (v. 8). That Judah left his brothers because of the pangs of guilt over the "death" of Joseph is a possibility. Chapter 38 also involves sibling struggles, first with Onan's refusal to honor his deceased brother (v. 9) and, second, the interloper Perez, whose internecine tussle compromised his brother's claim as "firstborn" (vv. 27–30). Since Judah left his father's house and married outside the family (exogamy), the author may be indicating that Judah jeopardized his place in Jacob's household. The word "to stay" *(nāṭâ)* appears again in v. 16, "he went over," where it describes Judah's solicitation of the harlot. The sojourn in Adullam will set in motion the events that result in his shameful conduct. "A man of Adullam" (lit., "Adullamite," vv. 1,12,20) refers to the Canaanite town near Beth-shemesh (modern esh Sheikh Madhkur), whose king was defeated by Joshua (12:15) and remembered especially for David's hideout (1 Sam 22:1; 2 Sam 23:13; 1 Chr 11:15; cf. *2 Mac* 12:38).[139] Ironically, the settlement lay within the tribal allotment of Judah (Josh 15:35; Neh 11:30). The name "Hirah" appears only in this chapter (vv. 1,12; cf. vv. 20–23).

JUDAH'S WIFE AND SONS (38:2–5). **38:2–5** The passage specifies the Canaanite lineage of his new wife (cp. Samson, Judg 14:1). This was a signal change in the endogamous preferences of the patriarchs, following the despised practice of Esau (e.g., 24:3–4; 27:46–28:2).[140] Joseph (41:45) and Simeon (46:10) also took foreign wives. Although she is unnamed, the text provides her father's name, "Shua" (*šûāʿ*, vv. 2,12; 1 Chr 2:3; see "Bathshua," 1 Chr 3:5).[141] The LXX has "Shua" as the name of the woman herself (vv. 2,12).[142] The word

---

[139] J. M. Hamilton, "Adullam," *ABD* 1.81.

[140] The marriage of the honored Judah to a Canaanite woman incited early Jewish interpreters (e.g., *Tg. Ps.- J.; Gen. Rab.* 85.4) to supplant "Canaanite" by the homonym כְּנַעַן, meaning "merchant" (e.g., Hos 12:7).

[141] 1 Chr 2:13 specifies Shua as a "Canaanitess," מִבַּת־שׁוּעַ הַכְּנַעֲנִית, "by a Canaanite woman, the daughter of Shua."

[142] Cf. the feminine form of the relative pronoun, ἧ ὄνομα Σαυα, "whose name was Saua"; v. 12 LXX reads accordingly, Σαυα ἡ γυνὴ Ιουδα, "Saua wife of Judah," versus the MT's "daughter of Shua."

šûā' means "cry [for help]" (*šw'* I; cf. *šûā'*, Job 30:24; 36:19);[143] it perhaps names an Asherite woman (but spelled *šûā'*, 1 Chr 7:32). Judah's progeny looked promising with the birth of three sons, Er, Onan, and Shelah.[144] Other notable patriarchs produced three sons (Adam, Noah, Terah). "Er" (*'ēr*, "watchful," *'ûr*), the eldest son of Judah, appears again in 46:12; Num 26:19; 1 Chr 2:3; it also is the name of his nephew (1 Chr 4:21). The name "Onan" (*'ônān*, "strength, vigorous" *'ôn*), the notorious second son, comes into view again with his brothers' names in 46:12; Num 26:19; 1 Chr 2:3. It is striking that in giving the genealogies of Judah's descendants, 46:12 and Num 26:19 can offer no descendants for Er and Onan (Num 26:19, "but they died in Canaan"). "Shelah" (*šēlâ*, "drawn out [from the womb]" *šālâ*) is the ancestor of the Shelanites (46:12; Num 26:20; 1 Chr 2:3; 4:21; Neh 11:5); the name also designates the father of Eber (spelled *šelaḥ*, cf. 10:24; see comments on 11:12–15).[145] "Kezib" (or Chezib), usually identified as the place Achzib (Tell el-Beidai) just west of Adullam (Josh 15:44; 19:29; Judg 1:31; Mic 1:14), was the birthplace of Shelah.[146]

JUDAH OBTAINS TAMAR (38:6).   **38:6**   In accordance with the custom of arranged marriages,[147] Judah acquired a wife for his son (e.g., 21:21; 24:2–4; Exod 2:21; Judg 14:1–3). Mention of Er as "firstborn" *(běkôr)* twice in vv. 6–7 brings to the fore the issue of family solidarity and inheritance. The appellative "Tamar" (*tāmār*, "palm tree," e.g., Exod 15:27) also names the daughter of David, who was the sister of Absalom after whom he named his own daughter (2 Sam 13:1 *passim*; 2 Sam 14:27). Tamar's ethnicity is undisclosed, but commentators often assume a Canaanite lineage since the text does not indicate an Israelite connection. Conversely, one could argue that the identification of Judah's wife as a Canaanitess (v. 2) means that the silence of the text for Tamar's ethnicity implies that she was Israelite. If she were of Canaanite background, matters were turning from bad to worse, since another generation would have married outside the Abraham family (e.g., Ishmael,

---

[143] *HALOT* 4.1444–45 notes the by-form שֶׁיַע, "help, deliverance"; cf. the sentence name אֲבִישׁוּעַ, "my father is help" (Noth, *Personnenamen,* 154). BDB 447 explains Shua from *y-š-'*, "to save, deliver."

[144] According to the MT's וַיִּקְרָא ("he named"), Judah names Er (v. 3), but his wife names the other children (vv. 4–5); the MT can be an indefinite construction ("who was named," NIV); SP, *Tg. Ps.-J.* harmonize the naming by reading וַתִּקְרָא ("she named") at vv. 3,29,30 (cf. NAB, NJB).

[145] Rabbinic midrash casts dispersions on the children, explaining the meaning of Er by עֲרִירִי, "childless," and Onan with עֳנָה, "afflicted" *(piel)* (*Gen. Rab.* 85.4; *Tg. Ps.-J.*); in *Tg. Ps.-J.,* Shelah is related to Aramaic שְׁלִי, "neglect, forget" (see Maher, *Pseudo-Jonathan,* 127–28, nn. 5,6,7).

[146] D. W. Manor, "Chezib," *ABD* 1.904. The LXX reads αὐτὴ δὲ ἦν ἐν Χασβι, "and she was in Kezib" (cf. NRSV, REB), rather than masc. וְהָיָה בִכְזִיב, "and he [Judah] was in Kezib"; or the NIV (NASB, NJPV, HCSB) renders Eng. neuter, "it was at Kezib." The LXX presupposes that all three sons were born in Kezib, "when she bore them (αὐτούς)" (Wevers, *Notes on the Greek Text,* 632).

[147] V. Hamilton, "Marriage (OT and ANE)," *ABD* 4.562–63.

Esau; also Simeon, 46:10). Joseph, too, will marry an Egyptian ("Asenath"), but the event is somewhat mitigated by his circumstances; she is a gift from Pharaoh (41:45). The text tends to veil his foreign marriage under the act of naming "Manasseh" and "Ephraim," whose meaning revealed the mind-set of Joseph (41:50–52; 46:20).

(2) Tamar's Threat to Judah's Sons (38:7–11)

7But Er, Judah's firstborn, was wicked in the LORD's sight; so the LORD put him to death.

8Then Judah said to Onan, "Lie with your brother's wife and fulfill your duty to her as a brother-in-law to produce offspring for your brother." 9But Onan knew that the offspring would not be his; so whenever he lay with his brother's wife, he spilled his semen on the ground to keep from producing offspring for his brother. 10What he did was wicked in the LORD's sight; so he put him to death also.

11Judah then said to his daughter-in-law Tamar, "Live as a widow in your father's house until my son Shelah grows up." For he thought, "He may die too, just like his brothers." So Tamar went to live in her father's house.

Although the Lord is responsible for the deaths of Judah's two eldest sons, Judah believes that Tamar somehow contributed to their deaths. Therefore he chooses to withhold his last son on the pretense that he is too young for marriage. The passage reports the divine judgments against evil Er (v. 7) and against the dishonorable Onan (vv. 8–10), which lead to the exile of Tamar (v. 11).

THE LORD KILLS ER (38:7). **38:7** The precise "evil" *(raʿ)* committed by Er is unstated (cf. "your wives will become widows," Exod 22:24[23]). The similar language, "evil in the eyes of the LORD," is a popular Deuteronomic phrase that describes many different illicit behaviors, especially idolatry (e.g., Deut 4:25; 17:2; Judg 2:11; 1 Sam 15:19; 2 Sam 12:9; esp. 1, 2 Kings). "To put to death" *(mût* in the causative stem) often describes God's judgment or capital punishment by human agency (e.g., Exod 4:24; Num 35:19,21).

THE LORD KILLS ONAN (38:8–10). **38:8–10** In accordance with the custom of levirate marriage ("brother-in-law"), Judah instructs Onan to have sexual relations with his deceased brother's widow. Deuteronomy 25:5–10 provides the codification of the practice, which is illustrated in the Judah-Tamar episode (cf. Luke 20:28).[148] The purpose for this practice was to "produce *[qûm]* offspring" in the name of the deceased (cf. Deut 25:5,7, lit., "to establish *[qûm]* the brother's name"). Onan, however, refused to impregnate Tamar, ejaculating on the ground *(coitus interruptus)* because he did not want to reduce his share of the family inheritance. He stood first in line after the death

---

[148] On the terms and interpretation of levirate marriage, see "Levirate Marriage" above.

of Er, and producing a son by his brother's widow would mean the loss of his new status as heir. His behavior possibly indicates that the men in Judah's household had struggled for supremacy, as we have found it commonly in the households of the patriarchs Isaac and Jacob. This family travesty results in the kindled anger of the Lord against Onan (v. 10).

JUDAH SENDS TAMAR AWAY (38:11).   **38:11**   Judah protects his sole remaining heir by sending Tamar home to her father's house (cp. Lev 22:13). By relegating her to the life of a "widow" (*'almānâ*), for whom special protections are necessary (e.g., Exod 22:22[21]; Deut 24:17–21), Judah puts her future at jeopardy with no husband or potential son to care for her (Job 24:21; Ps 94:6; Isa 10:12; Mark 12:40). He does so under the pretense of Shelah's adolescence, but he has no intention of subjecting his son to Tamar's string of misfortune. "For he thought" translates the verbal root *'āmar,* "to say," indicating interior dialogue, that is, he said to himself (e.g., 1 Sam 18:17). This is the narrative's way of explaining to the reader Judah's motivation for his peculiar behavior. He appears oblivious to the reasons for his sons' deaths.

(3) Tamar Deceives Judah (38:12–14)

¹²After a long time Judah's wife, the daughter of Shua, died. When Judah had recovered from his grief, he went up to Timnah, to the men who were shearing his sheep, and his friend Hirah the Adullamite went with him.

¹³When Tamar was told, "Your father-in-law is on his way to Timnah to shear his sheep," ¹⁴she took off her widow's clothes, covered herself with a veil to disguise herself, and then sat down at the entrance to Enaim, which is on the road to Timnah. For she saw that, though Shelah had now grown up, she had not been given to him as his wife.

38:12   Tamar herself sets about to remedy her situation because of two reasons. First, "after a long time" shows that Judah will not yield Shelah, although he had become of marriageable age (v. 14b). Second, Judah's wife has died, leaving Judah more vulnerable to a sexual encounter. After the proper period of mourning had ended, Judah returned to his daily activities, including the shearing of his flocks (e.g., 31:19; 1 Sam 25:4; 2 Sam 13:23). The contrast between the conclusion of Judah's bereavement and the widow's clothing of Tamar points out Judah's irresponsibility.[149] Joined by his Adullamite friend Hirah, Judah went northeast to nearby Timnah also in the southern hill country of Judah (Josh 15:57; not to be confused with the site at the northern border of Judah and Philistia, e.g., Josh 15:10; 19:43; Judg 14:1,2,5; 2 Chr 28:18).[150]

---

[149] Sarna, *Genesis,* 267–68.

[150] H. G. May, ed., *Oxford Bible Atlas,* 3d ed. (New York: Oxford University Press, 1984), 57,142; W. R. Kotter tentatively proposes another location generally in south Canaan ("Timnah," *ABD* 6.556–57).

38:13–14   When Tamar learned of Judah's journey,[151] she plotted to deceive her father-in-law (*ḥām*, v. 13) by changing her dress and meeting him along the road (v. 14). Mourning clothes were distinctive in appearance (cf. 2 Sam 14:2). That her new dress indicated that she was a harlot is possible (v. 15; cf. Prov 7:10), but more likely it was her location on the road that suggested her business (cf. Jer 3:2; Ezek 16:25). She stationed herself alone at the entrance to the town to ensure that she would encounter travelers (cf. Prov 8:3; 9:14; 2 Kgs 23:8). The veil was a common ornamental garment of women, which accentuated her attractiveness and often signified an elevated status (cf. Isa 3:18–23). Probably because she sat alone emboldened Judah to propose the tryst. By employing a "veil" (*ṣāʿîp*, cf. 24:65), she "covered herself" (*kāsâ*[152]) and wrapped herself up (from *ʿālap, hith.;* NIV, "to disguise herself"), effectively concealing her face. That she removed her mourning clothes and put on a veil contrasts her former state of bereavement and her new appearance.[153] A woman's veil was not the garment of a harlot but of a betrothed woman (e.g., see comments on 24:65; 29:21–25). Assyrian law forbid an unmarried woman from wearing a veil.[154] The irony of the veil was that it not only hid her identity but it also could have signaled that she had been given in pledge to another, namely, Shelah. Apparel is an important signal of social status, especially in the narrative of Joseph (see comments on 37:3).[155] The text's descriptions of her dress incognito—"she took off her widow's clothes" (v. 14) and "put on her widow's clothes again" (v. 19)—exhibited the depths of her humiliation. She set aside her widowhood for the demeaning status of a prostitute. The widow who has been mistreated by the men of her family uses the callous whim of her father-in-law to turn the tables on him. She chose "Enaim" (*ʿênayim*), meaning "eyes,"[156] to spring her trap. Its location is unknown, identified only as "on the road to Timnah" from Adullam (but cf. Enam in the territory of Judah, Josh 15:34). "Enaim" may have one of a number of potential wordplays when we remember that she veiled her identity, leaving exposed only her eyes, and the importance in the narrative of visual effects signaling sexual relationships

---

[151] הִנֵּה חָמִיךְ עֹלֶה, "your father-in-law is now going up"; the construction of הִנֵּה plus the ptc. indicates "vivid immediacy" (*IBHS* §40.2.1b).

[152] וַתְּכַס (piel); SP, Syr., *Tg. Onq.* indicate וַתִּתְכַּס (hithpael); cf. 24:65.

[153] See K. van der Toorn, "The Significance of the Veil in the Ancient Near East," in *Pomegranates and Golden Bells: Studies in Biblical, Jewish, and Near Eastern Ritual, Law, and Literature in Honor of Jacob Milgrom* (Winona Lake: Eisenbrauns, 1995), 330, 339 (esp. 327–39).

[154] MAL §40, *ANET* 183.

[155] See V. Matthews, "The Anthropology of Clothing in the Joseph Narrative, *JSOT* 65 (1995): 25–36.

[156] בְּפֶתַח עֵינַיִם, lit., "at the entrance of eyes"; many EVs read עֵינַיִם as a place name "Enaim" (e.g., NIV, ESV, NRSV, HCSB [note has "springs," from II. עַיִן, NASB). Syr., Vg., *Tgs. Neof., Ps.–J.* interpreted the expression as "at the crossroads" (cf. "in an open place," AV; "where the road forks," REB).

("saw," *rāʾâ*, vv. 2 ["met," NIV],14,15). The narrative's occupation with Judah's ignorance as a core idea comes into play here as well (see comments on v. 16).

(4) Judah Impregnates Tamar (38:15–19)

¹⁵When Judah saw her, he thought she was a prostitute, for she had covered her face. ¹⁶Not realizing that she was his daughter-in-law, he went over to her by the roadside and said, "Come now, let me sleep with you."
"And what will you give me to sleep with you?" she asked.
¹⁷"I'll send you a young goat from my flock," he said.
"Will you give me something as a pledge until you send it?" she asked.
¹⁸He said, "What pledge should I give you?"
"Your seal and its cord, and the staff in your hand," she answered. So he gave them to her and slept with her, and she became pregnant by him. ¹⁹After she left, she took off her veil and put on her widow's clothes again.

The passage describes the encounter (vv. 15–16) and the bargain struck, including Judah's items of pledge for payment (vv. 17–19).

JUDAH MISTAKES TAMAR FOR A HARLOT (38:15–16). **38:15–16**   The word rendered "prostitute" (*zônâ*, v. 15) is the usual term identifying a harlot (e.g., 34:31), although the root usage *(zānâ)* can include other forbidden heterosexual relations (Num 25:1; Judg 19:2).[157] In our passage *zônâ* might be interchangeable with the term *qĕdēšâ* (NIV, "shrine prostitute," see vv. 21–22 below) if the Adullamite's characterization of Tamar was literal rather than a euphemism for the demeaning term *zônâ* ("prostitute") (see below comments on vv. 21–22). The text admits that Judah unwittingly had sexual relations with his "daughter-in-law," fooled by her appearance (v. 16). His act transgressed sexual prohibitions stated later in levitical law (Lev 18:15; 20:12).

Judah is typically portrayed as ignorant of his circumstances and their unseen significance. The recurring terms "know" (*yādaʿ*, vv. 9,16,26) and "recognize" (*nākar*, vv. 25–26) bring this motif to the forefront. He wrongly ascribed to Tamar the reason for his sons' deaths (v. 11), not knowing that the Lord had punished them (vv. 7,10), and he does not understand why she required the particular personal items for a pledge (v. 18).[158] Judah's failure to "know" (*yādaʿ*, v. 16) her identity but his recognition ("recognize," *nākar*, v. 25) of his pledge echoes Jacob's ignorance of what became of Joseph, a ruse fostered by Judah and the brothers (37:32–33). Judah's lack of knowledge anticipates the motif of recognition in Joseph's court, for the brothers failed to "recognize" (42:8) and "know" (42:23) Joseph's identity. That Judah was unaware of her identity recalls Laban's deception of Jacob by giving him Leah

---

[157] Contrast נָאַף, "to commit adultery" (e.g., Lev 20:10); Hos 3:1–3 distinguishes prostitution (זָנָה) and adultery (נָאַף).

[158] Menn includes the vocabulary of sight, "to see" (vv. 2,14,15); בְּעֵינֵי יְהוָה, "the eyes of the LORD" (vv. 7,10); and הִנֵּה, "behold" (vv. 13,23,24,27,29; *Judah and Tamar,* 32, 40, 44).

(29:23–25) and the immorality of Lot's daughters, who tricked him during a drunken stupor, catching him unaware (*lōʾ yādaʿ*, 19:33,35). That the text comments "[Judah] did not sleep [lit., "know," *yādaʿ*] with her again" (v. 26) at the conclusion of his embarrassing confession provides a subtle allusion to his gullibility. In addition to the brothers and Jacob collectively, Judah's lack of knowledge provides a foil for the wisdom of Joseph, who is the interpreter of dreams par excellence and whose knowledge and insight gain him the upper hand over his siblings. His brothers meanwhile are dim-witted like Esau, unsuspecting of their host's identity and his knowledge of their conversations. Returning to our passage, for the word "went over" *(nāṭâ)* see comments on v. 1. Tamar plays out her role by asking for the appropriate payment, "What will you give *[nātan]* me?" This may be a play on the failures of Onan and Judah, the former who did not "give *[nātan,* "spilled," NIV] his semen" (v. 9) and the latter's son to whom "she had not been given" *(nātan,* v. 14).

JUDAH GIVES A PLEDGE (38:17–19).   **38:17–19**   Judah offers the promise of a "young goat" or "kid" (*gĕdî ʿizzîm,* v. 17). This was a handsome payment, a tender animal tasty for food (27:9,16; Judg 6:19; 13:15; 15:1; 1 Sam 16:20). Under the guise of securing a "pledge," Tamar achieved the true objective of obtaining proof of identity. "Pledge" *(ʿērābôn)* is another presage of the brothers at court when Judah "guaranteed" (from the related word *ʿārab*) his own life for the boy Benjamin's safety (43:9; 44:32; cf. Prov 20:16; 27:13). The "seal," "cord," and "staff" (v. 18) taken in pledge may have presaged the sibling tension over inheritance, which underlies the whole of the Joseph narrative, for they were unique to the owner. Tamar shrewdly requests the undeniable evidence of Judah's identity. Foolishly he yields his personal identifying credentials used in official transactions. The ancient cylinder "seal" *(ḥôtām/ḥôtemet)* was typically made of engraved stone that was rolled across soft clay and on pottery handles, leaving an authoritative and authenticating imprint (e.g., Exod 28:11; 1 Kgs 21:8).[159] The word may be a loanword from Egyptian *ḥtm* ("seal").[160] The earliest seals could bear distinctive designs that distinguished their owners, and later seals could exhibit the names of the owners. The cylinder seal may have a cord that enabled the owner to wear it around the neck. The stamp seal could be a finger ring, known as a "signet" ring (e.g., Jer 2:24; cp. *ṭabbaʿat,* "ring," 41:42). The word "cord" *(pātîl)* describes flexible material for tying, which had various purposes (e.g., Exod 28:28), probably used here for suspending Judah's seal. "Staff" *(maṭṭeh)* is the common term for a supporting rod, pole, or stick (e.g., Exod 4:2; 1 Sam 14:27). Its predominant usage means "tribe" (e.g., Num 30:1[2]). Like a walking cane, a staff was an important per-

---

[159] A. R. Millard, "חתם," *NIDOTTE* 2.324; B. S. Magness-Gardiner, "Seals, Mesopotamian," *ABD* 5.1062–64.

[160] Muchiki, *Egyptian Proper Names and Loanwords,* 246–47.

sonal item that travelers and shepherds required. The head of the staff could be marked with an inscription, such as the owner's name or tribe (e.g., Num 17:2[17]). The staff had a symbolic function at times, indicating a master's authority (e.g., Num 17:3[18]) and occasionally royal authority (cf. "scepter," Ps 110:2; Ezek 19:11).[161] On this latter point, Judah's staff could have hinted at a royal implication, but this is uncertain since different terms, "scepter" (*šēbeṭ*) and "ruler's staff" *(měḥōqēq),* describe Judah's future rule in 49:10.

The narrative reveals that Tamar became pregnant by that first and only act of intimacy (cf. v. 26b). This is one of many subtle indicators that divine providence superintended the events leading to her impregnation.

38:19 Tamar ends the ruse by changing her dress (v. 14). She achieved her mission without detection, meaning that only her pregnancy three months later gave her away (v. 24).

(5) Tamar Steals Judah's Pledge (38:20–23)

[20]Meanwhile Judah sent the young goat by his friend the Adullamite in order to get his pledge back from the woman, but he did not find her. [21]He asked the men who lived there, "Where is the shrine prostitute who was beside the road at Enaim?"

"There hasn't been any shrine prostitute here," they said.

[22]So he went back to Judah and said, "I didn't find her. Besides, the men who lived there said, 'There hasn't been any shrine prostitute here.'"

[23]Then Judah said, "Let her keep what she has, or we will become a laughingstock. After all, I did send her this young goat, but you didn't find her."

"Did not find [from *māṣāʾ*] her" appears twice, forming the boundaries of the unit (vv. 20,23). Judah sent the payment via his friend Hiram, who searched in vain for the woman (vv. 20–21); and he returned to Judah, reporting the failed attempt, for which Judah seemed satisfied (v. 23).

38:20–22 Judah fulfilled his promise, expecting to retrieve his pledge in turn (v. 20). As to why he dispatched Hiram to Enaim with his payment is unstated; perhaps Judah as an Israelite was embarrassed by such behavior, whereas the Adullamite was not (as) disturbed by the assignment. Although adultery (sexual relations with another man's wife) was sternly condemned in ancient Near Eastern societies (see comments on 20:9), there was greater acceptance of prostitution.[162] As it turned out, if Hiram had not gone in his stead, Judah probably would have had to subject himself to a public inquiry (v. 21). When Hiram asked of the town's men about (disguised) Tamar, he referred to her by the term *qědēšâ* rather than the typical term *zônâ* for "pros-

---

[161] D. M. Fouts, "מַטֶּה," *NIDOTTE* 2.924–25.

[162] E.g., Mesopotamian laws provided for the rights of prostitutes (e.g., MAL §§40,49,52, *ANET* 183–85); see E. Goodfriend, "Prostitution (OT)," *ABD* 5.506.

titution" in the narrative description of Judah's thought (cf. v. 15). Commentators[163] and translations (e.g., NASB, NRSV) usually distinguish *qĕdēšâ* as a technical term for a "shrine prostitute" (NIV). The precise meaning of *qĕdēšâ* (fem.), however, is now disputed (see above "Tamar and Shrine Prostitution"). Since it is apparent that Tamar did not practice cult prostitution in Enaim, what Hiram exactly had in mind must remain enigmatic. The local populace denied that such a person frequented the area,[164] heightening the mystery of her identity (v. 21). The ambiguity created by the use of the divergent terms *zônâ* and *qĕdēšâ* is one of many literary ambiguities in chap. 38 and the Joseph account. Hiram dutifully returned to Judah, reporting the futile results of his mission (v. 22); that he took the extra step to inquire of her whereabouts with the townsmen absolved him in his eyes, having made a reasonable effort to locate her.

38:23 Judah reveals his colors here. He reckons that his reputation will be soiled if it is learned that a prostitute outwitted him. If they pursue the matter again, they will be ridiculed (*bûz,* "laughingstock"; cf. Job 31:34). Since an effort had been made to meet his obligation, Judah was satisfied to let her keep the items. Probably, Judah was happy to forget this sorry episode, thinking that was the end of it.

(6) Judah's Threat to Tamar (38:24–26)

[24]**About three months later Judah was told, "Your daughter-in-law Tamar is guilty of prostitution, and as a result she is now pregnant."**

Judah said, "Bring her out and have her burned to death!"

[25]**As she was being brought out, she sent a message to her father-in-law. "I am pregnant by the man who owns these," she said. And she added, "See if you recognize whose seal and cord and staff these are."**

[26]**Judah recognized them and said, "She is more righteous than I, since I wouldn't give her to my son Shelah." And he did not sleep with her again.**

38:24 After three months Tamar's pregnancy became obvious to all. Such news would readily be passed along to Judah, for she evidently still had marital obligations to Judah's family. He had not released her to marry another, which later was an option provided in Deut 25:5–10. Since she was to live as a widow in her father's house (v. 11), implying that she was to abstain from sexual contact, the community concluded what was evident on the face of it: she had become pregnant by harlotry. The passage's reference to Tamar as "your daughter-in-law" *(kallāteka)* brought to the fore her accountability to Judah's family name. Judah self-righteously declared her fate. "Bring her out" *(yāṣā')* shares in the language of Deut 22:21 that

---

[163] E.g., Westermann, *Genesis 37–50,* 54.

[164] אַנְשֵׁי מְקֹמָהּ, "[he asked] the men of her place" (cf. NASB); most EVs read as אַנְשֵׁי הַמָּקוֹם, "men of the [or that] place" (cf. v. 22).

describes the penalty required of a promiscuous daughter. After discovery by her husband on their wedding night, she "shall be brought [from *yāṣā*] to the door of her father's house," where she is executed by stoning (Deut 22:21). The Deuteronomic instruction specifies that the guilty daughter must be brought to the door of her father's house and the townsmen must carry out the sanction. The demand for her death is not the offended father's decision but is the disposition of the town's elders. Since her act is deemed a "disgraceful thing" *(něbālâ),* it merits the sternest response due to its implications for the reputation of Israel (see comments on 34:7). This incident differs from Deuteronomy by Judah functioning as the sole judge in the matter, but the city's elders as in the Deuteronomy case carry out the sentence. Most striking is the call for Tamar's burning, which is rare in Mosaic law as a form of capital punishment; it is reserved for the heinous sex crimes of a man's marriage to his mother-in-law and the promiscuous daughter of a priest (Lev 20:14; 21:9; contrast stoning in Deut 21:21,24). Burning the body was an act of severe degradation (2 Kgs 23:16; Amos 2:1). The Code of Hammurapi (§§110,157) provides for the burning of culprits in the cases of a religious transgressor and a sexual offender.[165] Perhaps the essential idea behind death by fire for sexual offenses was purging the offense from the community (e.g., Josh 6:24; burned after stoning, 7:15,25).

38:25–26   At the critical moment, Tamar revealed the saving pledge by sending the items with a message to Judah (v. 25). Although Judah and the men of the city appear to have complete power over Tamar's fate, by her knowledge she maintains power over the bamboozled men. She did not make a direct charge but permitted Judah to draw the obvious conclusion. The language of the verse recalls the brothers' request of their father regarding the identity of the torn robe (37:32): "sent" *(šālaḥ)* and "recognize" *(nākar).* The motif of "recognition" recurs here (see comments on 37:32). Judah "recognized" them and admitted his guilt.[166] Judah's remark did not mean necessarily that her action was approved; rather, Judah acknowledged that her motivation was consistent with the purpose of levirate marriage, whereas Judah had attempted to circumvent the custom. That the text adds that he did not have sexual relations with Tamar again showed that the patriarch had repented of his behavior. Although the sexual encounter was wrong, Judah was not satisfied with acknowledging the obvious. He no longer is ignorant of his circumstances or their broader importance (see comments on vv. 15–16). Judah's insight into his guilt and the understand-

---

[165] *ANET* 170,173.
[166] On the difficulty of the Hb. translation, "She is more righteous than I" [v. 26], see "Levirate Marriage" above.

ing of the reason that lay behind it points ahead to the character transformation the patriarch will fully undergo. Unlike Reuben and his brothers, Judah perceives the more important underlying issues of their actions, bringing about favorable results (42:2; 44:18–34). As Noble summarizes, "Judah shows a remarkable ability to bring the heart of the matter clearly into view, and thereby to enable his present circumstances to be seen from a new perspective."[167]

(7) Judah's Sons by Tamar (38:27–30)

[27]When the time came for her to give birth, there were twin boys in her womb. [28]As she was giving birth, one of them put out his hand; so the midwife took a scarlet thread and tied it on his wrist and said, "This one came out first." [29]But when he drew back his hand, his brother came out, and she said, "So this is how you have broken out!" And he was named Perez. [30]Then his brother, who had the scarlet thread on his wrist, came out and he was given the name Zerah.

38:27 That Tamar had twins echoes the birth of Jacob and Esau, employing the exact words (25:24). Since the peculiar circumstances of their birth indicated that the younger superseded the elder, the happenings of Tamar's delivery become important to discerning the chosen successor to Jacob's position. The narrative implies that Judah is the successor in the sense that his descendants will rule over their sibling tribes (49:8,10; 1 Chr 5:2). The children's birth conveys the same rivalry that marked the chosen line in the lives of Abraham, Isaac, and Jacob.

38:28–30 The order of birth was paramount in the psyche of the Hebrews. So as to ensure that the firstborn was noted, since the birth of twins might compromise the firstborn's identity, the midwife ties a "scarlet thread" (*šānî;* cf. Josh 2:21) to the emerging hand of Zerah (v. 28). "This one came out first," spoken by the midwife, establishes the priority of the child. Although formally Zerah was the firstborn, inexplicably the child retracted his hand[168] and his twin came out. This unusual circumstance of his birth elicited the infant's name, "Perez" *(pereṣ)*, meaning "breach, break through." The explanation of the name makes this certain, lit., "What a breach *[pereṣ]* you have breached *[pāraṣtā]*for yourself!" The narrative clarifies that only after the birth of Perez did Zerah fully come forth, repeating the vital information that the infant bore the scarlet thread. "Zerah" *(zāraḥ),* meaning "dawning, shining," became the head of a Judahite clan (e.g., 1 Chr 2:6). The name was popular, found for an Edomite clan and king (36:13,17,33), an Ethiopian (2 Chr 14:9), a Simeonite (1 Chr 4:24) and Levite (1 Chr 6:21). Zerah, son of Judah, also occurs with his famous brother's in the lineage of Jesus (Matt 1:3).

---

[167] Noble, "Esau, Tamar, and Joseph," 240.

[168] וַיְהִי כְּמֵשִׁיב ("as he drew back," cf. GKC §164g).

3. Joseph in Egypt (39:1–23)

After recounting the disgraceful affair of Judah and Tamar (chap. 38), the narrator returns the reader to Joseph's situation: "Now Joseph had been taken down *[hûrad]*to Egypt" (v. 1; cf. 37:36). The place of chap. 39 in the Joseph account provides a significant stage in the development of Joseph's rise to power. The last two of the three symbolic "descents" that precede his ascension in the court of Pharaoh occur here: first was the lowering of Joseph into the wilderness cistern (cf. 37:24–25), second, his forced descent into Egypt (37:36; 39:1), and third, his incarceration in prison by Potiphar (39:20). Joseph's residence in Potiphar's household (39:1–19) and in Potiphar's prison (39:20–23)[169] must also be interpreted in light of Joseph's descent into Egypt (chap. 37) and Judah's descent ("went down," *wayyēred*) into Adullam (38:1). Judah's separation from his brothers was voluntary, whereas Joseph's was forced. At the level of human involvement, Joseph was in Egypt because of Judah. The pause in the narration of Joseph's life in Egypt by chap. 38 increases our interest in what became of Joseph, but, more importantly, the Judah-Tamar episode contributed to the broader concerns exhibited in the Jacob and Joseph narratives (see introduction to chap. 38). The chief ideas are divine promise and sovereign purpose, family inheritance, and personal moral transformation.

Rhetorically, the Joseph narrative often couples events, especially the double dreams of Joseph (chap. 37), the duo of the baker and butler (chap. 40), and the two dreams of Pharaoh (chap. 41). After the Judah-Tamar incident, chap. 39 provides the second story of a patriarch's temptation by a married woman.[170] That the two chapters share language and imagery underscores the contrast between the rival patriarchs (see Introduction to the Joseph section and to chap. 38). Judah and Joseph responded differently to their separations from their father. Judah's experience ended in disgrace (38:26), although God graciously provides descendants (38:27–30) despite Judah's sabotage of his future legacy (38:11,24). Joseph's rise in Potiphar's household and his virtue in resisting Potiphar's advances distinguish him from Judah and his brothers.

Our comments thus far arise from looking back at chaps. 37 and 38. Chapter 39 also looks ahead, forming the introduction to chaps. 39–41 that describe Joseph's experience in Egypt before the arrival of his brothers. Chapter 39 sets in motion and presages the positive events of chaps. 40–41 that narrate his elevation in the service of Pharaoh. His successes in the service of Potiphar show and explain the meteoric rise of the slave who becomes ruler (cf. 45:9). Moreover, as Sarna observed, Joseph's residence in Egypt signals the beginning fulfillment of the prophecy made to Abraham, "Your descendants will be strangers

---

[169] Cf. "captain of the guard," 37:36; 39:1; 40:3,4.

[170] Typically, interpreters have considered Tamar a foreigner, although the text does not state this unequivocally; if so, we can add that both chapters pertain to foreign women.

in a country not their own" (15:13).[171]

Theologically, chaps. 38 and 39 agree that the oversight of God in the lives of the patriarchs, which is common in the patriarchal narratives (e.g., 17:7; 21:22; 24:40; 26:3–4,24,28; 28:15; 31:3; 48:21), provides for both Joseph's and Judah's separations, though in very different ways. In Judah's case (after 38:10) the involvement of the Lord is only inferred from the narrative, whereas providential blessing is overtly stated in Joseph's sojourn. "The LORD was with Joseph" and its variation (vv. 2,3,21,23) encapsulate the message of the Joseph story as a whole, but the narrator makes this explicit observation in this chapter alone. We can go further by noticing that the distinctively Israelite name of God, *Yahweh,* occurs in the Joseph narrative only in this chapter, excepting 49:18. What the dreams (chaps. 37; 40–41) and their subsequent fulfillings imply (chaps. 42–45), Joseph's successes in Potiphar's household make plain. That is, the Lord God of Israel's fathers was enabling Joseph's ascent. The Lord ensured that Joseph's trials would redound to the good of others: "The LORD blessed the household of the Egyptian because of Joseph" (v. 5). What was true in the microcosm of Potiphar's house would be true on the wide stage of Pharaoh's kingdom and the world (41:57). This major development in the family of Jacob reflected the universal blessing: "All peoples on earth will be blessed through you" (12:1–3; cf. 18:18; 22:18; 26:4; 28:14). It is in accord with the blessing's universal aspect that the narrative exploits Joseph's role as the vehicle of divine grace that is bestowed on all nations. Joseph's achievements are not his own; they have divine reason. Joseph himself came to recognize that his suffering was for the ultimate good of saving family and nations (45:5–7).

Joseph's moral encounter with Potiphar's wife was also a trial for the youth because his fidelity to God was at stake: "How then could I do such a wicked thing and sin against God?" (v. 9). Ambrose observed the nexus between Joseph as ruler of Egypt and the moral incident in Potiphar's house: "But why should I enlarge on arrangements that pertained to a private house in the case of that slave [Joseph] who ruled an empire? It counts for still more that Joseph earlier ruled himself" (*On Joseph* 5.22). Joseph's remark implies that there was a standard of righteousness demanded by the God of his fathers (e.g., 15:6; 17:1; 20:6,9; 26:10; 44:16; 50:17). Like other ancient Near Eastern societies (see comments on 20:9), adultery was sternly condemned in Mosaic law, which required death of the transgressors (Exod 20:14; Lev 20:10). Joseph later strives to "forget" his father's house (41:41), but in his earliest days in Egypt the voice of his father's moral instruction commanded his attention. A rabbinic tradition reflects this thought when it attributes to Joseph's father the cause for his successful resistance: "[Joseph] saw [Jacob's] face before him and his blood

---

[171] Sarna, *Genesis,* 271.

cooled off" (*Gen. Rab.* 87.7; also *Soṭa* 36b; *Tanḥ.* 8–9).[172] Luther, too, surmised that Joseph's spiritual heritage made the difference in his decision: "And the Word implanted in the boy's heart by his father surely was completely pure and exceedingly fruitful."[173] What Joseph exhibited in fleeing the temptress demonstrates sage advice against such immoral entanglements: "But a man who commits adultery lacks judgment; whoever does so destroys himself" (Prov 6:32; also Prov 2:16–19; 6:23–35; 23:26–28; 1 Cor 6:18; cf. 2 Tim 2:22, "Flee the evil desires of youth").[174] Moreover, the depiction of Joseph's high moral character in this chapter is transparent when compared to the ambiguity presented in chap. 37.

COMPOSITION.   Two questions dominate the discussion of the literary history of this chapter. The first concerns the traditional pentateuchal sources and, second, the relationship of the Joseph account to Egyptian stories that appear to have bearing on the Hebrew tradition of Joseph in Egypt. Source critics usually assign the chapter to the Yahwist (J) and interpret it as a later addition to the Joseph story.[175] There is widespread agreement that the chapter is a literary unity. Humphreys represents the popular idea that chap. 39 is a late addition to the Joseph novella.[176] For him chap. 39's ending does not fit with chaps. 40–41. The style differs from chaps. 40–41, especially the regular occurrence of "Yahweh" in chap. 39. Chapter 39 seems incomplete, omitting the outcome of Potiphar's wife. The introduction of this story into the Joseph novella was to make an overt statement about divine involvement and to idealize the figure Joseph. For others, however, chaps. 39 and 40–41 evidence a unit that pertains to Joseph in Egypt, exhibiting an independent tradition from the family narratives in chaps. 37; 42–50.[177] The two Egyptian stories of chaps. 39 and 40–41 explain the rise of Joseph to his position of power. Coats views this as a "digression" in the family history that dominates chaps. 37–47. His analysis identifies three scenes in chaps. 39–41 that depend on one another: Joseph and Potiphar's wife, 39:1–20a; Joseph in prison, 39:20b–40:23; and Joseph before Pharaoh, 41:1–57. For this reason Westermann does not distinguish the literary history of chap. 39 from chaps. 40–41, rejecting the view that chap. 39 is late.[178]

---

[172] *Gen. Rab.* 87.5 explains that Joseph refused Potiphar's wife in part because of his fear of his father's rejection, like that of Reuben, who had committed adultery with Bilhah, losing his birthright. The midrash *Gen. Rab.* 87.1; 87.3 attributes some culpability to Joseph. God used this trial to humble Joseph. Rashi (on v. 6) questions Joseph's culpability, for he accepted the midrash that he primped himself. For Rashi, "after" (*'aḥar,*v. 7) means that immediately after his primping, God sent Potiphar's wife to trouble him.

[173] Luther, *LW* 7.54.

[174] von Rad notes the symbolic role of Potiphar's wife who in Proverbs is "the strange woman" enchantress (i.e., "adulteress," e.g., 2:16; 5:3,20; 7:5; 22:14; *Genesis,* 431).

[175] E.g., Gunkel, *Genesis,* 404–5; von Rad, *Genesis,* 364.

[176] Humphreys, *Joseph and His Family,* 202–5; Redford, *Joseph,* 181–82.

[177] E.g., Coats, *Genesis,* 276–84; Carr, *Reading the Fractures of Genesis,* 288–89.

[178] Westermann, *Genesis 37–50,* 60.

We have already addressed the connections of chap. 38 with that of chaps. 37 and 39, showing that the Judah-Tamar story is not a foreign composition imposed on the Joseph narrative as a whole (see introduction and chap. 38). That chap. 39 provides a "re-introduction" to the Joseph account is indicated by 39:1 and 37:26. Back referencing is a common literary technique, bringing forward important information necessary for understanding a new episode. The typical source division into an "Ishmaelite version" (J) and a "Midianite version" (E) is unnecessary (for discussion see "Composition" in 37:2–36 and comments on 37:25).[179] The close-fitting character of chap. 39 and chaps. 40–41 is made obvious by the common narrative plot of Joseph's ascension in the court of Pharaoh. The final paragraph of 39:20–23 provides an appropriate bridge to chaps. 40–41. Moreover, since the totality of chaps. 39–41 is necessary to the broader family narratives of chaps. 37(38) and 42–45, it is reasonable that chaps. 39–41 were presupposed by the family narratives of the brothers in Egypt, suggesting that they were not independent of the Joseph narrative as a whole. Coats admitted that as the broader narrative stands now, "The digression [chaps. 39–41] is fully integrated with the preceding and following elements in the Joseph story."[180] If chaps. 39–41 are so well integrated (and necessary) to the whole, the description of the unit as "digression" is not helpful. As for the relationship of chaps. 39 and 40–41, chap. 39 evidences its own narrative structure by the repeated phrase "The LORD was with Joseph and he prospered" and its variations (vv. 2,3,23), forming the beginning and end of the chapter. But as the symbolic presage of Joseph's rise to power in chaps. 40–41, the account of the seduction and imprisonment must have been written in mind of chaps. 40–41.

The second topic is the relationship of two notable Egyptian folktales, "The Tale of the Two Brothers" and "The Tale of Sinuhe," to the origin of the Joseph-in-Egypt narratives. The first concerns the motif of the adulterous wife in chap. 39, and the latter story informs the portrayal of Joseph as Egyptian courtier in chaps. 40–41. The first portion of the "The Tale of the Two Brothers" (late nineteenth dynasty, ca. 1215 B.C.) describes two brothers who live and work together in the elder brother's fields.[181] The younger brother is also a successful caretaker of the cattle. He returns to the elder's house to obtain seed, when the wife of the older brother seduces him but he repels her. After the wife produces false evidence against him, the older brother seeks to murder him but upon being forewarned by a cow escapes. Once the older brother confronts his brother, he is convinced of his brother's innocence and returns to kill his wife. Gunkel gathered far-ranging examples of stories that share the basic plot of an adulterous wife whose failed seduction of a handsome young man ends in false charges brought by the scheming siren.[182] "The Tale of Sinuhe" (twelfth dynasty, ca. 1930 B.C.),

---

[179] Gunkel explains that the redactor added 39:1 at inserting J's version of chap. 39 into E's story, equating "the Egyptian" of J with "Potiphar" of E's version (*Genesis*, 404).

[180] Coats, *Genesis*, 270.

[181] *ANET* 23–25; S. T. Hollis, *The Ancient Egyptian "Tale of Two Brothers": The Oldest Fairy Tale in the World* (Norman, Okla.: University of Oklahoma Press, 1990).

[182] Gunkel, *Genesis*, 406.

a funerary autobiography, describes the travels of the Egyptian official Sinuhe, who served "the Royal Wife of King Sesostris in Khenemsut."[183] With the death of King Amenemhet I, struggles at court led Sinuhe to flee to Syria-Palestine, where he came to reside at Upper Retjenu, gaining the favor of the local ruler Amunenshi. Sinuhe married the ruler's daughter, produced children, and became a prosperous man at court. In his old age he accepted the invitation from King Sesostris to return to Egypt, where he lived his final days as an esteemed courtier, receiving a proper nobleman's burial in a stone pyramid. The connections of the two Egyptian stories with biblical Joseph are the common motifs of an adulterous wife and of a successful courtier.

At one time it was commonplace to attribute borrowing to the biblical narratives, but scholars today largely accept a common cultural mileu as the source of the Hebrew story. Coats, for example, says "the narrative motifs were part of the culture that gave rise to the Joseph story."[184] Humphreys surmises that the biblical author of chap. 39 was cognizant of the Egyptian story when he penned the Joseph experience, giving it a decidedly Israelite theology (employing the name *Yahweh*).[185] He believes that "Egyptian traces" in chaps. 40–41 show that the author was aware of Egyptian practices but that the author's attention to dreams as the means of divine revelation is non-Egyptian in character, suggesting that the author was a foreigner who wrote his material outside Egypt for non-Egyptian readers.[186] Although the author of chaps. 39–41 may have been aware of the hero stories that exhibit these motifs,[187] of which the Egyptian versions are best known, the distinctive theological and historical character of the biblical accounts indicate that the author worked independently.

STRUCTURE.   The unit consists of three parts, forming a chiasmus. The motif of the Lord's presence and Joseph's subsequent successes establish the boundaries of the unit (vv. 2,3,23). The matching paragraphs (A and A') exhibit parallels of imagery and of language. Both paragraphs begin with Potiphar's actions: "Potiphar bought him" (v. 1), and "his master (Potiphar) took him and put him" (v. 20). The house and prison of Joseph's "master" (vv. 2,3,20) provides the two settings in which Joseph ascends. Potiphar is the "captain of the guard" in whose house and prison Joseph lives (39:1; 40:3). The explanation for Joseph's rise in both settings uses the similar language: "The LORD was with Joseph and he prospered" (v. 2); "the LORD was with him and . . . the LORD gave him success in everything he did" (v. 3); and "the LORD was with Joseph and gave him success in whatever he did" (v. 23). Joseph received "favor" *(ḥēn)* in "the eyes of" *(bĕʿênê)* Potiphar and of the prison warden (vv.

---

[183] *ANET* 18–19; also M. Lichtheim, *Ancient Egyptian Literature: A Book of Readings,* Volume I (Berkeley: University of California Press, 1973), 223–33.

[184] Coats, "Joseph, Son of Jacob," *ABD* 3.979.

[185] Humphreys, *Joseph and His Family,* 204–5; also Redford, *Joseph,* 91–93.

[186] Ibid., 165.

[187] Hoffmeier, *Israel in Egypt,* 82: "It could well be that some aspects of this widely dispersed Near Eastern literary pattern were employed by the Hebrew author(s) to cast the story of Joseph."

4,21). Similar language describes the delegation of responsibility to Joseph by Potiphar and the warden: "all (NIV, "everything") he owned"/"all that he owned"/"all that he owned" (NIV "had," vv. 4–5) and "all that was done there" (v. 22); "to his care" *(běyādô); "*Joseph in charge" *(běyad Yōsēp); "*under Joseph's care" *(běyādô,* vv. 4,22,23); and "he did not concern himself with anything" *(mě'ûmâ,* v. 6a) and "paid no attention to anything" *(mě'ûmâ,* v. 23).

A   Joseph Prospers in Potiphar's House (vv. 1–6a)
    The Lord Prospers Joseph (vv. 1–2)
    Potiphar Puts Joseph in Charge (vv. 3–6a)
  B   Potiphar's Wife Seduces Joseph (vv. 6b–19)
    Joseph Rejects Potiphar's Wife (vv. 6b–9)
    Joseph Flees Potiphar's Wife (vv. 10–12)
    Potiphar's Wife Deceives the Household (vv. 13–19)
A′   Joseph Prospers in Pharaoh's Prison (vv. 20–23)
    Potiphar Puts Joseph in Prison (v. 20)
    Jailer Puts Joseph in Charge (vv. 21–23)

The middle paragraph (B) explains the descent of Joseph, from Potiphar's house to Potiphar's prison. Verse 8 resonates the language found in A and A′: "With me in charge," he told her, "my master does not concern himself with anything in the house; everything he owns he has entrusted to my care." Another echo is "his cloak in her hand" *(běyādâ,* vv. 12–13), which is a subtle allusion to Joseph's supervision *(běyādô,* "in his hand" and variations, vv. 4,22–23), except Potiphar's wife. Beyond the same participants and plot line, Joseph's "cloak" *(beged)* holds this paragraph together. The term occurs six times (vv. 12[2x],13,15,16,18). Since the homonym *b-g-d* may refer to adultery (e.g., Jer 3:20; Mal 2:14), Sarna observes that "cloak" *(beged)* reinforces the idea of infidelity.[188] Potiphar's wife put forward the "cloak" as evidence of Joseph's attack. But as a wordplay on marital infidelity, the "cloak" symbolizes her unfaithfulness, which she clutches in her hand. This middle paragraph (B) contains terms typical of sexual relations. In addition to the obvious euphemism "go to bed/ sleep with" *(šākab,* "to lie with") for sexual relations (vv. 7,10,12,14), there also occurs "enter, go into" *(bô',* vv. 11,14,16,17[2x, "brought" in causative stem]) and perhaps "hand" for the male sex organ (vv. 8,12,13; cf. Isa 57:8[189]).

(1) Joseph Prospers in Potiphar's House (39:1–6a)

¹Now Joseph had been taken down to Egypt. Potiphar, an Egyptian who was one of Pharaoh's officials, the captain of the guard, bought him from the Ishmaelites who had taken him there.

---

[188] Sarna, *Genesis,* 274.
[189] J. N. Oswalt, *The Book of Isaiah Chapters 40–66* (Grand Rapids: Eerdmans, 1998), 480.

²The LORD was with Joseph and he prospered, and he lived in the house of his Egyptian master. ³When his master saw that the LORD was with him and that the LORD gave him success in everything he did, ⁴Joseph found favor in his eyes and became his attendant. Potiphar put him in charge of his household, and he entrusted to his care everything he owned. ⁵From the time he put him in charge of his household and of all that he owned, the LORD blessed the household of the Egyptian because of Joseph. The blessing of the LORD was on everything Potiphar had, both in the house and in the field. ⁶So he left in Joseph's care everything he had; with Joseph in charge, he did not concern himself with anything except the food he ate.

This unit reports the success the Lord gave Joseph (vv. 1–2), resulting in his rise to power as supervisor in Potiphar's household (vv. 3–6a). The psalmist recalled this moment in the history of Israel as the lamentable beginning of a glorious deliverance (Ps 105:17–18).

THE LORD PROSPERS JOSEPH (39:1–2). **39:1–2** Verse 1 back references 37:36 but here gives the transaction for Joseph from the perspective of Potiphar's purchase. The verse especially emphasizes his destination "Egypt" and that his descent was coerced. "Now Joseph had been taken down" *(hûrad)* and "who had taken him *[hôridūhû]* there" form the boundaries of the verse. Moreover, the two descriptions of his sale contradict the scholarly notion that the Midianites sold Joseph to the Ishmaelites first before their descent (37:36; 39:1). The terms "Midianites" and "Ishmaelites" were interchangeable in the author's mind, each passage stating specifically that they sold him directly to Potiphar. See more at comments on 37:36.

Verse 2 provides three observations on Joseph's status. First, "the LORD was with Joseph" occurs again in v. 21, drawing an explicit parallel between Joseph's success in Potiphar's house and his achievement in Pharaoh's prison. The expression "the LORD was with . . ." (v. 21; Josh 6:27; Judg 1:29) and its variants[190] indicate success, prosperity or victory. Second, "and [so] he prospered" *(maṣlîaḥ* from *ṣālaḥ,* "to succeed") spells out the effect of the former clause in the life of Joseph.[191] The same term occurs twice more in vv. 3,23, the latter occasion again drawing the parallel between his prison experience and his achievement in Potiphar's service. The word "success" also describes the servant in Abraham's house (24:21,40,42,56). Third, Joseph was a household servant, not a field hand. This gave Potiphar first-hand knowledge of Joseph's ability but also made him vulnerable to the sexual overtures of the wife of the house. Although Joseph will ascend in the eyes of the Egyptians, the passage does not let us forget that he was a slave to "his Egyptian master" (vv. 3–4; cf. v. 20).

---

[190] E.g., vv. 3,23; 26:28; Judg 1:22; 1 Sam 3:19; 1 Sam 18:12; cp. "God was with . . ." 21:20; Deut 32:12 (cf. Acts 7:9); and "The LORD his God was with . . ." 1 Chr 1:1; 15:9.

[191] *IBHS* §33.2.1a, *"and so* he *was* prosperous."

POTIPHAR PUTS JOSEPH IN CHARGE (39:3–6a). **39:3–4** Verse 3 provides the reason (protasis) why Potiphar highly regarded Joseph, placing him in charge of his affairs (v. 4). That "the LORD gave him success in everything he did" embellishes the report of the previous verse, making the Hebrew's ability inclusive. This measure of success corresponds to the comprehensive assignment that Potiphar gives him to oversee "everything he owned" (v. 4). This encompassing assignment for a slave was staggering, meriting four mentions of it in the chapter (vv. 4,5[2x],8). Precisely what he achieved and how it came to his master's attention is unstated, although "blessing" in Genesis typically involves material wealth (e.g., 24:35; 26:12; 30:27,30). We may surmise that the household operated smoothly and Potiphar increased his holdings. This role presages his future status as second to Pharaoh by accumulating unprecedented wealth for the king (41:49; 47:15–26). Repeatedly, the narrative indicates that the source of his achievement was a divine grant ("the LORD"), not a native intellect or ability. The purpose of enriching those whom Joseph served and of establishing Joseph's reputation, however, was not an end in itself. God's blessing of Joseph resulted in his rise to power where he could provide sustenance and salvation for his family and for many (50:20).[192] "And became his attendant" (*wayšāret;* lit., "served him") describes a personal subordinate (e.g., Josh, 24:13), the same position that Joseph initially held in Pharaoh's prison (40:4). The same term *šārat*("to serve, minister") often characterizes the priests and Levites in the service of the sanctuary (e.g., Exod 28:35 and *passim*). The second role of Joseph was overseeing Potiphar's business. That Potiphar "put him in charge" (*yapqidēhû,* v. 4) creates another literary parallel with his designated role in prison (*yipqōd,* 40:4). The word group *p-q-d* describes Pharaoh's overseers in Egypt (41:34).

39:5–6a These two verses repeat essentially what the author has already implied in vv. 2–4, but here the text is explicit: the Egyptian prospered "because of" *(biglal)* Joseph (v. 5). The temporal clause "from the time he put him in charge" indisputably ties the period of success with the appointment of Joseph (v. 5). Additionally, by the merism "in the house and in the field," the passage reinforces that the Hebrew slave supervised "everything" (*kol;* cf. vv. 22–23). In furthering the description of how Potiphar "left" (*'āzab,* v. 6a) all in Joseph's care, the text provides for a wordplay with Joseph's cloak, which he "left" (*'āzab,* vv. 12,13,15,18) when enticed by Potiphar's wife. The term "left" may be a double entendre, since it often describes disloyalty (e.g., 24:27; Deut 28:20; cf. comments on 2:24). Implicitly, the passage shows that Joseph rightly understood that despite his privileged place, Potiphar's wife was excluded from Joseph's indulgence, leading him to restrain himself from enjoying his master's wife. That "food" may be a

---

[192] On the significance of "favor in one's eyes," see vol. 1A, pp. 345–46.

euphemism for Potiphar's wife (cf. Prov 30:20) is supported by v. 9 (*Gen. Rab.* 87.6; Rashi); otherwise, his daily dietary needs must be in view, although it is puzzling why this responsibility was not Joseph's too.

(2) Potiphar's Wife Seduces Joseph (39:6b–19)

Now Joseph was well-built and handsome, ⁷and after a while his master's wife took notice of Joseph and said, "Come to bed with me!"

⁸But he refused. "With me in charge," he told her, "my master does not concern himself with anything in the house; everything he owns he has entrusted to my care. ⁹No one is greater in this house than I am. My master has withheld nothing from me except you, because you are his wife. How then could I do such a wicked thing and sin against God?" ¹⁰And though she spoke to Joseph day after day, he refused to go to bed with her or even be with her.

¹¹One day he went into the house to attend to his duties, and none of the household servants was inside. ¹²She caught him by his cloak and said, "Come to bed with me!" But he left his cloak in her hand and ran out of the house.

¹³When she saw that he had left his cloak in her hand and had run out of the house, ¹⁴she called her household servants. "Look," she said to them, "this Hebrew has been brought to us to make sport of us! He came in here to sleep with me, but I screamed. ¹⁵When he heard me scream for help, he left his cloak beside me and ran out of the house."

¹⁶She kept his cloak beside her until his master came home. ¹⁷Then she told him this story: "That Hebrew slave you brought us came to me to make sport of me. ¹⁸But as soon as I screamed for help, he left his cloak beside me and ran out of the house."

¹⁹When his master heard the story his wife told him, saying, "This is how your slave treated me," he burned with anger.

The unit describes the events that lead to Joseph's imprisonment. Joseph resists his master's wife, who is attracted to the handsome and popular young Hebrew (vv. 6b–9). After repeated rejections, she accosted Joseph, but he fled, escaping her grasp (vv. 10–12).

JOSEPH REJECTS POTIPHAR'S WIFE (39:6b–9). **39:6b** The text's comment on Joseph's pleasing appearance transitions the passage to the following scene of temptation. "Amid Joseph's many blessings, he suffers from one endowment too many, stunning beauty."[193] The language is photographic: Joseph was "well-built and handsome," lit., "fair with regard to form" (*yĕpēh tōʾar*) and "fair with regard to appearance" (*yĕpēh marʾeh;* cf. David, 1 Sam 16:12,18; 17:42). The feminine formula of the same expressions "beautiful with regard to form" (*yĕpat tōʾar*) and "beautiful with regard to appearance" (*yĕpat marʾeh*) portray the loveliness of a woman (e.g., 1 Sam 25:3; Gen 12:11), and the full description captures Rachel's attractiveness (29:17; cp.

---

[193] Wenham, *Genesis 16–50,* 374.

Esther, lit., "beautiful with regard to form and good *[ṭôbat]* with regard to appearance," Esth 2:7).

39:7–9 "After a while" indicates time for the passions to inflame (v. 7). "Took notice of Joseph" (lit., "lifted her eyes to Joseph") recalls Rebekah's first sighting of Isaac from afar (24:64). Joseph offered an explanation for his refusal of her solicitation based on three lines of argument: (1) the abuse of trust, (2) an offense against her husband, and (3) a sin against God. The Hebrew introduction has "he said to his master's wife" ("he told her," NIV, v. 8), emphasizing first his subservience to Potiphar and second that she is the possession of another man. "My master" on Joseph's lips reinforces his sense of duty to the man who has entrusted all to him. The expression "does not concern himself" renders the idiom "does not know" *(lōʾ yādaʿ)*, which may be a play on the same expression "to know" *(yādaʿ)* that metaphorically means having sexual relations (e.g., "knew *[yādaʿ]* his wife," 4:1). Joseph's line of defense is a reflex of the earlier commentary in v. 6, but here Joseph is explicit; as the man's wife, the woman was off limits. Potiphar's ignorance may be a secondary allusion to the recurring motif of Joseph's superior knowledge. Joseph's retort reaches the highest ethical plane: "How . . . could I do such a wicked thing and sin against God?" (v. 9). The rhetorical question highlights the absurdity of considering such a breach of moral conduct. The Hebrew "this great wickedness" ("such a wicked thing," NIV) has the same effect of underscoring the depravity of her illicit suggestion (cp. "this great guilt" at comments on 20:9). "Wickedness" *(rāʿâ)* also described the mental affections of prediluvian society (6:5), and it was the Mosaic penalty of death that removed "the evil *[raʿ]* from Israel" (Deut 22:22). But the crime is not against Potiphar alone; Joseph understood that this transgression offended God himself. The confession of David acknowledged the same (Ps 51:4[6]). Mosaic law required the death of adulterous offenders (Lev 20:10; Deut 22:22) since it was viewed as an offense against the Lord and not against the spouse alone. The law codes of Israel's neighbors permitted the death penalty too (cf. comments on 20:9) but often included a specific provision under which the offended spouse could pardon the wrongdoer.[194]

JOSEPH FLEES POTIPHAR'S WIFE (39:10–12). **39:10** Joseph was not deterred despite the daily pressure. "Day after day" *(yôm yôm)* expresses the distributive use of the repeated "day," that is, "every day." Temptation is not a part-time experience of the believer. Calvin commented, "Holy Joseph, therefore, must have been endowed with extraordinary power of the Spirit, seeing that he stood invincible to the last, against all the allurements of the impious

---

[194] E.g., Code of Hammurabi §129, *ANET* 171; see the discussion in H. O. Thompson, "Adultery," *ABD* 1.83–84.

woman."[195] The unusual expression "to lie beside [*ʾeṣel*] her" (NIV "to go to bed with her") rather than "to lie with her" (34:7; 39:14) may indicate a progression in her strategy, meaning to invite familiarity first and then sexual completion. The word "beside" occurs four times in vv. 10–18 and just once more in Genesis (41:3; cf. also the verb *ʾ-ṣ-l* in 27:36). Joseph wisely set a defensive boundary, refusing "even [to] be with her." Verse 11 suggests that his refusal "to be with her" meant he avoided being alone with her. Alternatively, the phrase means sexual intercourse, as in 2 Sam 13:20.

39:11–12 Verse 11 shows Joseph's innocence in the affair and his vulnerability to the mistress of the house. He was about his own business when circumstances provoked the woman's assault. This was the classic case of "she said, he said," for there was no witness to the incident. God alone was witness to what occurred. On one occasion he was working in the house alone, implying it was an exceptional situation in the house,[196] which despite his best efforts to avoid contact made him susceptible to her advances. She forced the incident by seizing his cloak and making the identical appeal for sexual relations. "Caught" *(tāpaś)* is the term that describes the violation of a virgin in Deut 22:28 (lit., "seizes her and lies with her"; NIV, "rapes"). The word "cloak" is central to the plot of the story, occurring six times in the chapter (vv. 12[2x],13,15,16,18). This term for "cloak" *(beged)* is the most often used (about 200x) and the most general term for clothing, referring broadly to a variety of garments, some sacred (e.g., Exod 28:2) and some common (Gen 28:20), worn by men and women.[197] It describes Tamar's "widow's clothes" (38:14,19). Joseph's special "robe" *(kĕtōnet)* given by Jacob is important in the development of the narrative (37:3,23,31–33). The idea of "clothing" in chaps. 37 and 39 has implications for Joseph's difficulties. The garment in both narratives is the specious evidence presented by his adversaries that results in his unjust imprisonments. That he "ran" *(nûs)* is also central to the case, the word occurring four times. His counteraction has become an example for all when subject to temptation of the passions (cf. 2 Tim 2:22). Wisdom especially warned the young against the ills of the "smooth tongue of the wayward wife" (Prov 6:24).

POTIPHAR'S WIFE DECEIVES THE HOUSEHOLD (39:13–19).   Scorned by the refusal of her prey, the woman sets out to retaliate against the vulnerable foreigner. She spreads her concocted story first to her household servants (vv. 13–15) and then rehearses the tale to her husband (vv. 16–18). Adding the narrator's account (v. 13) and the woman's repeated dissembling (vv. 14–15,17–18,19), Sternberg counts four reports of the seduction in the episode (vv. 11–12). He shows how each of her reports reinvents the "facts" and plays by subtle

---

[195] Calvin, *Comm.*, 297–98.

[196] *IBHS* §39.2.3b, *"while* none of the household staff . . ."

[197] R. L. Alden, "בֶּגֶד," *NIDOTTE* 1.595–97.

rewording to her audiences, creating the angry response she desires.[198] We will note her prevarications in the comments below.

39:13–15 When she realized that she had evidence to support her story, she set in motion the circumstances that victimized Joseph (v. 13). This incident is a sobering reminder of the wide destruction that the lying tongue produces (Prov 18:21; 26:28; Jas 3:6). "Look" directs the attention of the servants to the prima facie evidence (the garment). Potiphar's wife aims her attack at Joseph's "Hebrew" descent (cf. comments on 14:13), avoiding his personal name (cf. "Hebrew servant," v. 17) and exhibiting noted Egyptian anti-Semitism (43:1). This is a striking picture of the later enslavement of the Hebrews, who were deemed a burgeoning threat (Exod 1:8–16). The woman mitigates her charge against her husband here by the indefinite construction, lit., "he brought to us" (v. 14), but she is pointed when protesting her husband's involvement (v. 17). The phrase "to make sport of us" contributes to the us-versus-them cast of mind, setting the whole household against Joseph, who was a foreign interloper. Perhaps she hopes to fuel any existing jealousy the servants had toward their overseer. The woman was not claiming her offense was Joseph's ethnic identity foremostly, but rather his station in life. Intermarriage with foreigners was common in Egypt, but acceptance of foreigners required their assimilation into Egyptian culture. "Thus, we may regard the Egyptians more as cultural chauvinists than as racists."[199] "To make sport" (ṣaḥēq, piel) indicates derision (e.g., 21:9; Judg 16:25) but also has sexual implications (e.g., 26:8). Her insistence that she resisted ("screamed," vv. 14,15,18) exonerated her (cf. Deut 22:24–27). She repeated the lie, inventing the details to conform to the circumstance (v. 15). Together, the testimony of the master's wife and the exhibited cloak sealed Joseph's apparent guilt.

39:16–18 The same deceptive tact followed when reiterating the tale to her husband. She did not disturb the physical scene, keeping the garment at her side (v. 18). She repeated essentially the same commentary as before, but she bluntly burdened Potiphar with culpability for the crime, since he had elevated the "Hebrew slave" in the household (v. 17). She again indicates that Joseph was out of place, "You [Potiphar] brought [among] us." In other words, she blames Potiphar, and she implies that he had better do something about it. She explained that the slave ran, escaping at hearing her scream (v. 18). She cast Joseph in as poor a light as possible. First, he took advantage of the favor Potiphar had shown him, and second, Joseph was an inept rogue. She, on the other hand, was the innocent damsel in distress who valiantly screamed. Such provoking vividness in her lie inflamed the passions of the offended husband.

39:19 "His master" reinforces the idea of the power that Potiphar had

---

[198] Sternberg, *The Poetics of Biblical Narrative,* 423–27.
[199] S. T. Smith, "Race," *OEAE* 3.112.

over the life of Joseph, and their master-slave relationship exacerbated the alleged betrayal. She does not let this pass when she belittles Potiphar's lack of control and judgment ("your slave"). Moreover, that Joseph was a slave would have left him subject to Potiphar's disposal. The term for "anger" *(hārâ)* conveys an inflamed anger, that is, "he was enraged" (NRSV, NAB; "furious," HCSB, NJB, NLT). Only after hearing the emphatic accusation "*your* slave" (italics mine) does the master become incensed. His wife ignites his rage when she rubs the betrayal in his face. Since he "burned with anger," it is surprising that he did not demand Joseph's death. The hidden hand of God preserves the young man's life once again.

(3) Joseph Prospers in Pharaoh's Prison (39:20–23)

[20]Joseph's master took him and put him in prison, the place where the king's prisoners were confined.

But while Joseph was there in the prison, [21]the LORD was with him; he showed him kindness and granted him favor in the eyes of the prison warden. [22]So the warden put Joseph in charge of all those held in the prison, and he was made responsible for all that was done there. [23]The warden paid no attention to anything under Joseph's care, because the LORD was with Joseph and gave him success in whatever he did.

The narrative describes the result of the episode, placing Joseph in the king's prison (v. 20). The same language describing his ascent in Potiphar's house (vv. 1–6a) explains Joseph's favored status in prison (vv. 21–23). Despite the malicious intentions of the brothers or the manipulations of a scorned seductress, the Lord's purposes for Joseph prevail. "The human figures in the large biblical landscape act as free agents out of the impulses of a memorable and often fiercely assertive individuality, but the actions they perform all ultimately fall into the symmetries and recurrences of God's comprehensive design."[200] At the lowest point in his life, in the bonds of a foreign place, with no friend and no prospect of release, God initiated the steps that brought about deliverance for Joseph, his kin, and the world (cf. Ps 105:17–22).

POTIPHAR PUTS JOSEPH IN PRISON (39:20). **39:20** The stark contrast in Joseph's state between the beginning and end of the chapter is indicated by similar phrases: "in the house of his Egyptian master" (v. 2) and "in the house of the prison" (vv. 20,22, "in prison"/"in the prison," NIV). The expression for "prison," lit., "the round house" *(bêt hassōhar)* is unique to the Joseph narrative (vv. 20,21,22,23; 40:3,5). That Potiphar did not require the slave's execution has perplexed interpreters (cf. Deut 22:23–27). That Joseph escaped death at the hands of his brothers by the interventions of Reuben and Judah (chap. 37) may presage the same explanation in the case of Potiphar. We know that Joseph cried out for mercy from the pit (42:21), and we may surmise that he argued his inno-

---

[200] Alter, *The Art of Biblical Narrative,* 112.

cence with Potiphar. Perhaps Potiphar was already suspicious of his wife, especially when measured against the record of trust Joseph must have exhibited in the past. Another explanation offered is that the woman herself intervened so as to leave open the possibility of coercing Joseph into compliance during his incarceration (*Gen. Rab.* 87.10). Ultimately, in both the wilderness pit and in Potiphar's prison, the Lord's presence ("the LORD was with him") delivered the young Hebrew from death. That imprisonment is Joseph's "reward" for his uprightness must be interpreted in the wider scheme of God's purposes, for it is "at the nadir of his life" that Joseph comes "into contact with persons from the apex of Egyptian society."[201] Christian allegorists even saw Joseph's imprisonment with the two officials, the butler and baker (40:2–3), as a picture of Christ's passion. "Under the veil of allegory," it reveals "our Joseph, that is, Christ, as Isaiah says, 'was numbered among the transgressors'" (Isa 53:12; Quodvultdeus, *Book of Promises and Predictions of God* 1.28.40).[202]

THE JAILER PUTS JOSEPH IN CHARGE (39:21–23).   **39:21**   The parallel of this scene with the Potiphar scene is obvious, for example, both Potiphar and the jailer are identified as the *śar* ("chief") of the guard (v. 1) and of the jail (v. 21). Verses 21–23 are not, however, a pure repetition of vv. 3–4. The text elaborates on the earlier impression. "He [jailer] showed him kindness" *(wayyēṭ ʾēlāw ḥāsed)* recalls the former narrative and also anticipates the prison scene. The word translated "showed" *(nāṭâ)* repeats the verbal root translated "to stay" (38:1) and "went over" (38:16), bringing to mind the contrast in Judah's sordid behavior and that of Joseph, who had resisted self-indulgence. In the former narrative Potiphar extends "favor" *(ḥēn,* v. 4), but here the narrative reports that the Lord was the one who showed "favor" to Joseph. This coupling of human involvement and divine intercession reflects the author's theology, for it was ultimately the Lord who propelled Potiphar to bestow special privilege on Joseph. The word "kindness" appears again in Joseph's plea to the king's cupbearer, whose dream Joseph had favorably interpreted (40:14).

39:22–23   The text emphasizes, as in the earlier case (vv. 6,9), that nothing was withheld from Joseph's oversight in the prison. "All" *(kōl)* the prisoners and "all" activities fell under his supervision (v. 22; cf. vv. 5–6). The warden's motivation for endowing Joseph with exceptional authority ("the LORD . . . gave him success," v. 23[203]) was the same as that of Potiphar (vv. 2–3) and ultimately Pharaoh (41:38–41).

---

[201] White, *Narration and Discourse,* 256.

[202] *ACCS* 2.257.

[203] Wevers comments on the LXX's enhancement of v. 23: "What is fully evident from Gen's [LXX] rendering of this verse (and of v. 22) is its strong emphasis on the theme of the Joseph story, viz., that God was on the side of Joseph. Even in adverse circumstances he prospered. Though the MT also presents this theme, Genesis makes more of it by adding details, which enhance Joseph's superiority, and illumine the bright star of divine guidance under which he lived" (*Notes on the Greek Text,* 662).

4. Joseph, Savior of Egypt (40:1–41:57)

Chapters 40–41 narrate the emergence of Joseph from the dungeon of life to the heights of Egyptian rule. The idea of his transformation from slave to ruler dominates the episode. This turn in his fortunes is not surprising to the alert reader, given the earlier hints of change in the making. His youthful dreams showed the image of reversal in which the younger brother ascends over his elders (chap. 37). Also chap. 39 portrays his ascension in the house of Potiphar and in prison, a presage of greater things to come. That he resides in prison at the end of chap. 39 is mitigated by the narrator's repeated assertion that "the LORD was with Joseph" (vv. 2,23). As in the experience of Jacob (e.g., 28:15; 31:3,42; 35:3), we expect that the enabling presence of God will assure a favorable outcome for Joseph too. In Abraham's night vision the prediction of 15:13–16 expects an exile but one that will also be reversed. Joseph's slave-to-ruler story forecasts the national reversal of Israel, which emerges from captivity "with great possessions" (15:14). Joseph's "rags to riches" story fits the pattern that God has promised for Abraham's descendants. Joseph's rise points to the national dimensions that chap. 15 suggests. More is to come, but the informed reader can relax, knowing that God has already foretold just such deliverance for Israel's future. What the Lord accomplishes in the days of Israel's forefather Joseph, he can do again on the grand scale of a nation.

The means of his ascension, however, could not have been foreseen by the reader on the basis of Joseph's adolescent dreams (chap. 37). Unexpectedly, Joseph came to power by humble subservience to others. The events of chaps. 39–41 demonstrate that a facile explanation of reward and punishment, based on moral choices alone, is not adequate to understand God's relationship with his people (cf. comments on 18:19; 20:4). Joseph is the victim of Potiphar's wife and the negligent cupbearer, but in each case the result proves to be a stepping-stone. Strikingly, Joseph's greatest setback arose out of his greatest moral victory, when he resisted the advances of Potiphar's wife (chap. 39). There are few nobler lines in the Bible than his avowal, "How then could I do such a wicked thing and sin against God?" (v. 9). The cast of characters in Genesis generally receives their comeuppance, typically expressed through dramatic irony. For example, Judah's behavior toward Tamar met with a just requital (38:26), as did the brothers at the hands of (unrecognized) Joseph (44:16). The ambiguous picture of Joseph's character in chap. 37 (a brat? or an obedient son?) complicates our assessment of his victimization by his brothers. We are certain, however, about his virtue in chap. 39, leading to his imprisonment. The outcome in chap. 39 does not tally with the expectation of reward for Joseph's impeccable behavior. Yet the dissolution of Joseph's already difficult life, from slave to convict, worked to his advantage and to that of the Jacobite family— indeed to the countries of that whole region. The overriding issue in Joseph's

life of humiliation was the purposes of God for the salvation of Israel's forefathers and the nations (e.g., 12:3). As Waltke remarks, "The salvation of the
world depends on one descendant of the patriarchs."[204] We do not know
Joseph's interpretation of his difficulties, since the narrative does not provide
his opinion, other than his pleas of innocence (40:15). Joseph later expressed
understanding of the ultimate purpose for his suffering (45:5–8; 50:20). But to
conclude that human choice made no difference is to overstate the matter. The
muted voice of God in chaps. 40–41 indicates that the Lord works out his deliverance in different ways, both overtly, as in chap. 39, and opaquely, as in chaps.
40–41. The characterization of Pharaoh in chaps. 40–41 effectively illustrates
the human-divine confluence of events.[205] He is both powerful and impotent,
to be feared and to be manipulated. He acts decisively and timidly. Although he
is the subject of the dreams in chaps. 40–41, he is subservient to what the
dreams predict. In effect, as B. Green observed, "Pharaoh's actions are determined in realms beyond Egypt."

Moreover, the human tools of God's grace add strikingly to our knowledge
of the way God carries out his higher end. The Egyptians were a notorious
threat to the family of Jacob, beginning with Abraham and continuing in the life
of his descendants (15:13). Yet Egyptian officials and Pharaoh receive the gracious revelations of God, as had the non-Israelite king Abimelech (20:3). The
closest parallel to Joseph is the Hebrew captive Daniel, whose rise to stardom
in Nebuchadnezzar's kingdom came by his ability to interpret the dreams of
foreign rulers while in their charge. The common motif of Joseph's superior
knowledge comes into view again when Pharaoh's officials (40:8) and "magicians" (41:8,24) could not interpret dreams. That Pharaoh, perceived as the
divine Horus in Egyptian religion, should need an interpretive word reinforced
the message that only the God of the "Hebrew" Joseph could provide the
insight that Joseph had uniquely received (41:16,38–39). Joseph prefigured the
victors Moses and Daniel, the bookends of Israel's period of captivity, whose
wisdom prevailed over the Gentiles (cf. 1 Cor 1:18–2:16).[206] Joseph was a
divine gift to the court of the great foreign power. Joseph was "put" *(nātan)* in
prison (39:20–22) and "put" in charge over Egypt (41:41,43),[207] showing
God's gracious heart toward those outside the Abraham family. Ultimately, the
outsiders become beneficiaries of the promises through a right relationship
with the chosen family (e.g., 12:3; 18:18; 22:18; cf. 49:10). God's intervention,
though obscure to the Egyptians themselves, pacifies the enemies of Israel and

---

[204] Waltke, *Genesis*, 536.

[205] See B. Green, "The Determination of Pharaoh: His Characterization in the Joseph Story
(Genesis 37–50)," in *The World of Genesis: Person, Places and Perspectives,* JSOTSup 257 (Sheffield: Sheffield Academic Press, 1998), 150–71.

[206] Waltke, *Genesis*, 537.

[207] Ibid., 523.

sets the course for their deliverance. The apostle Paul discerned the weightier dimension of the promise when he commented that the outsiders became insiders when they put their trust in Abraham's descendant, Jesus Christ (e.g., Gal 3:8–9,14; Eph 3:11–14).

COMPOSITION.   The relationship of chaps. 40–41 and the preceding account of Potiphar's wife (chap. 39) was discussed in the introduction to the prior chapter. We have also addressed the role of chaps. 39–41 in the introduction to the Joseph narrative. Here we add a few brief remarks on chaps. 40 and 41 particularly. Gunkel, following the lead of Wellhausen, considered 39:20–41:57 to be made up of a combination of passages derived mainly from the Elohist (E) with snippets of the Yahwist (J), usually discernible where redundancies occur in the text.[208] In this opinion he reflected the typical source approach to these chapters. He viewed two different understandings of Joseph's position in prison as further evidence. In the J source he was the supervisor of all the prisoners (39:22), but in E he is the servant to the Egyptian officials in prison (40:4). Speiser differed from the old view by attributing chap. 39 to J and chaps. 40–41 to E, as essentially wholes, giving them two different authors.[209] Those who contended for two recensions of the Joseph narrative (the "Reuben" and "Judah" versions), such as Redford, who strongly rejected the source approach, nevertheless also viewed the chapters as containing two redactional strands. Thompson viewed chap 39 as made up of two variant stories of Joseph's entrance into the service of the "captain of the guard" (vv. 2,21–23) and "his master, the Egyptian" (Potiphar; vv. 2–20). He treated chaps. 40–41 as two stories bound by the same motif (interpreting pairs of dreams), but he is suspicious that the two were once told independently.[210] Carr viewed chaps. 39 and 40–41 as independent stories—though the nature of which, he says, we cannot characterize—that were taken up by the author of the early "prepromise" Joseph story around which he built the Joseph narrative. They are largely literary unities, showing small additions of the promise theme to connect them to the bulk of the story (e.g., 39:2–3,5–6a,21–23; 41:39–40). Others, such as Coats and Westermann, maintained that the fragments attributed to J were too slight to warrant the conclusion of a mixture of sources. Rather, the chapters exhibit the symmetry and cohesion of a literary unity, the product of one author.[211]

   We find that the coherence of chaps. 40–41, as evidenced by the same participants and progressive staging of the plot line, indicates a single author. As Wenham notes, the appearance of J-like elements in chaps. 40–41 (E) testifies to a

---

[208] Gunkel, *Genesis,* 411–21.

[209] Speiser, *Genesis,* 304, 316.

[210] T. L. Thompson, *The Origin Tradition of Ancient Israel,* JSOTSup 55 (Sheffield: JSOT Press, 1987), 122–23.

[211] Westermann, *Genesis 37–50,* 73, 85–86; Coats, in accord with his view of chaps. 37; 39–50 as largely that of J, believes that chaps. 39–41 show a single line of development, which has been well integrated into the whole by the author (*Genesis,* 264–65, 279).

"closer connection" with chap. 39 (J) than is widely acknowledged.[212] Chapters 39 and 40–41 have in common the vocabulary and motif of servanthood, eliciting from the reader a contrast between Joseph and the Egyptian officials. Among the vocabulary items are "serve" *(šārat),* occurring only in 39:4; 40:4 in Genesis, "master" *('ādôn,* 39:2 and *passim;* 40:1,7), "king" or "king of Egypt" in reference to Pharaoh (39:20; 40:1,5; 41:46), and words for "anger" *(yāḥar,* 39:19; *qāṣap,* 40:2; 41:10). The juxtaposition of chaps. 38 and 39 implicitly contrasted Joseph's behavior toward Potiphar's wife and Judah's treatment of Tamar. Chapters 39 and 40 create another contrast between Joseph's behavior toward his "master" *('ādôn,* 39:4,9) and that of the cupbearer and baker toward their "master" *('ādôn,* 40:1,4). Both Potiphar and Pharaoh were "angry" at their servants *(yāḥar,* 39:19; *qāṣap,* 40:2; 41:10), but in Joseph's case the anger is unjustified. The same was not true of the Egyptian officials, at least not for the baker, who met with the just consequences that we would have expected for Joseph, given the charge of rape.

Also the double dream motif, that is, the officials' two dreams (chap. 40) and Pharaoh's two dreams (chap. 41), are essential to the design of each chapter, showing a well-organized plan for the "twin" chapters. Together they reinforce the authenticity of the dreams as divine revelation (41:32) as well as exhibit the underlying theology of the chapters—the sovereign outworking of God's purposes for Joseph. This is accomplished overtly (e.g., "The LORD was with Joseph," vv. 2,23) in chap. 39; it is the counterbalance to chap. 37 as introduction, which only implies that the young Joseph's dreams are from the Lord. It is the observations of the narrator in chap. 39 that imply this divine dimension for the dreams of chaps. 37 and 40–41, so as to make clear from the narrator's perspective that Joseph's assessment that Pharaoh's dreams were divinely given was indeed correct. We can compare the overt statements of intervention in 38:1–10, which colors our understanding of 38:11–30 in which the Lord is not overtly said to be engaged. Also chap. 38 ends in the birth of children and so does chap. 41, which in their respective contexts indicate that the births were part of the grand plan. It is not happenstance in the mind of the author that two sons are born to Judah and also to Joseph. Moreover, the double dream motif relates chaps. 40–41 to Joseph's dreams in chaps 37, alerting the reader that the pre-Egypt dreams (chap. 37) find their realization not in Canaan, as we might have suspected, but in the land of Egypt by the unexpected means of a foreign court. Pharaoh unwittingly facilitated the salvation of Jacob's family and secured a future place for Israel to develop into a mighty people.

Since the few occurrences of the divine name *Yahweh* in the broader Joseph narrative cluster in chap. 39, source scholars deem this as crucial evidence that the source of this chapter differs from the "secular" telling of Joseph's rise at court in chaps. 40–41. This peculiarity is not to be taken as a sign of different authorship; rather, it is a feature of the literary tactic that the author utilizes to

---

[212] Wenham, *Genesis 16–50,* 380–81; he also observes that the reputed plot differences between chaps. 39 (J) and 40 (E) in Joseph's descent into Egypt and his standing in prison are better explained as plot development than competing sources.

convey his theology of human instrumentality. The Joseph narrative shows the human interpretations of events, events that are often left ambiguous as to their meaning for the participant (and reader) to ascertain. The chief case is the two dreams of Joseph in chap. 37; the text does not ascribe them to the Lord (the reader is predisposed to this assumption, especially given Jacob's experience, 28:10–22). The brothers thought not, and Jacob was not too sure what to make of them (37:11). We don't know Joseph's opinion, but the dreams' potential fulfillment must have left his consideration at some point because he later discerned their correlation with the brothers' arrival in Egypt (42:9). For the most part in the Joseph narrative, the name *Elohim* is employed, as we would expect, by the speakers when the setting is non-Israelite. Most often when the name of God (*Elohim*) occurs, it is in the speech of the participants, not the narration. The narrator does not insert himself, minimizing overt references to the intervention of God. He is satisfied with innuendoes, hints, and the like of God's intrusion because he wants to show that although God's work is not directly revealed, as in the cases of Abraham and Jacob, he is still very much at work in the life of the nation.

Finally, proposed discrepancies can be explained on exegetical grounds. The popular assumption that J and E conflict in their depictions of Joseph's supervisory roles is unnecessary (J, 39:22; E, 40:4). Genesis 40:3–4 clarifies that Joseph gave personal attention to the newly arrived Egyptian officials in addition to his oversight duties. The "captain of the guard" simply added the Egyptian officials to Joseph's responsibility (39:22). The "captain of the guard" (Potiphar? 37:36; 39:1) is assigning the same kind of work detail that Joseph undertook in Potiphar's charge.[213]

In our opinion chaps. 40–41 were penned in concert by the same person and in light of chaps. 37–39.

STRUCTURE. The unit consists of two parts that exhibit a similar narrative progression (40:1–12; 41:1–57). Together they advance the narrative from Joseph "in the house of the captain of the guard" (40:3) to the supplier of grain to the starving masses of "all the world" (41:57). "Some time later" (40:1) indicates a new stage in the story (e.g., 15:1; 22:1; 39:7). The time reference of "two full years" (41:1) binds the prison and royal court scenes, perhaps reinforcing the "two" dream motif of chaps. 40–41. The plot development of each episode builds on the revelation of two sets of two dreams (officials and Pharaoh) whose meanings are indiscernible to the recipients, leaving it to the Hebrew convict to interpret them. The dreams of the cupbearer and the baker (40:9–19) exhibit obvious parallels that tie the narrative together. These include the number "three" (vv. 10,16), the phrase "will lift up your head" (40:13,19), and the occupational motifs of food and drink for Pharaoh. The second set of dreams by Pharaoh (40:1–7,14–24) have two dreams so close in language and imagery that the king considered them one "dream" (sg.; 40:8,15,17). The man-

---

[213] Hamilton, *Genesis Chapters 18–50*, 475.

ifest connections include the number "seven" (41:2–7,18–30), the word "came up"/"growing" (*'ōlôt,* 41:2,3,5,18,19,22,27), and the words "gaunt, "thin," lean" (*daqqôt,* 41:3,4,6,7,23,24 and *raqqôt,* 41:19,20,27). The imagery of cows and grain in the dreams reflects the chief animal and agricultural features of Egyptian life.

After retarding the narrative by the two-year hiatus, the author describes Joseph's rise to prominence whereupon he undertakes the saving of Egypt and the "world" (41:57) from famine. Chapter 40's event makes possible the narrative advancement in chap. 41. That the cupbearer forgets the Hebrew slave creates a narrative tension that makes for good storytelling but, more importantly, infers that Joseph's deliverance from his dungeon will only be accomplished by the gracious involvement of God. The reader is encouraged to suppose that a change in the events of chap. 40 would have hindered the positive outcome of chap. 41. If Joseph had been released by the intervention of the cupbearer prematurely, the train of events would have been derailed. Chrysostom acknowledged this point: "As it was, however, the wise and creative Lord, who like a fine craftsman knew how long the gold should be kept in the fire and when it ought be taken out, allowed forgetfulness to affect the chief cupbearer for a period of two years so that the moment of Pharaoh's dreams should arrive and that by force of circumstances the good man should become known to the whole of Pharaoh's kingdom" (*Homilies on Genesis* 63.11–12).[214]

Thus chaps. 40–41 provide the "second floor" of the literary structure, resting on the foundation of chap. 39. In two chapters, in the space of two years (41:1), Joseph reaches the rank required if he were to assure the deliverance of his family. The final verse, "And all the countries came to Egypt to buy grain from Joseph, because the famine was severe in all the world" (41:57), alerts us to the imminent arrival of Joseph's brothers (chap. 42). The apostle Paul held the conviction that "all things work together for good," referring to the good of kingdom purposes. Although the suffering Joseph endured was evil in itself, it was one of many events that in the wisdom and mercy of God was used to accomplish the good outcome purposed for his people (cf. Rom 8:28).

(1) Dreams of Pharaoh's Officials (40:1–23)

[1]Some time later, the cupbearer and the baker of the king of Egypt offended their master, the king of Egypt. [2]Pharaoh was angry with his two officials, the chief cupbearer and the chief baker, [3]and put them in custody in the house of the captain of the guard, in the same prison where Joseph was confined. [4]The captain of the guard assigned them to Joseph, and he attended them.

After they had been in custody for some time, [5]each of the two men—the cupbearer and the baker of the king of Egypt, who were being held in prison—had a

---

[214]*ACCS* 2.262–63.

dream the same night, and each dream had a meaning of its own.

[6]When Joseph came to them the next morning, he saw that they were dejected. [7]So he asked Pharaoh's officials who were in custody with him in his master's house, "Why are your faces so sad today?"

[8]"We both had dreams," they answered, "but there is no one to interpret them."

Then Joseph said to them, "Do not interpretations belong to God? Tell me your dreams."

[9]So the chief cupbearer told Joseph his dream. He said to him, "In my dream I saw a vine in front of me, [10]and on the vine were three branches. As soon as it budded, it blossomed, and its clusters ripened into grapes. [11]Pharaoh's cup was in my hand, and I took the grapes, squeezed them into Pharaoh's cup and put the cup in his hand."

[12]"This is what it means," Joseph said to him. "The three branches are three days. [13]Within three days Pharaoh will lift up your head and restore you to your position, and you will put Pharaoh's cup in his hand, just as you used to do when you were his cupbearer. [14]But when all goes well with you, remember me and show me kindness; mention me to Pharaoh and get me out of this prison. [15]For I was forcibly carried off from the land of the Hebrews, and even here I have done nothing to deserve being put in a dungeon."

[16]When the chief baker saw that Joseph had given a favorable interpretation, he said to Joseph, "I too had a dream: On my head were three baskets of bread. [17]In the top basket were all kinds of baked goods for Pharaoh, but the birds were eating them out of the basket on my head."

[18]"This is what it means," Joseph said. "The three baskets are three days. [19]Within three days Pharaoh will lift off your head and hang you on a tree. And the birds will eat away your flesh."

[20]Now the third day was Pharaoh's birthday, and he gave a feast for all his officials. He lifted up the heads of the chief cupbearer and the chief baker in the presence of his officials: [21]He restored the chief cupbearer to his position, so that he once again put the cup into Pharaoh's hand, [22]but he hanged the chief baker, just as Joseph had said to them in his interpretation.

[23]The chief cupbearer, however, did not remember Joseph; he forgot him.

Chapter 40 introduces the king's cupbearer and baker, whose dreams are interpreted by Joseph. The officials are imprisoned by the king, where Joseph is assigned to serve them (vv. 1–4a). Each of the officials has a disturbing dream that prompts Joseph's assistance (vv. 4b–8). Joseph hears and interprets each dream, beginning with the cupbearer (vv. 9–15). Encouraged by the good report given the cupbearer, the baker requests Joseph's interpretation, but his is a prediction of his imminent death (vv. 16–19). The final verses report that the dreams were fulfilled just as Joseph had predicted (vv. 20–23).

CUPBEARER AND BAKER IMPRISONED (40:1–4a).   **40:1–2a** The chapter's events follow "some time later" (lit., "after these things"; see comments on 15:1; 22:1; 39:7), after Joseph had arisen in influence in the eyes of the prison warden (39:20–23). The interval of time is uncertain, though we know that Joseph's sale to Potiphar was at seventeen years old (37:2), and his rise to ruler over Egypt was thirteen years later at thirty (41:46). The two-year period between the events of chaps. 40 and 41 indicate Joseph was twenty-eight years old (41:1). The crime committed by the officials of Pharaoh's court started the series of interrelated events that eventually landed Joseph himself in the court of the king. The nature of the offense is conveyed only by the general term "offended" (*ḥāṭā'* "to sin, incur guilt," v. 1). The same term describes the threat of adultery by Joseph ("sin [*ḥāṭā'*] against God," 39:9) and by Abimelech against Sarah ("sinning," "wrong," 20:6,9). The passage rather reiterates against whom they had committed the offense, namely, "the king of Egypt . . . their master, the king of Egypt" (v. 1). The rare description "king of Egypt" for Pharaoh occurs where servitude is the focus (vv. 1,5; 41:46; cf. 39:20). Especially important to the account is the acuteness of the king's displeasure (v. 2; 41:10). "Was angry" (from *qāṣap*) translates a common word expressing God's or man's anger against malefactors (e.g., King Ahasuerus, Esth 1:12; cf. Exod 16:20; Lev 10:6; Deut 1:34). This explained their imprisonment and the eventual hanging of the baker. That the cupbearer was restored to his position must have been related to some unidentified exculpatory evidence. The text remarks on the elevated status that the two men held at court (vv. 2,7); the term "official" *(sārîs)* also described Potiphar's position (37:36; 39:1). From the beginning of Joseph's ordeal in Egypt, he toiled in the company of powerful administrators who observed his special gifts.

40:3–4a Verses 3–4a explain the circumstances that put together the slave Joseph and these two high-ranking officials. The phrase "captain of the guard" (vv. 3,4; 41:10,12) also described Potiphar (37:36; 39:1), suggesting they were one and the same, but there is no explicit indication in the narrative that Potiphar is in view here. That they were put "in the same prison," which is emphasized in the text,[215] implies that Providence lies behind the events (cf. 39:5,23). The description of Joseph's assignment as servant to the officers parallels his role in Potiphar's household (39:4; 40:4; cf. the same vocabulary, *pāqad*, "appoint," and *šārat,* "attend").

DREAMS IN PRISON (40:4b–8). **40:4b–6** A considerable period passed ("for some time") when the next providential event transpired (v. 4b). That the two men dreamt on the "same night" evidenced to them an omen that demanded an answer (v. 5; 41:11). The passage mentions that each man had his own dream and each dream required a separate interpretation. The "meaning" (NIV) of the dream is its *pitrôn* ("interpretation"); the word group *p-t-r* ("to

---

[215] בְּמִשְׁמַר בֵּית שַׂר הַטַּבָּחִים אֶל־בֵּית הַסֹּהַר מְקוֹם אֲשֶׁר יוֹסֵף אָסוּר שָׁם, lit., "in the custody of the captain of the guard, to the *prison* the *place* where Joseph was confined *there*" (italics mine); the recurring term מִשְׁמָר ("custody," 40:3,4,7,10; 41:10; cf. 42:17,19) probably distinguishes a special chamber.

interpret") exclusively appears in the Joseph narrative, describing the explanation of dreams. As a good attendant, Joseph probably was perceptive of the
moods of the men, observing that they were terribly distraught (v. 6).
"Dejected" translates the root word *zā'ap* (cf. Dan 1:10) used of a "raging" sea
(Jonah 1:5) and "raging" tantrum (2 Chr 26:19). Here their internalized anger
at failing to understand the dreams leads to their gloomy countenance. Moreover, unlike Pharaoh's dreams, the officials saw themselves as participants in
their dreams, which probably added to the angst they felt.

40:7–8 Joseph inquired why their faces are "sad" (v. 7; from *ra'*, "bad, sad,
unhappy"). A person's visage is generally thought to reflect one's attitude (e.g.,
Neh 2:1–3; Eccl 7:3; Mark 10:22). They explained their disappointment at having no one who could interpret their dreams (v. 8; cf. 41:16). In Pharaoh's court
such dreams received the consideration of professional counselors, but they are
cut off from the expertise that they had probably often witnessed. In ancient
thinking, dreams were the prime vehicle of divine revelations. Joseph acknowledges this but departs from the common viewpoint that professional magicians
were required to interpret the officials' dreams: "Do not interpretations belong
to God?" (v. 8). God, who gave the revelation, could provide the interpretation
to whomever he chose. Dreams were not the privilege of humans but the
domain of God. That Joseph requested to hear the dreams ("Tell me your
dreams,"[216] v. 8) implied that he could interpret them, if God so chose to reveal
their meaning to him. The recurring observation "The LORD was with Joseph,"
(39:2,23) by the narrator in the previous chapter has conditioned the reader to
assume that Joseph, too, knew that God was favoring him in everything he
attempted. Why not also in the matter of their dreams?

CUPBEARER'S DREAM AND ITS INTERPRETATION (40:9–15).   **40:9–11** In
retrospect the meaning of the dreams appears self-evident, but there are sufficient ambiguities to create divergent interpretations, if based on human ingenuity alone. The dream of a budding vine fits the cupbearer's occupation. The
imagery is one of abundance and involves groups of threes: (1) "three
branches," (2) which "budded," "blossomed," and "ripened" (v. 10), and (3)
the cupbearer "took," "squeezed," and "placed" (v. 11). Additionally, there
are three mentions of "Pharaoh" and "cup" (v. 11). "Budded" (*pāraḥ*, "to
sprout") also describes Aaron's rod (Num 17:20,23; cf. Song 6:11). The word
"blossomed" translates the literal "its blossoms *[nēṣ]* came out." The word
group *n-ṣ-ṣ* ("to bloom") refers to a plant's top growth (e.g., Song 2:12).
Finally, "ripened" *(bāšal)* typically refers to cooking meat (e.g., Exod 12:9)
and rarely of ripening produce (only Joel 3:13[4:13]). The dream depicted the
cupbearer with Pharaoh's "cup" *(kôs),* a drinking vessel (e.g., 2 Sam 12:3; Ps
23:5; Prov 23:31; cp. *gābîa',* 44:2), into which he "squeezed" (from *śāḥaṭ*) the

---

[216] סְפֶּרוּ־נָא לִי is terse, lit., "tell please to me."

juice of the matured grapes, placing the cup into the king's hand. The two-step activity portrayed the duties of the royal cupbearer, pouring and serving wine. (On the ornamented cup of sprouting *[peraḥ]* blossoms, see the molten sea at 1 Kgs 17:26//2 Chr 4:5.)

40:12–13 After learning the content of the dream, Joseph provides imme-diately its explanation (*pitrôn,* cf. v. 5). The decipherment of "three branches," symbolic of "three days," parallels as a time element the number of "seven" cows and "seven" sheaves representing "seven years" in Pharaoh's dreams (41:26–27). How did Joseph discern that three "days" were meant as opposed to another time unit? Apart from the explanation of divine revelation—that is, we are to understand that God told him—Joseph might have surmised that the imminent birthday of Pharaoh would require the skills of his chief officials. Commentators have suggested that the series of threes in vv. 10–11 (see above) suggests quick, imminent action.[217] The nature of the cupbearer's dream would appear on the surface to indicate a fortunate omen, and Joseph's interpretation agreed. The period of "three days" (v. 12) was sufficiently short to discover soon the efficacy of the Hebrew's ability. The expression "will lift up your head" (v. 13) has no correlation with a specific feature of the dream. The idiom "lift the head" *(nśʾ rʾš)* occurs three times at tactical points in the account, including the interpretation of each dream (vv. 13,19) and the narrative conclu-sion (v. 20). It describes one's show of favor toward another (e.g., Job 10:15; Ps 3:3; cf. 4:5–7, vol. 1A, pp. 268–69). The expression "to lift the head of *X*" describes the release of King Jehoiachin from incarceration, resulting in a state-sponsored stipend.[218] Although the idea of "release" for the expression's mean-ing fits the cupbearer's dream well (v. 13), it cannot have this narrow sense when addressed to the baker (vv. 19–20) since he was not judged favorably. Other suggested meanings of "lift the head" include "to summon, call into the presence of the king"[219] and "to count, take a census" (e.g., Num 1:2 and *passim*).[220] Verse 20's "among his servants" suggests that the meaning of the phrase is likely "to summon" before Pharaoh with the view of adjudication of their case. Joseph's use of the term when predicting the baker's outcome may yet have a third sense (see v. 19). Joseph continued, predicting that the cup-bearer will be restored to his original "place" (from *kēn,* "position"; cf. 41:13; Dan 11:7), meaning that he will be the "chief" officer once again (40:2). This

---

[217] E.g., Sarna, *Genesis,* 278. As was typical of Jewish midrash, the dreams were interpreted as indicative of the fortunes of Israel. The three branches refer to Abraham, Isaac, and Jacob, whose descendants will be enslaved by Pharaoh; but in the future three shepherds, Moses, Aaron, and Mir-iam, will deliver them (see *Tg. Ps.-J.; Tg. Neof.; Gen Rab.* 88.5).

[218] אֶת־רֹאשׁ יְהוֹיָכִין ... נָשָׂא, lit., "(he) lifted ... the head of Jehoiachin," i.e., released Jehoiachin (2 Kgs 25:27//Jer 52:31).

[219] On the Akk. equivalence *rêša našû,* see Hamilton, *Genesis Chapters 18–50,* 480, n. 19.

[220] On Akk. *rēšum našûm,* see Speiser, *Genesis,* 308.

full reinstatement will make Joseph's deliverance from prison possible. That Joseph added that the cupbearer "would put Pharaoh's cup in his hand" (v. 13) gave credence to his interpretation by tying his understanding to the particulars of the dream (v. 11). Joseph was able to discern which elements of the dream were to be taken symbolically and which literally. Since the interpretation matched the specifics of the dream and forecasted welcomed news to the cupbearer, Joseph's analysis must have been immediately pleasing.

40:14–15 Verses 14–15 evidence Joseph's confidence in his interpretation. He pleads with the cupbearer, once he has been restored to the court, to assist him in his predicament. Joseph's supplication is strongly worded: "remember me" *(qal, zākar),* "show me kindness" *('āśâ,* "to do, perform" with *ḥesed,* "lovingkindness, mercy"; cf. 39:21; 47:29), "mention me" *(hiph., zākar),* and "get me out" *(hiph., yāṣāʾ;* cf. 2 Chr 18:33).[221] This last term often is used to describe God's liberation of the Hebrews from the land of slavery ("will bring/brought you out," hiph. *yāṣāʾ;* e.g., Exod 6:6; 20:2). Joseph's plea may forecast Israel's release from Egyptian bondage.[222] The final entreaty places the responsibility in the hands of the cupbearer; he can spring Joseph from prison by making the most of his elevated position. Joseph is not satisfied, however, with the cupbearer reciprocating out of indebtedness. He bolsters his appeal by insisting on his innocence (v. 15). His imprisonment was a grave miscarriage of justice to begin with; the cupbearer's endeavor then would not only be fitting but also justified. Joseph succinctly but vehemently recalls his abduction ("I was forcefully carried off"[223]) and concludes that when he arrived "here" (Egypt) he was victimized again ("I have done nothing," i.e., "not anything," *mĕʾûmâ,* "anything," cf. 22:12). Although Joseph's recitation of his abduction did not mention the sale to Potiphar, as the narrative recounts in 37:28, there is no essential contradiction in the two memories. Kidnapping typically led to trade (cf. Deut 24:7; Amos 1:9), and since he was in Egypt, it was transparent that he had been sold. The phrase "from the land of the Hebrews" occurs only here and may refer to Canaan at large or to the central home-based locations of his ancestors—Hebron (Abraham) or Shechem (Jacob). His ethnicity as a foreigner ("Hebrew") was an important social consideration in the cupbearer's recollection to Pharaoh, especially since the identity of Joseph's deity and religion distinguished him (41:12; cf. 39:14,17; 43:32). Joseph's choice of the word "dungeon" *(bôr)* is the same word for the "cistern" in which his brothers confined him (37:20,22,24,28,29). In effect he was protesting that he had been wrongly incarcerated, from dungeon to dungeon! Such reprehensible mistreatment merited redress, which the cupbearer could facilitate.

---

[221] The verbal forms are perfects, having volitional force (cf. *IBHS* §3.2.3d; GKC §163d).

[222] Wenham, *Genesis 16–50,* 383.

[223] כִּי־גֻנֹּב גֻּנַּבְתִּי, *pual* infinitive absolute + *pual* perfect, expresses the intensity of the kidnapping; in Mosaic law "kidnapping" (גָּנַב) merited execution (Exod 21:16; Deut 24:7).

That Joseph did not indict his brothers or Potiphar's wife corresponds with the following silence of the text concerning the baker's crime. Either Joseph resisted the impulse to give a "bad report," as he had done in the past (37:2), or the narrator wanted the reader's attention on the more important impression of God's purposes working through his imprisonment.

BAKER'S DREAM AND ITS INTERPRETATION (40:16–19). **40:16–17** Encouraged by the good outcome of his companion's dream, the baker hastened to impart his tale (v. 16). The repeated phrase "on my head" forms the boundaries of the dream (vv. 16b,17b), pointing out the central feature of the dream. The mention of "head" alludes to the all-important expression "lift up the head," referring to the judgment of Pharaoh (vv. 13,19,20). The dream corresponded in several ways with the cupbearer's. Both have threes—three branches and three baskets; both dreams pertain to their respective occupations; and in both dreams the cupbearer and baker appear. The differences are significant too. In the baker's dream Pharaoh is not seen, the baker is not performing his duty, and there is nothing in the former dream corresponding to the birds of prey. The baker is totally passive. The vision of three baskets balancing on the baker's head paints an unusual sight and was perhaps comical to some readers. The term "baskets" *(sallîm)* is associated with baked goods (e.g., Exod 29:2–3), though not always (Judg 6:19).[224] The prolific number and variety of the items ("all kinds of baked goods") reflect what we know of Egyptian cuisine. From the top basket birds were feasting on the food designated for Pharaoh. The word for "bird" *('ôp)* is the general term, referring to clean and unclean species (e.g., Lev 20:25), but it may describe birds that feed off carcasses (e.g., Deut 28:26). Carnivorous birds dining on fallen corpses is a common prophetic image of God's judgment against the wicked (e.g., Jer 34:20; Ezek 39:17–20; Rev 19:17–18). The baker's vision of birds picking at the food brings to mind the disquieting episode of Abraham *('ayiṭ,* "birds of prey," 15:11). Since Pharaoh did not receive the baked goods prepared by the baker, unlike the dream of the cupbearer, the picture conveyed impending doom. Unlike Abraham, who in his vision dispersed the scavengers (15:11), the baker failed in his duty by leaving the food unguarded (e.g., 2 Sam 21:10; Jer 7:33).

40:18–19 The interpretation begins predictably and even comfortingly by the reappearance of the exact phrase in the favorable interpretation of the vine: "Pharaoh will lift up your head" (vv. 13,19). But a significant variance

---

[224] חֹרִי occurs only here, typically understood as "bread" (NIV, NASB, NRSV), perhaps "white bread" (HCSB; from חוּר, "to be pale, white," Isa 29:22; cf. Ar. *ḥuwwarā,* "white, white flour" *HALOT* 353; see Hamilton, *Genesis Chapters 18–50,* 481, n. 1 for more); others have "wicker," i.e., wicker baskets of bread (e.g., NIV note, NAB, NJB; Speiser, *Genesis,* 307; Westermann, *Genesis 36–50,* 77); LXX χονδριτῶν, "cakes of coarse grain" (LSJ); Syr. "of white things"; Vg. *farinae,* "of meal, flour" (see Wevers, *Notes on the Greek Text,* 670–71); a possible Egyptian association *(ḥr[.t]),* "a kind of cake," is uncertain (Muchiki, *Egyptian Proper Names,* 244).

in v. 19 gives the interpretation a startling change in meaning. The addition "from upon you" *(mēʿāleykā)* indicates a decapitation of the baker: lit., "Pharaoh will lift up your head from upon you." The NIV incorporates this interpretation by its nuanced rendering: "Pharaoh will lift *off* your head" (italics mine).[225] That the interpretation is negative is made obvious by the next phrase, "and hang you on a tree"[226] (NIV, cf. NASB, REB; "gallows," NJB). The notion of "hanging" after a decapitation appears contradictory.[227] Some commentators contend that "from upon you" must be a mistaken scribal addition,[228] derived from the same phrase at the end of v. 19, lit., "and the birds will eat your flesh from upon you"[229] ("eat *away* your flesh," NIV [italics mine]). The mention of "tree," however, may indicate impalement on a stake ("impale . . . on a pole," NIV note; cf. HCSB note, NRSV, NJPS, NAB, NLT) rather than hanging (cf. 2 Sam 4:12). The impalement of a corpse was commonly enough practiced and was considered frightfully ignominious (e.g., Deut 21:22–23; Josh 8:29; 10:26; 2 Sam 4:12; 21:12). The exegetical problem exists, however, only if a literal decapitation is meant. The phrase "from upon you" could be a rhetorical play on "lifting the head" in the former interpretation (v. 13) and is not to be pressed as a literal beheading.

Another surprising twist in the second interpretation was the identity of the baked goods eaten by the birds. The birds were both symbolic and literal, as was the cup in the first dream, but the baked products represented the baker himself (v. 19). Since the king did not enjoy the baker's food, the birds that stole away the king's food will feast literally on the exposed body of the Egyptian officer.

FULFILLMENT OF THE DREAMS (40:20–23). **40:20–23** The concluding verses detail the outcome, showing that the dreams came to pass "just as Joseph had said to them" (v. 22). The birthday celebration of Pharaoh gave the three-day period in the two dreams significance at first undetected by the reader and perhaps by Joseph (v. 21). The "birthday"[230] would necessarily require a "feast" *(mišteh,* "drinking banquet"; e.g., 19:3; Esth 1:3) that entailed both food and drink (v. 20). Hoffmeier has argued that Pharaoh's "birthday" is not the celebration of his physical birth but the celebration of his accession as the

---

[225] Cf. NRSV, "[He] will lift up your head—from you!—and hang you . . .," or "from off you" (HCSB).

[226] Cf. Esth 2:23, lit., "were hanged on a tree" (= "were hanged on a gallows," NIV).

[227] Sarna *(Genesis,* 279) notes that beheading employs the *hiphil* form ("remove") of the different verb סוּר (1 Sam 17:46).

[228] E.g., Westermann, *Genesis 37–50,* 77.

[229] וְאָכַל הָעוֹף אֶת־בְּשָׂרְךָ מֵעָלֶיךָ; the word מֵעָלֶיךָ, "from upon you," is absent in two Hb. MSS *(BHS)* and Vg.

[230] יוֹם הֻלֶּדֶת אֶת־פַּרְעֹה, lit., "on the day of Pharaoh's *having been caused to be born* [as an event]" *(IBHS* §28.1b); *hophal* infinitive construct הֻלֶּדֶת also occurs in Ezek 16:5, "on the day you were born," בְּיוֹם הֻלֶּדֶת אֹתָךְ.

divine son of Re. That accessions of new kings included the release of prisoners may give the background for Pharaoh's release of the cupbearer (cf. Jehoiachin, 2 Kgs 25:27).[231] In any case, a festive occasion of such importance meant the prospects of reinstating the chief officials who probably had contributed regularly to social gatherings. That the text specifies that the king "lifted up the heads" of the two officials alerts the reader to the moment of truth for Joseph's predictions, retaining some tension regarding the outcome of the baker.

Since this was done in the presence of the other members at court, the king's decision may have rested on some form of adjudication or competition. Verse 21 corresponds to the language Joseph used to predict the cupbearer's restoration (v. 13), manifesting the accuracy of Joseph's prediction, as we say, "to the letter." The narrative tension reaches its height at reporting the baker's demise (v. 22),[232] which came to pass in the same way Joseph had said (v. 19). The text gives no basis for Pharaoh's decision.[233] As for Joseph's lot, the final verse of the chapter would appear to seal his fortune (v. 23). The reverberation of the neglect of Joseph, "[he] did not remember" *(zākar)* and "he forgot him," sounds the certainty of his continued incarceration. For the cupbearer's neglect, the modern aphorism "Out of sight, out of concern!" aptly fits. The term "remember" echoes Joseph's impassioned request of the official, "remember me" and "mention me" (v. 14, both from *zākar*). The role of the word "remember" in Genesis, signaling God's faithfulness (8:1; 9:15,16; 19:29; 30:22; cf. 42:9), raises the question as to God's "remembrance" of Joseph. Hebrew narrative often leaves it to the reader to look beyond the human script for the divine hand that pens the events (e.g., Ruth 2:3; Esth 6:1–2; cf. 1 Sam 6:9). The issue of God's immanence finds its resolve in the cupbearer's admission of neglect and sudden remembrance ("reminded" *[mazkîr]*, 41:9). An ancient midrash said it well, "Said the Holy One, blessed be he, to him [cupbearer], 'You may have forgotten him [Joseph], but I have not forgotten him.' "

(2) Dreams of Pharaoh (41:1–57)

¹When two full years had passed, Pharaoh had a dream: He was standing by the Nile, ²when out of the river there came up seven cows, sleek and fat, and they grazed among the reeds. ³After them, seven other cows, ugly and gaunt, came up out of the Nile and stood beside those on the riverbank. ⁴And the cows that were ugly and gaunt ate up the seven sleek, fat cows. Then Pharaoh woke up.

---

[231] Hoffmeier, *Israel in Egypt*, 89–91.

[232] The *wāw* adversative sharpens the contrast of the officers' fates, וְאֵת שַׂר הָאֹפִים תָּלָה, lit., "but the chief baker he hanged."

[233] *Gen Rab.* 88.5 tied the cupbearer's dream to the future four redemptions of Israel, relating the four "cups" (vv. 1,13) to the four cups of the Jewish Passover. The baker's baskets, however, signified the kingdoms, ending with Rome, that will subjugate Israel. Thus the baker received the bad interpretation and fate (*Gen. Rab.* 88.6; also *Tg. Ps.-J.*).

⁵He fell asleep again and had a second dream: Seven heads of grain, healthy and good, were growing on a single stalk. ⁶After them, seven other heads of grain sprouted—thin and scorched by the east wind. ⁷The thin heads of grain swallowed up the seven healthy, full heads. Then Pharaoh woke up; it had been a dream.

⁸In the morning his mind was troubled, so he sent for all the magicians and wise men of Egypt. Pharaoh told them his dreams, but no one could interpret them for him.

⁹Then the chief cupbearer said to Pharaoh, "Today I am reminded of my shortcomings. ¹⁰Pharaoh was once angry with his servants, and he imprisoned me and the chief baker in the house of the captain of the guard. ¹¹Each of us had a dream the same night, and each dream had a meaning of its own. ¹²Now a young Hebrew was there with us, a servant of the captain of the guard. We told him our dreams, and he interpreted them for us, giving each man the interpretation of his dream. ¹³And things turned out exactly as he interpreted them to us: I was restored to my position, and the other man was hanged."

¹⁴So Pharaoh sent for Joseph, and he was quickly brought from the dungeon. When he had shaved and changed his clothes, he came before Pharaoh.

¹⁵Pharaoh said to Joseph, "I had a dream, and no one can interpret it. But I have heard it said of you that when you hear a dream you can interpret it."

¹⁶"I cannot do it," Joseph replied to Pharaoh, "but God will give Pharaoh the answer he desires."

¹⁷Then Pharaoh said to Joseph, "In my dream I was standing on the bank of the Nile, ¹⁸when out of the river there came up seven cows, fat and sleek, and they grazed among the reeds. ¹⁹After them, seven other cows came up—scrawny and very ugly and lean. I had never seen such ugly cows in all the land of Egypt. ²⁰The lean, ugly cows ate up the seven fat cows that came up first. ²¹But even after they ate them, no one could tell that they had done so; they looked just as ugly as before. Then I woke up.

²²"In my dreams I also saw seven heads of grain, full and good, growing on a single stalk. ²³After them, seven other heads sprouted—withered and thin and scorched by the east wind. ²⁴The thin heads of grain swallowed up the seven good heads. I told this to the magicians, but none could explain it to me."

²⁵Then Joseph said to Pharaoh, "The dreams of Pharaoh are one and the same. God has revealed to Pharaoh what he is about to do. ²⁶The seven good cows are seven years, and the seven good heads of grain are seven years; it is one and the same dream. ²⁷The seven lean, ugly cows that came up afterward are seven years, and so are the seven worthless heads of grain scorched by the east wind: They are seven years of famine.

²⁸"It is just as I said to Pharaoh: God has shown Pharaoh what he is about to do. ²⁹Seven years of great abundance are coming throughout the land of Egypt, ³⁰but seven years of famine will follow them. Then all the abundance in Egypt will be forgotten, and the famine will ravage the land. ³¹The abundance in the land will not be remembered, because the famine that follows it will be so severe. ³²The reason the dream was given to Pharaoh in two forms is that the matter has been firmly decided by God, and God will do it soon.

³³"And now let Pharaoh look for a discerning and wise man and put him in charge of the land of Egypt. ³⁴Let Pharaoh appoint commissioners over the land to take a fifth of the harvest of Egypt during the seven years of abundance. ³⁵They should collect all the food of these good years that are coming and store up the grain under the authority of Pharaoh, to be kept in the cities for food. ³⁶This food should be held in reserve for the country, to be used during the seven years of famine that will come upon Egypt, so that the country may not be ruined by the famine."

³⁷The plan seemed good to Pharaoh and to all his officials. ³⁸So Pharaoh asked them, "Can we find anyone like this man, one in whom is the spirit of God?"

³⁹Then Pharaoh said to Joseph, "Since God has made all this known to you, there is no one so discerning and wise as you. ⁴⁰You shall be in charge of my palace, and all my people are to submit to your orders. Only with respect to the throne will I be greater than you."

⁴¹So Pharaoh said to Joseph, "I hereby put you in charge of the whole land of Egypt." ⁴²Then Pharaoh took his signet ring from his finger and put it on Joseph's finger. He dressed him in robes of fine linen and put a gold chain around his neck. ⁴³He had him ride in a chariot as his second-in-command, and men shouted before him, "Make way!" Thus he put him in charge of the whole land of Egypt.

⁴⁴Then Pharaoh said to Joseph, "I am Pharaoh, but without your word no one will lift hand or foot in all Egypt." ⁴⁵Pharaoh gave Joseph the name Zaphenath-Paneah and gave him Asenath daughter of Potiphera, priest of On, to be his wife. And Joseph went throughout the land of Egypt.

⁴⁶Joseph was thirty years old when he entered the service of Pharaoh king of Egypt. And Joseph went out from Pharaoh's presence and traveled throughout Egypt. ⁴⁷During the seven years of abundance the land produced plentifully. ⁴⁸Joseph collected all the food produced in those seven years of abundance in Egypt and stored it in the cities. In each city he put the food grown in the fields surrounding it. ⁴⁹Joseph stored up huge quantities of grain, like the sand of the sea; it was so much that he stopped keeping records because it was beyond measure.

⁵⁰Before the years of famine came, two sons were born to Joseph by Asenath daughter of Potiphera, priest of On. ⁵¹Joseph named his firstborn Manasseh and said, "It is because God has made me forget all my trouble and all my father's household." ⁵²The second son he named Ephraim and said, "It is because God has made me fruitful in the land of my suffering."

⁵³The seven years of abundance in Egypt came to an end, ⁵⁴and the seven years of famine began, just as Joseph had said. There was famine in all the other lands, but in the whole land of Egypt there was food. ⁵⁵When all Egypt began to feel the famine, the people cried to Pharaoh for food. Then Pharaoh told all the Egyptians, "Go to Joseph and do what he tells you."

⁵⁶When the famine had spread over the whole country, Joseph opened the storehouses and sold grain to the Egyptians, for the famine was severe throughout Egypt. ⁵⁷And all the countries came to Egypt to buy grain from Joseph, because the famine was severe in all the world.

Chapter 41's events propel Joseph from the prison cell to the royal court, from prison clothes to the apparel of rulers, from the lowly station of slave to prisoner to ruler over all Egypt. Pharaoh's two dreams are recounted (vv. 1–7), and upon learning of them the king's cupbearer remembers the Hebrew interpreter of dreams whom he had promised to keep in mind (vv. 8–13). After Pharaoh retells the dreams to Joseph (vv. 14–24), he interprets the dreams that forecast the seven years of plenty and seven years of famine (vv. 25–36). The divine insight that he showed motivates the king to appoint Joseph second in command, bestowing on him all the proper accoutrements of the office (vv. 37–46). Joseph takes up the task by collecting and filling the store cities during the seven years of plenty (vv. 47–49). His increased stature is matched by his burgeoning Egyptian household with the birth of two sons, Manasseh and Ephraim (vv. 50–52). The final paragraph describes the salvation that resulted from the dreams given the king—Joseph provides grain to all the countries during the famine (vv. 53–57).

PHARAOH DREAMS TWICE (41:1–7). **41:1** A two-year period passed, giving Joseph ample time to despair over his state.[234] The narrative presents a word cinema of the king's dreams, as if they were taking place before the reader's eyes.[235] The significance of the Nile in the dreams was its centrality to the life of Egypt.[236] The word "Nile" (yĕʾōr) is the first of many Egyptian loanwords in this chapter (*itrw; Iteru* when the Nile not in flood), as we would expect, due to its technical description of Egyptian officials and practices. The Nile water system was the most conspicuous feature of Egypt's geography and the primary source of the country's economic and social stability. The Nile was deified in Egyptian religion (god Hap or Hapy when Nile in flood), and the appearance of the cows from the river may have suggested to Pharaoh a close connection to the gods. Pharaoh's state was responsible for maintaining the irrigation of the river system, distributing land grants, gathering taxes, and storing grain. Despite the success of natural irrigation and human engineering (dams, canals), high and low Niles occurred, producing famine and its ill effects on society. Significant inundations delayed the planting season that subjected tender sprouts to the cyclic hot winds (see *"khamsin"* below) that produced drought and famine.

41:2–4 His first dream entailed two sets of seven cows that emerged from the Nile. The grassy banks of the Nile provided a habitat for animals and

---

[234] Calvin interpreted Joseph's two years as a lesson "that nothing is more improper, than to prescribe the time in which God shall help us; since he purposely, for a long season, keeps his own people in anxious suspense, that by this very experiment, they may truly know what it is to trust Him" (*Comm.*, 312).

[235] The verbal sequence consists of participles, וּפַרְעֹה חֹלֵם וְהִנֵּה עֹמֵד, lit., "Pharaoh was dreaming and, behold, he was standing . . ."

[236] B. B. Williams, "Nile (Geography)," *ABD* 4.1112–16; K. W. Butzer, "Nile," *OEAE* 2.550.

birds.[237] The first set of well-fed cattle are seen feeding on the Nile's "reeds" (*ʾāḥû;* Egyptian *3ḥ[y]*, "plant"), representing a peaceful and thriving time (vv. 2,18; Job 8:11; cf. Hos 13:15, NRSV). The grasslands of the Nile flourished due to its annual flooding.[238] The second group that emerged was opposite in appearance, "ugly and gaunt,"[239] standing beside the healthy cows (v. 3). Unlike the fat specimens, these bony cows were not feeding on the grass. That the unsightly cattle stood beside the first group created a stronger contrast and naturally elicited a question about the relationship of the two groups. The sudden frightful consumption of the fair cattle by the emaciated was a disturbing sight that indicated a bad omen, probably the source of the king's temporary awakening (v. 4).

41:5–7 The second dream concerned a staple in Egyptian agricultural life, grain production. The narrative describes the dream as vividly present to the mind's eye.[240] The first set of seven "heads of grain" (*šibbŏlîm*) parallels the fat cattle in their appealing heartiness (v. 5; cf. Joseph's dream, "sheaves," *ʾălūmmîm,* 37:7). The word *šibbōlet* (cf. *sibbōlet,* Judg 12:6) refers to the seed atop the stalks of grassy cereal plants; it is that part of the plant that is cut and gathered (e.g., Job 24:24; Isa 17:5). The "stalk" (*qāneh,* "reed") is the stem of the plant. That they were sprouting from a "single stalk" testified to their potency. Because of its abundance in the Nile valley (Isa 19:6), the "stalk" ("reed") is associated especially with Egypt (2 Kgs 18:21//Isa 36:6; Ezek 29:6–7).[241] The second set of grain was scrawny due to the searing heat of the desert's blasting "east wind" (*qādîm,* v. 6; cf. Exod 14:21; Hos 13:15).[242] The scorched heads of grain correspond to the unsightly cows in the first dream. Although the ugly cows "ate up" (*ʾākal)* the fat ones (v. 4), the thin heads of grain "swallowed up" (*bālaʿ)* the plump grain (v. 7; cf. Exod 7:12; Num 16:30).

CUPBEARER REMEMBERS JOSEPH (41:8–13). **41:8** The king's "troubled" (*pāʿam,* v. 8) reaction parallels the anxiety exhibited by Nebuchadnezzar at his disturbing dreams (*pāʿam,* Dan 2:1,3). What especially frightened the king was the destruction of the fat and healthy by the ugly and thin. A subtle play of *parʿōh* ("pharaoh") and *pārôt* ("cows") may have contributed to his worry.[243] The rendering of "mind" for *rûaḥ,* meaning also "spirit" (also Dan

---

[237] H. G. May, ed., *Oxford Bible Atlas,* 3d ed. (New York: Oxford University Press, 1984), 21.

[238] Muchiki, *Egyptian Proper Names,* 238.

[239] רַקּוֹת, "gaunt, thin," occurs in vv. 3,4 describing the cows and in vv. 6,7,23,24 describing the heads of grain; רַקּוֹת, "lean" in vv. 19,20,27. SP and some MSS have רַקּוֹת at vv. 3,4; a confusion of ד and ר probably explains their difference. The LXX harmonizes the whole by the same term, λεπτός ("thin"; see Wevers, *Notes on the Greek Text,* 675–76).

[240] "He slept and dreamt . . . and *behold,* seven heads of grain *were coming up*" (*IBHS* §37.6d).

[241] J. K. Hoffmeier, "קָנֶה," *NIDOTTE* 3.942–43.

[242] Cp. the *khamsin (ḥamsîn),* the hot, dry wind that blows from the south and southeast from N. Africa and Arabia, destroying plant life (cf. Isa 40:7–8; Jer 4:11).

[243] Green, "The Determination of Pharaoh," 159.

2:1,3), focuses on the psychosomatic disturbance that arrested his sleep (cf. *pāʿam*, Ps 77:4[5]). This fretfulness caused him to call "all" his counselors to resolve the dreams' perplexities. The interpretation of dreams was native to Egypt from the earliest times. "Magicians" *(ḥarṭummîm)* were common in the courts of foreign kings (e.g., Exod 7:11; Dan 1:2; 2:2). The term is the Egyptian loanword *ḥr(y)-tp* ("who is upon, chief"), an abbreviation of the Egyptian term "chief lector priest," who also practiced the magical arts.[244] The training center for the craft was the "House of Life," where guidebooks for dream interpretation were produced.[245] These "dream books" are known from the twelfth dynasty, which involved the interpretation of dreams by discerning puns and symbolic images.[246] The Egyptian magicians of Moses' day were able by their "secret arts" to reproduce the miraculous works performed by Moses and Aaron (e.g., Exod 7:11) but not in all respects (e.g., Exod 8:14). Likewise, Joseph's ability surpassed Egyptian divinatory arts. The "wise men" *(ḥăkāmîm)* at court were most likely educated, intellectually capable advisers (e.g., Esth 1:13; Isa 19:11–12; Dan 2:12), and also they were believed to be gifted by the gods (e.g., 41:38–39; Dan 2:11; 4:18; 5:11). There was no guild of professional diviners in Israel, for magical means of prognostication were prohibited (Lev 19:26; Deut 18:10–12).[247] That none of the counselors provided an interpretation disconcerted Pharaoh. Judging by Nebuchadnezzar's skepticism of his counselors' integrity (Dan 2:6–12), such court sorcerers were typically quick on the uptake. The Hebrew text of v. 8 possesses a grammatical feature that may have been the source of confusion for the magicians. The Hebrew (MT) has "Pharaoh told them his dream (sg.), but no one could interpret them (pl.) for him" (cf. v. 15). Ancient and modern versions commonly harmonize the singular "dream" and the plural "them."[248] Sternberg, however, proposed that the incongruity is a rhetorical strategy of the narrator, indicating Pharaoh viewed them as one dream with one interpretation and the magicians considered them two dreams with two interpretations.[249] Joseph counted them as two dreams with unified meaning (vv. 25,27,32).

41:9–13 Upon witnessing the distress of his master, the cupbearer remembered his similar dilemma in prison (v. 9). The construction, lit., "my oversights I am remembering today,"[250] indicates that he is at that moment

---

[244] Muchiki, *Egyptian Proper Names*, 245.

[245] Hoffmeier, *Israel in Egypt*, 88–89; K. A. Kitchen, "Magic and Sorcery," *NBD* 769.

[246] R. K. Ritner, "Dream Books," *OEAE* 1.410–11.

[247] Sarna, *Genesis*, 282.

[248] MT, אֹתָם . . . חֲלֹמוֹ, "his dream (sg.) . . . them (pl.)"; SP (and EVs) prefers plural, "dreams," and LXX singular, "his dream . . . it."

[249] Sternberg, *The Poetics of Biblical Narrative*, 394–400.

[250] אֶת־חֲטָאַי אֲנִי מַזְכִּיר הַיּוֹם; cf. the present nuance of the participle "remembering" and the adverbial "today."

reconstructing what occurred in his prison experience. "My shortcomings" (*ḥēṭᵓ*, "sin") occurs at the head of the Hebrew clause, showing he readily acknowledged guilt for his oversight. Ironically, it was Joseph's refusal to "sin" (*ḥāṭaᵓ*) that landed him in jail in the first place (39:9). The cupbearer's condensed account (vv. 9–13) corresponds generally to the narration of the event in 40:1–5,8, though he omits the embarrassing picture of their sullen disposition (40:6–7). Moreover, he overlooks the details of the dreams (40:9–19) and directly recounts Joseph's involvement and the precision of his interpretations (vv. 12–13; 40:20–22). He may well have considered the contents of the dreams too somber a recollection, which he did not care to elaborate on to the already-agitated king. Mention of Joseph not by name but as "a young Hebrew" (v. 12) may have arisen by the cupbearer's memory of Joseph's story of abduction (40:15). Or what the cupbearer recalled clearest about Joseph was his elevated position ("a servant of the captain of the guard"), despite his outsider status. Here is another allusion to Joseph's resistance to Potiphar's wife, in which "Hebrew" as a foreigner she used in a demeaning way (39:14,17). The report by the cupbearer concludes by underscoring the accuracy of the outcome, "and things turned out exactly" (adverb *kēn* + verb *hāyâ;* cf. 2 Sam 13:35) as Joseph had predicted. The phrase may be a play on the cupbearer's restored "position" (*kannî* from the noun *kēn,* meaning "place, office"; cf. 40:13). The constructions in the cupbearer's speech describing his own restitution ("I was restored"[251]) and the hanging of the baker (". . . was hanged"[252]) are indefinite, i.e., the subject is not stated. Moreover, the word "baker" does not recur, only "him," referring back to v. 10. This was probably a delicate way of recalling the sensitive event, omitting the specifics of Pharaoh's command to execute the culprit. The text's parallel phrases telling the ending of the two officers heighten the life and death contrast.

PHARAOH DESCRIBES HIS DREAMS (41:14–24). **41:14** Verse 14 initiates the transformation of Joseph the Semite into Joseph the Egyptian. At the instruction of the king the attendants reverse Joseph's status, "quickly" (from *rûṣ,* "run," e.g., 18:2) ushering him from the dungeon of slavery to the presence of the king. The change in his slave's garments to a courtier's apparel portrays the magnitude of the change about to transpire in Joseph's fortunes. That he was "shaved" (from *gālaḥ*), probably the head as well as the facial hair, accorded with Egyptian custom (cf. Isa 7:20), although it was generally avoided in Hebrew practice since it was often associated with regrettable, personal circumstances (e.g., Lev 14:8; Jer 41:5). Baldness of the head (from *qārah,* "to be bald") commonly indicated shame or grief (e.g., 2 Sam 10:4; 2 Kgs 2:23; Amos 8:10). A change of clothes was deemed a prize that the royal

---

[251] אֹתִי הֵשִׁיב, lit., "me he restored."
[252] וְאֹתוֹ תָּלָה, lit., "and him he hanged."

house and the wealthy could afford (e.g., 45:22; Judg 14:1; 2 Kgs 5:23; cf. the plundering of Egypt, Exod 3:22).

41:15–16 Pharaoh's interview of Joseph recalls the slave's dialogue with the two officers in prison (see 40:8). Pharaoh uses the language of the two officials when describing his frustration (v. 15). He sketches the prison incident, which entailed the recitation of the dreams followed by Joseph's interpretation. Although the similarities in the two circumstances are apparent, Joseph is not presumptuous. His response to Pharaoh's probe, as in the first case, denied any special claims for himself. God is the sole source of dreams and their interpretations (v. 16; 40:8). "I cannot do it" is succinctly and pungently stated by one Hebrew word (*bilʿāday;* cf. v. 44).[253] That the king will receive the answer "he desires [*šālôm,* "peace"]" (or "favorable answer," NRSV, HCSB, NJB) does not mean that the interpretation is necessarily pleasant for the king; rather, God will give him the correct ("right," NAB) explanation that the king seeks and thus pacify his disturbed spirit (e.g., NLT, "will set you at ease").

41:17–21 Pharaoh's recitation of his dreams conforms to the narrative account in vv. 1–7 with minor differences and some commentary. For example, the expression "fat and sleek" in v. 18 reverses the description "sleek and fat" in v. 2; also the language translated "sleek" varies, employing synonyms.[254] Compared to the narrative in v. 3, the king's memory of the ugliness of the cows is heightened, adding "very" (*mĕʾōd*) ugly and "lean" (*raqqôt,* v. 19). Then he comments on the exceptional emaciation of the cows, unique to anything in Egypt he's known. Judging also by v. 20's reversal in the description of the thin cows ("lean, ugly," v. 20; "gaunt and ugly," v. 4), the king was especially alarmed by the skeletal appearance of the cattle. Their thin frame probably was made more obvious by the two sets of cattle standing "beside" one another (v. 3). Again Pharaoh adds his analysis of the matter, noting that the consumption of the fat beasts did not alter the appearance of the thin ones one bit (v. 21). The second dream varies only slightly in this second telling. "Full and good" (v. 22; cf. v. 7, "full") appears for "healthy [fat] and good" (v. 5),[255] the former description perhaps better fitted for ears of grain. Again the king's description is harsher in v. 23 (cf. v. 6), adding the detail "withered" (from *ṣānam,* "dry up, harden"). Verse 24 omits the more favorable words "healthy, full" (v. 7), satisfied with the single description "good."[256] The king concludes with his beginning: "but none could explain it to me" (v. 24 with v. 15; cf. 40:8; 41:8).

JOSEPH INTERPRETS THE DREAMS (41:25–36). **41:25–28** Joseph estab-

---

[253] בִּלְעָדָי, prep. בִּלְעָדָי ("not to") and the first person possessive suffix ("me"); SP, LXX, Syr. בִּלְעָדֵי אֱלֹהִים לֹא יַעֲנֶה, "without God an answer cannot be given" (see *BHS*).

[254] יְפוֹת מַרְאֶה, "beautiful in appearance" (v. 2); וִיפֹת תֹּאַר, "and beautiful in form" (v. 18).

[255] מְלֵאֹת וְטֹבוֹת, "full and good," v. 22; בְּרִיאוֹת וְטֹבוֹת, "fat and good," v. 5.

[256] הַשִּׁבֳּלִים הַבְּרִיאוֹת וְהַמְלֵאוֹת, "the fat and full heads," v. 7; הַשִׁבֳּלִים הַדַּקֹת, "the good heads" (v. 24).

lishes his interpretive framework at the start: first, the two dreams portray the "one and same" *('eḥād hû')* message and, second, God has made this event known in advance to Pharaoh[257] (v. 25). He repeats the principle in v. 26 *('eḥād hû')*, explaining the seven good specimens in each dream are seven years. And, correspondingly, the seven weakly ones represent seven years, but he specifies that they represent years of famine (v. 27). That the number seven indicated years versus days (40:12,18) would be obvious since the second dream portrays agricultural seasons. Joseph closes out the first portion of his interpretation by repeating the sentiment with which he started: God has revealed ("shown") this matter to the king (v. 28; cf. v. 25). Joseph insistently declares that the dreams and their interpretation come exclusively from God, authenticating his interpretation.

41:29–32 He now elaborates on the interpretation, clarifying that seven years of plenty will come to Egypt (v. 29). He reinforces the idea of "abundance" *(śābā', "plenty"; cf. Prov 3:10)* by the descriptive "great" *(gādôl)* and "throughout the land" *(běkol 'ereṣ, "in all the land")*. The term for "abundance/plenty" appears six times in the chapter (vv. 29,30,31,34,47,53). Verse 30 focuses on the subsequent "famine" *(rā'āb),* the word occurring at the beginning and end of the verse. The term appears eight times in the chapter (vv. 27,30,31,36,50,54,56,57). The severity of the famine is so awful that the years of plenty will fade from memory ("forgotten," *šākaḥ,* cf. 40:23), and it will "ravage" *(piel,* from *killâ,* "destroy," "finish off"; cf. Amos 7:2) the once-productive fields (v. 30). Verse 31 reinforces the extent of the famine ("so severe," lit., "very heavy/grievous," *kābēd . . . mĕ'ōd;* cf. 12:10; 47:4,13), reiterating that the good years will "not be remembered," lit., "known" *(niph.* from *yāda',* "know"). The gravity of the famine will so overshadow the fruitful years that they will not matter to the people in their suffering. Joseph provides a second interpretive principle: double dreams convey the assurance of their imminent fulfillment (v. 32). This would apply to Joseph's own dreams (37:6–9) and the two dreams of the imprisoned officials (40:8–19). The language "firmly decided" *(nākôn)* indicates that which is established, unfailing, proven (Deut 13:15; 17:4; cf. "support" *[nākôn]* pillars, Judg 16:26; "as surely as" *[nākôn],* Hos 6:3). "Soon" renders the participle "quick, hasten" *(piel,* from *māhēr;* cf. 18:6–7), suggesting that the period of fourteen years is underway.

41:33–36 Joseph exceeds the bounds of the king's initial request when he proceeds to advise what steps the ruler should take. "So now" *(wĕ'attâ[258])* introduces the logical consequence of the aforesaid interpretation (v. 33). Joseph profiles the résumé of the administrator who should be designated to

---

[257] The participle expresses imminence, אֵת אֲשֶׁר הָאֱלֹהִים עֹשֶׂה הִגִּיד לְפַרְעֹה, "God has told Pharaoh what he *is going to do*" *(IBHS* §37.6f).

[258] Occurs as often as twenty-six times in Genesis, eleven in the Joseph account (37:20; 41:33; 44:30,33; 45:5,8; 47:4; 48:5; 50:5,17,21).

lead the nation in coping with the coming disaster. A "discerning" *(nābôn)* and "wise" *(ḥākām)* man describes the sagacious in wisdom literature (e.g., "The wise in heart are called discerning," Prov 16:21; cf. Prov 10:13; Hos 14:10). The two terms can appear in parallel (Prov 17:28). Pharaoh must "put him in charge" *(šît)*, that is, separate out (30:40) the one who would be ruler (cf. Ps 8:7). Next, Pharaoh must delegate selected "commissioners" *(pĕqidîm*, cf. 2 Chr 31:13; Esth 2:3) to collect a tax amounting to one-fifth of the annual yield during the first seven-year period (v. 34).[259] (On the word *pāqad,* see 39:4, *hiph.,* "entrust to.") The three verbs "collect," "store," and "to be kept" constitute the subsequent stage in the agenda (v. 35; cf. vv. 48–49). The program of collection must have the full weight of royal authority (lit., "under the hand of Pharaoh"; cf. 2 Kgs 17:7) to be successful. That the grain would be deposited ("held in reserve," *piqqādôn)* in a number of store cities would expedite its distribution during the years of famine (v. 36). By this means they could stave off the destruction of the nation. "Ruined" *(niph.* from *kārat,* "cut off") translates the root term *(k-r-t)* that describes the destruction of life by Noah's flood (9:1); "cut off" often describes the sanction of death against a transgressor (e.g., 17:14; Num 15:13).

PHARAOH MAKES JOSEPH SECOND IN COMMAND (41:37–46). **41:37** The king and his advisers immediately recognized the wisdom of Joseph and welcomed his opinion (cf. 45:16; Esth 1:21).

41:38–40 The king concluded that only a person who possessed the "spirit of God" in measure could have discerned the significance of the dreams (cf. Daniel, e.g., 4:5; 5:11). In effect Joseph's blueprint for the chief administrator was his own résumé. "Wise and discerning" is the same phrase used by Joseph (vv. 33,39). So farsighted was Joseph's plan the king realized that no one but God could have made "all this known,"[260] making Joseph exceptional in the kingdom. That he bestowed the royal imprimatur on Joseph is underscored by the recurring introduction at each conferral: "Then [So] Pharaoh said to Joseph" (vv. 39,41,44). As in the case of Potiphar's house, Joseph received authority over the whole of the king's household (v. 40; 39:4). The second in authority to Pharaoh was the "vizier" *(t3ty [tjaty]),* the prime minister at the top of the administrative bureaucracy. The vizier's responsibilities typically included superintending the land and supervising the judicial system.[261] Joseph's authority appears to have extended to these traditional areas. We do not have sufficient data, however, to identify precisely what titular position

---

[259] וְחִמֵּשׁ, "and to take a fifth," a denominative verb (חָמֵשׁ, "five") appears only here; refers to Pharaoh, "and let him [sg.] exact a fifth" (NASB); LXX, καὶ ἀποπεμπτωσάτωσαν, "and let them [pl.] collect a fifth part," וְיִמְמְשׁוּ (see *BHS*).

[260] *IBHS* §27.5b interprets the verb as expressing permission, "Since God let you know all this . . ."

[261] D. A. Warburton, "Officials," *OEAE* 2.579.

Joseph held in Egyptian bureaucracy. That he married into the priestly caste, which was a commanding influence in Egyptian life, further enhanced his power. We can confidently say that Semites, at least persons bearing Semitic names, achieved high office in the Middle Kingdom, Second Intermediate, and New Kingdom periods. Hoffmeier has shown parallels between Joseph and to Aper-El, the vizier to Amenhotep III and Amenhotep IV (Akhenaten; fourteenth century).[262] In the vizier's funeral chamber (Saqqarah, east of Memphis, the chief cemetery for officials), we learn the Semitic names of his family members and their communal burial in coffins, which correlate with the practices of Joseph and Jacob (49:29–32; 50:2–3,12–14). This high-ranking Semite superintended the king's business in Lower Egypt. The wording "All my [Pharaoh] people are to submit to your orders" (v. 40) translates a difficult text, lit., "All my people will kiss *[yiššaq]* you on your mouth,"[263] probably expressing homage to Joseph as their lord (cf. Ps 2:12; also 1 Kgs 19:18; Job 31:27; Hos 13:2).[264] The king reserves, however, his royal prerogatives. "Throne" is a metonymy, referring to the rule of Pharaoh. Throughout the Joseph account, he exhibits a subordinate role to Pharaoh, never usurping Pharaoh's authority (e.g., 47:11,20; 50:4).

41:41–43 Nevertheless, the extent of Joseph's power will include the entire sphere of Pharaoh's realm. The phrase "charge of the whole land of Egypt" begins and closes vv. 41–43. So as to demonstrate Joseph's new authority, the king bestows on him the symbols of royal power (cf. Dan 5:16). By extending his signet ring to Joseph, the king offers the predominant sign of his reign (cf. Esth 3:10,12; 8:2,8,10; cf. *ḥôtām,* Jer 22:24; Hag 2:23). The term "signet ring" *(ṭabbaʿat),* found most often describing priestly and tabernacle decor ("rings," Exod 25–39), may be related to Egyptian *ḏbʿwt,* "seal, signet." He clothed him in costly "fine linen" *(šēš)* and adorned his neck with "a gold chain" *(rĕbid hazzāhāb;* cf. Ezek 16:11). The bestowal of the "fine linen" was a known feature of Egyptian investiture. The term for linen refers specifically to Egyptian linen (*šš,* "byssus"), the fabric used for crafting the tabernacle and priestly vestments (e.g., Exod 25:4; 28:5). That the Hebrew terms for "linen" were not employed (e.g., *bûṣ,* Ezek 27:16) suggests that the author knew early Egyptian practice well.[265] Babylon's King Belshazzar rewarded Daniel in the

---

[262] Hoffmeier, *Israel in Egypt,* 94–95.

[263] Ancient and modern versions reflect varied proposals: *Tgs. Onq., Ps.-J.,* "shall all my people be fed"; LXX, ὑπακούσεται, "will hearken to," see *q-š-b,* "give attention to, obey," cf. *BHS;* "shall order themselves" (NRSV; cf. NLT), i.e., arrange themselves, see *n-š-k* II, "to be armed," *nešek,* "weapons"; "all my people shall dart" (NAB), see *š-k-k,* "to rush, leap on."

[264] K. A. Kitchen ("The Term *n-š-q* in Genesis xli.40," *ExpTim* 69 [1957]: 30), on the basis of an Egyptian term, "kiss the earth," recommends, ". . . shall all my people kiss (the earth in submission)" (quoted in C. J. Collins, "נשׁק," *NIDOTTE* 3.197).

[265] Hoffmeier, *Israel in Egypt,* 92.

same fashion for the task of interpretation (Dan 5:29). Moreover, Pharaoh equipped Joseph with a chariot, either as his "second in command" or in a "second chariot (to his own),"[266] led by an entourage of runners (cf. 2 Sam 15:1; 1 Kgs 1:5).[267] The NIV's "Make way," which suits the context, translates the obscure Hebrew term *'abrēk*.[268] Other versions, ancient and modern, interpreted the element *brk* as "knee," thus "Bow the knee!" (NRSV, NASB; "bow down," NIV text note; "kneel down!" NLT).[269] Explanations involving Egyptian have been suggested, including *ib-r.k*, "attention!" (the Semitic loanword *brk*, "to pay homage," plus the prothetic *'aleph i*).[270]

41:44 The final word by Pharaoh on the matter of Joseph's commission asserts his own place as the ultimate authority ("I am Pharaoh," v. 44; cf. 2 Sam 19:43). Yet he does so to show again how expansive the rule of Joseph is, for the king is the sole exclusion to abiding by Joseph's decrees. "But without your [Joseph's] word" (*ûbil'ādeykā,* "without you") is the language Joseph used of himself when declaring God's exclusive ability to interpret dreams ("I cannot do it," v. 16). By the repetition of the term, the king in effect establishes Joseph on the highest plane, second only to Pharaoh. In Egyptian religion the living king of Egypt was the god Horus or the "son of Re," making his edicts inviolate. His chief role as the mediator between the gods and society was to maintain *maat,* that is, order in the land. Because of the king's human limitations, it was necessary to delegate officials to represent him in the breadth of the land.[271] Joseph, bearing the symbols of pharaonic authority, would oversee the grain industry. The expression "hand" and "foot" is a figure (merism), meaning that every activity must meet with Joseph's approval. Again, his sphere of dominion equates to "all" of the land.

41:45–46 The king completes the "Egyptianizing" of Joseph by renaming him and assigning an Egyptian wife from a prestigious priestly family (v. 45). The advancement of Semites, such as Joseph, is well attested in ancient Near

---

[266] בְּמִרְכֶּבֶת הַמִּשְׁנֶה אֲשֶׁר לוֹ, lit., "in the chariot of the second which (was) to him"; the difference in the translations rests with the antecedent of אֲשֶׁר, renaming either the "second" or the "chariot"; both perceptions might have been accurate, however, since the second best chariot probably belonged to Pharaoh too and was reserved for the second in command (cf. Wevers, *Notes on the Greek Text,* 695).

[267] SP, LXX, Syr. reflect the singular וַיִּקְרָא, "and he called out" *(BHS).*

[268] The LXX has καὶ ἐκήρυξεν ἔμπροσθεν αὐτοῦ κῆρυξ, "and a herald cried out before him"; HCSB, NJB, NAB transliterate the Hb., thus "they (servants) shouted out before him, 'Abrek!'"

[269] Aquila, γονατίζειν, "bow the knee" (cf. Wevers, *Notes on the Greek Text,* 695); Vg. *omnes coram eo genuflecterent,* "all should bow their knee before him" (see BHS). The targums interpret *'brk* as two terms (see McNamara, *Targum Neofiti 1: Genesis,* 188, n. 33): *'ab* ("father") and *rk* ("royalty," or "tender"), thus the heralds cry, "This is the father of the king!" *(Tg. Onq.;* cf. *b. Bat.* 4a) or "This is the father of the king, great in wisdom, tender *[rak]* in years!" *(Tg. Ps.-J.;* cf. *Tg. Neof.; Gen. Rab.* 90.3), the latter referring to Joseph's youth.

[270] Muchiki, *Egyptian Proper Names,* 236.

[271] U. Luft, "Religion," *OEAE* 3.143–45.

Eastern texts.[272] The etymological meaning of the four personal names in v. 45 are disputed among specialists but there is agreement that they are all Egyptian in character.[273] The more important aspect of the names is their evidence for dating the Joseph narrative (see Introduction). "Zephenath-Paneah" *(ṣāpĕnat paʿnēaḥ)* has been generally explained as equivalent to Egyptian "the god said, let him live" or "the god has said, he will live." Kitchen proposed "called *(I)pi-ankh,*" that is, "Joseph [who is] called *(I)pi-ankh* ["who recognizes life"]."[274] Muchiki also departed from the common view, commending "My provision is god, the living one."[275]

The most popular explanation for the Egyptian etymology of "Asenath" *(ʾasĕnat)* is *ns-nt,* meaning "she who belongs to Neith," the goddess of the cult center Sais. Kitchen suggested *Ius-en-at,* "she belongs to you [fem.]," on the order of the Egyptian pattern meaning "she belongs to me/to her father/to her mother."[276] (On the name "Potiphera," see comments on 37:36). The city "On" *(ʾōn)* was the prestigious religious center of Re and Atum, the Egyptian solar deities.[277] Remembered for its numerous obelisks, the Hebrew name *ʾōn* reflects Egyptian *ʾIwnw,* "city of the pillars." Jeremiah 43:13 has Hebrew *bêt šemeš* ("Beth-shemesh"), "house of the sun," comparable to the Greek name Heliopolis, "city of the sun." It was the location of the earliest temple dedicated to Re *(-harakhty).* Its theological tradition was one of the most influential throughout Egypt's long history, and the city's power was surpassed only by Memphis and Thebes. The ancient ruins of Heliopolis are located at Tell Hisn and el-Matariyeh in suburban Cairo, ca. seven to ten miles northeast of the city. Joseph's marriage into the priestly family probably was deemed an honor in Egypt's eyes but was a consternation to the rabbis who balked at his marriage to the daughter of a pagan priest. *Tgs. Onq., Neof.,* and *Ps.-J.* render "chief, master" *(rabbā)* for "priest," and Jewish midrash contended that Asenat was the daughter of Dinah and Shechem, giving her a Jewish heritage *(Tg. Ps-J.; Gen. Rab.* 89.2; *Pirqe R. El.* 36.272; 38.287–88). As the offspring of Asenath, the Joseph tribes of Manasseh and Ephraim were in part descended from Egyptian ancestry.

That Joseph "went throughout" Egypt (v. 45) symbolized the establishment of his rule, actualizing what the king had only declared. Verse 46 provides supplementary information, amplifying the remarkable achievement at his young age of thirty. This meant that Joseph ruled for eighty years (50:26). The Joseph

---

[272] For details see Hoffmeier, *Israel in Egypt,* 93–95.

[273] Ibid., 87.

[274] Kitchen, "Genesis 12–50 in the Near Eastern World," 80–84; id., *Reliability of the Old Testament,* 345–46; Hoffmeier, *Israel in Egypt,* 86.

[275] Muchiki, *Egyptian Proper Names,* 224–26.

[276] Kitchen, "Genesis 12–50 in the Near Eastern World," 84–85.

[277] K. A. Kitchen, "On," *NBD* 910; D. B. Redford, "Heliopolis," *ABD* 3.122–23.

narrative introduces Joseph as a lad of seventeen (37:2), thus making it thirteen years since his abduction from Canaan. "When he entered the service of Pharaoh" (v. 46) translates the figure of speech (metonymy), "When he stood *['āmad]* before Pharaoh *[lipnê parʿōh]*." That the narrative says that Joseph "went out *[yāṣāʾ]* from Pharaoh's presence *[millipnê parʿōh]*" gives a picture of the chain of command Pharaoh had established. "And he traveled *[ʿābar,*"to pass through"] throughout Egypt" varies from the parallel phrase in the previous verse by the addition of the verb "traveled." As this second-in-command "passed through" *(ʿābar)*the land, it was ironic that the former "Hebrew" *(ʿibrî,* 41:12) slave had become the master of the whole land.

JOSEPH FILLS THE STORE CITIES (41:47–49). **41:47–49** The previous verse describing Joseph's survey of the land transitions to the present passage regarding the store cities. In accord with Joseph's interpretation of Pharaoh's dreams, the land produced crops "plentifully" *(liqmāṣîm,* v. 47); the word *qōmeṣ* means a "fist(full)" (e.g., Lev 2:2; the verb *qōmaṣ,* "to grasp, enclose the hand"), indicating graphically the voluminous handfuls of grain piling up (e.g., "brought forth by handfuls," AV). The strategy for stockpiling was the deposit of grain in designated cities reaped from the fields adjacent to each city (v. 48). The process entailed the full seven years and involved every region of the land. The harvest was so enormous that documenting the yields became unfeasible (v. 49). The narrative portrays the unqualified abundance by a standard hyperbole: "Like the sand of the sea" that is "beyond measure." Here we have an allusion to the imagery describing the promise of innumerable progeny made to Abraham and Jacob (22:17; 32:13; cf. Jer 33:22; Hos 1:10[2:1]). (On the idea of an incalculable multitude, see 15:5; 16:10; 1 Kgs 3:8; 8:5; Ps 40:5[6].)

JOSEPH'S FAMILY (41:50–52). **41:50–52** Verses 50–52 provide supplementary information regarding Joseph's two sons. That the children came before the famine symbolizes the years of plenty that Egypt experienced (v. 50). The names of the two sons reflect the mind-set of Joseph toward his new life in Egypt. The naming formula, which includes the explanation for the name, is well attested in Genesis (e.g., 3:20; 4:25; 26:20). Commonly, the Israelite mother assigned the name of the child based on her interpretation or sentiment of the event (e.g., 4:25; cf. Exod 2:10; 1 Sam 1:20). Joseph, however, gives his sons Hebrew names whose folk etymology conveys his response to his Egyptian experience. "Manasseh" *(měnaššeh),* meaning "he who makes [someone] forget," is morphologically a *piel* participle from the verb "forget" *(nāšâ).* Joseph explains the name as a pun, commenting on his own experience: "God [*Elohim*] has made me forget *[naššanî] . . .*" (v. 51). "My trouble" *(ʿămālî)* refers broadly to Joseph's sorrow arising from his abduction and imprisonment. The same term describes the labor of the afflicted Hebrew slaves in Egypt (Deut 26:7; parallels *ʾāwen,* "sorrow," Num 23:21). In this way Joseph's forced servitude presaged Israel's life in Egypt. "And all my father's household" specifies the source of his sorrow, referring to sibling strife that led to his Egyptian slavery.[278] That Joseph made no attempts to learn about his family after his rise to power probably is explained by his desire to forget his past life. The LXX translators have "all the things pertaining to my father's house,"[279] toning down Joseph's neglect of his father's family circle. The name "Ephraim" *('eprāyim)* is a pun on the word "to bear fruit" *(pārâ):*"God *[Elohim]* has made me fruitful *[hiprānî]*" (v. 52). Although the name Manasseh has a negative connotation, Ephraim is positive in tone, referring to the birth of a second son. Joseph continues, however, the idea of his travail, referring to Egypt as "the land of my suffering *['onyî]*." The words "trouble" *('āmāl)* and "suffering" *('ŏnî)* are found in parallel (Ps 25:18). Jacob describes his servitude under Laban as "suffering" (31:42; also cf. 16:11; 29:32). The Hebrews' "misery" *('ŏnî)* in Egypt did not escape the attention of God (Exod 3:7,17; 4:31; Deut 26:7). The names of his sons probably reflected the ambivalence he felt toward the birth of his sons, which brought to mind his father and brothers. That Joseph considered his life blessed by God in Egypt and that he desired to forget his father's household may imply that he had neglected the promises made to the Fathers. However, it may be, in spite of all that had happened to him, that the realization of his boyhood dreams prompted his renewed vigilance for the promises and the family (42:9).

JOSEPH PROVIDES GRAIN (41:53–57). **41:53–55** The narrative reports that the ensuing events came about "just as Joseph had said" (v. 54). Because of Joseph's wise administration, Egypt alone among the neighboring nations escaped the famine by its food reserves. When the hungry Egyptians implored Pharaoh for food ("cried to," from *ṣā'aq,* v. 55), he instructed them to follow the direction of Joseph. The word "cried to" often indicates an appeal for relief in the midst of adversity (e.g., Exod 5:15, "appealed"), which is typically directed to God (e.g., Deut 26:7).

41:56–57 Depiction of the "famine" as extending throughout the land begins and closes v. 56. That Joseph provided "all" (absent NIV) the storehouses showed his benevolent intentions but also the depth of the famine.[280] The "famine was severe" translates "the famine grew" *(ḥāzaq,* "to strengthen, prevail, harden"), meaning that it became worse (cf. 2 Kgs 25:3//Jer 52:6; cp. NJB, "the famine had gripped the land of Egypt"). The final verse (v. 57) transitions the narrative to the descent of Joseph's brothers in chap. 42. They were among the many peoples from diverse parts of the Near East who bought grain

---

[278] Some medieval Jewish commentators suggested a hendiadys, "all the sorrow of my father's house" (cf. Sarna, *Genesis,* 289).

[279] καὶ πάντων τῶν τοῦ πατρός μου; cf. Wevers, *Notes on the Greek Text,* 700.

[280] MT אֲשֶׁר בָּהֶם אֶת־כָּל יוֹסֵף חַ וַיִּפְתַּח, "and Joseph opened all which was in them"; the EVs read with the LXX, Syr., "opened up all the granaries"; SP, *Tg. Onq.,* adds *br,* "all in which there was grain."

from Egypt.[281] "Because the famine was severe" *(ḥāzaq)* fittingly closes out the chapter, reiterating how dire the circumstances had become that the world faced. In retrospect Joseph could rightly say that God's wisdom had achieved "the saving of many lives" (50:20).

5. The Brothers' Journeys to Egypt (42:1–43:34)

The account of Joseph's rise in Pharaoh's court (chaps. 39–41) created a necessary interval in the family story of Jacob's household, explaining the rise of Joseph to power. Chapters 42–43 narrate the reunion of Joseph and his ten brothers, picking up the story line from chap. 37. Many of the same motifs in chap. 37 reappear in chaps. 42–43, such as a fractured family, a father's favoritism, a journey of brothers, deception, remembering dreams, superior knowledge (Joseph's), a lost brother (Simeon), a report, and an inconsolable father. As Humphreys observed, since chap. 37 Joseph has changed, but the family at the beginning of chap. 42 remains essentially unchanged.[282] The same circumstances of ten sons and a favored son persist (42:1–4). Jacob repeats the mistake of preferring the youngest son, and the brothers are as inept spiritually. Their two journeys to Egypt will show, however, that their outlooks toward one another and toward God are changing. The brothers will perceive that the hand of God is at work in the midst of their troubles, requiting them for their crime (42:28). Despite the father's early intransigence, he at last releases Benjamin into the care of Judah. This he interprets as acquiescence to the greater purpose of God whose will cannot be resisted (43:14). Yet God's mercy for which Jacob prayed was an irruption in unexpected ways. "Not only is God's timetable difficult for us to anticipate, God's methods may be difficult for us to recognize."[283] Joseph's steward refused to accept the returned silver, recognizing that it was God's blessing (43:23). And the Egyptian lord himself calls upon God to be generous to the youngest brother (43:29). What the brothers viewed as their demise works to their benefit.

EARLY JEWISH AND CHRISTIAN INTERPRETATIONS. The history of interpretation addressed the moral character of Joseph's brothers and delved into Joseph's true motives for the trials he imposed. Jewish interpretation generally improved the image of the nation's fathers. The house of Jacob was not starving, which would cast dispersion on God's promised provisions for Jacob (28:20–21). Genesis 42:1 was retold, "Why do you make yourselves conspicuous?" meaning that they had food despite the famine and should not stir up their rivals (Ishmael, Esau) to envy by flaunting it (e.g., *Gen. Rab.*

---

[281] "And all the countries came to Egypt," i.e., "all the inhabitants" (metonymy).

[282] Humphreys, *Joseph and His Family,* 42.

[283] J. Walton, *Genesis,* The NIV Application Commentary (Grand Rapids: Zondervan, 2001), 696.

91.2; *Ta'an.* 10b, Rashi; cf. *Tg. Neof.*). Also they set on their journey to Egypt for the nobler purpose of retrieving Joseph from slavery (e.g., *Gen. Rab.* 91.6; *Tanḥ.* 8; Rashi). In *Tg. Ps.-J.,* 42:28 reads, "What is this the Lord has done, even though there is no guilt on our part?" thus exonerating the brothers of the crime of theft. Jewish interpretation also depicted Joseph in a favorable light. Joseph's aloofness toward his brothers was tempered in the translation at 42:7, "And he considered what he should say to them" *(Tg. Onq.).* But *Tg. Neof.* has "he showed himself hostile," maintaining the tenor of the verse.[284] Early church fathers interpreted the tribulations imposed by Joseph on his brothers redemptively. By forcing the brothers to examine their attitude toward Simeon's imprisonment, it leads them to repentance for their past sins (Caesarius of Arles, *Sermon* 91.6; Chrysostom, *Homilies on Genesis* 64.11).[285] Calvin painted a positive picture of Joseph's behavior.[286] Joseph "tortured" his brothers, not for revenge but to learn if his brothers had repented. Also he feared that should the brothers discover who he was, they might commit another crime to protect themselves by killing Benjamin. His sternness had the positive benefit of encouraging their confession that was made possible by the indwelling Holy Spirit. Moreover, the returned money benefited Jacob, ensuring that he had funds for future food necessities.

Such microreadings of the chief participants fail to understand the wider purpose and goal of chaps. 42–43. The motives and actions of Joseph and his family members are not patterns to be copied or avoided. The author's goal is to show that God's designs for Israel's fathers are working toward the end of redeeming the household of faith. Testing produces spiritual reclamation (cf. Exod 20:20; Deut 8:16; Jer 9:7; Zech 13:9; Jas 1:2–3,12; 1 Pet 1:6; 4:12). The mending of the family is now underway. "The faith, penitence, tender emotions, and loyalty that unite a family are now being fashioned."[287] Whatever the motivations and faults of the broken family, the divine plan for the embryonic nation would be achieved. God superintended the good and ill choices made by the family—even by a recalcitrant old man, a harsh master, or blind siblings—to bring about the greater good. But these are not cardboard figures whose choices and emotions do not count. The emotions are real and run the full range, including fear, anger, levity, and weeping. If there is a message for the people of God to cling to from these events, it is found in the words of the steward: "Don't be afraid *[yārē'].* Your God, the God of your father, has given you treasure in your sacks" (43:23). The brothers and father "were frightened" *(yārē')* when they discovered the returned silver (42:18), and the brothers "were frightened" *(yārē')* in the house of the Egyptian lord (43:18). But

---

[284] Grossfeld, *Targum Onkelos,* 141, n.4.

[285] *ACCS* 2.276–77.

[286] Calvin, *Comm.,* 326–44.

[287] Waltke, *Genesis,* 550.

the steward comforted them (43:23, "It's all right," *šālôm*), and (the Egyptian) Joseph inquired after their well-being (43:27, *šālôm* [2x]).[288] Little did they realize that the Egyptian in whose hands were their lives was not foreign but their very brother, who was moved to tears over their family sorrows.

COMPOSITION.   Source critics believed that chap. 42, the first visit of the brothers to Egypt, was preeminently from the Elohist (E) with insertions from the Yahwist (J) document, the extent of which varied considerably among scholars. The chief evidence, which all source critics cited for dual sources, was the different versions of the discovery of the returned silver in the brothers' sacks. One account attributed it to one brother during the night's stop en route to Canaan (J, vv. 27–28), and the other version assigned it to all the brothers after their return to Jacob (E, v. 35; 43:21). Collaborative evidence put forward was the different lexical terms for "sack(s)" in the two versions: *śaq* in E (v. 35) versus the preferred *'amtaḥat* in J (vv. 27,28), which consistently occurs in J's narrative (chaps. 43–44). Chapters 43–44, the second visit of the brothers, were considered the product of the Yahwist primarily with some inclusions from the Elohist. The most obvious evidence of E in chaps. 43–44 is the assumption of Simeon's imprisonment, reflecting the account of E in chap. 42 (42:24,36; 43:14a,23b).[289] That the delay in returning to Egypt appears in 42:38 and 43:1–10 shows that the J source "knows nothing at all of a detention of Simeon,"[290] requiring the redactor to add 43:15,23b so as to connect the two versions. Those, however, who demur parallel sources behind chaps. 42 and 43–44 and contend for an essentially unified story show that the "unevenness" in the narrative is not contradictory due to documentary sources but can be explained on other grounds.[291] Coats and Westermann argued persuasively that chap. 42 exhibited a unified account made up of segments that had shifting settings between Canaan and Egypt.[292] Chapter 42 belongs to the main stream of the original Joseph story, relying on the rise of Joseph in the prior chapters and setting the scene for the family resolution in chaps. 43–45. Wenham cataloged many references in chaps. 43–45 to the first journey of chap. 42. He concluded that chaps. 43–45 were one unit and that the whole of chaps. 42 and 43–45 are by one author.[293] Although we prefer to distinguish chaps. 42–43 and 44–45 as two divisions,[294] since they show heightened similarity (see below), the cumulative effect is the same, namely, that chaps. 42–45 provide a smooth continuation of the primary theme (family strife) of the

---

[288] Westermann observes the importance of שָׁלוֹם, "peace," to the message (*Genesis 37–50,* 127).

[289] E.g., Gunkel, *Genesis,* 423–24, 428; Skinner, *Genesis,* 473–74, 479; Speiser, *Genesis,* 324.

[290] von Rad, *Genesis,* 382.

[291] E.g., Coats, *From Egypt to Canaan,* 36; Carr, *Reading the Fractures of Genesis,* 285–88.

[292] Westermann advocated three parts based on the journey and return of the brothers (vv. 1–5,6–24,26–38; *Genesis 37–50,* 103); Coats, *Genesis,* 285–88, proposed four "panels," segmenting vv. 27–28 (at the inn).

[293] In this Wenham (*Genesis 16–50,* 403–4, 419) agreed with Westermann (*Genesis 37–50,* 118–19).

[294] As does Rendsburg and Sarna, followed also by Waltke.

whole Joseph account.

Westermann effectively argued that the double accounts of discovery in chap. 42, the first by the anonymous brother at the overnight lodging (vv. 27–28) and the second by all the brothers and Jacob upon their return (v. 35), are potentially congruous with the brothers' statement to Joseph's steward in 43:21. The author focused on one brother's discovery in 42:27–28, after which all the brothers must have examined their bags, in accordance with their summary in 43:21. Further, concerning the difference in the terms for "sacks," Westermann answered that the criterion was unreliable for source division since both terms appear in 42:27 and since both words occur together in the Pentateuch only in the same context of the journeys to Egypt. But Westermann failed to explain adequately the different locations of the "discovery," the first on the road (42:27–28; 43:21) and the second in Canaan (42:35). Westermann relegated v. 35 to an interpolation, which was designed to show that Jacob, too, learned of the restored silver ("they and their father saw").[295] Verse 35, however, does not interrupt the flow of the narrative; the verse fits nicely in its place, elucidating why Jacob abruptly assails his sons in v. 36. The appearance of the money sealed the doom of Simeon in his mind, creating a disturbing reminder of Joseph's failure to return with his brothers. Sternberg has suggested that Jacob was afraid when seeing the money because he thought Simeon had been sold off, which he had secretly suspected all along was Joseph's end too.[296] Moreover, v. 35 cannot be a late addition since Jacob's instructions to return double the silver in 43:12 assumes v. 35 since he was fully aware of the discovery. More appealing is Sarna's explanation of v. 35, namely, that the brothers staged the discovery.[297] This does not alleviate the problem altogether but that the brothers waited until the bitter end to unveil the money and that they deceived their father in doing so is consistent with what we know of the brothers' devious temperament in the past. Yet since the narrator makes the description of the brothers' fright at the discovery of the silver, it suggests to the reader that the matter genuinely surprised them. If this is the case, what might this mean for the report in 43:21 to the steward? Their testimony to the steward can be taken as a summary, in which they telescoped the two events, treating the autonomous brother's incident at the lodge as representative of all the brothers. Finally, as Coats observed, the idea of a double discovery of the silver in chap. 42 coincides with the narrative pattern of chap. 42 in which it is said that Joseph "recognized" his brothers twice (vv. 7,8) and made two accusations of spying (vv. 9,14).[298] There is the doubling of the hostage motif, referring to Simeon and the youngest brother (Benjamin, vv. 19–20).

The problem passage of the brothers' delayed return, despite the incarceration of Simeon, can be mentioned briefly. According to source proponents, that Jacob

---

[295] Westermann, *Genesis 37–50,* 112–13; also Redford explained v. 35 as an interpolation, but 43:21 he imagined was the brothers' mistake brought on by the pressure of the situation (*Joseph,* 151).

[296] Sternberg, *The Poetics of Biblical Narrative,* 297–98.

[297] Sarna, *Genesis,* 296.

[298] Coats, *From Egypt to Canaan,* 66.

does not appear to know of Simeon's plight (43:38) signals another version of the story (J). The absence of concern for Simeon on Jacob's part, however, is better explained as Jacob's obsession with the sons of Rachel. Benjamin, therefore, "is the only one left" (v. 38) of the favored wife.

The conclusion we reach is that chaps. 42 and 43 are unified compositions (see Structure below), and those places of "unevenness" do not require a complex source or redaction history explanation.

STRUCTURE. The unit consists of two parts, recounting the first and second journeys of Jacob's sons to Egypt (42:1–38; 43:1–34; although the conclusion to the second journey occurs in chap. 45). Grammatically, the unit exhibits a smooth continuum by the use of pronouns "they" and "their father" in 43:2, whose antecedents are named in chap. 42.[299] Chapter 42 possesses four segments: (1) vv. 1–5 and (4) vv. 35–38 pertain to Jacob's decision to keep Benjamin in Canaan, and (2) vv. 6–28 and (3) vv. 29–34 describe the audience with Joseph and the brothers' report to Jacob of their journey. Genesis 42:1 reintroduces the main story line of Jacob and his sons in Canaan, which was last prominent in chap. 37. References to "Jacob," which occurs twice (but 1x, NIV), and to "his sons" (v. 1) recall the last scene in which we find Jacob and his sons, depicting the father's inconsolable sorrow at the loss of Joseph (37:34–35). Coats observed that chap. 42 complicates the plot initiated in chap. 37 by reversing the roles of the main players. Thus "the oppressed becomes the oppressor."[300] Chapters 38 and 39–41 established the setting for the reemergence of the protagonists (especially Jacob, Judah, and Joseph), whose reconciliation is the object of chaps. 42–45, climaxing in the revelation of Joseph to his brothers (45:1–15). Mention of "Egypt" and "famine" in 42:1–5 brings forward the immediate context of food distribution by Joseph in Egypt (41:56–57). Thus chap. 42 brings together the ideas of family and famine, known already from chaps. 37–41. The chapter begins with Jacob dispatching his sons to Egypt (42:1–5) and closes with his resolute refusal to send Benjamin with them on a second journey (42:35–38).

Chapter 43 consists of three segments: (1) a brief introduction (v. 1), (2) a description of Jacob's instructions to return, including Benjamin (vv. 2–14), and (3) the second audience with Joseph, including Benjamin (vv. 15–34). The second half of the unit (43:1–34) begins as did the first half (42:1–38) by referencing "famine" and "Egypt" (43:1–2). It, too, describes Jacob's instructions to obtain "grain" from Egypt for the starving family (43:2; 42:1–2). The author's penchant for doubling events in the Joseph narrative as a whole explains the paralleling of the first and second journeys in chaps. 42–43. What these two journeys have in common is the narrative

---

[299] Westermann mentions this in arguing against source division (*Genesis 37–50*, 120).
[300] Coats, *Genesis*, 285.

interest in the youngest son, Benjamin. The author's early attention on Benjamin's absence in the first journey (42:3–4) initiates the narrative arc that will end in the descent of Benjamin into Egypt on whom Joseph bestows special favor (43:34). Benjamin's absence and presence are critical to the development of chaps. 42–43. The reader cannot escape him. Even when he is absent in chap. 43, he is still influencing the direction of the chapter's unfolding. Moreover, the "food" image in chaps. 42–43 comes full circle, from famine to feast (42:1–5; 43:31–34). The conclusion of chap. 43, however, does not bring to a close the second journey of the brothers. Their return to Canaan will not be realized until 45:25–27. The next unit (chap. 44) focuses attention on the next complication in the plot, namely, the test Joseph establishes, which leads to the peak episode in chap. 45. As chaps. 42–43 involved an imprisonment (Simeon), chap. 44 presents the accentuated threat of Benjamin's imprisonment.

The two journeys of the brothers in chaps. 42 and 43–44 evidence parallels that contrast the two episodes.[301] The character of Jacob's instructions differs (42:1–2; 43:1–15). At first he was abrupt, demeaning, but after the troubling conclusion to the first journey he appeals to his sons and makes elaborate preparation for the journey. In the first journey he is resolved to retain Benjamin (chap. 42), but in chap. 43 he concedes to the Lord's will for his family. In the first journey the brothers seek out food but receive charges of spying that lead to guilt and confession. In the second journey they arrive seeking to justify their actions but are welcomed and face no charges. Their return trip shows the steward's involvement again (44:1; 42:25), who adds the accusing silver cup. First, Joseph threatens to imprison them, except one, but now he presents himself as the paragon of fairness, imprisoning only the guilty party. In the first journey they protest their innocence only to acknowledge their historic guilt (42:21). In Judah's speech they concede their historic guilt (44:16) and omit a plea of innocence.

(1) First Journey without Benjamin (42:1–38)

¹When Jacob learned that there was grain in Egypt, he said to his sons, "Why do you just keep looking at each other?" ²He continued, "I have heard that there is grain in Egypt. Go down there and buy some for us, so that we may live and not die."

³Then ten of Joseph's brothers went down to buy grain from Egypt. ⁴But Jacob did not send Benjamin, Joseph's brother, with the others, because he was afraid that harm might come to him. ⁵So Israel's sons were among those who went to buy grain, for the famine was in the land of Canaan also.

⁶Now Joseph was the governor of the land, the one who sold grain to all its people. So when Joseph's brothers arrived, they bowed down to him with their

---

301 Humphreys, *Joseph and His Family*, 44–48.

faces to the ground. [7]As soon as Joseph saw his brothers, he recognized them, but he pretended to be a stranger and spoke harshly to them. "Where do you come from?" he asked.

"From the land of Canaan," they replied, "to buy food."

[8]Although Joseph recognized his brothers, they did not recognize him. [9]Then he remembered his dreams about them and said to them, "You are spies! You have come to see where our land is unprotected."

[10]"No, my lord," they answered. "Your servants have come to buy food. [11]We are all the sons of one man. Your servants are honest men, not spies."

[12]"No!" he said to them. "You have come to see where our land is unprotected."

[13]But they replied, "Your servants were twelve brothers, the sons of one man, who lives in the land of Canaan. The youngest is now with our father, and one is no more."

[14]Joseph said to them, "It is just as I told you: You are spies! [15]And this is how you will be tested: As surely as Pharaoh lives, you will not leave this place unless your youngest brother comes here. [16]Send one of your number to get your brother; the rest of you will be kept in prison, so that your words may be tested to see if you are telling the truth. If you are not, then as surely as Pharaoh lives, you are spies!" [17]And he put them all in custody for three days.

[18]On the third day, Joseph said to them, "Do this and you will live, for I fear God: [19]If you are honest men, let one of your brothers stay here in prison, while the rest of you go and take grain back for your starving households. [20]But you must bring your youngest brother to me, so that your words may be verified and that you may not die." This they proceeded to do.

[21]They said to one another, "Surely we are being punished because of our brother. We saw how distressed he was when he pleaded with us for his life, but we would not listen; that's why this distress has come upon us."

[22]Reuben replied, "Didn't I tell you not to sin against the boy? But you wouldn't listen! Now we must give an accounting for his blood." [23]They did not realize that Joseph could understand them, since he was using an interpreter.

[24]He turned away from them and began to weep, but then turned back and spoke to them again. He had Simeon taken from them and bound before their eyes.

[25]Joseph gave orders to fill their bags with grain, to put each man's silver back in his sack, and to give them provisions for their journey. After this was done for them, [26]they loaded their grain on their donkeys and left.

[27]At the place where they stopped for the night one of them opened his sack to get feed for his donkey, and he saw his silver in the mouth of his sack. [28]"My silver has been returned," he said to his brothers. "Here it is in my sack."

Their hearts sank and they turned to each other trembling and said, "What is this that God has done to us?"

[29]When they came to their father Jacob in the land of Canaan, they told him all that had happened to them. They said, [30]"The man who is lord over the land spoke harshly to us and treated us as though we were spying on the land. [31]But we said to him, 'We are honest men; we are not spies. [32]We were twelve brothers,

sons of one father. One is no more, and the youngest is now with our father in Canaan.'

[33]"Then the man who is lord over the land said to us, 'This is how I will know whether you are honest men: Leave one of your brothers here with me, and take food for your starving households and go. [34]But bring your youngest brother to me so I will know that you are not spies but honest men. Then I will give your brother back to you, and you can trade in the land.'"

[35]As they were emptying their sacks, there in each man's sack was his pouch of silver! When they and their father saw the money pouches, they were frightened. [36]Their father Jacob said to them, "You have deprived me of my children. Joseph is no more and Simeon is no more, and now you want to take Benjamin. Everything is against me!"

[37]Then Reuben said to his father, "You may put both of my sons to death if I do not bring him back to you. Entrust him to my care, and I will bring him back."

[38]But Jacob said, "My son will not go down there with you; his brother is dead and he is the only one left. If harm comes to him on the journey you are taking, you will bring my gray head down to the grave in sorrow."

The first journey entails the descent of the "ten" brothers to Egypt for food (vv. 1–5) whom (undisclosed) Joseph charges with spying, keeping Simeon as a hostage in jail (vv. 6–28). The brothers report the calamity to Jacob and argue the necessity of Benjamin's return to prove their innocence to the Egyptian lord (vv. 29–34), but Jacob vehemently refuses Reuben's request (vv. 35–38).

JACOB SENDS THE "TEN" BROTHERS TO EGYPT (42:1–5). **42:1–2** In response to news of Egypt's grain (41:56–57; cf. Acts 7:12), Jacob chides his sons for their indecisiveness (v. 1). The same root term "see" *(rā'â),* translated "learned" and "looking at each other," occurs at the beginning and end of v. 1. His sons failed to notice what was obvious to Jacob. That Jacob could "see" despite his encroaching blindness (48:8) heightens the disparity. The brothers' incompetence contrasts sharply with Joseph's insight that foresaw the need to prepare for the famine. The verbal stem expresses reciprocal action, "looking at each other" (v. 1).[302] The Greek text renders the sense of the Hebrew by "idle, remiss" *(rathumeō).* The recurrence of "Egypt" in vv. 1–3 (3x) alerts the reader to the imminent and inevitable meeting of the brothers. The situation in Canaan had reached the most desperate condition of life and death: "so that we may live *[ḥāyâ]* and not die."[303] The Jacobites had no other option, if they wanted to survive (cf. 47:15,19,25). It is the same act of desperation that led Jacob eventually to release his son Benjamin into Judah's care to sojourn to Egypt (43:8), which was the additional obligation placed on

---

[302]וְתִּתְרָאוּ *hith.* imperfect; "look on one another," *IBHS* §26.2g.

[303] The construction (imperatives + imperfect) gives attention to the purpose of the exhortation (*IBHS* §34.6).

them by Joseph: "Do this and you will live" (*ḥāyâ*, v. 18). That the brothers sought food that only Joseph could supply to survive fulfills the purpose for his elevated position (cf. *ḥāyâ*, "preserve, revive," 45:7,27; 50:20).

42:3–4 That the text describes the sons as "Joseph's brothers" (v. 3) rather than "Jacob's/Israel's sons" (vv. 1,5) points up the past that had embroiled the family. The configuration of "ten" brothers is painfully drawn, since it reinforces the fragmentation and distrust that the family had experienced. The number of brothers anticipates the charge of spying and the tests Joseph will put to them (cf. 42:13; 42:32,38; 43:6–7; 44:20). Thus "but . . . Benjamin" (v. 4) clarifies that the eleventh brother did not leave his father's sight. Benjamin was "Joseph's brother" in a different sense from the other brothers; they shared the same birth mother, Rachel, implying that Benjamin held his father's special favor, as had Joseph. That Benjamin did not go "with his brothers" ("the others," NIV) painted logistically the dissidence that was characteristic of the family. Our narrator provides a hint at what is to come by explaining that Jacob's fear of "harm" (*ʾāsôn*) befalling Benjamin prevented the release of the boy (v. 4). "Harm" occurs five times in the Old Testament, three times in the Joseph story (vv. 4,38; 44:29). The latter two occasions, in the speeches of Jacob and Judah, echo our passage. The other two uses of the word "harm" describe physical injury against a pregnant mother's unborn child (Exod 21:22–23), an image that may describe Jacob's passion for his youngest boy. One implication of Jacob's decision is his distrust of his sons, since he viewed his sons as responsible for Joseph's "death" (cf. 42:36).

42:5 Nevertheless, the brothers "take their first step toward acting together."[304] They were "among those who went to buy grain" in Egypt (v. 5), showing that they were in a stream of refugees descending upon Egypt. That the brothers entered the city conspicuously as a group of ten in Semite apparel made the charge of spying by the "lord of Egypt" (Joseph) preposterous on the face of it.[305] Mention of famine in "Canaan" establishes the extent and severity of the famine (cf. 41:57; 43:1; 47:14–15). The same conditions prevailed in the times of Abraham who sought refuge in Egypt (12:10–13:1; cf. Isaac, 26:1).

JOSEPH RECEIVES THE BROTHERS (42:6–28). Joseph, as "governor of the land," meets the delegation of brothers but imprisons them as spies (vv. 6–17). He manipulates them by retaining Simeon in prison in order to force the return of Benjamin to Egypt (vv. 18–28).

Joseph Charges His Brothers with Spying (42:6–17). **42:6–8** This segment begins in v. 6 with old information, back-referencing Joseph's administrative role in Egypt (41:43,55–57). It provides background for understanding

---

[304] Waltke, *Genesis,* 544.

[305] Ephrem the Syrian, *Commentary on Genesis,* on 36.4 (see *ACCS* 2.275).

the scene, in which the brothers unwittingly submit to the undisclosed Joseph. Importantly, the text specifies that he personally oversaw the allocations of food,[306] putting him in direct contact with the brothers. The description "governor *[šallîṭ]* of the land" meant that Joseph had domineering power over all Egypt (cf. the verb *šalaṭ,* "lorded over," Neh 5:15; *šallîṭ* occurs 3x in Eccl 7:19; 8:8; 10:5).[307] That his brothers showed proper deference to the master of the land was expected, but the act of "bowing" *(ḥāwâ)* said far more than they realized. Their assent fulfilled the dreams of young Joseph, to whom the sheaves and stars "bowed down" *(ḥāwâ,* 37:7,9,10). Verses 7 and 8 possess another allusion to Joseph's dreams and their consequences by the words "recognized" and "pretended to be a stranger," both from the word *nākar.*[308] They recall the blood-stained robe "recognized" *(nākar)* by Jacob (37:32–33; cf. also *nākar,* 38:25–26). Hebrew *yitnakkēr,* "pretended to be a stranger," may be a play on *yitnakkĕlû,* "they plotted" (37:18). That Joseph spoke "harshly" *(qāšôt)* was the prelude to his charges against the brothers; this intimidated the brothers, which they recall to Jacob (v. 30). The related verbal root *qāšâ,* "hard, severe," appeared twice earlier, describing the birth of Benjamin (35:16–17). Joseph did not disguise his anger as he had disguised his identity. He may have concluded upon seeing the "ten" brothers that Benjamin's life was in question. Asking their country of origin provided confirming information that his identification was correct (v. 8). Thus the text notes he "recognized" them but reaffirms that they "did not recognize" Joseph. That the brothers are clueless to Joseph's identity and that he so easily manipulates them contributes to the picture of Joseph's wisdom against the ineptitude of his brothers.

42:9–14 "You are spies!" in vv. 9,14 forms the boundaries of the paragraph. Verse 9 shows that there was a connection between his memory of his dreams as a boy, which had inflamed their hatred for him (37:4,5,8), and his present charge of spying against his brothers (vv. 9,14,16,34). The word "remembered" *(zākar)* recalls momentous events in Genesis, when God brought about salvation (8:1; 9:15–16; 19:29; 30:22; cf. also 40:14,23). It was the memory of the cupbearer that led to the deliverance of Joseph

---

[306] The clause gives background information, using the *wāw* disjunctive: וְיוֹסֵף הוּא הַשַּׁלִּיט עַל־הָאָרֶץ. *IBHS* §16.3.3c analyzes the clause as adversative, i.e., "And the (other) sons of Israel went . . . but *Joseph* was the governor of the land" (vv. 5–6). This verbless clause with the pleonastic pronoun (הוּא) spotlights Joseph versus his brothers. A. Niccacci understands וְיוֹסֵף as a *casus pendens* (focus marker) and the clause as "marked" by the unexpected function of הוּא: "Now as for Joseph, it was he governor over the land . . ." ("Types and Functions of the Nominal Sentence," in *The Verbless Clause in Biblical Hebrew: Linguistic Approaches,* LSAWS 1 [Winona Lake: Eisenbrauns, 1999], 225, 227–28).

[307] H. J. Austel, "שָׁלַט," *TWOT* 2.929.

[308] וַיַּכֵּר *(hiph.),* "and he recognized them," and וַיִּתְנַכֵּר *(hith.),* "and he kept his identity [from them]."

(41:9). Despite his zeal to "forget" (41:51) his difficult past, he cannot escape it. It is facing his painful past that leads the way to his deliverance from the past. The term "spies" *(mĕraggĕlîm)* occurs here for the first of seven times in this chapter (vv. 9,11,14,16,30,31,34). In terse verbless clauses the parties make contrasting claims: lit., "spies [are] you" (vv. 9,14,16,34) and "honest [are] we" (vv. 11,31) and "honest [are] you" (vv. 19,33,34).[309] His accusation was that they had surreptitiously come to see where the "land is unprotected," lit., "the nakedness *['erwat]* of the land," a description that is unique to Genesis (vv. 9,12). This charge was a means of determining the character of his brothers, not personal retaliation. Eventually, he will put them in the same situations they once had faced and failed: the imprisonment of a brother and monetary gain (Simeon) and the opportunity to rid themselves of a rival (Benjamin). The brothers adamantly but politely ("my lord," "your servants") protest their innocence (v. 10). Their further response ties together their family's state of affairs ("all the sons of one man") and their claim as "honest men" (v. 11). They stated more than they knew since "we are all the sons of one man" could be taken to include the undisclosed Joseph *(Gen. Rab.* 91.7). They bumbled through the interview, hopelessly at a disadvantage to Joseph, who not only was all-powerful but also all-knowing. Unwittingly, they provided the grounds for the test that Joseph devised to prove their honesty (vv. 19,33,34). This, too, was part of his deceptive strategy because Joseph knew that they were truthful, but his purpose for the test had a hidden agenda. That the author never revealed Joseph's motives contributed to the mystery of Joseph's actions, actions that must have befuddled the brothers. Joseph's retort is equally emphatic, "No!" *(lō'),* reiterating the charge (v. 12). The brothers continued the same line of argument but added significant details, providing a snapshot of the family's history (v. 13). The "youngest is now with our father" must have given Joseph comfort that his brother was alive, but the solace was followed by the terse but painful remark "and one is no more" *(wĕhā'eḥād 'ênennû,* v. 13; cf. vv. 32,36). Their words drip with irony since they are kneeling before the one who was "no more." Joseph insists that they, despite their denial, are spies (v. 14). He rejects the reasoning of their pleas of innocence just as they had once rejected his plea from the pit (42:21).

42:15–16 So as to examine their claim, ostensibly Joseph proposed a test to expose the men's veracity. The purpose of the test is explicitly stated: "to see if you are telling the truth" (v. 16). "Truth" *('emet)* describes the veracity or dependability of the brothers' words. It occurs typically for

---

[309] Verbless clauses of "classification" describe the character of the group of which the individual is a member *(IBHS* §8.4.2a,e).

describing God's faithfulness (e.g., 24:27,48; 32:11) but also human fidelity (e.g., 24:49; 47:29; Exod 18:21). If they lied about their family, they had lied about being spies, but Joseph's test actually sought to ensure that Benjamin would be brought to Egypt and under his protective eye. Since their lives depended now on the well being of Benjamin, Joseph probably reasoned that Benjamin's life would be secure. The nature of the "test" in vv. 15–16 is expressed in an abbreviated form of an oath, that is, the curse is not specifically stated (e.g., 14:23; Num 14:23).[310] "As surely as Pharaoh lives" frames the oath in vv. 15–16, identifying the royal witness (cf. "as my lord the king lives," 2 Sam 15:21). In Egyptian practice the oath in the name of the king was the "Oath of the Lord."[311] The nature of the oath is Joseph's promise to prohibit the party from returning, except the youngest brother is escorted back to Egypt (v. 15). If the party fails to fulfill the obligation, the judgment "you are spies" stands (v. 16), implying that an unstated punishment (curse) will be imposed. The test pertains specifically to the "words" (claims) of the brothers (vv. 16,20). The term "tested" *(bāḥan)* appears only in 42:15–16 in Genesis. There are three terms for "test" in the Old Testament. The synonym *nāsâ* ("tested") occurs in the testing of Abraham (see comments on 22:1). It means to "put to the test" in the sense of discovering a person's veracity or an item through a concrete trial or hardship (e.g., 1 Sam 17:39; 1 Kgs 10:1).[312] The word *bāḥan* usually has God as its subject and thus conveys religious significance.[313] In this case, since the test is given as a (sacred) oath, the word *bāḥan* may have been preferred over other words for "test." The word the psalmist used to describe Joseph's "test" in prison was *ṣārap* (Ps 105:19), which means "to refine, purge" in the sense of removing impurities (e.g., Isa 1:25; Jer 6:27,29). It is also used to indicate the discovery of a person's fidelity (e.g., Ps 17:3). The word *bāḥan* may also have the nuance of purge (e.g., Job 23:10), and it often parallels *ṣārap*. e.g., Ps 66:10, "For you, O God, tested *[bāḥan]* us; you refined *[ṣārap]* us like silver" (also paralleled in Ps 26:2; Prov 17:3; Jer 9:6; Zech 13:9; for all three terms for "test," see Ps 26:2). The nature of the test may have this secondary sense, that is, refining the brothers through verifying their "words." That their words of innocence were already known to be true shows that the test by Joseph sought more. He wanted to learn if they had been truthful about his father and brother, but he

---

[310] T. Cartledge, *Vows in the Hebrew Bible and the Ancient Near East,* JSOTSup 147 (Sheffield: Sheffield Academic Press, 1992), 15–16; on Egyptian oaths, see J. A. Wilson, "The Oath in Ancient Egypt," *JNES* 7 (1948): 129–56; Cartledge, *Vows,* 91–99; and Wenham, *Genesis 16–50,* 407.

[311] Wilson, "Oath," 130–31, remarked that any oath in the name of a deity or king had the weight of legal force even if not formally declared in court.

[312] T. Brensinger, "נסה," *NIDOTTE* 3.111–12.

[313] M. Tsevat, "בחן, bḥn," *TDOT* 2.69–71.

also hoped the impact of the test elicited repentance over past sins.[314] Their confession in vv. 21–22 initiates them on the path to spiritual renewal and family reconciliation. By placing them in jail for three days, Joseph set them in the crucible of transformation.

42:17 When Joseph put them "all [together]" in jail for three days, he gave them ample opportunity to squabble over who would return to Canaan, leaving the others behind. The soul searching they underwent may well have been intensified by the three days of close quarters in the dungeon. There is no mention of anyone volunteering, as Judah did later (44:33). But the brothers will not be forced to make this decision after all (vv. 19,24).

Joseph Deceives His Brothers by a Test (42:18–28). **42:18–20** Yet Joseph also experienced change during the three-day period. Joseph showed the brothers leniency when he revised the conditions of the oath. Although the demand "do this and live" keeps the onus on their back (cp. Moses, Deut 30:15,19; cf. 2 Kgs 18:32), the test is expressed positively. This is their opportunity to survive as a family intact.[315] "For I fear *[yārē']* God" prefaces the plan, declaring his integrity and intention to fulfill his obligation (v. 18). The construction has "God" at the head of the clause, lit., "God *[Elohim]* I fear." Commentators dispute the precise intention of this phrase by Joseph. The expressions "fear God" and "fear the LORD" describe someone who worships the Lord (e.g., Deut 25:18; Josh 22:25; 1 Kgs 18:3; Eccl 12:13), but here the expression probably is equivalent to "a God-fearer" *(yir'at 'ĕlōhîm)*, referring to a person's moral conduct (cf. comments on 20:11; 22:12). This is someone who does not oppress a weaker person (e.g., Lev 19:14; Deut 25:18). Also this description by Joseph occurs for those outside the community of Israel (e.g., Job 1:1,8–9).[316] Yet the author of chaps. 42–44 constructs much of what is said and done between Joseph and the brothers to convey a double meaning. The implication one might draw from Joseph's protestation is that he was a person of integrity and the brothers were not. That the brothers immediately acknowledged their sin suggests strongly that they recognized the deeper meaning of his challenge to their integrity. From their perspective, the Egyptian lord presumably did not know their family secret, but in the ears of their conscience his words were the judgment of God against them. Moreover, by his assertion "I fear God," another implication was that even this foreign lord acted with more

---

[314] G. S. Smith proposed that the "test" (בָּחַן) was the purging of the brothers, the bridge episode between the "test" (נִסָּה) of Abraham (22:1) and the "test" (נִסָּה) of the nation (Exod 20:20; "'What Is This That God Has Done?' The Fear of God in the Joseph Narrative as a Precursor to Sinai," ETS Annual Meeting, November 2002; see R. W. L. Moberly, *The Bible, Theology, and Faith: A Study of Abraham and Jesus* [Cambridge: University Press, 2000], 81–84).

[315] Cp. the provision for the Kohathites in Num 4:19, וְזֹאת עֲשׂוּ לָהֶם וְחָיוּ וְלֹא יָמֻתוּ, lit., "this do for them so that they may live and not die."

[316] Moberly, *The Bible, Theology, and Faith,* 92–94.

780

fidelity than they had toward their own family.

Joseph changed the initial plan by releasing all the brothers except one who served as his hostage (vv. 19–20). This alteration had a dual effect. First, by keeping only one in prison, the majority of the caravan could return with foodstuffs for the awaiting family. Second, the new situation placed the brothers in the similar spot that they had faced with young Joseph. Once they had the food for which they came, they could return and lie again to their father, leaving their brother to languish in prison. Precisely how their failure to return with Benjamin would mean their death is unstated. Perhaps he assumed that they would eventually require more food during the famine, knowing that it would last seven long years and thus would be executed upon their return or would die by starvation in Canaan. "This they proceeded to do" *(wayyaʿăśû kēn)* shows their ready compliance; the word "this" translates *kēn,* perhaps a pun on the word *kēnîm,* "honest men" (v. 19). Their integrity and their lives were on the line with their agreement to accept the terms.

42:21–24 The brothers interpreted this trial as God's judgment, confessing their guilt (v. 21). "They said to one another" translates the same expression in v. 28 ("[turned trembling] to one another"), where it also prefaces their admission. Their response begins with the adverb "surely" *(ʾăbāl),* which most EVs understand as emphatic. Or it may be better rendered "but," expressing a strong contrast to their unstated assumption that they got off scot-free from their crime (e.g., 17:19).[317] "We are being punished" renders the piercing language "guilty [are] we" *(ʾăšēmîm[318] ʾănaḥnû).* They construed that their present "distress" *(ṣārâ; cf. 35:3)* was divine retribution for their disregard of Joseph's "distressed" *(ṣārâ)* cries for mercy. Although the earlier narrative did not detail the events of his internment, here we learn that he "pleaded" *(hith.,* from *ḥānan,* "be gracious, pity"; cf. 2 Kgs 1:13) with them without success. Reuben especially was exercised, believing he was vindicated (v. 22), since he alone had protested the brothers' deed (37:21–22,29–30). "Boy" *(yeled)* may only refer to Joseph's teen years (37:30) but may reflect an older sibling's way of thinking toward the youngest (cf. 44:20). (On the term "accounting" *[dāraš],* see 9:5 [vol. 1A, p. 403]). That the brothers "did not realize" (lit., "know," v. 23) that they spoke with Joseph contributes to the author's portrayal of them as spiritually blind. Joseph played his role flawlessly by feigning the need of an interpreter, giving him sway over the affair.[319] But Joseph could not mask his emotions as capably, and he "turned" *(sābab)* and "began to weep" *(bākâ,* v. 24). The former term *sābab* recalls

---

[317] I.e., "a reversal in expectations" *(IBHS* §30.3.5e).

[318] The word group *ʾ-š-m* may indicate "guilt" or the "penalty" for the given offense; cp. "we are guilty" (RSV) and "we are paying the penalty" (NRSV).

[319] A Jewish tradition identified Manasseh as Joseph's interpreter, who was the older son and presumably knew Hebrew and Egyptian *(Tg. Ps.-J.; Tg. Neof.; Gen. Rab.* 91.8).

Joseph's dream of the sheaves that "gathered around" *(sābab)* his sheaf and bowed (37:7). That Joseph had a soft heart for his brothers became increasingly evident despite the façade of his stern demeanor and harsh words (43:30; 45:14–15; 50:17). Once he had collected himself, he chose Simeon and bound him "before their eyes" (cf. 2 Kgs 25:7). Although the text permits that he commanded others to bind Simeon (e.g., NIV, NRSV, HCSB), it also naturally reads that Joseph himself tied up his brother (e.g., AV, NASB; cp. v. 25).[320] Simeon was born by Leah, her second son after Reuben. After overhearing that Reuben came to Joseph's defense (v. 22), Joseph may have passed over him, taking the second son in line (29:33). Moreover, there may have been a greater temptation to abandon Simeon by the others, presuming that Jacob would be less agitated about his detention, since Simeon had infuriated their father in the past (34:30; 49:5–7). A rabbinic tradition (e.g., *Tg. Ps.-J.*) assigned to Simeon more guilt for the conspiracy to kill Joseph (37:18–19, "they said to one another"), noting Simeon and Levi had conspired to slaughter the Shechemites (so Rashi; 34:13,25).

42:25–28 Joseph ordered the return of the brothers' silver in their sacks, along with the grain agreed upon (v. 25). This action can be interpreted in two opposing ways: first, he wanted to trump up evidence to sustain the charge that they were dishonest men, or second, he kindly returned their monies for the benefit of his father and family. This ambiguity reflects the mixed characterization the narrative projects for Joseph in general. Outwardly he is a hardened interrogator, but inwardly he is a broken-hearted brother whose emotions he must restrain. More likely, his action was to test the men, for he used the similar tactic in deceiving them a second time (44:1–2). The money proved to be a haunting fear for them, but they let down their guard when reassured that their gain was providential (v. 28; 43:18–23). Verse 26 describes straightforwardly the departure of the brothers, showing that they were oblivious to Joseph's hidden deed. Upon making camp that same evening, one of the party opened his sack to feed his beast (v. 27), discovering the returned silver. It matters little which brother opened his sack, for at their return they learn that all had their money returned (v. 35; on the problem of the sequence of events, see "Composition" above). The improbable discovery led the anonymous brother to blurt out what he found (v. 28). That the silver was in the same sack as the grain added to the surprise, since it would be astonishing that the two happened to be together in the same container, although Jacob will wish so (43:12). Dread fell upon them at the realization of their obvious plight. To the charge of "spies" could be added the allegation, "You are thieves!"[321] "Their hearts sank" renders the idiom "their hearts went

---

[320] וַיֶּאֱסֹר אֹתוֹ לְעֵינֵיהֶם, "and he [Joseph] bound him before their eyes."
[321] Westermann, *Genesis 36–50,* 112.

out" *(yāṣaʾ lēb),* meaning that they lost courage (cp. *yippōl lēb,* lit., "the heart falls," 1 Sam 17:32). That they "turned to each other trembling" *(ḥārad,* cf. 27:33; 1 Kgs 1:49) manifested a paralyzing fear. Their claims of innocence had been dramatically undone. The expression "to each other" recalls their earlier admission (v. 21; cf. 42:21), but now they explicitly attributed their calamity to God. "What is this that God has done to us?" indicates they believed that God had put them in peril (cf. 3:13; 12:18; 26:10; 29:25; Exod 14:11; Jonah 1:10).

THE BROTHERS REPORT TO JACOB (42:29–34). The brothers carefully crafted the report, omitting some of the more disturbing details (e.g., the three-day imprisonment), minimizing the impact of others, and exaggerating the positive where possible. First, they described the "man's" angry demeanor and accusation of spying (v. 30), followed by their avowal of innocence (vv. 31–3), and last, the conditions of the test (vv. 33–34).

42:29–32 When the brothers had returned to their father once before, they deceived him regarding Joseph (37:32). Now, however, the chastened brothers divulge "all" to Jacob (v. 29), that is, in the sense that they did not lie to Jacob. Unsuspectingly, they are reporting on Joseph ("the man who is lord over the land") again to their father, as they had at the first (37:32). The report first established the hostile conditions they had faced (v. 30; cf. v. 7), perhaps to impress upon their father the staggering power the man had over them. Twice "the lord over the land" occurred in their description (vv. 30,33). The report does not follow precisely the dialogue they had with Joseph (v. 31), reversing the order of explanation (cp. vv. 11,13). They mentioned the family's "twelve brothers" last (v. 32), though it was first in the original interview (v. 13). Another significant difference in the two accounts was referring to Benjamin last ("the youngest," v. 32) in this report instead of Joseph last ("one is no more," v. 13). They probably recognized after the fact that volunteering such information was unwise, which would expose them again to Jacob's ire. But it was necessary to admit it to Jacob, for they must convince their father to release Benjamin into their care.

42:33–34 They summarize the conditions of the test that Joseph had established (vv. 15–20). Twice "[so] I will know" *(yādaʿ)* describes the intention of the test, reminiscent of Abraham's test (15:12) and his servant's inquiry (24:14). The narrative presents Joseph as the one who "knows" more than any other person in the kingdom and certainly more than his brothers (e.g., 41:39; 42:8; 44:15), but in the matter of his brothers' integrity the question remains open in his mind. New to the former account of Joseph's speech is the invitation, if indeed they are proven trustworthy, to "trade" in the land of Egypt (v. 34). That the brothers concocted this incentive to persuade their father seems too trivial against the critical issue of releasing Benjamin into their care. Hebrew narrative does not require the initial account to provide a complete rendering of what transpired, or they may have extrapolated from the promise "you will live" (v. 18) the optimism of future trade relations. The word "trade" (*sāḥar,* or "move about freely," NIV note, NAB, NJB), however, brings to our mind the past crimes of the brothers who had murdered the Shechemites (34:10,21) and had sold Joseph to "merchants" (*sōḥărîm,* 37:28). The irony of the term in the mouths of the brothers is obvious. Their history testified that they are anything but honest men whose word can be trusted. As it turns out, Joseph keeps his word, ensuring that Jacob's family will have a permanent residence in Goshen (e.g., 45:10; 47:5–6,27).

JACOB REFUSES TO SEND BENJAMIN TO EGYPT (42:35–38). **42:35–36** Whatever success the brothers had achieved in their appeal to their father to this point, it immediately vanished when they opened their bags. The discovery of the returned silver in the belongings of each brother creates "fear" in them and their father. There may be a play by the similar language, pointing up the connection: "saw [the silver]" *(wayyir'û)* and "[they] were frightened" *(wayyîrā'û,* v. 35). The money might have alarmed Jacob who was suspicious that the brothers had killed or sold Simeon as they had done with Joseph (*Tg. Ps.-J.*; *Gen. Rab.* 91.9; Rashi).[322] Jacob's complaint that follows expresses the obvious; like their brother Joseph, Simeon too is lost (v. 36). The fact tersely and painfully uttered by Jacob, "Joseph is no more and Simeon is no more," argues against releasing Benjamin into their care. Jacob blames the brothers for his bereavement ("deprived," *šākal*), which explains why Reuben, the eldest son and presumably the most liable, makes his desperate proposal next (v. 37). Loss of children was the most woeful sorrow that a parent could experience in ancient Israel (e.g., Job 1:18–20; cf. 27:45; Lev 26:22). Here Jacob sounds despair, "Everything is against me!" but later sounds his impotence, "If I am bereaved, I am bereaved" (*šākal,* 43:14).

42:37–38 Reuben counters by offering also to become childless if he fails to return with Benjamin (v. 37). "Both of my sons" *(šĕnê bānay)* headlines his appeal, assuring his father of his sincerity (on the importance of "two sons" in the story, cf. 41:50; 44:27; 48:5). Reuben had four sons according to 46:9 (cf. 1 Chr 5:3). The twice-given phrase, "I do not/I will bring him back," evidences Reuben's determination. "Put to death" (*hiph.,* from *mût*) commonly describes killing for a wide-range of circumstances, such as execution for punishment (e.g., 18:25; Deut 13:9[10]; cf. *mût yûmat,* "to be put to death," e.g., 26:11; Exod 21:12). It is reminiscent of the threat against Joseph ("to kill him," from *mût,* 37:18). Here probably no more than hyperbole for dramatic effect was meant. It is true that Judah demanded the death

---

[322] Calvin, too, mentions that his behavior can only be explained that he was suspicious of his sons, especially when he credited to them his bereavement (*Comm.,* 348–49). Also Sternberg, *The Poetics of Hebrew Narrative,* 298–99, who elaborates on the different reasons for the sons' and Jacob's fear.

of Tamar, but that was because she was guilty of adultery in the eyes of the community (38:24). That Reuben or Jacob would have unrestricted power over innocent members of the family is doubtful, since there is no such provision in Hebrew law.[323] Execution typically involved community action, and there was prohibition against execution of innocent persons as proxy for the guilty (father and son are "to die for his own sin," Deut 24:16; see 2 Kgs 14:6 [but cf. 9:26]; Jer 31:30; Ezek 18:4,20). The argument in any case had no effect on Jacob, for it would be of no solace to the old man to carry out vengeance against his grandchildren. Jacob's refusal is stated stridently. The construction "my son will not go down there" (v. 38) is a strongly worded prohibition.[324] His explanation for his refusal was forcefully stated and reasoned, though no doubt stinging to Reuben. "My son" and "his brother" sound the closed circle of Rachel's two sons and their father. That Benjamin is "the only one left" states what the brothers had known all along: Benjamin was the only son who counted in their father's eyes. The term "harm" (*'āsôn*) occurs only five times in the Old Testament, three times in the Joseph narrative (42:4,38; 44:29; Exod 21:22,23). The Joseph incident continues to haunt the brothers, who have no convincing answer to their father's fears. The plural pronoun "you" in "you will bring my gray head down" refers to the whole cadre of brothers. "You will bring down" is a metonymy, indicating the effect of their grievous action, that is, they will precipitate his death. "Gray hair" (*śêbātî*) is a metonymy of adjunct, indicating the patriarch's old age (e.g., 15:15).[325] The idea of the patriarch's old age brings to mind the importance of Benjamin for his father since he was the last born. On this basis Judah will appeal to Joseph's compassion to release Benjamin since it will result in the death of his father (44:29,31). "Sorrow" (*yāgôn*) describes the mental torment that he as a bereaved father would experience (e.g., Ps 13:2[3]). The future of a father was lodged in his sons' prospects (cp. a father's "grief" [from related *tûgâ*], Prov 10:1; 14:13; 17:21).

(2) *Second Journey with Benjamin (43:1–34)*

¹Now the famine was still severe in the land. ²So when they had eaten all the grain they had brought from Egypt, their father said to them, "Go back and buy us a little more food."

³But Judah said to him, "The man warned us solemnly, 'You will not see my face again unless your brother is with you.' ⁴If you will send our brother along with us, we will go down and buy food for you. ⁵But if you will not send him, we

---

[323] MAL §2 reflects the same prohibition (*ANET* 180).

[324] The negative particle "not" initiates the clause, followed by the verbal imperfect: לֹא־יֵרֵד בְּנִי.

[325] E. W. Bullinger, *Figures of Speech Used in the Bible* (1898; reprint, Grand Rapids: Baker, 1968), 587.

will not go down, because the man said to us, 'You will not see my face again unless your brother is with you.'"

[6]Israel asked, "Why did you bring this trouble on me by telling the man you had another brother?"

[7]They replied, "The man questioned us closely about ourselves and our family. 'Is your father still living?' he asked us. 'Do you have another brother?' We simply answered his questions. How were we to know he would say, 'Bring your brother down here'?"

[8]Then Judah said to Israel his father, "Send the boy along with me and we will go at once, so that we and you and our children may live and not die. [9]I myself will guarantee his safety; you can hold me personally responsible for him. If I do not bring him back to you and set him here before you, I will bear the blame before you all my life. [10]As it is, if we had not delayed, we could have gone and returned twice."

[11]Then their father Israel said to them, "If it must be, then do this: Put some of the best products of the land in your bags and take them down to the man as a gift—a little balm and a little honey, some spices and myrrh, some pistachio nuts and almonds. [12]Take double the amount of silver with you, for you must return the silver that was put back into the mouths of your sacks. Perhaps it was a mistake. [13]Take your brother also and go back to the man at once. [14]And may God Almighty grant you mercy before the man so that he will let your other brother and Benjamin come back with you. As for me, if I am bereaved, I am bereaved."

[15]So the men took the gifts and double the amount of silver, and Benjamin also. They hurried down to Egypt and presented themselves to Joseph. [16]When Joseph saw Benjamin with them, he said to the steward of his house, "Take these men to my house, slaughter an animal and prepare dinner; they are to eat with me at noon."

[17]The man did as Joseph told him and took the men to Joseph's house. [18]Now the men were frightened when they were taken to his house. They thought, "We were brought here because of the silver that was put back into our sacks the first time. He wants to attack us and overpower us and seize us as slaves and take our donkeys."

[19]So they went up to Joseph's steward and spoke to him at the entrance to the house. [20]"Please, sir," they said, "we came down here the first time to buy food. [21]But at the place where we stopped for the night we opened our sacks and each of us found his silver—the exact weight—in the mouth of his sack. So we have brought it back with us. [22]We have also brought additional silver with us to buy food. We don't know who put our silver in our sacks."

[23]"It's all right," he said. "Don't be afraid. Your God, the God of your father, has given you treasure in your sacks; I received your silver." Then he brought Simeon out to them.

[24]The steward took the men into Joseph's house, gave them water to wash their feet and provided fodder for their donkeys. [25]They prepared their gifts for Joseph's arrival at noon, because they had heard that they were to eat there.

[26]When Joseph came home, they presented to him the gifts they had brought into the house, and they bowed down before him to the ground. [27]He asked them

how they were, and then he said, "How is your aged father you told me about? Is he still living?"

²⁸They replied, "Your servant our father is still alive and well." And they bowed low to pay him honor.

²⁹As he looked about and saw his brother Benjamin, his own mother's son, he asked, "Is this your youngest brother, the one you told me about?" And he said, "God be gracious to you, my son." ³⁰Deeply moved at the sight of his brother, Joseph hurried out and looked for a place to weep. He went into his private room and wept there.

³¹After he had washed his face, he came out and, controlling himself, said, "Serve the food."

³²They served him by himself, the brothers by themselves, and the Egyptians who ate with him by themselves, because Egyptians could not eat with Hebrews, for that is detestable to Egyptians. ³³The men had been seated before him in the order of their ages, from the firstborn to the youngest; and they looked at each other in astonishment. ³⁴When portions were served to them from Joseph's table, Benjamin's portion was five times as much as anyone else's. So they feasted and drank freely with him.

Due to the sustained famine (43:1), Jacob instructs his sons to return to Egypt for more grain, and reluctantly he acquiesces to Judah's request, releasing Benjamin into Judah's care (vv. 2–14). To their surprise, Joseph receives the brothers without recriminations, and Joseph shows favor toward Benjamin (vv. 15–34).

INTRODUCTION: FAMINE (43:1).   **43:1**   The severity of the famine was forecast in Pharaoh's dream (e.g., 41:27,30–31) and described in the narrative (41:54–57; cp. the same description of Abraham's descent, 12:10; cf. 26:1).

JACOB INSTRUCTS HIS SONS (43:2–14).   The section recounts the metamorphosis of Jacob's decision to release Benjamin into Judah's care. Jacob's instructions in vv. 2 and 11–14 envelop the contentious debate regarding Benjamin's leave to go, involving complaint and countercomplaint between father and son (vv. 3–7,8–10).

Jacob's Instruction to Return to Egypt (43:2).   **43:2**   Significant difference occurs in Jacob's attitude toward his sons here ("a little more food") than initially when he chided them for their indecision (42:1–2). Perhaps Jacob was more civil here because he knew that the brothers were right all along and because his request put their lives in jeopardy if they returned to Egypt without Benjamin.

Request to Take Benjamin (43:3–7).   **43:3–7**   Judah is the principal spokesman from this point onward in the narrative (v. 3), since Reuben's leadership had diminished to complaining (42:22) and his influence with his father was exhausted (42:37–38). A telltale sign of lost influence is a failed leader's gasping protestation, "I told you so!" Moreover, Judah's repentant attitude would prove to represent the whole group of siblings when he shows empathy for his father and Benjamin (44:31–34). Judah will eventually exhibit the self-sacrifice that genuine repentance requires of him. His eloquent plea is passionately delivered. There is no time to waste. The repeated condition set forth by the Egyptian man, "You will not see my face . . .," establishes the borders of Judah's entreaty (vv. 3,5), referring to the test of their integrity (42:15–20). Reference to "see my face" is language describing diplomatic audience (e.g., Exod 10:28–29; 2 Sam 14:24). Judah depicts Joseph's intensity by the construction "warned us solemnly,"[326] fortifying his contention that they had been clearly forewarned. According to the Egyptian's threat, if they return without Benjamin, they will be imprisoned for life. Thus Judah answers with his own precondition: only if Jacob permits Benjamin to accompany them will they carry out their father's wishes (vv. 4–5a). Jacob's response is a counterjab (v. 6), blaming the brothers for creating the impossible circumstances he faced ("bring trouble," from $r\bar{a}\,{}^{c}a^{c}$ cf. Moses, Exod 5:22–23; Num 11:11). This frustration with his sons' behavior recalls Jacob's lashing out against Simeon and Levi (*'ākar,* "brought trouble," 34:30). After his accusation, the brothers ("they") speak as one when they answer their father's unjustified grievance (v. 7). The group depicts the interrogation of the Egyptian more forcefully than first narrated, where they appear to volunteer the information (42:10–14). "Questioned . . . closely" and "how were we to know" express their intense objections to his complaint.[327] There is no hint in their report that they were ever suspicious of the motive of the Egyptian interrogator, who had shown such concerted interest in their father and brother.

Judah's Pledge for Benjamin (43:8–10). **43:8–10** Judah picks up his exhortation again from vv. 3–5, urging Jacob to stop his procrastination (v. 8) by cleverly repeating Jacob's own stated concerns (42:2, "live and not die"; cf. 42:20). He appeals further to his father's paternal sense of obligation for the welfare of the whole family, including the vulnerable children *(ṭap).* Jacob had once before displayed paternal protection toward the young (32:11; 33:1–2,13–14). Judah himself refers to Benjamin compassionately as "the boy" *(na'ar;* cf. Joseph, 37:2), revealing a caring stance toward the young. Judah "puts himself out on a limb," so to speak, when he offers himself as security for the boy. His language heightens the intensity of his personal resolve, lit., "I, I will become surety for him, from me . . ." Though the threat is not specific, we may surmise that at most Judah placed his own life at risk, and, at least, he agreed to bear the lifelong shame of failure (cf. 44:32). Reuben had earlier offered his two sons' lives as security, but theirs were not a sufficient guarantee for Jacob initially (cf. comments on 42:37). Now, how-

---

[326] Cf. the infinitive absolute + perfect, הָעֵד הֵעִד; cf. 1 Sam 8:9; Jer 11:7.
[327] Cf. the infinitive absolute + perfect, שָׁאוֹל שָׁאַל and infinitive absolute + imperfect, נָדַע יָדוֹעַ; *IBHS* §35.3.1g renders the modal imperfect, "How could we *possibly* have known that . . .?"

ever, the desperate circumstances of unrelenting famine changed the matter completely. The word rendered "guarantee" (from *ʿ-r-b*) is possibly an unintended echo of Judah's disgrace when he put up a "pledge" *(ʿērābôn)* for Tamar's services (38:17–18,20), for it was by her he fathered two sons.

Jacob's Further Instructions (43:11–14). **43:11–14** When Jacob at last concedes, he puts into action a plan of appeasement. He knows the value of a lavish gift (cf. Esau, 32:10), practicing the sage advice of Proverbs, "A gift opens the way for the giver and ushers him into the presence of the great" (Prov 18:16). The gift consisted of commodities (v. 11)[328] typically exported from Canaan (e.g., Ezek 27:17), recalling especially the products borne by the caravan of Ishmaelite merchants (37:25). It was imperative that the money owed the Egyptian be returned, which Jacob hoped ("perhaps," *ʾûlay*) was an unintentional error ("mistake," *mišgeh),* plus funds for the new purchase (v. 12). The reader knows that there is no mistake but rather a contrived plan, leaving the reader to wonder with the father and brothers how Joseph will respond upon their return to Egypt. The final directive concerned the most important cargo, Benjamin ("your brother," v. 13). That Jacob refers to the Egyptian as the "man" and Benjamin as "your brother" echoes the verbiage of Judah's plea (vv. 3,5,7). Jacob concludes by invoking God's "mercy" *(raḥămîm),* recognizing that the outcome lies in the hands of God alone (v. 14). Prayer for deliverance also preceded Jacob's confrontation with brother Esau (32:9–12[10–13]). (On the name "God Almighty" *[El Shaddai],* see the commentary Introduction.) Appropriately, this first occasion of "mercy" in the Bible appears in an invocation to God. The word occurs only twice in Genesis (vv. 14,30). Ironically, the answer to Jacob's plea, in which refers to (undisclosed) Joseph as "the man," is Benjamin's brother. Joseph's emotional eruption ("deeply moved," also from *raḥămîm*) evidences the compassion for which Jacob prayed (v. 30). Simeon remains nameless; he is only "your other *(ʾaḥēr)* brother" (v. 14).[329] A variant reading, "the one *[hāʾeḥād]* brother" (SP, LXX), echoes Joseph's initial demand for the return of Benjamin, where Simeon again is not named (42:19; cf. v. 24). Jacob concedes he is powerless ("if I am bereaved, I am bereaved") and acquiesces to God's will (v. 14; for "bereaved," see 42:36).

JOSEPH RECEIVES HIS BROTHERS (43:15–34). This segment recounts the second meeting of the brothers with the Egyptian in his house. Joseph takes steps to soften the brothers' defenses, so as to achieve the culminating deception. First, Joseph instructs the steward to prepare a state dinner (vv. 15–17).

---

[328] "Best products" (NIV, HCSB) or "choice fruits" (ESV, NRSV) translates the obscure term זִמְרָה; see "strength," i.e., "strength of the land" (cf. Exod 15:2) in *HALOT* 1.274.

[329] A Jewish interpretation understood his prayer as a divine prophecy, referring to Joseph as the "other" brother (e.g., Rashi); thus Simeon, who is "your brother," Joseph, the "other" brother, and "Benjamin" will all be released.

Second, the steward cheerfully accepts their explanation for the returned silver, even attributing it to divine benevolence, and releases Simeon to them
(vv. 18–24). Third, Joseph continues the goodwill, accepting the gift of the
men and inquiring about their father's well-being. Joseph, too, is softened by
the appearance of Benjamin, leading to an emotional exit (vv. 25–30). The
final scene depicts the Egyptian mysteriously seating the brothers by seniority
and unexpectedly lavishing gifts on the youngest (43:31–34).

Joseph Instructs His Steward (43:15–17).   **43:15–17**   Verse 15 reports
that the brothers carried out their father's instructions to the word, leading to
an audience with Joseph. At seeing Benjamin with them, Joseph proceeded to
treat them ostensibly well, instructing the steward to prepare his own gift for
the visitors (v. 16). All that followed hinged on Benjamin's presence. That
they are invited to eat with the lord of the land "at his house" must have given
rise to their fears of deception, since the privilege was probably exceptional
(v. 18). As we will discover, dining with the undisclosed Joseph will put them
at ease, disarming them to the trickery in store.

Steward Receives the Brothers' Gift (43:18–24).   **43:18–22**   The brothers imagine the worse when brought to Joseph's residence (v. 18). The
aggression they envision is described in three consecutive actions, "attack . . .
overpower . . . take." Among their ruminations about the returned silver, they
may have considered the possibility that it was not a mistake as their father
had hoped (v. 12) but a deliberate pretense for robbery. "Frightened"
described the same reaction of the brothers and Jacob to the discovery of the
money in their sacks (42:35). Although they had appeared with Benjamin
according to the Egyptian's request, they believed the unexplained money in
their sacks would lead to their enslavement anyway (cf. also 44:9). It was not
an unwarranted fear, for an attack in the privacy of a dining hall had the
advantage of surprise (e.g., 2 Sam 13:28). That the brothers remained suspicious of Joseph's ultimate intentions even after their reconciliation is revealed
by their alarm at the death of their father (50:18). Immediately, the brothers
make their explanation to the steward (v. 19), offering to return the mysterious money (v. 21). They couch their language so as to prove their innocence.
They begin with a courteous plea ("Please, sir," *bî ʾădōnî*) and go straight to
the motivation of their first visit, "to buy food" (v. 20). Their account varies
from the earlier narrated events, indicating that they all opened their sacks
and discovered their silver (v. 21). This is an example of telescoping two
events, the discovery by one brother the first night (42:27–28) and the later
finding by all upon their return to Jacob (v. 26). That the discovered silver
was "the exact weight" each man had originally possessed reinforced their
perplexity but also implied that they were victims. Moreover, the silver was
"in the mouth of the sack," meaning the money was not hidden from plain
view ("top," NRSV, REB). They hastened to add simply that they wanted to

make good on their word by returning the money. Addressing again the question of motivation, they explain that they also returned to purchase more food ("to buy food," v. 22), bringing the necessary monies. So as to drive home their innocence they insist that they don't "know" who would have done this to them. That they don't know and that Joseph and his steward do know add force to the motif of Joseph's knowledge versus the incompetence of the brothers (e.g., 41:39; 42:7–8).

43:23–24 The steward calms their anxiety by attributing their experience to God's good favor (v. 23). "Your God, the God of your father"[330] identifies the patriarchal heritage (26:24; 28:13; 31:29; 46:3; cf. Exod 3:6), and appears again in the brothers' confession to Joseph (50:17). "Treasure" *(maṭmôn)* typically refers to concealed wealth (e.g., Job 3:21; Isa 45:3; cf. "buried," from *ṭāmēn,* Gen 35:4). The steward's declaration "I received your silver," lit., "your silver came to me," answers for the brothers why they are welcomed ("It's all right," *šālōm*). The books were already balanced, and the implication is that they may retain the money as a divine gift. Proof that they were not in peril was the immediate presentation of Simeon. Moreover, the steward provides them and their animals the customary acts of hospitality (v. 24; cf. 24:32). All appeared to be working out better than they could have wished.

Joseph Receives Benjamin (43:25–30). **43:25** The subject matter of the brothers' "gift" *(minḥâ)* reappears (vv. 11,15,26).

43:26–28 The greeting includes two acts of homage to the lord of the land ("bowed down," vv. 26,28), returning us to the dreams of Joseph's youth (37:7,9,10; 42:6). Joseph, too, greets them with polite interest in their welfare (v. 27a), but his inquiry about their father is not perfunctory (v. 27b). That Jacob was "aged" explains why Joseph would raise the question about his father's condition. In their positive reply the brothers show proper deference to the Egyptian by speaking of their father as "your servant" and by prostrating themselves. "Bowed low to pay him honor" (v. 28) renders the complementary verbs "bowed down" *(qādad)* and "prostrated" *(ḥāwâ),* which often occur together to express homage to God (cf. 24:26,48) and occasionally reverence for royalty, as here (e.g., 1 Sam 24:8[9]). Now that Benjamin was with the ten brothers, the complement of "eleven stars bowing down" according to Joseph's dream finds its fulfillment (37:9).[331]

43:29–30 The text recognizes especially the unique relationship of Benjamin and Joseph, the brothers of the same mother ("his own mother's son"). (On "looked up and saw," v. 29, cf. comments on 18:2.) His question,

---

[330] The SP, LXX readings reflect אֲבֹתֵיכֶם, "your fathers," referring to all of their ancestors (cf. 15:15; 31:3; 48:21).

[331] At no place in the Joseph narrative does Jacob bow to Joseph, which would be an unexpected departure for a father toward a son (cf. 48:12), but the repeated references to Jacob as "your servant" would seem to satisfy the intention of the dream.

"Is this your youngest brother . . .?" (v. 29), does not require an answer. The invocation that Joseph confers on Benjamin must have struck the brothers as unexpectedly generous. That Joseph singled out Benjamin as the recipient of God's grace (from *ḥānan*) could have suggested to the brothers that Benjamin was the chosen successor to their father Jacob (cf. 33:5,11). "My son" indicates a benevolent relationship toward a subordinate (e.g., 2 Sam 18:22), which is the counterpart to "my father" as an expression of respect when addressing a superior (e.g., 2 Kgs 5:13; 6:21). The Egyptian's favorable disposition toward their youngest brother will appear again at the dining table (v. 34). If jealousy toward Benjamin had existed among the brothers, this special goodwill by so powerful a figure as the lord of the land would have surely chafed the men. The later arrest of Benjamin for the theft of the cup would have been viewed as a great boon to spiteful rivals. Whereas Joseph was able to control himself at the brothers' first visit (42:24), he became so overcome with his emotions at receiving Benjamin that he must hastily leave to avoid detection (v. 30). "Deeply moved" (*nikmĕrû raḥămayw*, lit., "his compassion grew hot"[332]) also describes the compassion of a mother for her son (1 Kgs 3:26) and of God for his people (Hos 11:8). The Joseph narrative often depicts Joseph weeping when restored to his family (45:14,15,29; 50:1,17; cp. 29:11; 33:4). If Jeremiah is the so-called "weeping prophet," Joseph is the "weeping patriarch."

Joseph Favors Benjamin (43:31–34). **43:31–34** The scene shifts to the dining table, where again Joseph favors his younger brother by lavishing food on his plate, five times greater than the others. The irony of the scene is that the same activity preceded the sale of Joseph by the brothers (37:25). A contrast between the brothers and Joseph in the narrative is the brothers' washing of feet (v. 24) and Joseph's washing away of tears (v. 31). The brothers are oblivious to the magnitude of the events at hand. "Controlling himself" translates *yith'apaq* (*hithpaal,* from *'āpaq,* "hold, be strong"), meaning he possessed restraint (e.g., Esth 5:10; Isa 42:14). This façade of self-discipline will at last break down when the brothers have passed the trial (45:1). The events of the meal convey symbolic meaning. The segregated seating of Joseph, the brothers, and the Egyptians reflected the low status of the Hebrews (v. 32). The author's explanation for the distinction informs the Hebrew reader of a ritual taboo in Egypt, which is explained further in 46:34 (cf. Exod 8:26[22]). That Egyptians exhibited such discriminatory practices has some corroboration in Herodotus's *Histories* (fifth century B.C.). Egyptians, according to Herodotus, would not eat or sacrifice cows, who were considered sacred, and for this reason they avoided cohabiting with Greeks (2.18,41; cf. 2.42,46).

---

[332] The *niphal* is ingressive-stative (*IBHS* §23.3c).

"Detestable" *(tô'ēbâ)* is a common term (117x),[333] meaning what is morally or ritually repulsive to God or to humans (e.g., Lev 18:22; Deut 7:25–26; Prov 6:16). This exclusionary policy toward the Jacobites will mean eventually the permission to establish their separate domain in Goshen (46:31–47:6). Moreover, by seating the brothers according to their order of birth, from the eldest to the youngest, Joseph symbolically recreated the tension of sibling rivalry that had led to the crimes against him and potentially against Benjamin.[334] The distinct term "firstborn" *(bĕkôr)* appears, unlike the generic word for "oldest" *(gādôl)* as in 44:12. The brothers were amazed at the coincidence, perhaps fearing that God's judgment was not yet satisfied. The root *t-m-h,* "to be astonished" (v. 33), often involves the sense of alarm (e.g., Isa 13:8). There was no explanation for this as there had not been for many of the puzzling events surrounding their visits to Egypt. The culminating act also symbolized events to come. The provisions of food and drink for the brothers came from Joseph's personal portion, signifying that he would be the source of the family's survival (v. 34; e.g., 45:11,18,20–21). The five additional portions for Benjamin have a parallel in the lavish gifts (five sets of clothing) that Egyptian Joseph bestows on the boy (45:22). The wine flowed and the brothers became merry, if not actually inebriated ("drank freely," from *šākar,* "to be drunk"). Joseph's actions could exacerbate any latent jealousy toward Benjamin. Through drink they become unguarded, readied by Joseph for the crowning ruse.

6. Joseph Tests the Brothers (44:1–34)

The final test begins in the same fashion as the first deception (42:25). Joseph instructs his steward to load grain in their bags, but this time the Egyptian's silver cup rests in Benjamin's pouch (44:1). The test is designed to expose without ambiguity the genuine attitude of the ten brothers toward their youngest, Benjamin. Sternberg comments that the device "consists in turning back the wheel of time to the original crime against himself [Joseph], with the circumstances reproduced and the ten ranged against Benjamin."[335] The Simeon imprisonment achieved the purpose of retrieving Benjamin. Joseph knew that the famine would last years longer and that the need for a return to Egypt was inevitable. He could with his own eyes see the condition of his beloved little brother. Now it was necessary to take the next step, increasing the pressure so as to pit the ten brothers against the one remaining obstacle to their father's

---

[333] M. A. Grisanti, "תעב," *NIDOTTE* 4.314.

[334] *Tg. Ps.-J.; Gen. Rab.* 91.6; 92.5; 93.7 maintain that Joseph pretended to use the silver divining cup to determine the birth order (cf. 44:2). According to Rashi, the seating also took in account their respective birth mothers (cf. *Gen. Rab.* 92.5), making the placing all the more astounding.

[335] Sternberg, *The Poetics of Hebrew Narrative,* 303.

favor. Cynically speaking, they could return to their father with a clear con-science, for indeed they had no control over Benjamin's fate in the hands of so despotic a ruler as the Egyptian master! God through this calamity had spoken, they could reason, for Jacob himself conceded that whatever the outcome it was of divine provenience ("If I am bereaved, I am bereaved," 43:14).

But Judah rose to the occasion, placing his life on the line, not firstly for the preferred brother but principally for the sake of his aging father. Judah refers to his "father" fourteen times in his speech,[336] showing a sympathy that melted the stern façade of the Egyptian lord (45:1–2). The contrast between the Judah of Joseph's abduction and the Judah of the present circum-stances could not be more stark. He stood to gain by accepting the Egyptian's judgment to incarcerate only Benjamin (44:17) as he had gained from Joseph's sale (37:27–28), or so he had thought. His self-serving plan resulted in a life of guilt that included his own sad experiences of losing sons and of suffering deception (chap. 38, Tamar). No more. Judah, faced with a second chance, seizes his opportunity for absolution. As Luther remarked, "They will confess more than they have committed."[337] Guilt-ridden persons are known to think, "If I had it to do over again . . ." What was Joseph's "cruelty" proved to be Judah's "cross" to bear. But unlike Jesus, who was innocent of wrong-doing, bearing the undeserved punishment of others (1 Pet 3:18), Judah was not innocent. Granted, he had not stolen and had no knowledge of the silver chalice, but he interpreted the judgment against the brothers as God's just ret-ribution for their unrequited crime against Joseph. Judah especially took the lead in doing away with his brother Joseph (37:26–28), and now he fittingly takes on the weight of the responsibility (43:9; 44:33).

The plea by Judah (vv. 18–34) is the longest speech in the narrative. It also contains the most extensive use of "second level" quotation (flashbacks), in which Judah recounts earlier dialogue. He revisits the first encounter of Joseph and the brothers (44:19–24) and subsequent interactions between Jacob and the brothers (44:25–29; cf. 43:2–5; 42:38). Judah's offer of surety for the life of Benjamin, for example, is told at a second level quotation, "I said, 'If I do not bring him back . . ., I will bear the blame'" (44:32; cf. 43:9). Especially significant is Judah's recollection of Jacob's sorrow over Joseph. Verse 28 contains a "third level" of embedded quotation when Judah quotes Jacob, who quotes himself, "I said, 'Surely he has been torn to pieces'" (44:28; cf. 37:33). The length and complexity of the Judah speech marks it as the important precursor to Joseph's climactic self-disclosure (45:3–4). The same root term, "approach, draw close" *(nāgaš),* in the narrative introduction to Judah's speech ("Judah went up to him," 44:18) and in Joseph's response

---

[336] Wenham, *Genesis 16–50,* 425.
[337] *LW* 7.365.

("'Come close to me' . . . and they came close,"[338] 45:4) connects the petition of Judah and the affective reaction of Joseph.

Judah is neither a hero nor a villain. The character of Judah is too real, too complex for such facile categories. One level of Jewish interpretation reversed the roles of Judah and Joseph, casting Judah in a superior position to Joseph. An extensive midrash and variations (e.g., *Tg. Neof.*; *Gen. Rab.* 93.6; Rashi[339]) depict Judah as a "roaring lion" (cp. 49:9) who reprimands the disguised Joseph, threatening him and Pharaoh with violence if he fails to pardon Benjamin. The point is that Judah is not submissive to Joseph in his Egyptian guise. Such efforts to paint Judah as a strong leader whose offspring are kings does not reflect the impression gained from Judah's speech. Neither is his voluntary offer of bondage a mere timely expediency.[340] Judah has undergone a moral reformation, not through a single event here or there but through the cumulative effect of life's vicissitudes. Christian author and speaker Catherine Marshall once observed, "No man can lead well until he has given himself to leadership greater than his own." This Judah did when he humbled himself before God and before the "Egyptian" whom he had victimized so long ago.

COMPOSITION.   The relationship of chap. 44 to the preceding chapters was touched upon in the introduction to chaps. 42–43. Source critics were in wide agreement that chap. 44 was largely of the same source as chap. 43 (J source plus E additions [43:14a,23b]).[341] The trend toward a unified Joseph story argued against parallel Yahwist (J) and Elohist (E) versions. Speaking on chaps. 43–44, Coats remarked: "The first part of the next scene [chaps. 43–45] offers no problem for source analysis. Gen 43–44 belongs entirely to J."[342] Westermann questioned Redford's supplemental theory, which identified chap. 42 as the "Reuben" version and chaps. 43–44 as the "Judah" revision. The insuperable problem according to Westermann is the Simeon imprisonment in chap. 42. It occurs only in the Reuben edition (E) (chap. 42), according to Redford's two-layer approach, but Simeon's detention is assumed in the Judah layer (J) (chaps. 43–44). Redford must excise the mention of "Simeon" in 43:14a,23b to sustain his thesis or posit a Simeon episode in J.[343]

Thompson also bucked the trend toward a single author view. He discerned what he deemed multiple plots that belied a unified story created by one author. He argued that the double motif of hidden treasure in the brothers' sacks in 42:25,27–28 and in 44:1–2 function differently. In the latter case the placement of the money in the sacks has no narrative purpose, for the search is solely con-

---

[338] NIV, "When they had done so . . ."

[339] For the many ancient Jewish citations, see McNamara, *Targum Neofiti*, 198, n. 10.

[340] Coats believes "he had no other viable choice" (*From Canaan to Egypt*, 47).

[341] E.g., Gunkel, *Genesis*, 427–28; Skinner, *Genesis*, 479.

[342] Coats, *From Canaan to Egypt*, 67.

[343] Westermann, *Genesis 37–50*, 119.

cerned with the silver cup. For Thompson the mention of the returned silver in chap. 44 is a secondary contrivance, transparently not part of the plot in chap. 44.[344] Rather than argue for two disparate plots, an exegetical explanation for the difference is more attractive. The returned silver in chap. 44 makes sense when we remember that the story consistently depicts Joseph's generosity toward his estranged family, such as his concern for their "starving households" (42:19). The inclusion of the money also contributed to the favorable mood that Joseph created for his visitors the evening before, disarming any latent suspicions. The interconnections between chaps. 43–45 are integral to a cohesive plot that is best explained as the product of a single author.

STRUCTURE. This unit falls naturally into two parts, in which the first part (vv. 1–13) establishes the background for the climactic part (vv. 14–34). The two parts flow naturally in a coherent sequence of events. The first describes the interaction of three character slots: Joseph, his steward, and the brothers (vv. 1–13). The steward is a minor character but a critical one, who serves as the linkage between the Egyptian master and the house of Jacob. He is the hands and the mouthpiece of Joseph. Joseph delivers two sets of instructions to his steward, and the narrative reports his strict adherence (vv. 1–3,4–6). Both paragraphs are set in the house of the Egyptian lord. In the subsequent two paragraphs the scene shifts to the dialogue of the brothers and the steward not "far from the city" (vv. 7–10,11–13). The brothers answer the steward's charge with a countercharge in the form of a proposal, which the steward accepts (vv. 7–10). The segment ends with the narrative report of the discovery of the lord's silver cup and the reaction and return of the brothers "to the city" (vv. 11–13).

The second part is set "in the house" and describes the dialogue between Joseph and Judah, the two chief characters of the chapter (vv. 14–34). The encounter has no intermediary, neither the steward nor the interpreter (cf. 42:23). Judah fills the slot of the collective brothers as a representative voice. The dialogue consists of uneven duration, allotting to Judah the longest speech in the Book of Genesis. The first round of speeches entails Joseph's accusation and Judah's concession to divine retribution (vv. 14–16). In the second round Joseph announces judgment against Benjamin, and Judah makes a sustained and passionate plea for leniency (vv. 17,18–32). Judah's argument divides into two stages. First, he recapitulates the salient dialogue of their first meeting and of the report to their father (vv. 18–32), fostering a tone of sympathy for the family's aged father. Second, Judah ends with a counterproposal to Joseph's judgment by offering to stand in for Benjamin's enslavement (vv. 33–34).

The chapter begins with Joseph's command, "Now Joseph gave these

---

[344] Thompson, *The Origin Tradition*, 126–27.

instructions" (v. 1). The verse assumes knowledge of the circumstances and persons in the prior chaps. 42–43. Chapter 44 narrates loosely related but new events. The Hebrew text indicates both continuity and discontinuity with the preceding chapter. The nonspecific subject, lit., "he gave" (NIV "Joseph gave"), assumes the continuation of 43:31–34. The reason that Joseph's name does not occur in the opening verse is because the new events require the reader's attention on the "steward," which appears at the head of the clause after the verb. The end of the chapter is the natural break provided by the termination of Judah's speech (44:18–34).

Among the chief links that hold the chapter together are the recurring narrative interests of Jacob and Benjamin. Although the name "Benjamin" appears but one time (44:12) and he never speaks nor is spoken to individually, he is introduced as early as Joseph's first speech (v. 2) and is the sustained interest in the development of the plot and the extensive speech of Judah (vv. 12–34). In addition to the ubiquitous third person pronoun references in the chapter, Benjamin is named "the youngest" *(haqqāṭôn,* vv. 2,12) or "youngest brother" *('aḥ haqqāṭôn,* vv. 23,26[2x]), "the one who was found *[nimṣā']* to have the cup" (vv. 16,17), "the boy" *(hanna'ar,* vv. 22,30,31,32,33[2x],34), "child" *(yeled,* v. 20, NIV "son"), "he is the only one of his mother left" (v. 20, NIV "mother's sons"), "two [sons]" (v. 27), "this one" (v. 29), and "his life" (v. 30, NIV "boy's life"). The lengthy epithet "the one who was found *[nimṣā']* to have the cup" (vv. 16,17) contains the key connecting term "find, found" *(māṣā'),* appearing repeatedly in both halves (vv. 8,9,10,12,16[2x],17,34). The "finding" of the silver cup leads to Judah's admission, "God has uncovered *[māṣā']* your servants' guilt" (v. 16). The search for the cup is paralleled by God's search of the brothers.

Another leading idea that binds the two parts of the chapter is expressed by the persistent word "servant/slave" *('ebed).* It appears most often in courteous address to Joseph, the Egyptian lord, referring to the brothers ("your servants," vv. 7,16,18[2x],21,23,31; "his servants," v. 19), to Jacob ("your servant my father," vv. 24,27,30; "your servant our father," v. 31), and to Judah ("your servant," vv. 32,33). The word also conveys the nuance of "slave" (vv. 9,10,16,17,33), which is the threat that hangs over the brothers. Another recurring item, though only appearing in the second part, is the term "father" *('ab),* which always refers to Jacob and occurs predominantly in Judah's speech (vv. 17,19,20[2x],22[2x],24,25,27,30,31,32[2x],34[2x]).

(1) Joseph Deceives His Brothers (44:1–13)

[1]Now Joseph gave these instructions to the steward of his house: "Fill the men's sacks with as much food as they can carry, and put each man's silver in the mouth of his sack. [2]Then put my cup, the silver one, in the mouth of the youngest one's sack, along with the silver for his grain." And he did as Joseph said.

³As morning dawned, the men were sent on their way with their donkeys.
⁴They had not gone far from the city when Joseph said to his steward, "Go after
those men at once, and when you catch up with them, say to them, 'Why have you
repaid good with evil? ⁵Isn't this the cup my master drinks from and also uses for
divination? This is a wicked thing you have done.'"

⁶When he caught up with them, he repeated these words to them. ⁷But they
said to him, "Why does my lord say such things? Far be it from your servants to
do anything like that! ⁸We even brought back to you from the land of Canaan the
silver we found inside the mouths of our sacks. So why would we steal silver or
gold from your master's house? ⁹If any of your servants is found to have it, he will
die; and the rest of us will become my lord's slaves."

¹⁰"Very well, then," he said, "let it be as you say. Whoever is found to have it
will become my slave; the rest of you will be free from blame."

¹¹Each of them quickly lowered his sack to the ground and opened it. ¹²Then
the steward proceeded to search, beginning with the oldest and ending with the
youngest. And the cup was found in Benjamin's sack. ¹³At this, they tore their
clothes. Then they all loaded their donkeys and returned to the city.

Joseph gives his steward two sets of instructions regarding his silver cup,
the first to plant the cup in the luggage of the youngest and, second, to pursue
and charge them with theft (vv. 1–2,4–6). Verse 3, which narrates the brothers' departure, links the two speeches. The boundaries of vv. 4–13 are the
brothers' exit from "the city" (v. 4) and the return of the brothers to "the city"
(v. 13). After the steward overtakes the brothers (vv. 4–6), they protest their
innocence (vv. 7–10), but upon inspection of the bags the cup is discovered
and the caravan returns to face the lord of the land (vv. 11–14).

THE STEWARD PLANTS THE SILVER CUP (44:1–3).   **44:1–3**   These
verses establish the circumstances for the disturbing events that follow.
Joseph instructed his custodian to fill the brothers' saddlebags with as much
grain as possible, return their "silver" to each one's bag, and finally plant his
"silver" cup in the bag of the youngest brother (vv. 1–2). "As much food as
they can carry" (v. 1) reflects the same personal concern that Joseph had
shown for their "starving households" (42:19). This feature is consistent with
the narrative motif of Joseph providing sustenance for his family and for the
world.³⁴⁵ That the text mentions twice that Joseph instructed the steward to
return the men's "silver" in the sacks (vv. 1,2) effectively ties this incident to
the first test (42:25). The term "to command" (ṣāwâ) introduces the first and
final tests (NIV "gave orders," 42:25; "gave these instructions," 44:1). The
weight of the bulging pouches probably gave the brothers the sense of generosity continued from the night before, encouraging a false impression of
security. "My cup, the silver cup" occurs at the head of the Hebrew clause,
drawing attention to its character. It is the personal item of the Egyptian mas-

---

³⁴⁵ Ibid., 131.

ter, and it is a valued article made of precious silver. The repeated references
to "silver" in vv. 1–2,8 contribute to the twenty appearances of the term in
chaps. 42–45, recalling for us the twenty pieces of silver for the purchase of
Joseph (37:28).[346] The term "cup" *(gābîaʿ)* is a chalice or goblet to be distinguished from *kôs,* the common word for drinking cup (e.g., 40:11; 2 Sam
12:3), by the chalice's flower-shaped interior and by its larger, bowl-like size.
It describes the flower-shaped cups of the tabernacle's lampstand (Exod
25:31–34; 37:17–20; but cf. Jer 35:5). We learn from the steward in v. 5 that
the cup had the dual purpose of drinking cup and divining device. Whether or
not the brothers actually had access to the cup does not ruin the ruse. Some
commentators speculate that Joseph used the cup in their presence the evening before (43:34b).[347] The men "were sent on their way," presumably by
Joseph, initiating the trap (v. 3). "Twenty years of unresolved conflict
between the brothers will be reconciled on this critical day of testing."[348] An
early morning departure fits an expected travel pattern (e.g., 21:14; 22:3;
24:54; 26:31; 31:55[32:1]), raising no reason for suspicion. That the brothers
did not check the bags demonstrated that they were completely taken in by
the goodwill Joseph had shown them.

THE STEWARD OVERTAKES THE BROTHERS (44:4–6). **44:4–6** Lest the
plan unravel prematurely, Joseph shortly dispatches his steward to overtake
them, for "they had not gone far" (v. 4). The steward is to deliver an interrogation, hurling two charges that assume the brothers know the crime (vv. 4b–
5a). "Repaid good for evil" does not describe merely ingratitude but describes
malicious exploitation of a person's kindness (e.g., 1 Sam 25:21; cf. Prov
17:13). The psalmist sharply reproached his enemies for such cruelty (Pss
35:12; 38:20[21]; 109:5; cf. Jer 18:20). In a reversal of the expression, Joseph
later exclaimed that God had exchanged evil ("harm") for good (50:20; cf.
Prov 14:19). What appeared to be evil proved to be the good, leading to the
salvation and reconciliation of the family.

The steward continues the allegation by a second question, referring to the
divination cup, although the brothers are ignorant of what he has in mind
(v. 5).[349] Divination is the practice of foreseeing the future or discovering
hidden knowledge. Hydromancy, the art of interpreting the liquids (water) in

---

[346] Sarna, *Genesis,* 303.

[347] "They, no doubt, all thought that Benjamin had actually stolen the cup; and the probability
of this guilt might be heightened by the circumstance of his having that very cup to drink out of at
dinner; for as he had the most honourable mess, so it is likely he had the most honourable cup to
drink out of at the entertainment" (A. Clarke, *The Holy Bible containing the Old and New Testaments,* 6 vols. (Nashville: Abingdon, 1960 [1833 original]), 1.247.

[348] Waltke, *Genesis,* 559.

[349] The LXX begins the verse with a preceding question: ἵνα τί ἐκλέψατέ μου τὸ κόνδυ τὸ
ἀργυροῦν, "Why have you stolen my silver cup?" so as to specify the charge, which in the MT
Joseph, according to his scheme, assumes they would know.

a cup or bowl, was widely practiced in the ancient Near East (other liquids included oil and wine). The common methods were interpreting the patterns of moving liquids or the patterns of floating objects in the liquid (cp. tasseomancy [tea leaf reading]).[350] That Joseph is said to use the cup for "divination"[351] (cf. comments on 30:27) is unexpected since this practice is outlawed in Israel (Lev 19:26; Deut 18:10). There is no instance of this practice in the Joseph narrative (cf. comments on 43:33), and since Joseph's wisdom relies on the interpretation of dreams, it is best understood as part of the elaborate ploy. The importance of the divination cup is its personal ownership by the Egyptian lord ("my cup," v. 2). By stealing the cup, the steward concludes, "This is a wicked thing you have done" (v. 5). Verse 6 is typical of good Hebrew narrative style, indicating that the messenger carried out his instructions.

THE BROTHERS ASSERT THEIR INNOCENCE (44:7–10). **44:7–10** The brothers answer that such a claim is preposterous (v. 7). "Far be it from your servants . . ." means that such a crime is out of character for them (cf. 18:25; 44:17). They thought they had already vindicated their character by returning the extra money returned in their sacks at the first journey (v. 8). Their indignant retort is logically sound: thieves don't return merchandise in order to steal. If they were thieves, it would have been self-defeating to return the silver, and since they had, it was irrational for them to steal now. So confident are they of their innocence that they boldly volunteer the worst of punishments—death to the culprit[352] and imprisonment for the others (v. 9; cp. Jacob and Rachel, 31:32). Moreover, they assume collective guilt, although only one among them would be found guilty. They stand or fall together, perhaps another sign of a rekindled family loyalty. Their assurance contrasts with the apprehension of imprisonment they had when first taken to Joseph's house (43:18). Ironically, they condemn themselves to the punishment that they all along feared. The steward readily accepts the principle of their offer, "Let it be as you say," lit., "according to your own words, let it be" (v. 10). Their proposed penalty, however, was too severe in the steward's eyes (as well as Joseph's, v. 17). Only the guilty party will be enslaved, and the others will be set free. The phrase "free from blame" translates *nāqî*, which can mean "exemption from obligation," that is, release (e.g., Deut 24:5), or "guiltless" in a juridical sense (e.g., Exod 23:7).[353] By employing the word

---

[350] E. Hostetter, "גְּבִיעַ," *NIDOTTE* 1.800.

[351] The construction is intensive (infin. absol. + imperf.), וְהוּא נַחֵשׁ יְנַחֵשׁ בּוֹ, lit., "indeed he uses it for divination."

[352] יָמֻת, "he will die" or "let him die," is often used of capital punishment (cf. 1 Kgs 1:52; Exod 21:28; Deut 13:10[11]), although it also describes divine retaliation (1 Sam 26:10); יוּמַת, "let him be put to death" (SP, *Tgs.*), indicates capital punishment (e.g., 26:11; Exod 21:12).

[353] M. C. Fisher and B. K. Waltke, "נָקָה (*nāqâ*)," *TWOT* 2.597–98.

"blame," the NIV suggests the latter nuance (cf. NASB, HCSB, NAB), whereas others permit the former by translating "set free [from servile obligation]" (e.g., NRSV; cf. REB, NJB, NLT). The fate of the perpetrator will mean his bondage to the steward, he himself most likely a slave. This menial status was similar to Joseph's circumstance in prison, serving the king's baker and butler (40:4).

THE STEWARD DISCOVERS THE CUP IN BENJAMIN'S BAG (44:11–13). **44:11–13** Their overconfidence fueled a speedy ("quickly") and complete ("each of them") baring of their possessions (v. 11), for the men had no reason to doubt their vindication. The servant was thorough and methodical, moving from the eldest's sack to the youngest's (v. 12). The process echoes the seating arrangement in Joseph's dining hall (43:33). We can imagine that with each sack's examination the brothers became increasingly more assured, but the steward knew what waited at the end of the line. He does not tip off the plot by going directly to Benjamin's bag but plays out the ruse in an Oscar-winning performance! "Searched" *(ḥāpaš)* describes Laban's rummaging through the baggage of Jacob's belongings for his *tĕrāpîm,* only to be fooled by Rachel (31:35). Here the outcome and deception are reversed. Jacob's sons, not the searcher, are deceived, and the search results in the successful retrieval of the planted object. "And he found the cup in Benjamin's sack" describes the regrettable end of the search, but it is narrated in a matter-of-fact fashion. The name "Benjamin" appears in the text at the finish of the verse, reinforcing the end result of the search (v. 12). No one "in the know," as we say, was surprised; the reader anticipates the outcome and the steward knows, but the brothers are utterly devastated by the unthinkable revelation (v. 13). The emotive outpouring of the brothers contrasts with the cold investigation by the steward. Spontaneously, the brothers "tore their clothes," which was the sign of deep emotional distress (e.g., Num 14:6). That all the brothers suffered such distress is a telling sign of the new sense of unity they had developed. They had already been informed that the innocent will be released (v. 10). Moreover, that they all return to Egypt underscores their commitment to Benjamin. The brothers are of one accord without any grumbling or dissent. For the victims of the ploy the polarities of human emotions have been reached, from the merriment of their successful journey to the woeful depths of their worst thoughts. The gesture of torn clothing recalls the (separate) events of Reuben and Jacob at each one's discovery of Joseph's demise (37:29,34). The narrative conveys again the irony of deserved punishment for the offenders. They were guilty but did not show remorse; now they are innocent and demonstrate deepest agony. The text straightforwardly describes what was inevitable from the start; each brother solemnly reloaded his donkey and the caravan returned intact (v. 13). If Jacob lost the whole household to slavery in addition to Benjamin, surely the old man would be as good as dead (42:38; 44:29,31). How much longer can the ruse continue short of crushing the family?

(2) Judah Pleads for Mercy (44:14–34)

[14]Joseph was still in the house when Judah and his brothers came in, and they threw themselves to the ground before him. [15]Joseph said to them, "What is this you have done? Don't you know that a man like me can find things out by divination?"

[16]"What can we say to my lord?" Judah replied. "What can we say? How can we prove our innocence? God has uncovered your servants' guilt. We are now my lord's slaves—we ourselves and the one who was found to have the cup."

[17]But Joseph said, "Far be it from me to do such a thing! Only the man who was found to have the cup will become my slave. The rest of you, go back to your father in peace."

[18]Then Judah went up to him and said: "Please, my lord, let your servant speak a word to my lord. Do not be angry with your servant, though you are equal to Pharaoh himself. [19]My lord asked his servants, 'Do you have a father or a brother?' [20]And we answered, 'We have an aged father, and there is a young son born to him in his old age. His brother is dead, and he is the only one of his mother's sons left, and his father loves him.'

[21]"Then you said to your servants, 'Bring him down to me so I can see him for myself.' [22]And we said to my lord, 'The boy cannot leave his father; if he leaves him, his father will die.' [23]But you told your servants, 'Unless your youngest brother comes down with you, you will not see my face again.' [24]When we went back to your servant my father, we told him what my lord had said.

[25]"Then our father said, 'Go back and buy a little more food.' [26]But we said, 'We cannot go down. Only if our youngest brother is with us will we go. We cannot see the man's face unless our youngest brother is with us.'

[27]"Your servant my father said to us, 'You know that my wife bore me two sons. [28]One of them went away from me, and I said, "He has surely been torn to pieces." And I have not seen him since. [29]If you take this one from me too and harm comes to him, you will bring my gray head down to the grave in misery.'

[30]"So now, if the boy is not with us when I go back to your servant my father and if my father, whose life is closely bound up with the boy's life, [31]sees that the boy isn't there, he will die. Your servants will bring the gray head of our father down to the grave in sorrow. [32]Your servant guaranteed the boy's safety to my father. I said, 'If I do not bring him back to you, I will bear the blame before you, my father, all my life!'

[33]"Now then, please let your servant remain here as my lord's slave in place of the boy, and let the boy return with his brothers. [34]How can I go back to my father if the boy is not with me? No! Do not let me see the misery that would come upon my father."

Judah and his brothers come again before the Egyptian lord (v. 14). Two rounds of speeches follow (vv. 15–16,17–34). The first round entails Joseph's interrogation (v. 15) and Judah's admission of guilt (v. 16). In the second round of speeches, Joseph assigns punishment (v. 17), and Judah makes an impassioned plea for mercy (vv. 18–34). Judah's plea involves two steps. First, in a prolonged and carefully crafted entreaty, he explains that the punishment against the young offender threatens the life of the innocent and aging Jacob (vv. 18–32). Second, in a brief but riveting conclusion, he begs Joseph to accept him in the place of Benjamin for the sake of his father (vv. 33–34).

JUDAH CONFESSES THEIR SIN AGAINST GOD (44:14–16). **44:14–15** The text indicates that Judah will now take center stage as the spokesman for the brothers (v. 14).[354] That Joseph was "still in the house" shows that he had expected a speedy return and no doubt was anxious for their arrival. The brothers' immediate collapse at the feet of the master acknowledged their total dependence on Joseph's mercy if they are to survive the allegation. The same term, "threw themselves [down]" *(nāpal),* describes the reaction in 50:18 (but there has "before him"), where they also admit, "We are your slaves." Here, however, they cannot speak before Joseph launches into his angry diatribe (v. 15). The author does not intend to depict the imagery of the dream scenes in which the sheaves and stars bow to Joseph. He prefers the word "fall [down]" *(nāpal)* to avoid "prostrate, bow in honor" *(ḥāwâ,* 37:7,9,10; 42:6; 43:26,28). As Waltke remarks, "The [brothers] are now desperate, not deferring."[355] Joseph's question is accusatory, paralleling the language of the charge delivered by the steward upon overtaking them (v. 5). The wording recalls earlier inquisitions concerning guilt in Genesis (3:13–14; 20:9; 26:10; 29:25). Moreover, Joseph belittled them for thinking that they could fool a man of his stature who knew the diviner's arts (v. 15).

44:16 Judah resigns that they cannot clear their name. After all, the cup was discovered in their possession. "Prove our innocence" *(hith.* from *ṣādaq)* is not the first time that the word was in Judah's mind (v. 16).[356] It is the same root word heard in his admission, "She [Tamar] is more righteous *[ṣādaq]* than I" (38:26). He admits their guilt, but he does not mean the charge of theft pending before them. For this allegation was not true. Rather, he has in mind the crime against their long-lost brother.[357] For Judah this mistaken charge against them is recompense for the crime they had not atoned for. There was no human explanation for the peculiar circumstances of the cup. God must have "uncovered *[māṣā']* your servant's guilt" (v. 16a).

---

[354] The verb וַיָּבֹא, "came in," is sg., focusing on Judah, versus the pl. וַיִּפְּלוּ, "they threw themselves [to the ground]"; Hamilton remarks, "The emphasis in this verse is not so much on the return of the brothers to Egypt as on the return of one brother—Judah" *(Genesis Chapters 18–50,* 564).

[355] Waltke, *Genesis,* 561.

[356] *IBHS* §18.3, "How can we justify ourselves!" (exclamatory use of מַה).

[357] This is true in context, but the vague confession leaves the possibility of other crimes too, including against Tamar, Bilhah, and Dinah (Shechemites; *Gen. Rab.* 92.9).

The occurrence of *māṣā'* ("to find") is a play on the discovery of the cup in Benjamin's bag ("who was found *[māṣā']* to have the cup," v. 16b; cf. *māṣā'* also in vv. 8,9,10,12,17).[358] He accepts what appears to be the inevitable punishment that he himself had recommended. The language underscores the collective guilt of the ten brothers ("we . . . we ourselves"), distinguishing themselves from Benjamin ("and the one . . ."). Sadly, Benjamin is an innocent bystander caught up in the crime of his siblings. (On the meaning of "guilt" *['āwôn],* see vol. 1A, p. 276; also comments on 15:16).

JUDAH ACCEPTS HIS PUNISHMENT (44:17–34).   After the Egyptian declares his judgment (v. 17), Judah initiates the longest speech in Genesis. He pleads for Jacob's life by explaining how the imprisonment of Benjamin would result in the old man's death (vv. 18–32). He concludes dramatically by offering himself to the master in place of Benjamin (vv. 33–34).

Joseph Announces the Punishment (44:17).   **44:17**   Joseph, however, pretends magnanimity when he protests that justice demands only an accounting for the boy (v. 17). Now the brothers face the "moment of truth" when they can either abandon their brother or save him. The contrast in outcome is heightened in the text, lit., "But as for you [pl.], go up in peace to your father" (v. 17).[359] Yet the offer of leniency for the brothers meant exactly what they would not do—face their father once again without their brother (cp. Reuben's sentiment, 37:30).

Judah Pleads for Jacob (44:18–32).   **44:18**   Judah again steps forward (*nāgaš*, "to approach," cf. 43:19), taking the lead (v. 18). On Judah's final answer to Joseph's leniency, Longacre observes that Judah's "counterploy . . . is an attempt to placate Joseph by wholesale capitulation . . . . is deferential to the point of groveling."[360] With good reason Judah shows special deference to Joseph, exceeding that shown toward the steward (cf. 43:20). The master had power over them equal to Pharaoh himself (lit., "like you like Pharaoh"). Judah may have risked impudence by his request (cf. Esth 4:11); thus he employs proper decorum by referring to himself in the third person when he seeks permission to speak ("let your servant speak"). "Do not be angry" *('al yiḥar 'appĕkā)* is the language of a subordinate beseeching God's or another's patience (e.g., 18:30; 31:35; Exod 32:22; Judg 6:39).

44:19–20   Judah reviews the first visit in which Joseph learned through questioning the brothers about their aged father Jacob and youngest brother Benjamin. This recounting (vv. 19–23) is the fourth version of their first visit, indicating the centrality of that episode (cf. 42:9–20,29–34; 43:2–14). In this account Judah reports that Joseph had initiated the questioning (cp. 43:7), but

---

[358] Hamilton, *Genesis Chapters 18–50*, 566.

[359] וְאַתֶּם עֲלוּ לְשָׁלוֹם אֶל־אֲבִיכֶם, the *wāw* disjunctive (contrastive), initiates the clause.

[360] Longacre, *Joseph*, 195–96.

he delicately omits the charge of spying that had dominated that interview (42:9,11,14,16; cp. also 42:30–34). Judah especially appeals to the sympathies of the master. "Aged father" (v. 20) is actually taken from Joseph's second inquiry (43:27), but "a young son born to him in his old age" is Judah's addition. The narrator describes Joseph's favored status similarly ("born to him in his old age," 37:3), but here Judah embellishes the youth of Benjamin by the construction "young son." Judah chooses the word *yeled* ("son," NIV), which may convey the tender sense of "child" (e.g., 21:8; 33:14; 37:20), thus "a little child of *his* old age" (NASB; "child," NRSV, HCSB, NAB, NLT; *paidion*, LXX). The construction also differs from the common expression "young son, youngest son," resulting in the translation "the son born to him in his old age *is young*."[361] Both the feeble age of Jacob and the youth of Benjamin call attention to their vulnerability. Judah elaborates on the sorrowful condition of the father. His favorite son was dead, and Benjamin was the sole survivor of their mother. Moreover, Judah underscores the tragedy by adding, "and his father loves him" (cf. 37:3). That Judah admits Joseph "is dead" makes explicit what is only euphemistically said before ("one is no more," 42:13,32). His candor here and his empathy for Jacob prove a remarkable change in the moral fiber of Judah and the brothers. Rather than resist the special love that Jacob has for Benjamin, he appeals to it as reason for mercy.

44:21–23 The linchpin of the test has been Joseph's demand for the appearance of Benjamin (42:15,20,34; 43:3,5,7), and Judah adds vividness in this version of the stipulation by "so I can see him myself," lit., "so that I may set my eyes on him" (v. 21). "Bring him down to me" (*hôriduhû ʾēlāy*, v. 21) ironically echoes the lament of Jacob, "You will bring my gray head down" (*wĕhôradtem ʾet śêbātî*, 42:38; 44:29). Judah reports a factor new to the first visit. The brothers immediately counter that Joseph's request would mean their father's death (v. 22). Their rejoinder begins with the negative "cannot" (*lōʾ yûkal*) followed by the gentler term "the boy" (*hannaʿar*, v. 22). But Joseph vehemently insisted, and Judah nuances the master's stern warning by featuring the boy's youth, further designed to create pity: "Unless your youngest brother . . . you will not see [Joseph's] face again" (v. 23; cf. 43:3,5).

44:24–26 After recalling the first visit to Egypt, Judah tells of the report to Jacob in Canaan (vv. 24–29). Referring to Jacob as "your servant my father" (vv. 24,27,30) continues the respectful tone toward Joseph but adds Judah's personal concern for Jacob (cf. vv. 32,34).[362] A significant omission in his account is the disheartening discovery of the returned silver and Jacob's

---

[361] I.e., the "adjectival present perfective," *IBHS* §30.5.3c; also Hamilton, *Genesis Chapters 18–50*, 567; and Wenham, *Genesis 16–50*, 415. The typical construction is the adjectives הַזָּקֵן (42:13,15,20,22,32,34; 43:29; 44:2,23,26; 48:19) or זְקֻנִים (9:24; 27:15,42; 1 Sam 16:11), but in 44:20 וְיֶלֶד זְקֻנִים the perfect verb, focuses more attention on the subject.

[362] Hb. MSS, SP, LXX, Syr. (see *BHS*) harmonize the text by אָבִינוּ, "our father," as in vv. 13,31.

harsh refusal to release Benjamin (42:35–38). He focuses on Jacob's compliance, though he is quick to point out that it meant jeopardizing his health and life. Verse 25 reports verbatim Jacob's instruction to return to Egypt for more food (43:2). The brothers refuse, except Benjamin returns with them (v. 26). Their answer possesses parallel elements for emphasis: "We cannot go down//we cannot see"[363] and "Only if our youngest brother is with us//unless our youngest brother is with us."[364]

44:27–29 Verses 27–29 give an account of Jacob's fear at losing the boy. Judah preserves the pathos of Jacob's avowal. He has compassion for his father as he gives the account of Jacob's sorrowful words, personalizing their relationship by "my father" (v. 27; also vv. 24,30,32,34) rather than "our father" (42:13,32; 43:28; 44:25,31). Jacob's statement is exclusionary, referring to Rachel as "my wife" and referring to Joseph and Benjamin as his "two sons." Joseph again is nameless, "one of them went away" (v. 28; cf. 42:13,32). "Torn to pieces" (v. 28) brings to mind Jacob's heartrending interpretation of his son's bloodstained robe (37:33). Judah's rendition includes the adverb *ʾak* ("surely"), which emphasizes the unexpected outcome of Joseph's travel.[365] Jacob kept the image of the torn robe in his mind's eye for twenty-two years. That Judah quotes the pitiable reaction to Joseph's death vividly impresses the extent of their father's grievous loss.[366] This is the first time that Joseph hears how his father learned of his death and his reaction to the news. That he "had not seen *[rāʾâ]* him since" (v. 28) reflects his one dying wish, "I will go and see *[rāʾâ]* him before I die" (48:11). Judah presents Jacob's final words (v. 29) as a collage of his rebuffs to the thought of releasing Benjamin (42:4,36,38). (On "to the grave [*šěʾôl,* Sheol]," see 37:35; 42:38; 44:29,31.) "If you take this one from me *[mēʿîm pānay]* too" (v. 29) may be a play on Joseph's warning "you will not see my face" (*pānay,* 43:3,5; 44:23,26); "from me," lit., "from my face," suggests that Benjamin must be seized from his father's "face" to be received before Joseph's "face" (cf. "so I can see him myself," 44:21).

44:30–32 Judah comes to the finale of his appeal in these verses, continuing his sympathy for his father (vv. 30–31). But also he admits his own personal calamity if the boy does not return (vv. 32–34). Judah again personalizes the situation, "When I go back . . . my father" (v. 30; cf. v. 32[367]). He reiterates the passion that his father has for the boy, intensified by the death of Joseph. "If the boy is not *[ʾênennû]* with us" (v. 30) contains a disquieting echo of Joseph, "who is no more" (*ʾênennû,* 42:13,32,36). The father and son

---

[363] לֹא נוּכַל לָרֶדֶת//לֹא נוּכַל לִרְאוֹת.

[364] אִם־יֵשׁ אָחִינוּ הַקָּטֹן אִתָּנוּ//וְאָחִינוּ הַקָּטֹן אֵינֶנּוּ אִתָּנוּ.

[365] *IBHS* §39.3.5d, n. 95.

[366] Humphreys, *Joseph and His Family,* 47.

[367] SP אָבִיו, "his father," harmonizes the pronoun with third person "servant."

have one heartbeat. "Bound up" *(qāšar)* means "tied up with" (e.g., 38:28; Deut 6:8; Josh 2:21) and metaphorically describes indissoluble love (1 Sam 18:1) or change in one's essential character (Prov 22:15). Judah predicts that his father's forewarning that he will die at the loss of Benjamin ("the boy isn't there"[368]) will surely come true and thus that the brothers will indeed have brought down his "gray head . . . to the grave in sorrow" (v. 31; 42:38). Judah next recalls his own personal liability, summing up his individual guarantee made to his father (v. 32; 43:9). The proviso, "If I do not bring him back *['ăbî'ennû]* to you" (v. 32) contains the similar sounding "my father" *('ăbî* [2x]), which produces a sound play.

Judah Offers Himself for Benjamin (44:33–34).   **44:33–34**   Judah concludes by proposing a substitution—his life for the boy's release (v. 33). Here is the moral high point of Judah's career. The request contains the polite verbiage of a subordinate's pleas for mercy (v. 33a). "In place of" *(taḥat)* translates the same term in 22:13, which describes the ram offered "instead of *[taḥat]* his son." Last, Judah explains (*kî*, "for") why he makes this desperate offer: he cannot (*pen*, "No!"[369]) return without Benjamin and see his father suffer (v. 34). Here, in emotional overload, he forgets formality (omitting "your servant," "my lord") and headlong makes his final objection.[370] "Misery" (*raʿ*, v. 34) is the same term used by Jacob when he describes to Pharaoh his troubled life ("difficult," 47:9). Once before Judah witnessed how the crushing news of Joseph's loss indelibly altered his father's spirit (37:34–35). Now he would rather suffer the remainder of his days as a slave than bear the blame of his father's dying grief.

7. Joseph Reveals His Identity (45:1–28)

"Now, finally, after such a long climb, the narrative has reached the climax."[371] The voice of this chapter realizes what the narrator and the reader have known from the outset, beginning in chap. 37 through the cryptic dreams of young Joseph. Our knowledge of what Joseph, the brothers, and Jacob underwent to come to this point of unveiling fuels the emotive power of this chapter. This sigh of "at last" is coupled with the incomparable expressiveness of the chapter. Delitzsch remarked, "Every word is as it were bathed in tears of sympathy, in the heart's blood of love, in the wine of rapture."[372]

---

[368] SP, LXX have אִתָּנוּ, "with us," as in v. 30 (v. 26[2x]), but the MT has the sharper expression כִּי־אֵין הַנָּעַר, "that the boy is not."

[369] On the clause introduced by פֶּן see GKC §152w: "I cannot see the misery . . ."; or "I fear to see . . ." (NRSV).

[370] Longacre, *Joseph*, 197.

[371] Gunkel, *Genesis*, 436.

[372] Delitzsch, *A New Commentary on Genesis*, 2.332.

What the dreams did not make known was that grace, love, and forgiveness—not submission enforced by power—achieved the benevolent outcome of the ruler over his subjects. The estranged "men" become Joseph's "brothers" again. That "his brothers talked with him" (v. 15), when before the brothers could not speak kindly to him (37:4), portrays the mending of the family fracture. Yet it is not Joseph who initiates the reconciliation. Remarkably, it is Judah's moving speech of self-sacrifice, of his love for his father and family (4:18–34), that incites Joseph to move the family beyond its pain of the past to a new beginning. As at the first of the story (chap. 37), Jacob and his relationship to his sons is front and center. The reappearing utterance "my father" (*'ābî*) by Joseph in his speeches (45:3,9,13[2x]) recalls Judah's speech based on this same relationship (*'ābî,* 44:24,27,30,32,34[2x]). Ironically, the first time Joseph spoke "my father" is when he declared he forgot Jacob ("all my father's household," 41:51). His son Manasseh (meaning "forget") would prove to be a reminder of God's inexplicable grace in the lives of Jacob's family members. He does not dwell on himself, but he immediately asks, "Is my father still living?" (v. 3). Only after the twice-repeated directive to "bring down" Jacob quickly (vv. 9,13) does Joseph permit his full attention to turn toward Benjamin and the others (vv. 14–15). After this the narrative returns to the subject of Jacob's descent by the intervention of Pharaoh when he formally extends the invitation to Joseph's family ("your father") to settle in Egypt (vv. 16–20). Here the narrative brings together two trajectories, the family story and the nation's story. The two are one and the same, implying that the events of Jacob's troubled family have a historic role. That the foreign king would give assistance to Jacob brings to mind the patriarchal promise of blessing for those who bless Abraham's family (27:29; cf. 12:3). The Hebrews were not interlopers but honored guests.

If the author were to speak only at the family and national levels, however, the reader may miss the overarching message that the narrative has addressed primarily by hint and innuendo. So as to ensure that the reader captures the purpose of his account, the author permits Joseph to voice his theology of disclosure. The author P. Éluard once remarked, "Another world exists and it is in this one."[373] Our author knows the other world, and he reveals it through the trappings of this world of sight and sound. Joseph discloses his knowledge to his brothers, and his brothers disclose their knowledge to their father. Joseph reveals his identity (45:3,4), relinquishing his power over his brothers by bringing them to the same level of knowledge that he and the reader have known. But this human disclosure can create only fear, astonishment, and possibly recrimination (vv. 3,5,24,26). What makes possible the alleviation of

---

[373] Quoted by J. Miles, "You Won't Believe Who I Just Saw!" *The New York Times Book Review* (May 11, 2003): 12.

anger, guilt, and vengeance is the "other world." Joseph has gained an insight that breaks the cycle of hatred and retaliation. He perceives a broader setting and meaning that transcends their behavior and feelings. "God sent me ahead of you" (45:5,7) dwarfs their part in this family trial, whether they are victims or victimizers (or both). How did Joseph come by this insight? We are not told directly. The answer resides in Joseph's earlier acknowledgment to Pharaoh that the future is known only to God, who alone interprets the significance of dreams (41:16). We must assume that Joseph came to this insight through divine revelation. This revelation came by the inspiration of the sage (cf. Ps 105:22), not through a direct revelation. By Joseph's recollection of his life's course in the context of his father's God, who made promises of presence and provision, he observed the higher purpose of saving others. There is not much ground for recriminations when our offenses are placed in the rising tides of God's gracious purposes (and his example, cf. Rom 8:29; Heb 2:11–12,17). Does this mean that Joseph indifferently dismissed their crimes? No, he will forever be "the one you sold into Egypt" (v. 4), but God's greater purpose of preserving life supplants any thought of revenge (cf. 50:19). Luther explains the lesson of our passage for the believer. That Joseph interprets the "death" of Jacob's favored son and the tortured existence of the patriarch as life and salvation demonstrates a faith in the power of God to transform human misery into wonder and salvation. Joseph's God is mysterious. Luther remarked on this passage: "I cannot escape or draw away that horrible mask which hides the face of God, but I must stay in darkness and in exceedingly dark mist until a new light shines forth. Thus, Jacob and Joseph had a very sad sight set before their eyes and hearts. But with that great joy God shows them His back! [Exod 33:22–23] Thus the affliction and ruin of their descendants in Egypt were most wretched, but the outcome of the trial was most glorious."[374] The challenge for the believer is to accept the efficacy of God's thoughts (Isa 55:8–9), waiting by faith for the dawning of the new day. We can be assured that in whatever path the Lord directs us, it will lead us to the same place, his heavenly household.

COMPOSITION. The old source school followed, for example, by Gunkel characterized the chapter as a comprehensive mixture from the Yahwist (J) and Elohist (E) documents. G. von Rad concluded that chap. 45 "reveals obvious traces of a combination of sources."[375] The chief indicators of two parallel accounts are the doublets. Joseph discloses himself twice (vv. 3a,4b); the brothers are twice instructed to tell Jacob of Joseph's importance in Egypt (vv. 9,13); Joseph and Pharaoh each give the command two times to return with Jacob to Egypt (vv. 9,13,18,19); Pharaoh does not know of Joseph's relations and where

---

[374] *LW* 8.33.
[375] von Rad, *Genesis,* 397.

they are to live (v. 1; cf. 46:31–47:3), but in contrast he knows of them in a different version (vv. 2,16,17,18); and last, they have carts for all their possessions (vv. 19,27; 46:5) and only donkeys (vv. 17,23) for a few of their holdings (v. 20).[376] Nevertheless, source advocates admit that the contents are difficult to separate confidently into their respective strands. Speiser suggested vv. 1–15,28 are J and vv. 16–27 are E, but he remarked, "It has seemed best to omit the usual source markers in the translation."[377] Redford denies that chap. 45 shows the classic formulation of two parallel documents, but neither does the text indicate a literary unity. On the criteria of the dual figures playing the "good brother" (Reuben/Judah) and the names of the father (Jacob/Israel), he divided chap. 45 into the original Reuben version (vv. 1–4,16–27) and two stages of embellishments by the redactors of the Judah additions (vv. 4–9,11–13,28) and Genesis as a whole (v. 10).[378] But these criteria have been rejected by many as unreliable for discerning sources or layers.

Since chap. 45 completes the account of the second journey (chaps. 42–45), it is best to view the author of the chapter as that of chaps. 42–44, who was aware of the family tension and the "Joseph in Egypt" narratives. Concerning the doublets noted by source critics, Coats finds that "none of the pairs can be defined as self-contradictory or even real doublets."[379] These doublets are better explained along exegetical lines rather than source division. On the double revelation of Joseph's identity (vv. 3–4), for example, Carr believes the repetition is a natural artifice, emphasizing the surprise and importance of the event for the account.[380]

We conclude that there is no compelling evidence that requires us to discern multiple sources or layers in the chapter. The unity of the text can be supported and sustained.

STRUCTURE. The boundaries of this chapter are Joseph's disclosure to his brothers (vv. 1–2) and Jacob's acceptance of Joseph's identity and survival (v. 28). Jacob's final exclamation, "I'm convinced! My son Joseph is still alive *['ôd . . . ḥay]*" (v. 28), brings the chapter full circle by resounding Joseph's disclosure, "I am Joseph! Is my father still living *[hā'ôd . . . ḥay]*?" (v. 3). The chapter consists of two parts (vv. 1–15,16–28). The first part continues the interaction between Joseph and the brothers at the Egyptian's house (44:14–34). After the first revelation of Joseph's identity (v. 1), his expression of "weeping" (*běkî,* v. 2; *bākâ,* vv. 14–15) marks the boundaries of the scene (vv. 2,14–15). The centerpiece of the first scene (vv. 3–13) consists of three segments. First, vv. 3–4 describe Joseph's disclosure, "I am Joseph" (v. 3) and "I am Joseph your brother" (v. 4). Second, vv. 5–8 entail his interpreta-

---

[376] Gunkel, *Genesis,* 434–35; von Rad, *Genesis,* 397.

[377] Speiser, *Genesis,* 341.

[378] Redford, *Joseph,* 170

[379] Coats, *Joseph,* 67.

[380] Carr, *Reading the Fractures of Genesis,* 285–86, but even he finds a potential P addition in the mention of the carts (vv. 19–21; pp. 106, n. 56, 271).

tion of his bondage, which is bounded by the word "now" (ʿattâ, NIV "now, so then," vv. 5,8). Third, vv. 9–13 recount instructions for the brothers concerning Jacob (vv. 9–13), which are bounded by the exhortations "hurry and go up" (māhēr ʿălâ; NIV "hurry back," v. 9) and "hurry and bring down" (māhēr yārad; NIV "bring . . . down . . . quickly," v. 13).

The second part (vv. 16–28) repeats the basic structure of the first scene. There are the identity of Joseph's brothers (v. 16), Pharaoh's instructions for the return trip (vv. 17–20), Joseph's reassurances (vv. 21–24), and the brothers' report to Jacob (vv. 25–28). The second part continues the setting in Egypt (vv. 1–24) but concludes in Canaan (vv. 25–28). The expression "the house of Pharaoh" (v. 16) picks up where "the house of Pharaoh" overheard Joseph's wailing (vv. 1–2). Pharaoh's speech adds to the benevolent promises of Joseph toward the brothers (vv. 17–20), bordered by mention of their geographical trek, to "the land of Canaan" (v. 17) and back to "the land of Egypt" (NIV "Egypt," v. 20). "Do this" (zōʾt ʿăśû, v. 17) introduces Pharaoh's instructions, and "So the sons of Israel did this [wayyaʿăśû kēn, v. 21]" introduces the next paragraph (vv. 21–24), in which Joseph observes the king's instructions by providing gifts for their journey. That Joseph "sent" them echoes his father's assignment undertaken by young Joseph initially (37:13–14), which resulted in the brothers' anger directed toward him. Thus the paragraph ends with the terse remark by Joseph, "Don't quarrel on the way!" (v. 24b), probably reflecting his continued concern for Benjamin. The final paragraph reports the brothers' return ("they went up," wayyaʿălû, v. 25), concluding the second journey begun in 43:15 ("they . . . down," wayyērĕdû). Their announcement, "Joseph is still alive!" (v. 26), initiates their report; and Jacob's acceptance, "My son Joseph is still alive" (v. 28), echoes their words.

(1) Joseph Makes Himself Known (45:1–15)

[1]Then Joseph could no longer control himself before all his attendants, and he cried out, "Have everyone leave my presence!" So there was no one with Joseph when he made himself known to his brothers. [2]And he wept so loudly that the Egyptians heard him, and Pharaoh's household heard about it.

[3]Joseph said to his brothers, "I am Joseph! Is my father still living?" But his brothers were not able to answer him, because they were terrified at his presence.

[4]Then Joseph said to his brothers, "Come close to me." When they had done so, he said, "I am your brother Joseph, the one you sold into Egypt! [5]And now, do not be distressed and do not be angry with yourselves for selling me here, because it was to save lives that God sent me ahead of you. [6]For two years now there has been famine in the land, and for the next five years there will not be plowing and reaping. [7]But God sent me ahead of you to preserve for you a remnant on earth and to save your lives by a great deliverance.

[8]"So then, it was not you who sent me here, but God. He made me father to Pharaoh, lord of his entire household and ruler of all Egypt. [9]Now hurry back to

my father and say to him, 'This is what your son Joseph says: God has made me lord of all Egypt. Come down to me; don't delay. ¹⁰You shall live in the region of Goshen and be near me—you, your children and grandchildren, your flocks and herds, and all you have. ¹¹I will provide for you there, because five years of famine are still to come. Otherwise you and your household and all who belong to you will become destitute.'

¹²"You can see for yourselves, and so can my brother Benjamin, that it is really I who am speaking to you. ¹³Tell my father about all the honor accorded me in Egypt and about everything you have seen. And bring my father down here quickly."

¹⁴Then he threw his arms around his brother Benjamin and wept, and Benjamin embraced him, weeping. ¹⁵And he kissed all his brothers and wept over them. Afterward his brothers talked with him.

The emotions of Judah's plea (44:18–34) spill over in the subsequent description of the frenzied events surrounding Joseph's self-revelation (vv. 1–15). "Weeping" envelops (vv. 1–2; 14–15) the disclosure (vv. 3–13), bringing the brothers who were formerly uninformed into line with Joseph's and the reader's knowledge. In a moment the Egyptian taskmaster transformed himself before their eyes into their brother, who was "resurrected" from the dead.

JOSEPH WEEPS FOR HIS BROTHERS (45:1–2).   **45:1–2**   Judah's penitent plea for his father brought uncontrollable tears to Joseph ("control himself," *hith.* from ʾāpaq, v. 1). Although he was able to maintain his emotions previously ("controlling himself," *hith.* from ʾāpaq, 43:31), he cannot sustain the ruse any longer. "But when he heard the heroic self-sacrifice of Judah (44:33) and realized all the affection of that proposal—a proposal for which he was totally unprepared—he was completely unmanned; he felt himself forced to bring this painful trial to an end."[381] Joseph demands privacy for this personal moment, clearing the room of his servants. Perhaps he did so in part because it was unwise for the master of the land to let his emotions run free. The exact Hebrew, rendered "Have everyone leave my presence!" (v. 1), is repeated in 2 Sam 13:9 but there leads to family mischief (Amnon and Tamar). Despite Joseph's precautions, however, his wailing was too piercing, so that "the Egyptians" (his attendants?) and "Pharaoh's household" took notice of it (v. 2). Evidently, the court's attendants reported the event to Pharaoh himself (v. 16). The departure of the Egyptians provides for a private family reunion, signaling that Joseph is again their Hebrew brother. Now, as the narrative moves to its most telling episode, the narrator who commonly refers to the brothers as "the men" (43:33; 9x in chaps. 43–44) speaks again of "his brothers" (vv. 1,3,4,15,24) and "Joseph's brothers" (v. 16).[382]

---

[381] R. Jamieson, "Genesis–Deuteronomy," in *A Commentary Critical, Experimental and Practical on the Old and New Testaments,* 6 vols. (Grand Rapids: Eerdmans, 1945 [1868–1870]), 1.254.

[382] Longacre, *Joseph,* 149.

JOSEPH COMFORTS HIS BROTHERS (45:3–13).   Joseph's speech is the
longest and the central interest of the chapter. Especially vv. 5–8 captures the
author's broader view of Joseph's life. That "God sent" Joseph (vv. 5,7) and
"not you" (i.e., the brothers, v. 8) is the theological persuasion of the author.
The promise of a bountiful life in "Goshen" is the foreshadowing of the
nation Israel in Egypt, where it multiplies and eventually emerges under the
direction of Moses (vv. 10–11; Exod 8:22; 9:26; cf. 47:27 with Exod 1:7).
The historical perspective and theological perspective merge in the speech of
Joseph, forecasting what is narrated in the Exodus account (chaps. 1–12).

Identifies Himself (45:3–4).   **45:3–4**   Joseph's declaration was simple
and raw, "I am Joseph!" (v. 3). His focus is neither on himself nor on the
injustice that he suffered. Rather, his father is his foremost concern, reflecting
his true attitude toward Jacob. This is the third time that Joseph asks about his
father's well-being (43:23,27) but here without the mask of his secret. His
emotions are freed to rush forward. "'My father . . . my father' [is] from first
(v. 3) to last [v. 13b] Joseph's dominating concern in this speech."[383] This
consistent worry over his father's condition reveals Joseph's compassion for
Jacob during the time of trial. At this point, the hearts of Joseph and Judah
(44:33) have become one toward their father and family. Yet the brothers are
too traumatized to answer. "Terrified" (*niph.,* from *bāhal*) here indicates the
panic that seizes a person when surprised by obvious doom (e.g., Judg 40:21;
Ps 45:5[6]).[384] The same term describes the visible alarm Saul exhibits at the
apparition of Samuel (1 Sam 28:21). The brothers are staggered "at his presence," not knowing what to make of this bizarre claim. Westermann commented that Joseph must "bridge the gap (between them)," for the brothers
remain unaware that "the scene changes from an event in Pharaoh's court to
an event in the family of Jacob."[385] So as to convince them he told them to
"come close," presumably to see him better, and he pointed to the event that
he and the brothers alone would have known, "the one you sold into Egypt"
(v. 4). That the command "come close" *(nāgaš)* is plural indicates all the
brothers are intended. Judah took the first step toward reconciliation by
approaching ("went up," *nāgaš)* Joseph with pleas for mercy (44:18). Now
Joseph facilitates the next step toward resolution of the long-standing breach.

Interprets the Divine Purpose (45:5–8).   **45:5–7**   "And now" *(wĕʿattâ)*
in vv. 5 and 8 forms the boundaries. Geography is important to Joseph;
"here" *(hēnnâ),* referring to Egypt, occurs three times in his speeches (vv.
5,8,13; also 42:15). He first eases the men's fears by urging them to look at
what happened to them in terms of God's purpose (v. 5). "Distressed" *(ʿāṣab)*

---

[383] Wenham, *Genesis 16–50,* 429.
[384] *IBHS* §23.3c, "They *became terrified* at his presence"; the *niph.* נִבְהֲל֖וּ is ingressive-stative
with a reflexive nuance.
[385] Westermann, *Genesis 37–50,* 142.

and "be angry" *(ḥārâ)* appear in tandem twice more, describing fierce personal displeasure (34:7 [Dinah's brothers]; 1 Sam 20:34). Joseph explains that the purpose of God, "to save lives" *(lĕmiḥyâ),* surpassed the malicious intent of the brothers. The word *miḥyâ* ("preservation of life"; cf. 2 Chr 4:12) is a metonymy, referring to the grain Joseph provided, sustaining existence in the midst of the famine (cf. "food," Judg 17:10). Joseph may be a Noah figure whom God called to "keep alive" *(lĕhaḥăyōt,* "preserve," 6:19–20) the animal world.[386] Joseph continues that the famine will endure five more years, undoubtedly dooming them to death if not for God's intercession (v. 6).

"But God sent me ahead of you" (v. 7a) reiterates Joseph's interpretation of his travail in Egypt. The term "sent" *(šālaḥ)* often describes someone dispatching a person on a mission (e.g., 28:5; Neh 6:5), as when God sends forth his prophets (e.g., Deut 34:11; Jer 19:14). Unknown to Joseph and his brothers, God had sent Joseph on a divine undertaking. The corresponding "human" perspective is Joseph's mission to find his brothers *(šālaḥ,* 37:13–14) when the anonymous "man" set him on the right course (37:14–17). Joseph gives two reasons for his travail: "to preserve . . . a remnant" and "to save your lives by a great deliverance" (v. 7b; NIV text note, "save you as a great band of survivors"; cf. NRSV). The language "remnant *[šĕ'ērît]* on earth" is unique, but the word group *š-'-r,* meaning "to be left over, remnant," is widely used in the Old Testament to indicate a nation's surviving residue (e.g., Jer 25:20; Amos 9:12), especially the survivors of Israel's purging (e.g., 2 Kgs 19:4//Isa 37:4; 2 Chr 36:20). The term *šĕ'ērît* in this context indicates two nuances. (1) The word refers to future "descendants" (2 Sam 14:7); the plural pronoun "for you" *(lākem)* shows that the descendants in mind are the offspring of Jacob's twelve sons. (2) The description "on the earth" sets the descendants in a wider context; Joseph viewed the families of Jacob as the surviving "remnant" of the world's populations (cp. the Noah imagery, v. 5). If the Jacobites fail to survive, the whole of the human family will die without salvation hope. Joseph's role as savior of the world from starvation typifies the salvation of the nations that the promises call for (e.g., 12:3). That Genesis is oriented toward the future also explains the importance of *šĕ'ērît* as "remnant" here, which anticipates the preservation and return of Jacob's descendants to Canaan (Gen 15:16–18; Deut 26:5–9; cf. Isa 11:11,16 *[š-'-r]).* The "remnant" theology of the prophets *(š-'-r,* e.g, Isa 4:3; Mic 2:12; Jer 31:7; Zech 8:11–12) envisions a future day of Israel's restoration to the land in an era of blessing (e.g., Amos 9:11–15; Mic 7:12; Zech 10:10). The early church applied the notion of a future restoration by means of a believing remnant to the spread of the gospel among the Gentiles (e.g., Acts 15:13–18; Rom 9:27; 11:5). The second purpose was to achieve a "deliverance" *(pĕlêṭâ),* that is, an

---

[386] Wenham, *Genesis 16–50,* 428.

"escape" from the famine (cf. Exod 10:5; 2 Sam 15:14). The two words "remnant" and "deliverance, escape" often occur together, sometimes in parallel (e.g., Isa 15:9; 37:32), describing survival in the face of annihilation (e.g., Esau, Gen 32:9; Isa 10:20).

45:8 Last, Joseph emphatically denies that the brothers were (ultimately) responsible for his enslavement; rather, it was God's doing for a purpose that transcended their jealousy (v. 8). The Hebrew construction strongly contrasts the responsibility of the two parties.[387] Joseph is not absolving the brothers by this declaration; their guilt is real (42:21; 44:16), but he looks to the higher purpose (cf. Jas 1:2–3,12; 1 Pet 1:6–7). Joseph confirms explicitly here what the author artfully inferred from the dream sequences (chaps. 37; 39–41), namely, that God superintended the rise of Joseph. He explains the esteem of his position by three descriptions. "Father to Pharaoh" indicates that he is a special advisor to the king (e.g., "a counselor to Pharaoh," NLT), as a father blesses and instructs his son (cf. 47:7). The term "father" may be used to refer to a person held in high regard, even by a king (e.g., 2 Kgs 6:21; cf. Judg 17:10; 18:19; 2 Kgs 5:13; Isa 22:1). "Lord *['ādôn]* of his entire household" means Joseph has total control of state affairs and treasury (cf. 41:40–44,55; 42:6). As "ruler *[mōšēl]* of all Egypt" (lit., "all the land of Egypt"), Joseph's commands are incontrovertible (cf. "lord *['ādôn]* over the land," 42:30,33). Judah expresses it best when he said, "You are equal to Pharaoh himself," lit., "for like you like Pharaoh" (44:18). The populace of Egypt submits itself to Joseph as "lord" (*'ādôn,* 47:18,25). As to lofty positions held by a Semite, there is ample evidence in Egypt of "Asiatics" achieving influential roles at court, including vizier.[388] Scholars dispute the Egyptian background of the titles in the Joseph narrative.[389] Hoffmeier rightly shows a cautious viewpoint: "I do not believe the present evidence allows us to come to any firm conclusions about the Egyptian equivalents of Joseph's titles, but the general impression is that the offices or rank mentioned in Genesis do reflect genuine Egyptian institutions."[390]

Instructs His Brothers (45:9–13). **45:9–11** Joseph instructs the brothers to deliver his message to Jacob, imploring his father to come down at once. The words "hurry . . . quickly" (both from *māhar*) in vv. 9 and 13 form the literary borders of his instructions. "Don't delay" reinforces his plea for expediency (v. 9b). What he once thought was impossible, to be reunited with

---

[387] לֹא־אַתֶּם שְׁלַחְתֶּם אֹתִי lit., "not you (pl.), you (pl.) sent me," heads the sentence, followed by כִּי הָאֱלֹהִים, "but God," with the adversative use of כִּי (GKC §163a).

[388] Kitchen, "Genesis 12–50 in the Near Eastern World," 86–88, lists many examples from several Egyptian periods; cf. Hoffmeier also at our comments on 41:38–40.

[389] Scholars mention, for example, the Egyptian title for Pharaoh who is called "father of (the) god," but a direct connection with Joseph's position as "father to Pharaoh" is uncertain, since the title referred to priest or king and Joseph is neither (Redford, *Joseph,* 191; Sarna, *Genesis,* 309).

[390] Hoffmeier, *Israel in Egypt,* 93.

his family, can now be realized immediately. The message bears signs of authentication (e.g., "your son Joseph," "my brother Benjamin," v. 12) so as to answer what would have been a natural skepticism on Jacob's part (v. 9). Also his appeal is personal in mood, for example, "come down to me" (v. 9b), "be near me" (v. 10), and "I will provide" (v. 11). He also directs the message personally to Jacob, using the second person singular ("you/your") repeatedly in vv. 9–11. He begins his message with the same thought of God's providence ("God has made me . . .," v. 9; cf. vv. 7–8). By stating the divine component in this fantastic turn of events, Joseph is acknowledging that only God can accomplish so great an outcome.

He further says that a settlement in the "region of Goshen" will be readied for Jacob, his household, and all his possessions (v. 10). Such an assembly requires significant territory and grazing land, which this region could sustain. The geographical location of Egyptian "Goshen" (not the Goshen of Joshua and Judah, Josh 10:41; 11:16; 15:51) remains disputed,[391] but the location likely was in the eastern Delta area (in the area of Wadi Tumilat). This area generally meets the requirements of Goshen as described in Genesis and Exodus. "Goshen" regularly occurs in the phrase "the land of Goshen" (*'eres gōšen*)[392] and is interchangeable with "the land of Rameses" (47:11), which suggests that "Goshen" was a region.[393] That Goshen has not yet been formally assigned by Pharaoh (46:34; 47:1–6) shows Joseph's advanced planning and expectations. During the famine, grazing would have been impossible; therefore Joseph clarifies that he "will provide" (v. 11, *pilpel,* from *kûl;* cf. 47:12; 50:21; 2 Sam 19:34) the sustenance needed. Not only must Joseph supply food for the remaining five years of the famine, he argues that it is imperative for Jacob to migrate to Egypt. Otherwise, the inevitable conclusion would mean poverty ("become destitute," from *yāraš*)—all would be lost—and the promissory blessing would be in jeopardy. Joseph knows that Jacob is in no hurry to leave (cp. 46:3), as he once had left the land of his father Isaac (27:43–44). Joseph, like Judah before him, must convince Jacob that the good of the family resides in faraway Egypt.

---

[391] For "Goshen" the LXX regularly reads "Gesem"; here the Gk. is ἐν γῇ Γεσεμ Ἀραβίας, "in the land of Gesem of Arabia" (also 46:34), in which "Arabia" identifies one of the nomes (provinces) in Egypt. See W. A. Ward, "Goshen," *ABD* 2.1076–77 and Wevers, *Notes on the Greek Text,* 761.

[392] 45:10; 46:28,29; 46:34; 47:1,4,6,27; 50:8; Exod 8:18; 9:26; an exception is Gen 46:28 in which "Goshen" occurs by itself but followed by "land of Goshen."

[393] That "Goshen" was also possibly a city, cf. 46:28,29 LXX, καθ᾽ Ἡρώων πόλιν εἰς γῆν Ραμεσση, "to the city of Heroon (=Pithom?) in the land of Ramesse" (46:28). See Wevers, *Notes on the Greek Text,* 787 and M. W. Chavalas and M. R. Adamthwaite, "Archaeological Light on the Old Testament," in *The Face of Old Testament Studies: A Survey of Contemporary Approaches* (Grand Rapids: Baker/Apollos, 1999), 73–74. On the problematic identity of the store cities "Pithom and Rameses" (Exod 1:11), see Hoffmeier, *Israel in Egypt,* 116–22.

45:12–13 The brothers, however, are not messengers only but also witnesses ("you," pl.; vv. 12–13). They are to testify to Joseph's identity (v. 12) and to his grandeur in Egypt (v. 13; cf. "eyes," "see," vv. 12–13). Rashi suggested that the specific naming of "Benjamin" was Joseph's way of counting all the brothers as equals. Since he favors Benjamin later (v. 22), the mention of him here probably reflects Joseph's continued interest in their shared bloodline. Benjamin would serve as the more effective witness in Jacob's eyes. Yet after twenty-two years and presumably the "Egyptianizing" of Joseph, it is unclear how the brothers, especially Benjamin, who must have been quite young, could "see" that he was their long-lost brother. "It is really I who am speaking to you," lit., "[it is] my [own] mouth that speaks to you" (v. 12; cf. Isa 52:6), motivated the Jewish targumists to include that he spoke Hebrew directly. Thus, by not using an interpreter (cf. 42:23), Joseph's native Hebrew proved that he was a member of Abraham's descendants.[394]

Joseph instructs them to recount to Jacob "all the honor" ascribed to him (v. 13). "Honor" translates *kābôd,* which means "wealth" in 31:1, but here Joseph probably has in mind his esteemed position as lord over Egypt (cf. 1 Kgs 3:13; 1 Chr 29:28). His upright conduct and dependence on God reaped the honor that the Lord graciously bestowed, illustrating the observation of the Hebrew sage: "Humility and the fear of the Lord bring wealth and honor and life" (Prov 22:4). His final instruction reiterates the first directive: "And bring down *[hôradtem]* my father here quickly" (v. 13b; cf. v. 9). The same word echoes Jacob's forewarning of his descent into the grave (Sheol) at the loss of Benjamin ("you will bring my gray head down," 42:38; 44:29).[395]

JOSEPH WEEPS WITH BENJAMIN (42:14–15). **42:14–15** Calvin remarked, "When [Joseph] reflects that their wickedness had been overruled by the wonderful and unwonted goodness of God, forgetting the injury received, he kindly embraces the men whose dishonor God had covered with his grace."[396] The description of their reunion distinguishes Benjamin again from his brothers. Benjamin reciprocates Joseph's act of affection by weeping (v. 14), whereas the other brothers are said to have "talked with him" (v. 15b). Typical public expressions of reunion included hugging the neck, kisses, and weeping (e.g., 29:11; 33:4; 46:29; Exod 4:27; 2 Sam 20:9; Song 8:1). That they only "talked with him" may reflect caution, showing that (unlike Benjamin) they are unprepared to accept his benevolence as genuine. At the death of their father, they reveal fear of Joseph's true feelings (50:15–18). Neverthe-

---

[394] Another Jewish means of tying Joseph to Abraham's identity was that after they drew "close" (v. 4), he exposed himself, and the brothers could "see" his circumcision (*Gen. Rab.* 93.10; *Tanḥ.* 5; Rashi).

[395] Hamilton, *Genesis Chapters 18–50,* 581.

[396] Calvin, *Comm.* 2.380.

less, the author is satisfied to show that reconciliation has occurred, indicated by the reversal of the early sign of family schism: "They hated him and could not speak a kind word to him" (37:4; cf. 45:3b).

(2) Jacob Hears about Joseph (45:16–28)

[16]When the news reached Pharaoh's palace that Joseph's brothers had come, Pharaoh and all his officials were pleased. [17]Pharaoh said to Joseph, "Tell your brothers, 'Do this: Load your animals and return to the land of Canaan, [18]and bring your father and your families back to me. I will give you the best of the land of Egypt and you can enjoy the fat of the land.'

[19]"You are also directed to tell them, 'Do this: Take some carts from Egypt for your children and your wives, and get your father and come. [20]Never mind about your belongings, because the best of all Egypt will be yours.'"

[21]So the sons of Israel did this. Joseph gave them carts, as Pharaoh had commanded, and he also gave them provisions for their journey. [22]To each of them he gave new clothing, but to Benjamin he gave three hundred shekels of silver and five sets of clothes. [23]And this is what he sent to his father: ten donkeys loaded with the best things of Egypt, and ten female donkeys loaded with grain and bread and other provisions for his journey. [24]Then he sent his brothers away, and as they were leaving he said to them, "Don't quarrel on the way!"

[25]So they went up out of Egypt and came to their father Jacob in the land of Canaan. [26]They told him, "Joseph is still alive! In fact, he is ruler of all Egypt." Jacob was stunned; he did not believe them. [27]But when they told him everything Joseph had said to them, and when he saw the carts Joseph had sent to carry him back, the spirit of their father Jacob revived. [28]And Israel said, "I'm convinced! My son Joseph is still alive. I will go and see him before I die."

After the private reunion in Joseph's house (vv. 1–15; cf. 44:14), the setting expands to include the Egyptian king and his house once again (v. 16). Joseph mediates the instructions of Pharaoh to the brothers (vv. 17–24), and the brothers carry the message of Joseph to their father (vv. 25–28). That Joseph conveys Pharaoh's message and that Joseph exceeds the offer of the king demonstrates his esteemed position, "father to Pharaoh" (v. 8). The additional use of the word "father," referencing Jacob in vv. 16–28, reflects the interface of these two elements that have shaped the moment, Joseph's Egyptian and Hebrew connections. Joseph is the ideal arbitrator between the ancient enemies of Israel and Egypt. Also in this segment the motif of plenty supplants the motif of famine. The reversal signals the new era of reconciliation among the parties. The family's restoration is a microcosm of the healing of the nations. Egypt's former disposition toward Abraham, when he was expelled (12:10–20), is inverted by Pharaoh's invitation for Jacob's sons to take up residence in Egypt.

JOSEPH RECEIVES PHARAOH'S INSTRUCTIONS (45:16–20). **45:16–20** That Pharaoh and his officials "were pleased" *(yāṭab)* at hearing of Joseph's reconciliation to his family probably reflects their indebtedness to Joseph (v. 16). The same term ("seemed good") describes Pharaoh's and the courtiers' satisfaction at Joseph's plan to preserve the kingdom (41:37). The intentional echo of 41:37 shows that the exceptional concessions made by the king to this Asiatic immigration are due to Pharaoh's high regard for Joseph. Verse 16 possesses the typical introduction to direct speech (lē'mōr, "saying"); thus the report's verbiage is quoted, "Joseph's brothers have come" (cf., e.g., AV, NLT, NRSV, NJPS, HCSB).[397] The use of the Hebrew name "Joseph" by the court (as in 41:55) rather than his Egyptian name[398] indicates that the court has always kept in mind the Semitic origin of Egypt's "savior."

Pharaoh directs Joseph to inform his brothers that they are to return to Canaan and retrieve their father and families (vv. 17–18). That the king says that they are to return "to me" echoes the personal appeals made by Joseph (vv. 4,9). Pharaoh's promise to provide "the best [ṭûb] of the land" is central to his speech, occurring twice (vv. 18,20; cf. 47:6,11; Isa 1:9; Ezra 9:12); in the second case Pharaoh heightens his generosity by adding "all" Egypt (v. 20). Joseph will send ahead a foretaste of this promise (v. 23). The "best" is described as the "fat of the land" (v. 18), an expression found only here; "fat" (ḥēleb) refers to the finest products of harvest (cf. Num 18:12; Deut 32:14; Ps 81:16[17]). The king's kindness includes Egyptian carts for easier travel, and he instructs them to travel light, easing their minds that all that is desirable for a new settlement is awaiting them (vv. 19–20). Mention of their "children" and "wives" conveyed the idea of a permanent settlement. It is the fulfilling of Judah's plea to escort Benjamin to Egypt, "so that we and you and our children may live and not die" (43:8; cf. 46:5; 47:12). The return with Benjamin forecasts the return of all the Jacobites at Judah's direction (46:28).

JOSEPH PROVIDES FOR JACOB'S JOURNEY (45:21–24). **45:21–24** The narrator recounts the compliance of Joseph and the brothers to the king's instructions, showcasing the favor that Pharaoh bestows on the Hebrews (v. 21). Joseph exceeds Pharaoh's directive by outfitting them with extravagant gifts of clothing (v. 22). He is not inhibited by threat of jealousy, since he liberally presents to Benjamin added wealth (cf. 23:15–16). The "five sets" of garments correspond to the five servings of food for Benjamin (43:34) and the five remaining years of famine (45:6,11). Joseph demonstrates that he is fully capable of performing the guarantees made to the family throughout the long famine. The term "clothing" (śĕmālōt) corresponds to the word for clothing torn by Jacob (37:34) and by the brothers (44:13). By this Joseph is declaring that the period of mourning is over. For

---

[397] Others prefer indirect speech, "that Joseph's brothers . . ." (e.g., NIV, NAB, NJB, REB, NASB).
[398] Observed by Hamilton, *Genesis Chapters 18–50*, 584.

his father's journey, Joseph equips him in lavish style, including ten male and ten female donkeys bearing "the best things of Egypt" (v. 23). The abundance of grain and foodstuffs reinforces the image of plenty that Joseph wants to illustrate (e.g., 41:49), so as to corroborate his message. Indeed, the appearance of the "carts" has the desired effect on the old man (v. 27). "Ten" especially recalls the first pilgrimage of the ten brothers whose goal was to purchase grain (42:3). Ironically, the much sought after food would be theirs in abundance by the most unexpected means and after the surprising ordeal of a great trial (42:25).

The final directive concerns their behavior on their journey home: "Don't quarrel *[rāgaz]* on the way!" (v. 24). What precisely is meant by this admonition is uncertain, although most commentators and EVs understand the idea as fraternal strife. The verbal root *rāgaz*[399] appears in Genesis only this once. The essential idea behind its varied meanings in the Old Testament (verb, 41x) is "shaking, trembling," as when the ground trembles during an earthquake (e.g., 1 Sam 14:15; Amos 8:8).[400] It describes shaking that manifests fear (e.g., Exod 15:14) or angry rage (e.g., Prov 29:9). Gunkel adopted the former idea, translating "Have no fear," by which Joseph means to alleviate their anxiety of retaliation.[401] This understanding finds some support from the reaction of the brothers at the death of their father, who fear Joseph's revenge (50:15–19). A popular rabbinic interpretation believed Joseph warns them not to take undue risks on their journey or abandon the journey out of fear of hazards (e.g., *Gen. Rab.* 94.2; Rashbam, Ramban).[402] Alternatively, the common rabbinic and Christian interpretation believed Joseph cautioned them against sibling rankling brought on by recriminations among the brothers (e.g., LXX *[orgizesthe]*; targums, esp. *Tg. Ps-J.;* Rashi, Ibn Janah.; Ephrem the Syrian; Chrysostom). This interpretation makes sense in light of the brothers' former behavior (cf. 42:21–22). Joseph realizes that "stirring up anger produces strife" (Prov 30:33). Joseph avoids laying blame on them for his tribulation, choosing to focus on the good that will emerge. He urges them to do the same (cf. Eph 4:32; Col 3:13). Joseph's desire is that the brothers make haste to retrieve his father (vv. 9,13), not impeded by any distraction. Additionally, he may have worried that the brothers in the midst of strife would choose to back out. In delivering the news of Joseph's survival, it will be necessary for them to confess their part in the "death" of their brother. By eliminating Benjamin, the brothers could continue their cover-up.

---

[399] אַל־תִּרְגְּזוּ is *qal* jussive, 2 mpl.

[400] M. van Pelt and W. C. Kaiser, "רגז," *NIDOTTE* 3.1045–46.

[401] Gunkel, *Genesis,* 438.

[402] For the ancient authorities listed here and below, see Sarna, *Genesis,* 370, n. 7 and *ACCS* 2.294–95.

THE BROTHERS INFORM JACOB (45:25–28). **45:25–28** The geographical references "Egypt" and "Canaan" in this paragraph are important to later Israel. Their brothers' travel prefigures the migration experienced by their descendants (v. 25). The narrator omitting their confession to Jacob suggests that the brothers followed the counsel of not condemning one another (v. 24).[403] The news of Joseph is too remarkable for Jacob to accept. Not only that he is alive, which is difficult enough to accept, but that he is ruler over Egypt is too far-fetched to contemplate. His sons underscore the incredulous report by the emphatic construction "In fact" (*kî*, "even, indeed," v. 26). They tersely report the announcement, lit., "still Joseph [is] alive" (v. 26). That they declare "he is ruler *[mōšēl]* of all Egypt" repeats Joseph's own self-declaration (v. 8) and renews our memory of the brothers' incredulity of Joseph's dream: "Will you actually rule *[māšōl timšōl]* us?" (37:8). But Jacob, the reader was told, "kept the matter in mind" (37:11). The amazing news leaves him emotionally depleted, lit., "[Jacob's] heart grew numb/weak" *(pûg, v. 26b;* NIV "stunned"; cf. Pss 38:8[9]; 77:2[3]; Hab 1:4). He has good reason (*kî*, "for he did not believe them") not to trust his sons ("believe," *hiph. he'ĕmîn,* cf. Judg 11:20; Jer 40:14).[404] Once Jacob hears details of Joseph's unveiling and takes in the Egyptian carts, his mental outlook is revitalized (v. 27; on "spirit," *rûaḥ,* cf. comments on 41:8). Chrysostom remarked, "This old greybeard, all stooped and bent, suddenly takes on new vigor and heart" (*Hom. on Genesis* 65.3).[405] That Jacob is here called "Israel" corresponds to the author's interest in the descent of the nation where Jacob's descendants will rise to prominence. "I'm convinced" renders the lone Hebrew word *rab,* meaning "much, many," that is, "enough [said]!" (v. 28). His exclamation, "My son Joseph is still alive," reverberates the brothers' announcement (v. 26), indicating his full acceptance of their claims concerning Joseph. "My son" *(bĕnî)* repeats his reference to Joseph for whom he wept: "In mourning will I go down to the grave to my son" *(bĕnî,* 37:35; cf. 42:38). God benevolently grants the patriarch the opportunity to "see" his son in this lifetime! The poignancy of the moment recalls Abraham's love for Isaac, "my son," whom God also preserved (22:7–8,12). Now he has no hesitation to take the long trek to Egypt, for he must see his boy. "I will go and see him"[406] expresses his deep-seated desire to see Joseph for himself (cf. "must go," NRSV, NJB, NAB).

---

[403] von Rad, *Genesis,* 409.

[404] The contrast of Jacob's skepticism at the report contrasts with Abraham's faith at hearing God's word (15:6), illustrating that the difference lies in the reliability of the source.

[405] *ACCS* 2.298.

[406] *IBHS* §34.5.1, cohortatives of resolve.

8. Migration of Jacob's Family to Egypt (46:1–27)

"My son Joseph is still alive" (45:28) reflects Jacob's inspiration to leave Canaan (vv. 1,5), but he can go no further than Beersheba, at the southern edge of the land, before he offers up sacrifices of worship (v. 1). Jacob knows that his future is in Canaan, the land promised him and his progeny (28:15; 31:13; 35:12). This is God's word to his fathers, but the course of events indicates that Egypt is also his destiny. The patriarchs knew the life of an alien (*gēr* from *gûr;* cf. 12:10; 20:1; 21:23; 23:4; 35:27). He answers the entreaty of God, "Here I am," (46:2), as had his grandfather Abraham (22:1,11; cf. Moses, Exod 3:4). Once before Jacob answered the clarion call of God's angel, who enabled him to prosper despite the hardship of Laban's demands (31:1). Jacob now travels in faith and pauses at the homesite of his father (Beersheba) to offer his worship of thanksgiving and show his submission to God's will. The deity is the "God of your father" (v. 3) who ensured that Isaac flourished though he was in the land of the Philistines (26:13). It too was a time of famine, and Isaac lived under the regime of a foreign ruler (26:1). Jacob's migration to Egypt is the objective of the three journeys recorded in the Joseph story. All that has preceded prepared the way for this celebrated event, one that was remembered for generations (Exod 1:6–8; Ps 105:17; Acts 7:9–18; Heb 11:22).

Jacob's worship is an act of declaration and petition. Like the transjordan tribes that erected an altar to claim their part in the covenant made to Israel (Josh 22:28), Jacob offers sacrifices while in the land to symbolize his continued place in the covenant made to his fathers. Jacob's worship precedes the revelatory speech of God. Jacob announced his intention, "I will go and see [Joseph]" (45:28b), but it will be to no avail if he is not accompanied by the Lord. The renewed promise of divine presence ("I will go down to Egypt with you," 46:4) is God's message to the patriarch, encouraging him to leave the land once again ("Do not be afraid . . .," v. 3). Why is Jacob afraid? Egypt represents danger, a threat to the patriarchal promises, beginning with Abraham (e.g., 12:10–13:1). The promise to Jacob recalls the ominous prediction given to Abraham, also in a night vision: "Your descendants will be strangers *[gēr]* in a country not their own, and they will be enslaved and mistreated four hundred years" (15:13).[407] God forewarned Isaac to avoid Egypt (26:2), and Jacob took this to heart. He cannot risk his family in Egypt, unless the Lord leads him.

In Egypt, Jacob and his sons will "become the great nation of God's promises."[408] The expanded list of descendants (vv. 8–27) is another example in

---

[407] "Do not be afraid to go down to Egypt because of the slavery which I decreed with Abraham" *(Tg. Ps.–J.).*

[408] Thompson, *The Origin Tradition,* 128.

Genesis of the theme of numerous descendants. The inclusion of the genealogy fits naturally in the passage, expressing in concrete terms the theophany's message: "I will make you into a great nation there" (v. 3). The list of Jacob's descendants who sojourn to Egypt anticipates the exodus of the nation when the Hebrews have grown to a throng threatening their host nation (Exod 1:7–11). The exodus narrative begins with a back reference to our passage (Exod 1:1–4). God assures the patriarch that the promise of old will be realized. Israel will prosper and the nation will remain intact, despite its subservience to Egypt. His promises are true and truly kept (Pss 105:19; 33:4; Phil 1:6). Calvin commented: "For it was, by no means, according to human apprehension, a likely method of propagating the Church, . . . that he (Jacob), being increased with a moderate family, should be shut up in a corner of Egypt, and that there an incredible number of people should spring up from this dry fountain."[409]

COMPOSITION. Many scholars have contended that the end of the Joseph story occurred with the denouement in chap. 45, explaining that chaps. 46–50 were secondarily inserted (anticlimax) to tie the Joseph story to the broader Jacob/Israel history (but see Coats below). Traditional documentarians maintained a mixture of the chief narrative sources the Yahwist (J) and the Elohist (E) in chap. 46, as was their standard approach to the patriarchal stories as a whole. J was predominate, but E was the redactor's preference for describing the theophany report (notice, e.g., "God" *[Elohim]*, 46:1b–5a). Traditionally, critics believed the J parallel to this Jacob theophany is the revelation given Isaac (chap. 26). Since critics presumed that P was responsible for the genealogies of Genesis, it was common to attribute vv. 5–6 to the priestly narrative, which introduces the name list of P (vv. 8–27). The genealogy shows signs, however, of having its own history before being appropriated by P.[410] Among those who departed from the standard source analysis of the Joseph section was Redford, who assigned 46:1–27 to his priestly "Genesis editor" of the exile. He argued, for example, that vv. 1–4 exhibit substantial difference with the Joseph story (chap. 45).[411] Westermann, who advocated the essential unity of the Joseph story (chaps. 37; 39–45), assigned most of chaps. 46–50 as an insertion, consisting of J and P. He detected remnants of the Joseph story in 46:5b,28–47:6,11–12,27a, describing the audience with Pharaoh and the settlement of Jacob in Egypt. Verses 1–5a exhibit a "fixed sequence," thus a unified narrative, which is well known from the itineraries in chaps. 12–36. Verses 6–27 are due to P, including the expansion in vv. 8–27.[412] Humphreys also viewed vv. 1–4 and 6–27 as additions to the original Joseph story, which were designed to integrate the Joseph story and the wider Jacob/Israel narratives.[413]

---

[409] Calvin, *Comm.,* 392.
[410] Gunkel, *Genesis,* 438, 466.
[411] Redford, *Genesis,* 18–22.
[412] Westermann, *Genesis 37–50,* 153–54, 158.
[413] Humphreys, *Joseph and His Family,* 196, 206–7.

Coats differed from others by extending the original Joseph pericope beyond chap. 45. He reasoned that 46:1–47:27 is the proper conclusion (anticlimax), although he alleged that there are obvious secondary parts (46:1b–4; vv. 8–27; 47:13–26). Like others, Coats observed that the theophany report (vv. 1b–4) is out of character for the Joseph story, reminiscent of earlier patriarchal narratives. He perpetuated the old assessment, however, when he tentatively assigned its original provenance to the Elohist. The genealogical list he deemed a redactional item that was integrated into the Joseph story by connecting it to the itinerary framework in vv. 5–7. The modifications of the stereotypical pattern in naming the Rachel descendants point to an adaptation of an originally independent list to the Joseph story (contrast Exod 1:2–4). The return to the itinerary report occurs in vv. 28–30.[414]

We find, however, that chap. 46 exhibits a much more unified text than has been thought. Coats rightly shows that chap. 46 presumes the account in chap. 45, continuing the basic narrative plot of Jacob's migration to Egypt under the supervision of Joseph and with the permission of Pharaoh. Wenham observed that chaps. 46–47 narrate the third journey of Jacob's family to Egypt but it differs from the former two journeys by three additions that lay emphasis on the move: the theophany justifying the journey (46:1–4), the names of those who migrated (vv. 8–27), and the famine in Egypt (47:13–26).[415] This new orientation is the logical extension of the former chapters of the Joseph narrative. Although Coats recognized that vv. 1b–4 differed in style and content from the typical Joseph narratives, he admitted that the "report bears directly on the Joseph story plot . . . it is not contradictory . . . it provides an early heuristic tool for interpreting the Joseph story."[416] The juxtaposition of vv. 1–7 ("I will go down to Egypt with you," v. 4a) and vv. 8–27 makes further sense when it is remembered that both pertain to accompanying Jacob to Egypt—the divine and human companions of Jacob.[417] Since the passage belongs to its narrative environment, it begs the question if its style is sufficiently different to require a different and later hand than the author of the Joseph narrative. The passage shows similarities with the putative J passages recognized by source critics (e.g., 12:1–3; 15:13–16; 26:23–25; 31:11–18),[418] implying that the author of 46:1–4 is the same. Moreover, the segregation of the theophany report underestimates the importance of Jacob's history for telling the Joseph account. The whole of the Joseph narrative pertains to the father Jacob, especially the speeches of Judah and Joseph in the prior chaps. 44–45. Even in chaps. 39–41 (Joseph in Egypt), the importance of Joseph's father and family heritage shows itself. The author of 46:1–4 gives an important continuation of how the Joseph episode impacted Jacob and his descendants. "Jacob's odyssey began at Beersheba (28:10); it fittingly concludes with a revelation at the same place."[419] That the author casts the

[414] Coats, *From Canaan to Egypt*, 48–51 and *Genesis*, 296–98.
[415] Wenham, *Genesis 16–50*, 437.
[416] Coats, *From Canaan to Egypt*, 49.
[417] Hamilton, *Genesis Chapters 18–50*, 599.
[418] Wenham, *Genesis 16–50*, 440.
[419] Sarna, *Genesis*, 312.

account in the traditional language and theology of the patriarchal narratives only shows that the author knows the former patriarchal narratives and makes use of them in showing that the Jacob itinerary has the same promissory importance as his movements in Paddan Aram and Canaan. It was commonplace for the patriarchs on their journeys, including Jacob, to offer worship to God (e.g., 28:10–22; 35:9–15). There can be little doubt that the list of names in vv. 8–27 is the integration, and probably an adaptation, of an imported source. Naming individuals, however, who made up the traveling party in Jacob's movements has a precedent (chap. 35:21–27; cf. also Esau, 36:2–8). That the author of the Joseph section would have the same interest in the future of the sons as the Jacob section, in which their births and names are recorded (chaps. 29–30), encourages us to view a continuity in the two narrative sections of Jacob and Joseph. The exact words of the heading, "These are the names of the sons of Israel," appear in Exod 1:1, indicating that the Genesis list anticipates the Exodus account of national Israel.

STRUCTURE.   The structure of this unit consists of two obvious parts, an itinerary describing Jacob's migration to Egypt (vv. 1–7) and an ancestral list, naming and accounting for those who resided in Egypt (vv. 8–27). The frame for the entire narrative is marked by the recurring idea of Jacob's movement from Beersheba ("So Israel set out with all that was his," v. 1) to the accounting of all who were in Egypt with him ("the members of Jacob's family, which went to Egypt," v. 27).

The itinerary possesses the typical language describing the patriarchs' journeys (see comments below). The place names "Beersheba" (2x), "Egypt," (4x), and "Canaan" (1x) provide the itinerary's trek. The literary margins of this first part describe the departure and arrival of Jacob: "So Israel set out . . ." (v. 1a), and "he took with him to Egypt . . ." (v. 7). The boundaries are more obvious in the Hebrew text, in which the clause ". . . he took with him to Egypt" in point of fact ends the first part (v. 7b). Verses 1–7 fall naturally into two segments. Verses 1–4 describe the intermediate stop at Beersheba, where the patriarch worships through sacrifice and receives a night theophany in which God repeats the promises of presence and land. Verses 5–7 continue and complete the itinerary. Although v. 1 broadly refers to all of his possessions, vv. 5–7 focus on his accompanying descendants, which is transitional to the specifics of the genealogy (vv. 8–27).

The genealogical list has a highly structured arrangement. The list as a genealogical record is in a segmented form, naming more than one descendant per generation (e.g., 10:1–32; cf. vol. 1A, pp. 298, 431–32). "These are the names of the sons of Israel . . . who went to Egypt" is the introductory heading to the whole (v. 8; cf. the same heading in Exod 1:1). A striking inclusion in the count is the deceased sons of Judah, Er and Onan, who obviously did not migrate (v. 12). Verse 27b provides the conclusion, "the members of Jacob's family, which went to Egypt." The four subdivisions name the descendants according to Jacob's wives: Leah (vv. 8b–15) and her servant

Zilpah (vv. 16–18); Rachel (vv. 19–22) and her servant Bilhah (vv. 23–25). The colophons of each subdivision identify the mother's status in the family and the number of children she bore (vv. 15,18,22,25). Zilpah and Bilhah have less status, since they were only handmaidens. Each handmaiden bore half the number of children as their mistress: Leah, thirty-three; Zilpah, sixteen; Rachel, fourteen; Bilhah, seven, giving a count of seventy. Variation from the fixed form in the Rachel group, as the favored wife, especially distinguished her and her sons. The final colophon to the whole genealogical list provides cumulative information: "Sixty-six" persons accompanied Jacob to Egypt, and "seventy" total family members resided in Egypt (vv. 26–27).

The stylized expression "the sons of . . ." *(běnê)* introduces the descendants' names (vv. 9,10,11,12[2x],13,14,16,17,21,23,24). The exception is the listing of Joseph's two sons in v. 20 (". . . were born to Joseph," *wayyiwwālēd lĕyôsēp*), which draws attention to their birth in Egypt. The colophons of the Leah and Rachel branches (vv. 15,22) are similar with two exceptions: the mention of Leah's group born in "Paddan Aram" and the mention of "sons and daughters" to accommodate the naming of Dinah.[420] In the Zilpah group there is the inclusion of "Serah," who is the "sister" of the four brothers born to Asher (v. 17). An important variation in the identities of the wives is the inclusion "wife" when describing Rachel (v. 19), implying the special esteem she held in her husband's eyes. The colophons for the Zilpah (v. 18) and Bilhah (v. 25) groups are the same, excepting the number of children each bore.

(1) Jacob's Descent into Egypt (46:1–7)

[1]So Israel set out with all that was his, and when he reached Beersheba, he offered sacrifices to the God of his father Isaac.

[2]And God spoke to Israel in a vision at night and said, "Jacob! Jacob!"

"Here I am," he replied.

[3]"I am God, the God of your father," he said. "Do not be afraid to go down to Egypt, for I will make you into a great nation there. [4]I will go down to Egypt with you, and I will surely bring you back again. And Joseph's own hand will close your eyes."

[5]Then Jacob left Beersheba, and Israel's sons took their father Jacob and their children and their wives in the carts that Pharaoh had sent to transport him. [6]They also took with them their livestock and the possessions they had acquired in Canaan, and Jacob and all his offspring went to Egypt. [7]He took with him to Egypt his sons and grandsons and his daughters and granddaughters—all his offspring.

Verse 1 describes the journey to Beersheba, the ancestral home of Isaac, where the patriarch worshiped "the God of his father." Verses 2–4 recount a

---

[420] Another variation in v. 22 (MT) is the passive form יֻלַּד, "who were born [to Jacob]" (cf. יֻלַּד, v. 27); Hb. MSS, SP, Syr. harmonize v. 22 with v. 15 by יָלְדָה, "she bore."

night vision, reminiscent of his revelatory dreams (28:12–15; 31:11–12), in which God instructs him to continue on to Egypt. Verses 5–7 narrate the obedience of Jacob, giving attention to the transport of "all his offspring" (vv. 6–7).

SACRIFICE AND VISION AT BEERSHEBA (46:1–4). **46:1** "Israel" heads off from Hebron (37:14) for Egypt by way of Beersheba, which formerly was the principal settlement of Isaac his father (26:23–33; 28:10). The importance of the name "Israel" is its national implications for the move of the family to Egypt. Interplay of the two names of the patriarch in vv. 2,5,8 exhibits his role as the eponymous ancestor of the nation. The origin of the name "Israel" (cf. comments on 32:28[29]) reinforces the promises and provision of God as the patriarch faces another challenge. "Beersheba" was important to Jacob's career as the place from which he departed for Haran. (On the meaning of the name "Beersheba," cf. comments on 21:31). It was on this first journey leaving his homeland that he first met with God in a dream and received the promise of a safe return (28:10–22). Jacob needs the same reassurance before he carries on, departing the land once again. Jacob illustrates the maxim, "Keep close to God, and then you need fear nothing" (Joseph Eliot). The telling of the event recalls the earlier theophanies made to Isaac at Beersheba (26:23–24) and to Jacob in Haran (31:11–13). The passage especially remembers Jacob's religious heritage by identification of the deity as "the God of his father Isaac" (v. 1; cf. v. 3). That he offered sacrifice to his father's God is an echo of Jacob's sacrifice to "the Fear of his father Isaac" (31:53), for these are the only two passages in which "sacrifice" *(z-r-ḥ)* is specifically stated in Genesis. Jacob recognizes the necessity of spiritual preparation for his journey to Egypt; he depends on the Lord to escort him as he had in his journeys to Haran and back (28:10–22; 31:3,13). Isaac built an altar at Beersheba (26:25), which Jacob may have refurbished for this occasion. Abraham too had called upon the name of the Lord at Beersheba (21:33).

46:2–3 This nocturnal event is the only place in Genesis that the mode is specifically said to be a "vision" *(mar᾽ōt*[421]*)* versus a night dream (20:3; 31:24; 40:5; 41:11) or simply an appearance in the night (26:24). Allusions to Abraham are also present, although subtle. The dual summons of God, "Jacob, Jacob . . ." (v. 2), recalls the test of Abraham at Moriah (22:11) and anticipates the call of Moses (Exod 3:4). "Here I am" was also Jacob's response to the call of the angel of God (31:11). Whereas the theophany at Bethel emphasized the location of the experience (31:11), here the text identifies the deity in terms of family heritage. The deity's self-identification in the vision ("I am God, the God of your father," v. 3) recalls again the night theophany made to Isaac at Beersheba, where the similar phrase appears (26:24; cf. Exod 3:6). "Do not be afraid" (v. 3) was also divine encourage-

---

[421] The plural indicates intensity, i.e., "[an important] *vision*," GKC §124e.

ment given to Isaac (26:24; cf. Abraham 15:1; also Isa 43:5; 2 Thess 3:3), and in both passages the promise of numerous descendants follows. Here, however, the phrase "make you into a great nation" is the exact terminology in the Abraham corpus (12:2; 17:20; 18:18; 21:18), though the promise of "a community of nations" had been made already to Jacob (35:11). That Jacob might hesitate to depart for Egypt may be tied to the difficulty his grandfather experienced (12:10–13:1) and also the direct prohibition Isaac received (26:2). His twenty-year hiatus in the land of Haran also may have made him timid about leaving the land of his fathers. "His heart would cleave to Canaan, which was his native land by nature and his true home by promise."[422]

46:4 Thus God eases Jacob's concerns by his twofold promise in v. 4. God promises to accompany him in both his descent and his return. The language "I will go down . . . with you" is reminiscent of the pledge "I am with you" (28:15) made at Bethel (cf. Isaac at Beersheba, 26:24). The promise of return, "I will surely bring you back again" (v. 4), also corresponds to 28:15. The emphatic construction ("surely") qualifies the descent into Egypt, assuring Jacob that he will return "again."[423] The patriarchs' God is an "I will" God. "As God has said, 'I will live with them and walk among them, and I will be their God, and they will be my people'" (Lev 26:12; Jer 32:38; Ezek 37:27; cf. 2 Cor 6:16). Moreover, that the Lord ensures that Joseph himself would be at Jacob's deathbed meant that Joseph was indeed alive, that he would be with Jacob till his death, and that Jacob would have also returned to the land (albeit in his casket). The Genesis account narrates the fulfillment of these predictions (cf. 49:33–50:14).

JOURNEY TO EGYPT (46:5–7).   **46:5–7** The redundancies in vv. 5–7 accentuate that Jacob's entire household migrated to Egypt. Verse 5 describes the family from the perspective of the sons ("their father . . ."), and v. 7 details the same from the standpoint of Jacob ("his sons . . ."). The phrase "Israel's sons" (i.e., "the sons of Israel," *běnê yiśrāʾēl*) appears here in reference to the actual eponymous fathers of the twelve Hebrew tribes (v. 5; e.g., 42:5; 45:21; 46:8; 50:25(?); Exod 1:1; 28:9; 39:6; 1 Chr 2:1). It is the common designation for "Israelites," referring to the population of the nation (e.g., 32:32[33]; Exod 2:23). The individual "Jacob" and the national nuance of "Israel" appear together to indicate that the migration of Jacob is in effect the movement of the embryonic nation. "Then Jacob left" translates the root *qûm* ("to arise"), which often signals an itinerary (e.g., 22:3; 24:10; 31:17; Exod 24:13). Credit again is attributed to Pharaoh for the employment of the carts (cf. 45:19,21,27), which were unusual for common travel (e.g., Num

---

[422] Delitzsch, *A New Commentary on Genesis*, 2.336.

[423] Imperfect + infinitive absolute, וְאָנֹכִי אַעַלְךָ גַם־עָלֹה, "I, myself, will also surely bring you up (again)"; cf. *IBHS* §35.3.1f.

7:3; 1 Sam 6:7). Verse 5 uses the terminology of Pharaoh's speech in 45:19 when referring to the "children" and "wives." All, the narrator implies, is going according to plan. That the full number of their "possessions" *(rĕkûš)* follows shows that they view their migration as long-term (45:20; cf. 12:5; 31:18; 36:6). The text of vv. 6 and 7 repeats the idea of the Jacobites' complete descent, lit., "And Jacob and all his offspring with him went down to Egypt" (v. 6), and "all his offspring he brought with him to Egypt" (v. 7). The "offspring" includes both men and women down to the present, third generation, namely, "all his offspring" (v. 7). The vocabulary of vv. 6–7 occurs in the descriptions of Abraham's movements (12:20; 13:1,6; cf. 31:18). Jacob's descent bridges the brief descent of Abraham and the prolonged settlement of national Israel. The word "offspring" *(zeraʿ)* is reminiscent of the thematic promise of many descendants (e.g., 12:7; 26:4; 28:13–14; cf. 48:4). It appropriately is transitional to the genealogical list of Jacob's descendants to follow (vv. 8–27).

(2) Jacob's Descendants in Egypt (46:8–27)

⁸These are the names of the sons of Israel (Jacob and his descendants) who went to Egypt:

Reuben the firstborn of Jacob.
⁹The sons of Reuben:
    Hanoch, Pallu, Hezron and Carmi.
¹⁰The sons of Simeon:
    Jemuel, Jamin, Ohad, Jakin, Zohar and Shaul the son of a Canaanite woman.
¹¹The sons of Levi:
    Gershon, Kohath and Merari.
¹²The sons of Judah:
    Er, Onan, Shelah, Perez and Zerah (but Er and Onan had died in the land of Canaan).
The sons of Perez:
    Hezron and Hamul.
¹³The sons of Issachar:
    Tola, Puah, Jashub and Shimron.
¹⁴The sons of Zebulun:
    Sered, Elon and Jahleel.
¹⁵These were the sons Leah bore to Jacob in Paddan Aram, besides his daughter Dinah. These sons and daughters of his were thirty-three in all.

¹⁶The sons of Gad:
    Zephon, Haggi, Shuni, Ezbon, Eri, Arodi and Areli.
¹⁷The sons of Asher:
    Imnah, Ishvah, Ishvi and Beriah.
    Their sister was Serah.

The sons of Beriah: Heber and Malkiel.

[18]These were the children born to Jacob by Zilpah, whom Laban had given to his daughter Leah—sixteen in all.

[19]The sons of Jacob's wife Rachel:
Joseph and Benjamin. [20]In Egypt, Manasseh and Ephraim were born to Joseph by Asenath daughter of Potiphera, priest of On.
[21]The sons of Benjamin:
Bela, Beker, Ashbel, Gera, Naaman, Ehi, Rosh, Muppim, Huppim and Ard.
[22]These were the sons of Rachel who were born to Jacob—fourteen in all.

[23]The son of Dan:
Hushim.
[24]The sons of Naphtali:
Jahziel, Guni, Jezer and Shillem.
[25]These were the sons born to Jacob by Bilhah, whom Laban had given to his daughter Rachel—seven in all.

[26]All those who went to Egypt with Jacob—those who were his direct descendants, not counting his sons' wives—numbered sixty-six persons. [27]With the two sons who had been born to Joseph in Egypt, the members of Jacob's family, which went to Egypt, were seventy in all.

The genealogy shows the fulfilling of God's promises of numerous descendants (e.g., 12:2; 15:5; 17:6,16; 18:18; 22:17; 26:4,24; 28:14; 32:12[13]; 35:11; 46:3; 48:4,19). That they are located in Egypt may be disturbing, except for the prior theophany in which God promises the return of Jacob to Canaan and presumably his family's descendants eventually too. The later readers of the account who knew of the return could take encouragement that the Lord keeps his promise to the patriarch and his descendants. The genealogy consists of a title (v. 8a) and closing colophon (vv. 26–27). The children born to each wife of Jacob distinguish the branches of the family: Leah (vv. 8b–15), her servant Zilpah (vv. 16–18), Rachel (vv. 19–22), and her servant Bilhah (vv. 23–25). (On the structure of the genealogy, see the discussion above.) The importance of the list is reflected by the many parallels to Genesis (Exod 1:1–7; 6:14–16; Num 26:5–57; 1 Chr 2–8). Genesis and Exod 1:1–7 focus on persons, while the other lists recognize the clans that these forefathers produced (especially the census list in Num 26).

JACOB'S GENEALOGY (46:8a). **46:8a** The title, "these are the names of . . .," is common (e.g., 25:13; 36:10; Exod 6:16) and is tailored for the historical context, "who went to Egypt." The title underscores the dual names of the ancestor Israel/Jacob by means of a chiasmus: (A) "the sons of Israel" (B) "who went to Egypt" (A′) "Jacob and his sons." Exodus 1:1 repeats the heading, connecting the action of Jacob and the future history of the nation.

LEAH'S CHILDREN (46:8b–15). **46:8b–9** The first group names Leah's children (cf. 35:22b–26). Genealogies often distinguish the "firstborn" *(bĕkōr)* son (e.g., 10:15; 25:13; 36:15). Reuben is typically remembered in this manner (e.g., 35:23; Exod 6:14; Num 1:20; 26:5), despite his crime against his father (35:22; 1 Chr 5:1). On the meaning of the names of Jacob's twelve sons, see their naming in comments on 29:32–30:24; 35:18.

The four grandsons of Jacob by Reuben are Hanoch, Pallu, Hezron, and Carmi. These descendants are noted also in Exod 6:4; Num 26:5–6; and 1 Chr 5:3. On the significance of the name *Hanoch/Enoch,* see the descendants of Cain and Seth (vol. 1A, p. 285 [4:17–18; cf. 5:18–24]) and Abraham's Midianite descendant (see comments on 25:4). *Pallu (pallûʾ* from *plʾ,* "marvelous, wonderful"?) was the father of a clan (Num 26:5) and an ancestor of the inauspicious rebels Dathan and Abiram (Num 26:8–10). *Hezron (ḥeṣrôn)* also fathered a clan (Num 26:6; cf. Hezron of Judah, 46:12). *Carmi (karmî* from *kerem,* "vineyard"?) produced the Carmite clan (Num 26:6; on Carmi of Judah [1 Chr 4:1], the ancestor of the infamous Achan, cf. Josh 7:1,18; 1 Chr 2:7).

46:10 Simeon's sons numbered six offspring who each produced clans (Exod 6:15; Num 26:12–13), except possibly Ohad. The third son, *Ohad (ʾōhad),* is absent in Num 26:12 and 1 Chr 4:24, meaning no clan bears his name. Ohad's offspring may have been absorbed by another clan (cf. 1 Chr 23:11), or was numerically insignificant.[424] *Jemuel (yĕmûʾēl;* Exod 6:15), whose meaning is uncertain, is "Nemuel" *(nĕmûʾēl)* in Num 26:12; 1 Chr 4:24. *Jamin (yamîn),* meaning in Hebrew "right hand, right side [i.e., favored, lucky side], or south," also occurs for a Judahite descendant (1 Chr 2:27) and a Levite (Neh 8:7). *Jakin (yākîn),* also spelled Jachin in EVs, means "let him [God] establish" *(hiph.* from *kûn)*; the name also identifies a priestly clan (1 Chr 24:17; the person named in 1 Chr 9:10; Neh 11:10 is disputed) and one of the two temple pillars (1 Kgs 7:21; 2 Chr 3:17). *Zohar (ṣōhar)* is "Zerah" in Num 26:13 and 1 Chr 4:24. Zohar is the name of the father of Ephron the Hittite (23:8; 25:9) and of a Judahite (according to the *qĕrê* reading, 1 Chr 4:7). Simeon followed the objectionable practice of Judah by marrying a Canaanite who bore the last-listed son, *Shaul* (38:2; 1 Chr 2:3; cf. 28:1,6,8). On the name Shaul, see the Edomite king in comments on 36:37.

46:11 Levi bore three sons whose descendants made up the three Levitical families (Num 26:57) of Israel who cared for the sanctuary (e.g., Num 3:17–39; 1 Chr 6:1–30; 23:6). *Gershon (gēršôn)* produced two clans (e.g., Exod 6:17; Num 3:18,21). The progeny of *Kohath (qĕhāt),* the grandfather of Moses (Exod 6:20; Num 26:58–59), were four families (e.g., Exod 6:18; Num 3:19), and *Merari (mĕrārî* from *mrr,* "strong"[425]) produced two clans (e.g., Exod 6:19; Num 3:33).

---

[424] C. F. Mariottini, "Ohad," *ABD* 5.9.
[425] *HALOT* 2.639.

46:12 The author notes especially the prodigious offspring of Judah (also the Chronicler, 1 Chr 2:3–4:23). He produced five sons, three by his Canaanite wife, Shua (38:2–5; 1 Chr 2:3) and two by his daughter-in-law, Tamar (38:6,27–30; 1 Chr 2:4). On the meaning of *Er, Onan,* and *Shelah,* see 38:3–4. Er is the name of Judah's firstborn (38:3,6–7; Num 26:19; 1 Chr 2:3) and also the name of Judah's grandson by Shelah (1 Chr 4:21; also the name of Joseph's ancestor, Luke 3:28). Onan is Judah's second son (38:4,8,9; Num 26:19; 1 Chr 2:3). The text by inference reminds us of the ignominious deaths of these two sons who died prematurely in Canaan and unlike their brother, Shelah, left no clans (Num 26:19–20; cf. 1 Chr 2:3). Even they, nevertheless, are listed with these who migrated to Egypt.[426] Shelah, not to be confused with the father of Eber (10:24; 11:12–15), was the son withheld from Tamar (38:5,11,14,26; 1 Chr 2:3); he produced five sons, the Shelanites (Num 26:20; 1 Chr 4:21–23). On the meaning of *Perez* and *Zerah,* see comments on 36:13 and 38:29–30 (cf. also Achan, descendant of Zerah, Josh 7:1,18,24; 22:20; Neh 11:24). Perez and Zerah produced clans (Num 26:20; cf. 1 Chr 9:4; 27:3; Neh 11:4,6; on Zerah son of Reuel, cf. 36:13,17,33 and Zerah of Simeon, cf. Num 26:13). History shows that despite the sordid events involving Perez's conception, he became the ancestor of Israel's greatest king (David, Ruth 4:12,18) and in the line of Jesus (Matt 1:3; Luke 3:33). Here the two sons of Perez are listed, *Hezron (ḥeṣrôn)* and *Hamul (ḥāmûl,* "spared, pitied," from *ḥāmal;* also 1 Chr 2:5; 4:1; on Hezron, son of Reuben, cf. v. 9). Hezron fathered a Judahite clan (Num 26:21), and two locations in the territory of Judah bear the name (Josh 15:3,25). Hezron's descendants included important clans in Judah (1 Chr 2:9–41). He was a noted ancestor of King David (Ruth 4:18–19; 1 Chr 2:10–15) and in the genealogy of Jesus (Matt 1:3; Luke 3:33). Hamul also was the ancestor of a clan (Num 26:21); a variant is "Hammuel" *(ḥămmûʾēl),* meaning "God *[El]* protects" (cf. 1 Chr 4:26), in SP and Syr.[427]

46:13 The four sons of Issachar became heads of four clans (Num 26:23–25; 1 Chr 7:1). *Tola (tôlāʿ),* meaning "worm, scarlet, crimson," was the father of six sons whose families contributed numerous warriors in the time of David (1 Chr 7:2–5). The name also identifies the famous Hebrew judge (Judg 10:1). *Puah (pûʾâ,* SP, Syr.; *pûwwâ,* MT[428]) exhibits various Hebrew spellings *(pūwâ* [Num 26:23]; *pûʾâ* [1 Chr 7:1; cf. Judg 10:1]). The appellative also names the father of the Hebrew judge, Tola (Judg 10:1). The name *Jashub (yāšûb,* "may he [God] return,"[429] from *šûb,* "to return") occurs in the

---

[426] C. F. Mariottini, "Er," *ABD* 5.21.

[427] Id., "Hamul," *ABD* 3.43.

[428] The EVs following the MT have "Phuvah" (AV), "Puwah" (NASB), or "Puvah" (NJB, NRSV, HCSB).

[429] "May (Yahweh) turn (to us again)," Noth, *Personennamen,* 199 and J. A. Fager, "Jashub," *ABD* 3.648.

SP and LXX, as it appears in Num 26:24; 1 Chr 7:1. The MT is *yôb,* that is, "Job" [AV], "Iob" [NASB]). The appellative also names a returned exile, husband of a foreign wife (Ezra 10:29). The last-listed son is *Shimron (šimrôn);* the name also identifies a Canaanite town (Josh 11:11; 12:20) and a site in the territory of Zebulun (Josh 19:15; cp. Shamir, Judg 10:1–2; and *šōmrôn,* "Samaria"[430]).

46:14 Zebulun's three sons fathered clans (Num 26:26–27). The meaning and identity of *Sered (sered)* is unknown. On the name *Elon* see comments on 26:34. The name *Jahleel (yaḥlĕʾēl* from *yāḥal,* "to wait") means "let him wait for God *[El].*"

46:15 The author identifies this group as the offspring of Leah's sons who were born in Paddan Aram. The total is thirty-three "sons and daughters," which is the largest number of descendants in the genealogical list. Mention of "Dinah" accounts for the inclusion of "daughters," although she is excluded from the total count. That the plural "daughters" occurs, although only one daughter (Dinah) is named, may indicate that the expression "sons and daughters" is a stylistic echo of the Sethite and Shemite genealogies (e.g., 5:4; 11:11). It is reasonable to assume that other, unnamed daughters were born to Jacob. Inclusion of Dinah brings to mind the trials that Leah's sons created for Jacob in Canaan (chap. 34; cf. 30:21).[431]

ZILPAH'S CHILDREN (46:16–18). **46:16** The handmaiden of Leah produced the second highest number of descendants. Gad was the most impressive progenitor of children, producing seven grandchildren for Jacob (v. 16). All six offspring produced clans (Num 26:15–18). *Zephon (šĕpôn/šĕpōn,* SP, LXX; Num 26:15; *ṣipyôn,* MT, "Ziphion" [AV, NASB, HCSB, NJB]) appears again in the toponym Baal Ziphon (Exod 14:2,9; Num 33:7). *Haggi (ḥaggî,* "feast [of God]"?) is related to the common word "feast" *(ḥag),* as is the better-known prophet, Haggai *(ḥaggay).* *Shuni (šûnî)* is unexplained. *Ezbon* (*ʾeṣbōn,* MT; *ʾeṣbaʿōn* = "finger," SP, Syr.) is "Ozni" (*ʾoznî,* "my ear") in Num 26:16; Ezbon is the name of one of Benjamin's grandsons (1 Chr 7:7). *Eri* (*ʿĕrî* from *ʿûr)* perhaps means "watchful" (cf. Er, 38:3). *Arodi (ʾărôdî)* is "Arod" *(ʾărôd)* in Num 26:17 (but "Arodi," SP, Syr.). *Areli (ʾarʾēlî)* appears only once and is unexplained.

46:17–18 Asher's lineage includes four sons, a daughter, and two grandchildren (v. 17; 1 Chr 7:30–31). Numbers 26:44–47 lists the clans his sons produced, excepting one (Ishvah). *Imnah (yimnâ),* if related to *y-m-n,* is similar to the name "Jamin" (v. 10). If from *mānâ,* "count, consign to," the mean-

---

[430] Westermann, *Genesis 37–50,* 153 and Wenham, *Genesis 16–50,* 443.

[431] Calvin, however, surmises that the mention of the daughter "Serah" (v. 17) shows that Dinah was named, not because of her dishonorable past, rather, the two women were included because they remained unmarried since no wives are included (excepting Jacob's; *Comm.,* 393).

ing is "May [God] allocate" or "[God] allocated."[432] It also names a Levite (2 Chr 31:14). The second and third names, *Ishvah (yišwâ)* and *Ishvi (yišwî)*, are suspiciously alike. Both are needed to maintain the count of "sixteen" descendants (v. 18). Although also named in the list of 1 Chr 7:30, "Ishvah" does not occur in Num 26:44, which suggests that a textual disturbance has occurred. Others add that the names are possible spelling variants referring to the same person. Another explanation is that Ishvi did not bear children and thus had no clan.[433] "Ishvi" is also the name of one of King Saul's sons (1 Sam 14:49 = Ishboseth/Eshbaal?). The last-named son is *Beriah (bĕrî'â, "outstanding"?*[434]), a name that also Ephraim gave to one of his sons; the popular etymology explaining Ephraim's choice of the name is the word "trouble" *(rā'â;* 1 Chr 7:23). Beriah also names a Benjamite descendant of King Saul (1 Chr 8:13,16) and a Levite (1 Chr 23:10–11). *Serah (ṣeraḥ)* is only the second daughter listed in this genealogy (Dinah); her name occurs in both parallel genealogies (Num 26:46; 1 Chr 7:30). The next generation includes two sons born to Beriah who also formed clans (Num 26:45). *Heber (ḥeber/ḥēber,* "companion," from *ḥābēr)* is a popular name, additionally the name of the Kenite husband of Jael (e.g., Judg 4:11), a Judahite (1 Chr 4:18), and a Benjamite (1 Chr 8:17). The lineage of the Asherites is traced through Heber's three sons exclusively (1 Chr 7:30–40). *Malkiel* (or Malchiel, *malkî'ēl),* meaning "my king is God *[El],"* fathered one son (1 Chr 7:31).[435] The total count for the Zilpah groups is sixteen persons (v. 18).

RACHEL'S CHILDREN (46:19–22). **46:19–20** The designation "Jacob's wife" is only used of Rachel in this genealogy (v. 19). The location of the birth of Joseph's children ("in Egypt") and the priestly bloodline of his Egyptian wife "Asenath" (v. 20) reinforce the historical peculiarity that Jacob's descendants were born outside Canaan (except Benjamin).[436] The LXX text includes five additional names, son and grandson of Manasseh (cf. Num 26:29[33, LXX]) and two sons and grandson of Ephraim (cf. Num 26:35–36[39–40, LXX]).[437]

46:21 The parallel Benjamite genealogies in Num 26:38–40 and 1 Chr 7:6–12; 8:1–5 possess differences from Genesis in names and order, numbers of sons, and familial relationships. The diversity may be attributable to scribal confusion, dual names for the same person, and difference in literary genre.

---

[432] *HALOT* 2.416.

[433] C. F. Mariottini, "Ishvah," *ABD* 3.522 and D. V. Edelman, "Ishvi," *ABD* 3. 522.

[434] Noth, *Personennamen,* 224, and Wenham, *Genesis 16–50,* 444.

[435] Cp. the personal name *Milkil* in the Amarna correspondence; see C. F. Mariottini, "Malchiel," *ABD* 4.486.

[436] On the names Ephraim and Manasseh and those of Asenath and Potiphera, see comments on 41:50–52.

[437] Wevers, *Notes on the Greek Text,* 782–83.

The problems are compounded by the variations among the ancient versions. The LXX has the same ten names that correspond to the ten sons recorded in the MT, but the family relationships differ; it has three sons, six grandsons, and one great grandson. The Genesis and Chronicles lists are formal genealogies, and Numbers is a census list. That the Genesis genealogy records ten "sons" *(bānîm),* whereas Numbers and 1 Chr 8 have five and 1 Chr 7 has only three, suggests that the generic meaning "descendants," instead of "sons," may be intended. The youth of Benjamin in the narrative makes it doubtful that the ten descendants are all yet born. The author included future offspring, implying that they existed by virtue of being in the loins of Benjamin (cf. Heb 7:10).[438]

The eldest, *Bela (belaʿ),* occurs in all of the Benjamite lists. On the popular name Bela, see commentary at 14:2 and 36:32. Bela was the father and grandfather of significant Benjamite clans (Num 26:38,40[MT]). *Beker (beker,* EVs "Becher"), meaning "young bull camel" *(bēker,* Isa 60:6), is absent in the parallel genealogies (Num 26:38; 1 Chr 8:1). He produced nine descendants (1 Chr 7:6,8); the name also specifies an Ephraimite clan (Num 26:35 [MT]). *Ashbel (ʾašbēl,* "with long upper lip"[439]) was also the progenitor of a family (Num 26:38). Although in the third position here, he is in the second position in Num 26:38 and identified "the second son" (omitting Beker) in 1 Chr 8:1. First Chronicles 7:6 differs from the parallel passages by "Jediael" instead of Ashbel.[440] The identity and family connection of the persons named *Gera (gērāʾ,* "sojourner [of God]"[441] from *gēr,* "sojourner") in the parallel Benjamite genealogies create special problems for scholars.[442] The name is absent in Num 26:38 and 1 Chr 7:6. Among the genealogies, 46:21 (MT) is the only passage that has "Gera" listed as a son of Benjamin. In 46:21, LXX and 1 Chr 8:3, Gera is the son of Bela, grandson of Benjamin. The name "Gera" occurs three times in 1 Chr 8:3,5,7. Outside of the Benjamite genealogies, Gera is named the father (or clan name) of Ehud the judge (Judg 3:15 = Ehud [1 Chr 8:7]?) and a Saulide, father (or clan name) of Shimei (2 Sam 16:5). Evidently Gera was a popular clan name in the Benjamite tribe. *Naaman (naʿămān* from *nāʿēm,* "to be pleasant"), meaning "pleasantness" or "beautiful,"[443] is also the name of Bela's son, thus Benjamin's grandson, who formed a clan (Num 26:40; 1 Chr 8:4,7). In 46:21, LXX he is Bela's son. Naa-

---

[438] Wenham, *Genesis 16–50,* 444.

[439] Arabic *ʾasbal,* see Noth, *Personnenamen,* 227; *HALOT* 1.92; Ar. *sabala,* "to hang down" (Hb. *šbl*) in *HALOT* 4.1393.

[440] S. S. Johnson proposes that the name change occurred because Jediael ("known to God"?) was more acceptable than Ashbel ("man of Baal"; "Ashbel," *ABD* 1.447).

[441] "Client of divine name," Noth, *Personennamen,* 148 in *HALOT* 1.201.

[442] See R. W. Nysse, "Gera," *ABD* 2.988–89.

[443] *HALOT* 2.706.

man is also the name of the leprous Aramean general (2 Kgs 5:1–27).[444] Of the four names *Ehi (ʾēḥî), Rosh (rōʾš),* meaning "head, chief," *Muppim (muppîm),* and *Huppim (ḥuppîm),* the first three occur only in this verse. In 46:21, LXX, however, these four names are the sons of Bela, thus grandsons of Benjamin. The parallel genealogy in Num 26:38–39 of "Ahiram, Shupham [or Shephupham], and Hupham" may provide alternative names to the same persons or the Genesis passage may exhibit textual confusion. First Chronicles 8 has "Aharah" (v. 1) in the place of Ahiram, and "Shephuphan" is the son of Bela (v. 5). Huppim (or Hupham, Num 26:39) generated a clan (1 Chr 7:12,15). *Ard (ʾārd)* is also the name of Bela's son, thus grandson of Benjamin, who produced a clan (Num 26:40; cf. "Addar," Num 26:44 [LXX]; 1 Chr 8:3 [SP, LXX], which shows the transposition of ר and ד).[445] In 46:21, LXX, Ard is the son of Gera.

46:22 Rachel's lineage contributed fourteen members to the Jacobite family.

BILHAH'S CHILDREN (46:23–25). **46:23** The only descendant named[446] for Dan is *Hushim (ḥūšîm),* who is probably "Shuham" *(šûḥām)* in Num 26:42, which occurred by the transposition of *ḥ* and *š.* The LXX has *Asom,* probably rendering *ḥašum* ("Hashum," NRSV). The same name appears for a clan of Benjamin (1 Chr 7:12; LXX *Asom*) and a wife in the Benjamite family (1 Chr 8:8,11; LXX *Osin*).

46:24 Naphtali was father to four sons who were the heads of clans (Num 26:48–49; 1 Chr 7:13). *Jahziel* (or Jahzeel; *yaḥṣĕʾēl* or spelled *yaḥṣîʾēl,* 1 Chr 7:13 from *ḥāṣâ* "to divide") means "May God *[El]* divide [i.e., distribute a share]." *Guni (gûnî,* "partridge"?[447]) is also the name of a Gadite (1 Chr 5:15). *Jezer (yēṣer* from *yāṣar,* "to form, fashion") means "what is shaped or formed," perhaps originally "Formed by God" (cf. 2:7).[448] The name *Shillem (šillēm)* is unstable in the ancient versions. He is Shillem in 46:24; Num 26:49, and is "Shallum" *(šallûm)* in the Chronicler's record (1 Chr 7:13). Shallum was a popular name, designating eleven persons in the Old Testament (e.g., 2 Kgs 15:10; Ezra 2:42).

46:25 In Bilhah's line are seven descendants, half the number of her mistress.

CONCLUSION (46:26–27). **46:26–27** The concluding verses are problematic for interpreters, since there are two related but different counts given (sixty-six and seventy), and it is uncertain how the author arrived at

---

[444] The name is attested as a personal name and as an epithet in Ugaritic and Mari (Amorite) texts (C. G. Rasmussen, "Naaman," *ISBE* 3.465).

[445] S. S. Johnson, "Ard," *ABD* 1.369.

[446] The plural "sons of Dan," בְּנֵי־דָן, although only one descendant is named, probably reflects the tendency toward uniformity of the list's pattern.

[447] Cp. Ar. *el jūnī,* "black-winged partridge," *HALOT* 1.184.

[448] Noth, *Personennamen,* 172, and C. F. Mariottini, "Jezer," *ABD* 3.849.

the two counts.[449] The double colophon is similar, but they possess a significant difference: "All those who went to Egypt *with* Jacob . . ." (v. 26, italics mine) versus "all the members of Jacob's family, which went to Egypt . . ." (v. 27). The number of those who migrated "with Jacob" was "sixty-six" (v. 26), and the total number of "Jacob's family" in Egypt was "seventy" (v. 27). The passage also explains the nature of the dual counts by specifying that only direct descendants are meant (lit., "those who came from his loins"; cf. Judg 8:30), not the wives of the sons (v. 26), and that the two sons of Joseph were born in Egypt and presumably residing in Egypt already (v. 27). The number seventy is the total count from the cumulative figures of the four groups provided in the genealogy, which takes into account Joseph and his two sons (v. 22; cf. Exod 1:5; Deut 10:22), but not Dinah and presumably not Jacob. The difficulty is identifying the four members that should be counted from sixty-six to raise the number to seventy. From antiquity to the present there has been a stream of proposals, most including Joseph and his two sons, but divided over the fourth person (e.g., Jacob, Dinah, Serah [v. 17], Jochebed [Num 26:59]). Probably the most imaginative and pious was the midrash (*Gen. Rab.* 94.9), suggesting that God himself was intended in the count of seventy (cf. "I will go down to Egypt with you," v. 4a). Although no proposal can be definitive, the number "sixty-six" may also be achieved by deducting the two deceased sons of Judah, Er and Onan (v. 12), and the two sons of Joseph, Ephraim and Manasseh, who were born in Egypt (vv. 20,27). The advantage here is the symmetry this count achieves, noting two sons each of the chief narrative figures, Joseph and Judah.

The number "seventy" has also been understood as a round number, symbolic of the community as a whole, corresponding to the "elders of Israel" (Exod 24:1,9; Num 11:16,24,25). Especially relevant to this proposal is the listing of seventy nations in the Table of Nations (10:1–32), indicating that the Jacob group is a representative nation of the world of nations whom the Lord will bless (e.g., 12:3; 18:18; 22:18). Since the author has specified "sixty-six," which does not indicate a symbolic figure, it is best probably to interpret the number "seventy" as a literal number also. "Seventy" persons (v. 27) should be taken as a modest number (cf. Deut 10:22). That these few became a burgeoning multitude reflected God's blessing of his people Israel (e.g., Exod 1:7,20; Num 22:5,11; Deut 1:10).

---

[449] The LXX tradition added five names in Joseph's line (v. 20), which requires a cumulative count of seventy-five (Exod 1:5, LXX; Deut 10:22, LXX; cf. Acts 17:14). Since the number sixty-six left a gap of nine, the LXX translators boosted Joseph's offspring to nine—all born in Egypt (see Wevers, *Notes on the Greek Text,* 786).

9. Joseph, Savior of the Family (46:28–47:12)

The narrative interest in the momentous reunion of Joseph and Jacob (46:27–28), so long anticipated in the story, is all but swallowed up in the larger context of the nation's descent into Egypt. Jacob's story is Israel's story. The description of Jacob's migration anticipates the four hundred-year sojourn in Egypt (15:13) that is the setting for the culminating exodus events (chaps. 1–12). Genesis 46:28–47:12 exhibits the salvation of Jacob's household that God swore to the patriarch: "I will go down to Egypt with you" (46:4). Jacob experienced the same preserving presence of God in his earlier sojourn in Paddan Aram, and the Lord was faithful to the promise of his return to the land of his father Isaac (28:15; 31:3,13; 32:9[10]). The psalmist's review of God's historic faithfulness toward Israel reflects on our present passage: "Then Israel entered Egypt; Jacob lived as an alien *[gār* from *gûr]* in the land of Ham" (Ps 105:23). Historically, the Fathers of Israel were remembered for their alien *(gûr/gēr)* existence, as transients in Canaan and in Egypt (e.g., Gen 17:8; 28:4; Exod 6:4; 22:21[20]; 23:9; Deut 10:19; 1 Chr 29:15; Ps 39:12[13]). Israel's historic confession expressed the nation's identity by celebrating Jacob's migration: "He went down into Egypt with a few people and lived *[wayyāgor]* there and became a great nation, powerful and numerous" (Deut 26:5). Israel's alien status in Egypt was a fitting metaphor for describing the otherworldliness ("aliens" and "strangers") of the Christian community (e.g., Eph 2:19; Heb 11:13; 1 Pet 1:1; 2:11).

This is how Jacob interpreted his life when reminiscing before Pharaoh: "The years of my pilgrimage *[mĕgûray]* are a hundred and thirty" (47:9). From beginning to end our passage concerns the pilgrimage and survival of Jacob and his descendants. All up to this point in the Joseph narrative has arranged for the salvation of Jacob's family; God established Joseph as ruler over Egypt, and now God ensures a safe and prosperous refuge (Goshen) under Joseph's care. The openhanded provisions made for Jacob contrasts with the taxation that Egypt's own populace underwent. The family's sojourn was both an old story and a new beginning. It was an old story because this was the experience of Abraham, who emigrated from the family homeland of Haran. But also it was a new beginning, for here they would form the nucleus of a nation and would experience at the end of their enslavement the mighty hand of God's salvation that would indelibly mark its personality. The fulfillment of God's word to Abraham was underway: "Your descendants will be strangers *[gēr]* in a country not their own" (cf. 15:13–16).

The flip side to Israel's story is the welcome that Egypt extended to their Father. Egypt's king received the Hebrews in an unprecedented fashion, pledging to them the "best part of the land" (47:6,11). Our passage transitions to the account of the Egyptians' submission to Joseph. Pharaoh and all of

Egypt by virtue of Joseph's administrative wisdom survived the grievous famine (47:13–26), illustrating the promise of blessing for the nations (e.g., 12:3; 28:14). The removal to Egypt, therefore, was not a hiatus in God's plan for the nation and for the nations, but it advanced the blessing God forecast for Israel and the nations. "Faith does not require external confirmation but believes God in spite of appearances" (J. Oswald Sanders). The author of Genesis never lets his readers forget that the adoption of Israel was for the purpose of offering salvation to "all the world" (41:57; cf. 11:1,9).

COMPOSITION. Source critics typically reconstruct a composite text for 46:28–47:27. There are differences among them in the details of source identity and the nature of those sources (documents or redaction layers), but they agree on the major components. In Gunkel's view, which is typical of the documentary approach, the dominant source is the Yahwist (J) document.[450] The lengthy discourse of Pharaoh's taxation policy in 47:13–26 is also J but displaced from its original position after chap. 41. Significant Priestly (P) intrusions are the list of names (46:8–27) and the account of Jacob in Egypt (47:5b,6a,7–11,27b). Seen as doublets, he assigned the audience of the five brothers with Pharaoh to J (vv. 1–5a,6b,12,27a) and the audience of Jacob to P (vv. 5b,6a–11,27b–28). Coats observed that 46:28–30 back references to the narrative framework of vv. 1a,5–7. The reunion of Joseph and Jacob in vv. 28–29 parallels that of the brothers in 45:14–15, providing for a close relationship in the structural framework. The narrative in 46:31–47:10 entails the audience that the family has with Pharaoh (J). According to Coats, 47:11–12 and v. 27a conclude the original Joseph story. The secondary insertion of 47:13–26 is an etiology for the tax system in Egypt. It has nothing to do with the family crisis, not even in the fashion of chaps. 39–41 that described the rise of Joseph, whose position was critical to the narrative's purpose.[451]

The passage shows stronger evidence of coherence and continuity than usually has been acknowledged. After the inclusion of the name list (46:8–27), it is expedient to back reference to 46:1–7, where it tells of Jacob's migration from the perspective of the family. The retelling in 46:28–30 complements the former narrative by telling of the descent and reunion with Joseph's participation, focusing on the reunion of father and son. The subsequent narrative of 46:31–47:12 continues the main story line without disruption. Some scholars, however, challenged the continuity of 46:1–12, contending for two sources (J and P) that tell of the two audiences with Pharaoh. That the audience with the brothers preceded the father is suspicious, it is reasoned, since Jacob would be expected to be received first. Also vv. 5–6 appear scrambled, since Pharaoh does not look as if to answer in v. 5 ("your father and your brothers have come to you") the petition of the brothers in v. 4 ("let your servants settle in Goshen"). The LXX exhibits a different order in vv. 5 and 6, resolving the tension. Among its differences from the MT, the LXX transposes parts of vv. 5 and 6 so as to make Pharaoh's answer fit

---

[450] Gunkel, *Genesis*, 438, 442, 468.
[451] Coats, *From Canaan to Egypt*, 51–53.

the context smoothly ("settle them in the land of Goshen," v. 5, LXX [v. 6a, MT]).[452] However, alternative explanations for the response of Pharaoh to the brothers have left vv. 1–6 in one unified piece.[453] Pharaoh answers the brothers by instructing Joseph directly in the steps to implement their request for asylum in Goshen, since Joseph is the facilitator of the audiences, both for the brothers and for Jacob (vv. 2,7).

That the audience of Jacob with Pharaoh (vv. 7–10) is a secondary P insertion depends too much on the assumption that P alone was interested in the age of Jacob and that P interjected the foreign notion of Jacob "blessing" the king. The arrangement of the brothers who enter first followed by Jacob is an effective means of heightening Jacob's prestige, not diminishing his position. Joseph is an ambassador who introduces the entourage (brothers) prior to the appearance of the tribal head (Jacob). Moreover, this arrangement delays the more important encounter of the two nations' leaders. That Jacob "blessed" the king fits with the thematic promise of blessing for the nations in the patriarchal narratives, which is not a distinctive P characteristic (e.g., 12:3). The concern of Pharaoh was the occupation of the brothers, especially since he had in mind future employment for the heads of their families. He probably concluded that as brothers of Joseph, perhaps they too exhibit his competency and spiritual ennoblement. Pharaoh's interest in Jacob as the aged patriarch of the tribe, however, was the high regard the king held for longevity's wisdom.

STRUCTURE.   This unit consists of three parts, which narrate the arrival and establishment of Jacob's family in the land of Egypt through the auspices of Joseph. The beginning of the unit is made obvious by the prior close to the genealogy (46:26–27) and by the new subject matter, "Now Jacob sent . . ."[454] (46:28). The ending of the unit at 47:12 is evidenced by a new episode that begins in 47:13,[455] which describes Joseph's administration of the stored grain. The borders of the present passage describe the family's arrival in "Goshen" (46:28) and the provisions made by Pharaoh and Joseph "in the best part of the land, the district of Rameses" (47:11–12). Coupled with the emphasis on the land tenure of the family is the role of Joseph as mediator who ensures that Jacob's household survives the famine. The passage begins and ends with the family's dependence on Joseph. Jacob dispatched Judah to direct them "to Joseph" (46:28), and Joseph "provided . . . all his father's

---

[452] Cf. NAB: "Pharaoh said to Joseph, 'They may settle in the region of Goshen; and if you know any of them to be qualified, you may put them in charge of my own livestock'" (also see NJB).

[453] E.g., Westermann, *Genesis 37–50*, 168–69; Sarna, *Genesis*, 319; and Hamilton, *Genesis Chapters 18–50*, 607–8.

[454] The initial *wāw* disjunctive signals a new episode: וְאֶת־יְהוּדָה שָׁלַח, "*Now* [Jacob] sent Judah . . ." (46:28 italics mine).

[455] The *wāw* disjunctive initiates a new episode: וְלֶחֶם אֵין בְּכָל הָאָרֶץ, "*Now* there was no food in the land" (47:13); the NIV interprets the *wāw* as adversative, "There was no food, *however,* in the whole region" (italics mine).

household with food" (47:12). Repeatedly, the narrative and the speeches of
Joseph refer to the family bond from the perspective of Joseph: "his father"
(46:29,31; 47:7,11,12[2x]); "my father" (46:31; 47:1); "his brothers" (46:31;
47:2,3, 11,12); "my brothers" (46:31). Pharaoh also refers to Joseph's guests
as "your father and your brothers" (47:5,6). Joseph's lofty position in Egypt
made the survival of Jacob possible.

The first subunit (46:28–34) sets up the second and third subunits, namely,
the two audiences of the brothers (47:1–6) and of Jacob with Pharaoh (47:7–
10). Embedded in the narrative frame (46:28; 47:11–12) are three dialogical
scenes. (1) Jacob, who alone speaks, receives Joseph (vv. 29–30), and Joseph
instructs his brothers (vv. 31–34). (2) Pharaoh receives the brothers (47:1–6),
in which the king and brothers dialogue about their occupation (vv. 3–4), and
the king instructs Joseph (vv. 5–6). (3) Pharaoh receives Jacob (vv. 7–10), in
which the king and the father dialogue about his age (vv. 8–9).

The word "Goshen" marks the boundaries of the first subunit (v. 28[2x],
34; also v. 29). The centerpiece of the preparations is the moving reunion of
father and son, which occurs in "Goshen" (vv. 29–30). Joseph wept and Jacob
spoke, now ready to die after seeing his son once more. The extensive and
detailed instructions of Joseph to his brothers follows, coaching them in how
to answer the king in order to receive "Goshen" as their homestead (vv. 31–
34). That the "men are shepherds" (v. 32) is critical to their appeal for
Goshen, "for all shepherds are detestable to the Egyptians" (v. 34). The second subunit focuses on the all-important meeting of the brothers and the king
(47:1–6). The segment opens with a succinct description of their livestock
and "everything they own," which they brought from "Canaan" to "Goshen"
(47:1). It ends with Pharaoh's permission to dwell in "Goshen" and invitation
to supervise "my own livestock"[456] (47:6). Their occupation as shepherds
(47:3,6) and their Asiatic home ("Canaan," 47:1,4) advanced their case, since
the Egyptians preferred segregation from shepherds. The third segment
describes the settlement and provision of the family in the land of their
choosing (47:7–12). As he had presented his brothers to Pharaoh, Joseph ush-
ered Jacob into the presence of the king (vv. 7–10). Afterward Joseph "settled" and "provided" for his father and family in the land (vv. 11–12).

(1) Joseph before Jacob (46:28–34)

**[28]Now Jacob sent Judah ahead of him to Joseph to get directions to Goshen.
When they arrived in the region of Goshen, [29]Joseph had his chariot made ready
and went to Goshen to meet his father Israel. As soon as Joseph appeared before
him, he threw his arms around his father and wept for a long time.**

---

[456] Cp. "all which belonged them," וְכָל־אֲשֶׁר לָהֶם (47:1) and "livestock which belong to
me," מִקְנֶה עַל־אֲשֶׁר־לִי (47:6).

[30]Israel said to Joseph, "Now I am ready to die, since I have seen for myself that you are still alive."

[31]Then Joseph said to his brothers and to his father's household, "I will go up and speak to Pharaoh and will say to him, 'My brothers and my father's household, who were living in the land of Canaan, have come to me. [32]The men are shepherds; they tend livestock, and they have brought along their flocks and herds and everything they own.' [33]When Pharaoh calls you in and asks, 'What is your occupation?' [34]you should answer, 'Your servants have tended livestock from our boyhood on, just as our fathers did.' Then you will be allowed to settle in the region of Goshen, for all shepherds are detestable to the Egyptians."

The passage describes the preparations for the family's royal audience with Pharaoh. After Judah announces the arrival of the family in Goshen (v. 28), Joseph hurries to meet his father where they reunite after twenty years of separation (vv. 29–30). Joseph instructs his brothers in what to say to Pharaoh so that they will gain Goshen for a settlement (vv. 31–34).

JUDAH PREPARES THE WAY (46:28). **46:28** The new episode begins with "Judah" at the head of the clause, who continues as the lead figure among the brothers. As in previous episodes, Judah is the go-between for Joseph and his father. That Judah, who disrupted their union (37:26), should facilitate the reunion of father and son is most fitting.[457] The language "sent" *(šālaḥ)*[458] recalls when Jacob sent Joseph to learn about his brothers (37:13–14), but now the matter is reversed when Jacob sends the brothers, represented by Judah, to meet Joseph.

The NIV's "to get directions" *(hiph., lĕhôrōt*[459]*)* loosely translates a difficult construction. The word typically means "to teach, instruct" someone or something; the absence of an object here makes the text suspect. Ancient and modern versions strived to improve the text so as to make better sense, influenced by v. 29,[460] but the Hebrew (MT) though unusual is not too difficult to accept. The text probably means that Judah was sent ahead to notify Joseph of their imminent arrival in Goshen (cf. REB, "to advise him," i.e., Joseph); thus Joseph responded to the news by immediately departing for

---

[457] Sarna, *Genesis*, 317.

[458] The subject of the verb is indefinite, שָׁלַח לְפָנָיו, "he sent before him"; EVs add "Jacob" or "Israel" to identify the agent.

[459] לְהוֹרֹת, *hiphil* infinitive construct from ירה, "throw, cast, shoot" *(qal)* and "teach, instruct" *(hiph.)*.

[460] SP, Syr., לְהֵרָאֹת, "to appear [before him]," as in v. 29, וַיֵּרָא אֵלָיו, "he [Joseph] appeared before him [Jacob]." But NJB understands Judah, not Joseph, is the subject: "so that Judah might present himself to Joseph in Goshen" (v. 28). The LXX, συναντῆσαι αὐτῷ (= לְהִקָּרוֹת לְפָנָיו? BHS), "to meet him," i.e., "so that he [Joseph] might meet him [Jacob] in Goshen" (v. 28, NAB), as in v. 29: וַיַּעַל לִקְרַאת יִשְׂרָאֵל, "he went up to meet Israel."

Goshen to welcome his father (v. 29).[461]

JOSEPH APPEARS TO JACOB (46:29–30).   **46:29**   As to whether Joseph himself or a servant at his command (NIV, "had his chariot made ready") set his mount cannot be known, although Joseph is the grammatical subject ("Joseph hitched his horses," NAB). Omitting any reference to an assistant has the same effect, namely, the haste at which Joseph rushed to Goshen. That Joseph "made ready" (*ʾāsar,* "to hitch," v. 29) his chariot is an echo of the prison scenes where the same word describes Joseph's imprisonment ("confined," 39:20; 40:3,5) and of his brothers ("kept/stay in prison," 42:16,19; "bound," v. 24). By God's superintending grace, these confinements led to this momentous reunion of father and son. Reference to the alternate name "Israel" (vv. 29–30) may be an allusion to the wrestling incident with the man of Peniel (32:28[29]; see below), but here the author probably prefers it because of its national implications. Israel and his sons in effect are the embodiment of future Israel whose audience with Pharaoh has historical and international significance.

The word "appeared" (*wayyērāʾ,* v. 29) describes divine theophany in Genesis (e.g., 12:7; 17:1; 26:2,24; 35:9; cf. Exod 3:2). It is one of several expressions in the verse that conveys subtly the presence of God in this meeting. "And [Joseph] went [up] to Goshen" describes the topographical ascent of Joseph that commonly depicts the geographical return of the patriarchs from Egypt to Canaan (e.g., 13:1; 50:7). Yet the same word "went up" *(wayyaʿal)* also describes the ascent of God following a theophanic message (17:22; 35:13). Moreover, "since I have seen your face" (not in NIV) in v. 30 recalls the vision of the Lord at Peniel (32:31[30]), to which the patriarch alludes when he meets Esau, saying, "To see your face is like seeing the face of God" (33:10). This reunion with Joseph bears for Jacob the same divine significance as his reunion with Esau.

For the expressions of affection in v. 29, see comments on 33:4; 45:14. The phrase "for a long time" (*ʿôd,* v. 29) reinforces the larger narrative's depiction of Joseph's strong attachment to his father (50:1). The similar description of Joseph's embrace with Benjamin does not have the adverb *ʿôd,* indicating the stronger affection for Jacob. The LXX text understands the adverb *ʿôd* as meaning Joseph expressed excessive weeping (also Rashi).[462]

46:30   That Jacob does not reciprocate with equal passion is a striking departure from his temperament (cf. 29:11; 33:4; 37:4). It is as though Jacob's twenty years of grief have left him without tears to give. Jacob ver-

---

[461] Delitzsch argues for this view (referring to usage in Exod 35:34; *A New Commentary on Genesis,* 341). On the location of "Goshen," cf. comments on 45:10.

[462] καὶ ἔκλαυσεν κλαυθμῷ πλείονι, "and he wept with great weeping" (Wevers, *Notes on the Greek Text,* 788); the LXX elsewhere renders similarly the verb בכה ("wept") and infin. absol. בָכֹה (κλαυθμῷ ἔκλαυσεν, Isa 30:19, LXX; κλαύσατε κλαυθμῷ, Jer 22:10, LXX).

balizes the depth of his ordeal; it has been a matter of life and death for him (v. 30; 45:28). "I am ready to die"[463] expresses the final relief of his heart-wrenched desire (cf. Luke 2:29–32). Any parent who has lost a child by abduction lives with an open wound; not knowing a child's fate makes the trial's sorrow unspeakable. The possibility of seeing Joseph again ("still alive," from ʿ*ôd ḥāy*) was the chief reason that Jacob had lived, and likewise Joseph had worried that Jacob might not "still be alive" (from ʿ*ôd ḥāy,* cf. 43:27,28; 45:3).

JOSEPH INSTRUCTS HIS BROTHERS (46:31–34). **46:31–34** Joseph explains to his brothers the plan for approaching Pharaoh. First, he will inform Pharaoh that his instructions have been fulfilled (45:16–20), meaning that Joseph's father and brothers have arrived (v. 31). At that time he will make clear that the family practices animal husbandry, implying that expansive grazing areas are required (v. 32). The two descriptions of their occupation, "shepherds" *(rōʿê ṣōʾn)* and "keepers of livestock" *(ʾanšê miqneh)* are not contradictory[464] nor evidence of a clever cover-up of their profession.[465] The terms are effectively interchangeable in which the broader term "keepers of livestock" means that they herd small cattle as well as sheep.[466] The brothers readily acknowledge their occupation, answering, "Your servants are shepherds" (47:3). That they have brought "everything they own" also necessitated more territory. Moreover, as foreign shepherds the Egyptians would want the Hebrews segregated (v. 34b). This strategy will encourage Pharaoh to grant them the land of Goshen that Joseph had already anticipated (45:10; 46:28–29). Second, he instructs them in what to say to Pharaoh's inquiry regarding their occupation as shepherds (vv. 33–34). The purpose in answering that their family heritage was always shepherding was to ensure that Pharaoh would conclude that they were best suited for this livelihood (cf. "livestock," *miqnēh,* e.g., 31:9,18; 33:17; 46:6). This would avoid any concern of Pharaoh's that the family has ambitions beyond settlement in Goshen. Theirs is not a household of kings, despite Joseph's high office. But Joseph's eye is ultimately on the future of Israel's descendants who would one day return to their father's land. Joseph explicitly mentions to his brothers the reason for his instructions: it will mean a settlement in Goshen, detached from mainstream Egyptian life, which culturally avoided mixing with animal keepers ("detestable," *tôʿēbâ,* v. 34; cf. comments at 43:32).

---

[463] אֹמֻתָה, cohortative of resolve (GKC §108a).

[464] Coats, *Joseph,* 51.

[465] Gunkel, *Genesis,* 440–41.

[466] The passage shows a chiasmus: shepherds (v. 32), livestock (v. 32), livestock (v. 34a), shepherds (v. 34b).

(2) Joseph's Brothers before Pharaoh (47:1–6)

[1]Joseph went and told Pharaoh, "My father and brothers, with their flocks and herds and everything they own, have come from the land of Canaan and are now in Goshen." [2]He chose five of his brothers and presented them before Pharaoh.

[3]Pharaoh asked the brothers, "What is your occupation?"

"Your servants are shepherds," they replied to Pharaoh, "just as our fathers were." [4]They also said to him, "We have come to live here awhile, because the famine is severe in Canaan and your servants' flocks have no pasture. So now, please let your servants settle in Goshen."

[5]Pharaoh said to Joseph, "Your father and your brothers have come to you, [6]and the land of Egypt is before you; settle your father and your brothers in the best part of the land. Let them live in Goshen. And if you know of any among them with special ability, put them in charge of my own livestock."

After the audience Joseph has with his father, he arranges for an audience of his brothers with Pharaoh (vv. 1–2). The king inquires about their livelihood, as Joseph has anticipated, and the brothers acknowledge that they are alien shepherds seeking refuge (vv. 3–4). The king instructs Joseph to provide for his brothers in Goshen (vv. 5–6).

JOSEPH PRESENTS HIS BROTHERS (47:1–2). **47:1–2** According to plan, Joseph announces the arrival of his family (v. 1; 46:31–32). The goal from the outset in Joseph's dealings with Pharaoh was to win the pasturage of Goshen (cf. 45:10; 46:34). Joseph chose "five" of his siblings to represent the family before Pharaoh (v. 2).[467] Joseph may have reduced the number of brothers in order to allay any potential fears toward a burgeoning tribe. The identity of the "five" is unimportant to the author.[468] The number "five" reminds us of Joseph's favoritism expressed toward Benjamin (43:34; 45:22) and the five years of famine that remained (45:6,11).[469] By Joseph informing Pharaoh that the tribe waits in Goshen, perhaps he wants to plant the idea in the king's mind. The text's description of their interview, that Joseph "presented them" (v. 2, from *yāṣag*), also expressed Judah's oath to "set" Benjamin before Jacob (43:9).

THE BROTHERS REQUEST SETTLEMENT (47:3–4). **47:3–4** The king first inquires about the brothers' station in life ("occupation," v. 3), just as Joseph anticipated (46:33). The brothers for all intents and purposes follow Joseph's instructions, though here they directly request Goshen for their set-

---

[467] Either the selection occurred after the announcement to Pharaoh (v. 1), or the verb לָקַ֫ח is a pluperfect, "had taken" (e.g., NJB, NAB, REB).

[468] A Jewish midrash explained that Joseph chose the five weaker brothers (Zebulun, Dan, Naphtali, Gad, and Asher) so as to avoid the five's conscription into the king's army (e.g., *Tg. Ps.-J.; Gen. Rab.* 95.4).

[469] "Five" has been understood as a round number for a "few" (e.g., NJPS, "several," 43:34).

tlement. They show the proper protocol toward the king (e.g., "your servants"). "Shepherds" in the original text is the first word of their answer to
Pharaoh's inquiry (v. 3). They also pointedly note their family's solidarity,
lit., "both *[gam]* we, both *[gam]* our fathers." That they describe their purpose
in coming to Egypt as sojourners (v. 5, "to live here awhile," from *gûr*) due to
"severe famine" *(kābēd hārā'āb)* brings to mind Abraham's earlier descent
due to famine (12:10, from *gûr;* cf. also 20:1; 21:34; 35:27) whose movement
prefigures his descendants' migration (15:13; 23:4, *gēr,* "stranger"). They
imply that the famine was more intense in Canaan, forcing them to search out
new pastureland. They are thinking long term, since it is likely that Goshen
could not immediately support their flocks due to Egypt's own dearth. It is
understood that in the interim they will be dependent on Pharaoh's goodwill.
They show, however, no interest in or potential of jeopardizing the king's
future regime.

PHARAOH INSTRUCTS JOSEPH (47:5–6). **47:5–6** Ancient and modern
commentators have struggled over the suitability of Pharaoh's answer ("Your
father and your brothers have come to you," v. 5) to the brothers' question in
v. 4 (see the discussion of the LXX variant above under "Composition").
Some have understood this as textual confusion created by the fusion of two
different accounts (J and P). Because the brothers have already met with Pharaoh (vv. 1–4), it is unreasonable for him to inform Joseph of the family's
arrival. But Pharaoh is stipulating the basis for the kindness he extends to the
brothers: "[Since] your father and your brothers have come to you . . ." (v. 5).
The king's generosity toward Jacob's family is due to Joseph's kinship (cf.
"your . . . you," vv. 5–6). The foreigner's show of hospitality places him in a
positive light, which contrasts strikingly with the Pharaoh of bondage "who
did not know about Joseph" (Exod 1:8). Pharaoh provides Joseph's family
complete discretion in selecting "the best part of the land," as he had promised (45:18), but his language is probably ceremonial (e.g., 13:9; 20:15) since
he designates Goshen, in accord with their previous request (v. 6). Yet Pharaoh goes beyond Joseph's requests by extending employment opportunities.
Perhaps he reasoned that God's blessing also rested on Joseph's brothers, as it
did with Joseph, guaranteeing his herds success. "Special ability" translates
'anšê ḥayil, lit., "men of competence/means"; the same phrase describes
clever officials and exceptional combatants (e.g., Exod 18:21,25; 2 Sam
11:16). These men will be promoted to "keepers" (NIV "in charge," from *śar*)
of the royal holdings; the same term describes Pharaoh's "officials" (12:15;
"taskmasters," Exod 1:11).

(3) Jacob before Pharaoh (47:7–12)

**⁷Then Joseph brought his father Jacob in and presented him before Pharaoh.
After Jacob blessed Pharaoh, ⁸Pharaoh asked him, "How old are you?"**

⁹And Jacob said to Pharaoh, "The years of my pilgrimage are a hundred and thirty. My years have been few and difficult, and they do not equal the years of the pilgrimage of my fathers." ¹⁰Then Jacob blessed Pharaoh and went out from his presence.

¹¹So Joseph settled his father and his brothers in Egypt and gave them property in the best part of the land, the district of Rameses, as Pharaoh directed. ¹²Joseph also provided his father and his brothers and all his father's household with food, according to the number of their children.

The next audience with Pharaoh is the appearance of Jacob (vv. 7–10), during which the senior Jacob "blessed" the king (vv. 7,10). In vv. 11–12 Joseph establishes the family in the region of Rameses, according to Pharaoh's directions (vv. 11–12). Joseph is the chief facilitator: "Joseph brought his father [v. 7] . . . Joseph settled his father [v. 11] . . . Joseph also provided his father . . ." (v. 12). By granting an audience, Pharaoh's show of hospitality reflects his recognition of Jacob's tribal importance.

JOSEPH PRESENTS HIS FATHER (47:7a).   **47:7a**   That Joseph "presented" (*hiph.* from *ʿāmad;* cf. Num 27:22) Jacob before the king indicated a formal audience with the ruler (v. 7; cf. "stood before," from *ʿāmad lipnê,* e.g., Exod 9:10; 1 Kgs 1:28).

JACOB BLESSES PHARAOH (47:7b–10).   **47:7b**   That Jacob "blessed" Pharaoh upon his arrival and departure from the king forms the boundaries of the unit (vv. 7b,10). Although "blessed" may be a formal greeting or farewell, in Hebrew culture such formalities assumed an underlying religious significance (e.g., 31:55[32:1]; Ruth 2:4).[470] The significance of Jacob's blessing is a departure from earlier patriarchal contacts with foreign rulers. Although officials enjoyed the blessings that accrued from their relationships with the patriarchs, such as Potiphar (39:5), there is no other record of a direct blessing of a foreigner by a patriarch (cp. Abraham prayed, 20:17). This implies that Jacob was superior (cf. 14:19; Heb 7:7), perhaps accepted by Pharaoh because of Jacob's role as tribal head and of his senior age (v. 8). The polite relationship Jacob has with Pharaoh differs from the hostilities that Abraham and Isaac endured in foreign lands. The implication is clear: the Lord is with Jacob in this land as he is with Joseph. Egypt is a place of refuge for the Hebrews.

47:8–10   The king's inquiry into Jacob's age reflects the value that ancient Near Eastern cultures placed on longevity (v. 8). In Hebrew culture the esteem held for the aged was related to the assumption that the old had received divine favor (e.g., Lev 19:32; Ps 128:5–6; Prov 17:6; Zech 8:4) and possessed wisdom (Job 12:12; 32:7; Ps 105:22). The repeated mention of the patriarchs' ages points toward divine approval (e.g., 23:1; 25:7; 35:28–29;

---

[470] M. Brown, "ברך," *NIDOTTE* 1.766.

47:28; 50:22; cf. "good old age," 15:15; 25:8). The absence of respect for the aged was evidence of a decadent society (Deut 28:50). In the Semitic world, kinship-based societies elevated the old members to leadership positions. The concomitant importance of lineage reinforced the value attributed to the fathers of societal units, whether they were households, clans, or tribes.[471] Since Hebrew society was also patrilineal, the ruling "elders" *(zāqēn)* were typically older fathers (e.g., Exod 3:16; Deut 19:12). The term *zāqēn* also describes officials in Egypt (50:17) and in Moab and Midian (Num 22:4,7).

A Hebrew idiom expressing a person's age, lit., "the days of the years of your/my life," occurs three times in the dialogue (vv. 8–9). It appears, for example, in Barzillai's reply to David that at eighty years of age he is too old to accompany him to the capital city (2 Sam 19:35). Jacob, on the other hand, at 130 years shows a hearty resilience to have made this journey (v. 9).[472] Jacob describes his life in terms of his forefathers' days whose longevity exceeded his own (Abraham, 175 yrs. [25:7]; Isaac, 180 yrs. [35:28]; cf. Moses, Deut 34:7). Jacob will live seventeen more years under the auspices of his son (47:28). The implications of Jacob's answer testified of the Lord's favor toward the family. But he also admitted that his life was "difficult" *(rāʿîm,* "unhappy, misery"; cf. Ps 90:10). Jacob, in this reflective mood, recognized that his life had been scarred by the treachery he suffered at the hands of others—a just sentence for his early days of trickery (against Esau). Further, he describes his life and that of his ancestors in terms of their itinerant status as aliens in the world ("pilgrimage," *māgôr;* cf. *gēr,* "stranger"). There is a sobering humility about his answer to the king (cf. 23:4,7). He shows proper decorum toward his host, although he avoids the submissive language "your servant" (cf. 46:34; 47:3,4). In contrast, in speaking to Esau he referred to himself as "your servant" (33:4,5) and approached his brother by bowing (33:3). Jacob "blessed" *(bārak)* the king again at his leaving (v. 10), reinforcing the goodwill that the Egyptians and Israelites initially experienced. Perhaps for the Hebrew slaves of later Egypt, the king's acceptance of their ancestor Jacob showed that the Hebrews had the right to exist unmolested. God's hand of blessing was upon their ancestors, which even the nations had recognized and to which history had given evidence (e.g., Exod 1:7).

JOSEPH ESTABLISHES JACOB (47:11–12). **47:11–12** By settling the Jacobites in a land of their own "property" *(ʾăḥûzzâ,* "possession," v. 11), the imagery foreshadows the establishment of Israel in Canaan for a possession (e.g., 17:8; 48:4; Deut 32:49). Again the passage states that this land grant

---

[471] M. R. Jacobs, "Leadership, Elders," in *Dictionary of the Old Testament: Pentateuch* (Downers Grove: InterVarsity, 2003), 516.

[472] Joshua was deemed "old and advanced in years" (Josh 23:1–2), dying at 110 years (Josh 24:29).

was from Pharaoh himself (47:6). That Joseph "provided" (*pilpel*, from *kûl*, v. 12) necessities for the entire assembly ("all his father's household") fulfilled his promise (45:11), a pledge that he would reiterate to his brothers (50:21). (On the meaning of "father's household," cf. comments on 12:1.) That the provisions include the "children" (*ṭāp*[473]) points ahead to future generations. It is also an echo of Judah's fear for the survival of the family and "children" (43:8), a fear that Joseph alleviates (also 50:21). This generosity contrasts with the treatment received by the families (and "children," *ṭāp*) of the Egyptian populace (v. 24).

"In the land of Rameses *[ra'mĕsēs]*" identifies the region of Goshen (cf. comments on 45:10). Ironically, it became known for the store city "Rameses" erected in the area by their descendants under Egyptian slavery (Exod 1:11; 12:37; Num 33:3,5). The identity of the city Rameses is Pi-Ramesses (= modern Qantir, sixty-five mi. northeast of Cairo) in the area between Qanti and el-Khata'na in the northeast Delta region.[474] The site was the royal residence of the Ramesside dynasty of the nineteenth and twentieth dynasties (1295–1065 B.C.). Rameses II especially engaged in elaborate building projects in the area (1279–1212 B.C.), but building occurred earlier in the Middle Kingdom period (2106–1786 B.C.) at Tell ed-Dab'a (=Avaris, capital of the Hyksos, 1640–1530 B.C.), the southern part of Pi-Ramesses. Despite its importance to the nineteenth dynasty, the appearance of "Rameses" in Genesis and Exodus may be due to a later scribal updating of the location's original name and need not be an indicator of a late date for the events described.[475] Alternatively, some scholars explain that names like Rameses existed during the Hyksos period, long before the nineteenth dynasty, and may well reflect the original name of the site.[476]

10. Joseph's Administration in Egypt (47:13–31)

After Jacob's settlement in the land of Goshen (46:28–47:12), the narrative returns to the topic of the famine in Egypt and Canaan (47:13–26). The account traces the emerging famine (41:53–57), describing the starvation of the Egyp-

---

[473] לְפִי הַטָּף, the phrase, lit., "by the mouth of the little ones," is exceptional; some EVs include the wives in the expression, thus the general expression "their dependents" (NRSV, HCSB, NLT), or "down to the youngest" (NAB), "down to the least" (NJB), "down to the little ones" (NJPS).

[474] E. B. Pusch, "Piramesse," *OEAE* 3.48–50; M. Bietak, "Dab'a, Tell ed-," *OEAE* 1.351–54; E. F. Wente, "Rameses," *ABD* 5.617–68; Hoffmeier, *Israel in Egypt*, 117–18.

[475] See Hoffmeier, *Israel in Egypt*, 121–22.

[476] E.g., E. Merrill, *Kingdom of Priests: A History of Old Testament History* (Grand Rapids: Baker, 1987), 70–71; W. C. Kaiser Jr., *A History of Israel: From the Bronze Age Through the Jewish Wars* (Nashville: Broadman & Holman, 1998), 74–75.

tians. In contrast to the Egyptians and Canaanites, the family of Joseph is insulated from the harshest effects of the famine. They prosper under the patronage of Joseph (v. 27). The Hebrews do not lose their possessions or fall into slavery, whereas the Egyptians are slaves to the king through Joseph's handling of the royal granaries. After describing the "death" of the land, the narrative relates the preparations for the death of Jacob (vv. 27–31). Joseph accepts the oath imposed by his father, promising to return Jacob's body to Canaan for burial. What these two passages have in common is their attention to life and death. The populace pleads with Joseph for seed, "so that we may live and not die" (v. 19; cf. vv. 15,25). The "life" (v. 28) and imminent death of Jacob ("When the time drew near for Israel to die," v. 29a) precipitated his request to be buried in his ancestral sepulcher (vv. 29–31; cf. 49:29–31; 50:5–14). Despite the unrelenting famine, the Egyptians have a future, and the Hebrews even prosper in the midst of the famine. Although the masses survive ("You have saved our lives," v. 25a) and the Jacobite families prosper ("acquired property," v. 27b) in Egypt, Jacob knows that the future of his people lies in Canaan. He trusts that God's word will come to pass ("I will surely bring you back again. And Joseph's own hand will close your eyes," 46:4; cf. 48:21). Moreover, Joseph in both incidents is the facilitator of the two requests, first for the people's need for grain and second for the burial of his father. Joseph fulfills his obligations, responding to the impoverished people and honoring his father's final request. The author of Genesis reiterates by three burial reports that the Hebrew sojourners can look to the realization of the promises only after they have returned to Canaan (47:29–30; 49:29–31; 50:5–14; cf. 48:21).

There are two problems that the interpreter faces when considering the agrarian policy described in 47:13–26. First, there is the question regarding the Egyptian origin and authenticity of the system that the narrative portrays. There is no precise correlation between the description of Joseph's policy and what we know of Egyptian agrarian practices in a particular period. The closest correlation are texts of the second and first millennia from Mesopotamia, especially from ancient Emar (Tell Meskéné) dating to the thirteenth century.[477] There are, however, general lines of agreement between chap. 47 and known Egyptian practices.[478] In almost all periods, the state and temple primarily owned the land in Egypt, and Egyptian kings regularly imposed tax obligations on landowners and temple holdings from earliest times. From as early as the Old Kingdom there were periods, however, when priestly hold-

---

[477] Chavalas and Adamthwaite, "Archaeological Light on the Old Testament," 76–77, and V. A. Hurrowitz, "Joseph's Enslavement of the Egyptians (Genesis 47:13–26) in the Light of Famine Texts from Mesopotamia," *RB* 101 (1994): 335–62.

[478] Some historians and commentators, e.g., Speiser (*Genesis*, 353), as a point of comparison, remark that after the expulsion of Hyksos rule, Pharaoh (who was god) appropriated private land for the crown (ca. 1550).

ings or other special interests (tax-free zones) were exempted. That the temple was excluded from the one-fifth duty and was not supervised by Joseph (vv. 22,26) does not necessarily mean, however, that priestly holdings were exempted from all taxation.[479] The best sources for Egypt's taxation system come from the New Kingdom period, which give evidence of a complex bureaucratic system of collecting the annual general levy and occasional unscheduled levies by the power of the vizier. Local governors collected taxes for the central bureaucracy. The Wilbourn Papyrus, for example, from the time of Rameses V (1160–1156) reports that for large landowners, there was a thirty percent charge on the harvested produce and seventy percent returned to farmers for their own needs.[480] All in all, we cannot confidently utilize the account for dating Joseph's period or for the time of writing. The second millennium attestation of famine texts involving enslavement (Mesopotamia) at least shows that the practice was known early. Moreover, the general correlation with Egyptian economics at a minimum indicates that the Hebrew author did not freely imagine the agrarian reforms, especially since they differ from Israelite practices. In Israel families exclusively possessed and farmed their own lands before the period of the monarchy (e.g., 1 Sam 8:10–18; cf. 1 Sam 17:25; 1 Kgs 4:7; 12:4; 2 Kgs 23:35). Moreover, the projected royal tax in Israel was half (ten percent, 1 Sam 8:15,17) that in the time of Joseph (twenty percent, vv. 24–26); the standard religious duty in Israel was ten percent (Lev 27:30–32; Deut 14:22–25; the precise relationship of the triennial tithe [Deut 14:28] to the annual tithe is unclear). The year of Jubilee, at least ideally, ensured that the land remained under the auspices of the original family, who was viewed as a tenant in the land, which was exclusively owned by the Lord (Lev 25; 27).

Second, commentators have questioned the ethics of the policy that Joseph carried out, which involved the enslavement of the general Egyptian populace (On the textual problem see comments on v. 21.) Two stages of acquisition by Joseph in behalf of the king occur: first, the people (including Canaan, v. 15) give their money and livestock for grain in the beginning year (vv. 14–17); and second, they barter their land and their freedom in the second year (vv. 18–21). The future arrangement involved a form of land tenure in which the state provided seed and the debtor returned a fifth of the yield to Pharaoh (vv. 20–26). On the first matter, some commentators have charged that Joseph oppressed the Egyptian people by his bartering schemes, which led to the forfeiture of all possessions and ended in servitude to the crown.[481] Apologists for Joseph's behav-

---

[479] K. A. Kitchen, "Joseph," *NBD* 659.

[480] S. L. D. Katary, "Taxation," *OEAE* 3.351–56; E. Bleiberg, "Taxation and Conscription," in *Encyclopedia of the Archaeology of Ancient Egypt* (London/New York: Routledge, 1999), 761–63.

[481] Y.-W. Fung, *Victim and Victimizer: Joseph's Interpretation of His Destiny* (Sheffield: Sheffield Academic Press, 2000).

ior often note, however, that the crown's confiscation was incremental, and the populace itself proposed the exchange of land and liberty for food (v. 19). Debtor's slavery was commonplace in the ancient Near East that typically showed stages of severity from forfeiture of land to indebtedness requiring the sale of dependents. Laws and royal reforms attempted to curtail the practice and its excesses. Both Egyptian and Mesopotamian slavery differentiated generally between formerly free people who became debt slaves and foreigners (usually war captives) who were bought and sold as chattel. Mesopotamian laws and contracts indicate that creditors obtained the service of the debt slave until the debt was covered,[482] but chattel slaves belonged to their owners without much chance of release.[483] Although we cannot know from Genesis, there is reason to believe that the voluntary submission of the people assumes that the enslavement was not permanent (cp. the law established by Joseph, 47:26).

After the money of the people ran out, they desperately turned to Joseph for a solution, and he proposed their livestock. Their relieved response shows their gratitude to Joseph's acquiescence to their requests ("You have saved our lives," v. 25). Although Joseph acknowledges that he "bought" the people and their land for Pharaoh (v. 23), what follows is an informal agrarian pact, not treatment of the people as chattel (vv. 24–25). Since they agree to the proposal (v. 25), the arrangement is close to tenured farming, meaning that the farmer has access to the land and its produce and makes an agreed return to the owner.[484] Moreover, the one-fifth tax, leaving four-fifths to the workers, is generous compared to what is known elsewhere in the ancient Near East. This passage cannot be used as a justification for slavery or the charge that the Bible promotes slavery. It must be interpreted, as in the case of the slavery texts of the Pentateuch and New Testament (e.g., Exod 20:20–21,32; Eph 6:5–8) in light of the cultural norms of the time. There is a trajectory within Scripture itself toward better treatment of slaves which, taken to its logical

---

[482] G. C. Chirichigno notes especially the Old Babylonian *mēšarum* edicts and the Laws of Hammurabi §§116–17 and the Laws of Eshunna §LE 39 (*Debt-Slavery in Israel and the Ancient Near East,* JSOTSup 141 [Sheffield: JSOT Press, 1993], 55–144 [143]).

[483] Israelite practice recognized the need for similar restraints (e.g., Exod 21:2–6,20–21,26–27; Lev 25:39–55; Deut 15:12–18; 2 Kgs 4:1–7; Jer 24:8–16; Neh 5:1–13). Although biblical laws are not always clear to interpreters as to whether reference is made to debt slaves or chattel slaves, there are indications that Hebrew society recognized a difference (cp. "Hebrew" slave, e.g., Exod 21:2–6; Deut 15:12; chattel slave, e.g., Lev 25:44–45). See Chirichigno, *Debt-Slavery,* 145–85.

[484] Similar (but not the same) to this practice is modern usufructuary in which land is sold to another person but specific rights of usage (e.g., water rights) are *not conveyed* to the new owner. In the case of Joseph, however, the people do not retain rights of usage; rather, Joseph benevolently grants them rights of usage. The NJB probably attempts to mitigate the idea of slavery: "While the people he reduced to serfdom . . ." (v. 21).

conclusion, ultimately provides the basis for the end of the practice.[485]

We might also add that the exception made to temple lands (vv. 22,26) shows that Joseph's action was not a crass land grab without regard for Egyptian tradition and society's welfare. What Joseph established not only saved the people from starvation but also provided a system whereby they could live securely once the famine abated. The passage does not present Joseph as a brutal taskmaster, such as we see in Pharaoh's policy of Exodus 1, but portrays him as a conscientious overseer. The point of the author's inclusion of the agrarian reforms is to show that Joseph, who was subservient to an Egyptian overlord, has now become the overlord of the Egyptians.

COMPOSITION. The unit consists of two parts: the agrarian policy established by Joseph (vv. 13–26) and Jacob's burial instructions (vv. 27–31). Documentarians usually posited two sources (Yahwist [J] and Elohist [E]) for 47:13–26, assigning the majority (if not all) to J because of the content's association with 41:55–56 (J). Gunkel, for example, believed that it originally followed on 41:55–56 but was displaced to accommodate chronological concerns.[486] Coats, on the other hand, who viewed the Joseph story as a unified novella, attributed the tax etiology to J as an addition to the conclusion, created solely for etiological purposes.[487] For Coats the Joseph story ends in 47:27, forming the closure to the matching inclusio 37:1. Since scholars typically observe that 47:13–26 "makes no real contribution to the Joseph story," they consider it secondary, "isolated and extraneous."[488] As an etiology, explaining the origins of Egypt's legislated tax system ("still in force today," 47:26), it is unrelated to the family story of Joseph, even distinctive from the "Joseph in Egypt" narrative in chaps. 40–41. Why then was it attached to the family narrative? Some explain that the redactor added it to the original account to attribute greater stature to Joseph as a wise administrator to whom the Egyptians are indebted.[489] Redford concluded that it was an Israelite etiology that exhibited "mild amusement and pride" that Egyptian economy relied on Hebrew genius.[490] From the perspective of the entire Joseph account ("*tôlĕdōt* of Jacob," 37:2–50:24), it is not intrusive but logically brings to conclusion the wider concern for Jacob and his sons' destiny in Egypt.[491] Van Seters tentatively proposes that the passage is a late midrash that the (exilic/postexilic) Yahwist created (due to his etiological interests). It serves as a contrast with the

---

[485] See W. J. Webb, *Slaves, Women and Homosexuals: Exploring the Hermeneutics of Cultural Analysis* (Downers Grove: InterVarsity, 2001). Although Mesopotamian laws show humane reforms of the institution of slavery, the Israelite laws distinctively elevate the status of slaves by extending to them some rights and privileges of citizens (e.g., Exod 12:44; 21:23–27; Lev 25:6; see Chirichigno, *Debt-Slavery,* 177, 185).

[486] Gunkel, *Genesis,* 442–43.

[487] Coats, *Genesis,* 299.

[488] Coats, *From Canaan to Egypt,* 53.

[489] von Rad, *Genesis,* 410.

[490] Redford, *Joseph,* 182.

[491] Thompson, *The Origin Tradition,* 121.

Hebrew enslavement in Exodus 1 and the brothers' submission to servitude in 50:18–19.[492]

Verses 13–26, however, are not an "appendage,"[493] having nothing to do with the Joseph family. After dealing with the famine in his family, the passage turns attention to Joseph's success in behalf of the state for the provision of the Egyptian people. The taxation of the Egyptians is a "foil"[494] for the special benevolence Pharaoh and Joseph show toward the Israelites. Humphreys has shown the linkage between chaps. 40–41 and 47:13–26 through the provision of a one-fifth tax (cf. *ḥ-m-š* in 41:34; 47:24,34), which was recommended to Pharaoh by Joseph in chap. 41 and realized in behalf of Pharaoh by Joseph in 47:13–26.[495] Yet why should 47:13–26 occur in its present location, although it logically follows on chaps. 40–41? The strategy the author uses requires its present placement. Chapters 39–41 describe the rise of Joseph by which he accomplishes the salvation of his family as played out in chaps. 42–46. The perpetuity of the provision made for Jacob and family in 47:1–12 indicates that the family will survive the remaining years of the famine. But the rise of Joseph told in chaps. 40–41 was also divinely arranged for the deliverance of Egypt ("God has shown Pharaoh what he is about to do," 41:28). That denouement has yet to be told. The detailed accounting in 47:13–26 of the severity of the famine and of the tax code established by Joseph satisfies the narrative expectation of the salvation of Egypt. Both halves of 47:1–12 and 47:13–26 complete what the earlier narratives have left unfinished: 47:1–12 completes chaps. 42–46, and 47:13–26 completes chaps. 41–42. This effectively interlocks the two plot elements that make up the story, the account of the family schism and the rise of Joseph in Pharaoh's court.

As for the genealogical notice and burial request of Jacob (47:27–31), the consensus among scholars is that the passage is a combination of two sources. Verses 27a,29–31 are J (cp. "thigh" ritual in 24:2[J]), and vv. 27b–28 exhibit the signs (vocabulary, age notice) typically indicating the priestly source (P). In the totality of the narrative conclusion, Coats and Westermann agree that 47:29 begins the complex unit of 47:29(28)–50:14, consisting of many disparate parts. The death and burial of Jacob, however, anticipated in 47:27–31, continues what has long been expected by the many allusions to Jacob's well-being in the Joseph narrative (e.g., 37:35; 42:38; 43:27–28; 45:3,28; 46:4). From the beginning of the story to the end, the age of Jacob has been of interest in the development of the plot (37:3; 43:27; 44:20; 48:10). Wenham observes that 47:29–31 conforms to the ending of the former two journeys in which there is a reference to Jacob's death (42:38; 45:28).[496] As Coats observed, the framework of chaps. 47:28–50:14 involves the death scenes and the carrying out of the burial of Jacob

---

[492] Van Seters, *Prologue to History,* 318.

[493] Westermann, *Genesis 37–50,* 173–74.

[494] Carr includes 47:13–27 in the original Joseph account (*Reading the Fractures of Genesis,* 276).

[495] Humphreys, *Joseph and His Family,* 146.

[496] Wenham, *Genesis 16–50,* 438.

(47:29–31; 48:1,21; 49:29–33; 50:4–14).[497] Especially the deathbed setting dominates the final activities of Jacob, which in each case Joseph figures prominently. Jacob instructs Joseph in anticipation of his death (47:29–31), blesses Joseph's sons (48:1–22), and blesses all twelve sons, making Joseph the prominent recipient (49:1–33). Therefore the concluding paragraph (47:27–31) of our present unit is transitional and preparatory for the main issue that remains in the Joseph narrative. The "father-son" motif has been critical to the development of the Joseph narrative and rightly ends with Joseph carrying out his father's wishes to the letter. All that remains in Genesis is Joseph's deathbed remarks and his body's disposition (50:15–26). The age notices of Jacob (47:28) and of Joseph (50:22,26) bracket the final activities that lay the groundwork for the future return to Egypt and the blessing there that Jacob predicted (48:21; 49:1–33; 50:5) and Joseph repeated (50:24–25). The age notices and deathbed scenes are part and parcel of the Joseph narrative, expected in the author's development in the story.

STRUCTURE.   The borders of this unit are marked. The beginning construction, "[Now] there was no food in the land" (v. 13a; cf. comments there), indicates a different subject, although not describing altogether new information. Verse 13 reaches back to the summary narration of the famine's rise (41:54–56), reintroducing the famine but detailing the famine's severity and effects. The immediate context of Israel's safety (vv. 11–12) provides the foil for the threatening situation faced by the Egyptians in vv. 13–26. The end of the unit occurs in v. 31. The stereotypical phrase starting chap. 48, "Some time later"[498] (v. 1), often announces a new subject (cf. 22:1,20; 40:1; 1 Kgs 21:1).

The passage falls naturally into two parts, distinguished by content and literary genre. As the first part of the unit, vv. 13–26 report the economic response of Joseph, who represents the crown, to the increasingly grave famine. The etiological aspect in v. 26 ("a law . . . still in force today") couches the report from the author's long-range perspective. The second half, vv. 27–31, consists of mixed literary forms. A summation statement (v. 27) and an age notice (v. 28) introduce the dialogue involving the oath sworn by Joseph, who represents the totality of the sons (vv. 29–31). The beginning and the end of vv. 13–31 concern the land and the life-and-death circumstances of the inhabitants. The land of Egypt is dying and the inhabitants with it; Joseph, on the other hand, answers the people's pleas and saves them from starvation. Jacob, too, is dying, and Joseph answers Jacob's request by swearing to save his father from the ignominy of burial in a foreign land.

The first subunit consists of an introduction (v. 13), followed by progressive steps that lead to the acquisition of all the land for Pharaoh and a new law (v. 26). Narration encompasses (vv. 13,26) embedded dialogue between

---

[497] Coats, *Genesis,* 301–2.
[498] וַיְהִי אַחֲרֵי הַדְּבָרִים הָאֵלֶּה, "after these things" (48:1).

Joseph and the populace interspersed with narrative description.

introduction: severity of the famine (v. 13)
   narrative: Joseph receives money for food (v. 14)
      dialogue: people's request for food (vv. 15–16)
   narrative: Joseph receives livestock for food (v. 17)
      dialogue: people's request for food and seed (vv. 18–19)
   narrative: Joseph accepts enslavement for food (vv. 20–22)
      dialogue: people's agreement to bondage (vv. 23–25)
conclusion: a new law (v. 26)

As for the progression in the narrative, Joseph first sells grain for silver in the first year, forwarding the proceeds to Pharaoh (v. 14). Second, he offers to exchange grain for their livestock during the second year (vv. 15–17). Third, he receives their property and accepts the people's serfdom, excepting priestly holdings (vv. 18–22). And, finally, Joseph institutes a tenant arrangement, deriving one-fifth of the produce for the realm (vv. 23–26).

The second subunit begins with summary statements in vv. 27–28, returning to the idea of Israel's longevity in Egypt. Verse 27 describes the permanency and population growth of the Israelites in Egypt (v. 27). Verse 28 parallels v. 27 in its introduction: "Now the Israelites settled in Egypt" (v. 27a)//"Jacob lived in Egypt . . ." (v. 28a). Verse 28 concerns the man Jacob, whose life continued seventeen more years in Egypt, implying the same notion of Israel's permanency in the land. Verses 29–31, however, reverse the idea of permanency when the passage jumps ahead to Jacob's last wish for his body to be transported to Canaan. The dialogue between Jacob and Joseph entails a ritual sign ("put your hand under my thigh," v. 29) and oath ("promise . . . swear," vv. 30–31) to which Joseph agrees ("I will do as you say. . . . Then Joseph swore to him . . .," vv. 30–31). This subunit (vv. 27–31) transitions to the deathbed scene in chap. 48 in which Jacob blesses his grandsons, Manasseh and Ephraim.

(1) Joseph Procures Land for Pharaoh (47:13–26)

[13]There was no food, however, in the whole region because the famine was severe; both Egypt and Canaan wasted away because of the famine. [14]Joseph collected all the money that was to be found in Egypt and Canaan in payment for the grain they were buying, and he brought it to Pharaoh's palace. [15]When the money of the people of Egypt and Canaan was gone, all Egypt came to Joseph and said, "Give us food. Why should we die before your eyes? Our money is used up."

[16]"Then bring your livestock," said Joseph. "I will sell you food in exchange for your livestock, since your money is gone." [17]So they brought their livestock to Joseph, and he gave them food in exchange for their horses, their sheep and goats, their cattle and donkeys. And he brought them through that year with food in exchange for all their livestock.

[18]When that year was over, they came to him the following year and said,

"We cannot hide from our lord the fact that since our money is gone and our livestock belongs to you, there is nothing left for our lord except our bodies and our land. ¹⁹Why should we perish before your eyes—we and our land as well? Buy us and our land in exchange for food, and we with our land will be in bondage to Pharaoh. Give us seed so that we may live and not die, and that the land may not become desolate."

²⁰So Joseph bought all the land in Egypt for Pharaoh. The Egyptians, one and all, sold their fields, because the famine was too severe for them. The land became Pharaoh's, ²¹and Joseph reduced the people to servitude, from one end of Egypt to the other. ²²However, he did not buy the land of the priests, because they received a regular allotment from Pharaoh and had food enough from the allotment Pharaoh gave them. That is why they did not sell their land.

²³Joseph said to the people, "Now that I have bought you and your land today for Pharaoh, here is seed for you so you can plant the ground. ²⁴But when the crop comes in, give a fifth of it to Pharaoh. The other four-fifths you may keep as seed for the fields and as food for yourselves and your households and your children."

²⁵"You have saved our lives," they said. "May we find favor in the eyes of our lord; we will be in bondage to Pharaoh."

²⁶So Joseph established it as a law concerning land in Egypt—still in force today—that a fifth of the produce belongs to Pharaoh. It was only the land of the priests that did not become Pharaoh's.

This pericope moves from problem ("the famine was severe," v. 13) to resolution ("a law concerning the land," v. 26). Joseph provides security for Jacob's family (vv. 11–12), and he supplies continued existence for the Egyptians. Joseph's foresight enriches the house of Pharaoh, and his benevolence saves the Egyptians. Joseph opens the royal granaries, selling food for silver (vv. 13–14), exchanging grain for livestock (vv. 15–17), obtaining the estates and servitude of the people (vv. 18–22), and initiating a statute of perpetual land tenure (vv. 23–26).

JOSEPH SELLS FOOD (47:13–14). **47:13–14** Verse 13 initiates a new episode,⁴⁹⁹ providing background information. The verse back references to 41:54–56, which summarizes in general what is detailed in the present narrative. Twice in v. 13 the dire state of affairs is attributed to "famine" (cf. Abraham and Isaac, 12:10; 26:1). That the famine was "severe" *(kābēd)* is a recurring idea in the Joseph narrative (43:1; 47:4; cf. 12:10), but here in fulfillment of Pharaoh's dream (41:31), it is said to be "very *[mĕʾōd]* severe." So as to reinforce the point, the author observes there was "no food" (v. 13) in the "whole" region, specifying that Egypt and Canaan "wasted away"

---

⁴⁹⁹ *Wāw* disjunctive initiates the new scene, וְלֶחֶם אֵין בְּכָל־הָאָרֶץ, "Now there was no food in all the land" (v. 13).

(lāhâ[500]*)*. Repeatedly in the narrative the contiguous regions of "Egypt and Canaan" are specifically named (vv. 13,14,15; Acts 7:11). These are the two geographical foci of the Joseph account.

Again the text shows the scope of the famine by reporting the people's desperation, for he "collected all the money that was to be found" (v. 14) in the two territories. The word "found" *(māṣā)* often describes gathering up of money, food, and elusive captives (e.g., Judg 20:48; 1 Sam 21:3[4]; 2 Kgs 12:18[19]), which involves seeking them out. The sense is that the people fervently rummage for money, "bringing every last penny."[501] "Collected" *(lāqaṭ)* describes gathering up a variety of physical objects (e.g., "stones," 31:46) but especially the retrieval of foods including the gleaning of grain (e.g., Ruth 2:2; cf. Exod 16:4; Lev 19:9–10). The synonym "gathered" *(qābaṣ)* in the earlier description of collecting grain in the storehouses (41:35,48) commonly describes the assembling of people (e.g., 49:2). The appearance of *lāqaṭ* is more appropriate to the gathering of money, but it also may express a subtle irony since the people had no produce to "glean" from their wasted fields and vineyards. Since later Joseph distributes seed for planting (v. 23), he shows confidence that ultimately substantial productivity will return according to Pharaoh's dream (41:27,30,54). In the meanwhile Joseph manages in the name of Pharaoh all matters pertaining to the distribution of the stored grain, ensuring that the king receives the proceeds.

JOSEPH BARTERS FOR LIVESTOCK (47:15–17). **47:15–17** The duration of the famine exceeds their money and thus the whole of the region ("all Egypt") is dependent on Joseph's mercy. "Why should we die before your [Joseph] eyes?" is the rationale that the Egyptians make to Joseph for continuing the distribution of grain (v. 15). He can benefit from their penniless condition if they can come to an agreement. Joseph arranges for a bartering of their livestock for food (v. 16). Verse 17 specifies the kind and range of animals that they trade, showing that the retaining of valuable work animals was of no benefit to them ("all their livestock," v. 17b). The mention of "horses" is especially telling, since it was a valuable beast associated with Egyptian aristocracy, war, and international trade (e.g., Deut 17:6; 1 Kgs 10:28–29; Eccl 10:7; Isa 31:1,3). The picture of Joseph enriching Pharaoh's treasury at the people's expense can be interpreted as cruel, but the author has shown that Joseph's actions are tempered by mercy. He is said to have "brought them through" *(piel, from nāhal)*, a term that can indicate a gentle leading of the weak to a place of respite (e.g., 33:14; Ps 23:2; Isa 40:11; 51:18). There is no temptation to hoard the grain for himself and Pharaoh's needs alone; Joseph recognizes that providing for the

---

[500] וַתֵּלַהּ, from the word לההּ ("languish, faint"), occurs only here, probably a bi-form of וַתֵּלָא (לאה, Job 4:5), "to become tired, weary" (BDB 529).

[501] Wenham, *Genesis 16–50*, 448.

people is God's purpose for him (45:5; 50:20; cf. "You have saved our lives," 45:25). Moreover, he trusts in God's revelation that the famine will cease at the appointed time, enabling him to gauge wisely the allocated amounts. "That year" indicates that they would not have survived much longer without Joseph's forethought and tolerance. The significance of "that year" (v. 17) and "the following year" (lit., "the second year," v. 18) is uncertain. Since the people and Joseph speak of seeding the ground (vv. 19,23), the two years in view may suggest the final two years of the seven-year famine.

JOSEPH OBTAINS PROPERTY AND PEOPLE (47:18–22). **47:18–19** The people approach Joseph in the subsequent year, acknowledging that they cannot negotiate with leverage since he knows that they have nothing left, only themselves ("our bodies") and their lands (v. 18; cf. *gĕwîyâ*). They depend on his goodwill. The passage strengthens the idea of their desperate condition by wordplay. The word group *t-m-m,* translated "was gone" (v. 15), "was over" (v. 18a), and "is gone" (v. 18b) also describes the Hebrew community perishing (e.g., in the desert, Num 14:33). The word for "body" *(gĕwîyâ)* may be used of living persons, as in our passage (cf. Neh 9:37), but it typically expresses a "corpse, dead body" (e.g., 1 Sam 31:10). We can also mention a possible double entendre by the money that was "was gone/used up *['āpēs]*," described earlier in vv. 15–16. The word *'āpēs* can also convey the sense of human destruction ("come to an end," Isa 16:4; "will vanish," 29:20[502]).

The terms "buy" *(qānâ)* and "sell" *(mākar)* appear together (vv. 19–23), describing commercial dealings involving property or persons (e.g., Exod 21:2,7–8; Lev 25:14–16 and *passim*).[503] The reversal of Joseph's status as slave and now ruler over the Egyptians (vv. 23–26) shows an unexpected extension of his dreams to include not only his family's submission but also the submission of Egypt, a foreign power (cp. 15:13). Israel remembered Egypt as "the house of slavery" (NIV "land of slavery," e.g., Exod 13:3; Deut 15:15; Jer 34:13); but when recalling their ancestors, they saw that God had freed Joseph and had honored him by establishing him over Egypt (Ps 105:21–22; Acts 7:10; *1 Mac* 2:53). The Lord turned the tables on Israel's enemies when the slaves plundered the Egyptians (Exod 3:22; 12:36). The people plead that it will give Joseph no benefit to watch them perish (v. 19). They propose voluntary servitude so that they might survive the ordeal. Their request includes "seed" whereby they can work the land, looking ahead to the end of the famine. Seeding the ground in the time of famine would possibly

---

[502] כָּלָה//אָפֵס ("consume, cease") and תמם ("complete, perish"; Isa 16:4); and כָּלָה//אָפֵס and כָּרַה ("cut off"; Isa 29:20; V. Hamp, "אָפֵס," *TDOT* 1.361–62).

[503] But not always as slaves (e.g., Ruth 4:5,9–10); קנה ("buy, acquire") appears (as in the Mishnah) in a marriage contract when it involves a commercial arrangement. See D. H. Weiss, "The Use of QNY in Connection with Marriage," *HTR* 57 (1964): 244–48; E. F. Campbell, *Ruth,* AB (Garden City: Doubleday, 1975), 145, 147, 159.

delay the total erosion of the land, otherwise allowing it to become "desolate" *(šāmam)* through neglect (e.g., Lev 26:22–43). Alternatively, the people may mean that their deaths would lead to the destruction of the land, making the new landholdings useless to Pharaoh's future household.

47:20–22 Verses 20–22 summarize the outcome of the transaction, clarifying that the bargain was inclusive and that it was the consequence of an unusually relentless famine ("severe," *ḥāzaq,* cf. comments on 41:47). Verse 20 describes the purchase of the land, and v. 21 focuses attention on the people.[504] Repeatedly the passage says that the purchases are for Pharaoh's treasury, not Joseph's personal enrichment (vv. 19,20[2x],23,24,25,26[2x]).

The translation of v. 21 is troublesome, as the diverse readings among the versions show. The MT, followed by many EVs (e.g., AV, NASB, HCSB, REB, NJPS), says Joseph "moved them [i.e., the people] into the cities."[505] The SP, LXX (and perhaps Vg.), followed by other EVs (e.g., NIV, NRSV, NAB, NJB, NLT), read "he made them slaves."[506] Either reading makes sense in the context, though the latter corresponds well to the topic of servitude in v. 19. Yet since the text addresses the usage of the land in vv. 20,22, it is also sensible for the passage to tell what became of the population inhabiting the newly acquired parcels (MT). That such a mobilization of the population was temporary or limited in its extent is suggested by the tenant farming that is called for (vv. 19,23). "From one end of Egypt to the other" expresses the breadth of influence that Joseph exercised over the region. An important exception to this pattern is the priests, who do not dispose of their land, since they receive a regular food "allotment" (*ḥōq,* cf. "regular share," Exod 29:28) from Pharaoh's assets (v. 22). Israel's means of supporting the Levites and priests was through the sacral tithe provided by the people (e.g., Num 18:21–32). Also the Levites were assigned cities (with pasturelands) rather than extensive land parcels (e.g., Num 35:1–8; Deut 18:1–8).

JOSEPH TAXES THE PEOPLE (47:23–26). **47:23–26** By obtaining the people and their lands, Joseph in the name of Pharaoh establishes a tenant relationship, in which they can farm the land for sustenance (v. 23). Joseph's declaration of possession and provision in v. 23 echoes the requests of the people themselves in v. 19. The passage portrays Joseph as a compliant partner in assisting the destitute, not an oppressive schemer. (On the significance of "bought you," see v. 19.) The state provides the "seed"[507] (v. 23) and receives

---

[504] וְאֶת־הָעָם הֶעֱבִיר אֹתוֹ, "As for the people, he (moved or enslaved) them" (v. 21); the object is prominent by its beginning location in the clause and the resumptive pronoun (אֹתוֹ). GKC §143c.

[505] הֶעֱבִיר אֹתוֹ לֶעָרִים, lit., "he relocated them to the cities."

[506] הֶעֱבִיד אֹתוֹ לַעֲבָדִים, lit., "he enslaved them as slaves."

[507] "Here is seed for you" renders the puzzling Hb. הֵא לָכֶם זֶרַע; the particle הֵא, whose meaning is uncertain, occurs here and Ezek 16:43 (see *IBHS* §40.2.5d).

a portion of the income (v. 24). "When the crop comes in" *(tĕbûʾâ,* v. 24) is a common term describing the regulations of harvest among the Israelites (e.g., Exod 23:10; Lev 25:3–22; Deut 14:22). The amount of one-fifth (cf. 41:34) is another similarity to the Hebrew practice pertaining to the laws of restitution and redemption when a fifth of the value was added to the total worth (e.g., Lev 5:16,24; 27:13–31). In this case, however, the fifth is a royal tax (cf. 41:34–37; 2 Kgs 23:35; Amos 7:1; Neh 5:4), not a cultic requirement. That the people are permitted to keep four-fifths shows the crown's generosity,[508] enabling them to do more than survive the economically hard time (v. 24). The misappropriation of taxes was a constant threat to the general public, which typically led to oppression of the underclass (e.g., 1 Kgs 4:7–28; 12:1–24; Amos 5:11). That the people consider Joseph a savior ("you have saved our lives") should mitigate our modern sensitivity to Joseph's action (v. 25). The Egyptians gladly submit to Joseph's plan, which accomplishes the bond service that they themselves initially propose (v. 19). (On the phrase "find favor," see vol. 1A, pp. 345–46; cf. comments on 6:8.) Verse 26 provides a summary conclusion, adding that the arrangement was a perpetual "law" ("statute," *ḥōq*). This same term describes the fixed "allotment" for the priests (v. 22). "Still in force today" renders the common phrase "to this day" *(ʿad hayyôm hazzeh,* 26:33; 32:32[33]), indicating that the practice continued to at least the time of the author's writing.

(2) Joseph Promises Jacob (47:27–31)

[27]Now the Israelites settled in Egypt in the region of Goshen. They acquired property there and were fruitful and increased greatly in number.

[28]Jacob lived in Egypt seventeen years, and the years of his life were a hundred and forty-seven. [29]When the time drew near for Israel to die, he called for his son Joseph and said to him, "If I have found favor in your eyes, put your hand under my thigh and promise that you will show me kindness and faithfulness. Do not bury me in Egypt, [30]but when I rest with my fathers, carry me out of Egypt and bury me where they are buried."

"I will do as you say," he said.

[31]"Swear to me," he said. Then Joseph swore to him, and Israel worshiped as he leaned on the top of his staff.

The concluding narrative unit reports again of the successful settlement of the Israelites, adding that their number grew in Egypt (v. 27). An age notice for Jacob follows, indicating that he, too, achieved a long and successful life in Egypt (v. 28). In anticipation of his death and burial, Jacob imposes an oath on Joseph, who swears to bury him in Canaan (vv. 29–31). Despite the entrench-

---

[508] Sarna remarks that under Hammurabi the tenured farmer paid two-thirds to one-half of the produce after deducting expenses; interest rates on money advanced was commonly one-fifth and on loans for crops was one-third (*Genesis,* 322); *1 Mac* 10:29 speaks of a third of the grain and half the fruit trees for mortgage.

ment of the Israelites in Egypt, Jacob's request signals that the future of the nation is in Canaan.

ISRAEL RESIDES IN EGYPT (47:27–28). **47:27–28** These two summary verses describe the inhabitance of Egypt by "Israel" (v. 27) and by the person "Jacob" (v. 28). The parallel language beginning the two verses reinforces the importance of Jacob as father of the nation, which continues to be in view in the passage: "Israel settled in the land of Egypt"//"Jacob lived in the land of Egypt." Moreover, following the singular "Israel settled" are plural verbs ("acquired . . . were fruitful and increased . . ."), referring to the descendants of the eponymous head. The Israelites "acquired property" (*'āḥaz,* cf. 34:10) through the benevolence of Pharaoh because of the esteem that Joseph gained. That they "were fruitful and increased greatly" expresses the Genesis theme of blessing (1:22,28; 9:1,7; 17:6,20; 28:3; 35:11; 48:4). Despite their foreign residence, the Lord maintains his commitment of blessing to the patriarchs. The same can be said of Jacob in his youth when his sojourn in Paddan Aram resulted in numerous descendants and wealth (32:10[11]). The prosperity of Israel in Egypt, however, also sounds an ominous note in anticipation of Israel's bondage, when Pharaoh feared their number and believed that their population would spill beyond the region of Goshen (Exod 1:7–13; cf. Gen 15:13).

Despite the long period anticipated ("four hundred years," 15:13), theirs is a provisional residence in Egypt (15:14; 46:4) as Jacob's burial request signifies (v. 28). His seventeen years in Egypt under Joseph's care echoes the seventeen years of Joseph when the Joseph narrative began (37:2). Even if one were to believe in advance that the outcome of Joseph's separation from his father would land them in Egypt together once again, how it came about could hardly be imagined. These two verses that review the past but also anticipate the future transparently exhibit the benevolent and guiding hand of God in the lives of this father and son. Jacob's shorter age of 147 years contrasts with the longer lifespans of his ancestors (cf. comments on v. 9; cf. vol. 1A, pp. 334–35 at 6:3). Mention of his age at death is given much earlier in the narrative than the narration of his death (49:33), which departs from the pattern for reporting the deaths of Abraham (25:17) and Isaac (35:29). The context of chap. 47 makes its inclusion here effective, since the chapter describes the fate of the descendants in the land. Jacob's fate is not in the land of Egypt. "Egypt was to Jacob and his family what the ark was to Noah—a temporary shelter from the disaster on the outside."[509] Stating in advance his death and burial indicates the importance they hold for the remainder of chaps. 48–50.[510]

JOSEPH SWEARS TO RETURN JACOB (47:29–31). **47:29–31a** Jacob's insistence upon the return of his body to the family burial site at Machpelah

---

[509] Hamilton, *Genesis Chapters 18–50,* 625.
[510] Sarna, *Genesis,* 323.

forecasts the destiny of his descendants who will be restored to the land. The seriousness with which Jacob holds this request is the oath that he implores Joseph to assume. Jacob recognizes that he is dependent on Joseph's goodwill; therefore he politely makes his petition ("If I have found favor," v. 29; cf. 18:3; 30:27; 33:10; 50:4; Exod 34:9). The rite of oath and the language of the verse manifestly mimic Abraham and his servant (chap. 24), whose commission from Abraham also pertains to the future of the promises. In that case Isaac could not leave the land, and in this case Jacob cannot be kept from the land.[511] The petitionary character of Jacob's request is reflected by the jussive form of the verb, "Do not bury me [*'al nā' tiqběrēnî]*/in Egypt." Jacob describes his death by a common euphemism, "rest(ed) with my/his fathers" (v. 30; e.g., Deut 31:16; 1 Kgs 2:10), which emphasizes his solidarity with his ancestry. "Bury me where they are buried" further indicates his commitment to his kinship (cf. Ruth 1:17; 1 Kgs 13:31). Joseph agrees to the request, using a standard phrase expressing full concurrence, "as you say" (lit., "according to your word," *kidbārekā;* e.g., 30:34; 44:10; Exod 8:6). Jacob then implores him to utter the ritual oath, which Joseph promptly fulfills (v. 31a). The narrative describes the oath in typical oath formulae, "Swear [from *šaba*] . . . [he] swore [from *šaba*]" (e.g., 21:23–24; 24:9; 25:33; 31:53; 1 Sam 24:21–22[22–23]).

47:31b The description of Jacob's reaction poses translation problems. The first question is the sense of *ḥāwâ,* meaning either "worship" or "bowing" (i.e., resting on, leaning on). The NIV's "worshiped" (cf., e.g., NASB, REB, NLT) interprets *ḥāwâ* as the technical use of the term, that is, bowing before God (e.g., 24:26; Deut 17:3).[512] Others have a neutral rendering, "Israel bowed himself" (NRSV; cf. NAB, NJB, NJPS), which permits either worship of God, or a show of respect toward Joseph (HCSB), or simply that he steadies himself because of his frailty.

The second difficulty in the verse is the variant readings *miṭṭâ* (MT), meaning "bed," or *maṭṭeh,* meaning "staff" (LXX, *rabdos;* Heb 11:21), that is, he bowed on his staff or on his bed. That he worshiped the Lord on his bed has a parallel with David's deathbed prayer (also *ḥāwâ,* 1 Kgs 1:47–48),[513] but that Jacob already addressed his son as a superior, "If I have found favor in your eyes" (v. 29), suggests that he is bowing before Joseph here.[514] Possibly, the

---

[511] On the ritual of the oath, see comments on Abraham and his servant at 24:2,9; the language "kindness and faithfulness" appears in the same incident; see comments on 24:27,49 [cf. 32:10(11)]; also for "kindness" in pledges and petitions, see 19:19; 21:23; 24:12,14,27; 39:21; 40:14.

[512] Cf. Vg. *adoravit Israhel Deum* ("Israel worshiped God").

[513] Delitzsch, *A New Commentary on Genesis,* 2.356.

[514] R. de Hoop contends that Jacob bows to Joseph; he translates Jacob bowed "to the head of the tribe [הַמִּטָּה]," meaning he acknowledged Joseph as his successor ("'Then Israel Bowed Himself . . .' (Genesis 47.31)," *JSOT* 28 (2004): 467–80. That the Hb. word has its secondary meaning "tribe" here is unlikely, and the singular "tribe" to stand for all twelve tribes is dubious.

"bowing" is a fulfillment of Joseph's dream (37:9–10).[515] In the next scene Jacob revitalizes himself ("strengthens himself," *hith.,* from *ḥāzaq*) in his "bed" *(miṭṭâ)* when he prepares for Joseph's imminent visit (48:2). This scene supports the notion that in the present verse Jacob was too feeble to stand or bow before Joseph, requiring the armrest of his bed. If Jacob is not merely propping himself up in bed, what the text indicates is the humility of Jacob. Hearing Joseph's oath relieves his anxiety and engenders gratitude.

11. Jacob's Blessings (48:1–49:28)

The last days of Jacob continue the thematic elements of Genesis: the promises of blessing, progeny, and land. The proliferation of blessings for his family dominates—blessing for Joseph's house, Ephraim and Manasseh (48:1–22), and blessing for the whole of the twelve tribes of Israel (49:1–28). It is appropriate that the end of Genesis should draw to a close with repeated references to the thematic word of the book (*b-r-k,* "to bless"). Moreover, Jacob's life especially exhibits the blessing that God promised the fathers (49:26). The Lord "blessed" Jacob at Bethel and promised him a multitude of descendants and the land of Canaan as an everlasting possession (48:3–4). He is the progenitor of a prolific and prosperous family, and even at this late hour he increases his descendants through the adoption of Joseph's sons (48:5–6). Although he will die in Egypt, he has not relinquished Canaan. The land remains his possession by promise so that he by faith bequeaths an extra portion to Joseph (48:21–22). The blessings of Jacob were not restricted to one appointed successor (cp. 21:12; 27:37–38). He bestowed blessing upon all "twelve" tribes (49:28), even those who had troubled Jacob (Reuben, Simeon, and Levi, 49:3–7). Jacob humbly recognized that, despite his elevated stature as the namesake of the nation, he was but the channel of divine blessing, not its source. When Jacob bestows blessing on Joseph's sons, he grants Ephraim a greater role than the elder Manasseh. This motif of the younger son receiving greater favor than the elder is vital to the history of the patriarchs, especially in Isaac's blessing of Jacob (25:23; 27:29,37). By repeating the practice of blessing the younger over the elder, Jacob is carrying out the divine will, recognizing that the divine intention of blessing surpasses the practice of human convention (48:19–20). Although he was the recipient of the promissory blessing, he could not control its future. This was God's provenience.

Judah as the future ruler of the twelve tribes (49:8–12) matches the interlude in chap. 38, where he is the focal figure in the sordid story of Tamar. Judah's transformation in the Joseph story comes to a high point in Jacob's recognition of Judah as Israel's royal tribe. Despite his favor for Joseph,

---

[515] Sailhamer, "Genesis," 268.

Jacob bestows on Judah the imprimatur of the prophecy. The emphasis on Judah (49:8–12) and Joseph (49:22–26) exhibits the future of Israel. The blessings balance the prominence of Joseph as the recent leader of his family and the prominence of Judah in the future who will produce the nation's kings. These two sons who play strategically in the descent of Israel into Egypt, which saves the nation, will dominate the future history of Israel in the settlement and the monarchy periods. Judah takes center stage in the conquest and provides the greatest kings, David and Solomon, during which the nation enjoys its greatest prosperity (cf. the submission of the northern tribes, 2 Sam 19:20). Out of the Davidic household will emerge the messianic king (e.g., Ps 2; 89; Isa 11:1–16; Jer 33:15; Amos 9:1–14), who is Jesus of Nazareth (Luke 1:32–33; Rom 1:3; Rev 22:16). This one tribe maintains its ruling class until the destruction of Jerusalem in the sixth century. It, moreover, is the chief building block for the restoration after the exile. Matching the tribe to the south is "the house of Joseph" in the north (Josh 18:5; Judg 1:22; Zech 10:6). The tribes of Ephraim and Manasseh are the most numerous and prosperous in the northern tribes (Hos 13:1). The "house of Joseph" could refer to the whole of the central highlands and northern regions of Israel during the time of Solomon (1 Kgs 11:28). The first royal interloper in Israel's history, Jeroboam I, was an Ephraimite (1 Kgs 11:26–14:20; cf. 2 Sam 20:21). The Ephraimites exercised rule from the towering capital city Samaria (Isa 7:9), whose role in the north matched Jerusalem's prominence to the south (e.g., Mic 1:5). God favored Judah over Joseph (Ps 78:67), although Joseph was still loved as though the "firstborn" of the Lord (Jer 31:9). The future for the tribes of Joseph and Judah, however, is restoration under the rule of the Davidic king (Isa 11:10–13). Judah has precedence as the bearer of the ruling "scepter" (49:10).

The last days of Jacob also display his enduring faith. Chrysostom speaks of "the eyes of [Jacob's] mind," who although blind physically saw the future by faith (*Hom. on Genesis* 66.9). Jacob exhibited a strong finish in his race of faith, placing his confidence in God's promises despite appearances (48:21–22; cf. Acts 20:24; 2 Tim 4:7). The goodness of God surprised Jacob's eyes of faith by enabling the sightless father to "see" again Joseph's face and his children too (48:10–11). Moreover, Jacob received a preview of the lives of his descendants at his deathbed blessing (49:1–28), anticipating the tribes' settlement in the land and the budding of a kingdom under Judah's royal descendant (49:10). Jacob therefore bequeathed to his children a future that would shape their character and destiny as a people "in days to come" (49:1).

The deathbed blessings of Jacob reflect striking contrasts in chaps. 48–49. His blessing for the future life of Ephraim and Manasseh (48:15–20) is followed by Jacob's acknowledgment of his imminent death (48:21). The contrast of life and death is set in bold relief by the scene of the dying patriarch, who predicts a fruitful and abundant life for his choice son Joseph (49:22–26). The passage also perpetuates the contrast of bless and curse, which has been central to the development of the book's plot. Simeon and Levi receive their father's "curse" (49:7), a castigation harsher than that leveled against Reuben for his crime of incest. Jacob mitigates the judgment somewhat by condemning their action ("their anger"), not directly denouncing them as persons (contrast 3:14; 4:11; 9:25). The judgments against Reuben and Simeon and Levi show that the sons' behavior impacted the future of their descendants.

The oppression of Joseph alluded to by the patriarch reflected the family schism that threatened the future of the promises. The twelve sons could not have become the historic "twelve" tribes of Israel, if God had not delivered Joseph from the clutches of his brothers and Egyptian bonds. This evidence of God's grace fuels the optimism of chap. 49, in which the recitation of blessings manifests God's conquest over the sinful inventions of humanity.

As we would expect for a deathbed scene, the chapters contain both retrospect and prospect. He remembers God's promises to him at Bethel (48:3–4) and his father (48:16), which establish the basis for his look toward the future for Joseph's household (48:5–6,15–16) and for the descendants of the twelve tribes (chap. 49). Within the Blessing of Jacob, the two aspects recur. In the context of looking ahead, the blessings recall the moral transgressions of the elder sons (Reuben, Simeon, and Levi) and the strife Joseph endured in the past (49:24). Because of Jacob's God, the blessings Jacob had received, and the faithfulness of the promises, Jacob could optimistically point ahead to the prosperous future that the tribes will enter.

COMPOSITION. Scholars have commonly analyzed 47:28–49:28 as a highly composite text, consisting of the traditional Pentateuchal sources (J,E,P) or of a base text expanded by supplemental layers (e.g., Judah layer).[516] For traditional source critics, doublets and contradictions, such as the double introduction of Joseph's sons (vv. 10b[J],13[E]), elicited the isolation of the two principal

---

[516] For a detailed study of the history of the interpretation, see R. de Hoop, *Genesis 49 in Its Literary and Historical Context*, OtSt 39 (Leiden: Brill, 1999), 366–450; also J.-D. Macci, *Israël et ses tribus selon Genèse 49*, OBO 171 (Fribourg: Universitätsverlag/Göttingen: Vandenhoeck & Ruprecht, 1999). Among the multiple source proponents were, e.g., Wellhausen, Gunkel, Skinner, von Rad, and more recently H. Seebass, *Geschichtliche Zeit und theonome Tradition in der Joseph Erzählung* (Gütersloh: Gütersloher Verlagshaus Gerd Mohn, 1978); id., "The Joseph Story, Genesis 48 and the Canonical Process," *JSOT* 35 (1986): 29–43; H.-C. Schmitt, *Die nichtpriesterliche Josephsgeschichte*, BZAW 154 (Berlin: de Gruyter, 1980); and L. Schmidt, *Literarische Studien zur Josephsgeschichte*, BZAW 167 (Berlin: de Gruyter, 1986), 121–295. Among those who propose a tradition-history analysis (supplementary layers) are Redford, *Joseph;* W. Dietrich, *Die Josephserzählung als Novelle und Geschichtsschreibung: Zugleich ein Beitrag zur Pentateuchfrage*, BThSt 14 (Neukirchen-Vluyn: Neukirchener Verlag, 1989); and N. Kebekus, *Die Josefererzählung: Literarkritische und redaktionsgeschichtliche Untersuchungen zu Genesis 37–50*, Internationale Hochschulschriften (Münster: Waxmann, 1990).

sources, J and E. The criterion of the patriarchs' dual names identified the major sources, "Israel" in the Yahwist and "Jacob" in the Elohist. Commonly, the funeral instructions in 47:29–31 are attributed to J. Variance in the extent of E detected in chap. 48, if any, has made for differences among scholarly reconstructions. However, there continues general concurrence on the identity of the P material (47:28; 48:3–6; 49:1,28–33), which was later added. Chapter 49 (as with chap. 38) continues to be widely believed to have been a tradition that was independent of the sources of the Joseph story. As for the genre of the chapter, H. Gressmann's form critical study (1914) established the standard opinion today that chap. 49 is a collection of originally separate and independent "tribal sayings" that were composed and later inserted into the Joseph story.[517] Although most scholars acknowledge at least some progressive literary layering, most also agree that chap. 49 possesses elements of very old Hebrew poetry. The poem reflects the period of the settlement, when the tribes had formed a quasi-national entity, although the present composition itself is dated after the eighth century. Based on the early poetry of chap. 49 and the divine names and epithets (e.g., *El Shaddai*, 49:25[518]), D. N. Freedman contended that the collection came from late patriarchal times but in its present form reflected the historical situation of the eleventh century.[519]

There are also mixed explanations as to the development of the deathbed and burial scenes of chaps. 47:28–50:14 in their relationship to the Joseph story and the Jacob cycle as two originally separate entities. Generally, critics interpret the scenes as metaphors of the political situations during Israel's monarchy at the time of their composition. The consensus has been that the episodes betray two primary historical perspectives, an earlier northern version that promotes Joseph's tribes (probably from the area of Shechem, 48:22) and a southern version that promotes Judah (cf. cave of Machpelah, 49:30).[520] The present textual arrangement hints at the competition between Joseph and Judah as ruler over the brothers, resulting in Judah receiving the superior imprint in 49:10 ("scepter").

Coats and Westermann represent those who hold to the unity of the Joseph story but view chaps. 48–49 as made up of parts. Coats proposed that the conclusion of the original story was 47:27. The subsequent 47:28–50:14 entails a series of add-on scenes with the common theme of Jacob's last days.[521] The deathbed scenes in 47:29–31 and 49:29–50:14 create a framework in which three distinct

---

[517] E.g., J. C. de Moor, "Genesis 49 and the Early History of Israel," in *Past, Present, Future: The Deuteronomistic History and the Prophets*, OtSt 44 (Leiden: Brill, 2000), 176–98 (179–84), who argues from "comparable tribal sayings in Arabian oral poetry" (179).

[518] Reading Hb. MSS., SP, LXX, Syr.

[519] D. N. Freedman, "Divine Names and Titles in Early Hebrew Poetry," in *Pottery, Poetry, and Prophecy: Studies in the Early Hebrew Poetry* (Winona Lake: Eisenbrauns, 1980), 85–88.

[520] De Moor, e.g., identifies all the sayings as premonarchial, except parts of Judah (vv. 8–12); the picture of the tribes is sociologically akin to the Apiru of Canaan in the late second millennium ("Genesis 49," 184–96). The earliest configuration of the tribal sayings reflected Joseph's preeminence but historically with the rise of the Judean royal house, the sayings were recast and incorporated into the Deuteronomistic History (p. 187).

[521] Coats, *Genesis*, 300–303, 309–10.

narrative segments appear. The first is Jacob's adoption of Joseph's two sons (48:1–12), his blessing for Ephraim and Manasseh (48:13–20), and his tribal blessings (49:1–28). He and many other critics find these elements to be independent narratives that have been gathered under the heading of Jacob's final acts. Each segment shows signs of growth in the tradition. J probably is responsible for integrating the elements in the framework. The composition of chap. 49 indicates an early memory of the tribes before the twelve-tribe list was fixed. For Westermann, however, the Joseph story can still be discerned in the parts of chaps. 46–50. These final five chapters possess the two endings of the two independent narratives of the Joseph story and the Jacob story. The Joseph story was inserted into the Jacob story, maintaining both endings in the present arrangement. Chapters 48 and 49 consist of a complex of independent units. Chapter 48 has four autonomous units (vv. 1–12,13–20,21,22) whose origins for the most part are unknown. In vv. 1–12 the priestly tradition interrupts the narrative in vv. 3–7 (P), describing the adoption of Joseph's two sons. Verses 13–20 continue the blessing, explaining the primacy of the younger son Ephraim. Verses 15–16, the blessing of Ephraim and Manasseh, interrupt the flow of the account, since the objection by Joseph logically occurs before the blessing is uttered. Verse 20a also is an addition. Finally, vv. 21–22 are two independent appendages, consisting of a promise and a land grant. The inheritance addition in v. 22 is "quite foreign to the context."[522] Chapter 49 consists of two different parts: the framework of vv. 1a,28–33 derives from P, and the collected sayings, the "Blessing of Jacob" in 49:1b–27, are a later supplement. The framework in vv. 1a,28b–33 are part of P's original conclusion to the Jacob narrative. The P account of Jacob's blessing, death, and burial consists of the following: 49:1a introduces the blessing, instructions for burial, and death in 49:28b–33; and 50:12–13 narrates the burial as obediently carried out by his sons. Westermann explains that the redactor preserved two accounts of Jacob's request of burial in Canaan (47:29–31; 49:29–32) and the carrying out of the burial (50:3–14; 50:12–13) when he interfaced the Joseph narrative with its account of Jacob's death and burial into the broader patriarchal cycle of Jacob, which contains its own version (P). The "Blessing of Jacob" in 49:1b–27 is a later addition, unrelated to the Joseph story or the patriarchal history of Jacob. He deems the original settings of the tribal sayings to be the occasions when the tribes convened and shared information about one another. The sayings only afterward were given a theological significance.

Carr, too, discerns several layers in chaps. 48–49, which reflect the steps in the protracted development of Genesis. Genesis 48:1–2,8–14,17–20 contributes to the prepromise Jacob-Joseph complex of stories. This original chap. 48 formed an inclusio in the composite account that began in chap. 27, producing parallels in the stories of Ephraim over Manasseh and Jacob over Esau. Genesis 49:1b–28 exhibits the later Judean revision of the complex, giving preeminence to Judah, from the perspective of the Southern Kingdom. Even the original chaps. 48 and 49:1b–28 are clearly secondary, since they interrupt the nature of the deathbed scene in 47:31 and 50:1–11,14. The "proto-Genesis" form of the work included

---

[522] Westermann, *Genesis 37–50*, 192.

the supplements of 48:15–16,21–22, which tie Joseph to the broader patriarchal promises made to Abraham. The priestly additions included 48:3–6 and 49:1a,29–33. To the priestly redactor Carr assigns 48:7.[523] R. de Hoop's study discerns two "tendencies" in 47:28–49:33 (i.e., "The Deathbed Episode").[524] The passage exhibits a "pro-Joseph" layer and a later "pro-Judah" layer. Here de Hoop shows some agreement with Redford's interpretation, but he rejects there was a "Reuben" version. The tension in the Joseph story is the competition between Joseph and Judah, not Reuben. The "pro-Joseph" story appears in substantial parts of 47:29–48:22, which describe the funeral instructions for "Israel" (47:29–31), the introduction of Joseph's two sons (48:1a,2b,8–11), the blessing on Joseph (48:12,14aA,15aA), and "Israel's" gift of Shechem (48:21–22). The "pro-Judah" adaptation diminished Joseph's position by Jacob's adoption of Manasseh and Ephraim (48:3–7), leaving Joseph without a legacy, and by bestowing a blessing on them (48:9bB,13,14aB.b,15aB–20). The "testament" of 49:1–28 is not extraneous but part of the Judah adaptation, reducing Joseph's importance and elevating Judah. The Deathbed Episode legitimizes the reign of Judah during the period of the United Monarchy, when Judah ruled over the northern tribes. The earlier "pro-Joseph" version comes from the Late Bronze Age or early Iron period. One other significant departure by de Hoop from the standard interpretation is the denial of priestly additions in the passage.

There are substantial reasons, however, for recognizing the logical consistency of the text. Exegetically, alternative explanations show that the doublets are not inconsistent repetitions. Verses 8–14, for example, describe the introduction of Joseph's sons to Jacob for blessing, although he has already known of them (46:5). That Jacob was said both to be blind and yet can see (vv. 10–11) adds to the problem. The coherency of the text can be maintained when we understand that Jacob's blindness was not absolute, only impaired—perhaps better than Isaac's vision. The double introduction is the nature of a formal presentation in the rite of blessing (cf., e.g., 27:18).[525] Also the appearance of two blessings in our passage corresponds to the double blessing of Esau/Jacob by Isaac. Wenham argues for the coherence of 48:1–50:14 on the basis of parallels in Genesis.[526] He shows that chaps. 48–49 have a parallel in 27:1–28:5, where two blessings also occur. In both cases the patriarch bestowing the blessings (Isaac and Jacob) is blind and the blessing of the younger son (Jacob, Ephraim) is met with protest, which the patriarch dismisses and then offers up his second blessing. Moreover, he argues for type scenes and similar patterning in the endings to the Abraham and Jacob patriarchal cycles (e.g., chaps. 22–25; chap. 35; chaps. 48–49). Further, the use of the names "Jacob/Israel" has been largely undermined as a dependable criterion of discerning specific sources. Chapter 48's unexpected use of "Israel" in the putative E document (vv. 8a,11,21), which critics typically employ as a sign of J, calls for another explanation. One might contend for a

---

[523] Carr, *Reading the Fractures of Genesis,* 210–11, 253–55.

[524] de Hoop, *Genesis 49,* 451–621.

[525] Sarna, *Genesis,* 327; and Hamilton, *Genesis Chapters 18–50,* 633–35.

[526] Wenham, *Genesis 16–50,* 460–62.

redactor's motive for exchanging the names when splicing his sources, but it can also be attributed to the author, who highlighted Jacob's position as ancestor of the nation by using "Israel" when the patriarch pronounced the blessing on the fathers of Israel's tribal descendants.[527]

As for chap. 49, the genre is "blessing" according to the text's understanding of itself in 49:28. Attempts to find comparable tribal sayings in the ancient Near East have been so far unsatisfactory. The assumption that the chapter is secondary is not well founded. De Hoop, for example, argues persuasively that the chapter fits well in context.[528] The blessings (49:3–27) without their context in the deathbed setting (47:29–48:22; 49:29–33) have no clear purpose. Moreover, links in chap. 49 to earlier accounts would have no background if the blessings were originally independent. The significance of the terms "sons of Jacob" and "Israel, your father" (49:2) are not self-evident, requiring a preunderstanding of their unity as twelve sons born to one ancestor, which is known from the birth narrative and the genealogical listings (29:31–30:24; 35:23–26; 46:8–27). Additionally, the five sons who receive more attention are those who are important in the Jacob and Joseph narratives (Reuben, Simeon and Levi, Judah, and Joseph), and the same order of their birth appears as in the birth narratives. The cryptic descriptions of the crimes committed by Reuben, Simeon, and Levi against their father are only understandable if they had the broader context of Jacob/Israel's family history. Furthermore, the blessing's internal pattern shows a logical plan of presentation that suggests it was a coherent artifice from its inception (see "Structure" below).

STRUCTURE. The unit consists of two scenes, Jacob's deathbed blessing of Joseph's two sons (48:1–22) and his blessing of all twelve sons (49:1–28). Two sets of instructions concerning his burial enclose the scenes (47:29–31; 49:29–33).[529] There is progression in the two burial scenes; 47:29 announces the patriarch's impending death and 49:33 describes it.[530] The stock phrase "Some time later" (48:1) distinguishes this as a new scene. The summing up of the twelvefold blessing in 49:28, "All these are the twelve tribes of Israel," brings the two complementary scenes of blessing to their close. The first blessing pertains only to the two sons of Joseph, and the second is a blessing conferred on all twelve sons. The deathbed setting of Jacob provides the same context for both scenes. The theme word "bless" *(b-r-k)* also holds the two scenes together. The verb *(brk)* appears eight times (48:3,9,15,16,20;

---

[527] de Hoop acknowledges the limits of the dual names as a reliable criterion but pointedly rejects the alternative that the names were due to the author, since in his opinion the renaming of Jacob in 32:22[23]–32[33] is not authentically historical, exhibiting the union of two different persons or peoples into one (*Genesis 49*, 427–30).

[528] Ibid., 349–50.

[529] de Hoop (*Genesis 49*, 318) displays four scenes in chiastic relationship: (A) instructions for the funeral (47:29–31) (B) adoption and blessing (48:1–22)//(B′) blessing (49:1–28) (A′) instructions for the funeral (49:29–33).

[530] Westermann, *Genesis 37–50*, 197.

870

49:25,28[2x]), and the noun *(běrākâ)* occurs six times (49:25[3x],26[2x],28).

Chapter 48 clearly consists of three parts. The same setting of Jacob's imminent death stands behind the three parts. (1) Verses 1–12 describe the preparatory steps for the blessing of the two sons, in which a formal adoption occurs. (2) Verses 13–20 describe the blessing of Ephraim and Manasseh, in which Ephraim is declared superior to the older brother Manasseh. (3) Last, in vv. 21–22 Jacob bequeaths land in Canaan to Joseph. Dialogue especially characterizes chap. 48, beginning with anonymous messengers (vv. 1–2) and followed by the speeches of Jacob and Joseph, linked occasionally by brief narrative interludes and introductions (vv. 3–22). Jacob's first speech recalls key events in his past travels, including an embedded quote (v. 4), citing the divine promise made at Luz and his memories of Rachel's passing (vv. 3–7). When Jacob "saw" the boys, he asked, "Who are these [boys]?" (v. 8b), prompting Joseph and Jacob's round of dialogue about the ensuing blessing for his sons (vv. 8–12). Verses 13–16 entail the description of Jacob's laying on of hands and the oracular blessing itself. When Joseph "saw" the unorthodox crisscrossing of his father's hands, another round of exchange occurs, regarding the priority of the younger son (vv. 17–20). Jacob's final pronouncement describes the inheritance that awaits Joseph in Canaan (vv. 21–22).

Chapter 49 has a prose frame: "Jacob called for his sons and said: 'Gather around . . .'" (v. 1a) and "All these are the twelve tribes . . ." (v. 28). The fusion of the individual twelve sons and their tribal entities is evidenced by the frame's references to "sons" and "tribes." Poetic verse makes up vv. 2–27, in which v. 2 is an introductory invocation ("Assemble and listen, sons of Jacob"), and vv. 3–27 provide eleven distinctive segments, each given to a particular tribe, excepting Simeon and Levi, who are treated together. The pattern of the tribal blessings follows a chiastic configuration, named according to birth mother, but she is not named in chap. 49. This can only be known from the narrative account (29:31–30:24) and the two earlier genealogies (35:22b–26; 46:8–27). The Leah and Rachel tribes form the outer elements; the inner elements are their concubines, with Bilhah's two tribes outside of Zilpah's two tribes:

> Leah (vv. 13–15)
>> Bilhah (vv. 16–18)
>>> Zilpah (vv. 19–20)
>> Bilhah (v. 21)
> Rachel (vv. 22–27)

The Leah tribes are Reuben, Simeon and Levi, Judah, Zebulun and Issachar (vv. 3–15). The arrangement of Zebulun and Issachar reverses the birth order portrayed in the birth narratives and in the listing of Jacob's descendants (cp.

30:18–20; 46:13–14). The inclusion of a punishment for Reuben and Simeon/ Levi distinguish their blessings from the others. Only Simeon/Levi receive an antiblessing ("Cursed be their anger," v. 7a). Bilhah's sons Dan (vv. 16–18) and Naphtali (v. 21) encircle Zilpah's children Gad (v. 19) and Asher (v. 20). Rachel's sons Joseph (vv. 22–26) and Benjamin (v. 27) constitute the last named.

The blessing segments are typically brief, usually possessing one pronouncement for each tribe. In conformity with the Joseph narratives, however, the chief sons Judah and Joseph receive multiple descriptions (also Dan). The blessing of Judah is also made distinctive by identifying him as the recipient of the ruling "scepter" (v. 10). The blessing of Joseph especially alludes to the narrative story of his ordeal and ultimate ascension over his brothers, naming him the "prince among his brothers" (v. 26). Unlike the list of those who descended with Jacob to Egypt in 46:8–27, which gives partial counts according to the descendants of each mother, only a cumulative tally of "twelve tribes" occurs in chap. 49, as it does in 35:22–26, announcing "twelve sons" (36:22b). A significant distinction of chap. 49 is its view toward the sons as the progenitors of "tribes," whereas 35:22b–26 and 46:8–27 emphasize the sons as individuals. The attention on the fathers of "tribes" is appropriate for the future orientation of a blessing: "so I can tell you what will happen to you in days to come" (v. 1b). Other features of the Blessing of Jacob are the use of animal imagery (e.g., vv. 9,14–15,27) and wordplays on the names of the tribes (e.g., vv. 16,19).

(1) Jacob Blesses Joseph's Sons (48:1–22)

[1]Some time later Joseph was told, "Your father is ill." So he took his two sons Manasseh and Ephraim along with him. [2]When Jacob was told, "Your son Joseph has come to you," Israel rallied his strength and sat up on the bed.

[3]Jacob said to Joseph, "God Almighty appeared to me at Luz in the land of Canaan, and there he blessed me [4]and said to me, 'I am going to make you fruitful and will increase your numbers. I will make you a community of peoples, and I will give this land as an everlasting possession to your descendants after you.'

[5]"Now then, your two sons born to you in Egypt before I came to you here will be reckoned as mine; Ephraim and Manasseh will be mine, just as Reuben and Simeon are mine. [6]Any children born to you after them will be yours; in the territory they inherit they will be reckoned under the names of their brothers. [7]As I was returning from Paddan, to my sorrow Rachel died in the land of Canaan while we were still on the way, a little distance from Ephrath. So I buried her there beside the road to Ephrath" (that is, Bethlehem).

[8]When Israel saw the sons of Joseph, he asked, "Who are these?"

[9]"They are the sons God has given me here," Joseph said to his father.

Then Israel said, "Bring them to me so I may bless them."

[10]Now Israel's eyes were failing because of old age, and he could hardly see.

So Joseph brought his sons close to him, and his father kissed them and embraced them. ¹¹Israel said to Joseph, "I never expected to see your face again, and now God has allowed me to see your children too."

¹²Then Joseph removed them from Israel's knees and bowed down with his face to the ground. ¹³And Joseph took both of them, Ephraim on his right toward Israel's left hand and Manasseh on his left toward Israel's right hand, and brought them close to him. ¹⁴But Israel reached out his right hand and put it on Ephraim's head, though he was the younger, and crossing his arms, he put his left hand on Manasseh's head, even though Manasseh was the firstborn.

¹⁵Then he blessed Joseph and said,

"May the God before whom my fathers
  Abraham and Isaac walked,
the God who has been my shepherd
  all my life to this day,
¹⁶the Angel who has delivered me from all harm
  —may he bless these boys.
May they be called by my name
  and the names of my fathers Abraham and Isaac,
and may they increase greatly
  upon the earth."

¹⁷When Joseph saw his father placing his right hand on Ephraim's head he was displeased; so he took hold of his father's hand to move it from Ephraim's head to Manasseh's head. ¹⁸Joseph said to him, "No, my father, this one is the firstborn; put your right hand on his head."

¹⁹But his father refused and said, "I know, my son, I know. He too will become a people, and he too will become great. Nevertheless, his younger brother will be greater than he, and his descendants will become a group of nations." ²⁰He blessed them that day and said,

"In your name will Israel pronounce this blessing:
  'May God make you like Ephraim and Manasseh.'"

So he put Ephraim ahead of Manasseh.

²¹Then Israel said to Joseph, "I am about to die, but God will be with you and take you back to the land of your fathers. ²²And to you, as one who is over your brothers, I give the ridge of land I took from the Amorites with my sword and my bow."

Jacob's ailment provides the background for the patriarch's last days in which he provides for his heirs. Joseph and his sons Ephraim and Manasseh visit the patriarch, who adopts his grandsons as full heirs (vv. 1–12). The patriarch blesses the sons, giving priority to the younger Ephraim, despite Joseph's protest (vv. 13–20). Last, Jacob reiterates that he is about to die but prophesies that God will return Joseph to Canaan, and he bestows a land grant to Joseph (vv. 21–22).

JACOB ADOPTS EPHRAIM AND MANASSEH (48:1–12). The boundaries of this segment are the actions of Jacob and Joseph: Jacob "sat up" (v. 2), and Joseph "bowed down" (v. 12). Prompted by Jacob's illness, Joseph brings his sons to receive a blessing (vv. 1–2). Jacob establishes the basis and names the terms of the patriarch's adoption of Ephraim and Manasseh (vv. 3–7). The formal presentation of the heirs follows (vv. 8–10). The scene closes as it began with courtesy shown toward the patriarch (vv. 11–12).

Joseph's Visit (48:1–2). **48:1–2** Jacob's ill health gives the occasion for the blessings bestowed in chaps. 48 and 49.[531] The final three appearances of Jacob in the narrative have him on his deathbed ("bed," *miṭṭâ,* see comments on 47:31; 48:2; 49:33). The final days of a patriarch are a decisive phase in the life of the family when he provides for future heirs (chaps. 24; 27). The bestowal of blessing by a dying patriarch had irrevocable authority (25:5; 27:36–37). "Some time later" (v. 1) is nonspecific (cf. 22:20; Josh 24:29), but judging by 47:28 it probably was approaching seventeen years since Jacob's arrival in Egypt. This episode naturally occurred sometime after the previous scene, describing Joseph's oath to bury Jacob in Canaan (47:29–31). The implication of the present arrangement is that the end is near, and Joseph matches Jacob's request for burial with his own for a blessing on his two sons.

The description of Joseph's meeting with Jacob has the semblance of a formal audience. The indefinite Hebrew construction, rendered in the passive voice ("was told"), suggests that messengers were involved in arranging the meeting. Although it is unstated in the text, Jacob understands Joseph's purpose for the visit. He expects his father to give his two sons, especially his eldest (Manasseh), the patriarch's deathbed approval, perhaps as Jacob's successor. The language "your father" (v. 1) and "your son" (v. 2) reinforces the significance of the visit and the blessing that ensues. Jacob reflects the importance of the summit when he "rallied his strength" (*hith.* from *ḥāzaq*); the word *ḥāzaq* describes a person's fresh strength of purpose (e.g., Judg 20:22; 1 Sam 30:6). Isaac, too, strengthened himself with a meal before dispensing the blessing (27:25).[532] The mention of "Israel" (v. 2) suits the national implications of the blessing. That he "sat up" in bed at Joseph's appearance probably reflects the importance of the event at hand.[533] Delitzsch remarked, "The interchange of the names [Jacob and Israel] is not everywhere so significant as here. Jacob lies down sick, Israel draws himself up."[534]

Terms of Adoption (48:3–7). **48:3–4** The version of the promises that Jacob utters for Joseph draws especially on his own experience and that of the

---

[531] Hb. description is vivid, הִנֵּה אָבִיךָ חֹלֶה, "Your father is *now* sick" (*IBHS* §40.2.1b).

[532] Wenham, *Genesis 16–50,* 463.

[533] Rashi explains that despite his position as father, Jacob showed respect for Joseph as ruler.

[534] Delitzsch, *New Commentary on Genesis,* 2.357.

chief patriarch Abraham. Jacob recalls the promises made to him upon his return to Bethel (Luz) from Paddan Aram when "God Almighty appeared" and "blessed" the patriarch (35:9–15). (On the meaning "God Almighty," see comments on 17:1; cf. also 28:3; 43:14.) Although commentators often claim that vv. 3–6 interrupt the narrative, vv. 3–4 fit well by giving the basis for Jacob's authority to extend the blessing to others. Formal blessing typically includes allusions to the historic promises made earlier (e.g., 24:7; 28:3–4; 48:15). In remembering the blessing at Bethel, Jacob omits reference to the change of name "Israel," which was central to that occasion (35:10; 32:28[29]). Here, however, his focus is the promise of progeny (35:11), in anticipation of the blessing that he bestows on Joseph's two sons ("may they increase greatly," v. 16). At Bethel the promise was uttered in the form of a divine exhortation ("be fruitful," "increase"), imitating the blessing at creation (1:22,28; 9:1,7). Here the language specifically attributes the benefits to God's direct involvement ("I am going to make you . . . I will make you . . . and I will give," v. 4). The phrase "community of peoples" echoes Isaac's invocation at Jacob's departure from Canaan (28:3), a fitting synonym for the language "a community of nations" (35:11). Jacob foresees multiple nations formed by Joseph's sons (v. 19). Jacob omits, however, the mention of a royal progeny ("kings will come from your body," 35:11), for although this was true of Abraham (17:6,16) and Jacob, the throne is reserved in Jacob's tribal blessings for Judah (49:10; cf. Ps 78:67–68). The land promise in 35:12 is slightly altered in this recital by the addition "an everlasting possession," which was previously heard in the covenant of circumcision (17:8). That the promise is "an everlasting possession" *(ʾăḥūzzat ʿôlām)* contrasts with the temporary possession ("property," *ʾăḥuzzâ,* 47:11; *ʾāḥaz,* 47:27) of Goshen granted by Joseph.[535]

48:5–7 Jacob claims the sons of Joseph as his own, making them full recipients of his inheritance on the same order as Jacob's other sons (vv. 5–6). "Now then" *(wĕʿattâ,* v. 5) shows a logical connection with the preceding account of the promise made to Jacob. Since Jacob is the recipient of the inheritance, he has the authority to adopt Joseph's offspring. Jacob names "Reuben and Simeon" (v. 5b) as points of comparison because they were his two eldest sons, who stood sequentially in line to receive the inheritance, indicating that Ephraim and Manasseh will have full status as Jacob's sons (not merely grandsons), receiving their rightful legacy. The repetition of "mine" *(lî)* reinforces the new standing that Ephraim and Manasseh receive. This adoption extends to Joseph's first two sons only, not those Joseph may produce subsequently; future offspring will not have their brothers' elevated status, meaning that their inheritance will fall under the territorial designations of Ephraim and Manasseh

---

[535] Sarna, *Genesis,* 325.

(v. 6; Josh 14:4). By this arrangement, Jacob ensures that the ordered lines of inheritance will not be jeopardized in the future.

Historically, the tribes of Ephraim and Manasseh continue to be known as the sons of Joseph. As tribal units, the descendants of the two sons will establish the inheritance of their father (e.g., Num 26:28; Deut 33:13–17; Josh 17:17). Since Joseph is the recipient of Reuben's right of inheritance as the firstborn, according to the Chronicler, the sons of Joseph also receive firstborn rights as the *adopted* sons of Joseph (1 Chr 5:1–2). The mention of Reuben and Simeon possibly conveys another meaning, since these elder brothers did not succeed their father due to discrediting themselves (cf. comments on 49:7). The implication may be that Ephraim and Manasseh too will not ascend to the highest rank, safeguarding the esteemed place of Judah (49:10). The Chronicler recognizes this when he notes the rule of Judah's tribe, despite the elevation of Joseph and his sons. The blessing of Joseph shows the preeminence of Joseph over his brothers in the immediate context, but the blessing of kingship reserved for Judah projects that he will take the lead among the tribes (cp. "your father's sons will bow down to you," 49:8 with 37:7,9,10; 42:6; 49:26).[536] The adoption of Ephraim and Manasseh as the "sons of Jacob/Israel" also had implications for the configuration of the "twelve tribes of Israel." The diverse tribal lists in the Old Testament exhibit fluidity in the count and arrangement of the tribes, probably reflecting changing historical circumstances.[537] "Joseph" appears in the blessing of chap. 49, but the Blessing of Moses counts twelve tribes by deleting Simeon and dividing the house of Joseph into Ephraim and Manasseh (Deut 33:17). In the idealized count presented by Ezekiel (47:13–14), the land divides into twelve equal allotments with two going to Joseph, since the tribe of Levi receives no portion (44:28).

In addition to the memories in vv. 3–4, v. 7 further justifies what Jacob demands in vv. 5–6. The construction in v. 7, "As I was returning . . .," contrasts the positive condition of Joseph's household and the sorrow of Jacob's experience.[538] The expression "to my sorrow" renders the poignancy of the memory, lit., "Rachel died upon me."[539] The rationale for this adoption is the premature death of Rachel, the favored wife (v. 7; 35:16–20). Since Rachel had no more children, Jacob counted the sons born to Joseph as his own by proxy, immediately multiplying her tribes.[540] The locations of the events

---

[536] Walton, *Genesis,* 712.

[537] F. S. Frick, "Tribes, The," *HBD* 1096.

[538] וַאֲנִי בְּבֹאִי, lit., "As for me, when I came . . ."

[539] BDB 753; AV, "by me" and NKJV, "beside me."

[540] Luther comments that the divine promise of "many" descendants refers to children born by Rachel, therefore making it necessary for Jacob to adopt her grandchildren to realize the promise (*LW* 8.156–57).

recounted by Jacob are important to the author too. Jacob mentions "Egypt" twice (once in NIV) when describing the birthplace of Ephraim and Manasseh (v. 5). This corresponds to the author's interest shown in the genealogical table naming Jacob's descendants (46:15,20). Jacob's review of the location of Rachel's death and burial (v. 7) utilizes language occurring in the narrator's description (35:16,19). Remembrance of Rachel's tomb was important to Jacob in this family moment and, no doubt, to Joseph, her son, but more is in mind here. The future tribes of Ephraim and Manasseh lay within Canaan, not Egypt, where Rachel had given her life in childbirth and where the promissory blessing that Jacob bestows will be realized.

Presentation of Ephraim and Manasseh (48:8–10).   **48:8–9** Verses 8–12 appear to continue directly on the visit described in vv. 1–2. Jacob's question "Who are these?" creates a problem with vv. 3–7 in which the patriarch has already initiated adoption proceedings of Ephraim and Manasseh, whom he calls by name (v. 5). How can he not know the identity of those who stand before him? Wenham observes that since Joseph's response to the question does not name them, Joseph assumes that Jacob knows whom he meant when he identifies them as "sons" (v. 9).[541] If the account is chronologically ordered, Jacob's troubled vision may explain his question (v. 10). Or it may be a formal preface to an official utterance. Since the description of Jacob's blessing on Ephraim and Manasseh in many respects shows parallels with the blessing spoken by Isaac (e.g., both patriarchs are blind), perhaps "Who are these?" corresponds to the similar prelude to Isaac's conferral of blessing ("Who are you?" 27:32). Alternatively, the passage may have a topical arrangement, in which vv. 3–7 is a dialogue from an earlier time.[542] The proposal of adoption would not be new to Joseph, therefore, and would explain why he visited the sickly patriarch expecting his sons to receive a blessing.

When identifying the two as his sons, Joseph attributes them to God's gift (v. 9), as did Leah and Rachel acknowledge their children born in Paddan Aram (29:33; 30:6). Jacob, too, had interpreted his children as the gracious gift of the Lord (33:5; cf. 30:2). Joseph's comment "that God has given me here" (Egypt) indicates again the location of their birth. God's graciousness extends beyond the borders of Canaan (cf. 41:50–52). Jacob zealously volunteers, like his father before him, to bless the offspring before he dies (cf. 27:7).

48:10 Verse 10 provides the background information that explains the behavior of the parties during the meeting.[543] Jacob's vision is fading, leaving him dependent on others, which precipitates Joseph bringing forward his sons twice (vv. 10,13). Joseph assumed due to his eyesight that his father

---

[541] Wenham, *Genesis 16–50*, 464.

[542] וַיֹּאמֶר יַעֲקֹב can be a pluperfect, "Jacob had said" (Waltke, *Genesis,* 595).

[543] The *wāw* disjunctive initiates the clause, giving supp. information, וְעֵינֵי יִשְׂרָאֵל כָּבְדוּ, lit., "Now Israel's eyes became heavy" (ingressive-stative verb, cf. *IBHS* §30.5.3b).

erred when delivering the blessing on Ephraim (v. 18). The description "old age" *(zōqen)* underscores the last days of Jacob's life and the weight of his final acts. With old age came the possibility of blindness (e.g., 1 Sam 3:2; Eccl 12:3). Some EVs suggest that the blindness was functional, not absolute (e.g., "could hardly see," NIV, NLT; "could not see *well,*" NAB [italics mine]). By reiterating that he "could not see,"[544] the text emphasizes Jacob's limitations. Jacob's loss of sight reminds the reader of Isaac's failing eyesight (27:1) and Jacob's deception of Isaac (27:1–29), drawing a contrast between the virtue of Joseph and that of his father in his youth. There is no trickery here; both Joseph and Jacob have suffered the cruel consequences of deception. As with Isaac years earlier, Jacob must rely on touch and smell. Joseph pushes his sons forward so the old man can grasp them, whereupon he affectionately kisses them before the blessing (cf. 27:26–27; cp. 33:4).

The Adoption Concluded (48:11–12). **48:11–12** Jacob recognizes that this occasion was a purely divine gift, since he did not expect to be reunited with Joseph and certainly would never have expected to see his grandchildren. "To see *[rĕ'ōh]* your face again" brings to mind the events of Jacob's reunion with Esau, which he also appears to attribute to God (33:10). The root word "see" *(rā'â)* occurs again in the verse, probably a continuing play on his visual impairment. The common English vernacular "God has allowed me" or "let me" is not as forceful as the original construction, lit., "God has shown me" (*hiph.,* from *rā'â*).[545] God enabled Jacob to see Joseph and his sons before he was totally blind. That Jacob referred to the boys as "seed" *(zeraʿ),* translated "children" (NIV), instead of identifying them as "sons" *(bānîm)* echoes the promissory formula given to the Fathers (e.g., 12:7; 17:19; 22:17–18; 26:24; 28:13–14). Jacob fully believed that his son was dead (37:33–35; 42:36; 45:26), as did the brothers (42:13,32), and therefore he had no reason to look forward to seeing his son again. "Expected" (from *pālal*) means to assume, make an assessment, or judge a matter (cf. the noun "assessment," *pālîl,* Exod 21:22; Deut 32:31; Job 31:11).[546] The Hebrew sage crystallized what Jacob, father and grandfather, had experienced: "Children's children are a crown to the aged" (Prov 17:6; cf. Ps 128:6). Now Jacob's life was complete. He had expected to die at the loss of Rachel's sons (37:35; 42:38; 44:29,31), but God thought otherwise.

The text vividly details the proceedings of the adoption so that the reader can imagine the drama of Jacob's unorthodox blessing. Joseph is the choreographer of the event, withdrawing his sons so that he can stretch out[547] in rev-

---

[544] לֹא יוּכַל לִרְאוֹת (cf. Eli, 1 Sam 3:2).

[545] LXX, ἔδειξέν μοι ὁ θεός, "God has shown me"; AV, "God hath shewed me."

[546] *HALOT* 3.932–33; R. Schultz, "פלל," *NIDOTTE* 3.627–28.

[547] MT, וַיִּשְׁתַּחוּ, "and (Joseph) bowed down"; one Hb. MS, SP, LXX, and *Tg. Neof.* have the plural, וַיִּשְׁתַּחֲווּ, "they [Ephraim and Manasseh] bowed down."

erence before the patriarch (v. 12). The notion of "knees" (from *berek*) in the scene alludes to the sons' birth and descent, for "knees" appears in an idiomatic expression for childbirth, that is, "bear upon the knees" (cf. comments on 30:3; 50:23; Job 3:12). It can be likened to the placement of the hand at the thigh, which symbolizes the procreative powers of Jacob (47:29; cf. 24:2,9). Since Joseph "bowed" before Jacob, the picture reverses Joseph's dream (37:10). This surprising act of humility by the Egyptian ruler acknowledges the superiority of his father's mediation of God's promises.[548]

JACOB BLESSES EPHRAIM OVER MANASSEH (48:13–20). The names "Ephraim" and "Manasseh" form the boundaries of this segment (vv. 13,20). Jacob places his hands upon the sons, showing preference to the younger Ephraim (vv. 13–16). Joseph attempts to correct what he perceives as his father's error, but Jacob refuses (vv. 17–20).

The Blessing (48:13–16). **48:13–14** Joseph positions the boys facing Jacob so that his right hand of favor would predictably touch the elder Manasseh (v. 13). Unexpectedly, by "crossing his arms,"[549] Jacob rests his right hand on the "younger" son Ephraim (v. 14). The unorthodox nature of Jacob's hands requires the narrative's repeated description of "right" and "left."[550] "Younger" (*ṣāʿîr*) brings to mind the oracle predicting Jacob's ascendancy over the elder Esau (25:23), but in this case the younger is only said to be "greater" (v. 19), not the lord of the older son (27:37). The reference to Manasseh as "firstborn" (*bĕkôr*) recalls the treachery to which Isaac and Esau succumbed (27:19,32).

48:15a That the preface to the blessing has "he [Jacob] blessed Joseph" is perplexing at first thought, since we would expect "Ephraim and Manasseh." The LXX solves the tension by reading "them" *(autous)*, referring to the boys in lieu of "Joseph" (cf. NAB). More likely "Joseph" is the proper textual reading. Verses 16 and 20 make it clear that while directed also to Joseph, the blessing pertains solely to his sons ("may [God] bless these boys," v. 16a; "he blessed them that day," v. 20). Mention of Joseph, too, is understandable since his lineal connection is cause for the blessing.

48:15b–16a The invocation for blessing is the first petition, which begins with a description of God, describing him in three lines (vv. 15b,15c,16a). (A) Jacob focuses on the spiritual heritage of the family, which involves God's protective relationship of his forefathers and of himself (v. 15b). The imagery is the picture of sheep walking ahead of the shepherd,

---

[548] Waltke, *Genesis,* 598.

[549] שָׂכַל II, "to lay crosswise" *(piel)* occurs only here (BDB 968; cp. Ar. *šakala,* "to tie together animal's legs and Ar. *šikāl,* "rope," *HALOT* 3.1329), which is the interpretation of LXX, Syr., Vg. But *Tg. Onq.* and Rashi interpreted it from שָׂכַל I, "to be prudent," thus "he shrewdly directed" his hands (cp. Ar. *šakila,* "to become dark and doubtful," *HALOT* 3.1329).

[550] Sarna notes the "precision of language" (*Genesis,* 327).

who from behind drives and oversees the care of the flock (cp. 32:19[20]; 33:14).[551] "Walked" (*hith.*, from *hālak*, v. 15a) echoes the covenant admonition made to Abraham, "Walk before me [God] and be blameless" (17:1; cf. 24:40). The idiom "walk before *X*" exhibits multifaceted emphases: a faithful lifestyle (e.g., see comments on 5:22; 6:9; 2 Kgs 20:3//Isa 38:3) and the enabling presence and provision of the Lord (e.g., Lev 26:12; Ps 56:13[14]; Zech 10:12). This description especially suits Abraham's experience, since his life was made distinct by the repeated divine directive, "Go!" or "Walk!" (from *hālak;* 12:1; 13:17; 17:1; 22:2). Westermann observed the significance of the verbal form, "walked" (perfective): "The whole life of Abraham and Isaac is described as a path before God, as a path vis-à-vis God. This includes every conceivable relationship to God, every event mutually affecting the patriarchs and God."[552] (B) The second line moves from the past to Jacob's personal history. By the image of a shepherd, Jacob describes the enduring care that the Lord showed him throughout his perilous life "to this day" (v. 15b). Unlike the former sheep-shepherd imagery, in which the shepherd follows, the picture of Jacob and God is the shepherd preceding the flock. Jacob had no life outside of divine oversight, beginning with Rebekah's womb (25:23).[553] A prominent motif in the Jacob narratives is the attending presence of God in the travels of the patriarch (28:15,20; 31:3,42; 35:3; cf. 48:21).[554] Jacob knew firsthand the commitment that a faithful shepherd exhibited toward his flock (e.g., 30:31,38–41; 33:13–14). The imagery of gods and rulers as shepherds was common in the ancient Near East, reaching back as early as the third millennium.[555] Jacob employs the appellative "Shepherd" *(rō'eh)* when naming the Lord in 49:24. The imagery of shepherd and sheep depicts the deliverance of the new nation from Egypt (e.g., Exod 15:13,17; Ps 78:52–55,70–72). The prophets when depicting the divine Shepherd describe the personal care the Lord gives his people (e.g., Isa 40:11; Jer 23:4; Ezek 34:16).

(C) Last, Jacob depicts God as his delivering "Angel" (i.e., messenger, *mal'āk*, v. 16a). What precisely Jacob refers to or whether he is speaking only generally cannot be confidently determined. He may have in mind the role of angels in the "bookend experiences" of his exile from Canaan—first at Bethel (28:12) and then upon his return when he encounters Esau (32:1[2]). Since he mentions "harm" *(ra')* here, he may imply the dream that God gave Laban,

---

[551] P. van Hecke, "Shepherds and Linguists: A Cognitive-Linguistic Approach to the Metaphor 'God is Shepherd' in Gen 48.15 and Context," in *Studies in the Book of Genesis: Literature, Redaction and History*, BETL 155 (Leuven: Leuven University Press, 2001), 479–93.

[552] Westermann, *Genesis 37–50*, 190.

[553] Hamilton, *Genesis Chapters 18–50*, 637.

[554] van Hecke, "Shepherds and Linguists," 492.

[555] J. W. Vancil, "Sheep, Shepherd," *ABD* 5.1187–90.

warning him against harming Jacob ("bad," *ra*ʿ, 31:24). It was the "angel of God" who provided the means of escaping Laban's grip (31:11). These intriguing episodes indelibly marked the patriarch's view of his God whose messengers superintended his dangerous journeys. "Delivered" translates the important theological term *gōʾēl* ("redeemer"), occurring only here in Genesis. Exodus uses the word group *(g-ʾ-l)* to describe God's deliverance of Israel out of Egypt (6:6; 15:13). Especially important is its usage in Mosaic law, which explains the role of the human *gōʾēl*, a Hebrew kinsman who rescues a relative (e.g., Lev 25; 27:13–33; Num 35:12–27; Deut 19:6–12). Thus the divine *gōʾēl* is related to his people by covenant and intervenes in the face of dire circumstances to save them where they cannot save themselves (e.g., Ps 106:10; Isa 41:14; cp. "shepherd"//"redeem," Jer 31:10–11). The Mosaic community would have understood that the God of redemption whom they served was the same Lord who delivered their ancestor Jacob from his trials in and outside the land when he faced the likes of Esau and Laban as well as the local Canaanite populations (31:32; 32:11[12]; 34:30).

48:16b–16c   After the formal request for blessing, the second petition pertains to the sons' future identity and unity (v. 16b). "Called by my name" and variations on the phrase indicate a relationship that conveys solidarity. When a woman takes her husband's name, there is meaningful existence by virtue of her relationship and identity with her husband, without which she suffers shame and isolation (Isa 4:1). When used of God the phrase identifies the covenant people (e.g., Deut 28:10; 2 Chr 7:14; Isa 43:7; 48:1). Jacob's plea is that the descendants of Joseph, despite their Egyptian origins, will never lose sight of their distinctiveness as the sons of "Israel," whose forebears were the recipients of God's promises. This contrasts Joseph's earlier sentiments, who sought to forget his "father's household," naming his first child accordingly (cf. Manasseh, 41:51).

In the third petition, Jacob invokes the historic patriarchal promise of a mighty progeny (e.g., 17:2; 22:17; 26:4; 35:11; cf. Exod 1:9). This fits well with the naming of Ephraim ("double fruitful," cf. 41:52), which was ultimately realized by the burgeoning tribes of Ephraim and Manasseh (Deut 33:17; Josh 17:14–18). The word "to increase" (v. 16b) is a hapax legomenon from the verbal root *dāgâ;* if related to the word *dāg/dāgâ,* meaning "fish," the sense of the expression *(yidgû lārōb)* is "to become/grow into teeming multitudes" (NAB, NJB). Isaac offered up the similar blessing for Jacob (28:3).

The Younger Son above the Older (48:17–20).   **48:17–19**   The description "When Joseph saw *[raʾa]*" is an ironic play on Jacob's blindness, who though virtually blind has divine insight that the seeing Joseph does not. Moreover, "he was displeased" [with Jacob] translates the literal "it was evil *[raʿaʿ]* in his eyes." The disapproval of Joseph toward the patriarch's crossing of his hands is predictable, since patrilineal descent in Israel often gave priority to the firstborn son (v. 17). It, however, is typical in the experience of the patriarchs that the younger son displaces the older. "Displeased" translates the word *(rāʿaʿ)* that also describes Abraham's paternal concern for Ishmael's care ("distressed," 21:11–12). Joseph attempts to right what he thinks is an old man's confusion when he "took hold" *(tāmak)* of his father's arms. The root word describes the supporting of Moses' uplifted arms (Exod 17:12) and the grasping of a spindle stick (Prov 31:19). At the same time, Joseph emphatically snaps at Jacob by the expressive negative "No, my father!" (NIV) or "Not so, my father!" *(lōʾkēn,* v. 18; cf., e.g., Exod 10:11; Ps 1:4). Although Joseph interprets Jacob's hands as misguided, his hands acted upon his wiser impulse.

Jacob, however, cannot be dissuaded, for it is not his decision but ultimately God's, as it was in his own case (25:23; cf. Num 23:19–20,26). He is equally emphatic in answer to Joseph's protestation ("I know," twice; "he too," twice; v. 19), assuring him that Manasseh too will produce a "people" that is "great" (v. 19). By a division of the inherited blessing between Ephraim and Manasseh (v. 19), the patriarch alleviates a father's anxiety about the eldest's future (cf. 17:20; 21:18–21; 27:36–40). Ephraim, however, will be more numerous (cf. Num 2:18–21; Deut 33:17), fathering a "group of nations" *(mĕlōʾ haggôyim)*.[556] This expression occurs only here, although it rings similar to the promise made to Abraham ("a father of many nations," 17:4–6) and repeated to Jacob ("a community of nations," 35:11). Alternatively, it has been rendered "a whole nation in themselves" (REB; cf. *mĕlōʾ rōʿîm,* "a whole band of shepherds," Isa 31:4).

48:20 Jacob completes the final stage of blessing begun in v. 8. His blessing builds on the idea of the sons' powerful descendants. Jacob predicts that the two tribes will become so celebrated as to be the subject of a traditional benedictory saying (cp. Ruth 4:11–12). The Hebrew text has the singular "by you," which refers to Joseph as in v. 15. The virtual union of the sons with Joseph permits Jacob to refer to them under the auspices of their father.[557] The narrative reinforces the outcome of the episode by the apt phrase "Ephraim ahead of Manasseh" (v. 20). The antecedent of "he put . . ." may be an intentional ambiguity, referring to either God or Jacob.

JACOB BEQUEATHS LAND TO JOSEPH (48:21–22). After providing for the heirs Ephraim and Manasseh, Jacob predicts that God will return Joseph

---

[556] Although in the wilderness census Manasseh's clans outnumbered Ephraim's (Num 26:34), eventually Ephraim's power outstrips Manasseh (Delitzsch, *New Commentary on Genesis,* 2.362); Ephraim is the center of Jeroboam's Northern Kingdom (1 Kgs 12:25) and represents the whole of the north, paralleling Judah to the south (e.g., Isa 11:13; Hos 5:5).

[557] The LXX, ἐν ὑμῖν, reads plural "you" (cf. v. 15), and the LXX (Syr.) has passive εὐλογηθήσεται Ισραηλ, "shall Israel be blessed" (יְבֹרַךְ); *BHS* proposes תְּבָרֵךְ, *hith.,* "bless itself" (e.g., "by you shall Israel bless itself," NJB).

to Canaan (v. 21), and the patriarch assigns him a choice piece of land for an additional inheritance (v. 22).

48:21–22 Jacob underscores that his death is imminent ("I am about to die," v. 21; cf. 50:5,24)[558] to prepare Joseph as his successor who will care for the family in his absence. He leaves with Joseph what he had discovered in his trials and what Joseph had already experienced: "God will be with you." This article of faith (and its variations, e.g., "God is with you," "I am with you") is a repeated thesis in the patriarchal narratives, stated by God (26:24; 31:3; cf. Exod 3:12), the narration (21:20; 39:2–3,21,23), by foes (21:22; 26:28), and by the patriarchs themselves (24:40; 28:20; 31:5,42; 35:3). Calvin comments here, "Nay, until our faith rises to lay hold on those things which are removed afar off, we know not what it is to set our seal to the word of God."[559] The plural pronouns of "with you," "take you back," and "your fathers" (v. 21) show that Joseph is representative of all the Israelite tribes who are in mind. To be sure, Jacob repeats the divinely spoken phrase "the land of your [pl.] fathers" of the instruction given him prior to when he returned to Canaan from Paddan Aram (31:3; cf. Deut 30:5). Jacob's prediction forms the basis for Joseph's admonition to the Israelites to return his bones (50:24–25). Joseph and his subsequent generation all die in Egypt, but it is only Joseph's bones that are returned (Josh 24:32).

Verse 22 contrasts Jacob's part and that of God's described in v. 21.[560] So as to show his full confidence in God's provision for his descendants' future return, Jacob bequeaths a portion of land to Joseph personally (v. 22a, "to you," sg.). Although Jacob does not currently possess the land, he believes by divine right that the land is his to bestow. Jacob exercises his personal privilege, leaving a tract of land that he captured from the Amorites. Genesis does not record this incident, if a specific war is intended (more below). The verse contains two difficult phrases variously understood. (1) "As one who is over your brothers" (NIV) translates the Hebrew closely,[561] indicating that Jacob rewards Joseph in his role as ruler over his brothers (e.g., KJV, NAB). Alternatively, several EVs understand the phrase to mean that Joseph received an additional possession, "one portion more than your brothers" (cf. NASB, NRSV, NLT). The common point is that Jacob showed favor again toward Rachel's son. (2) More uncertain is the meaning of the Hebrew word behind the NIV's (also REB) rendition "ridge of land" (*šĕkem;* cf. "one mountain slope," RSV, HCSB). The Hebrew word is literally "shoulder, back" (e.g., 9:23; 21:14) and here interpreted metaphorically by many EVs as a "portion" of

---

[558] The construction is a future instans use of the participle, הִנֵּה אָנֹכִי מֵת, lit., "behold, I am [about to] die."

[559] Calvin, *Comm.,* 434.

[560] The verse begins וַאֲנִי נָתַתִּי לְךָ, meaning, "On my part, I [now] give to you . . ."

[561] אַחַד עַל־אַחֶיךָ, lit., "one over your brothers."

land (cf. AV, NRSV, NJPS, NLT). The Hebrew word is also the place name "Shechem" and has been interpreted accordingly (e.g., LXX, NAB, TEV). If not actually Shechem, the term may be a double entendre, meaning a land tract like that of Shechem (cf. NJB, "I give you a Shechem"). Joshua 24:32 reports the burial of Joseph at Shechem, but there in accord with 33:19 the acquisition is attributed to the land purchase from Hamor. In our passage Jacob says he obtained the possession through hostilities. He may have in mind the Dinah incident in which Simeon and Levi killed the Shechemites by the "sword" (34:26) but which at the time he denounced.[562] Most likely he mentions "Amorites" as a general term for Canaanite populations, if this incident with the Shechemites is meant, since Hamor and Shechem were Hivites (34:2; see 10:17, vol. 1A, pp. 456–57). Whatever he has precisely in mind, he uses the possession as evidence of God's future provision of the land for Israel (cp. Josh 24:12). The possession was won after a hard-fought battle, thus was a prized acquisition belonging to Jacob. "Bow" and "sword" are a common word pair, indicating instruments of war (e.g., Josh 24:12; 2 Sam 1:22; Ps 44:6[7]; Isa 21:15).[563] The memory possibly prefigures the return of the Israelites, who according to divine direction (e.g., 15:16–21; Exod 23:23; Deut 7:1) drive out the local Amorites (cf. Judg 1:35). It was from Shechem that the land was distributed among the tribes (Josh 24:1).

(2) Jacob Blesses His Sons (49:1–28)

[1]Then Jacob called for his sons and said: "Gather around so I can tell you what will happen to you in days to come.

**[2]"Assemble and listen, sons of Jacob;
  listen to your father Israel.**

**[3]"Reuben, you are my firstborn,
  my might, the first sign of my strength,
  excelling in honor, excelling in power.
[4]Turbulent as the waters, you will no longer excel,
  for you went up onto your father's bed,
  onto my couch and defiled it.**

**[5]"Simeon and Levi are brothers—
  their swords are weapons of violence.
[6]Let me not enter their council,
  let me not join their assembly,
  for they have killed men in their anger
  and hamstrung oxen as they pleased.**

---

[562] Jewish midrash and commentators assert that Jacob battled the Amorites at Shechem, following the Dinah incident (e.g., *Gen. Rab.* 80.10; 97.6; Rashi).

[563] Avishur, *Word-Pairs,* 258.

⁷Cursed be their anger, so fierce,
  and their fury, so cruel!
I will scatter them in Jacob
  and disperse them in Israel.

⁸"Judah, your brothers will praise you;
  your hand will be on the neck of your enemies;
  your father's sons will bow down to you.
⁹You are a lion's cub, O Judah;
  you return from the prey, my son.
Like a lion he crouches and lies down,
  like a lioness—who dares to rouse him?
¹⁰The scepter will not depart from Judah,
  nor the ruler's staff from between his feet,
until he comes to whom it belongs
  and the obedience of the nations is his.
¹¹He will tether his donkey to a vine,
  his colt to the choicest branch;
he will wash his garments in wine,
  his robes in the blood of grapes.
¹²His eyes will be darker than wine,
  his teeth whiter than milk.

¹³"Zebulun will live by the seashore
  and become a haven for ships;
  his border will extend toward Sidon.

¹⁴"Issachar is a rawboned donkey
  lying down between two saddlebags.
¹⁵When he sees how good is his resting place
  and how pleasant is his land,
he will bend his shoulder to the burden
  and submit to forced labor.

¹⁶"Dan will provide justice for his people
  as one of the tribes of Israel.
¹⁷Dan will be a serpent by the roadside,
  a viper along the path,
that bites the horse's heels
  so that its rider tumbles backward.

¹⁸"I look for your deliverance, O LORD.
"Gad will be attacked by a band of raiders,
  but he will attack them at their heels.

²⁰"Asher's food will be rich;
  he will provide delicacies fit for a king.

²¹"Naphtali is a doe set free

that bears beautiful fawns.

²²"Joseph is a fruitful vine,
  a fruitful vine near a spring,
  whose branches climb over a wall.
²³With bitterness archers attacked him;
  they shot at him with hostility.
²⁴But his bow remained steady,
  his strong arms stayed limber,
because of the hand of the Mighty One of Jacob,
  because of the Shepherd, the Rock of Israel,
²⁵because of your father's God, who helps you,
  because of the Almighty, who blesses you
with blessings of the heavens above,
  blessings of the deep that lies below,
  blessings of the breast and womb.
²⁶Your father's blessings are greater
  than the blessings of the ancient mountains,
  than the bounty of the age-old hills.
Let all these rest on the head of Joseph,
  on the brow of the prince among his brothers.

²⁷"Benjamin is a ravenous wolf;
  in the morning he devours the prey,
  in the evening he divides the plunder."

²⁸All these are the twelve tribes of Israel, and this is what their father said to
them when he blessed them, giving each the blessing appropriate to him.

The words "Israel your father" and "Israel . . . their father" mark the framework of the unit (vv. 1–2,28). The blessings of each tribal son are the central
segment (vv. 3–27). The patriarch calls for the gathering of the "sons of Jacob"
for his official blessing (vv. 1–2), presumably pronounced from his deathbed
(48:2,21; 49:33). The concluding verse summarizes the character of the preceding blessings, identifying the sons as the "twelve tribes of Israel" (v. 28).

CALL TO ASSEMBLE (49:1–2). **49:1–2** Admonition from father to son
exhibits the parental role of instruction (e.g., Ps 34:12; Prov 4:1; 5:7), but v. 1
gives the exhortation ("listen," from *šěmaʿ*) a prophetic tone as well (e.g., Isa
48:14, "Come together . . . listen"). The context is the issuance of Jacob's last
words on his deathbed (v. 33; cf. Deut 33:1). The term "gather around" *(ʾāsap)*
occurs figuratively for the death of Jacob in vv. 29,33. The expression "in days
to come" *(běʾaḥărît hayyāmîm)* reinforces the composition's orientation to the
future.⁵⁶⁴ The same language in the prophets announces the events of Israel's

---

⁵⁶⁴ On the significance of this passage for the structure and eschatological orientation of Genesis, see vol. 1A, pp. 46–47.

future restoration and preeminence (e.g., Isa 2:2; Dan 10:14; Hos 3:5).

REUBEN (49:3–4). **49:3–4** The oracle consists of two tricola. Verse 3 focuses on Reuben's favored position as "firstborn" in whom was invested the vigor ("might," *kōaḥ*) of his procreative powers ("strength," *'ôn*; cf. Deut 21:17; Job 40:16; Ps 78:51). He was superior ("excelling," *yeter,* cf. "beyond measure," Isa 56:12 [NRSV]) to his brothers in esteem as the firstborn. The term "honor" (*śĕ'ēt,* i.e., exaltation) is also used of God's majesty (e.g., Job 31:23). Yet he lost this place of dignity because he defamed his father's honor through sexual relations with his concubine wife (35:22).

His deed is likened to "turbulent" *(paḥaz*[565]*)* waters (v. 4), that is, reckless behavior (cf. ptc. from *p-ḥ-z,* Judg 9:4; Zeph 3:4), costing him his stature as the responsible eldest son (cf. Isa 57:20).[566] "You will no longer excel" (from *y-t-r*) reverses Reuben's former prestige (cf. v. 3, "excelling," *yeter* [2x]). His crime is sexual defilement (*piel, ḥillēl,* "defile, pollute, desecrate"), violating the purity of his father's concubinage. The parallel terms "bed" *(miškāb*[567]*)* and "couch" (*yāṣûa',* cf. 1 Chr 5:1) describe the place of sexual relations and thus are metaphorical in meaning and need not be taken literally, that is, Jacob's own bed. The Hebrew of v. 4c is difficult, generating a number of alternative readings, both ancient and modern. The MT has literally "then you defiled my couch; he went up,"[568] which has been retained by some EVs, rendering it "then you defiled [it]—he went up to my couch" (e.g., AV, NASB). The troublesome syntax and the change from "you" to third person "he" have encouraged alternative readings by EVs (including NIV).[569] The shift in person from "you" to "he" is not exceptional, however, in poetry.[570] First Chron-

---

[565] The noun form פַּחַז (MT) occurs only here (BDB 808); SP, LXX, Syr., *Tg. Onq.* reflect second masculine singular פָּחַזְתָּ, "You are turbulent" (see *BHS*). M. O'Connor, *Hebrew Verse Structure* (Winona Lake: Eisenbrauns, 1980), 170, reads infin. *pḥz,* used as a finite verb, "You are as unsteady as water."

[566] R. de Hoop ("The Meaning of *pḥz* in Classical Hebrew," *ZAH* 10 [1997]: 16–26) contends for "deceive, act untrustworthy" (Jer 15:18; Job 6:15), thus translated "deceptive like water" (de Hoop, *Genesis 49,* 86).

[567] Hb. plural מִשְׁכְּבֵי אָבִיךָ, "the beds of your father," may indicate the parts that constitute the whole (a "surface plural," GKC §124b); F. Cross and D. N. Freedman emend מִשְׁכָּבַי, "my bed" (*Studies in Ancient Yahwistic Poetry,* SBLDS 21 (Missoula: Scholars Press, 1975), 78). Cp. plural מִשְׁכְּבֵי, "to lie with," Lev 18:22; 20:13, which also describes a deviant sexual practice.

[568] אָז חִלַּלְתָּ יְצוּעִי עָלָה.

[569] Two readings are: (1) second person: τότε ἐμίανας τὴν στρωμνήν οὗ ἀνέβης, "then you defiled the bed, whereupon you went up" (LXX, cf. e.g., NIV, NRSV); and (2) the emendation, יְצוּעַ יַעֲלָה, lit., "the couch of [his] doe," in which "doe" refers to the concubine (as in Prov 5:19; see M. Dahood, "Hebrew-Ugaritic Lexicography III," *Bib* 46 (1965): 319; O'Connor has, "You profaned the couch of your father's beloved" (*Hebrew Verse,* 170); and Hamilton, *Genesis Chapters 18–50,* 645, n. 8.

[570] A. Berlin identifies the contrast in person as a morphological parallelism (e.g., Song 1:2; *The Dynamics of Biblical Parallelism* [Bloomington: Indiana University Press, 1985], 40–41).

icles 5:1 has "couch" as the object of defiled: "when he defiled his father's couch" (NIV, "marriage bed"). The object "my couch" may be gapped in the matching colon: "then you defiled my couch//[to my couch] he went up."

SIMEON AND LEVI (49:5–7). **49:5–7**   In the opening couplet of the oracle (v. 5), Jacob addresses the two together as "brothers," which probably alludes to 34:25 that recounts how "Dinah's brothers" attacked the town Shechem. That they were the blood brothers of Dinah (by Leah) explained why these two were especially outraged at her defilement, and for this reason Jacob views them as a pair of culprits. The primary problem in connecting this blessing with the Dinah-Shechem incident is the absence of hamstrung oxen in chap. 34. On the contrary, the passage says that the brothers confiscated the animals (34:28).[571] Among the resolutions is the ancient interpretation (e.g., Tgs., *Gen. Rab.* 108.5; Syr., Vg., Aquila and Symmachus) that understood the text as "wall" *(šûr)* instead of "bull" *(šôr)* and "uprooted" *('āqar,* "to pluck, root up"; cf. Zeph 2:4; Eccl 3:2) for "hamstrung" (MT, *'iqqēr, piel,* "to hamstring"). Thus, in their anger they pulled down the city's wall. Alternatively, some modern interpreters have understood "bull" as a figure representing Hamor (meaning "donkey"), Shechem, or for Jacob.[572] This animal figure has been found to refer to princes or noblemen in Ugaritic usage and for a leader in Deut 33:17 (Joseph) and Ps 68:30[31]. If Jacob is intended, the sense is that he became hampered by his sons' actions, opening himself to attack from his neighbors (cp. the sound play *'ākar,* "make trouble" in 34:30 and the root *'āqar,* "hamstring"). The simplest proposal is the brothers subsequently debilitated the oxen after their capture, since they were primarily shepherds, not farmers or cattlemen. Jacob seized upon this unrecorded incident as a signal evidence of the brothers' measure of "senseless brutality."[573] Thus by merism (human and animal), Jacob condemns their wanton attitude toward life.

The translation "their swords" *(mĕkērōtêhem)* is uncertain as a unique expression,[574] departing from the typical term for "sword" *(ḥereb),* which occurs in 34:25–26. The proposals for the meaning of the term are legion, and this wide diversity of opinion is reflected in the varying ancient and modern

---

[571] Moreover, one could press that there is a discrepancy between the mention of a "man" (אִישׁ) killed in v. 6 and the many Hamorites that the brothers murdered. The singular "man" and "bull" are easily explained as collective singulars, i.e., meaning the plural number "men" and "bulls."

[572] For bibliography see de Hoop, *Genesis 49,* 99–101, who contended for bull = Shechem. O'Connor, *Hebrew Verse,* 171, following F. I. Andersen, reads "ox, strong one," thus creating the parallel: "They murdered a powerful one *['yš]'//*"they hamstring a powerful man *[šwr].*"

[573] Waltke, *Genesis,* 606.

[574] MT, מְכֵרֹתֵיהֶם, derived from כרה, "to dig," i.e., with a weapon? Or כרר, "to dance, to round" (occurs once as *pilpel* in 2 Sam 6:14,16), i.e., to bore out a hole with a weapon? (see Delitzsch, *A New Commentary on Genesis,* 2.371).

translations.[575] The context recommends an instrument that was employed for bloodshed (NJPS has the generic "their weapons"). The popular rendering "sword" (e.g., NIV, NASB, NRSV) is fitting, but commentators ponder if the traditional rendering "sword" was unduly influenced in the past by the word's similarity to the Greek noun meaning "sword, dagger" *(makaira;* as in, e.g., *Gen. Rab.* 99.7; Rashi). Since the etymology remains disputed, the puzzle of the word's meaning will continue. In the description "weapons of violence,"[576] the word "violence" *(ḥamas)* is broadly used for violent behavior (e.g., 6:11,13) and may refer specifically to criminal homicide (e.g., Judg 9:24; Joel 3:19[4:19]).

Verse 6 consists of a quatrain, in which the first couplet describes Jacob's disassociation from the brothers and the second couplet provides the reason for their father's rejection. That he refuses their "council" *(sôd,* cf. Ps 83:3[4]; Jer 15:17) and "assembly" *(qāhāl,* cf. Ps 26:5) means that he disavows their wicked deeds (v. 6a). "Let me not . . . let me not . . ." renders lit., "let not my soul *[nepeš]* . . . let not my glory *[kābôd]* . . ." (MT; cf. NASB).[577] The verse

---

[575] de Hoop (*Genesis 49,* 101–9) offers a thorough discussion; or see the summaries of Hamilton, *Genesis Chapters 18–50,* 648–49, n. 4 (who opts for כרת, "to cut a covenant," thus "their covenanters"); and Wenham, *Genesis 16–50,* 473–74 (who translates "they are equipped"). AV's "[instruments of cruelty are] in their habitations" (i.e., houses) reflects מְכוּרֹה, "place/land of origin" (Ezek 16:3; 21:35; 29:14), cf. *Gen. Rab.* 99.7; Rashi; Ibn Ezra; see *Tg. Onq.,* "[they performed mighty feats] in the land of their sojourning" (rendering Hb. בְּאֶרֶץ מְגוּרָתָם[?]; see Grossfeld, *Targum Onqelos,* 158 n. 7). LXX has the perplexing συνετέλεσαν ἀδικίαν ἐξ αἱρέσεως αὐτῶν (from תרר, "choice"?): "[Simeon and Levi] completed the injustice by their choice" (see Wevers, *Notes on the Greek Text,* 822). de Hoop adapts M. Dahood's suggestion of a "knife (for circumcision)" (so NAB) from כרת, "to cut" ("*mkrtyhm* in Genesis 49,5," *CBQ* 23 [1961]: 54–56). *HALOT* 2.582 has "plan, recommendation" (*mekērâ* from מכר II [*mak(a)ra,* "to plan, counsel"]). Also the root *m-k-r,* "to sell," thus "their wares" (Speiser, *Genesis,* 365; Sarna, *Genesis,* 334); and Ethiopic *m-k-r,* "to advise, counsel," thus "their counsels" (so NJB, REB; see J. Barr, *Comparative Philology and the Text of the Old Testament* [Oxford: Clarendon, 1968], 57).

[576] SP, LXX suggest כִּלּוּ, "they completed," for MT's כְּלֵי, "vessels, utensils" (NIV "weapons").

[577] By synecdoche נֶפֶשׁ ("my soul") refers to the whole person, thus "my being," "my life," "me," or "I" (cf. vol. 1A, pp. 196–99); the parallel term כְּבֹדִי ("my glory") has the same sense of "life/person" (cf. Ps 8:5[6]). "Glory" (כָּבוֹד) parallels "life/person" (נֶפֶשׁ) in Ps 7:5(6); also see where כָּבוֹד refers to the whole or inner person (Pss 16:9; 30:12[13]; 57:7–9[8–10]; 108:1[2]). But instead of "glory," the LXX's τὰ ἥπατά μου reads כְּבֵדִי, "my liver, inward parts," referring to the inner person; cf. the parallel terms כָּבֵד ("liver")/נֶפֶשׁ ("life") in Lam 2:11–12. This solves an apparent gender incongruity in the MT created by the masc. noun כָּבוֹד ("glory") and the fem. verb תֵּחַד ("be united") instead of masc. יִחַד; the fem. כָּבֵד ("liver") agrees with the gender of the verb. Cf. יחד SP, LXX (ἐρείσαι, "support, stay") in *BHS.* For discussion of suggested emendations to the MT, see Hamilton, *Genesis Chapters 18–50,* 649, and for the LXX text see Wevers, *Notes on the Greek Text,* 822–23. The MT, however, can stand since אַל־תֵּחַד can be second person masc. ("may you not be united") and "glory" in the vocative case; alternatively, some sustain the MT by proposing that the fem. form of the verb is due to attraction to the preceding and parallel fem. verb תָּבֹא, "enter."

can also be interpreted as direct address: "O my soul, come not . . . O my glory, be not . . ." (cf. AV, RSV, NLT; cp. "Why are you downcast, O my soul?" Ps 42:5[6]; also Ps 103:1; 104:1).[578] The explanation for Jacob's disavowal is the brothers' irrepressible violence against man and beast (v. 6b). "Anger" (ʾap) parallels "as they pleased" (from rāṣôn), suggesting that "pleased" means here their unbridled self-indulgence ("just for sport," NLT), fueled by revenge. The "ox" (šôr) was a valuable commodity used as a work animal and beneficial for livelihood (e.g., Exod 23:12; Deut 15:19; 25:4; Job 24:3). Jacob depicts the brothers as wanton abusers, lacking regard for life.

Jacob's final utterance for them is his most strident (v. 7). Using a curse formula (ʾārûr, "cursed'; cf. 3:14, vol. 1A, p. 244), he invokes divine revenge against the brothers' "anger" (ʾap) and "fury" (ʿebrâ), that is, those who commit the anger. The latter term may be used of divine (e.g., Ps 78:49) or human wrath (e.g., Ps 7:6[7], where "anger" and "fury" also occur in parallel; Prov 14:35). His vivid language heightens the imagery of ruthless violence by the descriptive terms "fierce" (ʿaz, "strong") and "cruel" (qāšâ); "cruel" derives from the word group (q-š-h) that portrays a "hardened heart" (e.g., Prov 28:14) or "stiff-necked" recalcitrant (e.g., Deut 10:16; also Rachel's "difficult" labor, 35:16–17).[579] The sense that Jacob "will divide" (ḥālaq) and "disperse" (pûṣ, "to scatter") their descendants is due to the failure of the tribes to obtain a distinct land region in future Israel.[580] The word ḥalaq describes land allotment among Israel's tribes (e.g., Josh 13:7), and pûṣ bears the negative meaning of scattering under judgment (e.g., Babel, 11:4,8,9; cf. Deut 4:27). Historically, the Levites did not receive land tracts but forty-eight cities (e.g., Num 18:23–24; 35:1–8; Josh 21:1–45), and the Simeonite holdings were within the boundaries of Judah's territory where their identity eventually was absorbed by the larger Judahite tribe (Josh 19:1–9; Judg 1:3; 2 Chr 15:9). The parallel language "in Jacob" and "in Israel," referring to the territory of national Israel, reinforces the identification of the patriarch as the nation's paternal namesake.

---

[578] By reading the nouns as direct address, the gender agreement in MT is also resolved. The second fem. sg. form, תָּבֹאי, if defectively spelled according to early orthography, would not have the final vowel marker yod (î) as in the MT, thus agreeing with the vocative use of the fem. noun נַפְשִׁי ("O, my soul"). This parallels תֵּחַד, when interpreted as second masc. sg., which agrees with the masc. כְּבֹדִי ("O, my glory"). See Cross and Freedman, *Ancient Yahwistic Poetry,* 79 (who prefer כְּבֵדִי, "liver," as in the LXX).

[579] Reinforcing the intensity, NIV (also NAB, NJPS) plausibly interprets the accompanying כִּי as asseverate, "so fierce . . . so cruel."

[580] J. Fleishman, on the basis of ANE legal texts, contends that Simeon and Levi lose their inheritance due to the shaming of their father ("Towards Understanding the Legal Significance of Jacob's Statement: 'I will divide them in Jacob, I will scatter them in Israel' [Gen 49,7b]," in *Studies in the Book of Genesis,* 541–60); in particular they injure Jacob's honor by the retort, "Should he have treated our sister as a prostitute?" (34:31), impugning the moral character of the household.

The two names form a common word pair in Hebrew verse.[581]

JUDAH (49:8–12). Second in length to the Joseph oracle is the Judah blessing. The pronouncement depicts Judah as stalwart as a lion, which is the reigning tribe over his "brothers" (vv. 8–9). The reign of the tribe is without end, and a future descendant, to whom the "nations" will submit, bears all authority (v. 10). Historically, this verse provides for the Davidic dynasty (e.g., 2 Sam 7:13–16), which created the messianic expectation in Israel. The oracle has been notoriously difficult in the history of interpretation, and the literature is immense.[582] Early Jewish interpretation commonly applied the passage to the Jewish Messiah (e.g., 4Q252; *Tgs.*; *Gen. Rab.* 98.8; *b. Sanh.* 98b; *Tanḥ. Wayyeḥi* 10),[583] and in the Christian community interpreters related it to David and Jesus Christ.[584] Early Christian exegetes tied many details of the prophecy to aspects of Christ. The notion of submission and praise in v. 8, for example, refers to the Lord's spiritual triumph over wicked powers and the apostles' praise of the Lord Jesus. Ambrose, among others, interpreted the washing of the robe in wine (v. 11) as depicting the flesh (= robe) of Jesus, whose baptism at the Jordan washed away sin (*The Patriarchs* 4.24). Especially important to Christian exegesis was the description of tethering the foal to the vine (v. 11), which forecasted the triumphal entry of Jesus into Jerusalem (Luke 19:30–34). The vine, in accord with Jesus' declaration "I am the true vine" (John 15:1), represents Christ and the donkey, and its foal bound to the vine is the Gentiles and the Jews who respond to the gospel (Chrysostom, *Homilies on Gen.* 67.9; Rufinus, *The Blessings of the Patriarchs* 1.11). When commenting on v. 10, Calvin offered a lengthy refutation of Jewish opponents to the Christian interpretation of the passage.[585] He observed that Judah remained a united tribe despite its oppression and emerged from the exile as the embodiment of the nation. The splendor of David's kingdom indeed diminished, but the preeminence of Judah among his brothers remained and found its fulfillment in the coming of Christ. Luther, too, scolds Jewish and Christian interpreters who are satisfied with pinning this prophecy to David alone, asserting that Christ is "Shiloh," whom all

---

[581] O'Connor observes that "Jacob//Israel" is "the classic example of social organization binomination [splitting up a personal or geographic name]," naming Yahweh's people (*Hebrew Verse*, 375).

[582] For thorough discussions of the literature, see Skinner, *Genesis*, 520–24, and de Hoop, *Genesis 49*, 122–48.

[583] R. Syrén, *The Blessings in the Targums: A Study on the Targumic Interpretations of Genesis 49 and Deuteronomy 33* (Åbo: Åbo Akademi, 1986), 131. On the Qumran text 4Q252 and its messianic titles "Messiah" and "Branch of David," see J. VanderKam, "Messianism in the Scrolls," in *The Community of the Renewed Covenant* (Notre Dame: University of Notre Dame Press, 1994), 211–34 (esp. 215–18).

[584] *ACCS* 2.325–35.

[585] Calvin, *Comm.*, 2.452–60.

nations will worship, and the symbolic language of the foal tied to the vine depicts the church, which becomes "drunk" on the Holy Spirit.[586]

49:8–9 Verse 8 is a tricolon; cola one and three pertain to Judah's superiority over his brothers, and the middle colon describes his victory over enemies. "Your brothers" and "your father's sons" exhibit the parallelism of cola one and three. The imagery of submissive brothers and defeated enemies in v. 8 recalls the blessing bestowed on Jacob by his father Isaac (27:29). The second person pronoun ("you," "your") dominates v. 8, beginning with the independent pronoun "you" *(ʾattâ)*: lit., "Judah, as for you." Just as the second person "you" distinguished Reuben as the firstborn (v. 3), the second person here distinguishes Judah from his brothers. The term for "praise" *(yādâ;* "will praise you," *yôdûkā)* is a play on the name "Judah" *(yĕhûdâ)* as was the explanation by Leah in naming the child (29:35). The term "praise" also differentiates Judah since the word is rarely directed toward humans (Job 40:14; Pss 45:17[18]; 49:18[19]). The repetition of the sounds *y* and *d* continues by "your hand" *(yādĕkā;* cf. "hand" and "foes" in Moses' blessing of Judah, Deut 33:7). Suppressing the "neck" *(ʿōrep)* of an opponent meant that the enemy was overcome, having succumbed to the superior power of the victor (cf. Job 16:12). The term also describes the flight of an enemy whose fleeing "back" *(ʿōrep)* evidences defeat (e.g., Exod 23:27).[587] That the "father's sons will bow down" (from *ḥāwâ)* to Judah is an unexpected twist since Jacob had raised the question of Joseph: "Will your mother and I and your brothers actually come and bow down to the ground before you?" (37:10).

The quatrain in v. 9 presents the first of several animal images describing Judah: a fearless "lion" returns from successfully snagging its prey. Lions stalked their prey and dragged the victims to their lairs, where their young devoured them (Jer 4:7; Isa 5:29; Nah 2:11–12[12–13]; Amos 3:4).[588] Three of seven Hebrew words for "lion" appear in this single verse. There may be a sense of movement or growth by Judah in the verse by the change in lion imagery from a young "cub" *(gûr)* to a "lion" *(ʾaryēh).*[589] This would correspond with the development of Judah in the narrative who emerges from the pack of brothers as their leader and spokesman. Viewed as the mightiest beast (Prov 30:30), the lion as a symbol for royalty was widespread in the ancient Near East, including Israel's rulers and princes (e.g., Ezek 19:1–9; Zeph 3:3; cf. Solomon's throne, 1 Kgs 10:18–20). The lion became a symbol of Judah's King David and the Messiah (e.g., Rev 5:5; *4 Ezra* 11:37; 12:31; *Gen. Rab.* 98.7). The Blessing of Moses also

---

[586] *LW* 8.245–52.

[587] A second term for "neck" (צַוָּאר) occurs, which under a yoke indicates submission (e.g., Esau, 27:40; cf. Deut 28:48).

[588] G. J. Botterweck, "אֲרִי," *TDOT* 1.374–88 (382).

[589] de Hoop, *Genesis 49,* 140.

depicts the tribes Gad and Dan as lions (Deut 33:20,22). Judah is like a "lion's cub" *(gûr ʾaryēh),* exhibiting youthful vigor and aggression (cf. Deut 33:2,20; Ezek 19:2–5). Perhaps Jacob flatters himself when he mentions "my son," suggesting that he is the mighty father of the cub. Fresh "prey" *(ṭerep)* dangles from the cub's jaws upon his return to his parents' lair (cf. Num 23:24).[590] This scene of a lion's prey brings to mind Joseph's blood-drenched coat "torn to pieces" *(ṭārōp ṭōrap;*37:33; 44:28), making the chief sons, Joseph and Judah, a victim and a victimizer.[591] In addition to the frequent word *ʾaryēh* is the word *lābîʾ,* meaning "lion" or "lioness," depending on the context; in our passage it is probably "lioness," forming a word pair with the male "lion" (see Num 23:24; 24:9; Joel 1:6; Nah 2:12[13]; cf. Job 4:10–11). The description of the lion is one readied to attack: "he crouches" *(kāraʿ)* and "lies down" *(rābaṣ).* This latter word describes the typical pose of a lion lying quietly in wait, which is ready to pounce once aroused (cf. 4:7, vol. 1A, p. 270; Ps 104:22). A lion is noted for its stealth (Ps 17:12) and its paralyzing roar over its prey (e.g., Isa 5:29; Amos 3:4,8; Ps 22:13[14]). Balaam fittingly describes the Israelites in the same manner, using the near exact language (Num 24:9a). The description "rouse" *(hiph.* from *qûm)* is not the common word for awaken (cf. *ʿûr,* e.g., Job 3:8) and occurs in the same sense only in Num 24:9a. The semantic parallel in Num 23:24, "to lift up oneself" *(hith.* from *nāśāʾ),* that is, to stir up oneself, appears in Balaam's earlier description of the Israelites, who like a lion are not satisfied until they drink the blood of their victims.

49:10 The next portrayal of Judah describes him as ruler bearing the king's "scepter" *(šēbeṭ).* The "scepter" symbolizes the monarchy that will be Judah's inheritance (e.g., Num 24:17; Pss 2:9; 45:6[7]; Amos 1:8), which was historically realized in David's kingship (e.g., 2 Sam 7:8–16; Ps 89:3–4,20[4–5,21]). The kingdom is a permanent possession that "will not depart *[sûr]* from Judah," as it was promised to David's lineage in Nathan's oracle *(sûr* [2x] in 2 Sam 7:15; cf. Ps 89:33–37). The parallel expression, "ruler's staff" *(mĕḥōqēq),* describes a commander's mace (e.g., Num 21:18). Or it may refer to an authoritative leader (e.g., Judg 5:9,14; Isa

---

[590] The NIV's "return" renders עָלִיתָ, lit., "you have gone up"; alternatively, the sense may be that the cub has "grown up" on prey (cf. Ezek 19:3; Isa 53:2).

[591] Jewish Tgs. and commentators (Rashi) interpret מִטֶּרֶף בְּנִי as "from the prey of my son," i.e., "From the prey of my son Joseph you went up and were exalted, from the tearing of Tamar you went up and were exalted *(Gen. Rab.* 98.7). In both cases Judah intervened to deliver Joseph and Tamar from death (Grossfeld, *Targum Onqelos,* 162, n. 17). The LXX, ἐκ βλαστοῦ υἱέ μου ἀνέβης, "from a tender shoot, my son, you grew up," suppresses the picture of a vicious Judah (see Wevers, *Notes on the Greek Text,* 825).

33:22), which was the understanding of most ancient authorities on 49:9.[592] The psalmists designate Judah himself as God's "scepter" *(měḥōqēq;* 60:7[9]; 108:8[9])*.* The same term "ruler" *(měḥōqēq)* appears in the Mosaic blessing of Gad in Deut 33:21. "Between his feet" has been interpreted as a euphemism for sexual parts (cp. "from between her feet" = womb, Deut 28:57; cf. Isa 7:20; Ezek 16:25),[593] meaning here sexual potency (e.g., LXX *mērōn,* "thighs" [see 24:2,9; 47:29]; also interpreted as euphemism in Tgs.; Vg.; cf. "his descendants," NLT).[594] That the euphemism refers to female parts, however, creates difficulty for this interpretation. If it is a euphemism, the import is that Judah will always have a royal progeny.

The latter half of v. 10 is difficult because of the interpretation of Hebrew *šylh* (vocalized *šîlōh* [with *yod*] in the MT,[595] i.e., transliterated "Shiloh" [AV, NKJV, NASB]), whose meaning is uncertain. Both ancient and modern interpretations reflect a wide diversity of opinion. We will summarize the chief interpretations.

1. The least likely meaning of Hebrew *šylh* is the town name "Shiloh," thus "until he [Judah] comes to Shiloh." In this case "Shiloh" is understood as the destination of the future ruler. Shiloh was located in the tribal territory of Ephraim and was the religious center where the tabernacle resided until the town's destruction in 1050 B.C. (e.g., Josh 18; 1 Sam 1–4). Thus, in this view the blessing predicts Judah's leadership role in the settlement of the land (e.g., Judg 1:1–2), or it points beyond to the expansion of Judah's dominion over the northern tribes during the monarchy.[596] The difficulty is the unconventional spelling of the town's name in our text, since its common spelling is *šilōh* (without *yod*). Also, although the people did gather at Shiloh for the distribution of the land (Josh 18–19), the word "nations" (*'ammîm,* "peoples") in our text probably refers to foreign nations. There is no evidence that Judah exercised rule over the "nations" during the settlement period, unless

---

[592] מְחֹקֵק, *poel* participle from חָקַק, "to decree," thus interpreted as "king, ruler" who enacts edicts (LXX; Vg.; 4Q252; Rashi). The LXX parallels ἄρχων (= שֹׁטֵ?), "judge, ruler," and ἡγού-μενος (= מְחֹקֵק), "ruler." Other ancient authorities (CD VI, 7; Syr.; *Gen. Rab.* 98.8; *Sanh.* 5a; Ibn Ezra) interpret מְחֹקֵק as "scribe, teacher" derived from חָקַק, "to inscribe (a חֹק, "statute, ordi-nance"; cp. "a lawgiver," AV, NJKV). *Gen. Rab.* 98.8 identifies שֹׁטֵ as the institution "Sanhedrin" and מְחֹקֵק as "two clerks of the judges"; the Tgs. at Num 21:18 and Deut 33:21 associate מְחֹקֵק with the person "Moses." *Tgs. Ps.-J.* and *Neof.* include "kings" and "scribes," maintaining both interpretations. See Syrén, *The Blessings in the Targums,* 54–55; McNamara, *Targum Neofiti,* 220, n. 23.

[593] רֶגֶל ("foot, feet") is euphemistic for bodily functions (Judg 3:24; 1 Sam 24:3[4]; 2 Kgs 18:27; V. Hamilton, "רֶגֶל," *NIDOTTE* 3.1048).

[594] The SP reads דְּגָלָיו, "[between] his banners"; cf. Num 1:52; Song 2:4.

[595] שִׁילֹה, *kěthîb;* שִׁילוֹ, *qěrê.*

[596] E.g., see Delitzsch, *A New Commentary on Genesis,* 2.380–83; and J. Lundblom, "The Political Background in the Shilo Oracle," in *Volume de Congres Strasbourgh 1956,* VTSup 4 (Leiden: Brill, 1957), 138–47.

one counts the defeat of the indigenous Canaanite population (Judg 1). It was not until the era of David that Judah extended its dominion beyond its borders. Moreover, Judah's kings did not achieve hegemony at Shiloh, and the departure of the tabernacle (1 Sam 6–7) made the town politically unimportant during the era of Israel's kings.

2. More attractive to many scholars is the division of the Hebrew consonants into two well-known words: *šylh* becomes *šay lōh,* meaning, "tribute to him," thus "until tribute comes to him" (NRSV), that is, to Judah. This interpretation was proposed by some medieval Jewish commentators, but it underwent a rebirth in recent times.[597] The antecedent of the phrase "to him" is "Judah" appearing in v. 10a. The word "tribute" *(šay)* also occurs in Pss 68:29[30]; 76:11[12]; and Isa 18:7, which describe gifts offered by the nations to the all-powerful Lord—a picture that suits the imagery of our passage well. Instead of tribute "comes" *(bô᾿)* as in our passage, however, the verb is "bring, carry" *(yābal)* in the parallel passages.[598] The attraction of this view is the retention of the MT's text without a major disturbance. Also the reading parallels agreeably with the following line (v. 10b). The "obedience" of the nations is expressed through the presentation of royal tribute. This interpretation, which several EVs have adopted (NAB, NJB, NRSV, NJPS), has no serious flaw that rules it out as a possibility.

3. The word *šylh* is understood as the proper name of a person, transliterating the Hebrew "Shiloh," thus "until Shiloh come(s)" (e.g., AV, ASV, NKJV, NASB). Jewish midrash that interpreted "Shiloh" as a person identified him as Israel's future messiah (e.g., *Gen. Rab.* 98.8; *b. Sanh.* 98b; also Rashi). Other than the general tenor of the passage, there is no reason, however, to identify "Shiloh" with the messianic king. Opponents notice that Shiloh does not occur as a messianic title elsewhere in Scripture and point to something like "peacemaker" *(Šālôm)* as a more appropriate title for the messiah king (e.g., Mic 5:5[4]).[599] Also unlikely is emending the text to "his ruler" *(mōšĕlōh),* thus "until his ruler comes."[600] Although this fits the context nicely and has support from Mic 5:2[1] ("ruler over Israel"), the proposal requires unnecessary change to the text, and there is no textual support for it in the ancient witnesses.

---

[597] E.g., *Yalkut Shimoni* 160; Rashi includes this view as possible; see W. L. Moran, "Gen 49,10 and Its Use in Ez 21,32," *Bib* 39 (1958): 405–25, whose preferred rendering includes interpreting "come" (יָבֹא) as passive: עַד כִּי־יָבָא שַׁי לֹה, "until tribute is brought to him" (see Cross and Freedman, *Ancient Yahwistic Poetry,* 83). Among modern commentators are Speiser, Sarna, and Wenham.

[598] de Hoop shows why the lexical variation should not preclude this view (*Genesis 49,* 130).

[599] Delitzsch, *A New Commentary on Genesis,* 2.381–82; and Skinner, *Genesis,* 522.

[600] מֹשְׁלֹה, *qal* active participle מֹשֵׁל + third masculine singular suffix.; e.g., see Westermann, *Genesis 37–50,* 218 and von Rad, *Genesis,* 425.

4. Most commendable is the alternate Hebrew textual reading (in Samaritan and MT MSS) *šellōh* (or *šellô*), meaning "to whom it belongs," thus "until he comes to whom it [i.e., scepter] belongs."[601] This reading occurs in the Qumran text 4Q252 and in the chief versions (LXX,[602] Syr., Tgs.). Many EVs prefer this interpretation of the text (NIV, RSV, REB, NLT). Ezekiel 21:27[32] is the first known "interpretation" of our text, alluding to 49:10 when referring to the future, rightful successor to the wicked Zedekiah of Judah.[603] The future ruler envisioned in 49:10 will receive the scepter ("it"), which represents the kingdom. Some ancient witnesses possessed translations that reflected both the person messiah and the kingdom translations in combination (e.g., 4Q252; Syr.; Tgs.), whereas *Gen. Rab.* (97.10; 99.8) keeps them separate.[604] The text 4Q252 has "until the messiah of righteousness, the branch of David, comes, for to him and to his descendants the covenant of the kingship of the people has been given for the generations of eternity" (col. 5.3–4).[605] The targums and Jewish midrash also provided an explicit messianic paraphrase, for example, "until the Messiah comes, to whom belongs the kingdom . . ." (*Tg. Onq.;* see also Tgs. *Ps-J., Neof.*). Two interpretations are united here. "Messiah" interprets *šîlōh* as a person, and "to whom belongs the kingdom" reflects the alternate reading *šellōh*.[606] The problem with reading "to whom it belongs" *(šellōh)* is, if original, it does not explain the development of the erroneous *šylh*. The advantages of following this reading are the wide support of the textual witnesses and the minor textual disturbance.

The interpreter must decide if the passage refers to the historical figure David and his dynastic legacy or if it looks to the far horizon of the perfect messianic ruler. The word "until" does not mean that the role of Judah's house ceases with the coming of the king. The word "until" *('ad kî)* does not always indicate a break from the preceding action, but it may indicate continuity with the past action and which reaches a fuller expression.[607] The coming of King David follows the template in part and cannot be denied its place

---

[601] שֶׁלֹּה (or שֶׁלֹּו) from אֲשֶׁר לֹו, i.e., the relative pronoun + preposition + third masculine singular suffix., lit., "which belongs to him."

[602] ἕως ἂν ἔλθῃ τὰ ἀποκείμενα αὐτῷ, "until there should come the things laid up [i.e., held in reserve] for him," translation by Wevers, *Notes on the Greek Text,* 826.

[603] עַד בֹּא אֲשֶׁר־לֹו הַמִּשְׁפָּט, "until he comes to whom it rightfully belongs" (NIV, Ezek 21:27[32]), or for a nonmessianic interpretation, translated "until he [Nebuchadnezzar] comes to whom the judgment belongs," see D. Block, *The Book of Ezekiel Chapters 1–24,* NICOT (Grand Rapids: Eerdmans, 1997), 683, 692–93.

[604] See the discussion in Syrén, *The Blessings in the Targums,* 56–58,131 and Grossfeld, *Targum Onqelos,* 158, 163, nn. 25–26.

[605] Translation by VanderKam, "Messianism," 215.

[606] Syr. also reads "until the One, whose it is, will come," translation by Syrén, *The Blessings in the Targums,* 57.

[607] GKC §164f.

as a partial fulfillment of the blessing. But the intimation of an idealized permanent, universal reign must also look to the perfect eschatological figure, David's Greater Son. The Christian interpreter, who identifies the king of our passage explicitly as Jesus of Nazareth, therefore can agree with the historian that the Davidic monarchy must be initially in view and also can agree with ancient Jewish interpretation that our text requires a messianic fulfillment.

The word "obedience" *(yiqqĕhat)* occurs here and in Prov 30:17 (if not emended).[608] The tenor of the verse indicates that the people "obey" by submitting to the scion of Judah. "Nations" translates the plural term "peoples" *('ammîm)*, whose usage can refer to foreign nations (e.g., 27:29; Deut 32:8) as well as descendants of Abraham (e.g., 17:16; 48:4). The earlier mention of Judah's fellow kinsmen by "brothers//your father's sons" (v. 8) makes it likely that a worldwide dominion is in mind here—imagery that suits the messianic king (e.g., Pss 2:8; 72:8,11; Isa 11:10,12; Mic 5:4[3]; Zech 9:10).

49:11–12 The subsequent verse by hyperbole depicts Judah (or his royal offspring) as a prosperous husbandman, producing an extravagant harvest of grapes (v. 11). The metaphor of a rich grape harvest indicating wealth is common (e.g., 27:28,37; Deut 8:8; 33:28; Amos 9:13). The word pairs in v. 11 that parallel the general term and the specific term (particularizing) heighten the desired effect of extravagance. The visage of a "donkey" *('ayir,* male donkey) harnessed to a "vine" *(gepen),* even a "choice vine" *(śōrēqâ;* cf. Judah as *śōrēq,* Isa 5:2; Jer 2:21), conveys the picture of a successful harvest. A donkey so tied will consume the vine's grapes and even the vine itself, thus showing that due to the owner's wealth he has no regard for the vine.[609] This is advanced by the mention of "his colt [of a she-donkey]" *(bĕnî 'ătōnô);* the young "colt" signals vigor, corresponding to the "cub" lion in the former metaphor (v. 9). Also the female *'ătôn* was a valuable animal, suggesting affluence (cf. 12:16; 32:16[16]; 45:23; Judg 5:10) and perhaps royalty (cf. Zech 9:9; Matt 21:2 pars.). The final couplet of v. 11 depicts the extravagant use of crushed grapes for washing clothes. The parallelism gives the general term for garments *(lĕbûš),* followed by the unique word "robes" *(sût).*[610] That wine can be substituted for wash water demonstrates the excess of the

---

[608] יִקְּהַת is defined by Akk. and Ar. cognates (E. H. Merrill, "יִקְּהַת," *NIDOTTE* 2.518–19; "obedience" *HALOT* 3.430). Perhaps influenced by the messianic expectation of the verse (Wevers, *Notes on the Greek Text,* 826), the LXX (Syr., Vg.) προσδοκία reflects תִּקְוָה, "hope, expectation" from קָוָה, "to look for, wait for"; cf. קִוִּיתִי in 49:18; see Isa 51:5, יְיַחֵלוּן אִיִּים אֵלַי, "the coastlands (i.e., nations) will wait for me."

[609] Or, as Rashi comments, the picture is of a donkey loaded with produce gathered from one luxuriant vine.

[610] Like the Gk. περιβολή, which is a covering garment, most EVs have "robe(s)" (or "vesture," ASV, RSV). *Tg. Onq.* understands the red-stained garments as the purple robes of the messiah's royalty, whereas *Tgs. Ps.-J.* and *Neof.* view them as drenched red from the blood of the messiah's slaughtered enemies.

owner's grape harvest. Or, alternatively, the vat of berries produces juice-soaked garments when trampling out the grapes (cf. Isa 63:2).[611] The richly colored expression "blood of grapes" indicates a sumptuous crop (cf. Deut 32:14). Verse 12, expressed as a couplet, continues the idea of prolific harvest by describing the appearance of its effects on the man. So rich and abundant is the wine that he has produced, his eyes are "darker" (*ḥaklîlî*; cf. *ḥaklîlût*, Prov 23:29[612]) than the wine itself, and his teeth glisten whiter than milk against his red-stained lips.[613] The images of wine (vineyard) and milk portray prosperity (e.g., Deut 32:14; Isa 55:1).

ZEBULUN (49:13). **49:13** Although Issachar preceded Zebulun in birth by Leah as her fifth and sixth sons (30:17–20; cf. 35:23; 46:13–14; Exod 1:3), Zebulun is first in our text and in the Blessing of Moses (Deut 33:18). The priority of Zebulun in Israel's era of settlement and early monarchy partly explains the reversal of order (e.g., Num 34:24–25; Josh 19:10,17; Judg 4:6,10; 5:14–18; 6:35; 1 Chr 12:33).[614] Also it held a strategic location in the terrain of northern Israel; it was a target of invading troops, such as Assyria in the eighth century. It became (with Naphtali), however, the site of salvation in Isaiah's prophecy of God's deliverance (Isa 9:1–2 [8:23–24]). Isaiah's prophecy points to Jesus' initial Galilean ministry, where Nazareth and Capernaum were located (Matt 4:15–16). The subject is Zebulun's setting by the seashore, which ostensibly, unlike the other blessings, says nothing about its character or contribution. Yet since Zebulun's tribal boundaries were land-locked (Josh 19:10–16), the unexpected association with sea trade comments favorably on the entrepreneurial spirit of the tribe. The Blessing of Moses also draws attention to the affluence that the sea provided Zebulun and Issachar (Deut 33:18–19). Our text twice identifies the location at the shoreline in parallel expressions: "shore of seas" (*lĕḥôp yammîm*, "seashore," NIV) and "a shore for ships" (*lĕḥôp ʾŏnîyôt*, "a haven for ships," NIV). The mention of the north Phoenician seaport Sidon is understandable since it was an important international venue on the Mediterranean coast. Because of its preeminence, "Sidon" in our text probably represents the whole of the Phoenician seafaring enterprise (10:15,19) for which Sidon and Tyre were famous (e.g., Isa 23:2,8; Zech 9:4). The question that remains is in what way Zebulun could be said to

---

[611] Freedman suggested dyeing the vestment in a rich, perhaps royal, red (see O'Connor, *Hebrew Verse*, 173).

[612] For חַכְלִילִי and חַכְלִלוּת cf. Akk. *ekēlu*, "to be dark." *HALOT* 1.313 by means of metathesis derives the word from כָּחַל, "to paint [the eyes]," rendering "sparkling" in our text (cf. Ezek 23:40; *HALOT* 2.469); see the commentaries, e.g., Waltke, *Genesis*, 609, n. 19, and Wenham, *Genesis 16–50*, 479.

[613] The prep. מִן of מִיַּיִן and מֵחָלָב is the comparison use, "darker than wine" (e.g., NIV, NRSV) or indicates source (e.g., "from," NASB); the latter rendering, "red" or "darkened with wine" (RSV, NJB), also indicates excess and describes drunkenness in Prov 23:29–30.

[614] Sarna, *Genesis*, 338.

"live" at the seaside and that its "border" extended to Sidon, since its territory did not border the Mediterranean. This description is more appropriate for Asher, whose allotment lay west of Zebulun along the Mediterranean and north of Zebulun extending to Phoenicia (Josh 19:24–31). Also the portrayal of Asher's seaside location in the Song of Deborah (Judg 5:17) is similar to what we find for Zebulun in our passage. Yet the text's association of Zebulun with the coast may be justified when it is remembered that major thoroughfares for trade bordered and traversed Zebulun (to Acco), making the sea "nearby" to Zebulun's citizens (perhaps with Issachar, Deut 33:18–19) for developing commerce and manning Phoenicia's vast maritime industry.[615]

ISSACHAR (49:14–15). **49:14–15** The poetic stanza consists of a couplet (v. 14) and a quatrain (v. 15). Issachar is neither attractive nor fortunate. As a "rawboned" *(gerem)* beast, it exhibits a lean, bony structure, hardened by its labor (v. 14). The word *gerem* conveys the idea of "strong" (Job 40:18; Prov 25:15), thus a "strong donkey" (e.g., NIV text note; NASB, NRSV). The Hebrew word translated "saddlebags" *(mišpĕtayim)* occurs again in Judg 5:16 (NIV, "campfires") and possibly Ps 68:13[14] *(šĕpatayim;* NIV, "campfires"). Its meaning is uncertain. As a dual form, and given the image of an animal, "saddlebags"[616] is preferred (NIV, NAB, NJPS, HCSB).[617] Other EVs opt for "sheepfolds," that is, animal pens (NJB, NLT, REB, NASB, NRSV), perhaps influenced by the contexts of Judg 5:16 and Ps 68:13[14], where "sheepfolds" fits. One suggestion for the puzzling usage is that the same word conveys both meanings.[618] The image of "lying down" *(rōbēṣ)* conveys a welcomed respite from the animal's fatiguing load (e.g., Exod 23:5; Num 22:27; also see 29:2; but cf. the lion Judah, v. 9; see comments on 4:7). Thus it enjoys repose nestled beside the baggage (AV, "burdens") or as a companion with the idle sheep (cf. Ps 23:2). Verse 15 describes, however, the surprising outcome.

---

[615] D. A. Dorsey, "Zebulun," *HBD* 1158, and *The Roads and Highways of Ancient Israel* (Baltimore: Johns Hopkins University Press, 1991), maps 5,10; and J. J. Bimson, ed., *Baker Encyclopedia of Bible Places* (Grand Rapids: Baker/Leicester: InterVarsity, 1995), 312. Moreover, the southern boundary of Zebulun was the Kishon River, which, although the boundary did not extend the full distance of the Kishon, connected with the Mediterranean at Mt. Carmel (see Z. Kallai, *Historical Geography of the Bible: The Tribal Territories of Israel* [Jerusalem: Magnes Press/Leiden: Brill, 1986], 181–83).

[616] "Saddlebaskets," *HALOT* 2.652.

[617] Perhaps spurred on by the geographical description of Zebulun, some versions gave topographical interpretations. The LXX has ἀνὰ μέσον τῶν κλήρων, "between the allotments" and *Tg. Onq.* "between the boundaries," suggesting the terrain of Issachar's land was situated between other tribal territories (LXX; cf. *Tgs. Ps.-J.* and *Neof.*) or bounded by two plains *(Tg. Onq.). Gen Rab.* 98.12 compared the shape of a donkey to the terrain of Issachar's land with its mountain in the center flanked by "the valley of Akleslo and the valley of Jezreel" (see Grossfeld, *Targum Onqelos,* 167, n. 38).

[618] de Hoop *(Genesis 49,* 155–56), follows J. C. de Moor, "Donkey-Packs and Geology," *UF* 13 (1981): 303–4 and "The Twelve Tribes in the Song of Deborah," *VT* 43 (1993): 491, n. 33.

Although the setting ("resting-place," e.g., Num 10:33; Ps 23:2) is deemed "good" *(ṭôb)* and "pleasant" (from *nāʿēm,* "to be pleasant, delightful"), the animal submits to servitude. The "shoulder/back" *(šěkem)* naturally bore the weight of the cargo (e.g., 21:14); the word metaphorically describes the hardships suffered by God's people under tyrannical rule (e.g., Ps 81:7; Isa 9:3; 10:27). "Burden" (from *sābal,* "to bear," e.g., *siblâ,* Exod 6:6–7) and "forced labor" *(mas,* e.g., Exod 1:11) here indicate corvée labor. The blessing implies that to remain in its fertile territory Issachar submitted to Canaanite lordship, referring to the settlement period. During the eighth to sixth centuries, the tribes to the north unwillingly fell subject to occupying forces.

DAN (49:16–18). **49:16–17** This stanza consists of two bicola (vv. 16–17) and a closing tricolon (v. 18).[619] Verses 16 and 18 form the boundaries of the stanza, both pertaining to deliverance from enemies—Dan who defends "his people" (v. 16) and the Lord who is Israel's defender (v. 18). The middle verse describes the aggression of Dan (v. 17), presumably defending his people. The nature of the Dan pronouncement is paradoxical, like its role in the history of Israel. The Danites exhibited remarkable achievements and dismal failures. Although the second most numerous tribe in the wilderness (Num 2:26; 26:42), it was too weak to secure its designated allotment (Josh 19:47). Oholiab, a Danite, notably assisted Bezalel in the construction of the sanctuary (e.g., Exod 31:6; 36:1), yet it was a Danite who notoriously profaned the name of the Lord (Lev 24:11). The Danite migration resulted in a crushing victory over the Canaanite population at Laish (Judg 18:27–29), but its first order of business was the establishment of an idolatrous cult (vv. 30–31). Although Samson's victories over the repressive Philistines were unprecedented, he was morally impotent and was duped by a cunning woman (Judg 16:19–21).[620] The same mixed message occurs in Jacob's blessing. The positive view of Dan appears in the Blessing of Moses, who characterizes Dan as a "lion's cub" (Deut 33:22), the same metaphor that depicts the esteemed Judah (49:9). In Jacob's blessing, too, Dan is successful, despite its precarious position, but its vulnerability prompts Jacob's outburst for divine intervention (v. 18). This unique interlude of prayer in the poem distinguishes Dan's dangerous life in the land of promise as representative of what Jacob's tribal descendants will face.

By a play on the name "Dan," as in his naming (see comments on 30:6), Jacob predicts that he will "provide justice" *(yādîn,* from *dîn,* "to judge, contend") for his own people, "as one of the tribes of Israel" (v. 16). "His peo-

---

[619] O'Connor separates v. 16, interpreting the subject as "Yahweh"; the idiom עַמּוֹ דִּין most often refers to God, and דִּן is a defective spelling for דִּין, "judgment," thus "He governs his people Israel according to one judgment" (*Hebrew Verse,* 174, 427).

[620] Jewish tradition (e.g., Tgs., *Gen. Rab.*) identified the viper in this saying as Samson, who bites the heels of the Philistine warriors.

ple" probably refers to his own tribe as opposed to the whole of the Israelite confederacy (cf. Judg 5:17). The picture of the Danites during the settlement period shows the tribe looking after its own interests as a small tribal unit (Josh 19:47; Judg 1:34–35; chap. 18). That it is identified as "one of the tribes of Israel" reinforces the inclusion of Dan in the covenant nation, despite its insignificance and independence. M. O'Connor observed that of the animals named in the Blessing of Jacob, the snake is the only one that lives alone.[621] Dan's move to the far north put it at a great distance from the center of Israel's life. The transjordan tribes reflect the same angst due to the Jordan that hindered their inclusion (Josh 22:24–29). Dan is likened to a snake that effectively brings down a horseman, probably to be understood as an interloper (v. 17). The usual word for "snake" *(nāḥāš)* is matched by the rare term "viper," occurring only here *(šĕpîpōn,* "horned snake"?[622]). The imagery of a small, obscure snake that strikes ("bites," *nōšēk)* an unsuspecting passerby illustrates the stealth of this lethal opponent (e.g., Jer 8:17; Amos 9:3). The tactic of surprise attack brought down the more prosperous but trusting city Laish (Judg 18:7,10,27). A reflex of the garden imagery (3:15) is apparent, where snapping at the "heel" injures the victim (cf. Gad, v. 19). Moreover, "heel" *(ʿāqēb)* in vv. 17,19 recalls the play on Jacob's name (25:26; 27:36). The picture of Dan is not as victim but victimizer, like the serpent in the garden or Jacob the deceiver.

49:18 The final colon turns suddenly from the description of Dan's character to Jacob's direct address to the Lord, expressing his resolve to trust in the Lord's future deliverance. For this reason, scholars often consider v. 18 as a late gloss. Yet it functions effectively in its present place, since the Dan blessing (also Gad, Joseph) alludes to danger. At foreseeing the distress of Dan, Jacob admits the vulnerability of his descendants when he spontaneously appeals to the Lord as his true and trusted source of salvation.[623] That the language is known in Psalms (e.g., 130:5; 119:81) should not automatically rule out the blessing as part of the original composition. The Blessing of Jacob shows autobiographical reflection (vv. 3,4,7,9), and thus it is not out of character for the poem to include Jacob's prayer in first person. It was when Jacob faced personal danger (Esau) that he prayed, seeking God's deliverance (32:11[12]). "Look for" *(piel,* from *qāwâ)* is the language of a hopeful poet and prophet (e.g., Ps 25:3,5,21; Isa 51:5). This verse is the first occasion of the general term for "deliverance" *(yĕšûʿâ)* in the Old Testament. A prominent use of the term is the physical salvation granted Israel from its enemies (e.g., Exod 14:13; 15:2; Deut 32:15). Isaiah 33:2 unites both terms, "We long

---

[621] O'Connor, *Hebrew Verse,* 429.

[622] BDB 1051; NASB, "horned snake," NAB, "horned viper."

[623] According to *Gen. Rab.* 98.14, Jacob turned to the Lord when he foresaw that Samson, i.e., the snake that defeats the Philistine riders, had died and therefore could not be the messiah.

for [from *qāwâ*] you . . . our salvation [from *yĕšûʿâ*] in time of distress" (also Isa 59:11). As the patriarch pleads for the Lord to save his descendants from oppressors, the psalmists and prophets also call for the Lord's deliverance (*y-š-ʿ*, e.g., Ps 44:4[5]; Jer 31:7).

GAD (49:19). **49:19** Jacob's couplet heaps up the sounds *g* and *d* in three plays on Gad's *(gād)* name: *gĕdûd . . . yĕgûdennû . . . yāgūd*.[624] He reverses the favorable meaning of Gad received at birth ("What good fortune!" cf. comments on 30:11) to the misfortune brought on by a "band" (*gĕdûd* from *gādad;* e.g., 1 Sam 30:8,15,23) of invading marauders. But he is resilient, "attack[ing]" (*yĕgûdennû* from *gûd,* cf. Hab 3:16) those who "attack" *(yāgūd)* him.[625] That Gad strikes at the "heel" (*ʿāqēb*[626]) shows that the enemy is in flight, vulnerable from the rear (cf. v. 17; Lam 5:5). Gad (Num 32:33; Josh 13:24), located in the region of "Gilead" (Josh 20:8; 1 Sam 13:7; 2 Kgs 10:33), was vulnerable to encroaching forces (e.g., Judg 11; 1 Kgs 22:3; 2 Kgs 10:33).[627] Along with Reuben and the half-tribe of Manasseh, Gad was sandwiched between the Moabites to the south, the Ammonites to the east, and the Arameans to the northeast. As a consequence of their wars for survival, the Gadites became renowned warriors (e.g., 1 Chr 5:18; 12:8,12). Mention of the enemies' "heels" infers that their tactics were stealth and surprise. The Blessing of Moses exhibits the same perception of Gad, which is likened to a ferocious lion (Deut 33:20). Targumic midrash explained the verse in terms of Gad's assistance to their brethren tribes in capturing Canaan (e.g., Num 32:16–32; Josh 22:1–6).

ASHER (49:20). **49:20** This couplet plays on the sounds *m* and *š*, initiated by the opening word *mēʾāšēr* (MT), lit., "from Asher . . ." The adjective "rich" (*šĕmēnâ*, "fat") immediately follows in the construction, describing the produce of Asher's fields (e.g., "fat land," i.e., "fertile," Num 13:20). Thus he can afford the "delicacies fit for a king" (*maʿădannê melek,* cf. Lam 4:5). When used metaphorically, the word "delicacies" means the "delight" (gratification) of the inner person (Prov 29:17). According to Moses' blessing, Asher will enjoy favor with his siblings, prosperity, and security (Deut 33:24–25). How appropriate for Asher, whose birth made "happy" *(ʾōšer)* his mother Leah (by Zilpah, 30:13; 35:26)! Yet the history of Asher indicates unhappy times that Jacob's blessing may hint at. Joshua 19:24–31,34 describes Asher's territory in

---

[624] NASB shows the play by "raid": "As for Gad, raiders will raid him, But he will raid at their heels."

[625] This retaliatory attack is sharply expressed by the *wāw* disjunctive, גָד יָגוּד, "but he will attack."

[626] αὐτῶν κατὰ πόδας (= עֲקֵבָם?, "their heels") LXX, Syr., Vg. *(BHS),* deriving the *mem* from מֵאָשֵׁר by redividing the text.

[627] The Mesha stone mentions the defeat of Gad by the Moabite king (ca. 840–830); for the text see *ANET* 320, lines 10–13.

the western hills of Galilee, as a narrow strip traversing from Mount Carmel in the south along the coastal plain of Acco to Sidon in the north in the plain of Phoenicia. The coastline of Acco provided many harbors by which Asher could enrich itself through trade (Judg 5:17). Rich fertile land provided olive trees (cf. "bathe his feet in oil," Deut 33:24) and vineyards. Mention of the "king," however, may have a double significance. Although the land could produce the finest menu (cf. 1 Kgs 4:7), the tribe's failure to expel the Canaanites (Judg 1:31–32) and its vulnerable location made it subject to Phoenician interference (cf. "Cabul," Josh 19:27; 1 Kgs 9:11–13). Its provisions for the king, therefore, may imply foreign subjugation or at least compliance (cf. Deborah's critique, Judg 5:17). Nevertheless, any negative tone in the blessing is muted by the glowing expectation of Asher's future achievement.

NAPHTALI (49:21). **49:21** This bicolon likens Naphtali to the sure-footed hind (*'ayyālâ,* e.g., 2 Sam 22:34) that is noted for its calving (e.g., Job 39:1; Ps 29:9; Jer 14:5). Here the doe is unencumbered, free to roam (Hab 3:19) and presumably propagate. The LXX interprets the Hebrew quite differently, understanding *'ē(y)lâ,* "oak, terebinth" (e.g., 35:4). The root word of "set free" *(šělūḥâ* from *šlḥ)* can refer to spreading limbs (e.g., Isa 16:8); thus the metaphor is "a spreading stock/stem" *(stelexos aneinmenon;* cf. REB, "a spreading terebinth"). The second colon is difficult in the MT, "who gives beautiful words *['imrê]*" (v. 21b), which is followed by some modern EVs (AV, ASV, NKJV, NASB). More likely is "fawn" (cp. "lamb," *'immar,* Ezra 6:9,17; 7:17), which is adopted by most EVs (e.g., NIV, NAB, NJB, NLT, NJPS, NRSV, HCSB). Again the LXX translators differed by the translation "giving beauty by its fruit" (v. 21b); their interpretation fits their image of a luxuriant tree (v. 21a).[628] The common idea of these diverse opinions is the prosperity of the tribe. The allotment of Naphtali lay in the upper Galilee, west of the lake of Galilee, extending northward along the Jordan River (Josh 19:32–39). The importance of the lake is indicated by its mention in Moses' blessing too (Deut 33:23). Its southern boundary was Zebulun and Issachar, and its western border was Asher. One of the distinctive features of Naphtali in the giving of the tribal inheritances is the absence of a northern border specifically delineated. This unrestricted northern frontier may be reflected in Jacob's picture of the hind unfettered to roam where it pleased. Naphtali possessed remarkable natural resources that made for a beautiful and bountiful land,[629] truly one "full with the blessing of the LORD" (Deut 33:23).

JOSEPH (49:22–26). The longest oracle of the twelve falls naturally into three parts: Joseph's prosperity (v. 22), protection (vv. 23–24), and blessings (vv. 25–26). What is said of Joseph applies to his sons Ephraim and

---

[628] Wevers, *Notes on the Greek Text,* 831.
[629] P. H. Wright, "Naphtali," *Dictionary of the Old Testament: Pentateuch,* 587–88.

Manasseh in light of their adoption by Jacob (48:5,20), especially Ephraim, who was the chief of the northern tribes (e.g., Isa 7:17; Hos 5:5).

49:22 Joseph's affluence in this tricolon is likened to "a fruitful vine" *(bēn pōrāt*[630]*)*. A vibrant stream ("spring," *'ayin*) feeds the plant, and its branches (lit., "daughters," *bānôt*) extend over (lit., "march," *ṣā'ad*) an enclosure ("wall," *šûr*). The picture is a prodigious tree whose enclosure cannot accommodate the thriving plant. The rendering "a fruitful vine" translates the vocalized MT and is followed by most EVs (e.g., NIV, NASB, NRSV). The ancient witnesses regularly reflect this interpretation, although they depart significantly in the remaining part of the verse.[631] The metaphor alludes to Joseph's most prodigious descendant, "Ephraim" ("double fruitful"), whose name was explained by the same verbal root *pārâ* ("to be fruitful," 41:52). Moreover, in the context of blessing Joseph's sons (chap. 48), the text recalls God's promise to "make [Jacob] fruitful" (48:4).

There are problems with the text as it stands, however, and alternative interpretations of the Hebrew have been proposed. Because plant imagery is not used elsewhere in the Blessing of Jacob and animal metaphors dominate, many commentators prefer the interpretation "wild donkey" *(pere')*[632] instead of "fruitful" *(pōrāt)*: "Joseph is a wild colt/ass" (e.g., NIV text note; NAB, NJPS). Also "daughters" *(bānôt)* indicating a plant's "branches"[633] and the idea of "climb over" or "run over" for *ṣā'ădâ* are distinctive uses that raise doubts.[634] The word *ṣā'ad* means "to march, step," and when used figuratively it describes a person's lifestyle (e.g., Prov 4:12).[635] Support for animal imagery is the same metaphor in Hosea that compares Ephraim to a wild donkey *(pere'*; also cf. the verb *p-r-'*, 13:15).[636] A donkey image is not exceptional and appears earlier describing Issachar (v. 14, with the synonym *ḥămōr;* cp. "Hamor," 34:2). Further, the syntax matches v. 9a, describing

---

[630] בֶּן פֹּרָת, lit., "son of a fruit-bearing one"; the genitive פֹּרָת is *qal* active participle feminine singular from פָּרָה, "to be fruitful," indicating the quality (cp. בֶּן קֶשֶׁת, "son of a bow" = an "arrow," Job 41:28[20]; see GKC §128v).

[631] E.g., the LXX prefers a literal rendering of בֵּן, "a grown son is Joseph" (Gk. υἱὸς ηὐξη-μένος Ιωσηφ), and interprets פֹּרָת also from "to be fruitful" (פָּרָה). Its understanding of the following two cola differs: "a grown up son is Joseph, an envied grown up son, oh my youngest son, return to me." For a full discussion and translation, cf. Wevers, *Notes on the Greek Text*, 831–32.

[632] Understanding פֹרת as the feminine form of פֶּרֶא, "wild ass" (e.g., 16:12; Job 39:5).

[633] Two alternatives to בָּנוֹת צָעֲדָה (lit., "daughters march") are the similar Ar. *banāt ṣa'dat*, "wild asses," or reading בְּנָוֶת, "in the meadow" (cf. בְּנָוֹת BHS), i.e., "in the meadow [the donkey] steps."

[634] On the plural feminine subject ("daughters") with a feminine singular verb ("march"), see examples in GKC §145k.

[635] V. Hamilton, "צעד," *NIDOTTE* 3.824.

[636] Another proposal of animal imagery is "cow, heifer," interpreting פֹרת as the fem. bi-form of פָּרָה, "she-ass" (32:16; cf. Israel the stubborn heifer, Hos 4:16; Ephraim the heifer [עֶגְלָה], Hos 10:11); Moses' blessing depicts Joseph as a "bull" (שׁוֹר). See de Hoop, *Genesis 49*, 187–90.

Judah as a lion's cub.[637] If animal imagery is correct, the idea of a "wall" *(šûr)* does not fit the picture of an undomesticated animal, attracting further speculation that the word may be "bull, ox" *(šôr)* or the place name "Shur" (cf. 16:7,12).[638] If "wall" is retained, the animal imagery requires a "terraced hill" (NIV text note) or "hillside" (e.g., NAB, NJPS). Although the option of a donkey is plausible, the motivation for departing from the MT is largely the exception of plant imagery in chap. 49. Yet plant imagery commonly represents the prosperity of a person or a nation (e.g., Pss 1:3; 128:3; Jer 17:8; Ezek 19:10; Dan 4:11), which in this case would effectively depict the historical expansion of the Joseph tribes beyond their bounds (e.g., Josh 17:14–18). Hosea also compares Ephraim to vegetation "planted in a pleasant place" (9:13). Although "daughters" as branches and "climb" or "run on" for "march, step" are difficult, the metaphorical nature of the verse invites creative use of language and should not be quickly dismissed.

49:23–24 The mood of the oracle changes abruptly from prosperity to danger. The couplet in v. 23 describes "archers" *(ba'ălê ḥiṣṣîm,* i.e., "possessors of arrows") who attack Joseph. Three conjoined verbs in rapid fire detail the action of the archers, lit., "they treated him bitterly" *(mārar),* "they shot" *(rābab,* cf. Ps 18:14[15]) arrows,[639] and "they hated him" (NIV, "with hostility," *śāṭam;* cf. Ps 55:3[4]). The nature of the "arrows" probably is figurative for the opposition to Joseph, perhaps slanderous charges *(Tgs. Ps.-J., Neof.; Gen. Rab.* 98.19; cf. the figure of arrows for slander, Jer 9:3[2],8[7]; Prov 25:18; 26:18–19). The identity of the "archers" is uncertain, referring to all or any one of Joseph's many opponents.[640] The last term *śāṭam* also describes the sibling hatred Esau had toward Jacob for his treachery ("held a grudge," 27:41) and the hidden hatred the brothers feared Joseph held against them ("holds a grudge," 50:15). Therefore Joseph's brothers most likely are the "archers" in Jacob's oracle whose hatred fueled their vehement attack against him (cf. 37:4,5,8).

Nevertheless, the Lord sustained Joseph, enabling him to prevail in the conflict (v. 24). The quatrain of v. 24 continues the imagery of the "archers" in the prior verse, depicting Joseph with a bow that "remained steady" *(ʾêtān,* "ever-flowing, enduring"), that is, was firmly held or was strengthened. The

---

[637] Hamilton, *Genesis Chapters 18–50,* 679, n. 2.

[638] Sarna remarks that word plays and allusions in vv. 22–24 may obliquely refer to the Ishmaelites who sold Joseph to Egypt (37:25,28; *Genesis,* 343); the birth narrative of Ishmael includes a "spring" at the site "Shur" (16:7), where the angel's oracle describes Ishmael as a "wild donkey" (16:12), and Ishmael becomes an archer (21:20).

[639] MT, וְרֹבּוּ (from רָבַב, "to shoot"); but SP, LXX (ἐλοιδόρουν), וַיְרִיבֻהוּ, (from רִיב, "to dispute," "they quarreled with him" (so *Tgs. Ps.-J.* and *Neof.;* Rashi).

[640] E.g., the Egyptian wise men, *Tgs. Ps.-J.* and *Neof.;* Simeon and Levi, *Tg. Onq.* (see Grossfeld, *Targum Onqelos,* 170, n. 56), and the brothers (Rashi).

essential meaning is Joseph's stamina in the face of the onslaught.[641] Moreover, his "strong arms [lit., "the arms of his hands," *zĕrōʿê yādāyw*] stayed limber *[wayyāpōzzû]*." The same root term *(pāzaz,* "to be supple, agile") occurs once more, describing the "leaping" of David's dance (2 Sam 6:16). In other words, his arms were lively and graceful, facilitating the bow's repeated volleys.

The concluding couplet of the verse explains that God was the source of Joseph's survival (v. 24cd).[642] By stacking uniquely these divine names and epithets in vv. 24–25, the author intensifies the point. By this means the author signals that the blessing of Joseph as the leading tribe is the "strategic point" in the chapter to demonstrate the overshadowing rule of Israel's God.[643] The divine names and epithets, however, have been a source of difficulty for ancient and modern interpreters. The word "hand" *(yad)* in the phrase "hand of the Mighty One of Jacob" is a play on the same word in the prior clause referring to Joseph: "the arms of his hands" *(zĕrōʿê yādāyw).* Thus the Lord's power underlay the strength of Joseph's "hands" (cf. Ps 44:3). The oracle identifies the Lord by three epithets. The first epithet describes the Lord's power to save. The names "Mighty One of Jacob" *(ʾăbîr yaʿăqōb,* Ps 132:2,5; Isa 49:26; 60:16) and its variation "Mighty One of Israel" *(ʾăbîr yiśrāʾēl,* Isa 1:24) occur collectively six times in poetic texts. Apart from this first occurrence, it always is in apposition to the divine name *Yahweh.* The title is reminiscent of the divine epithet "the Fear of Isaac" *(paḥad yiṣḥāq,* Gen 31:42,53). The adjective *ʾăbîr* denotes "strong, powerful" (6x), as does the related adjective *ʾabbîr* (17x total) that describes, for example, a mighty horse (Judg 5:22), powerful men (Job 24:22), and a stout (Ps 76:5[6]) and stubborn (Isa 46:12) heart.[644] The word *ʾabbîr* (with doubling *[dagesh]* of *b)* means "bull" (6x), such as "the strong bulls of Bashan" (Ps 22:12[13]), but our passage does not require the epithet "bull" (translated "the

---

[641] But the LXX and some modern interpreters understand that the possessor of the "bow" in v. 24 is the "archer" in v. 23 (see NIV text note; e.g., Speiser, *Genesis,* 368; Wenham, *Genesis 16–50,* 485–86). Since the Hb. singular ("his bow") can be collective or distributive in meaning, the MT does not require emendation and can be interpreted as the archers' bows: thus "each one's bow" (NAB) or "their bows" (NJB) remained rigid (i.e., lost flexibility). Since the SP agrees with the MT, the LXX is likely an interpretation of the same text tradition (see Wevers, *Notes on the Greek Text,* 832; de Hoop, *Genesis 49,* 195), not based on a different Hb. text (as *BHS* proposes: καὶ συνετρίβη = וַתִּשָׁבֵר ["were broken"] instead of וַתֵּשֶׁב ["remained"]; καὶ ἐξελύθη = וַיָּפֻזוּ ["weakened"] instead of וַיָּפֹזּוּ ["agile"]; see also Hamilton, *Genesis Chapters 18–50,* 678, nn. 9–11).

[642] Each of the clauses introduced by the prep. מִן is causal, "because . . . ," or means, "by . . ." (on this use of the prep., cf. *IBHS* §11.2.11d).

[643] M. Saebo, "Divine Names and Epithets in Genesis 49:24b–25a: Some Methodological and Traditio-Historical Remarks," in *History and Traditions of Early Israel: Studies Presented to Eduard Nielsen,* VTSup 50 (Leiden: Brill, 1993), 115–132 (esp. 130–31).

[644] R. Wakely, "אָבִיר," *NIDOTTE* 1.232–43.

Bull of Jacob"), which has cultic nuances of the fertility bull in ancient religion.[645] This purported rendering does not correspond well to the context that seeks to distinguish the ancestral God of Jacob from the deities of Canaan.[646] The second appellative, "Shepherd" (ptc. *rō'eh*), depicts divine provision. It is a fitting reminder of Jacob, who earlier had acknowledged that the Lord was "[his] shepherd" in his blessing for Joseph (48:15; cf. Pss 23:1; 80:1[2]; Heb 13:20).[647] Shepherd imagery is used of Israel's king, who was designated by God to "shepherd" *(rā'â)* the nation (2 Sam 5:2; e.g., Jer 31:10), which leads naturally to the mention of Israel in the third appellative. "Rock *['eben]* of Israel" communicated the constancy and security of divine support. This divine title with the word *'eben* ("stone"; "Stone of Israel," AV, NJB, NASB) appears only here (cf. Isa 28:16). The common expression for Israel's "Rock" when referring to deity is *ṣûr* (e.g., Deut 32:15,18,30,31; 2 Sam 22:3//Ps 18:2[3]). The same appellative "Rock of Israel" but with the term *ṣûr* occurs twice more (2 Sam 23:3; Isa 30:29). The individual affirmation, "my Rock," may vary in Hebrew terms for "rock" (e.g., *sela'* and *ṣûr*, Pss 18:2[3]; 40:2[3]). Generally, *'eben* refers to natural, precious, or hewn "stones," whereas *ṣûr* indicates rock formations or boulders. Because of the unique title "Stone of Israel," many emendations have been proposed, including deleting the word.[648] Yet Jacob's unusual use of "stone/rock" *('eben)* may be an allusion to the "stone" *('eben)* he erected at Bethel (28:11,18,22; 35:14; cf. 31:45–46) and therefore should not be confidently emended. As "Shepherd" was an allusion to his own experience with God, "Rock" echoed his reliance

---

[645] Cf. Jeroboam's calves (1 Kgs 12:25–33). M. S. Smith argues that the epithet "Bull of Jacob" refers to the Canaanite deity El that was head of the pantheon of Israelite deities, including El, Yahweh, Baal, and Asherah (*The Early History of God: Yahweh and the Other Deities in Ancient Israel,* 2d ed. [Grand Rapids: Eerdmans/Dearborn: Dove, 2002], 47–53). As with many scholars, he interprets שָׁדַיִם וָרָחַם as female epithets, "Breasts and Womb," perhaps referring to the goddess Asherah. Also see A. H. W. Curtis, "Some Observations on 'Bull' Terminology in the Ugaritic Texts and the Old Testament," in *In Quest of the Past,* OtSt 26 (Leiden: Brill, 1990), 17–31.

[646] For arguments for the epithet "Strong One," see de Hoop, *Genesis 49,* 195–98.

[647] The MT's מִשָּׁם רֹעֶה, "from there the Shepherd," is difficult to understand; the sense of "there" perhaps reinforces the source is God. Alternatively, it has been repointed, מִשֵּׁם רֹעֶה, "by the name of the Shepherd" (Syr., *Tg. Onq.;* cf. NRSV; REB; NJB, HCSB). The word pair "hand" (יָד) and "name" (שֵׁם) occurs in Isa 56:5 (also cf. 44:5); see Avishur, *Word-Pairs,* 127, 675 and S. Talmon, *"Yad Wašem:* An Idiomatic Phrase in Biblical Literature and Its Variations," *HS* 25 (1984): 8–17. But for this meaning the construction בְּשֵׁם is expected (see Delitzsch, *A New Commentary on Genesis,* 2.394; Sarna, *Genesis,* 343). The LXX text differs at many points in vv. 24–25 but here supports the reading in MT: διὰ χεῖρα δυνάστου Ιακωβ ἐκεῖθεν, "by the hand of the mighty one of Jacob, from that place . . ." (see Saebo, "Divine Names," 117–18).

[648] E.g., BHS, מִשֵּׁם עֹזֵר יִשְׂרָאֵל, "from the name of the Helper of Israel" (cf. "Ebenezer," 1 Sam 7:12); Freedman understands אֶבֶן יִשְׂרָאֵל as plural אַבְנֵי יִשְׂרָאֵל (prosthetic *'aleph*), "the sons of Israel," thus "from the Shepherd of the sons of Israel" ("Divine Names," 87); the REB deletes "stone," thus creating a balanced parallelism between the cola: "by the power of the Strong One of Jacob //by the name of the Shepherd of Israel."

on the faithful God who rescued him from danger and returned him to his father's house. The parallel names "Jacob" and "Israel" are another instance of the common word pair and an example of binomination (i.e., split into two names; "Jacob-Israel," cf. v. 7cd).

49:25–26 Verses 25 and 26 are heavy, consisting of ten cola. The word group "bless" *(b-r-k)* appears six times in these two verses, implying by dense repetition that God has in store a superabundance of blessings. The term "bless" is key to the whole of Genesis and occurs the last time in Genesis in the summary verse, which applies to all the brothers (v. 28 [3x]). Here the repeated "blessings" distinguish Joseph's household from his siblings.

Verse 25a and 25b continue the description of Jacob's savior, who is "your father's God *(El)*" and "the Almighty" *(Shaddai)*. (For more on the importance of the expression "your father's God" and its variations and the meaning of *Shaddai*, see comments on 26:24 and introduction, s.v., "The Names of God.") The mention of "your father" reinforces the motif of inheritance that the whole of the Blessing of Jacob assumes. "God Almighty" *(El Shaddai),* which is split into two names (binomes[649]) in the parallel cola here *(El//Shaddai),* is the divine title distinctive to the God of the patriarchs (Exod 6:3).[650] That the singular "you" occurs in "[God] helps you" and "blesses you" stresses the personal relationship of deity and family member. The term "help" *('āzar)* occurs here for the first time in the Old Testament. It is well known as an element in names referring to God, for example, "Ebenezer" (1 Sam 7:12). Typically, the word group *'-z-r* describes military assistance (e.g., Josh 10:4; Isa 41:10) or personal assistance (e.g., Ps 30:11; Isa 50:7,9), both human and divine. Particularly forbidding to the victim is when there is "no one to help" (e.g., 2 Kgs 14:26; Pss 22:11[12]; 72:12).

The remainder of vv. 25cde and 26 describe the "blessings" *(birkōt)* intended for Joseph. The invocation in our passage calls for the common venues of blessing, including rainfall and the birth of children (e.g., Lev 26:4–5; Deut 7:13; 28:4,12). "Heavens above" and "the deep *[tĕhōm]* below" is a merism (indicating inclusiveness), drawn from creation imagery (1:1–2; 7:11; 8:2), promising abundant waters (on the similar language, see the Blessing of Moses, Deut 33:13). "Blessings of the heavens" calls to mind Isaac's blessing

---

[649] O'Connor, *Hebrew Verse,* 177, thus "from the god of your father, El-Shaddai, who helps you" (p. 373).

[650] The parallel שַׁדָּי וְאֵת ... אָבִיךָ מֵאֵל is difficult, and ancient versions (Hb. MSS, SP, LXX, Syr.; cf. *BHS*) erroneously have שַׁדָּי וְאֵל, thus "by the God of your father . . . and El Shaddai" (cf. NJB); that Shaddai may occur alone, see e.g., Num 24:4,16; Ruth 1:20. Many EVs indicate source ("from, by") or cause ("because"), thus "by/because of the God of your father . . . and by/because of the Almighty" (e.g., AV, NIV, NASB, NRSV); this is explained as (1) the continued influence of the prior prep. מִן on וְאֵת (e.g., Wenham, *Genesis 16–50,* 486) or (2) the occasional meaning "from" by וְאֵת (e.g., Hamilton, *Genesis Chapters 18–50,* 682 n. 18).

of Jacob: "May God give you of heaven's dew" (27:28; Deut 33:13; cf. Tgs.). The description of the subterranean blessing, "that lies *[rōbeṣet]* below," repeats the term *(r-b-ṣ)* describing the crouching lion (Judah, v. 9) and donkey (Issachar, v. 14). "Breasts" and "womb" speak of birth and the nurturing of an infant until the time of weaning (e.g., Job 3:11–12; Ps 22:9–10[10–11]; Isa 28:9). The judgment of God may involve the want of children, thus "wombs that miscarry and breasts that are dry" (Hos 9:14). The words "heaven" *(šāmayim)* and "breasts" *(šādayim)* and "deep" *(tĕhōm)* and "womb" *(rāḥam)* create a sound play between the cola, reinforcing the promised bounty of fertile land and numerous population. Moses' final benediction for the tribe of Joseph contains an echo of v. 25ab (Deut 33:13).

The final verse of the Joseph oracle possesses five cola (v. 26). Cola one to three describe the magnitude of the blessings invoked by the patriarch.[651] He remarks that his own experience, "the blessings of your father," exceeded even those of the "ancient mountains." "Ancient mountains" *(harărê ʿad)*[652] is the translation of the LXX and is preferred by many EVs (e.g., NIV, NJB, NAB, NLT, NRSV). This parallels nicely "age-old hills" *(gibʿōt ʿōlām)* in the next colon (cp. "ancient mountains"//"age-old hills," Hab 3:16[653]). The blessing of Moses for Joseph exhibits similar language (Deut 33:15). The enduring and alluring mountains produced lush vegetation that nourished society and created an aesthetically pleasing response (e.g., Pss 72:3,16; 80:10[11]; Amos 9:13; Ezek 34:14). The mountains were viewed as foundational to the whole of the natural world (e.g., Deut 32:22; Jonah 2:6) and were virtually indestructible (e.g., Isa 54:10), except by God himself (e.g., Ps 104:32).[654] However, the MT's reading, "[the blessings] of my progenitors *[hōray]*"[655] has its representatives (e.g., NIV text note; AV; "my ancestors," NASB, NJPS, HCSB). It corresponds well with the motif of Jacob's ancestral heritage in v. 25 ("your father's God"). In this rendering, Jacob is recognizing that his benefits exceeded those of Abraham and Isaac. He probably has in mind his wives, twelve sons, and numerous possessions obtained in Paddan Aram (33:5–15).[656] According to either interpretation, Jacob is acclaiming this present

---

[651] Redividing the text of v. 26, Freedman (*Divine Names,* 87) reads גִּבֹּר וְעַל as the divine titles "Warrior and Exalted One" (cf. divine גִּבֹּר, Ps 24:8; Isa 10:21; Ug. divine epithet, *ʿal* and Deut 33:12).

[652] The LXX, ὀρέων μονίμων = עַד הַרְרֵי (cf. *BHS*), in which עַד is the noun "perpetuity" (instead of the MT's prep.; see below).

[653] גִּבְעוֹת עוֹלָם//הַרְרֵי־עַד.

[654] S. Talmon, "הַר *har;* גִּבְעָה *gibhʿāh,*" *TDOT* 3.427–47; M. Selman, "הַר," *NIDOTTE* 1.1051–55.

[655] The MT, הוֹרַי עַד־תַּאֲוַת (from הרה, "to be with child"), lit., "the progenitors of me, as far as the boundary"; here the MT interprets עַד as the prep., "as far as, up to."

[656] Rashi observes that the land promise to Jacob is boundless (28:14), exceeding that made to Abraham ("all the land that you see," 13:14–15) and Isaac (26:3).

blessing bestowed on Joseph surpasses those of the past, whether of the ancient mountains or of their fathers.[657]

The word "bounty" in the phrase "bounty *[ta'ăwat]* of the age-old hills" (NIV) is another disputed word in the text, impacting the interpretation of the verse. In this understanding, the noun *ta'āwâ* (verb *'wh*) denotes "desire, delight," meaning here the good things that are "desired" (cf. 3:6; Num 11:4; see "bounty/bounties," NIV, NRSV, NJB, REB, HCSB; "delights," NAB). This interpretation creates a parallel for "blessings" in the previous cola.[658] Alternatively, the word may mean "boundary," related to the verb *t'h*, "to draw a line, mark out" (*piel*, Num 34:7,8,10), thus "up to the utmost bound *['ad ta'ăwat]* of the [everlasting hills]" (e.g., AV, NLT, NASB, NJPS).

Verse 26de culminates in a final plea, beseeching God that all these benedictions come to pass. The (almost) exact language occurs in Moses' prayer in Deut 33:16b. The NIV translates "on the brow of the prince *[nĕzîr]* among his brothers," understanding *nāzîr* ("one separated," from *nāzar*, "to separate, consecrate") in the sense of a ruler (also NAB, NLT, REB; HCSB; cf. Lam 4:7).[659] The same term names the "Nazirite" who undertakes the Nazirite vow of consecration (e.g., Num 6:2; Judg 13:5). The related noun *nēzer* means a "crown" worn by a king (e.g., 2 Sam 1:10) or priest (e.g., Exod 29:6). The word *nāzîr* does not ever refer to a king, although here it indicates eminence (e.g., "who was set apart," NRSV; "the elect," NJPS). There is no conflict between Judah, who bears the "scepter" of kingship (v. 10), and Joseph, who was superior to his brothers in their respective positions in Egypt. Jacob recognizes Joseph as the distinguished member of the brothers who receives greater blessing because of his role as ruler in Egypt. "He who was once separated from his brothers through spite is now separated from his brothers by blessing."[660]

BENJAMIN (49:27).　**49:27**　Benjamin is the youngest of the twelve (35:18; 42:13) and appropriately the subject of the final stanza in the oracle. The stanza consists of another animal metaphor; he is a "ravenous wolf" *(zĕ'ēb)* that shreds *(yiṭrāp,* "devours," NIV) its victims (cf. Ezek 22:27). The

---

[657] G. Rendsburg proposes that the word has a double meaning: "ancestors," paralleling "fathers" in the previous colon and "mountains," paralleling "hills" in the following colon ("Janus Parallelism in Gen 49:26," *JBL* 99 [1980]: 291–93).

[658] The LXX, accordingly, has εὐλογίαις ("blessings") for הֹרֲ֫תַ.

[659] The versions show two interpretations of רֹֽזיִנ: (1) ruler over his brothers, e.g., LXX, ἐπὶ κορυφῆς ὧν ἡγήσατο ἀδελφῶν, "upon the head of the brothers whom he led" (notice that the LXX interprets the blessings as resting on the brothers, see Wevers, *Notes on the Greek Text,* 835); also translated "consecrated one, crown, prince," *Tgs. Ps-J.* and *Neof.;* Syr.; (2) or "separated from, distinguished among" his brothers, e.g., *Tg. Onq.;* Vg.; also Rashi; for EVs, see NIV text note; NASB, RSV, NRSV, NJB. Syrén (*The Blessings in the Targums,* 60–61) shows that the LXX at Deut 33:16 takes the second interpretation, and the rabbis in *Gen. Rab.* 98.20 know both interpretations (i.e., "he was in fact an actual Nazirite" and "you are the crown of your brothers").

[660] Hamilton, *Genesis Chapters 18–50,* 686.

word group *ṭ-r-p* ("to tear, rend") appears in Jacob's imagination of Joseph's destruction by ferocious animals (37:33; 44:28). The noun *ṭerep* ("prey") occurs in the animal imagery of Judah's blessing (v. 9; cf. Gad in Deut 33:20). Reference to "morning" and "evening" is a merism, showing that the wolf is continually on the prowl. So numerous are the victims the morning hours are spent gorging on the night's "prey" (*'ad,* e.g., Isa 33:23). The LXX brings out the nuance of the meaning by its rendering, "He shall eat still in the morning."[661] The "evening wolf" is the most deadly (cf. Hab 1:8; Zeph 3:3), and after the kill it parcels out the carcass. The brutal picture of Benjamin's future is surprising since he, though important to the narrative plot, is a completely passive character in the Joseph narrative. He is depicted oppositely in the Blessing of Moses (Deut 33:12), where he is at rest in the safety of the Lord. The picture of Benjamin's aggressive character predicts the military feats of the Benjamites during the settlement and early monarchy periods, despite their small size as a tribe (1 Sam 9:21; Ps 68:27[28]; see e.g., Judg 3:15; 5:14; 20:21; 1 Sam 9:1; 2 Sam 2:25). The warriors of Benjamin were renown for their skill as left-handed marksmen (Judg 20:15–16; 1 Chr 12:2) and for their bravery (1 Chr 8:40).

CONCLUSION (49:28).   **49:28**   The final verse of the section is the closing narrative frame, providing a conclusion to the patriarch's deathbed benediction. Verse 28b reiterates that the pronouncements are "blessings." Three times the word group *b-r-k* ("bless") occurs. The structure of v. 28b reinforces this:

He blessed them, each one according to his blessing, he blessed them.[662]

The summary statements in v. 28 make three points. First, all the "twelve tribes of Israel" received recognition, including the discredited sons (Reuben, Simeon, and Levi) and the less significant sons in the narrative. The ideal figure of "twelve" for the member tribes of the nation is achieved by naming Joseph in lieu of his two sons Ephraim and Manasseh. Elsewhere the number "twelve" is accomplished by omitting one tribe (e.g., Levi, Num 1; 13; Simeon, Deut 32; Dan, Rev 7:5–8) and naming the two tribes of Joseph's house.[663] Second, the blessing had the authority of "their father" Jacob, who alone could pass on the blessings promised to the fathers. Third, the blessing each son received was "appropriate" (lit., "according to his blessing") to each tribe's role in the nation. The Blessing of Jacob, therefore, reinforces the unity of the future nation but also discriminates among them, realizing that each tribe will have its distinctive story.

---

[661] The LXX, ἔτι ("still") interprets עַד as the adverb עֹד (עוֹד).

[662] The parallel verbs "bless" are the same root but the different forms imperfect (+ *wāw*) and perfect: בֵּרַךְ . . . וַיְבָרֶךְ (for this feature in poetry and prose, see Berlin, *Dynamics of Biblical Parallelism,* 35).

[663] Delitzsch, *A New Commentary on Genesis,* 2.398–99.

12. The Death and Burial of Jacob (49:29–50:14)

The story of Joseph has come full circle with the mourning of Jacob by his once lost son, Joseph, for whom he had inconsolably lamented (cf. 37:12–36). Joseph is not alone, however. A concatenation of Jacob's other sons, Hebrew households, and Egyptian households lament the passing of Israel's father. The vocabulary in 50:10–13 offers a brief lexicon of terms for mourning, including "lament" *(sāpad, mispēd),* "mourning" *(ʾēbel),* and the etiology of the toponym "Abel Mizraim," meaning "the Mourning of the Egyptians."[664] That the word group "bury, burial" *(q-b-r)* occurs fifteen times in this episode reflects the central interest of the narrative, but the burial alone is not the primary attention. It is the place of burial that furnishes the author's message. The site of Machpelah in Hebron, its history of acquisition by Abraham, and its occupants begin and end the episode (49:29–32; 50:13). As the family "possession" *(ʾăḥuzzâ,* 23:4,9,20), the burial plot represented the land as the "everlasting possession" *(laʾăḥuzzat ʿôlām,* 17:8) promised Abraham and his descendants. That possession was claimed by Jacob symbolically by his entombment at the "burial place" *(laʾăḥuzzat qeber,* 49:30; 50:13) of his forefathers. Although the burial episode would appear to be about the past, it projects the future as did the orientation of the blessings in chaps. 48–49. The future is secured by Jacob/Israel's God and his promises, not the patriarchs themselves. All Israel can look beyond the grave to the life in the land that awaits them. The congregation of the Egyptians, Hebrews, and nearby Canaanites is a metaphor of the exodus and settlement of Israel in the land. The Israelites, bearing the gifts of Egypt and carrying the Egyptian sarcophagus of Joseph's bones, establish themselves in the land at the awe and fear of the Canaanites (Exod 3:22; 15:14–16; Deut 26:8). For the Christian reader, Jacob's confidence in the future is familiar and Joseph's mourning is understandable. Yet the Christian has more reason to trust in a life that is beyond the grave, and therefore Christian mourning is free from anxiety about the future by the knowledge of the resurrection. Chrysostom remarked on the difference in Joseph's response to death and that of the Christian: "Today, on the contrary, thanks to the grace of God, since death has been turned into slumber and life's end into repose and since there is a great certitude of resurrection, we rejoice and exalt at death like people moving from one life to another" *(Homilies on Gen* 67.17).[665]

COMPOSITION. The analysis of this passage is integrally related to the analysis of the prior deathbed scenes in 47:29–31 and 48:1–49:28 (see *ad loc.*). Source scholars typically discern multiple underlying documents in the present passage. Gunkel identifies the combined Yahwist and Elohist (JE) strands for

---

[664] R. W. L. Moberly, "Lament," *NIDOTTE* 4.866–84 (869).
[665] *ACCS* 2.350.

49:33ab; 50:1–11,14–26, based on vocabulary and doublets in vv. 2–11. Verse 10, for example, contains two notices of lament. The J strand includes the brothers in the burial processional and return (vv. 7–8,14,22a), whereas in E they do not appear to have made the journey (vv. 9,15–21). The periods of forty days and eleven days in vv. 10–11 (E) differs from the seventy-day mourning in v. 3b (J).[666] Also, according to most critical scholars, the Priestly version (P) of Jacob's final blessing, death, and burial occurs in 49:1a,29(28b)–33 and 50:12–13, as part of P's genealogical framework of the patriarchal narratives. The references in 50:12 to Jacob ("his sons," "for him," "he had commanded") refer back to 49:33, not to the immediate context where the name Jacob does not occur. Also 50:13b uses the same descriptions as 47:29–30, suggesting to scholars that the P account has been integrated into the Joseph story and shows some dependence on it.[667]

Westermann's reconstruction of the sources for this unit emerges from his intricate theory of the makeup of chaps. 46–50. They consist primarily of the union of two independent narratives, the Joseph story and the Jacob story. Each story possessed a report of Jacob's death and burial. The redactor retained both endings, creating an inclusion: 47:29–31 and 49:28b–33. The Joseph narrative in 50:1–14 describes the burial in Canaan. Joined to this Joseph narrative was the priestly contribution. The priestly hand produced the account of the death and burial in 49:33 and 50:12–13, which was blended into the Joseph story. Two groups of expansions followed, entailing the blessing of Joseph's sons (48:13–22), the Blessing of Jacob (49:1b–28a), the reconciliation of the brothers (50:15–21), and Joseph's last days (50:22–26).[668] Coats has a simpler explanation, since he views the Joseph story as a unity that continues up to 47:27. Thus 47:28–50:14 are add-ons that are held together by the same setting of Jacob's last days.[669]

Regardless of what resources were available to the author, Wenham has shown, however, that the events of Jacob's last days in the Joseph narrative (48:1–50:14) parallel the arrangement of the closing events in the Abraham and Jacob narratives. Further, he warns that the isolation of the P-passages (49:1a,29–33; 50:12–13) from the Joseph narrative depends on the assumption that P occurs in the burial notices at Machpelah (23:1–20; 25:9–11).[670] Identifying 50:12–13 as P, based on the antecedent "Jacob" in 49:33, is too narrow a basis for proposing a separate P-source. The presence of Jacob, although his name does not occur in 50:1–11, is obvious and is assumed throughout. The whole of 50:1–14 presupposes and naturally follows on the death report in 49:33.

STRUCTURE. The unit consists of two parts: the first describes Jacob's appeal for burial in the cave of his fathers and the narration of his immediate death (49:29–33), and the second describes the mourning of Joseph and the sub-

---

[666] Gunkel, *Genesis,* 450, 462, 469–70.

[667] Carr, *Reading the Fractures of Genesis,* 95–96; Westermann, *Genesis 37–50,* 202.

[668] Westermann, *Genesis 37–50,* 197, 211–14.

[669] Coats, *Genesis,* 300–303, 309–10.

[670] Wenham, *Genesis 16–50,* 462.

sequent burial preparations and processional to Canaan (50:1–14). The boundaries for this unit are subject to different interpretations. This is because 49:29–33 is transitional in character and therefore can conclude the prior unit and introduce a new unit. The term "gather" *('āsap)* at 49:1,33 begins and ends the chapter. The dual burial instructions in 47:29–31 and 49:29–33 have been understood as forming the borders of an entire unit. The word "gather," however, marks the boundaries of 49:29–33: "I am about to be gathered" and "he was gathered." Also the word "give instructions" *(ṣāwâ)* forms an inclusio at 49:29 and 33. Further, it is best to interpret the request "bury me *[qibrû]* with my fathers" (49:29) as the initiation of a new unit that has its closure with the accomplishment of the request, twice mentioned in 50:14, lit., "to bury *[liqbōr]* his father after he buried *[qobrô]* his father." What gives 49:29–50:14 its cohesion is the repeated topic of the patriarch's burial. The word group *q-b-r* ("bury") occurs fourteen times in nineteen verses (49:29,30,31[3x]; 50:5[3x],6,7,13[2x],14[2x]). The geographical notices also contribute to the organization of the unit. The pattern is from Egypt to Canaan and back to Egypt. "Egypt" appears in the beginning and concluding verses (49:29; 50:14), and references to the "cave" of "Ephron the Hittite" are at the margins (49:28; 50:13).

After the interlude of blessings declared for Joseph's sons (chap. 48) and the whole of the twelve tribes (49:1–28), the present narrative reaches back to the burial instructions in 47:29–31 by reiterating the patriarch's request in 49:29–33. His instructions assume the same context of Jacob's final deathbed words that begin in 47:29. The burial episode of the patriarch begins with Joseph's mourning, which can only make sense when read with the prior verse. The subunit follows logical progression: customary embalming and mourning for an important dignitary (vv. 1–3), Joseph's request of Pharaoh to bury the patriarch in Canaan and the promise to "return" *(šûb;* vv. 4–6), the funeral procession (vv. 7–13), and the "return" *(šûb)* by the brothers to Egypt (v. 14).

(1) Final Words and Death (49:29–33)

[29]Then he gave them these instructions: "I am about to be gathered to my people. Bury me with my fathers in the cave in the field of Ephron the Hittite, [30]the cave in the field of Machpelah, near Mamre in Canaan, which Abraham bought as a burial place from Ephron the Hittite, along with the field. [31]There Abraham and his wife Sarah were buried, there Isaac and his wife Rebekah were buried, and there I buried Leah. [32]The field and the cave in it were bought from the Hittites."

[33]When Jacob had finished giving instructions to his sons, he drew his feet up into the bed, breathed his last and was gathered to his people.

The word "instructions" *(ṣāwâ)* forms the boundaries of 49:29–33. Jacob gives "instructions" to his sons for burial (vv. 29–32), and the narrative reports his death after the "instructions" (v. 33).

BURIAL INSTRUCTIONS (49:29–32). **49:29** In anticipation of his death,

Jacob elaborates on his initial burial instructions to Joseph (cf. 47:29–30) to explain further the significance of his request. In this case, however, the audience is *all* his sons (pl. verb, "bury me"; cf. v. 33, "to his sons"). "Gathered to my people"[671] (v. 29) expresses the family solidarity that underlies his argument that follows (on this idiom, see Abraham at comments on 25:8 and v. 33 below); "with my fathers" reinforces his central concern. The location of the burial site and its history are repeatedly stated (vv. 29,30,32) so as to impress upon Joseph the importance of the precise burial location. It follows the same description found in chap. 23. On the location Machpelah, see comments on 23:17–20.

49:30–32 Jacob adds how the cave came to be owned, indicating that the family plot came by a legitimate business arrangement initiated by Abraham (v. 30). References to the act of purchase and the original Hittite owners form the boundaries of these verses (vv. 30,32). It was not a matter of conquest or squatter's rights; the Hittite owner, authenticating the purchase, granted Abraham a deed of ownership duly witnessed (23:17–18,20). The ancestral burial site symbolized the beginning realization of the land promise made to Abraham, which was repeated to Isaac and Jacob. Jacob, who had spent so much of his life outside the land, could always look to the cave at Machpelah as the permanent evidence that his destiny and that of his descendants were in Canaan. His insistence on burial in Canaan conveyed to his descendants his unyielding faith in God's promise for the future prosperity of the family. His faith encouraged Joseph and his brothers to instruct their children in the promise of the land (50:24–25; cf. Heb 11:21–22). The term "there" *(šammâ)* occurs three times in vv. 31–32, drawing further attention to the place of burial. Who was buried at Machpelah, however, was important too (25:9–10; 35:29). He names the historic figures of the family's ancestry, including the matriarchs Sarah (23:19), Rebekah, and his wife Leah. By naming the ancestors Jacob reinforces the necessity of his burial in the same location as Abraham and Isaac. It was appropriate that Jacob too should rest at Machpelah, giving the burial occupants the historic symmetry of "Abraham, Isaac and Jacob" (50:24; cf. Exod 2:24). With his interment the patriarchs of the nation have their final rest, gathered together with their wives who produced the families of Israel's ancestors. A significant omission is Joseph's own mother Rachel, whose burial near Bethlehem, however, was equally marked by a pillar as to place (35:19–20). Neither the deaths nor burials of the mothers Rebekah and Leah are detailed in the narrative as are Sarah's and Rachel's. Moreover, neither Joseph (Josh 24:32) nor his brothers (we may surmise) were buried in the sepulcher. That Jacob desired his place with his fathers, despite lying beside the remains of Leah, may be a symbolic gesture of the family's unification.

---

[671] אֲנִי נֶאֱסָף, "I am about to be gathered"; the participle expresses imminent action.

JACOB'S DEATH (49:33). **49:33** The benediction for his sons and the final instructions regarding his burial permitted Jacob to take his last breath in peace. The verse contains stock phrases describing death and burial (e.g., 25:8,17; 35:29; Ps 104:29). "Drew [his feet] up" and "was gathered [to his people]" translate forms of the same root verb *'āsap,* "to gather, remove, gather in." The drawing up of his feet "into the bed" recalls Jacob's posture, "sat up on the bed" (48:2), when his instructions began. Strikingly, "he died" is absent,[672] although it appears in the stereotypical pattern occurring in the obituaries of Abraham and of Isaac (25:8; 35:29; cf. 25:17). That the patriarch calmly retracted his feet, accepting his destiny, and that the author omits "and he died" elevates Jacob's confidence in the future. He is not dead but asleep, waiting for the realization of the promises (cf. 1 Cor 15:20; 1 Thess 4:13). Calvin commented, "We shall not deem it grievous to leave this failing tabernacle, when we reflect on the everlasting abode which is prepared for us."[673] "Gather" is reminiscent of his last will and testament when he assembled his sons in anticipation of his death (49:1; 48:21). The customary expression "gathered to one's fathers" meant that Jacob was united with his dead ancestors (see v. 29 above; e.g., Judg 2:10; 2 Kgs 22:20//2 Chr 34:28; cf. Isa 57:1). The imagery is the deposit of human remains with others in a collective burial site (cf. Jer 25:33). This set phrase also describes Moses' anticipated death (Num 27:13; 31:2; Deut 32:50). On the significance of "breathed his last," that is, "perished" (from *gāwaʿ),* see vol. 1A, p. 366 (comments on 6:17).

(2) Burial of Jacob in Canaan (50:1–14)

¹Joseph threw himself upon his father and wept over him and kissed him. ²Then Joseph directed the physicians in his service to embalm his father Israel. So the physicians embalmed him, ³taking a full forty days, for that was the time required for embalming. And the Egyptians mourned for him seventy days.

⁴When the days of mourning had passed, Joseph said to Pharaoh's court, "If I have found favor in your eyes, speak to Pharaoh for me. Tell him, ⁵'My father made me swear an oath and said, "I am about to die; bury me in the tomb I dug for myself in the land of Canaan." Now let me go up and bury my father; then I will return.'"

⁶Pharaoh said, "Go up and bury your father, as he made you swear to do."

⁷So Joseph went up to bury his father. All Pharaoh's officials accompanied him—the dignitaries of his court and all the dignitaries of Egypt— ⁸besides all the members of Joseph's household and his brothers and those belonging to his father's household. Only their children and their flocks and herds were left in Goshen. ⁹Chariots and horsemen also went up with him. It was a very large company.

¹⁰When they reached the threshing floor of Atad, near the Jordan, they

---

[672] *Tg. Neof.* supplies "and died."
[673] Calvin, *Comm.,* 473.

lamented loudly and bitterly; and there Joseph observed a seven-day period of mourning for his father. ¹¹When the Canaanites who lived there saw the mourning at the threshing floor of Atad, they said, "The Egyptians are holding a solemn ceremony of mourning." That is why that place near the Jordan is called Abel Mizraim.

¹²So Jacob's sons did as he had commanded them: ¹³They carried him to the land of Canaan and buried him in the cave in the field of Machpelah, near Mamre, which Abraham had bought as a burial place from Ephron the Hittite, along with the field. ¹⁴After burying his father, Joseph returned to Egypt, together with his brothers and all the others who had gone with him to bury his father.

Genesis 50:1–14 divides into four stages: the mourning for Jacob and the embalming of the body (vv. 1–3), the permission granted Joseph by Pharaoh to bury Jacob in Canaan (vv. 4–6), the funeral processional (vv. 7–13), and the return to Egypt (v. 14). Westermann observes that Joseph's request in v. 5b presages the following segments: "let me go up" (vv. 7–11), "bury my father" (vv. 12–13), and "return" (v. 14).[674] Joseph is the focal character who directs the postmortem proceedings. The account characteristically describes the events in terms of Joseph's actions (e.g., "Joseph threw himself," "directed," "said," "went up," "burying," "returned") and relationships (e.g., "his servants," "his father," "my father," "house of Joseph," "his brothers," "with him"). Verses 2 and 11 provide brief observations on the reactions of the Egyptians and Canaanites. The perspective widens only in vv. 12–13 when "his sons" (i.e., Jacob's) are said to have accomplished their duty. The word *bākâ*, translated "wept," "mourned," frames vv. 1–3. Dialogue between Joseph and the king dominates vv. 4–6. The geographical movements from Egypt to Canaan to Egypt give structure to vv. 7–14. "Joseph went up" (*'ālâ*) and "his sons carried him [Jacob] up" (*nāśā'*) enclose vv. 7–13. Last, v. 14 narrates that "all who had gone up" (*wĕkol hā'ōlîm*) returned with Joseph.

MOURNING FOR JACOB (50:1–3). **50:1–3** Joseph's deep-seated affection for his father is captured in three concrete actions toward Jacob's lifeless body: "threw himself upon," "wept over," and "kissed" him (v. 1). The depth of his grief exceeded his passionate reunion with his father at Jacob's coming to Egypt (46:29; cf. Benjamin, 45:14). That he fell upon his "father's face" (NIV, "his father") and "kissed" the dead are actions occurring only here in the Old Testament. The typical expression describes a person who "falls on another's neck" and "weeps on the neck," presumably when the two parties are standing in an embrace (e.g., 33:4; 45:14; 46:29). Mention of the patriarch's "face" recalls the promise in 46:4: "Joseph's own hand will close your eyes."

Joseph ordered his "physicians" (lit., "healers," *rōpĕ'îm*) to mummify the body. "Embalm(ed)" (from *ḥānaṭ*) occurs twice in this verse and once more in

---

[674] Westermann, *Genesis 37–50*, 200.

50:26; the adjectival form *(ḥănûṭîm)* occurs in v. 3. The embalming of Jacob
and Joseph are the only two cases in the Bible. Verse 3 provides the detail that
the embalming procedure required forty days. The customary Egyptian
mourning rites involved seventy days, probably to be understood to include
the aforementioned forty-day period. Embalming does not require such an
extensive period, and therefore the period probably included public ceremonial rites and honors. The days of bereavement corresponded to the number in
Jacob's family who descended into Egypt (46:27; Exod 1:5). That the patriarch underwent embalming and that the Egyptians declared a formal period
of mourning speak to the prestige Jacob and Joseph held. Hebrew practice
was the burial of the dead, not embalming, and the period of mourning varied
from seven days (50:10; 1 Sam 31:13) to thirty days (e.g., Moses, Deut 34:8;
Aaron, Num 20:29). Embalming was practiced throughout Egypt's history
and was a religious rite probably related to Egyptian beliefs about the after-
life. Anubis (Gk.), known as the "jackal-headed god," was the earliest Egyptian deity *(Inpw)* of the dead and embalming, although Osiris, who was the
embalmed god, took predominance as the god of the dead. Essentially,
embalming was designed to retard the normal processes of putrefaction of the
corpse. Methods varied from simply wrapping the body in resin-soaked linen
to the elaborate procedures of disemboweling the corpse, collecting the
organs in containers, and filling the void with linen. That the practice was primarily religious in character questions the accuracy of Egypt's physicians'
involvement as recorded in 50:2.[675] Perhaps Joseph wanted to distance the
mummification of Jacob from the beliefs of Egyptian religion, yet at the same
time attribute national honor to his father by involving the physicians instead
of or in addition to the customary role of the priests.

PERMISSION FROM PHARAOH (50:4–6). **50:4–6** At the appropriate time,
Joseph enlisted Pharaoh's courtiers ("court," lit., "household," *bayit*) to obtain
the king's permission to bury his father in Canaan (v. 4). On the formality of
the expression "if I have found favor," see comments on 18:3 (cf. 47:29). As to
why Joseph himself does not have the audience with the king may be related to
cultic impurity (e.g., Num 19:11,14,16) or mourning taboos (Esth 4:2; *Gen.
Rab.* 100.4) since he handled his father's remains.[676] Joseph wisely appeals to
the sympathies of the king by recalling Jacob's dying wish, taken under oath
(v. 5; cf. 47:31; 49:29–32). The repetition of "my father" in the Hebrew text
frames Joseph's request (v. 5). Joseph discreetly does not mention Jacob's
resistance to the notion of burial in Egypt. There is no record of Jacob hewing

---

[675] R. N. Jones, "Embalming," *ABD* 2.490–96 (493).

[676] Delitzsch remarks that Joseph could not approach the king "unshorn and unadorned" (*A
New Commentary on Genesis,* 402).

a burial chamber (*kārâ,* "to dig"[677]), but we may assume he (or those at his command) did in concert with the burial of Leah (v. 5). A separate "tomb" is not meant; rather, he probably refers to a chamber in the tomb's cave. The text emphasizes Jacob's planning and involvement in preparing the burial receptacle, lit., "in my grave which I dug for myself . . . bury me" (v. 5; cf. 2 Chr 16:14). Perhaps Pharaoh could appreciate the request of one who had prepared a tomb, since many Egyptian kings studiously engaged in the same project throughout their lives. "Now" (*wĕʿattâ,* v. 5b) introduces the trifold request of Joseph and presumes the argument of the foregoing explanation. So as to clinch the argument, Joseph assures the king that he "will return" once the task is accomplished (v. 5b). That Pharaoh might restrain Joseph reflects the value the king placed on his second-in-command (cf. 41:39). Permission appears to hinge on the king's respect for the solemnity of the oath ("to swear," *šābaʿ*) that Joseph undertook (vv. 5–6; cf. 50:25).

FUNERAL PROCESSION TO CANAAN (50:7–13). **50:7–9** The magnitude of the processional testified to the stature accorded Jacob. His funeral stands in stark contrast to the modest interments of Abraham and Isaac by their sons (25:9; 35:29). God took one man and prepared a nation in the making, a people who had the attention of the king of Egypt. The word "all" occurs three times in vv. 7–8, indicating by hyperbole the inclusive nature of the entourage. That the Egyptian "dignitaries" (*zĕqēnîm,* "elders," v. 7b) included those in and outside the court of Pharaoh showed widespread respect for Joseph's family in Egypt. The number also involved the "household" of Joseph, thus his attendants as well as family (v. 8). The "brothers" (and we may assume their households) and those who were in the "household" of Jacob completed the processional (v. 8a). In effect, all who were able and necessary accompanied Joseph, leaving behind the "children" and livestock (v. 8b). By leaving behind their valued children and possessions, Joseph signaled to Pharaoh that he and family would return in accordance with his promise (v. 5). Moreover, the measure had the practical effect of sparing the weaker members the arduous journey (cf. 33:13). Jacob's request was no small endeavor for Joseph and his attendants to carry out. Furthermore, the mention of "Goshen" recalls Pharaoh's bequest to Joseph, indicating the tract of land belonged to the Hebrew tribes. Pharaoh's benevolence and Egypt's pomp and ceremony faded under a new regime (Exod 1:8), but the memory of the grandeur served as an encouragement to generations of Hebrew slaves who traced their heritage to Jacob.

Last, v. 9 mentions the military arm of the delegation made up of "chariots" *(rekeb)* and "horsemen" (*pārāšîm,* "horse, horsemen"; cf. "charioteers," NRSV, NAB). Egyptian war chariots were especially formidable in Egypt's

---

[677] *Tg. Onq.* interprets the word as "prepared" a burial place, since it would not do for Jacob to be a grave digger (Grossfeld, *Targum Onqelos,* 175, n. 3).

long history of power (e.g., 1 Kgs 10:29; Isa 31:1). The accompaniment of Egyptian chariots in the eyes of later Israel would have brought to mind the salvation of God at the Red Sea (e.g., Exod 14:6–28; 15:19; Deut 11:4; Isa 43:17). That the chariots accompanied the return of Jacob's household to Canaan forecasts the eventual return of the bones of Joseph and the families of Jacob's descendants who escaped Egyptian persecution (Exod 13:19; Josh 24:32). After detailing the members of the traveling party, the text concludes the matter by stating the obvious: "It was a very large company" (v. 9). The context of the military description gives "company" *(maḥăneh)* a military nuance, which describes the opposing camps *(maḥăneh)* of Egypt and Israel at the sea (Exod 14:19–20,24). The expression "very large" *(kābēd mě'ōd)* describes other important convoys (Exod 12:38; 1 Kgs 10:2//2 Chr 9:1). Jacob's immigrant "company" *(maḥăneh)* at his first return to Canaan from a twenty-year exile in Paddan Aram was also impressive (32:10[11]; 33:8).

50:10–13 Upon approaching Canaan, the group paused at the "threshing floor *[gōren]* of Atad," or "Goren-ha-Atad" (e.g., NAB, NJB, NJPS) for seven days of "mourning" *('ēbel*, vv. 10–11; cf. 27:41; also Deut 34:8). A seven-day period of mourning was a common practice (cf. 1 Sam 31:13//1 Chr 10:12; Job 2:13; Ezek 3:15–16; *Jdt* 16:24; *Sir* 22:12) and as a Jewish rite is customary today. The location of "Atad" is unknown. "Atad" *('āṭād)* itself means "bramble, thornbush, buckthorn" (Judg 9:14–15; Ps 58:9[10]), yielding the translation "the threshing floor of the bramble." The NIV translates "near the Jordan" for the ambiguous *bě'ēber hayyardēn,* lit., "beyond the Jordan"; the phrase can refer to the east or west side of the Jordan depending on the viewpoint of the speaker (e.g., Deut 1:1; 11:30; Josh 12:1,7). If the location is east, then their route was the circuitous trip around the southern end of the Dead Sea, making it generally the same trek that Israel in the wilderness will take, carrying the bones of Joseph.[678] In this case the processional would have crossed the Jordan River and proceeded south to Hebron. Or, alternatively, it is reasonable that Atad was on the western side of the Jordan since the shortest route from Egypt to Canaan is along the plain of the Philistines (Exod 13:17).[679]

The text describes the intensity of the collective lament, lit., "they mourned *[wayyispědû]* there a mourning *[mispēd*[680]*]* great and very grievous *[wěkābēd mě'ōd]*" (v. 10). The NIV translates "and bitterly" for the phrase *wěkābēd mě'ōd*, which occurred in v. 9, translated "very large." The large funeral atten-

---

[678] Hamilton, *Genesis Chapters 18–50*, 697. W. H. Shea contends for the transjordan route, proposing that Atad was near the Jabbok River and thus the route would have commemorated Jacob's return from Paddan Aram (32:22), including stops at Shechem (33:18), Bethlehem (35:19), and Hebron (35:27; "The Burial of Jacob," *Archaeology and Biblical Research* 5 [1992]: 33–44).

[679] Sarna proposes Tell el-'Ajjul for Atad, known to be an Egyptian possession, which is four and a half miles southwest of Gaza *(Genesis*, 349), but A. Kempinski has identified it as Sharuhen (Josh 19:6; "'Ajjul, Tell El-," *NEAEHL* 1.49).

[680] The cognate accusative noun reinforces the verbal idea (GKC §117p–q).

dance created a conspicuous sight and sound. On the word "mourn" *(s-p-d)*, see comments on 23:2 (cf. *sāpad//yālal* and *mispēd//ʾēbel*, Mic 1:8). The response of the local Canaanite populace reinforces the idea of intense mourning (v. 11). The striking sight of such a throng in Egyptian pageantry for the sake of a Hebrew's burial raised special notice among the Canaanites. The memorializing of the place by the new name "Abel Mizraim" (i.e., "the mourning of the Egyptians," *ʾābēl miṣrayim*) arose from this unique occasion: "The Egyptians are holding a solemn ceremony of mourning" *(ʾēbel kābēd zeh lĕmiṣrayim)*. A subtle wordplay may be in the name "Abel" between the words *ʾēbel* ("mourning") and the word *ʾābēl,* meaning "stream, brook, watercourse," which appears only in place names (e.g., Abel Shittim, Num 33:49). If so, the site may have originally included the name "Abel" and was renamed "Mourning of the Egyptians." The expression "inhabitants of the land" (NIV "who lived there") also describes the indigenous populations of Canaan (cf. 34:30; 36:20; Num 33:52). That the Canaanites acknowledge the event foreshadows the submission of the Canaanites during the Conquest (e.g., Num 14:14; Josh 2:9; 9:24). For Hebrew readers the recognition of Jacob/Israel by their archenemies, the Egyptians and Canaanites, may well have portrayed the future succession of the Israelites.

The text (vv. 12–13) confirms the adherence of Jacob's sons to his request (49:29–32) by describing the journey on to Machpelah in Hebron. (On the stock phrase and variations "so [they] did," *ʿāśâ kēn,* cf. 42:20; 45:21.) The word "to command" *(ṣāwâ)* repeats the description of the patriarch's "instructions" in 49:29,33. Verse 12 is reminiscent of Noah's and Moses' obedience "as God commanded" (6:22; cf. Exod 7:6; 39:32,42; 40:16). Finally, v. 13 describes the interment by repeating the language of Jacob's request (49:29–32), giving attention to the precise burial location in conformity with earlier descriptions (e.g., 23:9,17,19–20; 25:9; 49:29–30). The repetition of Jacob's words highlights the careful compliance Joseph and his brothers gave to Jacob's dying words. The importance of mentioning the purchase of the site by Abraham is the right of ownership that the Hebrews claim in the midst of their Canaanite neighbors. Although Jacob left Canaan for the refuge of Egypt, he never conceded his possessions to others (e.g., 48:22). The land was the promissory gift from God, not to be dismissed (48:3–4).

RETURN TO EGYPT (50:14). **50:14** The verse concludes the episode with the recession of the funeral party. Mention of Joseph, his brothers, and "all the others" shows there were no stragglers, fulfilling Joseph's promise to Pharaoh (v. 5). The MT text twice mentions the burial: lit., "to bury his father, after he had buried his father" (cf., e.g., AV). The redundancy[681] reflects the magnitude of the event in the eyes of the narrator.

---

[681] The final clause in the MT אַחֲרֵי קָבְרוֹ אֶת־אָבִיו, "after he had buried his father," is absent in the LXX.

13. The Final Days of Joseph (50:15–26)

The final episodes in the life of Joseph bring to conclusion the Book of Genesis with his words of reconciliation to his troubled brothers (vv. 15–21) and his words of instructions for his burial (vv. 22–26). What the two episodes hold in common is the idea of loyalty. The brothers' fear questions the depth of Joseph's loyalty to them as siblings. At the death of Jacob they worry that Joseph's desire for vengeance will be unleashed against them. They hope to act preemptively by volunteering to serve him as slaves. Although the overture is rejected by Joseph, the depiction of the brothers abasing themselves at Joseph's feet fulfills the two dreams of Joseph at the outset of the story (37:2–20). There is no overt recognition by the brothers or Joseph of this. The narrator leaves it to the reader to recognize the significance of their submission for the symmetry and irony of the account. The hidden hand of God can again be detected, leaving this parting statement for the theology of the book. Joseph's dreams do not show the outcome of the brothers' submission, preserving the tension until this moment when Joseph fully and finally resists their offer of servitude. The dreams therefore depict the superiority of Joseph as the lord over the brothers, but not a picture of slaves. The people of Egypt had become enslaved to Joseph, but not his father and brothers. He refused to take advantage of their vulnerability. Mosaic legislation prohibited exploitation of one's fellow Hebrew by enslaving them (Exod 21:16; Lev 25:39–43; Deut 24:7). Joseph shows himself again to be an upright man who exhibits the features of a loyal covenant-keeper.

The eminent fourth-century Christian poet, Ephrem the Syrian, commented on Joseph's forgiveness of his brothers and his acceptance of God's will for his life (50:20). "Joseph wept and said, 'Do not be afraid of me, for although your father has died, the God of your father, on account of whom I will never strike you, is still alive" (see comments on Gen 44:2).[682] Ephrem's imagination captured the import of Joseph's answer to his troubled brothers. Joseph's forgiveness arose from his commitment to God. He offered a similar explanation in rebuffing Potiphar's promiscuous wife: "How then could I do such a wicked thing and sin against God?" (39:9). The issue included loyalty to Potiphar and, in this case, to his father Jacob; but much more importantly, Joseph makes clear that he resists indulging his vices because of his commitment to the Lord God. For him to retaliate against his brothers would be to undercut the gracious ends of preserving Joseph, for Joseph's sojourn was "to save [their] lives by a great deliverance" (45:7) and "the saving of many lives" (50:20).

---

[682] *ACCS* 2.350–51.

Since Joseph shows loyalty to his brothers and the family's unity has been preserved, it is fitting that Joseph makes a request that presumes the loyalty of the brothers and their descendants to him. He seeks to be returned to Canaan in accordance with the request of Jacob (47:29–30; 49:29–32). By making provisions for the future interment of his remains in Canaan, Joseph demonstrates his loyalty to the family and to the covenant God of his father. The family enjoys here a unity of identity and purpose that will be rarely experienced by the future descendants of the tribes. Thus in the midst of the foreboding aspects of Joseph's imminent death and the slavery under Egyptian rule that follows (Exod 1:8), the author has provided a hopeful note on the future. Together, as a united family, they will survive the ordeal of Egypt and return as God had first shown Abraham (15:16). This unification of brothers contrasts with the beginning of human history when sibling strife resulted in Abel's murder. Thus the twelve sons experienced divine grace that superseded the temptations of murder and vengeance that would have threatened the promissory blessing.

COMPOSITION.   There is wide agreement among critical scholars that Gen 50:22–26 completes the whole of the Joseph narrative and is patterned on the report of Jacob's death. Genesis 50:15–21 gives a variant (secondary) resolution to the sibling conflict in the Joseph story. The documentarians interpret 50:2–26 as a complex of the traditional sources Yahwist (J), Elohist (E), and Priestly (P). Gunkel, for example, determined that 50:2–11 and 14–26 were primarily the result of the combined sources JE. Verses 12–13 are by the hand of P. Evidence of the dual sources is E's account (vv. 15–21) of the brothers' reaction at learning for the first time of their father's death and burial. According to J, however, the brothers were present at the burial of their father in Canaan (vv. 8,14). Evidence of J and E also appears in vv. 22–26. J occurs in vv. 22a,26b, and perhaps v. 22b. Verses 24–25 (E, as in 48:21) recast the final words of Jacob (47:29–31[J]; 48:21–22[E]).[683] Coats analyzed 50:15–26 as made up of two parts, a restatement of the end of the Joseph story (50:15–21; cf. 47:27) and the death report of Joseph (50:22–26).[684] These two come from the final redaction of the patriarchal story chaps. 12–50, not from any source. They give closure to the Jacob-Joseph narratives and the patriarchal story as a whole. It is not the result of multiple sources, and the context is the present one alone. These two units were added to bring the story of Jacob's death (47:28–50:14) into the wider tradition about Jacob and his sons. Genesis 50:22–26 points backward to the Joseph story and the Jacob death report and points forward to the exodus and the conquest. Westermann differed from Coats by seeing the end of the original Joseph narrative at 50:14a. For him, 50:15–21 completes the Joseph narrative by the redactor's insertion of the brothers' reconciliation, to which was later added an epilogue giving the final remarks on Joseph's life (vv. 22–23) and his final words (vv. 24–26). These two expansions are two separate conclusions that

---

[683] Gunkel, *Genesis,* 462.
[684] Coats, *Genesis,* 311–15.

have been joined together, as shown by the repeated age notices ("one hundred and ten years"). The epilogue by reporting Joseph's last days concludes the patriarchal history.[685] Carr understood 50:14–21 as the conclusion to the "pre-promise Joseph story" that gives the final reconciliation of the brothers. The story has no necessary connection with a future exodus motif. Verses 24–25 are a revision of the non-P Jacob-Joseph story, which looks back to the covenant promise and oath to return to Canaan (15:14–21; 22:15–18) and looks ahead to the exodus sojourn (e.g., Exod 13:19; Josh 24:32). The priestly addition includes the death and burial account of Jacob (vv. 12–13) and the settlement notice for Joseph (50:22a) as P does with the earlier patriarchs (e.g., 13:12; 21:21; 25:11; 36:6–8; 37:1). Also vv. 22b–23,26a are P, providing a link between Joseph and the exodus. Last, v. 26 is a late revision of P, showing interest in the coffin ("ark") in contrast to his bones (as in v. 25).[686]

We find that vv. 15–21 are a literary unity that exhibits a logical progression in the plot. It is not necessarily an alternative tradition to the earlier episode of Jacob's burial, where the brothers are specifically said to be present in Canaan (vv. 8,14). Verse 15 does not say the brothers were ignorant of their father's death. The verb "saw" means that the brothers realized the implications of his death for them. The author contrasts the reaction of the Canaanites in v. 11 to the burial of Jacob ("When the Canaanites . . . saw") and the brothers. Verse 15 is to be understood as antecedent or contemporaneous with the burial processional. This indicates that they talked worriedly among themselves about what lay ahead upon their return to Egypt. Thus they sent a messenger to Joseph and initiated negotiations. Moreover, vv. 15–21 are not anticlimactic to the Joseph story, although their reconciliation occurred in 45:1–11. By intentional lexical allusions to the earlier account in chap. 45 (e.g., vv. 5,8; 50:19–21), the present episode recasts their reconciliation in a new context—the absence of Jacob. The tension of sibling rivalry reappears so as to show the genuine largesse of Joseph and the permanent security for the brothers that the hero provided. For this reason, 50:15–21 intentionally reaches back to the inception of the rivalry by contrasting "spoke kindly to him" (v. 21b) to "could not speak a kind word" (37:4b). The brothers "cast themselves down," showing the ultimate fulfillment of Joseph's dreams. But Joseph refuses to take advantage of them. Their earlier, indignant questions—"Do you intend to reign over us? Will you actually rule us?" (37:10)—are answered here in the negative by Joseph. Whereas Joseph exercised control over the Egyptians and their lands, he resists this gain over his brothers. This episode then is necessary to prove the schism at last was fully healed. Now Joseph (and the reader) can give his full attention to the future, which explains the subject matter in vv. 22–26. The double references to his age (vv. 22,26) are not unavoidably evidence of two different sources but are a rhetorical inclusio, distinguishing the final paragraph. The age of the patriarch provides a link with the future settlement of Canaan led by Joshua (cf. comments on v. 26).

---

[685] Westermann, *Genesis 37–50*, 208, 212–13.
[686] Carr, *Reading the Fractures of Genesis*, 109–10, 166–67, n. 40, 272.

STRUCTURE. Genesis 50:15–26 divides easily into two parts. (1) Verses 15–21 return to the subject of the family schism whose resolution is processed again. The literary boundaries are the fear of Joseph's retaliation ("What if Joseph holds a grudge," v. 15) and Joseph's benevolent response ("spoke kindly to them," v. 21). The scene consists of the brothers' preemptive pleas for forgiveness (vv. 15–18) and Joseph's tearful reassurance of provision for the brothers' families (vv. 19–21). That Joseph "spoke kindly" recalls the sibling enmity ("could not speak a kind word to him," 37:4) that began the conflict. (2) Verses 22–26 contain an obituary (vv. 22–23), the final words of Joseph (vv. 24–25), and his death (v. 26). The word "Egypt" and the repeated notice of Joseph's age ("a hundred and ten years," vv. 22,26) frames vv. 22–26. Verse 22 describes his life in Egypt (*wayḥî*, "he lived"), and v. 26 reports his death in Egypt (*wayyāmot*, "died"). His request to return his "bones" to Canaan resounds the similar oath of Joseph to his father (47:29–31). Thus 47:29–31 and 50:24–25 enclose the last days of the chief protagonists Jacob and Joseph. We conclude, therefore, that vv. 15–21 and 22–26 form a unified narrative, providing an appropriate conclusion.

(1) Joseph Reassures His Brothers (50:15–21)

[15]When Joseph's brothers saw that their father was dead, they said, "What if Joseph holds a grudge against us and pays us back for all the wrongs we did to him?" [16]So they sent word to Joseph, saying, "Your father left these instructions before he died: [17]'This is what you are to say to Joseph: I ask you to forgive your brothers the sins and the wrongs they committed in treating you so badly.' Now please forgive the sins of the servants of the God of your father.'" When their message came to him, Joseph wept.

[18]His brothers then came and threw themselves down before him. "We are your slaves," they said.

[19]But Joseph said to them, "Don't be afraid. Am I in the place of God? [20]You intended to harm me, but God intended it for good to accomplish what is now being done, the saving of many lives. [21]So then, don't be afraid. I will provide for you and your children." And he reassured them and spoke kindly to them.

After the death and burial of Jacob, the brothers admit their fear of Joseph's revenge and offer themselves as slaves in exchange for clemency (vv. 15–18). Joseph answers with disappointment at their fears and pledges to safeguard the family (vv. 19–21).

PLEAS FOR FORGIVENESS (50:15–18). **50:15–16** The death of Jacob had a bearing on the outlook of the brothers, fearing that Joseph held a deep-seated "grudge" (*śāṭam*, v. 15; cf. 49:23) despite his earlier assurance of pardon (45:5–7). Their fear of retaliation was not irrational. Although Esau nursed his anger ("grudge," *śāṭam*, 27:41), his regard for his father restrained a vendetta against Jacob. The angry response of Esau sharply contrasts with Joseph, who rose above personal revenge, viewing their lives in the vista of God's better purposes. The text does not say "all" of Joseph's brothers (cp. 45:15), which exempts Benjamin, who had no reason to fear. The offending brothers strongly word their worries (presumably) to one another (v. 15b). The text can be understood in one of two ways. The NIV's "what if" translates the particle *lû*, interpreting their worries conditionally—maybe he will hold a grudge and maybe not (cf. AV, NRSV, NAB, NJB, REB, NJPS).[687] The particle can also be emphatic,[688] making a positive statement in earnest: "Indeed, Joseph holds a grudge against us!" The common point of the two interpretations is the brothers continue to fear the consequences of their crimes. Perhaps Joseph's trickery continued to haunt them, producing insecurity in their relationship. We might also notice that prior to this incident (v. 17) nowhere in the text do the brothers ask for or receive an explicit statement of forgiveness from Joseph. To them it is inconceivable that Joseph would not require some penance on their part. There was no ostensible reason for the brothers to be suspicious of a hidden vendetta, but their guilt remained a heavy burden, which probably fueled their misgivings (cf. 42:21–22; 44:16). They admit again to themselves "all the wrongs" (*rā'â*, "evil," vv. 15,17; cf. "harm," v. 20) they committed against Joseph. The language, "pays us back in full," forcefully expresses the dread of their deserved requital.[689] The expression uses the word "return" (*šûb, hiph.*), which creates a play on Joseph's "return" (*šûb, qal*) from Egypt in the previous verse.[690] The final confession "all the wrongs we did to him" translates the word *gāmal*, meaning what one "deals out" requires appropriate recompense, whether for good or evil behavior (vv. 15,17; cf. 1 Sam 24:18; also noun *gĕmûlâ*, 2 Sam 19:37; Isa 59:18; Jer 51:56).

The brothers, probably too frightened to face Joseph, "sent word"[691] (*wayṣawwû*, lit., "they commanded," v. 16) by an intermediary. That the brothers' message has "your father" rather than "our father" draws attention to Joseph's obligation as a son, not as a brother. As to whether the brothers fabricated this story, we can't judge other than by Joseph's apparent acceptance of it.

50:17–18 Verse 17 possesses two voices: the postmortem report of Jacob's message (v. 17a) and the subsequent appeal of the brothers themselves (v. 17b). The former gives the basis for the latter's request and provides incentive for Joseph to respond favorably. Their plea essentially imitates the words of their father's message: lit., "I beg you [Joseph], please

---

[687] In this case the apodosis is absent (see GKC §159y).

[688] On the emphatic *lamed*, see *IBHS* §11.2.10i.

[689] Infinitive absolute + imperfect construction, הָשֵׁב יָשִׁיב לָנוּ, lit., "returning he will return to us," i.e., "he will repay us in full" (e.g., NRSV, NASB); see this meaning of שׁוּב in Prov 17:13.

[690] Hamilton, *Genesis Chapters 18–50*, 699, n. 4.

[691] LXX, παρεγένοντο (= וַיִּגְּשׁוּ ?), "they approached" (e.g., NRSV, NAB; cf. vv. 17–18; see *BHS*).

forgive the transgressions of your brothers" and "Now, please forgive the transgressions of the servants of the God of your father." The message begins with the interjection of entreaty, *ʾānnāʾ*, "please" or "I beg" (absent NIV; e.g., see the exclamation at Exod 32:31; 2 Kgs 20:3), followed in the Hebrew text by the request "forgive!" (imper. *śāʾ*, meaning "bear away, lift," indicating "forgiveness"; e.g., Exod 32:32). On the idiom *nāśāʾ ʿāwôn*, see 4:13, vol. 1A, p. 276. The vocabulary of the message draws on the semantic field of sin: "sins" (*pešaʿ*, "transgression, rebellion, crime"), "wrongs" (*ḥaṭṭāʾt*, "sin"), and "so badly" (*rāʿâ*, "evil, harm"). The appearance of these three standard terms for "sin" occurs only in this verse. "Sins" translates the noun *pešaʿ*, which generally means an "offense"; here the nuance of the term is that the brothers committed a breach in their relationship with Joseph as siblings.[692] "Sins" and "wrongs" are terms that occurred together in Jacob's angry rebuff of Laban's charges of offense against him (31:36). Here, however, the brothers cannot so excuse themselves but readily acknowledge their mistreatment of Joseph, hoping for clemency. The clause "they committed" repeats the term *gāmal* found in their admission in v. 15 ("we did to him").[693] The noun rendered "badly" *(rāʿâ)* occurs three times in this scene (vv. 15,17,20), meaning "harm, abusive." The word reaches back to the beginning of their schism, when Joseph produced a "bad report" *(dibbātām rāʾâ,* 37:2). By calling on Joseph to forgive, Jacob does not treat lightly the reality of their cruelty but exposes its heinous nature. Thus, if they are to have reconciliation, Joseph's absolution is required since they have no excuse.

We noted above that to their father's message—which comes as if from the grave—the brothers add their own emotional plea. They astutely emend the message of Jacob, referring to themselves as "the servants of the God of your father" (v. 17b). This recognition of the deity echoes 46:3 ("I am the God, the God of your father") when the Lord promises to make of Jacob a "great nation" (cf. 12:2; 26:24; 28:13–14; Exod 3:6; Deut 26:5). The brothers therefore are appealing to the divine purpose for their descent into Egypt and to the hope that their father had for the family. By elevating the basis for their plea, they hope to take advantage of Joseph's keen sense of loyalty, not only to Jacob but also to the God that Jacob has so faithfully served. The brothers have duly noted their crimes, and by humbling themselves ("servants") they exhibit sincere remorse for their deeds. When Joseph heard their fearful pleas, he "wept" as he had at Jacob's death (v. 1; cf. 42:24; 43:30; 45:14–15; 46:29). He was brokenhearted, probably realizing that their estrangement was not yet fully healed. Why did his father not trust him? Why did the brothers still fear

---

[692] E. Carpenter and M. Grisanti, "פֶּשַׁע," *NIDOTTE* 3.706–7.

[693] The clause כִּי־רָעָה גְמָלוּךָ is causal, "because they did you wrong."

him? The text again echoes the fractious past by the remark, "When their message came . . ." *(bĕdabbĕrām,* v. 17b), recalling when in seething anger at young Joseph "they could not speak *[dabbĕrô]*a kind word to him" (37:4b).

Verse 18 describes the brothers' contrition who, after the messengers,[694] enter the scene casting themselves at Joseph's feet ("threw themselves down before him") and volunteer their servitude. This episode replays the arrest scene in which the brothers concede that they are the Egyptian lord's slaves ("threw themselves . . . before him," 44:14; cf. vv. 16,33). Moreover, it brings to mind the dreams of the young Joseph (37:7,9). Even in the midst of their anxiety about the future, the brothers' actions unwittingly testify to the providence of God in the life of their family and descendants.

PROMISE OF PROVISION (50:19–21). **50:19–20** Joseph's response crystallizes the theology of the Joseph narrative as a whole (cf. Prov 19:21). F. W. Faber remarked, "God's will does not come to us in the whole, but in fragments, and generally in small fragments." First, Joseph acknowledges that he is not in control of history's measures (v. 19). "Don't be afraid" (vv. 19,21) echoes the comfort sounded by Joseph's chief servant, who recognized God's intervention in events (43:23; cf. 15:1; 21:17; 26:24; 35:17; 46:3). "Am I in the place of God?"[695] is the same exclamation a frustrated Jacob answered to Rachel's complaint (30:2). Divine purpose prohibits Joseph from exacting personal vengeance, even if he wanted to (cf. Lev 19:18; Deut 32:35; Ps 94:1; Rom 12:19). This is the role of God; Joseph cannot usurp deity's designs (cf. Num 23:19–20; 24:13). Second, Joseph explains that God transformed their evil intention into good, achieving the deliverance of many peoples (v. 20; cf. Prov 16:9). His opening words create a parallelism, which heightens the contrast between human and divine intentions, lit., "You yourselves intended against me harm *[rā'â]*/God intended it for good *[lĕṭōbâ]*."[696] The nature of their "intended" *(ḥāšab)* harm is well illustrated by Saul's "plan" *(ḥāšab)* to murder David (1 Sam 18:25b).[697] Joseph supports his reasoning by pointing

---

694 וַיֵּלְכוּ גַּם־אֶחָיו, "then his brothers also came."

695 כִּי הֲתַחַת אֱלֹהִים אָנִי; the introductory כִּי is asseverative, "Indeed, am I . . . ?" or explanatory, "For am I . . . ?" (AV, RSV, NASB). The LXX's τοῦ γὰρ θεοῦ εἰμι ἐγώ, "for I am God's," meaning his servant, answers the question rather than translates it; cf. *Tg. Onq.,* "I am one who is in reverence of the Lord" (see Grossfeld, *Targum Onqelos,* 174, and Wevers, *Notes on the Greek Text,* 850).

696 וְאַתֶּם חֲשַׁבְתֶּם עָלַי רָעָה אֱלֹהִים חֲשָׁבָהּ לְטֹבָה; the SP, LXX exhibit the contrast by the adversative *waw,* "but God" (SP, וְהָאֱלֹהִים; LXX, ὁ δὲ θεός).

697 On the word group "calculate, plot," see J. Hartley, "חשׁב," *NIDOTTE* 2.303–10. For the construction "to plot evil against," see, e.g., Ps 21:11[12]; Jer 48:2; cf. the cognate construction of verb + accusative noun "plan" in Ezek 38:10, וְחָשַׁבְתָּ מַחֲשֶׁבֶת רָעָה, "you will devise an evil scheme." Also consider the evil "intentions" (מַחְשְׁבֹת) of prediluvian humanity (6:5). Joseph and Jeremiah were both naive toward their enemies ("they plotted schemes against me," כִּי־עָלַי חָשְׁבוּ מַחֲשָׁבוֹת [Jer 11:19]).

to the many peoples that Egypt's storehouses have sustained ("what is now," *kayyōm hazzeh;* cf., e.g., Deut 2:30; 1 Sam 22:8). The "good/evil" motif that recurs throughout Genesis (see Introduction) fittingly makes its last appearance in Joseph's humble interpretation of his troubles. What became of Joseph in Egypt was the handiwork of God, too great for him to have accomplished alone (cf. 2 Kgs 5:7). Evil succumbs to God's gracious purposes in behalf of his creation. This theology is exhibited in our passage by Joseph's assessment of his purpose in Egypt, for "the saving *[ḥāyâ]* of many lives" (v. 20b). The language recalls his first assessment at the brothers' reconciliation: "But God sent me ahead of you . . . to save *[ḥāyâ]* your lives by a great deliverance" (45:7). In our passage "many lives" appears to include the Egyptians and other peoples who had sought refuge in Egypt from the famine.

Joseph concludes his speech (v. 21) by promising to perpetuate the necessities of life that he had afforded since Jacob's arrival in Egypt (45:11; 47:12), noting especially that he himself will see to this (lit., "I myself will provide *['ānōkî 'ăkalkêl],*" *pilpel,* from *kûl*[698]). Although the seven-year famine was over (45:10–11), Joseph had continued to ensure the preservation of the tribal families. The acquisition of land (Goshen) by the Israelites appears to have been exceptional at that time (as with the Egyptian priests, 47:20–27). Joseph is saying that the death of his father will not change his benevolence toward them. The narration confirms Joseph's calming demeanor ("reassuring," *piel,* from *nāḥam,* "comfort"; cf. 24:67; 37:35). On the expression "spoke kindly," see comments on 34:3.

(2) Joseph Instructs His Brothers (50:22–26)

[22]Joseph stayed in Egypt, along with all his father's family. He lived a hundred and ten years [23]and saw the third generation of Ephraim's children. Also the children of Makir son of Manasseh were placed at birth on Joseph's knees.

[24]Then Joseph said to his brothers, "I am about to die. But God will surely come to your aid and take you up out of this land to the land he promised on oath to Abraham, Isaac and Jacob." [25]And Joseph made the sons of Israel swear an oath and said, "God will surely come to your aid, and then you must carry my bones up from this place."

[26]So Joseph died at the age of a hundred and ten. And after they embalmed him, he was placed in a coffin in Egypt.

JOSEPH'S OLD AGE (50:22–23). **50:22–23** Joseph's age, "a hundred and ten years," forms the boundaries of the verses. Verse 22 mentions the longevity of Joseph's residence in Egypt and that of his father's family, an indication of the Lord's enduring provision. Moreover, the implication of the verse is that Joseph and Jacob's family did not return to Canaan again. This is

---

[698] The verb כוּל occurs three times in Genesis, always in the *pilpel* stem (45:11; 47:12; 50:21).

one of many narrative features anticipating the introductory event in the Book of Exodus. That Joseph lived the ideal life span of one hundred and ten years, according to the Egyptian viewpoint, coincidentally adds to the high esteem the narrative ascribes to him (cf. Joshua below, v. 26; for one hundred and twenty years, see Moses, Deut 31:2; 34:7 with Gen 6:3).

The subsequent verse reinforces the impression of blessing (v. 23). Joseph lived to see his offspring down to the "third generation" (*šillēšîm*, "third") by Ephraim's lineage (v. 23), which referred to Joseph's great-grandchildren or possibly great-great-grandchildren.[699] Such long life was considered a special benevolence from God (e.g., Ps 128:6; Job 42:16). The word "third" appears in the conventional phrase "to the third and fourth generation," also describing longevity (Exod 20:5; 34:7; Num 14:18; Deut 5:9). Additionally, mention of Joseph's great-grandchildren by "Makir" (v. 23), the son of Manasseh (Num 26:29), achieves the same purpose of demonstrating good, long life. The influential tribe of Makir (e.g., Josh 17:1; Judg 5:14) produced the numerous and powerful Gileadites (e.g., Num 32:39; 36:1–10). The significance of "Joseph's knees," if used in the same way as 30:3 (see comments), indicates formal adoption or at least informal guardianship by Joseph. Since the Joseph narrative intentionally parallels Jacob and Joseph in other matters (e.g., embalming, sworn oath for burial), it is not unthinkable that Joseph, as did Jacob (48:5), adopted his descendants.

JOSEPH'S LAST WORDS (50:24–25). **50:24–25** "I am about to die" (*'ānōkî mēt*) sets the scene and importance of Joseph's prediction of the Israelites' return to the land. The same prospects of Israel's future entry into the land accompany Jacob's and Moses' anticipation of death (48:21; Deut 4:22). Reference to "his brothers" does not require that all eleven are alive and present; the phrase has a rhetorical purpose, showing that Joseph views the surviving brothers and/or the brothers' children as one and the same (cf. below "sons of Israel," v. 25). The presence of "his brothers" at his last utterance gives the Joseph story a fitting symmetry, for it was they who heard his first predictions (37:5–10). Moreover, the image of "his brothers" present at Joseph's death gives solemnity to his passing, like that of Abraham, Isaac, and Jacob when each one's sons attended his death and burial. Although he will not live to participate in the return, Joseph confidently declares that the Lord will lead their descendants. Joseph could not appeal to the authority of a direct word from God. Unlike Jacob (48:3–4) there was no divine epiphany

---

[699] The MT has לְאֶפְרַיִם בְּנֵי שִׁלֵּשִׁים, "by Ephraim children of the third [generation]," i.e., Joseph's great-great-grandchildren; however, ancient versions SP, LXX, Syr., *Tgs. Onq.* and *Ps.-J.* have בָּנִים שִׁלֵּשִׁים, "third-generation children," meaning Joseph's great-grandchildren, which corresponds to Joseph's great-grandchildren by Manasseh's line (v. 23b). GKC §128v recommends a genitive of group (class) reading MT as "sons belonging to the third generation," i.e., Joseph's great-grandchildren.

for Joseph. He relied on the witness of his father and trusted in the promised word. "Will surely come to your aid" renders the idiom "he will surely visit *[pāqad]* you."[700] The word group *p-q-d* often describes God's intervention, bringing about harm or good (e.g., Deut 5:9; Ruth 1:6; Ps 106:4). The similar wording in Exod 3:16 ("I have watched over you") describes God's watchcare over the suffering Israelites in Egypt, precipitating their deliverance and return. The subsequent clause "and [he will] bring you up" (*hiph.* from *'ālâ*, "to go up") becomes a repeated phrase, recalling the redemption of God's people out of Egypt (e.g., 1 Sam 12:6; 2 Kgs 17:36; Jer 16:14–15; 23:7–8; Hos 12:13[14]). Another oft-repeated phrase in Scripture "Abraham, Isaac and Jacob" (and its variations) occurs for the first time in our passage. This celebrated reference to the Israelites' progenitors is reflected in the common Deuteronomic phrase pertaining to the gift of land, "which [God] swore [*nišba'*, "swear"] to your fathers" (and its variations, e.g., Deut 1:8). The divine oath made to Abraham confirmed the promises to the faithful and loyal patriarch (22:16, "I swear by myself"). The naming of the three patriarchs bridges Genesis and the episode when the Lord reveals himself to Moses, commissioning him to realize what Joseph here has predicted (Exod 3:6,15,16; 33:1).

Out of his certainty in the promises made by God's "sworn oath" (*qal, šāba'*) to his forefathers (v. 24), Joseph requires the Israelites to "swear an oath" (*hiph., šāba'*) to return his remains to Canaan (v. 25). Jacob had put Joseph under the same obligation (47:27; 50:5–6), but in this case the return of Joseph's body is not immediate. There is no evidence of formal mourning, no pomp and circumstance. Joseph's faith enables him to wait—an exemplary act of faith celebrated by the writer to the Hebrews (11:22,39). When God fulfills his promise, the Israelites must do the same in returning Joseph's body. This was Joseph's statement of faith in God's word when he insisted that he accompany those returning to the land. Joseph's identity and that of his sons were bound up in the pledge made to his forefathers, not in his Egyptian past or present. The final words of Joseph look to the future, as every believer's should. Intuitively, the author refers to "his brothers" (vv. 18,24) as "the sons of Israel" when referring to the future of the nation. The author wants to keep before the reader that these figures were national ancestors; the narrative is not merely a family story but part of an epic account of Israel's past. It will be the brothers' descendants who will carry out this charge. Joseph repeats the prediction that the Lord will liberate them and when that moment comes, they must transport his "bones" with them.[701] This demon-

---

[700] Infinitive absolute + imperfect, פָּקֹד יִפְקֹד אֶתְכֶם.

[701] Here reference to Joseph's "bones," despite the embalming of his body, is appropriate as a common metaphor for a corpse in Hebrew thought (e.g., 1 Sam 31:13; 1 Kgs 13:31).

stration of Joseph's faith was not forgotten, for Moses fulfilled the wish of Joseph, recalling the words of the patriarch (Exod 13:9).

JOSEPH'S DEATH (50:26). **50:26** The final verse of the book summarizes what the passage has already informed the reader regarding Joseph's end, adding that his mummified body was deposited in a "coffin in Egypt." Jacob and Joseph are the only two biblical persons who were embalmed (vv. 2,26). His age at one hundred ten years matches the life span of Joshua (Josh 24:29; Judg 2:8), which makes for an interesting happenstance since Joshua, successor to Moses, must have overseen the final journey of Joseph's sarcophagus (Exod 13:19). Their burials in Canaan are recorded in the same passage (Josh 24:32). Joseph and Joshua are the bookends of Israel's sojourn in Egypt. The mention of "Egypt" as the final word of Genesis prepares the way for the events that follow in the Book of Exodus. Although the promise to the patriarchs was not yet fulfilled, and indeed appeared very far from ever being accomplished, the Book of Genesis is calling on the reader to take up the faith of Joseph in the promises made to the Fathers.

Selected Bibliography

Aalders, G. C. *Genesis*. 2 vols. Grand Rapids: Regency Reference Library, 1981.

Alexander, T. D. "Genesis 22 and the Covenant of Circumcision." *JSOT* 25 (1983): 17–22.

_____. "Lot's Hospitality: A Clue to His Righteousness." *JBL* 104 (1985): 289–91.

_____. "From Adam to Judah: The Significance of the Family Tree." *EvQ* 61 (1989): 5–19.

_____. *Abraham in the Negev: A Source-Critical Investigation of Genesis 20:1–22:19*. Carlisle: Paternoster, 1997.

Andersen, F. I. "Genesis IV: An Enigma." Pages 497–507 in *Pomegranates and Golden Bells: Studies in Biblical, Jewish, and Near Eastern Ritual, Law, and Literature in Honor of Jacob Milgrom*. Winona Lake: Eisenbrauns, 1995.

Biddle, M. E. "The 'Endangered Ancestress' and Blessing for the Nations." *JBL* 109 (1990): 599–611.

Blenkinsopp, J. "Abraham and the Righteous of Sodom." *JJS* 33 (1982): 119–32.

Brown, W. P. *Structure, Role and Ideology in the Hebrew and Greek Texts of Genesis 1:1–2:3*. Atlanta: Scholars, 1993.

Bruce, F. F. "The Bible and the Environment." Pages 15–30 in *The Living and Active Word of God: Studies in Honor of Samuel J. Schultz*. Winona Lake: Eisenbrauns, 1983.

Bruckner, J. K. *Implied Law in the Abraham Narrative*. JSOTSup 335. Sheffield: Sheffield Academic Press, 2001.

Calvin, J. *Commentaries on the First Book of Moses, Called Genesis*. 2 vols. Grand Rapids: Eerdmans, 1948.

Carr, D. M. *Reading the Fractures of Genesis: Historical and Literary Approaches*. Louisville: Westminster John Knox, 1996.

Cassuto, U. *A Commentary on the Book of Genesis*. 2 vols. Jerusalem: Magnes/Hebrew University, 1961–1964.

Chavalas M. W., and M. R. Adamthwaite. "Archaeological Light on the Old Testament." Pages 59–96 in *The Face of Old Testament Studies: A Survey of Contemporary Approaches*. Grand Rapids: Baker/Apollos, 1999.

Clines, D. J. A. *The Theme of the Pentateuch*. Sheffield: Sheffield Academic Press, 1997.

Coats, G. W. *Genesis with an Introduction to Narrative Literature*. FOTL. Grand Rapids: Eerdmans, 1983.

_____. "Lot: A Foil in the Abraham Saga." Pages 113–32 in *Understanding the Word*. JSOTSup 37. Sheffield: JSOT Press, 1985.

_____. "A Threat to the Host." Pages 71–81 in *Saga, Legend, Fable, Tale, Novella: Narrative Forms in Old Testament Literature*. JSOTSup 35. Sheffield: JSOT Press, 1985.

Cohn, R. L. "Negotiating (with) the Natives: Ancestors and Identity in Genesis." *HTR* 96 (2003): 147–66.

Curtis, E. M. "Structure, Style and Context as a Key to Interpreting Jacob's Encounter at Peniel." *JETS* 30 (1987): 129–37.

Delitzsch, F. *A New Commentary on Genesis*. 2 vols. 1888 repr. Edinburgh: T&T Clark, 2001.

De Hoop. R. *Genesis 49 in Its Literary and Historical Context.* Leiden: Brill, 1999.

De Vaux, R. *The Early History of Israel.* Philadelphia: Westminster, 1978.

Dozeman, T. B. "The Wilderness and Salvation History in the Hagar Story." *JBL* 117 (1998): 23–43.

Fields, W. W. *Sodom and Gomorrah: History and Motif in Biblical Narrative.* Sheffield: Sheffield Academic Press, 1997.

Fishbane, M. "Gen. 25:19–35:22, The Jacob Cycle." Pages 40–76 in *Text and Texture: Close Readings of Biblical Texts.* New York: Schocken Books, 1979.

Fokkelman, J. P. *Narrative Art in Genesis: Specimens of Stylistic and Structural Analysis.* Assen and Amsterdam: Van Gorcum, 1975.

Frymer-Kensky, T. "Patriarchal Family Relationship and Near Eastern Law." *BA* 44 (1981): 209–14.

_____. "Law and Philosophy: The Case of Sex in the Bible." *Semeia* 45 (1989): 89–102.

Garrett, D. A. *Rethinking Genesis: The Sources and Authorship of the First Book of the Pentateuch.* Grand Rapids: Baker, 1991.

Goldin, J. "The Youngest Son or Where Does Genesis 38 Belong." *JBL* 96 (1977): 27–44.

Grossfeld, B., ed. *The Targum Onqelos to Genesis.* Wilmington: Michael Glazier, 1988.

Gunkel, H. *Genesis.* Macon: Mercer University Press, 1997.

Hamilton, V. P. *The Book of Genesis Chapters 1–17.* NICOT. Grand Rapids: Eerdmans, 1990.

_____. *The Book of Genesis Chapters 18–50.* NICOT. Grand Rapids: Eerdmans, 1995.

Hasel, G. F. "The Meaning of the Animal Rite in Genesis 15." *JSOT* 19 (1981): 61–78.

Helyer, L. R. "The Separation of Abram and Lot: Its Significance in the Patriarchal Narratives." *JSOT* 26 (1983): 77–88.

Hess, R. S. *Studies in the Personal Names of Genesis 1–11.* AOAT 234. Neukirchener-Vluyn: Neukirchener Verlag, 1993.

Hess, R. S., G. Wenham, and P. Satterthwaite, eds. *He Swore an Oath: Biblical Themes from Genesis 12–50.* Cambridge: Tyndale House, 1993.

Hess, R. S., and D. T. Tsumura. *I Studied Inscriptions from Before the Flood: Ancient Near Eastern, Literary, and Linguistic Approaches to Genesis 1–11.* Winona Lake: Eisenbrauns, 1994.

Hoerth, A. J., G. L. Mattingly, and E. M. Yamauchi, eds. *Peoples of the Old Testament World.* Grand Rapids: Baker, 1994.

Hoffmeier, J. K. "The Wives' Tales of Genesis 12, 20, and 26 and the Covenants at Beer-Sheba." *TynBul* 43 (1992): 81–99.

_____. *Israel in Egypt: The Evidence for the Authenticity of the Exodus Traditions.* Oxford/New York: Oxford University Press, 1997.

House, P. R. *Old Testament Theology.* Downers Grove: InterVarsity, 1998.

Hughes, R. Kent. *Genesis.* Wheaton: Crossway Books, 2004.

Humphreys, W. L. *Joseph and His Family: A Literary Study.* Columbia: University of South Carolina Press, 1988.

_____. *The Character of God in the Book of Genesis: A Narrative Appraisal.* Louisville: Westminster John Knox, 2001.

Kidner, D. *Genesis.* TOTC. Chicago: InterVarsity, 1967.

Kikawada, I. M. *Before Abraham Was: The Unity of Genesis 1–11.* Nashville: Abingdon, 1985.

Kitchen, K. A. "Joseph." Pages 656–60 in *The New Bible Dictionary.* Grand Rapids: Eerdmans, 1962.

_____. *Ancient Orient and the Old Testament.* Chicago: InterVarsity, 1966.

_____. *On the Reliability of the Old Testament.* Grand Rapids: Eerdmans, 2003.

Lambe, A. J. "Genesis 38: Structure and Literary Design." Pages 102–20 in *The World of Genesis: Persons, Places, Perspectives.* JSOTSup 257. Sheffield: Sheffield Academic Press, 1998.

Lambert, W. G., and A. R. Millard, eds. *Atrahasis: The Babylonian Story of the Flood.* Winona Lake: Eisenbrauns, 1999.

Le Tellier, R. *Day in Mamre and Night in Sodom: Abraham and Lot in Genesis 18 and 19.* Leiden: Brill, 1995.

Long, V. P., D. W. Baker, and G. Wenham, eds. *Windows into Old Testament History: Evidence, Argument, and the Crisis of "Biblical Israel."* Grand Rapids: Eerdmans/ Cambridge, U.K., 2002.

Longacre, R. *Joseph: A Story of Divine Providence—A Text Theoretical and Textlinguistic Analysis of Genesis 37 and 39–40.* Winona Lake: Eisenbrauns, 1989.

Luther, M. *Luther's Works: Lectures on Genesis.* 8 vols. St. Louis: Concordia, 1958–1966.

Maher, M., ed. *Targum Pseudo-Jonathan, Genesis.* Collegeville, Minn.: Liturgical Press, 1992.

Malamat, A. *Mari and the Early Israelite Experience.* Oxford: British Academy, 1989.

Mathews, K. "Genesis." Pages 140–46 in *New Dictionary of Biblical Theology.* Downers Grove: InterVarsity, 2000.

_____. "The Table of Nations: The 'Also Peoples.'" *SBJT* 5 (2001): 42–56.

Matthews, V. H. "Pastoralists and Patriarchs." *BA* 44 (1981): 215–18.

_____. "The Wells of Gerar." *BA* 49 (1986): 118–26.

McCarter, P. K. "The Historical Abraham." *Int* 42 (1988): 341–52.

McComiskey, T. E. "The Religion of the Patriarchs." Pages 195–206 in *Law and the Prophets.* Nutley, N.J.: Presbyterian and Reformed, 1974.

McConville, J. G. "Yahweh and the Gods in the Old Testament." *EuroJTh* 2 (1993): 107–17.

McNamara, M., ed. *Targum Neofiti 1, Genesis.* Collegeville, Minn.: Liturgical Press, 1992.

Menn, E. M. *Judah and Tamar (Genesis 38) in Ancient Jewish Exegesis.* JSJSup 51. Leiden: Brill, 1997.

Merrill, E. *Kingdom of Priests: A History of Old Testament Israel.* Grand Rapids: Baker, 1987.

Millard, A. R. and D. J. Wiseman, eds. *Essays on the Patriarchal Narratives.* Winona Lake: Eisenbrauns, 1983.

Millard, A. R., J. K. Hoffmeier, and D. W. Baker, eds. *Faith Tradition and History: Old Testament Historiography in Its Near Eastern Context.* Winona Lake: Eisenbrauns, 1994.

Millard, A. R. "A New Babylonian 'Genesis Story.'" *TynBul* 18 (1967): 12–18.

Miller, J. E. "Sexual Offenses in Genesis." *JSOT* 90 (2000): 41–53.

Miscall, P. D. "The Jacob and Joseph Stories as Analogies." *JSOT* 6 (1978): 28–40.

Moberly, R. W. L. *The Bible, Theology, and Faith: A Study of Abraham and Jesus.* Cambridge: Cambridge University Press, 2000.

Morschauser, S. "'Hospitality,' Hostiles and Hostages: On the Legal Background to Genesis 19.1–9." *JSOT* 27 (2003): 461–85.

Neusner, J., ed. *Genesis Rabbah: The Judaic Commentary to the Book of Genesis.* Atlanta: Scholars Press, 1985.

Noble, P. "Esau, Tamar, and Joseph: Criteria for Identifying Inner-Biblical Allusions." *VT* 52 (2002): 219–52.

Noort, E. and E. Tigchelaar. *The Sacrifice of Isaac: The Aqedah (Genesis 22) and Its Interpretations.* Köln: Brill, 2002.

O'Brien, M. A. "The Contribution of Judah's Speech, Genesis 44:18–34, to the Characterization of Joseph." *CBQ* 59 (1997): 429–47.

Pagolu, A. *The Religion of the Patriarchs.* JSOTSup 277. Sheffield: Sheffield Academic Press, 1998.

Parry, R. "Feminist Hermeneutics and Evangelical Concerns: The Rape of Dinah as a Case Study." *TynBul* 53 (2002): 1–28.

Pritchard, J. B., ed. *Ancient Near Eastern Texts Relating to the Old Testament.* Princeton: Princeton University Press, 1969.

Provan, I. W., V. P. Long, and T. Longman. *A Biblical History of Israel.* Louisville: Westminster John Knox, 2003.

Rashi. *The Torah with Rashi's Commentary. Genesis.* Vol. 1. Brooklyn: Mesorah Publications, 1999–2001.

Redford, D. *A Study of the Biblical Story of Joseph (Genesis 37–50).* Leiden: Brill, 1970.

Rendsburg, G. A. *The Redaction of Genesis.* Winona Lake: Eisenbrauns, 1986.

Rendtorff, R. *The Problem of the Process of Transmission of the Pentateuch.* Sheffield: JSOT Press, 1990.

Rooker, M. "Genesis 1:1–3: Creation or Re-Creation?" *BSac* 149 (1992): 316–23 (Part One) and 411–27 (Part Two).

Ross, A. P. *Creation and Blessing: A Guide to the Study and Exposition of Genesis.* Grand Rapids: Baker, 1988.

Rowton, M. B. "Dimorphic Structure and the Problem of the 'Apiru-Ibrim." *JNES* 35 (1976): 13–20.

Sailhamer, J. "Genesis." EBC. Grand Rapids: Zondervan, 1990.

Sarna, N. *Genesis.* JPST. Philadelphia: Jewish Publication Society, 1989.

Sasson, J. M. "Circumcision in the Ancient Near East." *JBL* 85 (1966): 473–76.

Selman, M. J. "The Social Environment of the Patriarchs." *TynBul* 27 (1976): 114–36.

Sheridan, M. *Genesis 12–50.* ACCS 2. Downers Grove: InterVarsity, 2002.

Skinner, J. *A Critical and Exegetical Commentary on Genesis.* ICC. 2d ed. Edinburgh: T&T Clark, 1910.

Speiser, E. A. *Genesis.* AB. Garden City: Doubleday, 1960.

Sternberg, M. *The Poetics of Biblical Narrative: Ideological Literature and the Drama of Reading.* Bloomington: Indiana University Press, 1985.

Syrén, R. *The Forsaken First-Born: A Study of a Recurrent Motif in the Patriarchal Narratives.* Sheffield: JSOT Press, 1993.

Terino, J. "A Text Linguistic Study of the Jacob Narrative." *VE* 18 (1988): 45–62.

Thompson, T. L. *The Historicity of the Patriarchal Narratives: The Quest for the Historical Abraham.* BZAW 133. Berlin: de Gruyter, 1974.

Tonson, P. "Mercy without Covenant: A Literary Analysis of Genesis 19." *JSOT* 95 (2001): 95–116.

Tsumura, D. T. *The Earth and the Waters in Genesis 1 and 2: A Linguistic Investigation.* Sheffield: JSOT Press, 1989.

Van Seters, J. *Abraham in History and Tradition.* New Haven: Yale University Press, 1975.

_____. *Prologue to History: The Yahwist as Historian in Genesis.* Louisville: Westminster John Knox, 1992.

van Wolde, E. J. *Words Become Worlds: Semantic Studies of Genesis 1–11.* Leiden: Brill 1994.

_____. "Telling and Retelling: The Words of the Servant in Genesis 24." Pages 227–44 in *Synchronic or Diachronic?* Leiden: Brill, 1995.

Vawter, B. *On Genesis, A New Reading.* Garden City: Doubleday, 1977.

von Rad, G. *Genesis*. OTL. Philadelphia: Westminster, 1961.

Warning, W. "Terminological Patterns and Genesis 38." *AUSS* 38 (2000): 53–68.

Waltke, B. K. *Genesis: A Commentary*. Grand Rapids: Zondervan, 2001.

Weisberg, D. E. "The Widow of Our Discontent: Levirate Marriage in the Bible and Ancient Israel." *JSOT* 28 (2004): 403–29.

Wenham, G. J. *Genesis 1–15*. WBC. Waco: Word, 1987.

_____. *Genesis 16–50*. WBC. Dallas: Word, 1995.

_____. *Jesus and Divorce*. Carlisle: Paternoster, 1997.

_____. "Pondering the Pentateuch: The Search for a New Paradigm." Pages 116–44 in *The Face of Old Testament Studies: A Survey of Contemporary Approaches*. Grand Rapids: Baker, 1999.

Westbrook, R. "The Purchase of the Cave of Machpelah." *Israel Law Review* 6 (1971): 29–38.

Westenholz, J. G. "Tamar, *QĔDĒŠÂ, QADISˇTU*, and Sacred Prostitution in Mesopotamia." *HTR* 82 (1989): 245–65.

Westermann, C. *Genesis 1–11, A Commentary*. Minneapolis: Augsburg, 1984.

_____. *Genesis 12–36, A Commentary*. Minneapolis: Augsburg, 1985.

_____. *Genesis 37–50, A Commentary*. Minneapolis: Augsburg, 1986.

Wevers, J. W. *Notes on the Greek Text of Genesis*. Septuagint and Cognate Studies 35. Atlanta: Scholars Press, 1993.

White, H. C. "Reuben and Judah: Duplicates or Complements?" Pages 73–97 in *Understanding the Word*. Sheffield: JSOT Press, 1985.

Whybray, R. *The Making of the Pentateuch*. JSOTSup 53. Sheffield: JSOT Press, 1987.

Wilson, R. R. *Genealogy and History in the Biblical World*. New Haven: Yale University Press, 1977.

Winnett, F. V. "The Arabian Genealogies in the Book of Genesis." Pages 171–96 in *Translating and Understanding the Old Testament*. Nashville: Abingdon, 1970.

Wright, G. R. H. "The Positioning of Genesis 38." *ZAW* 94 (1982): 523–34.

Wyatt, N. "The Story of Dinah and Shechem." *UF* 22 (1990): 433–58.

Youngblood, R., ed. *The Genesis Debate: Persistent Questions about Creation and the Flood*. Grand Rapids: Baker, 1990.

Selected Subject Index

Person Index

940

Selected Scripture Index

947